Weitere Werke von Gerd. W. Goede im Oldenbourg Verlag

Goede, Wirtschaftsenglisch-Lexikon,
Englisch-Deutsch · Deutsch-Englisch
2. Auflage (2 Bände im Schuber)

Goede, Lexikon des Internationalen
Handels,
Englisch-Deutsch · Deutsch-Englisch

Marketing-Lexikon

Marketing Dictionary

Englisch-Deutsch
Deutsch-Englisch

Von

Gerd W. Goede

R. Oldenbourg Verlag München Wien

Die Deutsche Bibliothek - CIP-Einheitsaufnahme

Goede, Gerd W.:
Marketing-Lexikon : englisch-deutsch, deutsch-englisch = Marketing dictionary / von Gerd W. Goede. – München ; Wien : Oldenbourg, 1998
ISBN 3-486-23945-7

Rosenheimer Straße 145, D-81671 München
Telefon: (089) 45051-0, Internet: http://www.oldenbourg.de

Gedruckt auf säure- und chlorfreiem Papier
Gesamtherstellung: Druckhaus „Thomas Müntzer“ GmbH, Bad Langensalza

ISBN 3-486-23945-7

To

Iris

with hearty thanks

for support, encouragement,

understanding, care, and

love.

The aim of marketing is

to make selling superfluous.

Peter F. Drucker

When business is good

it pays to advertise;

when business is bad

you`ve got to advertise.

Anonymous

VORWORT

Marketing ist allgegenwärtig - Produzenten, Groß- und Einzelhändler, Dienstleistungsunternehmen, öffentliche und private Institutionen, Vereine, Regierungen und unzählige Einzelpersonen beschäftigen sich mit Marketing und wenden es an, um ihre mannigfaltigen Ziele, Zielgruppen und Zielmärkte zu erreichen und ihre offerierten Waren und Dienstleistungen attraktiv, erschwinglich und verfügbar für tatsächliche und potentielle Käufer zu machen.

Marketing genießt auch eine Schlüsselstellung in unserer Gesellschaft - jeder Konsument, jeder Anbieter, die Medien, die Geschäftswelt, die Wirtschaft, unsere Lebensstile, unsere Bedürfnisse, unser Wohlbefinden, der Grad unserer Zufriedenheit, usw., werden direkt oder indirekt von Marketingaktivitäten beeinflußt.

Das vorliegende Lexikon bietet dem Leser eine gründliche, umfangreiche, aktuelle, gut verständliche, präzise und informative Darstellung der Marketingterminologie und der Marketinginhalte.

Das Lexikon umfaßt ca. 6.500 Hauptbegriffe. Da zahlreiche Begriffe in Mehrfachbedeutungen auftreten, werden auch diese definiert.

Der zweite Teil des Buches enthält die deutschen Fachtermini (ca 9.600) mit ihren englischen Entsprechungen in einem alphabetischen Glossar.

Im Anhang befinden sich ca. 1.300 alphabetisch geordnete Abkürzungen.

Dieses Nachschlagewerk ist hilfreich und nützlich für:

- jeden Konsumenten

- Fach- und Führungskräfte aus Marketing und Werbung, z.B. aus den Bereichen Industrie, Handel, Dienstleistung, Bankwesen, Versicherung, Transportwesen, usw.;

- Professoren und Studenten an Universitäten, Fachhochschulen und Berufsakademien;

- Lehrer und fortgeschrittene Schüler an wirtschaftsorientierten Gymnasien, Fachschulen und Berufsschulen;

- Übersetzer und Dolmetscher;

- alle an Marketing und am Wirtschaftsgeschehen Interessierte.

Mein besonderer Dank gilt:

Meinen Eltern, Margarete und Walter Goede, und meiner Schwester Ilka Annegret für die gewährte Unterstützung, ihre Geduld und ihr Verständnis.

Für Beratung und sonstige hilfreiche Aktivitäten danke ich ganz herzlich:
Herrn Dr. Phil. Andrew Hunter Lee (sprachliche Beratung), Frau Helga Schnur (Sekretärin), Herrn Bernd Baumann (DV Berater), Herrn Dr. Eckhard Gnädig und Herrn Diplom Volkswirt Martin M. Weigert, Cheflektor beim Oldenbourg Verlag.

Gerd. W. Goede

FOREWORD

Marketing is all around us - manufacturers, wholesalers and retailers, service firms, public and private institutions, clubs, governments, and all kinds of individuals study and use marketing to reach their manifold objectives, target groups and target markets and in order to be able to make their offered products and services attractive, affordable and available to actual and potential customers.

Marketing also enjoys a key position in our society - every consumer, every supplier, the media, the business world, the economy, our lifestyles, our needs and wants, our well-being, our degree of satisfaction, etc, are directly or indirectly influenced by marketing activites.

The intention of the present dictionary is to provide the reader with an in-depth, comprehensive, up-to-date, clear, concise and informative exposition of the terminology and contents of marketing.

This dictionary comprises approx. 6,500 main terms. As many of the terms have more than one meaning, the most widely used and accepted meanings have been included.

The second part of the dictionary lists a German-English glossary of approx. 9,600 terms in alphabetical order for reference.

The appendix lists approx. 1,300 marketing abbreviations in alphabetical order.

This reference book will undoubtedly be useful and beneficial to:

- Every consumer;
- Managers and trained staff involved in marketing and advertising, eg in industry, commerce, the services sector, banking, insurance, transport, etc.;
- Professors and students at universities, professional and commercial colleges and institutes;
- Teachers and advanced students at commercial schools and trade-oriented high schools;
- Translators and interpreters;
- All those interested in marketing and economic problems.

My particular thanks goes to:

My parents, Margarete und Walter Goede, and my sister Ilka Annegret for their encouraging support, their patience and understanding.

Finally, I would like to express my deep thanks to the following for their counsel, generous support, encouragement and other helpful undertakings:
Andrew Hunter Lee, Ph.D. (language consultant), Ms Helga Schnur (secretary), Mr Bernd Baumann (DP consultant), Dr. Eckhard Gnädig and Diplom Volkswirt Martin M. Weigert, Senior Editor at the Oldenbourg Verlag.

Gerd W. Goede

A

À la carte — nach der Speisekarte

The practice of an advertiser to buy in marketing services when needed from a number of suppliers rather than relying on just one agency over a period of time.

Abandonment — Patentaufgabe

Also called abandonment of patent.

The cession of patent rights or of similar rights (e.g. rights to trademarks).

Abatement — Herabsetzung, Minderung, Nachlaß

An allowance or reduction, e.g. the abatement of the purchase price.

Abbroachment — Aufkaufen großer Mengen zum Wiederverkauf zu überhöhten Preisen

The buying up of goods at wholesale to control the supply of these goods and then resell them at much higher resale prices.

ABC classification — ABC-Kundeneinstufung

The classification of customer accounts within a sales area into groups according to their size and potential, and, therefore, their importance. This system is often used to determine a salesperson`s call frequency.

ABC method — ABC-Methode (Aufmerksamkeit, Nutzen, Abschluß)

A sales method, where the customer's attention (A) is attracted, the salesman then shows the product's benefits (B) to the customer, and finally closes (C) the deal.

Abeyance order schwebender Werbeauftrag

An order for commercial radio or TV time in a time period that is not available when the order is placed.

Above-the-line Verkaufsförderung durch normale Werbemaßnahmen

Also called above-the-line advertising or promotion.

This is advertising in media (eg newspapers, magazines, TV) that pay commissions to the ad agencies that provide them with business.

The promotional expenses associated with any form of direct advertising, usually the media used are: press, television, radio, cinema, and posters.

Note: advertising which involves indirect promotion, for example, direct mail, exhibitions, demonstrations, point-of-sale material, is known as below the line promotion.

Above the line cost Produktionskosten für Werbung

Any cost involved in the production of advertising.

Abscissa Abszisse, X-Koordinate

The horizontal line (or X-axis) on a two dimensional graph.

Absolute cost advantage absoluter Kostenvorteil

Advantages possessed by established firms who are able to sustain a lower average total cost than new entrants regardless of size of output.

Absolute liability Gefährdungshaftung, verschuldensunabhängige Haftung

Also called liability without regard to fault, strict liability or liability based on causation irrespective of fault.

Liability without fault.

Absolute monopoly reines, vollkommenes Monopol

Also called perfect monopoly or pure monopoly.

A situation in which only one producer or supplier has total control over the output of one product or service for which there is no substitute.

Absorption Übernahme
Gesamtausgaben der Inländer für Güter und Leistungen

The taking over of something, e.g. costs, freight charges, etc.

The total spending of a country's residents on domestic and foreign goods and services.

Absorption costing Vollkostenrechnung

Also called full absorption costing, full costing or total costing.

The charging of all variable and fixed costs to operations, processes or products, whether they can be traced to a product directly or not. Apportionment (allocation) of overheads follows some reasonable convention, but is of necessity arbitrary. Thus, stocks and output are valued on a total cost basis.

Absorption point Marktsättigungspunkt

Also called market saturation point.

A point indicating that a market is now saturated.

Absorption pricing Vollkostenpreisgestaltung

A pricing strategy where all costs are recovered in the price for a product.

Abstinence Abstinenz, Zurückstellung, (Konsum)Aufschub

The sacrifice of current consumption to increase future consumption.

Abstinence theory of interest Abstinenztheorie des Zinses

A theory which states that the rate of interest is the reward for choosing to abstain from consumption.

Abuse of power Machtmißbrauch

The misuse of power.

Accelerated development beschleunigte (Produkt)Entwicklung

The process of speeding up the development process of new products, e.g. by eliminating unnecessary steps or by minimising decision-making procedures.

Accelerating inflation zunehmende Inflation

An increasingly sharp rise in the rate of inflation.

Acceleration principle Beschleunigungsprinzip, Akzelerationsprinzip

Also called accelerator principle.

It measures the relationship between the demand for consumer and producer goods. Changes in consumer demand induce accelerated changes in demand for producer goods (capital goods). The theory states that the level of investment depends upon the level of consumption.

Note: A rise of 20 percent in consumer demand can increase industrial demand by as much as 200 percent within the immediately following period. A decrease can cause an equally significant decrease.

Accelerator Akzelerator

This explains how higher consumption can lead to higher investment. The ratio between the change in the rate of growth of consumption and the change in investment is the accelerator.

Acceptable price range akzeptable Preislage

The prices buyers are prepared to pay for certain goods or services.

Acceptable quality level (AGL) ausreichendes Qualitätsniveau, Gutgrenze

The maximum amount of defectives (faulty units) that will be accepted in the output from a production process.

Acceptance (acc, acce) Akzeptanz
Zuschlag
(Waren)Annahme

In marketing, the acceptance of a product in the market.

The acceptance of a bid or tender. Also called award of contract or accept a bid (tender).

The acceptance of goods delivered by the seller. The acceptance of goods should not be confused with their mere receipt.

Acceptance of goods Warenannahme

The situation when the buyer accepts the goods delivered by the seller and agrees to pay for them; or if after a reasonable time the buyer has done nothing to refuse them, he is considered to have accepted them and must therefore pay for them.

In marketing, the willingness of consumers to buy a product.

Acceptance of offer Angebotsannahme, Vertragsannahme

Also called acceptance of contractual offer.

A declaration of willingness to enter into an agreement and thus the unconditional assent (ie the offeree must accept all the terms) by the offeree of an offer which has been made to him by the offeror.

Acceptance of order Auftragsannahme

The agreement, either verbally or in writing, to deliver or produce goods or to carry out a service.

Acceptance of proposal Vertragsannahme
Angebotsannahme

A declaration of willingness to enter into an agreement.

The acceptance of an offer.

Acceptance sampling Stichprobenentnahme bei (Waren) Annahme

A quality control based on taking a sample from a consignment to test that good quality has been delivered.

Access Einstiegszeit

In television programming, the time segment prior to prime time.

Access barriers Zutrittsbarrieren

Factors such as tariffs, legal and other restrictions which prevent potential market participants from purchasing or selling certain products.

Access to the market Marktzugang

Also called market access.

The ability to enter a market, acquire and maintain the legal right to sell in that market.

Accessibility (Markt)Zugänglichkeit

The ability of a market to be reached and served by a seller or producer.

Accession Neuanschaffung

The act of coming into the possession of something.

Accessory advertising Ergänzungs-, Randwerbung, ergänzende/flankierende/ unterstützende Werbung

Additional advertising for a product or service that supports a current ad campaign.

Accomodation Entgegenkommen Unterbringung

The doing of a favour or a kindness.

A place to live in or sleep in, e.g. a hotel.

Accomodation desk Kundenschalter, Informationsschalter

A counter in a large store or department store for customer accomodation on such things as store information, exchanges, refunds, etc.

Accordion insert Leporello, Leporellofalzbeilage

An advertising brochure or leaflet included or attached inside a magazine, that opens like the folds of an accordion, i.e. a zigzag, accordion-like fold permitting it to be extended to its full size with a single pull.

Account (A/C, A/c, a/c, acct) Kunde Geschäftsbeziehung

A customer or client.

A business relationship, i.e. a relationship between one party and another.

Account conflict Interessenkonflikt einer Werbeagentur

A situation in which an advertising agency obtains an offer to carry out advertising which is similar to that of an existing client/account.

The opposing interests that occur when an advertising agency accepts competing clients/accounts.

Account executive (AE) (Werbe)Kontakter, Sachbearbeiter eines Werbeetats Kontaktgruppenleiter

A person in an advertising agency or department who supervises the planning and preparation of advertising and who is reponsible for the overall managing of a client's requirements. Also called account director, account handler, account manager, account supervisor or client-service executive.

The group head of a number of account executives, i.e. the person to whom the account executives report. Also called account manager or account supervisor.

Account manager (AM) Kundenbetreuer (Werbe)Kontakter Kontaktgruppenleiter

Also called account executive (AE).

A sales representative responsible for a major customer or a group of customers.

An employee in a company responsible for the managing of a customer`s requirements.

An executive in an advertising agency responsible for the overall managing of a client`s requirements.

The group head of a number of account executives.

Account objectives Kundenziele

The specific aims and sales goals for a specified period which a salesperson wants to achieve for an account/customer for which he/she is responsible.

Account penetration ratio Kundenpenetrationsrate

The percentage of customers/accounts from which orders were received. This figure shows whether a salesperson is working his/her territory thoroughly or whether he/she is simply "milking" major customers.

Account purchase(s) (A/P) Einkaufs(ab)rechnung eines Kommissionärs

When a commission agent has purchased goods on the market for his principal, he renders to the latter an account purchase, giving details of the quantities bought and the prices paid. Expenses and commission are then added, and the amount is settled.

Account rendered laut erteilter (früherer) Rechnung

Words that often appear on a statement of account to indicate a previous invoice that has already been dispatched to the customer.

Account sales (A/S) Verkaufs(ab)rechnung eines Kommissionärs

A statement of sales rendered by an agent to his principal, showing the amounts received by the agent, expenses deducted, his commission and the amount due or remitted.

Account supervisor Kontaktgruppenleiter

An advertising agency employee responsible for overseeing the work of one or more account executives.

Acculturation Akkulteration, kulturelle Anpassung

The process of learning and adopting the social values, norms, life styles, behaviours, etc of another group of people or of people in another culture.

Achieved penetration (Markt)Penetrationsgrad, Grad der Marktdurchdringung

A degree indicating the extent to which a market has been penetrated.

Achievement of objectives Zielerreichung, Zielrealisierung

Also called accomplishment of goals.

A goal or goals that have been successfully accomplished.

Acknowledg(e)ment (ACK, acktg) Bestätigung

Also called confirmation.

An act of acknowledging.

A report to the sender that the thing (e.g. the shipment) he has sent has arrived.

Acknowledg(e)ment of order Auftragsbestätigung

Also called confirmation of order.

The acknowledgement letter follows an order; it lets the customer know the order has arrived safely and generally indicates the order number and the date, but does not constitute an acceptance, and the legal consequences of an acceptance do not therefore follow.

Such letters are usually fairly brief, and in some cases a preprinted postcard or a standard letter may be used, with a few details typed or written in, e.g. phrases which clarify the legal position - such as "our formal acceptance will follow in a few days".

ACORN ACORN (Wohngegend-klassifikation)

Acronym for A Classification Of Residential Neighbourhoods.

A concept based on the belief that people living within close proximity will have similar behaviour or purchasing patterns. ACORN classifies all households into geographic, socioeconomic, and demographic segments based on neighbourhood of residence.

For example, households can be classified into market segments such as:
1. modern family housing for manual workers, 2. modern housing for higher incomes, 3. rural areas, 4. low income areas, 5. traditional high status suburbia, etc.

Acquisitive society Erwerbsgesellschaft

A society in which people are constantly encouraged to possess things; some economists argue that this attitude is the driving force for economic activity.

Across the board (Werbe)Sendung, die täglich oder werktäglich (meist von montags bis freitags) vom selben Sender zur selben Uhrzeit ausgestrahlt wird

Also called across-the-board broadcast or program(me).

A broadcast or commercial run on radio or TV daily or on workdays, usually from Monday to Friday.

Act break Rundfunk-, Fernsehpause

The interruption of a radio or TV program(me) by commercials, station breaks, etc.

Action programme Marketingplan, Handlungsprogramm

Also called action plan.

A detailed plan showing how major marketing tasks will be managed and carried out, who will do them and when in order to achieve the company`s marketing objectives. Also called marketing plan.

An agency`s strategy adopted to best position and sell the goods and services of a client.
There are three primary objectivies: 1. to satisfy the needs of the marketplace; 2. to secure an advantage over competitors; 3. to create profit.

Active market lebhafter Markt

A market in which there is a lot of buying and selling.

Activity report Tätigkeitsbericht

Reports requiring salespeople to provide details of their sales activities within a given time period, e.g. the number of calls (visits) made, dealer meetings attended, etc.

Actual buyer-reader tatsächlicher Kaufleser

A person actually buying and reading a publication.

Actual cash value angemessener Marktpreis

Also called current cash value or fair market value.

The reasonable cash price that something will bring on the open market.

Actual non-buyer reader Zweitleser, tatsächlicher Nichtkauf-Leser

A person who has not bought a publication but reads it.

Actual product Produktinhalt, Produktkern

Also called formal product or tangible product.

The characteristics of a product, ie a product`s parts, styling, quality level, brand name, features, packaging, and other attributes that combine to deliver core product benefits.

Actuals effektive Ware, physische Ware (Warenbörse)
sofort verfügbare Ware

Physical commodities which may be purchased on the commodity exchange and delivered at once. Also called spot goods.

Merchandise and other items available for immediate purchase and subsequent sale.

Ad columns Anzeigenteil (einer Seite oder Zeitung)

Also called advertisement or advertising columns.

In a newspaper or magazine, the page(s) or section(s) consisting of advertisements.

Ad noting Werbemittelbeachtung

The activity of taking notice of or perceiving advertisements by individuals, the ad noters/ad noting audience.

Ad playback Erinnerung an den Inhalt einer Werbeanzeige

Also called advertisement or advertising playback.

The ability of ad noters to recall the ad message of a particular advertisement.

Ad valorem (AV, ad val) dem Werte nach

According to the value and not to the weight or quantity. Ad valorem tax, ad valorem duty, etc. is charged on the value of the goods. Value-added tax (VAT) is the best-known ad valorem tax.

Ad valorem freight Wertfracht

Freight rate based on percentage value of goods shipped.

Ad-A-Card/Ad-a-card perforierter Abreißgutschein

A perforated tear-off coupon attached to advertisements, e.g. in newspapers or magazines, to induce reader response.

Adaptation Adaptierung, Anpassung
angepaßtes, überarbeitetes Stück

The use of a basic idea but with minor changes, as in an advertisement, for other media, eg posters.

A thing which has been adapted.

Adapted marketing mix angepaßtes Marketingmix

In international marketing, a producer`s strategy to adjust his marketing mix elements to each international target market, bearing higher costs but hoping for a larger market share and return.
Companies that operate in one or more foreign markets must decide how much, if at all, to adapt their marketing mixes to local conditions.

Adaptive control system anpassungsfähiges Kontrollsystem

A marketing control system which allows for changes to be made to marketing goals/objectives during a planning period as well as to the performance to meet the objectives.

Adaptive inflation Anpassungsinflation

Also called adjustment inflation.

The future rate of inflation is based on the inflationary experience of the recent past. As a result, once under way, inflation feeds upon itself with, for example, wage increases which take into account the expected future inflation rate which, in turn, leads to further price rises.

Adaptive new product angepaßtes, erweitertes, verändertes Folgeprodukt

An adaptation of an existing product. The adaptive new product either can be a replacement for an existing product or it can be an addition to the existing product line (the latter is known as product differentiation).

Adaptive selling angepaßter Verkauf

In personal selling, a salesperson´s strategy of altering selling behaviours during a sales interaction due to changes in the selling situation in order to maximise effectiveness.

Add-on sale Anschlußauftrag

Also called loading.

The sale of additional goods or services to a recent buyer.

Added buyer effect käuferfreundlicher Kaufanreiz

An inducement (incentive to buy) given to a potential customer. For example, a lower price for a good attracts new buyers into a market, increasing their quantity demanded.

Added value product Mehrwertprodukt

A product, usually a branded product, that offers some additional benefit which differentiates it from its competitors. When building new brands, producers try to endow each one of these with a distinctive personality which is designed to set it apart from competitive brands.

Note: these additional benefits enable products to acquire an added value because consumers perceive them as an extra worth. Thus, companies can raise the price-pain limit as consumers are willing to pay more for what they regard as the better branded product.

Additional markon/mark-on zusätzlicher (Preis)Aufschlag

A further increase in a retail merchandise price, often done during periods of peak demand.

Additive Additiv, Zusatz

Chemical substance which is added, especially to food to improve its appearance, taste or smell, or to prevent it from deteriorating.

Address (ADD) Adresse, Anschrift

A writing on a letter or envelope showing where the letter is to be sent, i.e. the designation or place of delivery (contains details of street, town, district, and country).

Address coding guide (ACG) Postleitzahlenbuch

A publication containing post/zip codes.

Address line Anschriftenzeile

In an advertisement or other promotional material, the part containing the advertiser`s address, or the address to which any enquiries should be sent.

Addressee Empfänger, Adressat

Also called receiver or recipient.

The name of the person or company to whom a letter or parcel is being sent. The receiver of merchandise is called consignee; the receiver of money is called payee or remittee (transferee); and the receiver of a loan is called borrower.

Addressee unknown Empfänger unbekannt

A situation where an addressee whose name and address on a letter or parcel is not known by the deliverer (eg postman) and cannot be reached at this particular address.

Addresser Absender/in, Adressant/in

A person, company, or the like who sends a piece of mail.

Adequate distribution angemessene Warenverteilung

The availability of a product in the shops to meet demand, e.g. produced by advertising. The manufacturer may induce shopkeepers to stock goods, for example, by offering: special discounts, special display material, assistance with local advertising, sales promotion, etc.

Adequate sample adäquate Stichprobe

A sample large enough to minimise chance as a factor affecting the analysis of data obtained from research.

Adflation Anzeigeninflation
Kosteninflation für Werbung

Adflation = advertising + inflation.

A situation which occurs when the audience is flooded/swamped with advertisements.

A situation where advertising costs are constantly rising or rocketing up.

Adjacency angrenzendes Programm
Werbespot am Anfang
oder Ende einer Programmsendung

A radio or TV programme immediately preceding or following another programme on the same station.

In commercial advertising, the time period (usually two minutes) that precedes or follows network broadcasts. Also called commercial break position.

Adjusted selling price (ASP) berichtigter Verkaufspreis

The current selling price minus profit margin and selling expenses.

Admail Couponwerbung

This service enables advertisers to give a local address in their advertisements and to have replies redirected to their head office. It can be combined with the freepost service.

Adman Werbefachmann

Also called advertising man, adperson or advertising person.

A colloquial term for a man who works in advertising.

Admass Reklamevieh

Admass = advertisement + mass.

The masses of a society who believe in and are greatly influenced by advertising.

Administered price Richtpreis, regulierter Preis

A price which is set and kept constant for a period of time. The price tends to be cost determined and is set by "price makers" or "price setters".

Administered price theory Theorie der administrativen Preise

A hypothesis expressed by an American statistician during the depths of the Depression (the period 1929 - 1933). The hypothesis states that firms with market power (i.e. market leaders) may set prices by administrative action, rather than the free play of market forces, and keep them constant for a time period despite changes in input prices and/or demand.

Administered pricing administrative Preisfestsetzung

A pricing strategy where the firm establishes the price and buyers can either buy or not buy at this price. The price established covers costs and a profit margin.

Administered vertical market system verwaltete(s) vertikale(s) Kooperation, Marketing

Also called administered VMS.

A vertical marketing system that coordinates successive stages of distribution.

In this distribution channel, the flow of products from producer to end consumer/user is controlled by the power and size of one member of the distribution channel and not through common ownership or contractual ties. Thus, producers of a top brand can obtain strong trade cooperation and support from resellers, eg with regard to displays, shelf space, promotions, and price policies. Similarly, large and powerful retailers can strongly influence producers that supply the products they sell.

Adopter Akzeptierender, Werbeerfüller

A customer deciding to purchase/buy a new product regularly.

Note: customers adopting an innovation are often classified into five groups:
1. innovators, 2. early adopters, 3. early majority, 4. late majority, 5. laggards.

Adoption (of a product) — Akzeptanz, Adoption, Annahme (eines Produktes)

An individual`s (adopter`s) decision to become a regular buyer and user of a particular product; ie the person decides to choose one product over another.

Adoption curve — Adoptionskurve(nlinie)

A line or curve on a graph showing how many customers adopt, ie buy, a new product at various time periods after the launch/introduction date.

Adoption process — (Produkt)Annahmeprozeß

Also called adoption sequence.

The mental process an individual goes through from first hearing about a product until it is finally adopted. Thus, the various stages - (product) awareness, interest, evaluation, trial and adoption - which consumers go through in their decision-making process. This process varies greatly by individual, product and the effectiveness of the diffusion process.

The adoption process itself is composed of five sequential stages:

1. awareness stage (in this stage the consumer is exposed to the new product idea but is not yet really interested in it);
2. interest stage (in this stage the consumer seeks more information about the product);
3. evaluation stage (now the consumer mentally assesses the information received and decides whether or not to try it);
4. trial stage (the consumer uses or tries the new product to determine its suitability);
5. adoption stage (the consumer decides to continue using the new product).

Since individuals go through this adoption process at different times, there are five categories of adopters:

1. the innovaters (they first pass through the stages of the adoption process);
2. the early adopters;
3. the early majority;
4. the late majority;
5. the laggards (they are the last ones going through the process).

Adpage/ad page — Anzeigenseite
Seite, auf der eine Anzeige steht

Also called advertising page or advertisement page.

A page in a publication only consisting of advertisements.

In a publication, a page where an advertisement is shown.

Adpage audience — Leserschaft einer Anzeigenseite

Also called advertising page audience.

The number of persons who have seen and possibly read an advertisement.

Adpage exposure (APX) — Anzeigenseitenkontakt

The frequency at which readers are exposed to an average adpage in a newspaper or magazine.

Adrate card — Anzeigenpreisliste, Werbepreisliste

Also called advertising rate card or rate card.

A price list showing the prices for the use of different advertising media.

Advance — Anzahlung
Preisanstieg

A part-payment/downpayment to the supplier of goods.

A price increase.

Advance canvass — Vorausbesuch (von Einzelhändlern bei Werbekampagne)

A number of visits to retailers in a specific area to obtain their support for a future promotional campaign.

Advance freight (AF, adv frt) — Frachtvorauszahlung

Freight paid in advance, ie before delivery of the actual goods.

Advance order — Vorausbestellung

An order placed ahead of the time when delivery is desired.

Advancing market — Markt mit steigendem Preisniveau

A market in which demand for a good greatly exceeds its supply. Therefore the prices are rising.

Adventure — (gewagtes) Unternehmen, Spekulations-, Risikogeschäft

A commercial undertaking of a speculative nature.

Advertised brand — Marke, für die geworben wird

A branded article, usually a consumer product, which is advertised heavily.

Advertised price — (Werbe)Grundpreis angekündigter Bezugspreis

In broadcasting, the cost to advertise a product. The price the advertiser has to pay depends on the advertising frequency and the total ad time purchased, ie the volume.

In an advertisement or commercial, the price stated which the buyer has to pay

Advertisement (ad, advert) — Anzeige, Werbung, Reklame

Also called ad or advert. When an advertisement appears in the broadcast media (TV and radio) it is called commercial or broadcast advertising.

An informational notice appealing to a mass audience through the communications media for the purpose of calling attention to a product, service, event or organisation in order to inform or arouse a desire to purchase or support a product, service, event or organisation or to influence consumer behaviour.

Advertisement manager Werbeleiter bei einem Werbeträger, Leiter der Anzeigenabteilung Anzeigenleiter

The head of the sales department of a media organisation, eg a publishing company. He is the person responsible for selling advertising space.
Note: in commercial television, advertisement managers are called sales managers.

The person in charge of the advertisement section of a newspaper or magazine.

Advertisement size Anzeigengröße

An advertisement should be as large as necessary to communicate the unique selling proposition, USP (i.e. the unique benefits of the product) while positively impacting the brand image. On new products, this requires at least a one-half page advertisement. Once the USP has been sufficiently exposed to a large percentage of the market or target group, eighth or quarter page advertisements can be used.

Advertiser Anzeigenkunde, Inserent Werbeagentur

A person or company who advertises, and who ultimately pays the bill.

An advertising agency.

Advertising (ad) Werbung, Reklame

Advertising is non-personal communication directed at target audiences through various media in order to present and promote products, services and ideas.

Furthermore, it spreads information or awareness to create, increase, or at least maintain, the sales of a product or service. This can be achieved in two different ways. Firstly, ad can be used to inform consumers of the existence and location of the product(s) to which it is directed. Secondly, ad can influence the nature of the consumer's preferences to the benefit of the firm's products.

No aspect of the promotion mix affects an individual more than advertising, as each individual is constantly exposed to advertising. Many firms rely heavily on advertising as the primary element in their promotion strategy. The primary components of advertising are media and message. Such media as radio, television, magazines, newspapers, direct mail, outdoor, and transit are selected in the light of the message to be communicated, the budget and the target audience.

There are numerous reasons why someone advertises. In short, the advertiser wants to make known what he has to sell or what he wants to buy.

More special and specific reasons for advertising are listed below:
1. to announce a new product or service;
2. to expand the market to new buyers;
3. to announce a modification;
4. to announce a price change;
5. to announce a new pack;
6. to make a special offer;
7. to invite enquiries;
8. to sell directly;
9. to test an ad medium;
10. to announce the location of stockists;
11. to obtain stockists;
12. to educate consumers;
13. to challenge competition;
14. to remind;
15. to retrieve lost sales;
16. to please stockists;
17. to please the salesforce;
18. to recruit staff;
19. to attract investors;
20. to export;
21. to announce trading results; etc.

Note: the amount that should be spent on advertising depends of course on the strategic objectives of the firm.

Note, by law, advertisers must:
1. avoid false or deceptive advertising, 2. not make false claims, 3. avoid false demonstrations, 4. not create advertisements that have the capacity to deceive, even though no one may actually be deceived, 5. avoid bait-and-switch advertising that attracts potential buyers under false pretenses, 6. not advertise for dangerous or unhealthy products (in most countries e.g. tobacco), particularly in places frequented by children or adolescents.

Types of advertising are, for example:

Competitive ad: This is aimed solely at consumers and tries to persuade them to buy the advertiser's product rather than his competitor's by assuring them that it is better. Also called comparative ad, comparison ad or persuasive ad.

Generic ad: All the producers in one industry combine to advertise the product in general rather than their own particular brands (e.g. "Drink more milk"). Also called cooperative ad or joint ad.

Informative ad:
All ad is informative to some extent, in that it is informing people that a product exists etc.

Advertising agency Werbeagentur

In general, a service firm which will undertake market research for companies wishing to advertise; it will create, produce and distribute ads using suitable media.

There are three basic types of agency:
1. the full-service agency (this provides a client with services in copy, media, promotion advice, research, consumer packaging, design, public relations, and publicity);
2. the specialty service agency (this type of agency specialises in one or two services);
3. the in-house agency (it is part of a particular firm and may perform all or some advertising services).

Advertising allowance Werbenachlaß, -rabatt, -zuschuß

Payments or price reductions paid or granted by manufacturers to retailers or dealers to reward them for participating in advertising programmes.

Advertising and demand Werbung und Nachfrage

Successful advertising can increase demand dramatically by increasing the brand awareness, strengthening the brand image, stressing the advantages of the product or giving a tired product a new lease of life by creating a new image.

Advertising and market share Werbung und Marktanteil

New brands with a small market share tend to spend proportionately more on advertising and sales promotion than those with a large market share because:

1. new brands need more advertising and sales promotion because they need a certain minimum level of exposure to measurably affect purchase habits;
2. beyond a certain level of advertising expenditure, sales or the market share begins to decrease no matter how much is spent on advertising.

Advertising and the consumer Werbung und der Verbraucher

Advertising affects everyone´s daily life and influences many purchases. In the USA, for example, average citizens are exposed to about 300 advertisements a day from all types of ad media. Thus, advertising affects the TV programmes people watch, the content of the newspapers they read, the medicines they take, etc. But nevertheless, advertising cannot change strongly held values and attitudes deeply rooted within an individual. However, advertising may succeed in transforming a person´s negative attitude towards a product or company into a positive one and thereby change the customer´s buying behaviour. Moreover, advertising reinforces positive attitudes toward brands, and consumers with a high degree of brand loyalty are least susceptible to the influences of advertising for competing products.

Advertising announcement Werbeansage, Werbedurchsage

A brief spoken ad message, especially a radio or TV commercial.

Advertising appeal Anziehungskraft der Werbung

The ability of an advertisement to attract customers and match their wants.

Advertising artist Werbegraphiker

A person creating artwork, eg drawings, layouts, which are used in advertisements.

Advertising Association (AA) Werbefachverband (GB)

In GB, a national body representing the interests of advertisers, ad agencies and media owners.

Advertising audience Werbepublikum

Also called advertising noters.

The readers, listeners or viewers taking notice of advertisements.

Advertising audit Werbeleistungsüberprüfung

Formal examination of all ad activities and ad effectiveness, sometimes carried out by independent auditors.

Advertising believability Glaubwürdigkeit der Werbung

Also called advertising credibility.

The degree to which advertisements and their messages are perceived as true and honest by ad noters.

Advertising bill Werbeplakat, Werbeanschlag

Also called bill, billboard, placard or poster.

An advertisement in the form of a poster.

Advertising budget Werbebudget, Werbeetat

Also called advertising appropriation.

The amount of money an advertiser sets aside for spending on an advertising campaign (i.e. the combination of advertisements, run in the various ad media for varying periods).

When setting an ad budget, the following factors should be considered:
1. The stage in the product life cycle: new products usually need larger budgets to build awareness and to gain consumer trial. If you are entering a new field, you should spend more on advertising than the average of the top two leaders for the first two or three years after market entrance.
2. The market share: high-market share brands usually need more ad spending than low-share brands do;
3. Competition and clutter: a brand must advertise more heavily in a competitive market with high ad spending. If your company has already obtained a share of the market (eg 20%) and wants to maintain that share, then it should spend slightly above (eg 22%) its percent share of the market on advertising.
4. Advertising frequency: the more repetitions that are necessary to present the brand´s message to consumers, the higher the ad budget must be;
5. Product differentiation: a brand requires heavy advertising if it closely resembles other brands in order to set it apart; less advertising is required if the product differs greatly from competitive products.

Some of the most common methods of determining ad budgets are as follows:
1. As a percentage of sales: sales may relate to overall turnover, or to revenue received for individual products or groups of products. But this advertising-to-sales ratio reflects the low sales of a new product and the high sales of an established mature product. Thus, it should only be used as a guideline.
2. On the basis of competitive ad spending: this method is very unrealistic because no two companies are pursuing identical objectives from an identical base line of resources, market standing, or other factors.
3. As a cost of achieving a given objective: this is a very logical approach, at least to fix minimum and maximum limits, despite the difficulties of setting obejctives and measuring their attainment.

Note: the size of the budget will, in practice, very largely determine the selection of the media.

Setting the advertising budget is one of the most difficult decisions in marketing, since the amount of advertising impacts sales while its cost affects profitability.

Advertising campaign Werbekampagne

A coordinated advertising or publicity drive to promote and sell a product or service.

A series of advertisements with a common selling theme.

Advertising carryover Langzeitwirkung der Werbung

The situation where the ad impact can be seen a longer period after the release of the ad message or the end of an ad campaign.

Advertising claim Werbebehauptung

A statement made in advertising about the benefits, characteristics, and/or performance of a product or service designed to persuade the customer to buy the product or service.

Advertising contract Anzeigenvertrag, Werbevertrag

An agreement between a seller of advertising time and space and an advertiser.

An agreement between a retailer and a supplier of goods, eg a producer, stipulating that the retailer will advertise the goods for a consideration.

Advertising control Überprüfung der Werbung

Legislative measures, statutory regulations and self-regulations applied to prevent abuses in advertising.

Advertising copy Anzeigen-, Werbetext

The text of an advertisement.

Advertising costs Anzeigenkosten, Werbekosten

The costs incurred for advertising.

Advertising Council of America | Organisation zur Förderung von Werbung für Angelegenheiten des öffentlichen Interesses (USA)

In the USA, a private and nonprofit organization of advertisers, advertising media and advertising agencies that develops and runs social advertising campaigns such as "Keep America Beautiful", "Go to College", or "Say No to Drugs".

Advertising customer | Anzeigenkunde, Werbekunde

Also called advertiser.

The person or firm placing an advertisement.

Advertising decision process | Werbeentscheidungsprozeß

Ad decision making is a process consisting of five steps: 1. ad objectives setting, 2. budget decision, 3. message decision, 4. media decision, 5. ad effectiveness evaluation.

Advertising department | Werbeabteilung, Anzeigenabteilung

A company`s department which is responsible for a number of advertising and promotional activities such as: press, outdoor, TV, radio, cinema, trade, institutional, etc advertising. Furthermore, it may create, print and despatch direct mail; provide point-of-sale (POS) material; support sales promotions and merchandising; furnish showrooms and display centres; arrange window dressings; organise sales conferences; sponsor special events, eg sport events or pop concerts; run contests; show films; book exhibitions and fairs; arrange demonstrations, etc.

The department of a newspaper or magazine responsible for advertising; often divided into display and classified advertising. Also called advertisement office.

Advertising effectiveness | Werbeerfolg

Also called advertising efficiency.

The degree to which the aims of advertising have been achieved; usually measured by increases or decreases in sales, brand awareness, brand preference, consumer enquiries stimulated by the ad, consumer opinions on the ad, etc.

There is a wide variety of approaches to evaluation, including enquiry tests, recall tests, and market tests.

Advertising elasticity Werbeelastizität

It measures the responsiveness of the sales (sales revenues) of a particular good or service to a change in its advertising expenditure. The formula is:

$$\text{advertising elasticity} = \frac{\text{percentage change in sales}}{\text{percentage change in advertising expenditures}}$$

Advertising evaluation Werbungsevaluierung, Beurteilung/ Bewertung der Werbung

The evaluation of both the communication effects (called copy testing) and the sales effects of advertising.

The communication effect can be measured either before or after an ad is printed or broadcast, and it reveals whether or not an ad is communicating well.

As sales are affected by many factors besides advertising, eg product features, price, availability etc, it is often difficult to measure the sales effect. One way of measuring it is to compare past sales with past advertising expenditures.

Advertising expenditure Werbeaufwand, Werbekosten

Also called advertising expense.

The amount of money spent on advertising a product on television, in newspapers and journals, on radio, by posters, billboards, etc.

Advertising exposure Werbemittelkontakt

The presentation of advertisements to an audience, eg readers, listeners or viewers.

Advertising functions Werbeaufgaben

There are several major functions of advertising:

1. to make the complete sale of the product by having such an impact that the consumer will purchase the product without any additional stimulus (this is often the case with lower priced consumer goods);
2. to assist in the sale of the product with the major impetus for the sale being the display of the product, point of sale (POS) materials, and the salesperson;
3. to obtain requests for further information;
4. to reinforce the purchase decision of the consumer.

It is the aim of advertising to affect sales positively by producing a positive company and brand image.

Advertising hoarding Werbeanschlagfläche

A billboard or other surface onto which advertising posters are stuck.

Advertising lineage/linage Umfang des Anzeigenteils einer Publikation

The number of lines of advertising carried in a publication in a given issue.

The volume of advertising columns in a publication in a given issue.

Advertising location Werbestandort (Außenwerbung)
Anzeigenposition (Druckmedien)

In outdoor advertising, the place where an advertisement is shown.

In print media, the position of an advertisement, eg an island/solus position in a newspaper or magazine.

Advertising manager Werbeleiter
Werbeleiter bei einem Werbeträger

A manager in charge of advertising a company's products or services. He/she reviews and approves advertising plans and is responsible for the execution of advertisements. He/she also manages the advertising department. Also called ad director, marketing services manager or sales promotion manager.

His/her main responsibilities are:
1. to cooperate with the production and marketing manager,
2. to determine the advertising budget,
3. to control ad expenditure,
4. to cooperate with the ad agency,
5. to control all advertising activities and materials,
6. to assess the results of advertising, etc.

An advertisement manager.

Advertising medium Werbeträger, Werbemittel

Also called advertising vehicle.

The forms of media used to carry advertisements. The choice of media depends upon the product and the audience the ad is aimed at. The media include radio, television, newspapers, journals, posters, hoardings, etc.
Note: the plural is media.

Advertising message Werbebotschaft, Werbeaussage

The message a company is trying to communicate in an advertisement. Creative ad messages can be more important to advertising success than can the amount of money spent. Advertising can only be successful if commercials gain attention and communicate well. As consumers are bombarded with ads, good advertising messages are especially important in today`s costly and cluttered advertising environment.

To gain and hold attention, ad messages must be well planned, imaginative, entertaining, and rewarding to consumers.

Advertising mix Werbe(mittel)mix, Mischung der Werbemittel

The advertising mix is an element of the promotion mix which is an element of the marketing mix.
Elements of the ad mix are: 1. radio, 2. television, 3. newspapers, 4. magazines, 5. direct mail, 6. outdoor ad, 7. transit ad, 8. message, 9. ad budget, 10. cooperative ad., etc.

Advertising novelty Werbeartikel

Also called giveaway (article) or promotion article.

Cheap gift carrying advertising message, brand name or symbol. For tax purposes, it must not exceed a certain value.

Advertising objective Werbeziel, Zielsetzung der Werbung

Also called advertising end or advertising goal.

General advertising objectives are: to create, increase, or at least maintain, the sales of a product or service.

In detail, an advertising goal is a specific communication task to be accomplished with a specific target audience during a particular time period. Objectives can be stated in such terms as products to be sold, the amount of trial purchases, the amount of repeat purchases, audience members reached, the frequency with which audience members are reached, and percentages of the audience made aware of the advertising or the product.

Advertising objectives can be classified as to whether their aim is to: 1. inform, 2. persuade, 3. remind.

Possible advertising objectives are:
1. Information:
a. to inform potential/prospective customers of a new product or service;
b. to indicate new uses of an existing product;
c. to inform the market of a price change;
d. to explain how the product works;
e. to give information about desirable qualities of a product;
f. to provide technical information about the product;
g. to give information on special offers;
h. to promote the environmental aspects of the good; etc.

2. Persuasion:
a. to alter consumer behaviour;
b. to encourage consumers to increase the frequency of their purchases;
c. to create the belief among consumers that a brand is the leader in its field;
d. to stimulate impulse purchases;
e. to build (up) a brand preference;
f. to induce the customer to buy now;
g. to change the customer`s perception of product attributes;
h. to encourage customers to switch to your brand;
i. to stimulate enquiries; etc.

3. Reminder:
a. to remind customers of an existing product in order to maintain loyalty against competing products;
b. to remind consumers that the product may be needed in the near future;
c. to remind customers where to buy the product; etc.

In 1961, the American management consultant Russel H. Colley listed 52 possible advertising objectives in his well-known "DAGMAR" model (note: the acronym Dagmar is derived from the title of his book "Defining Advertising Goals for Measured Advertising Results").

Note: the more precise the objectives are the easier it is to estimate the value of an advertising campaign and to design an effective campaign.

Advertising office Anzeigenannahme

The office dealing with advertising orders placed by advertisers.

Advertising penetration Werbedurchdringung, Werbepenetration

The percentage of a target audience reached by an advertisement or ad campaign, ie the degree to which people in a target market have seen and thus remember a particular advertisement.

Advertising pillar Litfaßsäule, Plakatanschlagsäule

Also called advertising post, or poster pillar.

A post used as a billboard, today usually illuminated. It was invented by Ernst Litfaß in Berlin, Germany, in 1855.

Advertising planning Werbeplanung, Medienplanung

Also called media planning.

The steps taken in planning an advertising campaign.

Possible steps may include:
1. identifying the target market, 2. establishing the ad objectives, 3. setting the ad budget, 4. developing the ad strategies, 5. selecting the appropriate media,
6. evaluating the advertising effectiveness, etc.

Advertising point (Haupt)Werbeargument

The most important thing, argument, statement or position used in an advertising message.

Advertising pretest Werbungs-, Anzeigenpretest

The test of an advertisement prior to a full scale testing programme. Pretests differ by medium.

Print pretesting, for example, works as follows:
1. test ads are placed into magazines, 2. the magazines are then circulated to consumers, 3. later the consumers are contacted and interviewed concerning the magazines and their ads.

Alternatively, recall and recognition tests can be used to determine advertising effectiveness.

Possible broadcast pretests are:
1. in-home tests (representative target consumers watch the commercials);
2. trailer tests (shoppers are shown test products and a series of commercials in a shopping center; then they receive coupons which they can redeem in the shopping center; by evaluating redemption, advertisers can estimate the commercial`s influence on purchase behaviour);
3. theater tests (consumers view a new film along with commercials; before and after the film respondents are interviewed on the varoius brands shown and resulting preference changes indicate the power of commercials);
4. on-air tests (respondents watch a TV programme during which the test commercial will be viewed; after the commercial is aired, respondents are interviewed about their commercial recall).

Advertising promotion Werbeförderung

The promotional activities made by the media to sell, increase sales, or improve the quality of advertising.

Advertising pros and cons Für und Wider von Werbung

Possible arguments in favour of advertising are:

1. it provides useful information about goods and services, 2. it helps customers to get the best bargains, 3. it stimulates competition, 4. it may lower the prices for goods and services, 5. it improves the quality of goods and services, 6. advertised goods create a freedom of consumer choice, 7. without advertising it would almost be impossible to launch new products, 8. it improves the living standard by making new developments quickly available to the public, 9. by stimulating demand, it creates investment, production and employment opportunities, 10. it pays for TV and radio programmes, and for magazines and newspapers, 11. it increases or at least maintains sales, 12. it leads to higher profits, etc.

Arguments against advertising may be:

1. it makes people buy things they do not really need, 2. it makes people buy things they cannot afford, 3. it is very expensive, 4. it may lead to higher prices, 5. it leads to non-price competition, 6. it is an unreliable guide as to value, quality and satisfaction, 7. the mass media are too powerful and control what people read, hear and watch, 8. people are brain-washed by ads, 9. ads may mislead the public, 10. advertising disregards ethics, 11. it interrupts programmes, 12. it leads to oligopoly and monopoly, 13. it is a waste of natural resources, etc.

Advertising quadrangle Werbeviereck

In advertising research, the idea that advertising communication consists of four elements:

1. the sender, ie the advertiser; 2. the advertising message; 3. the receiver, ie the audience; 4. the advertising medium/vehicle.

Advertising rate Werbetarif, Anzeigentarif

Also called adrate or advertisement rate.

The ad charges made by media owners for advertising space or advertising time.

Advertising reach Anzeigen-, Werbereichweite

The number of individuals or households being reached by an ad message.

Advertising regulations werberechtliche Vorschriften

Rules and conditions imposed upon advertising by media owners, trade associations, or government.

Advertising representative Anzeigenvertreter, Anzeigenagentur

A person or agency that sells advertising space for the print media.

Advertising research Werbeforschung

The analysis of a product or service to discover its marketable features.

The investigation of a market to evaluate a product´s buying potential.

The evaluation of the efficiency of an advertisement or of an ad campaign with regard to the ad objectives (e.g. to inform, to persuade, to remind) it is set to achieve.

The measurement of an advertisement´s actual success after it was used.

Advertising response Werbereaktion, Publikumsreaktion(en) auf Werbung

Also called response to advertising.

The reaction(s) to an individual advertisement or advertising campaign.

Advertising response function Werbereaktionsfunktion

The situation in which spending for advertising and sales promotion increases sales or the market share up to a certain level before diminishing returns set in. That is, sales or market share begins to decrease no matter how much is spent on advertising and sales promotion.

Advertising schedule Werbeplan
Insertionsplan, Anzeigenschaltplan

A detailed programme of planned advertising, showing the exact costs, timing, media selected, etc.

A detailed plan showing the timing of advertisement insertions.

Advertising section Anzeigenteil einer Zeitung/Zeitschrift

Also called adcolumns, advertisement or advertising columns.

In a newspaper or magazine, the columns or sections where advertisements are published.

Advertising slogan Werbeslogan

Also called adslogan.

Catchwords or phrases used in association with brand advertisements.

Advertising space Anzeigenraum

The part or pages available for advertising purposes in a publication.

The portion of outdoor or transit display areas that may be purchased for advertising.

Advertising space buyer — Inserent, Anzeigenkunde
Anzeigenexpediteur

An advertiser.

An individual or ad agency, responsible for timely and economical purchasing of media space. Also called space buyer.

Advertising specialty — Werbeartikel, Werbegeschenk

Also called advertising novelty, giveaway (article), promotion article or specialty.

Cheap, but often useful gift given to customers and imprinted with an advertising message, eg the advertiser`s name or the brand name, etc. Typical examples are ball pens, key rings, scribble pads, pens, calendars, matches, shopping bags, T-shirts, caps, coffee mugs, etc.

Such articles can be very effective because surveys have shown that the majority of all consumers could recall the advertiser`s name or message.

Advertising spending — Werbeausgaben

Also called advertising expenditure, ad expenses or ad outlay.

The amount of money actually spent on advertising. Advertising expenditures in relation to total marketing costs (ie the costs of physical distribution and promotion) vary very widely. For example, during the Olympic Games in Atlanta, USA, in 1996, advertisers had to pay US $ 500,000 for a 30-second TV commercial.

Advertising Standards Authority (ASA) — Werberat, Selbstkontrollorgan der Werbewirtschaft (GB)

An independent body set up to monitor the advertising industry and to ensure that its voluntary advertising codes work in the public interest.

Advertising strategy — Werbestrategie

An advertiser´s strategy indicating: 1. the competitive frame, 2. the target market, 3. the ad message to be used in an ad campaign for a specific product or service.

Advertising substantiation — Substantiierung des Werbeinhalts

The documentation by means of tests or other evidence of product performance claims made in advertising, e.g. to avoid deceptive advertising and to protect consumers.

Advertising supplement Werbebeilage

Also called stuffer.

An advertising item enclosed in an envelope, newspaper, magazine, free sheet, etc.

Advertising test Werbetest

Measuring the effectiveness of an advertisement or an advertising campaign.

Advertising theme Tenor der Anzeige/Werbung, Werbethema

Also called copy theme or platform

The main message in an advertisement.

Advertising threshold Werbeschwelle

The point at which a consumer is likely to become aware or conscious of an advertisement message so that he/she will respond to it.

Advertising time Werbe(sende)zeit

Also called air time.

The time on TV or radio set aside for advertising.

Advertising types Werbearten

There are a number of distinct and particular types of advertising, some of which call for different media.

Examples are:
1. accessory ad, 2. advocacy ad, 3. analogy ad, 4. announcement ad, 5. anticyclical ad, 6. appetizing ad, 7. arena ad, 8. bellwether ad, 9. buckeye, 10. buried ad, 11. burst ad, 12. camouflaged ad, 13. cinema ad, 14. classified ad, 15. comparative ad, 16. competitive ad, 17. cooperative ad, 18. customised ad, 19. deceptive ad, 20. dishonest ad, 21. display ad, 22 emotional ad, 23. extension ad, 24. exterior ad, 25 facetious ad, 26. false ad, 27. familiarity ad, 28 financial ad, 29. flighting , 30. foreign ad, 31. fraudulent ad, 32. generic ad, 33. global ad, 34. government ad, 35. group ad, 36. harmful ad, 37. hype, 38. identification commercial, 38. illuminated ad, 40. image ad, 41 indirect ad, 42 indoor ad, 43. industrial ad, 44. infomercial, 45. informative ad, 46. inside panel, 47. inside transit ad, 48. institutional ad, 49. integrated commercial,

50. intensive coverage, 51. knocking ad, 52. lifestyle ad, 53. line ad, 54. litter bin ad, 55. local ad, 56. low-budget ad, 57. maintenance ad,
58. misleading ad, 59. mood ad, 60. multimedia ad, 61. multiunit ad, 62. national ad, 63. negative ad, 64. newspaper ad, 65. on-pack promotion, 66. outdoor ad, 67. package ad, 68. personality ad, 69. persuasive ad, 70. piggyback commercial, 71. pioneer(ing) ad, 72. pre-selling ad, 73. prestige ad, 74. primary demand ad, 75. producer ad,
76. product ad, 77. public service ad. 78. pulsing promotion, 79. railroad showing,
80. repeat ad, 81. rear, 82. reason why ad, 83. recruitment ad, 84. reinforcement ad,
85. reminder ad, 86. retail ad, 87. rosy ad, 88. sale ad, 89. saturation ad, 90. screen ad.
91. seasonal ad, 92. selective ad, 93. sky ad, 94. slice-of-life ad, 95. soft ad,
96. specialty ad, 97. spectacular, 98. split run ad, 99. spot ad, 100. station poster,
101. subliminal ad, 102. sustaining ad, 103. tasteless ad, 104. teaser ad,
105. testimonial ad, 106. theater ad, 107. tie-in ad, 108. trade ad, 109. transit ad,
110. unfair ad, 111. unscrupulous ad, 112. utility ad, 113. vertical cooperative ad,
114. want-creating ad, 115. Yellow pages ad, etc.

Advertising wearout — Nachlassen, Verfall der Werbewirkung

A situation where an advertisement or advertising campaign is no longer effective. Some ads or campaigns wear out in a relatively short time, while others last for years.

Advertising-audience combination — Kombination von Hörern, Lesern, Zuschauern

The composition of an ad audience with regard to listeners, readers and viewers.

Advertising-to-sales ratio (A/S ratio) — Verhältnis von Werbeaufwand zu Verkäufen/Absatz/Umsatz

A marketing control figure expressing total advertising expenditure as a percentage of total sales revenue. This figure is used to determine whether the amount spent on advertising in a given period was excessive or whether the ad budget was appropriate.

Using the A/S ratio, the advertiser sets the new ad budget as a percentage of either last year`s sales (known as retrospective A/S ratio) or an estimate of next year`s (known as forecast A/S ratio). Note: the retrospective A/S ratio has a serious disadvantage because it can lead into a downward spiral: sales fall, next year`s ad budget is cut, sales therefore may fall further and the ad budget is then cut again, and so on.

Note: advertisers of fast-moving consumer goods (FMCGs) generally spend 10% of sales on advertising, advertisers of consumer durable goods spend about 5% and business-to-business (BTB) advertisers and retailers spend approx. 1% of sales on advertising.

Advertorial redaktionell aufgemachte Anzeige

An advertisement in a magazine or newspaper printed in such a way that it looks like an editorial or article. Advertorial is a combination of advertisement and editorial.

Advice note (AN) Versandanzeige, Versandavis

Also called advice, delivery note, despatch note, shipping note, forwarding advice, letter of advice, or advice of despatch.

A document informing a customer that his goods are on the way. It usually gives the date of despatch and the method of transport, and gives details of the goods, but not their price. The customer uses it in the same way as a delivery note to check the goods when they arrive.

Advice of arrival Eingangsanzeige, Ankunftsanzeige

Notification from the carrier to the consignee informing him that a consignment addressed to him is being held at his disposal at a specified point in the place of destination.

Advocacy advertising engagierte Werbung

Also called advocacy advertisement or issue-oriented advertising.

Advertising sponsored by any type of advertiser (eg businesses, consumer or interest groups, political parties) and used to present information or a point of view on a controversial public issue, idea or cause, such as the environment, taxes, education, etc.

Advertising by a company to express a particular point of view on a certain major issue, eg a food producer may condemn unhealthy additives in foodstuffs.

Aerial advertising Luft-, Himmelswerbung

Advertising message in the air usually carried over towns, eg the banners behind an aircraft, a slogan on a hot-air balloon or on an airship, a symbol on a helicopter, or ads written in white or coloured smoke against a blue sky by a skywriting aircraft.

Affinity marketing | Marketing, das auf ähnliche Beziehungen zwischen Anbieter und Konsument aufbaut

A marketing campaign jointly sponsored by a number of differing non-competing companies who have a particular interest or event in common, e.g. the Olympic Games.

Affluent charges | Umweltabgaben

Fees charged for the disposal of waste materials polluting the environment.

Affluent society | Wohlstandsgesellschaft

A society characterized by continuous prosperity, abundance of material goods, surplus, wealth, etc.

Affordable method | Festsetzung des Werbeetats nach dem Gesichtspunkt, welche Ausgaben man sich nach Festlegung aller anderen Budgetposten leisten kann, All-we-can-afford Methode

Also called all-we-can-afford method.

One of four common methods used to determine the total budget for advertising; the other three being the percentage-of-sales method, the competitive-parity method, and the objective-and-task method.

Many companies set their promotion budget at the level management thinks the company can afford, rather than with reference to the task the company has to achieve. Thus, the advertising budget is unrelated to calculation and the amount allocated is the amount that can be afforded. This method completely ignores the effect of promotion on the sales volume and often results in underspending on advertising (occassionally it may also result in overspending).

After-sales service | Kundendienst

Also called customer service or post-sales service.

That part of a business's activities devoted to the customer after the sale of goods. This may include provision of replacement parts, repairs, technical assistance, etc. Good after-sales service is an essential component of modern marketing methods.

Aftermarket/after market Folgemarkt, Anschlußmarkt

After the sale of a product or service, all those efforts which help to consolidate the sale, satisfy the customer, encourage recommendations and, if possible, secure regular or repeat sales.

The market for repairs, replacements, upgradings and other needs of equipment buyers.

Afternoon drive Stoßverkehrszeit am Nachmittag

Also called PM drive time.

In radio broadcasting, together with morning drive time (6.00 a.m. to 10.00 a.m) radio`s prime time. It is the time segment from 3.00 p.m to 7.00 p.m. Monday through Friday.

Age and life cycle segmentation Segmentierung nach Alter- und Lebenszyklus

The breakdown of a market into different age and life cycle groups. As consumer needs and wants change with age, some companies offer different products or use different marketing approaches for different age and life cycle segments.

But note: marketers should guard against age stereotypes because age is often a poor predictor of a person`s life cycle, health, work or family status, needs, buying power etc.

Age and life cycle stage Alters- und Lebenszyklusstadium

One of the many personal factors affecting consumer behaviour; the others being, eg economic situation, lifestyle, occupation, personality, self-concept, taste, etc.

As buyers` decisions are influenced by age and life cycle, people change the goods and services they buy over their lifetimes. For example, consumers` tastes in food, clothes, furniture etc is age related. Furthermore, buying is also shaped by life cycle stages, ie the stages through which people pass as they mature over time, eg young, middle aged or older.

Age group Altersklasse

The social group to which people of different age belong. Many products appeal more to people in one age group than another. People in different age groups, eg teenagers, people in their twenties or post-forties, have different needs and wants, as well as different opportunities to buy.

Agency (agcy, agy) Agentur

A business and the place of business of an agent.

Agency agreement Vertretungsvertrag

A contract between a company and an agency stating all the conditions (eg commission, credit terms, etc) the company grants the agency upon appointment.

An agreement between customer and advertising agency.

Agency commission Agenturprovision

Also called agency remuneration.

A commission ranging from 10% to 15% received by agencies from media owners on time or space booked.

Agency of record (AOR) federführende Agentur

An advertising agency, chosen by a client, served by two or more agencies, to buy media time and space.

Agency personnel Personal einer Werbeagentur

Also called agency staff.

The people working for an advertising agency, eg the account executive, the account director/manager, the marketing manager, the market research manager, the media planner, the media/space buyer, the copywriter, the copy chief, the creative director, the visualiser, the layout artist, the typographer, the finished artist (the person who draws or paints the final artwork), the scraper board artist (a specialist at producing a drawing, often based on a photograph), the production assistants, the production manager, the traffic manager, the finance director, etc.

Agency-produced program Agentursendung

A television or radio program produced by an ad agency and not by a radio or TV station or an independent production company. The program is sold to a station or network ready for presentation.

Agent (agt) Agent, Bevollmächtigter, Vertreter, Beauftragter, Makler, Kommissionär

A person or firm authorized expressly or impliedly to transact business for another, called the principal. Contracts and arrangements are binding on the principal, provided that they are made in the course of the principal's business and fall within the terms of the authority granted to the agent. His reward usually takes the form of a commission.

Types, for example, are:

1. Sole agent: is the only person or firm entitled to sell a particular product in a particular area.
2. General agent: has the general authority in all matters of a particular trade or business.
   Special/particular agent: is employed to act only in a particular transaction.
3. Universal agent: one with unrestricted authority.
4. Del credere agent: he guarantees payment for any business he arranges. For his work he receives a higher rate of commission.
5. Commission agent: he buys and sells for a principal. He buys and sells in his own name, receiving a commission for the contracts he has arranged.
6. Export and import agent.

Duties to the principal are, e.g.:

1. observe the agreement,
2. follow the principal's instruction (when not illegal),
3. always act in the interest of the principal,
4. not in any way compete with the principal,
5. account properly to the principal etc.

Agent middleman Handelsmakler

Also called agent intermediary

A person that helps a company to find customers, negotiates contracts and closes sales with them but does not take title to (does not own) the goods he exchanges. He only provides services to the buyer or seller in exchange for which he receives a commission.

A common type of agent middleman is the broker.

Agent's commission Vertreterprovision

Also called agency fee.

Money, usually a percentage of sales, paid to an agent by his company.

Aggregate demand (AD) — Gesamtnachfrage, aggregierter Bedarf

Also called composite, market, overall or total demand.

The total demand for goods and services in the economy. Several factors affect total demand: the size of the population; the average age of the population; the structure of the population and the distribution of income within the population.

Aggregate demand curve — Gesamtnachfragekurve

A curve showing how aggregate demand increases when the price level of all goods and services falls.

Aggregate monetary demand (AMD) — monetäre Gesamtnachfrage, Gesamtgeldbedarf

The total demand for the entrepreneurs' goods (Keynes).

The public spends all that they receive, so that the total monetary demand for goods and services is the same as the earnings. The entrepreneurs are therefore receiving back all they paid out.

Aggregate production (AP) — Gesamtproduktion

The total market value of goods and services produced.

Aggregate savings — volkswirtschaftliche Ersparnisse

The difference between total disposable income and total consumer expenditure in the economy.

Aggregate supply (AS) — Gesamtangebot, aggregiertes Angebot

Also called overall or total supply.

The total supply of goods and services in the economy to meet aggregate demand. It consists of domestically produced goods and services plus imports.

Aggregate supply curve Gesamtangebotskurve

1. In the short run: a curve showing how aggregate supply increases in the short run when prices go up but factor costs do not change.

2. In the long run: a vertical curve showing (when costs have adjusted to price changes) that aggregate supply equals the full-employment level of output, no matter what the price level is.

Aggregated rebate Treuerabatt

Also called loyalty discount, loyalty rebate, or fidelity rebate.

A rebate given to a customer who remains loyal to the producer.

Aggressive pricing aggressive Preispolitik

A pricing strategy which tries to undercut the prices of competitors in order to increase one`s market share.

Aging/ageing population alternde Bevölkerung

A population in which the average age is rising and the proportion of people over 60 - 65 is increasing. This may be caused by a falling birth-rate or a falling death-rate.

Agony column Seufzerspalte, persönliche Anzeige

The advertising columns in a newspaper or magazine where individuals advertise for personal reasons. Examples are personal desires or sorrows, lost items, etc.

Agricultural cooperative Agrargenossenschaft, landwirtschaftliche Genossenschaft

An organisation formed by farmers to achieve some or many of the advantages of large-scale marketing.

Agricultural show Landwirtschaftsausstellung

An indoor or outdoor exhibition showing farm equipment, supplies and services.

Agricultural subsidies Agrarsubventionen

Assistance payments by the government to farmers to raise their incomes while at the same time maintaining reasonable prices for farm (agricultural) products.

Agroindustry Agroindustrie

Agricultural activities on an industrial scale.

AIDA-model AIDA-Modell

The initials stand for: attention, interest, desire and action.

Advertisements and mailing shots should always follow the AIDA format. The rule means that the successful salesman needs to arouse the attention of the customer, make him personally interested in the offer, and increase his desire to buy the product, in order to stimulate him to the action of buying.

AIDAS model AIDAS-Modell

AIDAS is an acronym for attention, interest, desire, action, and satisfaction. The model is used in selling to produce a favourable response from a customer.

AIDCA model AIDCA-Modell

AIDCA is an acronym for awareness, interest, desire, conviction and action. The model is used in selling and shows an individual`s mental states which supposedly lead a potential customer to a buying decision.

AIDCAS model AIDCAS-Modell

The acronym for attention, interest, desire, conviction, action, satisfaction. An advancement of the AIDA model meaning that the successful salesperson has to:

1. arouse the attention of the customer, 2. interest him/her in the offer, 3. increase the desire to purchase the product, 4. convince the potential buyer of the product`s benefit, 5. stimulate the customer to the action of buying, 6. achieve the customer`s state of satisfaction.

Aide-memoire Fragebogen

Also called questionnaire.

In marketing, a questionnaire generally used when the questions to be asked are broad and fairly general.

Aided recall gestützte Erinnerung

A test to see how well someone remembers an advertisement by giving the respondent/interviewee some help.

Aids to trade Hilfsfunktionen des Handels

Also called ancillaries to trade.

Services which support trade, such as banking, insurance, advertising, etc.

AIO statements AIO-Aussagen

An individual`s statements concerning his/her attitudes towards, interests in, and opinions of, a product or service.

Air carrier Luftverkehrsgesellschaft
Luftfrachtführer

A company furnishing air transport, usually scheduled, between specified points. Also called airline.

An individual or company engaged in transporting goods for profit by air. Although air carriers are more expensive, their cost may be offset by quicker delivery times. Also called air freight forwarder.

Air transport Lufttransport

Transportation of goods and passengers by air.

Air transport is quick, suitable for perishable foods, lighter goods, flowers, etc and may cut costs on inland transportation and warehousing. On the other hand, air transport is very expensive and unsuitable for bulky or heavy goods. Furthermore, the goods have to be taken to the airport.

Airdate/air date Sendetermin, Sendezeit(punkt) (Radio, TV)

The date on which a radio or television commercial or programme will be broadcast (on the air).

The date of the first transmission of a commercial (campaign) on TV or radio.

Airfreight/air freight Luftfracht (sowohl als Ware, als auch als Gebühr)

Freight transported by aircraft. Also called air cargo or air shipment.

The cost of transporting goods by air. Also called air freight charges.

The transport of goods by air.

Airmail Luftpost

A (postal) system of sending mail by airplane.

Airtel Flughafenhotel

The colloquial short form for airport hotel.

Airtime/air time Sendezeit

The amount of time allocated to an advertisement (ad) on TV or radio.

The time of transmission of an ad on TV or radio.

Airtime blocked to advertisers für Werbung gesperrte Sendezeit

Radio or TV airtime which is not portioned to advertisers, and thus is blocked to them, e.g. newscasts.

Airtime buyer Sendezeitkäufer

A broadcast advertiser who buys airtime/air time to broadcast commercials on radio or TV.

Aisle Gang

The passageway between the shelves of products in a storeroom, a supermarket, etc.

Aisle arch Verkaufsreihenbogen

Display above the aisles of a retail store, supermarket or shopping center.

All news reiner Nachrichtensender

A radio or TV station that specialises in news reports.
Other specialisations may be: all talk, all classical, all country and western, all rock, etc.

All-in price Inklusivpreis, Gesamtpreis, Preis einschließlich aller Kosten

Also called all-in-rate or all-round price.

A price which covers everything in a purchase, i.e. it includes all extras which are in addition to the basic price, ie the product bought, packing, delivery charge, insurance, shipment, tax etc.

Allocation Zuteilung
Warenzuteilung
Frequenzzuweisung

The allotment of limited amounts of an item or items to purchasers, e.g. the allotment of shares.

The quantity of merchandise to be made available to a particular customer or market.

The range of wavelengths assigned to a radio or television station (i.e. a broadcaster).

Allocative efficiency Allokationseffizienz

The production of goods and services in that combination that maximizes the total satisfaction of consumers.

Allotment Zahl der Anschlagtafeln, die Anschlagwerbeunternehmen einem Werbetreibenden anbietet
Zuteilen von Anzeigenraum/Sendezeit bei Nachfrageüberhang

The number of poster panels offered to an advertiser by an outdoor advertising company.

The distribution of ad space or time for which there is an excess demand.

Allowance Rabatt, Preisnachlaß

Also called discount, deduction, or reduction.

A deduction from the price charged.

Alternate demand Ausweichnachfrage, konkurrierende Nachfrage

Also called alternative demand, competing demand, composite demand, or rival demand.

A situation in which two products are substitutes for each other, so that a movement in the price of one will affect the demand (and supply and price) of the other.

Alternate weeks (A/W, a/w) Werbung jede zweite Woche

An agreement between a radio or TV station, or a publication to run an advertisement or commercial for one week, skip a week, and then run it again for a week.

Alternative advertising media alternative Werbemedien

Advertising media different from the traditional media. Apart from the well-known ad media there is a growing number of alternative media. Examples are: video screens attached to shopping trolleys, TV screens at the checkouts, in-store video screens, signs atop parking meters, back seats of taxis, public elevators and escalators, restrooms, posters on litter bins, logos on contact lenses (first used by the German firm PUMA in 1996); logos on finger rings, necklaces, bracelets, watches, shirt collars, sunglasses and manifold forms of outdoor advertising providing an excellent way to reach important local consumer segments and thereby hitting selected consumers where they live, shop, work and play.

Alternative closing Alternativ-Verkaufsabschluß
Ja/Nein-Angebot

Also called alternative close.

When seeking an order, a closing technique in which a salesperson presents the potential buyer two alternatives to purchase in an attempt to obtain a commitment from the buyer to one (eg "the blue or the green"). That means each alternative involves a "yes", so avoiding a "no" to any alternatives offered.

Alternative cost(s) Alternativkosten,
Opportunitätskosten

Also called opportunity cost(s), real cost or use cost.

The cost of a commodity not in money but in terms of the alternative forgone. Alternative cost can only arise in a world where the resources available to meet wants are limited so that all wants cannot be satisfied. Clearly, in a real world of scarcity alternative cost is positive. It is different alternative costs ratios that give individuals a comparative advantage in one trade or another.

Alternative evaluation Alternativbewertung

In the buyer-decision process, the consumer`s evaluation processes enabling him to choose among alternative brands. Certainly, no simple and single evaluation process is used by consumers in their buying situations; instead, several evaluation processes are at work. For example, consumers will see a bundle of product attributes to which they will attach different degrees of importance. Furthermore, they will consider the product`s brand image and its utility.
But note: how consumers go about evaluating purchase alternatives depends on the individual consumer and the specific buying situation.

Amalgamation Unternehmenszusammenschluß,
Fusion(ierung)

Also called combination or merger. Similar terms include: acquisition, consolidation, and takeover.

There are various types of amalgamation:
1. Merger:
Two or more business units agree to merge/amalgamate into a permanent single undertaking. One of the merged firms continues in existence while the other loses its separate identity and is incorporated in the first.
2. Takeover:
One firm, without necessarily having the consent of the other firm, acquires sufficient shares to have a controlling interest. Also called absorption.

3. Acquisition:
One of the firms loses its identity and has been purchased by the firm that continues in existence.
4. Consolidation:
A completely new firm is created from the merged firms.

Ambiguous question zwei-, mehrdeutige Frage

A question, e.g. in a questionnaire, which is vague or misleading and which does not make it clear what information is required, and which can therefore be answered in many different ways.

Ambush marketing Windschattenmarketing

Linking a marketing campaign to a specific event, eg a pop concert or a sports event, which is sponsored by another company without paying a fee.

American Advertising Federation (AAF) Amerikanischer Werbefachverband

In the USA, an association of advertisers, ad agencies, media owners and others dealing with advertising. It promotes understanding of advertising´s value and supports higher professional standards.

American Marketing Association (AMA) Amerikanischer Marketingverband

In the USA, a professional organization, founded in 1937, for persons engaged in the practice and teaching of marketing. The members are committed to ethical professional conduct.

They must, for example: 1. not knowingly do harm; 2. adhere to all applicable laws and regulations; 3. be honest in serving consumers, clients, suppliers, and the public; 4. ensure that communications about offered products and services are not deceptive; 5. disclose all substantial risks associated with product or service usage; 6. avoid misleading or false advertising; 7. not manipulate the availability of a product for purpose of exploitation; 8. not engage in price fixing, etc.

American Selling Price (ASP) amerikanischer Verkaufspreis (US-Zollbewertung nach dem inländischen Verkaufspreis; nicht nach Incoterms)

The value on which the U.S. customs charges import duty on a product. This is the price charged by U.S. producers for similar goods, not the actual cost of the product to an importer.

Analogy advertising Analogiewerbung

A form of advertising where the advertised product is explained by drawing a comparison to another product.

Anchor store Absatzmagnet, Spezialshop als Anziehungspunkt

Also called anchor tenant.

A popular, major retailer located within a shopping mall or shopping center to attract customers, ie to draw traffic to the whole area.

Anchorman Anchorman, Moderator, Studioredakteur

A person who anchors/acts/serves a radio or TV programme of news, sports, etc.

The female term is anchorlady or anchorwoman.

Animatic Probewerbesendung, Testwerbesendung

A rough draft of a commercial generally used for test purposes only and thus shown to the advertiser for approval or amendment.

Animator Animateur Trickfilmzeichner

A person employed to organise entertainments or other activities for guests, e.g. in a holiday resort.

An artist who draws animated cartoons.

Anniversary sale Jubiläumsverkauf

Special offers made by firms celebrating a jubilee.

Announcement Werbesendung, Werbespot

Also called commercial.

A brief message (typically 10 seconds) that advertises a product, service, or idea. It is broadcast by TV or radio between program(mes) to capture the attention of the audience of both program(me)s.

Announcement advertising Einführungswerbung

Also called initial or launch advertising.

A commercial to introduce (launch) a new product onto the market.

Announcement effect Ankündigungseffekt, Signalwirkung

Temporary changes in economic variables as a result of the announcement of some new information. For example, increased fluctuations in share (stock) prices as a result of the Central Bank's announcement that it will change the discount rate.

Announcer (ann., anner.) Ansager/in

A person who delivers messages to a radio or television audience.

Annual Jahrbuch

Periodical which is published once a year, usually in the form of a reference book.

Annual discount Jahresrabatt, Jahresbonus

An allowance granted to advertisers who advertised in the print media or broadcasted commercials on radio or TV during the whole year, usually at least once a week.

Annual volume discount (AVD) Umsatzbonus, Mengenrabatt auf Jahresbasis

A discount granted if the sales within a year exceed a certain quantity or value.

Anonymous product testing anonymer Warenprodukttest

A number of different basic products is presented to testees in a common anonymous form for evaluation.

Ansoff matrix Ansoff-Matrix, Produkt-Markt-Matrix

Also called product/market matrix.

The most widely used framework for classifying product/market expansion strategies adopted by a firm in relation to the two key dimensions:
1. what the company sells, i.e. its products; 2. who it sells its products to, i.e. its markets.

According to Ansoff, the four strategies that companies can follow to generate intensive growth are:
1. selling existing products to existing markets (market penetration strategy);
2. selling existing products to new markets (market extension or market development strategy);
3. developing new products for existing markets (product development strategy);
4. developing new products for new markets (diversification).

Answer print (AP) Original(werbe)film

A filmed TV commercial which is presented to a client for review and approval before a final print is made.

Answerphone Anrufbeantworter

Also called answering machine, telephone answering machine or telephone recorder.

A machine answering and recording incoming calls and inviting callers to leave a message which can be played back at any time.

Anthropology Anthropologie (Lehre vom Menschen)

The science that studies the origins, physical and cultural conditions, biological characteristics, and social customs and beliefs of humankind.

Anticipated change erwartete (Ver)Änderung

A change that is foreseen by decision-makers, allowing them time to adjust.

Anticipated economic upswing erwarteter (Konjunktur)Aufschwung

An expected increase in the level of economic activity and economic growth.

Anticipated inflation erwartete Inflation

An increase in the general price level that is expected by decision-makers; past experience and current conditions are the major determinants.

Anticipating rebate Vorauszahlungsrabatt

An extra discount granted for paying a debt in advance. If a customer pays a debt in advance, he may receive an extra discount from the supplier.

Anticipation zusätzlicher Nachlaß

An additional reduction.

Anticompetitive practice wettbewerbswidriges Verhalten

Activities which may restrict, distort or eliminate competition in a market.

Anticounterfeiting Coalition Markenherstellerverband zur Abwehr von Plagiatprodukten

A coalition of a number of international companies seriously concerned with and affected by brand piracy or product counterfeiting established to fight and restrict these activities.

Anticyclical advertising antizyklische Werbung

Advertising which tries to counteract the trade/business cycles, ie firms advertise more heavily during a slump/recession in order to stimulate business activity and sales and they advertise less during a boom.

Antidumping Antidumping

A situation when an overseas supplier (exporter) dumps goods through an overseas importer at less than their normal value. In this event, a dumping or penalty duty may be levied (imposed) by a government to correct the imbalance and bring the price of the goods back to their correct value. Alternatively, the overseas supplier may be asked to amend his invoices to the correct value.

Antidumping law Antidumping-Gesetz

The laws passed by a government to protect local industries from dumping.

Antitrust Law Anti-Trust-Gesetz, Kartellgesetz (USA)

A (US) law to control the growth of market power exercised by firms, to encourage competition, to suppress monopolistic abuses and restrictive practises operated by firms, trusts and cartels. First law of this kind was the Sherman Anti-Trust Act of 1890 which made price-fixing illegal.

In GB: Monopolies and Mergers Act; in Germany: Gesetz gegen Wettbewerbsbeschränkungen/Kartellgesetz, in Australia: the Trade Practices Legislation.

Apparent defect offener, offensichtlicher Mangel

Also called apparent damage.

A damage which is noticed when the cargo is unloaded, it must be reported immediately.

Appeal Anziehungskraft, Reiz

The power or ability to attract.

Being attractive.

Appetizing advertising appetitanregende Werbung

Advertising which has an appetizing appeal, ie advertising that creates a desire to satisfy any bodily need or craving, eg for food or drink.

Applause mail Zustimmungspost

Letters or postcards received by a radio or TV station and which are favourable toward a programme, person, or commercial.

Applied research angewandte Forschung

Research that focuses on an existing problem by using current available information and knowledge.

Appointed dealer Vertragshändler

A retailer specially appointed by a manufacturer to sell his product(s) in return for quality of service and promotion of sales. The number of such dealers in an area, country or town is usually limited to one or a few to avoid or restrict local competition.

Approach Herantreten, Herangehen(sweise) Betrachtungsweise: Art und Weise, ein Problem in Angriff zu nehmen

The stage in the selling process in which a salesperson contacts a prospective customer/buyer to make an appointment, to present a product and to attract his attention and curiosity. During the approach step, the salesperson should know how to meet and greet the potential buyer and to get the relationship off to a good start.

The method of dealing with a problem or subject.

Appropriation of goods Konkretisierung einer Ware

Also called ascertainment of goods.

An act of identifying goods with a contract (e.g. by marks and numbers).

The act of putting aside goods for a special reason.

Arbitrary mark Phantasiename, willkürlich gewählter Markenname

Also called coined word.

A coined brand name for a product, ie a name that is catchy and can easily be remembered but has no particular relation to the product itself.

Arbitrary method gewillkürte Werbeetatfestsetzung, über den Daumen gepeilte Festsetzung des Werbeetats

Also called arbitrary determination method.

A method used for establishing an advertising or promotion budget. The budget is determined in an arbitrary manner, ie the company executives rely on their intuition and past experience in establishing the budget. Costs are estimated as there are no objective figures. Although this is a very unsophisticated method, more firms use this method than any other. A benchmark frequently applied is 10 percent of last year`s sales.

Area allocation Aufteilung des Werbeetats auf Werbegebiete

Also called area-by-area allocation (ABA) or market-by-market allocation.

The allocation of the ad budget according to different market segments.

Area manager Bezirks-, Gebietsleiter

A manager who is responsible for a particular area.

Area of dominant influence (ADI) Hauptsendegebiet

In television broadcasting, the geographic area dominated by a particular TV station.

Area sample Flächenstichprobe

The number of people or firms situated in any particular geographical area who are part of a research study.

Arena advertising Arena-Werbung

Advertising by posters placed around a sports stadium, e.g. a football stadium, or other such place in order to gain publicity from the spectators, but more importantly from the viewers of a TV broadcast.

Arrival notification form (ANF) (Fracht)Eingangsbenachrichtigung Warenankunftsavis

Also called arrival note or notice.

Advice to the consignee by the consignor of goods coming forward.

Arithmetic mean arithmetisches Mittel

A measure of central tendency which is obtained by adding up all the items being considered and dividing by the number of items. Note: in ordinary speech the word "arithmetic" is often omitted or it is referred to as the "average" only.

Arithmetic(al) progression arithmetische Folge

Also called arithmetic sequence.

A series of numbers or algebraic terms in which each element bears an additive relationship to its predecessor and successor. The numbers are arranged in increasing or decreasing order, the difference between each number and the next being always equal (e.g. 3, 6, 9, 12, 15, the difference being 3).

Armchair shopping/buying Katalog-, Bildschirmverkauf

Shopping without shops, i.e. buying from catalogues, direct mail shots, press advertisements, etc by using the post, telephone or fax, or via internet. This form of non-store retailing is becoming increasingly attractive as customers obtain realistic product presentations and can pay by the use of credit cards or charge cards.

Art director (AD) Art-Direktor, Chef-Layouter

An individual translating the ideas of copywriters into dramatic visuals called layouts. Thus, he is responsible for developing the general design and supervising the final artwork.

The person in charge of an art department.

Art sponsoring Kunstsponsoring

The use of sponsorship to support an artistic event, eg an opera or an art exhibition.

Article Artikel, Erzeugnis

A product or thing for sale.

Artificial obsolescence eingebauter Verschleiß, geplante Veralterung

A marketing practice which tries to cause dissatisfaction among consumers by deliberately trying to make old models seem out-of-date or obsolescent by launching new ones with changes and improvements which will attract the customers.

Arts sponsorship Kunst- und Kultursponsoring

Also called sponsorship of arts.

The sponsoring of the arts such as art shows, exhibitions, theatres, ballet, opera, symphony orchestras, pop groups, book prizes, etc by commercial organizations.

Artwork/art work Werbegraphik

In the short form also called art.

Any illustration such as a drawing, painting or photography used in the production of print advertising.

As from mit Wirkung vom/ab

Also called on and after or as of.

From a certain date onwards, e.g. from 3 May ...

As per laut, gemäß

According to, e.g. as per account, as per advice, as per agreement or as per order.

As seen wie besichtigt

Also called as is.

Goods offered for sale in the condition in which the buyer sees or has seen them. The seller makes no promise and bears therefore no liability concerning the condition of the goods.

Ascertained goods Speziessachen, konkretisierte Sachen

Also called specific goods.

Goods identified and effectively appropriated subsequent to the conlusion of a sales contract.

Asch phenomenon Asch-Phänomen

A behaviour pattern discovered by the American psychologist S.E. Asch, stating that an individual's purchase decisions are highly influenced by reference groups and group norms.

Note: the plural of phenomenon is phenomena.

Asked price Brief, Briefkurs, Angebotskurs

Also called ask price, asking price, ask, offering price, offered, offer price, price offered, rate asked, or sellers' rate.

The price at which a security or commodity is offered for sale on an exchange or in the over-the-counter (OTC) market.

Asking price geforderter Preis
Verhandlungsbasis (VB)

A price which the seller/vendor is hoping go get for his item being sold.

A commodity for sale at a particular price or near offer (ono).

Aspiration level Anspruchsniveau

This is the level consumers desire or expect to reach in class of product or service. Thus, they are often ambitious to own prestigious goods or brands.

Aspirational group soziale Zielgruppe

A group that an individual wishes to belong to sometime in the future.

Assembly shop Montagehalle

An area where complex machinery is put together from interchangeable parts of standard dimensions.

Assessment method Abschätzungsmethode (bei Werbeetatfestsetzung)

A method of dertmining an advertising budget based on a specific amount per item sold in the most recent budget period.

Assisted area geförderte Region

An area with particularly serious problems of unemployment and industrial decline. Industry in such areas receives government assistance to promote development and expansion.

Association (Assoc, assn) (Interessen)Verband

An organisation that protects the interests of its members but does not trade.

Association test Assoziationstest

A test used to discover the percentage of people who are able to identify brand names, logos, ad messages, etc.

Assorting Produktgruppierung, Sortimentsaufbau, Sortiments-, Warenzusammenstellung

The process of combining products into collections or assortments which buyers want to have available in one place, eg a department store.

Assortment display Sortimentsauslage

The display of all the goods a shop has for sale.

Assortment of goods (Waren)Sortiment

Also called assortment of merchandise or product range.

The variety of merchandise held by a manufacturer or a retail store to meet their customers' needs.

Assortment strategies Sortimentsstrategien

A reseller`s options available to determine his/her assortment/range of products and services he/she wants to carry. Assortments may be varied according to width (ie the number of different product categories which are represented in the assortment) and depth (ie the number of varieties, colours, or sizes represented in each category).

Asterisk law | Sternzeichen-Gesetz (USA) (vergleichbar mit Robinsonliste)

In the USA, a law which prohibits telemarketers to try selling to people who have indicated (by putting an asterisk against their names in the phone book) that they do not want to be approached by teleselling/telemarketing salespersons.

Asymptote | Asymptote

A line which continually approaches a given axis of a graph but which never quite meets it.

At a discount (AAD) | unter Pari/Nennwert Diskontpreis, mit Abschlag/ Skonto/Rabatt

Also called below par.

At a price lower than par value (face or nominal value) or lower than normal.

The sale of goods below the normal price. Also called at a discount price.

At best | bestens, billigst

Also called at market.

An instruction to a broker to obtain the best selling or buying price for a share, commodity, etc., without restricting him to a specific price.

Abbreviation for "at the lowest possible price", in the case of a buying order, and "at the highest possible price", in the case of a selling order. This instruction must be carried out at once, no matter what the current price.

At/in-home audience | Zuhause-Publikum; Publikum, das Zuhause ist

A term describing the people who read at home (at-/in-home readers), listen to the radio at home (at-/in-home listeners) or watch/view TV at home (at-/in-home viewers).

Atmosphere Atmosphäre

The designed environment that creates or reinforces the customer`s/client`s inclinations toward buying a product or service.

The effect that an advertising medium itself, through which the advertisement is presented, has on the audience.

Atmospherics Gestaltung des Firmenimages

Creating a particular image of a company through the design of the premises and products, the store decor, amenities provided, etc to attract customers.

Atomistic competition atomistische oder poly-politische Konkurrenz

A market structure in which many firms compete independently and which are unable to influence price and output perceptibly.

ATR-model ATR-Modell (Bewußtsein, Probe, Wiederkauf)

ATR = awareness - trial - repeat.

A model showing different effects of advertising on a consumer; 1. the consumer becomes aware of the product (awareness = A); 2. he buys it once to try it (trial = T); 3. he buys it again when he finds it satisfactory (repeat = R).

Attack strategy Angriffsstrategie, Offensivstrategie

A marketing strategy applied by a market challenger, ie a firm that occupies second, third and lower ranks in an industry, to attack the market leader and other competitors in an aggressive way for further market share and higher profit.

Basically, the challenger/aggressor can attack three types of firms:
1. the market leader,
2. equal competitors,
3. smaller competitors,

The aggressor/attacker can apply one of five possible attack strategies:
1. The frontal/head on attack:
   in this case, the aggressor attacks the rival`s/defender`s strengths rather than its weaknesses, eg it attacks the product, its price, its package and the discounts granted; the outcome of the combat depends on who has the greater strength and endurance.

2. The flank(ing) attack:
   the attacker will act as if it will attack the opponent`s/defender`s strong side but will actually attack its weak spots/blind sides. This strategy is particularly attractive if the aggressor disposes of fewer (financial) resources than the opponent and is more successful than the frontal attack because the aggressor focuses either on a geographic region or a market segment in which the competitor is underperforming so that it can fill the gaps and develop them into strong segments satisfying the customers` needs.
3. The encirclement attack:
   the aggressor launches an attack on several fronts at once so that the opponent must protect all its fronts simultaneously. If the aggressor manages to offer everything the opponent offers or more, its offers may be unrefusable. This strategy makes sense when the aggressor commands resources superior to those of the opponent.
4. The bypass attack:
   this is the most indirect strategy as the aggressor does not directly attack the opponent but bypasses it and attacks easier markets by diversifying into unrelated products or into new geographical markets for existing products, or by developing new technologies to supplant existing products of the competitor(s).
5. The guerrilla attack:
   a strategy particularly suitable to smaller aggressors who want to attack larger firms (ie David attacks Goliath). The aggressor intermittently attacks different narrow territories of the opponent, e.g. through selective price cuts, short but intense promotional campaigns, or occasional legal actions. Eventually the aggressor hopes to gain a permanent foothold on the respective markets.

Note: to be successful, the aggressor/challenger must combine these general strategies with several other specific attack strategies. These comprise the following:
1. price-discount strategy, 2. cheaper-goods strategy, 3. prestige-goods strategy, 4. product-proliferation strategy, 5. product-innovation strategy, 6. improved services strategy, 7. distribution innovation strategy, 8. manufacturing-cost-reduction strategy, 9. intensive advertising promotion, etc.

Attention (attn) Aufmerksamkeit, Beachtung

The careful consideration and treatment of something, eg a message conveyed to a reader, viewer or listener by an advertisement.

Attention getter Aufmerksamkeitserreger, Blickfang

Also called attention compeller.

Any person, visual sign or sound that attracts attention, i.e. more than passive notice.

Attention value Aufmerksamkeitswert

The extent to which an advertisement can obtain the attention of a reader, viewer or listener.

Attitude Einstellung, Haltung, Verhalten

A person's state of mind reflecting a positive or negative view about evaluations, feelings, actions and reactions towards people, objectives, certain things, ideas or events.

Attitude change Einstellungs(ver)änderung

The extent to which an individual`s attitude varies, eg as a result of advertising.

Attitude study Verhaltensstudie, Einstellungsstudie

Also called attitude survey.

A study designed to determine people's attitudes to or beliefs about specific factors. For example, a study conducted by advertisers to assess the effectiveness of advertising or to determine consumer opinions about and evaluations of a company, product, service, etc.

Attitude testing Einstellungsmessung, Verhaltensmessung

Also called attitude measurement.

A procedure to measure a person's views, e.g. on certain products, by assigning scores to various factors.

Attractive offer günstiges Angebot

A very favourable offer, ie the goods are sold at a low price.

Attrition loss (rate) Kundenverlust(rate)

The decrease in brand loyalty of consumers to a product, e.g. because of a desire for change or because of a price change.

Auction Auktion, öffentliche Versteigerung

Also called sale by public auction or vendue.

A public sale in which the competing bidder offers an increase on the price offered by a competitor.
The person who bids last, or bids the highest amount, is the purchaser. A sale is completed by the fall of the hammer; until then any bidder may retract his bid.

In a Dutch Auction, the auctioneer (a person authorized by licence to sell goods on commission at a public auction) commences by a high price, and gradually reduces it until an offer is made.

Auction house Auktionshaus

A company engaged in selling merchandise by auction. The products are displayed and sold for a commission.

Auction market Auktionsmarkt

Also called double auction market.

A market in which buyers enter competitive bids and sellers enter competitive offers simultaneously. The stock exchange is an auction market.

Auction sale Auktionsverkauf, Versteigerung

A public sale where items offered are sold to the highest bidder.

Auctioneer Auktionator/in

A person who conducts sales by auction.

Audience Publikum, Besucher
Audienz
Personen und Haushalte, die mit Werbemittel oder Werbeträger Kontakt haben
Hörer-, Leser-, Zuschauer(schaft)

The people watching a film or play, listening to a concert or witnessing any other presentation or performance.

A personal meeting of a formal nature.

In advertising, the total number of people who may receive an advertising message.

The total number of listeners (the listenership), readers (the readership) or viewers (the viewership) reached by the appropriate medium.

Audience accumulation — Nettoreichweite
Publikumskumulierung

The total audience reached by an advertising campaign, including broadcast commercials, newspapers, magazines, and outdoor advertising.

The increase in the total audience viewing a TV programme by including reruns in the count.

Audience composition — Publikumszusammensetzung

The classification of audiences, eg listeners, readers, viewers, by specific characteristics, usually demographic, e.g. age, sex, income, occupation, education level, etc.

Audience duplication — Duplizierung, Überschneidung, Überlappung von Hörern/ Lesern/Zuschauern

The extent to which the audience, ie listeners, readers, viewers, are reached more than once by the same advertisement or commercial appearing in different media.

The number or percentage of households or individuals reached by one programme or station that are also reached by other programmes or stations.

Audience flow — Publikumsfluß

The gain or loss of audience, ie viewers or listeners, during a TV or radio broadcast through turning on or off or through changing channels.

Audience gain/loss — Publikumszunahme, -abnahme

An increase or decrease in the total audience, ie listeners, readers, viewers.

Audience measurement — Hörer-, Leser-, Zuschaueranalyse; Messung des Publikums

Also called audience analysis.

Definition and quantification (either expressed as a percentage or as an absolute quantity) of the listeners, readers and viewers reached by a medium to determine the impact achieved by advertisements placed within the particular medium.

Audience profile — Publikumsprofil

The socio-economic characteristics of a readership, listenership, or viewership.

Audience quality — Publikumqualität

The kind and quality of the target audience to whom the advertisement(s) is exposed.

Audience rating — Einschaltquote

Also called program(me) rating or rating.

The audience, i.e. the number of people/households watching or listening to a TV or radio programme. The figure establishes the popularity of a TV or radio programme. Sometimes there is an audience flow, i.e. a gain or loss of audience during a programme.

Audience share — Publikumsanteil

The group of people who actually receive an advertising message.

Audimeter — Audimeter

A means for monitoring television audience data. An electronic device is placed on the television receiver in households recording the time the TV is turned on, the channel to which it is tuned, and the length of time it is tuned to each channel.

Audiovisual advertising — audiovisuelle Werbung

Advertising communicated by a combination of vision and sound, ie the advertisement can be seen and heard (eg a TV commercial).

Audiovisual sales aids — audiovisuelle Verkaufshilfen

Communication facilities combining visual and audial media, used by salespeople to stimulate and promote sales, e.g. at exhibitions.

Audit — Auflagenprüfung

In publishing, the examination of a publisher´s statements by an independent auditor regarding the circulation figures of a publication.

Audit Bureau of Circulations (ABC) — unabhängige Organisation zur Kontrolle der Auflagenziffern von Zeitungen und Zeitschriften

An independent body formed to provide data on media distribution for magazines and newspapers and which monitors, publishes and authenticates circulation of publications.

Audited circulation — kontrollierte, überprüfte Auflage

Also called certified circulation.

The circulation of a newspaper or magazine which has been certified by an independent body, eg the Audit Bureau of Circulations (ABC).

Augmented product — erweitertes Produkt, durch Zusatzleistung verbessertes Produkt, Produkterweiterung

A product built around the core and actual products but enhanced by the addition of related services and benefits, e.g. pre-sales and after-sales services, installation, maintenance, repair services, warranty, etc.

Austerity — Sparprogramm (selbstauferlegte Einschränkung)

Generally, a government and monetary policy that is deliberately deflationary and tries to restrain public and/or private expenditure (e.g. by higher taxes, higher interest rates, wage restraints, lower government expenditure) in order to reduce inflation, deficit spending or to solve balance of payments problems.

Austrian School Österreichische (Grenznutzen) Schule

A school of economic thought, founded in the late 19th century by the Austrian economists Karl Menger (1840 - 1921; he initiated the "subjectivistic revolution", reasoning that the value of a good was not derived from its cost but from the pleasure, or utility (satisfaction), the consumer can derive from it; this way of thinking led to the marginal utility theory); Eugen von Böhm-Bawerk (1851 - 1914; he helped to develop the theory of interest and capital, arguing that the price paid for the use of capital is dependent upon consumers' demand for present consumption relative to future consumption); and Friedrich von Wieser (1851 - 1926; he introduced the economic concept of opportunity cost).

Authorized dealer Vertragshändler

A retailer who has been given exclusive right by a producer (manufacturer) to sell a specific item or line of merchandise (product range, line of goods), usually in a defined geographical area.

Authorized distributor Vertragshändler

A party authorized to sell the product(s) of a company in a particular country. A single distributor may have such an authorization from a number of foreign companies simultaneously.

Auto-dial recorded message player (ADRMP) automatisches Selbstwähl- und Aufzeichnungsgerät, Werbeautomat

Also called automatic dialing and recorded message player.

A fully automated telemarketing system which self-dials numbers, plays a voice-activated advertising message, and takes orders from interested customers on an answering machine or by forwarding the call to an operator.

Automated warehouse automatisiertes Lager

Also called automated store.

Usually, a single-storied warehouse with advanced materials-handling systems managed by a few employees only. A central computer reads orders and directs lift trucks or robots to collect goods, moves them to loading docks, and issues invoices.

Automatic checkout machine (ACM) automatisches Scanner-Kassen-system, kundenbedientes Einkaufssystem

A system which allows customers to check themselves out of a shop/store by scanning their purchases with the point-of-sale (POS) system, entering their customer identification card, and receiving clearance to exit the shop.

Automatic identification automatische Warenerkennung

The mechanical identification of a product and the automatic entering of the data obtained into a computer; the most widely used method involves bar codes.

Automatic markdown automatische Preissenkung, Herunterzeichnung

A price reduction for merchandise which has been in stock in a retail store (retail outlet) for a longer period of time.

Automatic reorder automatische Nachbestellung

The ordering of goods or materials in accordance with an order system based on levels of stock on (in) hand.

Automatic vending Automatenverkauf

Also called automatic selling.

A system of retail selling in which goods are contained in and delivered by a coin- or note-operated machine (automatic vending machine). This method of retailing has inherent cost advantages over more labour-intensive methods.
Types of vending machines are, for example: package vendors for wrapped items, bulk vendors, bottle vendors and cup vendors.

Automatic vending machine Verkaufsautomat

Also called automatic vendor, coin-or-note-operated machine, dispensing machine, slot machine, or vending machine.

A machine which sells food, drinks, sweets, cigarettes, etc. when a coin or note is inserted.

Autonomous consumption autonomer Konsum

Consumption that is independent of income.

Autonomous expenditure(s) autonome Ausgaben

Consumption, investment, and government spending levels that are determined by variables other than income; e.g. consumption and investment may be affected by changes in interest rates.

Autonomous saving autonomes Sparen

Saving by households influenced by variables other than income, e.g. saving can be affected by increases in the rate of inflation (inflation rate).

Autonomous spending autonome Ausgaben

Also called autonomous expenditure.

Spending that is independent of the level of income and interest rates.

Autonomy Autonomie, Selbständigkeit

Independence or freedom with regard to will or actions either for individuals or organizations.

Availability Verfügbarkeit

The state of being obtainable or of being at hand. This is a necessary condition for the purchase of a product.

Available market frei verfügbarer Markt
zugänglicher (vorhandener) Markt

That part of a total market which shows interest in a product, can afford to buy it, and is not prevented by access barriers from reaching it. That means, the set of consumers who have interest, income, and access to a particular market offer.
Note: a prospective buyer may be a part of the potential market for a product (eg a Porsche) but has no interest or money to buy it. Thus, he is no part of the available market.

The part of the total (served plus non-served) market which could be served by the company within a specific period.

Average (av, avg) arithmetischer Mittelwert
Durchschnitts...

In statistics, the arithmetic mean.

To produce work or do something normally or usually; of an ordinary or usual kind of quality, etc.

Average audience (AA, aa) durchschnittliche Hörerzahl, Zuschauerzahl

The average number of listeners or viewers (households or individuals) of a radio or TV programme. The AA is of importance to sponsors.

Average audience rating durchschnittliche Einschaltquote

Also called AA rating.

A figure showing the average size of the radio or television audience on a minute-by-minute basis throughout the duration of a programme. This figure is compared with a basic figure, e.g., the number of persons the programme is able to reach.

Average cost pricing Preisbildung auf Durchschnitts-kostenbasis

A pricing policy where the average price of a product is based on average cost plus some level of markup.

Average cost(s) of production durchschnittliche Produktionskosten

The firm's costs per unit of output, calculated by dividing the total production costs by the number of units produced.

Average costs (AC) Durchschnittskosten, Stückkosten

Also called unit costs.

The total cost of production divided by the quantity produced. Thus, average total cost (ATC) may be written:

$$ATC = \frac{TC}{X}$$

where X is output and TC is total cost.

Average total cost (ATC) will be comprised of average fixed costs (AFC) and average variable costs (AVC). Thus ATC = AFC + AVC.

Average deviation mittlere Abweichung

Also called mean deviation.

In statistics, a measure of variation within a group of numerical observations, i.e., the average of the (absolute values of the) deviations of the observations from the group mean.

Average fixed cost (AFC) durchschnittliche Fixkosten

The fixed cost (FC) divided by the total number of units of output.

Average frequency durchschnittliche Kontakthäufigkeit

The average number of times a consumer will see an advertisement or commercial over a specified time period.

Average issue audience (AIA) durchschnittliche Leserzahl pro Ausgabe

Also called average issue readership (AIR).

The numer of people who read or look at an average issue of a publication, eg newspaper or magazine.

Average issue readership (AIR) durchschnittliche Leserschaft einer Publikation

The number of people who read or look at an average issue of a publication.

Average markon durchschnittlicher Preisaufschlag

Also called average markup.

The difference between selling price (eg $ 200) and price of goods to the store (eg $ 150) divided by the selling price and multiplied by 100 (ie the average markup is 25%).

Average price Durchschnittspreis

The arithmetic average of the current prices of a commodity.

Average propensity to consume (APC) (durchschnittliche) Konsumquote (C/Y)

That part of national income devoted, on average, by the nation's individuals to consumption of goods and services. In other words, the ratio of consumption expenditures to (disposable) income.

$$APC = \frac{\text{consumption}}{\text{income}}$$

Average propensity to save (APS) (durchschnittliche) Sparquote (S/Y)

The fraction of a given level of national income that is saved; or the ratio of personal saving to (disposable) income.

$$APS = \frac{\text{saving}}{\text{income}}$$

Average rate of taxation durchschnittlicher Steuersatz

Also called average tax rate.

The total tax paid by an individual divided by the total income upon which the tax was based.

Average revenue (AR) Durchschnittserlös, durchschnittlicher Ertrag

The total revenue obtained from the sale of a commodity divided by the quantity sold; in other words, it is the price per unit of the commodity.

Average total cost (ATC) durchschnittliche Gesamtkosten

Total cost divided by the number of units produced.

Award Angebotsannahme Auftragsvergabe

The acceptance of a bid or the assigning of a project on the basis of a made offer.

Awareness Markenbewußtsein

Having knowledge of a product. Awareness is achieved with advertising, by having the product on the shelf in the shops (i.e. merchandising) or by other means. Awareness of a product is a precondition of purchasing it.

Away-from-home audience Publikum, das nicht Zuhause ist

The away-from-home listeners, readers and viewers.

Axis Achse

A straight line that intersects with another straight line (the vertical or y-axis and the horizontal or x-axis) at right angles to form the reference point of a graph.

Note: the plural is axes.

B

Baby billboard Verkehrsmittelwerbung

Advertising in and on (public) means of transport/transportation.

Baby boomers Babyboomer

The generation of people born between 1946 and 1965, a period of explosive population growth and thus a period of growing markets. Today, the baby boomers are a prime target for marketers.

Back cover (BC, bc) Rückseite
letzte/vierte Umschlagseite, U4,
(Buch)Rücken

In advertising, the back page (inside or outside) of a magazine.

The outside back page of a book or magazine. When used for advertisements, this page is usually the most expensive of all covers as it is read by most readers. Also called fourth cover (4C).

Back order unerledigter Auftrag

Also called open, outstanding, or unfulfilled order.

An order received in the past and not fulfilled.

Back-haul rate Preis für Rückfracht

Transport charges which are lower for movement in one direction than in the other, since it is unlikely that there will be exactly equal demand for transport in both directions, so that excess capacity will exist on one route.

Back-to-back commercials unmittelbar aufeinanderfolgende Werbesendungen

Two or more commercials appearing one directly after the other.

Backdoor selling Verkauf unter Umgehung der festgelegten Absatzwege

Direct sales approach to a company's real decision-maker(s), by-passing the purchasing department.

Backer Geldgeber, Sponsor

Also called financier or sponsor.

An individual who backs someone, often financially.

Backfreight/back freight Rückfracht
Rückfracht, Rücksendung

Also called freight home, freight homeward, homeward freight or return freight.

The amount payable by the owner of a cargo when he is unable to deliver at the discharge point and has to return the cargo to the departure point. In other words, the additional freight chargeable on the return of goods.
This may be payment for:
1. the return of goods not accepted at the port of delivery,
2. the disposal of the goods if the consignee fails to take delivery,
3. transport beyond place of destination because of wrong case markings - but, if this is due to an error of the carrier, backfreight is not chargeable.

Note: backfreight is payable by the party responsible.

The cargo returned. Also called return cargo, return consignment or return(s).

Backhaul allowance Preisnachlaß für Selbstabholer

A price reduction granted to customers who collect (pick up) their goods from a seller's business premises to reflect his savings in freight charges.

Backhauling Transport von Rückfracht

Return-trip carriage of goods with what would otherwise have been an empty lorry/truck.

Backload Rückladung

Also called return load.

The return load in a transport unit, eg a truck.

Backlog Auftragsrückstand
Arbeitsrückstand

The value of unfilled orders placed with a company. Also called backlog of orders.

The accumulation of work which needs to be done. Also called backlog of work.

Backup space Mindestanzeigenraum, der belegt werden muß

The minimum advertising space that must be purchased in a newspaper or magazine.

Backward integration Rückwärtsintegration

Also called vertical backwards.

Acquisition or takeover by a company of another company which supplies it with raw materials or parts for manufacture. One type of vertical integration; a firm extends itself into a previous stage of the production process and thereby ensures a more certain supply of materials.

Backwash effect Aushöhlungseffekt

A situation which exists when the economic growth in one region of an economy has adverse effects on the growth of other regions. These effects usually consist of flows of factors of production (e.g. labour, capital) from slow growing to fast growing regions. There is a divergence in productivity between the different regions or countries.

Bad bargain schlechter Kauf, schlechtes Geschäft

Also called bad buy.

An item bought which is not worth the price paid for it.

Bad faith Bösgläubigkeit, böser Glaube

An intent(ion) to deceive or otherwise commit an unfair or wrongful act against someone.

Bag Sack, Beutel, Tasche, Tüte

A package or container made of cotton, jute, strong paper, plastic, cloth, linen, canvas, rubber, etc. for carrying items.

Bag-in-a-box Getränk im Karton, kartonierter Beutel

Liquids such as wine, lemonade etc sold in practical square packs. This is more convenient than selling in bottles etc although the waste rate is higher.

Baisse Baisse, Fallen der Kurse/Preise

Contradiction in the prices for securities, goods, etc.; a fall normally in the stock market; a slump, a price fall or collapse generally.

Bait Lockartikel, Lock(vogel)angebot

Also called leader or leading article; lowball or lure (collq.).

A very attractive article or service which is sold at cost or even at a loss to attract customers.

Bait advertising Lockvogelwerbung

Also called bait and switch advertising, loss leader selling or switch selling.

The practice of advertising a product or service solely in order to attract (to bait) customers to the shop, where they can then be persuaded to buy something else, i.e. a higher-priced article. The salesperson disparages or belittles the article advertised (the bait or loss leader), recommends the purchase of a more expensive article or indicates any other difficulties in connection with the purchase of this product.

Bait pricing Lockvogelpreisfestsetzung

A special pricing tactic that tries to get consumers into a shop through false, deceptive or misleading price advertising and then uses high-pressure selling to persuade consumers to buy more expensive products.

Balance due fälliger Betrag

A specific amount of money payable immediately or on a particular date.

Balanced economic growth harmonisches Wirtschaftswachstum

Economic expansion throughout a country at approximately the same rate.

Balanced stock ausgewogener Lagerbestand/ Warenbestand

A stock of goods at all prices to meet the customers' demand and satisfy their wants.

Bale Ballen (in einem Ballen enthaltene Warenmenge)

A package of soft goods (e.g. cotton, wool, etc.) tightly pressed together and wrapped in a protective material (e.g. canvas, tarpaulin), often bound up with iron strips.

Banded offer Combipack-Angebot

An offer where two items are sold together (i.e. in a banded pack), e.g. to get rid of another, usually less attractive product, or to launch (introduce) a new one or to increase sales. Banded packs are sometimes offered with the slogan "buy one, get one free".

Banded pack Banderolenpackung, Verbundpackung

A form of sales promotion in which consumers are offered a multiple package of products put together as a special sales offer at a reduced price.

Bandwagon effect Mitläufereffekt, Sogwirkung, Bandwagon-Effekt

Also called demonstration effect.

A buying climate in which the purchasing enthusiasm of some people spreads to others because they are "infected" by their enthusiastic behaviour.

Bangtail Briefumschlag mit Werbung auf der Rückseite
Briefumschlag, dessen Klappe als Bestellformular dient

A promotional envelope that shows an advertisement on the back.

An envelope with a perforated flap that can be used for placing an order.

Bank holiday Bankfeiertag

Public holidays on which banks and most other business organisations are closed.

In England and Wales these are New Year's Day (1 January), Good Friday, Easter Monday, May Day, late Spring Holiday (first Monday in June), late Summer Holiday (the Monday following the last weekend in August), Christmas Day (25 December) and Boxing Day (the first weekend after Christmas Day).

In Nothern Ireland, all the English holidays plus St. Patrick's Day (17 March), Easter Tuesday and 12 July. In Scotland, all the English holidays except Easter Monday and Boxing Day.

Bank marketing Bankmarketing

Marketing activities of banks in consideration of the special requirements necessary for them to reach private and professional customers and thus improve sales of their manifold services.

Banner Banner, Spruchband, Transparent

A cloth or other material stretched between two walls or buildings, flown from a light plane or airship, or hung over a street or entrance, carrying an advertisement message.

Banquet Bankett, Festessen

A large formal dinner for many people.

Bantam store — Geschäft für Bedarfsartikel mit langen Öffnungszeiten

Also called vest-pocket supermarket.

A small convenience store with a limited range of goods and open long hours or even 24 hours a day.

Bar chart — Stabdiagramm, Säulendiagramm, Histogramm

Also called bar diagram, bar graph, column diagram, or frequency bar chart.

A graphic display to enable comparisons to be made. Data can be plotted by time period as a series of bars, the length of each bar depending upon the value of the data represented.

Barcode/bar code — Balkencode, Strichcode

A universal product code (UPC), i.e. a series of thick and thin black lines identifying the product and providing inventory and pricing information that can be read by a barcode scanner/electronic scanner. The barcode is read at the retail checkout.

Barcode reader — Strichcodeleser

Also called barcode scanner.

A device for optical scanning of bar codes and translation of the coded information (e.g. prices or product descriptions) into digital signals reachable by a computer.

Bargain — Kaufvertrag
Gelegenheitskauf
Geschäft
günstiges Kaufobjekt, Schnäppchen

An agreement for the purchase or sale of anything.

An advantageous purchase, usually something bought cheap. Also called buy, chance bargain or job lot.

A piece of business, especially of buying and selling. Also called deal or transaction.

Something offered at a cheap or specially reduced price.

Bargain basement Abteilung für Sonderangebote

The below ground level floor in a shop where one can buy cheap goods, i.e. the goods are sold at a bargain price or bargain basement price.

Bargain counter Verkaufstisch/Theke für Sonderangebote

The counter in a shop where goods are sold cheaply.

Bargain hunter Schnäppchenjäger; jemand, der Sonderangebote sucht

A person who searches things, e.g. good quality items or securities, he can buy cheaply, i.e. at a bargain price.

Bargain offer Sonderangebot, günstiges Angebot

The sale of a particular type of commodity at a cheap or specially reduced price (the bargain price).

Bargain pack (Waren)Sonderangebot

An offer of a product, usually in a special pack or wrapper, at a reduced price for a limited time period. The producer hopes to win new customers to his brand.

Bargain price sehr niedriger Preis, Spottpreis, Sonderangebots-, Gelegenheitspreis

Also called bargain basement price or knockdown price.

An extremely low price.

Bargain sale Ausverkauf, Verkauf zu (stark) reduzierten Preisen Sonderangebot

The sale of (all) goods in a store at cheap or reduced prices. Also called clean-up sale.

The sale of particular goods at cut-rate prices. Also called premium offer or special bargain.

Bargain shopper Käufer von Billigangeboten

An individual who buys special offers.

Bargain store Billigpreisgeschäft

A store that sells merchandise at a supermarket price. The merchandise is often damaged or seconds and the quantities offered are frequently limited.

Bargaining Verhandeln, Handeln

Also called negotiation.

The offer and counter offer of a price for goods or services.

Bargaining has the following features:
1. at least two parties are involved,
2. the parties have one or more conflicts of interest,
3. the parties are in a temporary and voluntary relationship,
4. the parties want to reach a satisfactory solution,
5. all activities are sequential rather than simultaneous, as they usually involve the presentation of demands by one party and their evaluation by the other, followed by concessions and counterproposals.

Bargaining position Verhandlungsposition

The position or status of a person or group during a negotiation.

Bargaining power Verhandlungsstärke

The strength of one person or group when discussing prices, wage agreements or other matters.

Bargaining tactics Verhandlungstaktiken

The manoeuvres/maneuvers to be made at specific points in the bargaining process.

Barrel (brl, bl) | Faß, Tonne
Barrel (Hohlmaß)

A wooden or metal drum or container. Capacity 25/60 gallons. "Tight" barrels are for carrying liquids; "slack" barrels for dry contents; hoops strengthen the barrels. Also called cask.

Measure of capacity, GB: 163,656 l; US: 119,228 l; oil: 158,97 l.

Barrier to entry | Marktzutrittsschranke, Zugangsbeschränkung

Also called restriction of entry.

A market situation that impedes or prevents the entrance of new firms into an industry, e.g. government controls, insufficient demand, high capital investment costs, resistance of competitors, consumer preferences, patent rights.

Barriers to competition | Wettbewerbsbeschränkungen

Forces, ususally economic or technological conditions, which restrict market competition and thus make the entry of more firms to a market more difficult.

Barriers to trade | Handelshemmnisse, Handelsrestriktionen

Also called trade restrictions, trade barriers or trade bars.

Any action by the government of a country to restrict/limit or prevent the free flow of imports (and exports).

Barriers to trade between countries and the discouragement of international specialisation are erected for social and political as well as economic purposes. These arise for four reasons:
1. protecting domestic employment, 2. protection against "dumping", 3. infant industries and 4. strategic arguments.

Methods to restrict free trade are: tariffs, import quotas, subsidies, embargoes, currency restrictions, price controls, import permits, health and safety standards, packaging and labelling regulations, etc.

Barter Naturaltausch, Tauschhandel

A form of trading in which goods are exchanged directly for other goods without the use of money as an intermediary (e.g. eggs are exchanged for milk).

Barter agreement Tauschabkommen

Also called barter arrangement or barter deal.

An agreement to exchange goods by barter.

Barter economy Tauschwirtschaft, Naturalwirtschaft

Also called moneyless or nomoney economy.

An economy with no money, ie the exchange of goods for other goods is effected without the use of money as an intermediary.

Base Sitz, Standort

Also called headquarters, head office or main office.

The place where a businessman or company have their main office or factory.

Base price Grundpreis, Preis ohne Rabatte

The price at which a company expects to sell its product or service.
A base price can be lowered through the use of discounts, allowances and rebates.

Base rate Anzeigengrundpreis

The basic price for an advertisement.

Base stock eiserner Bestand

Also called base stock inventory, buffer stock, minimum inventory level, minimum stock, reserve stock or safety stock.

The minimum stock with which a business can operate. It provides a cushion against variations in demand or delays in supply.

Base year Basisjahr, Bezugszeitraum

Also called basal year or base(d) period.

The year from which changes in an index (e.g. the Index of Retail Prices) are calculated; the base year is usually given an index number of 100 and subsequent years are measured accordingly. Thus if the Retail Price Index (RPI) is quoted as 120 (1995 = 100), then 1995 is the base year.

Basic commodities Grundstoffe, Rohstoffe

Also called primary products or basic materials.

Products which are basic raw materials.

Basic export price Export-Basispreis

This is the export price in domestic currency required by the exporter if he is paid by the importer before shipment of the goods.

When quoting prices in an overseas currency, the exporter has to convert his basic export price in domestic currency (e.g. US dollars or deutschmarks) to the overseas/foreign currency concerned.

Basic needs Grundbedürfnisse

Also called basic requirements or wants.

Things such as, e.g. food, clothing, etc., which a person must have if he/she is to live.

Basic price Basispreis, Grundpreis

Also called basic price or basis price.

The price of a commodity or service without any extras.

The maximum of any commodity or service that the seller expects to obtain from a buyer. This price usually serves as the start point for sales negotiation. Furthermore, it is the price from which the seller calculates special discounts.

Basic rate Grundpreis, Basispreis

Also called basic price or basis price.

The price of a commodity or service without any extras.

Basic research Grundlagenforschung

Research undertaken to extend the boundaries of knowledge in any field or area without attempting to give immediate application to an existing problem.

Basing point Frachtbasis

Also called base point.

The point from which customers are charged freight costs, commonly one of the company's manufacturing plants.

Basing-point pricing Preisfestsetzung auf Frachtbasis

Also called base point pricing.

A geographic pricing strategy in which customers are charged freight costs from a base/basing point (eg the producer´s factory or a particular city) designated by the seller. The system ensures that final selling prices are identical irrespective of the customer location or freight costs/charges involved.

Basket Korb
Einkaufskorb

Container made from various materials (e.g. wood or paperboard) and having a carrying handle.

A shopping basket.

Basket of goods Warenkorb

Also called basket of commodities or set of commodities.

A "basket" which represents fairly the weekly consumption by a typical family.

Basket transaction Pauschalgeschäft

Also called lump sum transaction.

A purchase or sale of a group of assets for a lump sum.

Batch Los, Menge, Stapel
Serie, Charge

The quantity of material prepared or required for one operation.

A group of items which are made at one time or in a single processing (unit).

Batch costing Produktbündelrechnung,
Serienkalkulation

A calculation method used where the batch is regarded as the unit for costing purposes.

Batch number Chargennummer, Seriennummer

A number attached to a batch.

Battle of the brands Markenkampf

Keen or even cut-throat competition in the market between competing/rival brands.

Bauded pack Großpackung, Haushaltspackung

Also called giant package, giant-size pack, or jumbo package.

Two or more items bauded together and usually sold at a price cheaper than the sum of the individual items bought separately.

Bayes' rule Bayessche Regel

The rule states that when deciding between two or more alternative choices the alternative with the highest expectation should be chosen.

Beauty shot Nahaufnahme eines Produkts in der Fernsehwerbung

In a TV commercial, a close-up of a product, i.e. a moment when the camera focuses on the product.

Beginning inventory Anfangsbestand

Also called opening inventory or opening stock.

The inventory at the beginning of an accounting period.

The opening balance of the inventory account.

Behaviour scan Werbeerfolgskontrolle durch Scannersystem

A measure of consumer purchasing which tracks electronically each consumer´s purchases, item by item, over time.
Specially selected consumers shop with an ID card, which is presented at the checkout in scanner-equipped shops.

Behaviour segmentation Verhaltenssegmentierung, (Markt)Segmentierung auf Grund von Verhaltensmerkmalen

Also called behavioural or behaviouristic segmentation.

Division of a market into groups based on the status of consumers, their knowledge, attitude, use, or response to a particular product and their buying habits. Many marketers believe that behaviour variables are the best starting point for establishing market segments.

Behaviour(al) research Verhaltensforschung

Research into human behaviour, singly or in groups, particularly in connection with buying or consuming habits.

Behavioural change Verhaltensänderung

In marketing, getting customers to do, or buy, something which they have not previously done or bought. This usually means that consumer spending is going to be diverted from one thing to something else, but still generally within the same overall limit of spending.

Behavioural science Verhaltenswissenschaft(en)

It includes the study of sociology, psychology and anthropology and it is particularly useful to managers as it will aid their analysis of behaviour within their business organisation.

Belief Überzeugung

A thought, conviction, opinion that a person holds about something.

Believability of advertising Glaubwürdigkeit der Werbung

The extent to which an advertiser's claims and message are accepted as being true.

Bellwether advertising Leithammelwerbung, Schlüsselwerbung

Advertising activities carried out by a market leader.

Below the line promotion Verkaufsförderung durch indirekte Werbemaßnahmen, z.B. Nachlässe

A below the line promotion is one where the expenditure does not go into paid advertising media but covers the costs for other kinds of promotion such as coupons, self-liquidating offers, bargain packages, gifts, sampling, and merchandising and display.

Benchmarketing Benchmarketing, Basis-Ziel-Marketing

Marketing activities developing objective guidelines and target values which are comparable with those of other leading enterprises.

Benefit Nutzen, Vorteil

Something to advantage, interest or profit.

A feature or property (e.g. the quality) associated with a product or service that supplies satisfaction or need fulfillment to the consumer.

Benefit segmentation Nutzensegmentierung, Benefit-Segmentation

The division of a market into groups or segments on the basis of the particular benefits (eg low price, first-class quality) consumers seek and obtain from the product. As the benefits that customers seek are their product needs, customers are segmented directly according to their needs. But note: the segments must be accessible to the firms′ marketing efforts.

When a company uses this type of segmentation, it has to find:
1. the major benefits people look for in the product class, 2. the kinds of people who look for each benefit, 3. the brand that delivers each benefit, 4. the major competing brands delivering the benefits. Note: the company can also search for new benefits and launch brands that deliver them.

Note: Each benefit group has special demographic, behavioural, and psychographic characteristics.

Benefit-cost analysis (BCA) Nutzen-Kosten-Analyse

Also called cost-benefit analysis (CBA).

A process to determine the efficiency of a project by estimating each benefit and each cost. A project is said to be efficient if it generates more benefits than costs.

Best before date Mindesthaltbarkeit(sdatum)

Also called sell-by date or use-by date.

Date stamped on the label of a food product, which is the last date on which the product is guaranteed to be of good quality.

Best time available (BTA) günstigste Werbezeit

Instruction given by an advertiser to a radio or TV station to air/broadcast a commercial, at the discretion of the station, in the best possible time slot so that the commercial can reach the largest audience.

Bestseller/best seller Bestseller

Also called key item.

A product, e.g. a book, that among of those of its class sells very well at a given time.

Betting tax Wettsteuer

A tax on betting (e.g. on football pools) through bookmakers. Most forms of betting are taxed.

Bias Bias, Verzerrung, systematischer Fehler (Statistik)

Statistical term referring to errors in sample survey results. It is the difference between the expected value and the true value in a probability distribution.

Bid Gebot
Submissionsangebot

The offer of payment for an object which is for sale (especially at an auction sale). In other words the price or terms at which a person is willing to buy something. The seller may make an offer and a prospective buyer may make a bid. The bid cancels out the offer. Also called bid price.

A tender, ie an offer, usually in response to an advertisement, for the supply of specified goods or the performance of specified work at prices and under conditions set out in the tender.

Bid price Angebotspreis, gebotener Preis

Also called offer price, quoted price, or supply price.

The amount agreed between the seller and buyer for transfer of property in exchange for money.

Bid pricing Preisfestsetzung durch Submissionsangebot

A situation where prices are determined through sealed or open bids. Potential sellers are invited to state, either orally or in writing, what they will charge to provide a good or service. The sale is awarded to one of the bidders.

Bidder Bieter(in)

A person who makes a bid, often at an auction. There are two types, the highest and the lowest bidder.

Bidding Abgabe von Angeboten

A procedure which occurs where a number of potential suppliers are invited to submit a written bid, within the bidding period, for a contract.

There are two types: 1. closed bidding (bidding is restricted to certain suppliers) and 2. open bidding (bidding is open to any supplier willing to bid).

Big ticket customer Großkunde

Also called big customer.

A customer who places regular and larger orders or a customer who places a large-scale order (big ticket item).

Big ticket items teure Gebrauchsgüter

Items whose costs run into millions of dollars, deutschmarks, etc., e.g. aeroplanes and special machinery.

Big-ticket sale Großabschluß

A very large contract or the sale of big-ticket items.

Bilateral contract bilateraler, gegenseitiger, zweiseitiger Vertrag

Also called bilateral agreement, reciprocal contract or synallagmatic contract.

An agreement between two persons, companies or groups, usually based on the reciprocity principle. Both parties undertake mutual duties which are enforceable at law.

Bilateral monopoly bilaterales (zweiseitiges) Monopol

A market in which a single buyer faces a single seller.

Bilateral oligopoly bilaterales Oligopol

A market situation with a significant degree of seller concentration (like oligopoly) and a significant degree of buyer concentration (like oligopsony).

Bill Rechnung (für Dienstleistungen)
Rechnung (Restaurant)
Plakat

A bill is a statement of what someone owes to someone else. Bills are usually for services (e.g. bills for gas, telephone); but also for goods. Also called invoice or sales bill.

In a restaurant, the invoice which a customer receives. Also called check (US).

A notice or advertisement in the form of a poster. Also called billboard, poster, or placard.

Bill insert Werbematerial, das einer Rechnung beiliegt; Rechnung mit Werbebeilage

Also called bill enclosure, bill stuffer or statement stuffer.

A secondary document of a promotional nature, mailed along with an invoice to advertise a good or service.

Bill of charges Gebührenrechnung

Also called bill of costs.

A detailed account of charges made by a person or firm for work done.

Billable time berechenbare Zeit

The amount of time which may be invoiced for a service rendered.

Billboard Reklame-, Werbefläche

A flat surface or board, usually outdoors, on which large advertisements are posted.

Billed cost(s) in Rechnung gestellte Kosten

The price acutally charged by a seller, i.e. the price stated on the invoice/bill before deducting cash discounts, but after deducting any trade and quantity discounts shown in the price list.

Billhead | Rechnungsformular
Rechnungskopf

A printed form with a heading giving details of a company, e.g. name and address, etc., and used for bills/invoices when charging customers.

The invoice heading itself.

Billing | Ausstellen und Zusenden von Rechnungen
Umsatz einer Werbeagentur
Plakatwerbung

The American term for invoicing, i.e. the writing and despatching of invoices/bills.

The gross turnover of an advertising agency, normally per year.

Billboard advertising.

Billing date | Rechnungsdatum

Also called date of invoice or invoice date.

The date of an invoice or bill.

Bimonthly | Zweimonatspublikation

Also called semimonthly.

A publication issued every two months.

Bin | (Transport)Behälter, Kiste, Kasten
Lagerfach
Mülleimer, Papierkorb

A large container.

Container for bulk display of merchandise at the retail outlet, i.e. a separate section of shelves in a warehouse. In a shop, a container for storing things. Also called storage bin or storage slot.

A container for rubbish. Also called dustbin, waste-paper bin or waste basket.

Bin tag Kistenanhänger

Also called bin card.

A tag attached to a bin, case, container, etc., which identifies the contents, the quantity, etc.

Binder Umschlag, Aktendeckel

Also called cover, folder or jacket.

A loose cover or folder.

Binding agreement verbindliches, bindendes Abkommen

Also called agreement binding upon the parties.

An agreement between parties that they are under a legal obligation to adhere to an agreement, i.e. all parties signing the agreement (e.g. a binding contract) must do what is agreed.

Bipolar scale bipolare Skala

A scale used in measuring attitudes and opinions in questionnaires containing two extreme points within which an interviewee (respondent) can choose an answer.

Bird dog Kundenjäger, Kundenfänger, (Kunden)Werber, Anwerber

A person who is paid by someone to identify potential customers.

Birdyback Lufttransport von LKW-Containern

A transportation system where containers are transferred from truck to aeroplane.

Birth rate Geburtenrate

A measure of the number of children being born in any year in relation to the total size of the population. It is normally expressed as so many live births per thousand of the population.

Biweekly Zweiwochenpublikation

Also called semiweekly.

A publication issued every two weeks.

Black and white (B&W, B/W, b&w, b/w) Schwarzweiß

An advertisement printed only in one colour, typically black, on white paper. B/W ads are less expensive than colour ads.

B/W may also refer to artwork films, photographs, etc.

Black economy Schattenwirtschaft, Untergrundwirtschaft

Also called cash economy, hidden economy or underground economy.

Economic activity, usually between private individuals, that goes unrecorded in the official income statistics because payment is made in cash. Earnings have not been declared to the taxman and no VAT, income tax, or social insurance has been paid.

Grey market; a less extreme form of black market.

Black gold schwarzes Gold

Originally coal. Today, oil when it became a more important source of energy than coal.

Black market Schwarzmarkt

Wholly illegal and uncontrolled market which deals in scarce or stolen goods or foreign exchange. Goods and services are bought and sold in a way which is not allowed by law. A black (illegal) market exists where goods and services whose supply or price is controlled, are made available at inflated prices outside the intended controls. An undesirable method of business, allowing only a privileged few to purchase essentials/necessaries.

Black trading Schwarzhandel

Trading on a black market, ie an uncontrolled and illegal market.

Blacklist/black list Verzeichnis unsicherer Kunden
schwarze Liste

Also called denied list.

A list of traders to whom it is risky to grant credit because, e.g. they defaulted on payments, defrauded traders, etc. so that they are considered to be dishonest and not trustworthy.

A list of traders, countries, etc., with which a business is not prepared to trade, e.g. for political reasons.

Blackout Übertragungssperre

A situation excluding a live event, most frequently a sports event, from telecasting/televising, usually to heighten ticket sales. The exclusion may be lifted if the event is sold out by a certain date.

Blanket branding Markenfamilienbranding

The strategy of giving a line of products the same brand name.

Blanket contract Generalvertrag

An agreement between seller and buyer that creates a long-term relationship in which the seller promises to resupply the buyer as needed at agreed prices for a set time period. The seller holds the stock and the buyer orders with the seller when stock is needed.
Blanket contracting tightens the relation between seller and buyer and makes it difficult for other sellers to break in unless the buyer becomes dissatisfied with prices, quality, service, etc.

Blanket coverage Sättigungsreichweite
Zufallsstreuung

The ability of radio or TV stations to reach all locations within a given area.

Advertising to the general public and not to a particular target audience.

Blanket order Blankoauftrag, langfristiger Dauerauftrag (mit laufendem Abruf)

Also called blanket purchase order.

A standing order to supply specified goods over time (usually a year) or against which actual delivery volumes and be called for by the customer as required.
The order contains details on price, approximate delivery requirements and other terms of trading.

Blanket purchasing contract Gesamtabschluß

A sales contract/purchasing contract which obliges the seller to provide a certain amount of product each month during the year at one set price. Each year the contract and the price are renegotiated.

Blanket refusal allgemeine Ablehnung

A person's refusal to accept anything, although many different proposals have been made.

Blanket statement pauschale Aussage

A general statement.

Blending Mischen, Verschneiden

Mixing together different qualities of a product, e.g. wines, tea, coffee, etc., in order to make it more attractive to a potential buyer.

Blind advertisement Chiffreanzeige, Kennziffernanzeige

In personnel management, an advertisement in which the advertiser, i.e. an employer, does not reveal his name. A box number is provided for response.

In marketing, this is called box number advertisement or keyed advertisement.

Blind offer — verstecktes Angebot (in einem Werbeträger)

Also called hidden offer or buried offer.

An offer placed inconspicuously into the text of an advertisement. It calls for reader response to find out how closely the advertisement was read.

Blind test — anonymer (Waren)Test, Blindtest

Also called blind product test.

A test of a product in such a way that the consumer (ie respondent) is unaware of the brand and its identifying features (e.g. labels, packaging, style, etc.) - often in comparison with other similar competing products. Respondents will answer questions without bias or partiality toward the product.

Blister pack(age) — Sichtpackung, Folienverpackung

Also called bubble pack.

A package with a transparent plastic overlay affixed to a cardboard backing (backing sheet) for protecting and displaying a product.

In particular, these are used in the pharmaceutical industry for packing tablets, capsules etc.

Blockbuster — außergewöhnlicher Verkaufs- oder Werbeerfolg

An extraordinary success of a sale or an advertisement.

Blocked-out time — Sperrzeit für Werbung

TV or radio time that is not available for advertising.

Body copy — Textteil (einer Anzeige)

Also called body text or text.

The main text of an advertisement created to sell the product.

Body language Körpersprache

Non-verbal communication with other persons by means of gestures, movements, or physical postures of which the communicator is conscious or unconscious.

Bogus merchandise (Produkt)Fälschungen

Counterfeit products, i.e. imitated products designed to pass as an original.

Boldface/bold face (BF, bf) Halbfettdruck, Fettdruck

Also called blackface, bold type or bold.

A typeface that is darker and thicker than the rest of the text. It is used to call attention to certain words, headings, lines (boldlines) or ideas.

Bonus Bonus

Something extra or additional given freely.

Bonus circulation Extraauflage, Zusatzauflage

Newspaper or magazine circulation in excess of the figure guaranteed by the publisher to advertisers.
Note: the advertisers are not charged for the additional readership reached.

Bonus pack Zugabepackung

Also called bonus size package or extra sized pack.

A method of making a product more attractive to customers by selling a larger pack with an additional amount of the product but at the price usual for a standard pack.

Booking Buchung, Reservierung

The act of ordering a theatre performance, show, room, a seat, a table, etc.

Booking office Schalter, (Vorverkaufs)Kasse

A point of sale dispensing various types of ticket, e.g. theater tickets, travel tickets, etc.

Bookstand Bücherstand

Also called bookstall.

A small open bookshop, e.g. in a railway station.

Boom Boom, (Hoch)Konjunktur, starker Aufschwung

The expansionary phase of the trade cycle. During a boom, due to a rising demand for all commodities, production expands, prices and wages rise, and unemployment decreases. After full employment has been reached a boom will, unless checked, become inflationary.
A boom is opposite to a depression, recession, slump, or stagnation.

Boom in orders Auftragsschwemme

A situation, e.g. during boom years, when the number of incoming orders is continuously increasing.

Boom market Haussemarkt

Also called bull or bullish market.

A market in which demand exceeds supply (there is an excess demand) so that there is an increase in prices.

Boomerang effect Bumerangeffekt

A situation where a hard-selling advertisement for one product may induce the consumer, as a result, to deliberately buy a competitive product.

Booth Messestand, Marktstand, Bude Telefonzelle

An exhibition stand for the sale of goods or for display purposes, as at a market or exhibition. Also called stand.

A place from which one can telephone. Also called telephone booth, box or kiosk; call, coin or phone box; pay station.

Borax Plunder, billige, aber augenfällige Ware
aufdringliche Werbung

An article that appears to be of high quality but in fact is not.

Advertising used to sell borax and that is often aggressive, poorly designed and/or tasteless.

Boston Box Boston-Box, Boston-Matrix, Vierfelder-Portfolio-Matrix

Also called Boston Matrix.

A matrix developed by the Boston Consulting Group (BCG) which enables firms to classify their products on the basis of two key variables: relative market share and market growth. The matrix can be used to forecast the future market position of products within a product portfolio.

The matrix consists of four boxes containing stars, problem children/question marks, cash cows and dogs, i.e. the four basic products of the company.

Note: 1. Stars enjoy major market share in high growth markets; 2. cash cows are market leaders in low growth markets; 3. dogs are low market share products in low growth markets; 4. problem children have large potential in high growth markets, but need attention to build market share. The problem child product was introduced recently but has not yet established itself. If it passes through the growth stage successfully, it may become a "star" and then a "cash cow" as it reaches maturity. Once it passes into decline it becomes a "dog".

Bottle hanger Flaschenanhänger

A small advertising card which hangs round the neck of a bottle.

Bottleneck Engpaß, Engpaßbereich

That part of a production (manufacturing) process, etc., where production of goods or services is slowed down, e.g. by shortage of materials.

Bottleneck area Engpaßgebiet

An area of the economy where specific shortages occur, often because demand is unusually heavy.

Bottleneck inflation nicht-monetäre Nachfrageinflation

This type of inflation is a combination of both demand and cost inflation. It assumes rising costs and rising prices long before all resources are fully employed. The basis for this assumption is that specific shortages occur in some areas of the economy (the bottleneck areas) where demand is unusually heavy.
Effectively the idea of this type of inflation is an admission that models of an economy with resources in perfectly elastic supply are unrealistic.

Bottom Tiefpunkt, Tiefstand
Konjunkturtief

The very lowest point of something, e.g. of sales. Also called low.

A low point in the business cycle. Also called cyclical depression, economic low or trough.

Bottom line Endgewinn oder Endverlust
Wesentlichste, Wichtigste

The net profit or loss.

The deciding or most important factor.

Bottom price niedrigster, äußerster Preis

Also called rock-bottom price.

The lowest price of anything.

Bought-in parts (fremd)bezogene Teile

Also called bought-in supplies, bought-out parts, or purchased components.

Parts of a company's products which are bought from outside, i.e. from other companies.

Boutique Boutique

Shop carrying a range of trendy wear (up-to-date clothes).

Box (bx) Kiste, Kasten

A small case or container, which may be of wood, cardboard or metal, and may have a folding lid.

Box number Postfach
Chiffrenummer

A reference number used in a post office to avoid giving an address (e.g. our address is P.O. Box 357). Also called post office box (POB).

In advertising, a number to which replies to a newspaper advertisement should be sent. The advertisement is called box number advertisement or keyed advertisement.

Box office Kasse

The office of a cinema, theater, stadium, or the like, at which tickets are sold.

Box rate Container-Frachtrate

A freight rate for shipment of a full container, irrespective of the volume that it contains.

Box store (Verbraucher)Abholmarkt
Geschäft mit beschränktem Sortiment

Also called limited line store or limited-item store.

A supermarket similar to a warehouse, with nearly no service, where goods are sold from their original boxes. Box stores, first established in Germany, carry only fast-turnover products. They usually have only a limited number of brands and one size per item, with stockouts and changes in brands occurring often. Products are displayed in cut cartons and customers do their own bagging. Individual items are not priced and prices are very low.

Box success Kassenschlager

An item that sells extremely well or a film or theatre performance that attracts masses of cinema-goers or theatre-goers.

Box-Jenkins method Box-Jenkins-Methode

A qualitative forecasting technique, eg to forecast sales. The method produces information that allows for the particular model to be selected that best approximates the data. A model is tentatively identified, checked for accuracy, and then used to generate forecasts. The problem with using this forecasting method centers around the availability of information and the costs involved. This technique differs from other forecasting techniques inasmuch that it does not pick up a mathematical model on a priori basis.

Boxing department Verpackungsabteilung

Also called packing department

The department in a company where goods are packed for delivery.

Boxtop offer Verpackungsgutschein, (Treue) Prämie bei Verpackungsteileinsendung

In sales promotion, a producer's offer to a consumer of some kind of premium or refund, or a free gift, or reduced price item, in exchange for a boxtop as a proof of purchase of the producer's product.

Boycott Boykott

Refusal to have trade relations with a trader or a country.

Historical note: To boycott is to coerce by preventing any social or commercial dealings with a person, group or nation. The term dates from 1880, when this treatment was first used against captain Boycott, a land agent in Ireland.

Brainstorming Brainstorming (Methode zur Ideenfindung und Ideensammlung)

A technique for encouraging creativity and useful concepts for solving particular problems, usually through team or group discussions. The problems are considered from several points of view. The purpose of brainstorming is the creation of ideas, not their evaluation. Therefore all ideas should be considered, no ideas should be criticized, no idea is trivial or irrelevant. Brainstorming is an application of the principle that several heads are better than one.

Branch Filiale, (Zweig)Niederlassung, Zweigstelle

Also called branch establishment or branch office.

A local office of a bank, an insurance company, a large business, or a local shop of a chain store under the control of a head office.

Branch manager Geschäftsstellenleiter, Filialleiter

A person in charge of a branch.

Branch out diversifizieren

Also called to diversify.

To open another section of a business or to go into new markets with new products or services.

Branch store Verkaufsfiliale, Zweiggeschäft

A store owned by a parent store.

Branches of production Produktionszweige

There are four main branches of production. These are: extractive/primary production, manufacturing industries, commercial services and direct services.

Brand Warenzeichen, Handelsname
Markenartikel
eingebranntes Zeichen

Sometimes also called label.

A trademark, indicating the quality of a product or service. The brand image reflects the overall status of users' perceptions of a company's offering.

A good or service with a set of characteristics which clearly differentiates it from all other goods or services. Also called branded article or good.

A mark made/branded upon property to indicate ownership.

Brand acceptance Markenakzeptanz

The degree to which a buyer accepts a particular product, i.e. he/she might be prepared to buy it.

Brand advertising Markenartikelwerbung

Advertising, e.g. on TV or in the press, for a particular brand.

Brand awareness Markenbewußtsein, Produktbewußtsein

Having knowledge of the existence of a branded product (brand).

The percentage of persons remembering the name of a brand of product.

Buyers` identification with a product or service.

Brand category Markenklasse

Generic classification of products or services. Similar and competing products or services all fall into the same brand category, e.g. different types of perfumes or washing powders.

Brand choice Markenwahl, Kaufentscheid für ein Markenprodukt

The decision to select a particular brand from the variety of brands with similar composition, quality, performance or price characteristics and thus capable of satisfying the consumer´s wants and needs.

Brand competition Markenwettbewerb

Competition/rivalry between brands which can satisfy a consumer's wants almost equally.

Brand development index (BDI) Markenkonsumindex

A percentage of a brand´s sales in a geographic market in relation to the population in that market indexed to the national rate.

Brand differentiation Markenwarendifferenzierung

The degree to which a brand has managed to establish a unique image.

Brand extension Markenerweiterung

The use of a well-known brand name to launch (introduce, bring out) a new product into the market under a successful brand.

Brand image Markenbild (eines Produkts)

The image (mental picture) of a branded product in the minds of consumers. All characteristics (e.g. price, quality, utility, etc.) of that particular brand belong to the brand image. By advertising, a producer tries to create an acceptable image for his product so that more and more consumers desire his brand and prefer it to the other brands.

Brand indifference Markenindifferenz

A buying behaviour characterised by a low degree of brand loyalty.

Brand label Markenetikett

The label which gives the brand name of the product.

Brand leader Markenführer, Spitzenmarke

Also called major.

Product which holds the greatest single share of a market for all products of its type.

Brand loyalty Markentreue

Allegiance to a branded product, i.e. the loyalty by the customer to repurchase the product despite keen competition by other branded substitutes. Many firms use advertising in order to build this allegiance to their product. On the other hand it is generally considered that brand loyalty is reduced by price and promotional competition. Therefore the consumer must perceive that the brand offers the right combination of price and quality.

Brand loyalty segmentation (Markt)Segmentierung nach Markentreue

The breakdown of a market into a sub-market based on brand loyalty which shows the consumer´s amount of product satisfaction and his/her unwillingness to switch to competing products. Thus, this market is characterized by the consumers´preference for one product and their readiness to purchase that product on a regular basis.

Brand management Marken(produkt)management

An organization system in which responsibility for one product or group of products is delegated to a person or a group of persons if the sales volume warrants.

Brand manager Produktmanager (Verkaufsleiter für ein bestimmtes Produkt)

Also called product manager.

Executive responsible for the overall marketing and promotion of a specific brand.

Brand mark Firmen-/Warenkennzeichen, (Firmen)Logo, Markenzeichen

Part of a brand such as a symbol, logo, design, or distinctive colouring or lettering, or a combination of these, that cannot be spoken.
Examples are the three stripes of adidas, the roaring lion of Metro-Goldwyn-Mayer or the colours blue and white in the BMW logotype.
Note: a brand mark is not the same as a trademark.

Brand name Markenname, Waren-, Handelsbezeichnung

Also called trade name.

The name of a brand which may consist of a letter, a word or a group of letters or words.

Some of the world´s most powerful brand names in alphabetical order are:
Adidas, Audi, BMW, Coca-Cola, Kodak, McDonald´s, Mercedes Benz, Microsoft, Nike, Philips, Porsche, Sony, Toyota, Volkswagen, etc.

Brand name selection Markennamenauswahl

The selection of a brand name for a particular product. Certainly, there are many criteria that can be used in selecting and establishing a brand name; but the three most important ones are:

1. pronunciation (the name should be easily pronounced and in only one way);
2. connotation (this means that the name selected does not have to be directly related to the product, but it should not have an associated use that is incompatible with the product);
3. memorability (most desirable is a name that can be easily remembered).

In selecting a meaningful brand name, all geographic words and generic terms must be avoided.
Note: the brand name should be registered and protected through use.

Brand piracy Markenpiraterie

Also called faking of brands.

The counterfeiting (faking) of well-known brands, usually in foreign markets; but not all fakers are foreign. A certain percentage of fakes are made in the company's home country, usually by marginal producers who cannot make a profit legally.

Two of the main reasons that encourage brand piracy are:

1. branded goods are often of high esteem, particularly those of long standing; in the less developed countries (LDCs), goods from advanced countries, especially the luxury goods, serve as status symbols and most of the time are in short supply;
2. the technological knowledge required to produce a counterfeit product is readily available.

Three forms of piracy can be labeled:

1. imitation (the copying of an established brand);
2. faking (identifying the fraudulent product with a symbol, logo, or brand name that is very similar to the famous brand);
3. preemption (this is feasible in those countries where the law permits wholesale registration of brand names which can then be sold to those interested in counterfeiting or better still to the original company when it is ready to move into the country).

Needless to say, brand piracy can cause unfair competition to multinational corporations (MNCs) in many markets. Worse still is the export of the bogus/counterfeit product to the home market. MNCs have still little protection in the form of international laws to protect their brands overseas and the laws pertaining to brand piracy in many countries are loose, with little punishment for shady practices.

Brand positioning Markenproduktpositionierung

A brand's position in a market, so that it is recognized by the public and may have a high rating in terms of quality, reliability and status.

Brand preference Markenpräferenz

The degree to which consumers prefer one brand over another or consider it acceptable or unacceptable in relation to competitive brands.

Brand recognition Markenbewußtsein

The stage of a buyer's awareness of the existence of a particular brand.

Brand repositioning Markenneupositionierung

The changing or adjusting of consumers´ idea(s) of a brand by changing the product and/or its image.
Repositioning may be necessary because: 1. a competitor has launched a brand positioned next to the company´s brand, 2. customer wants have shifted.

When repositioning a brand, the marketer must be careful not to drop or confuse current loyal users.

Brand selection Markenwahl

The choosing of one brand from a set of alternative brands.

Brand share Marktanteil einer Marke

The market share of one brand as compared to the share of all competitive brands in the same category.

Brand switching Markenwechsel

Ceasing to buy a branded article and shifting to another, similar product of another brand, showing little brand loyalty.

Brand X Marke X

In comparative advertising, the unknown brand which is used in TV commercials as a comparison to the named brand being advertised.

Branded good Markenartikel

Also called brand; branded article, merchandise or product, or trademarked article.

Goods sold under brand names, i.e. these are goods that bear a producer's trade mark, trade name or brand, in order to distinguish them from similar goods made by others. If the name is registered under the Trade Marks Act, it is a trade mark, and no one else may use it; if the name is not registered, it is called a trade name or brand.

Branding Warenzeichenpolitik

A procedure adopted by competitive firms to distinguish their product(s) from those of their competitors.

Arguments in favour of branding are:
1. memory recall is facilitated (this may lead to more rapid buying actions or greater frequency of buying);
2. branding leads to a more ready product acceptance;
3. advertising can be directed more effectively;
4. display space is more easily obtained;
5. the importance of price differentials may be diminished;
6. brand loyalty may increase;
7. self-selection is facilitated;
8. persuasive personal selling activities may be reduced;
9. market segmentation may be easier;
10. selling costs decrease;
11. good brands build the corporate image;
12. more legal protection of unique product features; etc.

Note:
1. The relevance of branding does not apply equally to all products.
2. Branding is a very general term covering brand names, designs, trademarks, logotypes, etc.

Break Preissturz
Sendeunterbrechung für Werbung
Pause

A rapid and sharp price decline. Also called sharp drop-off/tumble in prices or slump in prices.

In advertising, the time period in TV or radio when commercials are to be transmitted.

A short interval for refreshment.

Breakeven — Geschäftsabschluß ohne Gewinn und Verlust, mit Plus-minus-Null arbeiten

Carrying on business so that neither profit nor loss is made.

Breakeven analysis — Break-Even-Analyse, Gewinnschwellenanalyse

The study of how costs and profits vary with the volume of production, using accounting methods of analysis. The breakeven sales volume is that which ensures that all fixed and variable costs are covered by income, neither profit nor loss being made, giving a particular selling price.

Breakeven analysis is an important analytical tool as well as a method for pricing a product. It gives a firm an idea of the profit potential as well as any safety margin (this is the level of sales in excess of the BEP) in achieving this profit at alterntive prices. Breakeven analysis is particularly useful when considering a price change.

Breakeven point (BEP) — Breakeven-Punkt, Gewinn- oder Ertragsschwelle, Kostendeckungspunkt, Nutzenschwelle

The volume of sales necessary to start showing profit, i.e. to enable both fixed and variable costs to be covered by total revenue. At this point (level) a company's or product's sales revenue equals its total cost and there is neither profit nor loss. All sales over the breakeven point produce profits; any drop in sales below that point will produce losses.
Note: the amount of sales needed for the company to break even varies with alternative prices.
The BEP can be calculated by using the following formula:
$P(x) = FC$ and $VC(x)$
where: P = price, x = breakeven point (in units), FC = fixed cost, VC = variable cost.

The point where all the money invested in a project has been recovered and the cumulative value of cash flow is zero.

Breakeven price — Breakeven-Preis, Kostendeckungspreis

The price at which the firm just covers its costs.

The price at which a given quantity of product needs to be sold to avoid any loss on the operations.

Breakeven pricing — Breakeven-Preisbildung

A cost-oriented pricing strategy where a firm tries to determine/fix a product`s price, at which it will break even or make the target profit it is seeking.

Breakeven quantity — Breakeven-Menge, kostendeckende Menge

The quantity of product sales needed to break even, or meet all the costs involved in producing the product.

Breaking bulk — Stichprobenentnahme
Zerlegen einer (Waren)Sendung

To open a consignment or parcel for the purpose of taking samples.

The practice of a wholesaler or middleman to buy in bulk, i.e. to take a large, economical shipment from a manufacturer and divide it into smaller units to sell to retailers for greater profit.

Breakthrough product — bahnbrechende Erfindung
bahnbrechendes Erzeugnis

An unique innovation that is mainly technical in nature.

A completely new product.

Bribe — Bestechungsgeld, Schmiergeld, "Entscheidungshilfe"

Also called bribe money, secret commission, graft, improper payment, payoff, slush fund or payola (coll).

Money offered to a person to persuade him to do something which he should not do. For example, a reward of money or goods paid secretly to influence the payee (ie the bribee) to grant rights or privileges to the payer (ie the briber).
Offering or accepting a special right or privilege is usually a criminal offence.

Bribery Bestechung

Also called corruption or illegal gratification.

The act or practice of giving presents (e.g. money or commodities) to somebody to persuade him to do something which is dishonest or even illegal; bribery is subject to penalty.

The act or practice of accepting a bribe.

Brief Kurzbericht

Also called condensed report or summary report.

A summary of the main details of something longer.

British Standards Institution (BSI) Britischer Normenverband

A voluntary, non-profit-making body established in 1929 and jointly financed by industry and the government. It seeks to improve, simplify and standardize industrial materials such as screw threads, methods of testing, standards of quality and performance.

British Week Britische Woche

The promotion of British consumer goods (consumption goods) at the point of sale (POS) in a selected location overseas. The aim is to achieve an interest in all British things.

Broad assortment breites Sortiment

Also called wide assortment.

A reseller's assortment strategy to carry a wide range of related product lines.

Broadsheet großformatiger Werbeprospekt, großes Faltblatt, Handzettel

Also called broadside or throwaway.

A printed promotional material, usually a very large folder with pages often as large as those of a newspaper, or folding out like a map, usually with one or two folds. The broadsheet is often used in direct mail when it is folded to compact size and it can also be used as a shop poster or window display.

Brochure Broschüre, Prospekt

Also called booklet, handout or pamphlet.

A booklet (often illustrated) consisting of a few pages in paper cover giving details of goods.

Broken lot nicht handelsübliche Losgröße
unvollständiger (Güter)Satz

Goods offered for sale in smaller than normal quantity.

An incomplete set of goods for sale.

Broken stowage Staulücke

In the stowage of cargo, space wasted by cargo of irregular-shaped packages and packages of uneven size or irregularity of cargo spaces.

Broker Broker, Makler, Vermittler

An agent, acting as intermediary, who buys and sells for a principal on commission. The commission (brokerage) is calculated as a percentage of the value of business done. He does not have possession of the goods, shares, or policies in which he deals, i.e. the broker never becomes owner of the goods and cannot act in his own name. However, there are exceptions: bill brokers and some commodity brokers do buy and sell for themselves.
There are many different types of broker such as brokers dealing with commodities (commodity brokers), stockbrokers, insurance brokers, foreign exchange brokers, import brokers, etc.

Brokerage (bkge) Maklergebühr, Provision, Courtage
Maklergeschäft

Also called brokage, courtage, brokerage allowance, brokerage commission or fee, or broker's commission.

The commission charged by a broker to his principal for the services in arranging a contract, i.e. for the carrying out of buying or selling of goods, shares, etc. It is usually a percentage of the monetary value of the business transacted.

Synonym for broking, i.e. acting as a broker.

Broking Maklergeschäft

Also called brokering.

The business of a broker.

Browngoods/brown goods braune Ware

A classification of durable consumer goods (durables, consumer durables) which includes TVs, radios and hifi equipment and recorders.

Bubble company Briefkastenfirma, Mantelgesellschaft (Schwindelfirma)

Also called dummy company.

A company that never had any real business, a company to defraud the public.

Buckeye geschmacklose Werbung

Tasteless advertising.

Budget Budget, Etat

A sum of money set aside for a future activity or project.

Budget account "offenes" Kreditkonto, Kundenkonto

Also called budget plan.

A form of charge account. A customer makes regular fixed payments to a retailer and is allowed credit up to a certain amount (e.g. 12 times the monthly sum being paid).

Budget constraint Budget-, Etatbeschränkung Budgetrestriktion

The limitation of the amount of income available to a household in a given period, disregarding the availability of borrowing.

Given a limited income and the prices of products, the constraint that separates the goods that the consumer can purchase from those that cannot be purchased.

Budget department Sonderangebotsabteilung

A department where goods are sold at cheaper prices, i.e. at budget prices.

Budget line Bilanzgerade, Budgetgerade, Isobudgetgerade

Also called budget constraint line, consumer or consumption possibility line, iso-expenditure line or price line.

In consumer theory, a straight line on a graph which shows all the possible combinations of goods that a consumer could buy with his income at given prices. The slope and location of the line are determined by the prices of the goods in question.

Built-in (automatic) stabilizer eingebauter (automatischer) Konjunktur-Stabilisator (der Wirtschaft)

Also called automatic fiscal stabilizer or built-in flexibility.

Policies (e.g. fiscal policies) which automatically dampen down cyclical fluctuations in the economy (e.g. a decrease in taxation will stimulate spending and thus stimulate the economy) without any direct action by government, firms or individuals.

Built-in obsolescence eingebauter Verschleiß, geplantes Veralten

Also called planned obsolescence.

The deliberate policy of making a product become rapidly out of date or unserviceable in order to ensure future sales.

Bulk business Massengeschäft

A business for everyone.

Bulk buying Massen-, Großeinkauf, Engrosbezug

Also called bulk purchase or volume purchasing.

Buying in large quantities; suppliers often offer goods at cheaper prices for large quantities. A bulk buyer/purchaser buys large quantities.

Bulk cargo (BC, b/c) Massenfrachtgut, Schüttgutladung

A cargo which consists of one commodity in an unpacked condition such as grain, oil or coal. Thus it can be shipped in a bulk container or directly in the hold of a ship.

Bulk carrier Massengutfrachter

A vessel built to transport dry or liquid bulk cargo, e.g. oil, iron ore, coal, grain, etc., which are not packed in containers. The freight per ton of cargo is lower.

Bulk discount (rate) Mengenrabatt

Also called bulk rate, quantity discount or volume discount.

Reduction on standard price in consideration of purchasing a large quantity of goods or services or a reduced charge for multiple purchases.

Bulk goods Massengüter

Also called bulk commodities.

Products or materials distributed in large quantities such as coal, grain and sand.

Bulk mail Postwurfsendung, Infopost

Also called bulk mailing, junk mail or unaddressed mail advertising.

Advertising material (e.g. leaflets) sent by mail to every household. Letters posted in bulk can qualify for rebates of postage.

Bulk shipment Massengütertransport

Also called bulk goods transport.

The shipment of large quantities of goods.

Bull Haussier, Haussespekulant

Also called boomer or bull operator.

A person who thinks prices will rise, e.g. prices for an individual share, bond, commodity, etc.

Bull market Haussemarkt

Also called bullish or boom market.

A market in which prices are rising, e.g. share prices or commodity prices. Bull markets usually last at least a few months and are characterized by high trading volume.

Bulldog edition Morgenausgabe

The early edition of a daily newspaper.

Bulletin Bulletin, Bekanntmachung

A short statement of news, events, alterations of policy and other matters, e.g. staff-promotions or transfers. It is therefore an effective form of communication. Copies are either handed to every member of staff (staff bulletin) or exhibited on bulletin boards (notice boards). A bulletin is often several pages long, whereas a notice is usually shorter and announces a particular event.

Bulletin board (BB) schwarzes Brett, Anschlagtafel große Werbewand

A board for the display of messages or information. Also called notice board.

In advertising, a large board for outdoor advertisements. Also called billboard or hoarding.

Bullish haussierend, auf eine Hausse hindeutend

A stock or commodity market term; when conditions suggest higher security or commodity prices a bullish situation exists.

Bunches Ausverkaufsware

Clearance items, e.g. at clothing shops.

Bundle (bdle) Bund, Bündel

Miscellaneous goods tied together and handled as a unit.

Buoyancy Kursanstieg auf breiter Front

A stock or commodity market situation in which prices rise.

Buried advertisement versteckte, vergrabene Anzeige; verstecktes Inserat

An advertisement in a newspaper or magazine that is hidden among other ads.

Buried position ungünstig/abseits plazierte Werbeanzeige

In advertising, a position in a publication considered unfavourable for an advertisement, e.g. because the surrounding material either has little attraction to the readership or distracts from the advertisement.

Burst stoßweise Werbung

Also called flight.

A large number of advertisements for a product or service placed over a short period of time. A period of advertising activity is followed by a period of inactivity.

Burst advertising phasenweise Klotzwerbung, stoßweise Werbung

Concentration of TV commercials into a short time period.

Bushel (bsh, bu, bush) Scheffel, Bushel (Hohlmaß)

A measure of capacity used for dry goods such as grain, fruit, etc.. In the UK it measures 36,37 l, in the US 35,24 l.

Business jede wirtschaftliche Tätigkeit Branche, Geschäftszweig

The practice of commerce; any form of trading; the activities of buying, selling or manufacturing goods or providing services.

An industry. Also called line of business.

Business address Geschäftsadresse

The address, i.e. the house number, street, town, postcode (zip code), state and country of a company.

Business barometer Konjunkturbarometer

Also called economic indicator.

Statistical indicators which reflect the market conditions.

Business call Dienstgespräch
Geschäftsbesuch

A discussion or phone call on business matters.

A person's visit to/call on to a company to talk to someone on business.

Business card Geschäftskarte, Visitenkarte

Also called calling card or visiting card.

A card showing the holder's name, firm, address, position, etc.

Business cycle Konjunkturzyklus, Konjunkturphase

Also called trade cycle; business, economic or production cycle; boom-slump cycle.

In general, a fluctuation in the level of economic activity; a boom is followed by a recession/slump, leading to a depression succeeded by further expansion.

Phases of the business cycle are: the upswing or upturn; the boom or prosperity; the downswing, recession, contraction or slump; the depression, stagnation or trough; and the expansion, recovery or revival.

In detail, a cycle in time, during which economic activity moves from an upswing or boom (high output, investment and employment) through a downswing or recession (a running-down period) to a depression or stagnation (low output, investment and employment) and then upward again to a recovery or expansion until there is a boom again. The whole cycle then begins again.

Booms and slumps occur as a result of natural economic forces which tend to occur cyclically; in other cases they are due to seasonal variations or are the result of stop-go policies of the government to fight inflation.

Business enterprise — Handelsunternehmen, Wirtschaftsunternehmen

Also called business; business or commercial undertaking; commercial enterprise.

An economic organisation dealing with all factors involved in the production of goods for profit or an organisation engaged in commercial activities.

Business environment — betriebliches Umfeld

The atmosphere and all the surroundings and conditions that directly or indirectly influence a business.

Business expenses — Betriebsausgaben

Money spent on running a business, not on assets or stock.

Business forecast(ing) — Unternehmensprognose Konjunkturprognose

Predicting the future development of a company or economy.

Business hours — Geschäftszeit

The time when a business is open. Also called office or opening hours.

The time when an office or bank is open. Also called office hours or banking hours.

Business indicators — Unternehmens-, Konjunkturindikatoren

Statistical data which have an effect on the level of business and economic activity.

Business lunch — Geschäftsessen

A meeting where people have lunch together to discuss business matters.

Business market — Absatzmarkt für industrielle Erzeugnisse

Also called industrial market.

A market consisting of individuals and organisations who buy products and services that will be used in manufacture or business, or eventually resold to other customers.

Business monitor — Marktbeobachter

Persons who assess market share trends in a large number of product fields and analyse the growth of existing and potential markets.

Business name — Firmenname

Also called company name or firm name.

The name under which a business is conducted.

Business paper — Wirtschaftszeitung
Verkaufsunterlage

A publication designed to appeal to the needs and interests of a specific occupation or industry. Also called trade paper, business publication, trade or technical journal. Examples are: The Financial Times (GB), The Wall Street Journal (USA), Handelsblatt (Germany).

The original sales documents, e.g. the sales invoice.

Business portfolio — Unternehmens-Portfolio

The collection of businesses and products that make up the company and that should best fit its strengths and weaknesses.

Business press — Wirtschaftspresse

Publications dealing exclusively with business subjects.

Business reply card (BRC) or envelope (BRE) (bezahlte) Rückantwort, Freiumschlag, Rückumschlag

A Post Office service whereby firms may relieve customers of the post of stamps wher returning specially printed (and reply-paid) cards or envelopes. To do so a licence must be obtained from the Post Office.

Business service Dienstleistung im gewerblichen Bereich

An expense item obtained from an outside supplier that does not become part of a final product, e.g. advertising, management consulting, maintenance, marketing research, etc.

Business site marketing Firmengelände-Marketing

Marketing activities undertaken by property/real-estate developers which involve developing, selling, or renting business sites for factories, offices, stores, warehouses, etc. The developers research companies′ land needs and offer them real-estate solutions, such as industrial parks, greenfield sites, new office buildings, shopping centres, etc.

Business startup loan Existenzgründungskredit

A special loan granted to encourage people to invest in new businesses.

Business statistics Geschäftsstatistik

The systematic collection, presentation, and interpretation of data related to business problems.

Business to business (BTB) advertising Werbung von Unternehmen zu Unternehmen

Also called industrial advertising.

The means by which one business promotes its goods or services to another. The opposite of consumer advertising.

Suitable media for the promotion of industrial products are:
1. industrial and trade press advertisements, 2. public relations, 3. sales literature, 4. direct mail, 5. trade exhibitions, 6. demonstration films and videos.

In consumer product advertising, it is often essential to establish a satisfactory brand image to achieve loyalty from consumers. With BTB/industrial advertising, the situation is quite different. Here, one is selling on the basis of quality, service and price and usually in that order. Industrial buyers have no option but to purchase such materials and components that their production departments require. Thus, advertising does not create the demand for industrial products but backs the other promotional tools.

Business to business (BTB) market — Absatzmarkt für industrielle Erzeugnisse

Also called industrial market.

A market consisting of individuals and organisations who buy products (consumable products and capital goods) and services that will be used in manufacture or business, or eventually resold to other customers.

Business transaction — Geschäft
Geschäftsvorfall

An agreement or deal made between the business and either another business or a person. Also called deal.

A transaction entered in the accounting records of a business. Also called accounting event or external transaction.

Business trip — Geschäftsreise, Dienstreise

Also called business travel.

A journey for business puposes, ie a trip to discuss business matters with customers/clients.

Buy one - get one free (BOGOF) — bei Kauf eines Produkts, gibt es ein weiteres kostenlos

A special offer made to consumers whereby on purchase of one product, another one is given free of charge.

Buy turnover — hoher Umsatz mit geringer Gewinnspanne

A situation where a firm makes a high volume of sales but makes only little profit.

Buy-back agreement Rückkaufvereinbarung

A provision in a contract under which the seller agrees to repurchase (buy back) the sold item at a stated price upon the occurrence of a specified event within a certain period.

Buyer Kunde, Abnehmer
Käufer
Einkäufer, Leiter des Einkaufs

The customer. Also called client.

Someone who buys. Also called purchaser or vendee.

The person within a company responsible for buying. Also called purchasing or buying manager, or buying agent.

Buyer behaviour Käuferverhalten

The decision processes and acts of people involved in buying and using products or services.

The purchase behaviours of producers, resellers, etc.

Buyer decision Kaufentschluß

A potential customer`s decision to buy a product or service.
The customer may be influenced to buy to a greater or lesser extent by any combination of the following:
1. performance of the product, 2. aesthetic design features, 3. packaging, 4. service facilities available, 5. advertising, 6. distinctiveness of the product (e.g. branding, quality), 7. price to the ultimate buyer, 8. credit facilities, 9. the opinion of others, etc.

Buyer dynamics Käuferdynamik

Situations where customers´ needs and preferences change so that sellers must modify or change their product(s).

Buyer rejection Käuferablehnung

A situation which occurs when buyers do not want the product or service regardless of the marketing efforts. Thus, products and services must be designed to match customer wants more precisely.

Buyer's expectation method Käufererwartungsmethode

A qualitative forecasting method where a buyer is asked to predict/forecast the amount he/she will purchase in a future time period. The accuracy of this method depends on the extent buyers have clearly formulated purchasing intentions and the means to implement these plans.
Note: this method is best used in forecasting sales of industrial goods.

Buyer's inertia Käuferträgheit

The tendency of any buyer to continue to buy what he has bought in the past.

Buyer's rights Rechte des Käufers

Once the buyer has purchased something the seller takes on obligations to him/her. These are set out in the Sale of Goods Act. They are as follows:
The goods must be:
a. of a merchantable quality,
b. fit for their purpose,
c. as described.

Furthermore buyers are justified in assuming that the shopkeeper either owns the goods or has the right to sell them.

If goods are faulty, the buyer's rights are any one of the following:

a. he can reject the goods and ask for compensation,
b. he may ask for the article to be replaced or repaired,
c. he may be given a credit note to buy something else (a buyer cannot be compelled to accept it).

None of these rights can be taken away from the buyer, even if he/she signs a document which appears to do so. Rights under the Sale of Goods Act do not apply to private sales, however.

Buyer's strike Käuferstreik

A buyer's refusal to buy/purchase goods, e.g. because prices are too high.

Buyer-decision process Käuferentscheidungsprozeß

The process by which buyers make their buying decision.
This process consists of five stages:
1. problem recognition (in this stage the buyer recognizes a problem or need because he/she realizes a difference between the actual state and some desired state);

2. information search (the consumer looks for more (detailed) information);
3. evaluation of alternatives (the consumer will evaluate competing brands);
4. purchase decision (the consumer decides to buy the product);
5. postpurchase behaviour (further actions taken by the consumer after purchasing the product; generally, these actions depend on whether the consumer is satisfied or dissatisfied with the purchase).

Note: As the buying porcess starts long before the actual purchase and continues long after, the marketer should focus on the entire buying process and not just on the purchase decision.

Buyer-oriented pricing käuferorientierte Preisgestaltung

A pricing strategy considering consumer perceptions of price and how these perceptions affect consumers´ buying decisions. Effective, buyer-oriented pricing involves understanding how much value (i.e. the benefits of having or using the product) consumers place on the actual or perceived benefits they receive from the product and setting a price that fits this value.

As consumers do use these values to evaluate a product´s price, they will not buy the product if they perceive that the price is greater than the product´s value, and they will buy it if they perceive that the price is below a product´s value.

Note: good pricing begins with analysing consumer needs and behaviours and consumers´ perceptions of the product´s value and price. Certainly, price must also take the other marketing mix variables into consideration.

Buyer-reader Kaufleser, Erstleser

A reader of a publication who has also bought it.

Buyer-readiness states Kaufbereitschaftsstadien

The stages potential buyers normally pass through on their way to purchase. The buyer may be in any or all of the following stages: 1. awareness, 2. knowledge, 3. liking, 4. preference, 5. conviction, 6. purchase.

Buyer´s risk Käuferrisiko

Risk taken by a buyer when accepting goods or services without a guarantee.

Buyers' market Käufermarkt

A market characterized by excess supply because of overproduction, or because there are too many sellers and not enough buyers, so that prices will fall and buyers are able to obtain favourable terms.

Buyers´ reactions to price changes Käuferreaktionen auf Preisänderungen

Any price change will affect buyers and lead to different reactions:

1. buyers are most price sensitive to products that cost a lot and/or are bought frequently;
2. buyers hardly notice higher prices on products that they buy infrequently;
3. a higher price (which normally deters buyers from purchases) may mean that the product represents an unusally good value, may become unobtainable and thus should be bought soon, or that the seller is greedy and is charging a price the market will bear;
4. a lower price may make the consumer believe that the product is about to be replaced by a later model, may have some fault, is not selling well, is of inferior/minor quality, etc.;
5. a lower price may induce the consumer to defer the purchase to the future because he is hoping that the price will come down even further.

Buying Kaufen, Einkaufen

Deciding the type and amount of goods to be purchased, followed by the actual purchase.

Buying agent Einkäufer, Einkaufskommissionär

Also called purchasing agent.

One who buys goods for his principal.

Buying behaviour Einkaufsverhalten

Also called buying habit.

The way in which people behave when deciding whether or not to buy a certain product or service and their personal feelings and thoughts which will affect their behaviour.

Buying by specification Spezifikationskauf

Also called sale to specification(s) or sale by description.

The purchase of materials or goods in accordance with one's own requirements precisely described in writing.

Buying center Beschaffungsgruppe

The decision-making individuals and groups (eg the actual users of the product, those who influence the buying decision, the ultimate deciders who make the buying decision, those who do the actual buying, etc) who play a role in the purchase decision process.

Buying decision Kaufentscheidung

Also called purchasing decision.

The different situations a buyer has to face before purchasing a product or service satisfying his need(s).
There are three main buying decisions:
1. product decision (i.e. which product can be bought with available funds);
2. brand decision (i.e. which of the competing brands will be bought);
3. supplier decision (i.e. which supplier will be selected).

Buying department Einkaufsabteilung

Also called purchasing department.

The department in a company which buys raw materials for production or merchandise for resale.

Buying incentive Kaufanreiz

A sales promotional aid to persuade a buyer to purchase a product or service, often in the form of a discount, gift, or bonus good (e.g. "buy one get one free").

Buying intent Kaufabsicht

Also called buying intention.

The intention of a potential buyer to buy. This by no means always leads to a sale.

Buying motives Kaufmotive

All those factors, e.g. price, quality, prestige, etc, within a buyer which combine to create a desire to buy.
Other possible motives are: to gain acceptance of a peer group, to satisfy a personal goal, to increase productivity, to reduce costs, to improve security, to be remembered, to be different, to take advantage of a new technology, to reach an organizational objective, etc.

Buying on time Kauf auf Raten, Abzahlungskauf

Also called instal(l)ment buying or purchase; colloquially: to buy on the never-never.

The buyer acquires goods with no or only a small downpayment. The remaining amount of the purchase price will be paid at regular intervals, ie the buyer pays in instal(l)ments.

Buying power index (BPI) Kaufkraftindex

An index of buying potential constructed from basic economic data. It gives an indication of the ability to purchase in certain areas and thus indicates the sales opportunities.

Buying process Kaufprozeß

The steps in a buying decision. There are five stages in the buying process:

1. need arousal (this is the recognition of a need which can come from within - e.g. we become hungry - or from outside forces - e.g. we see an advertisement - or it comes on the spur of the moment);
2. information search (you will either be in a heightened state of awareness and thus accumulate general information or you will be on an active search for information and thus go for more specific information);
3. evaluation (often the most critical point because the consumer has to be convinced of obtaining the best quality and most utility at a certain price);
4. purchase decision (despite a positive evaluation, the product may not be purchased because social factors, e.g. the reactions of others, or anticipated conditions, e.g. economic changes, may influence the purchase intention);

5. postpurchase (if you want to stay in business, you must also pay attention to the consumer's feelings after the purchase has been made).

Buying roles Kaufverhaltensrollen

Three buying roles are involved in each transaction; these roles are:
1. the consumer-buyers (these are the individuals who do the actual buying);
2. the purchase decider (this is the individual who actually makes the decision regarding which product or service is to be purchased);
3. the ultimate users (the individuals who actually consume or use the product).

Buying round Direkteinkauf

Also called direct buying or purchasing.

Buying direct from a producer and thereby excluding middlemen, e.g. a wholesaler.

Buying signals Kaufsignale

Verbal or nonverbal signs or indications telling the salesperson that the potential buyer is ready to buy.

Buying stimuli Kaufanreize

Possible stimuli inducing a potential buyer to purchase a product are:
1. the product which represents an economic utility to the buyer;
2. the packaging materials and the package`s design, colour, size, illustrations, brand name, logotype, copy and layout may considerably influence a buyer´s perception and purchase of a product;
3. the price which a firm sets for its product will affect both sales and profitability; under intensifying competition and falling disposable incomes, the price level becomes the decisive decision determinant; note: it is very important to a firm to study the price elasticity of its product;
4. advertising and promotion activities which should create favourable opinions and feelings about a company and establish favourable customer attitudes towards product quality, price, delivery, sales and technical services;
5. the distributive channels, eg whether products: a. can be bought directly from the producer, b. are made available through intermediaries such as retail outlets, c. are sold through home selling, d. are offered at discount stores or shopping centres, etc;
6. the company's corporate image may change a buyer's attitude to a product sold by the company, etc.

Buzzword Modewort, Schlagwort

A word or phrase that has come into vogue in popular culture or a particular profession.

Bybidder Scheinbieter

Also called mock bidder or straw bidder.

A person who deceptively bids at an auction in order to raise prices for the seller or the auctioneer.

Byproduct/by-product Nebenprodukt, Nebenerzeugnis, Abfallprodukt

Also called co-product, residual product or subsidiary product.

A secondary or incidental product which is produced in the course of manufacturing or processing a main product. If uses or markets for by-products cannot be found, they become waste-products (spinoffs).

Byproduct pricing Nebenproduktpreisbildung

A pricing strategy where the producer tries to fix/set a price for a byproduct that at least covers more than the cost of storing and delivering it to customers. If the seller manages to achieve such a price, this allows him to reduce the main product´s price and thus make it more competitive.

Note: if the seller cannot find a market for the byproduct (eg because it has no value) and if it is costly to get rid of it, this will greatly affect the main product´s price.

C

C-terms C-Klauseln

One of the four different categories of the Incoterms (1990), the others being the D-terms, the E-term and the F-terms.

The C-terms comprise: 1. CFR (cost and freight), 2. CIF (cost, insurance and freight), 3. CPT (carriage paid to), 4. CIP (carriage and insurance paid to).

Their common characteristics are:
1. main carriage is paid, i.e. the seller has to contract and pay for carriage to the named place of destination, but the risk of loss of or damage to the goods or additional costs due to events occurring after shipment or despatch fall upon the buyer;
2. the seller fulfils the contract in the country of shipment or despatch (thus, the C-terms evidence shipment contracts);
3. the C-terms contain two "critical" points, one for the division of costs and another one for the division of risks.

Cable television (CATV) Kabelfernsehen

A system of distributing television signals to households by cable. Cable subscribers can receive a wide variety of TV channels.

Calculation of profit(s) Gewinnberechnung, Gewinnermittlung

From time to time a business prepares a profit and loss account. This shows on the credit side all the revenue items, and on the debit side all the expense items. The difference between the two sides of the account is a profit or a loss (revenue > expenses = profit, expenses > revenues = loss).

Call Telefonanruf, Telefonat (kurzer) Besuch

A telephone call. Also called phone call.

A short visit, e.g. by a salesperson to a customer to gather information, make a sales presentation, secure an order, etc.

Call bird Lockartikel, Lockvogel

Also called bait, button, decoy, leader, leading article, loss leader, lowball, lure, price leader or stool pigeon.

A product offered at an invitingly low price, at cost or less to attract customers. For example, the use of low prices on items not normally purchased in large quantities, as a feature in advertising. The aim is to increase store traffic in the hope of selling regularly priced goods or something more costly.

Call cycle (Kunden)Besuchszyklus

Also called calling cycle.

The time period between a salesperson's visits to the same customer.

Call date Stichtag

The date on which a payment falls due (matures), a withdrawal will be made, an application has to be handed in or an order has to be placed at the latest, etc.

Call frequency (Kunden)Besuchshäufigkeit

The number of times (ie the number of sales calls) a salesperson visits a particular customer during a certain period of time.

Call letters (Rundfunk- und Fernseh-) Senderabkürzung

A number of letters used to identify a radio or TV station.

Call off as required Abruf nach Bedarf

A form of materials purchase in which a supplier is given a schedule of goods likely to be required over a future period. The actual number of goods are called off as and when needed by the purchaser.

Call purchase Kauf auf Abruf, Abrufauftrag

Also called call order.

The purchaser buys a certain quantity of goods but the actual number of goods are called off as and when needed by the purchaser.

Call rate (Kunden)Besuchsrate

The number of calls (ie personal contacts) made by a salesperson on customers or prospects in a specific period of time, eg per month. The salesperson usually writes a call report, i.e. an account of his visit.

Call report (Kunden)Besuchsbericht
Kontaktbericht, -memorandum

A report submitted by a sales representative to his/her employer, usually in writing, after visiting a customer or prospect.

A written record of a meeting between an advertiser and an ad agency, prepared by an agency employee and sent to all interested parties. Also called conference or contact report.

Call slip Vertreterbericht

Also called agent's report.

A salesperson's report stating details of his calls made to customers (ie his customer calls).

Call-charge indicator (Telefon)Gebührenanzeiger

Also called call meter or tollcharge meter.

A device connected to a telephone console which records the number of call charge units.

Call-off purchase agreement Abrufvertrag

An arrangement (i.e. a call order) by which the purchaser places a firm order for a specific quantity and reserves the right to request delivery of required quantities as and when he needs them.

Callback Rückruf
Kontrollinterview, Nachfaßinterview

The recall of defective products by a manufacturer, e.g. cars.

A term for a visit to an interviewee/respondent who has already been interviewed once or who was not available for interview at the first visit.

Caller Anrufer
Besucher

A person who telephones. Also called calling subscriber.

A person who visits, e.g. a company. Also called visitor.

Calling card Visitenkarte
Telefon-Kreditkarte

A card showing the holder's name, firm, address, position, etc. Also called business card or visiting card.

A credit card issued by a telephone company/corporation.

Calling cycle Kundenbesuchszyklus

The average period between calls on a given customer.

Camouflaged advertising Schleichwerbung, versteckte Werbung

Also called background, hidden or masked advertising.

Advertising for which the advertiser does not pay because his products are mentioned or shown on TV, e.g. during a special event or an interview, although he has not booked any advertising time.

Campaign Kampagne

Organized course of action, planned carefully to achieve predefined objectives, e.g. an advertising campaign or a sales campaign.

Campaign plan Werbekampagne-Plan

A plan featuring a particular company's proposals relative to the promotion of a product involving advertising (TV, radio, press, posters, etc.), product launch date, mail shots, etc.

Campbell Soup position Anzeigenposition rechts gegenüber der Kommentarseite

In an advertisement, a position on the first right-hand page following the main editorial section of a publication. Named after the Campbell Soup Company who prefers this position.

Can Kanister, Dose, Büchse

Also called tin.

A small metal container for holding food, liquid, etc.

Cancellation clause (CC) Kündigungsklausel

Also called termination clause.

Clause in a contract which states the terms on which the contract may be cancelled.

Cancellation of order Auftragsstornierung

A decision that an order already placed should now not be carried out/executed.

Cancellation of sale Wandlung (Rücktritt vom Vertrag)

Also called rescission of sale.

In case of a complaint, the buyer has the right to withdraw/rescind from the sales contract concluded with the seller.

Canned presentation stereotype Verkaufsvorführung

A salesperson's presentation of merchandise to a customer in a very stereotype manner. The sales presentation includes all the key selling points arranged in the order designed to elicit the best response from the customer.

Cannibalisation Kannibalisierungseffekt

Also called cannibalism.

A market situation in which the sale of a company's new product increases at the expense of an existing product within the same product line, usually because there is little differentiation between them. That is, the new product "steals" some of the sales of the existing product.

Canvasser Akquisiteur, (Direkt)Werber

Also called solicitor.

A sales representative or selling agent calling direct on users or consumers.

Capital goods Investitionsgüter, Anlagegüter

Also called equipment goods, industrial goods, investment goods, or producer goods.

Goods with a long life (e.g. machinery, factories, raw materials) not wanted for their own sake but made for the purpose of producing consumer goods and other capital goods. They are not used up in one accounting period and are usually depreciated over a period of years.

Capital-intensive technology kapitalintensive Technologie

A technology in which the amount of capital used per unit of output produced is relatively higher than the amount of other inputs used per unit of output.

Caption Überschrift, Titel
Bildüberschrift, Bildunterschrift, Legende
(Film)Untertitel

A heading or title, as of a chapter or page.

A title or explanation above, below or next to an illustration or photograph, especially in a magazine.

The text of dialogue projected onto a motion-picture or television screen.

Captive audience unfreiwilliges Publikum

An audience that is nearly unable to escape an advertising message, e.g. cinema audiences.

Captive market Markt eines monopolitischen Anbieters, monopolistischer Absatzmarkt

A market in which virtually no competition exists relative to the product offered. There are no substitute goods for the demanders. That means, one supplier has a monopoly and the buyers have no choice in deciding where to buy.

Car allowance (Kraft)Fahrzeugzuschuß

Also called vehicle allowance.

An additional amount of money paid to employees as compensation for the use of their own car instead of a company car, e.g. the payment of mileage.

Car card Verkehrsmittelposter

Also called baby billboard (colloq. USA)

Small poster displayed inside or outside a vehicle, e.g. a bus, taxi, train, underground train.

Carat Karat

A measurement of the purity of gold. A twenty-fourth part of a unit of pure gold. Eighteen carats, for example means, that the article consists of eighteen parts pure gold and six parts alloy.

Carboy Korbflasche

A very large glass container protected in a metal or wicker cage with soft packing between glass and cage.

Cardphone (Magnet)Kartentelefon

A speedy, convenient and efficient way of making calls without using cash. The user inserts a phonecard, dials the number required, and, once connected, units will be automatically removed from the phonecard.

Cargo (cgo) Ladung, Fracht(gut)

Also called freight.

Goods carried in a ship, aeroplane or other vehicle in return for payment of freight charges (freight or transport expenses). Plural = cargoes.

Cargo handling charge(s) (CHC) Verladungskosten

Also called loading charges or costs.

The charges raised on handling cargo at an airport, depot, port, warehouse, etc., based on tonnage, commodity type, etc.

Cargo manifest Frachtmanifest

The inventory of cargo shipped.

Cargo marking Frachtgutmarkierung

The marking of cargo packaging.

The marking code and handling symbol (e.g. fragile - handle with care) on packages, cases, crates, etc.

Cargo plane Fracht-, Transportflugzeug

Also called airfreighter or freight plane.

An aeroplane/airplane which carries only cargo.

Cargo ship Frachter, Frachtschiff

Also called cargo boat or vessel, freighter, transport ship or vessel.

A ship which carries only cargo and not passengers.

Cargo stowage Fracht(ver)stauung

The act or process of stowing cargo. The shipper must be aware of the principle of cargo stowage and must observe the stowage standards.
Basically there are five main factors to consider in the stowage of cargo:

1. the best possible use should be made of the available deadweight or cubic capacity - whether it is a container, road vehicle, railway truck (freight car), ship or aircraft;
2. the safety of the transport unit employed must be considered;
3. the merchandise must not impair the general safety of the transport unit and likewise it must not endager others;
4. cargo which is fragile, is liable to leakage, scratches easily, has strong odours or other special characteristics requires proper segregation,
5. finally, a proper segregation of different consignments for various destinations/areas/ports/countries must be made to prevent delay in distribution and avoid double handling.

Carriage (cge, carr) Transport, Beförderung
Fracht-, Transportkosten
Rollgeld

The act of carrying goods, especially for payment. Also called conveyance, haulage, shipment, or transportation.

The charge made for transporting goods from one place to another. Also called freight, freight charges, or transport expenses.

The carriage/freight charged for short distances. Also called cartage.

Carriage forward (carr fwd; c/f, C/F) Fracht zahlt Empfänger, unfrei

Also called freight collect or freight forward.

A price quotation for goods which does not include carriage (freight); cost of transport (freight charges) to be paid by the buyer of goods.

Carriage free (CF) frachtfrei, franko

Also called carriage paid (c.p., c/p, cge. paid), carriage prepaid, free of charge, freight paid or freight and carriage paid.

This means that the seller pays for carriage. At the price quoted, the seller will deliver the goods using his own transport system at no extra charge to the buyer.

Carriage inward(s) Bezugskosten, Eingangsfracht

Also called freight inward(s) or freight in.

Carriage costs for the goods which a supplier has delivered to the business, i.e. the payment for carriage on goods bought by a business.

Note: in a non-manufacturing business, carriage inwards is part of the trading account (shown on the debit side of the account).

Carriage outward(s) Ausgangsfracht, Transportkosten

Also called freight outward(s) or freight out.

Carriage costs on goods which a business delivers to customers, i.e. the payment for carriage on goods sold by a business.

Note: carriage outwards is an expense of the business in the profit and loss account (shown on the debit side of the account).

Carriage paid (C/P, carr pd, c/p) frachtfrei, Fracht bezahlt

Also called freight paid or freight prepaid.

The price quoted for goods includes the cost of carriage; the seller of goods pays for the cost of delivering them to an agreed delivery point at the place of destination, e.g. a local railway station (from that point the buyer has to bear all carriage charges) or to the buyer's premises (this is sometimes called carriage paid home).

Carriage paid to frontier frachtfrei (bis) Grenze

The seller pays carriage (freight charges) to the frontier and bears the risks of the goods until they have been delivered into the custody of the first carrier.

Carriage underwriter Frachtversicherer

An individual or insurance company who covers the freight charges.

Carrier Beförderungsunternehmen, Frachtführer, Spediteur
Versicherungsträger
Fluggesellschaft
Zustellbote

Someone who takes goods (or passengers) from one place to another, at his risk, for a reasonable fee. Also called carriage or transport undertaking.

An insurance company. Also called insurance carrier, insurer or underwriter.

An airline.

A person that delivers newspapers.

Carrier bag Tragetasche

Also called shopping bag.

Plastic, paper or canvass bag for shopping, often branded with a store or product name.

Carrier`s risk (C/R) Risiko des Spediteurs, Frachtführers

The carrier is responsible (liable) for any loss or damage in transit and therefore must pay for it.

Carry-through rate Durchlaufpreis

In radio and TV advertising, a situation where a higher time segment rate is charged when a broadcast programme spans two segments.

Carrying charges Lagerkosten
Speditionskosten

The cost of storing inventory from the time of purchase until the time of sale. Also called inventory carrying costs, carrying costs, holding costs, inventory costs, storage costs, warehouse or warehousing charges.

The forwarding expenses or charges.

Carryouts beim Kauf mitgenommene (nicht zugeschickte) Ware

Also called take-withs or take-aways.

Goods bought in a shop that are taken from the shop by the buyer and not delivered by the seller.

Carryover effect Übertragungswirkung, Carryover-Effekt

The effect of something carried over (postponed) to a later time.

Cartage (ctge) Rollgeld, Transportkosten Transport

The charge made by inland carriers for pickup and short distance carriage of goods. Also called carriage, drayage, or freight.

The act of carrying goods by road. Also called carriage, conveyance, haulage, or transport.

Cartel Kartell

An informal voluntary association of firms acting together to reduce or eliminate competition between themselves or from other firms.

They may, for example, agree to charge the same prices for their goods, keep the price of their products at an artificially high level (price(s) cartel, price fixing cartel, or price ring), limit their output on some quota basis (quota cartel), or allocate markets (market sharing cartel). In the worst cases they may conspire to prevent the entry of new firms to the industry.

Members of the cartel retain their identity and their independence, except in so far as they stick to the stipulated terms.

Cartels may be national or international (e.g. OPEC). In many countries most cartels are illegal and banned by law because they create monopoly conditions. A type of cartel which is allowed is the standardization cartel (it relates to uniform methods for the specification of goods and services).
The term cartel is of German origin.

Carter Fuhrunternehmer

Also called carrier, haulier, trucker or road contractor.

A person who transports goods by road.

Case Kiste
Schachtel

Strong container made of wood. For extra strength they may have battens, metal bands or wires. The inside of the case may be lined with various materials. Als called crate or packing case.

A box.

Cash Bargeld, flüssige Mittel
Kassenbestand
Barzahlung

Commonly, coin in the pocket and notes in the wallet.
Ready money in the form of bank notes and coin.
Bank notes and coin plus deposits at the banks.
Bank notes and coin plus documents (e.g. bills, cheques, drafts, bonds, etc.) payable on demand readily be turned into cash.

Cash in hand or a cash balance.

The term is also used for immediate payment as opposed to credit. Also called cash payment.

Cash and carry (C + C) Verkauf gegen Barzahlung bei eigenem Transport, Selbstabholung gegen Kasse
Cash und Carry - Geschäft

Buyers select their own goods from open displays, pay cash (usually at a discount) on exit and take the goods away in their own vehicles. The sellers offer neither credit nor delivery services and, as a result, operate on lower margins.

A cash-and-carry store/warehouse.

Cash and carry wholesaler Abholgroßhändler, Abholgrossist

A cash and carry store or warehouse which enables the retailer to make his purchases at the end of the working day at cut prices which helps the small retailer compete with the multiples (multiple shops or stores).

Cash before delivery (CBD) Barzahlung vor Lieferung

Agreement that goods purchased have to be paid (in) cash before they are despatched.

Cash before shipment (CBS) Barzahlung vor Versand

An agreement between seller and buyer that goods purchased have to be paid (in) cash before they are despatched. That means, when the goods are ready for despatch the buyer is asked to pay and the consignment is then sent (off).

Cash cow ertragsstarkes Produkt, "Geldkuh", Dukatenesel

A product or product line that continuously generates profit.

Products become cash cows once they hold a high market share in a low growth market. The large amounts of revenue can be "milked" to fund the development of question marks and the growth of stars.

Cash dealing Barverkauf

A sale done for cash.

Cash desk Kasse

Also called checkout, pay station, point-of-sale (POS) terminal or till.

Place in a shop/store where one pays for the goods or services bought.

Cash discount Barzahlungsrabatt, Skonto

Also called sales, settlement or straight discount, discount for cash or reduction for cash.

The difference between the amount actually received and the amount of the debt.

A reduction in the quoted price given by a creditor to the buyer in return for payment of the debt in cash, before a certain date or within a specified period of time. It is usually stated as a percentage ("2 % one month" printed on an invoice means that a discount of 2 % will be deducted if payment is made within one month; otherwise the customer has to pay the full amount). Note: "2/10" means 2 percent discount for payment before or within 10 days; "n/30" means that the customer must pay the full amount after 30 days. If the account is not paid within 30 days, interest may be charged.

Cash float Kassenbestand

A small amount of cash. In shops, each cash register (cash box or till) has a small amount of cash - a cash float - in it at the beginning of the day. The shop assistants need a cash float to give change to customers.

Cash flow forecast Cashflow-Prognose

The forecast of when cash will be received or paid out.

Cash in advance (CIA, cia) Vorausbezahlung, Vorauskasse

Cash payment made in advance of supplying (or producing) the goods. The most secure method of payment for a seller.

Cash in/on hand Bargeld(bestand), Barguthaben, flüssige Gelder

Banknotes/notes and coins in the possession of a person or firm.

Money in coins or banknotes/notes kept, e.g. in the till (cash box or cash register), to pay small debts.

Cash inflow Barmittelzufluß, Einzahlungsstrom

The flow of cash into an entity for a given period, resulting from transactions with parties external to the entity.

Cash less discount bar abzüglich Diskont/Rabatt

A phrase showing that payment has to be effected in cash, but discount may be deducted.

Cash memo — Kassenzettel (meist hand-geschrieben)

A note, usually handwritten on a printed form, given by a shopkeeper or salesperson to a customer as evidence of payment.

Cash offer — Barzahlungsangebot

An offer to pay in cash.

Cash on delivery (COD, cod) — Nachnahme, Barzahlung bei Lieferung, zahlbar bei Lieferung

Also called collect(ion) on delivery, charges collect, charges forward (ch.fwd.) or delivery versus payment (DVP).

Small value goods are sent by Post Office parcel post and are released only after payment of the invoice plus COD charges. The sender (often mail-order houses) must fill in the despatch document provided by the Post Office.

Some businesses and stores also provide a COD service, using their own delivery vans.

Cash on shipment (COS, cos) — Barzahlung bei Versand, Verschiffung

An arrangement which requires payment for goods when they are despatched (shipped) to the buyer.

Cash only — nur gegen Barzahlung

A phrase showing that payment can only be made in cash.

Cash order (co) — Barzahlungsauftrag

An agreement between seller und buyer stipulating that the order placed has to be paid (in) cash, i.e. the seller grants no credit.

Cash outflow — Kapitalabfluß, Auszahlungsstrom

The flow of cash out of an entity for a given period, resulting from business transactions.

Cash payment Barzahlung
Sofortzahlung

The payment in cash.

Cash payments include the following:
Cash with order (CWO), cash on delivery (COD), spot cash, prompt cash and net cash.

Cash price Barpreis, Barzahlungspreis

The price of goods paid for at the moment of sale.

Cash purchase Bareinkauf

Also called cash buying.

Cash purchases are goods which a business buys from a supplier, and pays for at once by cash or cheque.

Cash rebate verkaufsfördernder Rabatt

A rebate used by a producer to stimulate sluggish retail sales. The rebate is given by the producer through the retailer to the consumer who buys the product(s). For example, car producers use cash rebates at model year ends to stimulate automobile sales.

Cash receipt Kasseneingang, Bareinnahme
Kassenquittung

Also called till receipt.

The money which a business receives for cash sales or income which it has received in cash. Also called taking or cash taking.

A receipt which tells the customer how much he has paid. It varies in style and the information given but usually contains such information as the name of the supplying firm, the date, details of the sale, who sold the article, the VAT charged, the total bill, the amount tendered by the customer and the change due. Also called cashier's receipt.

Cash receipts journal Kasseneinnahmebuch

All transactions involving the receipt of cash are recorded in the cash receipts journal.

Cash refund offer Barerstattungsangebot, Barvergütungsangebot

An offer to refund part of the purchase price of a product to consumers who send a "proof of purchase" to the manufacturer, usually within a specified time. The manufacturer sends the refund directly to the consumer.

Cash register Registrierkasse

Also called cash till.

A machine in shops for cash that customers have paid for goods. It shows and adds the prices of items bought and has a drawer for keeping the cash received.

Cash sale Barverkauf, Bargeschäft

Also called cash transaction.

A sale (transaction) which a business makes to customers for cash or cheque (i.e. immediate payment). Payment and purchase occur simultaneously.

Cash terms Barzahlungsbedingungen

The payment of cash for the purchase of goods, usually before a certain date or within a certain period, e.g. cash payment within 10 days.

Cash voucher Kassenbeleg, Quittung

Also called bill, cash record, note of purchase, receipt or voucher.

A receipt for a stated sum of money paid in cash or by cheque for goods and services.

Cash with order (CWO, cwo) Barzahlung bei Auftragserteilung, zahlbar bei Auftragserteilung

Also called payment with order.

A sales term showing that payment has to be made in cash when the order is placed.

If unwilling to grant credit the seller will normally sell on a CWO basis. Unfortunately, in a competitive market it is not often that CWO can be arranged. But it may be possible to obtain a part payment with the order; this is common practice in

some markets and in some trades. CWO avoids any risk on small orders with new buyers and may even be asked for before production begins.
Note: this form of payment means that a buyer is extending credit to a seller - instead of vice versa, as is normal.

Cashier Kassierer, Bankschalterbeamter

Also called cash or counter clerk, collector or teller.

In the office of a business, in a bank, or in a shop, the cashier receives money, and also pays it out. Furthermore he is responsible for keeping a firm's cash book. A cashier does not sell goods or services.

Cashless shopping bargeldloses Einkaufen

Shopping where the customer pays by plastic money, e.g. credit card or EFTPOS (electronic funds transfer at point of sale).

Cask (ck, csk) Faß, Tonne

A barrel-like container for liquids; a very small barrel.

Casting off Satzumfangsberechnung (Druck)

In printing, estimating the space required to accommodate a given number of words of a certain typeface and size.

Casual customer Laufkunde
Gelegenheitskunde

A customer who has never bought in a particular shop before, but now does so because he spotted the shop and an interesting product. Also called off-the-street customer (collq.).

A customer who occassionally buys in a particular shop but is not a regular customer. Also called occassional customer.

Catalog(ue) (cat) Katalog, Verzeichnis, Prospekt

A list, often in alphabetical order, containing a description of goods, their purpose, and their prices, published to help customers who wish to place orders. Prices are usually included unless subject to frequent fluctuation, in which case they are printed on a separate price list.

Catalog(ue) buying — Kauf nach Katalog

The purchasing of goods from catalogue by direct mail, by telephone, by TV or through salespersons. Furthermore, there are catalogue (discount) stores where customers select goods from a catalogue, usually at very competitive prices.

Catalog(ue) exhibition — Katalogausstellung

A country's firms may test product interest in foreign markets, develop sales leads, and locate agents or distributors through catalog exhibitions. These exhibitions feature displays of a large number of a country's product catalogs, sales brochures, and other graphic sales aids at embassies and consulates or in conjunction with trade shows.

Catalog(ue) marketing — Katalogmarketing

A method of direct marketing, i.e. selling through catalogs/catalogues mailed to a select list of customers or made available in stores/shops.

Catalog(ue) showroom — Kataloggeschäft; Einzelhandelsvertriebsform, bei der das Sortiment im Katalog präsentiert wird

A retail shop that consumers visit to make actual purchases of articles described in catalogues available in the shop. These shops often sell a wide variety of high-markup, fast-moving, brand name goods at discount prices.

Catalog(ue) store — Katalogwarenhaus

Also called catalog company or house.

A company which sells goods by mail order (MO). In a catalog store operation, the catalog is sent to consumers (catalog buyers) who select the items and pick up the merchandise at the store. Some stores have showrooms where customers select merchandise directly from the catalog or from store merchandise.

Catching bargain — Rechtsgeschäft zu unfairen Bedingungen

Also called unconscionable bargain.

An unfair contract, often one in which one party has been taken advantage of by the other.

Catchment area Einzugsbereich, Kundeneinzugsgebiet

Also called trading area.

A district from which a business draws its customers and/or its staff.

Catchpenny (article) Schund(ware), Billigartikel, Ramsch

Also called rubbish or trash.

An article that is worthless or useless, but nevertheless appeals to buyers.

Catchphrase/catch phrase Schlagwort, Slogan

In advertising, a product slogan which is so popular that it becomes part of everyday language, at least for a specific time period.

Category Kategorie

Classification of things, persons, events, etc.

Category brand Artikelgruppenmarke

A brand name used on a common category of products. Firms that use a category name usually have several category brand names.

Caterer Lebensmittellieferant, Caterer

Person or company supplying food and drink, e.g. for parties.

Catering Catering (Lieferung von Fertigmahlzeiten)

Supply of food (normally ready to eat) and drink by a caterer.

Catering trade Bewirtungsgewerbe, Hotel- und Gaststättengewerbe

The trade that supplies food ready to eat and drink, especially the hotel and restaurant sector.

Cats and dogs Ladenhüter

Also called bad seller, non-moving item, non-seller, shelfwarmer, sticker, sleeper, unsaleable article or drug on the market.

Goods which do not sell well.

Caution marks Vorsichtsmarkierungen

Also called cautionary markings.

Specific markings and labels (sometimes in more than one language or in international symbols) placed on boxes and containers to inform the cargo handlers that they have to be very careful and observe certain precautionary instructions when handling the cargo.
Examples are: "Handle with Care", "Glass", "Use No Hooks", "This Side Up", "Fragile", "Keep in Cool Place", "Keep Dry", "Open Here", "Keep Frozen", "Radioactive", "Inflammable Liquid", "Poison", etc.

Caveat emptor Gewährleistungsausschluß, Mängelausschluß (des Verkäufers)

A Latin legal term which means literally "let the buyer beware". The doctrine that a buyer must bear any loss resulting from any failure to satisfy himself as to the nature and quality of the goods he buys. It is up to the buyer to examine what he is buying and make sure that it is of the standard required for his purpose. Once goods have been bought the buyer cannot expect regress. The seller is not obliged to volunteer information detrimental to the goods or services offered for sale, but he must answer relevant questions truthfully. Nevertheless, legislation in many countries protects the buyer against wrongful representation.

Today, caveat vendor is more and more applied.

Caveat vendor Sorgfaltspflicht, Gewährleistungspflicht des Verkäufers

Also called caveat venditor.

A Latin legal term which means literally "let the seller beware". In brief this means that the seller may be legally obliged to inform the buyer of any defects in his goods or services.

Ceiling price Höchstpreis

The highest price that can be obtained in the market.

Celebrity endorsement Werbung, in der eine prominente Person ein Produkt demonstriert

An advertisement in which a well-known and respected person demonstrates a particular product.

Census Volkszählung

Official count of a country´s population, including such data as the age, sex, occupation, etc.

Cent Hundertstel Währungseinheit (Cent)

Latin centum, 100.

A term used to denote a certain rate or ratio, being so much per hundred (e.g. 10 per cent).

In currency, cent is the name of certain small coins in various countries, being the hundredth of other coins (e.g. $ in the USA).

Centenary Hundertjahrfeier

A 100th anniversary.

Central business district (CBD) Hauptgeschäftsviertel

The center/centre of business activity in a city.

Central buying zentraler Einkauf, Zentraleinkauf

Also called central(ized) purchasing, centralised buying or consolidated buying.

Purchasing organized by a central office for all branches of a company. In larger firms a central buying department will usually handle all purchases. The buying department evaluates various products on the market and picks the most appropriate for the firm's purposes. A system of records enables supplies to be ordered as they are required, i.e. as minimum stock levels are reached.
Note: larger orders qualify for quantity discounts.

Central purchasing Zentraleinkauf

Also called central(ised) buying or consolidated buying.

Purchasing organized by one main office for all departments or branches.

Centrespread/centre spread doppelseitige Anzeige

The two facing pages at the centre of a periodical. Usually desirable for an advertiser since this position occupies one continuous sheet of paper, enjoying the advantages both of a solus/island position and extra size.

Centring (centering) Zentrierung

Putting a line of text in the middle of the screen or paper, between the margin settings.

Cents-off coupon Preisnachlaß-Coupon

A coupon attached to a product which grants the consumer a certain price reduction. It is a less expensive and usually less effective method of getting the customer to try a new product. However, coupons can be very effective in getting a consumer to buy the product again and thereby establishing a repeat purchasing behaviour and possibly a brand loyalty.

Cents-off offer Preisnachlaßangebot

A consumer sales promotion technique offering the potential customer a product for a discount off the recommended price.

Cents-off the label Preisnachlaß offeriert auf Produktetikett

A practice in which the price of a product is reduced which is indicated on the label. Rarely do cents-off promotions attract new customers, instead, they give present buyers a lower price and thus reinforce brand loyalty.

Certainty Gewißheit, Bestimmtheit, Sicherheit

In general, the state of being certain; or something certain.

In marketing, the subjective assurance of management that knowledge of the market derived from specified samples, market analysis or from other sources is or will be adequate to allow to act in the market.

Certificate of analysis Analysenzertifikat

In certain industries, an internal certificate given to products passing rigid (for example, laboratory) tests; this is usually marked on product packets for consumer reference (e.g. cosmetics, pharmaceuticals, health foods etc.)

In foreign trade, a document often required by importers, attesting to the quality or purity of commodities purchased overseas.

Certificate of manufacture Fertigstellungsbescheinigung Ursprungszeugnis

In foreign trade, a document signed by an exporter that goods ordered by the importer have been produced and set aside for shipment.

A certificate of origin.

Certificate of weight Gewichtsbescheinigung

A certified statement of the weight of a cargo.

Certification mark Gütezeichen

A mark applied to goods that attests a certain quality.

Chain store Kettenladen, Filialkette

Also called multiple shop or store.

A retail selling outlet belonging to a chain of businesses selling a wide range of goods. It may have grown from the expansion of a single shop or it can have been set up as a chain. The term is mainly used in the US.

Challenger Herausforderer

In marketing, a business which challenges other businesses which are already established in the market, e.g. by lower prices or aggressive advertising.

Chance Möglichkeit, Wahrscheinlichkeit

The probability or likelihood that an event will occur.

Change Wechselgeld
Kleingeld

An abbreviation of exchange.

When a person buys something for cash he will often give more than the price to the seller who will give him the change.

Change in demand Nachfrageänderung

Also called shift in demand.

A greater or smaller quantity of a commodity or service is demanded without any change in price having taken place. Causes may be: change of taste or fashion, changes in the prices of other goods, changes in the disposable incomes, etc.

Change in supply Angebotsänderung

Also called shift in supply.

A greater or smaller quantity of a commodity or service is supplied without any change in price having taken place. Causes may be: changes in the cost of production, changes in production methods, changes in the price of other commodities, etc.

Change machine Wechselautomat

A machine which gives small change for a larger coin or banknote.

Channel captain führendes Unternehmen in der Vertriebskette

The most powerful member in the distribution channel (consisting of producer, wholesaler and retailer), usually the producer. However, exceptions are possible, e.g. when the retailer is a leading department store or a chain store, whose buying power is very strong.

Channel of distribution Absatzweg, Vertriebsweg

Also called chain of distribution, distribution channel, distributive channel, marketing channel, or trade channel.

The marketing institutions through which goods are transferred from the original producers to the end users or consumers.

The traditional chain of distribution has been: producer - wholesaler - retailer - consumer. But today the producer may deal directly with either the retailer or the consumer, thus completely bypassing the wholesaler.

Channel strip Regalleiste, Werbeleiste

The front edge of a retail display shelf on which details of the products can be shown, e.g. price, weight, code numbers, etc or which can hold POS advertising.

Character Charakter

The aggregate of features and traits that form the individual nature of a person or thing.

Charge (ch) Gebühr, Preis

Also called fee or price.

An amount of money which a person must pay for certain services (e.g. bank charges).

Charge account ("offenes") Kreditkonto, Kundenkreditkonto

Also called budget account or credit account.

A credit facility granted by retailers to customers. The customer may buy goods up to an agreed value and pay for them at a later date. Normally the account must be settled within a given period and traders may charge interest on outstandings.

Charge card Kundenkreditkarte

Also called store card.

A form of credit card issued by retailers to enable customers to shop in their store(s). The card bearing the holder`s name and registration number enables the holder to buy goods and services with the price charged to his account with the card company. The holder (the charge or credit buyer) pays the company's account in full at agreed intervals.

Charges forward (ch fwd) (per) Nachnahme, Gebühr bezahlt Empfänger

Also called charges collect.

A condition of sale stipulating that the carriage charges on goods must be paid by the buyer (consignee) only on receipt of the goods.

Charges prepaid (ch ppd, cp) franko, Kosten vorausbezahlt

Under such a consignment term, the sender (consignor) is responsible for payment of the forwarding charges.

Charitable donation wohltätige (karitative) Spende

Also called charitable contribution.

An amount paid by a company to a charitable organisation.

Charitable society Wohltätigkeitsverein

Also called charitable institution, do-good organization (collq.) or benefit society.

A society formed for the relief of poverty, for the advancement of education, for the promotion of art, science, religion, etc.

Charity wohltätige Einrichtung
Wohltätigkeit

A not-for-profit organization which allocates resources to the poor. Often only called do-good organization.

The act of giving money and/or other help to the poor.

Charity marketing Wohltätigkeitsmarketing

Marketing where the emphasis is on accumulating human, financial and physical resources, and redirecting those resources to areas perceived by the community to need them.

Chart Diagramm, Grafik

Also called diagram or graph.

A diagram showing information as a series of lines, dots, blocks, etc; a popular method of presenting statistics.

Chaser Terminjäger, Disponent

Also called accelerator, expediter or progress chaser.

A person who has to check that orders are fulfilled on time or that work is being carried out on schedule.

Cheap brand Billigmarke

Also called down-market brand.

A branded product sold at a low price and usually of inferior quality.

Check Rechnung
Gepäckschein, Garderobenschein
Kontrolle

In the US, a bill, especially in a restaurant. Also called account or invoice.

In the US, a receipt or ticket for luggage or for clothes left in the cloakroom. Also called baggage check or tag, or (luggage) ticket; coat or hat check, checkroom or cloakroom ticket.

A control for the purpose of making sure of the correctness of an information.

Check room Garderobe
Gepäckaufbewahrung

A room where hats, coats, umbrellas, etc. may be stored.

The left-luggage office. Also called cloakroom.

Checker Kassierer(in)
Kontrolleur
Garderobenfrau
Gepäckaufbewahrer

In a supermarket or shop, the person who receives money. Also called cashier, cash clerk or teller.

A person designated by a firm to inspect (check) goods, shipments and other items.

An employee of a checkroom (cloakroom).

An employee of a left-luggage office.

Checkin Hotelanmeldung
Einchecken

The arrival and registration at a hotel.

The arrival and registration at the checkin counter of an airport.

Checkin desk/counter Abfertigungsschalter

Also called check counter.

Place where passengers give in their tickets for a flight and check in.

Checklist Checkliste, Kontrolliste

Also called tally sheet.

A list of things which have to be observed or checked when processing a particular task, eg when producing or packing goods.

Checkout Kasse (z.B. im Supermarkt)
Hotelabreise
Zeit, zu der ein Hotelzimmer geräumt sein muß

Cash till at a supermarket's or self-service store's exit where customers pay for goods bought. Also called checkout counter or point or cash desk.

The paying of the hotel bill on leaving the hotel.

The time at which a hotel room must be vacated. Also called checkout time.

Cherry picking Sonderangebotskaufen (das Herauspicken von Rosinen); preisbewußtes, wählerisches Einkaufen

A customer's behaviour to look for special bargains and shop around, i.e. to go to various shops or suppliers and compare prices before making a purchase or placing an order. Only a few, reasonably priced and very attractive items are bought or ordered.

Chickenfeed Kleingeld

Also called loose or small change.

The coins which a person carries around with him.

Chipboard Graupappe

Cheap quality cardboard made from wastepaper.

Choice (Aus)Wahl

The act of selecting among alternatives. This involves evaluating alternative actions or modes of behaviour and forming an intention or plan to engage in the selected action or behaviour.

Christmas Day erster Weihnachtsfeiertag

December 25, first day of Christmas.

Note: Boxing Day is the second day of Christmas.

Cinema advertising Kinowerbung

Slide or film presentation in the cinema is rather popular, particularly with local promotions. Local cinema advertising is usually limited to consumer goods and mainly competes with local newspapers. Slides make single announcements, usually during the film intervals and whilst the audience lights are on. Short films attract more attention because the audience usually considers them as part of the total performance. Although the costs of a film may be high, they can be adequately recouped if it is shown in several countries.

Circular letter Rundschreiben

Also called circular, newsletter or mail shot.

These are duplicated letters sent to several addresses, either addressed generally or individually.

Circulation Auflage, Auflagenhöhe

The number of copies of a newspaper or magazine successfully distributed and sold. Note: it should not be confused with readership.

Circulation area Verbreitungsgebiet
Sendegebiet

The geographic area covered by a newspaper, magazine, leaflet, etc.

The geographic area covered by a broadcast station.

Citizens Advice Bureau (CAB) Bürgerberatungsbüro

In the UK, a voluntary organization which assists people with their shopping and other problems.

Civic action group Bürgerinitiative

A group of people concerned with the well-being of the community.

Claim Mängelrüge, Reklamation
Behauptung
Werbebehauptung

A complaint.

The act of saying that something is true. Also called assertion.

A statement made in an advertisement asserting some positive aspect of the product´s performance or a benefit to be obtained from the use of that product.

Claims department Schadensabteilung

Also called loss department.

A department dealing with clients claims.

Class magazine Prestigezeitschrift

Also called special interest magazine.

A periodical intended for a readership, often with an above-average income, sharing a range of common interests.

Class market Markt für hochwertige Güter

Also called upend market or upscale market.

A market for exclusive and high-priced consumer goods. The opposite is a mass market.

Class rate Gruppenfrachttarif

The standard charge for the shipment of specific goods by a carrier.

Classical economics klassische (National)Ökonomie

The economic period from 1750 - 1850. The major economists were Adam Smith, Malthus, Mill and Ricardo. in general these economists believed that free competition ensured that the community as a whole benefited. As a consequence, they concluded government interferences should be kept to a minimum.

Classical economists Klassiker

Economists such as Adam Smith, Malthus, Mill, Ricardo, etc who focused their analyses on economic efficiency and production. With regard to business instability, they thought market prices would adjust quickly in a manner that would guide an economy out of a recession back to full employment. Their belief in the power of market forces led them to support laissez faire and they also supported the idea of free trade among nations.

Classification (cl, class.) Klassifikation

The process of arranging items or individuals into classes or groups.

Classified advertisement Kleinanzeige, rubrizierte Anzeige (Suchanzeige)

Also called classified, small, small ad, small space advertising or want ad(vertisement).

This is a special art in writing an almost telegram-like ad in a few lines, using an intriguing opening to catch the reader's eye, squeezing as much abbreviated but intelligible copy into as few lines as possible. Small ads are bought on a line-by-line basis and are mostly inserted by individuals. The impact of a classified is lost if the copy is too long. Classifieds are grouped together under identifying headings (e.g. cars for sale), i.e. they are subdivided according to the types of products and services offered or sought.

Classified catalog(ue) nach Produkten/Bereichen/ Fachgebieten gegliederter Katalog

A catalogue grouping articles into certain categories.

Classified directory Branchenverzeichnis, Branchenadressbuch

Also called classified telephone directory or yellow pages.

A publication listing products and companies, classified into specialized groups, and listed in alphabetical order.

Classified display advertisement rubrizierte Großanzeige

Also called display classified advertisement.

A combination of display and classified advertising whereby a classified ad is presented in a display size and format.

Classified section Kleinanzeigenspalte, -rubrik

Also called classified column.

That part of a newspaper or magazine reserved for classified advertising.

Clear räumen (Lager)
Kosten decken (Plus-minus-Null-arbeiten)
Reingewinn erzielen

To clear out the stock, i.e. to sell off goods, usually at a cheaper price, in order to get rid of old stock and to make room for new stock.

To clear one's costs or expenses, i.e. to make neither a profit nor a loss. Also called breakeven.

To make a profit, e.g. to clear 10 % or £ 2,000 on the deal = to make 10 % or £ 2,000 clear profit.

Clearance sale Ausverkauf, Räumungsverkauf

Also called clearance sale, cleanup sale or sales. If the shop is closed, it is also called closing-down or winding-up sale.

The sale of merchandise at reduced prices to clear surpluses or end of season stock.

Clerk (clk) Verkäufer(in)

Also called sales or store clerk, salesman, salesperson or shopman; sales girl, lady or woman; shopgirl or shopwoman. The British term is (shop) assistant.

A person who sells goods in a store/shop.

Client Kunde

Customer of a business. All the clients of a business are called clientele.

Client list Kundenliste, Kundenkartei

Also called customer file or customer register.

A list of the clients belonging to a particular company.

Client rough Rohlayout für den Kunden

A preliminary layout of an advertisement (ad) that is shown to a client for approval or amendment before the ad is prepared in final form.

Clientele Kundschaft

Also called clients, custom, customers or patronage.

The customers who regularly deal at one shop.

Clique Clique, Klüngel

An informal sub-group formed from members of a larger group. The group members often show behaviour patterns of superiority or exclusiveness.

Close price scharf kalkulierter Preis

A keenly calculated price.

Closed display Verschlußauslage, Warenauslage unter Verschluß

A display cabinet for merchandise, usually covered by glass, so that customers have no access to goods.

Closed indent Auslandsauftrag, den der damit betraute Kommissionär nur an den vom Käufer genannten Hersteller weiterleiten kann

Also called specific indent.

Export orders are often called indents; a closed indent specifies the name of the manufacturer from whom the goods are to be obtained.

An open indent leaves the selection to the agent.

Closed question Alternativ-Frage

Also called alternative or dichotomous question.

A question in a questionnaire to which an answer has to be selected from a provided list.

Closed-end question Frage mit vorgegebenen Antwortmöglichkeiten

Also called fixed-alternative question or structured question.

A question which allows a respondent to choose an answer from a given list, e.g. a questionnaire.

Closeout (Teil)Ausverkauf

Also called closeout sale, cleanup sale, clearance sale, closing out sale, sell-off sale, selling off or out sale.

The sale of goods at low prices to get rid of them in order to get room for new goods.

Closing Verkaufsabschluß, Abschluß eines Verkaufs(gesprächs)

Also called closing a sale or close.

The point in a sales presentation in which the salesperson tries to close the sale and thus asks the customer for an order, offers help to write up the order or indicates that the buyer will lose out if the order is not placed now.

Note: the salesperson should not fail to recognize the right moment to close the sale.

Closing bid letzte Gebot, Höchstgebot

The last bid or the bid which is successful (the highest bid) at an auction.

Closing date Anmeldeschluß, Einreichungsschluß letzter Termin

The final date upon which an application for a tender or an application for a job, etc., can be accepted. Also called deadline.

Latest date for cargo accepted for shipment by shipowners for specified sailing.

Closing inventory Endbestand

Also called ending inventory or closing stocks.

The book value of stock on hand at the end of an accounting period. At the end of this period it is shown on the balance sheet as an asset and then carried forward into the following period as beginning/opening inventory.

Closing technique (Verkaufs)Abschlußtechnik

A special technique of persuasion used by salespeople to close a sale. One strategy that is often used is the assumptive close. This involves asking the buyer questions such as "would you prefer the large or the small model" or "when would you like delivery of the goods", etc.

Note: by assuming that the order has already been placed, the salesperson makes it hard for the buyer to make a direct refusal.

Closing time Geschäfts-, Ladenschluß

Also called closing hours.

The time when a shop or office closes.

Closing-down sale Ausverkauf wegen Geschäftsaufgabe

Also called winding-up sale.

The sale of goods because of closing down, i.e. shop is closing forever.

Closure Betriebsstillegung, Geschäftsaufgabe
Beendigung, Schluß
Verschluß(vorrichtung)

The closing/shutting of a shop or factory.

Bringing to an end, e.g. a debate.

The means by which something is closed up, e.g. the top of a bottle or the cap of a can.

Cluster analysis Clusteranalyse

A method of statistical analysis whereby people or things are classified into groups according to certain characteristics.

Cluster sampling Stichprobenverfahren mit Klumpenauswahl (Statistik)

Also called nested sampling.

In statistics, this type of research generally uses different geographical areas that resemble the total population as far as possible, with a random choice being made among the areas (or groups or clusters). Each person in the selected area is then interviewed.

Clutter Anzeigenblock, Werbeblock

A condition that exists when a large number of advertisements or commercials are placed too closely together in space or time, all of which compete for the viewer´s or listener´s (limited) attention.

Coaster Untersatz
Bierdeckel

A small dish or mat, especially for placing under a glass, eg a beer glass.

Cobweb theorem Cobweb Theorem, Spinnwebtheorem

Also called cobweb model.

A dynamic model in which the supply of a good in this year is a function of the good's price in the previous year; the demand for the good, however, depends on the price of this year. An increase in demand will result in a rise in price. A favourable price for certain commodities may induce producers to increase their supply. The increased supply will bring about a fall in price. The fall in price may induce the producers to reduce their supply. The smaller supply will result in a rise in price. The cobweb theorem investigates these fluctuations. Its analysis is useful in showing that perfect competition leads to unstable prices.

Cocktail party theory of marketing Cocktail Party Marketing Theorie

A theory stating the importance of marketing relationships with infrastructure members in order to promote word-of-mouth reports about perceptions of a product. Cocktail party chats often influence important buying decisions.

Code Code, Schlüssel

The representation of data and programming instructions in symbolic form. Codes provide a unique identification for transactions and records and are used for recording data. Code numbers are a compact means of identification. There are several codes (e.g. zip code, ABC code) in use, and so it is necessary to specify which is employed.

Code dating Auszeichnung mit Verfalldatum

The practice of coding products to indicate the sell by date.

Code of Advertising Practice (CAP) Werberichtlinien, (ethische) Richtlinien für gute Werbung

A set of rules governing the publication of advertising, seeking to ensure that advertisements are legal, decent, honest and truthful.

Code of ethics Standesordnung, (beruflicher) Ehrenkodex

Also called code of professional ethics/guidelines.

The professional standards and rules of conduct established by professional organisations to guide its members.

Cognitive dissonance kognitive Dissonanz

A psychologically uncomfortable state that occurs in people´s mind when they receive information in discord with their own feelings. This state of mind can be changed by discrediting the credibility of the source or by changing one´s own position.

Note: feelings of dissatisfaction or uncertainty about a purchase can be attributed to cognitive dissonance. Almost all major purchases result in cognitive dissonance, or discomfort caused by postpurchase conflict. Consumers almost always tend to have second thoughts after important purchases.

Coincidence of wants Bedürfniskoinzidenz

In a barter agreement, it is necessary to find an individual who wants the good or service you desire to exchange for the good or service that you possess.

Cold call unangemeldeter Besuch

Also called cold calling.

A visit to a customer or prospect (potential or prospective customer) by a salesperson, without prior notice, in the hope of getting an interview or order.

Cold canvassing ungezielte Kundenwerbung

Calling on potential/prospective customers without knowing or assessing their needs and without any prearrangement.

Collapse Zusammenbruch
Kurs-, Preisverfall

Failure or ruin of a firm. Also called breakdown, crash, failure or ruin.

A sudden drop in prices, e.g. share prices (also called collapse of stock prices or stocks drawdown) or commodity prices (also called price collapse; decline, deterioration or fall in prices; crumbling of prices; markdown).

Collateral material zusätzliches Werbematerial

Also called collateral.

The ancillary material (advertising and promotional material) used to support and reinforce a media advertising campaign, such as leaflets, direct mail, booklets, catalogues, POP displays, presentation charts, news releases.

Collect call R-Gespräch

Also called reverse-charge call or transfer call (GB).

In the USA, a phone call where the subscriber, usually the person receiving the call, agrees to pay for the call.

Collection Abholung
Datenerfassung

The fetching of goods, e.g. from a warehouse.

In statistics, the collection of data.

Collection charge Abholgebühr

A charge made by a collector for collecting goods.

Collection on delivery (COD) Zahlung bei Lieferung, (gegen) Nachnahme

Also called collect on delivery (cod).

In the USA, a method of payment stating that the cost of merchandise and other charges are to be collected at the time the goods are delivered. In GB called cash on delivery (COD).

Cash is usually collected by the delivering agent, e.g. a postman.

Collective goods Kollektivgüter, öffentliche Güter

Also called communal goods or public goods.

Commodities not in private ownership but owned by the community as a whole.

Collective interest öffentliches Interesse

Also called public interest.

The interest of society at large.

Collusion (geheime) Absprache

Also called accord, agreement, arrangement or understanding.

Secret agreement between firms to cooperate in order to avoid competition.

Collusive tendering Anbieterabsprache, Preisabsprache bei der Abgabe von Angeboten

Also called collusive bidding, bid rigging, or common pricing.

The practice by firms competing for contracts of agreeing among themselves on the tender prices each will submit for a contract. The firms thereby effectively allocate contracts among themselves.

Colour chart Farbmusterkarte

Also called shade card.

A sheet or map showing the varieties of colour.

Colour supplement farbige Beilage, Farbbeilage

A colour insert supplied free of charge with a newspaper or magazine.

Colours and packaging Farben und Verpackung

Colours on packages are often chosen to attract attention as people associate specific colours with certain feelings and experiences. When selecting packaging colours, marketers must consider whether a particular colour will evoke positive or negative feelings when it is linked to a specific product. Marketers must also consider the target market and its reaction towards a particular colour, e.g. cosmetics for women may be sold in pastel packaging whereas men will probably reject this colour.

Combination rate Kombinationspreis

Also called combo rate.

A reduced rate offered to an advertiser for booking advertising space and/or time in two or more periodicals or broadcast stations, under a common ownership. This form of quantity discount may have to be negotiated.

Combination store Kombinationsgeschäft

This type of store has both a supermarket and a full-line drugstore with a common checkout area.

Combine Unternehmenszusammenschluß

Also called (business) combination, amalgamation, absorption, consolidation, integration, or merger.

A group of firms or companies under common control wielding considerable power in any one industry; the association is temporary or permanent.

Comeback

Rückforderung(sanspruch)
Comeback
schlagfertige Antwort

A customer´s entitlement to receive compensation in the case of a justified complaint or claim.

A return to the higher status, prosperity, or success of a former time.

A clever or effective rejoinder.

Comfort

Komfort

A state of ease and satisfaction of bodily wants.

Something that produces such a state.

Command economy

Planwirtschaft, Wirtschaftssystem mit zentraler Planung

Also called centrally directed economy, controlled economy, or planned economy.

In a command economy, the targets are set by the government according to its own judgement of what the objects of society are. The system ensures production of important and necessary commodities for all the people. The State plans the allocation of all resources from a central office. Economic activity is not left to private enterprise and the price system. In a large industrial country there is fairly obviously a limit to the extent to which detailed central planning and allocation of resources can be made.

Commerce (com)

Handel (Binnen- und Außenhandel)

Latin words "cum" - with, and "merx" - merchandise.

The wide complex field of economic activity concerned with the buying and selling of services and goods and their movement from producer to consumer (in the right place, the right condition, at the right time, in the right quantity, and at the right price). It includes trade and a number of aids to trade.

Commerce

Trade
- --- Domestic (home/internal) trade
  - --- Wholesalers
  - --- Retailers
- --- Foreign (overseas/external) trade
  - --- Imports
  - --- Exports

Aids of trade
- --- Transport and Communications
- --- Banking and Finance
- --- Insurance
- --- Advertising
- --- Warehousing

Commercial Werbesendung, Werbespot (Radio, Fernsehen)

Also called (advertising) spot or spot advertising.

Advertisement on radio or television.

Commercial agent Handelsvertreter

A person selling a company's merchandise or service for a commission.

Commercial artist Werbegraphiker

Also called industrial artist.

A person who designs advertisements, posters, etc.

Commercial audience Publikum einer Werbesendung

The television audience (viewership) or radio audience (listenership) that is actively viewing or listening to a specific commercial.

Commercial break Programmunterbrechung für Werbung, Sendepause für Werbung

A break/interruption in a television or radio program(me) in order to transmit a commercial, i.e. an advertising message.

Commercial counterfeiting Warenzeichenfälschung

The use of a successful competitor`s trademark or tradename to benefit form their name or reputation. The production or sale of goods defrauds the buyer/purchaser by falsely implying that the products are produced by a reputable producer/manufacturer and thus are the well-known first-class brands.

Commercial delivery Werbesendungsreichweite

The total radio and television audience that is actually reached by a particular commercial.

Commercial district Gewerbegebiet

A particular area of a town, often at the outskirts of the town, where there are many shops, offices and other commercial enterprises.

Commercial documents handelsübliche, kaufmännische Dokumente, Handelspapiere

The most common commercial documents, in alphabetical order, are: bill of exchange, bill of lading, certificate or origin, consignment note, credit note, customs declaration, debit note, estimate, inquiry, invoice, letter of credit, order, packing list, proforma invoice, quotation, receipt, reminder, service agreement, statement of account, etc.

Some of the documents listed contain much the same information. For instance, a packing list (or delivery note) is similar to a consignment note and both are very much like an invoice, the only difference being that neither of the first two requires a price to be shown.

Commercial goods Handelsware(n)

Goods and services used by companies in carrying on their businesses.

Commercial integration charge Sonderpreis für die Ausstrahlung einer Werbesendung in einem laufenden Programm

A fee charged an advertiser by a radio or TV station for including a commercial in its broadcast schedule.

Commercial invoice (comi) Handelsfaktura, Handelsrechnung

Also called trading invoice.

A claim for payment for goods under the terms of a commercial contract with the buyer. The invoice should include full details of the goods together with unit prices, totals, weights and terms of payment, value added tax (VAT), as well as packing details and shipping marks. Where there are several packages in one consignment, the invoice is usually accompanied by a packing checklist. The main purpose of the commercial invoice is to inform the buyer of the amount due.

Commercial law Handelsrecht

Also called mercantile law.

That branch of law concerning matters relating to commerce. It has its foundations in the general law of contract.

Commercial length Dauer einer Werbung im Fernsehen/Rundfunk

A commercial should be as long as necessary to communicate the unique selling proposition, USP (i.e. the unique benefits of the product) while positively impacting the brand image. On new products, this requires at least 30 second commercials or commercials up to one minute. Once the USP has been sufficiently exposed to a large percentage of the market or target group, shorter commercials can be used.

Commercial minute (Werbe)Sendeminute

One minute of radio or television time set aside for broadcasting commercials.

Commercial policy Handelspolitik, Wirtschaftspolitik Außenwirtschaftspolitik

The rules adopted by a country for the conduct or regulation of its economic policy. Also called economic policy or strategy.

In the US, the policy concerning importation and exportation of goods and services, excluding monetary and fiscal policy. Also called foreign or international economic policy, or foreign trade policy.

Commercial protection Zeitabstand zwischen Werbung für Konkurrenzprodukte

In the case of print advertisements also called competitive separation.

The amount of time (usually 10 minutes) or space between commmercials or advertisements for competing products or services, at the request of the advertiser.

Commercial quality handelsübliche, gängige Qualität

Also called current quality or good merchantible quality.

In a contract, this means that the good delivered must be up to the ordinary standard of quality.

Commercial risk betriebswirtschaftliches Risiko

A financial risk undertaken by an entrepreneur in the process of executing commercial activities.

Commercial services kaufmännische Dienstleistungen

Services which support trade, such as advertising, banking, insurance, etc.

Commercial transaction Geschäftsabschluß, Handelsgeschäft

Also called (business) deal or transaction.

A transaction where a seller offers a good or service to a buyer for money.

The vital stages in a commercial transaction are:
1. receiving an inquiry,
2. sending of catalogues/price lists,
3. return of the order,
4. preparation of goods for despatch,
5. despatch of the goods with a delivery note,
6. sending of an advice of despatch,
7. sending an invoice,
8. posting a statement of account,
9. receipt of the sum due in settlement.

Commercial travel(l)er Reisender, Vertreter

Also called traveller, travel(l)ing salesman or sales representative.

A person appointed to represent his firm, as agent or representative, by visiting customers and prospective customers and trying to get orders for the firm he represents. He is frequently paid a basic salary and, in addition, a commission on the value of the orders he takes.

Home sales are usually secured by commercial travellers who are allocated a territory which they cover at regular intervals.

Commercialization Kommerzializierung
geschäftliche Verwertung

Making something commercial in character, or making something profitable, or emphasizing the profitable aspects of something.

A stage in the development cycle for a new product which begins when the product is introduced into the market.

Commission (com(m)) Provision

The reward paid to an agent, factor or broker for his services, consisting usually of a percentage of the value of the transactions carried out for his principal.

Payment made to a salesperson by an employer and calculated on the basis of his sales.

Commission agent Kommissionär

Also called commission merchant or factor.

An agent who buys (commission buyer or buying agent) and sells (commission salesman) for a principal; such agents are common in foreign trade. He buys and sells in his own name, receiving a commission for the contracts he has arranged. In foreign trade there is an export and an import agent.

Commission manufacturer Zulieferer, Zulieferbetrieb

Also called component supplier, outside supplier, subcontractor, subsupplier or supplier.

A manufacturer who undertakes a single process of production on behalf of another firm.

Commission merchant Verkaufskommissionär, Konsignatar Kommissionär

A merchant who never holds any goods in stock but sells usually only to his customers by showing samples. Also called commission salesman, consignee, selling agent or factor.

A commission agent.

Commission sale Verkauf auf Kommissionsbasis

Also called sale on commission.

A sale of goods or services where the salesman is paid a commission.

Commitment Zusage, Verpflichtung

Also called obligation, promise, or undertaking.

Something to which one has committed oneself, which one is bound to do.

Commodity (coty) Wirtschaftsgut Ware

In economics synonymous with a good. Economic goods are useful and scarce things wanted by buyers. They are divided into two classes: commodities and services.

In commerce, an article of trade.

There are many varieties of commodity. They can be classified as: consumer(s') goods (e.g. foodstuffs), durable goods (e.g. kitchen appliances), producer(s') goods (e.g. machines), primary products (e.g. raw materials), secondary products (e.g. manufactured goods), tertiary products (e.g. services).

Commodity broker Waren(börsen)makler

A specialized agent who deals on commodity markets/exchanges and works for a brokerage.

Commodity exchange (CMX, comex) Warenbörse

Also called commodity market.

A trading centre where commodities are bought and sold. Many organizations specialise in one particular commodity (e.g. tea, coffee, cotton, rubber, nonferrous metals, etc.). It is not necessary for the commodities to be physically exchanged; only rights to ownership need to be.
There is a spot market and a futures market. The first is a market for immediate delivery and payment in cash of commodities and foreign exchange; the latter deals with futures contracts and enables dealers to hedge against spot price fluctuations.

Commodity futures contract Warentermingeschäft

A contract to buy or sell a precisely defined quantity and quality of a commodity in a given period. The price is stipulated at the time of transaction.

Commodity market Güter-, Rohstoff-, Warenmarkt
Warenbörse

A market typified by the homogeneity of products. The commodity markets provide the link between the producers of raw materials and manufacturers who use these raw materials.
There are a number of commodity markets. For example, markets for sugar, spices, cocoa, coffee, rubber, tea, wool, metal (eg copper, tin, lead, zinc), and diamonds, etc.

In most of the markets the commodities can be very accurately graded and described, so that dealing can take place without an actual inspection of the goods. Buying and selling is by brokers representing users and producers. These markets help to achieve stability in international commodity prices. Also called product market.

The commodity exchange itself, i.e. the place where people buy and sell products.

Commodity money Warengeld

A medium of exchange which is generally acceptable to the people concerned. Many different commodities (e.g. cattle, sheep, shells, rice, tea, salt, gold, cigarettes, etc.) have been used as money. These were gradually replaced by precious metals, especially gold and silver in the form of coins, and banknotes.

Commodity rate Einzelfrachttarif

Also called special rate.

A freight rate applied where freight is product specific and not based on volume or weight.

Commodity tax Warensteuer

A tax levied (imposed) on goods and services, such as value-added tax (VAT) or sales tax (ST).

Common carrier Spediteur, Transportunternehmen öffentliches Verkehrsunternehmen Datenübermittler

A carrier obliged by law to carry any goods offered to him (except dangerous articles) at a reasonable charge for delivery to any destination served by the carrier. With certain exceptions, e.g. Acts of God, inherent vice, fraud of the consignor, fault of the consignor, he is liable to compensate the owner for loss of or damage to the goods he carries.

A public enterprise which carries goods or passengers, and which anyone can use.

An organisation which provides communication services.

Common Market (CM) Europäische Gemeinschaft (EG) gemeinsamer Markt

The popular name for the European Community (EC). This was established in 1958 (by the Treaty of Rome) to promote the economic and political development of the six original member countries (Germany, France, Italy, The Netherlands, Belgium, and Luxembourg). In 1998 there are 15 member countries. Its aims are a common currency (Euro), the abolition of tariffs, a common agricultural policy, free trade, free capital transfer, and freedom for citizens of member countries to travel and work without restrictions within the Community.
Since 1 January 1993 known as the European Union (EU).

A market that removes all barriers on trade among members, harmonizes trade policies toward the rest of the world, and also allows the free movement of labour and capital among member nations.

Common pricing Preisabsprache

The illegal fixing of identical prices by several firms so that they all charge the same price.The prices for goods or services are fixed by verbal agreement between otherwise competing firms. Also called price fixing, price (fixing) agreement, price collusion or price rigging.

An agreement (usually illegal) between several contractors to quote stipulated prices when tendering for contracts. Also called collusive tendering, dummy tendering, or level tendering.

Communication Kommunikation

The process of imparting information from an information source to an information destination as a basis for control and decision making (e.g. the exchange of ideas, concepts, feelings, etc. between two or more persons).

There are various types of communication, e.g.: one-way, two-way, horizontal (exchange of information etc. among persons at the same level), and vertical communication (the persons act at different levels).

The basic elements of communication are: 1. information source, 2. message, 3. transmitter, 4. signal,
5. receiver, 6. information destination.

The systems in which information is communicated are very diverse and dependent upon circumstances. Information is of supreme importance in the industrial organization but it is useless unless communicated by the correct source to the correct destination by the most efficient means.

Communication effect of advertising Kommunikationseffekt der Werbung

The influence that an advertising activity might have, is having, or has had, on the consumers of a product advertised.

Communications mix Kommunikationsmix

There are four major means of communication from seller to prospective/potential buyer: 1. advertising, 2. personal selling, 3. sales promotion, 4. publicity.
All companies have to use one or more of these means of communicating with their market(s), and most companies use all of them, although in differing proportions.

Community shopping center lokales Einkaufszentrum

This type of shopping center usually contains between 15 and 50 retail stores and normally has a branch of a department store or variety store, a discount store, a supermarket, specialty stores, professional offices, and sometimes a bank.

Company car Firmenwagen

A car owned by a company and lent to an employee to use it as if it were his own.

Company image Firmenansehen, Unternehmensimage

Also called corporation image.

The image which someone has of a company when its name is mentioned; this can be positive or negative, weak or strong, etc. The company image can influence consumers' propensity to buy its products, to acquire shares, to join the company and in general, facilitate the company's business operations. Additionally, it may affect the company's goodwill when it is sold.

Company name Firmenname

Also called business, corporate, firm, trade or trading name, or name of the company.

In general, the name under which a person (eg a sole trader) or other businesses (e.g. partnerships and companies) trade and register.

A company has considerable freedom in its choice of name, but there are certain statutory obligations which must be observed.
A chosen name will be acceptable provided that:
1. it is not the same as, or too similar to, that of another company;
2. it does not contain words or phrases which are misleading or offensive;
3. it ends with the words prescribed by statute (e.g. the name of a public limited company must end with the words "public limited company" or the abbreviation PLC; the name of a private limited company must end with Ltd.).

Note: the word limited tells anyone that the shareholders have limited liability.

Company profile Unternehmensprofil

Facts about a particular company sufficient to identify and compare it with other companies, such as sales turnover, profit, product range, number of employees, market penetration, advertising budget, etc.

Company sales forecast Absatzprognose eines Unternehmens

The amount of sales a company expects to obtain during a given future time period in a specified area. The sales level can be expressed in amounts of money or in physical units; the latter is usually better because it does not reflect prices and price changes.

Company salespeople firmeneigenes Verkaufspersonal

Salespersons employed by a company to distribute the company's product(s). They will give a manufacturer's product(s) the utmost attention and thus do a better job of selling and representing a company than agents, brokers or representatives, who are usually used in the company's early low-volume years. Company salespeople should be used when larger sales volume warrants - prior to this stage the costs may be too high.

Company-owned warehouse firmeneigenes (Waren)Depot

A warehouse owned by a company so that goods can be transported directly to the customers, possibly by a company-owned freight carrier.

Comparative advertising vergleichende Werbung

Also called comparison advertising.

An advertisement which makes direct (or indirect) comparisons with competitive products or services.The advertiser is the manufacturer of the product that is found to be superior. The reference brand may be a previous product of the advertiser, an unnamed competitor`s brand, or a specific and named competitor`a brand.

Note: comparisons must not be misleading or deceptive and the advertiser must have evidence to substantiate/prove his claims/statements.

Comparative price Vergleichspreis

Statements in advertisements comparing specific prices with previous prices, other prices, or prices goods are estimated to be worth.

Comparative product analysis Produktvergleichsanalyse, vergleichender Warentest

Also called comparative product test.

The systematic comparison of products now competing in the marketplace or likely to do in the future, to show their relative success in matching customer need.

Comparison pricing Preisfestsetzung durch Produktvergleich

A pricing strategy in which the price for a new product is fixed by comparing the benefits it offers to those of rival/competitve products.

Comparison shopper Käufer, der Vergleiche anstellt

Also called comparative shopper.

Someone who studies competitive brands, gathers information on the price, quality, etc. before he purchases a product.

A shopper posing as a customer and investigating the merchandising and sales promotion activities of competing stores.

Comparison test Vergleichstest

Detailed comparison of competing products or services available on the market, often done by an independent third party.

Compensating payment Ausgleichszahlung

Also called compensatory payment or monetary compensatory amount.

The increase in income a buyer in a market would require to restore his demand to its former level after a price increase.

Compensation method Kompensationsmethode

In the selling process, a salesperson´s handling of a customer´s objection by admitting the validity of the objection, but at the same time pointing out some advantage that compensates for it.

Competing product Konkurrenzprodukt

Also called competitive or rival product.

Different products from different companies of similar quality which have the same use and are sold at similar prices. These products can be substituted for each other by the buyer, either partially or completely.

Competition Wettbewerb, Konkurrenz

In economics, competition exists wherever and whenever large numbers of buyers and sellers are in active contact with the intention of maximising profits and satisfaction and prices are allowed to be determined by the forces of supply and demand.

There are two main types of competition:
1. perfect competition,
2. imperfect competition.

Other forms of competition are:
3. free competition (no government interference, prices are free to move according to the forces of supply and demand);
4. monopolistic competition (there are only a few producers who can force buyers to accept their prices);
5. nonprice competition (rival sellers do not compete by price but by offering other attractions, e.g. better product quality, packaging, after-sales services, etc.);
6. unfair competition (competition that is not in accordance with accepted business behaviour or that is dishonest, e.g. secret discounts, false claims about product quality); etc.

In business, it is the activity in which firms engage to attract customers to their product or service including price differentials, advertising, after-sales service, etc.

The firms competing with one another.

Competition Act Wettbewerbsgesetz

Also called Unfair Trade Practice Act (US).

An act that checks anti-competitive behaviour, i.e. any practices which may restrict, distore or prevent competition. For example, the act prohibits the sale of branded and unbranded goods below cost when the intent is to eliminate competition or to injure a competitor.

Competition law Wettbewerbsgesetz

A country`s laws prohibiting trade practices which prevent, restrict or distort competition.

Competition orientated pricing wettbewerbsorientierte Preisbildung

Also called pricing at the going rate.

A pricing strategy commonly found in price sensitive markets. Firms have to charge similar prices, i.e. they tend to keep their prices very much in line with each other, because unless their product offers customers a significant benefit it canot command a higher price.

Note: the company considers costs and revenue secondary to competitors´ prices.

Competition types Wettbewerbsarten

There are a number of different types of competition, examples are:
1. cutthroat competition, 2. global competition, 3. illegal competition, 4. imperfect competition, 5. indirect competition, 6. national competition, 7. nonprice competition, 8. perfect competition, 9. price competition, 10. pure competition, 11. unfair competition, etc.

Competition watchdogs Wettbewerbshüter

Authorities that watch competition in their respective countries, for example, the Monopolies and Mergers Commission in GB, the Antitrust Division in the USA, the Federal Cartel Office (Bundeskartellamt) in Germany, etc.

Competitive advantage Wettbewerbsvorteil

Also called competitive edge.

Anything that gives a company an advantage over its competitor(s) in the market place. For example, superior customer service.

Competitive advertising Produkt-, Konkurrenzwerbung; kämpferische, aggressive Werbung, Überzeugungswerbung

Also called combative or persuasive advertising.

This type of ad emphasizes product benefits by establishing a distinctive position for one product compared to another one and is aimed solely at consumers; it tries to persuade people to buy the advertiser's product rather than his competitor's by assuring that it is better. Competitive ad is particularly associated with oligopoly competition.

Competitive bidding Submissionsverfahren

Also called tender procedure.

A procedure in which buyers request prospective suppliers to submit quotations or tenders for proposed purchase of goods or services or a contract.

Competitive demand Konkurrenznachfrage, konkurrierende Nachfrage

Also called alternate, competing, composite or rival demand.

Demand for competing/competitive products. Sometimes one commodity is a substitute for another, and an increased demand for one will lead to a reduction in demand for the other. Sometimes the purchase of one commodity, which is not a substitute, prevents the purchase of the other.

Competitive loyal treuer Konkurrenzkunde, konkurrenztreuer Kunde

People who buy a competitor´s product most or all of the time.

Competitive market Konkurrenz-, Wettbewerbsmarkt; freier, offener Markt

Also called free or open market.

A market characterized by competition, i.e. a market in which a very large number of buyers and sellers trade independently, and as such no one trader can significantly influence price (i.e. there is absence of market power). In such a market there is only one price for a given commodity at any one time and all buyers and sellers know the conditions on the market

Competitive parity method Competitive-Parity-Method (Methode zur Festlegung des Werbeetats, die sich an Konkurrenz orientiert)

A competitive-based method to determine an advertising budget by taking into account the advertising expenditures of competitors.

Possible disadvantages of this method are: 1. the marketing objectives of the different companies may differ; 2. the advertiser uses other companies´ past results, etc.

Note: as some companies may have a budget that is too high and others one that is too low, the industry average should represent an approximation of the optimum budget.

Competitive position Wettbewerbsposition

A company´s position in a market relative to its competitors.

A company may have one of the following positions:

1. Market leader: the firm enjoying the largest slice of the market and retaining its competitve position by expanding the total market or expanding market share at the expense of rivals, while protecting or defending the current market share by retaining its customer base.

2. Market challenger: these are the competing firms behind the market leader who are aggressively attacking rivals, including the market leader, to gain more market share.

3. Market follower: these firms have a low market share and few resources to challenge for extra sales and market share. Their main objective is to do as before and survive. In boom times they may benefit from the success of their larger rivals, but in recession or when faced with rivals´ product innovations, they often struggle to maintain their business.

4. Market nicher: these firms specialise in terms of market/product/customers by finding a small, profitable, safe, noncompetitive market segment which is of no or little interest to the market leader and challengers. Nichers are vulnerable to downswings, the entry of rival nichers and the attacks of the major players on the market.

Competitive price Wettbewerbspreis, konkurrenzfähiger Preis

Also called free market price.

A price that is kept low so that it can easily compete with the price of other rival goods or services . The price is either lower than those currently prevailing, or it is a similar price together with an additional incentive.

Competitive pricing Wettbewerbspreisbildung

Also called competitor or competition-oriented pricing.

The putting of prices on goods as to be able to compete with rival/competitive products. Many companies set/fix prices after careful consideration of competitive price structure. Policies may be formulated to sell above, below or in line with competitors/rivals.

Note: the problem here is that cost and profit structures will differ.

Competitive strategy Wettbewerbsstrategie

Planning of business objectives and policies intended to give a firm a competitive advantage over its competitors. That means the development of those elements of the firm`s overall corporate activities that relate to beating the competition in the field. To be able to formulate this strategy one should:
1. analyse the strengths and weaknesses of one`s own company and of its rivals;
2. identify the key success factors in markets in which the business is to operate;
3. precisely define consumer attributes, demands, attitudes and behaviour, etc.

Competitive supply Konkurrenzangebot, konkurrierendes Angebot

Also called composite or rival supply.

A number of commodities which are substitutes may provide a composite supply to satisfy demand, e.g. tea, milk, coffee, etc. provide a composite supply of beverages. Producers usually choose what they will produce, and to this extent the alternative outputs are in competitive supply.

Competitiveness Konkurrenz-, Wettbewerbsfähigkeit

Also called competitive strength.

The ability and degree of being competitive, eg of a company.

The ability of a country to compete economically with other countries.

Competitor Mitbewerber, Konkurrent, Konkurrenzunternehmen

Also called rival or contender.

A rival, ie in business a firm usually offering similar products or services to buyers/purchasers. Each competitor has a certain philosophy of doing business, a certain internal culture, and certain guiding beliefs. Some competitors live in relative accord with one another, others are constantly fighting with one another.

There are different types of competitors, e.g.:
1. the laid-back competitor (he does not react quickly or strongly to a given competitor move, e.g. because he feels that his customers are loyal or because he may lack the funds to react);
2. the selective competitor (he reacts only to certain types of assult, e.g. he might always respond to price cuts but not to changing advertising strategies);

3. the tiger competitor (he reacts immediately and strongly to any assult on his terrain and signals that he is going to fight to the finish if attacked);
4. the stochastic competitor (he does not show a predictable reaction pattern, he might or he might not retaliate on any particular event).

Competitor analysis Konkurrenzanalyse, Analyse konkurrierender Produkte

The analysis of competitor capabilities, intentions, plans, prices, types of products, product quality, market position, advertising budget, financial resources, etc. This may be necessary, e.g. to make a decision on entry into a product market.

Competitors´ prices Konkurrenzpreise

The prices of competitors and possible competitor reactions to our own pricing moves are external factors affecting our company´s pricing policy. On the other hand, our company´s pricing strategy may affect the nature of the competition we face. For example, if we follow a high-price, high-margin strategy, this may attract competition; if we follow a low-price, low-margin strategy, this may stop competitors or drive them out of the market.

Complaint Mänglerüge, Beschwerde, Reklamation

An expression of discontent/dissatisfaction made by a buyer to the seller if the goods delivered are defective, if the seller has delivered wrong goods, if the quality is not satisfactory, if the goods have been delivered damaged or late, if the prices charged are excessive or not as agreed, etc.
Despite all efforts and care in the execution of orders, not all orders are perfect when they are received, mistakes and defects may occur, and thus it may be necessary for the customer to complain about them. The most important thing is to complain immediately a defect or deficiency becomes apparent.
A complaint should indicate clearly what is wrong and should mention such details as order number, date of order, etc. to enable the seller to identify the consignment in question.
Complaints may be justified or unjustified. Whatever the case may be, complaints call for the utmost tact and restraint by both parties.

Complaints department Reklamationsabteilung

A company's department which deals with customers' complaints about its goods or services.

Complementary demand komplementäre, verbundene Nachfrage Komplementärgüternachfrage

Also called joint demand.

A demand for two commodities that are jointly needed because one commodity gives little or no satisfaction without the other. Sometimes two commodities may be so related that the demand for one affects the demand for the other (e.g. tea and sugar); an increase or a decrease in the demand for one product leads to an increase or a decrease in the demand for the other.
What effect such a change in demand has on the price of the commodities depends on the conditions of supply; the more inelastic the supply the greater the change of price.

Complementary goods Komplementärgüter, komplementäre Güter

Also called complements or joint goods.

A good which tends to be purchased when another good is purchased, since it complements the first good. Examples are cameras and films, petrol and motor cars, bread and butter - products in joint/complementary demand.
Note: these goods have a negative cross elasticity of demand.

Complete refund offer Rückgaberecht mit Gelderstattung

Also called refund offer or money back guarantee.

Offer by a seller to refund the total purchase price after a complaint by a customer.

Complete segmentation Abdeckung aller Marktsegmente

The division of a market into segments consisting of individual customers and tailoring a specific product and marketing programme to each as each has a different need.

Completely knocked down (CKD, ckd) vollständig zerlegt

Products that are shipped as kits of parts for assembly at their destination. This method reduces the freight charges and is sometimes used in foreign trade.

Complimentary ticket Freikarte

A free ticket, given as a present.

Compliments slip (comp slip) Beilegezettel mit Firmenaufdruck, Empfehlungskarte

Also called "with compliments" slip.

A card, usually showing the company`s letter-heading, with the words "With the compliments of ..." printed on it, followed by the name and address of the person or firm sending it. It is often enclosed with a consignment sent to someone to identify the sender, or it can be used to accompany a catalogue or any other item and obviate the need to write a covering letter. Sometimes the sender adds a short message and signs the card.

Component Bestandteil, Bauteil

Processed materials and manufactured parts, e.g. a piece of machinery, included in finished products.

Component supplier Zulieferer, Zulieferant

Also called outside supplier or supplier.

A firm that produces parts which are used by other producers to make finished products.

Composite demand zusammengesetzte Nachfrage, Gesamtnachfrage konkurrierende Nachfrage

The total demand for a commodity which arises when it is required for different purposes and will be the sum of the different demands, e.g. steel for ships, railways, refrigerators, etc. Also called aggregate, market, overall or total demand.

The demand for two or more products which are substitutes for each other. Also called alternate demand, competing demand, or rival demand.

Composite supply Gesamtangebot, zusammengesetztes Angebot konkurrierendes Angebot

The total supply of a commodity offered for different purposes. Also called aggregate, market, overall or total supply.

A number of commodities which are substitutes may provide a composite supply to satisfy a demand, e.g. tea, milk, coffee, etc., provide a composite supply of beverages. Also called competitive, composite or rival supply.

Computer-assisted interviewing (CAI) computerunterstützte Befragung

Interviewing method in which the interviewer reads the questions from a computer screen and enters the respondent's data directly into the computer.

Computer-assisted trading (CAT) computerunterstützter Handel

The use of computers by brokers and traders on a market, e.g. the commodity or stock market, to facilitate trading by displaying prices, recording transactions, etc.

Concealed damage versteckter Schaden

A damage to a product that is not visible or to the contents of a package that is in good order externally.

Concentrated marketing gezieltes, konzentriertes Marketing

Also called niche marketing.

One of the three main marketing strategies, the others being undifferentiated marketing and differentiated marketing.

A strategy adopted when a firm concentrates on selling to a small market segment or niche. Instead of going after a small share of a large market, the firm goes after a large share of one or a few submarkets. Thus, the firm can concentrate its limited resources on establishing a well-known reputation and dominant market position within its chosen niche. Furthermore, costs can be kept low because of the savings made as a result of specialization in production, distribution, and promotion.
If the segment is well chosen, it can be very profitable. On the other hand, the risks are higher because a particular market can turn sour or larger competitors may decide to enter the same segment.

Note: this strategy is commonly adopted by smaller firms who are unable to compete in the wider mass market.

Concentration ratio Konzentrationsmaß, Konzentrationsrate

The market share held collectively by the four leading firms in an industry. In other words, the total sales of the four largest firms in an industry as a percentage of the total sales of the industry.
Note: the higher the ratio, the greater is the market dominance of a small number of firms.

Concentric diversification — konzentrische Diversifikation

A growth strategy in which a company adds new, but related, products to its existing product line(s) in order to attract new customers.

Concept test — Akzeptanztest einer Produktidee

A market research technique to assess the reactions of consumers to a new product or a change to an existing product.

Concession — Konzession
Entgegenkommen, Zugeständnis

The right given by a manufacturer (ie licenser/licensor) of a product to a business (the concessionaire/licensee) to be the only seller of that product in a particular country or area. Also called licence, charter or commercial privilege.

The act of conceding; and the thing or point gained from somebody in this way.

Concession close — Verkaufsabschluß mit Zugeständnissen

In the selling process, a (small) concession given to a buyer in order to attempt him/her to place an order immediately.

Concessionaire — Konzessionär, Vertragshändler
Konzessionär

A person or firm who operates as a distributor with a special authority granted by the manufacturer to work in a particular market area, usually on a basis of exclusivity.

One who operates a business within premises supplied by another, e.g. someone who rents the concession in a sports arena to sell goods there.

Concessionary terms — günstige Bedingungen, Vorzugskonditionen

Special conditions granted to someone, e.g. a reduced price granted to a regular buyer. Or, when seeking an order, giving a potential buyer small concessions, e.g. delivery free of charge or a longer credit period, to the proposed deal so tempting an immediate favourable response.

Conditional offer bedingtes Angebot

An offer which is not firm. The offerer makes an offer to do something, e.g. to buy goods, provided that certain terms apply.

Conditional order bedingter Auftrag

An order for goods given by a prospective buyer, subject to agreed conditions.

An instruction to a bank to pay a certain sum provided that a receipt is obtained from the person to whom payment is to be made.

Conditional probability bedingte Wahrscheinlichkeit

In statistics, the probability that an outcome will occur if some other unpredictable event will occur.

Conditional sales contract Kaufvertrag unter Eigentumsvorbehalt

Also called qualified sales contract.

A sales contract subject to a condition precedent; the contract is to come into effect at once but the ownership is not to pass until a specified event (eg the payment of instalments) occurs.

Conditions of demand Nachfragebedingungen

Demand is not fixed, but varies with changing conditions. The chief factors affecting demand are: the price of the product; the level of income; tastes; prices of other goods; population; government policy; and seasonal factors.

Conditions of sale Verkaufsbedingungen (und Liefer-bedingungen)

Also called terms and conditions; or conditions or terms of sale and delivery.

The terms and conditions (e.g. credit terms, discounts) upon which goods are sold. They are brought to the attention of buyers and usually appear in the seller's printed price lists or in documents acknowledging orders.

Conditions of supply Angebotsbedingungen

Supply is not fixed, but depends on various conditions. The most important conditions are as follows: the techniques of production; the scale of production; the cost of the factors of production; government action; natural influences; the price obtainable on the market, and the price of other commodities.

Confirmation Bestätigung

Also called acknowledgement.

In general, the act of confirming or the state of being confirmed.

Confirmation of order Auftragsbestätigung

Also called or acknowledgement of order.

The business (the seller) sends it to the customer (the buyer) to inform him that the business has received his order and will deliver the goods or services.

Conformist Konformist

A person who behaves in the same way as others because he/she allows them to influence his/her attitudes, opinions, behaviour, etc. This may be due to a deep-lying weakness in someone's personality or to the power of pressure groups.

Conglomerate Konglomerat, Mischkonzern

Also called conglomerate company, merger or amalgamation; or diversifying merger.

A term of American origin for a holding company with a large number of (often undervalued) subsidiaries, especially those acquired through takeovers.

Companies having a wide range of products, not necessarily related to each other in any way selling to a wide range of unrelated markets. The intention of a conglomerate is to spread the risk so that if one part of the total suffers a fall in profits at least some of the others will prosper.

Conglomerate diversification konglomerate, laterale Diversifikation

A growth strategy in which a company wants to grow by adding totally unrelated products to its existing product line(s).

Conquest strategy Eroberungsstrategie

A marketing strategy whose main purpose is to attract new customers.

Conscious buying motives bewußte Kaufmotive

The reasons for buying that people are aware of and willing to express. One of the many motives influencing a buying decision.

Consecutive-weeks discount (CWD) Malrabatt für Werbung

A reduced rate granted to an advertiser who buys radio or TV time for a continuous period, usually 26 to 52 weeks.

Consideration Entgelt, Vergütung

The price paid. The money (or thing, right, etc.) which a person gives in exchange for goods or services.

Consign (ver-, über-, zu-)senden, abschicken übergeben, anvertrauen

To forward goods from one place or person to another. Also called send off.

To entrust goods to a carrier for transport.

Consignee Empfänger (von Waren), Destinator Verkaufskommissionär, Konsignatar

The receiver of goods. The sender/supplier is the consigner/consignor. Also called receiver or recipient.

In foreign trade, a party, especially a commission agent, receiving goods on consignment.

Consignment (consgt) (Waren)Sendung Konsignationsware Versand

Goods sent by the consignor to the consignee, ie a batch of goods consigned.

In foreign trade, goods transferred by the owner (the exporter, i.e. the consignor) to an agent (the consignee) for sale on commission at the best price possible. Ownership does not pass to the agent; the consignor (ie the exporter) keeps the ownership of the goods until the agent has sold them. Also called consigned goods, consignment goods, consignment stock or goods on consignment.

The act or process of sending goods to someone who will keep them or sell them. Also called despatch, delivery, or shipment.

Consignment account Kommissionskonto

This account is a record of all the money that the commission agent has received and the expenses he has paid for the consignment.

Consignment goods Kommissionsware

Also called goods on consignment or goods on commission.

Goods sent to an agent for sale on a commission basis.

Consignment sale Kommissionsverkauf
Konsignationsverkauf

Also called consignment selling or trade.

A transaction between a manufacturer and a distributor. The goods are sent to the distributor who takes possession but title remains with the manufacturer until the consignment is paid for.

In foreign trade, a transaction between an exporter and foreign agent or distributor. The material is shipped to the agent or distributor to be sold on behalf of the exporter who retains title of the goods until they are sold by the agent or distributor. Once sold, payment is sent to the exporter.

Consignment stock Kommissionslager
Konsignationslager

Also called commission stock; consignment store or consignor's inventory.

A stock of goods which a businessman (ie the consignor) places at the disposal of his domestic or foreign agent. The agent (ie the consignee) sells the consignment goods for the consignor's account.

Consignment trade Kommissionsverkauf
Konsignationshandel

Also called consignment sale or selling.

A transaction between a manufacturer and a distributor. The goods are sent to the distributor who takes possession but title remains with the manufacturer until the consignment is paid for.

In international trade, goods are sent by an exporter to a nominal importer in a foreign country, that nominal importer being, in fact, an agent of the exporter. Thus, the goods come into the physical possession of the agent whose duty it is to sell the goods on the exporter's behalf and remit to the exporter (i.e. the principal) the proceeds of the sale, less all expenses of handling, storing and transport, customs duties and fees and his commission.

Consignor/consigner Ab-, Ver- Sender (von Waren)
Konsignant, Kommittent

The person or company that consigns/sends goods. Also called sender.

In foreign trade, the owner of goods who sends them to an agent (the consignee) who has agreed to sell them for the owner (ie the consignor).

Consolidated shipment Sammelladung

Also called consolidation, mixed consignment, pooled consignment, joint cargo, grouped consignment or collective consignment.

Goods from different companies grouped together into a single consignment.

Consolidator Sammelgutunternehmen

A company which groups together various goods from different suppliers to form one consolidated shipment.

Conspicuous consumption Geltungskonsum

Also called ostentatious consumption.

The purchase of expensive goods or services to demonstrate one's wealth or prominent position rather than for the utility of the goods or services.

Constant Konstante, konstante Größe

A term which takes only a single numerical value; whereas a variable can take a range of numerical values.

Constant returns to scale konstanter Skalenertrag

A situation in which a given increase in all inputs leads to a proportional increase in output.

Consultative selling beratender Verkauf

In general, a sales practice of developing a relationship with customers and providing them with information that will help them solve their problems and achieve their goals.

In detail, a personal selling technique in which the salesperson assists the potential buyer to identify his needs and to find need-satisfactions in the product range offered. The salesperson identifies the prospect´s needs and recommends the best solution even if the best solution does not require the salesperson´s products.

Note: consultative salespersons become consultants, partners, and problem solvers for their customers.

Consumable supplies Hilfs- und Betriebsstoffe

Items that facilitate a company´s production and operations, but do not become part of the finished product.

Consumer Konsument, (End)Verbraucher

Also called end consumer, end user, final consumer, or ultimate consumer.

People who buy and consume (use or use up) final goods and services to satisfy their wants. They do not resell what they buy and they do not use it for manufacturing other goods.

Consumer advertising Konsumentenwerbung, Verbraucherwerbung

Advertising (ad) directed at the end/final/ultimate consumer of a product or service. The main function of consumer ad is to influence the customer's predisposition to buy the product before he walks into the shop.

Consumer advice centre Verbraucherberatungsstelle

A centre which provides information and advice to the consumer. This activity is called consumer advisory service or consumer counsel(l)ing.

Consumer behaviour Verbraucherverhalten

Also called buyer or consumption behaviour.

The way in which consumers react to certain situations in the market (e.g. price changes, changes in design, new product promotion, etc.). It is determined by economic, psychological and sociological considerations.

Consumer benefit Verbrauchernutzen

The value(s) a consumer or user derives from a product or service.

Consumer buying behaviour Verbraucherkaufverhalten

The purchasing behaviour of end/final/ultimate consumers, i.e. individuals and households, who buy goods and services for personal consumption.

Consumer complaint Verbraucherbeschwerde, Mängelrüge

An expression of dissatisfaction made by a consumer to the seller if the goods delivered or the services rendered do not come up to his/her expectations.

Such complaints provide one source of information about discontent and sellers should deal with legitimate consumer complaints promptly and courteously because negative consumer reactions, if allowed to spread, can have devastating consequences on future sales. On the other hand, consumers who obtain adequate redress often like a company and its products more than before.

Consumer contest Verbraucherwettbewerb

In consumer contests, individuals compete for prizes based on their analytical or creative skill.

Consumer cooperative (society) Konsumgenossenschaft

Any retail business owned by consumers who achieve ownership by investing capital which receives a fixed rate of interest while profits are distributed according to purchases. The members elect the management.

Consumer credit Verbraucherkredit, Konsumentenkredit

Also called small-scale credit.

Credit from banks, finance houses, pawnbrokers, moneylenders, and shops by way of personal loan, hire purchase, and credit cards for the purchase of consumer goods. The goods are often taken as security for the credit.

Consumer Credit Act Verbraucherkreditgesetz (GB)

The Act protects all borrowers in the personal sector up to a maximum amount and applies to bank lending, hire purchase, credit sale agreements, credit cards and private loans. All consumer purchases must indicate the true cost of a facility, and written agreements are required - this does not apply to overdrafts.

Note: when a borrower enters into an agreement he has a period of three days in which to change his mind.

In the UK, all institutions which are concerned with consumer credit services have to be licensed by the Director General of Fair Trading.

Consumer credit agreement Verbraucher-Kreditvertrag

A personal credit agreement between a debtor (the borrower) and a creditor (the lender) by which the creditor provides the debtor with credit (fixed sum or running account) not exceeding a certain amount.

Consumer demand Konsumenten-, Verbrauchernachfrage

The demand of consumers for goods and services.

Consumer dissatisfaction Verbraucherunzufriedenheit

The degree to which a consumer´s expectations are not fulfilled by a product or service.

Consumer durables Gebrauchsgüter, dauerhafte Konsumgüter

Also called durable consumer goods or durables.

Consumer goods whose useful life extends over a relatively long period, e.g. cars, refrigerators, TVs, etc.

Consumer expenditure Verbraucherausgaben

Also called consumption expenditure or consumer spending.

Aggregate personal expenditures on goods (durables and nondurables) and services to satisfy current wants.

Consumer finance company Spezialinstitut für Konsumentenkredite

A financial institution that grants short-term loans to individuals to finance consumption expenditure.

Consumer goods advertising Konsumgüterwerbung

Advertising designed to reach the buyers of consumer goods, i.e. the final consumers.

Consumer loyalty Konsumententreue

Also called customer loyalty.

The loyalty of customers to purchase the same consumer/consumption goods of one producer.

Consumer magazine Publikumszeitschrift

Also called consumer journal or publication.

A publication intended for the general public rather than for a trade or profession (i.e. a trade or professional magazine).

Consumer market Konsumgütermarkt

The market for consumer goods.

Consumer marketing Verbrauchermarketing

Marketing focussing on retail consumers and their needs.

Consumer non-durables Konsumgüter

Also called disposables or single-use goods.

Goods that are used up within a short time after purchase, e.g. drinks, food, etc.

Consumer panel Verbraucherpanel, Verbrauchertestgruppe

A representative group of consumers, selected either randomly or by the quota method, who are prepared to supply continuous information on a particular product or service and their buying habits.

Consumer preference Verbraucherpräferenz

The relative preference levels for available goods and services expressed by consumers.

Consumer pretest Verbrauchervortest

A test of advertising effectiveness that asks people to examine advertisements and rank them on their ability to capture and retain interest. To minimise the risk of spending money on ineffective ads, advertisers use pretests before running the ads.

Consumer price (End)Verbraucherpreis

The retail selling price for a particular product or service.

Consumer price index (CPI) Verbraucherpreisindex

Also called cost-of-living index, index of retail prices or retail price index (RPI).

An index to measure monthly or annual changes in the buying power of a country's currency (e.g. £, $, DM). The index represents the total cost of a selected market basket (basket of commodities) expressed as a percentage of the average cost of the same market basket in a previous period. The index is used as an indicator of changes in the cost of living and as a measure of inflation.

Consumer product classification Konsumgüterklassifikation

According to the behavioural classification system there are five types of consumer goods:

1. convenience goods (products that are bought immediately and frequently with little ongoing comparison of alternatives),
2. shopping goods (products that consumers will carefully compare before they purchase them; these goods may be homogeneous or heterogeneous),
3. specialty goods (goods which are very important to the consumer so that he/she will invest much time and effort before purchasing),
4. unsought goods (goods the consumer either does not know or has no interest in purchasing, thus the consumer must be informed about their availability and values),
5. services.

Consumer profile Verbraucherprofil

Significant demographic, psychographic and cultural details about consumers, such as age category, marital status, family composition, hobbies, education, income level, occupation, sex, area of residence, buying habits, hopes, aspirations, expectations for the future, etc.

Consumer promotion Verkaufsförderung beim Konsumenten, Verbraucher

Also called consumer sales promotion.

Externally directed incentives offered to the end/ultimate consumer. In other words, sales promotion desgined to stimulate consumer purchasing, including coupons, self-liquidating offers, bargain packs, giveaways, contests, demonstrations, premiums, prices-off, loyalty rebates, displays, quantity rebates, samples, trading stamps, etc.

These tools are designed to gain one or more of the following:

1. product trial,
2. repeat usage of the product,
3. more frequent product purchases,
4. introduce a new or improved product or packaging,
5. neutralize competitive advertising or sales promotions,
6. encourage consumers to purchase more of the product at a time, etc.

Note: consumer promotions are particularly beneficial in introducing a new product as they help consumers overcome their hesitancy about trying something new.

Consumer protection Verbraucherschutz

Laws and regulations designed to aid and protect consumers, eg with regard to purity, quality, safety, etc of products and services.

There are two broad reasons why consumers need protection. First, some producers are dishonest (e.g. produce unsatisfactory goods), second, it is impossible for the consumer to make an objective assessment of many of the goods he wishes to buy.

Therefore, a number of independent bodies (e.g. the Consumers' Association, the British Standards Institution) exist to watch over the interests of the consumers. Further protection is given by special Acts of Parliament, e.g. The Fair Trading Act, The Sale of Goods Act, The Unfair Contract Terms Act, The Trade Descriptions Act, The Food and Drugs Act, etc.

Consumer research Konsumforschung, Verbraucheranalyse

Surveys (e.g. by enquiry tests, aided recall interviews) amongst consumers to obtain information and assess demand for a particular product or service or for a range of products or services. In particular, research into the requirements, attitudes and opinions of consumers, why they buy goods, what goods they really want to buy, etc.

Consumer resistance Kaufunlust

A consumer's lack of interest in buying a product, e.g. due to high prices.

Consumer rights Verbraucherrechte, Konsumentenrechte

The generally accepted rights of consumers:

1. the right to safety (i.e. protection against the sale of goods which are hazardous to health or life);
2. the right to be informed (i.e. the right to receive true information and to be protected against fraudulent, deceiving and misleading advertising, labelling or other practices);
3. the right to choose (i.e. to have access to a variety of products at competitive and fair prices at a satisfactory quality);
4. the right to be heard (i.e. the right that consumer interests will receive consideration in the formulation of government policy).

Consumer Safety Act Gesetz gegen (Unfall)Gefahren für Verbraucher (GB)

In the USA called Consumer Product Safety Act.

An Act to protect consumers. In the UK, this Act gives the government power to make regulations governing goods which may injure or kill the public.

Note: in the US, there is the Consumer Product Safety Commission (PSC), a federal agency created to protect consumers aganst risks of injury from consumer products.

Consumer satisfaction Käuferzufriedenheit

The satisfaction or utility a consumer derives from the purchase and/or use of a product or service. Note: satisfaction of a consumer want is an essential part of marketing.

Consumer society Konsumgesellschaft

A society where consumers are highly interested in buying goods or services.

Consumer spending patterns Ausgabenstruktur, Kaufstruktur der Verbraucher

The distribution of consumer spending at different income levels on major categories of goods and services. Food, housing, and transportation use up most household income. However, consumers at different income levels have different spending patterns.

Economic variables such as income, cost of living, interest rates, tax burden, savings and borrowing patterns have a large impact on spending habits.

Note: Engel´s laws (named after the German stastistician Ernst Engel, 1821-1896) noted how people shift their spending as their income rises.

Consumer survey Verbraucherbefragung, Konsumentenbefragung

In consumer research, a technique in which a questionnaire is used to enquire about consumers´ attitudes, buying habits, buying motives, spending patterns, demand for specific products, etc. The survey is carried out among the actual or potential purchasers of a consumer product.

Consumer sweepstake(s) Verbraucherverlosung

A sales promotion method where contestants submit their names for inclusion in a drawing for prizes.

Consumer want Verbraucherbedürfnis

The conscious desire to acquire a product or service in order to satisfy a need or wish.

Consumer's preference Konsumentenpräferenz

Often called the determinant of demand. There is a scale of preferences for each consumer. High on the scale come the things needed most, or liked best, i.e. things which will give the greatest satisfaction. Lower on the scale come things the consumer will buy if income permits once all the more satisfying items have been bought. The consumer's preference may change and this will alter his expenditure patterns (spending habits).

Consumer's surplus Konsumentenrente

Also called buyer's surplus or surplus value.

This is the utility or satisfaction which the consumer receives but does not pay for, i.e. it is the price difference which a consumer obtains when he buys goods or services at a price below that which he would be willing to pay (e.g. an item costs £ 80 and some buyers, purchasing at this price, would have been prepared to pay £ 100, then they can be considered to have obtained a consumer's surplus of satisfaction. Clearly a consumer's surplus represents a loss to the supplier.

Consumer(s') association Verbraucherverband

Also called consumer organization.

An independent and non-profit-making consumer information institution. It conducts regular comparative tests of goods bought on the open market and publishes the results in magazines.

Consumer(s') goods Konsumgüter
Verbrauchsgüter, Gebrauchsgüter

Consumer goods are things in everyday use, such as food, clothing and household goods which are wanted for their own sake and which are capable of immediately and directly affecting present living standards via current consumption; they yield consumers satisfaction. Also called consumable goods, consumption goods or goods for consumption.

They consist of nondurable consumer goods (nondurables, consumer nondurables, single-use goods or soft goods) which have a relatively short life or are consumed in the act of being used and durable consumer goods (durables, consumer durables (CD) or hard goods) which have a much longer life.

Consumer(s') sovereignty Konsumentensouveränität

The power which consumers have to decide what goods and services shall be produced. Furthermore, they determine the quantities and the acceptable prices. For example, an increase in consumers' demand for a commodity will raise its price and so encourage producers to increase their production, and vice versa.
Note: consumer sovereignty exists only in a free market system.

Consumer-oriented marketing verbraucherorientiertes Marketing

A modern marketing concept based on the belief that the consumer is the most important part of the business, and that a company must first find out what the customer wants before providing a good or service. The company views and organises its marketing activities from the consumers´ point of view.

Consumerism Verbraucherschutzbewegung,
Konsumerismus

The movement by individuals and pressure groups intended to safeguard the rights of consumers and the view that efforts have to be made by or on behalf of consumers. The movement developed from the 1960s onward to press for various improvements in business practices and services in the interests of the consumer (e.g. consumer goods should be of good quality, safe to use, advertising should be honest, etc.). Furthermore, the consuming public has a right to be safe, to be informed, to choose, and to be heard.

Consumers and pricing Verbraucher und Preisbildung

The consumer really determines whether the price of a product or service is a good one. Therefore one should carefully observe and analyze the consumer's reaction to a particular price.
Note: a product having a high utility to the consumer can usually have a higher price than one that does not.

Consumption (C) Konsum, Verbrauch

The act of consuming, ie the using up of goods and services having an exchangeable value.

The amount consumed.

Consumption function Konsumfunktion

The relationship between consumers' expenditure (consumption expenditure) and income, that is C = C (Y). The assumption is that the level of income will determine the level of consumption.

Note: consumers' expenditure may be related either to national income or to disposable income.

Consumption patterns Konsumgewohnheiten

Also called consumption habits.

The buying and consumption habits of consumers.

Consumption statistics Konsumstatistik

A source providing data on the consumption of various consumer goods.

Consumption tax Verbrauchssteuer

A tax on the purchase of goods and services.

Container — Container, Behälter

A very large, robust, metal construction of standard shape and size into which goods are loaded to be transported by road, rail, sea or air. They may be watertight and airtight, and goods sent in them cannot be lost or stolen. Containers can make transportation very economical. In the mid-sixties, the Americans sent the first "container-liner" across the Atlantic. Also called lift-van.

Anything such as a barrel, bottle, box, can used for holding goods.

Container carrier truck — Containerstapler

A truck for lifting and carrying containers.

Container freight station (CFS) — Containerfrachtladestelle

Also called container base (CB).

The place for packing and unpacking LCL (less than container load) and FCL (full container load) consignments.

Container inspection report — Container-Abnahmebescheinigung

A document completed by the truck driver stating the state of containers deposited or received.

Container rate — Container(fracht)rate

The general practice is to formulate individual rates by container type, capacity, and the actual origin and destination of the merchandise. Different rates apply to full-container-loads (FCLs) and less-than-container-loads (LCLs); the cargo of the latter is usually assembled and stuffed into a container at a container freight station (CFS) with each individual consignment attracting separate rates.

In foreign trade, for example, the through rate for FCLs will embrace the inland transportation cost embracing collection and terminal handling expenses, but it will usually exclude customs clearance charges, demurrage, etc.

Container ship — Containerschiff

Usually a large ship built to transport cargo in containers. These ships are usually loaded and unloaded in container ports.

Container stuffing Containerbeladung

The process of stowing a container.

Container terminal Containerterminal, Containerdepot

Also called container yard (CY).

A collection and distribution point for FCL (full container load) containers, i.e. the place where containers are loaded onto or unloaded from ships, trucks, railway waggons or airplanes.

Containerization Containerverkehr, Transport in Containern
Umstellung auf Containerverkehr

A method of freight-handling in which general cargo is packed into standard-sized containers for transport by road, rail, sea, or air. The problem of having to load and unload at terminals has been reduced by containerization. Goods are packed into the container, which is then loaded onto the lorry, mechanically transferred from the lorry to the train or ship and later back to a lorry for final delivery. Only then the container is opened.

The introduction of containers.

Contest Wettbewerb

Also called competition.

A competition in which an individual is required to show that he/she is in some respect superior and for which prizes will be awarded.

Contestable market Markt ohne Zutritts- und Austrittsschranken

A market in which the costs of entry and exit are low, so that a firm risks little by entering or leaving.

Continuity of advertising Werbekontinuität

The speading of advertising evenly within a given period, i.e. the level of advertising activity is maintained at a continous and stable level.

Continuous billing fortlaufende Fakturierung, laufende Rechnungsstellung

The process of invoicing a customer throughout a business year rather than at a single time each month (i.e. monthly billing).

Continuous innovation permanente, stetige Innovation; laufende Erneuerung

Usually a slight modification of an existing product which is easily accepted by consumers because it does not require consumers to change their behaviour drastically.

Contra-deal Gegenseitigkeitsgeschäft

Also called reciprocal deal.

An agreement between two companies to supply goods or services from the one in exchange for goods and services of the other.

Contract date Vertragsdatum, (Vertrags) Abschlußtag

The date on which a contract is concluded and signed (if necessary).

Contract maintenance Wartungsvertrag

Also called maintenance, service or servicing contract; or service agreement.

A company undertakes to do on contract basis the maintenance of specified equipment, buildings, etc.

Contract of sale Kaufvertrag

Also called contract for sale or sales contract.

A contract in which the seller transfers, or agrees to transfer, the general property (i.e. the ownerhsip) in goods to the buyer for a consideration in money (the price). It may be made in writing (with or without seal) or by word of mouth (orally, verbally), or may be implied from the conduct of the contracting parties (the parties to the contract).

Contract price Vertragspreis

The sale price negotiated between seller and buyer.

Contract rate Kontraktfracht

Also called negotiated rate.

The freight rate negotiated between carrier and shipper for the transportation of a specific commodity.

Contract work Auftragsarbeit

Work done by a firm according to a written agreement.

Contraction of/in demand Nachfrageschrumpfung

A decrease in the quantity demanded resulting from a change in price (shown as a movement along the existing demand curve).

Contraction of/in supply Angebotsschrumpfung

A decrease in the quantity supplied resulting from a change in price (shown as a movement along a supply curve).

Contractionary phase Rezessionsphase, Abschwungphase

Also called contraction phase, phase of contraction or recession phase.

In general, a decline of economic activity in the business/trade cycle. In particular, the phase of the trade cycle following a peak and lasting to the next turning point or trough (the economic low, recessive dip).

Contractual sales force Provisionsverkäufer

Salespersons who are not paid representatives of a company but who sell for it on a commission basis.

Contribution Deckungsbeitrag (Kostenrechnung)

Also called contribution margin.

This is the difference between price and variable costs (P - VC). Each time we sell a product this difference contributes towards covering the fixed costs and, after that has been done, contributes to profit.

Contribution costing Deckungsbeitragsrechnung

Also called contribution analysis, contribution margin accounting, direct or marginal costing.

In cost accounting, a technique used to establish the contribution (margin) a product makes to the firm's profit and its contribution to fixed costs. The method includes only variable costs; fixed costs are excluded from the unit cost under this method.

Contribution margin (CM) Deckungsbeitrag

The price of a product minus its variable costs (P - VC).

Control group Kontrollgruppe

A group which is identical to another group being used for research purposes and which serves as a comparison.

Control question Kontrollfrage

In a questionnaire, a question designed to check the validity of answers to other questions.

Controllable costs beeinflußbare Kosten

Also called managed costs.

Costs that may be directly influenced within a given period of time; e.g. variable costs are controllable already in the short-term, whereas fixed costs are controllable in the long-term.

Controlled circulation (CC) Gratisverteilung, Freiversand

Also called qualified or nonpaid circulation.

Copies of a publication distributed free of charge to a specialist readership who are members of a particular profession or organisation.

Controlled economy gelenkte Wirtschaft

Also called directed economy, command economy, or planned economy.

A situation where the most economic activity is state run, i.e. directed by orders from the government.

Convenience food Fertiggericht

Also called instant meal.

Ready-prepared dishes ready for serving with little effort and time, e.g. tinned/canned meals.

Convenience goods Waren des täglichen Bedarfs (Verbrauchsgüter) Fertiggerichte

Non-durable consumer goods, especially consumer disposables, e.g. packaged foods.

Food products designed to save time and effort for the consumer. Also called convenience foods or fast foods.

Convenience sampling Ermessensauswahl

Also called judg(e)mental or nonprobability sampling.

A sampling procedure where the researcher selects people from whom information is the easiest to obtain (the convenience sample).

Convenience store Nachbarschaftsladen, kleiner Verbrauchermarkt

A limited-line store that specializes in convenience goods and fast service.

Conveyance Transport, Beförderung Transport-, Beförderungsmittel

The transport of goods by a conveyer/conveyor. Also called carriage or haulage.

A vehicle for carrying goods or people. Also called means of conveyance, transport or transportation.

Cooling-off law Gesetz über Vertragsrücktritt

A law permitting a buyer to withdraw from a contract within a specific period after signing the contract.

Cooling-off period Bedenkzeit, Rücktrittsfrist

A short time period during which the buyer of a good or service may void the sales contract if he/she changes his/her mind about purchasing the goods offered.

Coop coupons Co-op (Gemeinschafts) Coupons

A form of sales promotion where several manufacturers print and distribute their coupons together in one or more pages.

Cooperation Kooperation, Zusammenarbeit

Also called collaboration.

A working together for some purpose.

Cooperation agreement Kooperationsvertrag

An agreement between various firms or firms and a government to cooperate, eg in a joint venture.

Cooperative advertising Gemeinschaftswerbung
Verbundwerbung

Advertising where all the producers or retailers in one industry combine to advertise the product in general rather than their own particular brands, e.g. "Drink milk". The costs of advertising are shared between the advertiser, normally a trade association, and the individual businesses. Also called co-op advertising, association ad, collective ad, generic ad, joint ad, or tie-up ad.

Advertising where the manufacturer and a retailer or distributor share advertising efforts and costs.

Cooperative mailing Gemeinschafts(werbe)versand

Also called co-op mailing.

A pack of promotional material mailed to potential buyers by several noncompeting advertisers who target the same audience and are thus able to reduce mailing costs.

Cooperative society (coop) Genossenschaft

The co-operative movement began in Britain in 1844. A co-operative enterprise is a business organization which is collectively owned by those with a direct interest in the firm. They are self-governing. There are broadly two kinds of co-operative enterprise - producers' and consumers' co-operatives.

Consumers' cooperatives:
They are owned and controlled by the consumers of the firm's output. Membership is open to any person, and each member possesses one vote. Profits are distributed in the form of dividends in proportion to the amount of a member's purchases. Also called retail cooperative.

Producers' cooperatives:
Ownership and control rests with those who work in them (usually small manufacturers), and profits are shared.

Cooperative wholesale society (CWS) Zentral-, Großeinkaufsgenossenschaft

Also called wholesale cooperative.

An organization founded by the co-operative movement for producing and wholesaling. They have their own factories and transport to supply their retail societies (retail co-operatives). Profits are distributed to retail societies in proportion to their purchases.

Coordinated marketing koordiniertes, aufeinander abgestimmtes Marketing

Marketing where the various marketing functions such as sales force, advertising, marketing research, etc are coordinated among themselves.

The coordination of the marketing department with all the other departments in the company in order to achieve customer satisfaction.

Copy Werbetext
Kopie, Abschrift
Exemplar
Ausgabe
Ausfertigung

In advertising, the copy consists of the wording. Also called advertising copy.

A document which is made to look the same as another, e.g. a carbon copy or duplicate.

One book.

One newspaper or magazine. Also called issue or number.

An official document.

Copy clearance Drehbuch-, Manuskriptannahme

Also called continuity acceptance or clearance.

The approval of an advertisement or commercial after a review by media specialists in order to avoid misleading or offensive statements or ideas; violations of laws, regulations or self-regulatory standards; illegal or unsubstantiated claims.

Copy date Anzeigen(annahme)schluß

Also called copy deadline.

The date by which an advertisement has to be delivered to the publisher.

Copycat product Me-too Produkt, Plagiat

Also called me-too-product.

A slightly modified imitation of a newly launched product. These products are tending to appear increasingly rapidly after the original´s product launch.

Note: the "new" version should not be an exact copy of the competitor´s product.

Copyright Urheberrecht, Copyright

The sole right to produce or reproduce any particular literary, artistic or musical work, or to perform or display it in public. A copyright protects only the work itself and not the ideas behind it. Literary copyright endures for the author's life and for fifty years thereafter (in Germany this is 70 years); musical copyright exists for fifty years from publication. The first owner of a copyright is the person who creates the work. Copyright can be assigned to another party.

Copytesting/copy testing Copytesten

The pre-testing of an advertisement copy for print advertisements.

Copywriter Werbetexter, Texter

The person who writes the words of an advertisement and commercial; however, he will probably also think up the general theme and presentation of the advertisement or commercial.

Cordless telephone schnurloses, tragbares Telefon

Also called portable or stringless (tele)phone.

A telephone without a cord connected to the telephone network and able to be used within a certain range of a telephone socket.

Corner Aufkauf, d.h. den Markt aufkaufen (zwecks Monopolbildung)

Also called cornering.

To make a corner or corner the market is to buy up the whole exisiting stock of a commodity available at a particular time in order to control the price of it or to obtain a monopoly.

Corner shop Laden an der Ecke (Tante-Emma-Laden)

Also called ma-and-pa-shop or mom-and-pop store.

This is the most localised form of retailer, and offers the highest degree of personal service. However, because his turnover will be relatively small, his prices are likely to be higher than in many other forms of retail outlet.

Corporate (image) advertising Firmenimagewerbung

Also called image or institutional advertising.

A tool companies use to market themselves to various publics in order to convey a positive image or attitude about a firm, or to create a public awareness of a firm, or to build up or maintain a favourable image, or to shift its actual image toward a desired new image, or to counter events that might harm their image.

Note: its purpose is not to promote the sale of a product or service but to promote a firm in general.

Corporate design (CD) Gestaltung des Erscheinungsbildes des Unternehmens

The visiual elements, eg name, logo, layout of letterheads, product design, outward appearance of the company`s buildings, etc, used to distinguish a company from all others and to show who and what a company is.

Note: the CD is an important part of corporate identity (CI).

Corporate identity (CI) Corporate Identity (einheitliches äußeres Erscheinungsbild eines Unternehmens in der Öffentlichkeit)

Also called house style.

Characteristic, or uniform, style of design adopted by a company to keep its name and corporate image before the public.

Instead of branching individual products, companies sometimes create product-family images or a corporate company image associated with all products.

Reasons for developing corporate identities are:
1. the increasing importance of public relations - establishing the right relationships with governments, opinion-influencing pressure groups, local communities, factories, distribution centres;
2. the need to attract and retain investment;
3. the need to attract labour;
4. the growing realisation of the importance of good relationships with suppliers, etc.

Corporate image Unternehmens-Image

Also called organisation image.

The image or impression that a company has in the minds of the public.

Corrective advertising/commercial Richtigstellungsanzeige, -werbung, berichtigende Werbung

Advertisement or commercial that is run to correct a false, misleading or erroneous impression or claim created by earlier advertisements or commercials.

Correctness Korrektheit

A behaviour that is in accordance with an acknowledged or accepted standard.

Correlation Korrelation, Wechselbeziehung

A mathematical measurement of the relation between two variables.

Cosmetic marketing "kosmetische" Werbung

Cosmetic marketing is the recognisable part of marketing, comprising communications by advertising, selling and public relations.

Cost Anschaffungs-, Herstellungskosten
Preis
Kosten, Aufwand
kalkulieren

The sum of money spent to purchase or produce a product or service. Als called acquisition or initial cost; factory, manufacturing or production cost.

The (cost) price charged or paid for anything.

Cost is another name for expenses or expenditure.

A manufacturer costs/calculates his products.

Cost and freight, free out (C + F FO) Kosten, Fracht und Entladekosten bezahlt

A quoted price that covers the cost of the goods, freight charges, and unloading charges.

Cost based pricing kostenorientierte Preiskalkulation

A common pricing method that covers the costs of a product. During inflationary periods, there are often excalator clauses in contracts which increase prices automatically.

Cost comparison Kostenvergleich

Studying the relative costs of two or more alternatives.

Cost function Kostenfunktion

A function that defines the costs of different combinations of inputs for each level of output.

Cost of goods manufactured Herstellungskosten

Also called manufacturing, factory, production or processing cost(s), cost of manufacture, or cost of production.

The sum of all costs charged or allocated to products whose production is completed during a period.

Cost of goods sold (COGS, cogs) Einstandspreis (Kosten) der verkauften Ware, Wareneinsatz

Also called cost of sales.

The cost price of the goods that have been sold. It is calculated as follows:
cost of sales = opening stock + purchases - closing stock.

The figure is shown in the trading account.

Cost of living Lebenshaltungskosten

Also called living costs or expenses.

The amount of money that an individual or a family in a specified geographical area must spend on food, clothing and other things necessary to be able to maintain a certain standard of living. For each individual, his cost of living is the cost of having a particular standard of living. Changes in the cost of living would mean that he has to pay more or less (work or earn more or less) in order to be able to live in the same way.

Cost of living allowance Teuerungszulage

Also called cost of living bonus or dearness allowance.

Extra money paid, in addition to the normal salary, to meet/cover increases in the cost of living/living costs.

Cost of production theory Produktionskostentheorie

Also called theory of production cost.

The theory that the price of an article depends on its cost of production.

Cost per contact Kosten pro Kontakt

The cost of reaching one member of the target group.

Cost per inquiry (CPI) Kosten pro Anfrage

The cost of reaching one person who responds to an advertisement or mailing, calculated by dividing the promotion costs by the number of inquiries received.

Cost per order (CPO) Kosten pro Auftrag

Also called cost per sale.

The costs incurred in selling an item divided by the number of orders received.

A measure of the profitability of a particular promotion, e.g. mail order advertising. The sales value of the (mail) orders received is divided by the cost of the promotion for the items ordered.

Cost per rating point (CPR, CPRP) Kosten pro Einschaltprozentsatz

Also called cost per point (CPP) or cost per gross rating point (CPGRP).

The cost of a rating point for a commercial on radio or television.

Cost per thousand (CPT) Tausenderpreis (Werbung)

Also called cost per mill (CPM, CpM).

In advertising, a measure for comparing the cost effectiveness of media vehicles. Basis of calculation is the cost incurred for reaching one thousand recipients, i.e. readers, viewers, listeners, subscribers, etc.

The CPT of any advertising vehicle is computed by dividing the cost of placing a specific ad or commercial in the media vehicle by the vehicle´s audience size and multiplying the result by 1,000.

Cost plus (contract) Vertrag auf der Basis Selbstkosten plus Gewinnaufschlag

A contract based on cost-plus pricing. That means a contract between vendor/seller and vendee/buyer to supply specified work at the cost of production plus an addition for profit. This can either be an amount fixed when the contract is signed (a cost-plus-fixed fee, or CPFF contract); or an amount that is related to how well the work is performed in terms of total cost, timing, etc. (a cost-plus-incentive-fee, or CPIF contract).
Such an agreement is made only when the cost is not known at the time when the agreement is made. Where costs are known, a fixed price contract will be used.

Cost plus pricing Preiskalkulation durch einen Gewinnzuschlag auf die Selbstkosten

To set a selling price, firms have to calculate the cost of the product and then add a profit margin/markup.

Cost price Anschaffungs-, Herstellungspreis
Herstellungskosten
Einstandspreis

The price at which a producer/manufacturer or merchant buys materials, goods or services for production or resale.

The cost of production.

The price at which a retailer buys his products for resale.

Cost price squeeze Kosten-Preis-, Preis-Kosten-Schere

Also called cost price scissors or price-cost gap.

A firm's cost for making its products are rising but the prices it can charge for its products cannot be increased, e.g. because of keen competition.

Cost push inflation Kosteninflation, kosteninduzierte Inflation

Also called cost inflation or cost-induced inflation.

Increased costs which are caused by a rise in the cost of factors of production (e.g. a rise in the prices of materials or labour), not by increased demand, are passed on to the consumers in the form of higher prices. Faced with increased prices, consumers try to increase their income to maintain their living standard by demanding higher wages, which in turn increases costs. Therefore sometimes also called wage-push inflation.

Cost variance Kostenabweichung

The difference between standard cost and actual cost.

Cost(s) of production Fertigungs-, Produktions-, Herstell-, Herstellungskosten

Also called production cost(s), final manufacturing cost(s) or manufacturing cost(s).

The costs of making a product, i.e. the costs of converting factor inputs into higher value outputs of goods or services. The costs may include: material costs, labour costs, depreciation, lighting, heating, rent, taxes, administration costs, maintenance costs, etc.

In order to make a profit, a business must be able to sell its output at a greater price than the total cost of production.

Cost-benefit analysis (CBA) Kosten-Nutzen-Analyse

Also called benefit-cost analysis (BCA).

A technique for the evaluation and comparison of investment projects (particularly in the government sector). CBA takes into account all costs (financial and social costs) and all benefits (financial and social benefits) which accrue to society, whether actual payments or receipts are involved or not. The costs and benefits will be discounted to the present value. This form of analysis is most often used in connection with projects which have social as well as economic implications (eg new airports, motorways, etc.).

CBA is analogous in principle to the present value method of ordinary investment appraisal used by private firms, but whereas this method is interested only in monetary revenues and outlays (costs, expenditure) contingent on the project, CBA seeks to evaluate all phenomena associated with the project that can be said to have a utility or disutility.

Cost-of-living adjustment (COLA) Lebenshaltungskostenausgleich, Teuerungsausgleich

Also called cost-of-living escalator.

In employment, a clause in a wage agreement (collective bargaining agreement, union or wage contract), guaranteeing a wage/pay adjustment to reflect changes in the consumer price index (CPI) whenever inflation exceeds a predetermined rate. This measure ensures that the purchasing/buying power of employees will be maintained.

Cost-of-living index Index der Lebenshaltungskosten

Also called consumer price index (CPI), general index of retail prices or retail price index (RPI).

An index of essential, generally used commodities and services like bread, meat, clothes, heat, light, fuel, transport, household goods, etc. (a basket of goods). The items are weighted by their importance to a typical family. The total value of all the items is calculated and "converted" in terms of a base figure of 100 (the index number). It is possible to chart rises and falls in the cost of living with reference to this base. A rise in prices of 3 per cent will then give a new index number of 103.
What the index does not measure is changes in the standard of living, as it takes no account of changes in the general level of money incomes.

Costs and pricing Kosten und Preisbildung

The level of costs faced by a firm has an important influence on pricing decisions and is at times its main consideration.

Three common cost based pricing techniques are: 1. cost plus pricing, 2. breakeven pricing, 3. markup pricing.

Note: when all fixed and variable costs are added together, the firm´s total costs can be determined. Knowing these, firms can then set suitable prices for their products.

Cottage industry (industrielle) Heimarbeit, Heimindustrie

Also called home industry.

The production of goods in the homes of the workers.

Counter Ladentisch, Schalter

A table of flat surface in a shop or bank, behind which the shopkeeper or (bank) clerk stands to serve the customers.

Counter card Aufstellplakat, Tresenaufsteller

A POS sign, usually placed onto a counter, displayed in a shop window or affixed to a shelf, containing the name of the product and its price.

Counter offer Gegenangebot, Gegenofferte Gegengebot

The reply of a seller to an offer made by a buyer. The seller may reject the buyer's offer if he is not satisfied with the terms. The seller may make a counter offer on new terms which the buyer may accept. The final counter offer is regarded as the legal offer - all previous offers are ignored. Also called counter proposal.

The reply of a buyer to a seller's counter offer, if this is unacceptable to the buyer.

A higher bid, especially at an auction sale, in reply to a previous bid. Also called counterbid.

Counteradvertising freiwillige (oder gesetzlich erzwungene) Gegendarstellung in der Werbung

An advertisement launched to warn consumers of potential harm that can result from the use of a product.

Counterbid Gegen(an)gebot

At an auction, a reply to a previous bid.

Countercyclical economic policy antizyklische Wirtschaftspolitik

Also called anticyclical economic policy.

A policy that tends to move the economy in an opposite direction from the forces of the business cycle.

Note: such a policy stimulates demand during the contraction phase and restrains demand during the expansionary phase.

Countermand Abbestellung, Stornierung

Also called cancellation, counterorder, reversal or withdrawal.

The order that something already ordered should not be carried out, e.g. to countermand/cancel an order.

Counterpurchase Gegenkauf, Gegengeschäft (AuW)

A form of reciprocal trading. As a condition of obtaining an export order, the exporter undertakes to purchase goods or services from the importer's country at an equal or specified value. Counterpurchase normally involves two separate transactions, each under conventional financing arrangements. The government will usually nominate a list of products which can be purchased; many of them are not readily saleable on world markets.

Countertrade Kompensationshandel (internationaler Tauschhandel)

Also called counter trading.

This is a general term used to describe a variety of commercial arrangements for reciprocal international trade between companies or other organisations in two or more countries. The common characteristic of countertrade arrangements is that export sales to a particular market are made conditional upon undertakings to accept imports from that market.

Common forms of countertrade are: counterpurchase, barter, buyback, clearing agreement, offset trading, switch trading, etc.

Note: most exporters view countertrade as something to be avoided unless it is absolutely essential to obtaining the business; importers usually deslike it, too because it normally complicates and delays the purchasing transaction.

Other problems may be: 1. the products offered by the buyer country are often of inferior quality and therefore difficult to sell in world markets; 2. often the exporter knows nothing about the market for these products; 3. it is very difficult to establish an appropriate value for the products offered; 4. legal and financial problems.

Countervailing power — ausgleichende Marktmacht, Gegenmacht

A situation which predominates when the excessive market power of firms is counterbalanced by opposing market powers possessed by traders who sell to or buy from the former.

Country potential — Länderpotential

The market potential for a firm´s product or service in a given country based on such factors as population size, economic growth rate, real GNP, per capita income, distribution of population and income, consumption patterns, etc.

Coupon (c, cp) — Gutschein
Einsendeabschnitt (Werbung)
Kassenzettel (Beleg, Quittung)
Lebensmittelkartenabschnitt

Commercially a ticket/label that can be used by a consumer to obtain something either free or at a reduced price. Also called money-off coupon, token or voucher.

Part of a coupon(-response) advertisement, e.g. in a magazine, inviting the reader to fill it in and return it to the advertiser for further details, a sales call, or to place an order. Also called reply coupon.

A sales slip given with a purchase. A kind of voucher or receipt.

A certificate authorizing the purchase of rationed food.

Coupon (promotion) scheme — Werbekampagne über beigefügten Coupon

The product manufacturer supplies to the consumer a coupon which offers him a price reduction against the purchase of the product. The consumer redeems the coupon by presenting it to the shopkeeper at the time he makes his purchase. The retailer obtains from the manufacturer repayment of the value of the coupon.

A press advertisement in which a return coupon is provided, by means of which the reader may place an order, request further information, or a sales call. Also called direct response advertising or coupon(-response) advertisement.

Coupon advertisement Couponanzeige

An advertisement with a reply coupon attached which is to be returned to the advertiser for further information.

Coupon offer Gutscheinangebot

A method of sales promotion where potential customers are offered money-off coupons.

The coupons are: 1. distributed to selected areas by hand or mailed, 2. placed in newspapers, magazines, etc. Usually, the coupons are redeemed at the point of sale (POS).
Note:
1. coupon offers are the next best method (after distribution of free samples) of encouraging trial purchases for new and improved products;
2. distribution of coupons is expensive, whereas the placing of coupons in publications is less expensive;
3. redemption rates are low because customers have to make an effort to redeem the coupons;
4. coupons are disliked by retailers because of administrative work.

Coupon price reduction Preisnachlaß mittels Gutschein

A price concession given to customers by providing coupons of fixed value in order to encourage the initial and/or repeat purchase. The coupons may be printed on the pack, appear in a printed advertisement or may be distributed to households.

Coupon redemption Gutscheineinlösung

The use of a seller´s value coupon by a buyer at the time of purchase to obtain either a lower price or greater value than normal.

The act of accepting a coupon by someone, e.g. a retailer.

Couponing Verkaufsförderung mittels Kupon

In sales promotion, a technique that offers buyers a specified discount if they redeem a coupon.

Courier service Kurierdienst

A delivery service which is used for the speedy transportation of urgent documents, letters or small parcels between companies.

Courtage (court) Courtage

Also called brokerage or commission.

The commission charged by a broker.

Cover (Brief)Umschlag, Hülle
Einband, Umschlag, Titelseite

An envelope or wrapper.

The outer pages of a book, magazine (also called cover page), etc.

Cover page Titelseite, Umschlagseite

The front or back page of a publication.

Cover price Verkaufspreis einer Publikation

The selling price of a publication, e.g. a magazine, as shown on the front cover page.

Coverage Reichweite (eines Werbemediums), Marktabdeckung, Streubreite

The proportion (expressed as a percentage) of a target market (individuals or households) or particular geographic area reached by advertising.

Covering letter Begleitschreiben

Also called accompanying letter, cover letter, covering note or letter of transmittal.

A letter or note sent with a consignment or documents explaining why one is sending them.

Crash Crash, Zusammenbruch

A sudden and disastrous collapse in business activity, prices, security values, etc.

Crate (cr) Lattenkiste, (Latten)Verschlag (Flaschen)Kasten

Wooden, metal or plastic container in which goods are packed. It has a bottom and a frame, and is sometimes open at the top. Crates are often built for the particular thing (e.g. machinery) they have to carry. They often have a special bottom, called skid, to facilitate handling.

A small container to carry bottles.

Creative boutique Kreativ(werbe)agentur

Also called creative shop or hot shop.

An advertising agency offering advertisers creative solutions to their creative needs.

Creative director (CD) Kreativdirektor

In an advertising agency, the head of the creative department who is responsible for all creative aspects of all advertising campaigns.

Creative person kreativ Tätiger (in der Werbung)

In advertising, a person employed with creative work. The main creative people are as follows:
1. the copywriter who produces the copy platform or theme and the words;
2. the visualiser who creates the artistic presentation of the copy platform;
3. the typographer who specifies type and creates typographical design;
4. the layout person who is responsible for the layout;
5. the scriptwriter who composes the storyboard for commercials;
6. the producer.

Creative selling kreativer Verkauf

A selling technique, where the seller determines the buyer's needs and matches them with the products for sale.

Creative strategy in advertising Kreativstrategie, (Werbe)Zielkonzeption

In advertising, the decisions about what needs to be communicated (e.g. images, messages, associations, information, etc), how the communication will be effected, and what the communication is intended to achieve in terms of consumer behaviour.

Credit (Cr, cr) — Zahlungsziel
auf Kredit bzw. Ziel

The time period before payment on a transaction is required. Credit arises from an exchange of goods or services against a promise of payment in the future, i.e. payment is deferred until an agreed future date. Also called credit period, period of credit or payment, period or time allowed for payment, term of payment, or time allowance for payment.

To give credit (to sell on credit) is to deliver goods or perform work under an arrangement for payment to be made at a later date, which may or may not be specified. If no date is specified, payment must be made within a reasonable time. To buy on credit is to receive possession of the goods and to pay for them sometime after one has bought them. The seller becomes the creditor, and the buyer the debtor, until the money is paid.

Credit account — Kreditkonto, kreditorisch geführtes Konto

Also called charge account.

An arrangement between a retailer and (charge) customer whereby the latter is able to buy up to a fixed value of goods on credit in return for payment at agreed periodic intervals. A service charge is normally made as a percentage of the value of each purchase.

Credit advice — Gutschriftsanzeige, Gutschrift

Also called credit note (C/N), credit memorandum, credit memo, or credit slip.

A document sent by a seller to a buyer to notify an overcharge in the original invoice, or to reduce the amount owing because goods had been returned by the buyer.

Credit balance — Guthaben

An amount of money overpaid by a customer in an account, i.e. more money has been received than is owed and so the account is in credit.

Credit buying — Kreditkauf

Also called credit purchase, credit sale, installment sale (US) or hire purchase (GB).

Goods which a business (the credit customer) buys from a supplier on credit. To obtain goods on credit means to "buy now, pay later". There are various types of credit buying, e.g. hire purchase.

Credit call telephone Kreditkarten-Telefon

A telephone that accepts credit cards and charges the call to the caller's credit card.

Credit card Kreditkarte

Also called plastic card, bank or banker's card, or cash guarantee card.

In the 1960s banks and other financial institutions, such as special credit card companies (e.g. American Express, Eurocard, Diners Club, Mastercard or Visa) started a credit card scheme. The idea was to replace the need for cash when shopping. Credit cards provide a means of obtaining goods and services immediately but paying for them later.
Each cardholder is given a credit limit/credit line up to which he may purchase goods and services from establishments who are members of the particular scheme. The cardholder receives a monthly statement detailing his purchases and either pays in full within several weeks, thus incurring no interest charges, or makes a part payment, in which case interest is charged on the balance left owing. Some organisations charge annual subscriptions (a membership fee) and the cardholders have to settle their accounts each month in full.
The sellers are paid by the credit company, which receives a commission from them.

The card can also be used to draw cash from one of the banks in the scheme within the credit limit, but interest is charged on such encashments from the day they occur.

Each credit card bears the cardholder's name, his signature, the card number and the validity (e.g. valid thru 05-99).
If the cardholder wishes to pay by credit card, he presents the card to the salesclerk/shop assistant who will write out a sales slip (sales check or voucher), which shows the nature of the transaction, the amount due and the details of the cardholder's account, and which the cardholder has to sign. The salesclerk then hands a copy of the sales slip to the cardholder and sends the sales slip to the card issuer, who credits the shop's (the vendor's) account with the appropriate amount (less a percentage commission) and debits the cardholder's account.
The increasing use of credit cards is a step nearer the "cashless society".

Credit card call Kreditkarten-Telefonat

This service enables you to make calls from any telephone without making immediate payment. The calls are charged to your telephone account.

Credit customer Kreditkunde
Kunde, der in einem Geschäft ein Kreditkonto hat (d.h. der anschreiben läßt)

A customer who is allowed to buy goods and services and pay for them at a later date.

A borrower. Also called borrowing customer.

A charge customer.

Credit insurance Kreditversicherung

Insurance taken out by a creditor/seller against the default of a debtor/buyer.

Credit note (C/N) Gutschriftsanzeige, Gutschrift

Also called credit advice, credit slip, credit memorandum, or credit memo.

A document sent by a seller to a buyer to notify an overcharge in the original invoice, or to reduce the amount owing because goods, cases, etc. had been returned by the buyer. The invoice must never be altered; errors are always adjusted by the issue of another document - another invoice or a credit note.

A document sent by a bank to an account holder stating that the account has been credited with a stated amount.

Credit period Kreditlaufzeit, Laufzeit eines Kredits

Also called currency, term (of a credit), duration of credit, maturity period or life span.

The amount of time allowed to a credit customer before payment is due.

Credit sale Kreditverkauf, Zielverkauf

Also called charge sale or sale on credit.

Sales which a business makes to customers on credit, i.e. payment will be made later. Goods bought in this way become the buyer's property as soon as they have been delivered to him.

Credit sale(s) agreement Abzahlungsvertrag, Ratenkaufvertrag

An agreement for the sale of goods under which the purchase price or part of it is payable by instalments.
On payment of the deposit (first or initial instalment) the goods become the property of the buyer; the seller has no security for the goods. The buyer may dispose of the goods as he wishes. In this way the credit sale differs from hire purchase/installment buying. The seller/vendor grants the buyer/vendee a short-term loan. The buyer will of course remain liable for the balance of the purchase price.

Credit terms Kreditkonditionen

A variety of forms of credit granted to a customer, e.g. payment within thirty days or 2 % discount on payment within ten days (usually stated n/30; 2/10), etc.

Credit transaction Kreditgeschäft

Payment for goods or services is not made at the time of purchase.

Credit(s) outstanding Kreditstand, (eingeräumtes) Kreditvolumen (Kreditgrenze)

Also called line of credit.

The amount of money a company is prepared to allow a customer to owe at a particular point of time. It includes unpaid invoices, goods in transit and part-finished work.

Creditor Gläubiger, Kreditor

A person or business who is owed money or its equivalent by a debtor.

Creeping inflation schleichende Inflation

Also called persistent inflation.

A slow, but continuous inflation; a process of gently rising prices.

Crop restriction Erntebeschränkung

The reduction of farm surplus to raise farm income. Sometimes the government compensates farmers for the losses suffered.

Cross couponing (Werbung mit) Gutschein, der für ein anderes Produkt gilt

A coupon, e.g. on a pack, which can only be used for a different product.

Cross elasticity of demand Kreuz(preis)elastizität der Nachfrage

The responsiveness of demand for one commodity to changes in the price of another commodity. Percent change in quantity demanded of a good due to a 1 % change in the price of another good. The formula is:

$$\text{Cross elasticity of demand} = \frac{\text{\% change in quantity of A demanded}}{\text{\% change in price of B}}$$

In the case of substitutes cross elasticity will be positive - a change (increase/fall) in the price of B (e.g. butter) will be followed by a change (i.e. increase/fall) in the quantity of A (e.g. margarine) demanded. If a small change in the price of good B results in a large change in the quantity of good A (highly cross elastic), then goods A and B are close substitutes. On the other hand, goods that are in complementary demand (i.e. complementary goods, complements) will have a negative cross elasticity, since a fall in the price of one will cause an increase in demand for both, e.g. a fall in the price of petrol will increase the demand for petrol and for cars.

Cross licensing Lizenzaustausch, gegenseitige Patentgewährung

The exchange of technology, licences or patents by different firms.

Cross merchandising kombinierte Absatzförderung

The display of complementary merchandise, usually in a supermarket, at opposite sides of an aisle, in order to tempt a customer to cross over from one product to another and make an impulse purchase.

Cross-national advertising grenzüberschreitende Werbung

Advertising in one country which obtains some advertising coverage in neighbouring countries, e.g. advertising in Germany may obtain coverage in Denmark, the Benelux, France, Switzerland, Poland, etc.

Crowding-out Crowding Out, Verdrängungswettbewerb (des Staates)

A reduction in private spending (which is mainly financed by borrowing) as a result of an increase in government spending. There is heavy government borrowing at a time when businesses and individuals (the private sector) also want to borrow money. As the government can pay any interest rate it has to and individuals and businesses cannot, the latter are crowded out of credit and capital markets by high interest rates. Crowding out can thus cause economic activity to slow.

Cultural environment kulturelle Umwelt

The institutions and forces that affect a society´s beliefs, values, perceptions, preferences, and behaviours.

Note: 1. Each country has its own folkways, norms, and taboos. 2. Cultural factors exert the broadest and deepest influence on consumer behaviour; thus, the marketer must understand the buyer´s culture, subculture, and social class.

Culture Kultur

The set of basic beliefs, values, perceptions, wants, and behaviours characteristic of a particular society, social, ethnic, or age group. Many of these values are learned from family and/or are transmitted from one generation to another.

Culture lag Kulturgefälle

Also called cultural lag.

Slowness in the rate of change of one part of a culture in relation to another part, resulting in a maladjustment within society.

Cumulative audience kumuliertes Publikum

Also called cumulative reach, accumulative audience or cume.

The number of individuals or households in a target audience (ie the listenership, readership, viewership) reached without duplication by an advertising medium over a specified time period.

Cumulative quantity discount kumulativer Mengenrabatt

A price reduction granted to a buyer where the amount of the discont increases over time with the volume purchased.

Current cost Kostenaufwand in Marktpreisen oder in Wiederbeschaffungs-preisen, Tageskosten

The present price of an article.

Current demand laufende Nachfrage

The ongoing or most up-to-date demand for goods and services.

Current gross national product Bruttosozialprodukt (BSP) zu Marktpreisen

Also called current GNP, nominal GNP or GNP at market prices.

The money value of a country`s goods and services sold at current prices (market prices).

Current loyal treuer (Stamm)Kunde

People who buy a firm`s product most or all of the time.

Current price Tagespreis, gegenwärtiger Preis

Also called going price or prevailing price.

Today`s price for a commodity or service.

Current profit maximization gegenwärtige Gewinnmaximierung

A situation where a company wants to set a price that will maximize current profits. To achieve this, it estimates what demand and costs will be at different prices and chooses the price that will generate/produce the maximum current profit.

Current transactions | Leistungsverkehr (AuW)
laufende Geschäfte

All money payments made or received for goods and services imported or exported.

The present business transactions of a company.

Current value | Tageswert
Marktwert, Zeitwert

Also called market value or present value.

The value of an asset at the present date; it is in contrast to its value when it was bought.

The price at which something is traded on the open market.

Custom | Sitte, Brauch
Kaufgewohnheit
Kundschaft
Handelsbrauch
Kunde

Things which are usually done by people. Also called established behaviour or customs.

Practice of regularly buying goods from a business. Also called buying, consumer or shopping habit.

The persons who regularly deal at one shop. Also called clients, clientele, customers or (business) patronage.

Usage which is understood and recognized by persons connected with a particular trade. Also called business usage; commercial custom, practice or usage; trade custom or usage; or usage of the market.

A customer.

Custom marketing | kundenspezifisches Marketing

A marketing strategy in which a company attempts to satisfy the unique needs of every customer.

Custom-made spezialangefertigt, auf Bestellung/Kundenwunsch gefertigt

Also called custom-built, purpose-built, made-to-order, customized or tailor-made.

Made or designed to specific individual customer specification.

Customary price gewöhnlicher Preis

The price that consumers expect to pay for a certain product.

Customary pricing handelsübliche Preisbildung

A pricing strategy where certain goods are priced primarily on the basis of tradition.

Customer Kunde, Käufer, Abnehmer

Also called buyer, client, purchaser, shopper or taker; account (in advertising), depositor (in banking), market operator (on the stock exchange) or patron (in a restaurant).

A person or business which buys or orders goods or services from another business. There are cash and credit customers.

Customer care Kundenbetreuung

A concept giving the customer special significance and treatment, i.e. everyone in the company is customer focused, and thus thinks and acts with the customer in mind.

Customer orientation Kundenorientierung

A management approach indicating that a company is focused on the needs of its customers. Managers ask customers exactly what they need before starting production. The customer now comes before the production process, not after it.

Customer profile Kundenprofil

Description of a type of customer or a customer group based on various demographic, geographic and/or psychographic characteristics, e.g. age, education, gender, income, hobbies, area of residence, etc.

Customer records Kundendaten

Data stored concerning customers such as enquiries and orders received, complaints, deliveries, buying behaviour, payment methods, customer satisfaction, etc.

Customer satisfaction index (CSI) Kundenzufriedenheitsindex

A measurement of the degree to which customers are satisfied with a product or service bought.

Customer segment pricing Preisgestaltung nach Kundensegment

A pricing strategy where different customers pay different prices for the same product or service.

Customer segmentation Kundensegmentierung

The division of a market according to the characteristics of its customers, e.g. the company´s size, location, purchase behaviour, preferences, etc.

Customer service Kundendienst

Also called client service, after-sales service, post-sales service, sales service or servicing.

A continuing service of maintenance, repair, supply of instructions for use, etc. a retailer or manufacturer provides for his customers after a product or service has been sold.

Note : a service rendered before a good or service is sold, is called pre-sale service.

Customer service department Kundendienstabteilung

A company´s department handling complaints and adjustments, maintenance service, technical service, consumer information, etc. Thus, such a department may create consumer satisfaction and loyalty and may induce need changes in product design, quality control, etc.

Customer turnover Kundenfluktuation

Rate at which customers leave the market and have to be replaced, so that new first-time buyers can be reached.

Customer turnover may be unavoidable, for example, because people move to other areas or children grow up and their infant needs vanish.

Customer values Produktanwendervorteile

Customer value is the ratio of benefits to the sacrifice necessary to obtain those benefits. Note: it is the customer who determines the value of both the benefits and the sacrifices.

The components of customer value are:
1. perceived goods quality, 2. perceived service quality, 3. value-based prices.

Real customer value is defined by the customer, not the company. Customer value is created when customer expectations in each of the three areas are met or exceeded. This is necessary to achieve success in today´s highly competitive markets. To maximise customer value, a firm must know if it is meeting customers´ expectations. If a company fails to meet customer expectations in any one of the three areas, it is not delivering good customer value.

Customer's own transport (COT) Transport mit Kundenfahrzeug

In transport, this means that the customer collects or delivers to the container freight station (CFS), container yard (CY) or other specified point.

Customer-oriented personnel kundenorientiertes Personal

A company that is focused on customers must have employees whose attitudes and actions are customer-oriented because, in customers´ eyes, the employee is the firm. Thus, any person or department that is not customer-oriented weakens the image of the entire company.

Customer-owned goods (cog) kundeneigene Ware

Goods already paid for by the customer so that they are part of his property.

Customer-unfriendly packaging kundenresistene Verpackung

A form of packaging unintentionally making it difficult for the customer to open or unwrap a good.

Customised advertising kundenspezifische Werbung

Advertising uniquely designed for a particular customer to meet the requirements of various markets.

In international advertising, customisation may be necessary because of:
1. cultural differences between countries and/or market segments withing countries;
2. language translation difficulties;
3. differences in the educational backgrounds of target groups in various countries;
4. legal requirements in particular countries;
5. peculiarities in national attitudes toward advertising;
6. variations in living standards between countries;
7. different shopping habits and buying motives, etc.

The main problem with customisation is the additional cost of having to tailor advertising for various markets.

Customised marketing kundenspezifisches Marketing

The ultimate degree of market segmentation - each buyer is potentially a separate market. A seller's approach to satisfy each specific buyer, e.g. by designing a separate product and/or marketing programme for each buyer.

Cut price Niedrigpreis

Also called thrift price.

A price temporarily reduced to stimulate trade for a particular, e.g. new product, or the price of a call bird/loss leader.

A low price charged in order to penetrate the market, i.e. to achieve a high market share.

Cut price merchandise Niedrigpreisware

Goods, e.g. goods of inferior quality, sold at reduced prices.

Cutprice shop/store Niedrigpreisgeschäft, Billigladen

Also called discounter, discount house or discount store.

A shop that sells at unusually low prices and is thus well below the price level of its competitors. The shop operates on a relatively low markup and with a minimum of customer service.

Cutprice war Preiskrieg

Also called price(-cutting) war.

An extreme form of competition; the prices are reduced to the point where the weakest producer is driven out of business. In the short period consumers gain from price wars but ultimately they lead to quality reductions, low profits and investment.

Cutthroat competition ruinöse(r) Konkurrenz, Wettbewerb

Also called destructive or ruinous competition.

An extreme form of competition, existing usually when there are few suppliers (oligopoly) or only two suppliers (duopoly) in the market and where supply exceeds demand.
The product of each producer differs from the products of the competitors, often by little more than the brand name.
Cut-throat competition may take the form of a price war, where the weakest producer is driven out of business - hence the term cut-throat. Only the first producer who cuts prices is likely to achieve a gain and that only temporary, since after a time other producers also will cut their prices and thereby reduce all producers' profit margins. In such cases advertising becomes an alternative to price-cutting because advertising usually increases sales without reducing prices.

Cybernetics Kybernetik

In general, cybernetics is concerned with the theory of information flow in control systems. It may be defined as the science of communication, computation and control.

Cycle Zyklus, Kreislauf
Konjunkturphase, -zyklus

A regularly recurring series of events.

In economics, alternating periods of prosperity and depression, i.e. a period during which trade expands, then slows down and then expands again. In detail this means trade moves from a state of high activity (boom, prosperity) through a running-down period (downswing, recession, slump) to a state of low activity (stagnation, depression), then upward again (recovery, expansion) until there is a return to high activity again. The whole cycle then begins again. Also called business cycle, economic cycle or trade cycly.

Cycle billing über den Monat verteilte Rechnungsaufstellung

The preparation and despatch by a firm of customers' statements throughout a month. Note: many firms apply monthly billing.

Cycle time Zeit für Gesamtarbeitsvorgang

The time from when production begins until the good is received by the customer. Companies with faster cycle times than their competitors can earn profits faster and can increase growth.

Cyclic(al) business konjunkturabhängiges Geschäft

A business whose earnings, value or profit fluctuate widely according to variations in the economy or the cycle of the seasons: e.g. selling Christmas decorations is a cyclic(al) business.

Cyclic(al) industry konjunkturabhängiger Wirtschaftszweig

Industries which are affected by business cycles, i.e. they flourish or decline according to the overall performance of the economy.

Cyclical fluctuations konjunkturelle Schwankungen

Swings up and down in the state of the economy.

Cyclical indicator Konjunkturindikator

Also called (business) cycle indicator, business or economic indicator, or economic pointer.

Economic signs which have a relevance to how the business cycle moves; they measure the progress of the business/trade cycle.

D

D-terms D-Klauseln (Incoterms)

Also called arrival clauses.

One of the four different categories of the incoterms (1990), the others being the C-terms, the E-term and the F-terms.

The D-terms comprise: 1. DAF (delivered at frontier), 2. DES (delivered ex ship), 3. DEQ (delivered ex quay), 4. DDU (delivered duty unpaid), 5. DDP (delivered duty paid).

Their common characteristics are:
1. the seller is responsible for the arrival of the goods at the agreed place of destination;
2. the seller has to bear all costs and risks in bringing the goods to the named place (thus, the D-terms signify arrival contracts);
3. under DAF, DES and DDU the seller has to deliver the goods cleared for export but uncleared for import;
4. under DEQ and DDP the seller has to deliver the goods cleared for export and for import.

DAGMAR model DAGMAR-Modell

DAGMAR is an acronym for Defining Advertising Goals for Measured Advertising Results; the title of a book published by Russel H. Colley in 1961.

A method of measuring advertising effectiveness in which advertising objectives are turned into specific measurable goals, e.g. advertising awareness.

Dailies Tageszeitungen

Newspapers published at least five times per week (Monday to Friday).

Daily activities report Tagestätigkeitsbericht

A salesperson's daily report on calls, i.e. a record of his or her activities on a day-by-day basis, showing clients visited, products presented and outcomes.

Daily effective circulation (DEC) effektiver täglicher Werbemittelkontakt

The audience that has an opportunity to see (OTS) an outdoor advertisment during one day.

Daily rate Anzeigenpreis bei täglicher Inserierung

The price of advertising space in a daily newspaper for all editions published Monday through Friday or Saturday.

Daily report Tagesbericht

A statement made on a daily basis, e.g. by a salesperson on the sales made.

Dairy products Molkereiprodukte

Also called dairy produce.

Foods prepared from milk, including milk, butter, cheese, cream, yoghurt, etc.

Damage Schaden, Beschädigung, Verlust

Also called injury or loss.

Loss, deterioration, spoiling or breakage of goods or of property, or injury to persons.

Dangerous goods Gefahrgut

Also called dangerous cargo.

Hazardous goods such as explosives, gases, flammable liquids, flammable solids, oxidizing materials, toxic substances, radioactive materials, corrosives, etc.

Dangerous goods note (DGN) Gefahrgutschein

A document covering delivery of dangerous/hazardous cargo.

Dangling comparatives indirekt vergleichende Werbung

The advertising practice of implying a comparison between one's product and a competing product, without mentioning the comparison.

Data Daten, Angaben, Informationen, Unterlagen, Zahlenmaterial

A collection of figures, facts or information available for analysis. Examples of business data include hours worked by employees, number of units ordered by customers, national income, the retail price level, etc.

A general term for numbers, digits, characters and symbols which are accepted, stored and processed by a computer.

Data analysis Datenanalyse

The processing of research findings to summarise a situation, discover relationships between elements of the information and to draw conclusions from them to solve a problem.

Data bank Datenbank

Also called data base or information bank.

Collection of facts and information, usually held on computer, for the use by commerce, industry, government and or research bodies. The centralisation of information in a data bank avoids the duplication of data as the data is usually available to a large number of users by means of remote terminals.

Data carrier Datenträger

Also called data medium or recording medium.

A general term referring to a medium for recording data, e.g. magnetic tape.

Data collection Datenerfassung

Also called data capture, acquisition, gathering or recording.

The way of capturing or collecting data for the use within a computer system.

In marketing, the collecting of data by personal interviews, mail survey, telephone survey or focus group.

Data entry Dateneingabe

Also called data input.

The entry of data into a computer by an appropriate input device.

Data matrix Daten-Matrix

An array of value stored as a series of rows and columns representing variables and the values they may take.

Data processing (DP) Datenverarbeitung, Materialaufbereitung elektronische Datenverarbeitung

The operations performed on data in order to produce information or to achieve systematic recording, arranging, filing, processing, retrieving and dissemination of information relating to business operations. In an organization data must be gathered, processed, stored and reported for various reasons, e.g. to provide cost estimates. Such activities have value for decision-making, problem solving, business administration and business control. Also called data handling or information processing.

Electronic data processing (EDP).

Data protection Datensicherung, Datenschutz

The protection of data against alteration without some special procedure, unplanned modification, damage, or loss. Furthermore it must prevent unauthorised access to data elements, thus protecting the privacy of data according to prevailing needs (eg the Data Protection Act).

Data Protection Act Datenschutzgesetz

An Act to protect the privacy of personal data. The Act affects everyone involved in the processing of personal information.

Data sheet Datenblatt

Also called data specification sheet.

A sheet, usually A 4 size; it sets out factual or statistical information and data about someone or something, eg persons, components, materials, products, etc.

Data storage Datenspeicher

Also called data memory, data logger or memory bank.

Storage (memory) of data from where it may be retrieved upon request.

Database marketing Databasemarketing, computergestütztes Marketing

A computerized system to identify both customers and potential customers by name, and to use quantifiable information about them, e.g. their purchase patterns to define the best possible buyers and prospects (i.e. target markets) for a given offer at a given point in time.

Date code Haltbarkeitskodierung

A code showing the date (i.e. the sell-by date) by which a product should be sold or consumed.

Date coding Kennzeichnung mit Herstell- oder Verfalldatum

Practice of showing the manufacturing date or the date by which a product should be sold or used (up).

Date of invoice Rechnungsdatum

Also called billing date, invoice date or invoicing date.

The date on which an invoice or bill is issued.

Date of payment Zahlungstermin, -datum

The date on which payment, e.g. of an invoice, falls due.

The day on which payment is made.

Date of receipt Eingangsdatum

The date when something, e.g. a letter, is received.

Date of shipment Versandtag, Versandtermin

The date on which goods have to be dispatched/shipped.

Date terms Datumsbedingungen

The words "by", "to", "until", "till", "from", etc., applying to any date term (e.g. in a documentary credit) will be understood to include the date mentioned.

The word "after" will be understood to exclude the date mentioned. The terms "first half" and "second half" of a month should be taken respectively as meaning from the first to the 15th and from the 16th to the last day of each month, inclusive.

The terms "beginning", "middle" or "end" of a month should be taken as from the 1st to the 10th, the 11th to the 20th and the 21st to the last day of each month, inclusive.

Day trip Tagestour

Also called day excursion or day tour.

A tour which leaves in the morning and returns the same evening. The people doing the tour are called day trippers or day visitors.

Day-after recall (DAR) Day-After-Recall (DAR), Werbeerinnerung einen Tag nach dem Werbespot oder der Anzeige

A method of measuring the audience memory and the number of audience members one day after exposure to an advertisement or commercial.

Day-after survey Umfrage einen Tag nach Werbemittelkontakt

In advertising, a survey made 15 to 24 hours after publishing an advertisement or broadcasting a commercial.

Daylight saving time (DST) Sommerzeit

Also called summer time.

The time observed when daylight saving is adopted in a country. Daylight saving is the practice of advancing standard time by one hour in the spring of each year and of setting it back by one hour in the fall/autumn in order to gain an extra period of daylight during the early evening.

Daypart/day part (Sende)Zeitsegment

A time segment in the broadcasting day of a radio or TV station.
The daypart with the largest viewing audience is the prime time (8:00 p.m. to 11:00 p.m.; M-Sat). Other well-known dayparts for TV are: daytime (9:00 a.m. to 5:00 p.m.), late night (1:00 a.m. to ...).
Typical dayparts for radio are: morning drive (sign-on to 10:00 am), housewife (10:00 am to 3:00 pm), afternoon/evening drive (3:00 to 7:00 pm), night (7:00 pm to sign-off).

Days of grace zusätzliche Zahlungsfrist, Zahlungsaufschub

Also called grace period.

Days allowed for payment after it becomes due.

In credit cards, the time period in which interest is not charged on current purchases
Also called free period.

Dead bargain spottbillige Ware

Goods that are extremely cheap.

Dead freight (D/f) Leerfracht, Fehlfracht

Freight charges payable for cargo space booked but not used.

Dead horse bezahlte, aber noch nicht gelieferte Güter und Dienste vorausbezahlte Arbeit

Goods and services paid for in advance of production or performance.

Work which has been paid for but has yet to be completed.

Dead letter unzustellbarer Brief

A letter which cannot be delivered.

Dead letter office (DLO) Postamt für unzustellbare Briefe und Pakete

The department of the Post Office which deals with letters and packets which cannot be delivered (dead letters or packets).

Dead loss Totalverlust

A total loss.

Dead season tote Saison, Vor- und Nachsaison (Sauregurkenzeit)

Also called dull season or off season.

The time of year when demand is at its lowest, e.g. when there is a slump in tourism.

Dead stock Ladenhüter, unverkäufliche Waren totes Inventar

Unsaleable goods left on hand. In the USA also called frustrated goods.

Any form of capital not in use.

Deadheading Leerfracht

The movement of empty vehicles to a destination point.

Deadline (letzter) Termin, Stichtag, Schlußtermin
Einsendeschluß, Annahmeschluß

Also called time limit, target date or finish date.

Time by which one must do something or by which a particular stage of a job must be completed.

The closing date (e.g. for the sending of a letter or for an application).

Deal Geschäft
Abschluß, Übereinkunft
Sonderangebot

A business transaction.

Agreement reached between two or more parties to a contract.

A special offer.

Deal merchandise Sonderangebotsware

A specific product that a seller may offer at a reduced price or that may have been specially processed, or produced for a limited time period.

Deal-in Deal-in, Händlerabsatzförderung

A deal-in usually consists of an offer made by the manufacturer to the retailer of a price reduction for a specified period. This offer is conditional upon the retailer accepting an agreed minimum supply of the product.

Deal-out Deal-out, Verbraucherabsatzförderung

In a deal-out, a special attraction is offered to the consumer; e.g. he may purchase a desirable item at a reduced price upon presentation of some labels of the product or he may enter a competition with the chance of winning a special prize.

Dealer Kaufmann, Händler
Makler
Dealer

A person who deals, buys and sells, on his own account and not as an agent of another. Also called merchant or trader.

A dealer in foreign exchange, stocks and shares, etc. Also called broker.

A person who buys and sells drugs illegally.

Dealer aid Verkaufshilfe

Also called selling aid.

Any material, e.g. leaflets, samples supplied by the manufacturer to a dealer or retailer in order to assist him in his task of selling goods or services.

Dealer brand Hausmarke

Also called dealer's or distributor's brand.

A product specially packed and labelled and sold in the dealers`s/distributor's name and not in the producer's.

Dealer commission Händlerprovision

Also called dealer allowance.

A special price reduction given to a dealer by a producer.

Dealer imprint in Werbung eingedruckte Händleradresse

The name and address of a local dealer, printed on a national advertisement after it has been designed and printed by the manufacturer/producer.

Dealer listing Bezugsquellen- Händlernachweis (in einer Anzeige)

Also called dealer tie-in or tagging.

The naming in a product advertisement of certain dealers that sell the product.

Dealer magazine (Einzel)Händlerzeitschrift

External house journal aimed at dealers.

Dealer tie-in Bezugsquellennachweis
Koppelanzeige
Verbundwerbung

A list of local dealers in an advertisement paid for entirely by a manufacturer.

The support by a local retailer for a manufacturer`s advertising, e.g. through inserting advertisements in the local media referring to the ones of the manufacturer.

Advertising where the manufacturer and a retailer share advertising efforts and costs.

Dealer`s price Wiederverkaufspreis

The price at which a dealer resells a product.

Death rate Sterblichkeitsziffer, Sterbeziffer

Also called mortality rate.

The number of deaths is measured by the death rate, which is the number of deaths per thousand of population per year. A low death rate indicates that the average life expectancy is high.

Debit card Kreditkarte (Lastschrift-karte) zur direkten Abbuchung von Einzelhandelskäufen

A plastic card which allows a person to make a purchase that is paid for by a direct substraction from the person's (bank) account. Debit cards (e.g. Access, American Express, Diner's Club, Visa, etc.) can be used in much the same ways as credit cards, provided that there are enough shops, restaurants etc. that accept them. Debit cards cannot be used for extended credit, and full payment must be made on receipt of the bill.

Debit note (D/N) Debitnote, Lastschriftanzeige, Belastungsanzeige

Also called charge slip, debit advice, or debit memo.

In general, a document issued by one party to a transaction to show the recipient that his account has been debited with the amount shown.

A document similar to an invoice. A debit note is issued because an invoice should never be altered. It is sent by a seller to a buyer when it is intended to debit his account or when he has been undercharged on an invoice. Sometimes it is sent to the seller by a buyer who has returned goods or has been overcharged; but it is more usual for a buyer to ask for a credit note (C/N).

Debriefing Nachbesprechung

A discussion with or an interview of a participant after an activity to obtain useful information and to assess the results or success of the activity.

Debtee Gläubiger, Kreditor Forderungsberechtigter

Also called creditor.

A person or business to whom money is owed by the debtor who has received goods or services on credit.

A person to whom an obligation exists.

Debtor (Dr, dr) Schuldner, Debitor Verpflichteter

One who owes money to a business for goods or services which the business has supplied on credit.

One who is under some obligation to another. Also called obligor.

Deceit Betrug

Also called deception, fraud or misrepresentation.

Hiding the truth; making a false statement; making somebody believe something which is not true.

Deceptive advertising irreführende Werbung, Falschwerbung

Also called misleading advertising.

An advertising message that misleads a consumer about an important aspect of a product or service.

Deceptive mark irreführendes Warenzeichen

A trademark that looks similar to another, usually a registered or well-known trademark in order to make the potential buyer believe he is buying a particular brand.

Deceptive packaging Mogelpackung

Packaging which creates an impression that the enclosed material is more than what it really is, in terms of either size, quality or quantity. It may exaggerate package contents through subtle design, not filling the pack(age) to the top, using misleading label(l)ing, etc.

Deceptive practices irreführende Praktiken

Practices that lead consumers to believe they will get more value than they actually do. There are four types of deceptive practices:
1. deceptive advertising: advertising that makes false claims, misleading statements, creates false impressions or fails to make full disclosure in order to mislead consumers

2. deceptive promotion: promotion that overstates the product`s features or perfomance, lures the customer to the store for a bargain that is out of stock, etc.

3. deceptive packing: this includes exaggerating package contents through subtle design, not filling the pack(age) to the top, using misleading label(l)ing, etc.

4. deceptive pricing: this includes savings claims, price comparisons, two-for-one sales, false preticketing, "factory" or "wholesale" prices, etc.

Deceptive pricing irreführende Preisangabe

The pricing of goods or services in such a way as to mislead a customer. Possible examples are: savings claims, price comparisons, special sales, two-for-one sales, factory prices, wholesale prices, false preticketing, etc. These pricing strategies are unlawful if false or deceptive.

Deceptive promotion irreführende Verkaufsförderung

Promotion that overstates the product`s features or performance, lures the customer to the store for a bargain that is out of stock, etc.

Decider Entscheidungsträger, Entscheider

Also called decision maker.

A person who either has the authority to make a decision or the ability to influence decisions or members of a particular group.

In marketing, individuals who have the power and the responsibility to approve a product and select final customers.

Decision lag Entscheidungsverzögerung

Time lag/delay between the receipt of information (i.e. the recognition of the need for action on an economic problem) by a decision-maker and the taking of action on it.

Decision maker Entscheidungsträger

Also called decider.

The person who actually makes the decision(s), e.g. to purchase a product, to develop a product, to launch/introduce a new product or to build a new plant.

Decision support system (DSS) Entscheidungsunterstützungssystem

An interactive, flexible computerized information system that enables managers to obtain and manipulate information as they are making decisions.

Characteristics of DSS are:
1. managers give instructions and see immediate results without having to wait for reports;
2. the DSS can sort, regroup, total, average, and manipulate the data in various ways;
3. managers can isolate problems, probe for trends and ask "what if" questions.

Decline stage Degenerationsphase

The final stage of the product lifecycle (after introductory stage, growth stage and maturity stage). The sales of most products eventually decline. The sales decline may be slow or rapid; sales may plunge to zero, or they may remain at a low level and continue for many years at that level. Sales decline, e.g. because of technological advances, shifts in consumer tastes, increased competition, etc.
Possible outcomes of sales declines are: price cuttings, overcapacity, drops in profits and ultimately the withdrawal from the market.

Declining population rückläufige Bevölkerung

The total size of population falls because the death-rate is exceeding the birth-rate.

Decoder Dekodierer, Decoder

A device used to translate data from one coded form to another.

Decoding Dekodierung

In the communications process, the process whereby the receiver assigns meaning to the pictures and/or words of the sender in order to understand the idea or message being transmitted by the sender.

Decrease Abnahme, Rückgang

The act or process of decreasing; a gradual reduction.

Decrease in demand Nachfragerückgang

A fall in demand. Due to changes in the conditions of demand (e.g. taxation changes, a fall in income), the demand curve shifts to the left (i.e. to a new demand curve). Note: there is no price change.

Decrease in supply Angebotsrückgang

A fall in supply. Due to changes in the supply conditions (e.g. the costs of production, the prices of other goods), the supply curve shifts to the left (i.e. to a new supply curve). Note: there is no price change.

Decreasing cost(s) Kostendegression, abnehmende Kosten

Also called declining cost(s).

A situation where an increase in the scale of production results in a fall in the cost of each unit produced.

Decreasing returns (to scale) sinkender Skalenertrag

A situation occurring when all productive inputs are increased by a given proportion and output increases less than proportionally. Economies of scale cease to operate because of the counter-acting effect of increasing average costs and the resulting decrease in profitability.

Dedicated line fest geschaltete Leitung, Standleitung

A telephone line used only for a particular purpose.

Deduction Abzug
Rabatt, Nachlaß

Any amount deducted.

A rebate, ie an allowance of money in reduction of an amount to be paid. Also called allowance or discount.

Deep assortment tiefes Sortiment

A reseller's assortment strategy of carrying many variants of each product in his range.

Deep rooted demand tief verwurzelte Nachfrage

A consumer`s continuing product loyalty even if the product may have lost its competitive advantage or may no longer offer value for money.

Defamation Verleumdung, Rufschädigung

In law, the unjustified damaging of another person's reputation or slighting of his/her person by the publication of false statements either by word of mouth (slander) or in a more permanent form (libel).

Default in/of delivery Lieferungsverzug

Also called delay in delivery.

Failure to deliver goods or render services at an agreed date or within a specified period.

Default in/of payment Zahlungsverzug

Also called delay in/of payment.

Failure to pay a debt at an agreed date or within a certain period.

Defaulter säumiger Zahler, zahlungsunfähiger Schuldner

Also called defaulting debtor, or debtor in arrears or default.

A person who fails to pay a debt or meet a financial obligation.

Defective goods beschädigte, mangelhafte Ware, Ausschußware

Also called faulty goods or substandard goods.

Goods that are in a bad condition. If a business receives such goods it sends them back to the supplier who will then send a credit note for the amount on the sales invoice or he will replace the faulty goods.

Defense strategy Verteidigungsstrategie

A company`s (e.g. the market leader`s) strategy to protect its current market share against enemy attacks through good defensive and offensive actions.

Possible defensive measures are: continuous innovations, product improvements, improved customer services, competitive distribution methods, low prices, counterattacks, an offense against the enemy before it starts an offense against the company, strategic withdrawal (i.e. giving up weaker territories and promoting stronger ones), expansion of the market share, etc.

Note: the best defense is a good offense.

)efensive advertising Abwehrwerbung, defensive Werbung

\ company's advertising to combat the effects of a competitor's promotion.

Deferment Aufschub, Zurückstellung, Vertagung

\lso called postponement.

'utting back/deferral to a later date; to wait until later before doing something.

)eferred demand aufgeschobene Nachfrage

)emand for goods or services which cannot be satisfied because the goods or services are not available; but demand will be met if the goods do become available.

)eferred payment (D/P) Zahlungsaufschub, gestundete Zahlung
Ratenzahlung

\n undertaking to make payments at some future date.

\ kind of hire purchase arrangement or a credit sale.

)eferred payment agreement Abzahlungs-, Ratenzahlungsvertrag

\n arrangement which allows payments to be extended over a period of time or put off to a future date. Some traders allow their customers to have the goods at once and to pay for them afterwards, i.e. payment is deferred. Usually the buyer must agree to pay a definite sum on definite dates.
There are two kinds of agreements for deferred payments: hire purchase and credit sale agreement.

)eferred rebate Treuerabatt

Also called loyalty discount or rebate, fidelity rebate, aggregated rebate or patronage rebate.

A discount on purchases within a specified period granted to loyal customers and to encourage customers to remain with a particular supplier.

Deflation Deflation

This is the opposite of inflation. Deflation occurs when the purchasing/spending power of money rises and the general level of prices falls (called disinflation).

A situation deliberately contrived which brings about: a fall in prices and income, a fall in purchasing power and demand, a stagnation or reduction in economic activity, and unemployment. The value of the currency has been raised deliberately and the price level lowered.

It may be brought about by monetary policies (e.g. increases in the interest rates), and/or by fiscal policies (e.g. increases in taxation) or reductions in government expenditure.

Governments introduce deflationary policies in order to cut the level of imports and to stimulate exports (i.e. to improve the balance of payments) or to reduce the quantity of money in order to combat inflation.

In inflationary times deflation may seem to be quite attractive but, in practice, the effects of severe deflation are as damaging, if not more so, than the effects of inflation. If prices are falling all the time, it is difficult for a producer to recover the cost of goods he makes; wages and raw materials have to be paid for at today's higher prices, while sales will be made at tomorrow's lower prices. This situation increases the entrepreneurial risk, with the result that industrialists become more cautious and reduce output. Production falls, unemployment increases, demand therefore decreases and production has to be further reduced; a vicious circle has developed.

Deflationary gap deflatorische Lücke, Investitionslücke

Investment falls short of that required to restore full employment.

Deflationary policy Deflationspolitik

Policies towards diminishing the pressure on price rises by reducing demand, using tax increases or government spending cutbacks.

Del credere Delkredere

The risk of non-payment.

An amount added to a charge to cover the risk of non-payment. That means, an engagement made by an agent, in return for additional payment or commission, whereby he guarantees the payment to the principal for all goods sold on commission, whether or not he himself receives payment from the buyer.

Del credere agent Delkredereagent, Garantievertreter

An agent who, in return for an extra commission (the del credere commission), guarantees payment for the goods he sells for his principal.

Del credere commission Delkredereprovision

A commission, usually 25% of the selling commission, paid to a del credere agent for taking the risk of nonpayment by the buyer.

Delay in delivery Lieferungsverzug

Also called delayed delivery or default in/of delivery.

Failure to deliver goods or render services at an agreed date or within a specified period.

Delay in/of payment Zahlungsverzug

Also called delayed payment or default in/of payment.

Failure to pay a debt at an agreed date or within a certain period.

Delayed broadcast (DB) zeitverschobene Übertragung

The transmission of a radio or TV programme at some time after the original broadcast.

Delayed delivery verspätete Lieferung

Also called late delivery or lagged delivery.

The delivery of goods to the buyer after the date which has been agreed upon in the sales contract. If the delivery time was a condition, the buyer may reject the goods; otherwise the buyer may sue the seller for damages if he has suffered any loss due to late delivery.

Delayed response verzögerte Reaktion

A slower than expected response by customers or consumers to a company's activities, e.g. an advertising campaign.

Delayed-action advertisement Werbung, die zu späterer/ aufgeschobener Kaufhandlung führen soll; Werbung mit verzögerter Wirkung

An advertisement which attempts to influence consumer attitudes and preferences, thus helping to set the stage for a purchase.

Deletion Elimination, Eliminierung

Also called elimination.

A situation where a company removes an old product from the market as it has lost market share or as a new one is being launched.

Delivered price Lieferpreis, Preis frei Haus

Also called door to door price.

Ex works/ex factory selling price plus all costs involved in transporting the goods to the customer.

Delivered pricing Preisstellung frei Haus

The charging of a price for a product that includes the cost of transporting the product from the manufacturer to the customer.

Delivery (D, Dely, dely, Dy) Ab-, Aus-, Ein-Lieferung
Lieferung (das Gelieferte)
(Eigentums)Übergabe

The act of delivering, i.e. the transport of goods to a customer's address. Also called supply.

Part or all of an order, i.e. the consignment or shipment.

The physical handover (i.e. transfer of title or possession over something from one person to another) of a commodity to settle a contract.

Delivery address Lieferanschrift

The address to which a consignment is sent/delivered.

Delivery against payment (DAP) Wertnachnahme

Also called cash on delivery (COD), delivery versus payment (DVP) or payment on delivery (POD).

Payment in cash when the goods are delivered.

Delivery book Lieferbuch

A book containing brief details of the goods which the recipient/consignee signs when he receives them.

Delivery date (D/D, dd) Liefertermin, Lieferdatum
Abliefertermin

The day on which a business sends goods to a customer. Also called date shipped.

Sometimes it may mean the day when the customer receives the goods.

Delivery expenses Versand-, Lieferungs-, Zustellkosten

Also called delivery costs or charges.

The costs of sending goods from a business to a customer.

Delivery free Lieferung/Zustellung frei Haus

Also called free delivery or delivery free domicile.

Contract term in which the seller agrees to pay all delivery charges (costs or expenses).

Delivery instruction Liefervorschrift, Versandanweisung

Also called forwarding or shipping instructions.

Instructions given by the buyer to the seller how and when to deliver the goods ordered.

Delivery month Liefermonat

The month when goods have to be delivered.

Delivery note Lieferschein Versandanzeige

A document giving details of a consignment of goods and normally sent with the goods to enable them to be checked upon arrival. The signature of the receiver/consignee on the delivery note provides evidence of delivery. Also called delivery docket, note, sheet or ticket; receiving slip or ticket; or bill of sale.

An advice note which is sent from the seller to the buyer, indicating that the goods have been despatched. Also called advice of despatch or shipment, despatch note, shipping note, forwarding advice or letter of advice.

Delivery notice Lieferanzeige

Also called advice of delivery, advice note or delivery note.

A formal notice sent by the seller or carrier to the consignee certifying that delivery of something will occur on a certain date, or has already occurred.

Delivery of goods Warenlieferung

The transport(ation) of goods to a customer's address.

Delivery order (D/O) Lieferauftrag
Auslieferungsauftrag, -schein
Lieferschein

An order to deliver/supply goods.

A document addressed by the owner of goods to a warehouse keeper or other bailee instructing him to release specified goods, whether in whole or in part, to the bearer of the order, or to the party named thereon by indorsement.

A delivery note. Also called advice note.

Delivery receipt Warenempfangsschein,
Wareneingangsbescheinigung

Also called goods receipt.

A receipt signed by the consignee/receiver as proof that the goods have been delivered to him.

Delivery terms Lieferbedingungen

Also called terms of delivery.

The principal terms of delivery are: the 13 incoterms, loco, delivered docks, franco, free on board airport (foa), free on quay (foq), free on rail or truck (for/fot), free on wharf (fow), free out (fo), free in (fi), etc.

A quotation should say when delivery will take place:
1. Ready delivery: the goods will be dispatched as soon as the order is received.
2. Prompt delivery: delivery will take place within a few days of receiving the order.
3. Forward delivery: where the goods are not in stock and cannot be obtained in a short time the seller will quote "forward delivery", the actual date being communicated later.

Delivery time Lieferzeit

The number of days before something will be delivered.

Delivery van Lieferwagen

Also called delivery car.

A van that takes goods from a supplier to a customer.

Delphi method Delphi-Befragung

Also called Delphi technique; sometimes also called jury of expert opinion.

It is a commonly used qualitative method for forecasting new product sales or new developments involving a panel of experts in science and technology. Each member of the panel makes his or her own forecast and the different forecasts are assembled in a composite report which is then sent round the panel for comment. This process is then usually repeated until a reliable forecast is obtained. In essence, the approach pools the opinions of experts. This technique of forecasting was developed in the USA in the early 1960s.

Note: the term was derived from the famous Delphic oracle in ancient Greece.

Demand effektive Nachfrage
Nachfrage, Bedarf
(Auf)Forderung
(Kunden)Bedarf

The quantity of a commodity that will be bought at a particular price per time period.

A member of the public wishes to buy a good or a service and has the ability and willingness to pay for that good or service; it is always demand at a certain price. There is a demand for goods and services because they satisfy wants, i.e. they have a utility. The price is the most important factor which influences how much is bought; therefore, the higher the price the less we will buy; the lower the price the more will be bought.
Various other factors affect demand: our disposable income, the distribution of incomes, the prices of other goods and services, the degree of utility of the commodity, the tastes and preferences of the purchaser, the size and structure of the population and changing fashions.

In the theory of competitive markets, demand is one of the two factors that determine market price; supply is the other.

A letter from a business to a customer who has not paid what he owes. The letter requires the customer to pay what he owes immediately - a request for payment.

Number of orders placed or received.

Demand analysis Nachfrage-, Bedarfsanalyse

Study of demand for product or service in order to establish reasons for its success or failure or in order to discover how sales performance may be improved.

Demand and price Nachfrage und Preis

Generally, the lower the price of a commodity, the greater the quantity demanded and hence an increase in demand results - partly because more can be bought with the same money and partly because demand for similar, but more expensive, commodities may be transferred to the cheaper commodity. The higher the price the lower the demand.

There are, however, exceptions and sometimes demand increases as the price increases and falls as the price falls (e.g. as the consumer's income rises, he buys less of the cheaper goods and more of dearer substitutes).

Demand and supply Nachfrage und Angebot

The demand for a good is related to the price of the good. The supply of the same good is also related to the price of the good.

Generally, the higher the price the lower the demand but the greater the potential supply; the lower the price the greater the demand but the lower the potential supply.

Under perfect competition, price is decided by the interaction of demand and supply; thus the market price is that price which equates demand and supply (equilibrium price). Note: at this price the demand curve intersects the supply curve.

Demand creation Nachfrageschöpfung, Nachfrageschaffung

The creation of or increase in demand for goods or services among consumers or resellers, e.g. through price reductions or other promotional incentives.

Demand curve Nachfragekurve

Also called demand line.

A graph which shows how much of a commodity will be bought in a time period for a given price (i.e. it shows the relationship between the price of a commodity and the quantity demanded). It is usually shown as sloping downwards from left to right. The curve is almost always shown with price (the independent variable) on the vertical axis (y-axis or ordinate) and quantity (the dependent variable) on the horizontal axis (x-axis or abscissa). On each point of the curve, the consumer is in equilibrium and the value of the item equals its price.

Demand factors Nachfragefaktoren

The elements that determine the consumers` willingness and ability to pay for products or services, e.g. price, income, quality.

Demand fluctuation Nachfragefluktuation

The continuous or irregular changes, the ups and downs of demand levels.

Demand forecast Bedarfsprognose, Nachfrageprognose

The prediction of future demand at different selling prices

Note: in reality the variable factors are such that a good forecast will be accurate only to within, say, plus or minus 5%.

Demand function Nachfragefunktion

In general terms, the relationship between a consumer's demand for a good and all factors, i.e. the independent variables (e.g. the price of the good, the prices of other commodities, the consumer's income, the consumer's taste and credit facilities) affecting demand. If all factors are held constant (ceteris paribus), except one, it is possible to study how demand will vary with changes in that one element. This is represented geometrically by the demand curve.

The mathematical expression of the demand schedule in form of an equation, e.g. Qd = f (P, Y, Ps, t, etc.); Qd = quantity demanded, P = product price, Y = income, Ps = prices of other products, t = taste.

Demand management Nachfragesteuerung

The regulation of aggregate (market, overall, total) demand through the use of monetary policy and/or fiscal policy in order to minimise unemployment and curb inflation.

Demand oriented pricing nachfrageorientierte Preisbildung

A pricing method based on the level of demand for the product. This means, that the price is high when demand for the product is strong and the price is low when demand is weak.

Demand oriented production nachfrageorientierte Produktion

Production which particularly considers the level of demand for the product(s) produced.

Demand price Nachfragepreis

The price which buyers are willing to pay for a given quantity of a good or service.

Demand pull Nachfragesog

Also called pressing demand.

The result of demand stimulants applied in marketing; demand will increase.

Demand schedule Nachfragetabelle

A table giving the demand (X) for a commodity or service at various prices (Y); all other factors (e.g. the price of other goods, income, taste) which determine demand remain unchanged. The schedule relates to a specific period of time. From this information the demand curve can be constructed.

Demand shift Nachfrageverschiebung

Also called demand shifting or switching.

The change in demand for a product or service due to one or more reasons other than price.

Demand side economics Demand-Side Economics, nachfrageorientierte Wirtschaftspolitik

Also called demand side policies.

Policies trying to increase aggregate/total demand in order to cure economic problems and to achieve the macro economic objectives full employment, price stability, external balance equilibrium, economic growth and the redistribution of income and welfare.

Demand theory Nachfragetheory

That part of economics that deals with consumer buying habits and factors which determine demand.

Demand types Nachfragearten

There are a number of different types of demand, eg:

1. aggregate demand, 2. aggregate monetary demand, 3. alternate demand, 4. competitive demand, 5. complementary demand, 6. composite demand, 7. current demand, 8. deep rooted demand, 9. deferred demand, 10. derived demand, 11. diffused demand, 12. direct demand, 13. effective demand, 14. elastic demand, 15. erratic demand, 16. excess demand, 17. existing demand, 18. fluctuating demand, 19. homogeneous demand, 20. keen demand, 21. latent demand, 22. market demand,

23. monetary demand, 24. negative demand, 25. incipient demand, 26. industrial demand, 27. inelastic demand, 28.inverse demand, 29. joint demand, 30. overfull demand, 31. peak demand, 32. perfectly elastic demand, 33. perfectly inelastic demand, 34. persistent demand, 35. potential demand, 36. primary demand, 37. regressive demand, 38. rival demand, 39. slack demand, 40. selective demand, 41. volatile demand, 42. weak demand etc.

Demand-pull inflation — Nachfrageinflation, nachfrage-induzierte Inflation

Also called demand inflation, demand-led inflation, buyers' inflation or (incorrectly) demand-shift inflation.

An inflation induced by increased aggregate demand for goods and services due to increased incomes, low interest rates, etc. Demand exceeds the supply and the excessive demand will force up prices.

Demand-shift inflation — Nachfrageverschiebungs-Inflation, Inflation durch Nachfragestruktur-Veränderungen, nicht-monetäre Nachfrage-Inflation

Inflation as a result of a change in the structure of aggregate/total demand. Note: one or more of the determinants/conditions of demand changes, whereas prices remain unchanged.

Demarketing — Demarketing, Anti-Marketing, Reduktionsmarketing

Marketing aimed at reducing demand and/or limiting growth, e.g. by a company that is currently unable to serve its customers adequately or particularly by governments to conserve natural resources or to reduce the demand for products or services believed to be harmful to society.

Demassification — Demassifizierung

The move by the mass producers and the mass media from attempting to reach as many consumers as possible or the greatest possible audience to appealing to less consumers or smaller audiences who are often upscale.

Demographic segmentation demographische Marktsegmentierung

The dividing up of a market on the basis of socioeconomic characteristics, ie the breakdown of markets into specific groups having the same characteristics, e.g. according to income levels, age, sex, etc, of the potential customers.

Demographics demographische Merkmale

Also called demographic characteristics.

The characteristics of the human population such as age, sex, education, income level, geographical location, etc.

Demography Demographie, Bevölkerungsstatistik

The science of social statistics, particularly population statistics (e.g. birth rate, death rate, occupational distribution, etc.).

Demonstration Vorführung, Demo

Showing the product or service in action.

Demonstration effect Mitläufereffekt

Also called keep up with the Joneses or bandwaggon effect.

A theory stating that people buy products or services to impress or keep up with friends or other people, e.g. neighbours.

Demonstration model Vorführgerät, Vorführmodell

A product used to show it in action to the consumers, eg a car or other piece of equipment used in demonstrations and later sold off at a lower price.

Demurrage Lagergeld

Also called standage charge.

The amount of money paid by a consignee for occupying space at a warehouse beyond a specified period.

Denationalisation (Re)Privatisierung, Entstaatlichung

Also called privatisation.

Returning a nationalised enterprise back to free enterprise.

Density of population Bevölkerungsdichte

The number of inhabitants in a given area.

Department of Commerce Handels-, Witschaftsministerium (USA)

In the USA, the federal department established in 1913 to promote domestic and foreign trade.

Department of the Environment (DoE) Umweltministerium (GB)

The DoE controls policies for regional development, housing, new towns, construction, inner city matters, environmental protection, water, the countryside, conservation, historic buildings and ancient monuments, sports and recreation.

Department of Trade and Industry (DTI) Wirtschaftsministerium (GB)

Also called ministry of economic affairs.

A department of the British government with responsibilities for company and commercial law, industrial policy, foreign trade, consumer protection, science, technology and research, etc.

Department store chain Warenhauskette

A number of department stores belonging to the same company and forming a chain of businesses.

Department(al) store Warenhaus, Kaufhaus

Also called emporium (plural: emporia).

A large retail business divided into departments and selling a very wide variety of goods/merchandise. Each department specializes in a particular range of goods. It is really a number of shops under one roof. Because of the heavy fixed costs (e.g. rent, heating), it will only be profitable if the turnover is large.

Departure (dep) Abfahrt
(Neu)Anfang

The act of departing or starting, e.g. the departure time is 19:00 hours.

A new venture or a new type of business.

Departure date Abreisetag

The day on which a plane, ship, traveller or tour group leaves.

Departure lounge Abflughalle

A room in an airport where passengers wait to get on their planes after going through passport control and baggage/luggage check.

Departure tax Flughafensteuer

A tax payable at an airport by passengers leaving a country.

Dependency ratio Abhängigkeitsrate

The number of people, i.e. children under a specific age (14, for example) and older (age 65 and over) living in a country, divided by the total population. An increasing ratio indicates that a larger burden is being placed on the productive-age workforce.

Dependent population nicht erwerbstätige Bevölkerung

Those people in the total population who are not part of the working population (the workforce), e.g. children.

Dependent variable abhängige Variable

A statistical term describing a factor which changes as a result of another variable, which is independent. The variable on the left hand side in an equation. For example, in the relationship Y = f(x), Y is the dependent variable. The dependent variable is conventionally plotted on the vertical axis of a graph (Y-axis, side axis, ordinate); the independent variable is plotted on the horizontal axis of a graph (X-axis, bottom axis or abscissa).

Note: 1. read graphs from left to right; 2. think of the variable on the horizontal axis as "causing" the other variable (on the vertical axis) to change; 3. two variables are positively related to each other if they move together (both going up or both going down); 4. two variables are negatively related if one increases, the other decreases.

Deposit Anzahlung

Also called downpayment, first or initial payment.

A part payment or first instalment of the purchase price of goods.

Depot Depot, Lager(haus), Warenlager

A place of deposit for goods, a storehouse or warehouse.

Depressed market flauer, gedrückter Markt

Also called flat market.

A market with low sales, e.g. because there are more goods than customers, the customers have no spending power or the whole area suffers from a depression.

Depression Depression, Flaute

Sometimes also called business panic.

A prolonged and severe slump or stagnation of economic activity; more severe and long-lasting than a recession; a period of high unemployment, excessive supply, falling prices, rising welfare costs, deflation, public fear, drop in personal incomes, and a decline in investment. The low point is often called a slump.
Note: often booms and depressions succeed one another.

Depth interview offenes Interview, Intensiv-, Tiefeninterview

An informal conversation without a formal questionnaire between a market research interviewer and a respondent/interviewee in order to discover facts which might not emerge from direct questioning. The questions are answered freely.

Depth of a product mix Produktmixtiefe

The number of product items within each product line.

Derivative product abgeleitetes Produkt

A product constructed from existing products.

Derived demand abgeleitete, derivative Nachfrage

Also called derivate or indirect demand.

This is the demand for a commodity (especially a factor of production) or service because it is needed as a result of the demand for another commodity or service (e.g. the demand for labour is derived from the demand for the goods produced by that labour; the demand for machines depends on the demand for the goods the machines produce).
Note: the demand for almost all products is conditioned by the demand for others.

Descriptive billing ausführliche Rechnungsstellung

Also called descriptive invoicing.

A statement of account sent to a customer showing his purchases made during a specific period, the price and the date of the purchases although the original invoice is not included in the statement.

Descriptive label Pflichtetikett, Etikett mit Inhaltsangaben, produktorientiertes Etikett

A label on a product carrying information about the product's ingredients, composition, weight, nutritional value, etc.

Descriptive label(l)ing ausführliche Produktkennzeichnung

The use of descriptive information on labels, e.g. ingredients, size, weight, etc.

Descriptive statistics deskriptive Statistik

The process of collecting, classifying, summarizing, and presenting data to describe economic relationships.

Design Design
Entwurf
Gestaltung
Plan
Muster

In marketing, a term embracing all types of visual work.

Plan or drawing of something before it is made.

The way something is planned.

Plan or intention to do something.

A pattern on any material.

Designer product Designerprodukt

Elegant, expensive and often fashionable products created by well-known designers.

Desintegration Produkteinstellung zugunsten Fremdbezugs

A company`s strategy to stop producing certain goods and to buy them instead from a specialised supplier.

Desk research sekundärstatistische Auswertung, Schreibtischforschung

Also called armchair research.

The study of existing or published data ranging from external data and material to internal information. It is not always necessary to undertake original research.

Desktop publishing computerunterstützte Textgestaltung, EDV-Textanfertigung

Also called desktop editing.

In an electronic office, the use of personal computers to prepare documents combining text and pictures.

Despatch/dispatch Versand, Expedition

The act of sending goods to a certain place. The despatch of goods is authorised by the copy invoices, the delivery note and advice/despatch note. These are sent to the despatch department by the invoice clerk, and authorise the appropriation of goods to the order.

Despatch date Versanddatum

The date on which an article, eg a consignment, is sent to a receiver or destination.

Despatch department Versandabteilung

The department which packs and sends off goods to customers.

Despatch note Versandanzeige

Also called advice, advice note, delivery note, shipping note, forwarding note, or letter of advice.

A note from a seller to a buyer informing him that the goods ordered have been despatched.

Despatch rider Fahrrad/Motorrad-Bote

A cyclist or motorcyclist who delivers mail and parcels to customers in a town.

Despatcher/dispatcher Dispatcher, Expedient

Also called despatch or shipping clerk.

An agent responsible for efficiently routing and sending merchandise to its destined location.

Destination Bestimmungsort

Also called place of destination.

The place to which a seller agrees to deliver goods.

Detailer Kundenbesucher

A salesperson who visits customers, e.g. doctors, and informs them about new products or services and who promotes goodwill among them so that they may influence the purchase of the products or services represented by the detailer.

Determinants of demand Nachfragedeterminanten

The law of demand is qualified with the phrase "other things being equal" (ceteris paribus). Those other things are the determinants/conditions of demand.
These are:
1. income; 2. tastes and preferences; 3. prices and availability of related products or services (a. substitutes, e.g. coffee and tea; b. complements; e.g. bread and butter); 4. expectations about prices and income; and 5. number and structure of consumers. The price of the product or service is not a determinant.

When one or more of the determinants changes, the entire demand curve shifts to a new position, either to the left or to the right.
Note: if the price of the product changes, then the quantity demanded changes (i.e. increases or decreases). This change in quantity is shown as a movement along the existing demand curve.

Determinants of supply Angebotsdeterminanten

The determinants affecting supply are:
1. the costs of production (e.g. labour and material costs, administration, rent, etc.); 2. technology, including the scale of the firm and production (e.g. the introduction of mass production or microchips); 3. expectations (about costs, prices, sales, and profits; if the expectations are grim, the firm will cut production); 4. the price of related goods (a. substitutes, b. complements); 5. the number of suppliers.

When one or more of the determinants changes, the entire supply curve changes position, shifting leftward or rightward. This is known as a change in supply (an increase results in a rightward shift of the supply curve and a decrease leads to a leftward shift of the supply curve).
Note: if the price of the product changes, then the quantity supplied changes (i.e. increases or decreases). This change in quantity is shown as a movement along the existing supply curve.

Determinants of consumer demand Determinanten der Konsumenten-, Verbrauchernachfrage

People`s purchase behaviour will be determined by:

1. economic factors such as: the real disposable income, the price of the available products, basic personal perceptions of what constitutes good "value for money", the relative prices of substitute products and complementary products, etc;
2. behavioural factors such as: individual motivation and personality, culture, lifestyle, social class, groups, family life cycle, etc.

Detour Umweg, Umleitung

Journey away from the usual or planned route.

Development Entwicklung

The process of making use of research results to achieve the best production techniques, and to produce new and improved products at low costs.

Development area Entwicklungs-Fördergebiet

Regions of high unemployment. The government gives financial and other assistance to encourage the growth of industry in order to raise employment.

Development cost(s) Entwicklungskosten, -aufwand

Also called development expense or expenditure.

The costs incurred by a business on a product from the research stage to the stage of production.

Development department Entwicklungsabteilung

The department responsible for the development of a company's products or services.

Diadic (product) test Zweiprodukttest, Paarvergleich

Also called paired comparison test.

A product test in which respondents test and compare two products.

Dial(l)ing code (Telefon)Vorwahl

Also called area code.

A special series of phone numbers necessary to make a (phone) call to another town.

Dichotomous question Alternativfrage

In a questionnaire, a type of question that simply requires a "yes" or "no" answer. It can be extended to include a "don't know" or "no preference" response. Thus, the respondents are simply asked to indicate which of two alternative responses most closely corresponds to their position on a subject or product.

Difference Differenz, Meinungsverschiedenheit
Differenz, Unterschied (Betrag)

Quarrel or disagreement.

The amount by which one total fails to agree with another.

Differentiated marketing differenziertes Marketing

A popular marketing strategy where a company operates in most segments of the market but designs tailored programmes for each significantly different segment.

Differentiation Differenzierung, Spezialisierung

If commodities are exactly the same, these are known as homogeneous products; if not, as differentiated products. Differentiation may be based on certain characteristics of the product itself such as exclusive features, trademarks, singularity in quality, design, style, etc.

Diffused demand diffuse Nachfrage

A demand pattern in which consumer needs and desires for a good or service category are so diverse that clear segments cannot be identified.

Diffusion process Diffusionsprozeß

The manner in which an innovation (e.g. a new idea or product) spreads across a market group by group according to the readiness of each group to adopt it.

There are four basic elements in this process:
1. innovation (this is the new product idea as perceived by the firm, the buyer and the channels of distribution),
2. communication (this is necessary to inform the potential consumers about the product and make them consider purchasing it; the more communication in the form of advertising, sales promotion, etc. the faster the diffusion process will occur);
3. social system (i.e. all the individuals or firms in a defined market which are able to use the new product; the diffusion process is complete when all of them have adopted the product);
4. time (this refers to how long after introduction an individual or firm adopts a new product).

Note: the diffusion process is the cause of an adoption process.

Diminishing marginal utility abnehmender, sinkender Grenznutzen

If any commodity gives satisfaction, it is said to possess utility. As the quantity of any commodity increases, so does the satisfaction to be derived from it, i.e. the utility increases. However, the larger a person's supply of a commodity, the less satisfaction/utility he derives from an additional unit of it. The additional satisfaction obtained from the additional unit is called the marginal utility. The fact that, normally, as the supply of any commodity increases, the marginal utility decreases is known as the law of diminishing marginal utility.
Note: a minimum quantity of a good must be acquired before the law begins to operate.

Diminishing returns (law of) Gesetz vom abnehmenden Ertrag, Ertragsgesetz

Also called law of non-proportional returns or law of variable proportions.

The inevitable fall in the "marginal product" is described by the "law of diminishing marginal returns/productivity", usually called the "law of diminishing returns", or sometimes: "the law of variable proportions".

The law was first applied to land, but it operates in all branches of productive activity. The law states that: if, in a given state of technology , increasing quantities of a variable factor of production are used in conjunction with a fixed quantity of other factors, then, after a certain point, each additional unit of the variable factor will make a smaller and smaller addition to the total output.

Diminishing utility abnehmender Nutzen

A situation in which consumption of additional items of a good causes total utility to grow at an increasingly slower rate.

Dinks kinderlose Doppelverdiener, Ehepaare mit doppeltem Einkommen ohne Kinder

Also called dinkies.

Dinks = double/dual income, no kids.

A couple who are both wage earners and have no children, usually with a high level of disposable income. Thus, they are a highly sought after target group, particularly they are big buyers of luxury items and travel.

DIPADA DIPADA

A formula for creative selling. The dipada process has six steps: definition (D), identification (I), proof (P), acceptance (A), desire (D) and action (A).

Selling demands a careful definition of the customer's needs and desires (stage 1). After this follows the identification of these with the offer (stage 2). The identification leads naturally to proof (stage 3) and acceptance (stage 4), and then the salesperson finally creates such a strong desire to buy (stage 5) that he is able to close the sale with the customer's buying action (stage 6).

Direct channel direkter Absatzweg, Vertriebsweg

A distribution method where producers sell directly to final consumers; no middlemen/intermediaries are involved.

Direct close direkter (Verkaufs)Abschluß

In the selling process, a closing technique where the seller ends a sales talk straightforwardly, i.e. he simply asks the buyer for an order, e.g. by asking "How many will you buy?"

Direct competition direkte Konkurrenz

The activity of competitors who provide the same or similar products and services.

The competing firms.

Direct cost(s) direkte Kosten
Grenzkosten

The total of all the costs which are a direct part of the cost of a product. Direct costs include all items of cost other than overhead costs, e.g. direct materials, direct wages and direct expenses. Direct costs vary directly with the amount of work being done. Also called direct expenses, prime costs or variable costs.

Sometimes a synonym for marginal cost.

Direct costing Deckungsbeitragsrechnung
(Teilkostenrechnung)

Also called contribution analysis or costing, contribution margin accounting, marginal costing or variable costing.

In cost accounting, a method of producing a statement of variable costs which are directly attributable to a particular product. Fixed costs are excluded from the unit cost under this method.

Direct demand direkte Nachfrage

Demand for a product or service for its own sake, and not for what can be derived/obtained from it. Most consumer goods are produced and bought in order to satisfy a direct demand.

Direct dial(l)ing (Telefon)Durchwahl

Also called direct dial.

The making of a (tele)phone call without the assistance of an operator.

Direct distribution Produzentenhandel

Direct distribution involves selling directly to customers. This may be done directly from your home country or through a subsidiary or branch of your company overseas. Direct distribution can take many forms:
1. direct selling to end users; 2. direct selling to retailers or wholesalers; 3. direct selling to export merchants who buy from you at home and then export in their own rights.

Direct mail advertising (DMA) Post-/Direktversandwerbung, Direktwerbung durch die Post
Postwurfsendung

Also called direct mail, direct mailing, or (direct) mail shot.

Mailing of unsolicited advertisements (e.g. by means of brochures, circulars, fliers, letters, etc.) or any other promotional material by use of the postal service direct to selected customers or potential customers. It does not include hand-delivery or mail-drop door-to-door distribution. It is a means of selling goods by mail order. Use is made of mailing lists.

Advertising material (e.g. leaflets) sent by mail to every household. Also called bulk mail(ing), junk mail or unaddressed mail advertising.

Direct mail house Direktmarketingunternehmen

A firm which specializes in the supply of names and addresses of people who are likely to be interested in the purchase of various services or types of merchandise. Further services may include: preparation, design and printing of sales letters; addressing and despatch of letters; evaluation of the response obtained.

Direct marketing (DM) Direktabsatz, Direktverkauf

Also called direct sale or direct selling.

Selling directly from the producer to the end user (the final or ultimate consumer) without the use of any wholesaler, retailer or any other form of middleman/intermediary.

Direct marketing manufaturer Hersteller, der direkt an Endverbraucher verkauft

A manufacturer who sells directly to the ultimate consumer.

Direct product profitability (DPP) direkte Produktrentabilität

The profit on sale of a product after deducting the cost of the good and the expenses directly attributable to that specific product.

Note: applying the DPP enables a retailer to have a more optimal product mix and a better use of shop space.

Direct production Eigenproduktion, Selbstversorgung

The satisfying of a person's needs entirely by his own efforts, i.e. without help from any other person.

Goods created for immediate consumption.

Direct purchase Beziehungskauf, Direktbezug, Direkteinkauf

Also called direct buying or purchasing.

The buying of goods directly from the producer by bypassing the retail trade.

Direct question direkte Frage

In a questionnaire, a question which requires a specific response, ie either a Yes or a No answer, or a clear answer structured in a specific way.

Direct response (DR) Direktantwort, Echo auf Direktwerbeaktion

Marketing operations where the provider of goods or services seeks to generate sales through direct customer responses from press or TV advertising.

Direct response advertising | Antwortinserat; Werbung, die Umworbenen zu Antwort bzw. Reaktion veranlassen soll

Also called direct-action advertising, direct response marketing or direct response commercial.

Selling by means of press advertisements which invite a direct placement of orders. The advertising message is designed to urge the receiver to an immediate action, e.g. to return a coupon, make a phone call, inquiry or purchase.

Direct response selling | Einkauf/Verkauf durch Direkt/Sofortbestellung, Direct-Response-Verkauf

In retail trade, a system where customers order merchandise by telephone or mail and the seller despatches the goods directly to the customer's home. Thus, purchasing is made directly between the manufacturer or supplier and the customer. The offer of goods is made by means of direct mail and/or telephoning, by press, TV and radio advertising.

Direct response TV (DRTV) | Werbespots mit eingeblendeter Telefon-oder Faxnummer, so daß Zuschauer sofort Kontakt aufnehmen kann

A TV commercial inserting the telephone or fax number to enable the viewer to respond to the commercial immediately, e.g. to ask questions or place an order.

Direct services | Direktdienste

In most occupations workers cooperate to provide the final/ultimate consumer with the finished product. But in some occupations (e.g. doctors, teachers, police) the object is to offer a direct service to the community. These people have, of course, an indirect bearing on the production of goods.

Direct store delivery (DSD) | Lieferung frei Haus

Also called store door delivery.

The delivery of goods directly to the buyer`s door.

Delivery by a seller directly to a customer`s retail store.

Direct-action advertisement Kaufwerbung, auf direkte Reaktion(en) zielende Werbung

Advertisements designed to move consumers to take some immediate action, i.e. to buy a product or service.

Directions for use Gebrauchsanweisung, -anleitung

Also called directions.

Instructions explaining how to use a particular (usually technical or mechanical) product, eg a washing machine.

Director General of Fair Trading Leiter der Wettbewerbsaufsichtsbehörde (GB)

The head of the Office of Fair Trading. He exerts a tremendous influence on the conduct of retail trade and reviews the economic interests of the consumer.

Directory Adreßbuch
Telefonbuch
Branchenverzeichnis

A list of people or businesses with information about their addresses and telephone numbers. Also called address book.

A telephone directory. Also called telephone book or phone book.

A trade directory. Also called classified directory.

Directory advertising Adreßbuch-, Telefonbuchwerbung

Also called directory-type advertising.

Advertising that appears in a specialized directory (e.g. the Yellow Pages) classified according to some purpose.

Discharge Entladen, Ausladen, Löschen

The unloading of a vehicle.

Discontinuity Unterbrechnung

A situation which occurs when an established trend or pattern unexpectedly ceases to exist.

Discount (dis, disct) Skonto, Rabatt, Preisnachlaß

The amount deductible from the value of an invoice; there are various types of discount: eg cash discount, trade discount, quantity discount, etc.

Discount house Diskontgeschäft, Discounter

Also called discounter or discount store.

A retail business which sells (brandname) merchandise at a lower price than other retailers.

Discount period Skontofrist, Frist für Barzahlung

The period after a sale during which payment entitles the buyer to deduct any cash discount.

Discount piracy Diskontpiraterie

A situation where a customer takes unearned discount, i.e. he deducts a discount where he is not entitled to do so.

Discount table Diskonttabelle

A list accompanying a price list showing discounts for various prices and quantities.

Discount types Rabattarten

There are a number of different types of discount, eg:
1. annual discount, 2. annual volume discount, 3. bulk discount, 4. cash discount, 5. consecutive-weeks discount, 6. cumulative discount, 7. discount(s) allowed, 8. discount(s) received, 9. early order discount, 10. employee discount, 11. functional discount, 12. frequency discount, 13. jubilee discount, 14. promotional discount, 15. purchase discount, 16. quantity discount, 17. sales discount, 18. seasonal discount, 19. settlement discount, 20. special discount, 21. time discount, 22. trade discount, 23. vertical discount, etc.

Discount(s) allowed Kundenskonto (-skonti)

A business may allow its credit customers to pay less if they pay before a certain date. The discount allowed account shows on the debit side the amounts allowed during a financial period. The total amount is transferred to the profit and loss account as an expense.

Discount(s) received Skonto- (Skonti-), Diskonterträge

Also called discount(s) earned.

A business may receive a cash discount from its suppliers if it pays for its credit supplies before a certain date. The discount received account shows on the credit side the amounts received during a financial period. The total amount is transferred to the profit and loss account as income/revenue.

Discounter Discounter, Diskontwarenhaus

Also called discount house, discount store or discount warehouse.

A commercial retail or wholesale business with nearly no customer services selling goods directly to the public at keen (very low) prices.

Discretionary buying power frei verfügbare Kaufkraft

Also called discretionary spending power or purchasing power.

Amount of income left over after fixed regular outgoings have been paid and essential purchases have been made.

Discretionary goods | Nicht-Grundgüter, nicht lebensnotwendige Güter

Products other than clothing, food or shelter.

Discretionary income | frei verfügbares Einkommen

Also called disposable income.

The amount of money left over for household use after taxes and the purchase of necessities/necessaries.

Discretionary spending | Ausgaben zur freien Verfügung

The spending of money by a consumer on things which are not necessary, but which can be bought (or not) at his choice.

Discriminating monopoly | diskriminierendes Monopol

A situation where the sole seller (the monopolist) of a commodity charges different prices for it in different markets. A form of price discrimination.

Discrimination test | Unterscheidungstest

A product test designed to show how one product differs from a competitor's product.

Diseconomy | Kostenzunahme

Something that increases costs.

Disequilibrium | Ungleichgewicht, gestörtes Gleichgewicht

Also called imbalance.

A state of not being in equilibrium, e.g. an unbalanced state in an economy caused by changes in supply and demand or a balance of payments disequilibrium.

Dishoarding Enthorten (gehortetes Geld und zurückgehaltene Waren zirkulieren lassen) Lagerbestandsvermarktung

The opposite of hoarding. Money, stored goods and other valuables are brought back into circulation when the cause of the hoarding has passed away.

A company`s strategy of putting goods back onto the market when they have been hoarded or stored for some time or reason.

Disinflation Desinflation, dezelerierte Inflation

A mild form of deflation designed to slow down economic activity (e.g. by tax increases, cuts in government spending, high interest rates) without causing a severe depression.

Disparaging advertising herabsetzende Werbung

Advertising which criticizes and disparages a competitor's product or service.

Dispenser Verkaufsautomat stummer Verkäufer

A machine which automatically provides something, e.g. a drink or some food, often when money is inserted. Also called dispensing machine, vending machine or automatic vender.

Hanging cards from which small products can be pulled off or shelves from which products can be taken.

Dispersion theory Dispersionstheorie

The objective of some consumer goods companies to reach with their advertisement the maximum number of different, unduplicated units such as households in a particular interval of time.

Display — Aufstellung, Ausstellung von Waren, Warenauslage (Bildschirm)Anzeige

In retailing, an exhibition of merchandise, whether in store (in-store display) or in window (window display). Displays are arranged to catch the eye and attract attention in order to promote sales.
Note: manufacturers and retailers may have special display posters, stands, cards and other material designed for windows, counters, shelves, floors, etc.

Character or graphical displays on the surface of a video screen. When data is entered into a computer it is displayed on the screen.

Display advertisement — Großanzeige

Also called displayed advertisement.

Display advertising, i.e. advertising in a publication by using a large size.

Display advertising — Großanzeige, Großanzeigenwerbung

Also called display advertisement.

A large advertisement placed in a printed publication. In newspaper advertising, advertising that allows the advertiser to illustrate and explain his product or service so that he may attract the reader's attention. Also called full page advertisement. If the ad is placed in the centre of the publication, it is called centre-spread advertisement.

Freestanding advertisement which is exhibited in traffic areas.

Display allowance — Ausstellungsnachlaß, -rabatt, Displayvergütung

An allowance granted by a producer to a retailer in return for a display of the product in the retailer`s store, on the shelf or in the shop window.

Display article — Ausstellungsstück

Also called exhibit or showpiece.

A product exhibited/displayed, for example in a display cabinet or in a showroom, to show it to potential customers.

Display bin Auslagenbehälter, -kiste, Warenbehälter

Also called dump bin or dumper.

An open container containing merchandise which the customers can handle and examine before a purchase will result.

Display cabinet Auslagekasten, Schaukasten, Vitrine

Also called display case.

A type of cupboard or container with glass panels which businesses use to show their goods in the best way.

Display case Musterkoffer Ausstellungsvitrine, Schaukasten

A portable case carried by a salesperson and opened to show the merchandise within to customers. Also called sample bag.

A display cabinet.

Display outer Auslagekarton

Also called display carton or dispenser pack.

Carton containing small item goods, which can be opened and folded back so that the lid becomes a display, and the product is sold from the open carton.

Display pack Schaupackung, Auslagepackung, Präsentationspackung

Also called display box or display package.

Pack which, in addition to performing a packaging function, also serves as a means of displaying the product at the point of sale (POS).

Display position Auslagenposition

The position in which display material, e.g. display posters, appears in the retailer`s premises. The most desirable positions, from the point of view of achieving the greatest impact, may differ from shop to shop.

Favoured positions, for example, are: 1. the shop window, 2. the counter top, 3. the floor area close to the counter, 4. the shelves behind the counter, 5. areas close to the till, 6. aisles, etc.

Display stand Auslagenstand

Also called display unit.

A special stand which shows goods for sale.

Disposable income (DI) verfügbares Einkommen
Nettoeinkommen

The amount of money left to us after the necessaries/essentials of life have been paid for. Also called discretionary income.

ncome less tax payments. Also called net income, net earnings, income or receipts; earnings net of tax; residual income; or take-home income or pay.

Disposable pack(aging) Einwegverpackung

Also called non-returnable pack(aging).

A pack which can be thrown away when emptied.

Disposable personal income (DPI) verfügbares persönliches Einkommen

The amount of income available to households after payment of personal income taxes and social contributions.

Disposable product Wegwerfprodukt, Einwegware

A product designed for or capable of being thrown away after being used or used up, e.g. a plastic cup.

Disposables Wegwerfgüter

Articles designed for or capable of being thrown away after being used or used up.

Dissaving Entsparen, negative Ersparnis (Überschuß der Verbrauchsausgaben über die verfügbaren Einnahmen)

Also called negative saving.

Consumption in excess of income. Consumption financed out of wealth (e.g. savings) or by borrowing. Spending exceeds current income.

Distance freight Distanz-, Fernfracht

Freight charged on the distance over which the goods are transported.

Distant markets entfernt gelegene Märkte

These are markets which are further away form the home market. Usually, they are more costly to serve and more difficult to manage and control.

Distinctive competence Unterscheidungskompetenz

A company`s advantage over its competitors.

Distress merchandise Ware zu stark herabgesetzten Preisen

Goods sold at heavily reduced prices because they are or soon will be past the point where they can be sold at anything close to normal prices.

Distress sale Notverkauf

Also called emergency sale, fire sale, forced or panic sale; distress marketing or selling; or bailout.

The sale of goods at substantially low prices (distress merchandise) in a situation of emergency.

Distribution — Vertrieb, Distribution

The movement of raw materials to the places of production.

The allotment of goods by producers among consumers.

Distribution agent — Vertriebsunternehmen/r

Also called distributing agency.

Someone who combines the services of a commission agent with the carrying of stocks of the product and arranging for their physical distribution to the customers in his territory.

Distribution center — Absatzzentrum

A center/centre that has as its primary purposes the consolidation of shipments from different production points and the processing of orders and the shipment of products to customers.

It may be operated by retailers, wholesalers, manufacturers, or distribution specialists, and may also deal with the receipt, storage and redistribution of goods.

Distribution channel — Absatz-, Vertriebsweg

Also called channel of distribution, chain of distribution, distribution chain, distributive channel, marketing channel, sales chain or channel, or trade channel.

This term refers to the system of marketing institutions through which goods or services are transferred from the original producers to the end/ultimate users or consumers. The traditional route for consumer goods from the producer to the consumer, involving the commercial services provided by transport and warehousing, usually is:
producer → wholesaler → retailer → consumer.

Other patterns of distribution are:

- The producer sells all his goods to a wholesaler, the wholesaler sells direct to the consumers.
- The producer bypasses the wholesalers and sells to the retailers direct.
- The producer sells direct to the consumers.

The distribution method depends upon many factors; e.g.: the nature of the product, the scope of the market it is intended to penetrate, etc.

Distribution cost analysis Vertriebskostenanalyse

This concerns the distribution of goods and is the analysis of the differences of cost involved when various ranges of goods are distributed in different ways.

Distribution cost(s) Absatz-, Vertriebskosten

Also called distribution expense(s).

Costs (e.g. packing and transport) associated with transferring (distributing) goods from a supplier to the customer.

Distribution depot Auslieferungslager

A depot which is used as a reception point for merchandise, and from which the products are reforwarded to their final destination(s).

Distribution gap Vertriebslücke

Part of the market not yet reached by outlets or agents.

Distribution list Verteilerliste, Verteiler

Also called mailing list.

A notification stating the names of persons or departments who are to obtain a copy of a letter. The notification may read copies to: ..., or distribution or more commonly cc: (copies circulated to...). The list of those circulated should then follow.

Distribution management Vertriebsmanagement

The decision-making process of evolving the most ideal and acceptable method of distributing goods to (international) markets. Factors which feature prominently in the choices made include efficiency and quality of service.

The selection of the most acceptable channel of distribution will vary by circumstances. It will particularly involve cost, profitability, efficiency, volume of business, nature of cargo, value of cargo, loadability, transport mode options, transit times, timescale of cargo shipments, infrastructure in the seller's/exporter's and buyer's/importer's market, level of competition, potential of growth, distance of the market, distribution costs from the seaport or airport to the buyer's premises, sea and airport handling charges, import/export regulations, import/export documentation, exchange risks, economic and political risks, the shipper's profile, etc.

Distribution mix Distributionsmix

The particular combination of channels of distribution through which a producer distributes his products at any point of time.

Distribution network Vertriebsnetz

The number of points or warehouses from which goods are distributed.

Distribution planning Distributionsplanung, Vertriebsplanung

A systematic decision making which concerns/involves the physical movement of goods from producer to consumer and the transfer of ownership of these goods.

Distribution research Vertriebsforschung

This consists of: 1. channel research (this can help a company decide which channels to use for distribution of its produts) and 2. location research (concerns decisions about warehousing, inventory, and transportation).

Distribution structure Vertriebsstruktur

The methods and routes by which a producer's product reaches the consumer.

Distribution theory Verteilungstheorie

This theory refers to the sharing of the national income among the factors of production (land, labour, capital and enterprise). That means, the theory seeks to explain how the wealth created by production is distributed among various people having a claim on it: the workers, landlords, savers of money capital and the entrepreneurs.

Distribution(s) manager Vertriebsleiter

A company manager who is in charge of warehousing, transportation, order processing, distribution channels, dealer relations, etc.

Distribution-based pricing vertriebsorientierte Preisbildung

A pricing strategy designed to cover the costs associated with the shipment of goods to distant customers.

Distributive trade(s) Absatzwirtschaft (z.B. Groß- und Einzelhandel, Verteilergewerbe)

Also distribution system or marketing system.

The distributive trade provides the connecting link between producers and consumers. This is achieved through the commodity markets, wholesalers and retailers.

Distributor (Zwischen)Händler, Vertragshändler
Auslieferer, Verteiler
Grossist, Großhändler
Filmverleiher

A business which contracts to buy a firm's goods and services, and sells to third parties. An intermediary/middleman between producer and customer. Where the business is the only seller in a particular area, it is called sole distributor.

In transport terms, a business involved in distribution of merchandise.

A wholesaler who distributes the products to retailers.

Someone who distributes films.

Distributor brand Händlermarke

Also called middleman brand, own brand, private brand, private label or store brand.

A brand name owned and controlled by a reseller, e.g. a retailer or other distributor rather than by a manufacturer. A manufacturer sells the product to middlemen who give it a private brand. Note: the term applies only to the brand, not to the product or its contents.

Districentre Vertriebszentrum

A distribution centre run by transport operators which provides a total transportation service package geared to individual manufacturers and their customers' needs.

District manager Bezirksdirektor

A manager with responsibilities for a company's activities within a particular region or district.

Disutility negativer Nutzen

Also called negative utility.

The loss of satisfaction/utility resulting from having too much of a thing.

Divergent marketing getrenntes Marketing

A company`s marketing strategy to treat each of its products separately.

Diversification Diversifikation, Diversifizierung
Sortimentserweiterung, Diversifikation der Tätigkeit
Streuung der Anlagepalette

Expansion of a firm into an unrelated industry, i.e. large companies take over businesses with which they have nothing in common. The company extends its range of products and its activities. The intention is risk-spreading. Also called branching out or conglomerate merger.

Diversification also implies extending beyond the existing field of business, e.g. introduction of new products into existing markets (diversification of lines), or of existing products into new markets (diversification of activity).

The spreading of investments among different companies in different fields (diversification of investment).

Diversified growth diversifiziertes Wachstum

The growth of a company by diversification, i.e. sales are increased by introducing new products into new markets.

Divestiture Entflechung (Kartellgesetz)

In a merger/amalgamation, the sale of a company to meet the requirements of the antitrust laws.

Divestment Entflechtung (Kartellgesetz)
Veräußerung
Abstoßen, Ausgliederung

Also called devestiture.

Transfer of the ownership and control of part of a firm's activities to another, independent firm to meet the requirements of the antitrust laws. Also called break-up, demerger or trust-busting.

The selling of a part of a company.

The elimination of unprofitable products to achieve rationalisation of the product range.

DIY goods Heimwerkerbedarf

Also called do-it-yourself goods.

Goods produced for the do-it-yourself market and sold in a DIY store.

Do-it-yourself (DIY) store Heimwerkerladen

A large store specializing in selling materials for the repair, improvement and building of flats/apartments and houses, etc.

Docket Etikett
Warenbegleitschein

A short summary of contents attached to the outside of a packet. Also called label, tag or ticket.

A list of goods delivered.

Dog Produkt mit geringem Marktanteil und schwachem Wachstum ("armer Hund")
Produkt mit geringen Marktchancen

A product that has a low growth rate and a low market share. The opposite is a star.

A product with low market/sales prospects but retained in production for sentimental reasons.

Domestic appliances Haushaltsgeräte

Also called household appliances.

Devices/gadgets which are used in the household, e.g. dishwashers.

Domestic demand Binnennachfrage

Also called home or internal demand.

A country`s (eg Australia`s or Germany`s) or an economic union`s (eg the European Union`s) demand for goods and services, whether produced at home or abroud.

Domestic market Binnen-, Inlandsmarkt

Also called home, inland, internal or national market.

A country's home market.

Domestic marketing Inlandsmarketing

A company`s markteting efforts in its home country.

Domestic trade Binnenhandel

Also called home, local, inland or internal trade.

Trade which takes place within the country and which plays a paramount and critical role in the country`s economy. It relates to the purchase and sale of goods within the country and encompasses two important areas: 1. the retail trade, and 2. the wholesale trade.

Dominant firm marktbeherrschendes Unternehmen

A company that maintains a qualifying market share and exercises considerable market power in determining the supply terms of a product or service (e.g. smaller rivals comply with its prices).

Donation Schenkung, Spende

An asset or an amount of money given by one person (the donor) to another (the donee) without cost as a gift.

Donor market Spendermarkt

A market where the target audience is asked to donate money, goods, body organs, blood, etc to an organisation without receiving something in return.

Door drop Wurfsendung

The delivery of promotional material (e.g. leaflets or folders) by hand to each household in a specific area.

Door opener Werbegeschenk

An inexpensive gift given by a salesperson to a customer or prospect to gain his/her attention.

Door to door Haustürverkauf, Verkauf an der Haustür
Haus-zu-Haus-Lieferung

Practice of direct selling by calls upon households. Also called door-to-door sale or selling, doorstep selling, house-to-house sale or selling.

Transport service from the sender/consignor to the consignee/receiver. Also called door-to-door delivery or house-to-house delivery.

Door to door interview Zuhausebefragung

Also called in-home interview.

An interview made at an interviewee`s home. This interview method is often used because it eliminates group influence and offers a clear advantage when thoroughness of self-disclosure is important. In an in-depth interview of 45 to 90 minutes, interviewees/respondents can be probed to reveal their real aspirations, behaviours, feelings and motivations.

Door to door salesman Hausierer

Also called door-to-door peddler/pedlar.

A person who sells to the customer at his own front door.

Double coincidence Bedürfniskoinzidenz

A condition in a transaction in which each party wishes to trade exactly what the other party is offering in exchange.

Double page spread (DPS) doppelseitige Anzeige

Also called double spread, double, or two-page spread.

In advertising, two facing pages in a magazine or newspaper, used as if they were one single sheet.

Double pricing doppelte (irreführende) Preisauszeichnung

A method of showing two prices on a product in order to mislead consumers and make them believe that there has been a price reduction.

Double spotting Nacheinandersenden von zwei Werbespots

The broadcasting of two commercials one after the other.

Downpayment/down payment Anzahlung

Also called advance, first or initial payment, deposit, downpay, payment on account or prepayment.

A first/initial payment of the purchase price; often in connection with a hire purchase transaction/instalment sale.

Downsizing Downsizing, Verkleinerung, Miniaturisierung

An act of cutting back or eliminating levels, units, groups, or indivduals in an organisation.

Reducing the size of a business to meet a new, lower demand level.

Downswing Konjunkturabschwung, Flaute

Also called downward swing, downturn, contraction, decline in economic activity, or slump.

The phase of the trade cycle (business or economic cycle) during which business activity is falling, prices are declining, and unemployment is rising.

Downtown Geschäftsviertel, Innenstadt

The central business district (CBD) of a town.

Downward sloping demand curve fallende Nachfragekurve

A demand curve or line sloping downwards from left to right indicating that when the price of a good is raised, less of it is demanded; when the price is lowered, however, more of the good is demanded.

Downward stretching Produkterweiterung in den Niedrigpreisbereich, Produkterweiterung "nach unten"

The introduction of a new product into a product line at the lower priced end of the market.

Dozen (dz) Dutzend

A group of twelve or something containing 12 parts.

Note: a baker`s dozen is a dozen plus an extra unit as a kind of bonus to the buyer.

Draft (dft) Zahlungsanweisung
Entwurf, Konzept

A written order for the payment of money. Also called instruction or order to pay.

The first rough writing of anything; a rough plan. In GB also called draught.

Draw Kassenerfolg, Kassenschlager

Also called box office draw or hit.

A popular and successful entertainment attracting paying audiences and thus making a good profit.

Drip Tröpfelkampagne (Werbung)

An advertising campaign over a relatively long period of time despite a limited advertising budget.

Drip mat Getränkeunterlage, Abtropfmatte

Also called coaster.

A mat made of card, cork or metal for standing drinks on. They are used by brewers and other drinks producers because they are useful for POS advertising.

Drive Elan, Schwung

An energetic, eager, enthusiastic, vigorous and motivated way of working.

Drive time (Spitzen)Zeit, bei der Autofahrer Radio hört

A time segment in the daypart of a radio station when the majority of the audience are people listening to car radios on their way to or from work.
There are two drive times: 1. the morning drive, generally from 6:00 a.m to 10:00 a.m.; 2. the afternoon/evening drive, generally from 3:00 p.m. to 7:00 p.m.

Drive-in Drive-in

A place, e.g. a bank, restaurant or cinema where you can drive in in a car and withdraw money from your account, eat while sitting in the car or watch the film.

Drop Rückgang

A decline, e.g. in orders, earnings, output, sales, prices, profits, etc.

Drop shipment business Streckengeschäft

A business transaction where a drop shipper/desk jobber sells a product and arranges for the manufacturer to ship directly to the customer on the agreed terms and time of delivery. The drop shipper does not carry inventory or handle the product, but he assumes title and risk from the time the order is accepted to its delivery to the customer.

Drop shipper Großhändler für Streckengeschäft, Grossist ohne eigenes Lager

Also called desk jobber.

A wholesaler who takes bulk orders from customers and then orders the desired products from manufacturers who ship directly to the customers.

Drug in/on the market Ladenhüter

Also called shelf warmer or cats and dogs.

A commodity which is unsaleable, often because of an excess supply.

Drum zylindrischer Container, Trommel

A cylindrical container, usually made of metal or plastic, but sometimes wood or strong cardboard, for transporting liquids, powders, paint, chemicals, etc.

Dry goods Textilwaren
Trockenware

In the USA, fabrics, textiles, clothing and related materials. Also called drapery.

In GB, sometimes dry foodstuffs such as corn and other grains, coffee, sugar and tea.

Dry port Container-Bahnstation

A rail terminal located in an inland industrial and/or commercial area providing a direct link with one or more container ports.

Dual adaptation doppelte, duale Anpassung

A global marketing strategy whereby both the product and the promotional activities are adapted to foreign market conditions.

Dual distribution channel dualer Absatzweg

A company`s strategy to appeal to different market segments or to diversify business by selling through two or more separate channels.

Due date (d/d) Fälligkeits-, Verfall-, Erfüllungstag

Also called maturity date.

The date on or by which a bill, an invoice or a liability must be paid.

Due diligence gebührende, verkehrsübliche Sorgfalt

Also called customary or ordinary negligence.

The customary degree of care and caution expected of a person, especially as party to a contract.

Dues (Mitglieds)Beiträge
Gebühren, Abgaben

The sum of money paid, or to be paid, for membership. Also called contributions or subscriptions.

Money due for services. Any charges made, e.g. by port authorities (e.g. dock dues, port dues). Also called fees.

Dummy Strohmann
erster flüchtiger Entwurf, "Türke"
Nullnummer, Aufmachungsmuster
Schaufensterpuppe
Versuchspuppe

A person whose name is used in a sales transaction in order to hide the name of the actual principal. Also called strawman.

Simplified representation of a package or other promotional item.

A preliminary layout for a printed piece, such as an advertisement, booklet, brochure, poster, or other printed material, prepared prior to printing and showing the characteristics of its design. Also called mockup.

A representation of a human figure, as for displaying clothes in shop windows.

A model which looks like a person and which is used for safety and technical tests.

Dummy pack(age) Attrappe, Leerpackung,
Schaupackung

An empty pack(age) for display only, e.g. in a shop window.

Dump bin Wühlkorb

A container or large box which is filled with low-priced goods for sale. The merchandise in the display bin is dumped rather than stacked.

Dumping Preisunterbietung, Dumping

A severe price-cutting in order to force competitors out of the market.

Selling by a company of a surplus production to non-regular customers at a lower price than the regular/steady customers are charged.

In international trade, the selling of goods in foreign markets at lower prices than in home/domestic markets. Often the price does not cover the full cost of production, i.e. the goods are sold at a loss. Dumping may be practised in order to earn foreign exchange, to respond to a domestic recession or to use a longer-term strategy to penetrate foreign markets. Once a foothold has been gained, prices are raised to yield a profit. The practice of dumping is viewed as unfair trade and is prohibited by international trade agreements. It represents serious competition to the importing country which may take protective measures to cancel the price advantage.

Dunnage Packmaterial

Wood, mats, etc. used to facilitate stowage of cargo.

Duopoly Duopol

A market situation where there are only two suppliers of similar products. The two firms sell to a large number of consumers who are unable to affect the market price of the commodities and therefore cannot keep the market competitive.

Duopsony Duopson, Nachfrage-Duopol

A market situation with only two buyers. The opposite of duopoly.

Duplicated audience dupliziertes Publikum

The audience, i.e. listeners, viewers, readers, produced by duplication of media. This audience is reached more than once by the same advertisement or commercial appearing in different media.

Durables (langlebige) Gebrauchsgüter, Wirtschaftsgüter

Also called durable (consumer) goods or consumer durables.

Goods in the hands of the final ultimate/consumer that can be used again and again over a period of time (e.g. furniture).

Dust cover Buchhülle

Also called dust jacket.

A detachable paper cover or jacket in which a new book is normally issued and which often contains information about the book or its author.

Dutch auction Abschlagsauktion (Holländische Auktion, Versteigerung)

A form of auction. The auctioneer commences with a high price, and gradually reduces it until an offer/bid is made. There is no outbidding as in normal auctions. Note: US Treasury bills are sold under this system.

Duty free shop zollfreier Laden

A retail shop where goods are sold free of customs duties. Therefore the selling price may be fixed at a lower level. Most often located at air or seaports.

Duty of care Sorgfaltspflicht

Also called duty to take care.

A legal obligation which means that individuals or companies must not be negligent when dealing with others.

Duty-free goods zollfreie Waren

Also called uncustomed goods.

Goods that are not liable to customs duty.

Dwell time Anstehzeit, Wartezeit, Warteschlangenzeit

The amount of time customers spend on lining up/queuing.

E

E-term E-Klausel

One of the four different categories of the Incoterms (1990), the others being the C-terms, the D-terms and the F-terms.

The E-term is EXW (ex works).

Its main characteristics are:
1. it is the only term whereby the seller fulfils his obligation to deliver when he has made the goods available to the buyer at his premises;
2. the seller is not responsible for clearing the goods for export and import;
3. the buyer bears all costs and risks involved in moving the goods from the seller`s premises to a specific destination;
4. the term represents the minimum obligation for the seller.

Eagerness to buy Kauflust (Kaufbereitschaft)

Also called disposition, inclination or propensity to buy or purchase.

The tendency or willingness in human beings to buy/purchase. This is the basis of demand; it influences the price of a commodity.

Ear Titelboxanzeige, Eckplatzanzeige auf der Titelseite einer Zeitung

In advertising, the space next to the masthead on either corner at the top of a newspaper's front page.

Early adopter früh Akzeptierender, früh Nachvollziehender

A person who tries a new product early in its life cycle without waiting for its acceptance by a large number of people.

Note: early adopters follow innovators and precede the early majority.

Early cash recovery schneller Bargeldrückfluß

The rapid recovery of cash. A pricing objective which can be very beneficial especially for a small firm particularly in periods of high interest rates. Frequently, long term sales and profits must give way to the more immediate problem of economic survival. In this case, you can establish a lower price on one or more of the firm's products that will result in a rapid recovery of cash.

Early closing früher Ladenschluß

A situation where shops close by 13:00 hours on one weekday.

Early closing day Tag, an dem die Geschäfte nachmittags geschlossen sind

The weekday when most shops in a (smaller) town close in the afternoon.

Early fringe Spätnachmittagsendezeit, frühe Abendsendezeit

Also called early evening time or early off-peak.

On television, the airtime between 5:00 and 7:30 pm.

Early majority frühe Mehrheit (bei Einführung neuer Produkte)

Also called early followers.

People who adopt a new product only after it has been accepted by a large number of people, i.e. after it has become socially acceptable. The early majority like to await the outcome of product trial by the two earlier groups - the early adopters and the innovators.

Note: the early majority are faster in adopting a new product than the two next groups - the late majority and the laggards.

Early markdown frühe Preissenkung

A strategy to mark down prices early in the season or while the demand for the merchandise is still relatively active.

Early morning time Sendezeit am frühen Morgen

Also called early morning or breakfast.

On television, the airtime between 7:00 and 9:00 o`clock.

Early order discount Frühdispostionsrabatt

A discount granted to someone who orders a product immediately after receipt of the offer or at least within a certain period thereafter.

Early season Vorsaison

The time period preceding one of the four periods of the year - spring, summer, autumn, and winter. During an early season, many products or services are sold at reduced prices.

Earmark Merkmal, Kennzeichen

A distinctive mark or feature.

Earned income realisierter, verdienter Gewinn

Also called realized gain or profits, or earned revenue.

The profits received for goods or services delivered.

Earnest (money) Draufgeld
Draufgabe

Also called bargain money or token payment.

When making a contract, the amount of money given by a buyer to a seller to bind a bargain made orally. Also called forfeit money.

The extra quantity granted to the quantity agreed in the sales contract. Also called boot money.

Easy listening (EL) leichte Unterhaltungsmusik

A form of light music, often serving as background music, e.g in supermarkets.

Easy terms günstige Bedingungen

Also called reasonable terms.

A phrase stating that payment may be effected in small instal(l)ments and at reasonable terms.

Ecological forces ökologische Kräfte

Increasing pressures on companies relating to the protection and preservation of the natural environment. Forces to avoid ecological unconcern.

Ecology Ökologie

The advocacy of protection of the quality of the natural environment, e.g. the air, water, etc. from pollution or its effects. Many consumers are discontent with the traditional methods of disposal of waste products, the littering of the environment, the level of ozone in the air, the amount of pollution in the water, etc.

Economic activity Wirtschaftstätigkeit

The activities and interactions of economic performers, e.g. producers, labour and consumers. It has its origins in the wants of a community and its main purpose is the satisfaction of those wants. Activities include: production, consumption, exchange and distribution of goods and services.

The economic activity of any person or entity.

Economic behaviour wirtschaftliches Verhalten

The economic reaction, movement or trend to a specific economic policy or policies, e.g. in a particular area or industry.

Economic climate Konjunkturklima

Also called business climate.

The persisting state of an economy apparent in its general trends over a specific period of time.

Economic competition wirtschaftliche Konkurrenz

Economists recognize four basic models of competition:
1. monopoly (one firm controls the output and price of a product for which there are no close substitutes);
2. monopolistic competition (a relatively large number of suppliers offer similar but not identical products);
3. oligopoly (a small number of firms dominate the market for a good or service);
4. pure competition (a large number of sellers market a standardized product to a group of buyers who are well informed about the marketplace).

Note:
1. these models are mainly based on the number of competitors and the nature of the products produced.
2. the type of competition has a great effect on pricing strategies (e.g. in monopolistic competition no firm can raise prices much higher than the prices charged by competitors).

Economic consultancy Wirtschaftsberatungs-Unternehmen

An enterprise whose employees (economic consultants) provide economic advice for a fee.

Economic crisis Wirtschaftskrise

A state of economic and financial problems in a country or particular region.

Economic development Konjunkturverlauf

The course of a country's economic activity.

Economic efficiency Wirtschaftlichkeit, ökonomische Effizienz

Also called economic effectiveness or operational efficiency.

Economic efficiency relates overall input costs to output values. The lower the cost per unit of output, without sacrifice of standard of quality, in relation to the value or price of the finished product, the greater the economic efficiency.

Economic environment wirtschaftliche Einflußfaktoren

The key factors in a company`s economic environment are the nature and extent of competition, growth rates, living standards, tax rules, market opportunities, infrastructure, legal regulations, etc.

Economic expansion Wirtschaftswachstum

An economy characterized by positive growth rates and a high degree of economic activity.

Economic expectations wirtschaftliche Erwartungen

People`s anticipation of the way the economy is likely to develop in the future. For example, firms will not invest if they believe they will not get an adequate return; consumers will not buy enough goods, whatever the price level, if they believe that they might lose their jobs.

Economic forecast(ing) Wirtschafts-, Konjunkturprognose

Also called economic predictions.

The process of making predictions about future general economic and market conditions. Every unit in the economy makes some sort of forecast of important economic trends over the next few months. It is generally true that the smaller the unit the easier the forecast.
The problems facing those who seek to forecast the trends of the whole economy are complicated. There are two particular problems: the first difficulty is that any forecast has to be based on existing data, and the existing data are out of date and not necessarily absolutely reliable. The second difficulty is that predictions are often unreliable because the variables consist of millions of independent decisions which customers and clients make daily.

Economic freedom wirtschaftliche Freiheit

The right of individuals to pursue self-interest, to maximize income and material satisfaction, to choose one's occupation, to select and buy whatever goods or services are available, etc. Additionally, producers must have the right to open or end a business, to produce or sell goods and services, to employ people, to maximize profit, etc. It is an important feature of a free enterprise economy.

Economic good Wirtschaftsgut

Also called asset or (economic) commodity.

Any commodity or service which must be paid for in money in a monetary economy. Due to their limited supply economic goods (consumers' goods and producers' goods) present economic problems with regard to their production and distribution.

Economic growth Wirtschaftswachstum

Also called expansion of business activity.

The rate of expansion in the annual volume of production of goods and services achieved by a country from period to period. Usually a rise in the gross domestic product (GDP) at constant prices or an annual increase in gross national product (GNP) is regarded as indicating economic growth.
Growth may be measured by a variety of criteria, such as per capita improvement in living standards, growth in investment, etc.

Economic indicator Konjunktur-Kennziffer, Konjunktur-Indikator

Also called business cycle indicator.

Statistics which are sensitive to activities, changes and movements in the state of the economy. Such indicators include: the Wholesale Price Index (WPI), the Retail Price Index (RPI), statistics of unemployment, wage rates, terms of trade, industrial output, imports, exports, consumer spending, bankruptcies, stock indices, industrial production, etc. The measurements may be used to determine overall economic trends.

Economic instruments Instrumente der Wirtschaftspolitik

Also called economic tools or weapons.

In seeking to achieve the objectives of economic policy (eg economic growth, stable prices) a government can use a number of instruments which can be classified broadly as follows: direct controls, fiscal policy, monetary policy, and exchange rate policy.

Economic law ökonomisches Gesetz

An economic law is a generalisation which tries to explain relationships between certain phenomena, e.g. price and demand. An economic law is often prefaced by the phrase "other things being equal" (ceteris paribus).

Economic liberalism Wirtschaftsliberalismus

The doctrine which advocates the greatest possible use of markets and competition.

Economic life (wirtschaftliche) Nutzungsdauer

Also called effective, operating, service, serviceable, useful or working life.

The period over which a fixed asset or device works efficiently or profitably. Note: the physical life of an asset may be considerably longer than its economic life.

Economic loss Vermögensschaden
wirtschaftlicher Schaden

A loss of or damage to property. Also called actual loss.

A situation in which a producer/manufacturer does not earn the level of profit that would justify remaining in business.

Economic man homo oeconomicus, "der Wirtschaftsmensch" (der Mensch als wirtschaftliches Wesen)

A person who is completely rational in satisfying his wants, is always seeking the greatest reward at the least possible cost and who pays no regard to the interests or influences of others.

Economic marketing factors wirtschaftliche Marketingfaktoren

In addition to social, demographic, technological, political and competitive factors, marketing managers must understand and react to the economic environment.

The three economic marketing factors of greatest concern are:
1. the distribution of income (the higher the disposable income the more people can afford),
2. inflation (real wages and hence purchasing power go up when inflation stays down),
3. recession (when income, production, and employemnt fall, demand will fall, too).

Note: the problems of inflation and recession go hand in hand, yet recession requires different marketing strategies.

Economic model ökonomisches Modell

A simplified reconstruction of the economy based upon a stated set of assumptions. These models are used in teaching and in assessing the likely impact of economic decisions and policies.

Economic obsolescence wirtschaftliches Veralten

Obsolescence due to causes other than wear and tear. There is a loss in the value of an asset.

Economic order quantity (EOQ) optimale Bestellmenge, Losgröße

Also called economic lot size (ELZ), optimum lot quantity or optimum order quantity (OOQ).

That quantity of raw materials or items for direct resale which minimises the total cost of ordering and stocking. The quantity is regularly used and is usually ordered at regular intervals.

The minimum order value producing a profit for a supplier.

Economic planning Wirtschaftsplanung

The planning done by individuals or firms to achieve some economic goal.

The term is often restricted to state planning; e.g. the government controls output, price and wage determination or stimulates certain economic activities through taxation or monetary policy.

Economic policy Wirtschafts-, Konjunkturpolitik

Also called economic strategy.

A governments's strategy to achieve its economic objectives. The four principal aims of economic policy for all modern governments are:
1. economic growth, 2. full employment, 3. stable prices (i.e. no inflation) and
4. a balance of payments equilibrium (or surplus).
Furthermore the governments pursue: to improve the standard of living, to lessen economic inequality, to provide social security, and to maintain stability of the monetary unit.

Economic power Wirtschaftsmacht

A buyer or seller is said to have economic power if, by his own actions, he can influence the market price.

Economic price wirtschaftlicher Preis

From the manufacturer`s or supplier`s point of view, this is the lowest price he can charge if he wants to regain costs (both fixed and variable costs), and make a satisfactory profit.

Note: to achieve an economic price it may be necessary to cost very carefully the use of labour, raw materials and components.

Economic problem Wirtschaftsproblem

An economic problem deals with the allocation of scarce resources among competing ends. Economic problems arise because of scarcity; goods and income are scarce relative to wants: a choice must be made.

Economic process Wirtschaftsprozeß

The economic process consists of persons providing factors of production to firms in return for money incomes. The firms receive these factors of production, for which they pay; the firms produce goods and services whose total cost gives the money value of the total products produced; persons spend their incomes on the goods and services produced by the firms.

There are two flows in opposite directions: 1. a monetary flow (money flows from firms to persons and then from persons back to firms), and 2. a real flow (factors of production flow from persons to firms and then goods and services flow to persons).

Economic purchase quantity (EPQ) optimale Beschaffungsmenge

The quantity of items purchased for direct resale and minimizing the total cost of ordering and stocking.

Note: EPQ is used to distinguish between the economic order quantity (EOQ) of items that are purchased for direct resale and that of raw materials for goods to be manufactured within a company.

Economic report Konjunktur-, Wirtschaftsbericht

Also called market report.

A report to show the current economic position of a country.

Economic resources ökonomische Ressourcen

The factors of production: land, labour, capital and entrepreneurship.

Economic shopper wirtschaftlich denkender Kunde

Shoppers who try to maximize the ratio of utility and money spent.

Economic system Wirtschaftsordnung, -system

Also called economic structure.

The economic principles, laws and attitudes of a country. The particular economic system of any country will depend upon who owns its wealth (e.g. the means of production), the individual or the State, and who undertakes the entrepreneurial function.
There are some basic types of system:
1. free enterprise (laisser-faire) (there is free trade and market competition), 2. market economy (allocation, production and prices of goods rely upon market forces, i.e. buyers and sellers, supply and demand), 3. planned economy (government planning dominates the direction of econommic activity), and 4. mixed economy (market forces and government intervention participate in economic activity).

Economic tailspin konjunkturelle Talsohle

The bottom of economic activity.

Economic tort unerlaubte wirtschaftliche Handlung

In law, a name for various types of conduct by a tortfeasor aimed at causing damage to other companies.

Economic trading groups Wirtschaftsgemeinschaften

An association of countries, formed for the purpose of doing business together. One of the prime aims of these groups (e.g. ASEAN, NAFTA) is to remove trade restrictions (e.g. tariffs, quotas) amongst members.

Economic trend Konjunkturverlauf

Also called economic development.

The pattern of economic development for an industry, a region or a whole country.

Economic utility wirtschaftlicher Nutzen

The ability of a product or service to satisfy a customer's needs or wants.

Economic value to the customer (EVC) wirtschaftlicher Wert für den Kunden

The maximum price that will be paid by a customer who is fully informed about both the product and the corresponding offers from competitors.

Economic welfare Wirtschaftswohlstand

Those aspects of social welfare that can be measured by money. It means more, however, than material well-being. The economic welfare of people depends on the total volume of production (i.e. the size of the national income) and the distribution of the goods and services so produced among the people. If the volume of production increases more rapidly than the population there will be a rise in the average standard of living.

Economical use of resources sparsamer Ressourcenumgang

The using of resources as carefully and cost-effectively as possible.

Economies of scale Größenvorteile, Größendegression; Effektivitätszuwachs, Kostenersparnisse durch Erhöhung der Produktionskapazitäten

Also called scale economies.

Reduction of the costs of production of goods achieved by increasing the size of the producing entity and the quantity produced (the scale of the company's output is increased). Large firms, particularly those with high fixed costs, are able to take advantage of economies of scale, because increased output reduces the percentage of fixed costs to total costs. Economies of scale mean that as the scale of production is increased it is possible to improve the efficiency of factor inputs and so reduce the overall unit costs. As capital, labour, raw material and managerial inputs increase in scale overall costs fall. The potential for economies of scale is often the motive for mergers/amalgamations.
Economies of scale may be of two kinds - internal and external.

Economizer/economiser sparsamer, haushälterischer Mensch

A person trying to save money by intentionally reducing the amount that he/she is spending. When choosing among things that yield equal benefit, an economizer will select the cheapest option.

Economizing behaviour sparsames Verhalten

An individual`s behaviour to seek to accomplish an objective at the least possible cost. When choosing among things that yield equal benefit, an economizer will select the cheapest option.

Economy (econ) (Volks)Wirtschaft

The system of money, industry, production, distribution, producers, labour, consumers, etc in a particular country.

Economy drive Sparkampagne

A strong effort to save money, materials, resources, etc.

Economy size Groß-, Sparpackung

Also called bulk pack, catering or family size, or giant package.

A larger than usual size package in order to encourage an increase in consumption or to save costs (e.g. a hospital pack).

Ecosystem Ökosystem

Short for ecological system.

A system formed by the interaction of a community of organisms with its environment.

Edge of town location Stadtrandstandort

Firms away from the traditional central business district (CBD), i.e. firms located in the green fields close to outer ring roads and residential suburbs. In these areas rent is relatively low, sites are sufficient for large open-plan stores, the space needed to display stock and sell goods is obtainable and affordable, and large volumes of traffic can be attracted.

Editing Plausibilitätskontrolle

The critical checking of the results of a survey to confirm that data has been collected correctly and can now be published.

Edition (ed) Auflage, Ausgabe

Particular issue of a publication.

Editorial Leitartikel, Kommentar

Also called leader.

Leading article in a publication or broadcast presenting the opinion of the publishers or editors, or station owners or station managers.

Editorial ad redaktionell aufgemachte Anzeige

Also called advertorial, editorial advertisement or editorializing ad(vertisement).

An advertisement in a magazine or newspaper printed in such a way that it looks like an editorial/leading article or article.

Editorial alteration (EA) redaktionelle Änderung

A correction or change made by an editor.

Editorial copy redaktioneller Text

Also called editorial content or matter.

In a publication, all the printed material other than advertisements.

Editorial publicity redaktionelle Werbung

Space in a publication in which a company, product or service is discussed at the discretion of the editor.

Editorital mention Hersteller-/Produkterwähnung im redaktionellen Teil, Gratiserwähnung

Reference to a company or a product, favourable or otherwise, in the editorial columns of a publication.

Educational advertising belehrende Werbung

Advertising devoted to improving consumers' knowledge about a product or service; it involves some change in beliefs or attitudes, eg don`t drink and drive, safer sex.

Effect lag Wirkungsverzögerung

The time period between a change in policy and its intended result(s).

Effective cover wirksame Reichweite (Werbung)

Also called the 4 plus syndrome.

A situation where consumers of a target group will have seen the advertisement at least four times on average.

Effective demand (E) effektive, tatsächliche Nachfrage

Also called monetary demand.

Demand for consumer goods, services, investment goods and supported by the willingness and ability to pay, i.e. actual expenditure. E (effective demand) = C (consumption) + I (investment), i.e. E = C + I. Total effective demand determines the levels of output, income and employment. To an economist, demand is always effective demand.
Demand for a product or service is reflected in the demand curve/line.

Effectiveness Effektivität

In general, the extent to which a person or company attains their goals.

Effectiveness lag Wirksamkeitsverzögerung

The time it takes for an action to affect something, eg to increase sales.

The time it takes for government action to affect the economy.

Effector/effecter Ausführer/in, Vollbringer/in

A person or thing that effects something.

Efficiency Effizienz
Produktivität
Wirtschaftlichkeit
Rentabilität

The ability of a person or organization to work well, or to produce the desired result or the right work quickly or satisfactorily.

The relationship between scarce factor inputs and outputs of goods and services. Also called productivity.

The relationship between overall input costs and output values. Also called economic or operational efficiency.

The state of bringing profit. Also called profitability.

Efficiency rule ökonomisches Prinzip

Also called economic principle.

A principle that aims at achieving: 1. the maximum utility at given expenses or 2. a given utility at minimal expenses.

Ego Ego, Ich, Selbst

In general, the "I" or self of any person.

According to Sigmund Freud (1856-1939) one of the three dimensions of an individual`s psyche, the others being the ID and the superego.
The ego is the conscious, rational component of an individual`s psyche that experiences and reacts to the outside world and mediates between the demands of the ID and superego.

Note: in marketing, the ego, the ID and the superego are important as they help to explain people`s buying behaviours.

Eighty/twenty (80/20) rule — Achtzig/Zwanzig-Regel, 80/20 Regel

According to V. Pareto, the rule that a small percentage (20 %) of customers may account for a large percentage (80 %) of sales. See also Pareto's law.

Elastic demand — elastische Nachfrage

A situation where a given percentage change in price results in a greater percentage change in the quantity demanded. If the result is greater than 1 (> 1), that is, if the demand has changed to a greater extent than the price, the demand is elastic.

Elastic supply — elastisches Angebot

A situation in which a percentage increase in price attracts a greater percentage of goods and services offered to the market, i.e. the result is greater than 1 (> 1).

Elasticity — Elastizität

A measure of the percentage change in one variable (y) (i.e. the dependent variable) in respect of a percentage change in another variable (x) (i.e. the independent variable). Two common measures are the price elasticity of demand (elasticity of demand) and the income elasticity of demand.

Elasticity coefficient — Elastizitätskoeffizient

A measure of the degree of elasticity, calculated by dividing the percentage change in the quantity supplied or demanded by the percentage change in price. The coefficient is greater than 1 when supply or demand is elastic, less than 1 when supply or demand is inelastic, and equal to 1 when there is unitary elasticity.

Elasticity of demand (ED, Ed) — Elastizität der Nachfrage, Nachfrageelastizität

Also called demand elasticity or price elasticity of demand.

The law of demand states that a change in the price of a commodity will cause a change in the quantity demanded (e.g. when price falls, demand tends to expand and when price rises, demand tends to contract). Elasticity of demand relates to the extent to which a change in price will cause demand to change. Elasticity is therefore the degree of responsiveness of demand to price changes.

Elasticity of demand is calculated as follows:

$$\frac{\text{\% change in quantity demanded}}{\text{\% change in price}}$$

If the result is greater than 1 (> 1), that is, if the demand has changed to a greater extent than the price, the demand is elastic; if less than 1 (< 1), that is, the demand has changed to a lesser extent than price, the demand is inelastic. If the result is 1 then demand at that price is unitary.
The main factors which determine the elasticity for a given product at a given price are: its availability, the price of substitutes, the proportion of income spent on the good, the degree of necessity of the commodity, whether the good is a habit-forming product, etc.

Elasticity of demand ranges from perfectly inelastic demand to perfectly elastic demand.
Demand is perfectly (absolutely or completely) inelastic if the same quantity is demanded whatever the price (elasticity = 0).
Conversely, if demand is perfectly (infinitely) elastic, an infinitely small change in price results in an infinitely great change in demand; i.e. consumers cease to buy at all if price rises fractionally (elasticity = ∞, infinite).

Elasticity of expectation — Erwartungselastizität

A measure of the changes in prices of goods and changes in the quantitiy sold to the market stemming from expectations by consumers.

Elasticity of supply (ES, Es) — Angebotselastizität, Elastizität des Angebots

Also called supply elasticity.

The law of supply states that rising prices tend to expand supply, while falling prices tend to reduce it. Changes in supply are also evoked by changes in the state of demand. If the price of a good rises because of an increase in demand, then the supply extends.

Elasticity of supply is the degree of responsiveness of the supply of a commodity to changes in its price.
The formula for measurement is:

$$\frac{\text{\% change in quantity supplied}}{\text{\% change in price}}$$

If the result is greater than 1 (> 1), the supply is elastic; if less than 1 (< 1), the supply is inelastic; and if equal to 1, the elasticity is unitary.

'he factors affecting elasticity of supply are: the ease and the cost of attracting the ecessary extra factors of production in order to produce the extra supply, the time eriod involved, and the price of the commodity.

:lectric spectacular Lichtreklametafel

ı outdoor advertising, a large board on which the words and designs are formed by ghts.

:lectronic bulletin board elektronische Anzeigetafel

. computerized notice board on which users can leave messages for other users.

:lectronic data interchange (EDI) elektronischer Datenaustausch

:DI enables companies to communicate with their suppliers by exchanging messages etween computers.

:lectronic funds transfer (EFT) belegloser, elektronischer Zahlungsverkehr; EDV-Überweisungsverkehr

. system, developed in the USA, of automatic transfer of money transactions (from ne account to another) by electronic means, i.e. computer and telecommunications ystems. When paying for goods and services the customer inserts a personal plastic ard into an electronic device connected to a computer of the store's bank, which hecks the balance of his account, verifies his signature, debits his account and credits ıe account of the seller.

:redit transfers between financial institutions around the world are carried out by sing the Society for Worldwide Interbank Financial Telecommunications (SWIFT) etwork.

:lectronic funds transfer at he point of sale (EFTPOS) elektronischer Zahlungsverkehr in Verbindung mit einem POS-System (elektronische Abbuchung am Verkaufsortterminal, d.h.POS)

. system which allows the automatic transfer of money from a buyer to a seller of oods and services at the time and point-of-sale (POS). A method of paying for urchases with a plastic card which automatically debits the account of your choice vithout the need of a cheque or a credit card.

Electronic mail (E-mail, email) elektronischer Briefkasten/Briefverkehr, E-mail, elektronische Post

A high-speed transmission system for hardcopy messages from one location to anothe by means of computers with a printer at the receiving end. The message will be stored until the receiver chooses to read it.

Electronic media elektronische Medien

In general, electronic-based media, such as TV and radio.

Advertisements making use of neon signs or lights, and capable of movements by electric impulses.

Electronic point of sale (EPOS) Datenkasse, elektronischer Kassenterminal

The point in shops etc. where sales are charged automatically to a customer's bank account, and stock is controlled through the shop's computer at the same time.

Electronic point of sale (EPOS) system elektronisches Kassensystem

Also called computerized checkout system.

A system in which a cashier passes an item sold over or past an optical scanner readin product barcodes; then a computerized register instantly records and displays the sale.

EPOS systems enable firms to monitor exact consumer spending patterns, to prevent stock-outs and to have detailed sales data which add weight to negotiations with suppliers.

Electronic retailing elektronischer Einzelhandel, Einzelhandelsverkauf/-einkauf

Electronic retailing includes:
1. the twenty-four-hour shop-at-home television networks and 2. on-line retailing.

The shop-at-home television networks are specialized forms of direct reponse marketing. Special shows display merchandise, with the retail price, to home viewers. Viewers can phone in their orders directly on a toll-free line and shop with a credit card. These networks are able to reach every home that has a TV set.

)n-line retailing is a service offered to people with home computers and now includes ıe internet. It provides customers with a variety of information and shopping pportunities. Users buy the required hardware and software, pay a monthly fee, order ıe product directly from their computer screen and electronically transfer the proper mount of money from their bank account to the retailer`s.

lectronic shopping elektronischer Einkauf

'he buying of goods and services with a plastic card and the paying for the purchases ırough electronic funds transfer at the point of sale (EFTPOS).

)irect marketing through home computers, special television sets, the internet or elephones that link consumers with the seller`s (e.g. bank`s, producer`s, retailer`s, etc) omputerized catalogue by cable or telephone. Products can be compared, ordered and aid without leaving the home.

mbargo Embargo
Informationsstopp

n embargo prohibits the import or export of certain classes of goods, or the goods of particular country.

time period during which certain information in a press release must not be ublished.

mbryo (product) Produkt in der Entwicklungsphase

product in the development stage.

motional advertising emotionale, gefühlsbetonte Werbung

roduct advertising appealing to emotional desires rather than logic, economy or tility. It attempts to create moods that will subsequently be associated with the roduct or service. The opposite of rational advertising.

motional appeal gefühlsbetonter (Werbe)Appeal

n an effective advertising message one can distinguish three types of appeals:
. rational appeals, 2. moral appeals, 3. emotional appeals.

ositive or negative emotional appeals (e.g. humor, love, pride, joy, flar, guilt, shame, tc) attempt to stir up some positive or negative emotion that will motivate the prospect o purchase.

Emotional close emotionales Beenden eines Verkaufsgesprächs

A closing technique in which the salesperson attempts to get a positive response from a prospect by appealing to his/her emotions, e.g. pride, flar, joy, etc.

Empathy Einfühlungsvermögen

It is an important communication and management skill if a person is able and willing to understand and appreciate the feelings and thoughts of another person in a given situation.

Empirical data empirische Daten

Data based upon observation or experiment.

Empirical research empirische (Wirtschafts)Forschung

Study by observation and accumulated experience.

Employee discount Personalrabatt

A certain discount, e.g. 10%, from selling price offered by firms to employees.

Employee discount Personalrabatt

A reduction in the price of goods or services granted by an employer to employees as a benefit.

Empty nesters Eltern, deren Kinder ausgezogen sind

People whose children have left home.

Encirclement attack Einkreisungs-, Umzingelungsattacke

One of the five attack strategies used by competing firms, the others being: 1. the frontal attack, 2. the flank attack, 3. the bypass attack, and 4. the guerilla attack.

An aggressor`s strategy to attack opponents/competitors (or enemies) by launching an offensive on several fronts, so that the opponent must protect all its fronts simultaneously.

Note: this strategy makes sense when the aggressor commands resources superior to those of the opponent, i.e. he believes that his offers are unrefusable and thus will break the opponent`s resistance.

Encoding Verschlüsselung

In the communication process, the process of symbolizing the ideas into pictures and/or words so that the idea is communicable and understandable. Once encoded, the idea or message can be transmitted through some media and then decoded by the receiver.

End aisle display Warenstapel am Ende des Ganges

A premium display point in a department store or supermarket where products are stacked from floor to ceiling instead of being displayed in shelves.

End consumer Endverbraucher

Also called final or ultimate consumer; final, end or ultimate user.

A person or company that ultimately consumes a product or service.

End product Endprodukt, Enderzeugnis

Also called final product.

A manufactured product, i.e. a product made at the end of the production process.

End user Endabnehmer

Also called end consumer, ultimate buyer or consumer.

A person or firm that uses a good or service.

End-of-month (EOM) settlement Ultimoabrechnung

A firms`s policy to settle invoices at the end of the month, eg 2/20 EOM indicates that a 2 percent discount is given if the invoice is paid/settled within 20 days of the end of the month.

Ending inventory Schlußbestand

Also called closing stock or end-of-period inventory.

Goods on hand at the end of the accounting period. The opposite of beginning/opening inventory.

Endogenous variable endogene Variable

A variable (e.g. income, money supply, prices) whose value is determined within the framework of an economic model.

Endorsement advertising Leitbildwerbung

In advertising, the use of famous and qualified people (celebrities) to promote a product or service.

Engaged tone Besetztzeichen (Telefon)

Also called engaged signal or circuit-busy signal.

This is a repeated single tone, and means that the called telephone number is in use (the line is busy or engaged).

Engel's law Engelsches Gesetz

Also called law of consumption.

A law formulated in 1857 by the German statistician Ernst Engel (1821 - 1896).
The law of consumption states that poorer families and societies tend to spend a greater proportion of their incomes on food than well-to-do people. According to this law the proportion of income spent on food tends to decline as income grows.
Further findings are: when income increases, the percentage spent on housing and household operation remains about the same; but the percentage spent on all other items increases.
On the basis of this law the Engel curve (a line showing the relationship between a household's income and its consumption of a specified good over a period of time) has been developed, which is important for the analysis of household spending habits.

Enlargement Vergrößerung

The act or process of enlarging or expanding, eg the expansion of a firm.

Reproduction in size larger than the original, eg in photographic print, the reproduction of an original in larger size.

An enlarged form of something.

Enquiry/inquiry Anfrage

In general, a seeking or request for information.

In business, a person (the enquirer) makes an enquiry when he wishes to know more about goods or services before he decides to buy them. He obtains more information from the supplier and then decides whether to buy or not.
In an enquiry state simply, clearly and concisely what you want (e.g. a catalogue or price list). It can be sent on a special enquiry form or in the form of a letter; it can be made orally or in writing.
Note: an enquiry is without any obligation for the enquirer.

Enquiry follow-up Couponwerbung

An advertising technique employed in the mail order trade. An advertisement invites the reader to write to the manufacturer for further details. In response, the supplier sends a range of literature describing his product in detail.
Generally, the enquiry follow-up consists of: a sales letter, an illustrated leaflet, an order form, and a reply envelope, usually prepaid.

Enterprise zone Förderungsgebiet

A geographical area which is especially supported by the government in order to further its economic and industrial development. Usually, these are areas of physical and economic decay so that the firms in these areas enjoy special government benefits, e.g. exemption from certain taxes.

Entertainment expenses Bewirtungskosten
Unterhaltungskosten

Money spent on giving meals to business visitors.

Money spent on entertainment or amusement, especially a performance.

Entertainment industry Unterhaltungsindustrie

The sector of service industry that provides amusement and entertainment, e.g. cabaret, film, shows, theatres, TV, etc.

Entertainment tax Vergnügungssteuer

Also called entertainment duty; admission, amusement or cabaret tax.

A tax/duty imposed on most forms of entertainment, e.g. concerts.

Entrant Teilnehmer
neuer Konkurrent
neues Mitglied

A person who takes part in a competition or contest.

Someone who enters the market and thus becomes a competitor. Also called newcomer.

A new member, e.g. of an association or club.

Entrepot Umschlagsdepot, Handelszentrum
Transitlager

A centre for the distribution of goods.

A commercial port where previously imported goods are reexported, without the need to pass through customs control.

Entrepreneur Unternehmer(in)
dispositiver Faktor

Also called businessman, businesswoman, business entrepreneur, employer or undertaker.

Entrepreneur is a French word, which means "undertaker". He is the owner of the business, who contributes the capital.

The entrepreneur initiates production and decides upon how the other three factors (of production), land, labour, and capital, are to be employed.

He undertakes production in the hope of earning a profit. In doing so he performs two main functions. Firstly, he takes decisions on what, where and how to produce. Secondly, he is the risk-bearer. He thinks he can foresee the kinds of products which

are most likely to satisfy consumers' needs. The risks borne by him arise from uncertainty of future market conditions, and his success will depend upon his ability to forecast future demand.
If revenue from sales exceeds costs the entrepreneur will make a profit, but if costs are greater than receipts, he will suffer a loss.

Entrepreneur is the fourth factor of production that brings land, labour, and capital together in order to provide a good or service. Also called enterprise or entrepreneurship.

Entry Marktzutritt

A firm's entry to a new market.

Entry value Anschaffungswert

The value at which an asset enters the business, e.g. its purchase price.

Envelope Briefumschlag, Briefkuvert
Hülle, Umschlag

Paper cover for a letter. It bears two addresses, the address of the addressee (the envelope address) and that of the sender (the return address). The Post Office Guide gives detailed information on envelope addressing.

Any form of covering.

Envelope stuffer Drucksachenbeilage
Person, die Drucksachen beilegt

Advertising material which is attached to an invoice or letter and mailed/posted to customers in an envelope. Also called stuffer.

The person who places materials into envelopes.

Environmental analysis Umweltanalyse

The gathering and analysing of data, about a company`s external environment in order to identify trends and developments and their impacts on the company. The forces which must be considered are political, cultural, social, demographic, economic, legal, international and ecological factors.

Environmental conditions Umweltbedingungen

The conditions of the environment. Every area and nation has localised problems of water pollution, air pollution, derelict land, decaying inner cities, polluted beaches, etc. Note: the ministry of the environment is seeking to improve the quality of the environment.

Environmental management Umweltmanagement

The implementation of strategies that attempt to shape the external environment within which a firm operates.

The factors within the external environment that are important to marketing managers can be classified as:
1. social, 2. demographic, 3. economic, 4. technological, 5. political and legal,
6. competitive.

Environmental pollution Umweltverschmutzung

The introduction of harmful substances or products into the environment, e.g. the contamination of a lake with sewage.

Environmental Protection Agency (EPA) Umweltschutzbehörde (USA)

In the USA, an independent federal agency established in 1970 that regulates the amount of pollutants manufacturers can emit. It is concerned with air, water, radiation, solid waste, pesticides and toxic substances.

Environmental sponsoring Umweltsponsoring

Marketing activities which sponsor the environment and thereby promote a company's product or service.

Environmental tax Umweltabgabe

A tax on a polluter.

Environmentalism Umweltschutz(bewegung)

The public concern over protecting, enhancing, and improving the environment.

That part of consumerism that concentrates on ecology issues such as air, water, and noise pollution and the depletion of natural resources.

Environmentalist Umweltschützer

A defender of the environment, ie a person devoted to the protection of the environment.

Equation Gleichung
Gleichheit

An expression or a proposition, often algebraic, asserting the equality of two quantities.

The state of being equal, e.g. at the equilibrium price supply equals demand.

Equilibrium Gleichgewicht

Economists use the term equilibrium to indicate a state of balance in which there are no forces causing change in either direction.
For example, equilibrium exists at the point at which the amount of a commodity demanded equals the amount offered for sale.

Equilibrium output Gleichgewichtsmenge, -produktion

Also called equilibrium quantity.

In order to maximise profit, the equilibrium output of a firm will be where the difference between total revenue and total cost is greatest. This occurs where marginal revenue equals marginal cost.

Equilibrium point Gleichgewichtspunkt

The point indicating a situation in which the quantity and price offered by sellers/suppliers equals the quantity and price taken by buyers/demanders.

When we plot the demand curve and the supply curve for any good on the same graph, with price on the vertical axis (y-axis, ordinate) and the quantity demanded with the quantity supplied on the horizontal axis (x-axis, abscissa), these curves will in general intersect at one point - the equilibrium point. At this point supply equals demand.

Equilibrium price Gleichgewichtspreis

Also called market clearing price.

The price at which all commodity brought onto the market is bought, i.e. the price at which supply equals demand. This price occurs at the intersection of the supply and demand curves for the commodity.
Once the market price has been determined at this intersection, should the supplier raise the price, demand will fall and eventually in order to sell all his goods, he will have to reduce the price. Likewise, if price is decreased, demand will exceed supply and the price will be forced back to equilibrium level.
Equilibrium price is almost never the actual price existing at a given time. "Market price" is the actual price prevailing at any given time.

Equilibrium quantity Gleichgewichtsmenge

The quantity of a good that will be produced and sold when the market for the good is in equilibrium.

Equivalent-price strategy Wettbewerbspreisbildung, konkurrenzangepasste Preisstrategie

A "meeting competition" method of pricing, i.e. companies use price comparisons as the basis for pricing their own products.

Erratic demand unstete, launenhafte Nachfrage

A demand pattern for a product or service that is varied and nearly unpredictable, e.g. the demand for certain luxury goods or extremely fashionable items.

Error Fehler, Irrtum, Versehen

In general, an error is a mistake; an act involving departure from accuracy or truth; a difference between a correct amount and an incorrect amount; etc.

In statistics, the difference between an occurring value and its true or expected value. Types of errors are:
1. measurement error (there is a difference between the information desired by the researcher and the information provided by the measurement process, e.g. consumers state that they buy a product when they do not);
2. sampling error (occurs when a sample somehow does not represent the target population);

3. frame error (occurs when the sample drawn from a population differs from the target population);
4. random error (occurs because the selected sample is an imperfect representation of the overall population),
5. accidental error: people do not know that they have made a mistake.
6. arithmetical error: an error of addition, calculation, etc.
7. deliberate error: people know that they are doing something wrong.
8. error of decision: a wrong decision has been made.

Error rate Fehlerquote

The percentage of errors made, e.g. in the production of goods or in shipping merchandise to customers (eg wrong items or wrong quantity, etc.).

Escalation of prices Preiseskalation, gradueller Preisanstieg

A steady price increase.

Escalator card Rolltreppenwerbung, -plakat

Also called escalator panel.

Advertisements, usually posters, on either side of an escalator, eg in underground/subway stations.

Escalator clause Preisgleitklausel (Vertrag)

Also called escalating, fluctuating or rise-and-fall clause.

A clause in a contract which allows a price to rise above that originally agreed if costs increase.

Escalator panel Rolltreppenplakat

Posters displayed alongside an escalator.

Escalator pricing gleitende Preisfestsetzung

A pricing strategy in which the final selling price reflects cost increases incurred between the time when the order was placed and when delivery is made.

Essential commodities Notwendigkeitsgüter, lebensnotwendige Güter, Waren des täglichen Bedarfs

Also called essentials or necessaries.

Goods considered essential to maintain a minimum acceptable living standard.

Established product gut eingeführte(s) Marke, Produkt

Also called established brand.

A product or brand widely acknowledged and accepted in the market.

Estate income Vermögenseinkommen

Income originating from owning land or buildings.

Estimate Kostenvoranschlag (Angebot)
Schätzung
Schätzwert

Also called estimation.

An estimate is a quotation for making something or providing a service (e.g. a manufacturer may offer to build a machine for a certain price). The price is quoted in advance for a specific article or service. Also called cost estimate, quotation or quote.

An approximate calculation of the value of a quantity which cannot accurately be determined (e.g. costs, prices, etc.). Also called appraisal, assessment or valuation.

The estimated value. Also called appraised or assessed value, appraisement or valuation.

Estimated time of arrival (ETA) voraussichtliche Ankunftszeit

The predicted day and time of reaching a destination or receiver, e.g. the time when an airplane is expected to arrive.

Estimated time of departure (ETD) voraussichtliche Abfahrtszeit

The time when someone or something is expected to leave a place.

Estimator Schätzer, Taxator
Kalkulator

A person who works out the estimates. Also called appraiser, assessor, evaluator or valuator.

A person who calculates costs. Also called cost accountant, cost estimator, or costing clerk.

Ethical pricing ethische, moralische Preisbildung

A pricing strategy in which the demand for the product is inelastic and the seller is a professional who has a responsibility not to overcharge the client.

Ethics Ethik, Moral

A system or set of moral principles.

The rules of conduct and professional standards recognized in respect to a particular class of human actions or governing a specific group, culture, etc.

Ethnic media (Kommunikations)Medien für ethnische Gruppen, Minderheiten

The communications media, such as the press, radio or TV, designed to reach specific racial or nationality groups.

Euro ad(vertisement) Euro-Werbung

An advertisement (ad) designed to be used in all countries of the European Union (EU), e.g. advertisements for cars.

Eurobrand (product) Euro-Markenprodukt

A product that meets European standards, eg with regard to quality and safety requirements. Thus, a producer can produce a product in one state and sell it throughout the remaining European states without any mandatory modification. But some products will be modified to meet different consumer needs or to reflect cultural tastes, etc.
Note: to be able to manufacture a product of one specification enables the manufacturer to exploit the economies of scale in production, distribution and servicing the market to a greater extent. This may lower the unit costs which gives the entrepreneur more flexibility in his pricing strategy.

European article number (EAN) europäische Artikelnummer

In most industries, eg in the food or pharmaceutical industry, a barcode system applied by a number of European countries. EAN barcodes consist of vertical lines printed on articles, packages, price labels or coupons and can be read and decoded with a special scanner and associated software. They tell the check-out assistant the price of goods and record stock movements.

European domestic market (EDM) Europäischer Binnenmarkt

The total market of the member states of the European Union (EU).

European Union (EU) Europäische Union (EU)

Until November 1993 known as European Community (EC).

Since May 1994 the EU has consisted of 15 member states: Austria, Belgium, Denmark, Finland, France, Germany, Greece, Ireland, Italy, Luxembourg, the Netherlands, Portugal, Spain, Sweden, and the United Kingdom.

Evaluation Bewertung

In general, an act of evaluating or appraising, e.g. evaluating the value of something.

In marketing, one of the five stages in the buying process and often the most critical point because consumers evaluate the quality and characteristics of various products based on certain characteristics such as quality, price, design, product life, safety, strength, utility, etc.

Even numbers gerade Zahlen

Numbers which can be divided by two.

Evening drive (time) spätnachmittagliche/frühabendliche Spitzennutzungszeit von Autoradios

Also called drive time or afternoon drive.

On radio, the airtime between 3:00 and 7:00 pm.

Event Ereignis, Veranstaltung

In general, an occurrence of some importance, e.g. a sports contest.

Occurrences staged to communicate messages to target audiences, e.g. news releases, press conferences, grand openings, etc.

Events marketing Eventmarketing, Erlebnis-, Veranstaltungs-, Showmarketing

A promotional activity in which an organization stages an event to which customers and prospects are invited, e.g. a competition, a concert, a sports meeting, etc.

Every day (ED) jeden Tag (Insertionsanweisung)

An instruction given by an advertiser to broadcast or publish an advertisement every day.

Every other day (EOD) jeden zweiten Tag (Insertionsanweisung)

An instruction given by an advertiser to a publisher of a newspaper to insert an advertisement every second day.

Everyday low price (EDLP) täglicher Niedrigpreis, Dauerniedrigpreis

A price tactic of permanently reducing prices 10 to 15 percent below the traditional levels and maintaining those prices while eliminating discounts.

Evoked set erinnerte Marken-, Produktalternative

The subset of available brands of a product class which a consumer considers appropriate alternatives, and from which a choice is made.

Ex factory price Preis ab Werk

Also called ex works, ex mill or ex warehouse price.

A simple form of price quotation. The buyer, e.g. an importer, is presumed to have bought the goods right at the seller's (e.g. exporter's) factory. All costs and risks from thereon become the buyer's problem. This arrangement limits the seller's risk; however, a buyer may find an ex-factory deal very demanding.

Note: in international trade, it could prove difficult for the importer to arrange for transportation and to take care of the various formalities required.

Ex stock (ex stk, X stk) ab Lager

Also called ex store (X store), off the shelf, or ex warehouse (ex whse, X whse).

Goods ordered can be supplied quickly from stock. The seller has goods of the type required in stock and makes them available at a named store or warehouse. The buyer is responsible/liable from that point on.

Ex warehouse (ex whse, X whse) ab Lager
ab Werk

Goods ordered can be supplied quickly from stock. Also called ex stock (ex stk, X stk) or ex store (X store).

The same as ex works or ex factory.

Exception rate Ausnahmetarif

A lower rate charged for a particular service which can be negotiated or which is offered by the supplier.

In transport, special lower rates which can be negotiated or which are offered by the carrier in order to compete.

Exceptions to the law of demand Ausnahmen beim Nachfragegesetz

Situations which contradict the law of demand and which create the opposite of what is expected, i.e. when the price goes up, more is sold (not less).
There are three possibilities:
1. prestigious products: certain expensive products are sought after because of their high price, i.e. a drop in prices would cause demand to fall;
2. Giffen goods: these are inferior goods or basic foodstuffs consumed by people on very low income; the demand for these goods rises when the price rises and drops when the price drops;
3. price increases are expected: demand sometimes increases even though prices are rising because consumers think that they should buy before prices increase even further.

Excess baggage Übergepäck

Baggage/luggage which is heavier than the weight allowed as free baggage for a certain category of ticket. An extra payment is charged.

Excess capacity Überkapazität, freie Kapazität

Also called overcapacity or surplus capacity.

Existence of more productive capacity than demanded at any given time. As a result a proportion of the capacity available stands idle.

Excess postage Nachgebühr

An extra payment for sending mail which is heavier than the weight paid for.

Excess stock Überbestand

Also called excess of inventory.

In inventory control, the portion of stock on hand which is in excess of a predetermined maximum stock/inventory level.

Excess supply of money Geldüberschuß

A situation in which the actual money balances of individuals and firms are in excess of their desired level. Thus, they will increase their spending on assets and goods.

Excess(ive) demand Nachfrageüberhang, Übernachfrage

Also called excess in demand, overdemand, demand surplus or demand overhang.

Existence of more demand than presently existing productivity is able to satisfy. Demand is greater than supply. In competitive markets there will be upward pressure on prices.

Excess(ive) supply Überangebot, Angebotsüberhang

Also called oversupply, excess in supply, supply overhang or supply surplus.

A market situation in which supply exceeds demand at some given price. In competitive markets there will be downward pressure on prices.

Exchange (ex, exch) Aus-, Ein-, Umtausch Tauschgeschäft

The process of exchanging.

The exchange of goods for other goods, ie a situation where one gives something to someone, and receives something else in return. Both things are usually of equal value. Also called barter.

Exchange economy Tauschwirtschaft

Also called barter or nonmonetary economy.

An economic system where specialisation has been introduced. The exchange of goods for other goods is effected without the use of money as an intermediary. No price or value is set for any item involved. But for the smooth working of such a system money must be employed.

Excise Verbrauchssteuer

Also called excise duty or tax; consumer, consumption, expenditure, purchase or use tax.

Taxes imposed/levied on specified home-produced goods for consumption in the home/domestic market (e.g. alcohol, petrol, tabacco). Although the seller pays such a tax, all, part or none (depending upon the respective elasticities of supply and demand) is shifted on to the consumer. Such duties may be levied for revenue only or they may be levied to restrict the home consumption of the goods.

Excise drawback Rückvergütung von Verbrauchssteuern

A refund of the excise duty collected on goods made in a particular country but subsequently exported from it.

Exclusion of/from liability Haftungsausschluß

Also called exemption from liability.

A clause which excludes one party to the contract from responsibility for any losses arising in connection with that contract, no matter how caused.

Exclusive agency Alleinvertretung

Also called sole agency.

An agreement binding two parties, one as principal (usually a manufacturer), the other as exclusive agent, involving a product or a market, being limited in availability to the agent for a period. The agent benefits from the lack of competition, and the principal benefits from a greater sales commitment on the part of the agent.

Exclusive contract Ausschließlichkeitsvertrag

Also called exclusive dealing agreement or exclusivity agreement.

An agreement between manufacturer and retailer that prohibits the retailer or sole agent in a particular market from carrying the product lines of firms that are rivals of the manufacturer.

Note: such contracts are illegal when they lessen competition.

Exclusive distribution Alleinvertrieb, Exklusivvertrieb

A policy in which a producer grants one retailer or wholesaler the sole right to sell a product or product range within a specific geographical area. This type of distribution is particularly suited for some shopping goods and more expensive specialty goods.

Exclusive reader Alleinleser, Exklusivleser

A person being the only reader of a copy of a publication.

Excursion Ausflug, Exkursion

Short visit, often for one day only, returning to the place from which you left.

Execution of order Auftragsausführung

The seller executes/carries out the buyer's order by delivering the goods according to the terms of the contract.

Exemption from VAT Mehrwertsteuerbefreiung (GB)

Also called exempt rating or zero rating.

In GB, a situation where a business is not required to add VAT (value added tax) to its charges. On the other hand, it is unable to reclaim VAT charged to it.

Exemption from tax Steuerbefreiung

Also called tax exemption.

A situation where a person or company does not have to pay tax, in whole or in part, on certain types of income or property.

Exhibit Ausstellung
Ausstellungsstück, Exponat

A situation where a person or company does not have to pay tax, in whole or in part, on certain types of income or property.

Also called display.

An act or instance of exhibiting, e.g. factory products. Also called exhibition or exposition.

An object or a collection of objects shown in an exhibition, fair, etc.

Exhibition Ausstellung, Messe

Also called exposition, fair, or show.

Exhibitions present information connected with many aspects of the commodity such as production, maintenance of quality, after-sales service, etc.

Exhibiting is an expensive form of promotion. Its costs incorporate:
1. prior research on audience and exhibitors, 2. design of literature and exhibits,
3. booking space, 4. stand construction, 5. hire of apparatus, 6. hire of furniture,
7. samples, 8. travel and subsistence, 9. staff, 10. dismantling, 11. transport,
12. storage, 13. insurance, 14. miscellaneous.

Exhibition grounds Ausstellungs-, Messegelände

Also called fair grounds.

The place where an exhibition or fair takes place.

Exhibition hall Messehalle, Ausstellungsraum

Also called exhibition room.

A hall where goods are displayed so that potential buyers can look at them and decide whether they will buy or not.

Exhibitor Aussteller

A person or company which disposes of exhibition stands and exhibits, demonstrates or shows something, eg products, to an interested audience at an exhibition or fair.

Existence value Existenzwert

The satisfaction people can derive simply from knowing that something exists. Certainly, it is extremely difficult to measure such values.

Existentialism Existentialismus

A philosophical belief stressing that each individual is alone and completely responsible for his/her actions and choices.

Existing demand tatsächliche Nachfrage

A product or service bought to satisfy a particular need.

Exogenous factor exogene Bestimmungsgröße

Also called exogenous determinant.

Forces influencing an economy from outside, e.g. the weather.

Expansion Wachstum, Expansion
Unternehmenswachstum

A period of increasing economic activity. Also called growth.

The growth of a firm, e.g. by reinvesting profits, increasing capital, merging with one or more other firms, broadening the business activities, extending the territory, increasing output, etc. Also called corporate growth.

Expansion of demand Nachfrageexpansion

A situation which occurs when the amount demanded rises as price falls, i.e. all other factors affecting demand remain unchanged. Thus, an expansion of demand involves a movement along an existing demand curve. It is the opposite to a contraction of demand.

Expansion of supply Angebotsexpansion

A situation which occurs when the amount supplied rises in response to a price rise, i.e. all other factors affecting supply remain unchanged. Thus, an expansion of supply involves a movement along an existing supply curve. It is the opposite to a contraction of supply.

Expansion pricing Expansionspreisbildung

A price reduction that is part cause and part an effect of economies of scale.

Expectation of life Lebenserwartung

Also called life expectancy, expectation or span.

Average remaining life span for a person of a given age according to the statistical tables.

Expectations Erwartungen

The benefits or satisfactions which consumers hope to receive through consumption of specific goods or services.
Note: if goods do not come up to the consumers` expectations they will invariably fail.

Expected price erwarteter Preis

The price of a product which consumers consider corresponds/comes up to the product's true value.

Expediter/expeditor Disponent, Terminjäger

An individual who works to speed up the progress of something, e.g. a shipment for delivery.

Expenditure tax Ausgabensteuer

Also called outlay tax.

A tax (like VAT) on the expenditure of individuals or households. This form of taxation is often preferred by tax theorists to income tax, as it does not distort the incentive to work.

Expenditure-changing policies nachfrageverändernde Wirtschaftspolitik

Fiscal and monetary policies directed at changing the level of aggregate demand (AD) of the country.

Expenditure-dampening policies ausgabedämpfende Maßnahmen

Government measures (e.g. lowering government expenditure) designed to reduce the aggregate/total demand for goods and services in the community.

Expense account Spesenkonto

An account maintained by salespersons that includes travel, hotel and other expenses which they incur for business purposes and for which the are compensated by their employers.

Expense allowance Spesenpauschale, Spesenzuschuß

The compensation of employees, eg salespersons, by their employers for travel, hotel and other expenses which they incur for business purposes.

Expenses (exp) Kosten
Aufwand, Aufwendungen
(Geld)Ausgabe(n)

Also called costs.

The costs of doing business; that is, the costs that must be incurred in order for a company to generate revenue. Expenses mean overhead and running costs/costs of operation of the business. They can be subdivided into fixed expenses (e.g. rent) and variable expenses (e.g. telephone charges). Also called costs.

Expense is the amount shown on the debit side of the profit and loss account. The opposite of revenue.

A (cash) payment.

Experience Erfahrung

Something personally lived through or encountered.

Knowledge or skill gained from what one has done, observed, felt, etc.

Experience curve Erfahrungskurve

In general, a curve reflecting the fact that the costs of doing something tend to decrease as the organisation gains experience doing it.

In marketing, the experience curve depicts the inverse relationship between production costs per unit and cumulative production quantity.
Experience in this context is measured by the cumulative number of units produced to date. The experience curve for a product shows the way in which total unit costs will decline due to the combined impact of:
1. learning (i.e. the increasing efficiency of labour that arises chiefly from practice);
2. technological improvements (e.g. new production processes, resource mix changes, product standardization);
3. economies of scale (i.e. increased efficiency due to size).

To take advantage of the experience curve, a company must gain a dominant market share early in a product`s life cycle. An early market share lead, with the greater cumulative production experience that it implies, will place a company further down the experience curve than its competitors, i.e. unit costs are falling.

Note: the total value-added costs decline by a fixed percentage (usually 10% to 30%) each time the cumulative number of units produced is doubled.

Experience curve pricing Preisbildung mittels der Erfahrungskurve

A pricing method in which a firm sets the price sufficiently low (so that high cost competitors cannot match it) to induce a large sales volume which will lead to a greater market share and thus enable the firm to reduce its unit costs. This practice is possible when a firm gains cumulative production experience and is able to reduce its production costs at a predictable rate.

Note: this strategy takes into account the costs of competing firms based on their experience in producing goods.

Experience good Erfahrungsgut

A good which is usually purchased frequently by a consumer who acquires information on it through repeat purchases.

Experience qualities Erfahrungsqualitäten

In service marketing, the qualities of services that can be assessed only after purchase and consumption (eg courtesy, satisfaction, taste, etc).

Experiment Experiment, Versuch

Method of gathering primary data in which one or more variables are altered to measure their relative influence on another variable.

Expiry date Verfalldatum
Fälligkeitstag

Also called expiration date.

The date after which a product may no longer be sold. Also called sell by.

The date on which something falls due. Also called maturity date.

Explicit cost(s) effektive Kosten

The sum of money actually spent on a good or service.

Export and domestic marketing Export- und Inlandsmarketing

There are manifold differences between export and home marketing:
1. overseas markets often require a different product specification;
2. advertising principles and regulations may differ;
3. the customer profile is different in every country, taking into account income levels, taxation, living standards, culture, religion, fashion,etc.;
4. particularly in less developed countries, communications are poor so that promotional activities are restricted;
5. product pricing is different - when pricing a product for the overseas market, many extra elements will contribute to the price, e.g. delivery charges, insurance premiums, etc.;
6. payment terms are of special importance;
7. exchange rates have to be considered;

8. import/export procedures require special attention;
9. packaging and distribution costs are usually much higher;
10. retailing requires special attention, etc.

Export delivery Exportlieferung

The delivery of goods to a customer's address in a foreign country according to the terms of the export sales contract.

Export market Exportmarkt

Any country in which a foreign company agrees to sell its products which are produced outside the borders of the countries in which the products are being sold.

Export marketing Export-Marketing

The marketing of goods or services in a foreign country.

Export marketing strategy Export-Marketing Strategie

In general, the strategies applied to optimize a company's resources in the production and sale of products.
In particular, the strategies used are:
1. the selection of and operation in the most advantageous markets both short-term and long-term, and thereby maximizing profitability and market dominance;
2. determining the number of foreign/overseas markets in which the company should best operate (this will depend on the company size and resources, the servicing of the market, the compatibility of the market with the home market and/or existing other overseas markets, etc.);
3. deciding on the market entry mode (i.e. direct or indirect market entry);
4. determining the export price (the price will be influenced by the transportation costs, import tariffs, exchange rate fluctuations, level of competition, etc.; note: it is very unlikely that an exporter will fix the same price in all the overseas markets);
5. deciding as to which extent the marketing mix (i.e. the four Ps: product, price, place promotion) can be transferred from the domestic/home market to the overseas market.

Export price Exportpreis

The price for goods exported should include the following:
1. all costs and charges incurred by the exporter in producing or acquiring the goods (including preshipment finance costs);
2. any other charges for which the exporter is responsible under the contract of sale (e.g. insurance and freight charges for goods sold under CIF or CIP terms);

3. the exporter's profit margin;
4. costs (if applicable) of forward exchange contract;
5. interest to cover any post-shipment period;
6. local and overseas bank commission charges for which the exporter is responible.

Note: the first three items listed can be regarded as the basic export price.

Export price list Export-Preisliste

A list used in international trade which quotes the current prices of a company's products.

Export price quotation Exportpreisangebot

An export price may be quoted to the foreign/overseas buyer in one of several ways. Every alternative implies mutual commitment by exporter and importer and specifies the terms of trade. The price alters according to the degree of responsibility that the exporter undertakes, which varies with each alternative.
Possible ways of quoting export prices are: ex works (EXW); free alongside ship (FAS); free on board (FOB); cost, insurance and freight (CIF); delivered duty paid (DDP); etc.

Export pricing Export-Preisbildung

Also called export price fixing or formation.

The activity or process of setting export prices for a firm's products or services. Export pricing involves many considerations in price formulation.
The following factors will influence export prices:

1. production costs, 2. product design/modification costs, 3. packaging, 4. distribution costs, 5. transportation costs, 6. import tariffs, 7. market entry costs, 8. costs due to exchange rate fluctuations, 9. methods of payment, 10. payment terms, 11. promotion and selling costs, 12. the level of competition, 13. the prices of competitors, 14. government price controls, 15. the sales volume, 16. the market share, 17. the market place, 18. the range of products, 19. the spending power and the income level, 20. the markup/profit charge, 21. the buyer behaviour, etc.

In international trade, companies mainly follow two different pricing methods:
1. the cost approach and 2. the market approach.
Whichever approach is preferred, export pricing is affected by three factors:

1. the price destination (that is, who it is that will pay the price, e.g. the final consumer, independent distributors, a wholly owned subsidiary, a joint venture organization, or some other competent person);
2. the nature of the product (that is, whether it is raw or semiprocessed material, components, finished products; or services or intangible property, such as patents, licences, and the like);

3. the currency used for billing (that is, the currency of the importer's country, the exporter's home country currency, or a leading international currency).

A pricing choice in export pricing that a company must consider is whether to set a common price or different prices for domestic and international markets. Although some companies have common prices, most firms develop two price lists, one for the domestic and one for the foreign market. Usually, a margin is built into the price list so that, if necessary, it is feasible to adjust prices in response to local market conditions. A company may make sale on a spot basis or for future delivery. For sales on a spot basis, prices are determined according to the daily exchange rate at the time of the order. On orders for future delivery, a company may either quote at the current (exchange) rate or use a forward (exchange) rate. The final decision on the use of the exchange rate will depend on the company`s export risk and its past experience with exchange rates.

Export promotion Exportförderung

The activities undertaken by an exporter, by direct or indirect methods, to persuade general and specific buyers to purchase his products or services.
Export promotion may arise in one of the following ways:
1. supporting the sale of existing products or services in an established foreign market,
2. promoting the sale of new products or services in an established market abroad,
3. entering the overseas market through the promotion of an entirely new product or service,
4. informing and possibly educating dealers and users about the exporter's company and its objectives,
5. seeking to influence the customers' behaviour favourably towards the exporter and his/her products or services.

Factors determining the type of promotion are as follows:
1. the type of product involved and its retail price, 2. the cost of promotion, 3. the potential profitable market, 4. the level of competition (nos 1-4 are the most important factors), 5. the availability of monies for such a promotion (a product launch requires a larger budget), 6. the method of sale, 7. the type of market, 8. the result of market research, 9. the type of sales organisation required, 10. the size of the market and the market share expected to be gained, 11. demographical features, 12. political constraints, etc.
Note: successful promotion could involve more than one medium.

Measures, for example, subsidies or tax concessions, designed to increase the volume of exports of a particular country.

Export trade Ausfuhr-, Exporthandel

The sale of goods and services to parties located in other countries. Depending upon the location and the economic and technological development and progress of a country, the exports may consist of partly or fully manufactured goods, sophisticated plant and machinery, cars, electronic products, raw materials, agricultural products, foodstuffs, etc.

Export-led growth exportinduziertes Wachstum

The expansion of an economy, which is stimulated by an increasing export volume. This has multiplier effects on the whole economy.

Exposure Werbemittelkontakt
(An)Zahl der Werbeempfänger

Any opportunity for a listener, reader or viewer to hear and/or see an advertising message in a particular media vehicle. Also called advertising or media exposure.

The number of people able to perceive an advertising message.

Express contract ausdrücklicher Vertrag

A contract in which the contracting parties make oral or written promises. Contracts involving important dealings should always be express contracts.

Express delivery Eilzustellung

Also called express service.

Where it is urgent to send a letter or package more quickly, the letter or package may be delivered express post. An extra fee is paid at the time of posting.

There is also a private express service, e.g. UPS (United Parcels Service) or DP (Deutscher Paketdienst).

Express distribution Express-Vertrieb

The rapid movement of goods on a door-to-door basis providing delivery within a specified time frame.

Express post Eilpost, Eilzustellung

Also called express mail.

A fast messenger collection and delivery service.

Express warranty vertragliche Gewährleistung, Gewährleistung für zugesicherte Eigenschaften

A promise or statement of fact concerning goods made by a seller as part of a sales transaction with a buyer.

Extended guarantee/guaranty verlängerte Garantie erweiterte Garantie

A guarantee which applies past the expiry date of the original guarantee.

A servicing and maintenance cover offered by manufacturers to their customers for a specified additional period of time exceeding the original guarantee.

Extended marketing mix for services erweitertes Marketingmix für Dienstleistungen

Also called the 7Ps.

The standard marketing mix comprises the four Ps: 1. product, 2. promotion, 3. price, 4. place.

In addition to these standard 4 Ps, there are three additional elements for services:
1. process (i.e. the process of the transaction for service, e.g. friendliness of staff, flows of information, ease of payment, etc; these operational issues directly affect customer perceptions and satisfaction);
2. physical evidence/ambience (the "feel" is very much part of the service offer, i.e. the environment such as layout, decor, upkeep, noise, etc, in which a service is offered and consumed);
3. people (as most services require direct interaction between consumer and the service provider`s personnel, the level of human involvement must be given maximum attention in order to maximise the customers` satisfaction).

Extension ad gigantische Außenwerbung

Extremely large outdoor advertisements.

Extension of a contract Vertragsverlängerung

Also called renewal of a contract.

The continuation of a contract for a further time period.

Extension strategy Revitalisierungsstrategie

A selling strategy trying to extend the life of a product, e.g. by making small changes in it, finding additional uses for it or establishing new markets.

Note: the strategy can be implemented during the maturity or early decline stages within the life cycle.

Extensive decision making extensive Entscheidungsbildung

A most complex type of consumer decision making, used when buying an unfamiliar, expensive product or an infrequently bought product. The potential buyer spends a considerable time and effort on seeking alternative products, searching for information about them, and then evaluating them to determine which one will be most satisfying.

Extensive marketing flächendeckendes Marketing

A marketing strategy using a wide network of distributors and a great variety of promotional activities to reach as large a section of the market as possible.

Extensive selling extensiver Verkauf

A strategy of selling products through every conceivable distribution channel and promoting sales to every likely market segment.

Exterior advertising Außenwerbung

Also called outdoor advertising.

The use of posters, billboards, etc on walls, roofs, buses, lorries, trams, etc.

External demand Auslandsnachfrage

Also called foreign demand.

In general, a foreign country's demand for domestic goods or services.

In detail, the quantity of a commodity or service that will be bought at a particular price per time period by overseas buyers.

External diseconomies negative externe Effekte
externe Nachteile

The diseconomies available to a whole industry.

The adverse effects which the production activities of one company have on those of another company, i.e. the adverse effects outside the influence of a single company.

External economies positive externe Ersparnisse
externe Vorteile, Effekte

These are the savings/economies available to a whole industry and which any business entering the same type of work can take advantage of. The economies arise from large-scale production or from a particular location.

The beneficial effects which the production activities of one firm have on those of another firm, i.e. the beneficial effects outside the influence of a single firm. Also called external effects or externalities.

External environment betriebliches Umfeld

Also called business environment.

Primarily the economic, political, sociological and technological factors outside a company that influence it and interact with each other.

External report Bericht

A company report intended for outside information; it does not contain any sensitive information.

Extra dating Rechnung mit Sonderterminierung,
Rechnungsdatierung mit Extratagen

A method of invoice dating which allows the buyer a specified number of days before the ordinary dating begins. For example, a seller may offer the buyer the following terms: "2/10 - 30 days extra". This means that the buyer has 10 days plus 30 days, or 40 days, from the invoice date in which to pay the invoice/bill with the discount deducted.

Extractive industry Grundstoffindustrie

Also called basic or primary industry.

This covers industries engaged in making available raw materials and natural products, e.g. mining, fishing, agriculture.

Extras Nebenkosten

Costs for items which are not included in a price, e.g. packing costs or postage.

Extreme close-up (ECU) Großaufnahme, Nahaufnahme

Also called extra close-up (XCU).

The closest possible shot of an object or person, i.e. the principal subject dominates the picture.

Eye movement camera Augenkamera

Also called eye camera

A camera tracking the eye movements of people when they are reading a newspaper or magazine or watching a television advertisement. The position of the pupils is measured at short intervals by a beam of infrared light and is recorded onto a computer tape. When the tape is connected to a video one can see where the eyes were positioned on the page or TV screen and how long they stopped there. This eye-tracking test enables marketers to measure the impact of advertisements in terms of the attention they have attracted. Furthermore, it may reveal which parts of an advertisement have gained people`s attention and which have not.

Note: the main advantage of this observation method is that it measures what people actually do (i.e. their actual behaviour) rather than what they say they do (i.e. their claimed behaviour).

Eye-movement test Blickverlaufstest

In advertising, a test recording the movement of a viewer/beholder as he or she looks at an advertisement to find out which parts of the ad are of special interest.

Eyeblink test Blinzeltest

In advertising, a measurement indicating the reactions or emotions caused by a person looking at an advertisement or watching a commercial. A blink-meter measures the frequency of a person`s blinking, so giving indications of emotions, eg interest or arousal.

Eyecatcher Blickfang

A person or thing that attracts the attention of a viewer.

Eyewash Augenwischerei, Geschwätz

Exaggerated claims made for something, e.g. a product.

F

F-terms F-Klauseln

One of the four different categories of the Incoterms (1990), the others being the C-terms, the D-terms and the E-term.

The F-terms comprise: 1. FCA (free carrier), 2. FAS (free alongside ship), 3. FOB (free on board).

Their common characteristics are:
1. main carriage is unpaid, i.e. the seller is only obliged to deliver the goods to a carrier appointed by the buyer;
2. they require the buyer to clear the goods for import;
3. FCA and FOB require the seller to clear the goods for export, whereas FAS requires the buyer to clear the goods for export.

Fabricated parts vorgefertigte Teile

Industrial goods used in manufacturing without further changes in form.

Face-to-face interviewing persönliche Befragung

In questionnaires, a situation where the questions are put to a respondent/interviewee directly on a personal and one-to-one basis.

Face-to-face selling persönlicher Verkauf

Sometimes also called belly-to-belly selling.

Personal selling usually on a one-to-one basis, i.e. a personal meeting between seller and buyer.

Facelift/face-lift Modernisierung

Improvement or restyling of a product's design or packaging or of a company's image.

Facetious advertising — scherzhafte Werbung, Werbung mit ironischem Unterton

Advertising not meant to be taken seriously or literally. It may be amusing, humurous, or frivolous.

Facia/fascia — Firmenschild

Also called name plate.

The signboard of a business.

Facing — (Plakat)Anschlagfläche

Surface of a billboard.

Facing matter (FM) — Anzeigenposition gegenüber redaktionellem Text

Also called facing text, facing editorial or facing text matter.

In advertising, a preferred position for printed advertising in a newspaper or magazine or the positioning of an advertisement so that it appears opposite an editorial matter.

Facing page — gegenüberliegende Seite

The page opposite.

Facsimile — Faksimile, Kopie

An exact copy of writing.

Fact book — Informationsbuch, Produktinformation/-info

A book giving information, e.g. about a product, so that it can be used for reference.

Fact sheet Informationsblatt, Produktinformation

A printed sheet listing all features of a product and accompanying the product when it is sold.

Factor Kommissionär
Factor, Factoring Gesellschaft

Factors are agents concerned with the buying and selling of goods (particularly in the import and export trades) on behalf of their principals. They have possession of the goods. Although they do not own the goods, they can buy and sell in their own names. Their remuneration is by commission/factorage and, if they undertake to guarantee payment by buyers, an extra del credere commission. Also called commission merchant.

A factoring company.

Factor analysis Faktoranalyse

A statistical procedure trying to discover a few basic factors that may underlie and explain the correlations among a larger number of variables.

Factor cost Faktorkosten

Payments made to the various factors of production (land, labour, capital, enterprise) to produce a good or service.

Factor demand (Produktions)Faktornachfrage

The demand for the factors of production (land, labour, capital, enterprise).

Factorage Factoring-Provision

Also called factor's commission.

The commission collected by a factor.

Factoring Factoring(geschäft), Ankauf (und Bevorschußung) von Forderungen (aus Lieferungen und Leistungen), Debitorenverkauf

Factoring, although not concerned with long-term finance, is an important method for firms to economize on capital. Factoring means selling trade debts/accounts receivable for immediate cash to a factor who charges commis-sion/factorage. Most factors offer three basic services, although clients are under no obligation to take them all. The range of services provided by a factor is:
1. an accounting, credit-checking and debt collection service. The factor takes responsibility for all aspects of sales accounting within the business: this includes maintaining the sales ledger, sending out regular statements of account and collecting payments as they become due. The client has just one trade debtor, the factor, who is a prompt and regular payer.

2. credit insurance against bad debts, for approved debts. The factor guarantees full payment on approved sales to customers. The payment is made even if the customer is unable to pay as a result of insolvency.

3. the provision of immediate cash against invoices, up to 75 - 85 % of the face value of the invoices and, because of the credit insurance, a guarantee of payment of the remainder within an agreed period of time. Charges are made for this service but the increased liquidity position of a firm might nevertheless enable it to take advantage of discounts for prompt payment offered by its suppliers. Factoring of debtors (debts) can assist the cash flow of a business considerably. This finance is more expensive than the interest cost of a bank advance, but it will nevertheless be highly attractive if further bank credit is not available.

The charges made by the factoring company (factor) vary depending on the services used. Factoring is normally done without recourse, meaning that the factor cannot turn to the client (the seller) in the event accounts prove uncollectible - the factor assumes the risk of nonpayment.

Factoring is "disclosed" or "undisclosed" according to whether the supplier/seller has notified his customers that payment is to be made to the factor or not.
Other types of factoring are: nonrecourse, recourse, export and import factoring.

Factors affecting changes in demand — Faktoren, die Nachfrageänderungen bewirken

The price is the most important factor influencing demand.

However, there are various other factors which affect changes in demand:
1. the level of disposable income, 2. the distribution of income, 3. the prices of other goods and services, 4. the degree of utility of the commodity, 5. the tastes and preferences of the buyer, 6. the size and structure of the population, 7. habits, customs and fashions, 8. government influence, mainly through direct and indirect taxes, 9. seasonal factors, 10. the weather, 11. the introduction of new or improved products, 12. the impact of advertising, etc.

Factors affecting changes in supply — Faktoren, die Angebotsänderungen bewirken

The price is the most important factor influencing supply.

Other chief factors/conditions affecting supply are:
1. the costs of production, 2. the state of technological development, 3. natural influences, e.g. the weather, 4. political influences, e.g. taxes or subsidies, 5. the price of other goods, 6. changes in the price of raw materials, 7. the regulation of supply, e.g. by purchasing the surplus of a product and storing it in warehouses, etc.

Factory — Fabrik, Werk, Fertigungsstätte

Also called manufacturing plant, plant or works.

In a manufacturing business the factory is the building where goods are manufactured/produced, usually by the use of modern machines.

Factory outlet — Fabrikverkaufsstelle, Verkaufsfiliale eines Herstellers, Einzelhandels-Fabrikladen für Endverbraucher, Direktverkauf

An off-price retail shop that is owned and operated by a manufacturer and that carries his surplus, discontinued, or irregular goods. The outlet may also serve as an alternative channel of distribution. Sometimes, these outlets group together in factory outlet malls.

Factory sale Fabrikverkauf

The sale of goods to customers at the factory, usually at lower prices.

Fad Mode(torheit), Modewelle, Marotte

A temporary fashion, manner of conduct, etc, especially one followed enthusiastically by a group. Fads enter quickly, are adopted with great zeal, peak early, and decline very fast. Usually, they last only a short period because they do not satisfy a strong need or satisfy it well. Normally, fads appeal to people who are looking for excitement or who want to set themselves apart.

A popular product with a particularly short life cycle which is quickly adopted by a number of people, achieves peak sales in a relatively short time period, and thereafter rapidly declines in popularity. The time period is highly variable, and a fad can repeat at intervals of several years.

Fair Markt
Ausstellung, Messe
Jahrmarkt, Volksfest

A local market held at certain times of the year, especially for farm produce.

A large-scale exhibition of commercial and industrial goods (e.g. the Hanover Fair, the Leipzig Fair, the London Antiques Fair). Also called trade or sample fair.

A form of entertainment where one can ride on large, brightly lit machines, win prizes in games, enjoy other forms of entertainment, buy various kinds of candies or sweets, have meals, etc. Also called funfair or carnival.

Fair average quality (FAQ, faq) Faq-Qualität, Handelsgut mittlerer Art und Güte

Certain standards of quality are laid down to facilitate trading. In this case, the goods' quality will be equal to the average of recent deliveries.
Note: the basis of trading on commodity markets is by description, no samples being produced.

Fair deal faires Geschäft

An arrangement or deal where both parties are treated equally.

Fair market value (FMV) angemessener Marktpreis

Also called actual cash value.

The reasonable cash price obtained on the open market.

Fair price angemessener Preis

A price which is acceptable for both buyer and seller.

Fair trade beschränkter Schutzhandel, im Außenhandel Gewährung gegenseitig gleicher Bedingungen
vertikale Preisbindung (USA)

An international trading situation in which goods are exchanged on equal terms (duties and restrictions imposed by one country are met by reciprocal duties and restrictions by other countries).

Formerly, an agreement between American producers and retailers to restrict price cutting; retailers agreed to sell products at or above an agreed-upon price. The prohibition of resale price maintenance (RPM) eliminated fair trade pricing.

Fair trading lauterer Handel
lauterer Wettbewerb

The way of doing business which is reasonable and not unfair to the consumer(s). Also called fair dealing.

Regulation of anticompetitive practices, restrictive trading agreements, mergers and monopolies.

Fair Trading Act Gesetz gegen Wettbewerbs-beschränkungen (GB)

In the UK, consumers are protected by this Act. The Director General of Fair Trading has wide-ranging powers to control trading practices and commercial activities which are considered unfair to consumers. The Office of Fair Trading recommends government action when necessary, prosecutes traders who break the law and it made pricing of goods in shops compulsory.

Fair value angemessener Wert

The amount for which an asset could be sold by a knowledgeable, willing seller/vendor to a knowledgeable, willing buyer/vendee.

Fairness Gerechtigkeit, Fairness

Treating all sides alike, justly and equitably, not showing favouritism.

Faking of brands Markenartikelfälschung

The convincing or acceptable imitation of a branded article and the identification of the counterfeit product with a symbol, logo, or brand name that is very similar to the famous brand.

Fall Fallen, Sinken

A sudden drop, e.g. a drop in sales or a fall in the exchange rate; a loss of value, e.g. a fall in the gold price; something suddenly becoming smaller, e.g. a fall of profits.

Fall guy (der/die) Hereingefallene
Sündenbock

A person who was deceived in a business deal and is thus the victim.

A scapegoat.

Fall-back price Vorbehaltspreis

Also called reserve or upset price.

The lowest price which a seller is prepared to accept.

Fallacy Fehlschluß, Trugschluß
Irreführung

A deceptive, misleading, or false notion, belief, etc.

A misleading or unsound argument.

'allacy of composition Fehlschluß der Verallgemeinerung

'he incorrect assumption/belief that what is true for the individual is necessarily true ɔr a group or for all people.

'alse advertising irreführende Werbung

ʌlso called fraudulent or misleading advertising.

ʌn advertisement or commercial that is inaccurate and misleading in a material ɛspect.

'alse claim falsche Angabe

ıaccurate or untrue claim made, whether deliberate or unintended.

'alse pretences/pretenses Vorspielung falscher Tatsachen

Vilful misrepresentation for an ulterior motive, e.g. to cash a cheque by pretending ɔ be the payee.

'amiliarity advertising Vertrautheitswerbung; Werbung mit bekannten, vertrauten Marken

ʌdvertising aimed at maintaining the association between the product, package and rand name.

'amily brand Dachmarke, Familienmarke

'he same brand name used with two or more of the products a firm sells. The ıdividual members of the family carry individual brands to differentiate them from ther family members.

'amily budget Familienbudget, Haushaltsrechnung

ʌn account of family income which shows the way in which a family distributes its xpenditure on, e.g. food, rent, clothing, household goods, holidays, etc.

Family life cycle (FLC) Familienlebenszyklus

The stages, each with its own characteristics, which people pass through during the course of their lives, e.g. newly - married couples, etc.

Six well-known stages of family life based on demographic data are:
1. young single people, 2. young couples with no children, 3. young couples with youngest child under six years, 4. couples with dependent children, 5. older couples with no children at home, 6. older single people.
This grouping can be useful in advertising and marketing as each group has its own specific needs and interests.

Family packaging Produktgruppenverpackung

A whole range of products is sold in similar packaging.

Fancy article Modeartikel

Small but attractive and fashionable goods, typical of a particular time.

Fancy price Phantasiepreis, Liebhaberpreis, "Apothekerpreis"

An extremely and unreasonably high price for a product or service which is not at all justified.

Fare Fahrgeld, Flugpreis
Fahrgast
Essen, Speise, Nahrung

The price of personal transportation in a bus, train, airplane, or other carrier.

Types of fare are:
1. business fare (tariff for business class passengers), 2. concessionary fare (a reduced fare for certain types of passenger), 3. full fare (the full price payable by an adult), 4. half fare (half-price ticket for a child), 5. single fare/one-way fare (fare for one journey from one place to another), 6. return fare/round-trip fare (price for a trip from one place to another and back again), etc.

A paying passenger, i.e. a person who pays a fare. For example, a person who pays to be conveyed in a vehicle, eg a taxi.

Food, eg a good country fare.

Fashion Mode

A prevailing custom or style of dress, make-up, hair, etiquette, socializing, etc.

Fashion cycle Modezyklus

Progression of stages through which fashion proceeds over time. A fashion cycle comprises three stages:
1. distinction stage (ie innovators take up a new fashion),
2. emulation stage (ie early adopters copy the innovators),
3. economic stage (ie the fashion appears to be attractive to the mass market and manufacturers will rapidly bring out large quantities of similar articles at much lower prices).

Fast food Schnellgericht

Convenience and frozen foods. The food is already prepared and so is served quickly.

Fast freight Eilfracht, Schnellgut

Also called express freight.

A consignment which is conveyed/forwarded very rapidly, e.g. perishable goods.

Fast moving consumer good/product (FMCG/FMCP) schnell umschlagendes Verbrauchsgut

Any repeat-purchase consumer product found in the shopping trolley, usually low in price and branded, e.g. butter, milk, coffee, tea, etc.

Fast selling merchandise (FSM) Selbstläufer, Schnelldreher, schnellverkäufliche Ware

Also called fast moving merchandise or money spinner.

Articles which sell fast, i.e. which walk off the shelves at a fast clip, and thus increase profit.

Fault | (Sach)Mangel
Fehler
Verschulden

A defect or imperfection.

An error or mistake.

The responsibility for failure or a wrongful act.

Fax mailing | Faxversand

Direct mailing using a fax machine rather than the post.

Fear appeal in advertising | Angstappeal in der Werbung

Advertising messages which use fear as their focus, eg employed in advertisements seeking to discourage smoking or warning of the dangers of hard drugs.

Note: usually, a strong fear appeal is less effective than mild fear appeals.

Feasibility study | Durchführbarkeits-, Eignungs-, Projektstudie

A study carried out prior to a particular project to find out whether it is feasible, practical, or will be profitable.

Feature | Sonderangebot
Sonderangebotswerbung
Charakteristikum, Merkmal
(Sonder)Beitrag (Presse)
Hauptfilm

A special offer, ie something offered as a special or main attraction.

The use of advertising, displays, or other promotional activities, usually by a retailer, to attract a customer´s attention to a product, generally for a limited time period.

An important or prominent part of something, e.g. a product or service. Also called characteristic.

In the press, an article or story in a newspaper or magazine that deals with one subject in depth.

The main motion picture in a movie program.

Feature improvement

Eigenschafts-, Merkmalsverbesserung

A kind of product modification to attract new users and to inspire more usage. New features are added to a product so that its usefulness, safety, or convenience is expanded.

Federal Cartel Office

Bundeskartellamt (Germany)

Also called cartel office, competition authorities, Office of Fair Trading (GB), Monopolies and Mergers Commission (GB), Antitrust Division (US), Federal Trade Commission, FTC (US).

A Federal German agency, located in West Berlin, charged with protecting and furthering competition, control of mergers, banning most types of cartels, and suvervision of market-dominating enterprises.

Federal Trade Commission (FTC)

US-Wettbewerbs-Aufsichtsbehörde (Kartellamt)

The FTC was established in 1915 to prevent restraint of trade, unfair pricing and advertising, and to protect the system of free enterprise in a strong economy. It is the custodian of free and fair competition in the US.

Fee

Gebühr, Honorar
Gebühr

An amount of money which certain types of business charge their customers/clients for professional services (e.g. tax accountants, doctors, lawyers will charge a fee). Also called honorarium.

A sum of money paid for giving permission to use or do something, e.g. admission, entrance, parking, registration fee, etc.

Fee for service

Einzelhonorar
Zustellgebühr

Payment for a service performed. Also called individual fee.

A delivery charge.

Feedback Feedback, Rückkoppelung

Response or reaction to a message, indicating to decision-makers, executives or others how the message is being interpreted.

Feeder Zubringer

A branch of a main transportation line, e.g. a branch railway line, airline, canal, etc. linking outlying areas with the main line.

Festival Fest(tag)
Festival, Festspiele

A religious celebration which comes at the same time each year.

An artistic celebration or entertainment which is held regularly, eg the Munich Beer Festival.

Fictitious pricing Phantasie-, Scheinpreisgestaltung

The often illegal practice of announcing a price reduction when, in fact, there has been no reduction at all, e.g. now $ 149, formerly $ 300.

Field Bereich, Gebiet

Area of operations.

Field activated promotion (FAP) Verkaufsförderung, eingeleitet vom Außendienst

Sales promotion initiated by a sales representative and a retailer or store manager.

Field interviewer Außendienst-Interviewer

A person working as an independent contractor under a research company`s supervision and direction to contact and interview sample households.

ield order taker Außendienstmitarbeiter, der Auftrag/Bestellung annimmt

. salesperson who travels to customers regularly, checks inventory and writes up new rders. Sometimes, the salesperson also delivers and stocks the goods ordered for the ustomers.

'ield research Feldarbeit, Feldforschung, Primärforschung

.lso called field study, fieldwork, first-hand research, original or primary research.

'hat part of a market research survey involving contact with (potential) customers, r a representative sample of the population. Thus, the process of conducting esearch in the market place involving face-to-face interviewing, questionnaires, elephone interviewing, visits to buyers, sellers and users of a product or service to btain first-hand information about its current and future market.
'ield research has the advantage of being tailored to the company`s needs and rovides answers to specific questions, but the collection of such data is time onsuming and expensive.

'ield sales force Außendienst(verkaufs)personal, Verkaufsaußendienst

'eam of sales representatives, ie the salesmen or saleswomen working outside the ompany's offices or among the customers, i.e. in the field.

'ield sales manager Außendienstleiter

. sales manager who is in charge of a group of salesmen/saleswomen (the field sales orce) and thus supervises their outside selling activities.

'ield sales report Außendienstverkaufsbericht

eriodic reports by salespeople on their field activities, e.g. on the number of calls nade on particular days; sales made or not made, with some explanation; localised ompetitive activities; significant customer developments; details of complaints on, for xample, product performance, etc.

Field salesperson Außendienstverkäufer/in

A salesperson contacting and selling goods to customers in their place of business or home.

Field selling Verkauf durch Außendienstmitarbeiter

Face-to-face sales calls made by company representatives on customers in their homes or on their premises.

Field staff Außendienstmitarbeiter

Also called outdoor staff.

Company employees whose work is in the marketplace outside of the company office. The opposite of indoor staff.

Field warehousing loan Kredit, gesichert durch Warenlager

Storage of inventories used as collateral in a warehouse on the borrower's property.

Fifty-fifty (50 : 50) plan 50-50-Plan, Fifty-Fifty-Plan

In cooperative advertising, a system which fixes that the advertising costs are shared equally by a manufacturer and a retailer, ie 50% of the advertising costs incurred are paid by the manufacturer and the other 50% are borne by the retailer.

Figure code Zahlenschlüssel

A combination of figures as symbols.

File maintenance Dateipflege

The process of periodically updating files by adding, altering or deleting information.

Filing date Abgabefrist, Einreichungsfrist

The final date for acceptance, eg of documents.

Filler Füllanzeige
Füller
Lückenbüßer

An advertisement, usually preprepared by the publisher, used to fill empty space in a newspaper or magazine.

Something such as talk or music, etc, used to fill extra time in a radio or TV broadcast.

A person or thing that fills.

Filter question Filterfrage

In a questionnaire, a question designed to separate interviewees/respondents who are worth questioning further from those who are not.

Final consumer Endverbraucher

Also called ultimate consumer.

An individual acquiring goods and services for personal, family, or household use.

Final consumer`s decision process Endscheidungsprozeß des Endverbrauchers

The procedure by which consumers collect and analyze information and make choices among alternative goods, services, firms, people, places, and ideas.

This process consists of six basic stages: 1. stimulus, 2. problem awareness, 3. information search, 4. evaluation of alternatives, 5. purchase, 6. postpurchase behaviour.

Note: this process may be affected by demographics, social factors and psychological factors.

Final invoice Schlußrechnung

An invoice giving the full details of a consignment of goods, including the price per item, the total amount, the weight, etc.

Final price Endpreis

The price charged to the final/ultimate consumer.

Final product Enderzeugnis, Endprodukt, Fertigprodukt

Also called final good, end product, finished good or product, or manufactured product.

Products used for consumption and not utilized as input by firms in the production process.

Finance house Teilzahlungs-Kreditinstitut, Geldinstitut

Also called industrial bank, small loan company (for consumer credit) or commercial credit company (for business credit). When suppliers have their own finance houses, they are called captive finance company.

In GB, a financial institution which borrows money from banks and the public and provides funds for hire purchase agreements and other forms of instalment credit which are used to finance the purchase of both consumer and capital goods.

Finance lease Finanzierungs-Leasing, langfristige Vermietung von Investitionsgütern

Also called capital lease, finance equipment leasing, finance leasing, financial leasing, or full pay-out lease.

Finance leases are a method of providing finance for the supply of fixed assets to businesses. Instead of lending a business the funds necessary to purchase an asset, the leasing company (the lessor) buys the asset in its own name and leases it to the user (the lessee). The lessor attempts to recover the full capital outlay of the asset, together with satisfactory return, from a single lessee. The lease period will therefore cover most of the useful life of the asset, and the lessee is responsible for maintenance and repairs. The lessee obtains the use of an asset for a period of time, whereas the legal ownership of the asset remains with the lessor. (A lease is therefore distinct from a hire purchase agreement, where ownership eventually passes from the seller to the buyer at the end of the agreement).
Note: the lease cannot be cancelled.

Where the asset is not fully amortised during the lease period, the lease is called an operating lease.

Financial advertising Finanzwerbung

Advertising by companies who deal with financial matters.

Financial supermarket Finanz-Supermarkt

A company offering a great variety of financial services under one roof, thereby aiming to provide its customers with one-stop shopping.

Finder's fee Vermittlungsprovision

A payment to a person who brings a buyer and seller together.

Fineness Feingehalt

A measure designating the purity of precious metals, e.g. gold and silver.

Finish Verarbeitung(squalität)
Oberflächenbeschaffenheit

The quality of being finished or completed.

The surface coating or texture of paper, metal, wood, etc.

Finished goods Fertigerzeugnisse, -fabrikate

Also called finished articles, finished products, manufactured goods or manufactures.

Goods held by a business which are complete and ready for sale to its customers. The output of production which is saleable. A finished product to one firm may be the raw material for another.

Finished goods inventory Fertigwarenlager

Also called finished goods store.

The stock of finished products ready for sale.

Finished goods warehouse Warenausgangslager

Also called outgoing merchandise inventory.

The warehouse of finished goods ready for delivery to customers.

Firm market Markt mit stabiler Preisentwicklung, feste Börse

A market (e.g. the stock exchange) in which there are more buyers than sellers and in which prices remain steady or have an upward tendency.

Firm name Firmenname

Also called business, commercial, corporate or trade name.

The name under which a business is carried on.

Firm offer (fo) festes, verbindliches Angebot; Festangebot

Also called binding offer or firm quotation.

Every offer is firm (i.e. binding on the offeror) unless it contains a clause to the contrary. If a seller makes a firm offer, he promises to sell certain goods at a certain price subject to acceptance within a reasonable time, or within a specified time (e.g. "our offer is firm for 10 days only", or "we offer you firm until ...").
Like any other offer, it is not legally binding so that the offeror can withdraw/revoke it at any time before acceptance. Once the acceptance has been posted/mailed, the offeror (i.e. the seller) can revoke his offer only with the offeree's (i.e. the buyer's) consent.
Note: in the USA, a firm offer states in writing that it is irrevocable for a set time.

Firm order feste Bestellung Festauftrag

A written or verbal/oral order that has been confirmed/acknowledged and that is not subject to cancellation.

An order to buy or sell a security within a specified time period which can be executed without the customer's confirmation/acknowledgement.

Firm order date Auftragsannahme- und Kündigungsschluß

The date after which an order for advertising space or time cannot be cancelled, ie the advertising will run, no matter what.

Firm price Festpreis

A price quoted which cannot be changed by the maker, provided the offeree accepts it within a specified time period.

Firm sale Festverkauf

A sale at a fixed or agreed price.

First class mail Post erster Klasse (bevorzug abgefertigt)

In the USA, mail that receives the fastest delivery and costs the highest postage rate of the four classes of mail (first, second, third, and fourth).

First hand direktbezogen (Wareneinkauf)

Goods obtained directly from the producer.

First mover advantage Vorteil des zuerst Handelnden

In marketing, the advantage gained by a company which first sees a marketing opportunity or a market niche and immediately acts to acquire a major market share.

Note: this advantage is sometimes offset by a subsequent market entrant who has a greater capital or is able to learn from the mistakes made by the first mover.

First order Erstauftrag

Also called initial order.

An order placed for the first time and which opens up/starts business between two firms.

First proof — Rohabzug

The first print of an advertisement or publication, made for examination and correction.

First-come, first served method — Windhundverfahren (wer zuerst kommt, wird zuerst bedient)

A principle that the person who comes first will be served first; or orders will be carried out on a first-come, first-served basis.

First-half operating profit — Halbjahres-Betriebsergebnis

A company's operating profit in the first six months.

First-in, first-out (FIFO, fifo) — Fifo-Methode, "zuerst eingekauft, zuerst verbraucht" (Methode zur Bewertung der Warenbestände)

Also called last in still here (LISH, lish).

A method of valuing stock in a business. This method assumes that the earliest stock/inventory purchased or produced is the first to be sold. The closing stock/ending inventory therefore represents the most recent purchases or productions and the cost price would be related to current values. FIFO normally results, in times of rising prices, in a lower cost of goods sold figure (and therefore a higher profit figure) and in a higher asset valuation in the balance sheet.

First-time buyer — Ersterwerber

Also called first or initial buyer.

A customer who has bought something from a seller for the first time.

Fiscal drag — fiskalpolitische Bremse, fiscal-drag Effekt

A demand-decreasing effect associated with progressive income tax. At the same time as your salary is raised, inflation moves people into higher tax brackets so that after-tax incomes do not rise. Thus private consumption, spending and demand is dampened down. On the other hand government revenue may rise at a faster rate than government spending, so that the government may unintentionally develop a surplus which will also tend to decrease demand.

Fishy price gesalzener, saftiger Preis

A colloquial term for a very high price.

Fixed alternative Antwortvorgabe

n a questionnaire, a question in which the answers are limited to stated alternatives.

Fixed break Terminwerbung

Also called fixed spot.

A TV or radio commercial that is broadcast in a specific commercial break on a pecific day.

ixed budget starres Budget

A budget which remains unchanged during the budget period irrespective of the olume of output or turnover attained.

ixed charge(s) feste (Geschäfts)Kosten

charge that remains the same no matter how much or how little business a ompany does, i.e. any expense that does not vary with size of output or sales. Examples are rent, property insurance, bond interest, property taxes, administrative alaries, etc.

ixed cost(s) Fixkosten; feste, fixe Kosten

lso called fixed expense, committed cost, constant cost, nonvariable cost, standby ost, standing cost or unavoidable cost.

osts which do not vary in direct proportion to a firm's output. They are costs of the ndivisible factors and are incurred whatever the output; they remain constant (within relevant range and for a given time period) even if the level of production varies. xamples are rent, salaries, interest expense, insurance expenses, etc.
ote: fixed cost per unit changes as output changes.

ixed order system Bestellsystem mit Fixgrößen

system of arranging that recurrent orders are dealt with on an automatic basis within pecific limits. This avoids constant renegotiation of orders.

A system where an available product is stored at quantities to ensure that a minimum number is always present and that a maximum number is not exceeded. Also called maximum-minimum inventory control.

Fixed position feste Anzeigenplazierung
feste Werbesendungplazierung

In advertising, the placing of an advertisement in a fixed location in a publication specified by the advertiser. Furthermore, it is the space in a periodical occupied by one advertiser for two or more consecutive issues. Also called fixed location.

Broadcasting a commercial on TV or radio at a specific time of the day.

Fixed price contract Auftrag zu Festpreisen

A contract where the price to be paid is fixed before the work is commenced. There is no escalator clause.

Fixed price technique Festpreismethode

A pricing system in which the seller who offers a product or service sells at the announced price.

Fixed spot feste Werbesendungsplazierung,
Terminwerbung

A TV or radio commercial that is placed in a fixed position. To ensure this position the advertiser has to pay a premium. Also called fixed position.

A TV or radio commercial that is broadcast in a specific commercial break on a specific day. The advertiser has to pay an extra premium. Also called fixed break.

Fixed-time call (vor)angemeldetes Telefongespräch

For a fee, a telephone call which may be booked in advance.

Flagship Aushängeschild, "Paradepferd"

A key product in a product range, usually the big seller (money spinner, bestseller), on which the producer's reputation most depends.

The principal station of a television or radio network.

Flagship brand — Verkaufsschlager; Produkt eines Herstellers, das sich am besten verkauft

A manufacturer`s best known and best selling product.

Flanker brand — flankierende Marke

A line extension, i.e. a brand introduced into a market by a firm which already has a large market share in order to increase its share.

Flash pack — Sonderpreisverpackung, Blickfänger, Eyecatcher

A package on which a price reduction is printed very clearly. Flash packs are usually displayed at eye-level on the shelves to attract the attention of passing customers.

Flash sales report — Vorabverkaufsbericht

A daily report of the money value of sales made by each department of a retail store.

Flat rate — Pauschalpreis, Pauschalgebühr Anzeigenfestpreis

A charge which stays the same, at least for a particular period.

A flat rate is a uniform rate for advertising space or time.

Flatware — Eßgeschirr, Tafelgeschirr

Forks, knives, spoons, pieces of china, such as plates, etc.

Flea market — Flohmarkt

A market, often outdoors, consisting of a number of stalls selling cheap secondhand goods or used articles, curios and antiques, cut-rate merchandise, etc. People seem to love the experience of walking from vendor to vendor, bargaining for their purchases, and not being charged value-added-tax (VAT) or sales tax.
Flea marketing is now an established industry, often with its own publications.

Fleet Fuhrpark

The number of motor vehicles (usually more that ten) owned and operated by a company.

Flexible budget flexibles Budget

Also called variable budget or sliding-scale budget.

A budget which varies with the actual level of activity.

Flexible pricing flexible Preisgestaltung/ Preisfestsetzung

Also called multiple or variable pricing.

A pricing strategy in which the price charged for a commodity is open to negotiation between buyer and seller. This pricing strategy allows a seller to adjust prices based on the customer`s ability to negotiate or on his/her buying power. Thus, the seller charges different prices to different customers.

Flier/flyer Flugblatt

Also called handout.

A small handbill, ie a printed piece of paper, usually a single sheet, used as an advertisement.

Flight attendant Flugbegleiter

Air hostess or steward, who looks after passengers during a flight.

Flighting Phasenwerbung

Also called pulsing or pulsation.

The strategy of unevenly timed exposures of advertisements. That means, an advertising strategy that alternates periods, usually a minimum period of three weeks, of highly concentrated advertising with periods of no advertising at all.

Note: Any period of time during which the advertisements are appearing is called a flight, and a period of ad inactivity is known as a hiatus.

Flip chart Flipchart, klappbares Schaubild

A large white paper fold-over pad used for conveying messages and making presentations, e.g. in conferences, seminars, training courses, etc.

Float Wechselgeld in der (Laden)Kasse

Also called (small) change or petty cash fund.

A sum of money kept in a till/cash register to enable the operator to give customers change.

Floating-price technique variable Preismethode

A pricing method in which the seller who offers a product or service sells at a price that is negotiable.

Flood orders Auftragsflut

A large quantity of orders received by a firm within a short time period.

Floor Mindestpreis, untere Preisgrenze

Also called floor price.

The minimum price for certain commodities or services.

Floor manager Kaufhaus-Abteilungsleiter, Abteilungsleiter im Warenhaus Aufnahmeleiter (bei Film/Fernsehen)

In the USA, a department manager who is in charge of the sales department and its sales staff in a department store.

The member of the film or television production crew directing the activities in the studio by relaying commands from the director in the control room. Also called floor director.

Floor plan(ning) Finanzierung eines Warenlagers

A loan granted to finance a dealer's (merchandise) inventory. The dealer (i.e. the borrower) issues a trust receipt to the lender (usually a bank), and the lender is repaid when the inventory is sold. This kind of dealer financing is usually done only on goods for which a heavy consumer demand exists. Also called selling out of trust.

In financing, a method how retailers and wholesalers of capital goods can finance their trading stock/inventory. The finance provider acquires the trading stock from the producer and retains legal title until each item is sold, at which time title to the goods passes to the dealer and then to the buyer of the goods. Also called floor plan finance.

Floor price Mindestpreis

Also called fall-back, reference or reserve price. Note: at an auction, this price is also called knock(ed)-down price.

A minimum price for certain commodities, often set by the government.

Floor pyramid Warenstapel, Warenpyramide

In retailing, a type of POS advertising where the products for sale are displayed and stacked in the shape of a pyramid, approx. up to eye height.

Floor show Varieteevorstellung

A show performed by comedians, dancers, singers, stripteasers/strippers, etc in a bar, club, restaurant, etc.

Floor space Bodenfläche

The area of floor in an office, a shop or warehouse, e.g. 500 square meters.

Floor stand Bodenverkaufsständer, Warengestell

A display stand/display unit which stands on the shopfloor for the display of merchandise.

Floorwalker Ladenaufsicht

Also called shopwalker.

Store security officer, usually mixing with customers and attempting to spot shoplifters. Also called store detective.

A person who moves about a large shop (store), e.g. a department store, through various selling departments and assists customers in ways not handled by sales staff/personnel.

Flop Flop, Pleite, Reinfall

Also called lemon.

An activity, event or product which is a complete failure or has not been successful.

Note: there is a lemon-of-the-year prize for the worst car, refrigerator etc.

Flow of funds Geldstrom, Geldmittelbewegung Kapitalfluß

The transfer of money between the different sectors in the economy. Also called flow or movement of money.

The money inflows and outflows. Also called cash or capital flow.

Flow of goods and services Güter- und Leistungsstrom

The transfer of goods (goods flow) and services (transaction flow) between different sectors in the economy.

Flow of income Einkommenskreislauf

Also called circular flow of income.

A simple model illustrating the movement of resources between producers/businesses and consumers/households.

A number of flows comprise the flow of income. First, households (i.e. the owners of all factors of production in the economy) provide the factor services of labour, land, capital, and ownership to businesses (the flow of factor services). Secondly, in return, households receive paid wages, rent, interest, and profits (the flow of factor payments).

Thirdly, businesses provide goods and services to households (the flow of goods and services). Fourthly, households buy the goods and services (the flow of spending) in return.

Note: there is complete symmetry between the two sectors: households and businesses Each provides the other with some real resource (factor services, goods and services) and receives cash (factor payments, spending) in return; and each spends that cash on the supplies of the other.

Fluctuating demand schwankende Nachfrage

Demand which rises and falls sharply in response to changing economic conditions and consumer spending patterns.

Fluctuation Fluktuation, Schwankung

In general, a continuous or irregular change.
Examples are:
1. a rise or fall in the price of anything, e.g. fluctuation in share prices or in the rate of exchange.
2. the ups and downs of business activity and employment.
3. varying intensities of demand for a product or service.
4. changing quality levels, etc.

Fluff Patzer, Schnitzer
falsches Wechselgeld herausgeben

A mistake, e.g. in speech, an error or blunder.

Colloquially, to short change.

Fluid cash Tageseinnahme(n)

Also called day's takings, daily receipts, or daily returns.

The cash and cheques that are collected by a company in the course of daily business.

Fly posting unerlaubter (wilder) Plakatanschlag

Illegal fixing of (fly) posters on another's property.

'ly sheet Gebrauchsanweisung
Flugblatt, Reklamezettel

. sheet on which instructions or information are printed. Also called instruction ook(let) or instructions for use.

. printed advertising sheet. Also called flier, handout, handbill or throwaway.

'ly-drive holiday Fly and Drive, Flugurlaub mit vorbestelltem Mietwagen

Also called fly-drive package.

An arrangement where the traveller flies to an airport and has a rented car waiting for iim/her to pick up.
Note: the rent of the car is paid in advance as part of the package price.

'OB destination price Preis FOB Bestimmungsort

n geographic price quotations, a term used to indicate who must pay the shipping charges. In detail, it means that the seller bears the costs of shipping the merchandise o the customer`s destination.

'OB factory price Preis FOB Fabrik

n geographic price quotations, a term used to indicate who must pay the shipping charges. In detail, it means the price of the merchandise at the factory, before it is oaded onto the carrier`s vehicle, ie it excludes transport charges and the buyer must pay for shipping. Note: the seller completes his obligations by delivering the goods to he carrier.

Focus group Focusgruppe, Diskussionskreis

Also called discussion group.

n group discussions, a group of people from an appropriate target group brought ogether in a friendly atmosphere and encouraged to discuss attitudes, likes, dislikes, products, etc, to provide insights into consumer or user attitudes, behaviour and opinions. The group consists of seven to twelve people with desired characteristics brought together to discuss specific topics for an hour or more.

Note: focus groups are occasionally used to brainstorm new product ideas or to screen concepts for new products.

Focus of sale Hauptverkaufsargument

The most important claim(s) employed by a brand in its advertising or sales strategy.

Foil Folie

Often called tin foil or silver paper.

Thin film of metal, usually aluminium, used in packaging.

Folder Faltblatt

In advertising, a sheet of paper or board that can be folded once or more.

Foldout Faltanzeige

An advertisement in a folded page which opens out to show a much larger advertisement.

Folio Seitennumerierung, Paginierung
Blatt
Folioblatt (einmal gefalteter Druckbogen)

Numbered sheet of copy.

A sheet of paper.

A large printed sheet folded once in the middle.

Follow-the-leader pricing strategy Preisgestaltung, die Marktführer folgt

A pricing method where smaller companies copy the market leader's prices.

Follow-up Überwachung

In management, the function and process of examining and evaluating the extent to which specified goals, policies, procedures, standards or tasks of an organisation or department have been met.

Follow-up letter Nachfaßbrief

A letter sent to someone who has not reacted to the information and details given in a previous letter. For example, a sales letter sent to someone who has made an inquiry inviting the inquirer to make a purchase or to discuss in more detail points which had been raised earlier.

Follow-up quotation Nachfaßangebot

A quotation sent to someone who has not acted on the previous quotation.

Follow-up/on order Anschlußauftrag

Also called reorder; further, renewal, repeat or sequence order.

An order placed by a buyer as a result of a previous order. The salesperson follows up after the first sale to ensure customer satisfaction and repeat business.

Follower Marktfolger
Anhänger

A company which follows another into the market.

A person who supports or follows someone.

Following reading matter textanschließende Anzeigenposition

Also called following and next to reading (matter).

An advertisement placed immediately after and alongside a leading article/editorial to attract the attention of readers, whose eyes are said to migrate to the advertisement. Thus, in advertising, a preferred position for advertisers.

Font Schriftart

Also called fount.

The style of lettering available for use on a printer or typewriter.

Food additive Lebensmittelzusatz, Konservierungsmittel

Chemical substance added to food, eg one which is added to food to improve its appearance or to prevent it going bad.

Food and Drug Administration (FDA) Lebensmittelbehörde (USA)

Also called Food Office (GB).

In the USA, a federal agency that has the power to set standards for foods and food additives and to enforce regulations against selling and distributing adulterated, misbranded, or hazardous food and drug products. All new drugs must be submitted to the FDA for approval, and extensive laboratory tests must indicate their efficacy and safety.

Food and Drugs Act (FDA) Lebensmittelgesetz (GB)

Also called National Food Bill (USA).

In the UK, this Act makes it an offence to sell food or drink which is unfit for consumption; it controls the manner in which food and drugs are labelled and advertised; it lays down standards of composition and controls processing and it makes hygiene regulations. The Act is also concerned with the amounts of various ingredients found in food products.

Food court Lebensmittelviertel, "Freßviertel"

In a shopping center or shopping mall, a place where there are a lot of restaurants and food service facilities, usually with a shared eating area.

Foot (ft.) Fuß

A measure of length, being 12 inches long, or the third part of a yard, or 0,3048 meter.

Footing Einstandsgeld, Eintritt

Also called entrance money.

Entry money (to pay one's footing).

Footloose industries nicht standortgebundene Wirtschaftszweige

Industries which need no particular locations and thus can locate anywhere.

Footnote Fußnote

A note at the bottom of a page.

For acceptance within x days zur Annahme innerhalb x Tagen

An offer open only for the number of days stated.

For the account für/auf Rechnung

To buy goods for one's own account.

Force majeure höhere Gewalt

Also called Act of God, fortuitous event, superior force or power, or vis major.

A French term meaning: superior force. An accident or event that is the result of natural causes, without any human intervention, that could not have been prevented. For example, events beyond the control of the parties to a contract, such as natural disasters, earthquakes, strikes or war.

Forced choice method Zwangswahlverfahren

In statistics or marketing, a survey method of giving the respondent (interviewee) of a questionnaire a fixed set of responses to choose from.

Forced draugh/draft expansion beschleunigtes Wirtschaftswachstum

Also called accelerated growth.

Economic expansion accelerated by special government measures and/or strong external influences.

Forced sale Zwangsverkauf
Verkauf wegen Geschäftsaufgabe

Also called winding-up sale.

A sale not in the ordinary course of business, but a sale by order of court.

A closing-down sale.

Forced saving Zwangssparen

Also called compulsory or involuntary saving.

A form of saving which occurs because consumers are unable to spend their money on desired consumer goods because those goods are unavailable. In free markets prices of goods will rise and suppliers will increase supply.

Forcing Zwang zur Produktabnahme

A situation where a seller makes the supply of a desired product conditional upon the buyer accepting another product or products.

Forecast Prognose, Vorhersage

Also called prediction.

This is a semi-scientific prediction of the future. The reliability of a forecast depends on three factors:
1. the accuracy of the research information which is used in the calculation of the forecast; 2. the relevance of the information which is included; 3. the number of unknown variables which form part of the prediction.

There are three types of forecast which are important for businesses:
1. sales forecasts, 2. economic forecasts, and 3. technological forecasts.

Foreign advertising Auslandswerbung

Advertising placed outside the advertiser`s own country.

Foreign competition Auslandskonkurrenz

Also called competition from abroad and foreign competitors or rivals.

Competition caused by companies from abroad. If internal/domestic prices rise faster on average than those of foreign competitors, whilst exchange rates remain constant, our exports become less attractive in their markets, whilst the goods imported from these countries have a relative price advantage. Consequently, exports decrease and import spending increases (ceteris paribus) causing balance of payments difficulties.

Floating exchange rates tend to offset the relative price disadvantage, but a lower exchange rate inevitably causes import prices to rise, which may in itself contribute to further inflationary pressures.

Foreign customs ausländische Gewohnheiten, Sitten

Things which are usually practised by the population of a foreign country. A lack of knowledge and understanding about the customs, habits and laws of the importer's or exporter's country creates an extra degree of uncertainty between buyer and seller.

Foreign market entry Auslandsmarkt-Zutritt

Entering an overseas market, either by exporting, licensing, joint venturing or direct ownership.

Foreign sales agent (FSA) Auslandsverkaufsvertreter

An individual or a firm that serves as the foreign representative of a domestic supplier.

Foreign sector Auslandssektor

The part of a nation's economy that is concerned with importing and/or exporting goods or services.

Foreign trade Außenhandel

Also called external or international trade, external commerce, or overseas trade.

Commerce with other nations. This can be bilateral or multilateral.

Foreign trade - price quotations Preisangebote im Außenhandel

In foreign trade a number of charges arise in connection with the sale and delivery of goods. The basic price of the goods is their ex-warehouse price in the country of origin. To this the following five additions have to be made:

1. the cost of carrying the goods to the docks at the port of departure;
2. dock dues and any other charges for loading the goods on to the ship;
3. the freight charges for carrying the goods from the port of departure to the port of destination;
4. insurance of the goods while they are in transit;
5. the charge for carrying the goods from the port of destination to the importer's warehouse.

The various terms which are employed to cover these charges are the incoterms.

Forgetting rate Vergeßlichkeitsspanne

In media research, the rate at which memory of advertising is lost from one advertising period to another without continued reinforcement.

Forklift (truck) Gabelstapler

Also called fork truck, materials handling truck or industrial truck.

A small vehicle with two metal arms in front, usually driven by electric batteries, for lifting, stacking and carrying loads on pallets from one part of a factory or warehouse to another.

Formal sales training formales Verkaufstraining

A process used to give new salespeople product knowledge, selling skills, information on markets and competition, and familiarity with company policies and practices.

Format Anordnung, Aufmachung
Format

The layout and order of presentation.

Shape, size, or style of a publication.

DIN formats (e.g. paper) are accepted all over the world.

Former buyer ehemaliger, früherer Käufer/Kunde

An individual or firm who has bought one or more times from a seller but has made no purchase over the preceding 12 months.

Formula pricing Formelpreisbildung

A pricing strategy in which a predetermined formula is used to set/fix a product`s or service`s price. For example, a firm sets prices at 150 percent of direct labour costs plus 200 percent of material costs plus actual shipping costs. The main advantage of this strategy is its simplicity, whereas the main disadvantage is that it ignores demand and other market conditions.

Fortune 500 Liste der 500 größten US-Gesellschaften

A directory of the 500 largest US corporations, ranked by sales and published each year by "Fortune" magazine. A "Fortune" 100 company is one of the 100 largest.

Forty-eight sheet Achtundvierzigerformat

A very large poster, eg on bulletin boards (from: a height of 48 inches = 122 cm).

Forward (fwd) (ab-,über-,ver-) senden, befördern von heute an

To send (off), dispatch, ship or transport goods, e.g. from one location to another.

From this day forward.

Forward booking Vorbestellung, Vorausbuchung, Reservierung

Also called advance booking.

Reservations made in advance.

Forward contract Terminkontrakt
Warentermingeschäft

The purchase or sale of a specific quantity of a commodity, foreign currency, or security at the current price/spot price, with delivery and settlement/liquidation at a specified future time.

A financial instrument for deferred delivery of a given quantity of specified goods at a given price between the two parties named in the contract. Forward contracts are suitable for goods that can be graded (e.g. oil, grain, wool, sugar, coffee, cocoa, metal, etc.), the prices of all grades rising or falling together. By entering into forward contracts, the parties run the risk that prices may change to the advantage of one party and to the disadvantage of the other party to the agreement. Also called forward sale.

Forward cover Terminsicherung

Also called futures hedging.

A forward transaction intended to protect a buyer or seller of a commodity or financial instrument from unexpected price fluctuations.

Forward deal Termingeschäft, -handel

Also called forward dealing.

Trading in foreign currencies, goods or securities for delivery and payment at some date in the future.

Forward delivery (FD) Terminlieferung

Also called future delivery.

Delivery at some specified time in the future.

Forward market Terminmarkt

Also called futures market.

A market where dealers agree to deliver commodities or financial instruments at a fixed current price at a specified future date.

Forward price Preis für künftige Lieferung

The price quoted for future delivery.

Forward purchase Kauf zur späteren Auslieferung

Goods that have been bought for delivery at some agreed date in the future.

Forward transaction Termingeschäft

To buy or sell (goods, currencies or securities) in the future, with payment and delivery at that future date. But the price has been agreed upon at the time of signing the contract. The opposite of spot sale.

Forwarding Versand, Expedition,
Ab-, Ver-, Senden
Nachsendung

The activities (e.g. handling and processing documents) and procedures relating to the transport of goods. Also called despatch, sending off or shipping.

The sending of letters etc. arriving at a previous address to a new address (the forwarding address). Also called redirection.

Forwarding address Nachsendeadresse

In case of a postal instruction "please forward", this is the address to which a person's or company`s post/mail may be sent on by someone to the appropriate addressee.

Forwarding agent Spediteur

Also called forwarder or freight forwarder.

A person engaged in collecting, transferring, warehousing, and delivering goods. His work involves documentation and he has a specialised knowledge of transport and of export and import regulations and procedures. He acts as intermediary/ middleman between a consignor or consignee and a carrier; but usually he has his own vehicles and transports the goods himself. His remuneration is by fees (often linked to the invoice value of the goods) plus any commission allowed by transporters, insurers, etc.

Forwarding instructions Versandanweisungen

Also called shipping instructions.

Instructions given by the buyer to the seller showing how goods are to be shipped and delivered.

Four colour (4/c) advertisement Vierfarbenanzeige

An advertisement in the four major printing colours: red, yellow, blue and black.

Four Os vier O's für Marketingoperation

The abbreviations of the essential factors of a marketing operation, which are objects, objectives, organization and operations.

Four Ps vier P's des Marketingmix

The abbreviations of the principal factors included in the marketing mix, i.e. product, price, place and promotion. Note: sometimes an S is included for service.

Four-plus cover mehr als vier Kontakte (Werbung)

In advertising, a situation where the members of the target group will have seen an advertisement at least four times or more.

Fragile zerbrechlich

Easily broken, injured or destroyed. Fragile articles must be properly packed and marked "fragile, with care", "caution - with care", "handle with care", etc. Often symbols are used to indicate fragility.

Fragmentation Aufteilung einer Werbekampagne

The use of a number of different media for an advertising campaign, with no single medium used predominantly or heavily.

Franchise

Vertragsvertrieb,
Alleinvertriebsrecht
(mit Lizenz oder Konzession)

The privilege, often exclusive, granted to a distributor or dealer (i.e. the franchisee) by a franchisor to sell the franchisor´s products within a specified area. This type of trading agreement is often made between a supplier and a reail outlet whereby coopertion, support and promotional aids are provided by the supplier.

Franchise outlet

franchisierter Ortshändler

A business owned and operated by an individual who is a franchisee of a franchisor.

Franchisee

Franchisenehmer

A person or company to whom a franchise is granted. The franchisee agrees to operate the business according to a marketing plan substantially prescribed by the franchisor and he operates his business under a trademark or trade name owned by the franchisor.

Franchising

Franchising (Art von Filialsystem),
Lizenzkonzessionserteilung

Franchising is the process whereby the owner of a business (the franchisor) allows others to run it for him in return for certain payments. The franchisor supplies a name, products, services and general know-how and the franchisee contracts to use all or a major part of the franchisor's services in an agreed manner. The franchisee pays the owner a substantial sum for this privilege. There is an agreement that the franchisee pays the franchisor either by purchasing all materials from him or by paying a royalty (a fixed percentage of sales).
The franchisor (the parent company) has the advantage of attracting capital from enterprising individuals (the franchisees) and in effect receives a share of their profits; limits his capital involvement and his administration; the franchisee has the advantage of being able to use a well-known and widely advertised name, without having to build up his own reputation; he can receive cheap supplies; and obtain managerial advice and guidance.

Some retail outlets which look like mulitple shops are, in fact, franchises. Perhaps the most notable franchise company of all is Coca Cola.

Franchisor/franchiser Franchisegeber

The supplier in a franchise system, i.e. the company or person who licences a franchise. The franchisor grants the franchisee the right to distribute or sell certain goods or services.

Franco (fco) frei

Also called free.

A term used in quotations. It means the price quoted is inclusive covering all charges up to delivery at the buyer's premises. It is the seller who is liable for all costs of transport.

Franco domicile frei Haus

Also called free domicile, free house, free to the door or free delivered.

The seller undertakes to deliver the goods free/franco to the buyer's premises, wherever they may be.

Franking Freistempelung

Using a franking machine and printing the postage on mail/post to indicate that postage has already been paid in advance.

Fraud (arglistige) Täuschung, Betrug

A misrepresentation intended to deceive or cheat. Fraud is a crime, and every contract made where one of the parties is misled by fraudulent statements is void. Note: the representations made in the negotiations leading up to a contract must be true.

Fraudulent misrepresentation wissentlich falsche Angaben

In law, making a false statement with the intention of tricking someone.

Fraudulent trading unlautere Wettbewerbshandlungen

The carrying on of a business with intent to defraud creditors.

Free — uneingeschränkt, erlaubt
kostenlos, unentgeltlich

Not subject to any special restrictions or regulations.

Without charge/free of charge; not subject to payment.

Free advertisement — Gratisanzeige
Gratiserwähnung, Schleichwerbung

An advertisement published without charging the advertiser, e.g. an advertisement for charitable purposes.

The use of trade names instead of generic names in news copy. Also called free mention, puff, puff notice or plug.

Free competition — freier Wettbewerb, freie Konkurrenz

Competition between companies without government interference. Prices are determined by the free, unregulated interaction of supply and demand.

Free delivery — Lieferung frei Bestimmungsort

A service given free of charge (foc) by a seller to his customers, of carrying the goods they have bought and delivering them to the named place of destination.

Free delivery area — Freihauslieferungszone

An area within which the seller will deliver goods purchased to the buyer free of charge.

Free economy — freie Marktwirtschaft

Also called free enterprise economy or system; free or liberal market economy.

An economic system based on free competition. Prices are controlled only by the market forces of supply and demand. Furthermore, an economic system, characterised by non-interference by government, in which all wealth is owned by individuals and economic problems are solved by variations in supply and demand through the price mechanism.

Free gift Werbegeschenk

Also called advertising or goodwill gift, or giveaway.

A promotional gift; something given away to (prospective) customers without any charge; a method of inducing impulse purchases.
Free offer "mail-ins" are those where a gift is offered in return for the label or package; "on pack" means that the gift is attached to the product at the point of sale.

Free goods freie Güter
zollfreie Waren

Free goods are those which have no opportunity cost (e.g. air). As the goods are available in unlimited supply, they have no market price. The wants for these goods can be satisfied without forgoing any alternative goods. Also called free resource or common property resource.

In foreign trade, a term used for imported goods that are free of customs duty. Also called duty-free goods.

Free in and out (FIO, fio) frei ein und aus, frei laden und löschen (Lieferklausel/ FIO-Klausel)

Goods may be carried on FIO-terms. In charter parties (C/Ps), a term stating that cargo is loaded and discharged (unloaded) at no cost to the shipowner. The cost of loading at the loading port (port of dispatch or embarkation) is borne by the shipper and the unloading charges at the port of discharge (port of debarkation, disembarkation or unloading) are borne by the receiver/consignee of the goods.

Free in store (FIS) frei Laden, Geschäft

A phrase stating that the producer is responsible for all freight and delivery costs, i.e. the ordered goods are delivered freight free to the customer, i.e. the store where the goods are sold.

Free market economy System der freien Marktwirtschaft, marktwirtschaftliche Ordnung

Also called free economy or enterprise system, competitive or free market.

A commodity market in which prices are determined by supply and demand and traders are free of interference by government regulations.

Free market price freier Marktpreis

Also called competitive price.

The price of a product or service fixed by supply and demand and not by governmental control.

Free merchandise Warenzugabe, (Gratis)Musterquote Zugabe, Gratisware, Extraware statt Rabatt/Nachlaß

A type of sales promotion in which resellers are given a certain quantity of merchandise free of charge in return for an order exceeding a certain quantity, ie a manufacturer offers resellers free merchandise in lieu of quantity discounts.
For example, instead of giving a reseller a price reduction for buying a certain quantity of merchandise, the manufacturer may throw in extra merchandise "free", ie at a cost that would equal the price reduction.

Free of charge (foc) ohne Berechnung, kostenlos, gratis

A phrase indicating that no payment is to be made.

Free on aircraft (foa) frei Flugzeug

Under this cargo delivery term, the seller's duty is to deliver the goods to the airport at the named departure point and load them onto the airplane or helicopter.

Free on board at airport (FOA) FOB Flughafen, frei Flughafen

Also called free airport or FOB airport (FOBA).

A term that applies to airports and aircraft. The seller/exporter has to deliver the goods to the air carrier at the airport of departure and completes his obligations by delivering the goods to the nominated air carrier at the departure airport. The risk of damage to the goods is transferred from the seller to the buyer/importer when the goods have been so delivered. The buyer pays the air freight and insurance and all other cost following delivery of the goods by the seller to the nominated air carrier at the specified airport.

Free on board free off board (fob/fob) frei an Bord plus frei von Bord

Under this cargo delivery term, the seller's duty is to deliver the goods free on board (usually of a vessel); additionally he has to bear the unloading costs.

Free on quay (FOQ, foq) frei (auf) Kai

An export trade term. The seller is responsible for delivering the goods to the loading quay at the port of shipment/departure, but not for loading them onto the ship.

Free on rail / free on truck (FOR/FOT) frei/franko Waggon

Also called free on wag(g)on (FOW).

Under this cargo delivery term, the seller's/exporter's duty is to deliver the goods to the railway at the named departure point (the word truck refers to a railway waggon) and, in the case of "full loads", to obtain and load the wagon(s). The buyer/importer accepts delivery of the goods when they have been delivered to the railway, and the invoice and transport documents have been provided by the seller. The buyer must pay all charges and assume all responsibilities from that moment onwards.
Note: the terms should only be used when the goods are to be carried by rail.

Free on truck (FOT, fot) frei LKW (USA)
frei Waggon (GB)

In the USA, a pricing term indicating that the quoted price includes the cost of loading the goods onto the truck/lorry.

In GB, the same as free on rail (FOR, for).

Free sample Gratismuster

An example of an article given free to prospective purchasers so that they can examine and test it. The best way of introducing consumers to a product is to let them try it out free. The free samples are given at particular shops or they are sent to every household.

Free time gebührenfreie Ladezeit
Freizeit

The amount of time allowed by carriers free of charge (foc) for the loading or unloading of freight. After the expiration of this time, demurrage has to be paid.

The time a person can spend freely. Also called leisure or spare time.

ree trade Freihandel

.lso called liberal trade.

'he policy of allowing the free interchange of commodities between countries by the on-imposition or abolition of protective duties. The advantages of large-scale roduction can be enjoyed because there is a global/world market.

'ree trade area (FTA) Freihandelsgebiet, -zone

.lso called free trade zone (FTZ).

. defined area consisting of several countries in which trade is based upon the nrestricted exchange of goods. No customs duties are imposed (levied) on goods oing from one of the member countries to another. Free trade groupings are the :uropean Union (EU), North American Free Trade Agreement (NAFTA), the :ouncil for Mutual Economic Assistance (Comecon, was abolished in 1991); the .atin American Free Trade Association (LAFTA), the Central American Common /larket (CACM), the Caribean Community and the Common Market (Caricon), the :entral African Economic Community (CEAO), and the Economic Community of Vest African States (ECOWAS).
'he advantages of free trade areas stem from the increased market (population and urchasing power) which is made available to member countries.

'ree trade association Freihandelsgemeinschaft

\ group of countries having no import duties among member nations. Each country .as its own tariffs with non-member countries.

'ree trader Freihandelsbefürworter

\ person who is promoting free trade.

'ree trial kostenlose(r) Probe/Test, kostenlos zur Probe

:esting of an item, eg a machine, with no payment involved.

'reedom of choice Wahlfreiheit

n a free enterprise system, businesses are free to hire people, invest money, decide vhat to supply, purchase goods, choose markets where they wish to operate, etc.

Freephone/freefone gebührenfreier Anruf

A service offered by Telecom to companies by which potential customers who wish to answer an advertisement, ask for information or place an order by phone can do so by calling a certain number at the expense of the company.

Freepost Rückumschlagsystem (ohne Wertzeichen), Gebühr bezahlt Empfänger, unfrei

A firm wishing to obtain replies from others without putting them to the expense of paying postage may include, in its correspondence, a business reply envelope. The reply can be posted in the normal way but without a stamp. The firm receiving the mail pays postage on all the replies received.
For example, a potential customer can write to an advertiser to place an order or to ask for information to be sent, and the advertiser, ie the seller pays the postage.

Freesheet/free sheet Anzeigenblatt, Gratiszeitung

Also called advertiser.

A local weekly newspaper or magazine which is distributed free of charge and which is full of advertisements which are the sole source of their revenue. Most of the space in these publications is sold for advertising, leaving little room for editorial content.

Freestanding insert (FSI, fsi) lose Anzeigenbeilage, Werbebeilage

Also called freestanding stuffer or loose insert.

Brochures, leaflets and similar advertising material distributed with publications such as newspapers and magazines and inserted loosely within their pages.

Freeze Stop

Official action to fix prices of goods (price freeze) or wages (wage freeze) at a specific level, or within stated limits.

Freeze out Verdrängen von Konkurrenten

Also called drive out.

A situation in which a company successfully out-competes its competitors/rivals and freezes/drives them out of the market.

Freight (fgt, frt) Ladung, Fracht
Frachtkosten, Beförderungskosten
befördern, verfrachten

The cargo in any mode of transport transported for pay.

Charge for the transportation of goods. Also called freightage, freight charges, transport expenses or cost of transport.

The movement of goods by some means of transport.

Freight absorption Frachtkostenübernahme

A pricing term stating that the seller of goods does not charge a buyer for freight out.

Freight absorption pricing Preisstellung mit Übernahme der Frachtkosten

A geographic pricing strategy in which the seller absorbs all or part of the actual freight charges in order to obtain the desired business. This strategy is frequently used on competitive markets or for market penetration.

Freight all kind(s) (FAK, fak) Frachtkosten tarifunabhängig von Warenart

A freight rate that applies to all kinds of cargo irrespective of commodity type, i.e. the rate charged is not based on the individual commodity.

Freight car Güterwaggon

Also called goods waggon.

A railway wag(g)on for carrying goods.

Freight charge Frachtgebühr

Also called freigtage.

The amount of money charged for transporting freight.

Freight contract Frachtvertrag

Also called contract of carriage.

A contract made by a shipper/consignor or consignee of goods with a carrier for the carriage/transportation of cargo. The consideration paid to the carrier, either by the shipper or the consignee, is known as freight/freightage.

Freight costs Frachtkosten

Also called freight, freight charges or freightage.

The amount of money paid for transporting goods.

Freight depot Güterdepot, Güterniederlage

A central point where goods are collected before being shipped/forwarded.

Freight forward (frt, fwd) unfrei, Fracht gegen/per Nachnahme, Fracht zahlbar am Bestimmungsort

Also called freight collect or carriage forward.

An annotation to give evidence that freight has not been paid. Freight charges are payable at the place of destination, ie the customer pays for transporting the goods.

Freight handling facilities Güterverladeanlagen

The facilities and equipment necessary to load and unload goods.

Freight in and out Eingangsfracht und Ausgangsfracht

Also called freight inward(s) and outward(s), carriage inward(s) and outward(s), carriage in and out.

The carriage charges made by a carrier for transporting goods from a supplier to our business or from our business to a purchaser of our goods.

Freight invoice Frachtrechnung

A document sent to the shipper of goods, e.g. by a carrier or forwarder, and giving details of freight charges.

Freight list (Ver)Ladeliste

A list giving details of the goods carried.

Freight note Frachtrechnung, Transportkostenrechnung

Also called freight account or freight invoice.

An account (invoice) giving details of freight payable.

Freight payable at destination (FPAD) Frachtzahlung am Bestimmungsort

In transport, a term which indicates that the freight is payable when the goods have reached their place of destination.

Freight plane Transportflugzeug

An aircraft/airplane which carries goods, not passengers.

Freight prepaid (frt ppd) Fracht vorausbezahlt, frachtfrei

Also called carriage paid (C/P) or freight paid.

A term which indicates that the freight payable on the goods has been paid.

Freight prepayment mark Frankaturvermerk

A mark on post/mail parcels, cases, etc. indicating that postage or freight charges have been paid.

Freight rate Fracht-, Gütertarif

The charge for carriage. Some goods are charged on a weight basis, others on a volume basis, and valuable goods are charged on an ad valorem basis.

Freight station Güterbahnhof

Also called goods station.

The station from which cargo is transported by freight train (goods train, freightliner).

Freight train Güterzug

Also called goods train.

A train used for carrying goods.

Freightage Frachtkosten
Frachtgut
Frachtbeförderung, Verfrachtung

The charge for the transportation of goods. Also called freight, freight charges/costs, cost of transport or transport expenses.

The cargo carried in return for payment of freight.

The movement of goods by some means of transport.

Freighter Frachter, Frachtschiff, Frachtflugzeug
Befrachter
Absender, Verlader, Verfrachter

A vessel or aeroplane transporting goods.

The charterer of a vessel or aeroplane. Also called shipper.

One for whom freight is transported. Also called consignor or shipper.

Freightliner Containerzug

A train which carries goods in containers.

'requency (freq) Eintrittshäufigkeit
Häufigkeit
Kontakthäufigkeit
Insertionshäufigkeit, Werbungshäufigkeit

ı general, the rate of occurrence.

ı statistics, the number of times something happens during a given time period, e.g. ıe number of occurrences of a given type of event.

'he number of times a person, household, or member of a target market is exposed to a ıedia vehicle/advertising medium, ie sees or hears an advertisement during a ampaign.

'he number of times in the course of a year or some other specified period that an dvertiser runs an advertisement, e.g. a commercial appears two or three times on the ame hour TV show.

'requency discount Malrabatt

. discount granted to an advertiser for running a certain number of advertisements ·ithin a specified time period.

'requency distribution Häufigkeitsverteilung

. statistical table including the number of times an event occurs. It measures the elative frequency that a variable can take on a set of values.

'requent buyer programme Programm für häufigen Kunden

. form of consumer sales promotion, designed to create and reward brand loyalty mong consumers who might otherwise switch from brand to brand within a category. 'onsumers are rewarded for making multiple purchases of a particular good or service, g the frequent flier plans offered by airlines are good examples.

'requent flyer Vielflieger

. person who travels often (with the same airline), and thus receives a special 'eatment.

Fringe accounts Sekundärkunden

Customers making marginal contributions to a supplier´s turnover and who are not very profitable for the supplier.

Fringe time Sendezeit vor und nach der Hauptsendezeit, "Randzeit"

A period of time on radio and television which precedes and follows prime time and thus attracts fewer listeners or viewers.

Front cover Titelseite

Also called front or title page.

First page of a magazine, newspaper or journal.

Front desk Rezeption

Also called reception.

Reception desk at the entrance to a hotel.

Front end Kassenbereich
Frontwerbefläche

The checkout area at a supermarket`s or self-service store`s exit.

The advertising area under the front windows of a vehicle, eg a bus.

Front-end checkout Kundenkasse am Ladenausgang

The placement of checkout counters/cash desks near store/shop exits rather than near sales areas.

Fudge Anzeigenfehler

A mistake made in an advertisement.

Fulfil(l)ment Erfüllung

Carrying something out in a satisfactory way.

The state of being fulfil(l)ed.

Full board Vollpension

A special rate for guests staying at a hotel, who take all their meals there.

Full container load (FCL) Container-Komplettladung

A fully loaded container, either in weight or cubic measurement terms.

An arrangement whereby a shipper utilizes all the space in a container.

Full cost Vollkosten

The cost of a unit of output which includes the variable costs of production and an appropriate proportion of fixed (costs).

Cost of manufacture including direct costs and a proportion of indirect costs/overheads and arrived at by absorption costing.

Full cost pricing Vollkostenkalkulation

Also called markup pricing.

The firm estimates the average cost of producing the good and then adds on a percentage markup for profit.

Full disclosure vollständige Offenlegung

In advertising, a legal requirement to protect the consumer, i.e. all data necessary for the consumer to make a safe and informed decision has to be provided in a promotion message.

Full economy erweitertes Wirtschaftskreismodell

An economy which contains the following sectors:
1. households, 2. trading enterprises, 3. financial enterprises, 4. government,
5. overseas.

Full fare voller Fahrpreis

Ticket for a journey by an adult at the full price.

Full line Vollsortiment

Also called full range of products.

A complete range of products.

Full line forcing Zwang zur Abnahme eines ganzen Sortiments

A form of tying arrangement in which a full-line supplier insists that the retailer takes all his product lines and not just those which the retailer feels are good sellers.

Full-line department store Kaufhaus mit Vollsortiment

A department store which offers many different product lines, such as clothing, electrical goods, food, furniture, gifts, sporting goods, stationery, etc. and many different services, including delivery and credit.

Full-line discount store Discount-Geschäft mit Vollsortiment

This type of store/shop carries lines of products comparable to those of a full-line department store, although at lower prices.

Full-line discounter Diskont(waren)haus mit Vollsortiment

A full-line discount store offering consumers very limited service but carrying a broad assortment/range of well-known, nationally branded "hard goods".

Full-line supplier — Anbieter einer vollständigen Produktpalette

A firm supplying a complete assortment/range of products.

Full-line wholesaler — Großhändler mit Vollsortiment

Also called general merchandise wholesaler.

A wholesaler who stocks a full assortment of products within a product line. Typically, he only carries one or two lines of merchandise.

Full-page advertisement — ganzseitige Anzeige

Also called full spread.

An advertisement covering one complete page in a magazine or newspaper.

Full payment — Zahlung in voller Höhe

Also called payment in full.

Payment of all money owed.

Full price — voller Preis

The price with no discount.

Full-service advertising agency — Full-Service-Werbeagentur

An advertising agency that has the resources to offer its clients a wide range of services, including marketing research, planning and management; setting advertising objectives, developing advertising strategies, producing ad messages, merchandising, press and/or public relations, packaging, etc.

Full-service retailer — Full-Service-Einzelhändler

A retailer, e.g. a specialty shop, that provides a full range of services to shoppers, e.g. salespersons assist customers in every phase of the shopping process.

Note: more services result in much higher operating costs which are usually passed on to customers as higher prices.

Fullface envelope Briefumschlag ohne Fenster

Also called closed-face envelope.

An envelope without a window.

Functional costs aufgabenbezogene Kosten

Costs associated with a specific business activity, such as advertising, marketing, research, selling, etc.

Functional discount Funktionsrabatt, Handelsrabatt

A different discount granted to effect different prices for different customers.

A price concession granted to an intermediary/middleman for providing such services as storage, handling, and selling.

Functional modification funktionale (Produkt)Modifikation

Also called feature modification.

A change that affects a product`s convenience, effectiveness, safety or versatility, and thus making the product useful to more people and more competitve.

Functional product differentiation funktionale Produktdifferenzierung

A marketing strategy which ensures that a product has functional features that distinguish it from rival products.

Fungibles fungible, vertretbare Waren; Fungibilien

Also called fungible goods or merchantable goods.

Assets which individually are so similar so that they are not distinguishable from one another.

Future delivery Terminlieferung

Delivery of something at a later date.

Future shock Zukunftsschock

A phrase coined by the contemporary writer Alvin Toffler which describes a situation when people suffer disorientation and confusion because social, economic, political, technological and scientific change is happening very quickly.

Futures Termingeschäfte, Terminkontrakte Terminwaren

A "future" is a contract to deliver standard commodities or financial instruments in the future at a price fixed now. A futures contract takes the form of a fixed and binding contract, i.e. it obligates buyer and seller to fulfil the contract.
For some commodities the markets quote a number of prices, varying according to delivery date. There is, however, no intention of actually making a delivery. The contract will be fulfilled by paying or receiving the difference between the contract price and the then current price. Dealing in futures insures the buyer against a rise in prices and insures the seller against a fall in prices.

The commodities in futures contracts.

Futures price Terminkurs, Preis für Termingeschäft

The price of a commodity or financial instrument (e.g. a currency) determined on a futures exchange.

Futures trading Terminhandel

Purchasing or selling financial instruments or commodities for future receipt or delivery.

Futurology Zukunftsforschung

The study or forecasting of future trends or developments.

G

Gag Witz, (Werbe)Gag

A laugh-producing joke, a comical line or situation, or a device aiming at constant repetition etc.

Gallon (gal) Gallone

A measure of capacity, both for dry and liquid articles. One American gallon = 3,7853 l (liquid measure) or 4,405 l (dry measure).

Galloping deflation galoppierende Deflation

A high rate of persistent deflation, ie a situation where prices fall continuously.

Galloping inflation galoppierende Inflation

Also called hyperinflation; cantering, runaway, snowballing or raging inflation.

A very high rate of persistent inflation. Prices rise so rapidly so that the value of money declines to a fraction of its former value. People quickly lose confidence in the monetary system.

Galvanic skin response (GSR) Erregungsmethode, Galvanometermethode

Also called arousal method or galvanometric response.

A physiological testing technique in which the change in skin conductivity due to change in moisture content/perspiration is measured by a galvanometer in order to check a person`s reaction, interest or level of arousal caused by an advertisement.

Gamble (Glücks)Spiel
riskantes Unternehmen

To play a game of chance or skill for money; to take risks in the hope of gaining money or advantage.

Any business venture in which risk and uncertainty predominate. Also called speculative venture.

Game Spiel

A consumer sales promotion technique that requires consumers to take specific actions or use special skills to complete a project or activity with the goal of winning a prize.

Gameshow/game show Quizsendung, Radio/TV-Spielshow

A radio or television programme in which contestants answer questions or play games in order to win prizes.

Gap analysis Marktlückenanalyse,
Lückenanalyse

In general, gap analysis is used to investigate the difference between any target and any forecast.

A systematical study of markets and of all known consumer wants of a particular product category to spot any gaps which exist in a market and that is not at present being provided with a particular product or service. Such an analysis shows up where new products can be introduced/launched because they find and are capable of satisfying unfulfilled wants and demands.

Garbology Abfallwirtschaft, Müllkunde

The study of consumer behaviour and preferences for foods and products by examining disposed goods found in the garbage and trash to learn what it reveals about a society`s social or cultural patterns.

Gate money Eintrittsgelder, (Sport)Einnahmen

A name for the cash receipts from entrance fees/admission charges for sports events, etc.

Gatefold ausschlagbare Anzeigenseite, Titelseite

In magazine advertising, an inside page or cover that must be unfolded for viewing, giving the advertisement a much larger dimension than the regular-size page.

Gatekeeper Informationsregulator Pförtner

An individual who controls the flow of information from the mass media to other individuals.

A person who controls decision making within an organisation by controlling the purchase process, eg the buying/purchasing agent is often the gatekeeper between the ultimate/end consumer and the seller of products or services.

A person in charge of a gate, usually to supervise the traffic, through it or services.

Gaze motion Augenbewegung, Blickverlauf

Also called eye flow or eye movement.

The movement of a reader`s or viewer`s eyes.

Gem-triangle magisches Marketing-Dreieck

Gem = goods, enterprise, man.

As a salesman must be able to convince his customer, every selling activity must be founded on three things:
The salesman must believe in:
1. the goods he is selling, 2. the enterprise he represents and 3. himself, the man.

Gender segmentation Segmentierung nach Geschlecht

The segmentation of a market by gender, ie marketers consider the special concerns of gender groups. Marketers of products like clothing, cosmetics, personal care items, etc commonly segment markets according to gender.

General (economic) equilibrium allgemeines/totales (ökonomisches) Gleichgewicht

A theoretical situation where all markets in an economy are simultaneously in equilibrium, i.e. prices and quantities of goods and services do not change. Supply equals demand in all markets.

General agent (GA) Generalvertreter

Also called free agent, general representative or universal agent.

A person employed to conduct a particular business or trade within a specified area.

General cargo Stückgut(ladung)

Also called piece goods or less than carload lot (LCL).

Goods requiring less space when transported than that available in a single freight car, ie cargo made up of various types of goods.

General cargo rate (GCR) Frachtrate für Stückgut

These are the basic rates for general cargo and fall into three categories:
1. minimum charges, 2. normal rate (the 100 kg rate), 3. quantity rate (applicable on the various minimum quantities shipped), note: the charging a consignment at a higher weight rate is allowed if a lower charge results overall.

General delivery postlagernd

Also called poste restante or to be called for.

Mail delivery at post office to persons who call for it.

General interest magazine Publikumszeitschrift

Also called general magazine or general editorial magazine.

A magazine containing information with a broad appeal for a wide range of readers.

General merchandise wholesaler Gemischtwarengroßhändler

A wholesaler who handles a broad range of products, eg food and drug items, tools and other technical items.

General need description allgemeine Bedarfsbeschreibung

In industrial purchasing, the process by which the company describes the general characteristics and quantity of an item needed.

General offer öffentliches Angebot

An offer to the public at large.

General Post Office (GPO) Hauptpost(amt)

The main post office in a city with several branch post offices.

General price level allgemeines Preisniveau

Also called general level of prices.

A sort of average of the prices of all kinds of commodities (producers' goods and consumers' goods) and services.

General Retail Price Index (RPI) Einzelhandelspreisindex

The RPI is based on a large series of items (commodities and services) which go into the average basket bought by households. Items are chosen that can represent price movements of commodities and services as a whole. Because some items are more important than others, they are weighted. Prices for the RPI are collected from selected areas.
The main groups comprising the RPI are as follows: food, alcoholic drink, tobacco, housing, fuel and light, durable household goods, clothing and footwear, transport and vehicles, services, miscellaneous goods, meals bought and consumed outside the home.

Note: the RPI is an index of retail price changes and not a cost-of-living-index.

General sales manager Vertriebsdirektor, Verkaufsleiter

A senior manager with overall responsibility for sales activities such as developing sales policies, strategies and plans that support the overall marketing plan. Additionally, he may supervise all salespeople; however, if the number of salespeople is too high, supervision must be delegated to field sales managers. He may report to the marketing manager or directly to the chief executive officer (CEO).

General store Gemischtwarengeschäft

A small shop primarily selling a large range of merchandise, the most important being food.

General terms and conditions allgemeine Geschäftsbedingungen

Also called general standard conditions, general business/sales conditions, or standard terms and conditions.

The standardized contract items that permit the contracting parties to refer to a preestablished set of rules that can be incorporated into their contract.

Generation X Generation X, "die jungen Unbekannten"

People who are currently between the ages of 18 and 29. They are more materialistic than past generations but have less hope of achieving their goals because they began entering the workforce in the era of downswing, so they are likelier than the previous generation to be unemployed or underemployed. The members of generation X are a challenge for marketers; because of their high aspirations and low expectations they are particularly difficult to target.

Generic advertising allgemeine Produktwerbung

An advertisement or commercial focussing on the benefits that apply to all brands in a product category rather than to a particular brand. Familiar examples are: "Drink more milk", "Butter is good for you", "Drink German beer", etc.

Generic products weiße Ware, generische Produkte

Products which are not branded, are simply packaged, and are usually lower-priced than comparable brands.

Generic term Gattungsbezeichnung, Gattungsname, Oberbegriff

Also called generic name.

A name which is not registered and is applied broadly to a kind of product, eg aspirin, biscuits, instant food, margarine, petrol, etc.

In marketing, applied to brand names which have become adopted as the general descriptive term for a product (e.g. people may refer to a "Biro", a "Fön" (a German term) or a "Hoover", where the generic terms are ball-point pen, (electric) hair-dryer or vacuum-cleaner).

Generics Gattungssachen
Generika, generische Ware

Also called generic goods.

Products which are known by general names such as aspirin or cornflakes.

Imitations or copies of branded goods, particularly of drugs whose patents have expired, usually sold at lower prices.

Geocentric branding policy geozentrische Markenartikelpolitik

A worldwide branding policy which exists only for those brands that are acceptable worldwide.

Geocentric stage geozentrische Phase

In international marketing, the stage when a company coordinates its international marketing activities.

Geocentrism Geozentrismus

A company with a geocentric perspective tends to look at world markets as a whole, with no demarcation between domestic and international business. Its strategic focus will be global.

Geodemographic segmentation geodemographische Segmentierung

A marketing strategy combining geographic, demographic and lifestyle segmentations. It helps marketers practice micromarketing, ie it tries to reach potential customers who live in small geographic regions (eg neighbourhoods) or who have very specific lifestyle and demographic characteristics by tailor-made marketing programs.

Note: people with the same characteristics tend to have the same pattern of consumer behaviour and are thus inclined to buy the same thing.

Geographic grouping of countries geographische Ländergruppierung

A popular way of grouping nations is to classify them along regional lines. Many multinational corporations (MNCs) organize their worldwide operations into such regions as (Western) Europe, Latin America, Far East, Middle East, etc. Geographic proximity makes it easier to manage countries blocked together.

Geographic market concentration geographische Marktkonzentration

The concentration of a number of firms in a particular area; industrial markets tend to be geographically concentrated.

Geographic segmentation geographische Segmentierung

The division of a heterogeneous market into relatively homogeneous groups on the basis of area, region, state, country, etc.

Geographical concentration geographische Konzentration

Limiting of a sales or promotional campaign to a particular geographical area.

The degree to which consumers in a market are concentrated in a particular region or country.

Geographical pricing geographische Preisfestsetzung

A pricing method where prices differ in certain areas.

A pricing method in which customers bear the freight charges from the producer's location to their own.

Geometric mean geometrisches Mittel

Also called geometric average.

In statistics, an average obtained by multiplying together the n given quantities and taking the nth root of the product.

Geometric progression geometrische Folge

Also called geometric sequence.

A series of numbers, or algebraic terms, in which each element is greater than the one before it by a constant multiple, e.g. 2, 4, 8, 16, 32.

Geriatric products Geriatrika

Products, principally medical or pharmaceutical for the market directed at elderly persons.

Gestalt psychology Gestaltpsychologie

In psychology, a theory that says that each thing in a group of associated things must be considered in its relation to the whole group rather than merely as an independent object, because the whole has a meaning apart from its individual elements.
Thus, in advertising, the result of this theory is that a particular brand must be seen as a whole and not just as a total of its elements. Therefore, if one element is changed in any way or if a new element is added, the consumer`s perception of this brand may change radically, and he/she may not buy the brand any longer.

Gestation period Entstehungsperiode, Reifezeit, latente Periode

The length of time which elapses between an initial enquiry and the placing of an order. When dealing with capital goods this period can amount to several months or even a few years.

Get-acquainted discount Einführungsrabatt

Also called introductory discount.

A discount granted when introducing/launching goods on the market.

etup Aufmachung, Präsentation

lso called presentation.

istinctive packaging which identifies and characterises a product.

host shopper Testeinkäufer, Marktbeobachter, Ghostshopper

person appointed by a company to gather marketing intelligence, e.g. by monitoring ie presentations of competitors, purchasing competitors' products, attending trade hows, reading competitors' published reports, talking to competitors' former and resent employees, dealers, distributors, suppliers, etc.

iant retailer Warenkette, Warenkonzern

very large retailing group, eg a chain store or department store.

iffen goods minderwertige Waren, Giffen Güter

commodity for which demand increases as its price increases and vice versa (ie emand falls at lower prices). Demand does not follow the classical laws of supply and emand.
ıferior goods are often called "Giffen goods". This is the term applied usually to those asic foodstuffs consumed by people on very low incomes. The demand for these oods rises when the price rises. The reason for this phenomenon is that when the rice of the good rises, low income consumers maintain their former level of urchases, and finding that they can no longer afford other relatively more luxurious oods actually increase their demand for the inferior good. Similarly, the demand for iese goods falls at a lower price (people enjoy an increase in their real income so that iey can afford more expensive goods).
his behaviour was noticed by the economist Sir Robert Giffen (1837 - 1910).

ift Schenkung, Geschenk Zugabe

his is a gratuitous transfer of the ownership of property. Ownership passes when the onor delivers the goods to the donee. Also called donation.

ı marketing, an extra. Also called bonus, free gift or giveaway.

Gift shop Souvenirladen

A store which sells gifts.

Gift tax Schenkungssteuer

Also called tax on donations.

A tax levied on transfers of wealth between individuals, whether by gift during a person's lifetime or by bequest on death.

Gift voucher (Geschenk)Gutschein

Also called (gift) coupon, token or voucher.

A card, bought in a shop, which is given as a present and which must be exchanged in that shop for goods or services.

A document given to a customer as a special incentive to purchase, usually involving money-off against next purchase of qualifying brand, or providing an opportunity for a special purchase.

Giftwrapping Geschenkpapier
Geschenkverpackung

Decorative paper or other material used to wrap presents.

A service in a store for wrapping presents for customers.

Gimmick witzige, sensationelle Werbung

Also called hook.

In advertising, a trick to get attention, increase popularity or to establish identity for a product image. The idea or object is novel or highly unusual.

Give and take Kompromißbereitschaft

The practice of dealing by compromise or mutual concession in order to cooperate.

Giveaway/give-away Werbegeschenk
Werbezettel, Flugblatt
Radio- oder Fernsehprogramm mit Geschenken, Preisen

Inexpensive promotional piece (e.g. plastic flowers, small toys) distributed to prospective/potential customers. This is a method of motivating the consumer to buy one's brand in preference to that of competitors. Also called advertising, free or goodwill gift.

A leaflet. Also called flier, handbill or handout.

A radio or TV game show where a prize or gift is given away to contestants/competitors or the listenership or viewership (the listening or viewing audience). Also called giveaway program(me) or show.

Giveaway magazine Anzeigenblatt, Werbezeitschrift

Also called freesheet/free sheet.

A magazine depending entirely on advertising for its revenue and distributed free of charge.

Global advertising globale, internationale Werbung

Also called international advertising.

The worldwide use of advertising appeals, copies, messages, photographs, stories, and film and video segments.

Global brand Weltmarke(nartikel)

Products sold to world markets with the same brand name. The advantage of a global brand is that it usually enables an advertisement or image to be used worldwide, provided the ad slogans travel well.

Global company Weltunternehmen

A company that markets its products worldwide and permits only minimal adaptations to local conditions and tastes from one country to another. All its strategies such as financial, advertising, and marketing are global and leave little room for regional or national differentiation as to their products.

Global competition weltweiter Wettbewerb

A situation where firms from all over the world compete on a particular market. Firms are no longer able to worry about domestic competitors only, but must also compete with strong foreign competitors.

Note: often, a firm`s toughest domestic competition comes from foreign companies.

Global distribution weltweiter Vertrieb

The worldwide distribution of goods. As global trade becomes a more decisive factor in success or failure for firms of all sizes, global logistics become more important. For example, sellers, distributors and shippers must be aware of and familiar with the permits, licenses, tariffs, regulations etc that apply in foreign countries. Furthermore, they must consider the transportation infrastructure.

Global economy Weltwirtschaft

All national economies which are interrelated through trade, etc.

Global firm internationales Unternehmen

Firms operating in more than one country. These firms establish worldwide manufacturing facilities and apply global marketing policies and logistical systems. The companies recruit management from many countries, buy components and supplies where they cost the least, and invest where the expected returns are greatest. The global company sees the world as one market and thus gains advantages by planning, operating and coordinating its activities on a worldwide basis.

Global marketing globales Marketing

Marketing to target markets throughout the world, ie a marketing strategy addressing global customers, markets, and competition. The same or a very similar product is marketed to world markets with essentially the same promotion.

Global marketing standardization globale Marketingstandardisierung, globale Marktabdeckung

A company`s strategy of producing uniform products that can be effectively marketed across national boundaries. The strategy presumes that the markets throughout the world are becoming more alike so that globally standardized products can be sold the same way all over the world. Uniform production should enable companies to lower production and marketing costs, and increase profits.

Global player weltweit tätiger Multikonzern

In international trade, a multinational company (MNC) with many foreign subsidiaries playing an important role in international competition.

Global retailing globaler Einzelhandel

Retailing activities spanning national boundaries and addressing global customers.

Globalization Globalisierung

Increasing internationalization of all markets, industries and commerce.

A globalized firm markets standardised products in the same way all over the world. The marketing mix has been globalised as much as possible by employing standardised products, promotion campaigns, prices and distribution channels for all markets. Brand name, product characteristics, packaging and labelling are among the easiest marketing mix variables to standardise; price may be more difficult. More and more large firms offer globally standardised products such as electrical equipment, videos, films, soft drinks, rock music, cosmetics, sportswear, etc.
Note: for some products, a global marketing strategy, including advertising, seems to work well, while for other products strategies must accommodate local, regional and national differences.

Glossing Prestige-Preisgestaltung, Preisveredelung

A pricing strategy, which sets the price of a product or service above the going rate to promote the idea of status and prestige on the assumption that, in certain market segments, the price is taken by the customer to be a form of self-evaluation.

Glut Überangebot, Schwemme

Also called excess or excessive supply, or oversupply.

An excess supply/oversupply of a commodity or money.

Going rate geltender Preis

Also called current or ruling price.

Current price for a product or service.

Going value Markt-, Tages-, Zeitwert

Market value. Also called current or present value.

Gondola beiderseitig offenes (Waren)Auslageregal

Self service, space saving display shelf, eg in a supermarket, on either side of which shoppers are able to pass.

Good faith guter Glaube

Also called bona fides.

Fair business or private dealings undertaken honestly without intention to mislead or seek unfair advantage. When a contract is made it is presumed that people will deal honestly with one another.

Good merchantable quality and condition handelsübliche Güte und Beschaffenheit

In a contract, this means that the goods delivered must be up to the ordinary standard of quality and in their customary sound state.

Goods (gds) Güter, Waren

Also called commodities.

Generally, movable items offered for sale, e.g. by a merchant. Goods contribute directly or indirectly to the satisfaction of human wants.

Goods may be classified as:
1. free good: this is a good which possesses utility, but is in such abundant supply that it can be obtained freely with almost no effort or cost;
2. economic good: a good which possesses utility but is scarce relative to demand and is only obtainable at a price. These goods can be divided into consumption/consumer goods and investment/producer goods.

Goods and chattels Hab und Gut

Goods, possessions and property, belongings.

Goods and services market Güter- und Dienstleistungsmarkt

A market comprising all final user goods and services during a period.

Goods and services tax (GST) Waren- und Dienstleistungssteuer

In Australia and New Zealand, a consumption tax imposed as a value added tax on the supply of goods and services, based on the value/price of the commodity or service.

Goods depot Güterdepot, Warenlager

Central warehouse where goods can be stored until they are collected.

Goods on approval Waren zur Ansicht, auf Probe

Goods sent to a (prospective) customer who wishes to see them before deciding whether to buy. The vendor (seller) will allow the customer a stated number of days to make a decision. The customer must return the goods within the time allowed, otherwise he/she is presumed to have bought them and cannot afterwards compel the supplier to take them back. If he/she decides not to keep them, he/she must inform the supplier and return the goods.

Note: when the supplier sends for inspection goods not asked for, the customer is not obliged either to buy them or to return them, but he/she must take reasonable care of them until he/she receives the supplier`s instructions as to disposal.

Goods on consignment Kommissionsware
Konsignationsware

Also called goods on commission, consignment goods or consigned goods.

Goods sent to an agent for sale on a commission basis.

Goods sent by an overseas firm to an agent in this country for sale on its behalf. The goods are not sold to the agent but only transferred to him. He sells them, deducts his expenses and commission, and sends the balance to the overseas firm.

Goods received note (GRN) Warenannahmeschein

Also called receiving slip.

A document issued by a recipient (receiver/consignee) to record receipt of goods.

Goods received register Wareneingangsbuch

Also called goods bought ledger, or merchandise purchases book or journal.

It is usual to list all goods received on a goods received register after they have been received and checked. This register lists, in date order, all goods received - the number or quantity, the supplier, the date the goods were received, and a general description of the goods.

Goods receiving department Warenannahme

Also called goods inward office.

A company's department which accepts delivery of goods.

Goodwill Goodwill
(immaterieller) Firmenwert,
Geschäftswert

Goodwill - that part of the value of a business attributable to its reputations and connections.

"Cat goodwill" is goodwill attached to valuable premises and "dog goodwill" is based on the special knowledge or skill of the people running a business.

The seller of an old business will want to be paid not only for the net assets, but also for having saved the buyer the trouble of having to build up connections, i.e. for the goodwill. This goodwill has monetary value - but only when a business is sold. The amount to be paid for it is usually taken as being equal to the profits for one or more years. The value of goodwill may be nil if a business is unprofitable.

The goodwill may be in:
1. the name of the business (the name may be associated with a certain quality of goods);
2. the trademark (people may buy the goods because of the trademark);
3. the place of the business.

Note: goodwill is an asset, but appears in the balance sheet only when it has been bought and paid for.

Gossen's laws Gossensche Gesetze

The laws developed by H.H. Gossen (1810 - 1858). The first law states that the pleasure obtained from each additional amount consumed of the same commodity diminishes until satiety is reached. The second law states that once a person has spent his entire income, he will have maximised his total pleasure from it only if the satisfaction gained from the last item of each commodity bought is the same for each commodity. Gossen's third law, derived from the first two, states that a commodity has a subjective value, and the subjective value of each additional unit owned diminishes and eventually reaches zero.

Government and pricing Regierung und Preisbildung, regierungsabhängige Preisbildung

Governmental activities to influence pricing.

In international pricing, government rules and regulations pertaining to pricing should be taken into account in setting prices. Legal requirements of both the foreign government and the domestic government must be satisfied.

Government controlled pricing staatlich dirigierte, verfügte Preispolitik

A pricing strategy where the state establishes the price of a product. This pricing may occur in oligopoly situations (eg telephone, electricity, gas, etc); in times of national emergency; or when a sudden demand for an important good cannot be supplied and the price rapidly increases.

Government inflation Inflation durch Kreditaufnahme des Staates

Inflation caused by borrowing of the government and its agencies to finance their commitments. Public sector/government borrowing contributes to the increase in the money supply and contributes to demand inflation.

Government monopoly staatliches Monopol

A market in which the government is the only seller.

Government purchases Staatsverbrauch

Current expenditures on goods and services provided by the government.

Grade Güteklasse, Qualitätsbezeichnung
Rang, Stufe

Category of something which is classified according to quality.
Types of grade are:
1. top-grade (ie of best quality), 2. high-grade (ie of very good quality), 3. low-grade (ie not of very good quality). Also called grade level.

Level or rank.

Grade label Qualitätskennzeichen

A label, letter, mark, sticker, tag or symbol which identifies the quality of a product.

Grading Güteklasseneinteilung

Also called classification of goods.

The classifying of commodities, e.g. raw materials and foodstuff(s), into standard quality categories.
Note:where commodities can be easily graded, dealings in futures are possible.

Graft Bestechungs-, Schmiergeld

Also called bribe money, grease, payoff, sometimes also kickback or slush money.

Money or gifts to a person to persuade him to do something which he should not do.

Gramme/gram Gramm

A measure of weight. English pound, avoirdupois = 453.6 grammes; German pound = 500 grammes.

Grand total Endbetrag, Gesamtsumme

The final total made up by adding together several amounts or subtotals.

Grant Beihilfe, Subvention

A subsidy. A grant does not form part of some exchange but represents a one-way transfer payment.

Graph Graph, Grafik, grafische Darstellung, Diagramm, Schaubild
Kurve

A diagram showing, by a line or lines (often curved), the relation between quantities. We distinguish three main types:
1. line chart: by joining with a line given points which represent figures or values we can see clearly and instantly any upward or downward movement;
2. circle (pie, circular) chart: it can be used to show the parts/components that make up a given total; this is done by dividing the circle into segments;
3. bar diagram (bar graph or histogram): the bars can be drawn individually or they can be stacked, each in a different colour or pattern.

Also called chart or diagram.

In statistics and mathematics, a curve.

Grass fire Strohfeuer

Short-lived enthusiasm for something.

Grass roots volkstümlich, volksverbunden

Popular and widespread opinion: a grass-roots policy is based on what people actually think and want.

Gratuity Trinkgeld

Sum of money given to someone for a service. Sometimes people pay more than the full amount of the bill. The extra amount is the gratuity or tip.

Grays on the go "Alte mit Schwung"

Older people who are very active, travel a lot, dispose of a high disposable income and are thus willing to spend generously. Thus, these people form an important target group for marketers.

Great Depression Weltwirtschaftskrise

Also called world or worldwide depression.

The period of worldwide low economic activity and very high unemployment which characterised the years 1929 - 1935. International trade dwindled to small proportions. A depression of such length and severity had never previously been experienced.

Green currencies grüne Währungen

Money used to support farm prices.

Green label grüner Punkt

A label awarded to a product or packaging that is considered ecologically beneficial or nonpolluting.

Green marketing umweltfreundliches Marketing

A form of socioecological marketing whereby the goods and services sold, and the marketing practices involved in their sale, give special attention to the development, pricing, promotion, packaging and distribution of products that do not harm the environment. Increased environmental awareness has led to changes in production methods - from product design, materials (which should be biodegradable and/or recycable, less toxic, more durable) and packaging to promotion and selling messages, and even product disposal. The marketers of these products are considered to be environmentally responsible.

The vast majority of people are worried about the environment and most tend to blame businesses for the environmental problems they see. Although consumers also blame themselves, many still admit that they are not willing to pay more for safer products.

Note: in Germany, environmental groups have created a seal of approval, the Blue Angel and the "green spot" (in the UK: green triangle), to distinguish products that are environmentally friendly. Companies receiving this seal can use it in advertising and on packaging.

Critics believe that green marketing campaigns are nothing more than an attempt to capitalize on people`s concerns about the environment. On the other hand, around the world, consumers and marketers alike are taking steps to preserve the earth and its atmosphere.

reen tax Ökosteuer, Umweltsteuer

lso called environment tax (GB).

tax imposed/levied as an incentive to encourage industry and consumers to behave ways that are harmless to the environment.

reenback Geldschein (USA)

US dollar bill or any other paper money issued by the Federal Reserve Banks.

reeting Anrede
Gruß, Begrüßung
Grüße, Empfehlungen
als Briefschluß

n correspondence, this should be made just under the inside address. The usual reetings are: Dear Sir, Dear Madam, Dear Mr X, Dear Ms X, Dear Sirs, Gentlemen preferred in the USA), Mesdames, Ladies (only in the USA), Dear James, Dear Juliet. lso called salutation.

irst words used on seeing somebody. Expression or act with which somebody is reeted, e.g. "Good morning".

reetings (pl): kind regards, e.g. give her my kind regards.

reetings (pl): in correspondence, the complimentary close, e.g. Yours faithfully or ours sincerely.

rey/gray market grauer Markt

market where scarce items can be bought easily and quickly at a price well above he usual market price.

market for commodities that are either mimics or fakes/counterfeits.

market for the "over 60s", ie a market for various goods and services of interest to his age group.

he importing of particular goods by firms which have not been appointed by the roducer as official agents/distributors of the product.

Grid card Werbepreisliste

An advertising rate card indicating the fees for commercials.

Grocer Lebensmittelhändler

Also called provision dealer or victual(l)er.

Generally a retail trader in food.

Grocery store Lebensmittelgeschäft

Also called grocery.

A grocer`s store, ie a store selling food, drinks and other commodities.

Gross brutto
Gros

Without deduction, e.g. gross profit makes no allowance for selling expenses, gross weight makes no allowance for the weight of the container, wrapping, etc.

Numerically, 144 units or 12 dozen.

Gross amount Bruttobetrag

The total amount before deductions.

Gross audience Bruttoreichweite

In media research, the total number of individuals or households in a listening, reading or viewing audience without regard to duplication.

Gross circulation Druckauflage
Bruttokontaktsumme, -reichweite

The total sales of a publication before adjusting for unsold copies.

In outdoor advertising, the total number of persons passing an advertisement during a specific time period and having a reasonable opportunity to view the ad message.

·ross domestic capital formation Bruttoinlandsinvestitionen

.lso called gross domestic capital investment.

. country's expenditure on fixed assets (e.g. buildings, plant, machinery), either for :placing, or adding to, the stock of existing fixed assets.

;ross domestic expenditure (GNE) Bruttoinlandsausgaben

.lso called gross domestic spending.

ıross domestic expenditure = domestic capital formation (i.e. increase in investment at ome) plus consumption.

;ross domestic product (GDP) Bruttoinlandsprodukt (BIP)

he total value in money of all the goods and services produced in a country by ationals and foreigners (residents and nonresidents) in a particular year, but excluding et income from abroad. It is calculated at what is known as factor cost, that is, xcluding subsidies and taxes imposed on any goods or services. It may also be ıeasured at market prices.

;DP = GNP - net income from abroad.

'he deduction of depreciation converts GDP into net domestic product (NDP).

;ross income Bruttoeinkünfte
Bruttoverdienst, Bruttogehalt
Bruttoerlös

'he total of a taxpayer's income from any source.

'he total amount paid to an employee each month before any deductions for tax, ealth insurance, etc. Also called gross earnings or pay, or gross salary.

'he sales of merchandise net of returns and allowances.

Gross investment Brutto(anlagen)investitionen

Also called gross capital expenditure or formation.

The total production of capital/investment goods between one date and the next. If the depreciation and obsolescence for the period is deducted from the gross investment, one obtains the net investment.
When the gross investment is insufficient depreciation and obsolescence, a society is consuming capital. Such a falling level of capital stock will lead to a lower future output of goods and services.

Gross loss Bruttoverlust

When a business prepares a trading account, it has made a gross loss if the revenue from sales is less than the cost of sales.

Gross margin (GM) Bruttogewinn, Rohgewinn

The amount of money a seller makes, stated as a percentage of sales, after the cost of the goods sold has been subtracted.

Gross national expenditure Bruttoausgaben (volkswirtschaftliche Gesamtrechnung)

Gross national expenditure (at market prices) = public and private expenditure on consumption goods (at market prices) + investments (at market prices) within the economy. Expenditures on imports are included, but exports are not.

Gross national product (GNP) Bruttosozialprodukt (BSP)

Also called gross product.

The GNP is the total value of all final products and services (valued at market prices) produced by a country's economy within a particular period of time, usually a year. (Note: final means that intermediate inputs are excluded - no double counting; gross means before deduction of depreciation charges).

The GNP is the GDP (gross domestic product) to which is added income in the form o interest, profits and dividends from a country's investments overseas and similar payments for the investments of other countries in this country.

GNP = GDP + net income from abroad (the value of exports less the value of imports)

The estimates of GNP and GDP take no account of the fact that part of the country's output will be needed to make good the wear and tear and accidental damage to buildings, plant, machinery and vehicles, and to replace equipment that becomes obsolete. The net national product (NNP) is arrived at by deducting this depreciation from GNP.

The GNP may be measured in three ways:
1. the output method (establishes the output of every firm); 2. the expenditure measure (counts the money spent on goods and services); 3. the income method (establishes the incomes of the owners of factors of production).
Care must be taken to avoid double-counting. GNP comes to the same amount when determined by the three different methods.

But note: in our complex economy with its complications, the measurement of the value of goods and services is complicated for five basic reasons:
1. the problem of government involvement in the economy; 2. the problem of transfer payments; 3. the problem of unpaid services; 4. the problems of imports and exports; 5. the problems of timing.

The GNP growth rate is the primary indicator of the status of the economy.

The GNP at market prices is called the nominal GNP, the GNP at constant prices the real GNP (this may be calculated by applying a GNP deflator to the nominal GNP).

Gross national product (GNP) deflator Bruttosozialprodukt (BSP) Deflator

A price index that reveals the cost of purchasing the items included in the GNP during the period relative to the cost of purchasing these same items during a base year (eg 1996). Since the base year is assigned a value of 100, it indicates that prices have risen, as the GNP deflator takes on values greater than 100.

Gross night hour (GNH) Listenpreis für einstündiges Programm während Hauptsendezeit

The cost for sponsoring one hour of television or radio station prime time.

Gross opportunity to see (GOTS) Bruttokontaktwahrscheinlichkeit

In advertising, the number of opportunities an average member of a target audience will have to see the advertisements in an ad campaign.

Gross output Bruttoproduktion

The total quantity or value of goods produced by an economy, industry, firm, etc.

Gross profit Bruttogewinn

The difference between sales revenue and the cost of goods sold (e.g. the costs of depreciation, wages and salaries, rent of land or buildings, interest on capital and stock appreciation, etc.) i.e. the amount by which the selling price exceeds the cost price.

Gross profit percentage Bruttogewinnprozentsatz

Neither gross profit figures nor net profit by themselves are very meaningful. They should be seen in relation to the turnover (the net sales) of the business. Gross profit is the difference between the cost price and the selling price of the goods sold.
A useful figure is that represented by the gross profit percentage.

$$\text{Gross profit percentage} = \frac{\text{gross profit}}{\text{turnover}} \times 100$$

Gross rate Listenpreis für Werbung

Also called card rate.

The published price for advertising space or time.

Gross receipts Bruttoeinnahmen

Also called gross earnings or gross takings.

The total amount of money received before expenses have been deducted.

Gross sales Bruttoumsatz
Bruttoerlöse

Sales at invoice prices, not reduced by discounts, allowances or returns. Also called gross turnover.

The total revenue from sales in a specified period. Also called gross revenue.

Gross turnover Bruttoumsatz

Also called general turnover or gross sales.

Total turnover including value added tax/sales tax, discounts, etc.

Gross weight (gr.wt.) Bruttogewicht

Gross weight = net weight + tare.

Group Gruppe, Gruppierung
Konzern, Firmengruppe

A number of persons viewed as a collectivity. There are primary groups (the members interact on an informal face-to-face basis - e.g. the familiy), secondary groups (they have a formal structure), interest groups (persons who have socio-economic interests in common), occupational groups, income groups, age groups, etc.

A group of companies. Also called combine.

Group advertising Gemeinschaftswerbung, Gruppenwerbung

Advertising by a group of independent firms, eg retailers.

Group behaviour Gruppenverhalten

The forms of behaviour as a group member. An important change occurs when an individual becomes a member of a group. He seems to take on two personalities or roles, one as an individual when he is alone and the other as a group individual when the others are present or when he knows he has their support. The same principle applies to any group. As a member of a group the person loses some of his individuality, but he feels a new form of power through the strength of the whole group. The group influences his behaviour and the tendency for the group to stick together is very strong.

The forms of behaviour as a whole group.

Group discussion Gruppendiskussion

A survey method in which a number of people (in an organized discussion up to 15) led by a chairman discuss (usually for up to 30 minutes) some selected issue, e.g. the message contained in an advertisement or the merits, general competiveness, reliability of a particular product freely among themselves.
The participants in the group must, of course, have some experience of the issue, eg the product, and it is usual for them to be all of the same social class or group.
Such a method determines attitudes towards, and trends of, a particular issue or product in a specified market.
The recorded proceedings are then subjected to further analysis.

Group norms Gruppennormen

Forms of behaviour, ideals, or opinions that are expected within the group as being acceptable and desirable.

Group of solicitors Verkaufskolonne, Drückergruppe

A group of persons normally specialized in advertising and/or selling products, usually in open places.

Group selling Gruppenverkauf

A sales strategy where two or more manufacturers engage jointly to market their products. Each principal continues its own individual activity as a manufacturer of the same merchandise or product range, except that the goods may be modified or the range extended to meet special requirements, e.g. on overseas markets.

Groupage Sammelladung

Also called consolidation; consolidated, collective, grouped or mixed consignment; grouped load or joint cargo.

Small consignments are grouped with those from other consignors. It is possible to ship small lots more cheaply than if sent alone. Some consignors (e.g. exporters) can fill a container completely and thereby qualify for FCL (full container load) terms (these grant preferential rates of freight). However, in many instances, consignors will not be able to do this, so they must ship on LCL (less than container load) terms.

Groupage agent Sammelgutspediteur

An agent who consolidates consignments (either an internal or international consignment) to offer a carrier, for example, as full loads in a container (then called FCL), railway wagon, road vehicle, or other convenient transport unit.

Groupage rate Sammelladungs-Frachtrate

The freight rates for consolidated consignments.

Growth Wachstum

The rate of expansion of the gross national product (GNP) or the rate of expansion in the volume of production of goods and services of a country to meet final demands, e.g. goods and services for domestic consumption, capital goods for accumulation, export goods to pay for imports.
An acceleration of growth requires better management, better education and training of labour, higher capital investment, technological improvements, etc.
Economic growth is so important as it determines the standard of living. Also called economic growth.

The expansion of a business enterprise. Also called increase or expansion.

Growth area Wachstumsbereich

An area in which sales are increasing rapidly.

Growth company expandierendes Unternehmen

A company expanding its business activities.

Growth industry Wachstumsbranche, -industrie

An industry which is expanding rapidly.

Growth market Wachstumsmarkt

A market where sales increase rapidly. In general, firms prefer to invest in growth markets because these offer more potential for products to succeed than declining or static markets. Additionally, these markets are more attractive to firms who wish to improve the market share of their products.

Growth rate Expansions-, Wachstums-, Zuwachsrate

The percentage rate by which something increases, e.g. the annual increase in the output, sales, etc. of a business or whole economy.

Growth stage Wachstumsphase

The product life cycle stage in which sales rise rapidly and profits reach a peak. This stage is critical to a product`s survival because competitors are attracted to the growing market and the product has to compete with more products. Profits start declining as a few more competitors enter a highly profitable market that has substantial potential, driving prices down and creating the need for heavy promotional expenses. Thus, aggressive promotional pricing, including price cuts, is typical during the growth stage. Note: during the growth stage, a company should try to strengthen its market share and develop a competitive position by emphasing the product`s benefits.

The period during which industrial sales increase rapidly.

The period of economic growth.

Growth strategies Wachstumsstrategien

The means by which a company plans to achieve its main objective to grow in volume and turnover.
There are four broad strategies:
1. market penetration,
2. product development,
3. market development,
4. diversification.

Growth theory Wachstumstheorie

Also called theory of economic growth.

There are two main theories: the neo-classical theory and the Keynesian (and the neo-Keynesian) growth theory. The theories are concerned with analysing the determinants of the rate at which economies grow over time.

Growth-share matrix Growth-Share-Matrix, Marktanteil-/ Marktwachstum-Portfolio

Also called Boston matrix/box.

A matrix developed by the Boston Consulting Group (BCG) that explains how market share, market growth, and cash flows are related.
On the vertical axis, market growth rate provides a measure of market attractiveness.
On the horizontal axis, relative market share serves as a measure of company strength in the market.
By dividing the growth-share matrix as indicated, four product classifications can be distinguished: 1. stars, 2. cash cows, 3. questions marks, 4. dogs.

Guarantee/guaranty Garantieerklärung, Gewährleistung

Also called warranty.

A promise that a service will be performed faithfully. A promise, given by a producer to indemnify customers against faulty goods over a limited period of time (the guarantee or warranty period).

Guarantee fund Garantiefonds

A fund formed by regularly setting aside a portion of the profits to meet any exceptional losses or payments.

Guaranteed home impacts (GHIs) Mindesteinschaltquote

Also called guaranteed home impressions (GHIs) or guaranted home ratings (GHRs).

A minimum viewing rate guaranteed by a TV station to an advertiser. If the GHI is not achieved, the TV station has to adjust the advertising costs downwards.

Guaranteed price Garantiepreis

A price predetermined which farmers receive for specified agricultural commodities.

An assurance given by a producer to an intermediary that if the wholesale price of a product is lowered while the intermediary is still holding stocks, the difference will be refunded.

Guerrilla attack Guerilla-Attacke

An attack strategy applied by a market challenger/aggressor/attacker. The guerrilla attacker makes small, intermittent attacks on different narrow territories of the opponent in order to eventually achieve a permanent foothold on one or more territories.
Specific attack strategies may include activities which provide buyers with:
1. selective price cuts, 2. intense advertising and promotion, 3. cheaper goods, 4. prestige goods, 5. product innovations, 6. improved services, etc.

Note: normally, the guerrilla attack is practiced by a small undercapitalized firm against a large one.

Guesstimate grobe Schätzung

An approximation which consists of a guess and a calculated estimate.

Gummed address label Aufklebeadresse

An address label which has a sticky reverse (side) so that it can be stuck to an envelope, etc.

Gusset envelope großer Umschlag für Briefe

An envelope used for sending bulky enclosures that may be fastened by sealing, with a tuck-in pocket or with a metal fastener.

H

Habit Gewohnheit

Something that is done so often that it becomes a common practice.
One of the influences on demand. Consumers continue to buy the same quantity of a commodity as before despite a price change simply because they have acquired a buying habit.

Habit of consumption Konsum-, Verbrauchsgewohnheit

Also called consumption pattern.

The consumer`s practice of buying a particular product again and again by force of habit, without any conscious decision-making to buy or product comparison.

Habitual buying Gewohnheitskauf

A consumer`s practice of always buying the same product, especially where there is little or no difference between one brand and another with regard to price, quality, product or availability. Consumers have little involvement in this product category, ie they go to the shop and reach for the product out of habit, not strong brand loyalty.

Note: a habitual buying behaviour is usually practised with most low-cost, frequently purchased products.

Haggler Feilscher/in, Schacherer

A person discussing prices and terms and trying to make them more favourable, prior to concluding a contract.

Haggling Feilschen, Gefeilsche

Also called bargaining.

Individual bargaining between buyer and seller. To haggle means to argue about the price of something. In many countries you have to haggle before you buy anything.

Half board Halbpension

Also called demi-pension.

A special rate for guests staying at a hotel, who take breakfast and dinner at the hotel, but not lunch.

Half-height (H/H) container Halb-Container

A usually open-topped ISO container of standard length and width whose height is only four feet.

Half-page (double) spread halbe Doppelseite(nanzeige)

Also called horizontal half page.

In a publication, eg a magazine, an advertisement or editorial matter positioned on either the upper or lower half of each of two facing pages.

Hallmark/hall mark Gütesiegel, Feingehaltsstempel

An official mark or stamp indicating a standard of purity, genuineness, good quality, etc.

Halo effect Halo-Effekt, Ausstrahlungseffekt, Lichthofeffekt

The glory a new product gains from the reputation of an earlier product produced by the same manufacturer.

Hammer Zwangsverkauf
Versteigerung, unter den Hammer kommen

A forced sale.

To sell at auction; to come/go under the hammer.

Hand baggage/luggage Handgepäck

Small bags and cases which passengers may take onboard a plane.

Hand barrow Handkarren

Manual cargo or baggage handling operated wheeled equipment.

Hand pallet transporter Handhubrollwagen

Manual cargo handling equipment used to move pallets.

Handbill Flugblatt, Prospekt, Handzettel, Werbeblatt

Also called flier/flyer, handout or throwaway.

Form of printed advertising delivered personally into the hands of potential customers. Handbills are often left on the counter in retail stores, are distributed by hand on the street, or are left on parked cars.

Handbook Handbuch

Also called guide, manual, operator's manual, reference book or manual.

A small book giving guidance on a specific matter, e.g. instructions for use.

Handling Handhabung, Handling

The process by which something is treated, dealt with, delivered, packaged, transported, stored, etc.

Handling allowance Abwicklungsvergütung

A discount or other price reduction granted by a manufacturer to a distributor, wholesaler or retailer for dealing with merchandise requiring special attention.

Handling charges (Um)Ladekosten
Bearbeitungsgebühr

Charges made for loading and reloading goods. Also called loading charges.

A charge made for services rendered. Also called management charge or fee, processing fee or service charge.

Handout Werbeprospekt, Reklamezettel
Pressemitteilung
kostenlos verteilter Artikel

Low-priced leaflet for free distribution at exhibitions or for promotional purposes, especially at point-of-sale (POS). Also called handbill or throwaway.

A press memo. Also called press announcement or release.

A product distributed free of charge to potential customers for advertising and promotional purposes. Also called giveaway (article).

Happy hour Happy Hour; frühe Abendzeit, zu der Getränke in Lokalen reduziert sind

Time, usually in the very early evening, when a bar offers cheaper drinks, to encourage customers to come in early.

Hard goods Gebrauchsgüter, langlebige Konsumgüter

These are consumer durables such as furniture, televisions, appliances, building materials, etc.

Hard sell aggressiver Verkauf

Also called high-pressure selling.

A method of selling where salespeople persuade people to buy goods they had not thought of buying. The salesperson puts pressure on the potential buyer to make a commitment to purchase. Thus, buyers are talked into buying unwanted or unneeded things.

Hard sell advertisement aggressive Verkaufswerbung

Also called hard selling ad.

A hard sell ad often features a specific product or group of products and aims to engender the interest of potential consumers by means of detailed information with regard to quality or performance, accompanied by an invitation to the reader to write to the company for fuller details.

Hardware Hardware (EDV)
Eisenwaren, Metallwaren
Haushaltswaren

The machines used in a computer system, including the computer itself. A computer consists of a number of hardware units or devices, e.g. card reader, processor, tape decks and disc drives, printer and console units, etc. Also called computer hardware.

Metalware such as tools and building materials. Also called ironware or metalware.

Solid goods for use in the house, eg cutlery, frying pans or cooking pots.

Harmonization Harmonisierung

This means that all countries within the EU (European Union) must obey the same rules (e.g. harmonization of taxes), so that the free competition which is being encouraged will be fair competition, not unfair competition (e.g. dumping is a highly reprehensible practice).

Harvesting strategy Aberntestrategie

A strategy of deliberately cutting back expenditure of all kinds on a specific product (usually in the decline stage of its product life cycle, PLC) or part of a business in order to maximise profit from it.

Note: despite of this strategy, the product continues to lose market share and thus will eventually be withdrawn from the market.

Haulage Beförderung, Transport
Transportkosten

The transport of goods by road, rail or canal. Also called carriage, shipment or transportation.

The cost of transport. It does not cover the loading and unloading charges. Also called carriage, freight or transport charges, or transport(ation) costs.

Haulage contractor LKW-Transportunternehmen(r), Fuhrunternehmen(r), Kraftverkehrsunternehmen(r)

Also called haulage business or company, carrier, haulier, road or transport contractor, trucker, or trucking company.

A person or firm that owns lorries/trucks and makes special contracts of carriage/transport with his customers to carry goods by road. In long distance road haulage, the contractor usually has his own collecting depots at various strategic spots. The contracter is required to possess a carrier's licence.

Haulier Fuhrunternehmer, Transportunternehmer

Also called haulage or transport contractor, or road haulier.

A contractor undertaking the transport of goods by road.

Hawker Hausierer
Straßenhändler, fliegender Händler

Itinerant dealer who carries his goods for sale from place to place, using a van to bring goods to the customer's door. Also called doorstep salesman, huckster, pedlar, or peddler.

A person selling merchandise on the street. Also called street seller, trader or vendor; or itenerant salesman.

Hawthorne effect Hawthorne-Effekt

A psychological theory stating that the behaviour of an individual or a group will change to meet the expectations of the observer if they are aware that their behaviour is being observed. This behaviour was documented in the USA in the 1920s at a factory in Hawthorne.

Hazard Risiko
Gefahr
Glücksspiel

Circumstance which is likely to increase the possibility of a loss occurring or the size of such a loss. Also called peril or risk.

A danger.

A gamble. Also called game of chance or game of hazard.

Hazardous cargo Gefahrgut, gefährliche Güter(ladung)

Also called dangerous cargo.

Cargo that may be dangerous, e.g. explosives, chemicals.

Head tax Kopfsteuer

Also called poll tax.

A lump sum tax levied on all individuals, regardless of their income, consumption, wealth, or other indicators of economic well-being.

Head-on position Plakatanschlagsposition frontal zum Verkehrsfluß

Also called head-on location.

In outdoor advertising, an advertisement positioned in such a way that it faces oncoming traffic.

Head-to-head competition Kopf-an-Kopf Konkurrenz

A highly competitive situation, particularly under oligopolistic conditions, where the second or third leading company decides to challenge the leader.

Headed paper Papier mit Briefkopf

Headed paper is usually bond paper of superior quality. The information of the letterhead is printed on it.

Heading Briefkopf
Titel(zeile), (Titel)Überschrift

The letterhead is printed at the top of the letter sheet. It contains at least the firm's name, logo, and postal address. Other details, such as the directors, the registered office, the registered number, the telephone number, the fax number and the email address, are usually included as well (or shown at the bottom of the sheet). Also called letterhead.

Title of report or published matter. Also called caption, head or headline.

Headline Schlagzeile, Titelzeile, Titelüberschrift

Also called caption, head or heading.

Dominant line of type in printing (e.g. at the top of a newspaper) to attract attention.

Health food Reformkost, Biokost

Food with no additives or natural foods, such as cereals, yoghurt, dried fruit, etc, which are good for your health.

Heavy equipment Industriegüter

Capital goods normally bought by end user customers. The buyer treats them as an asset and thus depreciates them for tax purposes.

Heavy half gewichtige Hälfte

A market situation where a small number of customers make up more than half of the total demand for a product or service.

Heavy industry Schwerindustrie

Also called heavy manufacturing or smokestack industry.

An industry concerned with the production of heavy goods, e.g. machinery.

Heavy lift (H/l) Schwergut

A unit of cargo that cannot be lifted by normal gear.

Heavy user Großverbraucher

A consumer who buys more of a product or service than average. Market research shows that often a small percentage of consumers consumes a very large percentage of the total sales of a product or service.

Heavy viewer Dauerseher, Vielseher

An individual spending a lot of time watching TV.

Hedonism Hedonismus

The philosophy that all human action is motivated by pleasure, i.e. people do behave as pleasure-seekers.

Hedonist Genußmensch

A person believing that pleasure or happiness is the highest good. Thus, these people habitually seek pleasurable experiences and buy products and services which provide them with the most pleasure.

Heterogeneous cargo heterogene Fracht

A variety of cargoes (in a single consignment or freighting unit).

Heterogeneous commodities heterogene Güter

Goods or services which are not identical in the eyes of buyers. Heterogeneous products may be close but not perfect substitutes for each other.

Heuristics Heuristik

A trial and error technique of problem solving. The solution is discovered by evaluations of the progress made towards the final result. A method of learning by doing.

Hidden decision versteckte Entscheidung

Any decision taken automatically and without question.

Hidden defect verborgener, versteckter Mangel

Also called latent defect.

A defect which could not be noticed when the product was tested.

Hidden economy Untergrundwirtschaft

Also called black, cash, moonlight or underground economy.

A sector of the economy in which individual tradesmen deal directly with customers for cash, bypassing taxation. Not to be confused with a black market, which is illegal trade in goods in most cases produced legitimately.

Hidden inflation verdeckte, versteckte Inflation

Also called camouflaged, concealed, masked or suppressed inflation.

A hidden price increase. Generally, a reduction in the quality or quantity of a product or service while its price remains static/stable.

Hidden objection versteckter, verborgener Einwand

An unstated objection which a potential buyer has to a product offered by a salesperson.

Hidden persuader geheimer Verführer
versteckte, verschleierte Werbung

Persons, particularly psychologists, being involved in advertising and trying to manipulate and persuade consumers to buy. The term was created by the American journalist Vance Packard.

Popular term for abstract or subconscious appeals in advertisements or commercials.

Hidden price increase versteckte Preiserhöhung

A price increase which is not obvious at first sight. The price increase is not open because the value of the product has been decreased, eg by reducing its quantity or quality.

Hidden reminder verdeckte Mahnung/ Zahlungserinnerung

A reminder included in an offer or sales letter sent to a customer.

Hidden tax verdeckte Steuer

An indirect tax which is included in the price of a product or service and not separately shown (e.g. duties on alcoholic drink or on tabacco). The ultimate user is unaware of this tax.

Hierarchy of effects model Modell einer hierarchischen Abfolge von Wirkungen

An expanded version of the AIDA concept outlining the six-stage process by which consumers make decisions:

. Awareness: an advertiser must first achieve awareness with the target market because he/she cannot sell something if the market does not know that the good or service exists;
. Knowledge: as simple awareness of a brand seldom leads to a sale, the advertiser has to inform the target market about the product`s characteristics;

3. Liking: after the target market knows about the product, the advertiser must create a favourable attitude;
4. Preference: the advertiser must create brand preference by explaining his/her product`s differential advantage over competing brands; this is especially important if buyers are brand loyal;
5. Conviction: although potential buyers may already prefer the advertiser`s product, the latter may have to offer additional reasons and thereby convince the prospective to buy the new product;
6. Purchase: extra incentives such as displays may push the convinced prospective into purchase.

Hierarchy of wants — Präferenzordnung, Bedürfnishierarchie

Also called scale or order of preferences.

Wants can be ordered; there is a hierarchy of wants. Some wants, such as the need for food and drink, must be satisfied before others can be considered. This means that there is an irreducibility of wants in the sense that we must first satisfy some wants before attempting to satisfy others. In exercising choice an individual, firm or country attempts to satisfy the greatest number of wants starting with the most important and going down the hierarchy. If individuals are seeking to satisfy different wants then, given the existence of limited resources to satisfy those wants, there may be a conflict of interest which may be difficult to resolve.

High — Hoch, Höchststand

A high point or level, e.g. a new high in the business/trade cycle.

A market situation where prices are relatively high.

High density freight — Volumenware

Freight which has a high stowage factor and therefore rather bulky with a low weight but high cubic volume ratio.

High income countries — Länder mit hohem pro-Kopf-Einkommen

Countries whose income per capita/head are high compared to the rest of the world.

High involvement product sorgfältig ausgewähltes Produkt, High-Involvement-Produkt

A product or service which is purchased only after careful comparison with other products and thorough consideration. That means that the buyer spends considerable time and effort in searching for and evaluating the product prior to purchase. These products are seen as having important personal consequences, or as useful in achieving important personal goals.

High loader Fahrzeug mit Hubladebühne

A vehicle with a loading platform able to load or unload freight units to and from a loading bay.

High pressure selling aggressiver Verkauf

Aggressive selling activity (e.g. a high pressure sales talk) to achieve sales revenue irrespective of a consumer's real needs. Buyers are talked into buying unwanted or unneeded things.

High season Hochsaison

Also called peak season.

The period of the year when there is much business activity, eg because there are a lot of travellers, tourists, visitors etc.

High stowage factor hohes Staumaß

Cargo which has a high bulk to low weight relationship.

High technology Hoch-, Spitzentechnologie

Also called advanced technology or high tech.

More complex and advanced technology relative to the general level, e.g. computers, lasers, solar energy systems.

High-end market Markt für Käufer mit hohem Einkommen

A market for buyers with a high income level.

High-price strategy Hochpreisstrategie

Also called premium pricing.

A pricing method applied by a company which has decided to keep the price for its product high. This pricing strategy is appropriate in situations of inelastic demand.

Highest bidder Meistbietende(r)

Also called best bidder.

At an auction, the person who offers the most money to purchase a product.

Highlight Glanzpunkt, Höhepunkt

An important conspicuous, memorable, or enjoyable event, scene, part, or the like.

Highly-organised market bestens organisierter Markt

In such markets (e.g. the Commodity Exchanges, the Stock Exchanges) either buyer and sellers are brought together in the same building, or they are in easy touch with one another by computer, fax or telephone. Business is usually conducted according to a definite set of rules.

Hire purchase (HP, hp) Finanz-, Ratenzahlungs-, Teilzahlungskauf
Mietkauf

A form of consumer credit in which the buyer of a good or service pays the principa and interest in regular instalments over a period of time. Usually an initial deposit/downpayment is required.
A hire purchase sale is the combined hiring and selling of an article. The purchase price (plus interest) is paid in instalments and throughout the period during which these instalments are being paid, the goods remain the property of the seller; they a

erely being hired out by the seller to the buyer and they do not become the roperty of the buyer until all the instalments have been paid. If payments are not aintained the goods can be taken back by the seller.
a person enters into a HP agreement and sells the goods to a third party before ompleting payment he commits a fraud. Also called instalment buying or sale.

ote: with a credit sale, the goods become the legal property of the buyer at the eginning of the transaction. The buyer pays a deposit/initial instalment and the emainder by instalments. If payments are not maintained the goods cannot be taken ack by the seller and he must seek recovery of the monies via the courts.

contract for the hire of an asset which contains a provision giving the hirer the ption to purchase the asset upon fulfilment of certain conditions.

ire purchase company Teilzahlungskreditinstitut

company providing finance for hire purchase sales.

ire retailer Einzelhändler, der seine Ware vermietet

a hire shop the equipment hired is used on the retailer's premises (e.g. the underette enables customers to hire washing machines). The equipment is often sed for do-it-yourself activities.

istogram Histogramm, Stab-, Säulendiagramm

lso called bar chart, block or column diagram.

graphical representation of a frequency distribution or probability distribution in e form of bar graphs which represent specific values.

it rate Erfolgsquote

he rate at which a target is reached, eg the number of orders received by a lesperson relative to the company`s total number of orders received.

Hive off — Unternehmensbereich ausgründen, ausgliedern (abstoßen)

Also called to spin off.

The separation of functions within a company, or the splitting off of a complete subsidiary from a group operation, often to start a new firm or as part of a rationalisation process.

Hoarder — Hamsterer

A person who buys and stores something, eg food or money in case of need.

Hoarding — Horten, Hortung
Anschlag-, Reklametafel
Litfaßsäule

A tendency by the public to hold cash. Some people keep their savings in cash hidden in the mattress or under the floor boards. Money saved does not necessarily have to be put to work by being placed in a bank or by being invested. Money hoarded is lost to the economy and this can have a detrimental effect on the economy. If the desire to hoard increases the result will be that money incomes fall; if there is a fall in the desire to hold money, incomes will rise.

A very large board on which advertisements are stuck.

An advertising or poster pillar.

Hogshead (hhd) — großes Faß
Flüssigkeitsmaß

A large cask.

A liquid measure; 52.5 gallons in GB or about 238.5 litres, 62 gallons in the US or about 234.5 litres.

Holding gain/loss — Wertzuwachs/Wertverlust

A gain or loss made when the market value of an asset rises or falls (appreciates or depreciates) after it has been acquired. This may be realised by selling the asset or remain unrealised.

Holistic evaluation Globalbewertung einer Werbekampagne

The evaluation of an advertising or marketing campaign as a whole and not the evaluation of its individual parts.

Home audit Haushaltsbuchforschung

A research method whereby a panel of households keeps records of purchases of specified goods, usually fast moving consumer goods (FMCGs), over an agreed time period, so that these can be checked regularly for brand and quantity.

Home banking Home Banking (Bankabwicklung vom privaten Haushalt)

Also called video banking.

Computer terminals in customers' homes are linked to the bank's central computer. The service offers monetary transfers, bill payments, balance information, etc. This service was introduced in the United States in 1982.

Home consumption Inlandsverbrauch

Also called domestic consumption.

Goods and services consumed in a country, whether produced at home or imported.

Home market Binnenmarkt, Inlandsmarkt

Also called domestic market.

The market in a producer`s or supplier`s own country.

Home produce Inlandsware, heimische Ware

Also called home produced goods.

Products which are produced and sold within the country - neither exported nor imported.

Home sales Inlandsgeschäft, Inlandsumsätze

Sales in the domestic/home market.

Home shopping Home-Shopping, Tele-Shopping

A form of non-store retailing, ie customers buy products directly from their house, eg by using a computer (linked to the telephone which is linked to the store`s ordering department), a television (the articles are demonstrated on TV so that consumers can place telephone orders for direct-to-home delivery) or electronic catalogues.

Home station Lokalsender

Also called local channel/station

A radio or TV station licensed to broadcast within a specific geographic area.

Home trade Binnenhandel

Also called domestic trade, inland trade or internal trade.

All trade confined to a country, i.e. trade between buyers and sellers who are all in the same country.
Note: home trade may be protected from foreign competition by the application of embargoes, quotas and tariffs to imported goods.

Homogeneous cargo homogene(s) Fracht(gut)

Similar cargoes.

Homogeneous commodity homogenes Gut

Also called identical product.

If each unit of a product offered by competing suppliers is exactly the same, it is known as a homogeneous product. The consumers consider the goods or services as perfect substitutes, i.e. they have no preference for the products of particular suppliers.

Homogeneous demand homogene Nachfrage

A demand pattern in which consumers have relatively uniform needs and desires for a good or service category.

Honarium Honorar

Also called professional fee.

Amount of money paid to a person for his services.

Hook Aufreißer, Aufmacher, werblicher Aufhänger/Blickfang
Aufforderung an Hörer/Zuschauer, sich bei Sender zu melden
Aufforderung an Leser, sich zu melden
Prämie

In advertising, a thing or phrase that catches the reader`s, listener`s or viewer`s immediate attention.

In broadcasting, a giveaway offer made to listeners or viewers to incite their response in order to be able to estimate the number of listeners/viewers by the number of phone calls following the announcement.

In the print media, a means intended to stimulate an immediate response or enquiry.

In retailing, a premium offered to purchasers of a product or service (as an incentive to buy).

Hooker Händlereindruck

Also called dealer imprint.

The name, address and other details of a local retailer added to a manufacturer-prepared advertisement, leaflet, brochure, catalogue etc.

Horizontal diversification horizontale Diversifikation

A form of diversification which results when new products that are not technologically related to current products are introduced into new markets.

Horizontal expansion horizontales Wachstum

Expanding a business in the same product line it is producing or selling.

Horizontal integration horizontale(r) Integration, Zusammenschluß

Also called horizontal combination, combine or merger; horizontal expansion or lateral integration.

Horizontal integration occurs where firms producing the same product combine under the same management (e.g. the merger of two brewing companies). Advantages are, e.g.: materials required by a group of firms can be bought in bulk and sizeable trade discounts can be earned; savings may be achieved in the selling of the finished product; financial economies can result; production can be organised on the principle of the division of labour, etc.
Horizontal integration reduces the amount of competition, achieving some degree of monopoly.

Horizontal market horizontaler Markt

Markets cutting across several types of industries, so that various segments are covered.

Horizontal marketing horizontales Marketing

The development of existing markets.

Horizontal price fixing horizontale Preisabsprache

The practice whereby sellers of different brands of the same product make agreements to charge the same price to buyers, thereby controlling the market price. Usually, this practice is illegal.

Horse trading Kuhhandel

A colloquial term meaning that two contracting parties bargain hard with the result tha one party gives something in return for a concession from the other party.

Hospitality Gastfreundschaft

The friendly reception and treatment of guests or strangers.

Host country Gastgeberland

A country that provides services for a convention or a sporting event, e.g. the Olympics.

Hostess party selling Partyverkauf

A method of direct selling where a manufacturer`s agent sells certain goods at a party directly to the potential customers invited.

Hot shop (kleine) kreative Werbeagentur, Hot Shop

Also called creative hot shop.

An advertising studio that has specialised in creating novel and topical advertising copies and designs.

Hot selling area umsatzstarker Bereich

An area of top sales.

Hot-selling line Verkaufsschlager

Also called hot number (colloq.) or runner (colloq.).

A top selling article.

Hotline/hot line Hotline, Notfall-, Servicetelefon

A telephone number providing direct access to a company, professional service, or agency, eg for information, complaints or counselling.

House advertisement Eigeninserat, Eigenwerbesendung

An advertisement in a publication which is placed by the publication itself or a commercial on radio or TV placed by the radio or TV station itself.

House agent Grundstücks-, Immobilienmakler

Also called real estate broker or estate agent.

A person whose business is the selling and letting houses and flats.

House magazine Hauszeitschrift, Hausmitteilungen Werkszeitung

Also called house journal, house organ, company magazine or newspaper.

A private magazine not issued for profit; periodically published by a company for public relations and/or sales promotional purposes. The external house magazin is addressed to dealers or to users, customers and other outside readers, the internal magazine (also called staff magazine) informs employees of current company policy and is for employee motivation.

House style Hausstil

A company`s own design, eg a distinctive logotype, which is applied in all areas of its activities, such as letter headings, advertisements, packaging, vehicles, office decoration, etc.

House-to-house salesperson Direktverkäufer, Haustürverkäufer

A salesperson who is primarily selling direct to end/ultimate consumers in their homes.

House-to-house selling Direktverkauf (an Verbraucher)

Also called house-to-house sale or door-to-door selling.

Direct sale made by visiting customers at their homes with or without an appointment. Usually, small producers with a limited product range sometimes turn directly to the consumer.

Household (HH) Haushalt

Households are the owners of all factors (of production) in the economy; ie they provide the services of labour, land, capital, and ownership to business.

Households are production and consumption units.

In market economies households acquire income from the sale of labour services which is then used to finance household activities.

The behaviour of households affects the level of demand for goods and services and, through production, the level of employment.
Factors affecting the demand of households are: the tastes of the household; the price of other goods; the necessity of the commodity, and its alternatives if any; and the income of the household.
The proportion of income spent on certain goods falls as income rises (once basic necessities have been satisfied then increases in income are spent on other goods); the proportion of income spent on some goods rises as income rises (e.g. household durables, clothing).

Households reached | Gesamtzahl der erreichten Sendernetzhaushalte

Also called homes reached.

The number of households in the audience of a radio or TV station or programme reached during a particular time period.

Housewife time | Hausfrauensendezeit

In broadcasting, the time, generally the daytime hours between 10:00 am and 4:30 pm, when the majority of listeners or viewers consists of women over 16 years of age.

Hundredweight (cwt) | Hundredweight, (etwa) Zentner

A unit of weight; in Great Britain 112 pounds (lbs) or 50.80 kg, in the United States 100 lbs or 45.36 kg. A hundredweight is subdivided into 4 quarters (qrs), each containing 28 lbs.

Hurdle rate of return | erwartete Mindestrendite

The expected minimum rate of return of a proposed investment.

Hype reißerische, übertriebene Werbung

Overly enthusiastic advertising and promotion making excessive claims.

Hyperinflation Superinflation, Hyperinflation, rasende Inflation

Also called runaway inflation or galloping inflation.

Inflation which cannot be controlled. As inflation proceeds, the velocity of circulation (the rate of money turnover) increases to an even greater extent because holding money entails considerable loss. Saving ceases, people begin to lose confidence in the value of money, and there is an increasing anxiety to turn all cash into real tangible assets. The result is a steeper rise in prices.

Prices are rising faster and faster and the value of money (i.e. the purchasing power) is falling so fast that people are no longer prepared to accept money in payment for goods or services nor in settlement of debts. Debts dwindle away to almost nothing. The gains of debtors are, of course, the losses of creditors.

Government usually have no alternative but the introduction of a new form of currency.

Hypermarket Verbrauchergroßmarkt, Großmarkt, Hypermarkt

Also called superstore.

Hypermarkets are really "super supermarkets" (a larger form of supermarket). There is usually a minimum of 3.000 square metres of selling space. They consist of stores - usually at the edge of towns - providing easy parking, competitive prices, self-service and a wide range of goods (foods and non-foods). The hypermarket has become a leading form of retailing.

Note: unlike the chain store, the supermarket, and the discount store, all of which were American innovations, the hypermarket (hypermarche) originated in France.

Hypothesis Hypothese, Annahme

Something which is assumed in order to argue or explain; a theoretical explanation (e.g. saving is a function of disposable income).

I

Iceberg principle Eisberg-Prinzip

The concept that important business information is often hidden in summary data.

Psychological concept that only a small portion of desires is apparent and the big rest is hidden deep down under the surface.

Idea Idee, Gedanke, Denkmodell, Vorstellung

Any conception existing in the mind as a result of mental understanding, awareness, or activity.

A thought, image or notion.

Idea marketing Ideenmarketing

The marketing of an idea, either a general or a specific idea. Note: in a sense, all marketing is the marketing of an idea.

Ideal capacity Betriebs-, Kapazitätsoptimum

Also called maximum or practical capacity.

The absolute maximum number of units that could be produced in a given operating situation, if absolutely nothing goes wrong.

Identification (ID) Identifizierung, Identifikation

A person`s tendency to identify himself/herself with persons or things with whom he/she closely associates.

Identification commercial Identifikationseinblendung

Also called identification spot or sponsor identification (SI).

A 10-second TV commercial inserted at the beginning, the end or during a broadcast to mention the sponsor.

Identification of goods Warenbeschreibung

The description of the type of good.

Identifier Kennzeichen, Identifikator

A symbol whose purpose is to identify or name a set of data.

Idle capacity freie, ungenutzte Kapazität; Kapazitätsreserve

Also called spare capacity.

Productive facilities (e.g. machinery, plant) which are not used.

Illegal illegal, gesetzwidrig

Behaviour that is contrary to the principles of law.

Illegal competition unerlaubter Wettbewerb

Competition which either involves the commission of an illegal act, or which in some other way is contrary to certain regulations.

Illegal gift unerlaubtes Werbegeschenk

A free gift which is so valuable that it represents a threat to trade.

Illuminated advertising Leuchtwerbung

Advertisements which are lighted, eg by neon lights.

Illuminated display beleuchtete Auslage

A lighted display, either static, moving or flashing on and off. Its purpose is to attract the attention of passers-by and/or window shoppers.

Illustration Abbildung, Illustration, Anschauungsmaterial

Something that illustrates such as drawings, photographs, charts, graphs, tables etc, used to clarify, explain or demonstrate.

Image Image, Vorstellungsbild

A buyer's mental picture about an organization or its products, e.g. brand image.

Image advertising Imagewerbung, Goodwill-Werbung

Advertising activities concerned with the perception of the product rather than its specific benefits or attributes in order to create or enhance its image.

Advertising designed to emphasize the resources, skills, and/or character of a company in order to enhance its image. Also called corporate advertising.

Note: the image may be one of elegance, first-class quality, luxury, reliability, sophistication, etc.

Image change Imageveränderung

An advertising or marketing activity intended to change the image of a product or company.

Image differentiation Imagedifferenzierung

The difference consumers perceive between competing products which are nearly the same due to their different brand or company images.

Image pricing Imagepreisbildung

Also called prestige pricing.

A method of pricing a product according to its image. Usually, prices are set at a high level because buyers will associate a high price with superior quality and prestige.

Image study Imagestudie

The study how buyers of a company`s product(s) or investors in its stocks perceive the company in terms of characteristics that the buyers rate as important for their purchasing decision.

Imitation Imitation, Nachahmung
Kopie
Fälschung, Falsifikat

The act of imitating

A result or product of imitating, ie a thing which is a copy of an original.

A counterfeit.

Imitative strategy Imitationsstrategie

A company`s strategy of imitating/copying the strategies of other companies, eg imitating products, designs, packaging and/or selling strategies, etc.

Immaterial wants immaterielle Bedürfnisse

Also called non-material wants.

This term covers people's wants for services or invisible items such as leisure activities, educational and health services.

Immovables Immobilien, unbewegliches Vermögen

Real property that cannot be moved, e.g. land.

Impact (of advertising) Werbewirkung

The way in which an advertisement or promotional message affects the audience receiving it. To achieve the greatest impact the advertiser has to position his advertising so that the greatest number of potential buyers will be exposed to it, remember it, and be motivated to purchase the advertised good or service.

Impact lag Wirkungsverzögerung

The time period between policy changes and the time when the major effects of these changes occur. For example, the time required for the multiplier effect (i.e. the process by which a change in spending results in a greater change in income) to change employment, income, and production.

Impact scheduling Zusammenprallplanung, Wuchtplanung

Also called impacting.

In advertising, the running of the same advertisements or commercials close together and presenting them to the same audience in order to achieve a strong impression on the target audience.

Imperfect competition unvollständige Konkurrenz, unvollständiger Wettbewerb

The market situation where at least one trader can materially affect the market price of a commodity or service. This occurs where there is a breach of the conditions of perfect competition. There is a variety of situations between the two extremes of perfect competition and monopoly. In ordinary speech forms of very imperfect competition are described as monopoly. Imperfect competition exists in a great variety of forms, ranging from near-monopoly at one extreme to nearly perfect competition at the other.

Note: Actual conditions lie between the two extremes of perfect competition and monopoly.

Instead of many producers, as in perfect competition, or the single producer of monopoly, there may be only a few producers (when only a few firms compete, this is known as oligopoly) - their supply affects price; instead of a homogeneous commodity, products may be differentiated (product differentiation), giving rise to monopolistic competition; there may be restriction of entry of competitors into various lines of production either because of the size of the initial investment required or because of restrictive practices (the restriction of supply leads to monopoly profits).

Imperfect market unvollkommener Markt

An imperfect market exists whenever any of the conditions necessary for a perfect market (e.g. customers have full knowledge of the state of the market, any buyer may deal with any seller and vice versa, etc.) do not exist. In this market, some of the producers and/or consumers can materially affect the price and quantity of goods. Thus, actual markets are imperfect markets.

Imperfect oligopoly unvollkommenes Oligopol

A form of oligopoly where there is some degree of differentiation between the products.

Imperfection Mangel, Fehler
Fehlerhaftigkeit, Unvollkommenheit

A fault, eg in a product.

The quality or state of being imperfect.

Implementation Durchführung, Ausführung

The process of putting plans into action.

Implementation lag Ausführungs-, Durchführungsverzögerung

The time it takes, e.g. for the government, to implement a policy and take action.

Implied contract konkludent abgeschlossener, stillschweigender Vertrag

A contract created by the actions of one or more parties.

Import pricing Import-Preisfestsetzung

The activity or process of setting import prices for products or services imported from overseas. All import pricing is "what the market will pay". That means, consumer goods have to be retailed at a price which the customer will pay; raw materials must be at a price which will enable the end product to sell at a profit.

Note: goods or services purchased at prices expressed in foreign currency will, of course, be subject to exchange rate fluctuations; but the exchange rate can be covered in the forward exchange market by buying the currency forward. To avoid this additional operation, buying in domestic currency is much to be recommended.

Import-push inflation import-induzierte Inflation, importierte Inflation

Also called imported inflation.

The domestic rate of inflation is directly affected by the prices of imported goods. Import prices may rise as a result of inflation in other countries or because of a falling domestic exchange rate. Thus, rising import prices may raise the domestic rate of inflation directly (in the case of imported manufactured goods) or indirectly by raising industrial costs, which are passed on in the form of higher prices (in the absence of a profit squeeze).

Importer Importeur, Importfirma Importland

A person or firm that purchases goods or services from another country. Also called import firm or trader.

An importing country.

Improved product veredeltes Erzeugnis

A product that is not unique but is generally superior to many existing brands.

Impulse buyer Impulskäufer, Spontankäufer

A person making an impulse purchase, ie someone who buys on the spur of the moment, not because he/she intended to buy.

Impulse buying Impulskauf, Spontankauf

Also called impulse buy, impulse purchase, impulsive buying or spontaneous purchase.

A purchase made without careful prior consideration, i.e. on the spur of the moment; sometimes without apparent rational or logical justification. Shoppers buy goods in addition to those they originally intended to purchase (the use of clever display techniques may increase sales, e.g. sweets or candies are often strategically placed near checkouts where customers in the queue may be tempted). Point-of-sale (POS) advertising is often designed to stimulate the spontaneous/impulse purchase.

Impulse good Impulsware

Goods which are purchased spontaneously because of a sudden feeling or urge to have them, ie they are bought with little search effort and without any previous consideration.

In depth interview Tiefeninterview, freies Gespräch

A method of studying motives where the interviewer tries to get the interviewee/ respondent to talk freely about anything at all in order to create an informal atmosphere. Usually, the interviewer asks general, non-directed questions and then probes the interviewee`s answers by asking for clarification.
Note: this type of interview may last for several hours.

In depth study eingehende Analyse, Untersuchung

The process of studying and/or evaluating a particular problem, situation, area, etc. in depth involving usually some degree of research.

In stock auf Lager, vorrätig

Also called on stock, in store, on hand.

Goods available, ready for delivery.

In transit unterwegs, auf dem Transport

This term describes goods that have left the consignor's location and are en route to the place of destination.

In-ad coupon Herstellergutschein

A coupon contained in a printed advertisement. Such coupons are often used by retailers to attract customers.

In-country segmentation Segmentierung eines Auslandsmarkts

In international trade, the segmentation of a market within a particular country into a variety of submarkets or segments that vary substantially from one another. One may use simple demographic (e.g. age, income, sex) and socioeconomic variables (e.g. social class), personality, and life-style variables or situation-specific events (e.g. brand loyalty, use intensity) as the basis for segmentation.
The variable(s) should create segments where customers have similar responsiveness to some aspect of the marketer's strategy. Once segments have been formed, the next step is to decide which segment should be selected.

In-home interview Zuhausebefragung, Inhome-Befragung

An interview conducted at the interviewee`s/respondent`s home. The advantage of this technique is that group influence can be eliminated.

In-home media zuhause genutzte Medien

Media such as newspapers, magazines, radio and television which are read, heard or viewed in the home.

In-home retailing Inhome-Einzelhandel(sverkauf)

A method of selling via personal contacts with consumers in their own homes. The seller sends representatives to the homes of preselected prospects after having had an initial contact, eg by phone or mail.

Note: a variation of in-home retailing is the party plan (hostess party selling).

In-pack coupon eingepackter Gutschein, Coupon

A coupon enclosed in the package of a product and redeemable in a shop where the product named on the coupon is sold. The coupon may be redeemed either at a subsequent purchase of the same product, or on buying a different product.

In-pack premium eingepackte Zugabe, Packungszugabe

In sales promotion, a small gift or coupon (in-pack coupon) enclosed in the package of a product to stimulate consumers to buy it.

In-store card Kundenkreditkarte

Also called charge card or store card.

A kind of credit card which is issued to customers by retail businesses and is only valid for use in the store issuing the card.

In-store coupon Gutschein, nur einlösbar in bestimmtem Geschäft

A coupon which is only redeemable in a particular shop or an outlet of a chain store.

In-store demonstration Verkaufsdemonstration im Verkaufsladen

The demonstration of merchandise, eg the showing of how to use a product, by demonstrators in a shop, eg in large department stores or supermarkets that have a heavy consumer traffic. Often, producers offer discounts to dealers who will do in-store demonstrations.

In-store interview Käuferbefragung (vor, beim oder nach dem Kauf) im Geschäft

An interviewing method where the respondent is questioned in a shop, ie the point of sale (POS), either before, during or after shopping.

In-store promotion Ladenwerbung, Verkaufsförderung direkt beim Einzelhandel/im Geschäft Laden-Promotion

Also called in-store advertising.

Promotional activity located within a sales outlet, ie at the point of sale (POS).

In-store shop Geschäft im Geschäft

A firm specialising in a particular line of articles sets up a shop inside a major store. It contributes towards the rent and other overhead expenses according to the floor space occupied and its position. It provides its own stock and employs its own staff.

n-supplier etablierter Anbieter

\ well-known supplier from whom companies will purchase with confidence.

n-the-market traffic Verkehrsfluß innerhalb des Markts

n outdoor advertising, the traffic originating in the market in which the billboards and)anels operate.

n-theater test Studiotest

Testing a TV commercial by showing it to an audience and measuring their response)efore broadcasting it on TV.

Inbound telemarketing passives Telefonmarketing

Telemarketing in which a company receives telephone orders and enquiries from :ustomers, usually in response to an advertising or other promotional campaign. Often :oll-free telephone lines are used.

Incentive marketing Incentive-Marketing, Anreizmarketing

Selling of existing or specially produced or imported goods which companies may use is business gifts or as premium offers, free gifts, prizes or staff incentive awards.

Incentives to purchase Kaufanreize

Special additional reasons for making a purchase. In recent years they have assumed a najor importance in marketing activites.

There are two types of incentives to buy:
1. immediate incentives such as:
a. price reductions, b. bonus pack offers, c. home sampling, d. multi-pack offers, e. banded offers, f. premium offers, g. coupon offers;

2. delayed incentives such as:
a. send-away premiums, b. self-liquidating offers, c. competitions, d. refund offers, e. trading stamps, f. charity promotions.

Incidental music — Begleitmusik, musikalische Untermalung

Music that enhances the atmosphere of an event or situation, eg a commercial.

Incipient demand — beginnende Nachfrage, Nachfrage in der Vorphase

A situation where there is a projected need that will emerge when customers become aware of it sometime in the future.

Income (Y) — Einkommen
Gewinn
Ertrag
Bruttoeinkommen
Einnahme

The inflow of wealth accruing to an individual or a business over a period of time. Income is received as wages or salaries, rent, interest and profits from labour, business and professions or property. That part of income which is not spent has been defined as saving.

Another name for profit or earnings.

Any receipt of a revenue item is regarded as income.

Money received from all sources.

The receipts of a business.

Income and demand — Einkommen und Nachfrage

Income affects the type of products bought in that an increase in income is likely to lead to an increase in demand, especially for non-essential products. Whereas, when income is low, demand for non-essential items will decline.

Note: demand will only increase if real income (ie income expressed in terms of the goods it can buy) is high in relation to prices.

Income differential — Einkommensgefälle

The difference in income levels between different people, e.g. due to types of job or location.

Income distribution Einkommensverteilung

Also called earnings distribution or income transfer.

The way in which income is distributed throughout the various socioeconomic levels.

Income effect Einkommenseffekt

A situation meaning that, when prices fall, people can in effect buy the same goods for less, making them better off. This has the same impact as if their incomes had risen.

Income effect of a price change Einkommenseffekt durch Preisänderung

This means that a lower price for a good or service is like giving consumers more income. Some of this additional income may go for buying more units of the good and thus increasing its quantity demanded.

Income elasticity (of demand) Einkommenselastizität der Nachfrage

This is a measure of the response of demand to a change in income. Changes in incomes (as well as changes in prices) will affect demand. If income increases or decreases, demand changes in relatively large volumes.
If income elasticity of demand for a commodity is low it means that there will be little change in a consumer's demand for that commodity if income is either increased or decreased. If it is high, demand will change considerably following a change of income.
It is calculated by dividing the percentage change in demand by the percentage change in income.

$$\text{Income elasticity of demand} = \frac{\text{\% change in quantity (demand)}}{\text{\% change in income}}$$

As a general rule, necessities (e.g. food) tend to have an inelastic demand, whereas luxuries tend to have highly elastic demand.

Unlike price elasticity, which is almost invariably negative, income elasticity is generally positive; but inferior goods have a negative income elasticity.

Income mobility Einkommensmobilität

Movement of people`s income either up or down during a specific time period.

Income redistribution Einkommensumverteilung

The use of taxation or labor/trade union wage policies to ensure that the incomes of the richer people are reduced and those of the poorer are increased.

Income segmentation Segmentierung nach Einkommen, Einkommenssegmentierung

Dividing a market into different income groups. For example, some companies target affluent consumers, others target low-income consumers.

Income tax Einkommensteuer

A direct tax imposed by the government upon a person's total income, whether earned or unearned. Everyone is allowed to receive a certain amount of income free of tax; the remainder is then taxed on a sliding percentage scale (know as progressive tax).
Note: the tax on wages and salaries is deducted at source by employers. The income tax is the main source of revenue for the government.

Income tax allowance Einkommensteuerfreibetrag

Also called earned income tax allowance or personal allowance.

An allowance that is deducted from income before taxation.

Income velocity of circulation Einkommenskreislaufgeschwindigkeit des Geldes

Also called circular velocity of money.

Measurement of the rate at which money is circulating through an economy.

Incomes policy Einkommenspolitik, Lohnpolitik

A strategy aimed at directly holding down incomes and prices. The aim of such a policy is to curb inflation and to avoid unemployment. Without it, higher pay would lead to higher prices (ie inflation); it would also lead to some people "pricing" themselves out of the labour market and becoming unemployed.

Incoterms | Incoterms, Internationale Regeln für die Auslegung handelsüblicher Vertragsregeln; Lieferklauseln im Außenhandel

International Commercial Terms (Incoterms). Also called trade terms.

In order to overcome all the variations and different interpretations of price and transport costs that could appear on an invoice for overseas orders, the international trading community has developed a system of terms for internal use, called Incoterms. They are designed to standardize contract terms and thus make it easier to follow what obligations, expenses, risks or other elements of the export contract affect the invoice. They are published in a booklet produced by the International Chamber of Commerce (ICC), Paris.
At present there are 13 Incoterms with three-letter symbols to identify them. They are: 1. EXW (ex works); 2. FCA (free carrier); 3. FAS (free alongside ship); 4. FOB (free on board); 5. CFR (cost and freight); 6. CIF (cost, insurance and freight); 7. CPT (carriage paid to); 8. CIP (carriage and insurance paid to); 9. DAF (delivered at frontier); 10. DES (delivered ex ship); 11. DEQ (delivered ex quay (duty paid)); 12. DDU (delivered duty unpaid); 13. DDP (delivered duty paid).

The incoterms are grouped in four different categories:

1. the E-term: EXW; 2. the F-terms: FCA, FAS and FOB; 3. the C-terms: CFR, CIF, CPT and CIP; 4. the D-terms: DAF, DES, DEQ, DDU and DDP.

The mode of transport and the appropriate incoterm:
1. any mode of transport including multimodal transport: EXW, FCA, CPT, CIP, DAF, DDU and DDP;
2. air transport: FCA;
3. rail transport: FCA;
4. sea and inland waterway transport: FAS, FOB, CFR, CIF, DES and DEQ.

Increasing marginal cost | steigende Grenzkosten

The cost of each additional unit of a firm's output is greater than the marginal cost of the previous one.

Increasing returns | zunehmende Erträge

They occur when the expansion of a firm produces economies and greater efficiency. If a firm is below the optimum size expansion will show increasing returns.

Incremental cost Grenzkosten

Also called marginal cost (MC) or differential cost.

The change (increase and decrease) in costs resulting from the production of one additional or one less unit of output. A firm has to determine its marginal cost in order to decide whether or not to vary a rate of production.

Indent Auslandsauftrag, Indentgeschäft

Also called foreign order.

Export orders are known as indents. An indent may be open or closed.
1. Open indent: the agent receiving the order from an overseas principal can obtain the required goods from any producer he pleases.
2. Closed indent: this names the producer from whom the foreign buyer desires the goods to be bought.

Independent retailer selbständiger Einzelhändler

A retailer owning and operating one or more retail outlets which are not part of a larger retail organisation. He has complete control of his business.

Difficulties encounted by the small retailer include the following:
1. price competition from multiple chains, who enjoy bulk-buying advantages, 2. lack of specialist expertise, 3. lack of capital to invest in modernisation, 4. location-rent in shopping centres is very high, 5. loss of market share, etc.

Advantages the small retailer can offer may include:
1. personal relationship with customers, 2. location may be near to customer,
3. products sold may cater for more individual needs, etc.

Independent store unabhängiges Geschäft

A shop/store, eg a retail shop, which is owned by an individual proprietor and not by a chain store.

Independent Television (ITV) Zusammenschluß unabhängiger kommerzieller Fernsehstationen (GB)

In GB, the regional TV stations which compete with the national networks.

Independent variable unabhängige Variable

Also called argument.

Take the function q = f(p); q represents quantity and p represents price. The variable on the left-hand side is termed the dependent variable and the variable on the right-hand side the independent variable. The function shows that the quantity depends upon price.
It is mathematical convention to plot the dependent variable on the vertical axis (y-axis) and the independent variable along the horizontal axis (x-axis).

Index Index

In statistics, a measure of relative value, usually related to a base year. A well-known index is the Consumer Price Index (CPI).

Index linking Indexbindung, Indexierung

Also called indexing, indexation or value-linking.

The automatic adjustment of monetary awards (e.g. wages) or long-term contracts (e.g. insurance contracts) to maintain purchasing power and to take account of inflation. The value of these items grows in line with changes in price levels measured by means of the Retail Price Index (RPI). Indexing removes some of the injustices caused by continuing inflation.

Index number Indexzahl, -ziffer

Index numbers measure the average percentage change in the prices of a "set" of items calculated in relation to a base date.

For example, in order to measure changes in the value of money we use index numbers. This is a statistical device which involves selecting a base data, measuring prices at that date, and comparing them with prices at later dates. The base year is selected and given the number 100.

Index of industrial production Index der Industrieproduktion

An indicator of the overall state of the economy, showing the level of industrial production each month compared with the base year (= 100).

Index of retail prices (IRP) Index der Lebenshaltungskosten, Einzelhandels(preis)index

Also called Retail Price Index (RPI).

The purpose of this index is to measure the retail prices of a group of major consumer goods and services, the prices being weighted to allow for the relative importance of each item. Weighting takes into account what the typical family spends on each product. The weights are revised annually. The weighted price is assumed to be 100 at the base date. The current price of each item is expressed as a percentage of the original price.

Indexing Indexierung, Indexbindung

Also called indexation.

The automatic increasing of money values as the general price level increases, eg wage rates are often indexed.

Indicator Indikator

An instrument that indicates the condition of a special market, e.g. the stock market, or the economy as a whole. Indicators are observed in an attempt to forecast market conditions.

Indifference Indifferenz, Gleichwertigkeit

If an individual is indifferent then he neither prefers nor not prefers one good to any other good. His utility/satisfaction from good X is the same as his utility from good Y.

Indifference curve Indifferenzkurve

This is a curve (plotted on a graph) showing how the consumer reacts when faced by an alternative choice of commodities which give him the same level of satisfaction.

Indirect advertising indirekte Werbung, Werbung ohne direkte Kaufaufforderung

Advertising intended to stimulate purchase of a particular product or service at some future time.

Indirect competition indirekter Wettbewerb

Competition experienced by firms from firms in other industries making alternative items which can be bought instead of the own items produced.

Indirect cost(s) indirekte Kosten, Gemeinkosten

Also called overhead costs.

These are production costs that do not change very much (if at all) as production increases. They are not chargeable to a particular product. Examples are administrative and maintenance costs and rent.

Indirect exporting indirekter Export

Selling commodities to an overseas customer through a middleman. The role of a middleman is to reduce the element of risk, particularly for a first-time or temporary exporter.

Indirect marketing indirekter Absatz, Vertrieb

The sale of goods, e.g. by an exporter, through an intermediary/middleman; the seller/exporter therefore has less influence over the distribution arrangements.

Indirect production Umwegproduktion

Also called roundabout production.

Goods created to help further production.

Indirect selling indirekter Vertrieb

The sale of products to a customer through a middleman/intermediary who should satisfy the following three criteria:
1. he should be oriented to serving the market;
2. he should dispose of the requisite technical and other resources to help exploit your competitive advantage;
3. he should be as controllable as possible.

Individual branding individuelle Markenkennzeichnung

A company`s branding policy, ie a policy of naming each product differently by using separate, unrelated names. The major advantage of this policy is that if a company introduces/launches a poor product, the negative images associated with it will not spoil the company`s other products.

Individual location alleinstehende Reklamefläche

In outdoor advertising, a specific location used for a single billboard.

Individuals reached Gesamtzahl der Hörer/Zuschauer, die Sender/Programm hören/sehen

Also called persons reached.

The estimated number of listeners or viewers of a radio or TV station, or specific programme, reached during a specified time period.

Indivisible load nicht teilbare Ladung

A consignment of excessive weight or dimension so that it cannot be split and thus requires special handling equipment.

Indoor advertising Innenwerbung

The use of advertising material inside buildings and rooms.

Induced consumption induzierter Konsum

The increased purchases (i.e. the additional spending) which are derived from consumers as a result of increased income.

Induced investment induzierte Investition

That part of investment which is determined by changes in output, i.e. the investment produced as a result of increases in consumption, i.e. spending by consumers.

Industrial advertising Industriegüterwerbung, Investitionsgüterwerbung

Also called business-to-business (BTB) advertising or industrial goods advertising.

Advertising of industrial products such as components, equipment or raw materials to industrial users.

Industrial bank Teilzahlungs-Kreditinstitut

In GB, a hire-purchase house or finance company.

Industrial buyer gewerblicher Abnehmer

Also called industrial user.

A person or company purchasing industrial goods.

Industrial country Industrieland

This is a country showing the following characteristics:
1. high level of income per head, 2. low birth rates, 3. the majority of workers is employed in industry and in the services sector, 4. relatively low rate of unemployment, 5. excellent infrastructure, 6. high level of education, 7. a balance of payments equilibrium or a favourable balance of payments, 8. a high degree of international trade, etc.
Usually these countries export a large part of their goods and services to other industrial countries and less developed countries (LDCs).

Industrial demand industrielle Nachfrage

The market demand for industrial products.

Industrial goods Investitionsgüter

Also called capital or investment goods.

Goods sold to industry (e.g. machinery) and used in the production of other goods or services.

Industrial market — Industriegütermarkt

The market for customers who buy goods to be used in production.

Industrial market research — Marktforschung für Industrie-/ Investitionsgüter

Market research for industrial/capital goods. The provision of data and information will help to understand the market(s) in which a company is operating today and in which it may hope to operate tomorrow.
Thus, it should report on:
1. the nature of the products which are being supplied into these markets,
2. the size of the relevant markets,
3. the degree of competition prevailing on these marets,
4. trends in supply and demand,
5. the development of prices and profits,
6. technological developments,
7. substitute products,
8. changes in the structure of industries from which demand arises, etc.

Industrial marketing — Investitionsgütermarketing Industrie(güter)marketing

Also called business-to-business (BTB) marketing.

The marketing of industrial products, i.e. goods bought by producers to be used in production.

The marketing of goods or services in which the potential market comprises businesses rather than consumers, i.e. the general public.

Industrial park — Industriepark

Also called industrial estate.

An industrial complex, typically in a suburban area and set in parklike surroundings.

Industrial policy — Industriepolitik

A government`s policy to stimulate the development and growth of some industry, eg high-tech industry, in an industrial country.

Industrial process Herstellungsprozeß

The processes involved in producing goods, eg in a factory.

Industrial product Industrieerzeugnis

Products manufactured for the industrial sector of an economy.

Industrial product customers Industriegüterkunden

Industrial product customers can be subdivided into:

1. original equipment manufacturer, OEM (buys the product to incorporate it into another product), 2. user customer (uses a given product to make other products for either consumer or industrial product companies), 3. industrial distributor (a wholesaler who buys the products and resells them to other firms).

Industrial production Industrieproduktion

Production output of all industries in a country or of individual industries of marked significance to the economy. It is a major barometer of the general economic prosperity of the country and is usually produced monthly on an index basis (the industrial production index).

Industrial property gewerbliches Eigentum

Ownership of copyrights, patents, trademarks, know-how, and agreements relating to these.

Industrial research Industrieforschung

The process of conducting market research into industrial products such as machinery.

Industrial sector Industriesektor

That part of the economy consisting of industrial companies.

Industrial society Industriegesellschaft

A society characterized by the spread of advanced technology to all sectors of the economy.

Industrial store betriebseigene Verkaufsstelle

A shop owned by a company where only the employees of the company may purchase.

Industry Industrie
Wirtschaftszweig, Industriezweig

Firms concerned with the production of goods.

A particular branch of industry which is directed to the production of a given class of goods, e.g. cars, machine tools, aircraft, etc.

Inelastic demand unelastische Nachfrage

Demand is inelastic if it does not change at a proportionate rate with the rate of change in price. That means, the quantity demanded does not alter, or changes minimally, with a considerable price change.

Inelastic supply unelastisches Angebot

Supply is inelastic if the quantity of an item produced/offered does not alter, or changes minimally, with a price change.
Supply is inelastic if the elasticity is less than 1.

Inelasticity Inelastizität, Mangel an Anpassungsfähigkeit/Elastizität (Angebot, Nachfrage)

If a fairly considerable change in price makes little difference to the quantity demanded, then demand is said to be inelastic. Demand is perfectly inelastic if the same quantity is demanded whatever the price. Supply is perfectly inelastic if the same quantity is supplied whatever the price.

Inertia selling Trägheitsverkauf

Goods are delivered to people who have not ordered them. They are delivered on a sale-or-return basis. Legally, the recipient/consignee is not obliged to retain or pay for such goods. Often the goods are purchased simply because it is too much trouble to return them to the sender/consignor.

Infant Minderjährige(r)

Also called minor.

In law, a person under eighteen years of age.

Infant industry junge, unterentwickelte Industrie

Also called baby industry.

A young and growing industry, often not able to compete on equal terms with competitors from abroad. If this is the case, temporary protection (through import controls or subsidies) may be necessary.

Inferior goods inferiore Güter, minderwertige Ware

Also called poor man's goods or shoddy goods.

Inferior goods are those we buy when our income is relatively low; we will buy less when our income increases; inferior goods are considered in relation to the consumers's income.

Inflation Inflation

Inflation is an increase in the total supply of money and credit beyond the amount necessary to satisfy the needs of trade at the existing levels of prices. It is thus characterised by a fall in the value of money (ie the purchasing power) and rising prices. The standard of living falls.

According to the monetarist view of inflation, increases in the supply of money are automatically followed by decreases in the value of money.

There are various types of inflation, eg:
creeping inflation; cost-push inflation; demand-pull inflation; hyperinflation; imported inflation; suppressed inflation; bottleneck inflation; hidden inflation; wage inflation, etc.

There are some main causes of inflation:
heavy government expenditure not covered by taxation or by borrowing from the public (ie the quantity of money will be increased); attempting to maintain full employment by stimulating demand by an increase in the money supply. While acknowledging the importance of the money supply to the inflationary process it is useful to consider other powerful forces which make their contribution to rising prices: cost-push inflation and demand-pull inflation. It is clear that there is no one single cause of inflation.

Possible effects of inflation are:

1. prices rise, and those living on fixed incomes suffer a decline in their living standards;
2. profit margins increase nominally;
3. debtors stand to gain, while creditors lose;
4. saving is discouraged;
5. rising wage rates;
6. exports become more expensive (because of increased costs of production);
7. imports increase (because they are relatively cheaper than domestic products);
8. fears that moderate inflation will give way to very rapid inflation (this will give way to a complete collapse of confidence in the monetary unit);
9. some people who previously did not pay income tax, now have to pay tax (their income now exceeds a certain amount);
10. VAT which is a percentage tax increases automatically as prices rise;
11. an adverse effect on the balance of trade (exports will decrease and imports will increase), etc.

Instruments to control inflation are:
The restriction of credit (credit squeezes or freezes) is one step towards dealing with the problem. The traditional way of reducing inflation is to reduce the level of aggregate monetary demand (AMD) through monetary policy (high interest rates, lower bank lending, open market operations, etc.) and fiscal policy (lower government expenditure and higher taxes). Experience shows that such policies can be counter-productive.
Other remedies are: increased production; control of wages and prices; import restrictions; stimulation of saving; etc.

Monetarism (Milton Friedmann) holds that inflation can be reduced only by slowing down the growth of the money supply.

The term inflation should not be used where rising prices are merely indicating a revival from a depression - the term reflation is more appropriate. A retreat from inflation may be described as disinflation. Both reflation and disinflation signify a movement of credit and prices upwards or downwards.

Inflation and demand Inflation und Nachfrage

The level of inflation is very important to marketers. When inflation is high, the price of goods and services increases and the purchasing power of consumers declines correspondingly. Consumers will tend to postpone the purchase of non-essential items so that demand will fall. When inflation is at a low price level, purchasing power and demand remain more or less stable.

Inflation rate Inflationsrate

The rate of change in prices. The rate is usually calculated on an annual or monthly basis.

Inflation types Inflationsarten

There are many different types of inflation, eg:
1. accelerating inflation, 2. adaptive inflation, 3. anticipated inflation, 4. bottleneck inflation, 5. cost-push inflation, 6. creeping inflation, 7. demand-pull inflation, 8. demand-shift inflation, 9. disinflation, 10. galloping inflation, 11. government inflation, 12. hidden inflation, 13. hyperinflation, 14. import-push inflation, 15. mixed demand-cost inflation, 16. repressed inflation, 17. spiralling inflation, 18. structural inflation, 19. supressed inflation, 20. supply push inflation, 21. validated inflation, 22. wage-push inflation, etc.

inflationary gap inflatorische Lücke

In demand inflation, i.e. inflation caused by excess demand, there is the so-called inflationary gap. Generally demand inflation occurs when the economy is at or close to full employment. In such a situation, should the level of aggregate demand continue to rise, an increased output to meet this demand will not be possible since all the production factors are fully employed, i.e. aggregate demand exceeds aggregate supply. The result will be a gap between production and desired consumption; the consequence will be rising prices.

inflationary spiral Inflationsspirale

Also called wage-price spiral.

A situation in which price increases lead to demands for higher wages and salaries and other incomes (e.g. profits, dividends, interest and rent), which, when granted, increase costs of producers resulting in further price increases, and further wage demands. Wage and cost increases react on each other and so lead to spiraling inflation; i.e. currency rapidly loses value.

influencer Beeinflusser

A person whose views and advice have the power to influence other person`s final decision, eg the buying decision.

Infomercial Infomercial, werbliche TV-Information

Infomercial is formed from the terms information and commercial.

A paid for television programme pretending to be a genuine station programme. Marketers use a programme-length time period to advertise products and services in a show looking like a talk show. Infomercials are an attractive advertising medium because of the cheap airtime and the relatively small production costs. Furthermore, they are an ideal way of presenting complicated information to potential customers.

Note: infomercials often include a direct response offer to sell the advertised items directly to the public.

Informal economy Schattenwirtschaft

Also called irregular, second or unrecorded economy.

Businesses that usually deal in legal activities but are not registered with the government. Thus, they have no licences, often pay not taxes, offer no social security to their employees, etc.

Information agreement Preisinformationsabsprache (Kartell)

Also called open price agreement or price reporting agreement.

A situation where firms circulate price lists to others in the industry. This may be as effective in some circumstances as actual price-fixing agreements in preventing price-cutting.

Information office Fremdenverkehrsamt, Information

Also called information bureau.

Office which provides information, eg to tourists or visitors.

Information officer Pressereferent

A company or government employee whose job is to give information to the public or organisations.

Information search — Informationssuche

The activity of a potential buyer to seek as much information as possible to enable him/her to find the most appropriate seller and product.

Information seeker (IS) — informationsaktiver Verbraucher

A consumer actively seeking as much information as possible before making a decision to purchase.

Informative advertising — Aufklärungswerbung, informative Werbung

Also called informational advertising.

Advertising that informs consumers about a product or service, eg a product that has only recently been introduced/launched. Advertising either tries to persuade customers to buy a product (competitive ad) or it tries to supply information. In practice, it is often very difficult to distinguish between the two.

Informative labelling — Verpackungsetikettierung mit Inhaltsangaben und/oder Gebrauchsanleitung, aufklärende Etikettierung Herkunftsbezeichnung

Also called informational labelling or descriptive labelling.

Labelling designed to help consumers make a proper product selection, eg by stating additives, ingredients and other details, and lower their cognitive dissonance after the purchase.

Labelling designed to show a product`s origin. Also called origin marking.

Informative promotion — informative Absatz-, Verkaufsförderung

Informative messages try to convert an existing need into a want, or to stimulate interest in a new product. People will only buy a product if they are aware of it, know its purpose, understand its benefits and its positioning in the marketplace.

The goals and tasks of informative promotion include:
1. increasing the awareness of a new product,
2. informing the market about new product attributes,
3. suggesting new uses for a product,
4. informing the market of a price change,
5. correcting false impressions,
6. explaining how the product works,
7. describing available service,
8. building up a company image, etc.

Informative advertising is commonly adopted with newly-launchend products.

Infrastructure Infrastruktur

Roads, airports, waterways, railways, telecommunication systems, power distribution and similar elements basic to economic development. The efficiency of a country's economy is closely related to the quality of its infrastructure.

Inherent vice verborgener, versteckter Mangel

Also called hidden or latent defect.

A defect in the quality of goods or their packing which may contribute to their deterioration, injury, wastage and final destruction, without any negligence or other contributing causes.

Initial approach Erstkontakt

The first contact by a salesperson with a prospect, usually to arrange a meeting.

Initial purchase Erstkauf

The first-time purchase of a product or service.

Initial sale Erstverkauf

The sale of a product or service to a customer who has not previously bought the product or service, but who is now a prospect for repeat purchases. In other words, the first time sale by a seller and first time purchase by a customer.

Inland waterways Binnenwasserstraßen

The rivers and canals in a country used for shipping, e.g. the Rhine-Main-Danube (RMD) link canal, completed in 1992. It covers 3500 km of cheap inland waterways route between the North Sea and the Black Sea, and serves nine East and West European countries.

Innovation Innovation

Introduction of new thoughts, policies, products, new methods in production, distribution, management and organization or other change.

Innovative marketing Innovationsmarketing
innovatives Marketing

The process of introducing something new or unique to the market, e.g. a product, a sales method or an advertising technique.

A strategy through which a company continuously seeks to improve its products and marketing activities.

Innovative pricing innovative Preisbildung

A pricing situation where a new pricing composition arises in the market, e.g. in retail pricing the provision of an interest-free credit to the buyer of a household appliance or the offer of car dealers to accept trade-ins.

Innovative product development innovative Produktentwicklung

A situation where a producer creates a completely new product, e.g. decaffinated tea or electric cars with a range of 50,000 kms and speed of 150 kmh.

Innovator Innovator, Pionier

The first consumers to adopt a new product. They enjoy trying new products, tend to be venturesome, dispose of higher incomes and are more worldly. Furthermore, they rely less on group norms, are more self-confident and well educated.

Note: there are five categories of product adopters: 1. innovators, 2. early adopters, 3. early majority, 4. late majority, 5 laggards.

Input tax Vorsteuer

Also called prior turnover tax, pre-tax (input) or prior tax.

A businessman who buys goods or services from a supplier has to pay input tax which is levied on the value of the goods. The tax is charged by the supplier.

Inquiry test Anfragetest

A test based on responses such as inquiries about an advertisement or coupon returns to find out the effectiveness of advertising.

Insert Werbebeilage
Anzeige, Inserat
Werbebeipack
Werbeeinblendung
annoncieren

Piece of sales promotional material placed into the pages of a publication. Also called supplement.

An advertisement in the press.

Promotional material enclosed in letters and packages. Also called stuffer.

A commercial, especially for television, usually broadcast between programs and related to neither. Also called spot (announcement).

To place an advertisement.

Insertion order Insertionsanweisung, Anzeigenauftra

In press advertising, instructions given by an advertiser to a publisher specifying the size of the advertisement, its position and the date(s) on which it is to appear.

Inside back cover (IBC) dritte Umschlagseite

Also called third cover.

The page on the inside of the back cover of a magazine and a preferred advertising position.

Inside front cover (IFC) zweite Umschlagseite

Also called second cover.

The page on the inside of the front cover (front or title page) of a magazine and a preferred position for advertising.

Inside lag betriebliche Ausführungs-, Durchführungsverzögerung

Also called implementation lag.

The delay between recognition (recognition lag) of the need for an action and its implementation.

Inside order taker Verkäufer/in, die Bestellung im Geschäft annimmt

Salespersons who work in sales offices and receive orders by mail and telephone (telesales), or salespersons in retail stores who communicate with customers face to face and take orders over the counter.

Inside panel Reihenanschlag(swerbung)

In outdoor advertising, a set of panels erected as a group and facing the same direction.

Inside transit advertising Werbeplakatanschläge in Verkehrsmitteln

Advertisements posted inside transportation vehicles such as buses, taxis, trams, trains, and undergrounds/subways.

Inspection certificate Abnahmebescheinigung

A document issued by a reputable body and containing a certification of the quality of goods. It protects the buyer from purchasing goods of a quality inferior to that which was ordered (minor quality).

Instability Instabilität, Unbeständigkeit

The quality or state of being unstable, eg cyclical instability.

Instal(l)ment Rate, Raten-, Teilzahlung

The partial payment of a total sum. To pay in/by instalments means to pay what one owes in small amounts over a longer period of time.

Instal(l)ment buying Kauf auf Raten, Teilzahlungs-, Abzahlungskauf

Buying on time. The buyer acquires goods with no (or a small) down/initial payment. The remaining amount of the purchase price will be paid at regular intervals.

Instal(l)ment credit Teilzahlungskredit

Also called hire purchase credit or loan, deferred payment loan or deferred credit.

A system of credit whereby a loan to buy goods is repaid in regular instalments, covering both the original capital sum and interest.

Instal(l)ment selling Teilzahlungs-, Ratenverkauf

Also called installment sale.

The seller takes an initial deposit/downpayment and collects the balance of the selling price over an agreed period of time in fixed instalments. Property in the goods purchased usually passes on payment of the last instalment.

Installation Anlage
Montage

Nonportable industrial good, eg a machine, used in the production process and lasting for some years.

The act of installing.

Instant (inst) — laufender Monat; Fertig-, Lös-, Pulvergericht

A term designating the present month, e.g. on the 3rd inst.

Prepared products of high convenience value, especially foodstuffs.

Instantaneous audience rating — Moment-Einschaltquote

The number of listeners and viewers of a radio or TV programme or station at a particular moment of time.

Institutional advertising — Firmenwerbung, Firmen-Goodwillwerbung

A form of advertising designed to promote goodwill for a company or organisation rather than to promote a specific product or service. Thus, it promotes names, reputation, images, ideas or political issues.

Insurance marketing — Versicherungsmarketing

Specific marketing strategies applied by insurers in order to improve and increase their sales of insurance cover.

Intangible assets — immaterielle Aktiva, Anlagewerte

Also called intangibles.

Assets, such as goodwill, patents and trademarks, that cannot normally be sold on the market.

Intangible damage — immaterieller Schaden

Also called non-material, non-physical or nominal damage.

A damage not resulting in pecuniary/monetary loss.

Integrated commercial eingeblendete, integrierte Werbung/ Werbesendung Huckepackspot

Also called blended commercial.

A broadcast commercial that appears as part of the programme's entertainment so that no perceptible interruption of the programme takes place.

A commercial advertising more than a single product or service. Also called piggyback commercial.

Integrated growth integriertes Wachstum

A type of growth that a company can have within its industry.

A company can grow through: 1. vertical forward integration, 2. vertical backward integration, 3. horizontal integration.

Integrated marketing integriertes Marketing

The bringing together of all marketing activities of a company in order to have common or at least complementary marketing strategies, eg with regard to advertising messages and times, packaging, POS material, after-sales service, etc.

Integration Unternehmenszusammenschluß, Integration

Also called amalgamation, combination or merger.

Integration occurs when two or more firms combine/amalgamate to form one new firm Integration may be horizontal/lateral, vertical or conglomerate.

The main motives for integration are:
1. a greater share of the market, 2. greater power over suppliers and buyers, 3. rationalization of production, 4. an integrated research programme, 5. a more diversified range of products, 6. lower costs, etc.

Intense growth Intensivwachstum

A type of corporation growth that can occur when current products and current markets have the potential for increasing sales.

There are four main growth strategies: 1. market penetration, 2. market development, 3. product development, 4. diversification.

Intensive coverage — Intensivwerbung

Also called heavy drumbeating (collq.).

Frequent, large-scale advertising to fully cover a market.

Intensive distribution — Intensivvertrieb

The effort of a producer to merchandise and sell his product(s) through every suitable retailer. This method of distribution maximizes product exposure but gives the smallest amount of control to the producer since a large number of retailers are carrying the product. This form of distribution is appropriate for convenience goods because these are in keen demand and therefore must be available to consumers quickly and intensively.

Intent — Absicht
Vorsatz

Something that is intended, eg the original intent was to maximise profit.

In law, the state of a person`s mind that directs his/her actions towards an objective.

Intention to purchase — Kaufabsicht

Also called buying intent(ion).

The penultimate stage in making a purchase. As research has shown, the intention-to-purchase stage does not always lead to an actual sale because many variables may influence the final decision to buy, eg family pressure may force someone to rethink the intention, the preferred brand may turn out to be too expensive or, simply, the person`s moods, habits, aspirations, etc. may change, etc.

Intercept interview — Spontanbefragung, Straßenbefragung

An interviewing method in which an interviewer stops people, eg in a shopping mall, in order to ask questions.

Interfirm comparison — zwischenbetrieblicher Vergleich

A comparison of business results between businesses trading in a similar line of business.

Interline freight von mehreren Spediteuren beförderte Fracht

Freight moving from the seller to the buyer by means of two or more freight forwarders.

Intermarket segmentation Inter-Markt-Segmentierung

In international trade, the combination of market segments with similar social-economic-political perspectives. Groups of customers who are alike in different countries form segments which may be combined to form a viable intermarket segment.

Intermedia comparison Intermediavergleich

The comparison of different media before running an advertising campaign.

Intermediary Vermittler, Mittler Zwischenhändler

Also called middleman.

A person who maintains contacts between people, e.g. a broker or agent.

An organisation such as a wholesaler or retailer through which goods and services pas along the distribution channel from manufacturer to end user.

Intermediate product/good Zwischenprodukt

Goods transformed by production into other goods. These goods do not directly satisfy a consumer need. The finished product of one firm is often the raw material of another It is then referred to as an intermediate product.

Intermodal transport kombinierter Transport, multimodale Verkehr

Also called combined transport.

Different modes of (container) transport, i.e. transport by road, rail, sea and inland waterway.

Internal balance binnenwirtschaftliches Gleichgewicht

Also called domestic economic equilibrium.

A situation in which full employment and price stability are simultaneously achieved.

Internal environment interne Umwelt

Factors within an organisation which influence its activities and decision-making.

Internal market Binnenmarkt

The domestic/home market of a country.

The market of the member states of the European Union (EU).

Internal marketing innerbetriebliches Marketing

The managerial actions necessary to make all employees of the company understand and accept their roles in implementing the chosen marketing strategy. This means that all personnel must do their part to ensure that customers are satisfied.

International advertising internationale Werbung

Advertising on international markets. To be successful three major tasks must be observed:
1. the advertisements must be suitable for international markets;
2. the location and choice of the best media to carry the messages;
3. possibly, the selection and control of an advertising agency competent to undertake the work required.
Additional important factors which should be observed may include:
1. the advertising budget; 2. the extent of competition among businesses; 3. the level of consumer spending; 4. cultural, social, legal and other national differences; 5. the laws on advertising; etc.

Major advertising objectives might include the following:
1. increasing or at least maintaining sales; 2. obtaining new customers; 3. altering consumer behaviour;
4. capturing a certain market share within a specific period; 5. the creation of brand awareness and/or inducing consumers to switch brands; 6. persuading foreign partners to stock up with the advertised item; 7. defending an existing market; 8. improving the firm`s corporate image; 9. encouraging consumers to increase the frequency of their purchases, etc.

International Advertising Association (IAA) Internationaler Verband von Werbefachleuten

An association of international individuals involved in the advertising and marketing of goods and services on global markets, headquartered in New York and founded in 1938.

International marketing internationales Marketing

Also called global marketing.

Marketing the same or very similar product(s) to world markets with essentially the same promotion. The international marketer treats the world as one large market consisting of innumerable segments and, from the beginning, develops a marketing plan to meet the needs of those segments.

Advantages of international marketing are:
1. market entry costs can be reduced,
2. product(s) can be priced at a low and competitive level on a volume-sales basis,
3. economies of scale,
4. increased profitability,
5. scope for countering falling demand in one area by increasing demand in another.

Note: the export marketer, in contrast, seeks to increase abroad the sale of his company's product(s) which have already gained market acceptance at home, to maximise volume and thereby reduce his overall unit costs and increase profit.

International recession internationale Rezession

An international decline in economic activity. Usually a recession starts in one country and takes several quarters to move into other countries.
For example, it is said that European economies are affected by a United States recessionary trend after about six months.

International reply coupon (IRC) internationaler Rückantwortschein

Reply coupons can be bought at the post office and should be enclosed with the letter requiring a reply, together with an addressed envelope. The addressee can then exchange his reply coupon at his post office for the appropriate stamps of his own country which he then affixes to the addressed envelope.

International sales forecast internationale Absatzprognose

The projection of likely international sales over a specified future period. International sales forecasting is especially difficult because foreign political and legal structures can change overnight, foreign taxes can alter, consumer tastes can change suddenly, competing firms may change their prices, new firms may enter the market, new production techniques could become available, exchange rates may change, extra tariffs or import controls may be imposed, etc.

International Standards Organization (ISO) Internationaler Normenausschuß (ISO)

An international organization of national standards bodies, based in Geneva, Switzerland, and responsible for standardization. ISO sets worldwide standards in areas dealing with international commerce.

International trade internationaler Handel, Welthandel

Also called global trade or world trade.

International trade arises because countries differ in their demand for goods and their ability to produce them.

International trade is the process of buying and selling between buyers, sellers and merchants in different countries. As well as the normal problems of trade and commerce which arise in any type of business venture, there are several additional difficulties. These are: time and distance (the credit risk and transit time); movements in foreign exchange rates (the foreign exchange risk); differences in laws and customs; government regulations (e.g. exchange controls), etc.

Unfortunately, increased international trade has created important economic and political problems. The major economic problem relates to long-term imbalances between the imports and exports of some countries. A number of countries regularly import more than they export. Basically, when a country imports more than it exports, the difference is financed by international borrowing. This means that chronic net importers find themselves with huge foreign debts as interest payments and principal accumulate. A continued import surplus will be possible only if lenders continue to relend and, in effect, do very often not ask for repayment of the borrowings. In the long run, more and more debtor nations will no longer be able to finance net imports and the enormous losses of lenders due to defaults on previous loans to chronic importers may jeopardize the ability of lenders/banks to provide loans even to creditworthy foreign customers. This has important implications for the continued expansion of international trade.

Interpersonal communication interpersonelle Kommunikation

Direct, face-to-face communication between two or more persons.

Interview Befragung, Interview

Meeting to find out, by questions and answers, about somebody or about his views. The contact can be either face-to-face or through a communication medium (e.g. personal or group interview, postal questionnaire, telephone interview).

Interviewee Proband(in), Befragte(r), Interviewte(r)

Also called respondent.

The person who is being interviewed.

Interviewer Fragesteller(in), Interviewer

Person who conducts an interview with a respondent/interviewee.

Interviewer bias Interviewer-Bias; Verfälschung durch den Befrager/Interviewer

An inaccurate response from an interviewee/respondent that may occur when an interviewer fails to ask questions according to instructions, intentionally or unintentionally influences the person being interviewed, gives non-verbal signals, explains the questions to some extent, etc.

In research interviews, it is necessary that well-trained and qualified interviewers conduct the interview with total objectivity, so that interviewees are not influenced by any outside source in their responses.

Interviewing methods Befragungs-, Interviewmethoden

In a consumer survey, the methods of approaching respondents/interviewees such as: 1. the personal interview, 2. the group discussion/interview, 3. the postal questionnaire, 4. the telephone interview, etc.

Introduction Vorstellung
Einführung

The act of bringing people together and making them known to one another by name.

The act of bringing in for the first time, eg a new product. Also called launch.

Introduction stage Einführungsphase

Also called introductory stage or pioneering stage.

The first of the five stages of the product life cycle (PLC), the others being: 1. the growth stage, 2. the maturity stage, 3. the saturation stage, and 4. the decline stage.

The PLC begins with the product`s first appearance in the marketplace, when sales are zero or low and profits are zero or low because of high research and development costs, factory tooling, and high introduction costs such as advertising and marketing costs. As time passes, sales should increase and profits should also build up. During this stage potential buyers must be made aware of the new product`s features, uses and advantages; a primary demand for the new product must be created. Often, there is no or little competition and penetration or skimming prices may be appropriate.

Note: the failure rate for new products is quite high, many products never get beyond the introduction stage, and many are never launched commercially at all.

Introductory discount Einführungsrabatt

Also called get-acquainted discount.

A discount granted by manufacturers to retailers to induce them to introduce a newly launched product on the market.

Introductory offer Einführungsangebot

When launching/introducing a new or modified product, a special offer made to customers during a specific time period to induce trial purchases.

Intrusiveness Aufdringlichkeit, Zudringlichkeit

The level at which advertising is experienced as an intrusion and thus begins to have a negative effect. A phenomenon, particulary noticeable in TV commercials.

Invention Erfindung

The discovery of a new product or process.

Inventory (inv) Vorräte, (Lager)Bestände

Also called stock, stock on hand, or stock-in-trade.

Goods, eg in a shop or warehouse.

The value of a firm's raw materials, work in process, supplies used in operations and finished goods. American word for what are called "stocks" in Great Britain.

Inventory change Bestandsveränderung

Also called change in inventories or stock movement.

The amount of increase or decrease in business inventories/stocks during a specified period.

Inventory control Bestands-, Lagerkontrolle, Lagerwirtschaft

Also called stock control.

An internal system for keeping supplies of inventory/stocks at appropriate levels to meet production and sales reqirements. When management neglects the control of inventories, its operations and costs invariably get out of hand. Stocks which are not turned over represent capital tied up without return. Inventory control involves decisions about assortments, optimum ordering, maximum and minimum stock levels, materials control, stores records, storeroom management, etc.

Inventory costs Lager(haltungs)kosten

Also called inventory carrying costs or storage costs.

The costs of keeping stocks at the place of production and consumption.
These costs involve four basic elements:
1. the cost of capital tied up in inventories/stocks; 2. obsolescence, deterioration, insurance, etc.; 3. administration and handling; 4. warehouse accomodation.

Note: the cost percentage on the average stock value may be as high as 25 % per year, but much depends on warehouse location and size, plus type of commodity.

Inventory cushion Sicherheitsbestand

Also called inventory buffer or safety inventory.

A reserve in the inventory made for uncertainties in deliveries or sales.

Inventory management Lagerwirtschaft

Inventory management deals with stocking inventory to fill customer orders. It involves two decisions: 1. how often to order in a given period of time and, 2. how much to order. Thus, an optimum point must be found for the number of orders in a year and the size of each order.

Inventory turnover Lagerumschlag, Lagerumsatz

Also called inventory sales ratio, turnover inventories, merchandise or stock turnover.

The ratio of sales during a time period to inventory. This is equal to the number of times that inventory/stock is sold and replaced during an accounting period. A low turnover might indicate a company is carrying excess stocks of inventory, an unhealthy sign because excess inventory represents an investment with a low or zero rate of return.

Inverse demand inverse Nachfrage

A demand pattern in which the laws of supply and demand do not apply, ie when price increases, demand also increases.

Inverse relationship im umgekehrten Verhältnis

Also called indirect or negative relationship.

The situation when two variables move in opposite directions, e.g. as price increases, the quantity demanded decreases, and vice versa.

Investigator Befrager
Ermittler

A person involved in market research conducting, e.g. questionnaire interviews. Also called interviewer.

A person who investigates, i.e. examines in detail.

Investment goods Investitionsgüter, Produktionsgüter

Also called capital, industrial, producer, producers' or production goods.

Commodities (e.g. machines) which assist the production of other goods; they satisfy consumer wants indirectly.

Invisible earnings Einnahmen aus unsichtbaren Leistungen

Earnings from the provision of invisibles, ie services. They include interest, profits or dividends from investments in foreign enterprises, and currency earned by domestic individuals and companies in the provision of services to foreigners.

Invisible trade unsichtbarer Handel(sverkehr), Dienstleistungsverkehr

The import and export of invisibles, such as banking, insurance, shipping and other services.

Invitation to treat Aufforderung, ein Vertragsangebot abzugeben

When a person puts goods in his shop window, lists goods in a catalogue or advertises, with prices, he is not making an offer, but merely inviting the public to make offers to him. The person is not bound to sell to every person who wishes to buy and he is under no obligation to sell at the price indicated. He is merely asking people to make him an offer.

Invoice (inv) (Waren)Rechnung, Faktura

Also called account, (sales) bill or (sales) check.

An invoice is a document used to provide a summary of the transaction between the seller and the buyer. It shows the following details: the quantity, description of goods, prices, method of delivery, terms of payment, amount of trade discount, amount of VAT, etc. An invoice usually has an invoice number and an invoice date. The purpose of the document is to notify the buyer of the amount due. Futhermore, it is written evidence of a contract, and may be produced as evidence in the courts.

There are four main types of invoice: 1. pro-forma invoice, 2. commercial invoice, 3. certified invoice and 4. consular invoice.

Invoice address Rechnungsanschrift

The address to which an invoice is sent.

Invoice date Rechnungsdatum

The date on which an invoice (bill, check) is issued.

Invoice discounting Bevorschussung von Rechnungen

A service offered to smaller businesses. It is similar to factoring except that only the financing service is used; copies of invoices sent to customers are discounted with a financial institution. The trading company still collects the debts (accounts receivable, receivables) as agent for the financial institution and remits the cash on receipt.

Invoicing Abrechnung, Fakturierung

Also called billing.

The activity or process of issuing and sending an itemized bill/invoice for goods sold or services provided.

Involuntary attention unfreiwillige Aufmerksamkeit, Beachtung

The attention paid to advertising without deliberate intent or conscious effort.

Irregular customer Laufkunde, Gelegenheitskunde

Also called chance customer or street customer.

A casual customer, ie a customer who only buys occassionally or irregularly. Many firms depend on these customers, whereas others count on regular customers.

Island display alleinstehende Warenauslage

Also called island.

A freestanding retail store display accessible from all sides.

ISO 9000 ISO 9000, Qualitätsmanagement-Zertifizierungsverfahren

Standards for quality management established by the European Union (EU).

Issue Veröffentlichung, Auflage (Buch)

The publication of a book or magazine.

Issue reader Leser einer Ausgabe

The reader of a publication.

Italics Kursivschrift

Style of typography in which a particular typeface is sloping.

Item price removal Regalpreisauszeichnung, pauschale Preisangabe (ohne Etikett)

A practice whereby prices are marked only on store shelves or aisle signs and not on individual items.

Itemized invoice aufgegliederte, detaillierte Rechnung

An invoice listing each item separately.

Itinerant trader Hausierer, ambulanter Händler

Also called hawker or peddler/pedlar.

Persons who carry their goods around and sell them to the customer at his front door.

J

Jacket (Schutz)Umschlag

Also called dust jacket.

A protective outer covering, eg for protecting the binding of a book.

Jargon Fachsprache
Jargon, umgangssprachliche, ungepflegte Ausdrucksweise

This term is applied to specialist words used by experts (e.g. bankers, brokers) and unlikely to be known by ordinary people.

Language difficult to understand, because it is a bad form or spoken badly.

Jingle Werbesong; gesungene, musikalische Werbung

A musical commercial, often sung and characterized by a compelling rhyme scheme. It is usually used in conjunction with other advertising for a product or service.

Job lot Partieware, Ramschware
Kleinserie

A quantity of miscellaneous goods, usually of inferior quality, bought at a reduced price.

A small batch.

Job production Einzelanfertigung

Also called individual production.

Manufacture of a single product to customer's specification.

Job selling Ramschverkauf

The sale of unwanted goods, usually of inferior quality, at a low price.

Job shop Betrieb mit Kundenauftragsfertigung

Also called job order plant or make-to-order plant.

A business that manufactures products to customer order (job order production), i.e. it starts production after receipt of order.

Jobber Großhändler

A wholesaler who buys from manufacturers, importers and other wholesalers and sells to retailers.

Jobbing production Kleinserienfertigung (nach Kundenauftrag)

The manufacture of small batches of products to customer orders.

Joint cost Kosten der Kuppelproduktion

Also called joint product cost or related cost.

Costs arising simultaneously in the production of two or more commodities; but only costs incurred up the point of separation (the splittoff point) of the different products.

Joint costing Kuppelkalkulation

Also called joint product costing.

The process of allocating a particular cost to two or more finished products derived from the same raw materials.

Joint demand verbundene, komplementäre Nachfrage

Also called complementary demand.

This is the demand for two (or more) goods to satisfy a want. The goods are usually needed together because of necessity or consumer preference (e.g. sand, cement and gravel for making concrete). A change in the demand for one commodity is likely to be followed by a proportionate change in the demand for the other product (e.g. petrol/ gasoline and cars).

Joint marketing Joint Marketing, Kooperationsmarketing, Gemeinschaftsvertrieb

The collaboration with a larger company which has an overseas marketing organisation to distribute one's products.

Joint product Kuppelprodukt

Also called complementary product.

Commodities which are produced simultaneously from the same input by a joint process and in such a way that a change in the output of one of them necessarily changes the output of the other.

Joint sales organisation gemeinschaftliche Absatzorganisation

Also called joint selling company.

An organisation consisting of two or more businesses which disposes of a joint sales office, distributing warehouse, travelling salesmen, etc.

Joint supply verbundenes, komplementäres Angebot

Also called complementary supply.

The supply of two or more commodities that are produced together; i.e. one commodity cannot be produced without producing the other. An increase in the production of one will create a surplus of the other and a fall in price.

Joint venture (JV) Joint Venture, Gemeinschafts-unternehmen

A commercial undertaking by two or more parties (e.g. two independent companies or a company and a government) to work on a particular project together. Each party makes a substantial contribution. A joint venture differs from a partnership, which forms the basis for permanent cooperation. It may take various legal forms, although usually involves the creation of a separate, jointly-owned subsidiary.

Joint ventures provide a mutually beneficial alternative to domestic and foreign businesses to join forces. For all parties, the ventures are a means to share both capital and risk and make use of each other's strength. However, the major problem in managing joint ventures stems from one cause: there is more than one partner. Thus, to be successful, one of the partners must play the key, dominant role to steer the business to success.

Some advantages of joint ventures may be:
1. they are a desirable entry mode to enter attractive new markets overseas;
2. some foreign governments are more receptive to or require joint ventures;
3. countries with raw materials usually do not allow foreign firms to be active there other than through joint venture;
4. the entire risks are shared with one or more partners;
5. low cash requirements because know-how and patents, or both, can be considered a partial capital contribution;
6. easier access to a foreign market.

Jollies Jollies (betuchte ältere Menschen)

Jet-setting elderly people (oldies) with a lot of money (slang: with plenty of loot).

Journal Fachzeitschrift
Zeitschrift, Zeitung

A trade journal. Also called trade paper, professional or trade magazine.

A general term for any periodical publication.

Journey mapping Passantenzählung

The counting or estimating of how many people pass a poster site.

Journey order Vertreterauftrag

An order placed by the shopowner to the sales representative when visiting his shop.

Jubilee discount Jubiläumsrabatt

A special discount which may be granted on the celebration of any of certain anniversaries, as, for example, the 25th, 50th, etc.

Judgement sampling bewußte (Stichproben)Auswahl, Ermessensauswahl

The selection of samples on the basis of the researcher`s knowledge and judgement.

Jumble display Wühlkiste, Restposten-, Sonderangebotsauslage

Also called jumble basket.

A display bin at the point-of-purchase/sale (POP/POS) in which all items may be different but are priced the same.

Jumbo pack Großpackung

Also called bulk pack(age), family size pack(age) or multiple pack.

A package that tries to encourage the sale of small items in multiples; a number of items are packed collectively in a single wrapper (or banded together), and usually offered at an advantageous price.

Jumpy market stark schwankender Markt

A fluctuating market, ie a market with ups and downs.

Junk food Schundnahrung, Junk Food

Bad, commercially prepared food that is high in calories but of little nutritional value and containing few fresh ingredients, such as potato chips or candy.

Junk mail — Abfallpost, Papierkorbwerbung, Wegwerfpost, unerwünschte Werbedrucksache/Reklamesendung

Unsolicited commercial mail, as advertisements and requests for donations, mailed in bulk and usually thrown straight into the dustbin by the people receiving it.

Junk shop — Ramschladen

A shop selling trash, unwanted or worthless goods, at very low prices.

Junket — als Dienstreise deklarierte Vergnügungsreise

An expensive business and pleasure trip, paid for by a company.

Justification — Rechtfertigung

A reason, fact, circumstance, or explanation that justifies.

The act of justifying.

Just in time (JIT) — fertigungssynchrone Materialwirtschaft

An inventory management method derived from Japan in which needed raw materials inventory arrives exactly when it is to be used, ie just in time. This avoids the expense of and need for warehousing.

Just in time (JIT) production — JIT-Produktion

A method of producing goods only when they are wanted.

Just in time purchasing — beständelose, fertigungssynchrone Beschaffung, JIT-Beschaffung

The frequent ordering of supplies and products in small quantities timed precisely to coincide with the need for them.

Just noticeable difference (JND) kaum wahrnehmbarer Unterschied

The minimal difference that can be detected between two stimuli.

Just price angemessener Preis

Also called justified price.

This is a price that is judged morally correct, i.e. a fair market price an informed buyer will pay for a commodity or service.

K

Karaoke Karaoke

Entertainment, coming originally from Japan, where people sing to recorded music.

Keen competition harte(r), scharfe(r) Konkurrenz/ Wettbewerb

Tough competition; there is a competitive market.

Keen demand starke Nachfrage

Also called brisk, heavy or strong demand.

A great demand for a commodity or service.

Keen price sehr niedriger, scharf kalkulierter Preis; konkurrenzfähiger Preis

A low and competitive price.

Keep out pricing Preisfestetzung, die Konkurrenz vom Markt fernhält

A pricing strategy where large companies maintain very low prices to discourage smaller competitors and prevent them from entering the market, and thus protect their own market share.

Keg kleines Faß, Fäßchen

A small barrel.

A former unit of measure: 1 keg = 30 gallons (1 US gallon = 3.785 litres, in GB 1 gallon = 4,546 litres).

Key account Großkunde Hauptauftraggeber

In industrial marketing, a big customer (bulk buyer or large lot buyer), usually generating more than a prespecified annual sales level. Therefore, he receives special treatment from salespeople.

A major retailer, from the viewpoint of a producer/manufacturer or a distributor.

In advertising, a client who spends a great deal of money on advertising through one specific advertising agency.

Key account manager Key Account Manager

A manager dealing with and responsible for one key account and its particular needs and problems.

Key buying influencer (KBI) Schlüssel-Kaufentscheidungsträger, (Haupt)Meinungsmacher

Also called key decision maker (KDM).

The manager making the decision to purchase. Note: orders are often initiated by top management, whereas purchases are actually carried out by middle management. This means that the actual buyer does not really initiate the order and start the buying process.

Key customer wichtiger Kunde

A big customer who often is a bulk buyer.

Key element segmentation Segmentierung nach Schlüsselelementen

The segmentation of a market according to a product`s key element, eg value, high price, low price, usage, etc. Once the proper key element of segmentation is found, then the numbers of users can be determined.

Key industry Schlüsselindustrie

Also called bellwether industry.

An industry that is vital to the economy of a country (e.g., in Germany the automobile industry).

Key number Chiffre(nummer), Kennziffer

Also called key.

The number used in a keyed advertisement.

Key product Schlüsselprodukt, Marktführer

Products which are in the greatest consumer demand.

Key prospect potentieller (Groß)Kunde

A hopeful or promising potential customer.

Key success factors Haupterfolgsfaktoren

The essential elements that are absolutely necessary conditions for success, ie for achieving a specified goal.

Keyboard Tastatur

A set of keys, usually arranged in tiers, for operating a computer terminal, typewriter, piano or the like.

Keyed advertisement Chiffreanzeige

Also called box number advertisement or keyed insertion.

A print or mail advertisement with a box or reference number. This ad is designed to cause an enquirer to indicate the source of his/her information.

Keynes effect Keynes-Effekt

According to J.M. Keynes, the indirect effect on the demand for commodities resulting from a change in the general price level.

Keynes' theory of investment — Keynes' Investitionstheorie

According to Keynes, saving = investment; but the level of saving and investment is determined by the level of income. Aggregate saving will be determined by the level of peoples' income, since only those people will save who can afford to save.
At the same time investment is carried out by industrialists. They will only expand their productive capacity if there is a potential demand for the additional products.
According to Keynes, the level of investment will depend on the marginal efficiency of capital, which is really the marginal productivity of capital or profitability of new investment. Moreover, the potential demand depends on the level of income.

Keynesianism — Keynesianismus

A branch of macroeconomics developed by the British economist John Maynard Keynes (1883 - 1946) in the 1930s which showed that national income and employment are dependent on real investments and consumer spending.

Keynes believed that active government intervention in the marketplace was the only method of ensuring economic growth and stability. He essentially thought that insufficient demand causes unemployment and that excessive demand results in inflation. The government should therefore manipulate the level of aggregate demand by adjusting levels of government expenditure and taxation. For example, to avoid depression Keynes suggested increased government spending and easy money (i.e. low interest rates), resulting in more investment, higher employment, and increased consumer spending (which would in turn encourage greater investment and hence production).

Certain Western economists (particularly the monetarists) began to question Keynesianism in the 1970s because of the occurrence of stagflation.

Kickback — Schmiergeld

Also called boodle, bribe, palm grease, push or slush money, or graft.

An illegal payment made secretly by a seller to a person in order to obtain an order or contract unfairly.

King size — Großformat, Königsformat

An item which is larger or longer than the usual size, eg an extra large pack, container, carton, poster, etc.

King size poster großformatiges Plakat, King-Size-Plakat

A very large poster.

Kinky demand curve geknickte Nachfragekurve

Also called kinked demand curve.

The shape of a demand curve when any rise in price above the customary level will result in a sharp decline in demand. In other words, this demand curve is highly elastic for a price increase but inelastic for a price reduction.

Kiosk Kiosk
Telefonzelle

A small, freestanding unit, used as a newsstand, refreshment stand, information stand, etc.

A telephone booth.

KISS principle KISS-Formel

KISS = keep it short and simple or keep it simple, stupid.

In advertising, a theory which states that advertising has to be short, simple and easily understandable.

Kitemark Gütesiegel, Qualitätszeichen

A symbol on goods showing that they meet certain standards or requirements.

Kitsch Kitsch

Cheap and sleazy, usually worthless goods.

Knocked down (KD, kd) zerlegt

A term referring to shipments of equipment that are to be assembled by the receiver/consignee.

Knocked-down price — Mindestpreis, niedrigster/äußerster Preis

Also called knockdown price.

The lowest, minimum or rock-bottom price.

A seller's asking price that has been lowered for purposes of making the sale.

Knocking advertising — extrem übertriebene Werbung herabsetzende Werbung

An exaggerated, sometimes even unethical, advertising.

An advertisement in which one seller compares a product to the product of another or criticizes competing products or companies. Also called disparaging advertising.

Knocking copy — Werbeanzeige, in der ein Konkurrenzprodukt diskreditiert wird

An advertisement which deliberately exposes competitive products to adverse comparison.

Knockoffs — Knockoffs

Products which are almost identical, look-alike, copies of competitors` bestselling items.

Knockout price — Schleuderpreis

Also called knockdown, slaughtered or throwaway price.

A giveaway price.

Know-how — Know-how, Sachkenntnis(se)

Skill and knowledge acquired from study and/or experience, eg the knowledge of how to do something.

Know-how licence/license — Know-how Lizenz

An agreement through which one firm possessing technical know-how not covered by patents authorizes another to use it to produce goods and services.

Known damage festgestellter Schaden

A damage discovered before or at the time of delivery of a shipment.

Known loss erkannter Verlust

A loss discovered before or at the time of delivery of a shipment.

Kraft paper kräftiges Packpapier, Kraftpapier

Strong paper, usually brown, used in packaging.

L

Label — Etikett, Aufkleber, Anhänger, Schild(chen)

Also called docket, tab, tag, tally or ticket.

A piece of paper or other material (e.g. a card, tag or patch) fixed to a product or package in order to give it a particular identity, to show who it belongs to or where it is to be sent.

Label(l)ing — Etikettierung, Kennzeichnung, Markierung, (Waren)Auszeichnung

Putting a label on a product or package; often done in a special labelling department. The label can be used to facilitate the identification of a product by presenting the brand and a unique graphic design. Labels can describe the source of the product, its contents and major features, how to use the product, how to care for the product, nutritional information, etc.
Labelling is important for promotional, informational, and legal reasons; regulated by numerous labelling requirements or national and EU laws. For example, some laws require products to be labelled or marked with warnings, instructions, certifications, and identification of the manufacturer.

Laboratory method — Labor-Testverfahren, Studiomethode

The study of respondent reactions, eg to advertising, under artificial but controlled conditions.

Labour cost(s) — Lohn-, Arbeits-, Personalkosten

Also called employment, personnel or staff cost(s).

The sum total of wages plus salaries plus fringe benefits associated with a particular task, product or cost centre, or over a particular time period.

The expenditure on employee pay and benefits in a company.

Labour intensive arbeits-, lohnintensiv

The production of goods by employing a high proportion of labour to other factors of production, e.g. capital.

Labour theory of value Arbeitswertlehre

This theory states that the value of a commodity depends upon the amount of labour required for its production.

Lack of sales Absatzmangel

A situation where sellers have difficulties in selling their products or services.

Lading Ladung

The cargo in a vehicle or ship.

Lady of the house (loh) Hausherrin, Hausfrau

The female head of the household.

Lag (Wirkungs)Verzögerung, Lag

Lag means a delay, e.g. a delay in payment, a delay in performance, a decision lag or a time lag.

Laggard Nachzügler, Zauderer

Also called late adopter.

In the diffusion process, the last of the five categories of product adopters; the others being: 1. innovators, 2. early adopters, 3. early majority, 4. late majority.

Laggards are the last consumers to adopt a new product; sometimes they resist and never adopt the innovation. They are suspicious of new products, are tied to tradition and do not rely on group norms. By the time laggards adopt a new product, it has probably been outmoded and replaced by a newer product. Thus, marketers usually ignore them because they do not seem to be stimulated by advertising or personal selling.

Lagged response verzögerte Reaktion

A delayed response by consumers to an advertising campaign.

Laissez-faire/laisser-faire Laissez-faire, Wirtschaftsliberalismus

A policy, suggesting that government should not interfere with the economy. The adoption by Great Britain of this policy in the nineteenth century was largely due to the influence of Adam Smith (1723 - 1790).

Lame duck nicht lebensfähiges Unternehmen
lahmes Produkt

A business which cannot meet its obligations.

A product which does not sell very well.

Lapse Ablauf, Erlöschen, Verfall
kleiner Fehler, Irrtum
Zeitspanne

The termination of a right or claim through disuse or failure to meet standard obligations.

A small mistake, e.g. in writing.

A period of time.

Lapse of time Frist-, Zeitablauf

Also called expiration of time.

The expiry of a fixed time or reasonable time, e.g. in which an offer must be accepted.

Large-scale production Massenproduktion, Großfertigung

Also called high-volume or mass production.

The production of a commodity in large quantities, using capital-intensive methods of production. During the past hundred years there has been a tendency for firms to

increase in the scale of production. The main motive for expansion has been to increase profit by securing economies of scale. Large-scale production is sometimes thought to be undesirable as it tends towards monopoly.
The absolute limit to expansion will be the point where marginal revenue and marginal cost are equal, since any further expansion will result in less profit.

Last in, first out (LIFO, lifo) zuletzt herein (eingekauft), zuerst hinaus (verbraucht); Lifo-Methode der Vorratsbewertung

The latest units bought are the first to be sold. A method of stock/inventory valuation which assumes that stock is consumed in reverse order to its purchase or production. LIFO normally results, in times of rising prices, in a higher cost of goods sold figure (and therefore a lower profit figure) and in a lower asset valuation in the balance sheet.

Late delivery verspätete Lieferung

Also called delayed delivery or lagged delivery.

The delivery of goods to the buyer after the date which has been agreed in the sales contract. If the delivery time was a condition, the buyer may reject the goods; otherwise the buyer may sue the seller for damages if he has suffered any loss due to late delivery.

Late fringe Sendezeit von 23:00 Uhr bis Sendeschluß

Also called late off-peak, post peak time or late evening.

In the broadcast day, the time segment from 11:00 pm to 1:00 am or until sign-off.

Late majority späte Mehrheit

The fourth of the five product adopter categories; the others being: innovators, early adopters, early majority and laggards.

These are people who are quite sceptical about new products, but eventually accept them because of economic necessity or social pressure, eg because most of their friends have already adopted them and they want to conform to group norms.

Note: the late majority tend to be older and below average in income and education, and they do not adopt an innovation until it is in widespread use and is thoroughly accepted.

Latent defect verborgener, versteckter Mangel

Also called concealed, hidden or invisible defect.

A concealed, hidden or invisible defect that is not apparent on the face of a commodity, document, etc.

Latent demand latente(r) Bedarf/Nachfrage, Erschließungsbedarf

A situation where a particular need has been recognized, but no products or services have been offered.

Lateral diversification laterale, seitliche Diversifikation

Expansion of a firm by entering a new area of business activity not related to the present field.

Lateral integration laterale Integration

Also called lateral merger.

This is the diversification of products or amalgamation between firms having similar products sold in the same market. The goods do not directly compete with each other.

Lateral thinking Querdenken, unorthodoxe Denkweise

In problem solving, a way of thinking which involves changing established patters of thinking in order to achieve a breakthrough.

Launch Einführung

Also called introduction.

The introduction of a new product or service on to the market, usually accompanied by an advertising campaign.

Launch customer Erstbesteller

A customer who is the first to order a new product or service.

Launching costs Anlaufkosten

Also called starting costs.

Costs of publicity for a new product or service.

Launching party Einführungsparty

A party held by a firm to advertise the introduction of a new product or service.

Laundering of money Geldwäsche

The conversion of dirty money (ie money obtained illegally) into clean/white money by passing it through the hands of a third party (e.g. a bank) in an attempt to disguise its origins.

Law of comparative advantage Gesetz des komparativen Vorteils

A law stating that individuals, companies or countries are better off when they produce goods they have a comparative advantage in supplying.

Law of consumption Engelsche Gesetz, Konsumgesetz

Also called Engel`s law.

The law states that poorer families tend to spend a greater proportion of their incomes on food than well-to-do people.

Law of demand Nachfragegesetz

This law states that the lower the price, the greater is the quantity demanded; demand contracts as prices rise, ie the higher the price the lower the demand. There is an inverse relationship between quantity demanded and price, other things being equal (ceteris paribus).

But certain other factors also influence buying habits. These include our own income, the prices of other goods, our own tastes or habits, the necessity of the product, government policy, etc.

Law of diminishing marginal utility Gesetz vom abnehmenden Grenznutzen

Also called law of satiation.

This law states that the total utility of a stock of a commodity to a consumer increases at a slower rate than the stock increases, i.e. each additional unit yields less utility than previous units. The marginal utility of a commodity declines as one's supply of it increases until satiety is reached. The actual rate at which marginal utility declines depends on the usefulness of the commodity in relation to other commodities possessed and still wanted.
Note: a person's demand for anything depends on the marginal utility of the commodity to him.

Law of diminishing returns Ertragsgesetz, Gesetz vom abnehmenden Ertragszuwachs

Also called law of non-proportional returns.

This law shows how physical yields vary as factors of production are combined in different proportions.
If the input of units of one resource (the variable factor, e.g. labour) increases while the input of other resources (the fixed factors, e.g. land) remains unchanged then beyond a certain point output can only increase at a diminishing rate (ie the returns derived from the variable factor will decline). The law of diminishing returns can apply to all the factors of production.

Law of increasing returns Gesetz der steigenden (Grenz)Erträge

This law states that, up to a certain point, the addition of more labour and capital will probably produce a more than proportionate increase in output for a time, so that increasing returns will occur.

Law of large numbers Gesetz der großen Zahlen

In statistics, the principle that large samples are more likely to be representative of the population than small ones.

Law of supply Angebotsgesetz

This law states that rising prices tend to expand supply, while falling prices tend to reduce it.
But other factors also influence supply, e.g.: the prices of other goods, the prices of those factors that go into producing the good, the state of technology, natural and political influences, the scale of production, etc.

Law of supply and demand Gesetz von Angebot und Nachfrage

The demand for a good is related to the price of the good. The supply of the same good is also related to the price of the good.

Normally one can say: the higher the price the lower the demand but the greater the potential supply; and the lower the price the greater the demand but the lower the potential supply.

The market price or equilibrium (market) price (i.e. the price at which the quantity demanded of a good is exactly equal to the quantity supplied) will be fixed somewhere within the price range.

There are five laws of supply and demand:
1. the lower the price of a commodity the greater will be the quantity demanded;
2. the higher the price the greater will be the quantity supplied;
3. at the equilibrium price the quantity demanded will be equal to the quantity supplied;
4. an increase in demand will increase the price and the quantity supplied;
5. an increase in supply will reduce price but increase the quantity demanded.

These laws are a fair description of what happens in most situations; but there are exceptions, at least in the short term (e.g. a rise in price of a certain commodity might be accompanied by an increase in demand, if it is feared that the price will rise higher still for a long period; a fall in share prices may not be accompanied by an immediate increase in demand if potential buyers are confident that prices will fall lower still).

Layaway zurückgelegte Ware

The goods purchased are retained by the shop until the customer has paid for them. The customer often makes a downpayment.

Layout Entwurf, Skizze
Layout, Aufmachung

A plan, first draft, outline or blueprint.

The arrangement of words, pictures, illustrations, headlines, subheadlines, body copy, etc, eg of an advertisement, newspaper or magazine page.

Layout person Layouter

A person responsible for the creation and the visual arrangement of the various elements used in a layout, such as graphics, illustrations, drawings, or type elements. Finally, he/she is responsible for the production of the finished layout.

Lead time Bearbeitungszeit
Beschaffungszeit

The time between the beginning of a manufacturing function and its completion.

The time between the receipt of an order and its actual completion by delivery.

An estimate of such a length of time.

Lead user vorbildlicher Produktverwender

A small group of product users, usually early adopters of an innovation, who need new products before the general market needs or recognizes them. Thus, lead users can provide valuable information to the product developer and/or they can influence other purchasers` buying decisions.

Leader Leitartikel
Spitzenartikel, -ware
führender Artikel
Lockartikel
Frühindikator

The leading article in a publication. Also called editorial or leading article.

A product that has a large market share.

A product which sells best.

A commodity offered at an attractive price for the purpose of inducing customers into the store. Also called bait, call bird, leading article or loss leader.

A leading or cyclical indicator used to predict economic trends and events. Also called leading economic indicator.

Leader pricing Lockpreisstrategie,
Lockvogelpreisbildung

Also called loss leader pricing.

A pricing method attempting to increase customer traffic by selling a product at a low profit margin, near or even below cost, hoping that shoppers will buy additional items at normal prices once they are in the shop. Thus, the goal is not necessarily to sell large quantities of leader articles but to sell more items which are more profitable.

Note: leader pricing is normally used on well-known brands that consumers can easily recognize as bargains at the special price.

Leading economic indicator Frühindikator

Economic indicators that reach peaks or troughs before aggregate/total economic activity.

Leading question Suggestivfrage

Also called loaded question.

A question inviting only one response because it is framed in such a way that the respondent is strongly motivated to reply with that response.

Leaflet Flugblatt, (Falt)Prospekt, Werbezettel, Broschüre

Also called folder , flier/flyer, flysheet, handbill, or throwaway.

Printed piece of paper, single or folded over, containing an advertisement.

Leakage (lkg) Schwund
Leckage, Rinnverlust
Sickerverluste, Sickerquote

Loss of stock resulting from damage, theft or going bad.

An allowance made for waste or loss in liquids.

In economics, any allocation of income that is not directly spent on goods and services; includes savings and taxes.

Lean design Lean Design, Öko-Design

A cheap and environmentally friendly design.

Lean marketing Lean Marketing

Cost-effective marketing achieved through greater efficiency of the individual marketing activites or through abandonment of superfluous activities.

Lean production Lean Produktion, schlanke Produktion

Manufacturing processes that minimise or eliminate wastage of material and time by applying waste-saving measures while maximising the quality of output.
The measures used include:
1. just in time (JIT), 2. stock control, 3. shorter product development times, 4. quality circles, 5. flexible specialisation, 6. flexible working methods, 7. better use of personnel, and 8. the extensive use of robots.
Lean production was inspired by Japanese manufacturing firms.

Learning Lernen

The relatively permanent changes in thought and behaviour, immediate or expected, that result from information, experience and practice.
Note: almost all consumer behaviour results from learning.

Lease (le) Miete, Pacht, Vermietung, Verpachtung
Miet-, Pachtvertrag

A contract granting use of real estate, equipment, or other fixed assets for a specified time in consideration of a payment, usually in the form of rent. The owner of the leased property is called the lessor, the user the lessee.

The contract made when property is let on lease is called lease.

Leaseback Verkauf mit (gleichzeitiger) Rückmiete

Also called sale and leaseback.

A method by which a business can raise money to finance business operations or expansion. The business sells the property (land and buildings) which it owns to a finance or property company which agrees to lease it back to the business.

Leasehold Pacht-, Mietbesitz

The lease of property for a specified period. During the period of the lease the lessee will have use of the property, and will pay the lessor/landlord rent in consideration for its use. At the end of term the land reverts to the freeholder (the person who owns the property).

Leasing Leasing

Leasing is the method of paying for expensive items of plant, equipment, machinery, vehicles, etc., without the need of capital spending; instead of buying them outright, the business leases or rents them. Ownership of the assets remains with the leasing company, ie the lessor, while the lessee has the use of the assets for which he pays a rental charge. A fixed primary lease is established for a period of years, at the end of which there is normally an option to renew for a further period at a much reduced rental or an option to purchase. The terms of the leasing agreement vary according to the nature of the assets concerned and the parties involved but, in essence, there are only two basic types of leasing: operating and finance leasing.

The advantage of leasing to a business is that, once the first rental has been paid, the business has complete use of the asset without having to finance its acquisition out of valuable capital resources or to seek a loan to cover its cost. It is also a less risky method of finance on the part of lenders, as they continue to own the asset. Leasing is simple, tax-efficient (the full rental charged is an allowable deduction for income and corporation tax purposes) and inflation-proof.

Leave piece Werbematerial, das Vertreter beim Kunden läßt

Also called leave behind.

A leaflet, brochure, catalogue or other promotional material left with a potential customer by a salesperson at the conclusion of a sales call in order to keep the product or service in the mind of the customer.

Legal adviser Rechtsberater

A person advising clients about the law.

Legal constraints Rechtsbeschränkungen

The Government imposes many legal restrictions and requirements on business (e.g. manpower policies are influenced by legislation in health and safety, and employment protection; marketing policies are constrained by consumer protection; etc.).

Legal tender gesetzliches Zahlungsmittel

Also called lawful money or legal currency (l.c.).

Legal tender is money which, in law, is bound to be accepted as payment of a debt; a debtor can legally compel his creditor to accept this payment, i.e. the creditor has no legal justification to refuse payment when it is offered (tendered) to him.
Legal tender in the UK consists of Bank of England notes and coin, although there are limits to the amount of any one denomination that a creditor can be compelled to accept. Bank notes and £ 1 pieces are legal tender up to any amount (unlimited legal tender), fifty-pence pieces are legal tender up to £ 10, five-, ten- and twenty-pence coins up to £ 5 and bronze coins up to 20 p (limited legal tender). Scottish and Northern Ireland bank notes are not legal tender.

All legal tender is money; but not all money is legal tender. Thus, for instance, no one can be forced to accept payment by cheque or by postal order/money order as they are not legal tender, but a creditor may elect to do so.
Note: you may insist on payment in cash: notes or coin.

Legend Bildunterschrift, Bildtext

A short note printed below an illustration to explain it.

Lemon Zitrone

Goods sold that have significant quality defects creating difficulties for the consumer.

Less developed country (LDC) Entwicklungsland

Also called developing country.

This is a country showing the following characteristics:
1. low level of income per capita, 2. high birth rates, 3. the majority of the workers is employed in agriculture, 4. high unemployment, 5. a high level of illiterate people, 6. bad infrastructure, 7. a high amount of imports and a few items for export, 8. shortages of foreign exchange for purchasing imported industrial equipment, 9. low economic growth, 10. an unfavourable balance of payments, etc.

Less than carload lot (LCL) weniger als Wagenladung, Stückgut (Sendung)

Goods requiring less space when transported than that available in a single goods waggon.

Less than container load (LCL) Teil-Containerladung

A consignment of cargo that does not fill a container which is grouped by the carrier at the container freight station (CFS) with other consignments for the same destination.

Less than truckload (LTL) LKW-Stückgut

Goods requiring less space when shipped than that available in a truck loader.

Lessee Leasingnehmer

A person who has a lease or who pays money for a property he leases.

Lessor Leasinggeber

A person who grants a lease.

Letter of acceptance Annahmeerklärung

A letter which tells someone that something has been accepted.

Letter of acknowledg(e)ment Bestätigungsschreiben

Also called letter of confirmation.

When an order is received, the seller should send the buyer a written acknowledgement. It is advisable to repeat the most important points of the order in such an acknowledgement.

Letter of advice Versandanzeige

Also called advice note, advice of dispatch, forwarding advice, delivery note, dispatch note or shipping note.

A letter notifying dispatch of goods.

Letter of complaint Beschwerdebrief

A letter in which someone complains about something, eg the quality of a product.

Letter of enquiry Anfragebrief

A letter from a prospect to a seller enquiring about products, their prices, terms of delivery, payment terms, etc.

Letter of intent (L I, LOI) schriftliche Absichtserklärung

Also called letter of preparedness.

Any letter expressing an intention to take or not to take an action, sometimes subject to other action being taken.

Letter style Briefform
Briefstil

Firms use different styles of letter. Most are typed in block style: all typing starts at the left-hand margin; some use the indented style: the beginnings of paragraphs are set in a few spaces.

Business correspondence is still the chief basis of arrangements between businessmen. It has the merit that it is in permanent written form, and can be used as evidence in any dispute about arrangements. A business letter must be neat, clear, concise, correct, complete, consistent, courteous, and cautious.

Letterbox/letter box Briefkasten

Also called mailbox.

A public or private box in which mail is placed.

Letterbox company Briefkastenfirma

Also called nominee company or tax haven corporation.

A company without economic functions registered in a particular country solely for the purpose of avoiding or reducing taxation.

Letterbox marketing Briefkastenmarketing

Also called mailbox marketing.

Hand distribution of promotional material by putting it into potential customers` letterboxes/mailboxes.

Letterhead Briefkopf

Also called heading.

The heading of a business letter; it is usually printed at the head of the first sheet only. The letterhead includes the company's name, address, telephone and fax numbers, often the names of the directors, logotypes, symbols, slogans and other matters.

Letters patent Patenturkunde

Also called patent document.

A document issued by the patent office which confers patent rights on a person or business.

Level(l)ed time Normalzeit(verbrauch)

Also called normal time.

The average time taken for the performance of a given task.

Levy Abgabe, Steuer

A tax or duty, eg a duty applied to imports from another nation.

Liability losses Haftungsschäden

These are losses arising out of legal liability (e.g. employer's liability, product liability) for incidents involving injury to third parties (including employees) or damage to their property.

License/licence Genehmigung, Konzession, Zulassung
Lizenz

A document (e.g. a driving licence) showing that permission has been granted to someone (the licensee) by a competent authority (the licensor) to engage in an activity that could not legally be done without that document. Usually it is obtainable by paying a fixed sum of money.

A permission to exercise the licensor's patent rights.

License/licence agreement Lizenzvertrag

Also called license contract or licensing agreement.

An agreement under which a company (the licensee) is given the right to use another company`s (the licensor`s) patent or other right in return for a license fee. As a license agreement is an important step for a company, a competent legal adviser familiar with legislation should be employed. In foreign trade, he/she should be familiar with the legislation of both countries.

Among the points that should be covered in such a contract are:
1. legality in both countries; 2. the parties and their responsibilities; 3. the products, trademarks, patents, know-how, improvements; 4. territories, and exports to other countries; 5. finance: royalties, methods of payment, currency; 6. transfer of information; 7. patents: usage, quality control, etc.; 8. procedures for settling disputes; 9. applicable laws; 10. investment obligations; 11. restriction clause limiting the licensee to compete with similar products; 12. secrecy clause; 13. product pricing and supply; 14. duration of license; etc.

The selection and appointment of a licensee requires careful evaluation and the following points should be considered:
1. qualifications of the top management; 2. the previous three years' annual published accounts; 3. experience of the company; 4. current product range and product volume; 5. production and distribution facilities; 6. market share and marketing capabilities; 7. legal constraints; 8. general competitiveness; 9. any major shareholdings; 10. member of a trade association; etc.

Licensed production Lizenzfertigung

Also called production under license.

The production of goods by a licensee, eg in an overseas country, according to the conditions stipulated in a license agreement.

Licensee/licencee Konzessionsinhaber, Lizenzinhaber

A person or company to whom a licence/license is granted or issued.

Licensing/licencing Linzenerteilung, -gewährung

The issue of a licence that gives a company a right it would not otherwise have (e.g. a firm (the licensor) licences its patent rights to other firms (the licensees). A carefully worded licence agreement which includes licence fees should be made.

Licensor/licenser Konzessionsgeber, Lizenzgeber

A person or company granting or issuing a license to someone.

Lien Zurückbehaltungsrecht, Pfandrecht

Also called right of lien or pledge.

The right of a creditor to hold the property of a debtor until he has been paid. A lien may be either particular/special or general.

Life cycle Lebenszyklus

All products have both a beginning and an end. Almost all products are subject to a pattern of demand after which it starts, grows, stabilizes, then tends to decline and finally disappears.
The four main stages in the life cycle are: 1. introduction, 2. growth, 3. maturity, and 4. decline. Some products do not go through such a life cycle, e.g. some drinking glasses or knives. Also called product life cycle (PLC).

The life cycle of the firm. The theoretical life cycle of the firm reflects the product life cycle: 1. startup (experimentation stage), 2. rapid growth stage, 3. maturity stage, 4. decline stage.

Life cycle extension Verlängerung des Produktlebenszyklus

The extension of the product life cycle (PLC), ie the process of finding new uses for the same product by the same users.

Life expectancy voraussichtliche Nutzungsdauer
Lebenserwartung

The predicted useful service life of an item of equipment. Also called expected useful life.

The number of years an individual is expected to live, according to statistical estimates taking into account sex, physical condition, occupation, etc.

Lifestyle/life style Lebensstil

The preferred patterns of living as expressed in a person`s activities, eg how to spend time and money, interests, and opinions. It is a function of the person`s social and psychological factors and his/her demographic background.

Note: lifestyle characteristics are useful in segmenting and targeting consumers.

Lifestyle advertising Lifestyle-Werbung

A type of advertising where the product`s environment is more important than the product itself.

Lifestyle segmentation Segmentierung nach Lebensstil

The division of a total market into submarkets characterized by the consumers` lifestyles. A large heterogeneous market is subdivided into relatively homogeneous submarkets.

Light industry Leichtindustrie

Industry producing small products, eg books, clothes, tools, etc.

Light listener/reader/viewer seltener Hörer/Leser/
Fernsehzuschauer

Listeners whose radio listening, readers whose reading of publications, or viewers whose TV viewing is below average.

Likert scale Likert-Skala

A rating device frequently used in questionnaires in which respondents indicate their level of agreement or disagreement with a statement by choosing the most suitable response from a scale, eg strongly agree, agree, undecided, disagree, strongly disagree.

Limit (LMT) limitierter Auftrag

Also called limit or limited order.

An order in which the customer has set restrictions with respect to price.

Limit price Limitpreis, Eintrittssperrenpreis

The price which established firms within an industry set with the objective of preventing new entry into a market. The existing monopolist lowers his price (and increases output) to such an extent that no new entrant could possibly sell enough to cover its large initial costs.

Limited distribution eingeschränkter Vertrieb

The distribution of a product to one or more specific geographic areas rather than nationwide.

The distribution of a product only to specific shops.

Limited function wholesaler Großhändler mit keinem oder geringem Kundendienst, Abholgroßhändler

Also called limited service wholesaler.

A type of wholesaler who has eliminated or modified certain well-established functions, eg small quantity merchandise handling, transportation, credit, ordinarily performed by regular wholesalers in order to offer buyers lower prices.

Limited line department store Kaufhaus mit beschränktem Sortiment

A department store carrying a narrower range of merchandise, typically high-quality goods, than a full line department store.

Limited line retailer Einzelhändler mit beschränktem Sortiment

A retailer carrying only one line or a few related lines, but a large variety of products.

Limited response question Frage mit begrenzter Antwortmöglichkeit

In a questionnaire or survey, a question to which there are only a few possible answers, eg yes or no, or multiple choice.

Line Sparte
Sortiment, Produktpalette, Produktlinie

Line of business.

Items carried by a merchant, ie his range of products. Also called assortment, line of merchandise, product line, product group, or product range.

Line advertising Werbung für Produktgruppe

Advertising for a complete product line/range.

Line chart Linienschaubild

Also called line graph.

The most useful form of all charts. By joining with a line given points which represent figures or values we can see clearly and instantly any upward or downward movement. The time factor (e.g. months) is shown on the bottom line; the figures on the side line show the information intended to be given.

Line divestment Eliminierung einer Produktgruppe

Dropping or selling a product line, eg because it is not profitable anymore.

Line extension Sortimentserweiterung

Also called product line extension.

The practice of adding products to an existing product line in order to compete more broadly in the industry.

Line of business Branche

The type of business.

Line rate Zeilenpreis

In a publication, the charge per line.

Line simplification Rationalisierung einer Produktgruppe

Removing one or more products from a product line in order to update it, make it more attractive and profitable, etc.

Line spacing Zeilenabstand

The number of lines of space which appear between each typed line of text.

Lineage/linage Anzeigenraum
(Druck)Zeilenzahl

The total amount of advertising space in a print medium.

The number of lines run. Classified advertisements are often charged by the number of lines used.

List Liste, Tabelle, Verzeichnis

An ordered set of items of data.

List broker Adressenverlag

Also called list house, list supplier or mailing house.

A firm which compiles and sells mailing lists and prospect lists, eg of people representing specific markets or segments of a market, e.g. doctors, engineers, etc.

List price Listenpreis

Also called catalog(ue), posted or sticker price.

The basic, recommended or retail price published by the supplier which can be varied by possible discounts. Normally, the price that users or consumers are asked to pay for products.

Listenership (Radio)Hörerschaft

Also called broadcast or radio audience.

The listeners of a radio station or programme.

Literal (error) Schreib,- Tipp-, Druckfehler

Also called misprint.

A mistake (typographical error) in typing or printing.

Litter bin advertising Papierkorbwerbung

An advertising method where litter bins are partly or wholly used for advertisements.

Live customer aktueller Kunde
Stammkunde

A customer currently buying a product or service.

A regular customer.

Live program(me) Live-Sendung, aktuelle Sendung

A radio or TV program(me) that is presented as it is happening.

Live tag Direktansage

In broadcast, a live ending following a prerecorded commercial and giving information such as store addresses or prices, special offers, etc.

Loaded price hochgeschraubter Preis, gesalzener Preis

An extremely high price, eg due to a large extra payment for some service.

Loading (ldg) Auf-, Be-, Verladen, Befrachtung

To put something in or on something (e.g. on a lorry, on a ship) to be carried away.

Lobby Lobby, Interessenvertretung

A group of persons who try to influence legislators or other public officials to vote or act in favour of a special interest.

Local advertiser lokaler Werbungtreibender

A business, usually a retailer, that advertises in the local media.

Local advertising lokale Werbung

Advertising for a local business in a specific area, eg a city. Possible media include: the daily newspaper(s), the local radio or TV station, a shopper`s guide, the yellow pages, etc.

Local buying office Einkauf(szentrale) vor Ort

A buying office located in an overseas country. Many companies in foreign countries buy so much, e.g. from UK sources, that they find it financially advantageous to maintain buying offices in the UK. These offices try to obtain products at very competitve prices and look after affreightment, insurance and finance.

Local call Ortsgespräch

A telephone call made within a specified local area. It is cheaper than a long-distance or trunk call which is a call outside the local area.

Local market

örtlicher/lokaler Markt
Inlandsmarkt, Binnenmarkt

This is a market held in our market halls and squares, where the goods are actually exhibited for sale.

The domestic, home or inland market of a particular country.

Local press

Lokalpresse

Also called community press.

Newspapers circulating mainly within a small area, eg a city and its suburbs.

Local rate

Werbepreis für lokale
Werbungtreibende

The advertising rate charged by local media to local advertisers.

Local station

Lokal-, Regionalsender

A radio or TV station serving a specific market area.

Local tag

lokale Werbeansage

Also called dealer tag or dealer super.

An identification of a local dealer at the end of a recorded broadcast commercial.

Local time (lt)

Ortszeit

The time at a particular place or in a particular country.

Location

Standort, Lage

A place of settlement, activity, or residence.

Industry is localised/concentrated in certain areas and some areas specialise in certain types of industry. This is known as the geographical division of labour.

The need for selecting a business location arises when a new enterprise or branch is to be established, when a firm must move because it has outgrown its facilities or cannot obtain a new lease, or when an undesirable location is to be abandoned.

The ideal location is one that permits the lowest unit cost in the production and distribution of a product or service.
A wide variety of factors influence the decision to locate a plant, firm or industry. These include: proximity and size of the market; supply of raw materials; availability of labour; adequacy and cost of transportation; supply of land, power, water, etc.; suitability of climate; character of the community; etc.

Location pricing Preisfestsetzung nach Standort

A pricing strategy where different locations are priced differently, even though the cost of offering each location is the same.

Loco price Loco-Preis, Preis ab ...

A term often used in foreign trade. The local price, e.g. loco factory. The basic price of the goods is their ex-warehouse price (in the country of origin); no additions (e.g. the cost of carrying the goods to the docks at the port of embarkation) have been made. The seller's responsibility ceases once the goods are safely delivered to the appointed place.

Logistics Logistik

The planning, organisation, implementation, and coordination of the details of any operation. For example in business, the planning and organisation of the most feasible combination of resources, facilities, personnel and time needed to carry out the objectives and policies of a company.

The strategic activity involved in ensuring that the products offered actually reach the final purchaser.

Logo Signum, Logo

Also called logograph, logotype or trademark.

A trademark or easily recognised symbol used by a company as a mark on its products and in advertising, and incorporated into the firm's letterhead. Often consists of the company's name in distinctive lettering. Companies take care to register their logos to provide some protection against counterfeiting.

Long-standing customer Stammkunde

Also called regular or steady customer.

A customer who has been buying for a long time period.

Long-term economic forecast langfristige Konjunkturprognose

An economic forecast covering a number of years.

Loose insert lose (Werbe)Beilage

Advertisements loosely inserted within the pages of a publication.

Loss Mindererlös, Verlust
Verlust
Schaden

In trading, the condition where costs exceed revenue.

In accounting, loss is the opposite of profit.

A general meaning of loss is that a person no longer has something which he/she had in the past.

A damage or an injury.

Loss leader Lockvogel, Lockartikel

Also called bait, call bird, leader, leading article.

A product or service, usually a well-known brand, which is priced at, or even below, cost, in the hope of attracting additional customers (to increase store traffic) who may be induced to buy other things as well. Supermarkets and hypermarkets, often do apply this technique of selling.

Loss of customers Kundenabgänge

Losing customers, ie to have fewer customers, eg because of bad quality or service, high prices, unreliability, etc.

Loss of order Auftragsverlust

The state of not getting an order which was expected.

Lost and found office Fundbüro

Also called lost property office.

An office which collects objects which people have left behind and keeps them until the owners claim them.

Lot Lieferposten, Partie

In a consignment, a number of articles of the same kind.

Lottery Lotterie, Glücksspiel

A drawing of lots.

A method of raising money in which a large number of tickets are sold and a draw is held for prizes.

Anything which is decided by chance.

Lover price Liebhaberpreis

A high price paid for an item by a person who is in love with it.

Low density cargo Fracht mit niedrigem Staumaß

Freight cargo which has a low stowage factor but is usually very heavy.

Low end untere Preisklasse

A product classification indicating that the product or the product range is sold at a lower price level.

Low income country Land mit niedrigem Pro-Kopf-Einkommen

A country with an extremely low income per capita/head compared with other countries.

Low involvement product Produkt von geringer Faszination, wertfreies Produkt, Low-Involvement-Produkt

A product in which the potential buyer shows little interest, ie he/she buys it routinely or impulsively without much thought, search or purchase time.

Low pressure selling dezentes, unaufdringliches Verkaufen

Als called soft selling.

A selling approach in which the salesperson attempts to win the customer`s confidence and respect through subtle sales techniques.

Low season Nachsaison

The period of the year when there are few travellers or tourists. Usually, sales are declining and prices are falling, eg room prices.

Low-budget advertising Werbung mit kleinem Werbebudget

An advertising campaign financed by a small ad budget; thus, for example, the advertiser inserts a large number of classified ads.

Low-class magazine minderwertige Zeitschrift

A magazine of inferior quality.

Low-grade (l g) mindere Qualität

Of inferior quality.

Lowball Lockvogel

Also called bait or loss leader.

An article which is sold at a very low price, at cost or even at a loss to attract customers for the purchase of other, more profitable merchandise.

Lowercase (LC, lc) Kleinbuchstabe

Also called lowercase (lower case) letter.

Small letters of the alphabet of type or lettering.

Loyalty discount Treuerabatt

Also called loyalty rebate; aggregated, fidelity or patronage rebate.

A rebate granted to loyal customers with regular purchases.

Luggage Reisegepäck

Also called baggage.

Suitcases or bags for carrying clothes when travelling.

Luggage claim Gepäckausgabe

Also called baggage claim.

In an airport, the place where luggage comes off the plane onto a carousel where passengers can collect it.

Lull Flaute

Also called dullness, slack or sluggishness.

A period where there is little economic activity, eg demand is not brisk and sales are dull.

Lump sum Pauschalbetrag

An amount of money paid in a single payment to a beneficiary.

In transportation, the freight payable irrespective of the amount of goods loaded.

Lump sum freight Pauschalfracht

The amount of freight charges payable for the use of the whole or portion of a vehicle, e.g. a ship.

Luxury goods Luxuswaren

Also called fancy articles, luxuries or prestige goods.

These are goods which are not absolutely essential to meet the needs of a man.

Luxury tax Luxussteuer

Tax on goods considered non-essential, ie a tax on luxury goods.

M

Macrodynamics makrodynamische Analyse

Also called macrodynamic analysis.

The forces which influence the rates of increase or decrease of broad categories of demand (for example, for imports or exports, capital goods, etc.).

Macroeconomic aims makroökonomische Ziele

Macroeconomic policy tries to achieve certain objectives:
1. economic growth, 2. full employment, 3. balance of payments equilibrium, and 4. a low inflation rate. Other important aims are the redistribution of income and wealth.

Macroeconomics Makroökonomik

The study of an economy as a whole, rather than of individual buyers, sellers and firms; ie the study of aggregate economic activity and behaviour. In particular, it includes the determination of total output and employment as well as changes in prices (the rate of inflation). The use of money in the economy is also studied.
Note: macroeconomics relies on deductions from microeconomics.

Macroenvironment Makroumwelt

All the general environmental factors that may affect a company.

Macromarketing/macro marketing Makromarketing

The study of marketing processes, activities, and results from a broad perspective, eg marketing seen from a national perspective and thus focussing on marketing actions within a country's economy and its economic, cultural, social or political needs.

Macrosegmentation Makrosegmentierung

Division of markets into segments according to such general characteristics as geographic location, customer type, customer size or product use.

Madam Sehr geehrte Frau

The salutation "Dear Madam" is used to address both single and married women. "Mesdames" is the proper salutation when writing to two or more women. Madam Chairman is used when addressing a woman who is in the chair at the meeting.

"Made in" label Herstellungsetikett, "hergestellt" in Kennzeichnung

The identification of the country of origin on a product, eg Made in Germany or Made in the USA. Whether such labels are used may depend on:

1. the market for which the product is destined;
2. the laws requiring such identification (eg goods entering the USA must be identified by their origin);
3. whether the image of "made in" products is held in high esteem;
4. whether national sentiments favour locally produced products;
5. whether the "made in" label benefits the business; etc.

In the light of these factors, an international marketer may choose not to use the "made in" attribute as a regular practice.
Note: due to the internationalisation of production, large companies start using the "made by ...." label, eg "Made by Mercedes Benz".

Magazine Zeitschrift, Magazin
Warenlager, Magazin

A periodical publication, usually paperbound, containing miscellaneous editorial pieces, e.g. articles, illustrations, interviews, photographic essays, stories, etc. It may cater for special interest groups or it may be designed for the general reader. Additionally, magazines provide a lot of advertising space. Also called journal or periodical.

A place to store goods, eg a warehouse. Also called depot, depository, store, storehouse or warehouse.

Magazine advertising Zeitschriftenwerbung

Advertising in one of the various magazines. There are several types of magazines, e.g. trade journals, specific consumer magazines, more general consumer magazines. As magazines are specialized they can be very efficient in reaching specific target markets.

Magnate Magnat, Großindustrieller

Also called tycoon.

An important and rich businessperson, ie a person of great wealth and power.

Magnetic card Magnetkarte

A plastic card with a magnetisable surface on which data can be recorded.

Mail (ml) Post(sendung)

Also called post.

All types of written correspondence between persons, firms, etc. sent or received by post.

Mail box Briefkasten

Also called letter, pillar, post or posting box.

A box into which incoming mail is put, or a box for putting letters into for sending by mail/post.

Mail interview briefliche Befragung, Umfrage

Also called mail survey.

A survey method where questionnaires are sent to interviewees/respondents, who are encouraged to complete and return them. This type of survey is very suitable when the respondents are spread over a wide area and funds for the survey are limited. But, there may be the possibility of a low response rate or of misleading results.

Mail order (MO) Postversandauftrag, Postbestellung, Mail-Order

A selling method in which the product is promoted by either media advertising or direct mail and the potential buyer is invited to order by mail/post, or by telephone or fax. The goods so ordered are usually delivered through the mail or by a carrier, or sometimes through a local agent.

ıail order business Versand(haus)handel

ılso called mail order selling or mail order trade.

ıail order (MO), a direct marketing business, was originally developed in USA for the enefit of customers who lived far away from stores. This is a marketing method in ɿhich buying and selling is carried out by post/mail. The customers (the mail order uyers) send their orders to the seller (the mail order house or catalogue company) by ost and goods are delivered to the customer's home through the mail, by carrier direct :om warehouse or factory, or sometimes through a local agent.
'here is no personal contact between the seller and the buyer. The customer orders ither from an advertisement, usually including an order form, or from a catalogue. ometimes customers choose their products through local agents who visit their omes. Some mail order houses send out a direct-mail shot to their prospective and ɜgular customers.
ıs the goods are sent on approval, they can be viewed and handled before purchase; if ıe customer dislikes the goods, he can return them to the seller.
ayment is either cash with order (CWO), cash on delivery (COD), on account, or by ıstalment.

ıail order buying Versandbestellung

he purchase of goods by a mail order buyer through mail, computer, telephone, or ıx.

ıail order catalog(ue) Versandhauskatalog, Versandkatalog

. catalogue issued by a mail order house showing customers all the articles for sale.

ıail order house Versandhaus

lso called catalog(ue) company, catalog(ue) retailer or mail order firm.

company which sells goods by mail order.

ıail order retailing Versandeinzelhandel

form of non-personal and non-store retailing that involves selling by description ɜcause buyers do not see the actual product until it arrives in the mail. Orders are ɔmmonly placed by computer, telephone or fax.
ɜllers inform and contact buyers through direct mail, catalogues, TV, radio, ɜwspapers and magazines.

Mail order wholesaler Versandgroßhändler

A mail order house that sells through direct mail by sending catalogues to retailers or industrial buyers.

Mail questionnaire briefliche Befragung

Also called mail survey.

A questionnaire sent to respondents by mail.
Possible benefits are: relatively low costs, elimination of interviewers, centralized control, anonymity for respondents, etc.
On the other hand, mail questionnaires usually produce low response rates.

Mail shipment Postversand

The shipment of small quantities by surface, air or sea mail.
In overseas trade, a mail shipment must be within the size and weight limits of both countries. As the postal department will do the customs work for you, you do not have to pay for customs clearance; but you will still have to pay the customs duty if any is charged.

Mail(ing) shot Briefwerbeaktion

A single mailing of direct mail advertising literature and thus an advertising technique of attracting demand to increase sales.
The mail shot must stand alone to attract the sale as it is usually unpracticable for the product to accompany the advertising material.
Note: two mailings to the same list is known as a two-shot campaign.

Mail-in per Post angefordertes Werbegeschenk

Also called mail-in premium.

A free gift offered by firms, eg in advertisements, if consumers submit proof of purchase, ie consumers have to mail in to obtain the gift.
Note: a time or quantity limit should be printed on the offer in order to avoid disappointment among consumers if demand for the gift exceeds supply.

Mail-out Werbeversand

Promotional literature sent to prospects by direct mail.

Mailer Direktwerber
Briefwerbematerial

A direct mail advertiser.

A printed direct mail advertising piece.

Mailing Werbesendung

A number of leaflets, brochures, circulars, etc, mailed at one time to prospects.

Mailing list Adressenliste
Versandliste
Verteiler(liste)

Classified list of names and addresses to whom an organisation regularly sends some form of written communication.

A shipping list. Also called packing list.

A distribution list.

Mailing piece Postwurfsendung

Also called bulk mail, direct mail shot or mailshot/mail shot.

A letter, leaflet, postcard, order form or product sent through the post on a widespread basis.

Mailroom/mail room Poststelle, Expedition

Also called mailing room or department, or post room.

An office in a company where incoming mail is sorted and distributed and where outgoing mail is collected and mailed/posted.
The department also deals with mail passing inside a firm between departments.

Maintenance advertising Bestands-, Erhaltungswerbung

Advertising intended to maintain a product or service in the customers` mind, and thus keep the current sales level in a competitive market.

Maintenance bond Mängelhaftungsgarantie

A bond that guarantees against defects in workmanship or materials for a fixed period after completion of a contract.

Maintenance manual Wartungshandbuch

A booklet distributed to service personnel. It provides complete technical descriptions, fault diagnosis (US: trouble shooting), repair and overhaul, and routine maintenance procedures.

Major führendes Unternehmen
Volljährige(r)

A very large firm, a blue chip company.

A person above 18 years of age. The opposite is minor.

Majority Mehrheit
Volljährigkeit

The greater number, more than half.

Full legal age, in many countries the age of majority is 18 years. Also called full age or legal age.

Make Produktionsmenge
Herstellung, Produktion
Marke
herstellen, produzieren
verdienen

The quantity produced/made. Also called output volume or (volume of) output.

The manufacture or production of goods.

The brand; the type of product manufactured. Also called label or trademark.

To make, manufacture or produce a commodity.

To earn or to increase in value, e.g. to make a profit.

Make or buy decision — Entscheidung über Eigenfertigung oder Fremdbezug

When considering the acquisition of a new product, the decision as to whether to lease or purchase a product or to produce it internally.

Make-up — Umbruch

In a publication, the arrangement of material into pages.

Makegood (MG) — Ersatzinserat, Ersatzspot

An advertisement placed again in a magazine or newspaper, or a commercial rerun, free of charge, because of an error in running it the first time.

Maker — Hersteller

Also called manufacturer or producer.

A manufacturer, processor or producer of merchandise or products.

Managed trade — gelenkter Handel

Trade influenced and determined by political and economic powers and more dominant economic nations.

Any international trade that is impacted by nonmarket factors such as trade restrictions and other nontrade measures.

Management by objective(s) (MBO) — Management nach Zielvorgabe und Zielkontrolle (MBO)

A management technique whereby superiors and subordinates jointly establish quantified objectives (goals or targets) and the plans for attaining them within specified time-limits. MBO is concerned with results and their evaluation.

Mandatory blurb Warnhinweis, Pflichtwarnung, Mußwarnung

In an advertisement, an informative statement required by law, eg a health warning (also implying that the warning is usually ignored).

Manifest Ladeverzeichnis, -liste, Frachtliste, Manifest Passagierliste

A list of cargo carried by vessel or plane, listing the contents, value, destination, carrier and time a cargo is shipped. It is prepared and signed by the captain for presenting to port/airport and customs officials who may require it. Also called manifest of cargo.

A list of passengers on a plane or vessel. Also called passenger list.

Manil(l)a Hartpapier

Thick brown paper used to wrap commodities. Also used for envelopes, called manilla envelope.

Manual Handbuch, Leitfaden

A printed document or small book containing special instructions, e.g. an operating manual.

Manufactured goods Industriegüter, -erzeugnisse

Also called industrial products or goods, or manufactures.

Manufactured goods are the finished articles which, with the assistance of workpeople are worked up from the raw material.

Manufacturer (manfr, mf, mfr) Hersteller(firma), Erzeuger, Produzent

Also called maker or producer.

A person or firm who is engaged in the work of making finished or semi-finished goods from raw materials or from component parts.

Manufacturer brand Herstellermarke, Fabrikmarke

Also called manufacturer's brand.

A brand in which the registered name is owned by the company making the product. These brands are initiated by producers and ensure that they are identified with their products at the point of sale (POS). Usually, the producer distributes, promotes and prices the product.

Manufacturer's agent Handelsvertreter, Werksvertreter

Also called manufacturer's representative (MR).

A salesperson (or firm) who acts as an agent and represents one or more non-competing manufacturers/producers for a sales commission within an exclusive territory.

Manufacturer's guarantee Herstellergarantie

The manufacturer of goods assures the buyer of his goods a certain quality and fitness.

Manufacturer's liability Produzentenhaftung, Produkthaftung

Also called product liability.

The liability of a manufacturer of goods towards persons who may be affected or injured by his goods.

Manufacturer`s recommended price (MRP) empfohlener Herstellerpreis, Preisempfehlung des Herstellers

The price at which the manufacturer suggests the retailer should sell his product. Certainly, there is nothing to prevent retailers selling at lower prices if they want.

Manufacturing (mfg, manufg) Fertigung, Herstellung, Produktion

Also called production.

The making of goods from raw materials with the aid of tools and machinery. This is known as the secondary stage in production.

Manufacturing cost(s) Fertigungskosten

Also called production cost(s) or factory cost(s); sometimes also manufacturing expense.

The cost(s) of manufacturing a product; i.e. the cost(s) of direct materials, direct labou and factory overheads. Selling and other non-factory costs are excluded.

Manufacturing industry Fertigungswirtschaft, verarbeitende Industrie

Also called finishing or processing industry.

This covers firms engaged in using raw materials to produce manufactured goods. It involves changing the form of a commodity - usually by taking raw materials and processing/making them into finished products.

Manufacturing licence Herstellungslizenz

Also called licence to manufacture.

It is the custom of manufacturers to grant a license (ie a permit) to similar firms in other countries, to manufacture their products, using their trademark but not their name.

Manufacturing order Fertigungs-, Produktionsauftrag

Also called production order.

An order received by a company to produce a specific product.

Manufacturing overhead Fertigungsgemeinkosten

Also called factory overhead or expense, production overhead or indirect manufacturing costs.

All expenses arising from manufacturing activities except those of direct labour and direct materials. There are variable and fixed manufacturing overheads.

Margin

Grenzwert
Gewinnspanne
Handelsspanne
Bruttogewinn
Deckungsbeitrag

The margin is the point at which the consumer is indifferent as to whether he purchases any more or not. In making his decision, he compares the utility of the different commodities he can buy with a unit of money. At the margin, the consumer does not have to choose between several commodities; he has to choose between additions to and substractions from a given position, between a little less of one commodity and a little more of another. The unit of a commodity that a purchaser thinks is just worth buying has marginal utility, and the last unit bought is the marginal unit.

A margin of profit. Also called profit margin.

The operating margin. Also called price or trade margin.

The gross profit on sales.

The excess of sales price over a firm's variable costs. Also called contribution margin.

Marginal analysis Marginalanalyse, Grenzwertanalyse

A method of solving economic problems by using small steps and evaluating the costs and benefits of each marginal step.

Marginal benefit Grenzvorteil

The extra benefit received from one more unit of consumption, labour, production, or other control variable being increased. Similar to marginal utility.

Marginal buyer Grenzkäufer, Grenznachfrager

A buyer who will refuse to buy if the price is increased.

Marginal cost (MC) Grenzkosten

Also called alternative, differential, incremental or terminal cost(s).

The additional cost of producing an extra unit of output.

Marginal cost pricing Grenzkostenpreisbildung

Also called marginal pricing.

A pricing method which is based on the marginal costs of products and which can be used if the marginal costs are constant over the relevant range.
Note: it is less common in practice than full cost pricing.

Marginal efficiency of capital (MEC) Grenzleistungsfähigkeit des Kapitals

The rate of return/profits expected on an extra unit of capital. The marginal efficiency of capital decreases as the amount of capital increases.

Marginal factor cost (MFC) Faktorgrenzkosten

Increase in total cost when one additional unit of an input (e.g. one more unit of labour) is employed.

Marginal firm Grenzproduzent, Grenzbetrieb

Also called least efficient producer or marginal producer.

A producer who is just in the position to meet his production costs, with a small profit. If a firm persistently earns less than what is considered to be normal profit for the industry the entrepreneur will leave that industry. The marginal firm will thus be the one just capable of earning normal profit.

Marginal product Grenzprodukt

Also called extra product.

This is the additional product obtained from combining one more unit of the variable factor of production.

Marginal productivity Grenzproduktivität

Also called marginal productiveness.

The change in total output that results from employment of one extra unit of input.

Marginal profit Grenzerlös

Also called marginal revenue.

The increase in total profits that is obtained by producing an additional unit of output.

Marginal propensity to consume (MPC) marginale Konsumquote, Grenzkonsumneigung

The proportion of increases in income that is spent for consumption purposes rather than saved.

$$\text{MPC} = \frac{\text{change in consumption}}{\text{change in income}}$$

J.M. Keynes believed that the most important determinant in the decision to consume rather than to save is the level of income itself - Keynes said, as households' incomes rise, they are inclined to increase their consumption, but not by as much as the increase in their income. In other words, the MPC is less than one.

Marginal propensity to save (MPS) marginale Sparquote, Grenzneigung zum Sparen

The MPS is the change in total savings that is caused by a change in the level of disposable personal income. It is that proportion of an increase in income not spent on consumption. It is equal to 1-MPC (marginal propensity to consume).

Marginal purchase Grenzkauf

Product or service which a buyer thinks is only just worth buying.

Marginal rate of substitution (MRS) Grenzrate der Substitution

A ratio of the marginal utilities of two products. In other words, the rate at which a consumer is willing to exchange one product for another while maintaining a constant level of satisfaction.

Marginal revenue (MR) Grenzerlös

Also called marginal profit.

This is the additional revenue obtained by selling one more unit.

Marginal seller Grenzverkäufer

The seller who refuses to sell if the price is decreased.

Marginal unit letzte Produkteinheit

The marginal unit of anything is the last to be added or the first to be taken away from a supply. Marginal considerations concern the smallest possible increase or decrease in one's stock of a commodity. For example, the marginal unit of something is the smallest additional amount the consumer considers to be worth buying.

Marginal utility (MU) Grenznutzen

This is the satisfaction we receive from possessing one extra unit of a commodity, or the satisfaction we lose by giving up one unit.

Marital status Familienstand

The situation whether an individual is married, separated, single, divorced, widowed, or remarried.

Mark Marke, Markierung
markieren, kennzeichnen
Deutsche Mark
Finnmark

A sign put on an item to show something.

To identify something by a symbol or control key.

Money used in Germany, also called Deutschmark (DM).

A monetary unit used in Finland (markka).

Mark of origin Ursprungsbezeichnung, Herkunftszeichen

A marking on a product that indicates where the product was produced.

Markdown Preissenkung, Preisnachlaß

Also called price reduction or price cut.

A price reduction offered in order to stimulate sales.

Market (mkt) Markt, Handelsplatz
Börse
Nachfrage

A market is a place where buyers and sellers are in contact with one another for the purpose of trading a particular good or service, and for the fixing of prices. An equilibrium price is established when the same quantity is both demanded and supplied. The prices obtainable in one part of the market affect the prices paid in other parts.

There are various types of markets, e.g.: financial, labour, commodity markets; perfect, imperfect and highly-organised markets; the food or the drinks market, etc.

The theory of markets distinguishes between markets according to their structural characterisitics. The main distinctions are:
1. perfect competition (ie many sellers and many buyers), 2. oligopoly (ie few sellers and many buyers), 3. oligopsony (ie many sellers, few buyers), 4. bilateral oligopoly (ie few sellers, few buyers), 5. monopoly (ie one seller, many buyers), 6. monopsony (ie many sellers, one buyer), 7. bilateral monopoly (ie one seller, one buyer), 8. duopoly (ie two sellers, many buyers), 9. duopsony (ie many sellers, two buyers).

A stock exchange, commodity exchange, futures exchange, etc.

There is a market/demand for a particular commodity, e.g. for copper.

Market acceptance Marktakzeptanz

The condition in which a product or service satisfies a sufficient part of the market to continue production and possibly increase it.

Market accessibility Marktzugänglichkeit

A company's capability of effectively marketing and delivering product(s) to a defined market (segment).
Note: a market segment that cannot be profitably reached and served is of no benefit to the company.

Market analysis Marktanalyse

Also called market auditor marketing analysis.

The process of analysing the constituents of a specific market for a particular product or service.

The systematic understanding of the existing and potential market for a product or service, the provision of this information to management, and the making of recommendations on how customers` wants might be served.

Market behaviour Marktverhalten

Also called market conduct or market performance.

This is the aggregate behaviour of all the individuals purchasing a particular good.

Market capacity Marktkapazität

The ability of a market to absorb certain quantities of goods.

Market challenger Marktherausforderer

Also called runner-up firm.

In competitive markets, a competing company behind the market leader, ie a non-market leader which aggressively attacks rivals, including the market leader, to gain more market share and to dominate the market.
Note: usually, these players are number two, three or four in a market.

Market challenger strategies Strategien eines Marktherausforderers

The strategies of a market challenger to attack the market leader and/or other competitors. Possible attack strategies are:
1. the frontal attack, 2. the flank attack, 3. the encirclement attack, 4. the bypass attack, 5. the guerrilla attack.

Market concentration Marktkonzentration

The degree to which a relatively small number of firms dominates a large proportion of the market.

Market coverage — Marktabdeckung
Marktanteil

The number of available outlets that are selling a manufacturer`s brand in a given area. There are three typical forms of coverage:
1. exclusive distribution: the manufacturer sells the goods within a certain territory only through a single retailer or a limited number of retailers;
2. intensive distribution: there are many distribution outlets;
3. selective distribution: a limited number of outlets is chosen to sell the goods in a given market area.

A firm`s market share.

Market day — Börsentag, Markttag

The day when a market, e.g. the stock market, is regularly held.

Market demand — Marktnachfrage, Gesamtnachfrage

Also called aggregate, composite, overall or total demand.

The sum of individual demands for a commodity in a defined geographical area at a particular price in a specific time period.
Market demand is influenced by: 1. the size and composition of the population, 2. the distribution of income within the population and 3. individual demand.

Market density — Marktdichte

The number of prospects within a specific area, eg a square mile or kilometer.

Market development — Marktentwicklung

The expansion or growth of a specific market.

Market disruption — Marktzerrüttung

The difficulties in a home market as a result of a sudden increase in imports into that market.

Market diversification Marktdiversifizierung

A company strategy where the company seeks growth by adding products and markets of a kind unrelated to its existing products and markets.

Market dues Standmiete, Standgebühr

Also called stallage.

The rent payable for a market stall by a market stallholder.

Market ecology Marktökologie

The study of cultural, economic, political, and social environments of a country together with the effect(s) these have on a company's business policy.

Market economy Marktwirtschaft

Also called flexible price economy or market directed economy.

In a market economy, resources are privately owned and production decisions are made by private individuals and private firms acting in their own self-interest, in response to the forces of supply and demand.

Characteristics of the market economy are: the resources are allocated through a system of prices, private persons have the economic freedom to buy and sell as they wish; competition between firms will encourage low prices, economic efficiency and the invention of new products; unequal distribution of income, sellers tend to keep prices high and wages low, public goods will not be produced, resources may remain unemployed because firms as a whole consider that profit prospects are poor, etc.

Market entry Marktzutritt

The act of entering a market. Before entering a market, a firm should consider the following criteria:
1. the sales forecast, both short- and long-term;
2. the stability of the market, both in economic and political terms;
3. legal and political restraints;
4. the extent to which market research data on the potential market and its customers are available;
5. the degree of control in the areas of price, quality, marketing and distribution;
6. the profitability of the new market;
7. the relationships between the two countries; etc.

Market entry barriers Marktzutrittshindernisse

Any circumstance or event which inhibits or deters a firm from entering a market.

Market equilibrium Marktgleichgewicht

A market situation where producers produce exactly the quantity demanded by consumers. In any competitive market, the price will settle at a level that makes the quantities demanded and supplied equal. Conclusions about market equilibrium are sometimes called the "laws of demand and supply".

Market expansion Markterweiterung

A growth strategy in which a company targets products to new markets; develops new segments or totally new users.

Market factor analysis Marktfaktorenanalyse

A forecasting method which focuses on certain key market factors affecting the level of demand.

Market follower Marktfolger

Also called me-too company.

In a competitive market, a low share competitor without resources, market position, research and development to challenge the market leader or the market challengers for extra sales and market share. Its main strategy is to do as before and survive.

In a competitive market, a company content to maintain its existing market share behind the market leader. That means, this firm will not challenge the market leader and thus avoid direct competition, but will follow him, either closely, at a distance or occasionally.

Market forces Marktkräfte

The factors influencing the supply of and the demand for goods and services which are outside the control of business.
The markets which organisations serve are constantly changing. In order to survive, organisations have to react to market changes.
For example, the elements of risk and uncertainty which exist in business are primarily caused by the shifting nature of demand.

Market forecast — Marktprognose

The forecast of sales for a market during a given period, taking into account prevailing environmental circumstances. A market forecast plays an important role in formulating future strategy with regard to both the product and the market.
Market forecasting is a task which involves market analysis, market research and statistical processing, in addition to sound judgement and a good comprehension of the market.

Note: in international market forecasting, the forecaster(s) must be well acquainted with the economic, political, cultural and business background of the overseas market. Moreover, the forecast should reflect any likely change in exchange rates, import controls, more intense competition, changes in the delivery and payment terms, etc.

On the stock exchange, the forecast of prices.

Market forms — Marktformen

Market forms show the number of market participants on the supply side and the demand side. Simplified, we can say that there are three main types of market form:
1. the monopoly, 2. the oligopoly, 3. the polypoly.

Market leader — Marktführer

Also called market guide or top seller.

Brand, product or company which has the largest share in a market.

Market manager — Marktleiter

A manager who is reponsible for coordinating marketing efforts designed to reach a particular group of customers, ie he/she has to serve a specific market segment, not a particular product.

Market map — Marktstrukturkarte, Marktstrukturdarstellung

A chart showing the structure of a market, eg indicating the number and type of consumers, consumers` purchasing power, the activities of competitors or competition on a particular market.

Market mechanism Marktmechanismus

This mechanism assumes that potential buyers and sellers satisfy their needs and wants by the mechanism of price, especially if the products are identical.

Market niche Marktnische

A small market overlooked or ignored by market leaders/majors and therefore served by smaller firms or smaller divisions of larger companies.
An ideal market niche should be of negligible interest to large competitors, should have sufficient size, purchasing/spending power to be profitable and growth potential. The market nicher should dispose of the required skills to serve the niche effectively and has to specialise along market, customer, product, or marketing-mix lines.

Market nicher Nischenanbieter

A firm supplying to a narrow target market and specialising in a narrow product range. Nichers, eg Porsche, survive by finding a safe, small, profitable market segment which is not attractive for market leaders or market challengers.
The problem of market nichers is that they are vulnerable to market downswings, the entry of rival nichers and the sudden attention of the market leader or challengers.

Market overt organisierter Markt

Also called regular market.

A public market where goods are openly offered for sale.

Market penetration Marktduchdringung

A marketing strategy used by a firm to increase the sales of a product within an existing market by aggressive sales and marketing strategies.

The degree, usually expressed as a percentage, to which a product is sold in its present markets. Also called penetration of the market or sales penetration.

Market penetration pricing Penetrationspreisbildung

A pricing strategy which sets a low initial price for a new product in order to attract a large number of buyers and win a large market share.

Note: low prices increase the sales volume and a high sales volume causes falling costs which, in turn, lets the seller keep prices low, or even cut prices; this may help to keep out competitors.

Market place Markt

The place where goods are sold.

Market position Marktstellung

A company`s position in the market.

The position of a product or service within a particular market segment relative to those of competitors. Ideally, it should stand out from the competition and occupy a unique position (ie it should offer a unique selling proposition, USP) due to better quality, design, performance, reliability, etc.
A position is achieved:
1. by associating the benefits of a product with the needs or life style of the market segments;
2. the differentiation of the company´s offering from the competition by making or implying a comparison in terms of specific attributes.

Market positioning Marktpositionierung

A marketing activity which tries to place a product into a desired position in a specific market and to have it perceived in that way by consumers.

Market power Marktmacht

Also called discretionary power.

This means that an organisation is in a position to exploit its position as the sole demander or supplier, or one of the few demanders for or suppliers of a range of products.
For example, the firm manipulates prices, fails to pay on time, controls competitor's access to the marketplace, etc.

Market price Marktwert, Marktpreis, Tageswert Kurswert, Börsenkurs

The price at which something has just sold in a particular market. The market price of a product is determined by the interaction of the forces of demand and supply.

At the equilibrium price, the quantity the sellers are prepared to sell will equal the quantity the buyers wish to buy. If the price in the market is higher than the equilibrium price, sellers will be unable to sell all of their output, and this will induce them to lower the price. If the market price is lower than the equilibrium price sellers will soon sell out, and this will induce them to raise their price. In this way there is a tendency for the market price to approach the equilibrium price. Also called actual, current or ruling price, going or market rate, or present value.

The price of a commodity or stock sold on a commodity or stock exchange. Also called listed or quoted value.

Market pricing — marktorientierte Preisgestaltung
Preisbildung durch Marktmechanismus

Also called market determined pricing.

A pricing strategy which focuses on pricing from the viewpoint of the customer. First, an estimate is made of the acceptable price in the target market. If this price does not meet the company's profit objective, then the company can either give up the business or increase the price. Additional adjustments in price may be required to cope with competitors, host country government, expected cost increases, and other eventualities.

A pricing method where the seller does not have control of the price of each separate transaction and instead allows supply and demand to operate freely to determine the price. This type of pricing occurs in the commodity exchanges.

Market profile — Marktprofil

The basic features of a particular market, i.e. the facts about members of a particular market group sufficient to identify such members.

Market report — Marktbericht

Also called market letter or review.

A report describing the conditions of a particular market.

Market research — Marktforschung (Mafo)

Also called marketing research.

The process of making investigations into the characteristics of given markets in which a company is operating today and in which it may hope to operate tomorrow.

The five steps in market research are:
1. to define the problem, 2. to define the method of research, 3. to ask the questions and record the answers, 4. to decide what the answers mean specifically in terms of the defined problem, 5. to compile and present the report.

The object of market research is to secure information to help in formulating selling policies. It should include the measurement and analysis of markets, the study of advertising effectiveness, distributive channels, competitive products, and the buying habits of consumers. It should predict and monitor trends, both in supply and demand. It supplies regular information on prices and profits and on the development of substitute products.
Market research is also used to discover why consumers purchase the goods they do; it studies ways of packaging goods so as to make them attractive to the purchaser; and it makes sales forecasts.
Market research is conducted in several ways:
1. trained investigators/interviewers may be sent out to interview the customers (the interviewees or respondents), or
2. questionnaires may be sent through the post.

Despite the numerous benefits of market research, there are severe limitations in conducting market research:
1. time: a research project takes time to complete and consequently, by the time action is taken on the data, market situations, especially profile, competition and legislation might have changed and research data can become out-of-date;
2. commercial risk: as research merely collects information but does not formulate decisions, the management must draw its own conclusions and finally make its own decisions - thus research can reduce but not eliminate risk;
3. data collection: its accuracy largely depends on the method of collection used (e.g. personal interviews, mail or telephone survey, focus group);
4. conclusions: these can never be completely accurate because people can only express beliefs or intentions at any point in time and a subsequent change in circumstances can change their beliefs;
5. cost: as market research, especially field research, can be very expensive, it should be carefully costed and the benefits should be evaluated before conducting research;
6. personnel: the quality of the staff involved largely determines the quality of the survey; etc.

Note: 1. to monitor changing trends continuous research should be carried out; 2. the findings of the research project should be implemented in the company without delay.

Market resistance Marktwiderstand

The general reluctance of a market to accept a product or service on offer.

Market sales potential Absatzpotential eines Marktes

The maximum amount of product that can be sold in a given industry with maximum marketing expenditures under existing marketing mixes within a specific area and over a certain period of time.

Market segment Marktsegment

A group of buyers with similar purchasing characteristics.

Market segmentation Marktsegmentierung

The division of a total market into market groups (the sub-markets), differing in their characteristics of frequency of purchase, income, location, rate of product usage and other characteristics of behaviour such as influence by fashion, in order to direct marketing efforts towards the most income-maximising product mix, distribution and selling policy. By employing market segmentation, a firm tailors its products and marketing programmes to small sub-markets/segments, e.g. the youth market.

Market selection Marktauswahl

The process of choosing a particular market (segment) for the sale and promotion of a company's products. When selecting a market, the ultimate consideration must be the profit level on a both short- and long-term basis.

Additional important factors which should be considered are:
1. the market potential relative to the company's product(s); 2. the market profile; 3. overall marketing/promotion factors; 4. market accessibility; 5. the stage when the market will be in profit relative to the sales forecast and the investment return; 6. the company`s size and resources, including finance; 7. the compatibility of the market with the home market and/or existing overseas markets; etc.

Market share (MS) Marktanteil

Also called brand share, market coverage or share of the market.

A firm's percentage of its industry's total sales (either the number of units sold or the value of sales) during a period in a specified market (usually a national market).

Market sharing Marktaufteilung

Also called market allocation or division.

An arrangement between producers to avoid competition between them by sharing the market for their product. Each producer sells his product only in a particular area.

Market sharing cartel Gebietskartell

A type of cartel where the members agree to allocate markets among them. Note: this type of cartel is illegal.

Market size Marktgröße

The number of likely buyers and their income, purchasing power, socio-economic class and the country's gross domestic product (GDP).

Market skimming Marktabschöpfung(sstrategie)

A pricing objective where a high price is established to secure initial maximum profits. This high price is lowered at later stages as the market expands and competition arises. The initial high price skims the cream off those market segments which are less price sensitive and therefore do not mind paying a higher price to be one of the first to own the new product.

Market skimming pricing Abschöpfungspreisbildung

A pricing strategy which sets a high price for a new product to secure a quick return from customers who are willing to pay the high price.
Note: the company makes fewer but more profitable sales.

Market stallholder Inhaber eines Marktstandes

A retailer who hires a stall at a town holding its markets in the open air.

Market structure Marktstruktur

The pattern of a market formed by the number, size and distribution of sellers and buyers in a market.
Structural features having a major importance in relation to market behaviour/conduct include:

1. the degree of seller concentration, 2. the degree of buyer concentration, 3. the condition of entry to the market, 4. the nature of the product supplied. Note: market structure, in turn, is affected by market behaviour.

Market survey Marktumfrage

A report on market conditions.

Market target Käuferzielgruppe

An attractive market segment and its consumers who are the target of a firm`s marketing efforts.

Market test(ing) Markttest

The introduction of a new product into a market on a limited basis in order to test its acceptance before a full launch.

Market trends Markttendenzen

The course or tendency prevailing in a market.

Market types Marktarten

There are many different types of market, eg:
1. active market, 2. advancing market, 3. available market, 4. black market, 5. business to business market, 6. captive market, 7. class market, 8. commodity market, 9. competitive market, 10. consumer market, 11. contestable market, 12. depressed market, 13. distant market, 14. domestic market, 15. export market 16. firm market, 17. flea market, 18. foreign market, 19. forward market, 20. global market, 21. grey market, 22. high-end market, 23. highly-organised market, 24. home market, 25. horizontal market, 26. import market, 27. jumpy market, 28. local market, 29. mass market, 30. mature market, 31. merchandise market, 32. minimarket, 33. narrow market, 34. near market, 35. niche market, 36. not-for-profit market, 37. open market, 38. organised market, 39. perfect market, 40. potential market,41. producer market, 42. ready market, 43. reseller market, 44. restricted market, 45. terminal market, 46. thin market, 47. scattered markets, 48. sensitive market, 49. service market, 50. sluggish market, 51. soft market, 52. stable market, 53. steady market, 54. upmarket, 55. vertical market, 56. weak market, etc.

Market value (MV, mv) Börsenwert, Kurswert Markt-, Tages-, Zeitwert

Also called current market value or price, current value or price, market price, prevailing price.

The price of a commodity on the daily quotation, indicating the amount required for buying or selling.

The price the property will command on the open market, i.e. the highest price a seller is willing to accept and the lowest price a buyer is willing to pay. Also called fair market value.

Market(ing) analysis Marktanalyse

Also called market audit.

Market-driven economy marktwirtschaftlich gesteuerte Wirtschaft

An economy controlled by market forces rather than by government action.

Market-orientated firm absatz-, marktorientiertes Unternehmen

Also called marketing-oriented company.

A firm which is chiefly preoccupied by its market(s). This firm is usually in a state of competition with rival firms; its goods will be sold in a buyers' market, where the consumer to some extent is king. The market-orientated firm provides products or services which are appropriate to consumer needs.

Marketability Absetzbarkeit, Marktfähigkeit, Verkehrsfähigkeit

The speed and ease with which a particular asset can be sold and converted into cash.

Marketeer Marktverkäufer

A person who sells goods or services in or to a market.

Marketer Anbieter, Verkäufer
Marktteilnehmer

A person or firm that sells/offers goods and services in a market.

A market participant.

Marketing Marketing, Absatz, Verkauf, Vertrieb
Absatzlehre
Einkaufen

There is no single, universally agreed definition of marketing, but there are many definitions. Expamples are:
1. Marketing is a social and managerial process by which individuals and groups obtain what they need and want through creating and exchanging products and value with others.
2. Marketing is a term meaning the bringing together of sellers and buyers to complete transactions of sale and purchase of goods.
3. The activities that are concerned with acquiring and maintaining markets for a company's products and for ensuring that a company's output reaches those markets.
4. The management function responsible for identifying, anticipating and satisfying customer requirements profitably.
5. The activities that accelerate the movement of goods or services from the producer to the consumer or producer, including advertising, distribution, merchandising, product planning, promotion, research and development, sales, transportation and warehousing.
6. Marketing consists of the activities of buying, selling, transporting and storing goods. It also includes the provision of any after-sales service or pre-sales service.
7. Marketing is a positive business activity which establishes, develops and satisfies both customer needs and wants.

Whatever the formal definition, it is generally accepted that true marketing requires, on the part of the supplying organisation:
1. a genuine attention to customers' needs and wants (usually a specific target segment is selected);
2. satisfaction of those needs and wants at a profit;
3. orientation of the whole organisation towards the customer-satisfaction process.

Marketing includes such business activities as:
1. the planning and development of products that customers require, with appropriate packaging and support services (e.g. repair facilities);
2. the distribution of those products through appropriate channels, e.g. wholesalers, retailers, etc., which will provide the services required by the customers;
3. the establishment of prices which offer both value to the customers and a satisfactory profit for the supplier;
4. promotion of the products, including advertising, sales promotion, public relations and personal selling.

These four activities (often referred to as product, place, price and promotion) constitute the marketing mix.

The marketer must also take into account environmental factors (eg economic and technological development; social and cultural influences; political and legal decisions; business practices and institutions; competitive activity) over which he has no control (uncontrollables), but which will significantly affect the degree of success he achieves.

Three alternative basic strategies are open to any marketer:
1. undifferentiated marketing: a company offers a standard product and endeavours to attract the largest possible number of buyers with a standard marketing programme and thereby hopes to minimize both its production and marketing costs;
2. concentrated marketing: a company devotes its whole marketing effort to one market segment, or to a very few segments, i.e. the segment(s) it believes will prove most profitable;
3. differentiated marketing: a company segments its markets and operates in all or several segments of the market but modifies both products and marketing programmes to achieve maximum customer appeal within each segment.

The economic theory of marketing.

To go marketing or to do the marketing; i.e. to go shopping. Also called shopping.

Marketing agreement Vertriebsvereinbarung

A contract between two companies by which one company untertakes to market the other`s product(s).

Marketing and sales plan Absatzplan

A plan outlining the marketing/selling techniques and the programme covering a specified period to promote a particular product or service.

Marketing audit Marketing-Audit

A comprehensive, systematic, independent, orderly, and objective examination and evaluation of a company`s marketing environment, goals, strategies, activities, performance, and results. This is to determine problem areas and recommend improvements.

Marketing budget Marketingbudget

The amount of money allocated for expenditure on marketing activities such as advertising, sales and consumer promotion, etc in a specified period.

Marketing channel Absatzkanal, Vertriebskanal

Also called distribution channel or channel of distribution.

A group of individuals and organisations that direct the flow of products from producers to customers.

Marketing concept Marketingkonzept

The philosophy which states that an organisation should try to provide products that satisfy customers` current, broad and long-term wants and needs while meeting its own goals, eg to increase profits, market share, sales, or a combination of all three.

Thus, management has two main responsibilities:
1. remaining sensitive to market needs, ie they must be aware of the nature of market demand, and of changes that occur in it;
2. operations must be market-oriented, ie the marketing objectives must be achieved in a competitive and profitable manner.

Customer satisfaction is the major aim of the marketing concept. Thus, a company must:
1. find out what will satisfy customers, 2. create satisfying products, 3. continuously modify, alter and develop products that keep pace with customers` changing desires, needs and preferences.

If the company does not provide the would-be customer with:
1. the right product information; 2. the right product, accessible and available, 3. the product at the right time, 4. the product at the right price, 5. the right guarantees, eg after-sales service etc, then - in a competitive market - the customer will not buy the product.

Note: all marketing activities begin and end with the customer.

Marketing consultant Marketingberater

An independent marketing specialist hired by a firm to advise on a wide range of marketing matters.

Marketing control Marketingkontrolle

The process of checking and evaluating the desired results of marketing action plans, and taking corrective action to ensure that marketing objectives are achieved.

Marketing cost analysis Absatz-, Vertriebskostenanalyse

The breaking down and classification of costs to determine which are associated with specific marketing activities. This lets a company evaluate the effectiveness of an ongoing or recent marketing strategy by comparing sales achieved and costs incurred.

Marketing database Marketing-Datenbank

A set of organised data acquired through marketing research or a marketing information system (MIS) and used as an aid to decision making. The data is about individual customers or potential customers and can be used to provide helpful information on customers (eg charge account, cash or credit card customers), products or services.

Note: building up a rich marketing database takes time and involves much cost, but allows one to gain profitable new business by locating promising customers, anticipating customer needs, cross-selling products, and rewarding loyal customers.

Marketing decisions Marketingentscheidungen

These can be classified in three basic categories:
1. target-market decisions; 2. marketing-mix decisions; and 3. decisions to organise and control marketing activities.

Marketing department Marketing-, Vertriebsabteilung

The department responsible for carrying out the activites involved in identifying customers and their needs or wants, promoting the products or services offered to them and achieving sales. Furthermore, it may also be responsible for the physical distribution of the products and for aftersales service.

Marketing efforts Absatzbemühungen

Also called sales or selling efforts.

All marketing activities such as assessing customer needs, identifying target groups and markets, conducting market research, developing and modifying products, fixing prices, carrying out promotion and distribution, etc.

Marketing environment Marketingumfeld

Factors affecting the market which are external to the company's sphere of direct influence but which influence the company's behaviour.
The most important factors are: 1. economic development, 2. political decisions, 3. competitive activities, 4. the legal system, 5. moral values, 6. the economic system, 7. the level of income, 8. group influences, 9. cultural factors, 10. the consumer movement, 11. technological forces, etc.

Marketing information system (MIS) Marketing-Informationssystem

A set of procedures and methods for the collection, analysis, management and presentation of information gathered regularly from sources both inside and outside an organisation for use in making marketing decisions.
As such, an MIS provides information on prices, competition, sales, advertising and distribution expenses, etc.

Marketing infrastructure Marketing-Infrastruktur

The marketing infrastructure of a particular country is the sum total of the facilities and services available for marketing.
This includes the following country related items: geographical, cultural, economic and political factors; the media and marketing services that are available; the distribution systems, etc.

Marketing intelligence Marktinformationen

Information or data collected from external sources for a firm on a continual basis. They are used to aid decision-making or to monitor earlier decisions.

Marketing intermediary Absatzmittler

Also called marketing middleman.

Firms which assist in the flow of goods and services from producers to end/final users, ie firms which help to promote, sell and distribute the goods. They include agents, wholesalers, retailers, physical distribution companies, marketing service agencies, financial institutions, etc.

Marketing man Marketingfachmann

A marketing expert.

Marketing management Marketingmanagement

A process of setting marketing goals, the planning, organising, implementing, and controlling of marketing activities to meet these goals.

Marketing manager Marketingmanager

An individual responsible for formulating, planning, executing, controlling and evaluating the marketing activities of a company such as marketing research, product planning, pricing, distribution, etc.
Furthermore, he may be responsible for coordinating with other departments that perform marketing related activities, such as packaging, warehousing, order filling, shipping, design of new and improved products, billing, transportation, purchasing, maintenance and repair, warranty/guaranty fulfillment, technical assistance to customers, etc.
Note: the title marketing manager may also be used for jobs of lesser scope, e.g. the manager may only be in charge of a product line or a business segment.

Marketing mix Marketingmix, Marktplan

This is the planned mixture of marketing tools which may stimulate sales of a particular product in the target market. The market strategy consists of elements concerned with the product (e.g. price, quality), with channels of distribution, and with communications (e.g. advertising, public relations). The aim is to combine these elements in such a way as to achieve the profitable exploration of the market at minimum cost.

The 4 Ps: product, price, place, promotion

Marketing mix decisions Marketingmix-Entscheidungen

An integrated decision about: 1. the product to be offered; 2. its price; 3. its distribution; and 4. its promotion. These four decision-making aspects reinforce each other.

Marketing objectives Marketingziele

Also called marketing goals.

The specific, measurable aims or expected outcomes of a company's marketing activities in a given period. For example, this may involve increasing the market share from twenty to thirty per cent of a particular product or service.

Marketing orientation Absatzorientierung

To achieve marketing orientation, a company must fulfil four conditions:
1. the management thinking and decisionmaking must be outward looking based on its target groups and markets rather than inward looking based on internal views and pressures;
2. the managers must be prepared to contribute to the corporate marketing objectives and, in doing so, must be prepared to sacrifice to some degree their individual or departmental goals;
3. departments and divisions must be prepared to achieve a unity of purpose in order to achieve the corporate marketing objectives;
4. all of the staff, particularly the chief executive, must believe in and practice the marketing concept.

Marketing plan Marketingplan

A written document for implementing and controlling an organisation`s marketing activities involved in achieving a particular marketing goal. It may include an analysis of the current marketing situation, sales forecasts, production and profit targets, pricing policy, sales promotion, selling strategies, the marketing mix, expense budgets, etc.

Marketing planning Marketingplanung

The process that leads to the marketing plan and thus involves assessing marketing opportunities and resources, determining marketing objectives, and developing a plan for implementing and controlling the marketing activities necessary to achieve the objective(s).

Marketing policy Absatzpolitik, Vertriebspolitik

A company`s basic marketing attitudes and activities.

Marketing process Marketingsprozeß

In the past, the marketing process was bound up in the four Ps:
1. price, 2. place, 3. promotion, 4. product.
Today, additional factors influence the marketing process:
1. economic factors (eg the total supply available, the elasticity of demand, substitute products, the demand for related products, government policies and regulations, the general state of the economy, etc) which fall outside the control of the marketer,
2. skill factors (eg product introduction, modification or elimination; product knowledge; guarantees; afersales service; communication matters; the market environment; distribution matters, etc) which are under the control of the marketer.

Marketing research Marketingforschung

The collection, analysis, presentation, and interpretation of information related to a well-defined marketing problem or project. This means it comprises all research carried out in the interests of successful marketing, including market research, media research and product research.
Good marketing research involves a systematic approach to a problem and frequently contains five aspects:
1. research objectives and budget; 2. data availability; 3. primary research; 4. data analysis; 5. conclusions and recommendations.

Note: in practice, marketing research is used interchangeably with the term market research which is, however, narrower in scope.

Marketing service agency Marketingdienstleistungsagentur

Firms that support the marketing activities of sellers, eg marketing research firms, advertising agencies, media firms, marketing consulting firms, etc.

Marketing stimuli Kaufanreize

The main stimuli influencing a potential buyer such as:

1. the product itself as having utility, 2. the product`s quality, 3. the product`s prestige, 4. attractive packaging, 5. a fair price, 6. advertising, 7. the buyer`s attitute, etc.

Marketing strategy Marketingstrategie

In general, the broad principles by which a business expects to achieve its marketing objectives in a target market.

In detail, the determination of a company's marketing objectives and how these can be achieved (e.g. by acquiring a competitive company, by price reductions, product improvements, etc.), the selection of its target markets, the creation of an approriate marketing mix for each, and the allocation of the resources needed to achieve the goals desired.

Note: a marketing strategy is usually an integral part of a business strategy that provides broad direction to all functions.

Marketing types Marketingarten

These are a number of different types of marketing, examples are:

1. affinity marketing, 2. aggressive marketing 3. ambush marketing, 4. benchmarketing, 5. business site marketing, 6. catalog(ue) marketing, 7. charity marketing 8. concentrated marketing, 9. consumer-oriented marketing, 10. coordinated marketing, 11. database marketing, 12. divergent marketing, 13. domestic marketing, 14 email marketing, 15. events marketing, 16. global marketing, 17. green marketing, 18. horizontal marketing, 19. idea marketing, 20. inbound telemarketing, 21. incentive marketing, 22. industrial marketing 23. innovative marketing, 24. integrated marketing, 25. internal marketing, 26 internet marketing, 27. lean marketing, 28. letterbox marketing, 29. macromarketing, 30. mass marketing, 31. megamarketing, 32. micro marketing, 33. multinational marketing, 34. niche marketing, 35. nonprofit marketing, 36. nonstandardized marketing, 37. outbound telemarketing, 38. Pan-European marketing, 39. person marketing, 40. place marketing, 41. proactive marketing, 42. product differentiated marketing, 43. relationship marketing, 44. remarketing, 45. retention marketing, 46. reverse marketing, 47. selective marketing, 48. service marketing, 49. social marketing, 50. socioecological marketing, 51. standardized marketing, 52. synchromarketing, 53. target marketing, 54. undifferentiated marketing, 55. value-added marketing, 56. vertical marketing, 57. vacation marketing, etc.

Markup Gewinnaufschlag (in %) (Kalkulationszuschlag, Handelsspanne)

Also called margin.

The percentage profit which is added by a trader to his cost price in order to arrive at a selling price.

The difference between the selling price of a product and its cost to the seller.

Markup pricing Vollkostenkalkulation

Also called full cost pricing.

A pricing method that sets the price by adding a fixed percentage markup of product costs to the production and marketing costs.

Mart Markt

A place, market or trading center where goods are sold, eg a car mart.

Maslow's hierarchy of needs Maslows Bedürfnishierarchie, -pyramide

A theory developed by the American personality theorist A. Maslow (1908 - 1970). According to Maslow, only unsatisfied needs are prime sources of motivation (this means, for example, that only if you are hungry you will buy, grow, or even steal food to satisfy the primitive physiological need to survive).

Maslow suggested that there are five need systems which account for most of our behaviour. These he ranked in lowest (the most primitive and immature needs in terms of the behaviour they promote) to highest (the most civilized and mature needs) order with lowest needs coming first:

1. physiological needs (food, water, shelter, sex) which reflect the individual's concern for survival;
2. safety needs (protection, security, stability) reflecting concern for safety and the avoidance of harm;
3. social needs (affection, friendship, acceptance) representing the normal human desire to be accepted and appreciated by others;
4. ego needs (prestige, success, self-esteem) which motivate a person to be ambitious and always contribute his or her best;
5. self-actualization/self-fulfillment needs which show the ongoing striving to fulfill one's creative capacities.

According to Maslow, there is a natural trend in which individuals become aware of and therefore motivated by each of these needs in ascending order.

Note: Maslow did not believe that any need ever receives complete satisfaction; rather, he believed that some minimal degree of satisfaction is required to be able to move on to a higher need.

Mass communication Massenkommunikation

Communication to large audiences, eg through mass media such as television or newspapers.

Mass display Massenauslage

In retail trade, a large additional display of a product already on the shelf, so positioned that the majority of traffic will pass it.

Mass market Massenmarkt

A market where consumer goods can be purchased in some quantity by everyone. Usually, these goods are purchased frequently, ie there is substantial repeat buying.

Mass market product Massenmarktprodukt

Products designed to appeal to the majority of people.

Mass marketing Massenabsatzstrategie, Marketing für breite Zielgruppen

Marketing which aims at reaching large numbers of people.

Mass medium Massenmedium

Mass media, ie radio, TV and press are channels of communication which reach a very large market

Mass merchandising Massenmerchandising

A retailing strategy of using moderate to low prices on large quantities of merchandise, combined with heavy promotion, to stimulate and increase sales.

Mass production Massenfertigung, -produktion

Also called large-scale production or volume production.

Any system which aims at producing, with the fewest workers, the greatest output of identical/standardized goods. This has been made possible by modern machinery (e.g. automated machines, assembly lines, conveyor belts, etc.), which is costly and takes up a lot of capital. The bigger the output of a machine the less each article costs to produce.

It was first developed in the motor vehicle industry by Henry Ford. His definition reads: "It is the focusing upon a manufacturing project of the principles of power, accuracy, economy, system, continuity, speed and repetition".

Mass tourism Massentourismus

Tourism involving large numbers of people.

Masthead Zeitungskopf, Titelkopf einer Werbedrucksache

The standing heading of a newspaper, magazine or advertising matter.

Matched sample parallelisierte Stichprobe

A statistical sample that is the same as one or more others in terms of significant characteristics, eg size or demographics. It is used for test purposes, eg to compare reactions to different products.

Material (MAT, mat) Material
Stoff, Gewebe

Material usually means raw materials.

Material sometimes means fabrics like woollen or cotton cloth.

Material costs Materialkosten

Also called cost of materials.

That cost of a product which is due only to the cost of materials. Material used in business may be direct or indirect.
Direct materials are items which go into, and are easily traceable to, the product.
Indirect materials are items (e.g. lubricating oil) that either do not go into the product or are not easily traceable/chargeable to specific products.

Material wants materielle Bedürfnisse

These are wants for material goods.

Materials buyer Materialeinkäufer

Also called procurement officer.

An employee in a factory responsible for buying the materials needed for production.

Materials handling Materialtransport
Materialwirtschaft

The moving of materials to a factory and the moving of finished goods to customers.

Materials management.

Materials management Materialwirtschaft

Also called materials handling, inventory management, materials and logistics management, materials control system or materials management and control.

The activity of planning, organizing and controlling the use and flow of a firm's materials through a firm. It includes stock control, stockkeeping, production, materials handling, purchasing and distribution.

Materials price variance Materialpreisabweichung

The difference between what was actually paid for a given quantity of materials and the budgeted price, multiplied by the actual quantity of materials used.
The variance is favourable if the actual price is lower than the budgeted price, and unfavourable if the actual price exceeds the budgeted price.

Materials requirements planning (MRP) Materialbedarfsplanung

A technique for determining the quantity, quality, and timing of the components used in the production (manufacturing) process.

Mathematical pricing mathematische Preisbildung

A pricing method where the asking price is determined by taking cost and applying some kind of mathematical formula, usually a percentage markup, to arrive at the price.
This pricing method is simple to do and ensures that a profit is achieved. On the other hand, it may result in on uncompetitive price or may arrive at a price which is considerably below that of competitors\` or customers\` expectations, ie it may leave profit on the table.

Mature consumer reifer Verbraucher, Konsument

People who are 65 and older, ie seniors who dispose of a high disposable income and are thus a very attractive target group.

Mature economy reife Volkswirtschaft

The condition of a country's economy with a falling rate of population growth, falling share of national income used for new capital investment, accompanied by a relative increase of national income spent on the purchase of consumer goods.

Mature market gesättigter Markt

Also called saturated market or saturated demand.

A market where a product can no longer be sold because most customers have already purchased it. New customers are being found at a declining rate, if at all.

Maturity stage Reifephase eines Produkts

The stage in the product life cycle (PLC) in which the sales curve peaks and starts to decline as prices and profits continue to fall.

The market situation is as follows:
there is severe competition with many brands on the market, and competitors modify and improve their products to stay in the market. Anyhow, weaker competitors start dropping out of the market or switch their attention to other products. Producers who remain in the market must increase advertisting and dealer orientated promotions in order to maintain customer loyalty, the rate of repurchase and hence market share. New customers cannot be added indefinitely, and sooner or later the market approaches saturation.

Normally, this is the longest stage of the PLC.

Maximal awareness höchster Bekanntheitsgrad

A situation where a consumer is fully convinced by a product`s advertising and thus buys the product.

Maximum price Höchst-, Maximalpreis

Also called ceiling, highest, peak, premium or top price.

The highest price which a company can charge for its goods or services.

A statutory maximum price is designed to prevent the exploitation of the consumers. Statutory maximum prices result in excess demand.

Maximum stock level maximaler (Lager)Bestand, (Lager)Bestandsobergrenze

Also called maximum inventory level.

The figure set by the stockkeeper to indicate the upper limit of stock to be held at any time. The amount depends on various factors: e.g. the capacity of the stockroom, the rate of turnover, the period of waiting for orders to be delivered, etc.

Me generation Ich-Generation

People who practice a consumer lifestyle of being good to oneself.

Me-too product Me-too Produkt, Ich-auch Produkt, nachgemachtes Produkt

Also called copycat.

An imitation or copy of a successful product of a competitor.

Mean Durchschnitt, Mittelwert

Also called average.

The average of a list of figures. It is calculated by adding several figures together and dividing by the number of figures added.

Mean price Mittelkurs

Also called middle-market price, market average, mean course or rate, or middle rate.

The arithmetic mean of two given prices.

Measurability Meßbarkeit

The degree to which something can be measured, eg the size and purchasing power of a market.

Media Medien

Television, radio and the press, i.e. the means of communicating a message, e.g. about a product or service, to the audience (viewership, listenership, readership).

Media advertising Medienwerbung

Also called above-the-line advertising. This refers to the media of press, TV, radio, cinema and posters.

Below-the-line advertising include direct mail, exhibitions, demonstrations, point-of-sale/point-of-purchase, sales promotion, merchandising and sales literature.

Media budget Medienbudget

The marketing budget allocated to media advertising for a specific product or service in a particular time period.

Media buying Streuplanung

A media buyer`s activity of placing advertisements in the media on behalf of an advertiser.

In buying media, three main theories can be used:
1. frequency theory: you want the maximum number of impressions per 1,000 homes,
2. pressure theory: you want to achieve maximum efficiency,
3. dispersion theory: you want to reach the maximum number of different unduplicated homes within a specific time period.

Media event Medienereignis

A happening attracting the attention of the mass media.

Media mix Mediamix

Combination of media to be used for a promotional campaign. The choice of a particular media mix is typically based on cost per thousand (CPM), reach and frequency.

Media plan Medienplan, Werbeplan

Also called media schedule.

A plan that determines the exact media vehicles (e.g. TV, radio, press) to be used for an advertising campaign in such a way as to reach the potential markets and customers with maximum efficiency and minimum expense. Futhermore, it fixes the dates and times that the advertisements are to appear.

Media planner Medienplaner

A person working in an advertising agency whose work focusses on the formulation of a media strategy. His/her primary function is to match the target audience with the appropriate media.

Media presentation Medienpräsentation

The demonstration by the media (TV, radio, press) of a product or service to possible customers.

There are four basic factors to consider in the selection of the medium type:
1. characteristics: these are the qualities that the medium makes available to the product or service and its message; e.g. size of the advertisement(s); colour, sound, movement, demonstration of the product, etc.;
2. atmosphere: this derives partly from the medium itself and partly from the reader's, viewer's or listener's state of mind at the time of advertisement exposure; e.g. cinemas usually have a youthful, light-hearted atmosphere and are thus useful for products which target the youth adult market;
3. quantitative coverage: this needs market research to establish demographical, socio-economic classification, geographical distribution, etc.;
4. cost: the media plan must be reconciled to the advertising budget and the period of the campaign.

Media reach Medienreichweite

The size of audience (ie readers, listeners, viewers) exposed to an advertisement or commercial through a particular medium.

Note: it is difficult to measure reach precisely, eg because there are more readers per copy of a publication than the number of copies sold, or more/less viewers than the number of TV sets tuned to a programme.

Media selection Medienauswahl

The process of choosing the appropriate advertising medium to carry the ad message. The major steps involved are:
1. to decide on media reach, frequency and impact; 2. to choose among the media types (eg TV, radio, magazines, newspapers, outdoor, direct mail); 3. to select the best media vehicles (eg specific magazines, TV shows or radio programmes); 4. to decide on media timing.

Media vehicle Werbeträger

A specific medium for the transmission of an advertiser`s message, eg in the print media newspapers, magazines, billboards, direct mail; in the broadcast media TV or radio.

Median Median, Zentralwert

Point in the middle of a list of numbers.

Medical rep Ärztevertreter

A drug company`s sales representative who calls on medical practitioners to provide product information and other forms of assistance.

Megadealer marktbestimmendes Handelsunternehmen

A trading enterprise that is so large and powerful that it can influence the market happenings, eg competition, prices, terms of delivery and payment, etc.

Megamarketing Megamarketing

A type of marketing activity using economic, psychological, political and public relations skills as well as the marketing variables to gain the cooperation of several parties and pressure groups in the country.

Note: the American marketing academic Philip Kotler suggests that two more Ps must be added to the marketing mix: public relations (PR) and power.

Megastore Megaladen

A very large store, often selling goods at lower prices.

Memorandum sale Verkauf auf Kommissionsbasis

Also called consignment sale.

The sale of consigned goods whose title rests with the seller for a stated period. At the end of the period, unsold items may be returned to the seller, and the sold or held goods are invoiced to the buyer.

Mercantile agent Handelsagent, Absatzmittler

A commercial agent with the authority to buy or sell on behalf of his principal, usually in return for payment of a commission. He takes possession of the goods and acts in his own name when selling or buying the goods.

Mercantile law Handels-, Wirtschaftsrecht

Also called commercial law or merchant law.

That branch of law concerned with commercial transactions.

Mercantilism Merkantilismus

An economic thought prevalent in the seventeenth and early eighteenth centuries. Mercantilism was the product of nationalism, and the desire to develop national power. The essential thing was to achieve a "balance of payments", or rather an imbalance of payments (exports exceeding imports). In order to achieve this, tariffs were imposed to protect home export industries and exclude imports.
This form of protectionism was critized by later classical economists, such as Adam Smith (1723 - 1790).

Merchandise (M`dise, mdse) Handelsware, Ware(n)
Verkaufssteuerung, Angebots-optimierung

Goods that a business has purchased with the intention of reselling them without changing them.

Action to help retailers to sell products one has produced (e.g. by supplying point-of-sale advertising). Usually called merchandising.

Merchandise advance Warenlombard

Also called commodity collateral advance, goods advance or advance against merchandise.

This is a loan on the security of the goods which the buyer has purchased and it enables him to pay for the goods.

Merchandise inventory Bestand an Handelswaren

The goods on hand at the end of an accounting period.

Merchandise manager Leiter der Ein- und Verkaufsabteilung (eines Warenhauses)

An executive who is responsible for supervising the purchasing and selling activities in a department store/general store.

Merchandise mark Warenmarkierung

Marks, used for identification purposes, on the outside of cases, packets, bales, etc.

Merchandise mix Handelswarenmix

The basic variety, ie the breadth and depth of the merchandise inventory carried by a retailer.

Merchandise on call Ware auf Abruf

Goods which the buyer ordered some time ago but which have not yet been delivered because the buyer calls forward the quantities he needs from time to time.

Merchandise purchases Wareneinkäufe

The goods that a trading business purchases for the purpose of resale.

Merchandise returns Warenrücksendungen, Warenretouren

Also called goods returned or returns.

Merchandise returned to a business because of minor quality, wrong size or colour, or other defects.
Note: the seller will call these sales returns, while the buyer calls them purchase returns.

Merchandiser Merchandiser, Verkaufsexperte

A person who organizes the display and promotion of goods in a retail shop, to best advantage.

Merchandising Merchandising, Absatzvorbereitung, Warendarbietung, Angebotsoptimierung

Also known as the "silent salesman".

All sales promotion activities (e.g. display, packaging, pricing, special offers) related to selling a product or service at the right place, at the right time, in the right quantities, and at the right price. Merchandising is the means by which a manufacturer and his retailer combine their resources in the common aim to increase sales.

The purpose of merchandising is: to ensure that a product is widely available and prominently visible; to give customers information about, and easy access to, products near or at the point of sale/point of purchase. Failure to put the product in the right place at the right time frequently means no sale.
Merchandising may be carried out by supplier's salespersons (the merchandisers), store staff or jointly operated.

Merchant (mcht) Kaufmann, (Groß-, Einzel-)Händler

Also called trader, wholesale dealer, wholesaler, shopkeeper, or retailer.

A businessman who buys and sells goods without altering their physical form on his own account as a principal to the transaction and not as an agent. The commodity belongs to him.
A type of wholesaler or retailer who is not committed to handling goods from a particular supplier or selling to particular traders.

Merchant ship (M.sh.) Handelsschiff

Also called merchant vessel (MV).

A commercial ship engaged in the transport of goods.

Merchant wholesaler Großhandelsunternehmen

A business that buys goods from manufacturers and resells them to other businesses such as retailers, takes title to the goods and stores them in its own warehouse.

Merchantable quality handelsübliche, marktgängige Qualität

Also called commercial or good quality.

Goods are of merchantable quality if they are fit for the purpose or purposes for which goods of that kind are commonly bought. The goods must be of a quality sufficiently good to satisfy the purpose for which the buyer intends to use them; the goods must be free from defects and acceptable to a reasonable person.

Merger — Fusion, Unternehmenszusammenschluß, Verschmelzung

Also called amalgamation, business combination, combination or consolidation. The terms takeover, absorption and fusion are sometimes also used as synonyms.

Two or more companies combining/amalgamating to a new company.
Mergers fall into four main groups:
1. horizontal merger: the companies are engaged in the same stage of production;
2. vertical merger: the companies are engaged in different stages of production;
3. lateral merger:the companies produce goods which are related to each other but not in direct competition;
4. conglomerate/diversifying merger: the products of the companies are unrelated.

A merger by acquisition occurs when one firm absorbs another so that the latter ceases to exist. A merger by combination occurs when two or more firms join together to form a new firm.

The shareholders of the firms receive shares in the new company in an agreed proportion in exchange for shares in the old companies.

A merger may increase monopoly power but it may also take advantage of economies of scale.

Merit good — meritorisches Gut

Also called quasi-private good.

These are commodities (e.g. health and education) which should be available to individuals irrespective of their income.

Message — Nachricht, Information
Werbebotschaft

A set of verbal and/or nonverbal signs and symbols transmitted to an audience through a communication channel.

An advertising message.

Message effect — Werbewirkung

The effect of an advertisement`s or commercial`s message on the target audience.

Messenger (msgr) Bote, Kurier

Also called courier, despatch rider, delivery boy (or female messenger) or runner.

A person who carries messages or light goods between firms when the distances are short.

Microeconomics Mikroökonomie, Mikroökonomik

An economic theory that examines and explains the behaviour of the "small" elements of economics, i.e. individual persons, particular firms and households.
Topics that are dealt with include the analysis of the price mechanism, competition, the supply of and demand for goods and services, the allocation and efficient use of scarce economic resources, etc.

Micromarketing Mikromarketing

A marketing strategy particularly tailored to prospective buyers who live in small geographic areas or who have very specific lifestyle and demographic characteristics.

Microsegmentation Mikrosegmentierung

Division of macrosegments into segments based on the characteristics of decision making units within a macrosegment. Thus, the marketer can define the market segments more clearly and the target markets more precisely.

Middle-of-the-roader (MOR) Unternehmen mit breitgefächerter Marketingstrategie
breitgefächerter Radiosender

A market participant which does not pursue a clear marketing strategy.

A radio program trying to satisfy the taste of all listeners.

Middleman Mittler, Vermittler
Zwischenhändler

Also called intermediary.

An intermediary between buyer and seller (e.g. an agent or a broker). Anyone who comes between the producer of the goods and the final buyer can be termed a middleman. The wholesaler and the retailer are middlemen. The middleman is frequently blamed for the large difference that may exist between the factory price and the retail price; but each middleman has to make a profit. It may therefore be in the interest of the buyer and seller to "cut out the middleman" (as in mail order). Middlemen are useful in buying in bulk from producers, in stocking the goods, in marketing the products, in breaking bulk, etc.

Milking strategy — Melkstrategie, Gewinnmitnahmestrategie

Also called profit taking strategy.

A company`s marketing strategy trying to obtain the greatest possible profit from a product or service.

Mill pricing — Nettopreis-System

Also called factory pricing.

A pricing system in which the producer/seller quotes a price excluding of transport costs. The buyer has to pay for transporting the goods from the factory/mill to his premises.

Minimarket — Minimarkt

A very small self-service store.

Minimax principle — Minimax-Regel

In game theory, the principle of choosing options which minimise the maximum potential loss.

Minimerger — Kleinfusion

A merger/amalgamation between two small companies.

Minimum charge — Mindestgebühr, Mindestbetrag

The lowest fee or amount which will be charged.

Minimum manufacturing quantity (MMQ) minimale Losgröße

The theoretical minimum production which can be made economically acceptable for a product.

Minimum order Mindestauftrag

The smallest order, expressed in units or value, a seller is prepared to sell to an orderer.

Minimum price Mindestpreis, Minimalpreis

Also called knocked-down price; floor, lowest or reserve price.

The lowest price which a company can charge for its goods or services.

If a government feels that a price gives producers insufficient return on their investment it may establish a minimum price. The effect of this is to induce a greater output, but to reduce consumer demand. Statutory minimum prices lead to excess supply.

Minimum stock level Mindestbestand, eiserner Bestand

Also called minimum inventory level; base, reserve or safety stock; safety level; inventory buffer, cushion or reserve.

The smallest amount of any one particular stock item. Stocks held must not be allowed to fall below this level. When calculating the minimum stock level one has to consider the normal delivery period (i.e. the time gap between the ordering of the goods and their supply) and the quantity used (e.g. per day or week).

Minor Minderjährige(r)

Also called person of non-age.

A minor is a person under 18 years of age, and as such is not bound by contracts.

Misleading advertising irreführende Werbung, Falschwerbung

Also called deceptive, false or fraudulent advertising.

An advertisement or commercial that is misleading in a material respect.

Misleading price irreführender Preis

Prices which confuse or dupe consumers.

Misrepresentation falsche Darstellung, Falschdarstellung

Also called deceit, deception, fraud, misstatement.

The making of a false or fraudulent statement in order to induce someone to enter into a contract.
Legislation makes misrepresentation a criminal offence. Any contract entered into because of misrepresentation can be voidable, and the injured party can claim damages.

There are various types of misrepresentation, e.g.: misrepresentation of facts; fraudulent, innocent or material misrepresentation.

Missionary salesperson Verkaufsberater, Verkaufsmissionar

A salesperson who is employed by a firm and who calls on customers who do not buy his product but influence other people to buy it.

Mistake Irrtum, Fehler

Wrong action or wrong decision.

Mixed cargo Sammelladung

Also called consolidated shipment.

A consignment which contains a number of different commodities.

Mixed cost Mischkosten, teilvariable Kosten

Also called semivariable cost.

A cost composed of fixed and variable elements.

Mixed demand-cost inflation gemischte Nachfrage-Kosten-Inflation

A type of inflation consisting of elements of a demand-pull and cost-push inflation.

Mixed economy Mischwirtschaft, gemischtes Wirtschaftssystem

This economic system attempts to obtain the benefits of both the market and the planned economy, and the disadvantages of neither. There is considerable government interference in what is basically a market economy.
Most countries have mixed economies: ie private enterprise and government sectors exist side by side.

Mobile Deckenanhänger, Mobile

Also called dangler.

In POS advertising, a display piece suspended from the ceiling and moved by air currents.

Mobile exhibition mobile Ausstellung

A mobile vehicle fitted out like an exhibition stand which travels around to demonstrate a company's products.

Mobile shop fahrender Laden, mobile Verkaufsstelle

A van, specially set up in the form of a shop, owned by a trader who visits certain areas on certain days. By using a mobile shop a business can extend the area it serves and find more customers.

Mock auction Versteigerung mit Scheingeboten

An auction at which the auctioneer or the seller arranges for bids to be made that are merely intended to force up the price.

Mock purchase Scheinkauf

A potential buyer`s tactic to pose as a customer in order to obtain information about a competitor`s product(s) or plans.

Mockup Modell in Originalgröße

A model of a new product for testing or to show to prospective/potential buyers.

Mode of payment Zahlungsweise

The way in which a buyer pays, eg in cash or by credit card.

Mode of transport Beförderungsart

Also called mode of conveyance.

Goods may be transported/conveyed by road, railway, air or by sea. At times, the goods may be transported by two or more modes of transport.

The documents called for are:
1. if the goods are being despatched by post, you need a parcel post receipt;
2. if by air, an airway bill (AWB) is required;
3. if by sea, a (marine) bill of lading is required;
4. if by railway, a railway consignment note is required;
5. if by a road, a road consignment note is needed.

Model stock Idealbestand

The right goods at the right time in the right quantities at the right price.

Modified rebuy modifizierter Wiederkauf

A repurchase situation where the buyer wants some change in the original good or service, eg a new colour or design.

Mom and pop store Tante-Emma-Laden

Also called ma and pa corner store, corner store or family store. .

A small store, generally operated by members of a family with limited capital.

Monadic product test Einzel-Produkttest

Product test involving only one product.

Monetary demand monetäre oder effektive Nachfrage

Also called effective demand.

The level of overall demand for goods and services in the economy measured in terms of money.

Money back guarantee Rückerstattungsgarantie, bei Nichtgefallen Geld zurück

Also called satisfaction or money back.

A seller`s guarantee given to customers to pay back the purchase price if they are dissatisfied with their purchase.

Money illusion Geldillusion

People`s failure to realize that rising prices reduce the value of anything measured in monetary terms, eg savings and wages.

Money refund Geldrückerstattung

A relatively inexpensive sales promotion method where consumers submit proof of purchase to the manufacturer and are mailed a specific amount of money. Usually, manufacturers demand multiple purchases of the product before a consumer can qualify for a refund.

Note: as many customers perceive the redemption process as being too complicated, the response rate may be low and money refunds may have a limited impact on sales.

Money spinner Kassenschlager, Schnelldreher

Also called big seller.

An item which sells very well and/or which is very profitable.

Money value Geldwert

Also called monetary value, value of money, money's worth or cash value.

The value expressed in money terms.

Money-off coupon Preisnachlaßgutschein

A coupon in a publication or on a package, which has to be handed to the retailer in order to claim a discount on the purchase of the product.

Money-off offer Preisnachlaßangebot, Rabattangebot

In sales promotion, a special offer where buyers receive a certain amount off the regular price shown on the label or package.

Monopolies (and Mergers) Commission (MMC) Kartellaufsichtsbehörde, Monopolkommission (GB)

Also called cartel office, Office of Fair Trading (GB), Antitrust Division (US).

In the UK, a government-appointed body which looks into the activities of business units which may be behaving in ways that are against the public interest. The Commission investigates and reports on monopoly situations, prospective mergers that might produce a monopoly situation, and individual anti-competitive practices.

Monopolisation Monopolisierung

A kind of restrictive trade practice, i.e. it is a conduct aimed at preventing or eliminating competition in a particular market for goods or services by a large company which is in the position to control the market.

Monopolist Monopolist

A firm or person who has a monopoly. A monopolist may raise prices or restrict output almost at will - but his power depends on the elasticity of demand for his commodity or service. The more elastic the demand the weaker is the monopolist`s position.

Monopolistic competition monopolistische Konkurrenz

A form of imperfect competition.

A market in which there are many producers (and buyers) of differentiated products who can control the price within limits. The goods of the various producers are not perfect substitutes (ie the products are not homogeneous); each producer has a monopoly of his own product but competes with other producers making similar products.
Note: most competition is monopolistic competition.

Monopoly Monopol

Literally, this means a situation in which there is only one seller of a commodity or service. In practice, however, the word refers to any large firm or group which has a significant degree of control over price and total output of a commodity. A monopoly can exist only where the commodity being supplied has no close substitutes and the supplier is able to exclude competition. Thus, an absolute monopoly does not exist in the real world.

A monopoly situation exists if a single firm or a group of firms supplies more than one quarter of a particular good or service, or if more than one quarter of the supplies of particular goods or services are bought by one buyer.

A monopolist may raise prices or restrict output almost at will - but his power depends on the elasticity of demand for his commodity. The more elastic the demand the weaker the monopoly.

There are various types: absolute monopolies, natural monopolies, technological monopolies and statutory monopolies (these are established by the government; e.g. nationalized industries).

Monopoly power Monopolmacht

The ability of a firm to influence the market price of the commodity or service it sells.

Monopsonist Nachfragemonopolist

A monopsonist is a monopoly buyer, i.e. he is the only buyer of a commodity in the market.

Monopsony Nachfragemonopol, Monopson

A market on which a single buyer dominates though there may be several sellers. It is the counterpart to monopoly.

Monthly sales Monatsumsatz

The sales results of a particular company for a specified product or service within one month.

Mood advertising stimmungserzeugende Werbung

An advertisement or commercial designed to establish or intensify a particular atmosphere or audience attitude.

Mood music stimmungsvolle Hintergrundmusik

Background music used to establish or intensify a particular atmosphere or audience attitude.

Moral pricing moralische Preisbildung

A pricing strategy used when it is difficult to identify costs and where the product or service is socially or politically sensitive.

Morning drive (time) morgendliche Sendezeit während der Fahrt zur Arbeit

A daypart for radio, ie the time segment from sign-on or 6:00 am to 10:00 am, Monda to Friday. This time period is considered to be radio`s prime time because it draws the largest listenership.

Motivation Motivation

A psychological stimulus that activates or moves people towards (selected) goals. Motivation may be intrinsic or extrinsic. A number of theories have been put forward to explain motivation; most of these involve the idea of need identification and satisfaction.

Motivation research (MR) Motivforschung

Also called motivational research.

Market research that examines the psychological reasons and the real motives as to why people choose to buy one brand of goods rather than others. It provides indications of important motivational factors underlying purchasing and usage behaviour. Findings are used to make more effective promotional appeals and product formulations.

Motive Motiv, Beweggrund

The driving force that causes a person to act in a certain way or do a certain thing, eg to take action to satisfy specific needs.

Mountain Berg, Anhäufung

A pile or large heap. For example a very large stock of butter (butter mountain) or a mountain of debt (debt burden or mountain).

Liquids are referred to as lakes, eg wine lake.

Mov(e)ables bewegliche(s) Sachen, Vermögen, Mobilien

All property other than land, eg movable property such as money or securities.

Moving average gleitender Durchschnitt, Mittelwert

A sales forecasting technique that combines sales data from several of the most recent years and uses an average to forecast/predict next year`s sales. Furthermore, it averages out seasonal variations in the pattern of sales.

Multi-modal transport multimodaler Transport

A system whereby goods are moved by various modes of transport, such as road-sea-road transport (e.g. "roll on roll off" (RoRo) traffic) or road-sea-rail transport. Containerisation of cargo is usual.

Multi-product company Mehrprodukt-Unternehmen

A business producing two or more different products.

Multi-way packing Mehrwegpackung

Also called resuable or two-way package.

Package which can be used twice or several times.

Multibrand strategy Multimarkenstrategie

A company`s strategy to develop and sell two or more brands in the same product category in order to secure a greater market share and counteract brand switching.

Note: this is the only way to capture brand switchers.

Multichannel distribution — Mehrfachvertrieb, mehrkanäliger Vertrieb

A distribution method where a single firm establishes two or more distribution/marketing channels to reach various market segments.

Multilateral trade — multilateraler Handel

The alternative of bilateral trade is multilateral trade, where every country buys goods where they are cheapest and sells its exports wherever it can, each country's currency being freely exchangeable with another.

Multimedia — Multimedia

Also called mixed media.

The combined use of two or more media, as radio and TV. Often a primary medium supports a secondary medium, taking advantage of the benefits of each medium and increasing the overall exposure rate.

Multimedia advertising — Multimediawerbung

Advertising which uses a number of complementary media vehicles to increase awareness, coverage, credibility etc.

Multinational (company) — multinationales (internationales) Unternehmen

Also known as an international company.

This is a multinational company or corporation (MNC). The term is commonly used to describe holding companies with foreign subsidiaries.

Multinational marketing — multinationales Marketing

A complex form of international marketing in which an organisation engages in marketing efforts in many foreign countries.

Multipack Mehrstück-, Mehrfachpackung

Also called multiple pack or jumbo pack.

A package containing two or more products such as twin packs, six-packs or other forms of multipacks. For certain types of products, but not for all, multiple packaging is used to increase demand because it increases the amount of the product available at the point of consumption. Usually, the multipack is offered at an advantageous price.

Multipack offer Mehrfachpackungsangebot

In sales promotion, a special offer in which the seller offers an extra pack free of charge or at a reduced price, for each pack bought at full price.

Multiple Einzelhandelskette

Also called chain, multiple chain or retail(ing) chain.

An enterprise that owns and operates a number (ten or more branches) of retail outlets (multiple stores/shops or chain stores) selling one particular commodity (now called specialist multiple) or a wide variety of goods (now called variety chain store).

The emphasis is on cheapness and economies are attained by standardization so that each shop/store is a repetition of the same well-organised unit. Control is centralised, the general policy of the shop is laid down by the head office, and buying is done in bulk.

Multiple bar chart Mehrfach-Säulen-Diagramm

Also called compound bar chart or component bar chart.

Two or more sets of data are shown by the grouping together of several bars whose respective heights represent the value or size of the component.

Multiple branding Mehrmarken-Produkt

Also called multibrand product.

A company sells the same product, or similar products, under different brand names, all competing with each other.

Multiple choice question (Mehrfach)Auswahlfrage, Speisekartenfrage

Also called cafeteria question.

In a questionnaire, this type of question gives several possible answers, already formulated, to reflect varying shades of opinion and choice. The respondent (interviewee) may now choose a single answer from the several possible ones to indicate which comes closest to his point of view.

Multiple offer Multiangebot

An offer for sale of several products as a single purchase. This type of offer is particularly common in direct mail selling in order to reduce selling costs.

Multiple pack Mehrstückpackung, Multipack

Also called jumbo pack or multipack.

Such packs try to encourage the sale of small items in multiples; the items are packed collectively in a single wrapper and are usually offered at an advantageous price.

Multiple pricing Preisdifferenzierung, mehrstufiges Preissystem

Also called price differentiation.

A practice of charging different prices for the same product in different markets.

Multiple product announcement (MPA) Werbesendung für mehrere Produkte

A commercial which presents two or more products or services as a unit.

Multiple reader Mehrfachleser

A reader who reads a particular publication and one or more other publications of the same category.

Multiple readership Mehrfachleserschaft

More than one reader per issue of a publication, ie the secondary, tertiary and pass-along readers.

Multisegment strategy Multisegmentstrategie

A market segmentation strategy in which a company directs its marketing efforts at two or more segments by developing a marketing mix for each segment. This will lead to higher marketing costs because the strategy may require more research, different promotion and distribution methods, product modifications, etc.

Multiunit advertising Mehrproduktwerbung, Sammelwerbung

The practice of including two or more company products in a single advertisement to reduce media costs.

Mystery shopper Scheinkunde, Mystery Shopper

A person appointed by a firm to buy competitors` products in order to gather information on these products, the competitors` practices, services, discounts, etc.

N

Naderism Naderismus, Konsumerismus

A consumer movement created by the American lawyer Ralf Nader in the 1960s which produced some effective investigations and criticisms of unsatisfactory products, such as unsafe cars. Nader`s achievements included the Auto Safety Act, the Air Pollution Act, and that President John F. Kennedy declared that consumers have the right to safety and to be informed, to choose, and to be heard. This led to the founding of consumer organizations and magazines etc.

Name Name

A word or phrase by which a person, thing or firm is designated.
In business, different types of name are: 1. company name, 2. brand name, 3. trade name, 4. generic name.

Naming Namensgebung

Giving a name to someone or something.

In a world of so many names competing for attention, it is sensible to invent or adopt names for new companies or products that will strengthen the marketing strategy. When deciding on a new name, one should consider the following essentials; the name should be:
1. distinctive, 2. easily pronounceable, 3. memorable, 4. internationally acceptable, 5. helpful to assist the corporate image, 6. useable for advertising, etc.

Narrow market begrenzter, enger Markt
lustloser Markt

Also called inactive, thin or tight market.

A market in which only a small supply is available of whatever it is that market sells.

Securities or commodities market characterised by light trading.

Narrowcasting/narrow casting Zielgruppen-, Marktlücken-Kommunikation

Presenting advertising messages to relatively limited and well-defined audiences. Advertisers with specialised interests can narrowcast their messages rather than broadcast them. For example, broadcasting stations with specialised interests such as sports, news, movies, weather, etc, allow advertisers great selectivity in reaching their target audiences.

National account überregionaler Kunde

A customer of major importance, often with branches over an entire country. These accounts are often served by a separate salesforce because of their importance.

Note: a national account with an international scope is referrred to as a global account.

National advertising Werbung auf nationaler Ebene, landesweite Werbung

Also called general advertising.

Advertising operating on a nationwide basis, not just in particular areas.

National advertising rate Werbepreis für landesweite/nationale Werbung

The price charged for space and time by local media for national advertising.

National brand Herstellermarke

Also called manufacturer`s brand.

A product which is branded and advertised by its producer.

National call Ferngespräch

Also called long-distance call, toll call or trunk call.

A long-distance call by telephone.

National campaign überregionaler Werbefeldzug

An advertising or marketing campaign covering the entire country.

National competition nationaler Wettbewerb

The ability of a country's producers to compete successfully in/on the world markets and with imports in their own home markets.

National income (NI) Volkseinkommen, Nettosozialprodukt zu Faktorpreisen

National income is the monetary value of the flow of goods and services produced by an economy from economic activity over a period of time, normally one year.

Theoretically it can be measured in three ways:
1. it can be measured as the total output of goods and services of all domestic producers (output method);
2. by estimating the total income received by the factors of production (income method);
3. by calculating the total expenditure on domestically produced goods and services.

Since some goods and services are exported, exports must be added, but since some expenditure in the domestic country is on goods and services produced abroad, imports must be deducted. Furthermore, indirect taxation (e.g. value-added tax, VAT) is deducted and subsidies are added.

In any country the sum of the incomes in a given period is the national income; the sum spent on goods and services in a given period is the national expenditure; the sum of the value of all the goods and services produced in a given period is the national product. Hence, national income = national expenditure = national product.

National introduction landesweite (Produkt) Einführung

The immediate launch of a new product on a nationwide scale. This operation involves a high risk and a substantial investment in production and marketing.

National marketing manager nationaler Marketingmanager

A marketing manager who is responsible for the nationwide operations of a marketing division.

National output gesamtwirtschaftliche Produktion

Also called aggregate, overall or total output.

The total of consumer goods and services, plus the total of the producer goods created by the various firms in the industries of the nation. The figures are collected on a "value-added" basis to avoid double-counting.

National press nationale, überregionale Presse

Newspapers or periodicals distributed throughout the country.

National plan Volkswirtschaftsplan

An economic plan formulated by a government stating its economic development over a given time period.

National product Sozialprodukt

Also called aggregate output or economic pie (coll.).

The total market value of all goods and services produced in a country, less depreciation.

National sales manager nationaler Verkaufsleiter

A sales manager with responsibilities for the countrywide sales operations of a firm.

National wealth Volksvermögen

Also called national capital or social wealth.

The total money value of all goods and property in a country at a particular time. Only the value of real assets is included; paper money and paper titles (e.g. bonds, shares) must be excluded, since they merely represent government debt or simply claims to wealth.

Nationalised industries verstaatlichte Industrie

Nationalised industries are formed and controlled by the government taking over the assets of privately owned firms in return for compensation.

Natural barriers to entry natürliche Markteintrittsschranken

The difficulties for firms to enter an industry due to high capital requirements and raw material ownership.

Natural environment natürliche Umwelt

The physical forces in nature, such as climate, geographical location and natural resources, affecting a firm`s market(s) and/or marketing activities.

Natural monopoly natürliches Monopol

Certain goods and services are by their nature monopolies, e.g. electricity, gas and water supply.

Natural price natürlicher Preis

The central long-term equilibrium product price around which market prices fluctuate. The term was introduced by Adam Smith.

Natural resources natürliche Ressourcen

Natural resources covers such things as mineral deposits, sources of fuel and power, climate, fertility of the soil, fisheries around the coast, geographical advantages, etc.

Near markets nahegelegene Märkte

These are markets which are in the proximity of the home market. They are easier to serve, and to manage and control. Moreover, regular business and control systems are easier to set up; freight costs are lower and transportation time quicker. Furthermore, culture, infrastructure and ongoing developments are more familiar.

Necessaries Notwendigkeitsgüter, Güter des täglichen Bedarfs

Also called necessities, essential goods or essentials.

Goods needed and demanded by everyone, e.g. food, clothing and shelter. They are considered essential to maintain a minimum acceptable living standard. Some necessaries in an advanced affluent society may be considered luxuries in poorer countries.

Need Bedarf, (Grund)Bedürfnis
Mangel, Bedürfnis, Notwendigkeit

Something fundamental that is required by an individual for his survival, health, well-being or comfort. A need may be satisfied by any one of a large number of alternatives. Not to be confused with "want". Sometimes also called basic needs or basic wants.

A state in which something is lacking, required or necessary.

Need hierarchy Bedürfnishierarchie

Also called hierarchy of needs.

Preference order in which innate needs are satisfied. Some needs are stronger than others at particular times, in particular people, and in particular societies.

A. H. Maslow has set out a five-stage priority of human needs which account for most of our behaviour:
1. basic physiological needs (e.g. food, sleep, sex); 2. safety needs (self-protection against present and future dangers); 3. the need for recognition, for love and belonging; 4. ego-satisfying needs (e.g. desire for self-respect); 5. self-fulfilment needs (e.g. independence).

Business needs may be classified as follows:
1. basic needs (e.g. capital, profit, sales); 2. security (e.g. market share); 3. image (e.g. to customers and competitors); 4. goodwill; 5. achievement (e.g. independence).

Need satisfaction Bedürfnisbefriedigung

A situation where a customer`s needs are satisfied, ie the fulfillment of a want or desire to such an extent that a new need arises.

Needs Bedürfnisse

Basic economic requirements of food, clothes and shelter, but also wants which have become converted into needs, eg cars, TV sets, etc.

Negative advertising Negativwerbung

Advertising that focusses on pointing out undesirable aspects of competing products, firms, ideas, or companies.

Negative appeal negativer Werbeappeal

Also called negative advertising appeal.

An advertising message that does not point out the good qualities of a product or service but promotes the negative aspects of life when not using the advertised product or service.

Negative demand negative Nachfrage

A demand for products which consumers dislike and would prefer not to have to purchase, eg unpleasant medicine.

A consumer`s decision not to buy a particular product.

Negative income elasticity negative Einkommenselastizität

A situation where an increase in income results in a decrease in demand.

Negligence Fahrlässigkeit

Failure to use such care as a reasonable and prudent person would use under similar circumstances. Liability resulting from negligence may arise if someone fails to act in what the law considers to be a reasonable manner.
There are two types: 1. slight/ordinary negligence and 2. gross negligence.

Neglet of care Vernachlässigung der Sorgfaltspflicht

The act of giving not enough care or attention to people or things that are your responsibility.

Negotiated contract ausgehandelter Vertrag

A formal agreement for the sale or purchase of goods or services at a price agreed upon by both buyer and seller.

Negotiated price ausgehandelter Preis

A price obtained by negotiation. The purchaser is powerful enough to force the seller to accept prices lower than those usually charged.

Negotiated pricing Preisfestsetzung durch Verhandeln

A pricing strategy which determines the price a customer has to pay through bargaining even when there are stated list prices and discount structures.

Negotiation selling Verhandlungsverkauf

A selling approach in which the salesperson, through negotiation with a potential customer, acts as a councellor to assist the customer to find the best solution to a problem and thus establishes what product or service the customer really needs. Seller and buyer establish a form of partnership and attempt to produce a "win-win" outcome for both parties.

Neighbourhood shop Nachbarschaftsladen

A small convenience store clustered around a central supermarket.

Neoclassical economics neoklassische Ökonomie, Neoklassik (Lehrmethode)

Also called the marginalist school or neoclassical school.

A school of economic thought in the tradition of classical economics, that was founded in the 1870s. The founders (e.g. Böhm-Bawerk, A. Marshall, V. Pareto, L. Walras, K. Wicksell) used marginal analysis (ie the concepts of marginal utility and marginal productivity) to analyse the pricing of goods, services and factors of production in competitive markets.
The marginalists believed in the utility and profit maximizing behaviour of individuals and firms and that competition led to an efficient allocation of resources. Futhermore, they believed that government should not interfere with markets. Thus, in neoclassical theory the prices of factors of production are determined by the forces of demand and supply.

Note: these economic thoughts dominated from the 1870s to the 1930s, first replacing classical economics and then being considerably modified by Keynesian economics.

Net/nett netto

Figure remaining after all deductions and charges have been made from the gross amount.

The actual amount with no deductions allowable.

Net amount Nettobetrag

The amount of money which a person pays or receives for something after deductions or additions.

Net audience Nettonutzerschaft

The number of unduplicated homes, listeners, readers or viewers.

Net cash netto Kasse, bar ohne Abzug
netto Kasse

Net cash means the price when no deduction is permitted - that is to say, that the price given is the price for prompt payment without deduction. Usually the phrase is completed by adding a time limit, e.g. net cash 30 days.

The amount due after all deductions have been made.

Net circulation effektive Nettoauflage
Nettozahl der Personen mit Anschlagwerbemittelkontakt

Total sales of a publication after deduction of unsold copies.

Total number of persons viewing an outdoor advertisement within a given time period. Also called net advertising circulation (NAC).

Net cover(age) Nettoreichweite

The percentage of the target audience exposed at least once to a commercial or advertisement. A high net coverage is desirable when introducing a new product.

Net domestic product (NDP) Nettoinlandsprodukt

Also called net national product (NNP).

The gross domestic product (GDP) minus capital consumption.

Net earnings Netto-, Reingewinn

Also called net income or net profit.

The difference between total sales and total costs and expenses.

Net investment Nettoinvestition

Also called net asset formation.

Net investment = gross investment minus depreciation (which is equal to replacement investment).

Net investment is the net addition to the capital stock.

Net lease Netto-Leasing

Also called net leasing.

A lease stating that the lessee will bear all maintenance costs, insurance, and other expenses.

Net loss Netto-, Rein-, Bilanzverlust

A situation where the expenses of a business exceed its revenue/income for a financial period, usually a year.

Net margin Reingewinn

The difference between the received price and all costs, including overheads.

Net national income (NNI) Nettovolkseinkommen

NNI = gross national income (gross national product, GNP) at market prices minus depreciation, minus indirect taxes, plus subsidies.

Net national product (NNP) Nettosozialprodukt

This is a country's gross national product (GNP) minus depreciation of capital (capital consumption or depreciation). It considers the fact that part of a country's capital stock is used up in producing this year's output.

Net operating loss (NOL) Nettobetriebsverlust

Also called net trading loss.

The excess of business expenses over business income in a financial/fiscal year.

Net operating profit (NOP) Nettobetriebsgewinn

Also called net operating income (NOI) or net trading profit.

The excess of business income over business expenses in a financial/accounting year.

Net output Nettoproduktion

Also called net production.

The gross output of a firm or industry, minus the value of inputs supplied to it.

Net present value (NPV) Kapitalwert

Also called capital value or capitalised value.

The difference between the present values of an investment's expected cash inflows (ie its returns) and outflows (ie its costs). All inflows and outflows are discounted back to the present time by reference to the cost of capital.
An investment is acceptable if the NPV is positive.

Net price Nettopreis

A price less discounts, rebates or other allowances.

Net proceeds (np) Nettoerlös

The cash amount received from the sale of property after deduction of all costs incurred.

Net profit Reingewinn

Also called clear or pure profit, net earnings, net gain, net income, net proceeds, or net revenue.

This is the clear profit made when we have paid all the expenses of the business. Net profit = gross profit minus operating expenses. It represents the real gain of a business, available in the case of a company for distribution as dividend, and, in the case of a sole trader or partnership, as the reward of enterprise.

The profit as shown by a profit and loss account (P+L account).

Net profit percentage Nettoumsatzrendite, Reingewinn in Prozent

Also called net profit margin, net ratio or net earnings as percentage of sales.

Neither gross profit figures nor net profit by themselves are very meaningful. They should be seen in relation to the net turnover (the net sales) of the business.

$$\text{net profit percentage} = \frac{\text{net profit x 100}}{\text{net turnover (net sales)}}$$

Net purchases Nettoeinkaufswert

Purchases less purchases returns.

Net rating point (NRP) Nettoreichweitenprozentpunkt

One percent of the cumulative audience for a specific broadcast programme or commercial.

Net reach Nettoreichweite

The number of people reached by an advertising medium at least once.

Net tare Nettotara

The weight of an empty container, railway wag(g)on, trailer or other vehicle.

Net turnover Nettoumsatz, Nettoumsatzerlöse

Also called net sales.

Net turnover = gross sales minus sales returns, allowances, freight out, and sales discounts.

Net weight (nt wt) Netto-, Reingewicht

Also called net contents.

The weight of the contents only.

Net weight = gross weight - tare (the weight of the packing).

Never-outs Artikel, die immer auf Lager sein müssen

Commodities, eg key items or best sellers, that should never run out of stock because of continuous/current demand.

New buy Erstkauf
Neuproduktaufnahme

A buying situation requiring the purchase of a product for the first time.

New product neues Produkt

A product which may be new to the marketplace, the producer, the seller, or some combination of these.

When planning a new product, the firm has to consider at least the following items:

1. the need(s) statisfied by the product, 2. competing products, 3. similar products, 4. price thresholds, 5. the speed of market penetration, 6. the size of the market.

Note: new products may fail because:

1. managers may push a new product idea through in spite of negative market research findings,
2. the market potential is overestimated,
3. the actual product is not designed well enough,
4. the product is not advertised effectively,
5. the product is overpriced,
6. the product is incorrectly positioned,
7. the development costs are higher than expected,
8. competitors fight back harder than expected,
9. competitors develop a similar product at a faster speed,
10. rivals quickly imitate the new product and thereby shorten the new product`s life cycle, etc.

New user Neubenutzer/in, Neukonsument

A buyer who has been unaware of a product or has resisted it but now starts buying and using it.

New-to-the-world product Weltneuheit

A product serving a purpose for which no product has previously existed.

News agency Pressedienst, Nachrichtenagentur

Office which distributes news to newspapers, radio, television, and other institutions.

News release Pressenotiz

Also called press release.

An informational document on an event of timely value distributed by an organisation to broadcast stations, newspapers and magazines for public relations purposes.

Newscaster Nachrichtensprecher
Leuchtschriftnachrichten

A person reading the news on radio or TV. Also called newsreader.

Electronic signs, usually placed on high buildings in city centres, which spell out news flashes in lighted strips, interspersed with advertisements.

Newsletter Informationsbrief, -blatt
Mitteilungsblatt

Also called newssheet or information sheet.

A printed sheet or small newspaper giving news about a company.

Newspaper Zeitung

A publication containing news, opinions, features, advertising, etc, usually issued daily or weekly. Also called paper.

A business organisation that prints and distributes such a publication.

Newspaper advertising Zeitungswerbung

Advertisements placed in Sunday, local or national newspapers. Newspapers enable advertisers to advertise their product(s) and their stores and to target specific geographic markets. Furthermore, they are effective in informing consumers about retail store promotions and special sales.

Newspaper insert Zeitungsbeilage

Also called preprint.

A printed promotional enclosure in a newspaper.

Newsstand (N/S) Zeitungsstand, Zeitungskiosk

Also called news kiosk.

A retail outlet selling single-copy magazines and newspapers at the newsstand price, ie the nondiscounted basic rate, usually printed on the cover.

Next to reading (NR) neben Text, textanschließend

Also called next to editorial matter or next to reading matter (NRM).

An advertisement position immediately next to text instead of other advertising.

Niche Nische

Also called market niche.

A small market overlooked or ignored by market leaders and therefore served by smaller firms.

Niche marketing Nischenmarketing

Also called concentrated marketing.

A marketing segmentation strategy in which a firm concentrates on selling to a small specialized market segment or niche.

Niche marketing is the outcome of gap analysis and involves the promotion of new products or the developing of a new product within an existing product range already operative in the market. An example of the latter can be found in the car industry which finally realized that many (young) buyers are receptive to sports cars or convertibles.
Niche marketing involves innovation and shows the following features:

1. it gives the company a high market profile,
2. it permits premium prices - at least until keener competition arises,
3. due to the premium prices it allows an above-average markup,
4. it is a high risk area - thus effective market research and test marketing are necessary,
5. problems may arise in meeting excessive demand in the early stages of the product's life,
6. competitors may emerge and induce price wars.

Niche strategy — Nischenstrategie

A strategy employed by nichers who specialise in serving particular market segments that are of sufficient size and profitable enough while avoiding direct confrontation with major competitors.

Nicher — Nischenanbieter

Also called market nicher.

A firm whose products or services serve segments not being pursued by firms with larger market shares.

Nielsen rating — Einschaltquote, gemessen von der A.C. Nielsen Company (USA)

The percentage of US TV households watching a particular programme, calculated by the A.C. Nielsen Company.

No change forecast — unveränderte Prognose

A forecast assuming that there will be "no change". For example, managers involved in foreign currency-related decisions often refuse to make a forecast on future exchange rates and assume that it will be the same as the present one. In fact, they are making a forecast - that there will be no change in the exchange rate. It is a forecast of "no change".

No direct mail list Robinsonliste

A list of people who do not wish to receive any direct mail.

No show festgebuchter, aber nicht mitfliegender/reisender Passagier

A person who reserves space on an airplane, ship, train or road vehicle on a specified date, but neither uses it nor prior to despatch cancels the reservation.

No-name (product) markenfreies Produkt, weiße Ware

Unbranded lower-cost product found in super- and hypermarkets.

Nominal gross national product (GNP) nominales Bruttosozialprodukt

Current year output expressed in current year prices (e.g. 1997 production times 1997 prices).

Non-containerizable cargo nicht-containerfähiges Frachtgut

Cargo that cannot be transported in a container.
Non-containerizable cargo consists of:
1. rollable cargo with its own wheels (e.g. tractors, trucks), 2. cargo that is carried on trailers (e.g. boats, cranes), 3. special project cargo (e.g. aircraft wings, subway cars), 4. neo-bulk cargo (e.g. lumber, steel products).

Non-renewable resources nicht ersetzbare Ressourcen

Natural resources such as fossil fuels or metals which are exhaustible deposits of the earth`s surface.

Nonacceptance (Na, n/a) Annahmeverweigerung, Nichtannahme

Also called refusal, refusal to accept, refusal of acceptance, rejection or refusal to take delivery.

A wrongful neglect or refusal by the buyer to take possession of the goods from the seller.

Nonbuyer-reader — Zweitleser

Also called pass-along reader or secondary reader.

A reader who reads a publication but does not buy it.

Nondelivery — Nichtlieferung
Nichterfüllung

A wrongful neglect or refusal by the seller to deliver the goods ordered.

A wrongful neglect or refusal by the seller to transfer the possession/ownership of the goods to the buyer. Also called nonperformance or nonfulfil(l)ment.

Nondirective interview — nichtdirektive Befragung

An interview method using no preset questions and thus following no fixed pattern.

Nondurable goods — Konsumgüter, (kurzlebige)
Verbrauchsgüter

Also called consumer, consumption or consumable goods, or consumer nondurables. In the case of foodstuffs they are also called perishable goods or perishables.

Frequently purchased consumer goods that have a relatively brief lifetime, e.g. food, clothing, and which are quickly consumed or worn out; or become dated, unfashionable, or in some other way no longer popular.

Nonessential goods — nicht lebensnotwendige Güter

Also called nonessentials.

Commodities which are not necessary to maintain a minimum acceptable living standard.

Nonfamily household — Wohngemeinschaft (WG),
Hausgemeinschaft

A household consisting of singles or non-related individuals.

Nongoods service nicht güterbezogene(r) Dienstleistung, Service

Personal service offered by a seller which does not involve a good.

Nonmarket economy (NME) nicht-marktwirtschaftlich orientierte Wirtschaft

An economy where commercial activity is centrally planned.

Nonpackaged goods unverpackte Ware

Nondurable consumer goods which are not packaged.

Nonpayment Nichtzahlung

Also called default of payment or failure to pay.

Not paying a debt due.

Nonperformance Nichterfüllung

Also called nonfulfil(l)ment.

The failure of a contracting party to perform his part of the contract.

Nonprice competition außerpreislicher Wettbewerb

Concentration of competitive activity into sectors other than price.
It includes: 1. the use of advertising; 2. the offering of pre-sales and/or after-sales services, 3. improved guarantees and warranties for consumer durables; 4. the offering of favourable terms of credit; 5. competition in the style or the packaging of the products; etc.
The importance of nonprice competition was first recognized in the early 1930s.

Nonprobability sampling Ermessensauswahl

Also called convenience or judgmental sampling.

In statistics, the arbitrary process of selecting a sampling unit. That means researchers decide as to which members of a total population are representative.

Nonprofit marketing Marketing nichtkommerzieller Unternehmen, Marketing für gemeinnützige Zwecke

Also called non-business marketing or social marketing.

Marketing activities conducted by firms that operate in the public interest and do not seek financial profit. It tends to focus much more on ideas such as ecology, clean cities, energy conservation than on products. Thus, this marketing is used to increase the acceptability of social ideas.

Nonregular reader unregelmäßiger Leser

A person who reads a publication only occassionally.

Nonresponse Nichtbeantwortung

In a market research survey, a person`s act of not taking part, eg an interviewee`s refusal to be interviewed or his/her failing to return a completed mail questionnaire.

Nonreturnable packing Einweg(ver)packung

Also called disposable or one-way package.

Packaging which cannot be returned to the seller or producer once it has been used but is thrown away. The opposite of multi-way packing.

Nonseller Ladenhüter

Also called shelfwarmer, sleeper, slicker, or unsaleable article.

An article which does not sell at all but stays in the shelves.

Nonstandardized marketing nicht standardisiertes Marketing

In international marketing, a strategy that assumes each country or region is different and requires a distinct marketing plan.

Nonstore retailing Direktverkauf

The merchandising of goods by means other than retail shops. The seller reaches consumers and completes transactions, for example, through mail order, vending machines, telephone sales, door-to-door selling, catalogues, in-home retailing, etc.

Nontariff barriers (NTBs) nichttarifäre, zollfremde Handelshemmnisse

Also called non-tariff trade barriers.

Obstacles, other than tariffs, which restrict/hinder free trade. With the removal of commercial barriers (ie tariffs and quantitative restrictions), the significance of non-tariff barriers (e.g. discriminatory administrative practices, the insisting on different technical standards) to trade has increased.

Nonverbal communication nichtverbale Kommunikation

The transmission of a message from sender to receiver without using words.

Normal (Gaussian) distribution (Gauß'sche) Normalverteilung

Also called Gauss distribution.

In statistics, a term describing the commonest type of frequency distribution. It provides an exact measure of distances of the standard deviation from the arithmetic mean.
A symmetrical or bell-shaped curve when plotted on a graph and when the distribution of values is normal.

Normal good Normalgut

A good whose consumption changes directly with money income when prices remain constant. In other words, as people's incomes, other things being equal, rise, the demand for normal goods rises.
A good for which the income elasticity of demand is positive.

Normal price Normalpreis, marktüblicher Preis

Under normal market conditions, the price a buyer can expect for a product or service

Normative economics normative Wirtschaftswissenschaft

Economic theories which are not testable against facts alone, but including elements of opinion and social judgement.

Normative influence normativer Einfluß

The influence exerted on a person by a reference group to conform to its norms.

Norms Normen

Rules and guidelines setting forth proper attitudes and behaviours for specific situations.

Not otherwise specified (NOS) nicht anderweitig spezifiziert

A phrase relating to commodities not specifically named in tariffs or freight commodity classes.

Not-for-profit market gemeinnütziger Markt

A market which serves the society and thus provides services with varying but nonprofit goals. Examples are institutional markets such as hospitals, museums, universities, etc.

Note Anmerkung, Fußnote
kurzer Brief

A short comment or explanation apart from the text. Also called footnote.

A short letter.

Notice (not.) Information
Aufmerksamkeit
Ankündigung

Written or printed information about something. Also called information.

To bring something to someone's attention. Also called attention.

A formal declaration. Also called announcement.

Notice of acceptance Annahmeerklärung

Also called acceptance notice.

In general, information given to someone that something has been accepted, e.g. an offer has been accepted by the offeree.

Noticeboard schwarzes Brett

Also called bulletin board.

A board put up specially to allow (authorized) persons to pin up notices. Many noticeboards are nowadays electronic, e.g. in airports, stations, etc.

Noting score Beachtungswert

In print advertising, the percentage of the total number of readers who note an advertisement in a publication.

Novelty Neuheit
Scherzartikel

An article which is novel.

A small, decorative or amusing article.

Nuclear family Kernfamilie

The basic family unit with two parents and their children.

Nutritional labelling Nährstoffangabe, Zutatenangabe

The listing of a product`s nutrients on a label.

O

Objection (Kauf)Einwand, Bedenken

A concern or any form of resistance raised by a potential buyer to a salesperson.

Objective and task method Ziel-Aufgaben-Methode

A technique used to determine the promotion budget. Marketers first set the objectives that a promotional campaign is to achieve and then attempt to determine the tasks required to accomplish these objectives. The costs of all tasks are then calculated and added to arrive at the amount of the total budget.

Note: the major advantage of the most popular and most scientific method of setting a promotion budget is that: the objectives are defined, alternatives are analyzed, and the costs of each task are determined.

Objectives Unternehmensziele

The aims, goals or targets of a business, e.g. market standing, profitability, growth, productivity, etc.

Observation Beobachtung

A research method whereby situations of interest, eg the buying behaviour of consumers, are watched and the relevant facts, actions, or behaviours are noted.

Observation research Erhebungsforschung

A research method where data is collected by researchers watching people or events.

Obsolescence technisch-wirtschaftliche Überholung
vorzeitiges Veralten

The decline in value of a physical asset (e.g. a machine) from technological changes or changes in demand rather than deterioration/depreciation.

The outdating of a product or process.

Occasion segmentation Ereignissegmentierung, Gelegenheitssegmentierung

A type of behaviour segmentation, ie a market is divided into groups according to occasions when buyers get the idea to buy, actually make their purchase, or use the item bought.

Occasional customer Gelegenheitskunde

Also called casual customer.

A customer who is not a regular customer, but one who only buys or orders from time to time.

Odd lot Restpartie
Auktionsposten

A broken lot reduced in price.

A number of miscellaneous items for sale at an auction.

Odd pricing (Preis)Auszeichnung mit gebrochenen/ungeraden Preisen

Also called odd-even pricing or psychological pricing.

A selling technique using attractive and more acceptable prices (e.g. £ 9.99 rather than £ 10.00) in order to suggest a bargain. Note: the price is not necessarily a low price.

Odds and ends Kleinkram, Krimskrams
Ramschware

Also called job goods, junk, oddments or rummage goods.

Small articles which have little value.

Commodities that are being sold cheaply because they are left over or are parts of incomplete sets.

Odds sale Ramschverkauf

The sale of articles which are worthless, useless or considered as rubbish.

Off season tote Saison, Sauregurkenzeit Nebensaison, außerhalb der Saison

A time of the year where business is dull. Also called dead season.

In tourism, a less busy season, eg in some areas during winter, when there are fewer travellers.

Off shelf display Warenauslage außerhalb des Regals

In a store, the display of merchandise not in the store`s shelves but in another location.

Off-invoice Rechnungsabzug

Also called off-invoice allowance.

A price reduction granted by a seller to a buyer at the time of invoicing/billing.

Off-price label Preisschild mit Originalpreis und reduziertem Preis, Jetzt-Vorher-Preisschild

A label on a product which shows two prices: the original price and the reduced price.

Off-price shop Niedrigpreisladen, Discountladen

A shop that sells at prices far below traditional store prices because it pays cash for its stock and usually does not ask for return privileges.
Off-price shops often buy manufacturers` overruns at cost or even less, leftover goods, irregulars, absorb goods from bankrupt shops or buy unsold, end-of-season output. Merchandise styles and brands change frequently so that buyers can only purchase what is available or what they believe to be a good deal.
Note: merchandise is often higher-quality, current goods.

Off-the-page buying Kauf über die Druckmedien

The purchase of items which have been advertised and offered in newspapers or magazines. The advertisements usually explain the offer in detail and include an order form.

Offensive market strategy offensive Absatzstrategie, Marketingstrategie

In a competitive market, a challenger`s strategy to attack the market leader and/or other competitors in order to increase market share. Thus, the challenger must consider the strengths and identify a weakness in the leader`s and other competitors` marketing mix and develop a genuine corresponding strength.
Note, however: any attack should be on a narrow front only, ie on a front where the challenger obviously has an advantage.

Offensive marketing offensives Marketing

A marketing strategy characterised by a desire to be innovative, to assume market leadership and to respond to competitive moves with forceful counterattacks.

Offer (off.) Angebot

Also called quotation, quote or proposal.

A manifestation of willingness to enter into an agreement/contract. The offer usually comes from one potential party to a contract, the seller (ie the offeror). In order to be effective, it must be communicated to the other party, the buyer (ie the offeree).

The proposal/offer may be made verbally/orally or it may be made in writing - perhaps in a formal deed or just in a letter or on an order form - or it may be by a course of action.

An offer may be made to an individual, to a group, or to the world at large. In an offer to the world at large anyone may accept the offer.

An offer may be revoked at any time before the moment of acceptance by the offeree, but the revocation must be communicated to the offeree.
Once an offer has been made, the receiver of the offer has three choices:
1. he can reject the offer, 2. he can make a counter-offer, or 3. he can accept the offer.

Acceptance of the offer can bind the offeror; the acceptance must be in the same terms as the offer.

Offers may be submitted in answer to an enquiry (solicited offer) or on the seller's own initiative (unsolicited or voluntary offer). Unless otherwise indicated, the person (the offeror) making the offer is expected to keep it open for a reasonable time (firm offer). Should the offeror not want to be bound, he states that his offer is subject to confirmation or without engagement.

An offer is distinct in law from "an invitation to treat" (i.e. an "invitation to make offers"). The display of goods in a shop is an invitation to the customers to make offers to buy. It is not an offer to sell.

Offer for sale Verkaufsangebot

Also called sales offer.

An offer for the sale of goods or services.

Offer subject to confirmation freibleibendes, unverbindliches Angebot

Also called flat, free or open offer; not binding offer, or offer without engagement.

An offer made which does not bind the offeror.

Offer types Angebotsarten

There a number of different types of offer, eg:
1. attractive offer, 2. banded offer, 3. bargain offer, 4. blind offer, 5. cash offer, 6. cash refund offer, 7. counter offer, 8. firm offer, 9. general offer, 10. introductory offer, 11. multiple offer, 12. offer for sale, 13. offer subject to confirmation, 14. premium offer, 15. refund offer, 16. self-liquidating offer, 17. solicited offer, 18. special offer, 19. specific offer, 20. swap offer, 21. total offer, 22. trial offer, 23. unsolicited offer, 24. voluntary offer, etc.

Offer(ed) price Angebotspreis
Briefkurs, Angebotskurs (Bö)

The bid, quoted or supply price of a commodity.

The price at which a security is offered for sale. Also called asked price, price offered, rate asked or sellers' rate.

Offeree Angebotsempfänger

The person receiving an offer.

Offeror/offerer Offerent, Anbieter

The person making an offer.

Office of Fair Trading (OFT) Amt für Verbraucherschutz (GB)

The OFT was set up under the Fair Trading Act 1973. It is a government agency whose job is to keep watch on trading matters in the UK and to protect the consumer against unfair practices (e.g. the OFT may take legal action if a manufacturer tries to force retailers to sell his goods at a minimum price or if people try illegally to restrict competition).

Offpeak außerhalb der Hauptzeiten

A period when business is less busy.

Oligopolistic competition oligopolistische Konkurrenz

A competitive situation in which there are only a few sellers who have a large market share and are highly sensitive to each other`s marketing and pricing strategies.

Oligopoly Oligopol

A market in which there are a few large sellers but many buyers. A feature of oligopoly is that each seller must consider his competitors' price policy and marketing activities.
Two forms of oligopoly can be distinguished:
1. perfect oligopoly (the products are homogeneous) and 2. imperfect oligopoly (there is some degree of differentiation between the products).

Oligopsony Oligopson

A market in which there are few buyers but many sellers.

Omnibus agreement Globalabkommen

An agreement covering many different items.

Omnibus book Sammelband

A volume of reprints by a single author or on a single subject.

Omnibus survey Omnibus-, Mehrthemenbefragung

Also called multi-purpose survey.

A continuous survey, commonly organised by a marketing research agency, used to examine a number of topics together, eg buying habits, product and brand preferences, brand loyalty, etc.
Note: called omnibus survey because any marketer can buy in to the survey, for a fee, and add questions.

On account (o/a) gegen Kredit, auf Rechnung
als Teilzahlung

On credit terms, i.e. the buyer pays sometime after delivery. Also called open account.

In partial payment of an obligation.

On approval (on appro) zur Ansicht, auf Probe

A potential buyer receives goods from a seller on approval in order to decide whether or not he wishes to buy them. He may return the goods in perfect order without payment within a fixed period (the approval period) if he does not purchase them.

On consignment in Konsignation,
kommissionsweise

Goods that are entrusted to an agent (the consignee) to be sold for his principal (the consignor). If these goods (the consignment) are not sold within a specified period, they are returned to the owner (the principal). Payment is made for the goods sold. The agent receives a commission for the sales he has transacted.

On credit auf Kredit

Without paying immediately; a customer is given time before he has to pay.

On demand (O.D., o/d) auf Anfordern/Aufforderung/
Verlangen

On/at call whenever required; without any period of notice.

On offer im Angebot, zum Verkauf

Also called on sale

Goods for sale at a stated price.

On order (o.o., o/o) bestellt, in Bestellung auf/bei Bestellung

The goods are on order means that we have ordered them from our supplier but we have not yet received them.

The goods can be delivered on order, ie immediately after having placed the order.

On sale or return Verkauf mit Rückgaberecht

A method of sales promotion. Some firms, anxious to get sales at all cost, especially when business is slack, will send goods to the buyer, e.g. a retailer on the understanding that he is allowed to return them within a given period if he cannot sell them. Payment is made only if and when the goods are sold.

On site demonstration Vorführung vor Ort

The demonstration of a product to a potential customer on the premises of a satisfied previous buyer (ie a customer who is acting as an innovator).

On the air auf Sendung, Sendung läuft

An indication that broadcasting is taking place.

On-pack promotion Packungswerbung

Promotional material affixed to the package of goods in order to stimulate sales at the point of sale (POS) or to complement an advertising campaign.

One-off production Einzelfertigung

Also called individual, job, non-repetitive, single-unit or unit production.

A method of production in which a single item is produced according to customer specifications.

One-price policy Einheitspreispolitik

A pricing method where the same price is charged to all customers who purchase a good or service under similar conditions.

One-sided ad message einseitige Werbeaussage

An advertising message in which only the benefits of a good or service are mentioned.

One-stop shopping Einkauf alles unter einem Dach, Einkauf im Einkaufszentrum, One-Stop-Einkauf, Einkaufsbummel mit einem Parkhalt

Also called single-stop shopping.

A place containing many retail outlets where the customer may buy all that is required within one area.

One-to-one interview persönliche Befragung, Befragung unter zwei Paar Augen, Eins-zu-eins-Befragung

An interview in which one person (the interviewer) personally talks to the interviewee.

One-way bottle Einwegflasche

A non-returnable bottle.

One-way communication einseitige Kommunikation

A type of communication where the transmittor does not expect, and does not get, a response from the receiver. It is prevalent in organisations which are authoritarian in the way they deal with employees (authoritarian-style leadership).

One-way goods Einwegartikel

Goods or items which can only be used once before discarding, e.g. medical syringes.

Packaging units (such as plastic bottles etc.) which cannot be returned.

One-way package Einwegpackung, Wegwerfpackung

Packaging which cannot be returned to the seller or producer but has to be thrown away after use.

Online retailing Online-Einzelhandel

A two-way, interactive service offered to people with microcomputers by retailers. It provides customers who log on to online services with a variety of information and shopping opportunities.

Open account (O/A, o/a) offenes Konto
offene Rechnung

An account on which the final balance is yet to be paid. Also called credit or charge account.

In general, a credit relationship between buyer and seller - the seller sells on credit, the buyer pays on receipt of the invoice or after an agreed period of credit.

Open bid offenes Angebot

A type of bid pricing where several, but not all, sellers are asked to submit bids. Note: the amounts of the bids are made public.

Open dating offene, nicht kodierte Datierung; sichtbares Ablaufdatum, offene Haltbarkeit

Also called open-code dating, open-date labelling or date stamping.

In product labelling, the stating of the expected shelf life of a product, ie its sell-by date, in an uncoded form so that consumers can easily read and observe it.

Open indent Auslandsauftrag mit Herstellerspezifizierung; Indent, bei dem der Indentgeber dem Nehmer die Wahl der Lieferquelle überläßt

In export trade, an order from a foreign buyer to an agent who may choose any suitable producer or supplier for the supply of goods or services.

Open market freier, offener Markt

A market in which goods are available to be bought and sold by anyone who cares to. Prices on this market are fixed by the laws of supply and demand.

Open offer freibleibendes, unverbindliches Angebot

Also called flat offer, free offer, not binding offer, offer subject to confirmation, or offer without engagement.

An offer made which does not bind the offeror.

Open order unerledigter Auftrag offener Auftrag

A back, unfilled or outstanding order.

An order placed without price or delivery stipulations.

Open price agreement Preisinformationsabsprache

An arrangement between a number of firms to inform one another of details of the prices of their products and of future price changes.

Open pricing offene Preispolitik, Preisaustausch zwischen Konkurrenten

A pricing strategy where different companies attempt to achieve some cooperation and conformity in pricing their goods or services.

Open rate offene Frachtrate Anzeigengrundtarif

A freight rate that is not fixed and is therefore to be negotiated.

The basic rate without any discounts for a single advertisement or commercial. Also called base rate.

Open to offers Angebote werden entgegengenommen

A situation where a firm is waiting for offers and ready to discuss and negotiate the price.

Open-door policy Politik der offenen Tür

The policy of a country, allowing the goods from all other countries to be imported on the same terms. Furthermore, all foreign products receive the same treatment as domestic products.

Open-end contract Sukzessivlieferungsvertrag, Bezugsvertrag

Also called multiple delivery contract or continuing sales contract.

An agreement whereby a seller contracts to meet the buyer's requirements during a specified period and to deliver according to his wishes, e.g. to deliver by installments.

Open-end lease offenes Leasing

A lease agreement where the lessee pays to the lessor an additional amount at the end of the lease term, to cover any change in the value of the property. So the risk of decrease in value is placed on the lessee.

Open-ended question offene, frei beantwortbare Frage

In a questionnaire, a question which the respondent/interviewee may answer in his or her own words. This tends to produce a very wide range of answers and may prove difficult to classify. Thus, it is a type of question best avoided unless there are compelling reasons for its inclusion.

Opening Eröffnung

The act of starting a new business.

Opening bid erstes Gebot (Versteigerung)

The first bid at an auction.

Opening hours Öffnungszeiten

Also called business hours or hours of business.

Hours when a shop or business is open.

Opening stock Anfangsbestand

Also called opening or beginning inventory.

The value of stock at the beginning of a trading period. This is equal to the value of the closing stock of the previous trading period.

Operating leasing Operating-Leasing

Also called operating lease or service lease.

This type of lease is usually offered by the supplier (the lessor) of the assets which are to be leased. The lessor not only supplies the goods but also undertakes to service them and effect any necessary repairs. The lessor is the owner of the assets.

Operating manual Bedienungsanleitung

Also called operating or working instructions.

A book which shows how to work a machine.

Operating profit / loss Betriebsgewinn / Betriebsverlust

The profit or loss arising from trading, i.e. from normal operations of the business, not from extraordinary items.

Operating ratio Erfolgskennziffer

A ratio measuring the effectiveness of a company`s operations, eg operating expenses to net sales, gross margin to net sales, net profit to net sales, etc.

Operating statement Gewinn- und Verlustrechnung

Also called income statement or profit and loss (P+L) statement.

A company`s profit and loss statement, ie a financial statement which shows company sales and other income (on the credit side), cost of goods sold, and expenses (on the debit side) during a given time period, usually a year. The balance on the account is the profit or loss.

Operating supplies Betriebsstoffe

Also called factory supplies.

Consumable items that do not become part of the final product, eg lubricants.

Operations research (OR) Operations Research (OR), Operationsforschung

Also called operational research (OR).

OR represents the application of scientific and mathematical thought to business problems. OR demands a thorough study of the problem concerned, the construction of a model, and the manipulation of the model to produce an optimum solution. The purpose of OR is to help management determine its policy and action scientifically.

Opinion leader Meinungsbildner, -führer

Also called opinion former.

Persons whose opinions on new products or services have a great effect on other people. Therefore, it may be advantageous to direct advertising and other promotional activities to the opinion leader(s).

Opinion poll Meinungsumfrage

Also called public-opinion survey.

An opinion research method in which the views of the general public are ascertained by asking a representative sample group of people questions, eg on their opinion on a topical controversial issue of the day or how they intend to vote.

Opinion research Testbefragung, Meinungsforschung

Also called opinion poll or opinion survey.

Opinion research seeks attitudes or shifts of opinion, and questions usually require "Yes", "No" or "Don't know" answers.

Opportunity and threat analysis Marketing-Umweltanalyse

A company`s analysis of both the advantages and disadvantages in its environment in order to carefully estimate and plan its marketing activities.

Opportunity cost Opportunitätskosten, Alternativkosten, Kosten der entgangenen Gelegenheit

Also called alternative or economic cost.

This is the cost of a good or service in terms of the value of the next best alternative good or service that has been sacrificed to obtain it.
Opportunity does not mean how much money will be required to take an opportunity; it means how much money you have lost by taking one. If the alternative would have produced a higher return, then the opportunity cost is the difference between that figure and what you actually earned in the chosen activity.

Opportunity price Opportunitätspreis

The price where the buyer has the opportunity to choose either one or the other product but cannot afford both. Thus, he/she has the choice to decide between the desirable purchases, and the price may determine which desirable purchase has to be sacrificed.

Opportunity to hear (OTH) Kontaktwahrscheinlichkeit mit einer Radio(werbe)sendung

The number of people of a target audience who have an opportunity to listen to a radio programme or commercial.

The number of times a listener has the chance to hear a radio commercial.

Opportunity to see (OTS) Kontaktchance/Kontaktwahr-scheinlichkeit, etwas zu sehen

The number of people of a target audience who have an opportunity to see an advertisement or commercial. This can range from an OTS of over 90 percent for television to an OTS of less than 5 percent for cinema.

The number of times a person has the chance to see an advertisement or commercial.

Optimization Optimierung

The process by which the best solution or result may be obtained (ie the optimum).

Optimizer Optimierer

A customer who considers numerous suppliers, both familiar and unfamiliar, solicits offers and studies them carefully before selecting one.

Optimum order quantity (OOQ) optimale Bestellmenge

Also called optimal lot quantity or economic order quantity (EOQ).

The best amount/quantity of something to order.

The minimum order value producing a profit for a supplier.

Optimum population optimale Bevölkerungszahl

The number of people which, when combined with the other resources of land and capital, yields the maximum output of goods and services per head of the population.

Option to purchase/sell Kaufoption/Verkaufsoption

Giving someone the privilege of buying/selling something at an agreed price withing a specified time period.

Optional extras Extras, Sonderzubehör

Items which a customer can add to a product if wanted, eg a CD-player to a car.

Optional-product pricing Preisbildung inklusive Extras, Inklusivpreisbildung

A pricing strategy which states a price that covers the main product including optional or accessory products. For example, the sticker price of car dealers often includes many useful items, usually sold only as options.

Or near offer (ONO, ono) Verhandlungsbasis (VB)

The offeror indicates that he/she is prepared to accept a price which is slightly lower than the price asked.

Oral communication mündliche Kommunikation

Communication conducted orally, it may either be one-way (i.e. transmitting only) or two-way (i.e. transmitting and receiving).

Order (O, Ord, o) Auftrag, Bestellung

A request to make or deliver goods, or provide services. Orders are placed either in response to a quotation/offer or on the buyer's own initiative, without a preceding quotation.

An order should include the following essential points:
1. nature and quality of the goods; 2. quantity; 3. prices and discounts; 4. delivery date; 5. terms of delivery; 6. terms of payment.
According to law the buyer's order is an offer to buy and the arrangement is not legally binding until the seller has accepted the offer. After that, both parties are legally bound to honour their agreement.

The seller's obligations are:
1. to deliver the goods (the kind ordered, at the agreed time),
2. to guarantee the goods to be free from faults of which the buyer could not be aware,
3. to transfer ownership,
4. to accept payment, ie the sales/selling price.

The buyer's obligations are:
1. to accept the goods,
2. to pay for them at the time of delivery (unless there is an agreement to the contrary),
3. to check the goods at once (failure to give prompt notice of faults will be taken as acceptance).

The buyer is entitled to cancel his order at any time before it has been accepted by the seller.

If faulty goods are delivered, the buyer can demand either a price reduction, or replacement of the goods, or cancellation of the order. He may also be able to claim damages/compensation.

Orders can be placed orally/verbally or in writing and should be acknowledged straight away.

There are first or initial orders; repeat orders or re-orders; trial orders (small orders for testing purposes); advance orders (an order placed ahead of the time when delivery is desired); standing orders; and indents (ie foreign orders), etc.

When a covering letter is sent with an order form, essential details will be contained in the form and additional explanations in the covering letter.

Order book Auftragsbuch

Also called order register or job ledger.

A book containing a record of the orders obtained by a business.

Order cancellation Auftragsstornierung

The revocation of an order. The buyer is entitled to cancel/withdraw his order at any time before it has been accepted by the seller.
Note: if an order is to be cancelled after acceptance, the seller has to agree. But the buyer may, of course, cancel his order after acceptance if the seller fails to fulfil his contractual obligations.

Order card Bestellkarte

A reply card used to place an order by mail.

Order costs Kosten der Auftragsabwicklung

The expenses involved with order processing. This includes typing up the order, mailing it, filing a copy, checking to see that the delivered goods match the order, arranging payment, etc.

Order cycle time Auftragszyklusspanne

The time between placement of the order by the customer and the receipt of the merchandise.

Order filling costs Kosten der Auftragsabwicklung

Also called order handling costs or order processing costs.

All the costs incurred by filling/processing an order, eg warehousing, transportation, invoicing, payment collection, etc.

Order form Bestellformular

Also called order slip.

A document used to place orders on behalf of the business. It usually has an official order number.

Order fulfil(l)ment Auftragserfüllung

The supplying of goods or services which have been ordered.

Carrying out an order in a satisfactory way.

Order getter Auftragsbeschaffer

A type of salesperson who increases the firm`s sales by selling to new customers and by increasing sales to present customers. To achieve this goal, the salespersons have to recognise potential buyers` needs and then give them the necessary information.

Order getting Auftragsbeschaffung

An order getter`s activity to seek potential or present customers who will place an order. To obtain sales, an order getter must actively seek prospects, inform them about the product, and then persuade them to buy.

Order intake Auftragseingang

Also called order entry.

A customer`s placement of an order.

Order number Auftragsnummer

A reference number used by a firm to identify a particular order.

Order picking Zusammenstellung einer Bestellung

Collecting various commodities in a warehouse to make up an order which is to be despatched to a customer.

Order processing Auftragsabwicklung

Also called order filling, handling or procedure; or execution of order.

The series of tasks (e.g. to check the stocks, to deliver the goods) which must be carried out by the supplier on receipt of an order from a customer.

Order quantity Bestellmenge

Also called ordering quantity or order(ing) size.

The amount of goods ordered. The amount to order at any one time is guided by the economic order quantity (EOQ).

Order taking Auftragsannahme

Processing orders from customers who have decided they want to buy.

Order timing Bestellpunkt

Also called order or reorder point.

The inventory level that signals when more inventory should be ordered.

Order types Auftragsarten

There are a number of different types of order, eg:
1. abeyance order, 2. advance order, 3. back order, 4. blanket order, 5. cash order, 6. conditional order, 7. delivery order, 8. firm order, 9. first order, 10. follow-up/on order, 11. mail order, 12. manufacturing order, 13. minimum order, 14. indent order, 15. insertion order, 16. open order, 17. outsize order, 18. outstanding order, 19. part order, 20. purchase order, 21. repeat order, 22. rush order, 23. sales order, 24. sampling order, 25. shipping order, 26. shop order, 27. space order, 28. special order, 29. split order, 30. standing order, 31. telephone order, 32. trial order, 33. unexecuted order, etc.

Ordering cost(s) Beschaffungs-, Bestellkosten

Also called order or procurement cost(s).

All costs associated with the ordering of inventory, including clerical labour, forms, and processing costs.

The clerical cost of receiving an order.

Ordinate Ordinate

The vertical line (or Y-axis) on a two dimensional graph.

Organisational buying Firmeneinkauf

Purchasing done by organisations, eg for resale purposes.

Organised market organisierter Markt

In organised markets, buying and selling takes place in a recognised building, business is governed by agreed rules and conventions, and often only a limited number of recognised persons are allowed to engage in transactions. Generally the public are excluded. They are thus a very highly developed form of market, e.g. the stock exchange.

Origin Koordinatennullpunkt
Ursprung

The lower left-hand corner point at which the vertical (y-axis or ordinate) and horizontal (x-axis or abscissa) axes meet.

Something from which anything arises or is derived.

The first stage of existence.

Original Original

Something made for the first time and not a copy of something.

Original cost(s) Anschaffungskosten

Also called asset, first, historic, historical, initial, cost(s), or cost price.

All costs associated with the acquisition of an asset. That means the net invoice price of an asset plus all expenditures (e.g. customs duty, freight in, installation costs, legal fees) incurred in placing and preparing that asset for its intended use.

Original equipment manufacturer (OEM) Erstausrüster, Original Equipment Manufacturer (OEM)

A company which purchases industrial goods in order to incorporate them into other new and unique products that are sold to other businesses or final consumers.

Ostentatious consumption Geltungskonsum

Also called conspicuous consumption.

Comsumption for approbation instead of utility; thus consumers demand more when prices rise - an abnormal market behaviour.
This type of consumption is attributed to the American economist Th. B. Veblen.

Ounce (oz) Unze

A measure of weight; 1 oz = 28.35 grams (grammes).

Out of stock (o.s., o/s) ausverkauft, nicht vorrätig, nicht am Lager

Goods are not in the store when requested by a customer; the supplier is unable to supply from stock.

Out-of-stock costs Fehlmengenkosten

Also called stockout costs.

The costs incurred by not having a product in/on stock when a buyer wants to purchase it.

Outbid überbieten

Also called overbid.

To bid more or to make a higher bid, e.g. at an auction.

Outbound telemarketing aktives Telefonmarketing

A firm`s telemarketing activities carried out by trained salespeople who phone customers in order to obtain orders.

Outcome Ergebnis, Resultat

A final product or end result.

Outdoor advertising Außenwerbung, Plakatwerbung

Also called out-of-home advertising.

Advertising by means of posters, painted displays, billboards, spectaculars, illuminated signs, skywriting, minibillboards and other display advertising, eg in malls, on bus stop shelters, in sports arenas, in bus terminals and airports, on the side of cars and trucks, alongside highways, on walls and roofs, etc.

Outgoing invoice Ausgangs-, Verkaufsrechnung

Also called sales invoice.

The invoice issued by the seller of the goods.

Outgoing mail Ausgangspost

Also called outward mail or outgoing post.

Mail sent out from a business.

Outlet Absatzgebiet
Einzelhandelsgeschäft

A sales area or a retail store where goods or services can be sold.

Output (O) Output, Ausbringung, Produktion

Also called production.

All that is produced by an economic unit in a given time period.

Output and costs Produktion und Kosten

Provided that everything else remains constant then unit costs will fall when production/output increases.

Outsell höheren Umsatz haben als

To sell more than somebody else, e.g. A has been outselling B.

Outsize order (OS order) Riesenbestellung

A very large order.

Outsourcing Outsourcing

The process of obtaining, eg raw material, resources from external sources, rather than from within the company.

Outstanding order unerledigter Auftrag

Also called back order or unfulfilled order.

An order that still has to be delivered.

Outwork Heimarbeit

Also called indoor work, cottage industry or homework.

Work done by, usually unskilled, workers (the outworkers) at home.

Over-the-counter (OTC) rezeptfreie, nicht verschreibungspflichtige Medikamente; nicht ethische Arzneimittel

Pharmaceutical products not requiring a physician`s prescription, ie they may be sold over-the-counter, eg in a supermarket.

Overage Bestands-, Warenüberschuß Kassenüberschuß

A situation where physical inventory exceeds the book inventory figures.

A cash excess.

Overcharge (o/c) zu hohe Berechnung, zu viel berechnen

To ask a price for goods or services which is higher than the price stipulated. Overcharges are usually the result of errors and are therefore refunded to the customers. Usually, the customers receive a credit note (C/N).

Overdue überfällig

Also called past due.

Past the time when due for payment.

A situation where the consignment (or the plane or ship etc.) is late in arriving.

Overfull demand Übernachfrage, Nachfrageüberschuß

Also called excess or surplus demand.

A demand level that is higher than the one suppliers can or want to handle.

Overhead Gemeinkosten

Also called overhead cost(s) or overhead expense; indirect cost or indirect expense; or oncost.

The kind of costs which have to be paid regardless of variations in manufacturing or sales volume, e.g. rent, rates, postage, etc., and which are not directly chargeable to any particular unit sold or produced.

There are fixed overheads (e.g. rent) and variable overheads (e.g. telephone expenses).

Overheating (of the economy) Konjunkturüberhitzung

In an overheated economy, too much money is chasing too few goods, leading to price rises (ie inflation). The economy is expanding too rapidly and the country's productive capacity is usually nearing its limit.

Overland transport Überlandverkehr

Transport services provided overland, such as by rail or road.

Overpayment Über(be)zahlung, zu viel gezahlter Betrag

Amount of money received or paid that exceeds the amount due.

Overpriced zu teuer, überbewertet

More than most customers would be prepared to pay for a commodity, service or share.

Overproduction Überproduktion

Also called excess production or overrun.

A situation where the supply of a commodity is greatly in excess of effective demand.

Overrun Überproduktion

Excess production, ie supply of a product is exceeding effective demand.

Oversaving theory Überspartheorie

The theory that oversaving may result in underconsumption.

Overseas agent Auslandsvertreter

An agent in a foreign country who will market your goods for you, using his existing sales base to display and advertise the product. This is often done on consignment. The agent receives a commission and usually assumes the risks of non-payment by the customer; if he does so he is entitled to an extra commission called del credere commission.

Overseas shipment Auslandsversand

The shipment of goods to a foreign country.
When preparing to ship products overseas, the exporter needs to be aware of packing, labelling, documentation and insurance requirements, etc.
The exporter must be sure to follow all shipping requirements to help ensure that the merchandise:
1. is packed correctly so that it arrives in good condition;
2. is labelled correctly to guarantee proper handling of the goods and arrives on time at the right place;
3. is documented correctly to meet domestic and foreign requirements;
4. is insured against damage, loss, or pilferage.

Overseas trade — Außenhandel, Handel mit dem Ausland

Also called foreign trade.

Trade with foreign countries, eg to increase sales and profit.

Overseas visit — Auslandsbesuch

A businessperson`s visit to a company in a foreign country. Whenever a foreign trip is planned, it is imperative to determine its objectives clearly.

Overshopping — ruinöser Wettbewerb wegen zu hoher Ladendichte

Cut-throat competition because there are more shops/stores than are needed; there is a high density of shops.

Overstocking — zu hohe Vorratshaltung

Ordering and storing more than can be sold.

Overtrading — Liquiditätsklemme trotz hoher Rendite, zu starke Unternehmens-expansion (d.h. über durch Betriebskapital gesetzte Grenzen hinaus)

Trade beyond one's capital. A situation in which a business is aiming at a higher production and turnover than is justified by the size of its own working capital. The business expands in such a way and at such a rate that it has liquidity problems, even if it is highly profitable. Cash is not flowing in quickly enough to cover outlay (e.g. rent, wages, costs of materials, etc.). In other words, the inward cash flow is inadequate to service outward cash flow requirements.
Overtrading is generally regarded as one of the most common causes of business failure.

Ownbrand — Hausmarke

Also called house brand or own label.

Goods produced by a manufacturer to the specification of a large retailer who sells the goods under his own brand name.

P

Paasche index Paasche Index

A weighted price index invented by the German economist H. Paasche (1851 - 1925). The index is used to measure price changes over a period, usually a year.

Package (pkg) Kollo, Packstück
Postpaket, Päckchen
Packung
Verpackung
Radio/TV Programm (ohne Werbung)
Werbepaket

A container, as a box or case, in which something is packed. Also called parcel.

An object wrapped in paper or cardboard so that it can be sent by post. Also called parcel or packet.

A group of things tied together or a quantity of merchandise together with its wrapping, ie a number of a particular type of goods have been wrapped and are being sold together, eg a pack of chewing gum.
Other examples are: a six-pack (ie six containers of something, eg beer, wrapped and sold together), a twin-pack (ie two pieces wrapped and sold together, eg toothpaste), a multi-pack (ie several units of something wrapped and sold together, eg several packs of (paper) tissues). Also called pack or packet.

The packaging of objects, ie the protective materials in which they are wrapped before being sold.

A radio or TV program, exclusive of commercials.

A combination of radio or TV programs or commercials offered together to an advertiser, usually at a discount.

Package advertising Werbung in einem Programmpaket

Commercials run in a combination of radio or TV programs.

Package band (Packungs)Banderole

A strip of paper on which an advertisement, announcement, or special offer is printed and which is wrapped around a package.

Package car Waggon für Stückgutladung

A railcar loaded with several less-than-carload (LCL) shipments.

Package deal Pauschalangebot

Also called package offer.

An offer consisting of several parts or conditions. To reach an agreement, all conditions must be accepted. It usually involves concessions and compromises on all sides to arrive at an agreement.

Package delivery service Paketzustelldienst, Lieferdienst

A transportation service offering to move packages which conform to specified size and weight restrictions, either by ground or air.

Package enclosure Packungsbeilage

Also called package insert or in pack.

A free gift, coupon or other promotional piece enclosed in a product`s package.

Package freight Stückgutfracht

Merchandise shipped in less-than-carload (LCL) quantities.

Package holiday Pauschalreise

Also called package tour.

A holiday where the travel, accomodation and sometimes meals are included in the price and paid for in advance.

Package outsert Packungsanhänger

A separate piece of printed material attached to the outside of a package, eg to highlight a special offer.

Package plan Werbepaket

A combination of radio and TV commercial spots offered to advertisers at a special price.

Package store Spirituosenhandlung

In the USA, a store selling sealed bottles or cans of alcoholic beverages for consumption off the business premises.

Packaged good verpackte Ware

Goods packed and wrapped by the producer and usually sold through retail outlets.

Packaging Verpacken
Verpackung

Also called packing.

The activity of putting goods into the wrappers or containers and/or the operation by which commodities are made ready for transportation/carriage, storage and delivery.

The materials in which objects are wrapped before being sold. Packaging protects goods going long distances from damage in transit. While packaging is essential, much of it is thrown away after use, so that packaging materials (e.g. wrapping, containers) should always be kept as cheap as possible. But the goods must be properly protected. Furthermore, packing must be attractive to encourage sales. Also called make-up, wrappage or wrapper.

Packaging and labelling regulations Verpackungs- und Auszeichnungsvorschriften

Legal and other regulations concerning packaging and labelling of products, eg the materials necessary to protect certain products, or the wording required on a product or package.

Packaging design Verpackungsdesign

Also called package design.

Planning and creating the complete form and structure of a product`s package.

Product design is an important factor in market acceptance of a product. From the sales promotion standpoint, packaging design should consider the following points and perform at least the following functions:

1. each package must be so designed as having a good "eye appeal";
2. it must be robust and of convenient shape and size for both the distributor and consumer;
3. the materials used must be environmentally friendly/compatible and strong enough to withstand transit and handling;
4. the colours selected must be appropriate for the product;
5. the name display should be very prominent;
6. the description and instructions for use must be brief but clear;
7. the package should have a strong visual appeal;
8. cultural peculiarities must be observed;
9. the costs should be as low as possible;
10. offer convenience (eg with regard to handling, opening, storage),
11. reduce transport charges,
12. provide the opportunity for re-use,
13. create a favourable product image,
14. establish product differences,
15. promote the corporate identity,
16. attract customers,
17. be suitable for display on shelves or racks,
18. be recycable, etc.

Packaging mix Verpackungsmix

The mixture of packaging elements. The aim is to combine them in such a way as to achieve the greatest effect at minimum costs.
A good packaging mix is one that:
1. protects the product, 2. promotes the product, 3. facilitates the use of the product, 4. provides reuseable value for the customer, 5. satisfies legal requirements, 6. keeps the packaging costs as low as possible, 7. conveys the feeling of quality, 8. ensures that the brand name is easily readable, 9. gives an impression of appropriate size, etc.

Packer Packer/in
Verpackungsunternehmen
Verpackungsmaschine

A person who packs or wraps goods.

A firm which packs goods.

A machine which packs goods.

Packet Paket, Packung

A small parcel or pack.

Packing certificate Verpackungsbescheinigung

A certificate issued and signed by the shipper confirming to the shipping company and the master of the ship that the task of packing the goods and the container have been properly carried out. The document accompanies the goods throughout the voyage.

Packing charges Verpackungskosten

The costs incurred for packing goods, bags, barrels, boxes, cases, crates, containers, etc. The charges will reflect climatic, geographical, economic and cultural considerations.

Packing list Packliste, Versandliste

Also called packing note, packing sheet or packing slip; delivery note, despatch note, or specification.

This is a list of the goods despatched. It is enclosed with the goods and enables the customer to check off each item as he unpacks it and to make sure the order is complete.

Packing slip Packzettel

A list stating the goods which have been packed and indicating that they have been checked. The slip is enclosed with the consignment.

'acking station Packstelle

'he place in a company where the goods are packed for transport.

'age rate Preis für ganzseitige Anzeige, Seitenpreis

ı advertising, the price for a whole page in a publication.

'age traffic Lesevorgänge, Anteil der gelesenen Seiten einer Publikation

'he number of pages in a publication which have actually been read.

'aired comparison test Paarvergleichstest

'est in which respondents have the choice of comparing two products on the basis of ertain attributes which are common to both, thus arriving at the final choice.

'allet Palette, Laderost

ˎ transportable platform used for the mechanical loading, unloading and transport of ;oods. It is a wood or metal framework on which cartons or cases may be stacked and vhich can be picked up by a forklift truck or other mechanical device. Pallets may be eusable or expendable after one trip and are usually owned by the sender.

'allet load Palettenladung

ˎ large number of small boxes loaded on a single pallet.

'alletized consignment palettierte Warensendung

ˎerchandise loaded on pallets and usually covered with shrink-wrapping, ie with a ılastic foil.

Pamphlet Broschüre, Prospekt, Werbeschrift

Also called brochure, folder, handout or leaflet.

A small printed folder, sometimes with charts or photographs, used to promote a product, service, organization or idea.

Pan-European marketing gesamteuropäisches Marketing

A marketing strategy which treats Europe as a single market by selling the same product(s) in the same way throughout Europe.

Panel Testgruppe, Panel Diskussionsrunde

Representative sample of sellers or buyers who provide information on buying, media, consumption habits, etc. Panels are most frequently used in consumer marketing research.

A group of speakers at a meeting.

Panel of experts Expertengruppe

A group of highly qualified persons who give advice on a problem.

Panel research Panelforschung

Research in which the same interviewees/respondents give information on more than one occasion, usually regularly.

Panic buying Angstkauf, Panikkauf

Also called scare buying or purchasing.

A buyer`s behaviour to rush and buy something immediately, whether needed or not, eg because he/she fears that stocks may run out, or prices may rocket (shoot up, skyrocket).

Paper Zeitung

A newspaper, e.g. a financial paper.

Paper sizes Papiermaße

There are many sizes available. The most commonly sizes used are: A sizes (used for office paper); B sizes (used for larger sheets); C sizes (used for envelopes).

Paperboard Pappe

Also called cardboard.

A heavy, stiff, paper-like material, composed of layers of paper, waste paper, or paper-pulp compressed together.

Parallel position Parallelposition

Also called parallel location.

In outdoor advertising, an advertisement`s position parallel to a street or road.

Parallel pricing gleichgerichtete Preisgestaltung, Oligopolpreisbildung

An agreement between producers or traders of similar products to increase their prices by similar amounts at approximately the same time.

Parameter Parameter

A term used in mathematics and statistics. A quantity which remains constant in a given model, function or any other context (e.g. in the equation y = a + bx, x and y are variables and a and b are constants; i.e. a and b are the parameters of the equation).

Parcel delivery Paketzustellung

The delivery of parcels by rail, post or other organizations.

Parcel post Paketpost
Paketsendung

The post office operates a parcel delivery service for parcels up to a certain weight.

The package.

Parcel post receipt Postpaketempfangsschein

A document issued by the Post Office for goods (up to 20 kgs) sent by parcel post. It is both a receipt and evidence of despatch; but it is not a document of title. It is not negotiable and cannot be issued "to order". Goods are released only to the party offering proof of identity as the party named as consignee (receiver).

Parcel(s) office Paketannahme, Paketausgabe, Gepäckabfertigung

Also called parcel(s) receiving office or station.

Office were parcels can be handed in for sending by mail or train or where parcels may be collected/picked up on arrival by the receiver/consignee.

Pareto's law Paretosche Gesetz, Pareto-Effekt

Also called Pareto effect, law of the trivial many and the critical few or eighty-twenty (80-20) law.

The theory of Vilfredo Pareto (1848 -1923), an Italian-Swiss economist, states that there is a tendency for income to be similarly distributed among a population in all countries, regardless of different forms of taxation or their political systems. Only increased production will raise the incomes of the poorer members.

The Pareto (Paretian) optimum/optimality exists when the economy`s resources and output are allocated in such a way that no reallocation can make anyone better off without making someone else worse off. Pareto-optimality is a fundamental criterion in welfare economics.

Other applications of the law include the idea that in most business activities a small percentage of the work force produces the major proportion of output or that 80 % of sales by value will come from 20 % of the customers.

Parity pricing Paritätspreisfestsetzung

A pricing strategy which bases the local price of a commodity on an agreed international price where such exists.

Parity products Paritätsprodukte, gleichwertige Produkte

Products which are basically identical to each other apart from variations such as packing, price, advertising, promotion, etc.

Part delivery Teillieferung

Also called partial delivery, delivery by instal(l)ments or part(ial) shipment.

Delivering or shipping only some items of an order.

Part exchange (Kauf unter) Inzahlungnahme

A purchase where one gives an old product as part of the payment for a new one.

Part load Stückgut, Teilladung
Teilauftrag, Teillieferung

Less than a full load conveyed in a transport unit. In the case of a container it is usually termed "less than container load" (LCL).

A part-order or part delivery.

Part order Teilauftrag
Teillieferung

An order placed for only some items of a larger order.

The delivery of only some items of an order. Also called part(ial) delivery.

Part payment Teilzahlung

Also called partial payment or instal(l)ment.

A person or business pays only a part of an amount which he/it owes to a creditor. Part payment should be distinguished from payment on account/downpayment.

Partial sponsorship Teil-Sendefinanzierung

A radio or TV programme sponsored by more than one advertiser.

Particulars Einzelheiten, Angaben

Also called details.

Detailed facts or full information.

Partly manufactured goods/products halbfertige Waren, unfertige Erzeugnisse, Halbfabrikate

Also called semi-finished products, semi-manufactured goods, unfinished products, work-in process, goods or material in process, or work in progress.

Goods which a business is making but it has not yet finished.

Parts Teile

Fabricated items that are assembled into other products.

Party selling Party-Verkauf, Heimverkauf

A method of direct selling where prospective buyers are invited to parties. The merchandise is demonstrated to a group of the host`s or hostess` friends. The salespeople earn a commission on sales achieved.

Pass-along/-on reader Folgeleser, Mitleser, Sekundärleser

Also called secondary reader.

A reader of a publication who has not bought it, but has obtained it from someone who did.

Passing off Mimicry, Ähnlichkeitsstrategie, Fast-Nachahmung, "Mitreiten"

Packaging or naming a product in such a way that it resembles a famous brand, and is bought in mistake for this brand.

Patent (pat) Patent

A licence from the Patent Office giving the applicant (the patentee) the sole rights (the patent rights) to an invention or new process. The period covered by a UK patent is 16 years. The rules in other countries are very similar. The Patent Office also deals with the registration of trademarks and trade names.

Note: An invention is patentable if it is a useful, novel, and nonobvious process, machine, manufacture, or composition of matter.

Patent application Patentanmeldung

The activity or process of a prospective pantentee to apply for a patent at the patent office.

Patent infringement Patentverletzung

Also called infringement of patent.

The illegal production or sale of a product which is patented.

Patentee Patentinhaber

Also called holder, owner or proprietor of a patent.

A person or firm holding a patent.

Patentor Patentgeber

A person or firm granting a patent.

Patron (Stamm)Kunde
Gast
Förderer

A person who is a customer, especially a regular one, of a store, or the like.

A paying guest in a hotel.

A person who supports with money or efforts, eg a charity.

Patronage Kundschaft

Also called clientele or custom.

The customers, eg of a shop, considered collectively.

Patronage discount/rebate Treuerabatt

Also called loyalty discount.

A reward given to a loyal buyer by a seller for the regular purchase or use of certain products or services.

Patronage-oriented pricing Preisbildung, die sich an der Kundschaft orientiert

A strategy of setting prices for services at a level that will maximise the number of customers using the service.

Pattern (patt) Muster

A sample, a decorative design, a distinctive model or form.

Pattern book Musterbuch

Also called sample book or book of samples.

A book showing patterns of design, materials, etc.

Patterned interview strukturierte Befragung

In an interview, an interviewer`s practice to ask preset questions which follow a fixed pattern.

Pawnbroker Pfandleiher

Also called money-lender.

A person (the pawnee) who is licensed to lend money against the security of goods (called a pledge) deposited. The pawner/pawnor receives a pawn ticket or pawn receipt. The goods may be sold after a certain time if the loan (plus interest) is not repaid. The pawnbroker is also a dealer in second-hand goods (which he sells in a pawnshop).

Pawner/pawnor Pfandbesteller, Vorpfänder

In pawnbroking, the borrower who receives a pawn ticket from the pawnee.

Pawnee Pfandinhaber

A person who is licensed to lend money at interest to someone against the security of goods, ie a pledge, deposited.

Pay desk Kassenschalter, Kasse

Also called cashier's desk or teller's counter.

The place in a store where one pays for goods or services bought.

Pay TV Münzfernsehen, Pay-TV

Television programmes distributed over the air or by cable, for which subscribers pay on an individual programme basis.

Pay-per-view (PPV) Pay per View; Abo-TV, bei dem nur Einschaltzeit bezahlt wird

A TV service that charges viewers only for the programme watched.

Payable in easy terms zahlbar in bequemen Raten

A method of payment where the buyer may pay in small instalments.

Payable on delivery (pod) zahlbar bei Lieferung

Also called payment on delivery (POD).

Payment has to be made when the goods are delivered.

Payable on demand zahlbar bei Aufforderung/Verlangen

Payment must be effected when it is asked for.

Payment (PYT, payt, pt) Zahlung (bezahlte Summe)
(Be-, Ein-, Aus-) Zahlung

The amount of money which a person or business pays, wholly or in part, to someone else for goods or services.

The act of paying or being paid.

Payment after delivery Zahlung nach Lieferung

The goods are paid after they have been delivered (e.g. 10 days 2 %, 30 days net; 2/10, n/30).

Payment date Zahlungstermin

Also called date or day of payment.

The date on which a payment has to be made.

Payment in advance Vorauszahlung, Vorauskasse

Also called advance payment, prepayment, anticipation or anticipatory payment; if payment is made in cash or by cheque/check, it is also called cash in advance (cia).

Payment made in advance of the production or shipment of goods.

Payment in full Zahlung in voller Höhe

Paying the whole amount of money owed to someone.

Payment in kind (PIK) Sachleistung

Payment in the form of goods and services rather than with money.

Payment on account Abschlagszahlung, Akontozahlung

Also called downpayment.

A payment made by a debtor of only part of an amount owed, usually coupled with an agreement to repay the balance on a specified date.

Payment on invoice Zahlung bei Erhalt der Rechnung

Payment is due as soon as the buyer receives an invoice, which may be before the goods are delivered, or at the same time, or after they are delivered. This method is often used for a single sale.

Payment on open account Zahlung in offener Rechnung

In domestic trade, a credit relationship between buyer and seller, i.e. the seller sells on credit and the buyer pays on receipt of the invoice or after an agreed period of credit.

Payment on statement Zahlung bei Erhalt des Kontoauszugs

Payment is due when the buyer receives a statement (of account) or at an agreed later date.

Payment terms Zahlungsbedingungen, -modalitäten

Also called terms of payment.

The conditions agreed between parties for the payment of goods or services, e.g. due within 30 days and 2 % discount allowed if paid within 10 days. These terms are usually demanded or proposed by the seller and either they are accepted by the buyer or different terms are arranged by negotiation.
The main methods used are:
1. cash or payment with order; 2. cash or payment on delivery; 3. prompt cash; 4. payment after delivery; 5. payment on invoice or statement; 6. monthly or quarterly account; 7. open account; 8. transfer; 9. bill of exchange; 10. documents against payment or cash; 11. documents against acceptance; 12. letter of credit; 13. acceptance credit, etc.

Payphone Münzfernsprecher

Also called pay telephone.

A public telephone which is coin operated.

Peak business hours Hauptsgeschäftszeit

Also called peak hours.

Those hours of the day when certain activities are at their maximum.

Peak demand Spitzennachfrage

Also called top-out.

The period in which the maximum demand for a product or service is attained.

Peak period Stoßzeit

The time of the day or year when traffic, use, or demand is greatest and charges, fares, etc, are highest.

Peak price Spitzenpreis, Höchstpreis (Höchstkurs)

Also called highest or top price.

A very high price for a commodity, service or security which results from peak demand.

Peak time Hauptsendezeit

Also called peak viewing time (TV) or prime time.

The period of the day when the highest number of people are viewing TV or listening to the radio so that the highest price for advertising time is charged.

Peak year Spitzenjahr

A company`s successful or best year, eg because sales were top and/or profits very high.

Peanuts "Kleinvieh", lächerliche Summe, Pfennigbeträge

A negligible amount of something, usually money; a very small wage.

Pedestrian precinct Fußgängerzone

Also called pedestrian mall or shopping precinct.

That part of a town which is closed to traffic so that people can walk about and shop.

Pedlar Hausierer, ambulanter Händler

Also called peddler, doorstep salesman, hawker, huckster or itinerant peddler.

A pedlar is a trader who carries his wares about and sells to the customer at his own front door.

Peer group Peer Group

Also called friendship group.

Class of people who are held in high esteem by others, i.e. they regard them as their peers.

Pegged price subventionierter Preis

Also called supported price.

A subsidised selling price.

Pegging Preisstützung, Kursstützung

Also called price support or supporting the market.

Stabilizing the price of a security, commodity or currency by manipulating or regulating the market.

Pelmet Werbedeckenanhänger im Schaufenster

Promotional material attached to the top edge of a shop window.

Penalty Strafe

A punishment imposed for a violation of rule or law.

A loss incurred by nonfulfillment of an obligation.

Penetration — Durchdringung, Marktdruchdringung, Penetration
Marktanteil, Penetrationsgrad
Werbedurchschlagskraft

The share of a target market occupied by a brand or product, usually expressed as a percentage.

The percentage of individuals or organisations in a particular market who have bought a specific product in a given time period. Also called market share.

The effectiveness of advertising in reaching and persuading the advertising audience.

Penetration pricing — Penetrationspreispolitik

Exactly the opposite of price skimming.

The strategy to force a high market share through low prices. This pricing policy is often used when a new product is launched/introduced.

But this policy can only be valid if the market is very price-sensitive (a very important determinant of the product price), and/or if production costs fall significantly in line with volume increase, and/or if competitors will be discouraged.
If penetration targets are achieved and competitive activity has been restricted the problem of whether to raise prices (this is possible as there is a heavy demand for the product) or to reduce profit margins to intermediaries/middlemen might arise.

Note: penetration pricing does not employ profit maximization as the chief goal but focuses on the demand side of the market.

Penny (p) — Penny (Münze) (GB)
Centstück (USA)

The plural is pence (quantity) or pennies (individual coins).

A currency unit of the United Kingdom - one hundredth part of a pound (£).

A popular name for the one-cent coin of the USA.

Penny-off or penny-down-price — psychologischer, gebrochener Preis

The offering of an item a fraction below the calculated price to make it look cheaper, e.g. $ 9.99 (instead of $ 10.00).

Peoplemeter Zuschauerzähler

A device attached to a TV set that records the audience, the person who is watching and the channel to which the TV set is tuned.

Per capita pro Kopf

Per head, as in per capita income or per capita consumption.

Per capita consumption Pro-Kopf-Verbrauch

The total amount consumed divided by the number of people involved.

Per capita expenditure Pro-Kopf-Ausgaben

The total amount of money spent divided by the number of people involved.

Per capita income Pro-Kopf-Einkommen

Also called per head income.

The income per head/per capita, normally defined as the national income devided by the total population.

Per capita output Pro-Kopf-Leistung

The gross national product (GNP) of a nation divided by its population.

Per cent/percent (P/C) Prozent

Figure expressed as a part of one hundred, e.g. 10 % = 10/100.

Per mille (‰, per mil) Promille, vom Tausend

This means by the thousand, e.g. 10 ‰ = 10/1000.

Perceived purchase risk wahrgenommenes Kaufrisiko

The level of risk experienced by an individual when purchasing a product or service. The perceived risk may be physical (eg is the product safe?), financial (eg can I pay the instalments?), or social (eg am I showing off if I buy this product?).

Perceived value pricing (PVP) subjektive Preisbildung, Preisbildung aus Kundensicht, Preisbildung anhand des wahrgenommenen Wertes

This method is sometimes known as "what the market will bear".

A pricing method based on the product`s perceived value. This means that the firm sees the buyers` perception of value as the key to pricing rather than the product`s cost. Furthermore, this method ignores competition.

In order to maximize sales and profit we need to price within the perceived value price band. Pricing below the PVP band leads to a loss of sales and profit while pricing above the band leads to an even more rapid decrease in profit and sales.

Once the PVP is determined the price is then compared to cost to determine whether we will achieve a satisfactory profit level. If so,we can proceed and if not then we have to consider whether we want the business at that profit level, whether we can reduce our costs or whether we abandon the business.

Note: 1. to use this pricing strategy, the seller has to build up perceived value in the buyers` minds, 2. the seller has to accurately determine the buyers` perception of the offer`s value in order not to overprice or underprice the product.

Clearly the market leader always has the best perception of value because the best value gets the maximum sales.

Percent(age) of sales method Methode des erwarteten Umsatzes (bei Festsetzung des Werbeetats)

Also called percentage of anticipated turnover method.

The method of setting the advertising/promotion budget by forecasting sales for the next year and by making the budget equal to some percentage of that figure.

Percentage change Prozentsatzänderung

A change, eg in price or quantity, on a percentage basis of past data from one point in time to the next (or compared with a point in the past as reference).

Perception Wahrnehmung

The process of becoming aware of something.

Perceptual map Wahrnehmungslandkarte

Also called position map or connotative map.

A map or diagram displaying or graphing, in two or more dimensions, the location of products or brands in customers` minds.

Perfect competition vollständige Konkurrenz, vollständiger Wettbewerb

For competition to be perfect, the following conditions are necessary:
1. buyers regard the product as homogeneous (ie all sellers must be selling exactly the same kind of product);
2. there are a large number of independent actual and potential buyers and sellers (ie buyers and sellers must be unable to affect price);
3. there are no barriers to the entry of new firms (ie it must be possible for any firm to enter the market and add to the supply);
4. firms aim to maximize their profits;
5. consumers aim to maximize their utility and will have no undue preference for some goods;
6. there is perfect knowledge (ie transparency) on the part of buyers and sellers.

In conditions of perfect competition, entrepreneurs take it for granted that the price to be obtained for their goods will be the market price. They have thus no incentive to restrict output.

Perfect elasticity unendliche Elastizität

A situation which occurs when the quantity of goods supplied or demanded varies with no change in the price.

Demand is perfectly/infinitely price elastic if an infinitely small change in price results in an infinitely great change in demand, ie consumers cease to buy at all if prices rise fractionally.

Supply is perfectly price elastic if any amount will be supplied at the prevailing price.

Perfect inelasticity unendliche Unelastizität

A situation which occurs when the quantity of goods supplied or demanded does not change at all when price changes.

Note: 1. the demand curve shows up as a straight-line vertical demand curve;
2. the supply curve shows up as a straight-line vertical supply curve.

Perfect market Markt mit vollkommenem Wettbewerb

In such a market the buyer is indifferent from whom he buys and the seller is indifferent to whom he sells. In this market there is only one price for the same quality of similar goods.

Perfect oligopoly homogenes Oligopol

Also called pure oligopoly.

A market containing only a small number of producers who produce identical/homogeneous products. The only way producers can compete is by varying the price of their product. There is imperfect competition and only one price is possible in the market. A change in the price of one producer is followed by a change in the prices of the others (e.g. if the price of producer A is lowered, then the price of his competitors will also be lowered to maintain their sales; similarly, a rise in price by producer A would be followed by a rise in price of his competitors).
Generally, price leadership will be with the largest producer.

Perfectly elastic demand vollkommen elastische Nachfrage

Also called infinitely elastic demand.

If demand is perfectly elastic, an infinitely small change in price results in an infinitely great change in demand, ie consumers cease to buy at all if price rises fractionally (ie elasticity = ∞, infinite).
For example, when the coefficient of elasticity is infinite, a small increase in price leads to demand falling away to nothing.
Note: such a demand curve is shown as a horizontal line.

Perfectly inelastic demand vollkommen unelastische Nachfrage

Also called absolutely or completely inelastic demand.

Demand is perfectly inelastic if the same quantity is demanded whatever the price (ie elasticity = 0). A coefficient of elasticity equal to zero shows that the quantity demanded remains unchanged whatever the price.
Note: such demand curves are vertical lines.

Performance Gebrauchsfähigkeit
Aufführung

In marketing, a high level of capability in a product.

An entertainment presented before an audience.

Periodical Zeitschrift, Magazin

A publication which appears at regular intervals, e.g. weekly, monthly, etc.

Peripheral service Nebenleistung

Supplementary services that a company provides to its customers.

Perishables leicht verderbliche Güter

Also called perishable goods.

Food or other goods which can go bad easily.

Perished goods verdorbene Güter, Waren

Also called damaged or unsound goods.

Goods which have become commercially worthless, eg because they went bad, decayed, were ruined or destructed. .

Permanent-income hypothesis permanente Einkommen-Hypothese

Also called life-cycle hypothesis.

This theory states that household consumption expenditures are related to permanent income and are not affected by the current level of income.

Perpetual inventory permanente, laufende Inventur

Also called perpetual or continuous stocktaking; book, permanent or running inventory.

A stock control system involving constant checks on stock levels (either their quantity or value). Every inflow or outflow is recorded so that the firm knows the composition of its inventory at all times.

Persistent demand anhaltende, stetige Nachfrage

A market situation where there is a continuous or stable demand for a product or service.

Persistent dumping Dauerdumping

Aso called international price discrimination.

The continuous selling of goods in foreign markets at lower prices than in domestic markets.

Persistent inflation Dauerinflation, schleichende Inflation

Also called creeping inflation.

A slow, but continuous inflation; a process of gently rising prices.

Person marketing Personenmarketing, Werbung für eine Einzelperson

The marketing activites undertaken to create, maintain, or alter awareness, attitudes or behaviour favourably towards particular persons, eg celebrities such as politicians or entertainers.

Personal assistant (PA) persönlicher Assistent

A person who is appointed to help a manager or director.

Personal buying decision persönliche Kaufentscheidung

A buyer`s personal decision to purchase a product or service. A buyer`s purchase decisions are highly influenced by his/her unique set of cultural, social, psychological, and personal factors. The latter consist of the buyer`s personal characteristics such as age and life cycle stage, occupation, economic circumstances, lifestyle, personality, self-concept, etc.

Personal consumption expenditure privater Verbrauch

The aggregate/total amount spent each year by consumers to buy goods and services.

Personal interview persönliche(s) Befragung, Interview Vorstellungsgespräch

In market research, a direct form of investigation, in which an interviewer obtains information from selected respondents on a face-to-face basis, e.g. at their homes, in the street or at work. Normally, the interview is structured around a formal questionnaire.

Advantages of this interviewing method are:
1. the interviewer can encourage the respondent to answer each question in the questionnaire,
2. the interviewer can explain the reasons for the survey,
3. mistakes in answering the questions can be dealt with immediately,
4. a good interviewer can add assessments of the respondents
5. it yields a high percentage of acceptable responses,
6. there is a low refusal rate,
7. the information can be accurate, as the interviewer can immediately clarify misunderstandings or contradictory statements,
8. personal questions can be asked,
9. the interviewer can interfere when incorrect information is given deliberately, etc.

The drawbacks of the personal interview method are:
1. it is expensive,
2. there are difficulties in finding respondents who have the desired characteristics,
3. the interviewers themselves must be carefully selected,
4. the interviewer may influence the answers given,
5. the respondents may deliberately give incorrect or inaccurate answers,
6. the number of interviews per time period, eg a day is restricted, etc.

In personnel management, a formal meeting in which one or more persons assess the personal qualities of a job candidate. Also called interview or job interview.

Personal letter persönlicher Brief

In dircct mail, a letter containing the addressee`s name in the salutation and personally signed by the sender.

Personal selling persönlicher Verkauf

Selling to a customer by face-to-face contact between buyer and seller. This enables buyers to ask questions and salespeople to adjust their sales messages to suit the needs of particular buyers.

Personalised mailing personalisiertes Mailing

In direct mail, the mailing of letters to people by name.

Personality Persönlichkeit
(Waren)Profil

The distinctive character of an individual.

A famous or prominent person. Also called celebrity.

The distinctive character of a product.

Personality promotion Prominentenwerbung

Promotion which makes use of celebrities in order to market an idea, product or service.

Persons using television (PUT) Zahl der effektiven Fernsehzuschauer

The number of persons, expressed as a percentage, who are viewing television in a given area during a specific time.

Persuasive advertising überredende, überzeugende, aggressive, kämpferische Werbung

Also called combative or competitive advertising.

This type of advertising is aimed solely at consumers and tries to persuade them to buy the advertiser's product rather than his competitor's by emphazising the distinctive characteristics of his product. Persuasive ad becomes important in the competitive stage, where a company's aim is to build selective demand for a particular brand. Some persuasive ad has moved into the category of comparison advertising.

PEST factor PEST-Faktor

PEST factors cover political (eg stability), economic (eg infrastructure, taxation), social (eg lifestyles) and technological (eg research and development) factors which may effect decision-making, such as whether to launch a new product or export to a specific foreign country.

Petties kleine Auslagen

A term sometimes used on an invoice for minor charges made for various small items not separately enumerated.

Petty cash (P/C) kleine Kasse, Nebenkasse

A small amount of money kept in a business (often in a petty cash box) to pay small debts. The payments made are recorded in a petty cash book.

Petty cash voucher Barzahlungsbeleg

A receipt for payments of petty cash.

Phone book Telefonbuch

Also called telephone directory.

A book which lists names, addresses and phone numbers of people and companies.

Phonecard Telefonkarte

The card looks rather like a credit card and has charge units which are erased automatically from the track during the call. Phonecards can only be used with cardphones.

Physical distribution (PD) Warenverteilung, physische Distribution

The storage, handling and movement of goods within a company and their shipment to customers, via various channels of distribution. In other words, PD is concerned with getting the right product to the right place at the right time in good condition and at reasonable costs.

The four important aspects of PD are: 1. warehousing, 2. transportation, 3. inventory management, and 4. order processing.

Pickup and delivery service Abhol- und Zustelldienst

A service which takes goods from the warehouse and delivers them to the customer.

Picture card Bildkarte, Sammelkarte

In sales promotion, cards given with products in order to induce regular purchases and create brand loyalty. To encourage collection, albums can be bought or are supplied free of charge (foc).

Pie chart Kreisdiagramm

Also called circle, circular, sector or wheel chart or diagram.

A diagram showing the relative sizes of the components of some quantity by means of a circle cut up into sections of different sizes.

Piggyback (service) Huckepackladung
Huckepackverkehr, Kombiverkehr

In transportation, putting one load on top of another.

The transportation of lorry/truck trailers and containers on flat rail cars from terminal to terminal; a combination of rail and lorry cargo transport. Also called trailer on flat car (TOFC), rail transport of trailers or rail-trailer shipment.

Piggyback commercial Huckepackspot

A commercial advertising more than a single product or service.

Piggyback export scheme Huckepacksystem
Vertretung kleiner Firmen durch große (Außenhandel)

Also called piggybacking.

Large export firms, in cooperation with trade associations (e.g. the Confederation of British Industry, CBI), assist small firms unused to the export field.

A small company's products are exported by a larger company that carries complementary products.

Pigou effect Pigou-Effekt, realer Kassenhaltungseffekt

Also called real balance effect or wealth effect.

Named after the English economist A.C. Pigou (1877 - 1959), the Pigou effect describes the way in which the value of money varies in direct proportion to systematic movements in prices. According to Pigou, consumption is not solely a function of income. When the price level falls the real value of money increases and consumption may well increase. Thus aggregate demand may increase with falling prices.

An economy with flexible prices will therefore always return automatically to full employment in the long run. When unemployment exists, prices will decline, and holders of liquid money will be better off in real terms and increase their consumption, thus stimulating demand and increasing income and employment. This effect exists, but it has never been indisputably identified in action.

Pile of goods Warenstapel

A lot of goods put one on top of the other.

Pilferage geringfügiger Diebstahl

Stealing/pilfering in small amounts.

Pilot plant Pilotanlage, Versuchsanlage

Also called demonstration plant.

A small-scale production plant for a new product used to test methods of production and the marketability of the new product.

Pilot study Leitstudie, Pilotstudie

Also called exploratory or preliminary study.

A limited research untertaking designed as a preliminary test of the hypotheses and methods of a subsequent major project.

Pilot survey Probeerhebung

Also called exploratory survey.

Trial run for a survey or other research project to ensure that all aspects such as the sampling scheme, questionnaire and analysis work properly and as planned, and provide the required information.

Pint Pint, Pinte (Flüssigkeits-, und Trockenmaß)

A measure of capacity used for both liquid and dry goods.
One liquid pint = 0,57 litre (GB), 0,473 liter (US).
One US dry pint = 0,55 liter.

Pioneer pricing Pionierpreisfestlegung

A pricing method where a company sets the base price for a new product.

Pioneer(ing) advertising Initialwerbung, Einführungswerbung

Advertising that increases the primary demand for a product or service, ie advertising that converts nonusers into users.

A type of advertising that informs potential consumers about what a product is, what it can do, how it can be used, and where it can be bought.

Pioneering stage Einführungsphase

In the product life cycle (PLC), an early period during which the pioneers are trying to build primary demand for the new type of product.

Place Ort, Platz

A location or position.

In the marketing mix, one of the four Ps, the others being product, price and promotion.

Place marketing Standortmarketing

The marketing activities undertaken to create, maintain, or alter awareness, attitudes or behaviour favourably towards particular places or areas, eg holiday resorts.

Place of acceptance (POA) Annahmeort

The place where something is accepted, eg the place where goods are received for transport by a carrier.

Place of delivery (POD) Lieferort

Also called delivery place or point of delivery.

The place where freight/cargo is delivered. Often the place of fulfil(l)ment.

Place of destination Bestimmungsort

The final destination, ie the place to which a person or thing travels or is sent.

Place of final use Verbrauchsort

The place where goods, eg imported from abroad, are finally used up.

Place of fulfil(l)ment Erfüllungsort, Ort der Leistung

Also called place of performance.

The place where an obligation has to be fulfilled, e.g. in a sales contract the place where the goods have to be delivered.

Place of payment Zahlungsort

The place where something is or has to be paid by a debtor.

Place of receipt (POR) Empfangsort

The place where something is received.

Place of transshipment Umladeplatz

The place where goods are transshipped/reloaded from one vehicle to another.

Place utility räumlicher Nutzen eines Gutes

The value given to a product by virtue of the fact that is available at the place consumers want.

Placement test Laden-Test, Store-Test

Before launching a new product, a test where different versions of the product are tested in carefully selected shops (usually 10-30) and with different types of consumers to collect information on performance and attitudes towards them.

Plain cover neutraler Umschlag

An envelope with no company name printed on it.

Planned obsolescence geplantes Veralten

A company`s tactic to design and introduce a new product whose life cycle will be ended by the already-planned introduction of another product or model, short-run material wearout, style changes, functional changes, etc.

Planning Planung

Planning is a very essential element of management which is concerned with:
1. what is to be done, 2. when it is to be done, 3. where it is to be done, 4. who is to do it and 5. how it is to be done.

Planning forces management:
1. to think ahead systematically, 2. to prepare for unforeseen eventualities, 3. to clarify objectives, 4. to coordinate projects, 5. to decide on future activities in advance, 6. to recognise their own strengths and weaknesses, etc. Furthermore, planning might reveal: 7. duplications of effort, 8. avoid foreseeable pitfalls, 9. identify opportunities for greater efficiency and profitability, etc.

Plans should be as detailed as possible, necessary and financeable, but should not extend too far into the future since accurate prediction of the distant future is difficult or even impossible.

Possible forms of planning are: top-down planning and bottom-up planning.

Plant Betrieb(sanlage), Fabrik, Produktionsanlage, Werk

A plant is the physical unit (e.g. a factory) performing productive activities in the output of goods and services.

Plant capacity Betriebskapazität

Also called factory or operating capacity.

The entire production capacity of a plant.

Plastic money Kreditkarte, Plastikgeld

A term often used for credit cards or ATM (automated teller machine) cards.

Plateau pricing Durchschnittspreiskalkulation

A pricing method, where the seller sets a medium price for a product because some of the raw materials processed into it are subject to wide price fluctuations.

Pledgee Pfandinhaber(in), Pfandnehmer(in)

Someone to whom something is pledged.

Pledger/pledgor Pfandgeber(in), Pfandschuldner(in)

Someone who deposits personal property as a pledge.

Plug — Werbung für ein(e) neue(s) Produkt/Firma
Schleichwerbung

Advertising a new product or firm.

A free on-air mention of a product or firm.

Plunge in prices — Preissturz, Kurssturz

Also called collapse of prices; sharp or sudden fall in prices or quotations.

A situation where prices fall/plunge/plummet suddenly and very steeply.

Point elasticity — Punktelastizität

The point on the demand curve which denotes the amount demanded at a particular price. Theoretically elasticity should be measured at a particular price since elasticity changes with price.

Point of sale system (POSS) — Daten(erfassungs)kasse, POS-System

Also called POS system or POS terminal (POST).

An online electronic terminal located in a retail outlet that receives and stores bar code information derived from sales transactions and that allows for transfer of funds between accounts at the time of buying.

Point-of-purchase (POP) — Einkaufsort
Verkaufsförderungsmaterial

Place at which a purchase is made.

Promotional material used at the POP and designed to attract consumer interest or call attention to a special offer.

Point-of-purchase (POP) display — POP-Werbeauslage, Werbeauslage am Verkaufsort

Promotional display material set up at the retailer`s location to advertise the products, attract traffic, or induce impulse purchases.

Point-of-sale (POS) — Verkaufsort
Verkaufsförderungsmaterial

Place at which a sale is made, e.g. a retail sales outlet.

Promotional material used at the POS, e.g. posters, showcards, leaflets, etc.

Point-of-sale (POS) material — Promotion-/Verkaufsförderungs-material am Verkaufsort

Also called point-of-purchase (POP) material.

POS material consists of all kinds of promotional aids displayed in retail shops to promote sales of particular products.
There are: 1. internal and 2. external displays.
1. Internal displays may comprise:
showcards, mobiles, posters, pelmets, dump bins, wire stands, dummy packs, clocks, models, working models, illuminated displays, dispensers, display outers, window stickers, window displays, display racks, shelf edgings, cash mats, crowners, coasters, wrapping paper, carrier bags, menu cards, sales literature, etc.
2. External POS material may consist of:
billboards, shop facias, metal signs, flags, pavement standing signs, etc.

POS material helps to attract attention, to inform customers, and to encourage retailers to carry particular products.

Point-of-sale advertising (POSA) — Werbung am Verkaufsort, POS-Werbung

Also called POS advertising or point-of-purchase (POPA) advertising.

Advertising at the point of sale, i.e. the place at which the customer makes the ultimate decision to purchase: at the shop counter.

Point-of-sale terminal (POST) — Kassenterminal, POS-Terminal

Also called POS system (POSS).

An online terminal located in a retail shop that allows customers to use a plastic card to transfer funds from their bank account to that of the retail shop.

POISE POISE-Formel

In offensive marketing, a formula for marketing which is profitable, offensive, integrated, strategic, and effectively executed.

Political environment politisches Umfeld

Laws, regulations, pressure groups, etc that influence, restrict or prohibit activities in a given society.

Poll Befragung, Umfrage

Also called public opinion survey.

An investigation into what customers think on a certain product or service.

Pollution (Umwelt)Verschmutzung

Contamination of the air, water, land, or environment in which life exists.

Polypoly Polypol

A market where many sellers/suppliers and buyers/demanders meet.

Pool Kartell, Pool, monopolistischer Zusammenschluß

A type of monopoly. A combination, usually loose, sometimes temporary, of competitive firms for the purpose of control of prices, markets, output, etc. Their motivation is to lessen or eliminate competition.
Such poolings are generally outlawed by the Antitrust Law (USA), the Restrictive Trade Practices Act (GB), the Kartellgesetz (Germany), etc.

Pool selling Absatz durch ein Kartell

The sale of goods or services through a cartel.

Pooling of orders Zusammenfassen von Aufträgen, Auftragspoolung

An arrangement within a merger or cartel whereby all orders are dealt with and carried out from a central office.

Popular press Boulevardpresse

Publications that contain more entertainment than information.

Popular price gängiger Preis

Also called going rate or sal(e)able price.

A price intended to appeal to a majority of buyers.

Popular pricing populäre Preispolitik

A pricing technique which tries to fix prices (popular prices) appealing to a majority of buyers.

Population (Popn) Bevölkerung, Einwohnerzahl

The total number of persons inhabiting a country, city or any particular area.

Population characteristics Populationsmerkmale

Important marketing variables, including age, education, gender, income, marital status, nationality, race, religion, etc.

Portfolio analysis Portfolioanalyse

A company`s technique of individually assessing and positioning every business unit and/or product.

Positioning Positionierung

Also called market positioning.

Placing a product into its desired market position and to have it perceived in that way by consumers.

Positive income elasticity positive Einkommenselastizität

An income elasticity prevailing when an increase in consumers` income leads to an increase in demand.

Positive rate of time preference positive Zeitpräferenzrate

The desire of consumers for goods now rather than in the future. This means that people subjectively value goods obtained in the present or near future more highly than goods obtained in the distant future.

Post Post
Brief-, Postkasten
Postamt
versenden

The material sent or received by post. Also called mail.

A postal letter box/mailbox.

The Post Office.

To dispatch mail. Also called to mail.

Post Office (PO) Post

A means for transmitting information or payment from one person or firm to another. The first postal service in England was established as long ago as 1635, and in 1710 a post office was opened in London.
In addition to the ordinary postal service, the Post Office often provides in many countries a variety of other services, e.g.: express letters, business reply service, cash on delivery, registration of letters, recorded delivery, franking; postal orders, money orders, giro service, fax facilities, etc.

Post office box (POB) Postschließfach, Postfach

Also called PO Box or private box.

Mail is usually delivered to the addressee by the postman. Firms wishing to collect their mail at times convenient to them may do so through the private box service. This enables the firm to hire a box in the Post Office from which their mail can be collected. This service enables a firm to ensure that mail is collected, opened and distributed to departments early in the day.

Post office receipt Posteinlieferungsschein

Also called postal receipt or certificate of posting.

A transport document for goods despatched by parcel post. It provides details and confirmation of despatch of the goods.

Post paid freigemacht, frankiert

Also called post free or postage free or paid.

In a price quotation, postage is included in the price quoted and will be paid by the seller.

Postage Porto

Also called postal rate.

The amount of money one has to pay for the transport of letters and parcels.

Postage and handling (P+H) Porto und Bearbeitung

A charge made to cover the costs of postal delivery and its preparation.

Postage and packing (p&p) Porto und Verpackung

A charge made to cover the costs of postal delivery and packaging.

Postage book Portobuch

A book used to record postage. Today most firms use franking machines for their outgoing mail; but to record items which have not been franked firms often use a postage book.

Postage due Nachporto

Also called additional or extra postage, or surcharge.

An additional postage on mail which is collectible on delivery to the addressee.

Postage saver Drucksachenumschlag

Also called penny saver.

An envelope used for printed matter mailings.

Postal address Postanschrift

Also called inside address.

The postal address consists of the house number and street; place of destination; the name of of the county, state, or province; and the post/postal code (GB) or zip code (USA). Should the addressee have a post office box (POB), the POB number replaces the house number and the street.
Note: in foreign mail, the name of the country of destination should be added.

Postal charges Postgebühren

Also called mailing charges.

Charges for the mailing of letters and parcels.

Postal questionnaire Fragebogen, verschickt durch die Post; postalischer Fragebogen

Also called postal inquiry, mail interview or mail survey.

In marketing, an interviewing method where the questionnaire is sent out to respondents through the post/mail for self-completion and return.

Characteristics of this method are:
1. no need for trained interviewers,
2. much cheaper than personal interviews,
3. questions must be put in an elementary manner and require as little writing as possible on the part of the respondent (there is no interviewer to help),
4. questions usually require a simple "yes" or "no" answer, or the respondent is provided several alternative answers to each question and is asked to put a mark against the one he considers applicable,
5. only about one respondent in ten will take the trouble to respond.

Postal terms Posttermini

Special terms used by the post office.
Examples are: (by) Airmail; express delivery; poste restante (special delivery); printed matter; please forward; if undelivered, return to ...; urgent; personal (this letter may only be opened by the addressee); confidential; addressee unknown; cash on delivery (COD); excess postage; reverse charge; do not bend/fold; fragile; caution; return receipt; handle with care; declared valuation; return to sender; moved, address unknown; self-addressed or stamped and addressed envelope (SAE); postage; international (postal) reply coupon; under separate cover (by the same mail); post code (zip code, USA); post office box (POB, PO Box); etc.

Postcode Postleitzahl (GB)

Also called postal number, postal code or zip code (US).

A group of letters and figures included in an address to assist Post Office sorting.

Poste restante postlagernd

Also called general delivery or to be called for.

Letters and parcels to be called for may be addressed to any post office with the words "To be called for" or "Poste Restante" as part of the address. The letters etc. will be kept at the post office until collected by the person to whom they are addressed.

Poster Plakat, Poster
Absender

A placard displayed in public place. Poster advertising is very popular. Also called bill.

The sender, e.g. of letters or parcels. Also called consignor.

Poster plant Plakatwerbeunternehmen

A firm specialising in outdoor advertising.

Poster site Plakatanschlagstelle

A place where posters may be posted.

Postindustrial society nachindustrielle Gesellschaft

A society characterised by a rising professional and technical class and a change from a goods-producing to a service economy.

Postmark Poststempel

A mark stamped by the post office on a letter or parcel, showing the postage stamp, the time, date and place.

Postpurchase behaviour Nachkaufverhalten

A buyer`s behaviour after purchasing a product.
In the postpurchase period, the buyer may experience:
1. some level of satisfaction,
2. some level of dissatisfaction.

The buyer`s degree of satisfaction or dissatisfaction with the product will influence his/her subsequent behaviour, eg a satisfied buyer may repurchase the product, whereas a dissatisfied buyer will tend to make negative statements about the product. Other forms of postpurchase behaviour are the buyer`s use and disposal of the product.

Postsale service Kundendienst (nach dem Verkauf)

Also called customer service.

The service provided by a seller after the business transaction, eg processing a complaint.

Posttest/post test Posttest

Also called postcampaign test.

A way of testing and evaluating the effectiveness of advertising after an ad campaign.

Potential audience potentielles Publikum

The estimated maximum number of readers, listeners, viewers who have the opportunity of reading a publication, listening to a radio programme, watching TV or seeing an advertisement.

Potential customer Interessent, möglicher Kunde

Also called potential buyer, prospect, or prospective buyer or customer.

A person who could be a customer.

Potential market potentieller Markt
Marktpotential

A market which could be exploited in the future.

All the individuals and companies in a particular market who are interested in a product or service.

Potential viewer (PV) potentieller Zuschauer

The estimated maximum number of persons who have the opportunity of watching TV or seeing an advertisement or commercial.

Pound Pfund

A measure of weight; 1 pound (lb) = 16 ounces = 453,6 grammes (grams). Also called avoirdupois.

The currency unit (£) of Great Britain consisting of one hundred pence. £ is from the medieval Latin abbreviation of libra (plural of librum = pound). Also called Pound Sterling (£).

Some other countries also use the pound as their currency unit (e.g. Egypt (£ E), Malta (£ M), Cyprus (C £), etc.).

Poverty line Armutsgrenze

Also called poverty level.

The level of income at or below which people have the right to receive welfare benefits/public assistance.

Poverty trap Armutsfalle

A situation where an increase in money wages may result in a fall in real income. For example, as earnings rise entitlement to social benefit/welfare aid is either reduced or removed altogether.

Pre-delivery inspection (PDI) Kontrolle vor Warenabnahme

Inspection undertaken prior to taking delivery of the products.

Pre-selling advertising Werbemaßnahmen, die dem Verkauf vorausgehen

All advertising activities run before a product is launched upon the market.

Preapproach Besuchsplanung

In the selling process, the stage in which a salesperson prepares his/her actual meeting with a customer.

Preaudit Schlußprüfung vor Lieferung

The verification of sales transactions before delivery.

Precaution Vorsichtsmaßnahme, Vorsicht

Special care taken to prevent a loss, damage or risk.

Preclusive buying Ausschlußkauf

Also called preclusive purchasing.

The buying of materials to prevent someone else from buying.

Predatory dumping räuberisches Dumping, Eroberungsdumping

The strategy of temporarily selling exported products in another country below the normal price of the products in the exporter`s domestic/home market, with the aim of driving/freezing local producers or foreign competitors/rivals out of the market. After freezing rivals out of the market, the price is raised/increased to its previous level, ie the normal price charged on the exporter`s home market.

Predatory practices

Verdrängungswettbewerb

Also called destructive competition.

A pricing practice whereby a company reduces its prices and charges lower-than-normal prices for its products solely to drive/freeze rival competitors out of business.

Predatory pricing

räuberische Preisbildung, ruinöse Preisunterbietung, räuberisches Dumping

Also called predatory price cutting, discrimination dumping, predatory dumping or predatory price discrimination.

A pricing practice by which a company (the predator) charges lower (possibly unprofitable) prices and is thereby underselling/undercutting competitors/rivals in certain markets to drive/freeze them out of business, or to keep out new entrants to a market. Thereafter prices are raised again to exploit the market void of competition. Predatory price cutting is a means of establishing or maintaining monopoly power.

According to the OECD, predation is commonest where the predator firm operates in many markets and/or where competitors and national supervisory authorities do not have sufficient information to be able to prove that predation is taking place.

Note: predation in European Union (EU) countries can be illegal under the EU competition law, which prohibits unfair trading conditions and outlaws the use of unreasonably low prices. For example, Germany`s Unfair Competition Act outlaws prices that are so far below cost that they are clearly designed to force competitiors to leave the market through acts other than superior economic performance.

Prediction

Prognose, Vorhersage

The act of predicting, eg a future condition or occurrence.

Something predicted, eg future sales. Also called forecast.

Preference item

Präferenzgut

A customer's choice of a particular item even when similar items are less expensive.

Preference question Präferenzfrage

In a questionnaire, a questioning technique which provides information on the preferences of the respondent/interviewee. The disadvantages of this technique are that the preferences may not reflect purchase choice, and/or that they may present some confusion.

Preference scale Präfenrenzskala

Also called scale of preferences.

A scale of relative importance of various goods and services to an individual.

Preferred position Vorzugsplazierung

A specific placement of an advertisement in a publication or of a commercial on radio or TV. Many advertisers demand special positions and are prepared to pay higher rates.

Prefinancing Vorfinanzierung

Also called advance or preliminary financing.

Financing in advance.

Premium (Pm, pm, Prem.) von besonders guter Qualität
Preis

Of specially good quality and therefore sold at a higher price.

A prize.

Premium brand Markenerzeugnis hoher Qualität, Spitzenerzeugnis

Brand of a product that sells, usually because of higher perceived quality, at a higher price than other products.

Premium coupon Prämiengutschein

Coupons cut off the package and saved until a customer accumulates enough coupons to receive a refund or a more valuable item of merchandise.

Premium offer Sonderangebot

Also called bargain offer or sale, special bargain, or special offer.

Special offer (often a non-profit-making offer) of merchandise at a reduced price.

Premium pack Zugabepackung

A package of a product offering a premium, eg an in-pack or on-pack premium.

Premium price Höchstpreis
Spitzenpreis

Also called top price.

The maximum price.

A price above the normal price which emerges when goods are in short supply and demand is exceptionally heavy.

Premium pricing Höchstpreisgestaltung, Festsetzung von Prestigepreisen

Also called prestige pricing.

The fixing of prices at a maximum/premium price. Some prices are more attractive than others because they are higher; this commonly applies to luxury or top-of-the-range items, whose high price is thought by the purchaser to be a guarantee of high quality and prestige.

Premium product Zugabe(Produkt), Produktbeilage
Spitzenerzeugnis

A premium placed in the package of a product.

A premium brand, ie a product of higher quality sold at a higher price.

Prepaid reply card freigemachte, frankierte Antwortkarte

A stamped and addressed card which can be returned to a company without paying postage.

Prepared sales presentation vorbereitete Produktpräsentation

A structured or canned sales talk, ie the salesperson will tell a complete story about the product, will arrange all sales pitches in a logical and systematic order, and will address most or all potential objections.
Note, however: this form of sales presentation may not allow the salesperon to adapt the presentation to the prospect`s needs.

Prepayment Vorauszahlung

Also called advance payment, payment in advance, or anticipatory payment.

A payment that is made before goods or services have been delivered or received.

Prepricing Preisauszeichnung durch den Hersteller

Also called premarking.

The price marking by the producer or other supplier before the goods are delivered to the retailer.

Preprint order form vorgedrucktes Bestellformular

An order form listing all the seller`s items constantly available.

Preretailing Preisfestlegung bei Auftragserteilung

The practice of determining prices and stating them on a copy of the purchase order at the time an order is placed.

Presale service absatzvorbereitender Kundendienst

Services provided by a seller to a customer before a business transaction, eg the furnishing of information material.

Present value (PV) Marktwert, Zeitwert

The value something has now. Also called current, market or time value; or present worth.

The value today of a future payment disounted at some appropriate interest rate. Also called discounted value or time value of money.

Presentation Vorlage

Also called submission.

The submission of goods.

Presentee Person, der etwas vorgelegt wird

A person to whom something is presented.

Presenter Redakteur im Studio, Moderator
Person, die etwas vorlegt

A person who discusses news, sports events, or other topics on TV or radio. Also called a commentator.

A person presenting something to someone.

Preshipment inspection (PSI) Inspektion vor dem Versand

Inspection of goods at the supplying firm`s premises before shipping them to their final destination. Customers may insist that the goods purchased conform to a certain quality standard (e.g. ISO 9000) and/or rigid design specifications, and reserve the right to reject consignments not meeting the stated requirements.
Note: the document issued by an independent organisation and confirming that all is in order is known as a "clean report of findings".

Press Presse, Zeitungswesen

Printed publications, especially newspapers and periodicals.

Press advertising Werbung in Druckmedien

Also called print advertising

Advertising in the print media. A very popular method of advertising which may involve local or national, daily or weekly newspapers, consumer or trade magazines usually appealling to specific groups, technical journals (they are very specialized and primarily directed at the trader), freesheets (they feature primarily the advertisements which pay for the paper), etc.

Before determining whether a newspaper or magazine is suitable for promoting a specific product, one should consider their market and circulation. Furthermore, it is important to ensure the correct timing of the advertisements. Another feature of press advertising is that each paper usually has a readership factor of above one, and for journals and weekend editions it may be four or five. Hence, press advertisements have a life of several days and enable the readers to evaluate the message in depth.

Note: repeated presentation in the press tends to produce better results than isolated advertising.

Press conference Pressekonferenz

A meeting to which news reporters are invited to hear a statement about an event (e.g. a product launch, bankruptcy or takeover) and where the reporters can ask questions.

Press relations Pressearbeit

Process of keeping the press informed.

Press release Pressemitteilung

Also called press launch or news release.

A written statement of something sent to the press in the hope that it will be published by them.

Pressing order Eilauftrag

Also called express, rush or urgent order.

An order that must be supplied immediately.

Prestige advertising Prestige-, Firmenimage-, Repräsentationswerbung

Also called corporate, image, or institutional advertising.

Advertising run to create, improve or enforce a favourable image, either of the product or the company (or both) and, by constant repetition, to instil that image into the minds of its users or potential customers.

Prestigious product Prestigeartikel

Also called prestige product.

Certain expensive luxury products sought after because of their high price. Often the price tag is a central part of the attraction. Usually, a drop in price causes demand to fall.

Pretax income Einkommen vor Steuerabzug

Income before income tax has been deducted.

Pretax profit Gewinn vor Steuern

Also called profit before taxes.

The trading profit of a business after deduction of expenses but before deduction of taxes.

Pretest/pre-test Pretest

Also called acceptance test.

A test of a product, packaging, advertising, etc. before being put on the market.

Preventive maintenance vorbeugende Wartung, Instandhaltung

The regular maintenance of a particular item of equipment to ensure its reliability and a maximum of operational life of the equipment.

Preview Vorschau

The viewing of a commercial by a specially invited studio audience before it is broadcast.

Price (pr) Preis

The amount of money which the buyer of a commodity or service pays to the seller. Including any warranties, guarantees, delivery, discounts, services, or other items that are part of the conditions of sale and are not paid for separately.
Very broadly prices are generally set by the manufacturer and retailer. Theoretically, prices are determined by supply and demand.

Price adjustment Preisanpassung

Adapting a price to a new market situation or meeting the requirements or circumstances of specific buyers, eg by raising or lowering a price, or by granting allowances, discounts, etc.

Price and demand Preis und Nachfrage

The relationship between the price of a product and the demand for it. Generally, the lower the price of a commodity, the greater the quantity demanded; and the higher the price the lower the demand.

Note: sometimes, however, demand increases as the price increases and falls as the price falls.

Price and value Preis und Wert

This relation is best indicated by the phrase "value for money". It involves the utility o value of the product or service as perceived or viewed by the user in terms of the selling price.

Price awareness Preisbewußtsein

The degree to which buyers know the prices of other goods and services which they are interested in buying.

Price bundling Preisbündelung, Preiskoppelung

The sale of two or more products in a single package for a special price, eg the sale of computer hardware together with a maintenance contract, or the sale of an airline ticke together with a hotel room.

Price cartel Preiskartell

Also called price fixing cartel or price ring.

An informal voluntary association of firms acting together to agree to charge the same or similar prices for their goods or to keep the price of their products at an artificially high level. Members of the cartel retain their identity and their independence, except i so far as they stick to the stipulated terms.
This type of cartel is illegal and banned by law because it creates monopoly conditions.

Price ceiling Höchstpreis, Limitpreis, Preisobergrenze

A restriction imposed by the government that prohibits a price going above a certain level. A price ceiling set below the equilibrium price results in a shortage of the good.

Price changes Preisänderungen

These are either price increases or price reductions. Whenever a price change is to be made, consideration is needed as to how the change should be implemented. Generally, price increases will need to be announced differently than price cuts.

Price changes need to be made for a variety of reasons:

1. price increases are needed when costs go up, demand increases, product line balancing requires it, production capacity limits have temporarily been reached, etc;

2. price cuts can become necessary whenever it is judged that profits would be higher at a lower price, competitors cut prices, a price reduction is needed to maintain or increase market share, or there is a need to balance demand for slow-moving items.

Price code Preiscode

A code or symbol placed on a price tag to indicate the price payable.

Price competition Preiswettbewerb

A pricing strategy where a competitive price is used as the major means of differentiating the product of one company from that of a competitor. The competing firms seek to attract customers on the basis of price, rather than by the use of other marketing factors.

Price consciousness Preisbewußtsein

The degree to which buyers are sensitive to price differences between alternative products. Price-conscious buyers often shop around in order to be able to buy at the best possible price.

Price control | Preiskontrolle, Preisüberwachung, Preisbindung

Government activity of controlling inflation and increases in the cost of living by preventing or postponing the price increases of private firms, by limiting the ability of firms to pass on labour costs in higher prices, by holding the prices of nationalized industries artificially low, or by increasing subsidies.

The government may establish maximum or minimum prices.

Price cutting | Preisunterbietung Preissenkung

Selling goods or services at prices below the commonly accepted level. This might provoke a price war. Competitors will react by cutting their own prices so that everyone's price remains relatively the same except that now each producer will be selling at a considerably lower price than at the outset. Price cutting may prove advantageous if it causes a number of small competitors to cut their own prices below their break-even figure. Also called undercutting or underselling.

A price reduction. Several circumstances might lead a firm to cut its price, for example: keen competition, excess capacity, a falling market share, lower costs, etc. Also called price cut or markdown.

Price decision | Preisentscheidung

The act or process of deciding on the price for a product or service.

There are six occasions on which it is necessary to make price decisions. These are: 1. when introducing a new product, 2. when altering profitability objectives, 3. when substantial cost changes occur, 4. when entering a competitive tender, 5. when responding to a particular competitve activity, 6. when shortages or supluses occur.

Price determinant | Preisbildungsfaktor

One or more of factors affecting the final price of a product or service.

Price determination | Preisermittlung

Also called pricing.

The fixing of selling prices for a firm's products or services. Theoretically, prices are determined by the interaction of demand and supply in a market.

Price discrimination Preisdiskriminierung, Preisdifferenzierung

Also called price differentiation, discriminatory pricing or rate discrimination.

The charging of different prices for the same commodity or service to different markets or groups of consumers. The differences in price do not reflect cost differences.
Price discrimination is possible and profitable only:
1. where production is monopolistic and there are no close substitutes for the product;
2. where consumers are in separate markets and resale of the product is impossible;
3. where elasticity of demand for the product differs in each market.

Examples of discriminatory pricing are dumping (i.e. selling a product abroad at a much lower price than at home) and the use of different trade names to sell the same product at a range of different prices. Perfect price discrimination occurs when the seller prices each unit of output at its demand price.

The practice of charging the same consumer different prices for different units of the same good.

Price effect Preiseffekt

The effect of price changes on customers` buying habits. Thus, the total change in the demand for a good resulting from a change in its price while the consumers' money incomes remain unchanged. It is composed of the income effect and the substitution effect.

Price elasicity Preiselastizität

An economic theory that describes the degree of responsiveness to a change in price. The theory applies to demand and supply.

Price elasticity of demand Preiselastizität der Nachfrage

Also called demand elasticity or elasticity of demand.

The most commonly used elasticity measurement. It measures the responsiveness of the quantity demanded of a particular good or service to a change in its price. As price falls, demand tends to expand and as price rises, so demand tends to contract.

For example, a slight change in price may cause a big change in the quantity demanded; if so, demand is said to be elastic. On the other hand, demand may hardly alter at all as the result of a price change, and in this case demand is said to be inelastic.

The formula for the price elasticity of demand is:

$$\frac{\text{\% change in quantity demanded}}{\text{\% change in price}} \text{, i.e. } \frac{\% \Delta D}{\% \Delta P}$$

The higher the absolute value of elasticity, the more elastic demand is said to be.

Perfect price inelasticity of demand:

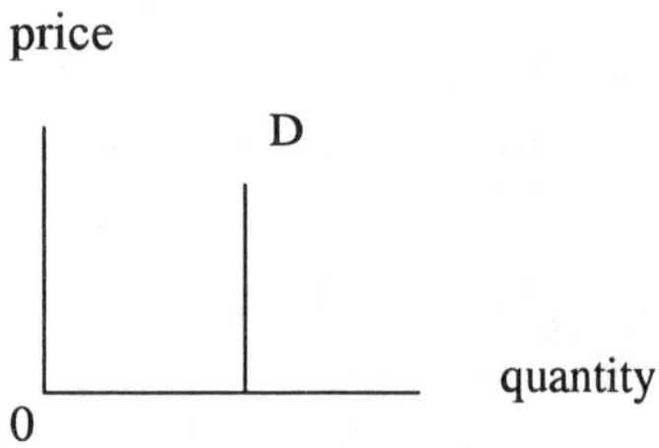

$$\text{price elasticity of demand} = \frac{\% \Delta D}{\% \Delta P} = 0$$

Perfect price elasticity of demand:

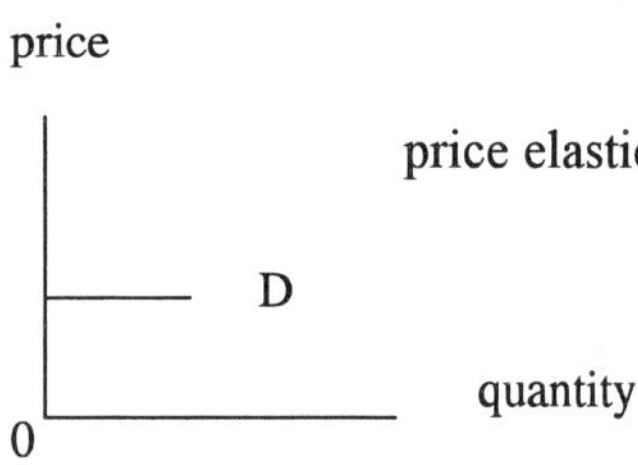

$$\text{price elasticity of demand} = \frac{\% \Delta D}{\% \Delta P} = \infty$$

Price elasticity of supply Preiselastizität des Angebots

Also called supply elasticity or elasticity of supply.

Price elasticity of supply is the responsiveness of supply to changes in price.

$$\text{Price elasticity of supply} = \frac{\text{\% change in quantity supplied}}{\text{\% change in price}}$$

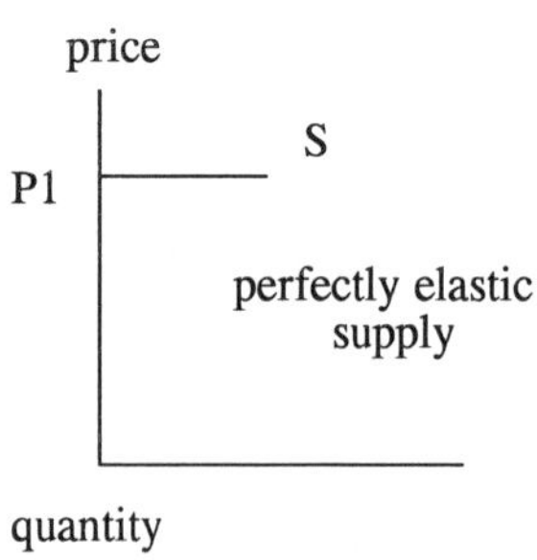

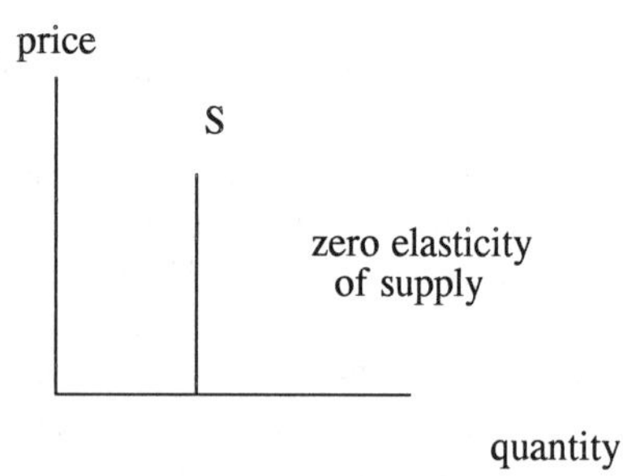

Note: perfectly elastic supply is rather improbable in real life; supply with zero elasticity is quite common in real life.

Price escalator clause Preisgleitklausel

Also called price escalation clause, escalator clause, rise and fall clause, or price redetermination clause.

In a contract, a clause that allows price adjustments, usually price increases.

Price fixing Preisabsprache
Preisbildung, Preisfestsetzung

An agreement between companies which are selling the same type of product or service to charge the same price for their competing products or services. Such an agreement is often illegal unless it can be proved that the public gains by it. Also called price (fixing) agreement or competition restricting agreement.

The activity or process of setting selling prices for a firm's products or services. Also called pricing, price formation or price setting.

Price floor Mindest-, Minimumpreis, Preisuntergrenze

Also called minimum-knocked down price.

A restriction imposed by the government that prohibits the price from falling below a certain level. A price floor set above the equilibrium price results in a surplus of the good.

The lowest possible price which is still profitable.

Price floor pricing Mindestpreiskalkulation

A form of cost-based pricing whereby a firm determines the lowest price at which it is still profitable to increase the amount of goods offered for sale.

Price follower Preisnachahmer

A firm that prices its goods or services by imitating/following the existing price leaders (ie firms that set the price).

Price guarantee Preisgarantie

The practice of sellers to guarantee their customers a certain price.

Price incentive Preisanreiz

In sales promotion, price reductions offered to consumers/users to encourage them to buy a particular product earlier or in larger quantities.

Price increase Preiserhöhung

Also called price hike, price rise, or markup.

A price change resulting in a higher price for a product or service.
Possible reasons for price increases are:
1. costs go up; 2. demand increases; 3. product line balancing requires it; 4. production capacity limits have temporarily been reached; 5. competitors raise their prices; 6. high inflation rates; 7. to protect profit margins that would otherwise be reduced by increasing costs; etc.
Price increases are always resented, however, there is a widespread acceptance of the belief that prices should move proportionately to costs. Thus, the existence of inflation makes it easier to explain and understand cost-induced price increases.

Although the standard method of raising prices is simply to raise the price, there are many other methods of increasing prices:
1. revising the various discounts granted; 2. changing the minimum order quantity; 3. changes in the terms of payment; 4. collecting interest on accounts receivable/outstanding debts; 5. writing escalator clauses into sales contracts; 6. reducing inventories; 7. unbundling (i.e., for example, charging separately for parts and accessories or for delivery and special services previously included in the price); 8. reducing the quality; 9. reducing the size or weight; 10. redesigning the product to make it less costly to produce; etc.

When price increases are necessary, the timing of these increases should be carefully considered. Furthermore, when a sizable price increase is to be made, or when continuing cost increases require frequent price rises, it is generally preferable to make a series of small increases during a time period than one or two large ones because such slight increases will be more acceptable and are less likely to be perceived by customers.

Price index Preisindex

A measure to illustrate the changes in the price of an individual good, or the average level of prices, from one period to another. The prices at a particular date (the base date) are quoted as 100. The prices of the following dates are then shown as percentage change (increase or decrease) of the base date. A well-known price index is the consumer price index (CPI).

Price inelasticity Preisunelastizität

A situation where buyers are price-insensitive, ie a situation where a percentage change in the quantitiy demanded is less than the percentage change in price.

Price leader Preisführer
Lockvogel, Lockartikel

In a competitive market, a firm whose prices set a lead for other firms in the market to follow. Normally, the price leader initiates price changes, and the other firms (the price followers) will follow.

In retailing, a product priced abnormally low in order to attract customers. Also called bait, leader, leading article or loss leader.

Price leadership Preisführerschaft

Where one firm is dominant in the market, price leadership may arise. The dominant firm's price is accepted as the market price by its rivals/competitors, who are aware that any attempt to undercut it may lead to a price war which would only benefit the dominant firm. Competition is shifted to nonprice elements (e.g. differences in design, styling or performance; special offers; guarantees; after-sales service; etc.).

Price level Preisniveau

Also called level or standard of prices.

The general level of prices (ie the value of money) at a particular time in comparison with the general level of prices at a specified base period.

Price lining Preislinie

A form of psychological pricing in which a company sets specific price points for a product line.

Price list Preisliste, Preisverzeichnis

Also called price catalog(ue), prices current or list of prices.

A list which quotes the catalogue number of a product and its current price. The prices remain in force for a period of time.

Price loco Loko-Preis

The price charged at the place of purchase.

Price maintenance Preisbindung (der zweiten Hand)
Preisstützung

Any binding agreement between producers or wholesalers and retailers not to sell goods below certain prices.
In Britain, Germany, the USA and many other countries, it is illegal for any supplier to impose minimum prices, except where RPM can be shown to be in the public interest. Also called resale price maintenance (RPM) or fair trade agreement (USA).

The support of certain prices above a minimum level through governmental regulations. Also called price support.

Price maker Preisfixierer

The price leader, ie the firm whose prices set a lead for other firms in the market.

Price marking Preisauszeichnung

Also called price tagging.

The marking of goods and services with price tags.

Price mechanism Marktpreis-Mechanismus,
Preissystem

Also called price system.

The mechanism which pushes prices up when demand is in excess and prices down when supply is in excess.
In the market economy goods and services are produced for profit and the amounts produced and consumed depend upon price - and prices are left to the determining forces of supply and demand. The price system can be viewed as a mechanism that allocates scarce goods and resources among competing uses by rationing them among buyers and sellers who are willing and able to buy and sell at the going market price.

Price mix Preismix

The total of different product prices a company offers to its customers, eg it may offer a range of different prices such as low, medium and high priced products.

Price negotiation Preisverhandlung

Form of price fixing based on the premise that the buyer is a price maker rather than a price taker.

Price objection Preiseinwand

A potential buyer`s objection made to a salesperson on the grounds of price, discounts, other allowances, freight charges and other charges.

Price off offer Preisnachlaßangebot

An offer which gives buyers a certain amount off the regular price shown on the price label or package.
This method is frequently used as an incentive for trying the product, stimulating sales or promoting products in off-seasons. However, frequent price off offers may cheapen a product`s image.

Price off promotion Verkaufsförderung durch Preisnachlaß

A promotion strategy which involves temporary price reductions to resellers with the intent that savings will be passed on to consumers.

Price out of market sich durch zu hohe Preise vom Markt ausschließen

Loss of business as a result of a firm's price(s) being higher than those of its competitors.

Price pack Sonderangebotspackung

Also called cents-off deal.

An offer to consumers of savings off the product`s regular price, marked directly on the label or package.

Price pegging Preisstützung

The maintaining of prices at a certain level.

Price plateau hohes Preisniveau, Höchstpreis

The price level which is accepted by buyers as being fair for a particular product or service.

Price quotation Preisangebot

Also called quote or quotation.

A statement of the current price and conditions upon which a seller is prepared to sell certain goods, or upon which certain services may be performed.
A common method of quoting prices is:
1. carriage paid (comprising the price of the goods including delivery to the buyer's premises),
2. carriage forward (being the price ex-works; the delivery charges have to be borne by the buyer).

In foreign trade, the basic price of the goods is their ex-works price in the country of origin. To this the following additions have to be made:
1. the cost of carrying the goods to the port of departure;
2. dock dues and any other charges for loading the goods on to the ship;
3. the freight charges for carrying the goods to the port of destination;
4. insurance of the goods while they are in transit;
5. the charge for carrying the goods from the port of destination to the importer's warehouse.

Price range Preisspanne, Preislage

Also called price gap, price differential or price spread.

Prices from the lowest to the highest available for a particular product or service.

Price reduction Preissenkung

Also called price cut, price cutting, markdown or roll-back.

A price change which leads to a lower price for a product or service. Usually price reductions are viewed positively by prospective buyers.

Possible reasons for price cuts are:
1. the company may judge that profits would be higher at a lower price;
2. competitors cut prices;
3. a price reduction is needed to maintain or increase the market share;
4. slow-moving items have to be sold;
5. the products have reached their maturity stage (i.e. sales growth slows or levels off) or their decline stage (i.e. sales decline) etc.

One should ensure that the price decrease is either large enough to be perceived as a lower price, or is advertised as such.

Note: sometimes buyers may perceive the price reduction as the result of a lowering of quality, an indication that a new formulation or model is about to be launched, or that prices may come down further and so it will pay to wait.

Price repression Preisneufestsetzung

Also called price suppression.

The activity or process of lowering prices due to changing market conditions.

The deliberate reduction of domestic prices when competing imports are sold at significantly lower prices than the domestically produced products.

Price ring Preiskartell

Also called prices cartel or price fixing cartel.

A loose association of firms which agree to charge the same price or a minimum price for their competing products or services. The purpose is to limit competition and so increase profits for all. Price agreements/fixings and price rings are a type of cartel and thus illegal in most countries.

Price scanner Preis-Scanner, Preisabtastgerät, Preislesepistole

Computerized optical reader that identifies bar codes on merchandise.

Price searcher Preissucher

A seller, eg a monopolist, with imperfect market information who tries to find the price that maximises profit. Trial and error are often necessary to find the appropriate price and the change in sales due to price changes.

Price sensitive product preiselastisches, preisreagibles Produkt

A product which reacts to price changes, i.e. it will not sell if the price is increased or it will sell if the price is lowered.

Price sensitivity Preisreagibilität

The buyers` reactions to different prices. According to Thomas Nagle there are nine factors affecting buyers` price sensitivity:

1. unique value effect: the more unique a product is the less price-sensitive buyers are;
2. substitute awareness effect: buyers are less price-sensitive when they are less aware of substitutes;
3. difficult comparison effect: there is less price sensitivity when buyers cannot easily compare the quality of substitutes;
4. total expenditure effect: the lower the expenditure is as a ratio to buyers` income the less price-sensitive buyers are;
5. end-benefit effect: buyers are less price-sensitive the less the expenditure is to the total cost of the end product;
6. shared cost effect: there is less price sensitivity when part of the cost is borne by another party;
7. sunk investment effect: buyers are less price-sensitive when the product is used in conjunction with assets previously bought;
8. price-quality effect: price sensitivity is lower when the product is assumed to have more quality, prestige, or exclusiveness;
9. inventory effect: buyers are less price-sensitive when they cannot store the product.

Price setting Preisfixierung, Preisfestsetzung

Also called price fixing or price formation.

The activity or process of setting selling prices for a firm`s products or services.

Price shading Preiszugeständnis

A demand oriented pricing tactic where salespersons deviate from the book/list price and use discounts to increase demand for one or more products in a product line.

Price skimming Abschöpfungspreispolitik

The strategy of charging the highest price the market will bear. Firms who adopt this tactic usually have identified a market cluster of customers with inelastic demand; the customers regard the high price as a promise of quality. Businesses who market a new product (e.g. an innovation with no immediate competition), often practice price skimming.
The strategy of price skimming does not employ profit maximization as its chief goal (but short-term profit-maximising pricing objectives are sometimes applied to recover costs quickly in conditions of uncertainty, or to compensate for high development costs), but focuses on the demand side of the market whereby it considers consumer tastes and price sensitivity as important determinants of the product price.

Price skimming makes sense under the following conditions:
1. a sufficient number of buyers have a high current demand;
2. the unit costs of producing a small volume are not too high;
3. the high initial price will not attract more competitors;
4. the high price supports the image of a superior product.

Note: the inherent danger of price skimming is that other firms may be attracted to the market.

Price stability Preisstabilität

A situation of stable prices. One of the aims of economic policy. In periods of rapid inflation, the government exercises a policy of price stabilization, i.e. it tries to keep prices at a stated level.

Price support Preisstützung

Also called price maintenance.

The maintenance of certain prices (e.g. of agricultural products) above a minimum level through governmental regulations.

Price tag Preisschild

Also called price label, price sign, price sticker or price ticket.

A label which shows the price of a product or service.

Price taker Mengenanpasser

Also called quantity adjuster.

The perfectly competitive firm is often referred to as a price taker. The firm's course of action is dictated by forces outside its control, i.e. by the industry. It is industry supply matched against market demand which determines the price at which the individual firm can sell its output. Each firm must accept the market price as something given and unchangeable by individual action - the market is the "price maker"; each firm is a "price-taker".

Price theory Preistheorie

Also called theory of price.

A theory concerned with the determination of prices in individual markets. The two components of price theory are the demand side and the supply side.

Price threshold Schleusenpreis, Schwellenpreis

A price below which demand for a product or service increases dramatically. Demand becomes so large that its total sales will be large enough in volume to interest many potential suppliers, and the market will be capable of large penetration.

The lowest and highest prices that buyers are willing to pay for a particular product or service.

Price types Preisarten

There are many different types of price, eg:
1. administered price, 2. advertised price, 3. all-in-price, 4. asked price, 5. average price, 6. bargain price, 7. base price, 8. basic price, 9. bid price, 10. bottom price, 11. breakeven price, 12. cash price, 13. ceiling price, 14. close price, 15. competititve price, 16. consumer price, 17. customary price, 18. cost price, 19. cover price, 20. current price, 21. dealer`s price, 22. delivered price, 23. demand price, 24. economic price, 25. equilibrium price, 26. every day low price, 27. ex factory price, 28. expected price, 29. export price, 30. fair price, 31. fancy price, 32. fictitious price, 33. final price, 34. firm price, 35. fob destination price, 36. fob factory price, 37. fall-back price, 38. fishy price, 39. floor price, 40. forward price, 41. free market price, 42. full price, 43. futures price, 44. import price, 45. just price, 46. keen price,

47. knocked-down price, 48. knockout price, 49. limit price, 50. list price, 51. loaded price, 52. loco price, 53. lover price, 54. market price, 55. maximum price, 56. minimum price, 57. misleading price, 58. natural price, 59. negotiated price, 60. normal price, 61. odd price, 62. offered price, 63. opportunity price, 64. parity price, 65. peak price, 66. pegged price, 67. penetration price, 68. penny-off/down price, 69. popular price, 70. premium price, 71. producer price, 72. psychological price, 73. purchase price, 74. real price, 75. recommended price, 76. reduced price, 77. relative price, 78. replacement price, 79. reserve price, 80. retail price, 81. rock bottom price, 82. quoted price, 83. selling price, 84. skimming price, 85. split price, 86. spot price, 87. sticker price, 88. softening price, 89. subjective price, 90. subscription price, 91. subsidised price, 92. suggested retail price, 93. supply price, 94. survival price, 95. target price, 96. total price, 97. trade price, 98. transfer price, 99. umbrella price, 100. unit price, 101. upset price, 102. wholesale price, etc.

Price variance — Preisabweichung

Also called price divergence.

The difference between actual unit price and standard/budgeted unit price.

Price variation clause (PVC, pvc) — Preisänderungsklausel, Preisgleitklausel

Also called price escalator or escalation clause, escalator clause, or rise-and-fall clause.

A clause found in a contract permitting one party to the contract to vary the price at a certain date and in specified circumstances in the life of the contract, usually increase it.

Price war — Preiskrieg

Also called pricing battle or price cutting war.

Competition between companies producing similar products in which each attempts to undercut/undersell the other's prices.

Price(s) subject to change without notice — Preis(e) freibleibend, unverbindlich; Preisänderung(en) vorbehalten

The offeror reserves the right to change the price of a good or service after having submitted his offer to the offeree, without notice.

Prices Act Preisauszeichnungsgesetz

The act requires retailers to mark unit prices on their goods. Unit pricing helps shoppers to make direct comparison of price and quantity.

Pricing Preisbildung, Preisfestsetzung

Also called price setting or fixing; price formation, or formation of prices.

The activity or process of setting selling prices for a firm's products or services. There is a difference between the total cost of a product sold on an ex-works basis and the same product sold on a delivered basis (the latter has to include such additional costs as freight, packaging, handling charges, etc.).

The traditional components for determining proper prices are costs, market demand, and competition. These categories are the same for domestic and foreign sales.

In domestic and in foreign markets, the price at which a product or service is sold directly determines a firm`s revenues. Thus, it is essential that a firm`s market research include an evaluation of all the variables that may affect the price range for the product or service. If a firm`s price is too high, the product or service will not sell. If the price is too low, domestic sales and/or export activities may not be sufficiently profitable, or may even create a net loss.

Decisive questions to guide pricing considerations for the seller or exporter are:
1. at what price should the firm sell its product?
2. does the price reflect the product`s quality?
3. is the price competitive?
4. should the firm pursue market penetration or market skimming pricing objectives?
5. what type of discount (eg cash, quantity, trade) and allowances (eg advertising, trade-off) should the firm offer its customers?
6. should prices differ with market segment?
7. what should the firm do about product line pricing?
8. what pricing options are available if our costs increase or decrease?
9. is the demand in the market elastic or inelastic?
10. how are prices going to be viewed by the foreign government?

Pricing and competition Preisbildung und Wettbewerb

The prices of competitive products establish the benchmarks for a pricing decision. Thus, a firm has to decide whether to meet, undersell, or oversell the prevailing market prices knowing that consumers will compare its price to the prices of competing products. Furthermore, a firm has to consider competitive reactions to a price change.

Pricing consumer goods Konsumgüterpreisbildung

There are two basic methods for a firm to calculate its prices for consumer goods:

1. The cost-plus method: one calculates the costs of the product and adds the profit margin considered necessary to cover fixed costs and provide an acceptable return on capital employed (ROCE).

2. The market approach: this method concerns itself with the price the customer is likely to pay. From this price, the costs of production and distribution are deducted. Provided the resultant figure (ie the gross profit) is considered satisfactory, the product can be offered to the market.
Note: if the gross profit is too low, costs must be reduced, or, if this is impossible, the product must be abandoned.
Note:
1. The price is a major element of the marketing mix, together with product, place and promotion.
2. Depending upon the nature of the product, in general terms high prices tend to deter demand, whereas low prices encourage it.
3. In many market segments, the market leader has already set a price level that both satisfies his profitability requirements and is acceptable to a majority of customers.

Pricing down Preisherabsetzung

The process of reducing a product's price.

Pricing methods Preisbildungsmethoden

There are a number of distinct and particular methods of pricing. Examples are:
1. bait pricing, 2. basing-point pricing, 3. bid pricing, 4. breakeven pricing, 5. buyer-oriented pricing, 6. byproduct pricing, 7. common pricing, 8. competition oriented pricing, 9. customary pricing, 10. customer segment pricing, 11. deceptive pricing, 12. demand oriented pricing, 13. escalator pricing, 14. ethical pricing, 15. experience curve pricing, 16. flexible pricing, 17. formula pricing, 18. freight absorption pricing, 19. image pricing, 20. keep out pricing, 21. leader pricing, 22. location pricing, 23. market penetration pricing, 24. market skimming pricing, 25. mathematical pricing 26. moral pricing, 27. negotiated pricing, 28. optional product pricing, 29. patronage oriented pricing, 30. perceived value pricing, 31. pioneer pricing, 32. plateau pricing, 33. price floor pricing, 34. product line pricing, 35. profit maximising pricing, 36. promotional pricing, 37. revenue oriented pricing, 38. sales based pricing, 39. sales-oriented pricing, 40. skimming pricing, 41. skim-the-cream pricing, 42. special event pricing, 43. status quo pricing, 44. survival pricing, 45. trial-and-error pricing, 46. umbrella pricing, 47. unbundled pricing, 48. unit pricing, 49. value-based pricing, etc.

Pricing objectives Preisgestaltungsziele, Preisbildungsziele

The goals, outcomes or results that a company can pursue through its pricing policy. The main objectives are:
1. survival (the main short-term objective if the company faces overcapacity, keen competition, or changing consumer wants; prices will often be cut, but have to cover variable costs and some fixed costs, because profits are less important than survival);
2. maximum current profit (to achieve this, the company tries to charge a price that will produce the maximum current profit, cash flow, or return on investment);
3. maximum current revenue (this can be achieved by setting a price that will maximize sales revenue, which should lead in the long run to profit maximization and market share growth);
4. maximum sales growth (to achieve this objective companies apply market penetration pricing, i.e. as they assume that the market is price-sensitive they set the lowest price and thereby hope to reach a higher sales volume which will lead to lower unit costs and thus to higher long-term profit);
5. maximum market skimming (the company sets a high price to skim/cream off the market and when sales slow down it lowers the price to attract customers belonging to the next price-sensitive layer);
6. product quality leadership (the company has to charge a high price to cover the high product quality and high research and development costs).

There are other pricing objectives that can also be employed.
These include:
1. product line promotion (i.e. one product is priced to stimulate the sales of another product or the entire product line), 2. market share, 3. meeting competition, 4. image, 5. balancing the demand for products in the line, 6. increasing sales to specific market segments, 7. profit maximization, 8. pricing at the high end of the price range, 9. profitability improvement, 10. achieving a specified return on investment (ROI), 11. price stability, 12. price cuttings to gain a temporary advantage, etc.

Note: when establishing or changing the price of a product, the company must carefully consider each of the fundamental three Cs of pricing - cost, competition, and the consumer.

Pricing orientation Preisbildungsorientierung

There are two main types of pricing orientation which companies mainly follow:
1. the cost approach:
   this approach involves first computing all relevant costs and then adding a desired profit markup to arrive at the price which is based strictly on costs; the final price emerges after making adjustments, dictated by considerations of government, competition, demand, company objectives, etc.;
2. the market approach:
   this approach focuses on pricing from the viewpoint of the customer.

Pricing policy Preispolitik

Also called price policy.

The main factors which will influence a company's pricing policy are:
1. the cost of the product; 2. the planned return on investment (RoI); 3. the company's need for liquidity; 4. the supply of similar products; 5. and the nature of demand and its elasticity.
The pricing policy of commercial organisations can be a constantly changing process.

Companies may adopt:
1. a high pricing policy to give a new product prestige;
2. a low pricing policy to obtain a high market share or a high degree of market penetration;
3. a policy of matching the prices of leading competitors.

Pricing review Preisüberprüfung

The process of reviewing prices, usually with a view to increasing them.

Pricing up Preisanhebung

The process of increasing a product's price.

Primary data Primärdaten, Urmaterial

Data which has been collected firsthand from consumers, viewers, readers, etc in order to meet current research objectives. The process of collecting this data involves conducting field research.

Primary demand Primärnachfrage

Consumer demand for a product category rather than for a particular brand within the category.

Primary demand advertising Produktgruppenwerbung

Advertising designed to increase the aggregate/total demand for a product or service, rather than for a particular brand.

Note: this form of advertising is often run by trade associations to promote their members` products.

Primary industry Grundstoffindustrie

Also called basic or extractive industry.

Industry dealing with basic raw materials.

Primary market Haupthandelsplatz

The principal trading market for a particular commodity.

Primary marketing area (PMA) Hauptabsatzgebiet
Hauptverbreitungsgebiet

The major area of sale for a product or service. Also called heartland.

A newspaper`s main area of editorial and advertising coverage.

Primary needs Primärbedürfnisse

Physiological needs, such as food, water, clothing, shelter, sleep and sex.

Note: people have two major types of needs, primary and secondary.

Primary package Grundverpackung

A product`s immediate wrapper or container.

Primary products Grund-, Rohstoffe

Also caled basic or primary commodities or raw materials.

Products which are basic raw materials.

Primary reader Erstleser, Primärleser

A subscriber, a purchaser or only a reader who is the first to look at the content of a publication.

Primary sector primärer Sektor

Economists often divide the economy into three main sectors:

1. The primary sector:it includes agriculture, forestry, fishing and the extractive industries.
2. The secondary sector: it includes manufacturing and construction.
3. The tertiary sector: it includes commercial services and services such as education and health.

Prime cost(s) (PC, pc) direkte (variable) Kosten, (Fertigungs)Einzelkosten Selbstkosten

In manufacturing, those costs which vary directly with the quantity produced, comprising expenses such as wages and materials (i.e. direct labour and direct materials) and other direct costs that can be identified with the actual product. It excludes overhead costs. Also called direct cost.

The costs involved in producing a product.

Prime market Hauptabsatzmarkt

The major area of sale for a product or service.

Prime time Hauptsendezeit

Also called peak viewing hours/time (TV) or peak listening hours (radio).

In radio and television the period of the day which attracts the largest audiences.

Principal market area Hauptabsatzgebiet

The chief place where products are sold, not necessarily the place of manufacture.

Printed matter Drucksache

Also called printed papers.

Any of various kinds of printed material that qualify for a special postal rate, eg catalogues.

Printer`s error (PE) Druckfehler

Also called misprint.

A mistake in printing.

Private brand Hausmarke, Händlermarke

Also called private label, house brand or own brand.

The own brand of wholesaling and retailing organisations. The products are supplied by manufacturers with special labels and packaging.

Private carrier Beförderungsunternehmer, privater Frachtführer

Also called transport company.

A carrier who carries under a private contract with those who wish goods to be moved.

Private enterprise (system) Privatwirtschaft, (freie) Marktwirtschaft

Also called free market economy.

One of the systems under which a country's economic activities can be organised. The essence of private enterprise is that each individual manages his economic life in whichever way he thinks fit. In such a system, price is the decisive mechanism by which it is decided what shall be produced.

Private sector privater Sektor

That part of the economy which is left to private enterprise.

Private siding privater Gleisanschluß

A railway siding situated on a company's private property.

Prize Preis, Prämie, Gewinn

A reward for victory or superiority, as in a contest, game or sweepstake.

Pro forma invoice (p/i) Proforma-Rechnung, vorläufige Rechnung

Also called pro forma/proforma account.

This is exactly the same as an ordinary invoice except that the words "pro forma", which mean "as a matter of form", are marked on it.
It is used to cover goods sent on approval, or on consignment; to serve as a quotation; to serve as a request for payment in advance if the goods are required (in this case the seller does not wish to grant the buyer credit terms).
It is also used when a copy of the original invoice is required for some purpose, e.g. to show the customs officers what goods have been exported.

Pro rata freight Distanzfracht

Also called distance freight(age), freight(age) by distance, or freight pro rata.

The proportion of freight charges due as a result of cargo being delivered to a place short of the place of destination.

Proactive marketing Proactive Marketing

An aggressive and ongoing marketing activity which anticipates market changes and alters the marketing mix to fit newly emerging economic, social, and competitive trends.

Probability Wahrscheinlichkeit

Also called likelihood.

Chance or likelihood of an event occurring, estimated as a ratio between the number of ways in which the event may occur and the number of ways in which alternative events may occur. Probability is usually expressed as a number between zero and one or as a percentage; thus a probability of zero indicates that an event will never occur and a probability of one means that it is certain to occur.

Probability distribution Wahrscheinlichkeitsverteilung

Graph or table showing the possible events that could occur and the chance associated with each. It can also be described by a function.

Probability sample Wahrscheinlichkeitsstichprobe

Also called random sample.

A sample in which each individual within a total population has an equal or known chance of being included in the sample.

Problem child Sorgenkind

Also called question mark or wild cat.

In the Boston matrix, products which show rapid growth but poor profit margins. They have a low market share in a high growth market. A problem child needs a great deal of cash and substantial marketing activities to maintain or increase market share in the face of keen competition. Without support, problem children eventually become dogs.

Problem-solving selling problemlösungsorientierter Verkauf

A selling technique in which the salesperson cooperates with the prospective buyer to evaluate alternative solutions to a specific problem, and to select the most suitable alternative.

Proceeds Erlös, Erträge

The result of a sale represented in money - the money received from a sale.

Process costing Divisionskalkulation, Stückkostenrechnung für Massenfertigung

Also called unit costing.

A costing system used for determining the cost per unit of output of mass produced products or services. The costs are computed through dividing total costs by total output.

Procurement Beschaffung, Einkauf

Also called buying, purchasing, resource acquisition or resourcing.

The act of buying or acquiring something, e.g. procurement of capital or labour, material procurement.

Procurement costs Beschaffungskosten

Costs which arise from ordering products.

Produce landwirtschaftliche Produkte, Agrarerzeugnisse

Agricultural products collectively.

Produce broker Produktenmakler

Also called merchandise broker.

A buying or selling broker (ie a commodity broker) on a produce/commodity exchange.

Produce exchange Produktenbörse

Also called mercantile exchange.

A commodity exchange mainly trading in perishable commodities.

Producer Hersteller, Produzent
Produzent

Someone who makes goods or services or creates economic value. Also called maker or manufacturer.

Someone who is responsible for bringing a film, commercial, television series, play etc before the public.

Producer advertising Herstellerwerbung, Produzentenwerbung

Advertising run by producers of goods and services.

Producer cartel Produzentenkartell

A unilateral agreement among producers of a commodity, or suppliers of a natural resource, to deal collectively as a group with the buyers for purposes of trading the commodity.

Producer goods Produktionsgüter, Investitionsgüter

Also called producers', production, capital, industrial or investment goods.

Goods that are used in the production of other goods, e.g. machinery, raw materials, partly finished goods, factory buildings, etc. Producer goods wear out or become out of date, and so have to be replaced.

Producer market Produzentenmarkt, Herstellermarkt

The portion of the business-to-business (BTB) market consisting of buyers that buy goods and services for use in producing other products, or for incorporation into other products.

Producer price Erzeuge-, Produzentenpreis

The price charged by a producer/manufacturer.

Producer price index (PPI) Erzeugerpreisindex

Formerly called wholesale price index (WPI).

This index is an average price of the prices wholesalers have to pay. It is often a useful indicator of future retail price rises, since wholesale price rises can expect to be reflected eventually in the retail price index (RPI).

Producer's surplus Produzentenrente

Also called producer surplus or employer's surplus.

The term was invented by the English economist Alfred Marshall (1842 - 1924) and means the difference between the market price that a producer receives for his product and the payment actually necessary to induce him to continue to produce.

Producers' cooperative Produktionsgenossenschaft

Also called production co-operative.

A form of business unit in which usually small manufacturers/producers are the owners. They combine to obtain the advantages of bulk buying and other services such as jointly owned machinery.

Product Produkt, Erzeugnis

Anything made by man or nature.

Output or end result of a production process.

In marketing, anything that can be marketed, including objects, services, ideas, personalities, etc. A product exists for the purpose of exchange in the satisfaction of individual or organizational objectives.

Product idea Produktidee

An idea for a new product, a product adaptation or a product modification that a firm can see itself offering to the market.

Product acceptance Produktakzeptanz

The degree of success of a product launch, i.e. the acceptance by the market place of a particular product. To find out how well a product is selling, the firm may carry out a product acceptance test (PAT).

Product acceptance test (PAT) Produktakzeptanztest

A test of the degree of acceptance of a product by consumers.

Product adaptation/adaption Produktanpassung

The modification of a product to meet new and/or different requirements either on the domestic market or on a foreign market.

For example, for a domestic company to enter a foreign market successfully, its product may have to be modified to conform to:
1. government product regulations (eg high or special tariffs), 2. price expectations, 3. geographic and climatic conditions (eg topography and humidity), 4. buyer preferences, 5. environmental requirements (eg low energy consumption), 6. the standard of living (eg due to a lower level of income less sophisticated products might sell better), 7. differences in the level of technical skill of operatives, etc.

Furthermore, modifications may be necessary to facilitate transport or to compensate for possible technical differences or packaging and design standards.
Note: the market potential must be of sufficient size to justify the costs involved in product adaptation.

Product advertising Produktwerbung

Advertising that promotes goods and services.

Product analysis Produktanalyse

An examination of a particular product or range of products in the market place to find out why it sells, who buys it, or which provides the best value for money.

Product attributes Produkteigenschaften

Distinctive tangible and intangible features of a product such as color, taste, smell, calories, fat content, texture, design, speed, convenience, safety, low maintenance costs, etc.
These attributes give the product its value to the user and influence his/her readiness to buy and the amount he/she is prepared to spend on it.

Note: advertising can affect the way consumers rank a product`s attributes.

Product characteristics Produktmerkmale

Attributes which buyers and sellers regard as important when determining the suitability of a product to satisfy their needs.
These characteristics may be classified as follows:
1. technical characteristics (e.g. material used, reliability, safety, etc.);
2. economic characteristics (a. non-price: e.g. servicing costs, running costs, etc; b. price: list and sale price, financing arrangements, discounts, etc.).

Product class Produktklasse

A range of products that are homogeneous or treated by consumers as substitutes for each other.

Product classification Produktklassifizierung

There are many methodologies for classifying products.

1. Products can classified into three groups according to their durability: a. nondurable goods, b. durable goods, c. services.

2. Consumer goods can be classified on the basis of buyer behaviour activities (ie consumer shopping habits); we can distinguish between:

a. convenience goods (goods on which the consumer purchases immediately and frequently with little ongoing comparison of alternatives and with the minimal amount of time, money, and effort possible); convenience goods can be further divided into staples, impulse goods, and emergency goods;

b. shopping goods (goods on which the consumer will expend time and effort in comparing and purchasing, he will particularly compare price, quality, suitability, and style); shopping goods can be further subclassified into homogeneous and heterogeneous goods;

c. specialty goods (goods with unique characteristics and/or brand identification; the products are so important to the consumer so that they are the most important element in the purchasing decision);

d. unsought goods (goods that the consumer either does not know anything about or has no interest in purchasing; the consumer therefore must be informed about their availability and their attributes and values).

3. Industrial goods can be classified as follows: a. materials and parts (noncapital goods), b. capital goods, c. supplies and services.

Product compatibility Produktkompatibilität

Tying a product to another in order to reduce competition, eg through producing computer software which can be used only on a specific computer model.

Product control Produktkontrolle

The control of a company`s products to ensure that they meet set quality standards.

The periodic control of a company's products to ensure that those which need improvement or change to meet the company's objectives (e.g. profitability) are changed, and that those which cannot meet those goals are eliminated.

Product copy produktbezogener Werbetext

That part of the advertising copy devoted to the product and claims.

Product cost(s) Herstellkosten

Also called cost(s) of production, final manufacturing cost(s), inventoriable cost(s), or processing cost (s).

Product cost(s) comprise direct materials, direct labour and factory/production overhead.

Product costing Stückkalkulation

The calculation of the costs of a product. The two main cost factors are: 1. direct and 2. indirect costs.
1. Direct costs embrace all those elements in the product manufacture including labour, raw materials, component parts, salaries, heating, lighting, etc and any other ancillary costs which could be directly allocated to the product.
2. Indirect costs (they are not chargeable to a particular product) embrace all those elements which can be identified with the production of the items, e.g. indirect labour, indirect materials and other indirect expenses such as administrative costs.

Product deletion Produktaufgabe

Also called product abandonment or product elimination.

The elimination of a product that no longer satisfies target market customers, is obsolete, reduces a firm`s profitability, creates losses, or transfers negative feelings to some of the firm`s other products.

Note: basically, there are two ways of abandoning a product: 1. to phase it out over a period of time, 2. to drop it immediately.

Product design Produktdesign

The combination of details and features of a product. Good design considers a product`s distinctiveness, functionality, usefulness, attractiveness, aesthetics, ergonomics, production costs, ease of production, distribution, service and repair, safety, saleability, etc.
Note: formerly, design followed the maxim "form follows function", today, design is a powerful competitive weapon which has to attract attention and win sales.

The process of designing a product.

Product development Produktentwicklung

The process of fulfilling marketing objectives by developing new products or modifying existing ones. This is done in order to maintain or increase sales or market share, or to add value and therefore price. Product development can be through marginal changes (low risk, small profit) or major innovations (high risk, high profit).

Product differentiated marketing produktdifferenziertes Marketing

A marketing strategy in which a firm disregards market segmentation but produces goods and services that differ from those available on the market.

Product differentiation Produktdifferenzierung

An attempt to create differences between products which are basically very similar, e.g. by advertising, design, packaging, branding, etc.
Producers often use packaging, labels or trademarks to help customers to differentiate between their products and the products of close competitors. This technique is known as branding.

Product disparagement Produktherabsetzung

The process of making false or deceptive comparisons or distorted claims concerning a competitor`s product.

Product elimination Produktelimination

Also called product deletion or product abandonment.

The elimination of a product that no longer satisfies target market customers, is obsolete, reduces a firm`s profitability, creates losses, or transfers negative feelings to some of the firm`s other products. Furthermore, the decision to drop a product releases resources that could be more effectively used in other ways.
Weak products, on the basis of estimated future profit and contribution to the product line, must be phased out to prevent dispersion and fragmentation of effort.
Additionally, the rapid change in marketing conditions requires continuous monitoring of products to weigh their relevancy in the light of new customer needs, competitive offerings, and environmental conditions.
Note: the elimination of weak products reduces the level of inventories at the domestic and international level.

Product elimination may occur at any time from shortly after launch (ie there is a new product failure) to many years later.
Basically, there are two ways of abandoning a product: 1. to phase it out over a period of time, 2. to drop it immediately.

Product evolution Produktevolution

The gradual change in a product to keep it competitive or enable it to enter a new market.

Product failure Produktmißerfolg

A situation where a new product fails or proves to be unsuccessful.
A new product may fail because:
1. managers may push a new product idea through in spite of negative market research findings, 2. the market potential is overestimated, 3. the actual product is not designed well enough, 4. the product is not advertised effectively, 5. the product is overpriced, 6. the product is incorrectly positioned, 7. the development costs are higher than expected, 8. competitors fight back harder than expected, 9. competitors develop a similar product at a faster speed, 10. rivals quickly imitate the new product and thereby shorten the new product`s life cycle, 11. there is excessive established competition, etc.

Product family Produktfamilie

All the product classes capable of satisfying a core need with more or less effectiveness.

Product feature Produkteigenschaft

Also called sales feature.

Benefits and attributes of a product which a company tries to point out to its customers to make them buy.

Product gap Produktlücke

Part of the market out of our reach due to inadequate product line.

Product idea testing Produktideenbewertung

The evaluation of a new product idea, usually by consulting experts and by interviewing a sample of consumers.

Product image Produktimage

The particular picture/image that consumers acquire of a company's product.

Product innovation Produktinnovation

The act of creating a new product or process.

Product knowledge Produktkenntnisse

A salesperson`s detailed knowledge of a product`s attributes, benefits and weaknesses necessary to convince a prospect to purchase.

Product launch Produkteinführung

Also called launch of a product.

The process of informing the market of a new product or service and their introduction on to the market, usually with some special promotional activity or campaign.

Product liability (P/L) Produkthaftung

The liability of a producer of goods to a third party (i.e. the purchaser and sometimes other users or even bystanders) for injury and damage caused by a defective product.

Product liability insurance Produkthaftpflichtversicherung

This type of insurance provides an indemnity to manufacturers and others against third-party claims for personal injury or damage to property which arise from the purchase or use of products.

Product liability law Produkthaftungsgesetz

A law which imposes some liability on a person or company associated with the design, production or sale of a product as a result of some attribute of the product, some loss or damage of the product or something the goods have done, have failed to do or may do or fail to do.

Product liability laws usually focus on laws which provide that the designer, producer or seller of a product should pay damages/compensation to a person who has suffered loss or damage which has resulted from something the goods have incurred.

Product life cycle (PLC) Produktlebenszyklus

The theory that all products follow a similar life course.

Each product goes through five stages:
1. pioneering stage (introduction stage); 2. growth stage; 3. maturity stage;
4. saturation stage; 5. decline stage.
The duration of each stage varies considerably. Prior to the introduction of a product to the market there is a development stage.
The product life cycle concept is useful in determining the time and cost of development projects in relation to the ultimate pay-off.

The PLC has four premises:
1. that products have a limited life;
2. that product sales pass through distinct stages, each stage having different implications for the seller;
3. that profits from the product vary at different stages in the life cycle; and
4. that products require different strategies at different stages of the life cycle.

Factors affecting the length of a product`s life cycle are:
1. durability (if the product need be bought only once, then market saturation can occur quickly),
2. fashion (fashionable products die rather quickly),
3. technology (a technological change can turn the customer away from a product that now seems obsolete).

Product life cycle (PLC) and profitability Produktlebenszyklus und Rentabilität

How close a firm will ever get to recovering its investment will depend on exactly what point it entered the life cycle of the product it is selling.
All products have a life cycle of growth and subsequent decline. At the stage of sales expansion, profit margins are often high, as the lead company uses prices to skim the market and rapidly recoup its expenditures before competitors begin to copy the product and enter the market. When product after product enters the market, profit margins begin to fall and the rate of sales expansion begins to slow down; then the market moves to saturation. At this point, the shake-out begins, and sales and profits start to decline. When a product begins to come to the end of its life cycle before full investment recovery has been achieved, the company faces a serious failure. If a cycle is shortening, it is important to recover investment as rapidly as possible.
Note: all products seem to pursue this cycle, although time-scales differ.

Product line Produktlinie, Produktgruppe

Also called product range.

A group of products having related characteristics or a common market and manufactured or distributed by a company.

Product line breadth Produktgruppenbreite

Also called product line width.

The number of product lines in a company`s product mix.

Product line depth Produktgruppentiefe

The number of different items within a product line.

Product line extension Produktgruppenerweiterung

The development of greater depth by adding new product varieties to the product line.

Product line pricing Preisbildung für eine Produktgruppe

The process of fixing/setting prices for an entire product group.

Product management Produktmanagement, -betreuung

All the management activities involved in looking after a firm`s products, including product planning, product ranges, product prices, product selling, etc.

Product manager Produktmanager

Also called brand manager.

The marketing executive with responsibility for a particular product.
Among his responsibilities are:
1. innovation of new products; 2. working with advertising agencies or departments; 3. developing any promotion deals needed; 4. determining the quality standards and price; 5. making forecasts on sales, cash flows, profits, etc.
If this manager handles a range of products, he is called product line manager.

Product market potential Gütermarktpotential

This is the total possible sales in the market for a type of product.
For a durable product, it is the number of relevant consumers; for a consumable product, it is the number of relevant consumers multiplied by the number of use occasions which arise per consumer per period (usually per annum).

Product market strategies Gütermarktstrategien

Marketing strategies considering the product and the market.
There are four basic strategies available:
1. market penetration, 2. market development, 3. product development,
4. diversification.

Product marketing Produktmarketing

The process or technique of marketing a particular product.

Product mix Produktmix

The total assortment of products (the product line or product group) a company offers. In its range of assorted items a company may offer low and high priced products, a wide variety of different items and/or a large number of quality or style variations.

Product modification Produktmodifikation

Any change to the attributes (eg colour, design, price, shape, style, weight, etc) of a product.
Product modification is often necessary to meet consumer preferences, differences arising from climatic or geographical conditions, differences in the level of technical skill of operatives, new or different legal requirements, e.g. on foreign markets, etc.

Product objection Produkteinwand

A prospect`s objection made to a salesperson on the grounds of product quality or other attributes.

Product orientation Produktorientierung

Also called production orientation.

A marketing philosophy based on the belief that a good product or service will sell itself. The firm`s internal capabilities, eg production techniques, efficiency, etc, are more important than the desires and needs of the target market(s). The orientation assumes that consumers will favour those products that are the most readily available at the most affordable prices.

Product performance Gebrauchsfähigkeit eines Produkts

The manner in which or the efficiency with which a product fulfills its intended purpose.

Product pioneering Einführung neuer Produkte

The launching/introducing of new products to the market.

Product placement Produktplazierung, Product-Placement

The placing of one`s own product in a television, film, or theater production. If the hero or heroine of a successful production uses the product several times, this is an effective form of advertising.
Note: certainly, the producer has to pay for the product to be placed in a particular scene.

Product placement test Einführungstest, Markttest

Also called acceptance test.

A product test in which a product is left with a potential user (e.g. a household) who tests its usefulness and value.

Product policy Produktpolitik

This policy is concerned with defining the type, volume and timing of the products (both existing and new products) a company offers for sale.

Product portfolio Produktbestand, Produktportfolio

Collection of products which are all at different stages in their life cycles but made by the same company. A company which offers several products has a product portfolio, each product involving a particular combination of risk and return.
Accordingly, products may be categorised as:
1. developing products: these are products which are increasing their market shares in expanding markets;
2. safe products: the firm depends on them for a steady cash flow;
3. declining products: they contribute little to company profits due to reduced demand, keen competition, etc;
4. high risk products.

Note: international businesses need balanced portfolios to avoid having too many high risk and/or declining products.

Product position Produktstellung

A product`s place in the minds of consumers and users relative to competing products.

Product positioning Produktpositionierung

The way consumers, users and others view competitive brands or types of products.

Product positioning is important to find out consumer needs and develop differentiated products and services which precisely match the purchasers' requirements. Positioning is not what you do to a product; it is what you do to the mind of the consumer. That is, you position the product in the mind of the consumer.

Positions depend on the nature of the product, competing products and how consumers see themselves. Companies normally wish to position their brands so as to make them appeal to a predetermined consumer group, which might require a promotional campaign to alter the ways in which an item is perceived by the target group.

Product proliferation Produktausbreitung, Produktproliferation

A situation where successful markets tend to become overcrowded by a large number of new product launches. Thus shopkeepers may have difficulties to find enough shelf space for all the products available and consumers may become confused by the large variety of products.

Product quality Produktqualität

The particular attributes of a product, its ability to perform its functions and its physical features. Thus, product quality may include: durability, reliability, level of performance, precision, ease of operation and repair, speed, flavour, ingredients, price (a high price signals premium quality), etc.

Note: firms must build quality into their products, must communicate product quality, and must control quality to support a product`s position in the target market.

Product range Sortiment

Also called product line, product assortment, assortment or range of goods, line of merchandise, or business mix.

All the products made and offered by a single firm.

Product recall Produktrückruf

The withdrawal and request for return of a product by a company in order to repair or replace it due to the detection of a defect which renders it unsuitable for the purpose for which it was sold.

Product research Produktforschung

Research activities attempting to discover what products or product ranges are required, or being bought by a market, industry, or type of customer, the specification and performance expected by customers, the price they are prepared to pay, the service facilities expected, etc. Last not least, researchers want to find out the products` market acceptance and market image.

Product research and development (PRD) Produktforschung und -entwicklung

Also called research and development (R+D).

Scientific activity which transforms a product idea into a technically sound and promotable product.

Product screening Produktvorprüfung , Produktauswertung im voraus

Process of testing all aspects of a potential product to ensure that it will fit the market, company and financial objectives and operational needs.

Product selection Produktauswahl

The activity or process of selecting a product that will sell.

Product specification Produktbeschreibung

In the industrial buying process, the stage in which the buyer decides on and specifies the characteristics for a product needed.

Product standardisation Produktstandardisierung

The making of products in standard parts, which can be used in many similar products. This will lead to cost savings and permits the realisation of economies of scale.

Offering a common product on a national, regional, or worldwide basis.

Product strategy Produktstrategie

A firm`s strategy of developing the most appropriate products for its target market(s).

Product test Produkttest

The testing of a product by allowing a sample of consumers to use and evaluate it without knowing which product it is.

Product trial Produktversuch

The rate at which consumers in your target market buy or try your product for the first time, eg 60% of coffee buyers tried your coffee and 10% of the trialists repurchased it.

Product value Produktwert

The value of a particular product, usually its market value. It may be required for customs or insurance purposes.

Product-market matrix Produkt-Markt-Matrix

A visual means of defining a business by its markets and by the products sold to these markets.

Production (Pn, pdn) Produktion, Fertigung, Herstellung
Output, Produktionsausstoß
Vorlage

Production is the creation of economic goods and services, i.e. the creation of utilities, for consumption purposes. Consumption is the final aim of production.
Production may be direct (i.e. the creation of utilities for immediate and final consumption; these goods are known as consumer goods), or indirect (i.e. the creation of goods for use in further production; these goods are known as producer goods).

Production also includes the distribution and sale of goods after their manufacture, since without these operations consumption would be impossible. Direct services too are regarded as forms of production.
The total volume of production thus becomes the total of all goods and services produced during a period.

The output of a factory, often expressed in units produced per hour, week, month or year.

The presentation of a document (e.g. a bill of exchange).

Production bonus Akkordprämie

An extra payment made for additional production, or for production exceeding standard output.

Production capacity Fertigungs-, Produktionskapazität

Also called output or productive capacity.

The maximum amount of production which can be achieved in a stated period with the equipment available.

Production coefficient Produktionskoeffizient

Also called technical coefficient.

$$\text{Production coefficient} = \frac{\text{volume of factor input}}{\text{volume of output}}$$

Production cost(s) Produktionskosten

The total of all the manufacturing costs.

Production cycle Fertigungszeit

Also called production period or time; manufacturing cycle, period or time; or production lead time.

The period of production time, from raw materials to finished product.

Production department Produktions-, Fertigungsabteilung

Also called product or production division; factory department.

The place where a company's goods, ie its finished products, are produced or prepared. It may be occupied in assembling together separate materials produced elsewhere, or it may be involved in organizing and controlling production taking place on the factory floor.

Production function Produktionsfunktion

The mathematical relationship between output of a company or economy and the inputs (e.g. capital, labour, raw materials, etc.) used to produce that output.

Economists tend to express the nature of the production process (i.e. the transformation of resources into goods) by means of a simple equation:

$Q = f(X_1, X_2, \ldots\ldots, X_n; T)$. This expression says that output, Q, is a function, f, of the inputs $(X_1,\ldots,X_n)$ and the prevailing state of technology or know-how, T. The most important item in the equation is the f-sign (representing function) which tells us that there exists a systematic relationship between inputs and outputs.

Production lag Produktionsverzögerung

The amount of time which elapses to change the output mix, for example as a result to price changes.

Production possibility curve Produktionsmöglichkeitskurve

Also called transformation curve.

A curve that shows the maximum amount of any two products that can be produced from a fixed set of resources.

Production sharing Produktionsaufteilung

A concept of international business and trade introduced by the American management expert Peter Drucker.

Production sharing means that manufacturing, assembly and marketing take place in different countries. Thus, a product is manufactured in one country, assembled in another, and marketed in a third.
For example, production sharing permits developed countries to turn to less developed countries where there is a surplus of cheap labour, qualified only for semiskilled or unskilled jobs, which can be employed in labour-intensive manufacturing.

Productive efficiency Produktivitätsoptimum

A situation where an increase in yield of one item results in a decrease of yield of another item.

Professional journal Fachzeitschrift

Also called scientific journal.

A magazine whose editorial content is designed for the members of a specific profession, eg doctors, lawyers, marketing specialists, personnel managers, etc.

Profit Gewinn, Erfolg

Also called earnings, income or surplus.

To the accountant, profit means simply the difference between total revenue and total costs. Profit = revenue - costs.

The purpose of business activity is to make a profit by supplying goods and services to consumers. This is done by buying goods at one price and selling them at a higher price. A rough indication of profits can be obtained by subtracting the cost of the goods from the money received from selling them.

Profit may be expressed as before or after tax.

There are various types of profit:
1. gross profit: the difference between turnover and the cost of the goods sold;
2. net profit: gross profit minus expenses (e.g. rent, taxes, wages, depreciation, etc.;
3. pure profit: this is what is left of the producer's income after all payments have been met;
4. normal profit: an acceptable return on capital invested - every enterprise must earn a reasonable reward for the capital invested in it, otherwise the capital will leave the industry and go to some alternative employment where the rewards for bearing uncertainties are better;
5. supernormal profit: any excess over normal profit; it encourages the movement of resources from activities in which below normal profit is earned;
6. trading profit: trading revenue minus trade expenses;
7. profit before tax: trading profit plus net non-trading revenue;
8. profit after tax.

As long as uncertainty exists there can be no general rate of profit, for profit will vary between different industries according to the extent of uncertainty in each line of production. Differences in profit between firms in the same industry are due to differences in the skill of entrepreneurs in bearing uncertainty. When "boom" times come the entrepreneur is able to make good profits, which rise faster than wages, rent or interest. When a "slump" arrives the reverse is true.

Profit based pricing objectives — gewinnorientierte Preisbildungsziele

A pricing strategy aiming at some type of profit goals: eg profit maximization, satisfactory profit, return on investment (ROI), early cash recovery, etc.

Profit impact of market strategy (PIMS) — Gewinnträchtigkeit einer Marktstrategie, PIMS

A research programme which provides reports on the products, the financial and market performance of a few thousand strategic business units (SBUs) representing several hundred firms. These reports assist firms in analysing marketing performance and formulating marketing strategies.

Profit margin Gewinnspanne

Also called margin of profit, margin over cost(s), markup, or operating margin.

That percentage of the selling price which represents a trader's profit. For example, if an article which costs £ 80 is sold at £ 100, the profit margin is

$$\frac{20}{100} \times 100 = 20\%$$

Profit maximising pricing gewinnmaximierende Preisfestlegung

A pricing strategy where the seller researches to find the likely level of demand at different prices and then calculates which is the most profitable.

Profit maximization Gewinnmaximierung

The hypothesis that all firms seek to maximize profits. That is, they produce the output at which the positive difference between total revenue and total costs is at a maximum. The output at which profits are maximized (or losses are minimized) is known as the equilibrium output of the firm.

From the point of view of marginal costs (MC) and marginal revenue (MR), profit maximization requires that MC = MR. To see why this is so, consider the following: each additional unit produced which adds more to a firm's revenue than to its costs will increase profits; so a firm will not forgo the production of any unit of output where MR is greater than MC. Conversely, if MC is greater than MR, the unit will detract from profits, so a firm will not wish to produce any unit where MR is less than MC. It follows, therefore, that profits will be maximized where the output is produced at which MR = MC.

Profit maximization is rejected in modern finance theory; today it is possible to assume that businessmen only aim to reach satisfactory levels of sales, profits, growth and security.

Profit oriented pricing gewinnorientierte Preisfestsetzung

A pricing strategy intended to maximize profit during a given time period. Profit oriented pricing of a product or service for a single market is different from, and simpler than, that for two or more market segments.
Note: there is no need to include fixed costs in the costs to be considered in setting profit maximizing prices. The price at which the greatest contribution to profit and fixed costs is realized will also be the point of maximum profit.

Profit percentage Umsatzrendite, Umsatzrentabilität

Also called percentage return on sales, or profit on sales.

This is obtained by the formulas:

$$\text{gross profit percentage} = \frac{\text{gross profit}}{\text{turnover (sales)}} \text{ X } 100$$

$$\text{net profit percentage} = \frac{\text{net profit}}{\text{turnover (sales)}} \text{ X } 100$$

Profit squeeze Gewinndruck

Profit decrease resulting from stable prices and increasing costs.

Profit taking Gewinnmitnahme

Also called realization.

The selling of securities or commodities after a sharp rise in price to cash in gains. Profit taking pushes down prices, but usually only temporarily.

Profit to sales ratio Verhältnis Gewinn zu Umsatz

The profit before tax expressed as a percentage of sales value.

$$\text{profit to sales ratio} = \left(\frac{\text{profit before tax}}{\text{sales value}} \text{ X } 100 \right)$$

Profitability Rentabilität

Also called rate of return on capital employed (ROCE), rate of profit or rate of profitability, return on investment (ROI) or profitable efficiency.

The state of bringing profit.

A measure of earnings. For example, the measure of the profit of a product in relation to the amount of money invested.

Profitability analysis Rentabilitätsanalyse

Also called return on investment (ROI) analysis.

An analysis designed to provide information on the profit performance of individual investments in order to determine appropriate corrective action.

Profiteer Geschäftemacher

A person who makes a profit on the sale of scarce or rationed goods.

Profits tax Gewinnsteuer

Tax to be paid on profits, nowadays called corporation tax.

Program station basis (PSB) Programmeinschaltquote eines Senders

The percentage of radio or TV receivers in a coverage area tuned in to a given program at a specific moment.

Progress payment Fortschrittszahlung, Abschlagszahlung

Also called progress billing or stage payment.

A payment made by a customer as work progresses instead of making full payment on completion.

Progress report Fortschrittsbericht, Lagebericht

A report on a particular situation, sent from time to time, informing someone of the progress made, eg in executing an order.

Projection Projektion, Prognose

Working out estimates of future developments based on the knowledge of past or present events.
Economists use econometric models to project gross national product (GNP), inflation, unemployment and many other factors.

Promoter Veranstalter, Promoter

One who shares the financial costs and risks of bringing about a special event, e.g. a pop concert.

Promotion Verkaufsförderung

Also called sales promotion.

The ways by which customers become aware of a product, including advertising, public relations, selling and merchandising. The aim is to increase sales.

Promotion manager Promotionmanager, Leiter der Verkaufsförderungsabteilung

A person responsible for a company`s promotional activities and campaigns.

Promotion mix Verkaufsförderungsmix

Also called promotional mix.

These are the tools available to a marketer to communicate.
They may be split into two major parts:
1. non-personal communication, which is "one-way" only (e.g. messages sent in print form);
2. personal communication, where "two-way" communication can take place by the interaction between people.

Promotion has its own mix consisting of:
1. the advertising mix (eg radio, TV, magazines, newspapers, direct mail, outdoor ad, etc.);
2. the personal selling mix (eg selection, training, compensation, control, territory; etc);
3. the sales promotion mix (eg coupons, premiums, samples, POP material, shows, contests, etc.);
4. the publicity mix (eg news and product releases, speeches, feature stories, etc).

Note: the marketing mix consists of:
1. product mix, 2. price mix, 3. promotion mix, 4. distribution mix.

Promotion research Verkaufsförderungsforschung

Research for advertising and personal selling.

Promotional activities Verkaufsförderungsaktivitäten

Activities that draw the attention of the trade, customers generally or even the entire public, to a firm's products or services. Such activities include exhibitions, displays, trade fairs, meetings for local businessmen, fashion shows, dinners, luncheons, press conferences, etc.

Promotional budget Verkaufsförderungsbudget

The amount of money set aside for expenditure on promotion within an accounting period.

Promotional discount Verkaufsförderungsnachlaß

A discount granted to middlemen for encouraging promotion and sales efforts.

Promotional pricing verkaufsfördernde Preisgestaltung

The temporary pricing of goods and services at lower-than-normal levels, and thus violating price norms to attract customers and force up sales. The motive for this pricing strategy may be to hold market position, make windfall profits, clear excess stock or fight a slack/sluggish demand.

Promotional tools Verkaufsförderungsmittel

Also called promotools.

Material used in promotion, such as mailing shots, on-pack premiums, display material, coupons, etc.

Prompt cash (payment) prompte Zahlung

Payment without delay. Goods must be paid for within a few working days of delivery or after receipt of a statement of account. The customer has reasonable time to examine the goods and to check the invoice.

It also means payment on or before due date.

Prompt day Abrechnungstag

The day upon which payment becomes due for the purchase of goods.

Prompt delivery (PD) sofortige Lieferung

Delivery within a few days of receipt of an order.

Prompt supplier Sofortlieferant

A supplier who delivers goods ordered immediately.

Prompted recall gestützte Erinnerung

In advertising, a test where the respondent is given some help to find out how well he/she can remember an advertisement.

Prompted response geleitete, gestützte Antwort

In market research, a situation where respondents are given some help in answering questions by providing them with a list of possible answers.

Prompts sofort lieferbare Ware

Goods which are on stock and can be delivered at once.

Proof of delivery Liefernachweis

The consignee usually signs on a delivery note and thereby acknowledges that the goods actually have been delivered and received.

Proof of purchase Kaufnachweis, Kaufbeweis

Evidence showing that an article has been bought, usually a receipt.

Some element of the product or package, eg a boxtop or label, used as evidence that the buyer has bought the product. The buyer may need it to receive a premium or refund.

Propensity to consume (C/Y) Konsumneigung
Konsumquote

Also called propensity to buy.

According to Keynes, the keenness of people to buy consumers' goods. This and personal income are the important factors influencing total consumption. Lower-income groups display a very high propensity to consume.

The functional relationship between a given level of income and consumption spending out of that income. The propensity thus is expressed as a percentage of consumption spending divided by income.

Proposal Angebot
Vorschlag

An offer, eg to sell goods.

A suggestion, ie either the act of suggesting or the state of being suggested.

Proposal solicitation Angebotseinholung

In the industrial buying process, a potential buyer`s invitation to qualified suppliers to submit proposals/offers.

Proprietary goods Markenartikel

Also called branded goods or products, proprietary products, or standardised goods.

Goods identified with a proprietary name. They are more or less standardised for selling price, for size, for appearance and for quality.

Prospect Interessent

Also called potential/prospective buyer or customer.

A person who may buy in future.

Prospect list Interessentenliste

A list of potential customers who are qualified to purchase a product or service, maintained for promotion in the hope that they will become customers.

Prospectus Emissionsprospekt
Prospekt

A document that has to be produced by a public limited company, plc (corporation, Corp.) when it offers its shares/stocks for purchase by the general public.

The prospectus must comply with the requirements of the stock exchange and is given to prospective buyers of the offering. It contains full details of the company's history, its present position and its future plans. False statements, even though made innocently, will be construed as fraud and entitle a subscriber misled by the information to claim damages against the issuers of the prospectus.

A folder or leaflet.

Prosperity Prosperität, Hochkonjunktur
Wohlstand

The uppermost phase of a business cycle. Also called boom, buoyancy or high economic activity.

The state of being rich. Also called affluence or wealth.

Protectionism Protektionismus

Also called protection.

The policy of fostering home industries. This may be done in various ways:
1. by prohibiting imports of competing products;
2. by imposing import quotas;
3. by imposing protective taxes on imports (foreign produced goods are made dearer, and, if the homemade goods can be sold for less, no one will buy the foreign goods)
4. by subsidizing home production.

Protection is necessary when it is not possible to correct the balance of payments without restricting imports.

Protective duty Schutzzoll

Also called protective tariff.

A customs duty levied/imposed on imports to discourage imports and to protect the home producers of similar products.

Prototype Prototyp

A first or experimental working model of something to be manufactured, usually on a large scale, that will help developers to examine its feasibility, costs, characteristics, design, etc.

Psychographic segmentation psychographische Marktsegmentierung

The division of a heterogeneous market into relatively homogeneous submarkets on the basis of people`s common lifestyles, eg activities, attitudes, beliefs, interests, opinions, personalities, etc.

Psychographics Phsychogramm, psychographische Merkmalsanalyse

Elements of the lifestyles of consumers, usually measured in terms of their activities, interests, opinions (AIO), likes and dislikes, etc.

Psychological price optischer, psychologischer Preis

Also called charm price or odd price.

A price which seems more attractive and acceptable to customers; but the price is not necessarily a low price. For example, £ 9.99 has greater "charm" than £ 10.00.

Psychological pricing psychologische Preisgestaltung

A pricing strategy that considers the psychology of prices, i.e. the price is used to say something about the product and is thus intended to influence the customers` perception of the actual price of the product. Two common forms of psychological pricing are odd-even pricing and prestige pricing.

Public domain (PD) urheberrechtlich nicht geschütztes Werk

Original material, such as literature or music, that has not been copyrighted or whose copyright has expired, and can therefore be used by anyone free of charge.

Public goods öffentliche Güter, Kollektivgüter

Also called collective or social goods.

These are goods which generally cannot be paid for directly by individuals and need, therefore, to be provided by the government, e.g. defence, police force.

Public interest group Bürgerinitiative

A pressure group lobbying government officials and putting pressure on managers to pay more attention to consumer rights, women`s rights, minority rights, etc.

Public relations (PR) Public Relations, PR-Arbeit, Öffentlichkeitsarbeit

Public relations is the art of communicating ideas and facts to promote friendly relations with the general public and public understanding, acceptance and appreciation of the objectives and aims of business. It tends to deal with issues rather than specifically with products or services. A public relations officer (PRO) (an educational and research specialist) is often employed to regulate contacts between the company and the public and to influence public opinion in favour of his company by various means of communication, such as newspapers, radio, TV, speeches, bulletins and exhibits.
Note: a good public image is essential to good marketing.

Public relations officer (PRO) Öffentlichkeitsmitarbeiter

A person responsible for public relations for a company, government, etc.

Public sale (P/S) Versteigerung, Auktion

Also called auction or sale by public auction.

A method of selling by letting potential buyers make bids (ie offers of money). The property is sold to the person who makes the highest bid.

Public sector staatlicher, öffentlicher Sektor

That part of the economy run by central or local government (authorities) and nationalized industries.

Public service advertising (PSA) Werbung zur Information der Öffentlichkeit

Advertising a public activity, programme or service.

Public utilities öffentliche Versorgungsbetriebe

Public undertakings which provide essential services rather than goods, e.g. electricity, gas, railway transport undertakings, waterworks, etc.

Publication Publikation, Veröffentlichung
Bekanntgabe, Veröffentlichung

A printed document sold or given to the public.

The act of publishing something.

Publication date Erscheinungsdatum

Also called date of issue.

The date on which a publication becomes available for sale to the public.

Publicity (pub) Werbung, Reklame
Publizität, Bekanntsein

The promotion concerning a firm and its product(s) made available to the public by various communication media, such as newspapers, radio, TV, etc.

Public notice, i.e. the state of being known to or seen by everyone.

Puffery marktschreierische, reisserische übertriebene Werbung; Superlativwerbung

Also called puff or puffing advertising.

Exaggerated advertising of one's own products or services. It often uses words such as "the best" or "the greatest".

Puffing marktschreierische Anpreisung

When advertising or selling a product, the legitimate practice of making obviously exaggerated claims which are not considered deceptive.

Pull date Frischhaltedatum (haltbar bis), Haltbarkeits-, Verfalldatum

Also called eat-by or sell by date.

The date stamped on (perishable) products after which they should not be consumed.

Pull strategy Pull-Strategie, Strategie des "Rausverkaufs"; Marketingstrategie zur Schaffung von Verbrauchernachfrage

Also called pulling strategy.

A producer`s promotion strategy (mainly by means of advertising and sales promotion) to persuade final consumers to buy a product or service and so "pull" them through the distribution channel to the point-of-sale (POS). This forces the channels of distribution to stock and supply the product in question. The product is pulled through the channel by consumer demand initiated by promotional efforts.

Pull-push strategy Pull-Push-Strategie

A combination of both pull and push strategies.

Pulling power Marktkraft, Werbekraft

The power of advertising and sales promotion to increase demand and sales.

Pulsing Phasenwerbung

Also called flighting or pulsation.

An advertising strategy of unevenly timed exposures of advertisements or commercials.

Pump priming Ankurbelung der Konjunktur/ Wirtschaft, staatliche Konjunkturförderung

Also called priming the pump. Sometimes also known as compensatory finance, deficit finance or deficit spending.

A government policy of public spending undertaken for the purpose of reflating the economy by stimulating demand in order to reduce unemployment. Personal incomes and consumption are increased and firms are encouraged to invest.
Pump priming was first attempted by the US government during the depths of the Great Depression in the 1930s.

Purchase contract Kaufvertrag

Also called contract of sale or sales contract.

A legal agreement between buyer and seller to buy specified goods under agreed terms and conditions.

Purchase decider Kaufentscheider

The person, eg the member of the family, who actually makes the decision regarding which product or service is to be purchased.

Purchase decision Kaufentscheidung

The final decision to buy a product or service.

Purchase discount (Einkaufs)Skonto, Barzahlungsrabatt (vom Lieferanten gewährt)

Also called cash discount.

A cash discount received by a purchaser. A term mainly used in the US.

Purchase frequency Kaufhäufigkeit

The number of times during a specific time period that the average buyer buys a particular product.

Purchase money Kaufpreis, Kaufsumme

Also called buying or purchase price.

Money paid to obtain ownership of property, ie the amount of money for which a product is bought.

Purchase order (P/O) Kaufauftrag, Bestellung

An agreement to buy. It stipulates the kind of material (description and quality), quantity, delivery date, where to ship, order number, discount, billing/invoicing instructions, and other terms. It is often drawn on a preprinted purchase order form.

The placement of an order should not be considered complete until an acknowledgement (of order) of it is received from the vendor/seller. Once accepted by the supplier/seller, the purchase order becomes a legally binding purchase contract.

Purchase pattern Kaufverhalten

The buying behaviour of consumers.

Purchase price Kaufpreis
Beschaffungspreis

The amount of money for which a product is bought. Also called purchase money or buying price.

The invoice amount of the product plus additional expenses, e.g. customs duties, insurance, packing, freight, etc. Also called supply price.

Purchase requisition Bedarfsmeldung,
Materialanforderung

A document sent to the purchase department; it indicates the quantity of specified goods which has to be ordered.

Purchase return(s) Warenrücksendung (an den Lieferer)

Also called return(s) outwards.

Goods bought by a business which are returned to the supplier because they are faulty or unsuitable. The returns are entered into the purchases returns book or journal (return(s) outwards book). The opposite of sales returns.

Purchase tax (PT) Verbrauchssteuer

Also called excise duty or tax; consumer, consumption or use tax.

A tax charged/levied on a wide range of mainly consumer goods. In GB, value added tax (VAT) came into effect in 1973 and replaced purchase tax.

Purchase(s) account Wareneinkaufskonto

Details of purchases are kept in a purchase account.
Purchases are shown on the debit side; goods returned to the supplier are shown on the credit side (if the business does not keep a separate purchases returns account). The transactions are recorded on the double-entry principle.

Purchase(s) allowance Preisnachlaß dem Käufer nachträglich wegen Beanstandung gewährt

A reduction in the invoiced price of goods purchased, usually granted because the goods have been returned to the seller, or, if kept by the buyer are not according to order. The seller usually sends a credit note (C/N) to the buyer.

Purchase(s) invoice Eingangsrechnung

An invoice received by the buyer from the supplier for the purchase of goods.
It gives full details of the nature and quantity of goods supplied, their price and the total amount payable. When it arrives, it is at once stamped with the time and date of receipt.
An invoice qualifying for cash discount (if paid within X days) receives priority treatment and is paid immediately.

Purchase(s) journal Wareneingangsbuch

Also called purchase(s) book.

A journal recording the daily purchases. It usually has a number of columns, e.g. date, supplier, invoice no, total amount, etc.

Purchaser (pchsr) Käufer, Erwerber Abnehmer

A buyer.

A buyer, client, consumer, customer or taker.

Purchases Anschaffungen, Einkäufe

Purchases is the general name for all items a business buys.
Three main kinds of purchases are made by firms:
1. purchases of current or fixed assets (e.g. machinery, vehicles, office equipment, plant);
2. purchases of consumable items (e.g. stationery for office use, packing materials);
3. purchases of goods for re-sale, or of raw materials for manufacture into goods for sale (these items are the source of the profits).

Purchases account Einkaufskonto

Also called purchasing account.

A company`s account showing the acquisition of merchandise for resale.

Purchasing Beschaffung, Einkauf, Beschaffungswesen

Also called materials management, logistics or procurement.

A function or process by which a firm acquires the factors necessary to produce and distribute goods or services.
Efficient procurement is achieved by purchasing the required quantity and quality of raw materials, parts, supplies, tooling, and equipment at the right time, from the right source and at the lowest prices (a low price is uneconomical if the required quantity is not received when needed or if the quality does not measure up to specifications, or if the supplier fails to make satisfactory adjustments for his errors - e.g. in delivery or price). Purchasing becomes particularly important, e.g. when the purchased items account for a high proportion of the product's unit cost or when the prices fluctuate widely.
Forms of purchasing are:
1. contract purchasing, 2. purchasing by requirement, 3. purchasing for a specific period, 4. market purchasing, 5. hand-to-mouth buying, 6. speculative purchasing, 7. just-in-time (JIT) purchasing, etc.

Purchasing activity Kaufvorgang

The process of buying a product or service. This activity can be broken into six stages: 1. awareness, 2. knowledge, 3. liking, 4. preference, 5. conviction, 6. purchase.

Purchasing agent Leiter der Einkaufsabteilung, Einkäufer Einkaufagent

A person in charge of a purchasing department/office. He prepares a budget to show the total purchases necessary to meet production or sales requirements; he endeavours to secure advantageous purchase prices, regular deliveries of goods meeting the required quality standards, and, a maximum turnover of inventories; he has to have a good knowledge of the selling or manufacturing processes of his firm and of the kinds of materials or commodities that are suitable. Also called purchasing officer or head of buying department.

A person who buys goods on behalf of someone else for a payment, usually a commission. Also called buying agent.

Purchasing department Einkaufsabteilung

The section of a company which is involved in the procurement of the company`s bought-in components or services, raw materials, equipment, etc. Furthermore, suppliers are located and selected, prices are negotiated and delivery is organised.

Purchasing manager Einkaufsleiter

The head of the purchasing department.

Purchasing power Kaufkraft

The value of money measured by the amount of goods and/or services it can buy at a given time. The amount of goods one can buy for say £ 1 will fall if prices rise; or increase if prices fall. In short: the value of money is inversely related to the price level. It is also the relationship between the supply of and demand for goods. For example, if the supply is great and demand is low, prices will generally fall. Also called buying power.

The power of persons having the money to buy goods and services. Also called spending power.

Purchasing power parity (PPP) Kaufkraftparität

The theory developed by the Swedish economist G. Cassel (1866 - 1945) that, when exchange rates are free to fluctuate, they will be determined by the relative purchasing power of the currencies in their home markets; there is a close relationship between the internal value of a currency and its external value.
For example, if the purchasing power of $ 1 in the USA is half of the purchasing power of £ 1 in the UK, the equilibrium rate of exchange is $ 2 : £ 1. If foreign exchange markets are operating freely, given amounts of different currencies should in theory be able to buy the same amount of goods.
Note: in reality, purchasing power has less influence on exchange rates than interest rates and other economic factors.

Pure competition reiner Wettbewerb, vollkommen homogene Konkurrenz

A theoretical rather than a real-life situation where firms are selling their product in a perfect market but buying their production factors in imperfect markets.
Note: in a situation of perfect competition both product and factor markets are perfect.

Pure monopoly reines, echtes Monopol

Also called perfect monopoly.

A single seller of a product or service for which there are no close substitutes. Thus, the monopolist can act without the possibility of any sort of direct competition.

Purpose-designed kundenspezifisch

Also called custom-built, custom-tailored, customized, made-to-order, tailored or tailor-made.

A product manufactured according to particular specified wishes of the customer.

Push money (PM) Verkaufsprämie Verkaufsförderungsprämie

Money paid, by a producer or retailer, to salespeople as a bonus when they sell specific products. Also called sales premium.

A special bonus paid by a marketer to a middleman`s, eg retailer`s, salespeople as an incentive to increase sales. Also called premium money.

Push strategy

Push-Strategie, Strategie des "Reinverkaufs"; Marketingstrategie, die den Handel zum Verkauf eines Produktes bewegen soll

A marketing policy which brings a product to the attention of the final/ultimate consumer through the cooperation of the distributive channels.That means, a producer attempts to push a product or service towards the consumer or attempts to persuade distributors (e.g. through trade allowances, pricing policies, inventory stocking procedures, etc) to take part in the marketing of the product, so "pushing" it through the distribution channel.

Pyramid selling

Schneeball-Vertriebs-System, Lawinensystem, Verkaufen nach dem Scheeballsystem

Also called multi-level distributorship.

A system of selling goods to the public by agents who help to establish a distribution network. The agents are originally customers, who then buy the rights to sell certain goods as well as a minimum quantity of the goods themselves. Many agents discover that there is little prospect of recovering their money (the payment made to the company for the right to sell its products) in the form of sales, and they concentrate on the recruitment of new agents, for each of whom they receive a cash payment. These newcomers, in turn, put down a payment to the company for the right to sell their goods and they too try to get their money back by recruiting others.
Success depends on selling to further people the right to sell the product and not to sell the product. As the system is open to abuse, it has been made illegal in many countries.

Q

Q rating — Einschaltquote von Hörern/ Zuschauern, die bewußt ihr Lieblingsprogramm eingeschaltet haben

The percentage of radio listeners or TV viewers who are listening/watching a particular programme because they regard it as their favourite.

Qualified acceptance — eingeschränkte Annahme

An offer that has been accepted, but not completely; thus a counteroffer to another's original offer.

Qualitative interview — qualitatives Interview, Intensivinterview

A detailed interview with a small number of respondents.

Quality (Q, qlty) — Beschaffenheit, Eigenschaft, Güte, Qualität

Standard of excellence that a thing or person has.
The quality of a product is defined by a set of specifications governing functional performance, composition, strength, shape, dimensions, workmanship, color and finish.
Quality is meaningful only in relation to the purpose and end use of the product. Good quality is attained when a product or a service fully satisfies the purpose for which it is designed.

Quality advertising — Qualitätsmarketing

Advertising targeted at a specific consumer profile.

Quality and price Qualität und Preis

The price of a product also depends on whether a firm wants to please a few quality-conscious customers by emphasizing quality or to sell a lot of a product by emphasizing low price. Emphasis on quality pays off because the relatively few customers are prepared to pay extra for the quality product. Consumers tend to judge the quality of a product by the price itself.
Note:
1. profitable small companies often focus on quality at higher prices rather than quantity at lower prices because, in order to make a profit, they must produce and sell more of a low-priced product;
2. firms with high-quality products also evaluate the importance of price in their marketing strategy.

Quality assurance Güte-, Qualitäts(zu)sicherung

The assurance that quality standards are agreed and met throughout the company, to ensure customer satisfaction. Factors that must be considered are, eg: the system of quality monitoring and control, the ability to deliver on time, the quality of materials and supplies, etc.

Quality certificate Qualitätszeugnis

Also called certificate of quality.

A certificate, issued by an independent third party, certifying that goods are of a required standard.

Quality competition Qualitätswettbewerb

Also called competition on quality or competition in terms of quality.

Competition where firms emphasize a superior, more attractive product, or better service than that offered by other products.

Quality control (QC) Qualitätskontrolle

The recognition and removal of identifiable causes of defects and variations from the set standards. It seeks to maintain high standards of quality by testing the product of a manufacturing process, either by testing every unit or by testing a random sample of each day's output. When a product is substandard, special techniques can be used for the systematic observation of quality; then corrective action can be undertaken. Proper standardization and effective control of materials, machines, and workmanship ensure uniform quality in the product.

Quality control seeks to reduce customer complaints, and wasted or rejected units of output. It is particularly important in mass production.

Quality controller Qualitätskontrolleur

A person checking the quality of a product before it is sold.

Quality market Qualitätsmarkt

A market in which the quality of the product or service matters more than the price.

Quality modification Qualitätsmodifikation

A change, eg by altering the materials or the production process, relating to a product`s reliability and durability.

Quality newspaper Qualitätszeitung

A nontabloid paper using a fairly developed command of the language and offering both news and comment.

Quality of life Lebensqualität

The sense of well being felt as regards one`s life, life style and standard of living. The most important factors influencing the quality of life include: health, income, education, safety, job satisfaction and security, wealth, recreation facilities, leisure time, etc. Certainly, the importance of these factors will vary by individuals and culture over time.

If businesses make available the products and services necessary to provide the desired standards of living and a satisfying quality of life at the right price and quality, and with no associated negative impact in such areas as the environment, then no problems arise.

Quality of life segmentation Segmentierung nach Lebensqualität

The grouping of markets or countries based on income per capita. This method assumes that market behaviour is directly related to income; an assumption which is very questionable.

Quantitative interview quantitatives Interview

An interview based on a statistically valid sampling of a target market.

Quantity (Q, qnt, qnty, qt, qty) Menge, Quantität
Unmenge

An amount, eg a quantity of sugar.

A large amount or number of.

Quantity advertising Quantitätswerbung

Advertising targeted at a larger audience than seen on TV.

Quantity demanded Nachfragemenge, nachgefragte Menge

The maximum quantity of a good buyers are willing and able to buy at a given price during a period of time.

Quantity discount Mengenrabatt

Also called bulk discount, volume discount, quantity allowance, or quantity rebate.

A price reduction, usually in percent, given for large orders/bulk orders. The greater the quantity bought, the cheaper the unit price. The discount is offered by suppliers in order to increase turnover. Most quantity discount arrangements apply to either single orders or single deliveries; but some discounts are paid retrospectively on the basis of orders received or goods delivered (then also called turnover bonus).

Quantity supplied Angebotsmenge, angebotene Menge
Liefermenge, gelieferte Menge

The maximum quantity of a good sellers are willing and able to supply at a given price during a time period.

The quantity of a good actually delivered by a seller. Also called quantity delivered.

Quarterly Vierteljahreszeitschrift

Publication issued four times a year.

Quasi retailing Quasieinzelhandel

Retailing relating to the sale of services rather than goods.

Query (Qy, qy) Frage, Erkundigung

A question or an inquiry.

Question and answer (q & a) Frage-und-Antwortspiel

An advertising method in which one consumer asks a question (eg about a product), and another (or others) answer(s) it.

Question mark Fragezeichen(produkt), Sorgenkind, Wildkatze

Also called problem child or wild cat.

In the Boston matrix, products that are in growth markets, but have a low market share and which are not very profitable. A question mark needs a great deal of cash and substantial marketing activites to maintain or increase market share in the face of keen competition. If nothing is done to change its market share, the question mark will remain a cash loser and, when growth slows down, become a dog.

Question types Fragearten

There are a number of different types of question, eg:
1. ambiguous question, 2. closed question, 3. closed-end question, 4. control question, 5. dichotomous question, 6. direct question, 7. filter question, 8. leading question, 9. limited response question, 10. multiple choice question, 11. open-ended question, 12. ranking (scale) question, 13. rating question, 14. semistructured question, 15. sentence completion question, 16. structured question, 17. unambiguous question, 18. unanswerable question, 19. unstructured question, etc.

Questionnaire Fragebogen, Erhebungsbogen

A base document for research studies containing both instructions which the interviewer has to complete for each respondent (interviewee or participant) interviewed and a set of questions seeking objective data or subjective opinion on a given subject.
In order to obtain the right answers, one must ask right and clear questions.
Questions may be:
1. closed-ended (i.e. answerable by checking one of several predetermined answers),
2. open-ended (i.e. respondents answer in their own words),
3. semi-structured (ie questions are structured but allow a certain amount of freedom in answering).
Note: 1. a specific set of objectives is essential, 2. a questionnaire should contain control questions indicating the reliability of the respondent.

The questions must be explicit, inoffensive and unambiguous. Generally, the "yes" or "no" or pre-choice type of answer produce the best results. The "yes" or "no" technique tends to aid classification of answers and thereby enables a more meaningful report to be produced. Futhermore, it is desirable that the questionnaire be tested in the field to eliminate any problems in its content which later could prove costly. Above all, the questionnaire should be so formed to produce all the relevant data required while maintaining confidentiality, for the respondent.
Before the final questionnaire is developed, the advantages and disadvantages of each should be carefully evaluated in terms of the problem being investigated.

Questionnaire design Fragebogengestaltung

After having decided on the size of the sample and the method of data collection, the questionnaire has to be designed.

There are three main types of questions:
1. Structured or closed questions. They demand short, specific answers and comprise dichotomous, multiple choice, checklist and recall questions, the Likert scale, the semantic differential and the ranking scale.

2. Unstructured or open questions. They allow respondents complete freedom to express their answers in any way they wish.
3. Semi-structured questions. These are structured questions which allow a certain amount of freedom in answering, eg as in sentence completion or word association.

When designing a questionnaire the following should be observed:
1. all the questions must be in a logical sequence;
2. the easiest questions should come in the early part of the questionnaire, whilst the more difficult and personal ones requiring some thought should be towards the end of the document;
3. the starting point must ensure that the matter under review is of concern to the respondent;
4. ask questions which the informant/respondent can answer from his own experience;
5. all irrelevant questions should be avoided as they might kill the respondent`s interest in the questionnaire;
6. the questions should not show any bias or prejudice, they should be impartial;
7. repeat questions should be omitted;
8. avoid leading questions (they lead respondents into answering a certain way),
9. avoid ambiguous questions (vague or misleading questions may be answered in many different ways),
10. avoid unanswerable questions,
11. avoid questions that respondents are unwilling to answer (eg personal questions),
12. keep your questionnaire as brief as possible,
13. ask short, easy-to-understand questions,
14. don`t provide motives for respondents to lie,
15. avoid complex words or phrases,
16. avoid unfamiliar words,
17. do not use questions that tax the memory too much,
18. each question should ask only one point,
19. avoid too wide a choice of answers, etc.

Queu(e)ing theory Warteschlangentheorie, Bedienungstheorie

Also called delay theory, theory of queues, or waiting line theory.

A theory based on the study of queues at a servicing facility (e.g. a bank or supermarket). Queues also occur very frequently in industry; e.g. partially processed parts may queue before the machine which will process them further.
Its object is to find out how to lessen the amount of time that customers have to queue and to find the state in which bottlenecks or queues are minimized.
Note: The American term for queue is line.

Queue Warteschlange

Also called (waiting) line.

A line of people waiting one behind the other.

A series of documents or telephone calls which are dealt with in order.

Quittance Schuld(en)erlaß, Entlastung (einer Schuld oder Verpflichtung) Quittung

Discharge from a debt or obligation.

A receipt. Also called bill or voucher.

Quota Quote

In general, a proportional part or share of a fixed total amount or quantity.

A restriction on international trade. There are import and export quotas.

A quota limits the quantity or total value of a particular commodity a country allows in from other countries (import quota) during a specified period. Import quotas may be imposed because of balance of payments difficulties. Export quotas may be imposed by a country heavily dependent on its export of primary products.

A production quota fixes the maximum amount of a commodity that an individual firm, e.g. a member of a quota cartel, or a particular country, may produce.

Quota cartel Quotenkartell

Also called commodity restriction scheme (US).

An agreement among firms to a specific industry by which each firm is assigned a portion of market demand. That means, a quota cartel is a cartel whose members agree to limit their output on some quota basis. All members keep their identity and their independence, except in so far as they stick to the terms agreed upon.
Note: this type of cartel is illegal.

Quota sample Quotenauswahl

A sample selected without regard to location, representativeness, etc by giving the interviewer a quota of a certain number of individuals with some specific characteristic(s).

Quota sampling Quotenauswahl, Quotenstichproben-verfahren

A sampling technique whereby a controlled sample (a quota sample) which is known to represent the special characteristics of the whole is selected.
A quota sample is made up of quotas or agreed numbers of people falling within age, sex, geographical areas, occupational groups, etc. The ratio of the sample to the whole is not significant. Whatever the number of items in the whole, a sample of between 200 and 3000 items would tend to reflect the characteristics of the whole. Certainly, the greater the size of the sample, the greater the accuracy.

Quotation (Quot, qu) Angebot
Kostenvoranschlag
Preisangabe

A detailed offer (e.g. containing quantities, prices, delivery dates, delivery terms, payment terms), in response to an inquiry, to sell goods at a price and under conditions that are stated. But it is not an offer in the legal sense that it is a promise to supply goods on the terms stated; a quotation is not necessary legally binding (i.e. if a seller quotes and later decides not to sell, the buyer has no legal remedy; but in practice the supplier will supply to protect his reputation).
Note: an offer may be firm for a stated period (firm offer) or it may not be firm (usually called a quotation). At all events, the terms 'quotation' and 'offer' are often used as synonyms. Also called quote or proposal.

A price estimate on a commercial project or transaction. Also called bid, (cost) estimate or quote.

A quotation of a price. Also called quote or quoted price.

Quoted price Kurs, Angebotspreis

The price of a particular security or commodity as it is quoted on an exchange. This price usually fluctuates from day to day.

R

Rack Regal, Gestell

Also called shelf or stack.

A frame, e.g. in a supermarket, to hold items for display.

Rack board Präsentationsgestell

A board on which articles can be displayed, showing their names and prices.

Rack folder Regal-, Ständerprospekt

A leaflet that has been folded so that it will fit into a rack/shelf designed for the display of such folders.

Racketeer Schwindler, Geschäftemacher

A person engaged in an illegal activity, eg someone who gets money in a dishonest way.

Rackjobber/rack jobber Regalgroßhändler, Service Merchandiser

Also called rack or service merchandiser.

An intermediary/jobber who specializes in providing a servicing function for food and non-food products, sold on a consignment basis. He delivers direct to the retailer without the need for storage facilities and takes over responsibility for maintaining stocks and display of particular product lines/product ranges on particular shelves/racks. He also takes back unsold items.

Radio advertising Rundfunkwerbung

Advertising on radio. Radio advertising is obtainable at reasonable rates and is thus useful for advertisers who cannot afford TV advertising, or who do not need it to sell their product(s). Radio is good during commuting hours and is good in reinforcing print or TV advertisements. Radio is especially effective when a catchy slogan or jingle can be developed.

Radio audience Rundfunkhörer(schaft)

Also called broadcast audience or listenership.

The total number of people listening to a particular radio programme. This number is very important because the fees for radio commercials are related to the listening audience, and duration and timing of the commercial.

Radio copy Radiowerbetext

The copy for a radio commercial. It should relate to the unique selling proposition (USP) and obtain the listener`s attention by voice, sound effects and jingles.

Note: impact is enforced when the USP is mentioned several times, eg at the beginning, in the middle and at the end of the commercial.

Radio household Radiohaushalt

Also called radio home.

A household owning any type of radio.

Radio rating point (RRP) Radioeinschaltquote

The number of listeners of a particular radio program or commercial as compared to the size of the potential listenership. One rating point represents 1% of the potential listenership. Thus, if a program had a rating of 15, it would mean that 15% of the potential listenership in a particular area had sets tuned in to that program or commercial.

Rail transport Bahntransport, Schienentransport

Also called railage, railroad or railway transport.

Transportation of goods by train. Note: there is an international document covering transport by rail throughout Europe: the CIM note which is effectively a railway consignment note.

Railroad showing Bahnwerbung

Also called station poster.

Posters exposed in a railroad/railway station or alongside a railroad track.

Rake off Preisnachlaß
Gewinnanteil
widerrechtliche Provision

A price reduction.

A share of profits.

A share of profits from a deal taken or received illicitly.

Ramp (Lade)Rampe

Also called loading ramp.

A raised platform from which it is easier to load goods onto a lorry/truck.

Random check Stichprobe

A check on items taken from a group without any special selection.

Random error Zufallsfehler

In statistics, an unpredictable error or mistake.

Random sampling | Zufallsstichprobenauswahl, Zufallsauswahl

Also called random selection.

In statistics, random sampling means that every item of the whole (ie the random sample) must have a full and equal opportunity of being chosen; this is almost impossible to achieve.

Random variable | Zufallsvariable

In statistics, a variable which takes on values according to its probability distribution.

Range | Bereich
Auswahl, Sortiment, Palette

The amount by which things, e.g. prices, vary from the minimum to the maximum.

The number of different products that are for sale and from which the customer can choose. Also called assortment (of goods), collection, choice, selection or line (US), e.g. product line.

Ranking question | Rangstufenfrage, Skalafrage, skalierte Frage

Also called ranking (scale) question.

In a questionnaire, a structured question used when researchers want to measure the strength of a respondent`s answer by fixed response choices. This questioning technique provides valuable information on relative consumer opinions on products or services. The respondent/interviewee provides a definite answer which yields information quickly.
For example, the technique can be applied as follows: rank in order from 1 to 5 (with one being the best and 5 the worst) your opinion of the following products. This technique neither provides any information on how good the best product is nor does i show relative difference between ranks of products.

Rate | Preis

Also called price.

The amount of money that is paid in exchange for goods or services.

Rate book Mediendatenbuch
Verkäuferhandbuch

A book stating rate cards for a number of advertising media.

A manufacturer`s manual listing products and their prices, given to the sales representative.

Rate card Anzeigenpreisliste, Werbepreisliste

Also called advertising rate list.

The price list issued by media owners showing advertising charges in various media, eg costs per page or per column cm for press, or for time slots on radio or TV or for cinema or outdoor advertising. In addition, the card will tell the advertiser other information such as the regulations governing the use of said time or space, copy regulations, kinds of products or services that are not acceptable for advertising in the medium, etc.

Note: production studios often publish rate cards listing their facilities and charges on a per hour or per day basis.

Rate cutting Frachtunterbietung

The process of cutting (freight) rates below the published tariff level in order to obtain business.

Rate discrimination Preisdiskriminierung

Also called price discrimination.

Charging different prices for almost identical goods or services to different buyers.

Rate of inflation Inflationsrate

Also called inflation rate.

The rate of change in prices. The rate is usually calculated on an annual or monthly basis.

Rate of return Rentabilität, Rendite

Also called (rate of) profitability, rate or return on investment (ROI), or return on capital employed (ROCE).

The measure of profitability which relates earnings/income to capital employed/invested. It is a ratio of profit and is calculated by measuring the earnings as a percentage of the capital invested.

Rate of return pricing Preisfestsetzung unter Berücksichtigung einer angemessenen Rendite

A method of price fixing which considers a planned rate of return on capital invested.

Rate of selling Absatzgeschwindigkeit

Also called rate of sales.

The speed at which products are sold.

Rate of turnover Umschlagshäufigkeit

Also called frequency of goods turnover, turnover rate or ratio, or stockturn rate.

The speed at which goods are sold. It is measured by the number of times a year that the average stock can be sold. To find the turnover rate, the stock in hand is averaged and divided into the sales at cost price.

$$\text{Rate of turnover} = \frac{\text{sales at cost}}{\text{average stock}}$$

This figure is meaningless by itself unless one is aware of the product to which it refers. However, whatever the product, the greater the rate of turnover, the higher the profits.

Rate war Preiskrieg

Also called price war.

A negative form of competition in which sellers sell their products below their costs in an attempt to drive competitors out of business.

Rating Einschaltquote, Erfolgskontrolle

The number of people listening (ie the listenership) or watching (ie the viewership) a radio or TV broadcast or commercial, usually expressed as a percentage.

Rating question Bewertungsfrage

A questioning technique which gives important information on relative feelings of the respondent/interviewee about various product attributes as it provides a wide range of responses for comparative purposes and does not force an arbitrary choice.
The technique works as follows:
on a scale from 1 to 9 (with 1 being "did not like it at all" and 9 being "liked it very much"), the respondent indicates his/her overall feelings about the product by marking the number that corresponds to his/her feeling. The problem with this technique may be that the distinctions on the scale may not be clear to the respondent.

Ratio Verhältnis

The relationship between one value and another.

Ratio analysis Kennziffernanalyse

The use of (financial) ratios to provide additional information and to assess a company's efficiency or to compare it with other companies.
Ratios can cover a wide range but might include, for example:
1. current assets to current liabilities (current ratio); 2. net sales to net working capital; 3. net sales to inventory; 4. current assets less stock to current liabilities (acid test ratio); 5. net profit to capital employed (rate of return on capital); 6. net or gross profit to sales (profit to sales); 7. liquid assets to current liabilities; 8. direct labour costs to indirect labour costs; etc.

Rational buying motives rationale Kaufmotive

Reasons for buying that are based on logic or judgement and not on emotion.

Rationalisation/rationalization Rationalisierung

The economic process of reorganizing resources, management structure, production, distribution, transport, etc. for the sake of maximum efficiency or economy (e.g. productivity improvements through replacing manpower by machinery).

Rationing Rationierung, Zuteilung

Also called allocation.

A system of distribution employed to limit the quantities of goods (the ration) that consumers are allowed to buy.

Raw data Rohdaten

Data which has not yet been arranged.

Raw materials Rohstoffe

Also called primary products.

Materials which are in their natural condition and have not been changed by processing. Raw materials are used to make products.

Reach Reichweite

The actual number of readers, listeners, or viewers in a medium`s audience who see or listen to an advertisement or programme at least once over some specified period.

Reach and frequency (R + F) Reichweite und Häufigkeit

The components used to figure out the gross rating points (GRPs) obtained by a broadcast media campaign.
Reach refers to the number of people reached by an advertisement, ie the people who will have at least one opportunity to see/hear (OTS or OTH) the advertisement. Frequency is the number of times each of these people is exposed to the advertising message. The product of reach and frequency is equal to the GRPs.

Read most Anteil gründlicher Leser

The percentage of the total readership who have read most of a publication or advertisement.

Reader Leser/in

A person who reads something, eg a book or newspaper.

Reader loyalty Lesertreue

Also called reader confidence.

The loyalty of a regular readership to a newspaper or magazine.

Reader profile Leserprofil

The set of demographic characteristics of the readers of various print media.

Reader response Leserreaktion

The actions taken by a reader of a publication or print advertisement, eg the placing of an order.

Reader service card Kennziffernkarte, Bingo-Karte

Also called bingo card.

A return postal card bound into a magazine and used by readers to request information or samples from various advertisers or companies mentioned in the editorial content. To receive the desired material, readers need only to mark off or encircle the proper numbers and return the usually prepaid card.

Readers per copy (RPC) Leser pro Exemplar (LpE)
Nummer (LpN)

The number of persons who read a particular issue of a publication. The number of readers is calculated by dividing the total readership by the publication`s circulation.

Readership Leserschaft, Leserkreis

Also called print media audience.

The number of people who read a magazine, newspaper, etc. (note: one person may buy a copy but many other persons will read it). The readership figure is anything from three to fifteen times greater than the circulation figure.

Readership study Leserschaftsuntersuchung

A survey of the characteristics of the readership of newspapers, magazines and journals.
These publications publish their circulation figures, but it is not the total number of readers that interests potential advertisers so much as how that readership is made up. They particularly want to know the breakdown according to age, social class, sex, occupation, residence, income, interests, hobbies, attitudes, etc.

Reading and noting Lesen und Sehen

The proportion of a publication`s readership who have noted and actually read a page or advertisement.

Reading time Lesedauer

Also called time spent reading.

The average time spent by the average reader of a publication on each issue.
Note: the more time to read the target readership will have, the more attractive a publication may be for an advertiser as the readers will also devote more time to its advertisements.

Readvertisement Zweitinserat

A second insert of advertisement.

Ready cash Bargeld

Money at hand, ie money which can be used for immediate payment.

Ready delivery Lieferung sofort nach Auftragseingang

The goods are in/on stock and can be delivered/despatched as soon as the order is received.

Ready market aufnahmefähiger Markt

A market with a high sales potential.

Ready sale leichter Verkauf

The sale of a product or service that is easily achieved.

Readymade Fertigprodukt, Fertigware

Something that is readymade, eg a garment or a piece of furniture that was made in advance for sale to any buyer.

Reaganomics Reaganomics

An economic policy named after the conservative US President Ronald Reagan. It applied supply side economics to run the US economy in the 1980s and attempted to stimulate the economy, for example, by reducing taxes, governmental interference in the market, and a switch in government expenditure so that more was spent on defense and less on social programs.

Real balance effect realer Kassenhaltungseffekt, Pigou-Effekt

Also called Pigou-effect or wealth effect.

The effect describes a situation where there is a change in the demand for commodities as a result of a change in the quantity of real money balances.
If an individual's real money balances exceed his immediate requirements he will increase his expenditure, thus reducing his real money balances. If his real balances are too low he will do the reverse. A change in the real quantity of money will thus affect demand.

Real cost Realkosten

The cost of a product or service in real terms, ie changes in the purchasing power are considered.

Real growth reales Wachstum

An increase in the output of goods and services measured at constant prices, ie after price changes have been eliminated.

Real income effektives Einkommen, Realeinkommen

Also called real earnings.

The income in terms of what can be bought with this income, i.e. the income corrected for inflation over time.

Real national income reales Volkseinkommen

The national income is the money value of goods and services available to an economy through its economic activity in a given time period. It is evident that, particularly in times of rising prices or inflation, the money value of these goods and services can increase without there necessarily being any real increase in the national income. Real national income must concern itself not simply with monetary values but with real values of the goods and services.

Real price tatsächlicher Preis

The nominal price of a good divided by a price index.

Real value realer Wert, Realwert

Also called actual value.

Real values abstract from inflation.

Real value of money tatsächliche/echte Kaufkraft, realer Geldwert

The price of money measured in terms of goods.

Realization Verkauf, Veräußerung

The selling/sale of assets, merchandise, securities, etc. for money.

Realized profit or loss realisierter Gewinn oder Verlust

Profit or loss resulting from the sale of an asset or security.

Rear Heckreklame

Also called rear-end display.

In transit advertising, the spaces available on the backs of buses, trucks and other means of transport for advertisement posters.

Reason why advertising begründete, rationale Werbung; Aufklärungswerbung

An advertising copy stating a fact about a product or service and then explaining why the claim is true.

Reasonable value angemessener Wert

A value placed on an asset that accurately reflects its worth on the open market.

Rebate Preisnachlaß, Rabatt

Also called deduction, discount or reduction.

An allowance/abatement made from an invoice/bill or in the price of goods, etc.

Rebuff schroffe Abweisung

A blunt refusal of a request, offer, etc.

Rebuy Anschlußkauf, Wieder(holungs)kauf

Also called repeat buying or purchasing.

The act of purchasing a product again.

Recall Rückruf

Also called callback.

The return of a distributed product, e.g. for exchange or repair (car factories sometimes recall defective cars). The manufacturer publishes a recall notice.

Recall test Gedächtnistest

A method of evaluating advertising effectiveness through the respondents` ability to recall advertising messages. The respondents are not shown the actual advertisement but instead are asked about what they have seen or heard recently.
Note: recall can be measured through:
1. an aided/prompted recall test, 2. an unaided/ spontaneous recall test.

Receipt (R, r, rcpt, rec) Empfang, Erhalt
Eingang
Quittung, (Zahlungs)Beleg

The act of receiving something, eg goods.

Something that is received, eg goods.

Written evidence or acknowledgement of payment. Statements of account and invoices are frequently stamped "Received with Thanks". Nowadays, however, receipts are usually issued only if a customer specifically asks for one. Also called voucher.

The letter R (for receipt) written on a cheque by an account holder indicates to the payee that a receipt is required.

Receipt of goods (ROG, rog) Warenannahme

Also called acceptance of goods.

The state of accepting goods.

Receipt of goods (ROG) dating Inkrafttreten der Zahlungsbedingungen ab Warenannahme

A sales condition under which the date for payment and the discount period are determined from the date the buyer receives the consignment, rather than from the invoice date. This method is primarily employed when great transport distances are covered.

Receipts Einnahmen
Lagerzugänge

Payments received. Also called proceeds, returns, takings or revenue.

Goods received on stock. Also called addition to stocks, incoming stocks, increase in stocks or inventory receipts.

Receiving date Empfangsdatum

The date on which something is accepted or received.

Recession marketing Rezessionsmarketing

Marketing during a period of economic recession in the home market and/or one or more of the major overseas markets. To redress the situation of falling sales, lower profits, higher fixed unit costs, lower production levels and a worsening cash flow situation, the marketeer should consider the following options:

1. evaluate the current situation and formulate a future marketing strategy;
2. examine the product range and establish their product life-cycle situation;
3. undertake market research to determine the future market profile and its constituents, e.g. total market value, competitors, pricing, import controls, exchange rates, trends, advertising, promotion, etc;
4. think of niche marketing;
5. advance the launch of new products;
6. review the advertising and promotion strategies;
7. critically review the pricing strategy;
8. review the packaging arrangements;
9. check the distribution arrangements; etc.

Reciprocal dealing Gegenseitigkeitsvereinbarung

Also called reciprocity arrangement.

An arrangement between firms whereby one firm agrees to buy from another on condition that the second one buys from it, ie they buy from and sell to each other.

Reciprocal transaction Kompensationsgeschäft

An agreement whereby one company agrees to purchase goods from a supplier provided he makes a return purchase of the buyer`s goods.

Reciprocity Reziprozitätsvertrag (AuW)
Geschäft auf Gegenseitigkeit,
wechselseitige Lieferbeziehung

An agreement between countries to charge lower import duties on each other`s goods.

The practice of placing orders with suppliers who are customers. The roles as seller and buyer are interchangeable, i.e. they buy from and sell to each other. Also called reciprocal buying or trading.

Reclos(e)able container wiederverschließbarer Behälter

A package or container which, after opening, can be resealed and reused.

Reclos(e)able pack wiederverschließbare Packung

A pack(age) which can be closed with a cap or lid.

Recognition lag Erkennungsverzögerung

A considerable amount of time elapses before a deviation from an economic situation, e.g. full employment, is recognized.

Recognition test Wiedererkennungstest, Recognition-Test

In print advertising, a method of measuring the effectiveness of an advertisement. The individual respondents are shown the actual advertisement and asked whether they recognise it. If they do, the interviewer asks additional questions to find out how much of the advertisement each respondent read.

Note: if the test provides a high degree of consumer recognition of the ad message, then the advertising is doing its job.

Recommended price (RP) empfohlener Preis, Richtpreis

Also called suggested price.

The producer supplies goods and recommends the retail prices at which they should be sold. There is nothing to prevent retailers selling at lower prices if they want. It is easy for consumers to be misled by the price markings on goods as they have no way of knowing if the recommended price has been artificially inflated so that retailers can cut prices.

Reconsignment Umleitung einer Warensendung

A route change made in a consignment before the goods have reached their place of destination.

Record Aufzeichnung, Verzeichnis

A written account of facts, events, business transactions, etc.

Record sales Spitzenumsatz

Sales which are higher than ever before.

Recovery (Konjunktur)Aufschwung, Wiederbelebung

Also called upswing, uptrend, upturn or revival.

Upward movement of the economy, i.e. an economic upturn, after a slump.

Recruitment advertising Stellenanzeige

Also called job or employment advertisement.

Advertising of open/vacant positions (vacancies), ie advertising to recruit/engage staff.

Recurring wants wiederkehrende Bedürfnisse

Wants that may be satisfied temporarily, but recur after a short time period, e.g. the desire for food.

Red herring (prospectus) vorläufiger Emissionsprospekt

Also called pathfinder prospectus.

A preliminary prospectus for a company share/stock issue, circulated before the price has been fixed. It contains all the details required by the Securities and Exchange Commission (SEC). Widely used in the USA to test the stock market's reaction to a proposed new issue of shares.

Red label Aufkleber für feuergefährliche oder explosionsgefährdete Stoffe

A label required on shipments of inflammable or explosive goods.

Redelivery Rückgabe, Rücklieferung

The return of a consignment to the party who originally delivered it.

Redemption Einlösung, Gutscheineinlösung
Einlösungsrate

The cashing in of coupons or trading stamps for a discount, premium, gift or stated product.

The percentage of coupons or trading stamps actually cashed in/turned in. Also called redemption rate.

Redistribution of income Einkommensumverteilung

Also called income redistribution.

Actions taken, e.g. progressive taxation, to reduce inequality of income.

Redistribution of wealth Vermögensumverteilung

Sharing wealth among the whole population.

Reduced price ermäßigter Preis

A price which has been lowered. When goods are offered at reduced prices, the previous price must have been charged for a continuous period of a certain number of days (eg in GB 28) within the last months (eg six months in GB). The aim of this law is to make illegal the practice of pretending goods are reduced in price when in fact they have been bought in for a special event.

Reduction Reduzierung, Verringerung
Rabatt, Nachlaß

The act of reducing or lowering, e.g. prices. Also called cutback, decrease or lowering.

The amount by which something is less or smaller. Also called discount, deduction, or rebate.

Reference book Nachschlagewerk

Also called reference work.

A book which is written on a particular subject and which is used for reference purposes, e.g. dictionaries, telephone directories, the yellow pages, etc.

Reference group Bezugsgruppe

Group of people who share some interest or purpose, interact, influence other persons` thoughts, or to which people turn in order to measure the acceptability of what they do.

Reference price Vergleichspreis

Prices, eg current or past prices, that potential buyers carry in their minds and refer to when they look at a specific product.

Referral selling Verkauf nach Weiterempfehlung

Selling to new customers who have been recommended by previous satisfied customers.

Refill pack Nachfüllpackung

A pack or container which can be filled again.

A material or the like which can replace something that has been used up.

Reflation Reflation

A mild form of inflation designed to gently stimulate the economy, usually by pumping in more money to encourage demand, production and investment in capital equipment. Action is taken to raise output to a level of full employment. Reflation accompanies the upswing of trade.
If reflation results in increasing demand which the domestic market cannot satisfy, then prices will rise and imports will increase.

Reflationary measure may be: increased government spending, lowered interest rates, and tax cuts.

Refund (refd) Rückerstattung, Rückvergütung

Also called reimbursement or repayment.

The paying back of money (e.g. he obtained a full refund when he complained about the product's quality).

Refund offer Warenangebot mit Rücknahmegarantie und Rückerstattung des Kaufpreises bei Nichtgefallen; Angebot zur Rückerstattung des Kaufpreises bei Nichtgefallen der Ware

Also called money back (guarantee) or cash-back offer.

An offer made by the seller to return the amount paid for an item to the buyer if he/she does not want to keep the item purchased.

Refusal to deal/sell Liefersperre

A situation in which a producer refuses to allow certain dealers to carry his products.

Regional issue Regionalausgabe

Also called regional edition or regional market edition.

A national newspaper or magazine that differs across geographic areas so that a publisher can vary the editorial content and advertisements. Thus, local advertisers can purchase advertising space separately to advertise in their own geographic area.

Regional segmentation regionale Segmentierung

The grouping of markets according to regions rather than country by country. Regional alliances, e.g. the EU or the NAFTA, create huge markets, facilitate cross-border transactions and enable companies based in the region to obtain economies of scale sufficient to make them competitive in the global market.

Register Register, Verzeichnis

A document, usually in form of a book, in which are recorded important details.

Registered design eingetragenes Gebrauchsmuster

A design which is legally registered thus providing protection against its unauthorized use.

Registered trademark eingetragenes, (gesetzlich) geschütztes Warenzeichen

A trademark which has been registered with the appropriate authorities in the user's country. Registration bestows the exclusive legal right to its use - no one else can use this trademark. Sign: ®

Regression analysis Regressionsanalyse

A statistical method of examining the relationship between one dependent variable, eg sales volume, and one or more independent variables, eg advertising expenditure, cost of salespersons.

Regressive commission regressive Provision

A sales commission where the rate paid decreases with the quantity of goods sold.

Regressive demand inverse Nachfrage, Nachfrage durch Wertzuwachs

A situation where at a certain price the quantity demanded is very small; at a higher price we would expect demand to be even less, but demand for the product is xceptional and increases when the price is raised.

Regressive supply inverses Angebot

A situation where the supply increases when the price falls (a situation which is not ery common).

Regular customer Stammkunde

Also called regular, regular patron; old or steady customer.

A customer who orders and reorders regularly.

Regular model Standardmodell

he main product in a firm`s product range.

Reinforcement advertising Festigungswerbung, Verstärkungswerbung

Advertising intended to assure current users that they have made the right choice to buy a particular product, and to tell them how to get the most satisfaction from the product`s use. The purpose of reinforcement ad is to make the positive product features stronger in order to prevent a loss in sales and to maintain market share.

Reject Ausschußteil, fehlerhaftes Stück

Also called defective item or unit, sub-quality unit, or waster.

A unit of output which fails to reach the required quality standard.

Reject shop Laden für zweite Wahl

A shop selling rejects, ie goods of substandard quality.

Rejection Ablehnung, Annahmeverweigerung

Also called refusal.

Refusal to accept something. For example, the refusal by the buyer to accept and pay for the goods; or the refusal by the offeree to accept the offer which has been made to him.

Rejects Ausschuß(ware)

Also called lost units or spoilage.

Incorrectly manufactured products that fail to meet quality control standards or that retailers will not accept for sale to final consumers.

Related display Auslage verwandter Produkte

The display of dissimilar but related products.

Related product artverwandtes Erzeugnis

Also called allied product.

Products which, although different, are connected by common basic components.

Relationship marketing Kundenpflegemarketing

A company`s marketing activity seeking to develop and maintain continuous long-term ties with its suppliers, distribution intermediaries, and customers.

Relative income hypothesis relative Einkommenshypothese

A theory of consumption and saving, developed by J. Duesenberry, stating that a person's consumption depends more on other people's consumption than on his own level of income (i.e. the poor will spend a higher proportion of their income than the rich). This hypothesis recognizes the "Keeping up with the Joneses" phenomenon. The theory is an alternative theory to the permanent-income hypothesis.

Relative market share (RMS) relativer Marktanteil

The market share (MS) held by a firm relative to its largest competitor. It is calculated by dividing the market share of a firm by the market share of its largest competitor.

Note: a firm should know the RMS held by each product in the product portfolio.

Relative price relativer Preis

The price of one good expressed in terms of another, rather than in money. Thus, good A's relative price tells how much of good B must be given to get one more unit of good A.

Relative product failure relativer Produktmißerfolg

A situation which occurs when a firm makes a profit on a product but the product does not reach its profit objectives and/or adversely affects the firm`s image.

Relaunch Wiedereinführung, Relaunch

Putting a product back on the market again, usually with some new feature, eg after the product has failed before.

Release Veröffentlichung
Gelder, Waren freigeben

The publishing of news. Also called press release.

The release of funds or goods.

Release note (RN) Freigabebescheinigung

A receipt signed by a customer acknowledging delivery of goods.

Reliability Zuverlässigkeit

The state or quality of being reliable. For example, the ability to perform a service dependably, accurately, and consistently.

Religious segmentation religiöse Segmentierung

The grouping of countries according to their religion, e.g. the Christian religions, Buddhism, Hinduism, Islam, etc.

Remainder Rest, Restbestand, Restbetrag

Also called residual amount or quantity.

What is left, e.g. a quantity of goods (the leftover stock) or an amount of money (ie a balance or residue).

Remarketing Remarketing

A marketing activity intended to encourage renewed use of a product in which market interest has dropped.

A marketing acitivity designed to reach the prospects who did not respond to the first sales effort.

Remarking Wiederauszeichnung

The practice of marking merchandise again, eg due to price changes.

Reminder advertising Erinnerungswerbung

Also called follow-up advertising or rememberance advertising.

Advertising used to remind the public that the product or service still exists, ie advertising devoted to overcoming memory lapse.

A campaign of brief mentions of a product that is assumed to be familiar to the audience.

Remuneration Vergütung, Honorar

Also called compensation or fee.

Payment for a service done.

Renewal Abonnementsverlängerung
Plakatauswechslung
Erneuerung

An order received from a current subscriber to renew his/her subscription.

In advertising, the replacement of a poster because it is damaged.

The act of renewing, the state of being renewed, or something renewed.

Reorder Nachbestellung

Also called repeat order.

The subsequent order of a product after its initial purchase.

Reorder quantity Bestellbestand, Meldebestand, kritischer Lagerbestand

Also called re-order level, reorder point (ROP), recordering quantity or protective inventory.

The quantity of materials, supplies, or merchandise on hand/on stock that signals the need to reorder. It is the sum of the minimum stock level and the expected usage during the reorder period.
The reorder quantity is a figure larger than the minimum stock/inventory level as it considers the delivery time.

Repeat advertising Wiederholungswerbung

Also called repetition or repetitive advertising.

The repetition of an advertisement or commercial a number of times. It is assumed to be necessary to repeat ads several times before there is a satisfactory probability that an acceptable proportion of the target audience will have seen it at least once. Furthermore, a prospective customer should have been exposed to advertising a certain number of times before being able to take it in fully.

Repeat demand Dauernachfrage

Consumer demand for goods or services which are purchased regularly, e.g. bread.

Repeat order Nachbestellung

Also called reorder, replenishment or supplementary order.

Ordering the same product or service with the same supplier.

Repeat purchasing Wieder(holungs)kauf

Frequent and automatic buying, ie without any conscious thought, of a product or service, usually for everyday use.

Repetitive manufacture/production Serienfertigung, Serienproduktion

Also called serialized manufacture or production, serial production, or series manufacture.

The production of one or more closely related standard items that generally go into storage from which sales are made.

Replacement Ersatz(stück)
Erneuerung, Umtausch

An item which replaces something.

The act of replacing.

Replacement demand Ersatzbedarf

Also called replacement needs.

Demand for consumer durables and industrial capital goods which are only purchased as replacements for worn-out or out of date items, ie depreciated or obsolete items.

Replacement good Ersatzware

A commodity replacing another one of the same kind.

Replacement lag Wiederbeschaffungsverzögerung

The amount of time which elapses to replace assets or to use up available inventories before new orders are placed.

Replacement price Wiederbeschaffungspreis

The price at which material identical to that which is to be replaced could be bought at the date of valuation. Note: this price differs from the actual cost price at the actual date of purchase.

Reply card Antwortkarte

Also called bingo card.

A card, sometimes prepaid, added to advertisements to encourage a reply.

Reply coupon (RC) Rückantwortschein

Also called reader reply form or card.

A coupon attached to an advertisement which has to be filled in and returned to the advertiser either placing an order or requesting further information. Use of a reply coupon is sometimes known as coupon advertising.

Reply paid envelope Freiumschlag

Also called postage paid envelope, return by stamped and addressed envelope (return by SAE), or stamped envelope.

An envelope that is addressed to the sender and already stamped.

Reply time Antwortfrist

The time period during which an offer made by the offerer to the offeree remains valid.

Report Bericht
Gutachten

A formal account of an investigation into a given subject. It must be accurate, clearly arranged, simple and easy to read. There are annual reports, audit reports, financial reports, marketing reports, research reports, etc. In many instances a report will include recommendations or suggested solutions.

An expert opinion. Also called expertise, official report or survey.

Repositioned product neupositioniertes Produkt

An existing product targeted at new markets or market segments. For example, a firm may reposition a brand from a unisex to a men`s or women`s brand.

Repositioning Neupositionierung, Umpositionierung

A firm`s conscious effort of changing consumers` perceptions of a product in relation to competing products, eg by a change in its advertising.

Note: changing demographics, declining sales, or competitors` actions often motivate firms to reposition established products.

Repossession Wiederinbesitznahme

The recovery of merchandise by the seller after delivery, owing to a customer`s failure to pay in full.

Representation Vertretung
Stellvertretung

An agency selling goods for a company. Also called agency.

The act of representing, or the state of being represented.

Representative (rep) Vertreter
Repräsentant

A person appointed to act for others.

A person who acts in the interests of the firm for whom he works within the country (note: an agent works for a firm abroad). He calls on customers and tries to get orders. He receives a commission on the amount of orders executed and gets a fixed salary. Also called sales representative.

A company which works for another company, selling its goods.

Representative office Repräsentanz

Also called agency.

An office established in a foreign country to represent a domestic company abroad.

Representative sample repräsentative Stichprobe

Also called average sample.

A quota sample including various elements of a population that are regarded as representative of the whole population.

Repressed inflation zurückgestaute Inflation

Also called suppressed inflation.

Inflation that would be much greater if the government were to remove controls on prices and wages. There is persistent excess demand for goods and services but prices are prevented from rising because of price and wage controls; consumers will not be able to satisfy their demand.

Repurchase (RP) Wiederkauf

The act of buying something again.

Repurchase cycle Wiederkaufszyklus

The period within which customers repeat their purchases. Products that are frequently purchased require high frequency advertising to remind consumers to buy.

Request for proposal (RFP) Aufforderung zur Angebotsabgabe

Also called request for quotation (RFQ).

In competitive bidding, a form sent to each qualified supplier on the bidding list for the particular product. The RFP includes the description and specification of the product, the product identification number, the quantity, the terms and conditions of delivery, the contract terms, and the due date of the bid. Normally, the contract is awarded to the lowest bidder.

Request(ed) circulation Frei-, Gratisexemplare
bestellte Exemplare

Copies of a publication which people receive free of charge but only on request.

The subscribed copies of a publication.

Requirements Bedarf

Also called demand.

Things which are needed.

Rerouting Umleitung

The activity or process of altering or amending the original route as specified on the consignment note or elsewhere so that a different route is to be followed.

Rerouting request Nachsendeantrag

A request made to the post office or mailing company to redirect/send on letters or parcels to the applicant`s new address.

Resale Weiterverkauf, Wiederverkauf

Also called reselling.

Selling goods which have been bought.

Resale price maintenance (RPM) Preisbindung der zweiten Hand,
vertikale Preisbindung

Also called vertical price fixing or resale price fixing.

RPM is the practice whereby the manufacturer fixes the prices at which retailers may sell his products. Today, the practice of RPM has been replaced by that of recommended prices.

Resale restriction Wiederverkaufsbeschränkung

A situation in which a producer stipulates to whom distributors may resell its products.

Research and development (R & D) Forschung und Entwicklung

Applying the findings of science and technology in creating improvements, new products, services and manufacturing processes.

Reseller market Wiederverkäufermarkt

A market consisting of firms that acquire goods and services in order to sell them again at a profit.

Reservation Buchung, Reservierung

Also called booking.

The process of booking, e.g. a seat on a plane, capacity on a transport unit, etc.

Reservation of title (RT) clause Eigentumsvorbehaltsklausel

Also called reservation of ownership clause, retention of title (RT) clause or retention of ownership clause.

In a sales contract, a clause to prevent title to the goods passing to the buyer until the seller has been paid for the goods. The seller retains the right to repossess the goods if payment is not received when agreed. With a simple RT clause the seller delivers the goods to the buyer but retains legal ownership of them until payment has been made.

Reservation price Mindestverkaufspreis

Also called minimum selling price.

The price below which the seller will not sell; he will sell, however, at any price above the reservation price.

Reserve price Mindestpreis

Also called fall back price; floor, lowest or minimum price, or upset price.

The minimum selling price, i.e. the lowest price an owner of goods is prepared to accept, e.g. used at auctions or when stock is being cleared at reduced prices.

Reshipment Wiederverladung
Wiederverschiffung
Umladung

The reloading of goods onto a vehicle.

The repeated shipment of goods.

The act or process of trans(s)hipping. Also called trans(s)hipment.

Resource-oriented industries rohstofforientierte Industrien

Industries that tend to locate near the source of the raw materials they use. Usually the costs of transporting the raw materials used by the industry are substantially higher than those for shipping/transporting the finished product to market.

Resources Ressourcen

Anything that can be used to satisfy a need. There are natural resources, e.g. ore; manmade resources, e.g. tools; renewable resources, e.g. timber; and nonrenewable resources, e.g. oil reserves.

Respondent Befragter, Proband

Also called interviewee or participant.

The interviewee, i.e. the person answering answers to research questions.

Response Antwort, Erwiderung
Reaktion

An answer, reply or rejoinder.

Any behaviour or reaction that results from a stimulus.

Response rate Antwortquote, Rücklaufquote

Also called rate of response, number of responses, cooperation rate or success rate.

A measure of advertising effectiveness, usually expressed in percentage terms; e.g. the number of completed questionnaires returned to those distributed, or in direct mail, the number of replies (eg an order or enquiry) per thousand; in other forms of advertising, the number of replies per insertion.

Restocking Lagerauffüllung, Lageraufstockung

Also called inventory accumulation, buildup, rebuilding, replenishment or restocking; refilling of inventory, or replenishment of stocks.

Ordering more stock in order to meet production or sales needs.

Restraint of competition Wettbewerbsbeschränkung

Also called restriction of competition.

Actions that may restrict, distort or prevent competition.

Restricted market beschränkter Markt

Also called reserved market.

A market in which producers agree not to sell more than a certain quantity in order to control and restrict competition.

Restrictions on trade Handelsbeschränkungen

Also called restraints of trade or trade restrictions.

Barriers which restrict trade, the main form of restrictions are:
1. tariffs (ie taxes on imported goods); 2. quotas (ie quantitative restrictions);
3. exchange controls; 4. subsidies to home produced goods.

Restrictive business practices (RBPs) restriktive Geschäftspraktiken

Acts of enterprises that limit entry/access to markets or indirectly restrict competition.

Restrictive practice(s) wettbewerbsbeschränkende(s) Verhalten

Also called restrictive trade practice(s) or restraint(s) of trade.

An arrangement between producers or suppliers of goods to restrict/limit competition among themselves, e.g. by enforcing minimum prices, controlling output and sharing markets. This practice is not in the public interest as it offends the rules of competition.

Restrictive Trade Practices Act (RTP Act, RTPA) Kartellgesetz (GB)

Also called Law Against Restraint of Competition.

In GB, the RTP Act protects the public from trade agreements which are against the public interest.

Retail advertising Einzelhandelswerbung

Advertising by retailers direct to consumers.

Retail audit Einzelhandelsbestandsaufnahme, Handelspanel

Also called shop audit.

A market research technique which studies a preselected sample of retail outlets to provide information on the sales volume, sales trends, stock levels, and promotional effectiveness of different brands during a given time period. Trained auditors regularly visit the sample shops to obtain such information.

Retail chain Einzelhandelskette, Detailhandelskette, Filialkette

Also called retailing chain.

A group of retail stores, centrally owned and managed, generally carrying the same kind of merchandise.

Retail cooperative Einzelhandels(einkaufs)-genossenschaft

Also called retailer cooperative.

A voluntary nonprofit-making buying organisation of independent retailers who buy jointly in order to enjoy quantity discounts, storage and shipping facilities, advertising, planning, and other functions.

Retail discount house/store Einzelhandelsdiscountgeschäft

Retail shops that offer their customers a fairly wide range of goods although they only stock the best selling lines. They purchase their stock in bulk direct from producers, and by keeping their costs as low as possible they are able to grant their customers substantial discounts. Sales are always on a cash basis, self-service is practiced, and customers make their own delivery arrangements.

Retail life cycle Einzelhandelslebenszyklus

The cycle of growth and decline that retailers go through.
This cycle includes four stages: 1. introduction, 2. growth, 3. maturity, 4. decline.

Retail marketing (Einzel)Handelsmarketing

Marketing activities of retailers in order to promote their sales.

Marketing activities of producers in order to reach and support the retail trade.

Retail mix Einzelhandelsmix

Also called retailing mix.

Those variables that a retailer can combine in alternative ways to form a strategy for attracting his consumers.

The retailing mix may consist of six Ps: the four Ps of the marketing mix - ie product, place, promotion, and price - plus personnel (ie customer service and personal selling) and presentation (ie layout and atmosphere). Other variables may include: advertising, promotion, store design, location, visual merchandising, etc.

Note: the combination of the six Ps and the other variables projects a store`s image, which influences consumers` perceptions.

Retail outlet Einzelhandelsgeschäft

Also called retail store, retail shop, retailing business, or retailing outlet.

A shop/store where goods are sold direct to the public, e.g. a supermarket.

Retail park Einzelhandelspark

The grouping together of freestanding superstores, eg DIY, grocery and clothing retailers, to form retail parks or villages located out of town but close to major roads and thus easily accessible to customers.

Note: some retail parks also provide shopping malls of specialty and chain stores and/or incorporate leisure facilities to cater for a family day out.

Retail positioning Einzelhandelspositionierung

A retailer`s decisions and activities which try to position himself, eg as a seller of high quality, premium priced products, providing many services, etc. This involves identifying an unserved or underserved market niche or segment, and serving it through a strategy which is visibly different from its competitors and thus creates a positive image in the minds of people in that segment.

Retail price Einzelhandelspreis, Ladenpreis

Also called shop price.

The price for which a shop sells goods, ie the price on leaving the retailer/final handler.

Retail price index (RPI) Einzelhandelspreisindex, Preisindex für Lebenshaltungskosten

Also called index of retail prices or general index of retail prices.

An index to measure inflation. The RPI is based on a "shopping basket" of goods and services bought by typical consumers and covers about 350 items, subdivided into eleven categories as follows:
food, alcohol, tabacco, housing; fuel and light; durable household goods; clothing and footwear; transport and vehicles; miscellaneous goods; services; and meals out.
Different sections have different weightings, since individuals spend less on some items than on others. The weights are revised annually.
The RPI measures the trend in price from a particular date (the base date). The prices of all the items selected for the "basket" at that base date are added together to give one total which is given the index of 100 (the base figure or base point). The current price of each item is expressed as a percentage of the original price.

Retail rep Einzelhandelsvertreter/in

Also called detail rep/man or field rep/man.

A manufacurer`s sales representative who calls on retailers to check sales, the condition and level of stock and to provide sales assistance.

Retail sales analysis Einzelhandelsumsatzanalyse

The process of analysing retail sales in a retail shop or group of shops. Analysis may be untertaken for an individual commodity, a product range, total sales, etc and for a particular time period, e.g. a month.

Retail salesperson Einzelhandelsverkäufer/in

A person employed in a retail store and selling goods and services to final/ultimate consumers.

Retail trade Einzelhandel

Also called retail business, industry or market; retail or retailing.

This market forms the last stage in the course of production, since on it the finished product is passed on to the consumer.
The simplest form is the street market. The permanent retail market is formed by the various kinds of shops (e.g. independent stores, chain stores, department stores,

supermarkets); other forms of retailing are mail order selling, mobile shops, door-to-door calls, travelling salesmen, vending machines, etc. But all perform the same functions: they provide goods that consumers want; at the right time, in the right place, and in suitable quantities.

The sale of goods to the final/ultimate consumer in small quantities by retail shops/stores, supermarkets, hypermarkets, chain stores, etc.

Retailer Einzelhändler

Also called retail dealer, merchant or trader; or single trader.

A businessman who owns a retail shop/store and who sells articles in small quantities. He is a middleman/intermediary and he performs functions for producers and wholesalers who provide him with goods and for consumers who buy the goods from him. Retailers exist to provide a link between the producers of goods and the consumers; they are the final link in the distributive chain/distribution channel.

Retailer coupon Einzelhändlercoupon

A coupon given to buyers by retailers. A sales promotion strategy used by retailers when price is the decisive factor for consumers` buying behaviour. Usually, retailers distribute a money off coupon through advertisements which is redeemable at a specific store.

Retailing Einzelhandel
Einzelhandelsverkauf

The retail trade.

The business activities involved with the sale of goods and services to the final consumer for personal, family, or household use. Thus, any transaction made by a seller with a final consumer, i.e. the activity of selling to buyers who are buying for their own ultimate consumption. Retailing thus includes all direct sales to the consumer from the producer whether through the producer`s own stores, independent stores, vending machines, door-to-door calls or direct mail.

There are five common problems each retailer encounters to some degree:
1. shoplifting (it can range to 10% of sales; dishonest employees account for about one half of the retail theft); 2. risk (e.g. the risk of not being able to sell the inventory profitably) 3. low productivity; 4. stock turnover problems; 5. perishable and damaged merchandise.

Retaliation Vergeltungsmaßnahme,
Retorsionsmaßnahme

Also called retaliatory action or measure, or reprisal.

Countermeasures taken by a company or country (the retaliator) in response to what are called inappropriate behaviours of a trading partner.

Retention marketing Stammkundenmarketing

Particular marketing activities focussing on regular customers.

Retention money einbehaltener Geldbetrag

Part of the agreed price for a contract which is retained by the buyer (the debtor) until the work is completed and the seller (the creditor) has fulfilled all his other contractual duties.

Retention of ownership Eigentumsvorbehalt

Also called retention of legal title, retention of title to ownership, reservation of ownership, reservation of right of disposal, or reservation of title.

Sales contracts often contain a retention of title (RT) clause which states that ownership cannot pass before payment of the purchase price.

Retention time Einprägungszeit

The length of time during which readers, listeners or viewers have an opportunity to hear/see (OTH/OTS) an advertisement or commercial.

Return (R, ret, rtn) Aufstellung, Bericht
Rücksendung, Retoure(n)
Bruttoumsatzerlös

A statement or report, e.g. the annual return.

Something sent back to the seller, e.g. goods because they are unsatisfactory or surplus. Usually used in the plural (returns).

The value of sales during a certain period. Also called gross sales revenue.

Return address Absenderanschrift

The address to which a mailing should be sent/returned if it cannot be delivered to the addressee.

Return call (Telefon)Rückruf

Also called ring-back.

A telephone call in reply to a phone call.

Return load Rückladung, -fracht

Also called back load or return cargo (r/c).

A back load arranged for a transportation vehicle, after delivering another load, in order to avoid its having to come back empty.

Return on capital (employed) (ROCE) Ertrag aus investiertem Kapital, Kapitalrentabilität

Also called return on capital invested or return on investment (ROI).

A ratio calculated by expressing the profit earned in a given period as a percentage of the owner's capital,

e.g. $\frac{10{,}000 \text{ (profit) x } 100}{100{,}000 \text{ (capital employed)}} = 10\ \%.$

The ratio is designed to show whether a businessman is justified in continuing his business or in closing it down.

Return on investment (ROI) Kapitalrentabilität

An American term used to mean return on capital employed (ROCE).

Return on sales (ROS) Umsatzrentabilität, Umsatzrendite

Net pretax profits as a percentage of net sales.

Return on time invested (ROTI) Rentabilität der investierten Zeit

A measure of the return in sales results of a measure of time spent to achieve those results.

Return receipt Rückschein

Also called advice of receipt (AR).

A card sent with registered mail for the recipient`s signature confirming receipt of the item. Thereafter, the card is returned to the sender.

Returned empties Leergut, Pfandware

Empty bottles or containers which can be sent back to the supplier.

Returns Retouren, Rücksendungen

Also called goods returned, returned goods, returned merchandise, returned sales, or sales returns.

Goods sent back to the seller. Goods sold are returned to the seller for various reasons, e.g. damage, excess delivery, wrong goods. This usually means that the seller will make out a new invoice and issue a credit note (C/N) for the goods returned.

Returns and allowances Rücksendungen und Nachlässe

Reductions in the invoice price of goods purchased or sold usually granted because the goods have been returned to the seller, or, if kept by the buyer, are not according to the order.

Returns to store Lagerretouren

Materials previously issued for processing, which have now been returned to the store.

Reusable container wiederverwendbarer Behälter/Container

A container that can be used again when empty.

Revealed preferences bekundete oder offenbarte Präferenzen

The revealed preference theory (first formulated by the American economist Paul A. Samuelson) states that the preferences which a household has already revealed will give a clue to its behaviour when prices change, and show what quantities it will demand in the new situation.

Revenue Umsatzerlös Ertrag

Income from the sales of products or services. Also called sales revenue.

In accounting, all items appearing on the credit side in the profit and loss account, eg from interest, sales earnings, etc.

Revenue-oriented pricing ertragsorientierte Preisbildung

A company`s policy of setting prices at a level that will maximise the surplus of income/revenue over expenditures.

Reverse charge call R-Gespräch

Also called reversed charges call, collect call or transfer charge call.

A caller asks the operator to connect him to a subscriber who pays for the call.

Reverse dumping negatives, umgekehrtes Dumping

The practice of selling goods abroad at a higher price than that charged in the domestic market.

Reverse marketing Einkaufs-, Beschaffungsmarketing

A market-oriented activity to procure goods or services.

Revocation Widerruf, Aufhebung

Also called cancellation, nullification, or withdrawal.

An act of revoking/withdrawing, e.g. to revoke/cancel an order.

Rework Nacharbeitung, Nachbesserung

Also called remedying the defect or subsequent improvement.

Corrective work which has to be done due to bad workmanship and to make goods saleable.

Right of resale Wiederverkaufsrecht

Also called resale right or right to resell.

An unpaid seller's right to resell goods to another person though he does not hold title to them.

Right of rescission Rücktrittsrecht (von einem Vertrag)

Also called right to withdraw from a contract, right of cancellation, or right to cancel a contract.

A right granted to consumers to void a contract within a certain number of business days with full refund of any downpayment and without penalty. The right is particularly designed to protect consumers from door-to-door sales and credit commitments.

Ring Kartell

Also called cartel.

A combination of firms organized for the purpose of controlling the market, e.g. particular areas, prices, etc.

Rise Anstieg, Erhöhung

An increase in something, eg in price or value.

Rival Konkurrent

Also called competitor or contender.

A person or company competing in the same market.

Rival commodity Konkurrenzerzeugnis, Konkurrenzprodukt

Also called rival brand or rival product.

Products or services that can easily be substituted for each other so that the price of one will affect the demand for the other, e.g. a price increase in product A will decrease the demand for x but increase the demand for product B.
The term was first used by the English economist Alfred Marshall (1842 - 1924).

Rival demand konkurrierende Nachfrage

Also called alternate demand, competitive demand, or competing demand.

The demand for products which are substitutes for each other, i.e. are able to replace each other. The products are competing to satisfy the market demand.

Rival product Konkurrenzprodukt

A competing product, often of nearly homogeneous brands.

Road show Verkaufsausstellung auf Rädern, Road Show

A promotional presentation touring on the road.

Road toll Mautgebühr, Straßennutzungsgebühr

Also called toll (rate).

A charge raised on road users. The charge raised on bridge users is called bridge toll.

Road transport Güterkraftverkehr, Straßengüter-transport

Also called freight haulage, road haulage or trucking.

Road transport continues to grow in volume. Cargo/freight is transported in large lorries/trucks to its destination without having to be unloaded in between (door-to-door service). For short and medium distances road haulage is a very speedy mode of transport; but it is not suitable for transporting goods of great bulk for long distances. Road congestion becomes more severe each year.

Robinson list Robinson-Liste

A mailing preference scheme whereby individuals may register with a national list of people not wishing to receive direct mail literature.

Robinson-Patman Act Robinson-Patman-Gesetz (USA)

In the USA, an act that prohibits price discrimination and other anticompetitive practices in business. For example, a discount to a large buyer has to be based either on differences in cost or be justified as a price to meet the low price of a competitor.

Robot Roboter

Any machine that performs jobs previously assigned to human beings, is self-operating and to some degree intelligent.

Rock-bottom price äußerster, niedrigster Preis, Schleuderpreis

Also called bottom price.

The absolutely lowest price.

Rocket sprunghaft ansteigen, in die Höhe schnellen (Preise)
haussieren (Wertpapiere)

Also called shoot up or skyrocket.

The prices of goods or securities rise suddenly and very steeply.

Role playing Rollenspiel

In sales training, an exercise in which one person acts the part of a salesperson and another the buyer to practise selling techniques.

Rollback Zurücknahme von Preiserhöhungen

The cutting/marking down of prices to an earlier, lower level, usually exercised by the government.

Rollout schrittweise Produkteinführung

The launch of a new product on a region by region basis. Once a new product has proved to be successful in test markets, it is then ready for national roll out. This means that the new product is introduced/launched first into one region, then some time later into a second region, etc. Thus, the firm can minimise risk and reduce investment in production and marketing. Furthermore, the firm has a chance to build up the necessary stock level to meet the rising demand for the product as the launch proceeds nationwide.

Rosy advertising Heile-Welt-Werbung

Cheerful, optimistic advertising showing a life with no problems and a bright and/or promising, ie rosy future.

Rough Rohlayout
Rohentwurf

Also called rough layout or (rough) dummy.

An unfinished layout of a print advertisement or an early version of a televison storyboard.

Rough draft Vorentwurf, erster Entwurf

Also called rough copy or preliminary draft.

A draft of a document which will be changed before it is complete.

Round figure gerundeter, runder Betrag

Also called round amount or round sum.

An amount nearest to a whole number (e.g. to round up/off from £ 348.50 to £ 350; or to round down/off from £ 351.22 to £ 350).

Rounding error Rundungsfehler

Discrepancy resulting from rounding up or down.

Rounding off Auf- oder Abrunden

A mathematical procedure which eliminates small insignificant numbers or decimals of numbers, by taking the nearest significant value, ie either to round up/off or to round down/off.

Route Transportweg
(Fahrt)Strecke, Route

The course or way that a consignment moves to get from one place to another.

The regular course taken by a transport service.

Routing order Leitbefehl, Vorschrift(en) über den Transportweg

Also called routing directive.

Instructions concerning the route by which the consignment is to be sent.

Royalty Lizenzgebühr
Autorenhonorar

The payment made to a patentee for permission to use his patent. Also called licence fee.

Payment made by publishers and producers to writers, composers, musicians or playwrights. Also called author's royalty.

Rummage Ramsch, Restwaren
Ausschußware

Miscellaneous articles, usually small and unimportant or of little value. Also called rummage goods, odds and ends, job goods, or odds and sods (colloq.).

Defective goods. Also called faulty goods.

Rummage sale Ramschverkauf
Wohltätigkeitsbasar

The sale of rummage, ie small, unimportant articles of little value. Also called jumble sale.

A sale of miscellaneous articles, especially items contributed to raise money for charity. Also called charity bazaar.

Run of business Konjunkturverlauf

Also called cyclical course, economic course, or path of the economy.

The economic course of the economy.

Run of paper (ROP) ohne Plazierungsvereinbarung

Also called run of press (ROP) or run of book (ROB).

An advertiser`s instruction to a publisher that the advertisement can be positioned/placed within the newspaper or magazine wherever the publisher decides. As the advertiser demands no special position, a lower charge is usually payable.

Run of station (ROS) ohne Sendezeitvereinbarung

Also called run of schedule or floating time.

An arrangement between an advertiser and a broadcasting station to transmit a commercial whenever it is convenient for the station, ie no specific day or specific hour has been reserved by the advertiser.

Run of week (ROW) im Laufe der Woche

An advertiser`s instruction to a publisher or broadcasting station to place the advertisement or transmit the commercial during a particular week.

Runaway inflation galoppierende, trabende Inflation

Also called hyperinflation; cantering, galloping, raging, rampant, snowballing, trotting inflation.

A very high rate of persistent inflation where prices rise rapidly so that the value of money declines to a fraction of its former value. People quickly lose confidence in their monetary system.

Runner Renner, Schnelldreher, ein sich schnell verkaufendes Produkt

Also called best selling item, hot selling line, or top selling product.

A best selling product.

Running cost(s) Betriebskosten

Also called cost of operation; operating cost(s), expenditure, expenses or overheads; operational cost(s), or running expenses.

Costs, e.g. rentals, taxes, wages, incurred in operating a business.

Running time Sendezeit

The total length of time that a TV or radio commercial or program actually runs.

Rural population Landbevölkerung

People living in the country, ie that part of the total population not classified as urban.

Rush order Eilauftrag

Also called express or urgent order.

An order which has to be carried out at once.

S

Sachet Sachet, Beutel, Briefchen, Päckchen

A small bag, case, envelope or package containing liquid, powder, or the like in sufficient quantity for one person at one time.

Sack Sack

A large bag made of strong paper, cloth, plastic, canvas, etc.

Safety Sicherheit

A state in which people are or feel protected, eg from the risk of injury.

Safety need Sicherheitsbedürfnis

In Maslow`s hierarchy of needs, one of the five need categories, the others being: physiological needs (these are the most basic human needs, such as needs for food, water, shelter), social needs (eg sense of belonging, love), esteem needs (eg self-esteem, recognition, status), self actualization needs (eg self-development).

Safety needs include security and freedom from pain and discomfort. Note: marketers often exploit these needs to sell their products and services.

Safety recall Sicherheitsrückruf

An advertised request by a company for the return of a particular product - either for repair, replacement or credit - when the product has turned out to be unsafe or defective.

Safety stock Sicherheitsbestand

Also called safety level of supply.

A higher level of inventory/stock kept on hand than is thought necessary to prevent stock outs, to meet unusually heavy demand, delays in supply, etc.

The optimum level of safety stock depends on the general demand and the standard of customer service to be provided. If the safety stock is inadequate, unreliable deliveries may cause lost sales.

Sal(e)able sample käufliches Muster

A product offered to prospective customers at a low price to demonstrate the product`s value or use and induce trial and future purchases.

Salability/saleability Verkäuflichkeit, Marktfähigkeit

The quality of a product which makes it easy to sell, i.e. the product is salable/saleable.

Sale Verkauf
Ausverkauf

The sale of goods is the chief activity of a trading company, and every aspect of a sale must be documented. The sequence of operations is as follows: 1. the enquiry, 2. the quotation, 3. the order, 4. the invoice.

An event, e.g. a closing-down sale or an end-of-season sale, in which a shop offers its goods at reduced prices in order to clear stocks.

Sale advertising Verkaufswerbung

Advertising, usually in the retail trade, which announces the sale of products at temporarily or permanently reduced prices.

Sale and leaseback/lease back Verkauf bei gleichzeitiger Rückvermietung an den Verkäufer

A transaction in which the owner (ie the seller) sells an asset to a buyer (often a finance company or leasing company) who agrees to lease it back to the original owner. The rentals and the sale price are usually interdependent as they are negotiated as a package and need not represent fair values.
If the leaseback is a finance lease, the transaction is a means whereby the lessor (ie the buyer of the asset) provides finance to the lessee (ie the original owner of the asset), with the asset as security. The seller can raise money because the capital tied up in the asset is released.

Sale by auction | Auktion, öffentliche Versteigerung

Also called sale at auction, public sale, auction (sale) or vendue.

A method of determining a commodity's price. There is one seller and a number of prospective buyers. The auctioneer offers an article for sale and asks for bids for it. Anyone desirous of purchasing it is then at liberty to make an offer/bid, and the article will eventually be sold to the highest bidder (the one prepared to pay the highest price).

Sale by description | Gattungskauf, Spezifikationskauf, Verkauf nach Beschreibung

Also called purchase by description, quantity sale or sale of unascertained goods.

Sale by description means that the buyer does not see the goods at the date of the contract but relies on the description alone.
Goods sold by description have to correspond with the description, and, if they are sold by sample as well as by description, it is not sufficient if the bulk of the goods corresponds with the sample if they do not also correspond with the description.

Sale by private treaty | freihändiger Verkauf (nicht durch Versteigerung)

Also called direct offering, open-market sale or sale in the open market.

On produce exchanges, commodities which can be graded (e.g. cotton, rubber, wheat), are sold by private treaty, that is, the seller and the buyer make a bargain with each other, or haggle.

Sale by sample | (Ver)Kauf nach Probe, (Ver)Kauf nach Muster, Musterverkauf

Also called purchase or sale on approval, or approval sale.

A sale made under the agreed condition (stipulated in the contract) that the quality and the state of the whole consignment must be at least as good as the quality and state of the sample.

Sale of Goods Acts (SGAs) Gesetze über den Warenkauf

In GB, these Acts formed the basis of consumer protection.
Under these Acts 1. goods must suit the purpose for which they are sold; 2. goods sold by description must fit the description; 3. goods sold by sample must correspond with the sample. If goods do not meet these requirements the buyer has the right to refuse the goods, to claim damages from the seller and to sue him for breach of contract in a civil action. The Acts were amended by the Supply of Goods Act.

Sale on approval (Ver)Kauf auf Probe,
Probe(ver)kauf,
(Ver)Kauf zur Ansicht

Also called approval sale.

The goods are delivered to a potential buyer under an agreement that he may test or use the goods for the purpose of determining whether or not he wishes to buy them.

The buyer may return the goods within the agreed period of time (approval period) even though they conform to the contract or, if no such period has been stipulated, within reasonable time. The return of the goods is at the seller's risk and expense. A buyer who keeps the goods beyond the approval period indicates that he has accepted (ie bought) the goods; now he cannot compel the seller to take them back.
Unless otherwise agreed, the risk of loss of, and the title to, the goods do not pass to the buyer until acceptance.

Sale or return (S/R, SOR) Kauf mit Rückgaberecht

A practice of selling in which the seller (a manufacturer or wholesaler) agrees to take back from the buyer (a retailer) any unsold goods, usually within a specified time; the buyer pays only for goods sold.

An agreement whereby goods are delivered to a person giving him the choice either to accept these goods, thus entering into a contract, or to return them to the seller without further obligation. Also called see-sale.

Sales Umsatz, Umsatzerlöse,
Verkaufserlöse
Absatz, Umsatz
Schlußverkauf

Money received for goods or services sold over a certain period; ie the value of goods or services sold.

In accounting, the total revenue received by a company from selling goods and services during a particular time period. Also called sales revenue.

The number of items, i.e. the quantity/volume sold. Also called sales volume or turnover.

The selling of goods at reduced prices for a limited time period in order to get rid of surplus stocks, etc. Examples are summer or winter sales. Also called end-of-season sale or seasonal closing-out sale.

Sales agency Verkaufsagentur

An independent person or firm appointed by a principal to negotiate on his behalf and to sell his products according to a laid down agreement.

Sales agent Handelsvertreter, Kommissionsagent

Also called selling agent

A person engaged in selling his principal´s product(s) or service(s), usually on a commission basis.

Sales aids Verkaufshilfen

Any elements of sales promotion such as brochures, catalogs, leaflets, samples, showcards, video tapes, etc which back up face-to-face selling activities.

Sales allowance Preisnachlaß

Also called price reduction.

A certain percentage or an amount of money granted to reduce the price for a good or service.

A lowering of a product's price which is granted when goods delivered are not entirely conforming to the customer's order.

Sales analysis Absatzanalyse, Umsatzanalyse Umsatzstatistik

The examination of sales to find out why goods have or have not sold well.

A diagram or table showing the main facts about the sale of goods.

Sales approach Art und Weise der Verkaufsanbahnung

A salesperson`s way to get in touch with a prospect. The three main ways to get a first interview are a letter, an unsolicited personal visit, and a phone call. The main goal of the sales approach is either to talk to the prospect or to secure a first appointment. The approach should always include an interest-capturing statement so that the prospect is willing to continue the conversation.
Note: an effective approach results in a personal meeting with a qualified prospective.

Sales aptitude Verkaufstalent

A salesperson`s ability and other personal characteristics to perform a given sales job.

Sales aptitude test Eignungstest für Verkaufspersonal

A test which applicants for positions in the sales force have to pass in order to determine their suitability.

Sales area Absatzgebiet

Also called sales territory.

The geographic area, the current and potential customers assigned to a salesperson.

Sales based pricing absatzorientierte Preisbildung

A company`s pricing strategy aiming at a high sales volume and/or increasing its share of sales relative to competitors.

Sales book Verkaufsbuch

The value of the sales book is that it shows a firm what has been sold over a period of time.

Sales branch Verkaufsniederlassung

A branch maintained by a company for the purpose of marketing its products at the wholesale level. It carries stocks of merchandise for delivery to customers.

Sales budget Absatzbudget, Absatzplan

An estimate of the probable future sales during a period of time, e.g. a week or month, etc. It shows the main source of a company's revenue.

Sales bulletin Verkaufsbulletin

A document prepared by a company`s sales department containing information of interest to the (potential) customers, e.g. new product launches, price changes, personnel changes, exhibitions, after sales service, etc. It is basically a sales aid distributed on a regular basis.

Sales call Vertreterbesuch

A visit to a (prospective) customer by a sales person.

Sales campaign Absatzkampagne, Verkaufsaktion

Also called sales drive or sales push.

Organised actions to achieve higher sales.

Sales cartel Absatz-, Vertriebskartell

Also called distribution or marketing cartel.

A cartel whose voluntary members agree to control the distribution of goods by making arrangements on the allocation of markets and on the terms of delivery and payment.

Sales chain Absatzkette

The passage of a product between producer and consumer or end user. The classic sales chain is that from producer to wholesaler to retailer to consumer. But today there are many variations (either extending or shortening the sales chain); for example, in the case of direct mail selling, the retailer (and the wholesaler) is cut out.

Sales closing Abschluß eines Verkaufsgesprächs

Also called sales close.

In the selling process, the activity of completing a sales talk with a customer in the hope of a getting an order.

Sales contest Absatz-, Verkaufswettbewerb

In sales promotion, a method to motivate distributors, retailers and salespeople to boost sales by recognising outstanding achievements. For example, if sales figures are improved by x percent, the top-achiever wins a trip to a special holiday resort.

Sales contract Kaufvertrag

Also called contract of sale, sales agreement, contract of purchase or purchase agreement.

A written or oral agreement made between two or more consenting parties to sell a product in return for the payment of money (the price). The seller transfers, or agrees to transfer, the general property (i.e. the ownership) in goods to the buyer and he may sue the buyer for the price if he fails to pay. The contract should contain the following essential factors: the type of goods, the quantity, the quality, the terms of payment, the terms of delivery, and details of packing and despatch.

Both parties (seller and buyer) have certain obligations:
The seller is required by law:
1. to deliver the goods specified in the contract at the agreed time; 2. to guarantee the goods to be free from faults (i.e. the goods must be in good condition); 3. to transfer the general property, ie the ownership, in the goods to the buyer; 4. to accept payment.
The buyer is required by law:
1. to accept the goods delivered provided they comply the contract; 2. to pay for them at the time of delivery, i.e. at once (unless there is an agreement to the contrary); 3. to check the goods at once.

Sales control Absatzkontrolle

The continuous and systematic check of a firm`s sales results in order to develop measures to fight sales declines and/or to improve sales.

Sales decline Absatz-, Verkaufsrückgang

A market situation in which sales are falling and will continue to fall.

Sales department Verkaufsabteilung

A department responsible for a company`s sales.

Sales discount Barzahlungsrabatt, Skonto Kundenrabatt

Also called cash discount.

A price reduction that is granted if payment is received within a specified period (e.g. ... less 2 % cash discount for payment within ... days or 2 % for cash).

A cash discount given by a seller to his customers.

Sales drive Absatzkampagne, Verkaufsaktion

Also called sales campaign or sales push.

A particularly active selling campaign to increase sales.

Sales effect of advertising Verkaufseffizienz der Werbung

The effect of advertising on sales. This effect can be measured by comparing past sales with past advertising expenditures. But note: sales are also affected by other factors, eg price, product features, and product availability.

Sales elasticity Verkaufselastizität

The ratio of relative change of sales volume to relative change of commodity price.

Sales engineer Verkaufsingenieur, technischer Kaufmann

A salesperson disposing of engineering knowledge or strong technical skills and thus qualified to sell highly technical or complex items.

Sales force/salesforce Außendienstmitarbeiter, Verkaufsstab Absatzorganisation, Verkaufs-organisation

Group of salespersons engaged in selling the firm's product(s), e.g. sales representatives.

The structure and distribution of the sales personnel to achieve sales goals. Also called sales or marketing organization.

Sales forecast Absatzprognose, Verkaufsvoraussage

Also called forward sales projection.

The projection of likely sales over a specified future period. It also predicts shifts in demand.

Sales giant Umsatzgigant

A firm achieving an enormous sales volume relative to competitors.

Sales goods Ausverkaufsware(n)

Goods reduced in price for quick clearance.

Sales incentive Verkaufsanreiz, Verkaufsprämie

A reward additional to salary or commission offered to a salesperson in return for achieving some predetermined sales goal.

Sales invoice Verkaufsrechnung

A document issued by the seller for a buyer who is buying goods or services on credit. It gives full details of the goods, the amount due, the date and number of the customer's order, the method of delivery, the amount of VAT (value added tax), and other information. Invoices are sometimes sent with the goods, but more usually by post separately from the goods.
If the buyer is a business it will treat this invoice as its purchases invoice.

Sales invoicing Fakturierung, Rechnungsstellung

The issue of a sales invoice in order to notify the customer of the amount he owes. Prompt rendering of the invoice promotes quick receipt of cash.

Sales journal Verkaufsjournal, Debitorenbuch, Kundenbuch

Also called sales book, sales ledger or sold ledger.

A book in which all the sales carried out by a business are recorded. It shows a firm what has been sold to a customer and what has been received from the customer (in the form of payments and returns).

Sales lead Verkaufshinweis

Pieces of information such as responses to advertising, enquiries, letters, etc that direct a salesperson to a prospective customer and may ultimately lead to a sales transaction.

Sales letter Werbebrief

A letter sent to selected types of customers for the purpose of interesting them in a product or service, or to remind them of its existence, or to persuade them that they need what you are trying to sell. Therefore, a good sales letter should arouse interest; create desire; carry conviction and induce action.

Sales literature Werbematerial

Printed material which serves to promote the sales of manufacturers, mail-order businesses, travelling representatives, wholesalers and retailers. It provides detailed information in a permanent and portable form.
The following are the chief kinds: brochures, calendars, catalogues, folders, leaflets, point-of-sale showcards, posters, wall charts, etc.

Sales management Vertriebsleitung
Verkaufsleitung

Also called marketing management.

The management activities involved in the storage, handling and movement of goods within an organisation and in their shipment/transportation to customers. Also called (physical) distribution management.

The management responsible for the sales department and the personal selling acitivities of the business. Furthermore, sales management includes the recruitment, training, motivation, compensation, organisation, evaluation and control of the sales force.
Sales management involves three interrelated processes:
1. formulation of a strategic sales program(me),
2. implementation of the sales program(me),
3. evaluation and control of sales force performance.

Sales manager Vertriebsleister
Verkaufsleiter

A firm`s distribution(s) manager.

An executive responsible for the activities of a company's sales department. His job is to analyse the market, to recommend selling strategies, to recruit the sales force, and to organize the activities of his team of salespersons to ensure their maximum effectiveness in promoting and maintaining a flow of orders from customers. His aim must be the highest appropriate sales volume at the lowest operational cost. Also called sales executive.

Sales manual Absatzhandbuch

A set of printed material containing product descriptions and related information issued to salespeople and customers.

Sales market Absatzmarkt

The market(s) on which producers or sellers sell or could sell their product(s) or service(s).

Sales maximization Umsatz-, Verkaufsmaximierung

A company`s efforts to maximize sales. As long as sales are rising, the company often ignores profits and competition.
Sales maximization can be effectively used on a temporary basis, eg to sell off excess inventory/stock or clear out old models before introducing the new ones.

Sales meeting Absatzkonferenz, Verkaufstagung

Also called sales conference.

A meeting of sales managers, salespersons and others to discuss sales results, future sales goals, or to train and inform them.

Sales mix Absatzmix

The combination of quantities of the various company products leading to a firm's total sales.

Sales negotiation Kaufverhandlung

The process of concluding a sale, either in a domestic market or in an overseas market. These negotiations require many skills and each situation requires a different strategy and varies by personal relationships, product/service, competition, market profile, after-sales service, and in foreign trade, culture, language, import regulations, etc.

The five basic steps in the sales process are as follows:
1. making contact with the potential buyer (e.g. through advertisements, exhibitions, visits);
2. arousing interest (the seller should quickly identify the buyer`s needs and problems and offer attractive solutions);
3. creating preference (the seller may have to deliver samples, arrange demonstrations and he must establish the strengths of his product and particularly emphasize the points which interest the buyer);
4. making a specific proposal (now the negotiations culminate and the seller offers a complete package including product specification, price, terms of sale, delivery date, etc; usually the seller gives a time limit on the quotation which should leave him some room for further changes);
5. closing the sale (i.e. the buyer accepts the seller`s offer).

Sales objective Verkaufsziel

A company`s goals to be realised in the process of marketing a product or service. It will be expressed in financial terms, quantity terms, market share, etc.

Sales office Verkaufsbüro

An office located away from the manufacturing plant and established to sell the manufacturer`s products. It carries no inventory and is owned and controlled by the manufacturer.

Sales order Bestellung, Verkaufsauftrag

An order received from a buyer asking the seller to sell goods to him/her.

Sales order processing Auftragsbearbeitung

Also called contract or order processing.

Administrative work involved in processing customers' orders, e.g. to issue all the necessary documents such as the acknowledgement of order, the despatch note, the delivery note, the invoice, etc.

Sales orientation Absatz-, Verkaufsorientierung

A philosophy assuming that:
1. buyers resist purchasing products that are not essential,
2. people will buy more goods and services if aggressive sales techniques are used,
3. high sales result in high profits.
Thus, to sales-oriented firms, marketing means selling things and collecting money.

Sales oriented pricing absatz-, verkaufsorientierte Preisbildung

A pricing strategy trying to increase a company`s market share, or its total value or unit sales.

Sales penetration Marktdurchdringung, Marktanteil

The degree to which a firm is achieving its sales potential. It is calculated as follows: sales penetration = actual sales : sales potential.

Sales pitch Verkaufsargument

In the selling process, a salesperson`s talks, statements, content and style of presentation made to persuade a prospective customer and overcome his/her buying resistance.

Sales planning Absatzplanung

The assessment of the present situation in a specific sales area, the setting of sales objectivies, the formulation of sales strategies, and the establishment of control and evaluation procedures.

Sales policy Absatz-, Verkaufspolitik

A company`s policies to promote and achieve marketing objectives.

Sales portfolio Verkaufsmappe

A briefcase, usually in ring-binder form, containing a set of items, eg price lists, photographs, samples, etc, which a sales representative can present to potential customers to support his/her sales arguments.

Sales potential Absatzchancen, Absatzmöglichkeiten, Absatzpotential

Also called sales opportunities, market potential or sales prospects.

The share of a market for a product or service that a company believes is achievable.

Sales presentation Produktpräsentation

In the selling process, a stage including the face-to-face discussion of the product, its benefits, available options and models, price, warranties, delivery, additional services, etc between the salesperson and the prospect, and a demonstration (if necessary).

Sales process Verkaufsvorgang

The process of selling a product or service. The five basic steps in the sales process are as follows:

1. making contact with the protential buyer (eg through advertisements, exhibitions, visits);
2. arousing interest (the seller should quickly identify the buyer`s needs and problems and offer attractive solutions);
3. creating preference (the seller may have to deliver samples, arrange demonstrations and he must establish the strengths of his product and particularly emphasize the points which interest the buyer);
4. making a specific proposal (now the negotiations culminate and the seller offers a complete package including product specification, price, terms of sale, delivery date, etc; usually the seller gives a time limit on the quotation which should leave him some room for further changes);
5. closing the sale (ie the buyer accepts the seller`s offer).

Sales promotion Absatzförderung, Verkaufsförderung

Any marketing activity concerned with the promotion of sales. Sales promotion supplements the process of advertising by reminding people, often at the critical decision-making stage, of the benefits of an immediate purchase.

Sales promotion may embrace the following marketing tactics:
free samples, price reductions, financing assistance, delayed payment, trading stamps, competitions, free gifts, premium offers (these offer an economic incentive to buy the product), coupons, sweepstakes/sweepers, etc.; but also product literature, display racks, trial product samples, free samples, exhibitions, demonstrations, displays at the point of sale, and sponsorships.

Sales quota Absatzquote, Verkaufsquote

The expected sales level for a product that a sales representative should achieve for a specific territory within a given time period. The sales level may be based on either unit sales or revenue.

Sales report Verkaufsbericht

A detailed report prepared by a salesperson on a particular visit to a customer or company. It will detail the nature of the visit, date and time, business secured and on what terms, name of salesperson, etc.

Sales representative (Verkaufs)Vertreter

A person who represents a company, usually within a geographic territory, and negotiates sales offers in the company's name.

Sales research Absatz-, Verkaufsforschung

A thorough examination of existing and past selling techniques and of field and office activities in order to discover means of improving sales force productivity and the firm`s competitive position in terms of market share and profitability. Such a survey would highlight the strengths and weaknesses of the sales system, e.g. it could reveal its cost-effectiveness (e.g. the cost of selling per unit), the competence of the salespersons, the performance of particular outlets, the necessity of after-sales-services, the need to change the distribution arrangements, etc.

Sales resistance Verkaufswiderstand, Kaufunlust

Also called sales apathy or sales opposition.

The rational or irrational opposition to buy a product or service.

Sales response (to advertising) Verkaufswirkung (der Werbung)

The development of a product`s sales volume in response to its promotion.

Sales returns book Retourenbuch, Warenrücksendungsbuch

Also called returns inwards book.

A book which records the returns of goods, e.g. because they are unsatisfactory or unsuitable. Each amount returned represents money owed by the seller.

Sales staff Verkaufspersonal

The people who sell goods or services to customers. Today, they occupy a key position in the marketing team and perform a variety of important roles:
1. they seek and acquire new customers, 2. approach these customers and make sales presentations, 3. obtain orders by matching the customer`s requirements, 4. establish long-term relationships with customers, 5. resolve problems and complaints, 6. call on customers regularly, etc.
To be successful in meeting their objectives, they should dispose of:
1. detailed knowledge of the product, 2. detailed knowledge of the customer`s needs and requirements, 3. an attractive and convincing personality, 4. the ability to motivate themselves and to work independently, 5. a sense of sales psychology, etc.

Sales talk Verkaufsgespräch

A conversation between two or more persons, the salesperson and the prospective buyer, intended to persuade the latter to buy a product or service.

Sales target Umsatz-, Verkaufsziel

A company`s sales objectives, either in quantitative or in value terms.

Sales tax (ST) Umsatzsteuer (USA)

Also called turnover tax.

In the USA, a tax levied by a state or municipality on the sale of goods.

The tax is levied at any level of distribution, e.g. the sales of producers are taxed when the items are considered to be completed goods; the sales of wholesalers are taxed when their goods are sold to retailers; retail sales are taxed when the goods are purchased by consumers.

Sales technique Verkaufstechnik

The methods used by salespersons to achieve their sales objectives.

Sales training Verkaufstraining

Formal or informal education in sales methods, product knowledge, sales talks, selling skills, time management, administrative work, customer service, etc.

The training of the members of the sales team (salesmen and saleswomen) should be continuous and not confined solely to induction training. Even experienced salespersons need refresher courses to add to their product knowledge and to improve their overall sales performance (e.g. a salesman must be shown how to present his range of products to his customers, how to plan his journeys and call frequencies, etc.).

Sales volume (Q) Absatz(menge), Umsatzvolumen

Also called volume of sales.

The quantity of goods sold.

Salescheck Kassenzettel

Also called salesslip.

A receipt issued by a store or other vendor showing the amount paid.

Saleslady Verkäuferin

Also called salesgirl, shopgirl or saleswoman.

A female salesperson.

Salesman Verkäufer

Also called salesclerk.

A male salesperson.

Salesmanship Verkaufskunst

The art of informing or persuading customers to buy or the art of selling.

Salesperson Verkäufer/in

A saleslady or salesman.

Salespersons have five major tasks in their daily work effort:
1. to persuade the customers of the benefits that they will gain by buying or using the company`s product(s).
   To be successful in this role they must take into account: a. sales aids, eg brochures, leaflets, technical data, success stories, etc; b. samples, eg to prove the validity of the claims made, c. presentations, eg the presentation of benefits which are meaningful to this particular prospect; d.knowledge of competition, eg to overcome objections resulting from competing products; e. enthusiasm, eg confidence in oneself and the product; f. value concept, eg to demonstrate prospects the product`s value and convince them that they really deserve to get the order.
2. to explain the policies and procedures of the company which will affect their mutual business relationship.
   The salespersons must ensure that the transaction is a mutually satisfactory one and that a successful sale does not conclude with this order. Thus, they should consider and fully explain: payment terms, delivery terms, warranties and guarantees, complaints procedures, special offers, company contacts, etc.
3. to inform the company of any factors in the marketplace which affect or impose modifications on the company`s marketing strategies.
   Thus, the salespersons should regularly report to the management, eg on the number of calls, the number of orders received, the value of orders received, complaints or comments about the company`s and competitors` actions and products, etc.
4. to create a company image in the customer`s mind that the company is an efficient, reliable, ethical firm best suited to satisfy the customer`s needs and expectations.
   In this connection, one must point out that the salesperson is the company in the mind of the customer and it is they who are the mainstay of the company`s reputation.
5. to assist customers in increasing their knowledge of the company`s product(s) so that they can gain the maximum benefits from the product(s).
   Thus, salespersons must ensure that the customers fully understand the operational, technical and other features of the product(s) so that they can maximise the benefit from their use.

Salesroom Verkaufsraum
Auktionsraum

The room where goods are sold.

The room where an auction takes place.

Sample Muster, Probe
Warenprobe
Stichprobe, Auswahl

On the commodity exchange, a small quantity taken from the bulk (i.e. a large quantity) of which it is representative (e.g. coffee, tea, wool) and used as an example of the bulk.

An example of a commodity, or the actual product itself, given to prospective buyers (usually free) to test a product's quality.

In statistics, a small group chosen from the whole for special study, e.g. a representative portion of a population to characterize a larger population.

Sample book Musterbuch

Also called book of samples.

A book showing samples of different products.

Sample copy Frei-, Probeexemplar

A free copy of a publication sent to prospective subscribers or advertisers.

Sample size Stichprobenumfang

In a survey, the number of units that supply information.

Sample survey Stichprobenerhebung, Repräsentativerhebung

A survey based on the examination of a typical part of the total group.

Sampling Stichprobenentnahme
(Waren)Probenverteilung

The statistical process of selecting a subgroup of a larger group of interest for the collection of information (e.g. attitudes, buying habits, etc.) which may be generalized to the whole group (if the research is correctly conducted).

The distribution of free samples to (prospective) customers in order to stimulate regular usage. This is not a method which recommends itself to a brand leader or a producer who already holds an appreciable market share, but for a producer new to a market there is considerable merit in the sampling method.

ṡampling case Musterkoffer

Also called sample bag.

A case used by salespersons to carry the samples of their products which they demonstrate to potential customers.

Sampling error Stichprobenfehler

An error that may occur when a sample drawn from a population somehow does not represent the target population.

Sampling fraction Stichprobenumfang

Also called sampling ratio.

In statistics, the proportion of a population size that is chosen as a sample.

Sampling order Probeauftrag

Also called tentative order or trial order.

An initial first/order for a small quantity of a product, made by a prospective/potential buyer to test the product. If the product meets his requirements he may place further orders.

Sandwich board Sandwich-Plakat, beidseitiges Werbeschild, Plakattafel

An advertising poster with signs in front and back and hung from the shoulders of a sandwich man.

Satisfaction Zufriedenheit
Befriedigung
Nutzen
Rückerstattungsgarantie

The state or feeling of being satisfied.

The act of satisfying.

The utility derived by a person from buying goods or services. Also called utility.

A money back guarantee.

Satisfaction of demand Bedarfsbefriedigung Nachfragedeckung

The state of meeting and satisfying demand for a particular product or service.

Satisfaction of wants Bedürfnisbefriedigung

Also called satiation of wants or subjective satisfaction.

Wants are defined as the goods and services which a person wishes to possess; that is visible items (eg clothes, food) and invisible items (eg education and health services).

Human wants are unlimited, in the sense that as soon as some are satisfied new ones emerge to take their place. It is the aim of production to satisfy as many of these wants as possible. However, people will never have all their wants provided for because there are not enough resources or factors of production (land, labour, capital, enterprise) to produce all the commodities which are wanted.

Satisficing Satisfizierung

A management behaviour which seeks to make satisfactory profits rather than achieve profit maximization.

Saturated home market gesättigter Binnenmarkt

A market situation where a company can sell no more in the home/domestic market and thus has to seek new markets abroad.

Saturation Sättigung, Saturierung

The act or process of saturating.

The state of being saturated, ie a stage where no more can be added or accepted.

Saturation advertising Sättigungswerbung

An amount of advertising above the standard levels of advertising coverage and frequency in order to achieve a maximum advertising impact.

Saturation of a market Marktsättigung

Also called market saturation.

A situation in which a market has as much of a product or service as it can sell. Once the saturation point is reached, the growth of demand slows down to levels determined by population growth and replacement.

Saturation point Sättigungspunkt

The point at which something is saturated, eg the point at which demand cannot be increased any further.

Say's law (of the market) Saysches Theorem

According to Jean-Baptiste Say (1767 - 1832), a French economist, supply creates its own demand, so that production itself stimulates a demand for what has been produced.
The law really means that the returns to the factors of production, wages, rent, interest and profit paid to produce the total output of goods, are just sufficient to purchase the total of goods produced. More production (supply) means more factor payments (income) and an increased ability to purchase (demand).

Scale of charges Gebührenliste

A list showing the charges for various services.

Scale of preferences Präferenzordnung (Hierarchie der Bedürfnisse)

Also called preference scale, order of preferences, set of preferences, or hierarchy of wants.

A scale of the relative importance of various goods and services to an individual. The making of a choice between alternatives implies that each individual has a scale of preferences (i.e. a sort of list of all his unsatisfied wants arranged in order of preference), placing those he considers more important or satisfying on top of his scale (necessities first, comforts next and luxuries last).
A person's scale of preferences will:
1. differ from those of other people because he has different likes and dislikes;
2. not remain constant but will change as time goes on;
3. affect his demand for commodities since it reflects the intensities of his wants.

Scale of prices Preistabelle

Also called price list.

A list showing various prices.

Scale of production Produktionsumfang

Also called scale of operations.

The word scale means size. Production can be on a small scale or large scale depending on the type of good being produced, technological factors (they affect supply) and market factors (they affect demand).

Scalp kleine Gewinnmitnahme

Also called scalping.

In general, a trade where a speculator enters into transactions to turn a quick and sometimes unreasonable profit.
For example, a scalper buys tickets at regular prices for a pop or sports event and when the event becomes a sellout, resells the tickets at the highest price possible.

Scanner Scanner, elektronisches Lese-, Abtastgerät

Also called bar code reader or bar code scanner.

An input device for the optical scanning of bar codes and transmission of the coded information to a computer.
For example in a supermarket or large shop the bar code on the product is moved over the laser scanner, which is under a glass window at the check-out till; the coded information (e.g. product description and price) is read and sent to the shop`s central computer. At the same time the customer can see the name and price of the product on a display screen. Finally, this information is printed on the receipt.

Large shops cannot function nowadays without computers. The check-out till not only takes the customer`s money but is also connected to the shop`s central computer. When an article is bought, information about the sale is sent to the computer which then immediately checks how many of the articles sold are left and decides when to order again.

Scarcity Knappheit, Mangel

Also called scarceness.

In economics, scarcity means limited in supply. In this sense all goods and services are scarce relative to the demand for them.
Human wants are nearly unlimited while resources are not, so that, no matter how much we produce, it is impossible to satisfy men's wants. Perhaps the major economic problem is that of scarcity; if scarcity did not exist, economic problems would not exist.

Scarcity value Seltenheitswert
hoher Preis für Mangelwaren

The value of something because it is scarce/rare and thus in keen demand.

The high price of a commodity that is limited in quantity, i.e. the supply of which is small or impossible to increase.

Scatter diagram Streudiagramm

Also called scattergram.

A graph on which the points are not connected by lines. The main purpose is to portray central tendencies, i.e. to show how the points form groupings and whether some points are scattered outside the groups.

Scattered markets verstreute Märkte

Markets which are spread over a large territory and thus can only be worked by firms disposing of an efficient distribution system.

Schedule Fahr-, Flug-, Zeitplan
Verzeichnis
Steuergruppe

A timetable, e.g. for planes or trains.

A list of details.

In the UK, a taxation class. Also called tax bracket.

Schmal(t)z Schmalz

Exaggerated sentimentalism, as in music or writing.

Scrambled merchandising gemischtes Merchandising, Gemischtwarenhandel

Also called scrambled retailing.

The contemporary practice of retailers to add dissimilar or unrelated products and product lines to an existing product mix in order to generate additional sales, i.e. a retailer offers goods for sale not normally offered by that type of retailer.

Screen advertising Kinowerbung

Cinema advertising.

Screening Screening

An early stage in the new product development process when new or modified product ideas are assessed to identify those that the firm might profitably develop. Products not meeting this and other essential criteria are thus eliminated at an early stage in their development. This helps to avoid unnecessary wastage of resources on ideas.
Note: most new product ideas are rejected at the screening stage.

Script Manuskript
Drehbuch

A manuscript, ie a written copy of an article or book before it is printed.

A written text of a play, show, motion picture, radio or TV program, or the like.

Scriptwriter Drehbuchautor

A person who writes scripts for a radio or TV programme or commercial.

Scrutiny Prüfung, Untersuchung

Also called examination.

A careful examination in detail.

Seal of approval Testsiegel

A symbol granted to a product by a test magazine stating that it has tested the product and found it satisfactory.

Sealed bid verschlossenes Angebot, Submissionsangebot in versiegeltem Umschlag

Also called sealed-tender (bid).

A method of competitive bidding and offering. Each potential supplier submits his bid in a sealed envelope. All bids/offers are opened at the same time and the bid of the lowest bidder/offeror will be accepted, provided that it meets all the necessary requirements. The price is fixed by the bidding process.

Season ticket Zeitkarte

A special ticket permitting usually unlimited travel between the points stated on the ticket throughout its validity, e.g. a month.

A ticket for a theatre, sports club, etc. permitting attendance at specified performances throughout the validity of the ticket.

Seasonal adjustment Saisonbereinigung

Changes made to figures to take account of seasonal fluctuations.

Seasonal advertising Saisonwerbung, saisonale Werbung

A strategy to run advertisements only during times of the year when the product or service is most likely to be used.

Seasonal discount Nachlaß außerhalb der Saison

A discount offered by sellers to encourage business during slack periods when there is slack/sluggish demand.

Seasonal fluctuation Saisonbewegung, Saisonschwankung

A variation in the demand for a product or service which depends or is influenced by the time of the year.

Seasonal product Saisonware

Products which are mainly sold within particular seasons of the year, eg skis in winter, and swimsuits in summer, Easter eggs on Easter, potted plants on Mother`s Day, etc.

Second zweite Wahl

A product of substandard quality.

Second class mail Post zweiter Klasse

In the USA, a mail service reserved for newspapers and magazines.

Second generation product Produkt der zweiten Generation

A product which evolves from one already on the market and finally replaces it.

Secondary data Sekundärdaten

Data of internal and external sources which already exists and may be used for an investigation but has not been collected for that specific purpose.
Data is generally classified as either primary or secondary.

Secondary industry verarbeitende Industrie

Also called industrial sector or manufacturing industry.

These industries manufacture the finished or partly finished commodities which satisfy human wants.

Secondary market Sekundärmarkt

In marketing, a market for commodities in which the producers of the commodities do not participate as sellers.

In general, any market in which commodities or titles to property are dealt outside a recognized or primary market.

Secondary meaning Zweit-, Spitzname

A nickname given to a brand either by the producer or the consumer and which may be registered as a trademark, eg Coke for Coca-Cola.

Secondary production Industrieproduktion

The production of manufactured goods rather than primary products (see primary production).

Secondary reader Zweit-, Folge-, Sekundärleser

Also called pass-along reader.

The readers of print media who obtain their copies from persons who have bought or subscribed to the publication.

Secondary research Sekundärforschung

Also called secondary market research.

The collection of marketing research data using previously published sources, such as trade statistics for a product or a country. Working with secondary sources is less expensive and helps the company to focus its marketing efforts. On the other hand, secondary research has its limitations, e.g. the most recent statistics may be relatively old or they may be distorted by incomplete data gathering techniques.

Secondary sector sekundärer Sektor der Volkswirtschaft, verarbeitende Industrie

Economists often divide the economy into three main sectors: 1. the primary, 2. the secondary and 3. the tertiary sector.

This sector consists of manufacturing and construction.

Secondhand dealer Gebrauchtwarenhändler

A dealer who sells secondhand goods, i.e. goods that have had one or more previous owners.

Seconds Waren zweiter Qualität, zweite Wahl

Also called rejects.

Goods which are of second-rate quality or below standard and therefore sold at a cheap(er) price.

Sector Bereich

The economic term for a part of the national economy (e.g. the private, the public, the goods or the money sector) or business activity.

Secular trend Langzeittrend

The regular, long-term movement of economic data, eg the rising or falling sales over a period of years.

Segment(al) reporting Berichterstattung über Teilbereich

Reporting on individual segments of a business's activities to obtain a segmental knowledge.

Segmentation Segmentierung

Also called market segmentation.

The breakdown of a market into sub-markets (which may be based upon age, income, leisure activities, sex, social standing, etc.) which have their own special requirements and characteristics and in which marketing factors such as price, quality, packaging, etc. may differ.

Segmentation types Segmentierungsarten

There are a number of different ways of dividing a total market into submarkets.

Examples are:
1. age and lifecycle segmentation, 2. behaviour segmentation, 3. benefit segmentation, 4. brand loyalty segmentation, 5. class segmentation 6. customer segmentation, 7. geodemographic segmentation, 8. income segmentation, 9. key-element segmentation, 10. lifestyle segmentation, 11. macrosegmentation, 12. microsegementation, 13. occasion segmentation, 14. psychographic segmentation, 15. sex segmentation, 16. spatial segmentation, 17. usage rate segmentation, 18. usage segmentation, 19. volume segmentation, etc.

Segmentation variables Segmentierungsvariablen

The factors by which market segments are formed, eg behavioural, demographic, geographic, psychographic or socio-economic variables.

Selective advertising gezielte Werbung

Also called selectivity advertising.

Advertising trying to reach a particular target group and intended to create a demand for a specific brand.

Selective demand selektive Nachfrage

Consumer demand for a particular product or service.

Selective distribution selektiver Vertrieb

A type of distribution where the producer selects only retailers who will provide a certain image or who will sell only certain merchandise, i.e. a product is distributed through a limited number of retailers in a given market area.
By using this method, the producer can avoid selling to retailers that are poor credit risks, make too many returns, place orders too small to be profitable, request too much service, etc.

Selective exposure selektiver Werbemittelkontakt

The choice made by listeners, readers, viewers of whether to listen to, read, or view a particular programme, commercial, etc.

As people cannot perceive every stimulus in their environment at one time, they use selective exposure to decide which stimuli to notice and which to ignore. A stimulus is more likely to reach awareness if its information helps to satisfy current needs.

Note: a consumer is exposed to over 150 advertising messages per day but notices only between 11 and 20.

Selective marketing differenziertes, selektives Marketing

Also called differentiated marketing.

A marketing strategy where a number of products or services are sold to selected market segments in order to increase total sales.

Selective perception selektive Wahrnehmung

The filtration process made by a reader, viewer, or listener to enable him/her to perceive only those stimuli which are rated subjectively as being of relevance.

Selective selling Vertrieb durch ausgewählte Händler, Auswahlvertrieb

Also called selective distribution.

Selling by more than one but less than all of the traders who are willing to sell a particular product. For example, a producer chooses retailers that will be permitted to receive his merchandise for sale. The traders must satisfy minimum requirements.

Self actualization need Selbstverwirklichungsbedürfnis

In Maslow`s hierarchy of needs, the highest level of need; the others being in descending order of importance: esteem needs, social needs, safety needs and physiological needs (the most basic human needs).

Self actualization refers to finding self fulfillment and self expression, ie the need for realising one`s true potential, for using one`s talents and capabilities in the most productive way. Maslow felt that very few people ever attain this level.

Self completion questionnaire schriftlicher Fragebogen, Fragebogen zum Selbstausfüllen

Also called self-administered questionnaire or self completion.

A questionnaire whose questions can be answered and filled in by the respondent without the assistance of an interviewer. Usually, it does not consist of more that ten main questions.

Self image Selbstbild, Eigenimage

Also called self concept.

The perceptions, ideas, attitudes and beliefs a person has of himself or herself. Note: to a great extent our behaviour is influenced by our self concept.

Self liquidating display Warenauslage zum Selbstkostenpreis

Display material provided by a manufacturer to a retailer in return for a payment covering the costs.

Self mailer Werbesache mit Rückantwort
Werbesache mit aufgedruckter Empfängeradresse, so daß sie ohne Umschlag verschickt wird

An advertisement or circular having a tear-off reply coupon.

A direct mail piece folded and printed in such a way so that it can be mailed without an envelope or wrapper.

Self regulation freiwillige Selbstkontrolle

A business`s or industry`s internal efforts to meet certain regulations and establish certain standards, eg quality standards.

Self sufficiency Autarkie, Selbstversorgung

Also called autarky or autarchy, or self-dependent.

A situation whereby a country or a person produces all or most of its needs without relying on other countries or persons, or other sources of supply.

Self-fulfilling prophecy suggestiv wirkende/sich selbst erfüllende Voraussage

A situation in which a person or company predicts something and ensures this by acting accordingly. For example, a firm predicts sales will decline and ensures this by reducing marketing activities.

Self-liquidating offer (SLO) Warenangebot/Zugabeartikel zum Selbstkostenpreis

Special offer or gift only made available to buyers of a specific product. A product manufacturer, having purchased in quantity a particular article, advertises it to the consumer at virtually cost price plus, eg a number of labels from his product.

The benefit to the consumer is that he is able to buy the article at a very low price; the manufacturer and the retailer benefit from the extra sales of the product which result from the consumer's additional purchases to obtain the necessary labels.
The offer is termed self-liquidating because the consumer's purchase of the article reimburses the manufacturer for his original outlay.

Self-liquidator Werbeartikel/Zugabeartikel zum Selbstkostenpreis

A gift, premium, or other reward offered to buyers by the seller at the seller`s cost price. Thus, these sales promotions generate enough income to pay for themselves.

Self-service store Selbstbedienungsladen

Also called self-selection store.

A retail selling arrangement where customers/shoppers have direct access to prepriced merchandise in shelves or other displays and pay for their purchases at particular cash tills or in total upon departure at the checkout/cash desk. The customer chooses the desired merchandise without direct assistance of sales personnel/staff.

Sell Verkauf

Also called sale.

The act of providing goods or services in exchange for money.

Sell by date Verfallsdatum (der Haltbarkeit)

In the case of food also called eat-by date or use-by date.

The date by which a product, particularly food, should be sold or consumed before it becomes unfit for use or consumption.

Seller Verkäufer, Veräußerer
Verkaufsschlager, Ware, die sich gut verkauft

A person who sells or agrees to sell (e.g. in a sales contract) goods or services. Also called vendor.

A thing that is easily sold and sells very well. Also called bestseller.

Seller's lien Pfandrecht des Verkäufers, Verkäuferpfandrecht

Also called vendor's lien.

The legal right of the seller, who is still in possession of the goods, to keep the goods until they have been paid.

Sellers over Anbieter-, Angebotsüberschuß

A market in which there are more sellers than buyers or simply a market in which there are still sellers after all the buyers have been satisfied.

Sellers' market Verkäufermarkt

A market in which demand is greater than supply, i.e. there is excess demand, so that there is a market imbalance and sellers may fix the prices and the terms of sale. Normally there are high or rising prices; but if, however, the prices become too high there may cease to be enough buyers and the market may change into a buyers' market.

Selling Absatz, Verkauf (als Vorgang)

In general, selling means convincing someone of the advantages of accepting your proposition - you sell an idea, not a product.

In marketing, selling is the process of persuading people to buy, initiated and perpetuated at either a personal or impersonal level but commonly confined to oral presentation in a conversation supported by visual aids.

Selling agent Verkaufsvertreter, Verkaufskommissionär

Also called sales agent.

A person who represents one or more manufacturers who normally produce complementary/joint goods. He takes on the whole marketing, controls selling, advertising, sales promotion and sometimes pricing, but usually holds no stocks. The selling agent usually works on a commission basis. Selling agents sometimes carry the risks of credit loss and are most commonly found where small manufacturers wish to be relieved of marketing responsibility.

Selling by description Kauf nach Beschreibung

The sale of goods on the basis of a descriptive representation and after inspection of a small sum of them.

Selling cost(s) Vertriebskosten
Vertriebsgemeinkosten

The cost(s) of transporting a firm's products to its customers. Also called distribution cost(s) or marketing cost(s).

The costs which are incurred in order to develop or widen the market for a commodity, i.e. the costs which can be directly attributed to sales activities/marketing but which cannot be allocated directly to a product. The main expenditure is on advertising, commercial travelling, market research, etc. Also called selling expenses, selling overheads, marketing overheads, or distribution overheads.

Selling in Hineinverkauf in den Handel

A manufacturer`s efforts to persuade a retailer to distribute, display and stock his products.

Selling off-the-page Selling off-the-page

A purchase made as a direct response to a press advertisement. The buyer/customer may have cut out a coupon and sent it off together with a cheque, or he may have placed a credit card order by telephone.

Selling overhead Vertriebsgemeinkosten

Also called selling expense(s), marketing overhead(s) or distribution overhead(s).

These are expenses to do with selling goods, ie these are costs which can be directly attributed to marketing/sales activities. They are costs which cannot be allocated directly to a product. Examples are: costs for advertising or market research.

Selling overseas Verkauf im Ausland

The sale of goods and services to foreign countries.
A number of factors must be considered when a company decides to sell abroad:

1. the type of product(s) involved; 2. the product quantity; 3. the potential annual income from sales; 4. the market profile; 5. the degree of competition on the overseas market(s); 6. the statutory regulations; 7. the long-term future of the market(s); 8 the economic and political situation in the country or countries; 9. the distribution costs; 10. financial assistance granted by the foreign governsment(s) when production or assembly is carried out overseas; 11. the selling techniques with regard to competition, price level, customer profile, profitability and product features; 12. market trends; 13. potential growth areas; 14. distribution, marketing, selling, trading regulations; 15. pre-sales and after-sales service; 16. export finance; etc.

Selling price Verkaufspreis
Abgabepreis, Ladenpreis

The price at which goods or services are sold to customers after deduction of any trade discount. The selling price to the seller is the same as the cost price or purchase price to the buyer.

The price at which a good or service is actually sold through a retailer. Also called retail price.

Selling process Verkaufsverfahren

The separate, but related, stages forming the activity of personal selling.
These include:
1. preapproach, 2. approaching potential customers, 3. determining customer wants, 4. giving a sales presentation, 5. answering questions, 6. handling objections, 7. closing the sale and, 8. post-sale follow-up.

Selling short Leerverkauf, Blankoverkauf, Windhandel

Also called short sale, short selling or shorting.

The sale of a security or commodity which the seller (the short seller) does not own. The seller does this in the hope to take advantage of an anticipated decline in the price so that he will be able to buy enough to cover his sale at a lower price before settlement is due, thereby making a profit. This is effectively a bear situation.

Selling space Verkaufsfläche

In a shop, the area used for merchandise displays, demonstrations of goods and interactions between salespersons and customers.

Selling syndicate Verkaufssyndikat

A joint selling organization for a definite but renewable period. The products are sold through one agency, an independently registered company.

Selling task Verkaufsaufgabe

A salesperson`s job activities, such as direct selling tasks (eg presenting a product to a prospect and taking an order), indirect selling tasks (eg mailing sales material to prospects) and non-selling tasks (eg writing a call report).

Selling technique Verkaufsmethode

The technique used in selling a product or service, e.g. direct selling or telemarketing.

Selling up Versuch, Kunden höherwertige Ware zu verkaufen; Verkauf nach oben

In the selling process, a salesperson`s practice of convincing a prospect to buy a higher-priced item than the one originally enquired about.

Sellout/sell out Ausverkauf

Also called clean-up sale, clearance sale, clearing sale, sell-off, selling out/off or closing-down sale.

The sale of all stocks or of a set of products.

Semantic differential Polaritätsprofil

A market research technique using rating scales of bipolar/opposite words, eg yes-no, good-bad.

Semantic differential question Polaritätsfrage

A structured question answered by indicating a point on a scale between two opposing statements. For example, "did you find the hotel comfortable .... uncomfortable?"

Semi-liquidator Teilkosten deckende Werbezugabe

Also called semi-self-liquidator.

A premium offer that is not fully self liquidating, ie the buyer has to pay part of the costs for the premium.

Semi-solus advertisement teilisolierte Anzeige

An advertisement sharing a page with other advertisements but which are not immediately next to it.

Semifinished products unfertige (halbfertige) Erzeugnisse, Halbfabrikate, Halberzeugnisse

Also called semi-manufactured goods, semimanufactures, partly finished products, unfinished products, or in-process items.

Products which are partly finished.

In the production process, components for assembly into major products.

Semistructured interview halbstrukturierte Befragung

An interview in which the interviewer uses some preset questions plus questions of his/her own choice.

Semistructured question halbstrukturierte Frage

Questions that include sentence completion items and word association tests.

Semivariable/semi-variable costs teilvariable Kosten, Mischkosten

Also called semi-fixed costs, borderline costs or mixed costs.

Costs that are composed of both fixed and variable cost components within a relevant range of production.
Such costs vary with production/output, but not in direct proportion to it. The costs are fixed for a given level of output and vary as different output levels are reached.

Sender Sender
Absender

In the communication process, the originator of the message.

A person or firm who sends something, eg a letter or parcel.

Sensitive market leicht, empfindlich reagierender Markt

A market, usually the stock market, in which prices move, i.e. increase or decrease, significantly in response to outside events, rumours, etc.

Sensitive products sensible Güter, Ware(n)

Products that are highly vulnerable to imported goods.

Sentence completion question Satzvervollständigungsfrage, Frage mit unvollendetem Satz

A semistructured question which has to be answered by completing a sentence.

Sequential sampling sequentielles Stichprobenverfahren

In statistics, a method of random sampling that continues until an adequate sample has been made (i.e. an undetermined number of samples are tested one by one) to validate or invalidate a hypothesis at determined confidence levels.

Service Gefälligkeit
Versorgung(sdienst)
Kundendienst
Dienstleistung
Wartung, Service

Work done by one person that benefits another, i.e. an act of helpful activity.

The supplying of utilities, commodities or other facilities that meet a public need, e.g. electricity, water, etc.

After-sales assistance provided by the manufacturer to maintain the quality of a product during its use. Also called customer service.

The work done by an employee, adviser, consultant, etc for customers.

The keeping of machines in good working order through overhauling, replacement of parts, and the like.

Service agreement Wartungsvertrag

Also called maintenance agreement or service contract.

A contract under which a supplier undertakes to maintain (service) equipment supplied for a stated period after sale or through a period of hire.

Service charge Bearbeitungsgebühr
Bedienungsgeld

A charge made for services rendered. Also called handling charge.

In hotels or retaurants, a charge (usually 10 % or 15 %) sometimes added to a bill to pay for the service.

Service department Kundendienstabteilung

An organizational unit that does not directly produce goods but is concerned with providing after-sales service to customers; e.g. it keeps customers' machines in good working order. Furthermore, the department may be involved with the handling of complaints which require tactful treatment to avoid temporary or permanent loss of goodwill.

Service desk Kundendienstschalter

In a store, a place where customers can exchange merchandise bought, receive information or make use of other services.

Service industry Dienstleistungsindustrie

Also called service economy.

The tertiary sector. An industry that provides a service such as advertising, the buying and selling of goods, banking, entertainment, finance, health, insurance, transport, travel, warehousing, etc, to another industry or the public.

Service level Servicegrad

A producer`s or seller`s efficiency in distributing goods.

Service life Nutzungsdauer

Also called economic, effective, operating, serviceable, useful or working life.

The estimated economic life of an asset to a business, which may be less than its physical life.

Service mark Dienstleistungsmarke

An identifying sign, symbol or mark used by a service provider. It performs the same function for a service as a trademark does for a tangible product. Thus, it can be registered.

Service market Dienstleistungsmarkt

The market for services, ie all organisations that buy in order to produce services.

Service marketing Dienstleistungsmarketing, Service Marketing

A form of marketing where the emphasis is on providing assistance, support or services to businesses, the general public or the government.

Service merchandiser Regalgroßhändler

Also called rack jobber.

A specialised full-service wholesaler who places sales racks or stands in retail stores, furnishes the racks or stands on which the products are displayed and charges the retailers, usually large supermarkets or chain stores, for what has been sold from the racks or stands.
Note: the rack jobber owns the goods on the racks and sells them on a consignment basis.

Service provider Dienstleistungsbetrieb, Dienstleistungserbringer

The person or firm providing a service.

Service quality Bedienungsqualität, Servicequalität

The standard of service provided by the seller to the customer.

Service sector Dienstleistungssektor

Also called tertiary sector.

That part of industry which offers services, such as banking, insurance, education, health, transportation, etc.

Serviceman Service-Mann, "Kundendienst"

A person or business who does the work of servicing.

Services Dienstleistungen

In an economic sense, services are any activities or tasks for which there is a demand and that are fulfilled by persons and/or organizations, and for the benefits of which consumers are prepared to pay a price as they satisfy their needs and wants.

Services are sometimes referred to as intangible goods/noneconomic goods which are usually non-transferable because they are consumed at the point of sale, e.g. a concert or medical care.

Note: a service may also take the form of a physical asset, e.g. the bank service to provide a cheque or statement of account; a service in which knowledge is imparted if freely transferable from one consumer to another, e.g. a tax advice.

Characteristics of the service sector, e.g. banking, business services, communications, distribution, insurance, etc., are: usually it is more labour-intensive and employs more capital per worker than the manufacturing sectors; trade in services is growing faster than trade in physical commodities and the export of invisibles is of growing importance.

Services rendered — geleistete Dienste, erbrachte Dienstleistungen

Also called services performed.

When a business receives an invoice for services provided it usually says "To (or for) services rendered".

Servicing — Wartung
Kundendienst

Work undertaken to keep equipment, machinery, a plant, etc. in good working order. Also called maintenance or upkeep.

All the work necessary to supply and dispatch goods ordered by a customer.

Setback — Rückschlag (Rückgang, Verschlechterung)

A small reduction in business activity, e.g. a setback in production.

Sets in use (SIU) rating — Einschaltquote

The percentage of radio or TV sets that are tuned in during a given time period.

Settlement — Begleichung, Verrechnung

Payment of an invoice (also called settlement of account), a bill, a debt, etc.

Settlement discount Skonto, Barzahlungsrabatt

Also called cash discount.

A discount given to debtors who pay their invoices promptly or within a specified time period, e.g. 2 % discount for payment within 14 days.

Seven Ps sieben Ps

The services marketing mix consisting of the 4 Ps: product, price, place, promotion; plus another 3 Ps: people, physical evidence, process.

Seven Sisters "sieben Schwestern"

Also called Big Seven.

These comprise the world`s seven largest oil companies: BP, Chevron, Exxon, Gulf, Mobil Oil, Shell and Texaco. In 1984 Chevron merged with Gulf.

Sex segmentation Geschlechtssegmentierung, Segmentierung nach Geschlecht

Dividing a market into different groups based on sex.

Sexy product attraktives Produkt

A very attractive and appealing product.

Shakeout Gesundschrumpfung
mäßiger Konjunkturrückgang

A process of natural selection, e.g. in industry many of the less profitable businesses are forced to leave the market so that only the profitable ones remain.

A moderate decline in economic activity (ie a downtrend or economic slowdown) with falling prices and increasing unemployment.

Share of audience Einschaltquote, Prozentsatz der Gesamthörer-/Zuschauerschaft

Also called audience rating or audience share.

The percentage of radio or TV sets in a coverage area that is tuned to a particular programme, radio or TV station during a given time period.

Share of mind Prozentsatz der Personen, denen eine Marke bekannt ist

The percentage of people who are aware of a particular brand.

Share point Anteilspunkt

A share equal to one percent of the total, eg one share point (1%) of the total market or readership.

Shelf Regal, Gestell

Flat piece of glass, metal, stone, wood, etc. attached to the wall or in a cupboard so that items for sale can be stored/shelved or displayed on it.

Shelf card Regalschild

Also called shelf label.

In a store, a display card attached to a shelf.

Shelf fee Regalgebühr

Also called slotting allowance or stocking allowance.

A fee paid by a manufacturer to a retailer for the provision of shelf space to display products.

Shelf filler Regalauffüller

A person responsible for filling the shelves in a shop to ensure that customers can buy the product.

Shelf life Lagerfähigkeit, Haltbarkeit, Verbrauchsfrist

Also called storage life or sell by date. In the case of food also called eat-by date or use-by date.

The tested or established period of time during which a product may stay on the shelf in a shop and still be good for use or sale (e.g. perishable goods such as milk etc. have a short-shelf life). Normally the goods bear a date code which indicates the date by which they should be sold or removed by the shelf filler.

Shelf marker Regalpreisschild

In a shop, a tag attached to a shelf and stating the price of a product.

Shelf pack Regalpackung

A container placed on a shelf.

Shelf pricing Regalauszeichnung

A situation where prices are not stuck onto individual products or packages, but printed on narrow strips which are stuck to the edges of shelves facing the customers.

Shelf space Regalfläche

The amount of space on a shelf available for merchandise.

Shelf strip Regalstreifen mit Werbung

A narrow adhesive strip printed with an advertising message and stuck to the edges of shelves facing the customers.

Shelf talker kleines Regalplakat

A printed advertising card or other sign that is attached to or hung from shelves or railings of display cases to call attention to a shelved product.

Shelf warmer Ladenhüter

Also called sleeper, slicker, nonmoving article, drug on the market, or unsalable article.

A commodity which does not sell at all but stays in the shelves.

Sheltered economy Subventionswirtschaft

An economy greatly supported by the payment of subsidies.

Sherman Antitrust Act (of 1890) Sherman Antitrust Act (USA), Sherman-Gesetz von 1890 (formales Kartellverbot), Kartellgesetz

Also called Anti-Trust-Law or Sherman Act.

In the United States action was taken against monopolies by the State as long ago as 1890 when the Sherman Act was passed declaring trusts to be an illegal form of business organisation. The Act made it illegal to monopolize trade and outlawed (i.e. declared illegal) all combination or conspiracy in restraint of trade or commerce. To strengthen the Sherman Act, the Clayton Act, 1914, (Clayton Antitrust Act) was passed (e.g., it outlawed price discrimination, to lessen competition, and tied contracts, in which a buyer or seller is forced to deal exclusively with a person; and it banned interlocking directorates and mergers designed to lessen competition).

In Great Britain action against monopoly was first taken in 1948 under the Monopolies and Restrictive Practices Act. Restrictive practices were further controlled by the Monopolies and Mergers Act (1965), and the Restrictive Trade Practices Act, 1976 (RTP Act), and the Resale Prices Act (1976).

In Germany, there is the Kartellgesetz/Gesetz gegen Wettbewerbsbeschränkungen (GWB).

Shift of demand curve Verschiebung der Nachfragekurve

Also called shift in demand or change in demand.

A demand schedule and matching demand curve show the relationship between price and quantities demanded when conditions of demand remain unchanged. It shows how demand changes when the good's price and only its price alters.

Changes in demand which occur even when the price remains constant are called shifts in demand.
A shift in demand is a change to a new demand curve and this is caused by a change in the conditions of demand (e.g. change of taste or fashion; more up-to-date commodities replace older things; changes in real incomes; changes in the prices of other goods; taxation changes, etc.) and not by a change in price of the commodity. A price change only produces an extension or contraction of demand and leads to a movement along an existing supply line or curve. When a shift occurs the whole relationship between price and demand changes, and a new demand line or curve is formed (e.g. increased income leads to increased demand for a commodity at each price and a new demand curve must be drawn to show the price-quantity relationship under the new conditions; the demand curve shifts to the right).

Note: We must differentiate between moving along a given demand curve and shifts in the position of this curve. Movements along a demand curve show changes in the quantity demanded as price changes with all conditions of demand unchanged (i.e. all other things remain equal). When any of the conditions of demand change, a new demand curve is required (the demand curve shifts to the left or to the right).

Shift of supply curve Verschiebung der Angebotskurve

Also called shift in supply or change in supply.

A supply curve shows the relationship between prices and the quantity supplied when the conditions of supply remain unchanged. It shows how supply changes when the good's price and only its price alters.

A shift in supply is a change to a new supply curve and this is caused by a change in the conditions of supply (eg costs of production, advance in technology, natural and political influences, the prices of other goods) and not by a change in price of the commodity. Even when the price remains constant, producers can change the amount they produce, i.e. there is a shift/change in supply.
For example, improvements in production can cause an increase in supply, i.e. the original supply curve (S1) shifts to the right and a new supply curve or supply line (S2) is formed, showing that more is supplied at each and every price. Conversely, inefficient management or industrial disputes/strikes can lead to a reduction in supply, i.e. the original supply curve (S1) shifts to the left and a new supply curve or supply line (S2) is formed, showing that less is supplied at each and every possible price.

Whenever a condition of supply alters, a new supply curve must be drawn to show the relationship between price and quantity supplied under the new conditions. Changes in the conditions of supply lead to shifts in the supply curve to either the right or left.

Note: We must differentiate between movements along a given supply curve or line (upwards or downwards) and shifts in the position of this curve or line. Movements show changes in the quantities supplied (extensions or contractions) as price alters with all conditions of supply remaining unchanged. Whenever the conditions of supply change, a new supply curve is required (either to the left or right of the original curve).

Shipment (shpt)	Versand, Verschiffung (Schiffs)Ladung, (Waren)Sendung

The act of sending/shipping goods.

The amount/quantity of goods sent/shipped. Also called cargo, consignment, freight or load.

Shipper	Absender, Verlader Spediteur

A firm or businessman who despatches goods.

A person or company whose business is to send goods (e.g. abroad) by air, rail, road or ship. Also called forwarding or shipping agent, freight forwarder, or forwarder.

Shipping	Versand

Also called forwarding.

The act or business of a person or firm that ships/forwards goods.

Shipping documents	Transportpapiere, Verschiffungs- dokumente, (Waren)Begleitpapiere, Verladepapiere

Also called shipping papers or transport documents.

The documents necessary depend on the mode of transport.
Common documents required are, for example: invoices, insurance cover notes, insurance policies, air waybills, combined transport documents (CT documents), railway consignment notes, marine bills of lading (B/L), e.g. clean B/Ls, dirty B/Ls, received for shipment B/Ls, consular invoices, certificates of origin, warehouse receipts, etc.

Shipping invoice	Versandrechnung

Also called shipment invoice.

A document prepared by the shipper giving details of the merchandise shipped and notifying the consignee of the amount due.

Shipping marks Markierungszeichen, Versandmarkierung

Identification marks put on chests, containers, etc. Every consignment must bear comprehensive shipping marks, details of which also appear on the invoice.

Shipping note (S/n) Versandanzeige

Also called advice note, advice of despatch, delivery note, despatch note, forwarding advice or letter of advice.

Written notice sent by the supplier to a customer giving details of goods ordered and shipped but not yet delivered. It states the date of despatch and may arrive before the goods.

Shipping order Versandauftrag

Also called despatch order.

An instruction of the shipper to the carrier for forwarding goods.

Shooting star Shooting Star, Senkrechtstarter

A person, eg a sportsman, actor, singer, writer, etc who has become very famous within a short time period.

Shop (kleines) Geschäft, Laden
Werkstatt, Werkhalle

A small retail business where goods are stored and sold. Also called store.

A location where production takes place. Also called workshop.

Shop assistant Verkäufer, Verkäuferin

Also called assistant, salesclerk, salesman, saleslady, saleswoman, salesgirl, salesperson, or counter jumper (slang).

Person employed, either full-time or part-time, in a shop to give advice and information, to serve customers and to complete the sale on behalf of the shopowner/shopkeeper, provided he is acting within the scope of his authority.

Shop floor/shopfloor Betrieb
Verkaufsfläche

Production or other factory working area.

The area of operation in a shop. Also called selling space.

Shop front Ladenfront

That part of a shop facing the mall or street, including the main entrance and windows.

Shop order Arbeitsauftrag, Fertigungsauftrag

Also called work order.

An instruction to a manufacturing department to make or assemble specified items.

Shop within a shop Geschäft im Geschäft, im Laden
vermieteter Laden

An independent retail shop operated within another larger shop, eg a department store.

Shopkeeper Geschäfts-, Ladeninhaber

Also called shopowner or store owner.

The person owning or running a shop.

Shoplifting Ladendiebstahl

Also called shrinkage.

Stealing goods from shops by customers and employees with the intention to evade payment. The person stealing the goods is called shoplifter.

Shopper Käufer, Ladenbesucher
Einkäufer

A person who is buying/shopping goods, or is about to buy goods, from a shop. Also called buyer, purchaser or vendee.

A person whose work is to buy goods for his employer. Also called buyer, buying agent, purchasing agent or officer, head of the buying or purchasing department.

Shopping Einkaufen
Einkäufe

The action of going to shops to buy goods, e.g. to go shopping around.

The goods that have been bought from a shop(s).

Shopping bag Einkaufs-, Tragetasche

Also called carrier bag.

A paper, plastic or canvass bag with handles, used to carry purchases.

Shopping basket Einkaufskorb

A basket for carrying purchases.

Shopping center/centre Shopping Center, (regionales) Einkaufszentrum

Also called shopping plaza.

A group of shops and service establishments of different kinds, often outside the centre of a town, to serve the interests of the local community.

A specially designed building in which a number of different shops are located.

Shopping channel Einkaufskanal

A television channel offering shop-at-home services. The merchandise is shown on the screen, and viewers can call a special number for ordering.

Shopping goods Shopping Goods, Güter des nicht täglichen Bedarfs; Konsumgüter, bei deren Auswahl und Kauf der Kunde kritische Vergleiche anstellt

High-priced consumer goods (especially consumer durables) that are purchased only after the buyer compares the offerings of more than one shop with regard to price, quality, style, suitability, etc.; i.e. the goods are not bought on impulse.

Shopping mall Ladenstraße, Geschäftsstraße, Einkaufsstraße

Also called shopping promenade or shopping street.

Enclosed street or area for shopping, with a variety of shops, banks, restaurants and other facilities.

Shopping newspaper Anzeigenblatt

Also called shopper, freesheet or throwaway.

A weekly newspaper for local shoppers, distributed free of charge and containing advertisements and information on local events.

Shopping precinct Einkaufsviertel, Geschäftsviertel

Part of a town which is closed to individual traffic so that people can make a shopping spree and shop.

Shopping spree Einkaufsbummel

A period of shopping, usually enjoyable and entertaining.

Shopping trolley Einkaufswagen

A metal cart used by buyers in a supermarket to carry their purchases.

Shoptalk/shop talk Fachgespräch

Conversation about work or business, sometimes using a specialised vocabulary.

Short delivery (SD, sd) unvollständige Lieferung

A delivery of goods that does not agree with the delivery note as, on arrival, some goods are missing.

Short haul (Güter)Nahverkehr

Also called short haulage or short haul goods transport.

The transportation of goods over a short distance, usually by small carriers.

Short range plan kurzfristiger Plan

Also called short-term or short-run plan.

A plan covering a period of one year or less.

Shortage Knappheit
Fehlbetrag, Fehlmenge, Defizit

Lack of something or not having enough. Also called scarcity.

The amount by which something is lacking or needed. Also called deficiency, deficit, short, shortfall or wantage.

Shortlanded cargo zu knapp gelieferte Ware

The quantity of cargo delivered is lower than the amount stated on the transport document, eg a bill of lading.

Shortlanding certificate Shortlanding Zertifikat

If a carrier discharges a consignment of lower quantity than stated on the transport document (eg a bill of lading), then the carrier should issue a certificate confirming the shortlanding. This certificate is necessary if the consignee wants to lodge an insurance claim to receive compensation for the missing cargo.

Show Ausstellung

Also called exhibition, exposition or fair.

An exhibition of something, e.g. a motor show.

Show house/flat Musterhaus/-wohnung

A house or flat built and furnished to show it to potential customers so that they are induced to buy similar houses or flats.

Showbill/show bill Werbeplakat
Werbeplakat fürs Showgeschäft

An advertising poster.

A poster advertising a theater performance, motion picture, musical, or other form of entertainment.

Showbusiness Unterhaltungsindustrie, Showgeschäft, Showbusiness

Also called show biz or entertainment industry.

The entertainment industry, as theater, motion pictures, television, radio, carnival, and circus.

Showcard Aufstellplakat

Advertising material, made of card or metal, at the point of sale (POS), generally placed on a counter. Showcards are often made as dispensers from which the product may be taken by the customer.

Showcase Schaukasten, Vitrine

A cabinet with a glass or clear plastic front, side and top to display products.

Showpiece Ausstellungsstück

Also called exhibit or display article.

Something exhibited or worthy of exhibiting as a fine example of its kind.

Showroom/show room Ausstellungsraum

A large room where goods are displayed for sale and where potential/prospective customers of a business may look at them before they decide to buy them.

Shrink wrapping Schrumpfpackung

A relatively cheap form of packing consisting of a plastic coating that conforms to the shape of the package when heated by the use of hot-air blowers/thermo guns. The goods to be covered are usually placed on a pallet and then covered with a film of plastic. It is very popular with air freight consignments and consolidated consignments.

Shrinkage Ladendiebstahl

Also called shoplifting.

Theft or pilferage by customers and employees.

Shut outs nicht verladene Güter

Cargo refused shipment because it arrived after closing date/closing for cargo.

Side position Seitenflächenposition

In transit advertising, the position of an ad poster on either side of the interior (usually above the window) or exterior of a transport vehicle.

Sign off Sendeschluß

On radio or TV, the end of a broadcast day.

Sign on Sendebeginn

On radio or TV, the time a broadcast day begins.

Silent close stiller Verkaufsabschluß

In the selling process, a salesperson`s technique of ending a sales talk by saying nothing and waiting for the prospect to make a response.

Silent salesperson stummer Verkäufer

All point-of-sale (POS) material getting the customers` attention.

Single European Market (SEM) europäischer Binnenmarkt

The SEM was established in 1993. The ojective of the SEM is to permit goods, services, capital and people to move freely between the member states of the European Union (EU).

Single column advertisement einspaltige Anzeige

An advertisement occupying one column in a newspaper or magazine.

Single line store Spezialgeschäft

Also called specialty store.

A retail shop offering only a selection (variety or range) of related merchandise.

Single price store Einheitspreisgeschäft

A type of off-price retail outlet offering consumers to buy anything in the store for a lump sum, eg $ 5 per article.

Single price strategy Einheitspreisstrategie

A firm`s policy of offering all goods or services at the same price (or perhaps two or three prices). This tactic removes price comparisons from the buyer`s decision-making process and enables the seller to apply a simplified pricing system.

Single product strategy Ein-Produkt-Strategie

A producer`s strategy to offer only one product variant, possibly with one or more options.

Single selling proposition wichtigstes, prioritäres Verkaufsargument

Out of all the benefits of a product, the salesperson selects the most important one for a particular customer and uses it as the best selling argument.

Single sourcing Single-Sourcing, Einzelbezugsquelle

A company`s action of buying all its supplies for a particular product or service from one source of supply. The buyer can concentrate on one supplier and thus exercise more power on it. On the other hand, the buyer relies on one source of supply. Thus, some buyers split their orders between two or more suppliers.

Single-person household Einpersonenhaushalt

A household occupied by one person only.

Single-use goods Konsumgüter

Also called consumer nondurables, nondurable consumer goods, or soft goods.

Consumer goods/consumption goods that are quickly consumed or used-up, e.g. food.

Single-zone pricing einheitliche Preisstellung frei Haus

Also called uniform delivered pricing.

A pricing method in which all customers pay the same freight charges regardless of their distance from the seller.

Site passage Zahl der an Außenwerbung Vorbeifahrenden

In outdoor advertising, the number of persons passing the viewing area of a poster site.

Situation analysis Situationsanalyse

The process of gathering past and present data on the firm`s internal strengths and weaknesses, as well as external opportunities and threats, in order to identify trends, forces, and conditions with the potential to influence the firm`s objectives.

Situation report (sitrep) Lagebericht, Zustandsbericht

A report on the current situation or circumstances.

Skim-the-cream pricing Abschöpfungspreisstrategie, Absahnpreisstrategie

Also called price skimming or skimming.

A pricing policy which sets a high initial price (the skim-the-cream price) for a new product. Makers of new products (e.g. in the fashion market) entering new markets generally use a skimming price technique. This allows them a high profit at a low manufacturing level - it is their hedge against things going wrong and the risk is thereby minimized.
The competitors bring the prices down as they copy their way into the market.

Skimming price Absahn-, Abschöpfungspreis

Also called creaming price.

A high initial price for a new product, either to recover costs quickly or to exploit demand and achieve high short-term profits.

Skimming pricing Hochpreisstrategie

A pricing strategy using high prices to attract the market segment more concerned with product quality, uniqueness, or status than price.

Sky advertising Himmelswerbung, Luftwerbung

Advertising messages displayed in the air, eg by small airplanes, airships or captive balloons. A very popular form of sky ad is skywriting where a brief message is written in the sky by an airplane using puffs of smoke to form the letters of the ad message.

Slack demand geringe, schwache, stagnierende Nachfrage

Also called laggish, slight, sluggish or weak demand.

A market situation where demand is decreasing or even low.

Slackness of business Geschäftsflaute, Flaute

Also called slack business, slack, slackness, or business slowdown.

A dull or inactive business, e.g. a slack period or season.

Slander Verleumdung

A malicious, false, and defamatory oral statement or report.

Sleeper potentieller Verkaufsschlager
Ladenhüter

A product that has not sold well so far but has the potential to become a runner.

A commodity which does not sell at all but stays in the shelves. Also called unsaleable article, non-moving item, shelf warmer or slicker.

Slice-of-life advertising Werbung, die ein Stück wirklichen Lebens zeigt, lebensnahe Werbung

Advertisements or commercials presenting the product or service in personal life situations and thus being used by ordinary people in very common and realistic settings or engaged in everyday activities.

Slide Dia

A photograph set in a frame to be projected and enlarged onto a screen for viewing by people.

Sliding commission angepaßte, gleitende (Verkaufs) Provision

A commission paid to salespersons depending on the quantity sold, ie the commission is paid at a changing rate.

Slippage rate Käuferanteil, der Gutscheine nicht einlöst

In sales promotion, the proportion of buyers who fail to redeem a coupon or premium received with the purchase.

Slogan Slogan, Werbespruch

In advertising and marketing, catchwords, short memorable phrases or sentences associated with a product, service or company. Slogans are used repeatedly and provide a very simple, direct form of message, making small demand on the reader, viewer or listener. Ideally, the product or the name of the advertiser should be stated in the phrase.

Slot | Platz, Stelle
Containerstellplatz
Geldeinwurf (Automat)
Schlitz

A place or position.

Space on board a vessel occupied by a container.

A narrow opening, eg one for receiving a coin in a vending machine.

A slit.

Slot machine | Verkaufsautomat
Spielautomat

A machine selling goods, e.g. food, drinks, etc., to customers who insert coins or notes into the machine's slot. Also called dispensing or vending machine, or automat.

A gambling machine operated by inserting coins into a slot and pulling down a long handle attached to its side.

Slow motion | Zeitlupe

The technique of showing a film at a speed slower than that at which it was shot.

Slow moving merchandise | schwer verkäufliche Ware

Goods which are difficult to sell. Thus, these goods are usually offered at reduced prices, eg in a clearance sale.

Slowdown in business | Konjunkturrückgang

Also called cyclical decline, downtrend, economic slowdown, slowdown in the economy or business slowdown.

A decrease in economic activity, e.g. a slowdown in investments which will lead to a slowdown in economic growth.

Sluggish market flauer, lustloser Markt

Also called dull or slack market.

A market with no or little business activity.

Slumflation Wirtschaftskrise mit Inflation

A period of declining economic activity and rapidly rising unemployment combined with inflation. The term is a combination of slump (reduced economic activity) and inflation (rising prices).

Slump starker Konjunkturrückgang, Depression
anhaltender Preis- oder Kursrückgang

Period of economic decline, recession, collapse and depression with falling production, low consumption, high unemployment, loss of trade, increased bankruptcies and liquidations. Prices tend to fall, confidence in the future is lacking, and investment is reduced. Also called depression or severe recession.

The Slump = the world economic crisis of 1929-1933. Also called the (Great) Depression.

Originally used to describe a stock market collapse.

Small advertisement Kleinanzeige

Also called classified advertisement, small ad or small-space advertisement.

A short advertisement bought on a line-by-line basis, mostly inserted by private individuals in a newspaper or magazine, e.g. asking for jobs, properties required or selling small items.
The advertisements are subdivided according to the types of products and services offered or sought.

Small profits, quick returns (SPQR) kleine Gewinne, schnelle Umsätze

When stock remains the same and the rate of turnover is increased, more can be sold in a given time. In order to speed up sales, prices may have to be lowered, so that the gross profit on each article is less. But if it is realized more quickly and made more times in the year, it will give a greater total profit. A policy of SPQR may pay better than one of big profits on each article, but slow returns (BPSR).

Smuggling Schmuggel, Schleichhandel

The taking of goods or currencies into or out of a country illegally, e.g. in order to avoid paying customs duties or because the goods are banned.

Snapper Snapper

An incentive, eg a coupon or premium, used to encourage customers to buy a product that is heavily advertised.

Sniffer Schnupperauslage

An advertising display in which fragrance is used to draw attention to the product.

Snipe Plakataufkleber

Also called overlay.

In outdoor advertising, a sheet containing additional information, eg a retailer`s name and address, usually pasted at the bottom of another larger poster.

Snob goods Snob-Güter

Also called Veblen goods (named after the American economist Th. B. Veblen, 1857 - 1929).

Goods for which the quantity demanded rises, when the price rises. Wealthy consumers might demand more in order to show off their status or wealth; some people derive utility/satisfaction from having a good which others cannot afford.

Soap opera Seifenoper, rührselige Familienserie

Also called soap, soaper or daytime drama.

A sentimental and melodramatic radio or television series centering around contemporary problems, family life and romance. So called because soap manufacturers were among the original sponsors of such programs.

Social indicator volkswirtschaftlicher Indikator

A index which tries to measure the degree of human welfare/well-being or quality of life in a given area. It is influenced by such factors as real income, employment, housing, educational and cultural facilities, transport services, recreational facilities and environmental pollution, etc.

Social marketing Nonprofit-Marketing, Sozio-Marketing

Also called cause marketing or societal marketing.

Nonprofit marketing activities designed to influence and/or increase the acceptability of social ideas.

Social needs soziale Bedürfnisse

In Maslow´s hierarchy of needs, the sense of belonging and love. These needs include the need for affection and the feeling of belonging to a group: eg family, social group, work group, etc.

Note: marketing managers probably appeal more to this need than to any other, eg ads for clothes, cosmetics and food suggest that buying the product can bring love.

Social performance Sozialverhalten

The patterns and roles of behaviour used by people as workers, family members, citizens, friends, etc and when they interact with others.

Social responsibility soziale Verantwortung

A person`s or firm`s concern for the consequences of their activities and as they might affect the interests of others. For example, in marketing, the recognition by marketers that the well-being of society and customer satisfaction are as, or even more, important as profits in determining marketing activities.

Social sponsoring Sozio-Sponsoring

The financing by a sponsor (eg a commercial bank) of all or some of the costs of charitable performances or societies in order to gain publicity and goodwill from its association with them.

Social system Gesellschaftssystem

The way a society is organised. There are three main social systems. At one extreme is the free-enterprise system (laissez-faire or capitalist system); at the opposite extreme is the command system (collectivist or socialist system); the mixed economy uses some elements of both.

Social values Gesellschaftswerte

The moral principles or standards of a society`s people. Values determine the modes of behaviour and help determine what an individual considers important and how he/she assesses other people`s worth. Values may influence work ethic, honesty, social responsibility, choice of career, etc.
Values change over time and may vary across industries and from nation to nation.

Socioecological marketing sozioökologisches Marketing

Marketing activities considering all the stages in a product`s life span from raw materials to the junkpile, and regarding the interests of all consumers influenced by the use of a good or service.

Socioeconomic groups sozioökonomische Gruppen

Also called social classes; in some countries also called castes.

The classification/grouping of the whole population into reasonably stable and long-lasting economic and social groups, ie groups according to income and position. The assumption behind such grouping is that those who fall within a classification will behave in a certain way. For example, members of a class or group place importance on similar things, live similar kinds of lives, are interested in similar pursuits, and value certain kinds of behaviour.
In some countries classes are very rigid, in others they are considerably flexible and fluid, but still definable.

In the USA, six social classes are usually identified:

1. the upper-upper class (it comprises less than 1% of the population; the members` wealth is inherited from previous generations and earned from investments; striving to get ahead is not part of their class ethic - they have already arrived);
2. the lower-upper class (the lower-uppers live on income earned through success and ability in business or the professions, are ambitious to attain upper-upper class status for their children and tend to be prominent in social, political and cultural affairs; some of the members personify the term "nouveaux riches", others are members of the "jet set");

3. the upper-middle class (it comprises about 12% of the population and its members are usually in the professions, support high culture and value well-furnished houses);
4. the lower-middle class (primarily composed of white collar workers and higher-ranking blue collar workers, comprises about 30% of the population);
5. the upper-lower class (comprises about 35% of the population, generally has little education and mainly works in unskilled manual jobs);
6. the lower-lower class (about 20% of the population, includes the rural poor, welfare recipients, the persistently unemployed, and the urban slum dwellers).

In GB, there is the following classification:
1. upper middle class (eg senior managers), 2. middle class (eg middle managers), 3. lower middle class (eg clerical staff), 4. skilled working class (professional workers), 5. working class (unskilled workers), 6. lowest or subsistence level (unemployed, casual workers).

Socioeconomic variables — sozioökonomische Variablen

Social and economic factors such as income, occupation, etc which indicate a person`s status within a society.

Soft advertising — umwelt- und verbraucherfreundliche Werbung
unaufwendige Werbung

Advertising that is nonpolluting and consumer-minded.

Inexpensive advertising, eg a small ad.

Soft market — rückläufiger Markt, Markt mit nachgebenden Preisen

Also called buyer's market.

A market (e.g. a soft stock market) where there is an excess of supply over demand so that prices have a declining tendency.

Soft sell(ing) — dezente, "weiche" Verkaufstechnik, zurückhaltendes Verkaufen

Sometimes also called low-pressure selling.

A selling technique whereby the salesperson persuades people to buy in an indirect, subtle, but convincing way and does not force them to do so.

Soft spot Schwachstelle

Also called potential trouble spot or weak spot.

A particular place which can easily be attacked or a particular weakness of character.

Soft terms günstige Bedingungen

Very favourable terms granted to a particular person or party.

Softening price abbröckelnder Preis

A price that is constantly decreasing/falling.

Softgoods/soft goods kurzlebige Verbrauchsgüter
Textilien

Usually fast moving consumer goods (fmcgs).

Textiles or merchandise manufactured from textiles.

Softs Weichwaren (kurzlebige Verbrauchs-/Konsumgüter)
Textilwaren

Consumer goods that are consumed, or used up, soon after they are bought, such as agricultural commodities. Also called consumer non-durables, soft commodities or soft goods.

Cloth of all kinds. Also called textiles.

Sole agent Alleinvertreter

Also called exclusive agent or sometimes sole distributor.

An agent who buys and sells in his own name and for his own account. He is the only representative of a manufacturer (his principal) in a particular territory, e.g. an overseas market. Often he will be responsible for maintaining stock levels to meet demand fluctuations and also be prepared to offer spare parts and an after-sales service.

Sole sponsor Alleinsponsor

An advertiser who exclusively sponsors a particular event or buys all the advertising time in a radio or TV broadcast.

Solicited offer verlangtes Angebot

An offer submitted by the offeror, i.e. the seller, in reply to an enquiry.

Solicitor Akquisiteur, (Direkt)Werber

Also called canvasser.

A sales representative calling direct on consumers or users.

Solus advertisement Inselanzeige, alleinstehende Anzeige/Werbung

Also called island advertisement.

An advertisement which occupies a solus or island position, i.e. it is separated from any immediate, especially competitive advertisement. A single advertisement on the page (e.g. the front page) likewise enjoys a solus or preferred position.

Solus site alleinstehende Außenwerbung

In outdoor advertising, a poster site with an isolated position, ie separated from any other poster.

Sound cargo unbeschädigte Ware

Cargo consisting of merchandise that is neither damaged nor defective.

Sounder Erkennungsmelodie, Sendermelodie

A brief musical passage played by a radio station to identify it.

Source — Quelle, Ursprung
Bezugsquelle
Nachrichtenquelle

The thing or place where something comes from or has been obtained.

A manufacturer or supplier from whom goods have been obtained. Also called source of supply.

A source of information.

Source credibility — Kommunikatorglaubwürdigkeit

In personal selling, the believability of the salesperson.

Space — Anzeigenfläche, Anzeigenraum
Reklamefläche, Werbefläche
(Werbe)Sendezeit,
Frachtraum, Laderaum

In advertising, the pages or parts of pages in newspapers and magazines which can be used for advertisements. Also called advertising space.

In advertising, the hoarding or billboard available. Also called advertising space.

Advertising time in the broadcast media.

The room in which goods are transported. Also called cargo or freight space.

Space allocation — zugewiesene Regalfläche

In a retail store, the amount of shelf space reserved for a particular product.

Space arbitrage — Arbitragegeschäft unter Ausnutzung von Preisunterschieden auf verschiedenen Handelsplätzen zum gleichen Zeitpunkt

Arbitrage that consists of taking advantage of different market prices on different trading locations.

Space broker — Anzeigenagentur, Anzeigenvermittler, Kontakter

Also called media broker.

Independent person or agency dealing with buying advertising space or time in the media and reselling it to advertising agents or advertisers at a profit.

Space buyer — Anzeigen(ver)mittler, Kontakter Inserent

In advertising, a person in an advertising agency, responsible for buying space or time in the media on behalf of his client. Also called media buyer.

An advertiser in the media.

Space charge — Belegungspreis

Alsoc called space rate.

The charge made for all types of advertising space.

Space order — Anzeigenauftrag

In the media, an advertising order placed by an advertiser.

Space position value (SPV) — Werbewert eines Standorts

In outdoor advertising, the value of an advertising position with regard to the visibility of the poster panel and its vicinity to competing advertisements.

Space salesperson — Anzeigenaquisiteur

A person selling advertising space in the media to advertisers and ad agencies.

Spatial segmentation — geographische Segmentierung

Also called geographic segmentation.

The division of a market into submarkets on the basis of area, district, region, state, etc.

Special Sondersendung

A radio or television program that is not broadcast on a regular basis but on a one-time basis.

Special delivery Eilzustellung

Also called express delivery.

A very fast delivery performed by the Post Office or a private mailing firm. An additional fee has to be paid.

Special development area besonderes Entwicklungsgebiet, Fördergebiet

Also called assisted area.

A particular region where a government wants to encourage industrial and commercial development by offering special financial incentives to investors.

Special discount Sondernachlaß

A discount granted to special groups of final users or on special occasions.

Special enquiry/inquiry bestimmte Anfrage

Also called specific enquiry.

A potential customer/buyer asks a supplier/seller to submit a detailed offer, including the terms of payment and delivery.

Special event pricing Preisbildung für eine Sonderveranstaltung

A pricing strategy used for seasonal or special situations. The price is coordinated with advertising or sales promotion for the special event. Note: whenever there is a sales lag, special event pricing may help to increase sales and revenue.

Special interest magazine Spezialzeitschrift

Also called specialized or selective magazine.

A magazine published for people with special interests.

Special offer Sonderangebot

An article or service offered for sale at a reduced price.

Special order Sonderauftrag, Sonderbestellung

The goods ordered are to be manufactured specially for the buyer (the orderer) and are not saleable in the ordinary course of the seller's business.

Special position Vorzugsplatz, Vorzugsplazierung

Also called preferred position.

A specified location for a radio or TV commercial, or for an advertisement in a newspaper or magazine, eg on the inside or outside cover. An extra charge is usually made.

Special modification Sondermodifikation

A deliberate and planned change which in some way exceeds the usual standard or is exceptional in character, quality, etc.

Special price Sonderpreis

Also called preferential price.

A very favourable price granted to special groups of buyers.

Specialist shop Fachgeschäft

Also called single-line retail store or specialty store.

A retail outlet that offers a large selection/assortment in a limited/narrow line of merchandise. Specialist shops (e.g. video and record shops, men's and ladies' wear stores) can provide customers with more information and a better service.

Specialty advertising Geschenkartikelwerbung

Advertising by printing messages, logos and/or trade names on lower-priced articles to be given away, or sold, if possible, to customers. These articles may include calendars, matches, key rings, pens, caps, T-shirts, etc.

Specialty good/product hochwertige(s) Gut/Ware

Goods with unique characteristics and/or brand identification for which many buyers are willing to make a special buying effort. The buyers of these goods rarely make comparisons. A Porsche, for example, is a specialty good.

Specialty-merchandise wholesaler Fachgroßhändler, Großhändler mit beschränktem Sortiment

Also called limited line wholesaler.

A full-service wholesaler concentrating on a relatively narrow product range with an extensive assortment within that range.

Specific offer bestimmtes Angebot

A precise quotation by the seller with the intention to obtain a contract.

Specific tax spezifische Steuer

Taxes on goods and services are either specific or ad valorem.
Specific taxes are levied in terms of a fixed amount of money upon a particular good or service, e.g. £ X are levied on each bottle of champagne.

Specification Spezifikation, Beschreibung
Packliste
Ausfuhrerklärung, Exporterklärung
Patentschrift

A detailed information about the work to be done and materials to be used in the completion of a task. It is often associated with a price quotation or the goods to be supplied.

A list of the articles contained in a particular package or container. Also called packing list, packing sheet or packing slip.

A list containing details of goods exported. Also called export declaration.

A very detailed written statement of a patent. Also called printed patent specification.

Spectacular große, aufsehenerregende Werbung

A very large outdoor advertising display located in or around large metropolitan areas, eg Piccadilly Circus, London. The advertisement is presented by using neon or electric lighting, moving parts, flashers, lavish colours, and/or other special effects.

Speculative buying Spekulationskauf

Speculative buying/purchasing is an attempt to gain considerable profits by buying an excess of materials, securities, etc. at greater than normal risk when prices are considered to be at a low point. Unlike market buying, it makes price trends the primary factor in buying and gives less regard to the strict/material requirements of the business so that large losses may arise. In the case of material buying there is danger of obsolescence of material, large investments in inventory, etc.

Spendable earnings (frei) verfügbares Einkommen, Nettoeinkommen

Also called spendable income, personal disposable income, disposable personal income, take-home pay or net wages.

The gross wages/salary less deductions for taxes and social insurance, i.e. the amount available for spending.

Spending pattern Ausgabenstruktur, Kaufstruktur

The proportion of total expenditures made by households at different income levels on goods and services, such as food, housing, transportation, clothing, health care, entertainment, personal care, education, etc.

Note: according to Engel`s laws, people shift their spendings as their income rises.

Spending power Kaufkraft

Also called buying or purchasing power.

The amount of money a person can spend on goods or services.

The amount of goods or services that money can buy at a given time.

Spending split Ausgabenaufteilung der Marketingausgaben

The allocation of expenditures to the key marketing elements: advertising and sales promotion.

Spiff Verkaufsförderungsprämie

Also called push money (PM).

Cash or other incentives paid to a producer`s or retailer`s salespersons to motivate them to promote and sell their products or services.

Spinner Drehständer

In a shop, a revolving stand on which products are displayed.

Spinoff/spin-off Nebenprodukt

Also called byproduct (by-product), residual or subsidiary product.

A product that arose as a byproduct of another.

Spiralling inflation sich spiralenförmig nach oben bewegende Inflation

A type of inflation where price rises make employees demand higher wages which then increase prices again - higher prices induce higher wages, higher wages induce higher prices, etc.

Split consignment Sammelladung/Warensendung, die am Bestimmungsort an verschiedene Empfänger verteilt wird

A consignment of goods which is split at the place of destination and distributed to different consignees. Note: do not confuse a split consignment with a groupage consignment.

Split load gespaltene Ladung

Cargo in a single shipping unit which has more than one place of destination.

Split order Auftrag zu verschiedenen Kursen zu kaufen/verkaufen

A large order for a commodity or security that is separated into smaller units which are sold or bought over a lengthy time period in order to avoid substantial price fluctuations.

Split price gespaltener, unterschiedlicher Preis (auf verschiedenen Märkten)

Also called differential price.

The practice of producers or traders of charging different prices for the same product in different marktes. Sometimes the products are branded or packed differently.

Split run advertising Anzeigen-Split

In press advertising, the placement of two or more different versions of an ad for the same advertiser in different issues to test the effectiveness of one ad against another.

Spoilage Ausschuß
Materialabfall

Goods that are not up to standard and are sold for disposal value.

Materials wasted or spoiled during production process.

Sponsor — Geldgeber, Sponsor
Jemand, der Radio- und Fernsehprogramm finanziert und dafür Werbung betreiben darf

A person or company which pays to help someone or finances all or some of the costs of particular events, e.g. sporting events or musical concerts, in return for advertising rights.

A company which gives financial support to a radio or television programme, in return for the right to advertise its products during the programme.

Sponsored event — durch Werbung finanziertes/r Ereignis, Wettbewerb

The financing by a sponsor (e.g. a car producer) of all or some of the costs of sporting events (e.g. horse races, tennis tournaments), musical concerts, art shows, research grants or other activities in order to gain publicity and goodwill from its association with them.

Sponsored program — durch Werbung finanziertes Programm

Also called sponsored broadcast.

A radio or TV program paid for (ie sponsored) by one or more advertisers.

Sponsored television — durch Werbung finanziertes Fernsehen

Television broadcasting financed by advertising.

Sponsorship — Sponsoring, Mäzenatentum, Schirmherrschaft

The act of sponsoring, i.e. a form of advertising in which a company offers funding to a group, club, sporting or entertainment event, etc in return for a range of promotional opportunities. The prime objective is to increase sale of the sponsor`s product(s) or service(s).

Spontaneous recall spontane Erinnerung

A respondent`s ability to remember things heard or seen without any help by the interviewer.

Sporadic dumping gelegentliches Dumping

The occasional sale of a commodity at a lower price abroad than in the home market in order to sell an unforeseen and temporary surplus of the commodity abroad without having to reduce domestic prices.

Sports sponsoring Sportsponsoring

The sponsoring of a sporting event by one or more sponsors, eg the Tour de France, the Admiral`s Cup or the Australian Open.

Spot sofort lieferbar, sofort zahlbar
Werbespot, Werbesendezeit

A condition stating that the goods must be delivered or paid within two working days from the date of the deal.

A single radio or television advertisement appearance. Also called time slot.

Spot advertising lokale Radio-, Fernsehwerbung
Werbung, die zwischen Programmsendung ausgestrahlt wird

Also called spot campaign.

A commercial broadcast on a local radio or television station.

A commercial broadcast between programs.

Spot buy Kauf von Werbesendezeit bei Lokalsender

The purchase of commercial time on a local radio or TV station.

Spot commercial kurzer, eingeblendeter Werbespot (im Radio oder Fernsehen), Werbeeinblendung

Also called spot announcement.

A brief commercial inserted between portions of a radio or TV programme.

Spot delivery sofortige Lieferung (gegen Kasse)

Immediate delivery against payment of cash.

Spot display Einzelauslage von Waren

In retail trade, the individual display of single items.

Spot payment sofortige Zahlung

A situation where a buyer pays immediately.

Spot price Spotkurs, Kassakurs, Lokopreis

Also called cash price, loco price or warehouse price.

In commodity markets, the price quoted is for spot/immediate delivery with immediate payment and for goods where they lie, i.e. their delivery is at the buyer's expense.

Spot radio/television Werbung in lokalen Radio-/Fernsehsendern

Commercials broadcast on local radio or TV stations.

Spot sale Kassageschäft

Also called cash sale, spot trading or spot transaction.

A deal made on the commodity, foreign or stock exchange which is for immediate cash payment and for immediate delivery.

Spread

Differenz zwischen zwei Preisen, Marge
Handelsspanne, Verdienstspanne
doppelseitige Anzeige
ganzseitige Anzeige

The difference between two prices.

The difference between the cost price or purchase price and the selling price, i.e. the profit margin. Also called margin, operating margin, price margin or trade margin.

In advertising, two facing pages in a publication over which one advertisement is printed. This advertisement enjoys a solus/island position. If the pages are in the centre of the publication, the advertisement is known as a centre spread. Also called double-page spread or double truck.

In advertising, a single page advertisement.

Stabilisation of the economy

Konjunkturstabilisierung

Policies designed to stabilise the business/trade cycle and level out unemployment and inflation through fiscal and monetary instruments.

Stable market

fester Markt

A market situation where sales volume shows little change when prices change.

Stable price level

stabiles Preisniveau

A market situation where prices remain relatively unchanged over a time period.

Stacking

Stapelung

The placing of cargo on top of one another in aircraft, ship or truck hold; container or warehouse, etc.

The placing of cargo units on top of one another, e.g. the stacking of containers in ship holds.

Stagflation Stagflation

Stagflation implies that there is no growth in the economy, i.e. there is stagnation, and at the same time inflation and unemployment are rising, so that a lower living standard must result for those on fixed incomes. A crucial obstacle when fighting stagflation is that fiscal and monetary policies aimed at stimulating the economy and reducing unemployment only intensify the inflationary effects.
The term was coined in the 1970s when there was a heavy increase in oil prices imposed by the OPEC; this raised price levels while slowing down economic activity.

Stagnation Stagnation, Flaute

An economic situation implying that there is only low economic activity and therefore no or only minimal economic growth.

Stall holder Standinhaber, Budeninhaber

Also called stall keeper.

In covered or outdoor markets, someone who holds a stall to sell his/her goods, eg fruit and vegetables, clothing and other articles.

Stamp Rabattmarke

Also called trading stamp.

A stamp issued by a retailer and given as a premium to a customer. The stamps may be exchanged for cash or for goods.

Stamped addressed envelope (SAE, sae) adressierter Freiumschlag

An envelope with your own address written on it and a stamp stuck on it to pay for return postage.

Stamped envelope Freiumschlag

Also called postage-paid or reply-paid envelope.

An envelope handed out to someone which has been franked or which bears a stamp to indicate that postage has already been paid.

Stand (Messe)Stand, Verkaufsstand
Haltestelle

A place where a company's goods are shown and sold, e.g. at an exhibition or fair. When setting up a stand, the following basic steps apply:
1. you must know how to set up a stand so that all the elements "on stage" can be presented effectively;
2. make sure you have a good location with enough space to present an imposing foreground;
3. ensure an excellent stand administration, ie make sure that there are no delays in setting up the stand and that the staff is motivated and friendly, acquainted with the products and able to speak the local language;
4. exhibits are not lost or coming late; etc.

Also called stall.

A place where buses or taxes/cabs regularly stop and wait. Also called stop.

Stand out test Augenfälligkeitstest

A test which wants to find out how well a product packaging stands out or catches the eyes of the shoppers.

Standard cost Plankosten, Sollkosten

Also called attainable, budget(ed), estimated, forecasted, planned, predicted, scheduled or target(ed) cost.

In cost accounting, the planned cost, e.g. of making a unit of production, operating a department or carrying out an operation in the factory, under specified conditions of working.

Standard costing Plankostenrechnung, Sollkostenrechnung

A method of comparing actual costs with standard costs. Any variance (i.e. the difference between the two types of cost) is noted and carefully analysed.

Standard deviation (SD) Standardabweichung, mittlere quadratische Abweichung

Also called mean square deviation.

In statistics, a measurement of the extent of variability (or dispersion) in a data set. It is based on the difference between each value in the data set and the mean of the group.

Standard Industrial Classification (SIC) Branchenklassifikation
Produktklassifikation

In the USA called Standard Industrial Classification System (SICS).

A numbering system for the classification of industries and enterprises, used for statistical purposes.

A standard numerical code system used to classify products and services.

Standard label Gütesiegel (auf Produkten)
TÜV-Zeichen, TÜV-Plakette

There are a number of institutions which allow manufacturers to display a symbol on their products to show that the goods meet its standards, e.g. the standards of quality or safety.

A special label or tab attached to a device (e.g. electrical) or machine (e.g. car) to indicate it has been tested (by an institute) and is safe for use.

Standard letter Einheits-, Standardbrief

A letter typed or printed in the same format and containing the same message to be sent to various recipients.

Standard newspaper Standardzeitung, Zeitung im Normalformat

Also called standard-size newspaper.

A newspaper of the standard size.

Standard of living (SOL) Lebensstandard

Also called living standard.

A measure of welfare of a nation's inhabitants. Conventionally, a rise in the national income is seen as an indication of a rise in the living standard. But the national income figure must be related to the size of population; thus average income per head is a better indication of well-being. To indicate the current living standard, the average personal disposable income might even provide a better indication. However, a person's living standard also depends upon the quality of his working life, the quality and quantity of goods and services he is able to buy, the quality of social security, etc.

Standardization cartel Normen- Typenkartell

A legal type of cartel which relates to uniform methods for the specification of goods and services.

Standardized advertising standardisierte, genormte Werbung

In international advertising, the standardization of advertising messages for common application in all countries. This means that the world is treated as one market and any apparent regional, cultural or national differences are ignored. The firm`s output is promoted in exactly the same way in all countries. This means that consumers with the same attitudes and buying habits are targeted in each nation.

Some arguments in favour of standardization are:

1. it requires less marketing research (than customisation);
2. it is convenient and cheap;
3. it demands less creative effort;
4. a single message can be devised for use throughout the world;
5. lifestyles and consumer behaviour are increasingly homogeneous (especially in developed countries) and therefore people respond similarly to the same advertising messages;
6. more and more people, regardless of the country or city in which they reside, follow the same working, shopping, living and travelling routines and thus buy and enjoy the same products;
7. youth culture is remarkably homogeneous across nations, ie young people read the same sorts of magazines, watch comparable TV programmes and wear the same types of clothes;
8. worldwide there is a growing number of consumers who are interested in value for money products;
9. the high number of new product introductions and faster turnovers require international messages;
10. many products possess the same characteristics wherever they or sold;
11. the company can adopt a uniform marketing mix throughout the world;
12. the company is able to create an international corporate identity (CI).

Standardized marketing standardisiertes, genormtes Marketing

In international trade, a marketing strategy in which a firm uses a common marketing plan for all countries in which it operates.

Standardized marketing mix standardisiertes Marketingmix

In international marketing, a company`s strategy to use basically the same marketing mix worldwide. Standardization of the product, advertising, distribution channels, and other marketing elements promise the lowest costs because no major changes are necessary to suit the needs of most consumers all over the world.

Standards Normen

Agreed and accepted values, practices, conventions etc. for carrying out business, technical or other activities.

Standing order (STO, s.o.) Abonnement
Kauf auf Abruf

An agreement made between a company and an individual for the purchase of a newspaper, magazine, etc. Also called subscription.

An order which calls for goods to be delivered in specified quantities at certain intervals until further notice. The buyer may also call forward the quantities he needs from time to time. Also called call purchase.

Staple Massenerzeugnis, Stapelware

Also called staple commodity or product.

Products which are essential and in constant demand, e.g. basic food or raw materials.

Star Spitzenunternehmen/Spitzenprodukt, Produkt oder Unternehmen mit starkem Wachstum und großem Marktanteil

A high-growth and high-share business or product which often needs heavy investment to finance its rapid growth. Stars are usually subject to competition but are very profitable.

Using the two dimensions growth and market share, businesses and products can then be classified into four categories: 1. stars, 2. cash cows, 3. question marks, 4. dogs.

Star piece Superprodukt

An item selling extremely well.

State-planned economy staatlich gelenkte Wirtschaft

Also called state-controlled economy.

In such an economy the state decides what shall be produced, how much shall be produced and how to allocate the productive resources among the various producers. Today, there is neither a free economy nor a completely state-planned economy. In all of them there is a public sector and a private sector.

Stated objection angegebener, erklärter Einwand

In the selling process, the prospective buyer`s reason given for not accepting the product offered. Note: the stated objection often conceals the true objection.

Statement Kontoauszug, Rechnungsaufstellung, Abrechnung

Also called statement of account.

A document sent by a supplier to his customers, at monthly intervals, setting out: the balance brought forward from the previous statement (if any); invoices and debit notes on the debit side; payments and credit notes on the credit side; the balance still outstanding.

Static economy statische Wirtschaft

An economy which does not grow or decline significantly over a time period.

Station break Sendepause

An interruption in a radio or TV program or the time between programs, usually used for commercials.

Station identification (SI) Senderzeichen

The specific identification letters of a radio or TV station.

Station poster Perronanschlag, Bahnhofswerbung, Haltestellenwerbung

Advertising posters displayed in bus, railway and underground/subway stations, and airline terminals.

Statistical error (SE) statistischer Fehler

In a survey, the difference between results achieved when using a sample and the results achieved when using the whole population.

Statistics statistische Daten, Statistik
Statistik (als Wissenschaft)

Numerical data acquired, e.g. by observations, measurements, experiments, etc., for the purpose of drawing conclusions or forecasts from them. The data may be presented in tabular, graphical, diagrammatic or pictorial form.

The science of facts in the form of numbers.

Status product Statusprodukt

Also called prestige or prestigious product.

Certain expensive products sought after precisely because of their high price. Once the necessary status symbol image has been created, price increases do not cause demand to fall.

Status quo pricing Status quo-Preisbildung

A passive pricing strategy that seeks to maintain current prices or simply to meet competitors` prices.

Status symbol Statussymbol

An object by which the social or economic status of the possessor may be determined, eg a prestigious product bought more for purpose of ostentation than for its utility.

Statutory liability gesetzliche Haftung, Haftpflicht

Also called legal liability.

A liability that has been created by legislation.

Statutory monopoly staatliches Monopol, Staatsmonopol

Also called state monopoly.

A monopoly established by the government.

Steady market fester Markt

A market situation where demand for products and services continues in a regular way.

Sticker Aufkleber
Ladenhüter

In marketing, a label, poster or other printed sheet or plastic used as an advertisement medium for display purposes, e.g. on windows. Also called self-adhering label.

An unsaleable article. Also called shelf warmer or slicker.

Sticker price Ladenpreis

The price of a product as shown on the price tag.

Stock (Lager)Vorrat, Lagerbestand

Also called stock in or on hand, stockpile, store, supply or holding. In the plural form also goods on hand or inventory.

A quantity of something, e.g. materials, work-in-progress/process, finished goods, supplies or merchandise held for sale, that is stored for use as the need arises.
In the plural form (stocks) it means the total amount or total value of a firm's stocks of materials, finished goods etc.

Stock account Warenbestandskonto

Also called inventory account.

An account in which a business records the value of its opening stock, the receipts and issues of stock, and the closing stock.

Stock appreciation Wertsteigerung von Vorräten

The increase in the nominal value of goods as a result of a rise in prices during a time period. For example, goods produced early in the year and valued at £ 10 at the time of production, may be worth £ 12 by the end of the year.

Stock control Lagerwirtschaft, Lager(bestands)-kontrolle

Also called inventory management.

The application of management techniques designed to determine and implement the best levels of stocks, e.g. raw materials or finished good stocks.
A stock control system must be able to give information about:
the quantities in stock; the maximum and minimum limit for stocks; how much to order and how frequently; the ordering time; the amount of money and space tied up in stocks, etc.

Stock depreciation Wertminderung von Vorräten

Also called stock loss.

The reduction in value of stock kept in a warehouse, e.g. as a result of falling prices.

Stock rotation Lagerumschlag

The process of moving stock.

Stock shortage Bestandsfehlmenge, Minusbestand

Also called inventory shortage.

A condition that occurs when the real value of inventory/stocks is less than that shown on the inventory books/stock books. Any stock shortages will be the result of: poor stock control, shrinkage or wastage.

Stock size stets vorrätige/(lager)gängige Größe

The normal size of a product, eg shoes or shirts.

Stocking agent Vertreter mit eigenem Lager

An agent who stocks commodities, provides storage and handling facilities, but does not take title to the goods. He receives a commission on sales plus a fixed sum to cover handling and storage.
The opposite term is a non-stocking agent.

Stockist Fachhändler

A person who runs a retail shop/store and specialises in one particular line of products, often high-quality products.

Stockist agency Fachhändler mit größeren Auslieferungslagern

An agency stocking commodities. The agent fixes the selling price - the difference between buying and selling price covers cost and profit - and undertakes to buy larger amounts of stocks for his own account. This could significantly improve sales turnover where the goods are such that the demand is always for prompt delivery.

Stockless buying/purchasing beständelose, fertigungssynchrone JIT-Beschaffung

Also called just-in-time (JIT) purchasing.

Buying and obtaining delivery of goods required for production on demand. The supplier/seller is responsible for holding stock so that the buyer can reduce his storage/carrying cost.

Stockout Fehlbestand

The condition of having no stocks of particular goods or materials.

Stockout cost(s) Fehlmengenkosten

Also called out-of-stock cost or cost of not carrying.

The additional costs a company has to bear because products are out of stock. These include direct costs due to lost sales and indirect costs due to the loss of dissatisfied customers.

Stockpiling Bildung von Vorratslagern (besonders durch den Staat) Warenbevorratung

Also called stocking-up.

The building up of reserves of strategic raw materials or other essential commodities, usually by the state, for use in a shortage or national emergency.

The situation in which persons or firms buy multiple units of products to hoard them for future use.

Stocktaking Bestandaufnahme, Bestandsermittlung

Also called inventory taking.

Physical counting of trading stock/stock on hand.

A company's periodic checking, listing and valuation of all materials currently held in stock for the purpose of correcting records for stock control and for the compilation of the trading account and the balance sheet.
Preparations for stocktaking often start weeks before the actual date; goods are arranged in their respective classes, measured, weighed or counted.
There are two main methods of stocktaking: 1. perpetual inventory and 2. yearly stocktaking.

Stockturn (rate) Lagerumschlag, Umschlagshäufigkeit

Also called rate of turnover, rate of stockturn, stock turnover(rate), inventory turnover, turnover of stock or turnover rate.

The number of times the value of average inventory (stock-in-trade or stock on hand) is used and replaced over a stated period, e.g. a year or month. Is is calculated by dividing the net sales of the firm, i.e. the sales at cost price (selling price cannot be used because of the element of profit) for the period by the average value of its stock-in-trade (inventory) during that period and expressed as a "times", e.g. 12 times per year; if the average amount of inventory held is valued at £ 5.000 and the stockturn for the year is 12, then total net sales (net turnover) will be £ 60.000. The higher the figure, the better.

Stopper — Blickfang in Anzeige oder Verkaufsraum

An eyecatcher in an advertisement or salesroom.

Storage — Lagerhaltung, Lagerung
Lagerraum, Lager
Lagergeld, Lagergebühr, Lagermiete

The act of storing goods. The holding of goods for future use. Almost any product may require storage at a particular time for various reasons, e.g. the goods are produced seasonally but consumed continuously. Also called stockkeeping or warehousing.

The space for storing goods. Also called stockroom, storeroom or warehouse.

A charge made for storing goods. Also called storage or warehouse charges.

Storage capacity — Lagerkapazität

The amount of stock/inventory that can be stored in a warehouse.

Storage charge(s) — Lagergeld, Lagergebühr(en)

Also called warehouse charge(s) or storage.

A payment made to or charged by a business which stores commodities in its storeroom/stockroom.

Store — Laden, Geschäft
Lager, Lagerraum

A shop, ie an establishment where merchandise is sold, usually on a retail basis.

A place where goods and materials can be stored/stocked. Also called storeroom, stockroom, storage or warehouse.

Store / door delivery Lieferung frei Haus

The free of charge transportation of goods to the consignee`s premises.

Store audit Einzelhandelsbestandsaufnahme, Handelspanel

Also called retail audit.

A market research method by which a research company regularly checks preselected stores to provide information on the sales volume, sales trends, stock levels of different brands to manufacturers on a subscription basis.

Store demonstration Vorführung im Geschäft

The demonstration of products held in a store.

Store image Geschäftsimage

Also called store identity.

The consumer perception of a store, ie the total of what buyers think about a store. Note: this may not correspond with reality.

Store layout Ladenanordnung

The arrangement of the interior of a shop or department or the grouping of merchandise so that customers can easily move through the shop and the goods are attractively displayed.

Store loyalty Geschäftstreue, Ladentreue

A customer`s behaviour to shop regularly in a specific shop.

Store promotion Verkaufsförderung im (Einzelhandels)Geschäft

A variety of promotional activities within retail stores.

In international marketing, promotions staged in favour of consumer goods and services from one or more countries. It is an effective way of market entry or further consolidation of an overseas market.

Store traffic Kundenverkehr, Ladendurchlauf

The flow of customers through a shop, ie the number of people coming into or passing through a shop.

Store-redeemable coupon Gutschein, der im Geschäft eingelöst wird

A coupon issued by a manufacturer that can be redeemed in any store selling the product.

Storecard (Kunden)Kreditkarte für Einkauf in bestimmtem Geschäft

A store card is a form of credit card issued by retailers to enable customers to shop in their store(s) without paying in cash. Customers often get an interest-free credit for a number of weeks. All large department stores issue storecards.

Storehouse Lagerhaus

Also called storage building or warehouse.

A building in which things are stored/stocked.

Storekeeper Lagerverwalter, Lagerist

A person who owns or operates a store/storeroom.

Storeroom Lager(raum)

Also called stockroom, storage or warehouse.

A room where stores are kept/stored.
The storeroom should be functionally arranged with adequate aisle space, handling facilities, light, and ventilation. Sufficient room should be provided for receipt, inspection, and issuance of materials. The storage equipment (e.g. racks, forklifts, etc.) should be suitable for the types of items carried and the storeroom should provide the required storage capacity, flexibility, protection, durability and safety.

Storyboard (Werbefilm)Drehbuch, Storyboard

A sequence of illustrations of the key scenes in a planned cinema or TV commercial. As it visualizes the commercial, it can be used for client approval. Furthermore, it may help to estimate the costs for the commercial and it may point out flaws.

Stowage (auf)gestaute Güter, Ladung
Stauen, Stauung, Verstauung
Laderaum
Staugeld, Staugebühr

Cargo that is properly stored.

The act of stowing cargo.
Basically there are four main factors to consider in the stowage of cargo:
1. the prime consideration is the safety of the transport unit employed which may be a container, vessel, aircraft or road vehicle;
2. the best possible use should be made of the available deadweight capacity or cubic capacity in order to avoid broken stowage;
3. cargo which is fragile, spoils very easily, is liable to leakage, is liable to sweat etc. requires proper segregation;
4. different consignments for various destinations, ports, countries must be separated from one another in order to prevent delay in distribution and avoid double handling.

The space for stowing cargo. Also called loading space or cargo hold (ships).

The charge made for stowing cargo.

Straight commission Provision auf Verkaufsbasis

A form of sales compensation where a salesperson`s earnings are directly related to sales. Each increment of sales increases the commission.

Straight rebuy direkter Anschlußkauf, unmodifizierter Wiederkauf

A routine reorder in which the customer buys the same goods on the same terms, often in the same quantity, from the same seller.

Straight salary Grundgehalt

A sales compensation in which a salesperson receives a flat salary but no or low commission on sales.

Strategic business unit (SBU) strategische Geschäftseinheit (SGE)

The key businesses making up the company. An SBU is a unit of the company, e.g. a department, a division, a product line within a division, a market segment, sometimes a single product or brand, or a subsidiary that has a separate mission and objectives and can be planned independently of other company businesses.
Usually, an SBU is set up as a separate profit center, with the manager in charge of it responsible for its profit performance.

Strategic planning strategische Planung

The process of determining the company`s objectives and actions, the strategies to achieve them, who is responsible for carrying them out, when and where they will be carried out and how they will be coordinated.

Strategy Strategie, Marschroute

A plan or method for achieving a company`s major goals, eg to offer the right products to the right markets at the right time with the right quality and at the right price.
Coherent and well-prepared business strategies enable the company`s management to coordinate its diverse activities more efficiently, to allocate its resources more effectively, to monitor and control its activities, to react to changes in competitors` behaviour accordingly and in time, to compare results against predetermined targets, etc.
The clearer the strategy the more obvious the objectives, eg the size of the market share and the net profits, that need to be attained for its successful implementation.
Note: a firm without a strategy is ill-prepared to adapt its activities to meet the demands of rapid environmental change.

In international marketing, the following strategic decisions are highly relevant:
1. the products the firm will supply; 2. the market(s) in which the business is to operate; 3. quality and price levels; 4. how to finance foreign operations; 5. how to sell the product(s) abroad; 6. how to promote the product(s); etc.

Stratified sample geschichtete Stichprobe

The population of interest is divided into homogeneous subgroups according to a common characteristic, and a probability sample is then conducted within each group.

Street market Straßenmarkt

An outdoor/open-air market held in specific streets of a town where a variety of goods is sold by street traders.

Strict liability Gefährdungshaftung, verschuldensunabhängige Haftung

Also called absolute liability, liability without regard to fault or liability based on causation irrespective or fault.

Liability imposed on a party which commits a tort and causes a damage, even when that party has exercised reasonable care or is unaware of his negligence or fault. For example, in some countries product liability is regarded as strict, so that injured parties can claim damages without having to prove fault on the part of the insured.

Stripping Containerentladen

The action of unpacking/unloading a container.

Strong market lebhafte Nachfrage

A market on which there is a heavy demand.

Structural inflation strukturelle Inflation

Increasing prices caused by a heavy demand (demand-pull inflation) or cost pressures (cost-push inflation) in a key industry, even when the economy's total demand is in balance with its total supply.

Structured interview strukturierte Befragung

An interview that requires the interviewer to ask carefully worded, preset questions and follow a fixed pattern to ensure consistent and comparable data.

Structured question strukturierte Frage

A question that demands brief and specific answers.

Structured questionnaire strukturierter Fragebogen

A questionnaire in which the questions and the answers are highly predetermined so that the interviewer and the interviewee are rather restricted in asking and answering questions.

Stuffer Anzeigenbeilage, Werbebeilage

Also called insert, free-standing insert or stuffer, giant insert, newspaper stuffer, sheridan stuffer or supplement.

Sales promotional material placed into the pages of a publication or enclosed in an envelope.

Stuffing Containerbeladen
Füllen, Beladen
Füllmaterial
Einkuvertieren

The action of loading a container.

The act of a person that stuffs.

A material used to stuff something.

Putting a letter or document into an envelope.

Stunt spektakuläre Werbeaktion
Kunststück

In advertising, an unusual or risky show or entertainment to attract public attention to a particular product or firm.

An exciting performance displaying a person`s (stuntman`s/stuntwoman`s) skill or dare, eg for use in a cinema film or commercial.

Subagent Untervertreter

Also called underagent.

An agent appointed by another agent who is acting for the principal.

Subcontract/sub-contract Subunternehmervertrag, Unterauftrag, Zuliefervertrag

A contract in which one party, the contractor, employs another firm, the subcontractor, to carry out work which is part of a main contract.

Subcontractor Subunternehmer

A firm doing work for a main contractor.

Subculture Subkultur

A group that shares the values and beliefs of the larger society but also disposes of distinctive practices and preferences.

The cultural patterns distinctive of such a group.

Subhead(ing) Untertitel

In general, a smaller heading which comes under the main heading/headline.

In print advertising, a line of copy that is secondary in importance to the headline, but that attracts the reader`s attention by adding a new idea to the headline.

Subject to (prior) sale Zwischenverkauf vorbehalten, freibleibend

A condition in an offer to sell stipulating that the offeror can withdraw/revoke his offer if the property offered is sold before the offeree has accepted the offer.

Subjective price subjektiver Preis

A consumer`s perception whether he/she considers a good`s or service`s price as high, low, or fair.

Sublease Untervermietung, Unterverpachtung

Also called derivative lease or underlease.

A lease that is given by a person or company (the sublessor) who is already the lessee of the property under a headlease. The person or company which takes a property on a sublease is called subtenant or sublessee.

Subliminal advertising unterschwellige Werbung

An advertising message presented below the level of consciousness intended to influence opinion without the audience being consciously aware of it. The message is disguised and so brief (no more than 10 seconds in length) so that it cannot overtly be seen or heard.

Film or television advertising whereby messages are flashed so rapidly (i.e. for a small fraction of a second) that the watcher/viewer is not conscious of seeing them but is nevertheless subconsciously influenced. A form of advertising normally banned by advertising codes as it is in effect a brainwashing technique.

Subscriber Abonnent/in

A person who subscribes, eg to a newspaper or magazine, cable TV, a series of concerts or theater performances, etc.

Subscriber trunk dialling (STD) Selbstwählferndienst

Also called direct distance dialing (US).

A telephone service which enables the telephone subscriber to dial direct to numbers abroad.

Subscription Abonnement
Beitrag

The right to receive a publication or cable TV service, attend a series of concerts or theater performances, etc, for a sum paid.

The sum paid in advance for a series of a newspaper or magazine, or the contribution paid to a club, etc by a subscriber.

Subscription circulation Abonnementsauflage

Also called subscribed circulation.

That part of a publisher`s circulation that is sold to subscribers.

Subscription price Subskriptionspreis

A special price offered to a buyer of an article, eg a new book, provided he places his order within a certain period.

Subscription television (STV) Abonnementsfernsehen

A pay television service provided for a monthly fee.

Subsidised price subventionierter Preis

A form of controlled price which is kept low by government subsidy (paid out of taxes), eg to support the poorer consumer or to encourage the production of certain goods by paying the producer a certain subsidy.

Subsistence allowance Tagegeld (für Geschäftsreisen)

Also called subsistence money or daily allowance.

Money (usually a fixed sum per day) paid by a company to an employee who is travelling on business to cover his daily expenses, e.g. for meals and hotels.

Subsistence economy Bedarfsdeckungswirtschaft, Bedarfswirtschaft

A type of economy which supplies only survival needs, e.g. food, clothing, shelter, etc.

Subsistence level Existenzminimum

Also called minimum survival needs.

The minimum living standard (for survival), i.e. the lowest standard compatible with existence.

Substantiation Glaubhaftmachung, Substantiierung

A consumer protection requirement requiring an advertiser to be able to prove all the claims he makes in an advertising message, eg through test results.

Substitute good Substitutionsgut, substitutives Gut

Also called substitute or competitive good.

A substitute good is one that can replace another to the satisfaction of the consumer, more or less serving the same purpose as the original good, e.g. margarine can replace butter. The majority of goods available to the public are substitute goods.

Substitution effect Substitutionseffekt

Price changes (with money incomes constant) have two effects:
1. an income effect and 2. a substitution effect.
For example, a fall in price leads to an increase in real incomes as the consumer is able to buy as many goods as he did at the previous price and still has money left to spend on extra goods, i.e. demand will increase. Part of this increase in demand may thus be ascribed to the income effect. The remainder of the increase in demand is attributable to the substitution effect, i.e. the tendency of the consumer to increase purchases when the commodity price falls as it then represents a better bargain when compared with other goods (as the commodity is a substitute for another commodity).

Suburban center Vorstadtzentrum

Large shopping centers in the suburbs of larger towns. Generally, they are near or on major road intersections.

Suggested retail price (SRP) empfohlener Abgabepreis, Richtpreis

Also called recommended retail price (RRP).

The price recommended by a producer or other seller to a retailer.
With most products the producer or seller has no legal right to force retailers to sell at this price - some charge more and some charge less.

Summary report Kurzbericht

Also called summary statement, abridged report, brief or summary.

A brief but detailed report on something, e.g. a meeting.

Summative close Kaufabschluß mittels Zusammenfassung aller Argumente

In the selling process, a salesperson`s method of ending a sales talk by summarizing the product`s benefits and asking for the sale.

Summer sale Sommerschlußverkauf

Also called summer closing sale.

The selling of goods at reduced prices for a limited time period at the end of the summer season in order to get rid of surplus stocks.

Sunday supplement Sonntagsbeilage

A separately printed publication included with a Sunday newspaper.

Sunrise industry Hochtechnologie-, Zukunftsindustrie, aufstrebende Industrie

An industry in the forefront of technological developments and which may become a large industry in the future.

Sunset industry Altindustrie; absterbende/niedergehende Industrie

An older industry which is in decline, usually because of obsolete technology, decreased demand for products, etc.

Supernormal profit Übergewinn

Also called excess profit or super profit.

Any excess over normal profit, i.e. the amount of profit required to keep a business in a particular line of production.

Superette Superette

A small supermarket.

Superior good superiores Gut

Also called normal good.

Goods and services that are demanded in larger quantities as incomes rise, holding prices constant. A majority of goods are superior goods.

Supermarket Supermarkt

A large retail self-service store where goods are prepacked, labelled and well displayed for the customer to examine. Skilled labour and hence service facilities are kept to a minimum; staff is needed only to replenish the display racks with merchandise drawn from the storeroom; cashiers check the goods purchased and collect the money. No personal selling of any kind is required. The main advantages of supermarkets are the great variety of goods offered and the keen price level; often they use cut prices and special offers to stimulate trade.

Small supermarkets are often called superettes, large ones superstores and very large ones hyperstores.

Superprofit außergewöhnlicher Gewinn

A profit exceeding the normal economic profit.

Supersite Großanschlagsfläche

In outdoor advertising, a very large billboard hoarding for posters.

Superstore Superstore, SB-Warenhaus, Verbrauchermarkt

A very large, diversified self-service supermarket that sells a broad range of food and nonfood items.

Supplementary service Zusatzservice

A service provided by a company that supports or enhances the core service offered.

Supplier Lieferant, Lieferfirma
Zulieferer, Zulieferbetrieb
Anbieter

A person or business who supplies goods or services. Also called seller, supplying firm or vendor.

A firm supplying components to a prime/general contractor or producer. Also called component or outside supplier, or subcontractor.

In economics, someone who supplies/offers goods or services. The opposite is a demander.

Supplier credit Lieferantenkredit

Also called trade credit.

The granting of credit terms by a seller to a buyer.

Supplier evaluation Lieferantenbeurteilung

A purchasing technique applied by buying departments trying to establish, in quantifiable terms, a supplier's total capability to supply their requirements - at the right time, at the right quality and at the right price.

Supplier management Lieferantenmanagement

An industrial or other buyer`s attempt to influence the policies of particular suppliers to improve their service quality.

Supplier search Lieferantensuche

In the buying process, the situation in which the buyer tries to find the most appropriate seller.

Supplier selection Lieferantenauswahl

In the buying process, the stage in which a prospective buyer reviews the various offers and finally selects the most appropriate supplier.

Supplier's quality inspection certificate Qualitätsabnahmebescheinigung des Lieferers

A signed declaration by the seller (eg an exporter) that the goods have been inspected before despatch and are of a quality in accordance with the contract of sale/sales contract. A commercial document often issued in foreign trade.

Supplies Zulieferungen

Components supplied by a supplier belonging to the components supplying industry.

Supply (S, sy) Angebot
Lieferung, Be- und Anlieferung
Vorrat
Versorgung

The second of the two forces, the other being demand, which influence the market price of a commodity or service. The supply of a commodity or service is that quantity which sellers/suppliers are prepared to sell at a certain price, in a given period of time. The supply of a commodity does not comprise the entire stock in existence, but only the amount drawn into the market by the price ruling at the time. The quantity that suppliers are prepared to sell at each price will change if the factors affecting supply change.

The chief factors affecting supply are:
the price of the commodity (the price affects the prospects of profitability and profitability will encourage the supplier to produce the supplies required); the conditions of supply (i.e. the costs of production, the state of technological development (improvements in technology will reduce costs), natural influences (e.g. the weather), political influences (e.g. taxes or subsidies) and the prices of other goods (e.g. if the prices of other goods rise the producer might switch to the good whose price has risen as he assumes higher profits)). The most important influence is the price; other things being equal, more of a commodity will be supplied if the price rises.

The second law of demand and supply states that the higher the price, the greater the quantity that is supplied. But another law states that an increase in supply will reduce the price of a commodity and lead to an increase in the quantity demanded. The price at which demand and supply are equal is the equilibrium price. At this price the same quantity will be supplied as is demanded.

There are five laws of supply and demand:
1. the lower the price of a commodity the greater will be the quantity demanded;
2. the higher the price the greater will be the quantity supplied;

3. at the equilibrium price the quantity demanded will be equal to the quantity supplied;
4. an increase in demand will increase the price and the quantity supplied;
5. an increase in supply will reduce price but increase the quantity demanded.

The delivery of goods or services by a seller (the supplier) directly to a buyer. Also called delivery.

The availability of goods needed for a certain purpose, e.g. the goods needed by a company to run its business.

Providing something which is needed, e.g. gas or water supply by public utilities.

Supply access Angebotszugang

Assurances that importing countries will, in the future, have fair and equitable access at reasonable prices to raw material supplies and other essential imports.

Supply and demand Angebot und Nachfrage

The market forces that in a free market economy determine the price (the market price) of a product or service. At one price, and at only one price, the quantity the sellers are prepared to sell/supply will equal the quantity the buyers wish to buy/demand. This price is called the equilibrium price.

Supply and price Angebot und Preis

Normally, a supplier is prepared to supply more when the price is high (second law of supply and demand) than when the price is low. However, this is not always possible since the supply of some goods is strictly limited (e.g. Picasso paintings) and with others it takes a good while to be able to increase the supply.

Supply contract Liefervertrag

Also called supply agreement.

A contract between supplier and buyer to supply/deliver goods.

Supply curve Angebotskurve

Also called supply line.

A curve on a diagram showing the quantity of a commodity supplied at different price levels (the price on the vertical or y-axis, the ordinate, and the quantity supplied on the

horizontal or x-axis, the abscissa), if the conditions of supply (e.g. the costs of production) remain unchanged.
Note: a change in the conditions of supply will shift the position of the supply curve, either to the right or left.

The supply curve normally slopes upwards from left to right, i.e. the curve obeys the second law of supply and demand, in other words, it indicates increased supplies coming on to the market as prices rise. Supply extends as price rises, and contracts as price falls. Extensions and contractions of supply depend on price alone; they are not changes/shifts in supply.
A change/shift in supply is a change to a new supply curve and this is caused by a change in the conditions of supply (e.g. an advance in technology, an increase in the production costs, an increase or decrease in the prices of other goods, etc).
It is usual to label the supply curve SS.

Supply inflation — Angebotsinflation

Sustained inflationary processes are inseparable from monetary expansion. On this view, many economists call increases in the supply of money (induced by the central bank) the principal direct determinant of inflation. Accordingly, control of the money supply is the obvious way of stopping inflation.

Inflation induced by increased prices without reference to demand, eg price increases due to higher interest rates or wage increases. Also called supply push inflation

Supply price — Angebotspreis
Lieferpreis

The price at which something is offered to a potential/prospective buyer. Also called bid, offer or quoted price.

The price at which a particular quantity of a commodity is supplied/delivered.

Supply push inflation — angebotsinduzierte Inflation,
Angebotsinflation

Also called sellers' inflation.

An inflation induced by increased prices without reference to demand, e.g. producers (or the government) increase their prices due to wage increases, higher import prices, higher interest rates, or higher profits.

Supply schedule Angebotstabelle

A schedule is simply a list or table of figures. A supply schedule is a table showing the quantity of a commodity or service that will be supplied at different price levels; all other conditions which determine supply, eg the production costs or the prices of other goods, remain unchanged.
The schedule relates to a specific period of time and provides the basis for the supply curve for a commodity.

Supply shift Angebotsverschiebung

Also called shift in supply.

Increase or decrease in supply of a product caused by a change in any factor other than the price of the product.

These factors include: the costs of production, the state of technology, natural influences, political influences and the prices of other goods.

A shift in supply implies that more or less of a particular product is supplied at each and every price.
Note: whenever the conditions of supply change, a new supply curve is required, either to the left (ie less is supplied) or right (ie more is supplied) of the original curve.

Supply shortage Lieferengpaß

A situation where a company, e.g. a producer or wholesaler, is unable to supply/deliver at the moment.

Supply side economics Supply-Side Economics, angebotsorientierte Wirtschaftspolitik

Also called supply side policies.

From World War II to the late 1970s governments concentrated upon demand side policies (ie Keynesian policies), i.e. aggregate demand, to cure economic problems and to achieve their macroeconomic objectives full employment, price stability, external balance/external equilibrium, economic growth, environmental protection and the redistribution of income and welfare. Supply side policies were disregarded.

Supply side policies concentrate on increasing the supply or output of the economy by encouraging factors of production and enterprise to increase effort, efficiency and hence output. Supply side policies are directed towards improving all aspects of industrial performance. These policies are designed to make the markets (i.e. the markets for land, labour, capital and enterprise) work better.

The measures taken include the following: encourage the mobility of labour, improve staff training, relate wage increases to productivity, reduce strikes and their impact, lower tax rates on personal incomes and business profits (this will result in a great increase in industrial investment in producer goods not in demand for consumer goods; and it is this investment that is the real driving force behind the economy), increase the degree of competition in labour and product markets, phase out investment subsidies, privatise/denationalise nationalised industries, restrict the growth of money supply to control inflation, encourage investments, etc.
Supply side economics believes:
if workers and companies are free to operate according to market forces, then overall output will increase and employment will result; the volume of money should grow in line with the growth of output generated by capital accumulation and labour force growth; flexible wages (supply side economists believe that much unemployment is due to workers refusing to accept a lower real wage and thus they are voluntarily unemployed) and prices will automatically ensure full employment and an appropriate level of aggregate demand.

Monetarists (the term monetarism was introduced by Karl Brunner in 1968), e.g. Milton Friedman, believe in supply side incentives to increase output and thus pursue classical economic beliefs in the free market in accordance with J.B. Say's (French economist, 1767 - 1832) dictum that supply creates its own demand.

Supply side policies are intended to achieve growth in the economy not by increasing demand (which monetarists believe will only result in inflation) but by increasing productivity and therefore the supply of goods and services available.

The reasons for the increased emphasis on supply side policies were the failure of demand policies of the 1960s, the rise of monetarism based upon neo-classical views of the economy and the adoption of these policies by like-minded governments (e.g. in GB the conservative government under M. Thatcher). In the early 1980s these policies gained prominence with the election of the conservative US President Ronald Reagan (the policy was then labelled "Reagonomics", a doctrine complementary to monetarism).
Supporters of supply side economics are called supply-siders.

Suppressed inflation zurückgestaute Inflation

Also called repressed inflation.

A condition in which effective demand is greatly in excess of supply, but the effect on prices is dampened temporarily or completely halted by government action, e.g. rigid price controls.

Surcharge Aufpreis, Aufschlag
Zusatzsteuer

A charge over and above the normal price of something; an extra charge.

A surtax, ie an additional tax on something already taxed.

Surface mail gewöhnliche Post

Also called ordinary mail.

Mail sent by land or sea.

Surplus Überschuß
Angebotsüberschuß

An excess over that which is needed or owed.

An excess of supply: this occurs if the price is above the equilibrium price.

Survey Erhebung, Umfrage
Überblick, Übersicht

In statistics, the evaluation, analysis and description of a population based upon a sample drawn from it.

A general or comprehensive view of something, e.g. the work done.

Survival pricing Überlebenspreisbildung,
Existenzerhaltungspreisbildung

A fundamental pricing strategy where prices are so fixed as to enable the firm to survive at least in the short run. In times of overcapacity, keen competition, or changing consumer wants, survival may become the firm`s major objective. As profits are less important than survival and inventories/stocks must be sold, the firm will often cut prices.

Note: in the short run the firm will be able to continue in business if its prices cover variable costs and some fixed costs.

Sustained growth stetiges Wachstum

Also called sustainable or steady growth.

A steady rate of economic growth that can continue for a long time period.

Sustaining advertising Stabilisierungs-, Stützungswerbung

Advertising intended to maintain the demand for a product or service rather than creating or increasing it.

Swap offer Umtauschangebot

An offer made by the seller to the buyer that he/she can exchange the goods within a specific period.

Swatch Muster(streifen)

A sample of cloth or other material.

A sample of anything, eg a colour swatch.

Sweepstake Wettbewerb mit Verlosung, Gewinnspiel, Lotterie

Also called sweeper or lottery.

A form of consumer sales promotion in which entrants fill out a form to enter a random draw so that they can win prizes if their names are drawn. That means winners are chosen purely by chance. The aim of a sweepstake is to create consumer involvement with a product and thus encourage consumption of the product.

Sweetener zusätzlicher Anreiz

An additional incentive to do something.

Sweetheart contract Freundschaftsvertrag, Geschäft unter Freunden

A contract placed by a buyer with a seller because of their close or special relationship.

Switch selling — Köderwerbung, Lockmittelwerbung, Lockvogelwerbung
Lock(vogel)angebot

Also called bait advertising, bait and switch, bait and switch selling or loss leader selling.

A very cheap, or sometimes non-available product is advertised and put on offer in order to attract potential customers to the shop, eg a supermarket. Usually, customers buy additional products.

A selling technique in which a low-priced item is offered as a bait to customers who are then pressured by the salesperson to buy a higher-priced item.

Switcher — Umsteiger

A type of consumer who switches from one product to another, ie a consumer who buys a variety of products in the product category.

SWOT analysis — SWOT-Analyse

Also called situation analysis.

A method of finding out how well a business is doing by examining its strenghts (S), weaknesses (W), business opportunities (O) and threats (T). The analysis includes an examination of both the internal factors (to identify S and W) and external factors (to identify O and T). Knowing exactly what each of these are for your business, one has the key to the present and the future.

Synchromarketing — Synchromarketing

A marketing technique intended to shift the demand pattern so that it equates more suitably with the supply pattern.

Syndicate — Konsortium, Arbeitsgemeinschaft
Verkaufs-, Absatzkartell

A temporary combination of businessmen or companies working together for the financing and completion of some specific project or to reach a certain business aim, e.g. to control the market in a particular commodity.

A joint selling organization. Also called marketing cartel.

Syndicated market research gemeinsame Marktforschung

The costs and results of market research are shared by a number of companies.

Synergy Synergy

Sometimes known as the " 2 + 2 = 5 effect".

Producing greater effects by joining activities or forces than by acting separately. Thus, synergy occurs when the combination of separate parts makes up a whole greater than the sum of these parts.

Systems seller Systemanbieter

A seller who sells a number of different products which have some functional relationship jointly, and not separately.

Systems selling Systemverkauf

The sale of goods plus related services by one vendor/seller. The advantages for buyers are that they only have to negotiate with one firm, and that they can rely on compatibility between various parts and components.

T

Table Tabelle, Übersicht

A list of figures or facts laid out in columns and rows.

Tabloid kleinformatige Zeitung, Groschen-, Sensations-, Boulevardblatt
kleinformatige Anzeigen-/Werbebeilage

A popular and sensational newspaper with a page size smaller than that of the standard newspapers; it typically contains sensational stories and news in condensed form, with a great many photographs. Also called Yellow Press.

A preprinted advertising insert of some pages only designed for insertion into a newspaper. Also called tabloid insert.

Tabulation Tabellarisierung
Tabelle

Arranging facts or figures shortly and clearly in a list, table or column.

A table, list or schedule.

Tactical planning taktische Planung

Planning to utilise resources or to achieve specific objetives in the most effective and efficient way, considering prevailing conditions.

Tag Etikett, Anhänger
kurze Absage am Ende einer Fernseh- oder Radiosendung

A label (eg of paper or plastic) on a product or package that shows its price, identifies its contents or serves as an advertising medium. Also called label or ticket.

A short announcement made at the end of a broadcast programme or commercial.

Take | Einnahme

Money received in a shop in return for the sale of products or services.

Take-and-pay contract | Langzeitliefervertrag mit Zahlung bei Lieferung

An agreement between a buyer and a seller that obligates the buyer to purchase a specified minimum quantity of a product or service over a specified period of time, and payment to be made upon delivery.

Take-down | Erfüllung

The time when a deal is actually performed, such as when goods have been both delivered and paid for.

Take-or-pay contract | Langzeitliefervertrag mit unbedingter Zahlungsverpflichtung

An unconditional agreement to make periodic payments of a certain amount over a specified time period whether or not the product is delivered or the service provided. An agreement used as a basis for financing a project.

Takeaway | Imbißstube, Restaurant für Außer-Haus-Verkauf
Speisen zum Mitnehmen

Also called takeout or carryout.

A shop or restaurant where you can buy takeaway food.

Hot food which you buy in a takeaway to eat it elsewhere, often at home.

Takeover time | Übernahmeperiode

The time period for a new, usually superior, product to go from 10 % to 90 % displacement of an older, usually inferior product.

Taker Abnehmer, Käufer

Also called buyer or purchaser.

A person who wants to buy.

Taking delivery Abnahme

Accepting receipt of goods from someone, usually documented by any form of receipt or acknowledgement.

Takings (Bar)Einnahmen

Also called cash receipts or earnings.

Especially in retailing, the total amount of money which a shop receives from cash sales for a period, e.g. a day.

Talk show Talkshow

Also called chat show.

A radio or television show in which a host interviews or chats with guests, frequently celebrities; sometimes with entertainment.

Tallyman Inhaber eines Abzahlungsgeschäfts

A businessman who sells goods on credit for payment by instalments.

Tare (tr) Tara, Verpackungsgewicht

The weight of the case, container, wrappings, or other packing materials, etc. in which the goods are contained, i.e. gross weight - tare = net weight (i.e. the actual weight of the goods themselves).

Tare weight Verpackungsgewicht, Taragewicht Leergewicht

The weight of the packaging material and/or the container without the weight of the goods it contains.

The unladen weight of a transport vehicle.

Target Ziel

A target is the precise restatement of an objective (which is often stated in rather general, broad terms), often given in figures. For example, it may be a company's objective to increase its turnover; restated as a target this might be "to increase the turnover by 10 % within the next two years".

Target audience Zielpublikum, Zahl der Adressaten

Also called target group.

A particular group of people or a market segment at which a specific promotional campaign is aimed.

Target group Zielgruppe

Also called target audience.

A group of people that an advertiser wants to reach by using advertising material.

The group of (potential) customers whose needs and wants a company wishes to satisfy.

Target group index (TGI) Zielgruppenindex

A report compiled from the returned questionnaires of a random sample of respondents on their use of hundreds of products and thousands of brands.

Target market angestrebter Markt, Zielmarkt

In marketing, also called market segment or segment.

The market on which a company plans to sell its products or services, e.g. the overseas market.

The group of potential/prospective customers which a company is attempting to reach. Also called target group.

Target marketing zielorientiertes Marketing

A firm`s marketing efforts which are concentrated on a clearly defined market.

Target price

angestrebter Preis
Richtpreis, Zielpreis

In marketing, the price which is desired to reach.

The basic price of a commodity established by a government from time to time. The price is intended to be an average price that will be fair to the producer. Thus subsidies are provided to guarantee the target price. Also called guide price.

Target pricing

Gewinnzielkalkulation

Also called target return pricing.

A method of calculating prices to reach a profit objective. Target pricing is aimed at securing in a given time period a predetermined rate of return on investment (ROI). To reach this objective one must calculate an average markup on average costs and simultaneously project sales revenue at various stages of the product life cycle (PLC).

Besides, target pricing demands accurate forecasting and accurate costing in terms of levels of output and marketing costs (distribution, sales or selling costs). Thus, target pricing wants to stabilise prices and yet achieve a given ROI over the product life (though at particular points of time the return will be high, at others low).

Tariff

Zoll
Zolltarif
Gebühren, Kostentarif, Steuersatz
Preisverzeichnis
Tarif
Speisekarte

Taxes or duties imposed/levied on imports when they enter the importing country. Tariffs can be specific (i.e. the duty or tax does not vary with the value of the goods) or ad valorem (i.e. the duty or tax is expressed as a percentage of the import price). Tariffs are impediments/barriers to free trade between countries in that they make foreign goods uncompetitive with similar home-produced goods or discourage the purchase of certain goods, in order to protect domestic industries. Also called customs duty.

The rate of duty to be paid for importing products.

Any scale of prices or charges, or of tax rates.

A list of the scale of charges for something, e.g. in a hotel for rooms and service.

In transport, a table of freight or passenger rates charged by a transport company.

In a restaurant, the bill of fare. Also called menu (card).

Tariff barriers tarifäre Handelshemmnisse

Any tariff (ie tax) imposed on imports by a country (sometimes there is also a tax on exports), regardless of its legitimacy, that prohibits, restricts or impedes the free flow of goods and services.
There are many reasons for imposing tariffs/customs duties on other countries' exports, i.e. on our imports:

1. to protect home/domestic industry from foreign competition;
2. to protect the balance of payments;
3. to maintain full employment;
4. the need for the government to raise revenue.

Whatever the reason for imposing a tariff may be, there are three effects:

1. tariffs reduce the benefits from international trade;
2. as taxes increase the price, exporters have more problems to sell their goods;
3. foreign trade is complicated since the customs authorities require documentation to be able to charge the correct amount of duty.

Task method Ziel-Aufgaben-Methode

Also called objective-and-task method.

A method of calculating the advertising budget by relating it to the estimated costs of achieving specific marketing goals.

Tasteless advertising geschmacklose Werbung

Any advertising message that either offends or embarrasses the receiver(s) (ie the audience), either because of the topic or the way in which it is presented.

Tax exemption Steuerbefreiung

Also called immunity from taxation or tax; tax concession or exclusion; exemption from tax.

A situation where a person or company does not have to pay tax, in whole or in part, on certain types of income or property.

Tax impact Steuerwirkung

The effect of a tax upon production and consumption of the good being taxed.

The effect of a tax upon an economic process, such as consumption or production.

Tear-off coupon Abreißgutschein

A coupon which can be pulled or torn off a product.

Tearsheet/tear sheet Belegseite für Werbungstreibende

An advertisement clipped or torn from a publication and sent to an advertiser as evidence of its insertion.

Teaser Teaser

An advertisement on an envelope that lures readers to open the letter, eg by offering a bonus, gift, or the like.

Teaser ad(vertisement) Neckwerbung, Neugier weckende Werbung, Teaser

Also called teaser.

A commercial or promotion designed to arouse curiosity in the audience. Also called hooker.

A brief advertisement designed to tease the audience by offering only bits of information without revealing either the sponsor of the ad or the product, service or event being advertised. The purpose of teaser ads is to arouse curiosity and draw attention to the ad campaign that follows (ie the teaser ad is its frontrunner).

Technical forecast technische Vorhersage

A method of forecasting that uses historical price patterns as the sole determinant of forecasting future prices or exchange rates.

Technical rally markttechnische Erholung

On a stock or commodity market, a rise in prices resulting from a shortage of stocks or commodities.

Technical salesperson technische(r) Verkäufer/in

A salesperson with a high degree of technical or scientific expertise so that he/she can provide qualified advice on product application, product features, installation, maintenance, etc.

Technological life technologische Nutzungsdauer

The estimated number of years of a piece of equipment before it becomes obsolete due to technological changes.

Technological monopoly Technologiemonopol

A monopoly resulting from the application of new technology.

Technology Technologie

The branch of knowledge that deals with applied science, engineering, the industrial arts, etc.

The application of knowledge, scientifically derived or otherwise, to the creation or modification of useful products or processes, ie for practical ends.

Telecommunication(s) Telekommunikation

The sending and receiving of messages over great distances, especially by telephone, computer, radio, television and telgraph.

Technology assessment Technologiebewertung

Also called technological assessment.

The evaluation of the introduction, modification, or development of a technology with regard to its social, economic and environmental impacts.

Technology licensing Technologie-Lizenzvergabe

A contractual agreement in which the licensor`s patents, trademarks, copyrights or know-how may be sold or otherwise made available to a licensee for compensation (known as royalties) negotiated in advance between the parties involved.

Telemarketing Telemarketing, Telefonmarketing

Also called telephone marketing, telesales, telephone selling or teleselling.

A cost effective method of using the telephone for the promotion, sale, and solicitation of goods and services, and for maintaining contact with existing customers.

A form of direct marketing which has three components:

1. the preparation: the teleseller needs a list of potential and regular customers and should know the best time to call them;
2. the call: the teleseller will be more successful if he calls people who have requested information, who have already done business with his company or who have received a letter stating that you will be calling;
3. the follow-up: the teleseller has about 45 seconds to stimulate his interlocutor to want to continue the conversation.

Telemarketing is used in both industrial and consumer marketing:
In industrial marketing, the telephone call is used essentially as a substitute for a sales call at the customer`s place of business.
In consumer marketing, in-store retailing is replaced by direct contact with the customer via telephone.
Note: the call may have been dial(l)ed by a computer and the sales message presented by a trained salesperson. The order is taken and the product shipped directly to the customer.

Telemarketer Telefonmarketer, Telefonkontakter

A person selling goods or services by telephone, maintaining contact with existing customers, or trying to establish business with potential customers.

Telephone (tel) Telefon

Also called phone.

A device for sending and receiving the sound of the voice by electrical signals; the most popular telecommunications device.
There is a range of telephones available, for example: the standard telephone; the press-button telephone; the payphone; the wallphone; the callmaker (enables pre-selected numbers to be dialled by pressing a button); the extension phone; the car telephone, the portable telephone, the viewphone, etc.

Telephone alphabet Buchstabiertafel
Telefonalphabet

Also called spelling table.

The telephone alphabet is used when spelling names or giving information over the telephone. In GB, the following could be used: A (Albert or Andrew); B (Barry or Benjamin); C (Charles or Charlie); D (David); E (Edward or Eric); F (Frank or Frederick); G (George); H (Harry or Henry); I (Ian or Isaac);J (Jack or John); K (Keith or King); L (Lion or Lucy); M (Mark or Mary); N (Nellie or Nine); O (Oliver or Orange); P (Peter); Q (Queenie or Quick); R (Robert); S (Simon or Sugar); T (Tommy or Trevor); U (Uncle); V (Victor or Victory); W (Walter or William); X (X-Ray); Y (Yellow); Z (Zebra).

In Germany: A (Anton); Ä (Ärger); B (Berta); C (Cäsar); CH (Charlotte); D (Dora); E (Emil); F (Friedrich); G (Gustav); H (Heinrich); I (Ida); J (Julius); K (Kaufmann); L (Ludwig); M (Martha); N (Nordpol); O (Otto); Ö (Ökonom); P (Paula); Q (Quelle); R (Richard); S (Samuel); Sch (Schule); T (Theodor); U (Ulrich); Ü (Übermut); V (Viktor); W (Wilhelm); X (Xanthippe); Y (Ypsilon); Z (Zacharias).

In USA: A (Abel); B (Baker); C (Charlie); D (Dog); E (Easy); F (Fox); G (George); H (How); I (Ikon or Item); J (Juliett or Jig); K (King); L (Love); M (Mike); N (Nan); O (Oboe); P (Peter); Q (Queen); R (Roger); S (Sugar); T (Tare); U (Uncle); V (Victor); W (William); X (eks); Y (Yoke); Z (Zebra).

International: A (Amsterdam); B (Baltimore); C (Casablanca); D (Denmark); E (Edison); F (Florida); G (Gallipoli); H (Havana); I (Italia); J (Jerusalem); K (Kilogramme); L (Liverpool); M (Madagaskar); N (New York); O (Oslo); P (Paris); Q (Québec); R (Roma); S (Santiago); T (Tripoli); U (Upsala); V (Valencia); W (Washington); X (Xanthippe); Y (Yokohama); Z (Zürich).

A person spelling the name "Ron" would spell it as Robert for R; Oliver for O; Nelly for N.

When dictating numbers you read the numbers in pairs counting from the last figure. The number 29351 would be given as two, nine three, five one. A double number at the beginning is always read separately; 33475 would be given as three three (or double three), four seven, five. Nought is given as zero. Double numbers are normally given separately.

Telephone answering machine Anrufbeantworter

Also called answerphone, answering machine, telephone answering and recording machine or telephone recorder.

A machine answering and recording incoming calls and inviting callers to leave a message which can be played back at any time.

Telephone calls record book Belegbuch für Anrufe

A book used to enter all outgoing official (and personal) calls, particularly trunk calls, in order to identify telephone expenses.

Telephone directory Telefonbuch

Also called telephone book or phone book/directory.

A book that contains information about telephone services and lists subscribers in alphabetical order. Customers who do not want their telephone number published for whatever reason are ex-directory and their details are known to Telecom only.
There are various types of directories, e.g.: the Yellow Pages, a classified telephone directory (contain details of a wide range of goods and services offered by subscribers); Business Directories (list businesses in alphabetical order); and Telephone Dialling Codes (provide details of national and international dialling codes).

Telephone directory advertising Telefonbuchwerbung

Advertisements placed in telephone books.

Telephone interview telephonische Befragung

In market research, a form of investigation, in which an interviewer obtains information from telephone subscribers who are asked a set list of questions.
Note:

1. subscribers often refuse to answer telephone requests for market research information,
2. the costs per interview are low,
3. a relatively large number of interviews can be conducted within a short time period,
4. interviewers can be located in one place,
5. only short questionnaires are feasible.

Telephone marketing Telemarketing, Telefonmarketing, Telefonverkauf

Also called telemarketing, telesales, telephone selling or teleselling.

Selling operation by telephone. The telephone is used to contact existing and potential customers and to solicit orders without any personal selling calls.
The main advantages are: quick advertising and assessable results; rapid contact over a wide market; cost advantages.

Telephone order Telefonauftrag

An order placed or received by telephone.

Telephone rates Telefon-, Fernsprechgebühren

Also called telephone charges.

The cost of a telephone call depends on the following: a private line or a public telephone; the distance over which the call was made; the time of day or week. There are peak rate calls, standard rate calls and cheap rate calls.

Telephone survey telephonische Befragung

Also called telephone interview.

Market research by telephone to question consumers with regard to purchases of certain goods, e.g. cars or household goods. The method is comparatively cheap, immediate responses can be obtained and the interviewer can telephone a large number of respondents/interviewees in a fraction of the time it would take to make personal visits to their homes. But often people dislike being telephoned by complete strangers asking them questions, e.g. on their age and occupation, and interviewers are likely to meet with an immediate rebuff.

Telephone transfer telefonische Überweisung

The transfer of money from one account to another, or from payer to payee made by telephone order, rather than traditional written documents.

Teleshopping Teleeinkauf, Teleshopping

A service offered by stores and mail order houses which enables customers to order goods for delivery over the telephone, by means of a television screen and a personal computer.

Teletext Bildschirmtext (Btx)

A service broadcast by television which provides all kinds of up-to-the-minute pages of information on many subjects (such as news and sports results) on the TV screen. It is like a televised news magazine.

Television advertising Fernsehwerbung

Also called TV advertising/commercial.

Television advertising has a captive audience in homes, regardless of age, religion, sex or class. TV can employ the audio message with sound effects, visual effects, animation, colour and a musical background, possibly even its own jingle.

The commercial is usually based on "30 second spots", but other rates apply. The rates depend on the time of the day or programme and the likely viewership. It is essential that the commercial is well thought-out and professionally produced.

There is no better media than television (TV) when the average money amount of product or service purchased is substantial or the product needs good visual display to be understood. Since there are millions of people watching TV, the cost per thousand (CPT) viewers in TV is lower than in any other media for large markets.

In most countries, television relies heavily on advertising revenues. But the amount of advertising time allowed on television is regulated in most countries. Thus, the increasing demand for time to broadcast commercials has led to a dramatic rise in the cost of TV advertising. Prime time is peak viewing time and this commands the highest rates.

Television household (TVHH) Fernsehhaushalt

A household with one or more TV sets.

Television marketing Fernseh-Marketing

A form of direct marketing, where the marketer uses the television to market goods or services to the ultimate consumers through direct-response advertising or home shopping channels.
TV is being used in two ways:
1. direct marketers broadcast commercials in which they describe their product, and the customer can call a toll-free number and order the advertised item;
2. an entire programme is devoted just to selling assorted merchandise.

Television rating (TVR) Fernseheinschaltquote

Also called TV rating, audience rating or viewing rate.

A unit of measure which shows the relative audience or viewership achieved by a TV programme, commercial or station. For example, one TVR represents 1 % of the total TV audience (the universe). The figures can be expressed for various population subgroups, e.g. homes, housewives, children, teenagers, etc.

Ten (:10) 10-Sekunden-Werbung

A ten second cinema, radio or television commercial.

Tender Submissionsangebot
Angebot, Offerte

An offer, usually in response to an advertisement, for the supply of specified goods or the performance of specified work at prices and under conditions set out in the tender. The tender is often made in competition with other tenderers and is made on the advertiser's own forms, which set out the terms in detail. When the tender is accepted by the tenderee, i.e. when the tenderer obtains the tender award, it results in a binding agreement. Also called bid.

An offer to supply goods. Also called offer.

Tender cash an Verkäufer gegebener Geldbetrag
zur Zahlung der Ware

The amount of money given to the seller or cashier for payment of goods or services.

Tender documents Ausschreibungsunterlagen

Also called tender specifications.

Documents required by the tenderer to make a bid for a contract.

Tenderee Submissions-, Angebotsempfänger

A person or company receiving a tender from a tenderer.

Tenderer Bieter, Submittent

Also called bidder.

A person or company making a tender.

Tendering Angebotsabgabe

A method of purchase. The seller, ie the tenderer, makes a bid (called tender) which cannot be changed, once made. Usually, but not necessarily, the lowest bid is the one accepted by the prospective buyer, ie the tenderee.

Tent card Klappkarte, Tischkarte

An imprinted and folded card that is readable on either side of the fold so that it can stand free on a table top, counter or other flat surface. It is used for the display of a POP ad (point-of-purchase advertisement).

Terminal Umschlagplatz, Umladeplatz

Also called reloading or transfer station, or transhipment point.

A place where interchange (reloading, transhipment) facilities exist, e.g. a seaport; railway, airport or road haulage depot.

Terminal market Terminmarkt, Warenterminbörse

Also called forward or futures market.

Commodity market that deals in the sale of goods for future delivery.

Termination of offer Erlöschen eines Angebots, Angebotsbegrenzung

An offer may come to an end by:
1. revocation (the offeror has the power to withdraw his offer at any time before it has been accepted by the offeree);
2. rejection (to be effective the rejection of an offer must be communicated to the offeror; any attempts by the offeree to change the terms of the offer amounts to a rejection);
3. operation of law (e.g. if the offeror dies or becomes insane before the offer has been accepted; when the offer specifies a time within which it may be accepted, it comes to an end at the expiry of the stipulated time).

Terms Bedingungen, Bestimmungen
Honorar, Gebühren
Zahlungsbedingungen
Preise

Rules or conditions, e.g. the conditions of a loan or contract, the terms of supply or demand, the terms of payment or delivery, etc.

A fee for professional services. Also called honorarium.

The terms of payment.

The price charged by a seller for the supply of goods including discounts and bonuses.

Terms and conditions Verkaufs- und Lieferbedingungen

Also called conditions of sale or conditions of sale and delivery.

In sales contracts, the arrangements on which the seller is willing to sell his goods. They are usually printed on his price lists and invoices.

Terms net Netto-Zahlungsbedingungen

Terms of sale that indicate that no cash discount is allowed.

Terms of credit Kreditbedingungen

The terms on which credits are granted.

Terms of delivery Lieferbedingungen

Also called delivery terms.

The terms of delivery specify the time, place, and mode of delivery of goods. Furthermore, they indicate whether the sender/consignor or the receiver/consignee shall pay the delivery charges, or whether the charge shall be divided between them. Who is to pay the charges is laid down in the delivery terms quoted in the sales contract between the two parties.

The following are a few examples of terms of delivery as they may be used in domestic trade:

1. at present our delivery time is x weeks;
2. delivery is to be made not later than ... or by x May;
3. delivery can be effected within x weeks or immediately after receipt of order;
4. please arrange the goods to be forwarded by air, rail, road, ship;
5. carriage forward (ie the consignee pays the delivery charge);
6. carriage paid (ie the sender or consignor pays the delivery charge);
7. loco (ie the buyer has to bear the transport costs);
8. franco or free domicile (ie delivery free of any charge to the consignee's premises);
9. S and S = station to station (freight charges include the transport from one railway station to another, but no cartage); etc.

In foreign trade, there is a wide range of internationally recognised terms of delivery which not only determine the responsibilities of the buyer and seller for the payment of the delivery charges/expenses involved but also establish the points at which the titles to the goods change hands. To overcome any difficulties in interpreting these terms used in foreign trade contracts, a set of international rules have been agreed by the member countries of the International Chamber of Commerce (ICC). These rules are known as Incoterms. Naturally, other terms do exist.

Terms of payment (ToP)

Zahlungsbedingungen
Zahlungsziele, Zahlungsmodalitäten im Außenhandel

Also called payment terms.

The conditions for paying something. The terms of payment specify the time of payment, the method of payment, and discounts, if any. The terms are negotiable between the contracting parties and may be laid down explicitly and in detail in the sales contract.
Goods may be purchased on any of the following terms:
1. cash payment; 2. cash with order (CWO); 3. cash on delivery (COD); 4. prompt cash (payment within a few days); 5. monthly account; 6. spot cash (the buyer must pay for the goods when he takes possession of them); 7. hire-purchase terms; 8. credit terms (e.g. payment within 30 days); 9. cash against documents (CAD); 10. open account terms (settlement is made on the basis of statements of account sent by the supplier); 11. on invoice; 12. documents against payment (D/P); 13. documents against acceptance (D/A); 14. downpayment; 15. payment in instalments; 16. deferred payment; 17. credit card, etc.

The payment methods in international trade.

Terms of sale

Verkaufsbedingungen
Preisforderung

The responsibilities of the buyer and seller in a sale, including:
the conditions of a sale, such as the price, the seller's given time to pay an invoice, other special credit arrangements, guarantees, arrangements for return of goods, etc.

The basic price asked for something offered for sale.

Territorial planning

Routenplanung

A salesperson`s activities of planning customer calls and routes.

Territory manager Gebietsleiter

Also called area manager, regional manager or division area supervisor.

A manager responsible for a particular area/territory within a company organisation structure. He/she must analyse, plan, implement, and control all sales activities within his/her sales area.

Tertiary reader Drittleser, Zufallsleser

A reader who casually reads a publication, e.g. during or while waiting for some other activity, usually outside the home, eg at the dentist or hairdresser.

In the magazine trade, readers of this type are collectively called the "waiting-room public".

Tertiary sector tertiärer Sektor, Dienstleistungsbereich

Also called tertiary industry or service producing sector.

A tertiary sector is a service industry. Unlike the primary sector (which produces raw materials) and the secondary sector (which manufactures products from raw materials), the tertiary sector provides services to industry or to the consumer.

Test case Testfall

In commerce, a test to find out if something is working well or is possible.

Test drive Probefahrt

The driving of a vehicle, before buying it, in order to evaluate its performancc and reliability.

Test market Testmarkt

A city, region, state or country used to test the market reactions to a new product or marketing campaign before full commercialisation begins.

Test marketing Durchführung von lokalen Markttests

A well-established device to test the public accetability of a new product or the likely response to changes to existing products. Because the costs involved in a test marketing are only a fraction of the costs of a national campaign, this method provides a comparatively cheap way in which to detect defaults in the product or its promotion and to correct them.

A new product may be test marketed in a limited but representative area of the country (the test market), thus avoiding the costs of a full-scale launch. This procedure enables the company to obtain an indication of the likely market acceptance. The reactions of consumers in that area are studied with a view to ascertaining the likely sales in the whole country. At the same time an attempt is made to assess the amount of advertising that will be necessary.
The value of test marketing is hotly disputed; its supporters believe it is the only means to protect a company from irreparable damage; others say that it warns competition and that local areas do not accurately mirror the national market.

Testimonial Anerkennungsschreiben

A letter appraising the qualities of a product or service.

Testimonial advertisement Testimonialanzeige, Affidavitanzeige

An advertising technique using written recommendations from satisfied buyers of a product, such as prominent persons, who claim that they use and like the product and thereby favourably influence potential buyers to buy it, too.

Theater advertising Kinowerbung
Theaterwerbung

Advertising by cinemas and by film or slides in cinemas. Also called cinema advertising.

Advertising in and by theaters. Also called theater publicity.

Theater test Studiotest

Also called in-theater test, laboratory test or studio test.

In TV commercial testing, a technique in which test participants view the commercials in a studio or theater/theatre setting.

Thematic apperception test (TAT) thematischer Apperzeptionstest (TAT)

A test used to uncover attitudes or reactions to a brand or advertising promise by showing vague stimuli or a series of pictures to respondents who are asked to complete or provide a story about these stimuli or pictures.

Theme Erkennungsmelodie, Kennmelodie

Also called theme song or signature (tune).

A recurring melody identifying a radio or TV program or an advertiser`s product or service.

Theory of consumer behaviour Theorie des Verbraucherverhaltens

A theory concerned with how consumers allocate their income in buying goods and services. A basic assumption is that consumers seek to maximise satisfaction/utility.

Theory of market structure Marktformenlehre

This theory distinguishes between markets according to their structural characteristics, in particular the number of buyers and sellers involved. Thus, market situations may be classified as follows:
1. perfect competition, 2. oligopoly, 3. oligopsony, 4. bilateral oligopoly, 5. monopoly, 6. monopsony, 7. bilateral monopoly, 8. duopoly, 9. duopsony.

Theory of price determination Theorie der Preisbestimmung

The theory states that prices are determined by the point of intersection of demand and supply curves, since at this point the quantity supplied equals the quantity demanded and hence there is no tendency for prices to alter.

Theory of the second best Zweitbest-Theorie

This theory states that if all the conditions required to maximize social welfare or reach Pareto optimum cannot be satisfied, trying to satisfy as many of these conditions as possible does not necessarily or usually lead to the second best welfare position.

Theory of value Werttheorie

There are various theories of value. In general, explanations of what determines the value of different commodities. If defined in terms of money, value determines price.

The two main notions of value are:
1. value is determined by the utility it gives a consumer and is reflected in the demand for it (high utility, high value);
2. value is determined by the cost of producing the commodity and is reflected by the supply of it (high cost, high value).

The classical economists (e.g. Adam Smith, David Ricardo) determined the value of a commodity by its costs of production.

The neoclassical economists (e.g. Alfred Marshall) of the late nineteenth century focused on the determinants of market price and concentrated on the utility of a commodity. According to Alfred Marshall (1842 - 1924; one of the chief founders of the school of neoclassical economists), the market price was determined by the interaction of demand and supply. If value is taken to mean the determination of price, it depends on the relation between demand (based on marginal utility) and supply (based on the costs of production).

Thin market begrenzter, enger Markt

Also called narrow, tight or weak market.

An inactive market, i.e. a market in which there are few bids to buy and few offers to sell, or both. Prices in thin markets generally are more fluctuating than in markets with great liquidity.
The term may be applied either to the market as a whole, or to a particular commodity or security.

Third class mail Postgut dritter Klasse (USA)

In the USA, an inexpensive mail delivery service for bulk mail such as catalogs and other direct mail items.

Third country Drittland

A non-EU state.

A country which is not a member of an economic union.

Third cover (3C) dritte Umschlagseite

Also called inside back cover.

The inside back cover of a magazine; a preferred position for placing advertisements.

Third party access (TPA) Zugang durch Dritte

The right of a third party to use a supplier`s facilities against payment of a fee.

Thirty (:30) 30-Sekunden-Werbung

A commercial of a timelength of 30 seconds.

Three Ls drei L`s

The abbreviations for luxury, leisure, and longevity. These three factors are confronting a society after a period of long-lasting economic growth.

Three-letter code Drei-Buchstaben-Abkürzung

A very popular and catching form of abbreviation, consisting of three letters only.

Through rate Durchfracht
Durchfrachttarif

The total cost of transporting goods when two or more carriers are used.

A transit rate applying on a through shipment between two points.

Throwaway Reklamezettel, Werbezettel, Handzettel

Also called handbill, broadsheet, dodger, flyer/flier or leaflet.

A single sheet of paper imprinted with an advertising message or announcement of a special sale or event. Frequently, they are distributed by hand on the street, left on parked cars or they are left on counters in hotels, stores, etc. for customers to pick up while shopping.

Ticket Fahrkarte, Flugticket, Eintrittskarte Etikett

A small piece of paper giving permission to the person to travel on a passenger transport mode or to enter a cinema, theatre, sports ground etc.

A small piece of paper or plastic showing the price of a commodity in a shop. Also called label or tag.

Ticket agency Fahrkartenverkaufsstelle, Vorverkaufsstelle

A shop which sales tickets, e.g. bus, train or theatre tickets.

Tie out Wettbewerbsverbot

A contractual agreement prohibiting firms to sell other products than those of the contracting party, ie the supplier of the goods.

Tie-in advertisement Koppelungsanzeige, Kombinationswerbung

A print advertisement (ad) that relates to other advertising, e.g. a retailer runs an ad in conjunction with a producer's ad for a product carried in the store.

Tie-in advertising Koppelungswerbung, Verbundwerbung

Advertising where two or more firms advertise for their different products in one advertisement.

Simultaneous advertising through two or more media, eg on television and in magazines, usually using the same motif or slogan etc.

Tie-in sale Koppelungsgeschäft

Also called tie-in transaction.

A sale in which the buyer contracts to purchase some extra, often unwanted, item in addition to the required goods or services as one product or service cannot be bought without the other.

Tie-on label Anhängezettel

A label with a string which is tied onto a product or other item.

Tied company lieferantengebundenes Unternehmen

A company which is tied to a particular supplier.

Tied industry standortgebundene Industrie

Industries that have little choice of location as they are tied to their raw materials or other conditions, e.g. climatic factors.

Tied shop Geschäft mit Bindung an eine Lieferfirma

A shop which agrees to sell one particular brand of goods or the products of one particular firm.

Till Ladenkasse
Geldkassette

The money drawer in a shop`s cash register. Also called register.

A box in which money is kept. Also called money box.

Till forbid (TF) bis auf weiteres

Also called till cancelled, till countermanded, or till further notice.

A standing order (SO) for goods or services until told to stop.

An advertiser`s instruction to a media vehicle to run an advertisement or spot until countermanded.

Till money Kassenbestand
Tageseinnahmen

Money kept in the till of a business. Also called counter money, cash (balance), cash in/on hand, cash assets or holdings, money in cash or hand.

In GB, the total cash taken during a day by a business, especially a retail shop. Also called takings.

Time bar Ausschlußfrist

Under a contract, a clause which limits the time within which action may be taken.

Time buyer Funkmedienkontakter

An executive in an advertising agency who chooses and buys radio and television time.

Time discount Mengenrabatt
Malrabatt

A discount granted to advertisers by radio and television stations.

A reduction of the advertising rate granted to advertisers who make quantity purchases of time. Also called quantity discount.

A frequency discount granted to advertisers who run a certain number of commercials within a specified time. Also called frequency or quantity discount.

Time lag Wirkungsverzögerung, zeitliche Verzögerung

Also called operational lag.

The delay between the occurrence of an event and its effects on the company or economy. In other words, a time period which elapses before the effect of an action, e.g. an interest rate cut or a tax increase, becomes apparent.

Time limit Frist, Zeitlimit
Termin

The period of time, e.g. as provided by the contract, during which something should be done or completed.

The date by which something has to be done. Also called appointed day or time, deadline or target date.

Time management Zeitmanagement

The perception of time as a valuable asset and the task of efficiently allocating blocks of time to certain tasks in order to maximise productivity.

Time of delivery Liefertermin, Lieferfrist, Lieferzeit

Also called delivery time.

The date on which or the period within which something will or has to be delivered.

In the performance of a sales contract, the seller must have the goods ready for collection or deliver them at the time fixed in the contract. If no time is fixed he must have them ready for collection or deliver them within a reasonable time. If he fails to do so, the buyer may refuse to accept delivery. The buyer may, however, give the seller further time for delivery.

Time preference Zeitpräferenz

The relative evaluation of present versus future goods. According to the Austrian economist Eugen von Böhm-Bawerk (1851-1914), most individuals value present consumption more highly than future consumption and prefer a sum of money now to an equal amount at a later date (when interest rates are low) but are more willing to save when interest rates are high.

Time segment Sendezeitsegment, Zeitsegment

Also called daypart.

The time periods into which a broadcasting day is divided, eg prime time, morning drive, or late night.

Time slot Werbesendezeit

On radio or television, a specific time period reserved for broadcasting a program or commercial.

Time spent listening (TSL) Radiohörzeit

Also called listening time.

The time, measured in quarters of an hour, which an average person spends listening to the radio during a specific time period.

Time spent reading (TSR) Lesedauer

Also called reading time.

The time spent by the average reader of a newspaper or magazine on any given issue.

Time spent viewing (TSV) Fernsehzeit

Also called viewing time.

The time spent by the average viewer in watching television during a specified time period, eg per day or month.

Time utility Zeitnutzen, Zeitvorteil

The usefulness gained when something of value is received at the time it is wanted. It may be measured by the price premium which the consumer is willing to pay for such immediate availability.

Time-based competition Produktkonkurrenz unter Berücksichtigung des Faktors Zeit

A product policy that focuses on the rapid development of new products. Thus, firms might prefer to produce new products faster rather than make them better or more cheaply. In today`s highly competitive world, new products need not only to possess novel and attractive features in order to succeed, but they must also be introduced quickly as many consumers are willing to pay premium prices for recently developed items. Product life cycles are shortening and the costs of rapid new product developments may be extremely high and the administrative procedures necessary for time-based competition may be complicated.

Time-out Zeitbegrenzung

The limitation of time available to someone.

Timelength Zeitdauer einer Werbesendung

Also called commercial length.

The length, eg 30 seconds, of a radio, television, or cinema commercial.

Timing Timing, Terminierung, Zeitwahl

The selection of the best time for saying or doing something in order to achieve the desired effect, e.g. the appropriate timing of an exporter to enter a new market and later move into other segments, or the timing of a manufacturer to introduce/launch a new product on/to the market with some special campaign or activity.

Tip Trinkgeld
Tip, Hinweis, Wink

Money given to someone who has rendered a service, over and above the bill. Also called gratuity.

A piece of information about what may happen passed to someone who is interested.

Tip in eingeklebte (Werbe)Beilage

An extra advertising page or a return card glued into a publication.

Tip on (Werbe)Aufkleber

An item, eg a coupon or reply card, glued to an advertising page or any other promotion piece such as a catalog(ue), book or magazine.

Title Titel (Buch, Film, etc)

The name of a specific publication, book, film, play, etc.

Title corner Titelbox-, Zeitungskopfanzeige, Eckplatzanzeige auf der Titelseite

Also called ear, earlug or ear space.

In advertising, a small space on either side of the title at the top of the frontpage of a newspaper.

Title music Titelmusik

The musical theme that is used with the titles of a television program or motion picture.

Token

Beweis
Andenken, Souvenir
Gutschein

Something offered or taken as evidence or proof.

A souvenir, ie a usually small and relatively inexpensive article given or kept as a reminder of a place visited, an event, etc. .

A card bought in a shop, used instead of money and given as a present which must be exchanged in that shop for goods, eg a book, flower or gift token.

Token payment

Draufgabe
Draufgeld
erste Ratenzahlung, kleine Teilzahlung
symbolische Zahlung

The extra quantity granted to the quantity agreed in the sales contract. Also called bargain money.

When making a contract, the amount of money given by a buyer to a seller to bind a bargain made orally. Also called earnest money or token money.

An initial payment of a small part of an amount owed to show that one agrees to pay the whole amount. Also called first or initial installment or part(ial) payment.

A small payment requested to show that something is not given away free of charge.

Toll

Straßen- und Brückenbenutzungsgebühr, Maut
Fernsprechgebühr

A charge made at a tollgate for using certain roads (toll-roads, toll-ways, turnpike roads), bridges (toll bridges) or tunnels.

In the USA, a charge made for a toll call (long distance call, trunk call). A toll charge meter (call-charge indicator) records the number of call charge units.

Tombstone advertising

Emissionsanzeige

An advertisement placed in newspapers by issuing banks in a public offering of new securities, ie in a new issue. It gives basic details about the issue, lists the underwriting group members or syndicate members involved in the offering and clearly states that the ad is informational only and not itself an offer to buy or sell. It often has a black border.

Top left/right position Anzeigenposition links/rechts oben

An advertisements`s position on the left or right side of a page.

Top of mind Spitzenbekanntheit

In advertising research, the first brand or advertisement that comes to a respondent`s mind in reply to an appropriate question.

Topout Spitzenbedarf, Spitzennachfrage

Also called peak demand.

The peak period of demand for a product or service, after which demand decreases.

Torture testing Bruchprobe

A product test where products are pushed to their limits, or breaking point.

Total Gesamtbetrag, Gesamtsumme

Also called grand total, sum total or total amount.

The sum after adding everything up, e.g. if you add 3 + 5, the total is 8.

Total audience (TA) Gesamtzahl der Leser
Gesamtzahl der Hörer/Zuschauer

The entire readership of a publication.

The number of people or the percentage of the population in a given geographic area that has listened to or viewed a particular station or program for at least six minutes.

Total circulation Gesamtauflage

The total number of copies of a publication distributed, ie all the copies sold to subscribers and single copy buyers, plus the courtesy copies.

Total cost(s) (TC) Gesamtkosten

Also called overall costs or total outlay.

The total costs of a firm consist of total fixed cost(s) plus total variable cost(s). It is an assumption of perfect competition that total costs include normal profit, that is, a return to the entrepreneur which is sufficient to keep him in business.
Total costs will always rise as output rises.

Total distribution costs Gesamtvertriebskosten

The costs of all parts of physical distribution, ie warehousing, materials handling, inventory control, order processing, and transportation.

Total market potential gesamtes Absatz-, Marktpotential

The total possible sales of a product by all competitors.

Total offer Gesamtangebot

A complete package offered to a customer, ie an offer including details on the product or service itself, its price, terms of delivery and payment, promotion, etc.

Total order cycle Gesamtauftragszyklus

The period elapsing between the receipt of an order and the actual delivery of the goods. To be able to estimate the duration of the total order cycle, one must break the order cycle down into subdivisions for order processing, documentation, warehousing, packaging, loading, unloading, intermediate handling, and final delivery.

Total price Gesamtpreis

The total amount payable for a product or service.

The total sum payable by the buyer under a hire purchase agreement.

Total quality management (TQM) Total Quality Management, umfassendes Qualitätsmanagement

A management philosophy attempting to fully satisfy customers in an effective and efficient manner. It is thus necessary to establish a culture of quality affecting the attitudes and actions of every employee. Additionally, it requires a customer focus, a commitment from top management, an emphasis on continuous improvement, and support and involvement from suppliers and distribution intermediaries.

Causes of poor quality could result from bad leadership, poor teamwork, lack of employee commitment and motivation, psychosocial problems, cultural differences, technical inadequacies, etc.

Note: the key idea in TQM is that quality is important at every step of the production process; thus, TQM strives to eliminate defects from the beginning.

Total revenue (TR) Gesamtumsatzerlös

The total receipts of a company from the sale of a particular output, i.e. the price per unit multiplied by the quantity sold (TR = price x quantity sold).

Total utility Gesamtnutzen

This is the total satisfaction we derive from the possession of a commodity. Usually total utility will continue to rise as we acquire more and more of the same goods. But there might come a point with many commodities where total utility has reached a maximum and a further supply will have not further positive effect.

Tourism Fremdenverkehr, Tourismus

A tertiary industry catering for individuals travelling within their own country or overseas
Today, tourism is an important source of income and employment. For some countries, tourism is a valuable source of export income.

Tourist marketing Tourismus-, Touristik-, Fremdenverkehrsmarketing

Marketing activities of, for example, tourist offices, regional and national tourist associations, hotels, restaurants, travel agencies, tour operators, airlines, holiday resorts, etc.

Traceable costs zurechenbare Kosten

Also called allocable/allocatable, apportionable or separable cost(s).

Costs that can be directly associated with and assigned/allocated to specific cost centers.

Trade Handel
Handelsware
Beruf
Branche, Wirtschaftszweig
Handwerk
Kundschaft
Außenhandel
Geschäft
Naturaltausch
Wertpapierhandel

The business of buying and selling commodities or services. Also called commerce.

Stuff, material or commodities for buying or selling ("This product is from the medical trade").

An occupation or employment.

A particular branch of commercial activity. Also called industry.

A manual occupation that requires particular training and a high degree of skill. Also called craft.

A firm's customers.

Trade with other countries. Also called foreign or overseas trade.

In the USA, a bargain. Also called deal or transaction.

The exchange of goods and services without the use of money. Also called barter.

The buying or selling of securities. Also called securities trading.

Trade advertising Händlerwerbung

Advertising directed at wholesalers and retailers rather than the general public.

Trade allowance Wiederverkäuferrabatt

Also called trade discount.

A price reduction offered by manufacturers to middlemen such as wholesalers and retailers. These middlemen receive a reduction for performing a specific service, eg for allocating shelf space for a new product, or for ordering during special periods.

Trade association (TA) Unternehmerverband, Fachverband

A group of firms in the same trade formed to represent, safeguard and promote their mutual interests at all levels. It acts as a pressure group on behalf of the member firms.

Trade catalog(ue) Geschäftskatalog

A publication describing products and products lines, and providing general information, eg on ordering and payment terms, distributed by a producer or dealer.

Trade character Warenzeichenfigur

A brand mark that is personified, ie animals or human characters used to characterise a product, eg the black and white dogs for Black & White Whisky, the Michelin Man, the roaring lion of Metro-Goldwyn-Mayer, etc.

Trade credit Warenkredit, Lieferantenkredit

Also called commodity credit or supplier credit.

The facility by which a company which purchases goods is allowed to delay payment for the goods it has bought. The buyer does not pay as soon as the goods are delivered but pays in arrears, i.e. he is in effect receiving a loan from his supplier.
During inflation it is profitable to delay the payment of creditors, and, of course, the money acquired in this way does not bear interest.

Trade custom Handelsbrauch

The custom how things are done in a particular trade.

Trade cycle Konjunkturzyklus, Konjunkturphase

Also called business cycle, economic cycle or boom-slump cycle.

The fluctuations of economic activity between boom and slump, the period between the booms being on an average five years. The trade cycle is characterized by: a decline from boom to slump followed by a period of depression (the downward part lasts on average some four and a half years), followed by a slow recovery (lasting about three and a half years).

Trade Description Act (TDA) Gesetz über Warenbeschreibung (GB)

In GB, this Act makes false and misleading statements about goods (e.g. labels on packets must give a true description of the contents) and services and the use of a trademark registered by another firm illegal.
For example, it is an offence to pretend to lower prices by crossing out high prices which were not charged for at least a certain number of days.
This Act lays down heavy penalties for traders who deceive the public.

Trade directory Branchenverzeichnis, Bezugsquellennachweis

Also called trade register or yellow pages.

A publication giving the names and addresses of companies operating in a particular field.

Trade discount Nachlaß (vom Listenpreis)
Händlerrabatt, Wiederverkäuferrabatt
jeder Nachlaß über 2 % Skonto

A deduction made by a manufacturer or wholesaler from list prices which represents the retailer's gross profit margin. That is, the difference between the retailer's buying price and his selling price, i.e. his markup. Also called functional discount.

A reduction in the normal selling price of goods given to a person or firm who will resell the goods.

Any deduction of more than 2 % from the price offered to customers. The size of the discount may depend on the size of the order, the importance of the customer, etc.

Trade fair Fachmesse, Fachausstellung

Also called trade exhibition or trade show.

A place where a firm can promote a particular product or range of products to a very receptive audience of visitors, who usually come with the firm intention of placing orders. Furthermore one can find out what one's competitors are offering.

Trade journal Fachzeitschrift

Also called trade magazine, professional (e.g. medical) or technical journal.

Publications dealing with business or other professional subjects.

Trade list Geschäftskatalog

A directory listing companies in a single country across all product sectors or companies in a single industry across all countries.

Trade mission Handelsmission

A group of businessmen who make a short visit to another country to establish and develop trade between the two countries.

Trade press Fachpresse

Newspapers or magazines dealing with professional subjects.

Trade price Großhandelspreis, Wiederverkäuferpreis

The price of a commodity charged by a wholesaler or any other reseller.

Trade promotion (Absatz)Förderung beim Handel

Sales promotion aimed at retailers, wholesalers and other distributors by giving them incentives to promote and increase sales.

Trade reference Firmenreferenz, Handelsauskunft

A company seeking credit terms from a supplier may be asked for a trade reference, i.e. to furnish another supplier's name with whom he has dealt previously and who is willing to comment on his creditworthiness.

Trade secret Betriebs-, Geschäftsgeheimnis

A particular knowledge, e.g. the process of making a product, known only to the company and to no one else. It should not be told to others without the firm`s permission.

Trade show Fachmesse, Handelsmesse

Also called trade fair.

An exhibition at which sellers display their products, usually once a year, for the benefit of visiting buyers and for taking orders. Therefore, they cater mainly for trade buyers, although the general public may be admitted on certain days.

Trade statistics Handelsstatistik

The listing of all the relevant trade figures in a country.

The indication of total exports or imports by country and by product.

Trade terms Verkaufsbedingungen
Handelsbedingungen
Incoterms

The responsibilities of the buyer and seller in a sale, including: the conditions of a sale, price, the seller`s given time to pay an invoice, other special credit arrangements, guarantees, arrangement for return of goods, etc. Also called terms of sale.

A scale of discounts granted by a wholesaler to retailers. A phrase often used is: "please supply at best trade terms", that is, at lowest prices and highest discounts.

The incoterms.

Trade usage Handelsbrauch, Usance

Also called usage of the market.

A well-established custom of a particular trade or industry which governs the rights and duties of the parties dealing in that environment.

Trade-in in Zahlung gegebener Gegenstand

A commodity or an old asset exchanged in part consideration or part payment of a purchase of new goods or a new asset, e.g. if you buy a new car your old car will be accepted as a trade-in.

Trademark/trade mark (TM) Warenzeichen, Handelsmarke

A unique name (the tradename), symbol, logo, etc., registered in the trademark register for the exclusive use of one firm to distinguish its products from all others (identified by the symbol ® for registered).
A trademark is given legal protection and thus is protected from infringement by competitors. But TMs also protect the public because consumers who bought a particular product can usually feel confident that they received the product they desired.
A trademark normally has to be registered separately in each country where it is used.

Trademark imitation Warenzeichenimitation

The attempt to take advantage of the reputation of another supplier by the production of similar products under similar or even the same brand names, with similar packaging and labelling.

Trademark piracy Markenpiraterie

The registration of brand names with the aim of selling them back to the companies that have originated them, if and when such firms wish to enter the market.

Tradename/trade name (TN) Markenname
Handelsname
Firmenname
Firmenzeichen

A name applied to a product supplied by one company that does not have the exclusive character of a trademark.

The name by which an article is known to the trade.

The name under which a business advertises, operates and sells its product(s).
A name can be registered if there is not already a similar company with a similar name operating.
Registration prevents other companies from using the same, or similar, names and ensures that the owner of a business can be located if, for example, one of its products causes harm to someone.

A trademark that is used to identify a product.

Note: it is wise to pick a short, easy-to-remember name.

Tradeoff — Tradeoff, Austauschbeziehung

This means that activities which provide benefits also incur disadvantages and vice versa, or the exchange of one benefit at the sacrifice of another.

Trader — Geschäftsmann, Händler, Kaufmann
Außenhändler

A person whose business is to buy and sell goods with his own money and for his own profit, often a shopkeeper. Also called tradesman.

A person whose job is to buy and sell products in large quantities, especially by trading with other countries. Also called merchant.

Trading — Handel

Also called dealing.

The business of buying and selling goods and services.

The amount of business done in a certain period.

Trading account — Betriebskonto, Betriebsergebnisrechnung, Erfolgskonto

The trading account determines the gross profit or gross loss on trading for the year, i.e. the difference between sales (on the right-hand side) and the cost of goods sold (on the left-hand side). For a manufacturing business the cost of goods sold is derived from the manufacturing account; for a trading business, it is simply the total cost of goods bought from suppliers during the year.

Trading area Absatzgebiet

Also called sales area.

The geographic areas where goods are sold, and in which there is a brisk demand for them.

Trading business Einzelhandelsbetrieb

Also called retail business or retail establishment.

A business organized for the primary purpose of selling a product or a group of products, usually to the final/ultimate consumer.

Trading down Versuch der Umsatzsteigerung durch Senkung der Preise, Trading-down

A company's policy to achieve a high(er) turnover by selling cheaper and/or lower quality products than the products it has sold in the past, sometimes accompanied by less customer services.

Trading estate Industriegelände
Geschäftsviertel, Einkaufszentrum

Area of land, usually outside a town, set aside for commerce and industry. Also called industrial estate or industrial park.

A shopping centre.

Trading loss Betriebsverlust, negatives Betriebsergebnis

A situation where a firm`s operating expenses exceed its operating revenue.

Trading partner Handelspartner

A firm or country trading with another, usually by preference or from experience etc.

Trading profit Betriebsgewinn, -überschuß, positives Betriebsergebnis

Also called earnings from operations, earned surplus or operating profit.

The surplus earned from normal business transactions, i.e. the difference between operating revenue/income and operating expenses/costs in the main commercial activities of the firm in a given period, usually a year.

Trading stamp Rabattmarke

Also called discount ticket.

Special stamps given by traders to customers at so many per pound, dollar, franc, deutschmark, etc spent. The trader uses them as means of increasing sales and the customer saves them and later exchanges them either for cash (the cash redemption value must be shown on the stamp) or for goods.
Trading stamps are thus a kind of discount.

Trading stock Warenbestand, Warenvorrat

A company`s stock on hand, ie the goods held for sale.

Trading up Versuch der Umsatzsteigerung durch Erhöhung der Preise, Trading-up Sortimentsaufwertung

The attempt of a salesperson who shows a medium-priced product first and then offers a better quality at a higher price or a larger quantity than the potential customer had originally intended to buy to increase his sales.

A company's launching of new products that are distinctly more expensive than the products it has sold so far to achieve a high(er) turnover and to secure exclusive customers and high profit ratios.

Whether such a strategy is really successful depends on the individual circumstances; furthermore there is always a danger that the company will be unable to shed its image of being a seller of "cheap" and lower quality products.

Traffic

Verkehrsaufkommen
Verkehr (Güter, Personen)
jede wirtschaftliche Tätigkeit
Handel
Kundenverkehr, Besucherfluß
Markt

The amount of vehicles moving along roads, or the amount of airplanes, trains or ships moving along a route.

The business of transporting passengers or freight/cargo by railway, road, water or air.

Any commercial activity.

Any trade, usually illegal.

The total number of persons who enter a store or the total number of persons or cars who pass the frontage of the shop whether they enter or not.

Traffic in the meaning of market, especially in the phrase "take what the traffic will bear".

Traffic count

Verkehrszählung

The counting of persons or vehicles passing a specific point during a particular time period; very important in outdoor advertising.

Traffic department

Versandabteilung
Terminabteilung
Warenauslieferungsabteilung eines Warenhauses

The traffic department is charged with handling all matters dealing with outgoing shipments. To obtain economical and reliable shipping, it selects the type of shipping service (e.g. railway, lorry, airplane) and the specific carriers on the basis of the lowest freight, best care of goods, etc., prepares packing instructions, transport documents, etc.

The department responsible for progress control and for the meeting of deadlines.

The department of a large store responsible for the delivery of goods to customers.

Traffic manager Versandleiter
Terminüberwacher

The head of a traffic department responsible for the movement of goods.

The person responsible for progress control and for the meeting of deadlines.

Transaction Geschäft, Transaktion

Also called deal or operation.

A business deal that usually involves an agreement to provide goods or services for the payment of money.

Transaction cost(s) Transaktionskosten

The cost(s) associated with carrying out a particular transaction, e.g. brokerage.

Transfer (TRF, trf) (Eigentums)Übertragung
Transfer
Abziehbild

The act of transferring ownership from one person to another.

The transfer of a person or thing, e.g. the transfer of a football player from one club to another.

A design, drawing, etc. transferred from one surface to another. Also called decal or decalcomania.

Transfer charge call (TCC) R-Gespräch

Also called collect call, reverse-charge call or transferred charge call.

A telephone call where the costs of the call are transferred to the called number (the recipient) if the call is accepted when the operator offers it. An extra fee is payable for this service.

Transfer of ownership Eigentumsübertragung

The act of transferring or shifting the ownership of something from one person to another.

Transfer price Verrechnungspreis

Also called transfer cost.

A price that is charged on goods sold between business enterprises that are related to each other through stock ownership, such as a parent and its subsidiaries or subsidiaries owned by the same parent. Transfer prices are used where each entity is managed as a profit centre and must therefore deal with the other internal parts of the multientity company on a market basis.

Such a price may also be charged between departments/divisions of the same company.

Transfer pricing Festsetzung von Transferpreisen

Deciding on the price of goods or services that are exchanged between various divisions of a decentralized organization. Transfer pricing is essentially the pricing of goods, services and know-how traded between various subsidiaries and related companies in a multinational corporation (MNC) so as to reduce the group`s global tax liability by concentrating income in low tax countries and expenses or losses in high tax countries.

Transfer pricing is one of the trickiest problems in management which has no perfect solution. If you charge only costs, that removes any profit incentive from the supplying division - and it makes it impossible to judge whether it should be making the thing at all. If you go to the other extreme and charge a true market price, you forfeit the advantage of having an in-house supply - and (because you apply your own markup on a higher base) you may push the final/ultimate price to the consumer up to uncompetitive levels. Most companies opt for a solution somewhere between the two extremes. There is no single transfer price that will please everybody - that is top management, the selling division, and the buying division.

Transit advertising Verkehrsmittelwerbung

Also called transport or transportation advertising.

The practice of carrying a message, e.g. on posters, on the inside or outside of transportation vehicles (i.e. buses, cars, railways, taxi cabs) and their stations.

Transit time Beförderungszeit

The total time a carrier needs to transport a product from one place to another.

Transnational corporation (TNC) transnationale Gesellschaft multinationales Unternehmen

A company owned and managed by nationals in different countries.

A multinational enterprise.

Transparency Transparenz

Also called transparence.

The quality or state of being transparent. For example, the extent to which agreements and practices are open, clear, measurable, and verifiable.

Transport Transport, Beförderung

Also called transportation.

The conveyance of persons, goods or materials from one place to another. Transport is the moving link in the distributive chain. Entrepreneurs are concerned with getting their products to their customers at the right time and at the right price. Without an adequate transportation system, commercial activity is impossible.
The particular mode of transport employed depends on: distance, nature of the goods, urgency, value, risk of damage, cost and buyer's instructions.
Transport modes are: rail, road, ship, air, hovercraft, ro-ro, etc.

Transportation charges Transportkosten

Also called carriage; freight; carrying, freight or transport charges; transport(ation) costs; transport expenses or costs of transport.

The costs of carrying goods or materials from one place to another.
Transportation charges are of two types. Charges for transporting merchandise to the company are freight in (freight inward or carriage inward). This will be an additional cost of acquiring the goods. Outward bound charges to transport goods the firm sold are freight out (carriage outward).

Transhipment/transshipment (transhpt.) Umladung

Also called reloading or reshipment.

The process of transferring (loading or discharging) freight/cargo from one transport mode, e.g. a railway wagon, vessel or aircraft, to another. A transhipment charge arises when cargo is transhipped en route to continue its transit.

Travel agency Reisebüro

Also called travel bureau.

A business which arranges journeys, holidays etc. for other people.

Travel agent Reisebüro
Reiseveranstalter

A travel agency.

A person or company acting on behalf of third parties, e.g. airlines, in selling package tours. Also called tour operator.

Travel allowance Reisekostenzuschuß

Also called travelling allowance or fares allowance.

Money which an employee is allowed to spend on travelling for business purposes.

Travel expenses Reisekosten, -spesen

Also called travel(l)ing expenses.

Money spent on travelling and hotels for business purposes.

Travel supplement Reisebeilage

A separately printed publication informing readers about travel, accommodation and the like, and added to a newspaper or magazine.

Travelling salesman Reisender, Vertreter

Also called commercial traveller or sales representative.

A person appointed to represent his firm by visiting customers and trying to obtain orders from them. Usually, he receives a basic salary plus a commission on the value of the orders he takes.

Tray pack Schaukarton; Packung, die durch Deckelabnahme zu Regalauslage wird

A carton that can be converted into a display unit by folding back or removing its top so that it fits into a shelf or on a counter.

Trend Trend, Entwicklungsrichtung

The general course or prevailing tendency.

Trend analysis Trendanalyse

A forecasting method in which specific statistics are analysed in order to identify trends, eg sales trends.

Trial Versuch, Probe

A test to see if something is good or suitable.

Trial and error pricing probeweise Preisfestsetzung

A pricing strategy where a company fixes a particular price to test its suitability. If it proves to be suitable the price will remain, if not, it will be changed.

Trial buyer Erst-, Probekäufer

A person who makes an initial purchase or a trial purchase.

Trial mailing Probe-Mailing, Probeversand

In direct mailing campaigns, these are mailings sent out to test the response to alternative offers.

Trial offer Probeangebot

Also called free trial offer or free examination offer.

An offer that allows a first-time buyer to examine, use, or test a product for a short period of time before deciding to purchase it (or return it). Or it may grant the first-time buyer a special reduced rate, e.g. a trial subscriber may obtain a reduced rate for his trial subscription.

Trial order Probeauftrag

Also called tentative order.

A small order, placed to test and judge the value or quality of a commodity, before placing a substantial order.

In the case of a trial and return order, the customer (the trial buyer) can check the goods and keep them for a trial/probation period.

Trial purchase Erstkauf, Probekauf

A small initial purchase of or order for a product by a trial/first-time buyer to test its suitability, quality, value, etc.

Trial sample Probestück

A small piece of a product or chosen item used to enable potential customers to test it.

Trial size Probepackungsgröße

A product package of small size, often used as a sample or sold at a lower price to attract potential customers and induce them to test the product.

Trial subscription Probeabonnement

The subscription of a newspaper or magazine at a special reduced price and/or for a short period by a trial subscriber.

Trolley/trolly Einkaufswagen

A small metal cart used by customers in supermarkets for carrying their bags and purchases.

Trotting inflation trabende Inflation

Also called galloping or runaway inflation.

A very high rate of persistent inflation. As prices rise rapidly, people lose confidence in the monetary system.

Troubleshooter Störungs-, Fehlersucher

An expert in discovering and eliminating the cause(s) of trouble in the operation of something.

Trough Konjunkturtief, Talsohle

Also called bottom, bottom of economic activity, cyclical depression, economic low, low point in the cycle.

The bottom of the business/trade cycle contraction, i.e. of a recession or depression - the point at which recovery begins.

Truck Lastkraftwagen (LKW)
offener Güterwagen

A large motor vehicle for carrying goods and materials. Also called lorry (GB).

In GB, a freight car having no top. Also called gondola car or open goods waggon.

Truckage Transport durch Bahn und LKW
Frachtkosten

The transportation of cargo by railway or truck.

The charge made for conveying/transporting goods by railway trucks and other trucks. Also called carriage, freight or freight charges.

Trucker-owned warehouse (Waren)Depot eines Güterverkehrsunternehmens

A warehouse owned by a trucking company and from where goods are distributed to another firm`s customers.

Trunk call (TC) Ferngespräch

Also called long-distance call or toll call.

A telephone call made to a subscriber outside the caller's local area.

Trust — Kartell
Trust

A term used in the USA for a cartel.

Any combination of competitors to fix prices, eliminate competition and control the market.

A large company or group of companies exercising monopolistic control over production and distribution of some goods and services.

Trustbusting — Zerschlagung von Trusts, Monopolen, usw.

The efforts of governments and trust busters to prevent monopolistic abuse (the main evils of monopolies are: higher prices, lower output, bigger profits) and, in some cases, to prevent mergers or takeovers that create dominant firms.

In Germany, the Bundeskartellamt (Federal Cartel Office) can ban restrictive practices and mergers; in Great Britain there is the Office of Fair Trading (OFT); and in the USA the Federal Trade Commission in cooperation with the Antitrust Division of the Department of Justice is the "watchdog of competition".

Tube card — U-Bahn-Plakat

In the USA also called subway card.

Advertising posters hanging on the walls of underground stations or inside underground trains.

Turn — Handelsgewinn, Marge
Umsatz

The difference between a buying and selling price where business done has resulted in a profit. To "make a turn" means to buy and sell at a profit. Also called dealing profit, trading profit or spread.

The short form for turnover.

Turnaround — Trendwende

Also called trend reversal.

A recovery, e.g. in business sales; or a change from loss to profit, etc.

Turnaround time Umschlagzeit, Verweilzeit

The time it takes to get a job done and deliver the output, ie the time between job submittance and receipt of results.

Turnkey/turn-key contract Vertrag, der die vollständige (schlüsselfertige) Projektdurchführung verlangt

A contract in which the customer commissions a specialist firm to carry out a complex project so that the customer only has to "turn a key" to set it working. There is no further commitment beyond satisfactory completion of the project.
Payment for a turnkey operation usually is in stages, as a project develops. It is common for 10 to 25 percent to be made as the down payment, another 50 to 65 percent to be paid as the contract progresses, and the remainder to be paid once the project actually is operating in accordance with the contract.
Because of the usual long time periods between conception and completion, the performing company should apply escalation clauses or cost-plus contracts.

Turnkey project schlüsselfertiges Projekt

A project for which a contractor undertakes to deliver a fully operational and tested facility.

Turnover (t.o.) Umsatz
Umschlag

The total amount of goods or services sold over a certain time, usually expressed in terms of value, sometimes also in terms of units sold.
The value of sales made is the gross turnover; the amount of gross turnover less goods which have been returned (returns inwards, sales returns) is the net turnover. Net turnover therefore means the amount of effective sales. Also called billings or sales.

The number of times average stock/inventory is sold during a given period, e.g. a year.

Turnover bonus Umsatzbonus

Also called turnover allowance.

A quantity discount paid retrospectively on the basis of orders received or goods delivered.

Turnover rate Umschlagshäufigkeit

Also called frequency of goods turnover, turnover rate or ratio, or stockturn rate.

The speed at which goods are sold. It is measured by the number of times a year that the average stock can be sold. To find the turnover rate, the stock in hand is averaged and divided into the sales at cost price.

$$\text{Rate of turnover} = \frac{\text{sales at cost}}{\text{average stock}}$$

This figure is meaningless by itself unless one is aware of the product to which it refers. However, whatever the product, the greater the rate of turnover, the higher the profits.

Turnover tax Umsatzsteuer, Bruttoallphasenumsatzsteuer

Also called cascade tax or cumulative all-stage turnover tax.

An indirect tax, typically on an ad valorem basis.
The turnover tax is a multi-stage sales tax, i.e. it is a tax levied by the government on a product or service at each stage of production or distribution. The value taxed at each stage includes the tax paid at earlier stages, which means that tax is paid on tax.

Turnround mittlerer Lagerumschlag

The value of goods sold during a specific time period, eg a year, divided by the average value of goods held in stock.

Twenty (:20) 20-Sekunden-Werbung

A twenty second cinema, radio or television commercial.

Twenty-four hour recall Werbeerinnerung nach max. 24 Stunden

Also called day after recall (DAR).

The extent to which a target audience can remember an advertisement after 24 hours.

Twenty-four-hour trading Handel rund um die Uhr

Also called all-day trading.

A firm is open day and night, eg 24-hour trading in supermarkets.

Twin pack Doppelpackung

A retail product package made up of two containers of the same product packaged together and usually offered at a discount price.

Two colour (2C) advertisement Zweifarbenanzeige

An advertisement printed in two colours, usually black plus one other, or two colours other than black.

Two-page spread doppelseitige Anzeige

Also called double-page spread (DPS).

An advertisement covering two facing pages in a newspaper or magazine.

Two-way communication zweiseitige Kommunikation

A type of communication where the transmitter gets an instant response from the receiver, thereby enabling a proper conversation to take place.

Tycoon Industriemagnat, Tycoon

A businessman who has made a great deal of money and thus is potentially influential.

Tying contract Koppelungsvereinbarung

Also called tying arrangement.

A condition of sale requiring the buyer of a particular product to purchase another, perhaps undesirable, product (often complementary to the first product), e.g. a service contract for a machine purchased.
Tying arrangements are generally illegal and act as a barrier to entry by denying new firms access to the market.

Typeface Schriftart

The style and design of letters, numerals and other symbols, eg Times Roman.

U

Ullage Schwund, Flüssigkeitsverlust

The difference between the capacity of a cask/barrel and its contents due to loss of liquid by leakage, evaporation, etc.

Ultimate user Endverbraucher, Letztverbraucher

Also called end consumer, final consumer or ultimate consumer.

Not necessarily the ultimate buyer but someone who actually consumes or uses a product or service.

Umbrella brand Dachmarke

A brand name placed on all products sold by a firm. A company`s original strong brand name is transferred to a number of other products, thus saving the cost of developing new brands from scratch.
A well-known umbrella brand is Yamaha, a brand name under which hifi equipment and motorcycles are sold.

Umbrella pricing Dachpreisstrategie, Spitzenpreisstrategie

In oligopolistic markets, a pricing strategy applied by larger firms. These firms set their prices at a level high enough to allow smaller inefficient competitors charging lower prices to operate profitably and remain in business.

Umbrella promotion Umbrella-Promotion

Promoting a theme covering a number of different products produced or sold by the same firm.

Unadvertised product Produkt, für das keine Werbung gemacht wird

A product that is not advertised, eg propagated by word of mouth.

Unaided recall test reiner Gedächtnistest

Also called pure or spontaneous recall test.

A research technique used to test the effectiveness of advertisements and commercials and to find out whether respondents are familiar with a particular brand name, slogan, etc. The respondents/interviewees are allowed to answer the questions without guidance or assistance of the interviewer; they are not prompted in their responses as they are in aided recalls.

Unambiguous question eindeutige, unzweideutige Frage

A question which clearly indicates what information is required, eg in a questionnaire.

Unanswerable question nicht zu beantwortende Frage

In a questionnaire, specific and detailed questions which respondents cannot be expected to know or remember.

Unascertained goods Gattungssachen, Gattungsware

Also called fungible or generic goods, fungibles or unspecified goods.

Goods which are not actually identified and agreed upon at the time of the contract, e.g. goods of a particular type or goods where the contract relates to part of a larger quantity of goods.

Unavoidable costs fixe Kosten, Fixkosten

Also called capacity, constant, fixed, nonvariable, standby, standing or volume costs/expenses.

Costs which do not vary in direct proportion to a firm's output. They are costs of the indivisible factors and are incurred whatever the output; they remain constant even if the level of production varies.

Unbalanced growth ungleichgewichtiges Wachstum

Also called unsteady growth.

Economic growth in which certain sectors of the economy grow faster than others.

Unbundled pricing bündelfreie, ungebündelte Preisfestsetzung

A pricing strategy that breaks down prices by individual components and allows the buyer to decide what to purchase.

Uncontrollable cost(s) nicht beeinflußbare Kosten

Costs which have to be met by a company but which are outside its control, e.g. changes in the exchange rate.

Uncontrollable variable nicht beeinflußbare Variable

Forces outside the firm over which managers have little or no control, at least in the short term.

Undeliverability Unzustellbarkeit

A situation in which something is undeliverable to a receiver, eg because the address is invalid or incomplete.

Under separate cover mit gleicher/getrennter Post

Also called by the same mail/post, or by separate mail/post.

A phrase indicating that something is sent the same day as the accompanying/covering letter but in a separate envelope or package.

Under-the-table money Schmiergeld

Also called bribe money, graft, kickback, palm grease, slush money or payoff.

Money given to someone secretly to persuade him (the payee) to do something he would not otherwise do, e.g. to grant rights or privileges to the payer.

Underbidder Unterbieter; jemand, der auf einer Versteigerung zu wenig bietet

At an auction, a person who bids less than the actual buyer. The opposite of overbidder.

Underclass unterpriviligierte Klasse

Also called the underclassed.

Economically and socially disadvantaged people in a society. A social class consisting of persons living in persistent poverty and social isolation. These people must count their cents or pennies even when making the most basic purchases.

Underconsumption theory Unterkonsumtheorie

Just as too much of certain goods may be consumed, so it is possible for too little of many other goods to be consumed (according to the prevailing aims and values of society). Such underconsumption may be general (a household underconsumes generally when its means are inadequate to finance a certain living standard) or specific (i.e. a household consumes too little of those goods and services which benefit everyone).

According to the underconsumption theory, this lack of spending by the public (due to low wages or excessive savings) leads to a depression.

Underlease/under-lease Untervermietung

Also called sublease/sub-lease or derivative lease.

A lease given by someone who is already the lessee of the property under a headlease.

Underpayment Unterbezahlung

A payment that is too little, often due to a mistake, e.g. only £ 300 is paid instead of £ 330 for goods delivered. The seller may either bill/invoice again for the remaining amount, accept the amount received as full payment, or proportionately reduce the service or goods to be delivered (if possible).

Underselling Preisunterbietung

Also called undercutting.

A situation where a firm sells its goods more cheaply than its competitors.

Understored zu wenig Geschäfte haben

The opposite of overstored; ie a market situation where there are too few stores to provide the market satisfactorily.

Undertone Marktstimmung, Börsenstimmung

Also called general mood of the market.

The underlying tendency of market prices and the current feeling that influence the actions of buyers and sellers in/on the market, particularly on a commodity exchange or stock exchange. The undertone may be weak, steady or strong.

Undertrading Erzielung zu niedriger Umsätze

Insufficient trading either to generate a profit or obtain an adequate rate of return.

Underwriting Übernahme der Fernseh- und Rundfunkfinanzierung durch Nicht-werbeträger

In media, the process of providing financial support for a TV or radio programme without the larger money investment involved in sponsorship or advertising.

Undifferentiated marketing undifferenziertes Marketing

Also called mass or unsegmented marketing.

A basic marketing strategy.
A firm using an undifferentiated marketing strategy views the total market for a product or service as one big target market with no individual segments. The firm assumes that all customers in the market have similar needs that can be satisfied with a single marketing mix.

Note:
1. an advantage of this strategy is the potential for saving a lot on production and marketing;
2. a disadvantage is that there are few markets where a single product or service is satisfactory for all;
3. with no competition, the firm may not need to tailor marketing mixes to the preferences of market segments;
4. when undifferentiated marketing is inappropriate, marketers use market segmentation to try to improve customer satisfaction.

Another two basic strategies are open to any marketer:

1. concentrated marketing: a company devotes its whole marketing effort to one market segment, or to a very few segments, i.e. the segment(s) it believes will prove most profitable;
2. differentiated marketing: a company segments its markets and operates in all or several segments of the market but modifies both products and marketing programmes to achieve maximum customer appeal within each segment.

Undifferentiated product undifferenziertes Produkt

Products which are identical and have no unique feature to differentiate them from others on the market.

Undisclosed factoring stilles, verdecktes Factoring

Also called confidential factoring, non-notification factoring or invoice discounting.

Factoring can be on a notification, or a non-notification basis. In the latter case, the client's (the seller's) debtors are not notified and the client collects payment as agent for the factor/factoring company and remits payments to the factor as they are received.
Factoring is normally done without recourse, meaning that the factor cannot turn to the client (the seller) in the event accounts prove uncollectlible - the factor assumes the risk of nonpayment.

Undue influence unzulässiger Einfluß

Unfair pressure put on someone, eg on a prospect to buy a product.

Unduplicated audience Nettoreichweite

Also called net audience, cumulative audience or net reach.

The number of different persons or households exposed to a particular advertising medium, at least once during a specific time period.

Unearned income Besitzeinkommen, Einkommen aus Vermögen

Income from investments or property (eg dividends, interest, rent), rather than from salary, wages or other employee compensation. Also called unearned revenue or property income.

Unearned increment unverdienter Wertzuwachs

An increase in the value of an asset because of changing economic or social conditions beyond the owner's control.

Unethical marketing practices unmoralische Marketingspraktiken

Marketing practices violating moral principles, such as:
false or misleading advertising, unfair manipulation of customers, lies told to customers in order to make the sale, price deception, unfair remarks about competitors, exploitation of underprivileged people, bribery, unsafe products, etc.

Unexecuted order noch nicht ausgeführter Auftrag

Also called back order.

An order that has yet to be supplied

Unfair competition unlauterer Wettbewerb

Also called dishonest trading or unfair methods of competition.

In general, a company's attempts to do better than another company by using unfair trade practices, e.g.:
wrongly criticising a competitor's products; unfair, untrue, or misleading advertising; too closely imitating a competitor's trademark, product, package, etc. in order to take away its business (also called passing off); pirating a product; selling below the cost of manufacture; dumping; etc.
In many countries there are laws to prohibit unfair trade practices.

Unfair trade practices unlautere Wettbewerbshandlungen

Also called fraudulent trading.

Discriminatory commercial activities and false representations and misleading conduct of various kinds. Examples are: unfair subsidies, dumping, the sale of counterfeit products/fakes, etc.

Uniform Commercial Code (UCC) Uniform Commercial Code (UCC) (USA)

In the USA, a code adopted by most states providing consistency in commercial law and dealing with all the aspects of commercial transactions and other commercial matters; eg all sales have an implied warranty under the UCC.

Uniform delivered pricing einheitliche Preisstellung frei Haus

Also called uniform delivery pricing or uniform geographic pricing.

A pricing method whereby all products are sold at the same delivery/delivered price, i.e. identical prices are charged to any destination.

Uniform price Einheitspreis

In domestic trade, a price which is the same on all markets.

A price which is the same for the same type of product and which is set by a government for price control purposes.

In international trade, a standardized price, i.e. a price which is the same in the markets of various countries. A firm, essentially in a monopoly or differentiated oligopolistic situation may price its products uniformly on a global scale.

Unique selling proposition (USP) einzigartiges, einmaliges Verkaufsargument

In 1960 a leading advertising man named Rosser Reeves published a book titled "Reality in Advertising" in which he outlined the unique selling proposition, USP.

USP is a creative strategy based on some point of physical differentiation of the product (ie the product itself must offer a feature, unavailable in others).

This strategy is best suited to durable goods (where the differentiation cannot be easily and quickly matched by competitors), presented to the consumer in a meaningful and persuasive way (ie the offering should present a benefit based on a specified reason, with this reason being so dramatically presented that consumers believe that the benefit will be obtained upon product purchase - consumers must desire the product).

According to Reeves, USP cannot be developed for all products, and those without them are doomed to failure.

There are three general principles behind USP:
1. uniqueness (ie the offering needs to be unique in being the sole source of the offered benefit);
2. selling (ie the consumers must desire the product);
3. proposition (ie the message should clearly indicate that the promised benefit will be obtained upon product purchase).

Unit Einheit, Stück

Any division of quantity as a standard of measurement or of exchange, e.g. a single product for sale or the unit of a country's currency such as a dollar, deutschmark, pound, yen (a monetary unit or unit of currency).

Unit billing Sammelrechnung

A list of all purchases by a customer, prepared on a single statement or invoice.

Unit contribution margin Deckungsbeitrag pro Ausbringungseinheit

Unit contribution margin = unit selling price - unit variable cost.
For example, the sales price is £ 50 and the unit variable cost is £ 30, then the unit contribution margin (CM) is £ 20. This means that each unit sold contributes £ 20 toward the fixed cost or profit.

Unit cost(s) Stückkosten

Also called cost per unit (CPU), cost per unit of output, piece costs, costs of article produced or unit production cost.

The total costs (ie total variable costs and total fixed costs) of producing a number of units of a product over time divided by the number of units.

Because of fixed costs, unit cost(s) will depend on the level of production as well as on the quantities of material and labour used. It is the unit costs rather than the total costs which give a better representation of the efficiency of a company.
There is a relationship between unit costs and the unit price: unit costs + % profit = unit price.

Unit costing Stückkostenrechnung

Also called item, process or product costing; sometimes also single costing or output costing.

Practice of determining the cost per unit of output of a product through dividing total costs by total output. This method of costing is used where manufacture/production is continuous and the unit of cost is identical throughout.

Unit labour cost(s) Lohnstückkosten

Also called unit wage cost(s) or unitized labour cost(s).

The labour cost(s) needed for one unit of a particular product.

Unit load Einheitsladung, Unit-Load

Also called unitized load.

Containerised or palletised traffic. The principle is that one large unit is speedier and easier to handle than numerous smaller items.

Unit of production Fertigungseinheit, Produktionseinheit

Also called production unit, unit of manufacture, unit of product, unit of output or work unit.

A separate piece of a product or a single product produced by a manufacturer.

Unit pack(ing) Einzelverpackung

Pack which contains only one product or unit.

Unit price Stückpreis

The price charged per unit of a product.

Unit pricing Einheitspreisbildung

A pricing method where each product`s price is expressed per unit of measure (eg gramme, pound, liter), as well as by total value. This enables consumers to compare price per quantity for competing products and for varying sizes of the same product.

Unit production Einzelfertigung

Also called individual, single unit, single-item or unique unit production.

The manufacturing/production of products one at a time.

According to Peter F. Drucker (US management consultant), there are three major systems of production: unit production, process production and mass production.

Unitary elasticity (demand) Elastizität = 1 (Nachfrage)

Also called unitary demand elasticity or unit elasticity.

A situation where in response to a given percentage change in the market price of a good, there is an equal (and opposite) percentage change in the quantity demanded.

Unitised cargo Einheitsladung

Also called unitized load.

Grouped cargo carried in pallets, containers, etc.
The main advantages are:
1. faster handling of fewer items making for quicker turnround of carrying vehicles, ships, aircraft; 2. reduction in labour costs (offset in some degree by heavy investment in equipment); 3. greater security; 4. less packing materials; 5. better freight rates.

Universal agent Generalvertreter

Also called free or general agent.

An agent who has (unlimited) authority to represent a business within a specified area.

Universal product code (UPC) UPC-Strichcode

A number (a barcoded identification number) used to identify a product (a barcoded product). The code is printed in a series of vertical parallel bars (the barcode) which can be read by an electronic scanner, or a barcode reader/scanner, for example at a supermarket checkout. Retailers use the UPC code to identify products and prices and to maintain a record of goods sold.

Universe Grundgesamtheit

Also called (parent) population.

In market research, the whole group or population of people or items within a defined boundary from which a sample is drawn, and which it has to represent, eg the total number of families with two or more cars.

Unladen weight Leergewicht

Also called deadweight (dwt), empty or unloaded weight.

The weight of a vehicle without its load/cargo.

Unlawful act unerlaubte, rechtswidrige Handlung

Also called illegal act, tortious act, wrongful act, tort or wrong.

An act against the law or an illegal act.

Unloading Entladen, Abladen, Löschen
Abstoßen von Wertpapieren
Niedrigpreisverkauf

The taking of goods off a vehicle, e.g. a ship. Also called discharge.

The selling of securities which do not seem attractive in order to avoid a loss due to a falling market.

The practice of putting on the market large quantities of a certain product at a low or concessionary price.

Slang for dumping, i.e. the selling of goods at lower prices than those charged on/in the domestic market.

Unmerchantable goods unverkäufliche Ware

Also called unsaleable goods or dead stock.

Goods that cannot be sold because they are in any way below the usual standard (e.g. of substandard quality) or not in their natural sound state.

Note: shares/stocks that are unsaleable are called sour stock.

Unpaid copy Freiexemplar

A copy of a newspaper or magazine distributed free of charge or at a lower price.

Unplanned economy freie (Markt)Wirtschaft

Also called uncontrolled economy, free or liberal market economy, or private enterprise.

A capitalist society based on private ownership. In this system, the use of resources is controlled by price movements. These movements are due to the actions of millions of people whose purchases and use of services affect supply and demand. As the consumer is very important, the producer tries to satisfy his needs; as there are numerous producers, there is keen competition so that the quality of the commodities is high and prices are reasonable.

Unprompted response spontane Antwort

In an interview, an answer to a question given by a respondent without any aids to memory.

Unsolds an den Lieferanten zurückgegebene (nicht verkaufte) Waren

Goods that are returnable to the supplier by a retailer as he could not sell them, e.g. newspapers.

Any goods returned to a supplier who has supplied them on sale or return.

Unsolicited goods unaufgefordert zugesandte, unbestellte Waren

Goods which have been sent to someone who has not requested or ordered them; the sender (the supplier) cannot demand payment for them.
If the recipient receives goods in this way and does not wish to keep them it is the sender's responsibility to retrieve them within a certain time; if he does not collect the goods, they become the receiver's/recipient's absolute property.

Unsolicited offer unverlangtes Angebot

Also called voluntary offer.

An offer sent to a customer who has not made an enquiry.
Unsolicited offers are often made to regular customers to inform them of a special opportunity (e.g. special offers), to customers who have not placed orders for a long time, or to potential customers to create new business.
Voluntary offers are often made in the form of sales letters.

Unsolicited testimonial unverlangte Empfehlung, Referenz

A letter of recommendation praising a product, person, or firm sent by a person without having been asked to write it.

Unsought goods verstecktes Produktpotential, nicht bewußte/bekannte Waren; latent vorhandene Waren

These are goods that the consumer does not know about or knows about but does not normally think of buying, e.g. new products. Consequently, the consumer must not only be informed about their availability but he must also be presented with the attributes and value of the goods through unique advertising and personal selling efforts.

Unstructured question unstrukturierte Frage

A question allowing the respondent a great deal of freedom and creativitiy in constructing answers.

Unstructured questionnaire unstrukturierter Fragebogen

Sometimes also called depth interview.

A questionnaire in which the interviewer knows the key points that should be investigated in depth, but is free to ask questions about the survey subject in a form and manner that seem appropriate to have a detailed discussion of a major factor without influencing the respondent by asking specific questions. Guided discussion is more important than question-and-answer.
But note: 1. the free-flowing verbal answers are difficult to analyse and interpret, 2. incorrect interpretations may occur, 3. an inexperienced interviewer may forget to ask important questions.

Unstuffing Entladen eines Containers

Unloading cargo from a container.

Update Aktualisierung

A new or current information added to something to make it up to date (update it).

Upgrading Verbesserung des Warensortiments

In retailing, the offering of a greater assortment/product range and superior goods to customers.

Upmarket Markt der gehobenen Preisklasse

A market dominated by higher prices and thus appealing to high-income consumers.

Upper class Oberschicht

One of the various social classes consisting of the very rich and the well-to-do.

Upper-lower class obere Unterklasse, Arbeiterklasse

Also called working class.

In the USA, one of the various social classes, comprising about 35% of the population. Its members have little education and mainly work in unskilled manual jobs. Marketers know that shoppers of this class have a high degree of brand loyalty and frequently buy impulse goods.

Upper-middle class obere Mittelklasse

In the USA, one of the various social classes, comprising approx. 12% of the population. Its members usually work in the professions, such as law, medicine or science. Marketers know that these people strongly support education and culture, value a comfortable, well-furnished house, and purchase quality items.

Upper-upper class obere Oberklasse

In the USA, about 1% of the population who have inherited their wealth.

Uppercase/upper case (UC) Großbuchstabe(n), Großschreibung

Also called uppercase letters or capital letters.

The capital letters of the alphabet, as compared to the small letter (lowercase, lower case, LC).

Upscale gehobene soziale Oberschicht

Persons at the upper end of a social or economic class, such as people with high incomes, high levels of education, or professional status.

Upscale consumers Verbraucher höherer Einkommensschichten

Also called upend consumers.

Consumers who dispose of an income which is above average. Therefore, they often buy upmarket products on class/upscale markets.

Upset price Mindestpreis (bei Versteigerungen)

Also called floor price or reserve price.

At an auction, the lowest price a seller is prepared to accept for an article being auctioned. It is the beginning price asked prior to public bidding.

Upstick/up stick Kursanstieg

A minor rise in price or value, e.g. a slight upstick in the Deutschmark or an increase in a stock quotation.

Upswing Konjunkturaufschwung, Aufschwung (scharfer) Anstieg (z.B. Preis, Kurs)

One of the phases in a typical business cycle characterized by an upturn/recovery in the level of economic activity and economic growth.
A recovery from a slump may arise for a variety of reasons but once under way, business confidence will grow and generate aggregate demand, which may come about autonomously or be induced by expansionary fiscal policy and monetary policy. Investment, production, employment, profit, incomes and consumers' spending will all begin to rise; but prices begin to rise slowly, too. An upswing can lead to a boom. Also called recovery, upturn, upward phase, cyclical or economic upswing.

Movement of prices, quantities, etc. that has changed to an upward direction, e.g. there was an upswing in the price of houses or shares, in the output of cars or in demand. Also called upturn.

Uptrend Aufwärtstrend, Aufwärtsentwicklung

Also called upswing ur upturn.

Improvement of some general kind, e.g. in sales, economic activity, etc.

Upward direction in market prices, the price of securities, commodities, etc.

Upward mobility vertikale Mobilität

Also called vertical mobility.

Movement from one socioeconomic class to a higher one, eg with regard to income, education, material goods, lifestyle, etc.

Urgency close Verkaufsgeprächsabschluß mit Kaufaufforderung

In the selling process, a salesperson`s technique of ending a sales talk or presentation by suggesting a reason for ordering now or soon, eg by stating that prices will be going up shortly.

Usage of the market Handelsbrauch

Also called usage of the trade; business, commercial or trade usage; custom of the trade; customary practice; mercantile custom.

Accepted manner of commercial dealing.

Usage pull verkaufsfördernde Wirkung der Werbung

The ability of advertising to persuade people who see or hear the advertisements to buy the advertised product or service.

Usage rate Verbrauchsrate

A measure of the quantity of a product sold or consumed within a specific time period.

Usage rate segmentation Segmentierung nach der Verbrauchsrate

The division of a market into segments according to the amount of the product bought or consumed, eg by light users, medium users, or heavy users. Marketers often focus on heavy users because they account for a sizable portion of all product sales.

Usage segmentation Segmentierung nach Gebrauchsnutzen

The division of a market into segments according to the type of use customers will make of the product.

User Anwender, Benutzer

Persons who actually use the purchased product.

User charge Benutzungsgebühr

Also called user fee, occupancy or usage charge.

A specific sum that users (or consumers) of a service have to pay to receive that service.

User customer Weiterverwender

The user customer is one who uses a given product to make other products for either consumer or industrial product companies.

User friendliness Benutzerfreundlichkeit

A state of being easy to maintain, operate or use.

User's guide Benutzerhandbuch

Also called user's manual, operator's manual, set of instructions.

A book showing someone how to use something.

Utilitarianism Utilitarismus

A moral philosophy concerned with maximising the greatest good for the greatest number of people. Thus, utilitarians select actions and options promising the best results for all people affected.

Utilities Versorgungsbetriebe

Also called public utilities.

These are industries which provide the most basic services such as water, gas, electricity, etc.

Utility Nutzen
Nützlichkeit

The amount of satisfaction derived by a person from buying goods or services. As people have individual tastes and preferences, utility varies from person to person. Utility is subjective in that it denotes someone's personal estimate of satisfaction; therefore utility as such cannot be measured in absolute terms, but for practical purposes the utility of a good to a particular consumer can be gauged by how much he is prepared to pay for it as compared with other things (but note: a rich man may be prepared to pay much more than a poor one for a certain article - but it does not follow that he will get greater satisfaction from it). Furthermore it will vary for the same person at different times, i.e. utility is not constant. Also called satisfaction, pleasure, or benefit.

Note: Utility is not always synonymous with benefit. To say that a thing has utility for a consumer does not necessarily mean that he will derive benefit from it - there are many things which satisfy consumers' desires and yet undoubtedly do harm them, e.g. drugs.

Usefulness, ie the state of being practical, helpful or advantageours, eg for some specific purpose.

Utility advertising — Produktnutzenwerbung, Werbung für Versorgungsgüter

Advertising which particularly points out the utility of a product or service.

Advertising for supply goods, such as electricity or gas.

Utility function — Nutzenfunktion

A preference function stating on what a consumer's satisfaction/utility is dependent. Generally, it is expressed as follows: U = f (x, y, ...). This shows a consumer`s utility as a function of the quantities of goods X, Y, ... that he/she consumes.

Utility goods — Gebrauchsgüter

Basic goods that are needed for everyday life.

Utility maximization — Nutzenmaximierung

An economic theory that seeks to explain consumer behaviour; it is the aim of the consumer to purchase those goods that enable him to achieve his highest possible level of satisfaction/utility among all the goods available to him and which he can afford.

The economic problem of consumers is that they have only a limited amount of income to spend and therefore cannot buy all the goods they would like to have. Therefore, demand theory assumes that the goal of the consumers is to select the combination of goods in line with their preferences that will maximize total utility or satisfaction.

Total utility is maximized when the ratios of marginal utility to price for all goods consumed are equal, e.g. for two goods X and Y, total utility is maximized when:

$$\frac{\text{marginal utility of X}}{\text{price of X}} = \frac{\text{marginal utility of Y}}{\text{price of Y}}$$

In other words, utility maximization is a state of consumer equilibrium. Given a fixed/limited income and fixed prices, we spend our money (e.g. dollars) in order to realize an equilibrium of marginal utility per monetary unit (per dollar) for all items purchased.

V

Vacation marketing Urlaubsmarketing

Also called holiday marketing.

Marketing activities carried out by travel agents, airlines, hotels, vacation resorts, governmental agencies, etc in order to attract vacationers/holidayers to cities, entire nations, resorts, sights, spas, states, etc special events, etc.

Vacillating customer unentschlossener Kunde

A customer unwilling, or unable, to determine own needs when presented with positive proposition (offer).

Valid contract rechtsgültiger, rechtsverbindlicher Vertrag

Also called binding contract.

An agreement signed by both contracting parties that meets the requirements of law and is therefore in force.

Valid objection berechtigter Einwand

A truthful objection raised by a potential purchaser to a good or service offered by a salesperson.

Validated inflation in Kauf genommene Inflation

Inflation which is allowed to persist because the money supply is expanded at the same rate as inflation.

Valorization behördliche Preisfestsetzung

The placing of a value on an article or service by government regulation at a level that differs from market price.

Valuable cargo wertvolle Ladung

Cargo of high value, e.g. diamonds, gold, platinum, pearls, rubies, etc.

Valuables Wertgegenstände

Also called objects of value.

Any property which has monetary value and which could be sold for a lot of money or pledged as a security, e.g. gold or precious metals, securities, etc.

Value (val) Wert, Tauschwert
Geldwert, Vermögenswert
Gebrauchswert
Nutzen
(angemessener) Marktpreis
Kaufkraft

The power an article or commodity has to exchange itself for other goods and services, either in units of money or in quantities of goods. Also called value in exchange (a term used by Adam Smith).

What an article or commodity is worth. This may be what something costs, what it would cost to replace it, what it would bring on the open market, etc. Also called worth.

The quality of being useful, i.e. the amount of satisfaction that is obtained from an article, commodity or service. Here value is considered only in relation to its usefulness to man, not to its price. Also called usefulness or value in use (a term used by Adam Smith).

The quality of satisfying man's wants. Also called satisfaction or utility.

The price at which an asset passes from a willing seller to a willing buyer (frequently the basis for tax assessments). Also called fair market value or actual cash value.

The value of money, i.e. what money will buy at any given time. Also called buying power, purchasing power or spending power.

Value added Wertschöpfung

Also called added value, increase in value, real net output or value creation.

The difference between the selling price of a company's product and the cost of the bought-in components, i.e. the value which a company adds to a bought-in product by its own efforts (ie the manufacturing and administrative costs, interest payments and profit).

Value added marketing Werterhöhung durch Marketing

Also called value marketing.

A marketing strategy emphasing that a company should invest most of its resources into value-building investments. In relation to pricing this means that the modern customer does not only examine closely what the money buys, but what are the best buys from the viewpoint of value for money. Thus, value marketing delivers a combination of fair pricing, quality and good service.

Note: many promotional activites raise sales in the short run but add little to value.

Value added tax (VAT) Mehrwertsteuer (MwSt)

An indirect tax levied by a government at specified rates on the value added to a good or service from primary production to final consumption.

The tax is based on the difference between the sale price of the goods and services (outputs) and the cost of bought-in inputs. At each point of exchange the tax is passed on in the form of higher prices. The final amount of tax is added on to the selling/sale price of the good or service and is passed on to the buyer. That means, each registered trader sells his outputs at a price increased by the appropriate percentage of VAT. He is then liable to the fiscal authorities for the payment of the tax obtained from his customers, but he is allowed to deduct any VAT that he has had to pay to his suppliers (i.e., his input tax) from his overall VAT liability, which, in certain cases, may result in a refund. His customers do likewise, and so on down to the final consumer. Thus, if a manufacturer buys raw materials, he will pay VAT at this stage; when he, in turn, sells to a wholesaler, VAT is levied on the difference between the sums paid for the inputs (his purchases) and the outputs (his sales). Businesses do not bear any VAT included in the invoices for the inputs which they buy from suppliers, but act as collecting agencies. Being at the final point in the chain of exchange, VAT is ultimately borne by the final consumer, who is unable to shift the tax.

Some goods and services are zero-rated, i.e. they are not subject to VAT (e.g. exports), some are exempt from VAT (i.e. VAT is not charged on the sales; examples are banking and insurance, education and health services), and some are subject to special rates. Exporters do not charge VAT to their customers; imports on the other hand, are subject to import VAT (plus customs duties, if any).

VAT is levied in all EU member states, in Japan and in many other countries but not in the USA, which have sales tax (ST). Australia, New Zealand and Canada have GST (goods and services tax).

Value adding reseller (VAR) Wiederverkäufer, der den Produktwert erhöht

Resellers, usually retailers, who modify products or provide additional services to offer tailor-made solutions to customers.

Value analysis (VA) Wertanalyse

Also called value engineering.

A formal approach to identifying and eliminating costs of products or services that are not necessary. Furthermore, one is looking at alternative materials and methods to get the best product at the lowest cost.

Value and price Wert und Preis

Value and price are not equivalent terms.
Price reflects value, not so-called "intrinsic value", but value in exchange. Therefore, value may be considered as the power of a commodity or service to attract other commodities or services in exchange for itself. Price is the market value of the commodity or service, i.e. value translated into monetary terms.

Value based pricing Wertschöpfungskalkulation

Also called value pricing.

A price setting process based on the value the product provides to the potential customer. This pricing strategy is used by a firm which is customer-driven. Thus, when setting the price, it starts with the customer after which the competition is considered. But, as customers evaluate the value of a product (not just its price) relative to the value of competing products, value pricing must also determine the value to customers of competing products. Therefore, the product`s price is set at a level that seems to be a good price to the customer when compared with the prices of alternative products.

Note: value pricing offers the right combination of quality and good service at a fair price.

Value in exchange Tauschwert

The amount of money or goods actually paid for a product or service.

Value in use Gebrauchswert

Also called service, user or utility value, or practical value.

The usefulness of an item to its user as opposed to its market value. The opposite of value in exchange.

Value paradox Wertparadoxon

Also called paradox of value.

The value paradox is the apparently illogical assignment of value to an article or commodity. For example, water is cheap though it is indispensable while diamonds, which are "useless", are expensive. Water has a higher value in use (user value) than diamonds and diamonds have a greater value in exchange than water. An article may be valuable in terms of exchange, but totally worthless in terms of use or vice versa.

Valued customer geschätzter Kunde

A customer whose interests and requirements must be given priority.

Values Wertvorstellungen

Shared principles and standards of what is acceptable and unacceptable, good and bad, desirable and undesirable, right and wrong, etc.

Values and lifestyles (VALS) Zielgruppeneinteilung nach Wertvorstellungen und Lebensstil

A classification system for segmenting consumers into groups on the basis of their values, attitudes, demographic characteristics and lifestyles.

Vampire video Werbung, die so gut ist, daß sie die Aufmerksamkeit vom Produkt auf sich lenkt

An advertisement that is so overwhelmingly eye-catching that it draws attention away from the product and focuses it on itself. The reader or viewer is left not with an impression of the product, but with an impression of the performance surrounding it.

Probably originated from an advertising campaign for the apéritif "Fernet Branca" involving a vampire scene.

Vaporware erfolgversprechendes, aber nicht auf den Markt gebrachtes Produkt

A promising product that is announced and promoted while it is still in development but fails to come to market.

Variable Variable, Veränderliche

A number that may take different values in different situations and that may be dependent or independent. For example, the quantity of a commodity demanded will change according to its price.

Variable cost(s) variable, veränderliche Kosten

Also called variable charges or variable expenses.

Costs which vary in total in direct proportion to the volume of production of a business within a relevant range. The main ones are raw materials, wages and power.

There are four different types:
1. proportional costs (variable costs change in step with volume of output; variable cost per unit is constant);
2. degressive costs (e.g. output increases by 50 %, variable costs increase by 30 %);
3. progressive costs (e.g. output increases by 40 %, variable costs increase by 60 %);
4. regressive costs (variable costs fall in absolute terms when output increases).

Variable markup variabler Gewinnaufschlag

A cost-based pricing strategy where separate product or service categories receive different percentage markups.

Variable pricing freie, variable Preisgestaltung

Also called flexible pricing or variable price formation.

A marketing strategy that allows a different price to be charged to different customers or at different times.

Reasons for variable pricing are: 1. the granting of cash, quantity or trade discounts; 2. "off-peak" or "out-of-season" pricing.

Variable pricing is most commonly applied to products (or services) with known variable time demands. It may be used to take advantage of extra profit at peak periods or to reduce production and overhead costs by stimulating demand in non-peak periods.

Variance | Abweichung
Streuung, Varianz

In general, the state of one thing being different from another.
In cost accounting, the difference between a standard/predicted cost and the comparable actual cost incurred. In budgeting, the difference between budgeted and actual results, or between planned costs/revenues and actual costs/revenues, etc.

In statistics, a measure of dispersion of probability distribution. Also called dispersion.

Variety chain store | Niedrigpreis-Kaufhaus-Kette

This type of store lies between the multiple store and the department store. The range of goods stocked is limited but there are many departments. By buying in very large quantities, prices can be low and the quality of the products can often be controlled. Examples are Marks and Spencer (GB) and F.W. Woolworth Ltd. (USA).

Variety reduction | Sortiments-, Typenbeschränkung

Also called product mix reduction, streamlining of the range of goods or reduction of types.

The reduction or elimination of certain products, product ranges, components or materials which are uneconomic or whose elimination will produce cost benefits.

Variety store | Kleinpreisgeschäft,
Niedrigpreisgeschäft

A retail store that sells a wide range/assortment of low-priced, popular merchandise. The services given are restricted; the selling staff merely take payment and wrap the articles (in the USA).

Variety-seeking buyer | abwechslungsuchender Käufer

A purchaser characterized by low involvement, little brand loyalty and regular brand switching occurring in order to experience diversity in consumption over time and not because of dissatisfaction.

VAT included | einschließlich Mehrwertsteuer/
Umsatzsteuer

A price quotation including value-added-tax (VAT).

Veblen effect Vebleneffekt

Also called conspicious consumption effect.

A theory of consumption created by the American economist Thorstein B. Veblen (1857 1929). The Veblen effect suggests that the quantity demanded of a particular commodity varies directly with a change in price - as price increases, demand increases (an abnormal market behaviour) because consumers practice conspicious/ostentatious consumption or because they believe that a higher price is evidence of better quality (whereas a falling price is considered as a deterioration in quality).
Note: one of the laws of supply and demand states that as price increases, the quantity demanded falls.

Vehicle Fahrzeug, Beförderungsmittel
Ausdrucksmittel, Medium
Werbeträger

Something which can be used as a means of transport for persons or goods, especially one with wheels, e.g. a bus, car, cart, lorry/ truck, etc.

Somebody or something through which feelings, thoughts etc. can be expressed.

Any medium, eg a newspaper, poster, radio or TV programme, used for advertising. Also called advertising medium or vehicle, media vehicle, or medium.

Vendee Erwerber, Käufer

Also called buyer or purchaser.

Someone to whom something is sold. A term especially used in law.

Vending machine Verkaufsautomat

Also called automatic vending machine, vendor, robot salesman or dispensing machine.

A self-service outlet, open day and night, making goods available when a coin or note is inserted. Vending machines are used to sell drinks, food, refreshments, tickets, etc. and help to increase a retailer's sales and save time in handling goods and receiving payment. The machines contain only a small quantity of goods, and therefore require frequent restocking.
Note: a vending machine operation usually needs about a 55 percent markup.

Vendor/vender Verkäufer
Straßenverkäufer
Lieferer, Lieferant
Verkaufsautomat

Someone who sells something; i.e. a seller of goods or services. A term especially used in law. Also called seller.

In street marketing, a retailer of merchandise, especially one without an established place of business. Also called sidewalk vendor or street vendor.

An individual or company which supplies goods to a customer. Also called seller or supplier.

A vending machine.

Vendor rating Lieferantenbeurteilung

Also called vendor appraisal or supplier evaluation.

A customer ranking of a supplier's performance and reliability in meeting delivery promises, quality standards, etc.

Vendor's lien Zurückbehaltungsrecht des Verkäufers

Also called vendor's retaining lien or vendor's right of retention.

A seller's legal right to retain (or reclaim) possession of property sold to a buyer if the buyer falls behind in payments.

Venture risikoreiches Unternehmen

A business, or a business deal, involving potential risk, which is accepted in the expectation of making a (greater) profit.

Venture team Innovationsteam, Projektgruppe

Also called project team.

An independent group of key people from various departments of a company formed to take responsibility for specific new product developments that may be aimed at new markets. The team is responsible for all aspects of a product`s development, such as research and development, production, finance, marketing, etc, and its members stay with the project until it is abandoned or the new product is introduced to the market.

Venue Schauplatz, Austragungsort

A place where a public event or meeting, e.g. sports meeting, happens.

Verbal contract mündliche(r) Vereinbarung, Vertrag

Also called oral agreement or contract, or viva voce agreement.

An arrangement agreed by word of mouth (orally or verbally) and not set up on paper/in writing.

Note: to be able to show proof, a contract should be in writing, but a verbal contract, even on the telephone and not necessarily confirmed in writing, may be held to be a legal contract on the grounds that there was implicit intent to enter into a contract.

Verification Bestätigung, Beglaubigung (Nach)Prüfung

Evidence/proof of the accuracy or truth of a statement. Also called attestation, authentication, certification or legalization.

The act of verifying or being verified.

Vertical cooperative advertising Gemeinschaftswerbung eines Herstellers mit seinen Händlerkunden

Advertising in which the manufacturer and his retailers and/or wholesalers share the advertising costs.

Vertical discount Malrabatt für häufige Werbung in einer festgelegten Zeitperiode

Also called repeat (advertising) rebate.

In advertising, a reduced rate for the purchase of several radio or television time slots to be broadcast at intervals within a set time period, eg a week.

Vertical half page hochformatige Halbseite

A magazine advertisement occupying the vertical half of a page.

Vertical integration vertikale Verflechtung

Also called vertical merging.

An amalgamation/merger made by two or more firms carrying out different stages of production within the same industry.
One firm controls successive stages of production, which might otherwise be independent, in an industry. The control of successive stages of production distinguishes it from diversification, in which the firm controls other apparently unrelated firms, i.e. the inputs of one are not the outputs of another.
If the dominant firm is gaining control of one of its raw material suppliers or one of the firms that supply its components, we call it backward integration/vertical backwards (it occurs when it is essential to secure certainty of supply in periods of scarcity or high demand).

Forward integration/vertical forwards occurs if the dominant firm is gaining control of one of the firms which buys its products. Forward integration tends to occur when demand is not certain and the producer wishes to obtain guaranteed market outlets.

Vertical integration may be advantageous because it enables the dominant firm to reduce its production and distribution costs by linking together successive activities.

Vertical market vertikaler Markt

Markets where products and services are sold to companies who are all within the same industry.

Vertical marketing vertikales Marketing

The marketing activities of opening up new markets rather than expanding existing ones.

Vertical marketing system (VMS) vertikales Marketingsystem

An organised, structured and unified marketing channel in which producer and intermediaries work closely together, and all distribution activities are coordinated in order to facilitate the smooth flow of goods and services from producer to end user and to achieve efficient, low cost distribution.

Vertical price fixing vertikale Preisbindung, Preisbindung zweiter Hand

Also called resale price maintenance (RPM).

A practice, usually illegal, in which the manufacturer fixes the price at which a retailer may resell the product. Today, this practice has been replaced by that of recommended prices.

Vertical publication Branchenpublikation

A publication edited for people working in specific professions or industries, or belonging to special interest groups or lifestyles.

Viability wirtschaftliche Existenzfähigkeit

Also called economic viability.

The ability of a person or country to support itself, or of a company or product to survive in a market (and generate profit).

Video conference Videokonferenz

A teleconference conducted via television equipment. Persons in different locations are able to confer with one another, each remaining in his or her own location.

Video exhibition Video-Ausstellung

A video tape presentation prerecorded in sound and vision and distributed to selected posts for display. These tapes take the place of live product demonstrations, enabling the exhibitor`s products to be explained, demonstrated, and sold more economically.

Video phone Bildschirmtelefon

Also called video telephone or viewphone.

A facility where a small television screen allows speakers to see each other during a telephone conversation.

Videotex Bildschirmtext, Videotext

Also called broadcast teletext or videotext, teletext or viewdata (in GB).

A service by which information stored in page form on a computer is broadcast or can be accessed by telephone and is shown on the screen of a TV in the home. Companies use this service to advertise their products and/or to enable potential buyers to place orders and pay for them by transmitting a credit card number or bank account number.

Viewer Fernsehzuschauer
Zuschauer

A person watching/viewing a television programme (the TV broadcast). Also called televiewer.

A person who views. Also called spectator/spectatress, looker-on or onlooker; in the plural also audience.

Viewer rating (Fernseh)Einschaltquote

Also called viewing rate, audience rating or share of audience.

The number of individuals (the viewing audience) watching a commercial or other television broadcast.

Viewers per household (VPH) Fernsehzuschauer pro Haushalt

The average number of persons watching television in a household, often classified by age and sex.

Visit brief Kunden-Info, Instruktionen vor einem Kundenbesuch

A short account of the chief objectives of a customer visit, together with pertinent data based upon the customer's record. It may include details of the particular market area covered by the customer and information about the customer's special needs, and even his personality, his particular problems of finance, transport, warehousing or marketing may be analysed.
Before making the actual call the executive reads through the visit brief and recalls the relevant points. He then enters the interview knowledgeable about the customer's needs and makes a more impressive impact on him.

Visiting card Visitenkarte

Also called business card or calling card.

A card on which is printed a person's name, address and telephone number, his/her position and the company he/she represents.

Visual Verbildlichung einer Werbeidee
Layoutskizze

A drawing or illustration of an advertisement used as one of the first rough layouts.

The designer responsible for producing visual ideas is called a visualizer.

Visual aids visuelle Verkaufshilfen

Any form of visual material, such as posters, photographs, videotapes, etc. used in sales promotion.

Visual display unit (VDU) Bildschirmgerät, Sichtgerät

Also called visual device or terminal.

A unit (similar to a TV screen) which enables characters and graphics to be displayed on a screen.

Visualizer Visualiser, Ideengestalter

A person responsible for producing visual ideas for advertisements.

Voiceover/voice over (VO, v/o) Sprechertext, Off-Kommentar (Werbetext des nicht sichtbaren Erzählers in TV-/Kinowerbung)

Also called off-screen narration.

In a TV or cinema commercial, the commentary spoken by a narrator, and not by any of the characters appearing on the screen, who is heard but not seen.

Volatile demand schwankende Nachfrage

A demand for goods and services frequently fluctuating for various reasons.

Volume (vol) Umsatzvolumen
Volumen
Buch, Band

The number of units (the total amount or quantity) traded during a specified time period. Often also called turnover or volume of business.

The amount of space occupied by something, usually shown in cubic metres, etc.

A bound book, especially one of a series of several such books, e.g. one of a three-volume book.

Volume discrepancy Mengenabweichung

Any difference between two quantities. For example, the difference between the amounts produced by suppliers and the amounts demanded by consumers.

Volume of business Umsatzvolumen

Also called turnover.

The number of items, ie the total quantity, sold during a specific time period.

Volume production Massenproduktion

Also called mass production.

The production of goods in large quantities, especially by machinery.

Volume segmentation Segmentierung aufgrund des Absatzvolumens, Volumensegmentierung

The division of a market into segments according to the volume consumed by individuals or groups of individuals in order to develop differentiated marketing strategies for heavy and light users.

Voluntary chain freiwillige Handelskette, Zusammenschluß von Einzelhändlern

Also called voluntary group.

An association of independent small retailers who undertake to buy all their supplies from "the parent wholesaler", whilst retaining individual ownership and control.

Due to their collective purchasing power they obtain bigger discounts so that they can compete on more equal terms with the multiple shops. Furthermore, the "parent wholesaler" supplies them with display material, advertising material under a group name, special offers, advice on merchandising, layout, equipment, stock ranges, accounting, etc.
Voluntary chains came into existence some time after the end of World War II.

Voluntary offer unverlangtes Angebot

Also called unsolicited offer.

An offer on the seller's own initiative in an effort to create new business. Voluntary offers are a form of sales letters and therefore have the same objective and often take the form of offers of free samples, goods on approval, special discounts and so on. The person making an offer should win the reader's interest at once, otherwise his letter will quickly disappear into the waste-paper bin.
Note: offers may also be submitted in reply to an inquiry (solicited offer).

Voluntary self-control freiwillige Selbstkontrolle

In advertising, a system of self-control practiced by advertisers and advertising agencies to ensure that advertisements and commercials conform to a defined code of practice.

Voucher (vou) Gutschein
Quittung, Rechnungsbeleg, Bon
Eintrittskarte

A paper which is given instead of money and which may later be used to claim goods or services, e.g. a gift voucher/token or luncheon voucher. Also called coupon or credit note.

A document which shows that a certain amount of money was paid. Also called acquittance or receipt.

An admission ticket. Also called entrance card or ticket.

W

Wage inflation Lohn(kosten)inflation

Also called wage-cost inflation or wage-push inflation.

An inflationary situation in which increasing wages are not offset by increasing productivity so that costs rise which will lead to higher prices for goods produced.

To be sure, a continued rise in money wages is invariably involved in every process of inflation, since if money wages did not rise, the rise in the price level could not continue beyond a certain point, whatever the nature of the forces underlying the price rise. But a distinction can be drawn between a situation in which the rise in wages reflects the forces making for the rise in prices and one in which the rise in wages causes the rise in price to take place, i.e. in which the rise in wages is primary and the rise in prices secondary.

Wage-price spiral Lohn-Preis-Spirale

Also called inflation or inflationary spiral.

In a period of inflation, the granting of higher wages is followed by the manufacturers increasing their prices for their products which in turn leads to increases in the cost of living. Increased prices through increases in wages induce further increases in prices and then lead to further demands for increased wages, and so on.

Wage-push inflation Lohninflation, Lohndruckinflation

Also called wagc inflation, wage-induced inflation or wage cost inflation.

An inflationary situation in which increasing wages are not offset by increasing productivity so that costs rise which will lead to higher prices for goods produced.

Waiting line theory Warteschlangentheorie, Bedienungstheorie

Also called queueing theory.

In operations research (OR), a quantitative technique for balancing services available with services required. It evaluates the ability of service facilities to handle capacity and load at different times during the day.

Its main task is to calculate the costs of having people, or materials or whatever, wait in a waiting line/queue against the cost of service to eliminate that waiting line. Other objects are to identify, illustrate, analyse, understand and influence the characteristics of waiting lines/queues, whether of people (eg at bank tellers or in supermarkets), materials, work-in-progress, etc.
Furthermore, it wants to find the best way of planning the sequence of events so that the length of waiting line can be minimised (eg by decreasing the average service time) and bottlenecks can be avoided.

Note: 1. The fact that there are periods when there are no waiting lines at all when service facilities are idle, must be taken into account. 2. Thus, one has to optimise service time, waiting time and the cost of resources, eg for extra teller positions or service counters in a supermarket or bank.

Walk-in — Laufkunde
ungeladener Besucher

A customer who walks into a shop from the street without an appointment. Also called chance or street customer.

A person who visits another person without an appointment.

Wall banner — Wand-Spannplakat

An advertising banner suspended from a wall.

Wall chart — Wandschaubild, Wandüber-
sicht(stafel)

A chart fixed to a wall in order to convey information, e.g. the location of staff, sales figures, visually at glance.

Want ad — Kleinanzeige, Rubrikanzeige
Stellenanzeige

A brief advertisement in a newspaper, magazine, or the like, subdivided according to the types of products or services offered or sought. Typical want ads are offers of or requests for jobs, apartments, houses, cars, etc. Also called classified or small ad(vertisement).

A job advertisement. Also called employment ad.

Want creating advertising bedürfnisweckende Werbung

Advertising carried out to create new wants.

Want creation Maßnahmen zur Ankurbelung der Nachfrage

The stimulation of demand by monetary (eg lowering interest rates) and fiscal (eg cutting taxes) policy, e.g. to keep up the level of employment or to reduce the unemployment rate/jobless rate.

The stimulation of demand through mass advertising media in order to increase a company's or industry's sales. Latent consumer needs are converted into conscious wants.

Wants Bedürfnisse

Also called wants and needs or tastes and preferences.

The desire for goods and services to satisfy a human need or wish. All living things have wants, e.g. air, food, water.
The wants of man in modern society are many, varied and complex, e.g. clothing, housing, cars, television, education, medical care, etc. The attempt to satisfy wants forms the basis of all economic activity.
Wants are expressed in the marketplace not by need or desire but by willingness and ability to purchase the good or service in demand. That means, only those wants are of economic importance that are backed up by the purchasing power necessary to satisfy them, and it is these wants that are the basis of effective demand.
Wants vary from person to person, from community to community, from one period to another and from generation to generation.

Warehouse (whse) Lagerhaus, Lager
Warenlager

A building or room in which companies can store their wares (goods, commodities, merchandise), usually in large quantities, before they deliver them to their customers, in conditions that protect them from the weather and from thieves. Also called stockroom, storeroom or storehouse.

A place of deposit for goods until they can be moved into a shop for sale. Also called depot, magazine, stockroom or storeroom.

Warehouse capacity Lagerkapazität

The space available in a warehouse/storeroom to warehouse/store goods.

Warehousing Lagerhaltung

Also called stockkeeping.

The storing of goods in a warehouse for the following reasons:
1. most goods are produced ahead of demand, and warehouses are required for storage during the interim period;
2. many commodities are seasonal and therefore they are warehoused until required throughout the year;
3. to avoid large fluctuations in prices; without large buffer stocks in warehouses, a sudden increase in demand would lead to scarcity and a rapid price increase.

Warrant Lagerschein
Garantie

A receipt that describes goods held in a warehouse. Also called warehouse certificate or warehouse receipt.

A guarantee/guaranty, ie a promise that something will be done or will happen, eg a promise by a firm to repair or change a product that develops a fault within a particular time period. Also called warranty.

Warranty Garantie(erklärung), Gewährleistung

Also called guarantee/guaranty.

A warranty in ordinary commercial contracts is a guarantee, i.e. the seller (the warrantor or guarantor) assumes responsibility for the quality or performance of the goods sold. That means, the seller guarantees that the goods purchased will perform as promised, or a refund will be given, an exchange made, or a repair done at no charge.

For example, the warranty that a new car is in roadworthy condition means that any defect will be remedied by the seller, but the contract of sale still stands. The buyer has the right to sue for damages but cannot return his car and demand his money back.

Note: warranties are effective for a limited time period and usually include limitations that exclude defects not caused by the manufacturer.

Wastage Verschleiß
Vergeudung, Verschwendung

The deterioration of machinery or property. Also called wear (and tear).

The act of wasting or being wasted. Also called waste.

Waste Materialabfall
Abfall
Verschwendung, Vergeudung

Material lost in a manufacturing process.

Material already used and no longer needed.

The act of wasting or being wasted. Also called wastage.

Waste circulation Fehlstreuung, Streuverluste

Also called circulation waste.

The readers, viewers or listeners in an advertiser's audience who are not potential customers for the product or service being advertised.

Advertising for a product or service in an advertising medium in an area where the product or service is not offered.

Wasting asset Wirtschaftsgut mit begrenzter Nutzungsdauer

Also called limited-life asset.

A fixed asset which gradually depreciates.

Watermark Wasserzeichen

A mark made on some papers by manufacturers to distinguish their papers from those of other manufacturers.

A mark in banknotes.

Waybill (WB, W/B)) Frachtbrief
Luftfrachtbrief
Versandanzeige
Passagierliste

A paper which accompanies goods on transport. Also called consignment note.

An air consignment note. Also called air waybill (AWB).

An advice of despatch.

A list of passengers.

Weak demand schwache Nachfrage

A market situation where the demand for products and services is lagging or sluggish.

Weak market schwacher Markt

A market which his constantly in danger of collapsing, e.g. due to an unstable government and/or a weak economy. Prices tend to fall.

Wealth Wohlstand
Vermögen
Reichtum

The usual meaning of wealth (Old High German, OHG, welida = riches) is prosperity.

Articles which have value, are limited in quantity (i.e. scarce) and which can be exchanged for a money price.

The stock of net assets owned by someone.

A large amount of money.

Wealth may be classified as follows: 1. private (e.g. one's house), 2. social (e.g. public buildings), 3. personal (one's skills), 4. material (e.g. machinery) wealth.

The state of being rich, of having a great store of valuable possessions. Also called affluence or riches.

Wealth effect Realkasseneffekt, Pigou-Effekt

Also called real balance effect or Pigou effect (after the English economist A.C. Pigou, 1877 - 1959).

The process by which falling interest rates and slowing inflation produce a rise in spending. Simply expressed, the wealth effect states that if you feel wealthier, you will spend more money and thereby increase consumption.

Weekend special Wochenend(sonder)angebot

In retailing, merchandise sold at a special price from Thursday through Saturday.

Weekly Wochenblatt

A newspaper or magazine which is published once a week.

Weight charge Frachtkosten nach Gewicht, Gewichtsfracht

The charge for carriage of goods based on their weight.

Weight list Gewichtsliste

A list stating the total or partial weight of a shipment or merchandise.

Weight note Gewichtsbescheinigung

A commercial document declaring the weight of the goods of a consignment.

Weight/measurement (W/M) freight Fracht nach Gewicht/Maß

A freight rate that is quoted on a basis of weight or measurement, ie the rate quoted by the forwarder will be applied either per kg/ton (weight) or on cubic metres (measurement), whichever will produce the greater revenue.

Weighted index Bewertungsindex

An index where some important items are given more value than less important ones.

Welfare Wohlergehen
Sozialhilfe

The well-being of people. It includes material wealth, health, happiness, wellbeing and many other qualities which are virtually impossible to measure.

Financial or other assistance given to those in poverty or need. Also called public relief.

Wet goods Flüssigware

Goods sold in liquid form.

White goods weiße Ware

Household appliances such as cookers, dishwasher, freezers, refrigerators, washing machines, etc, that are often finished in white; today also in colour.

Household goods, as bed sheets and towels, formerly white but today ususally coloured.

No-name products.

Whiteboard Whiteboard, weiße Tafel

A white board on a wall which can be written on using coloured pens.

Wholesale price Großhandelspreis

The price a wholesaler charges when he sells products to a retailer.

Wholesale price index (WPI) Index der Großhandelspreise

The monthly measure of wholesale prices.

Wholesaler Großhändler

Also called wholesale dealer.

A person owning a warehouse and who acts as the middleman/intermediary between manufacturer/producer and retailer. The wholesaler is one link in the chain of distribution.

His main functions are:
1. to economise in distribution, that is, to buy in large quantities from the producer and to sell in smaller quantities to retailers (breaking bulk);
2. to warehouse goods, i.e. to hold stocks to meet sudden increases in demand;
3. to give credit to retailers although paying his own suppliers promptly;
4. to grade and pack some goods;
5. to pass information between producer and retailers;
6. to help to develop new markets;
7. to brand and advertise goods;
8. to sell goods from small producers under his own brand name;
9. to provide storage facilities for both manufacturer and retailer so that their costs of warehousing are reduced, etc.

Wholesalers must know where to buy their commodities in the quantities and in the quality they want, and they must also know when to buy them so as to be able to obtain them at the lowest prices.

Wholesalers may be broadly divided as follows:
1. traditional wholesalers, i.e. those who operate solely as wholesalers; they can be subdivided into general wholesalers (they stock a wide variety of goods) and specialist wholesalers (they limit their activities to particular types of goods);
2. wholesalers who for a period own and warehouse goods, but carry out no process in connection with them;
3. wholesalers who own and store goods and prepare them for sale;
4. wholesalers who combine wholesaling with manufacturing and/or retailing.

Today, the function of the wholesaler is often undertaken by manufacturers who sell directly to consumers and by retailers who buy directly from manufacturers; therefore, wholesaling as a separate activity is declining.

Wholesaling Großhandel

Also called wholesale business or wholesale trade.

Wholesale trade includes establishments or places of business primarily engaged in selling merchandise to retailers, to industrial, commercial, institutional, or professional business users or to other wholesalers. Any sale made to anyone except the final consumer is a wholesale transaction.

Width of product mix Produktmixbreite

The number of product lines a firm offers.

Width of product range (Produkt)Palettenbreite

The number of different products a firm offers.

Wildcat Wildkatze

Also called problem child or question mark.

A product showing rapid growth but poor profit margins. It has a low market share in a high-growth market, which means it incurs a lot of marketing effort and thus needs a great deal of cash.
Note: without this cash support, the wildcat eventually becomes a dog.

Willingness to spend Ausgabebereitschaft

People`s readiness to spend money on goods or services. Factors which may influence people`s willingness to spend are:
1. their ability to spend, ie their buying power, 2. the product`s price and its price relative to the price of substitute products, 3. the amount of satisfaction received form a purchase, 4. the product`s features, such as quality, 5. general expectations about future employment, income levels, prices and economic conditions, etc.

Window banner (Schau)Fensteraufkleber, Schaufensterplakat

Also called window bill, window card, window streamer, window sticker or window strip.

An advertising poster in a shop/store window.

Window display Schaufensterauslage

Goods shown or exhibited in a shop`s window to impress and attract customers.

Window dressing Schaufensterauslage Schaufenstergestaltung, -dekoration

The displaying of goods in a shop window in such a way as to impress and attract customers. Also called window display.

The process of arranging and presenting goods in a shop window by a window dresser/trimmer to best advantage to impress and attract customers. Also called window trim or window trimming.

Window poster Schaufensterplakat

Posters of various size stuck onto the inside or outside of shop windows.

Window shopping Schaufensterbummel

Visiting shops and looking at window displays without an immediate intention or inclination to buy.

Windowshopper Schaufensterbummler

A person looking at articles displayed in shop windows without making any purchases. Note: the verb is to window shop.

Winter sale Winterschlußverkauf

The selling of goods at reduced prices for a limited time period at the end of the winter season in order to get rid of surplus or out-of-date stocks.

Wire stand Verkaufsständer aus Draht

In a shop, a metal stand usually self-standing and portable, often bearing the name plate of the supplier, used to hold goods.

With compliments slip Empfehlungskarte, Empfehlungszettel

Also called company note paper.

A little slip of paper which stands in the place of the more time-consuming letter. The amount of room allows for only one or two sentences.
Its layout should include the company logo, name, address and contact details. Furthermore, it will bear the words "With Compliments".
There are no real conventions as to how to write a message on a "With Compliments" slip. There is never a need for an attention line, subject line, reference data, etc. It is sometimes signed by the sender.
It usually performs one of two functions: 1. it provides a personal touch to accompanying material and thus is just a way of saying "Hi"; 2. it explains something, probably about accompanying material.

With-pack premium Produkt mit Zugabe, Extraangebot

A free or low-cost premium either inside the package of the product or attached to its outside, offered to buyers of a particular product.

Without engagement freibleibend

Also called subject to change without notice, or subject to confirmation.

A term used in an offer when an offeror quotes prices of goods liable to fluctuate suddenly so that he does not want to be bound. The price quoted is the market price at the moment, but the quotation is not binding on the offeror.

Womens`s magazine Frauenzeitschrift

A magazine designed primarily to service a female readership.

Word association Wortassoziation

In a questionnaire, a list of words to which respondents are asked for feelings, or other words, associated with the listed words.

Word-of-mouth(WOM)-advertising Mund-zu-Mund-Werbung, Mundreklame

Advertising communicated from one satisfied customer to another person, e.g. a friend, who may be a potential customer for the same product or service. Strictly speaking, this is not really advertising.

Work in progress/process (WIP) unfertige Erzeugnisse, Halberzeugnisse, Halbfabrikate

Also called goods in process, material in process, partly finished goods, or semi-finished products.

Inventory/stock-in-trade in an intermediate stage of production, i.e. at a stage between raw materials and finished goods. The products are partially completed at a specified date, usually at the end of a financial period.

Working class Arbeiterklasse

Persons working for wages, especially in manual labour.

Works visit Betriebsbesichtigung

Also called factory tour or plant visit.

Visit to a production plant to provide visitors, eg salespeople or potential customers, with authentic background knowledge.

World brand Weltmarke

Also called global brand.

A brand selling in most countries of the world.

World price Weltpreis

Also called global price.

The price at which a specific commodity is selling internationally under market conditions in effect at the time of the sale.

Wrapping paper Packpapier
Geschenkpapier

The paper put round something, usually a product, to cover and protect it. This paper is often printed with advertising messages.

Special paper for wrapping presents.

X Y Z

X-axis X-Achse

Also called horizontal axis or abscissa.

The horizontal axis in a coordinate system.

X-press callmaker Telefon mit Wahlwiederholung und Nummernspeicher

A special type of telephone. The X-press callmaker can store up to X numbers of the operator's choice using push buttoms instead of a dial.

Y-axis Y-Achse

Also called vertical axis or ordinate.

The vertical line forming a right angle with the horizontal axis (x-axis) in a coordinate system.

Yard (yd) Yard (Längenmaß)
Lagerplatz

A measure of length equal to three feet (ft) or 36 inches (in);
1 yard (yd) = 0,914 metres (m).

An enclosed place for the storage of materials. Also called storage yard.

Yearbook Jahrbuch

A book published annually, usually in the form of a reference book, containing information, statistics, etc. about the past year.

Yellow page advertising Werbung in den Gelben Seiten

Advertising carried out on the Yellow Pages.

Yellow Pages Branchenfernsprechbuch, Branchenverzeichnis

A special telephone directory printed on yellow paper. It lists addresses and telephone numbers of local firms alphabetically classified by business or profession and publishes details of a wide range of goods and services offered by subscribers.

Yellow press Regenbogenpresse, Sensationspresse

Also called tabloid or yellow journalism.

Sensationalized and exaggerated journalism.

Yield Ertrag, Gewinn

The proceeds of a transaction or the profit made by a firm.

Youth market Jugendmarkt

The market for young persons, ie teenagers and young unmarried adults. Today, this is a very important market as young people dispose of enormous financial resources.

Youthfulness Jugendlichkeit

A state of youth and a desire to look younger, more vital and attractive, healthier, fitter, etc. In marketing, an important cultural value given particular value.

Yuppie Yuppie

The term is derived from young urban professional; came into vogue in the 1980s (first used in the USA) and describes young career-minded, fashionable persons having relatively high incomes and education, seeking instant success and well connected on Wall Street, in the City of London or on other stock exchanges. Their life-styles are upwardly mobile and they represent a target audience for firms selling prestige items, such as Porsche cars and Boss men's wear.

Other popular terms are: Buppies or bups (black upwardly mobile professionals), Dinks (double income, no kids), Dobies (daddy older, baby younger), Mobies (mummy older, baby younger), Flyers (fun loving youth en route to success), Hanks (health and nature keeper), Limers (less income, more excitement), Woopies (well off older people), Yollies (young old leisure living people), Yuppie-dinks (young urban professional people, double income, no kids), etc.

Zapping — Umschalter, d.h. Fernsehzuschauer, der häufig das Programm wechselt häufiges Umschalten des Fernseh-Programms/Kanals

Also called channel flicking or channel zapping.

A term used for TV viewers who switch over to other channels during the commercial breaks.

The act of using a remote control to change TV channels, e.g. when a commercial begins.

Zero — Null (Zahl oder Zeichen)

The number or figure 0.

The noun nought (naught).

Zero economic growth (ZEG) — Nullwachstum

Also called zero growth.

A situation where there is no economic growth at all. This means that the rate of expansion of the national income or the increase in the total volume of production of goods and services of a country is zero during a specific time period.

Zero elasticity — Nullelastizität

Zero elasticity means E = 0. A situation where demand for a product or service is not affected by changes in income.

Zero rating — Mehrwertsteuerbefreiung

Also called exemption from VAT (value added tax).

A relief from VAT. This means that a trader does not have to charge VAT to a customer. But note: if the supply is zero-rated the trader may recover the VAT which he has paid on his inputs (the input tax); if the supply is exempt from VAT he may not.

Zero-base(d) budgeting Null-Basis-Budgetierung, ZBB-Planung

A financial management technique to formulate budgets; one develops next year`s budget without reference to last year`s budget. The ZB budgeter must start from the assumption that no budget for the function being budgeted exists, or ever has existed. Thus there is zero cost. Therefore ZBB requires managers, when preparing their budgets, to define their targets sharply and to justify all their expenditures from the zero level rather than simply asking for the previous year`s budget which is then suitably updated.
The purpose of ZBB is to identify and remove inefficient or obsolete activities within the firm. Certainly ZBB is more time-consuming than traditional budgeting where the budget is based on the previous year`s budget which is then amended.

Zip code Postleitzahl (USA)

ZIP is an acronym for Zone Improvement Plan. In GB and Canada called post code/postcode or postal code.

In the USA, the zip code is the standard abbreviation for postal purposes and normally appears as two letters indicating the state, followed by five numerals (the five-digit code), e.g. MA, 02181 (MA = Massachusetts).
The United States is divided into 10 large geographical areas, indicated by the first ZIP code digit (0 to 9). The second and third digits are used to divide states; the fourth and fifth digits represent local delivery areas.
The original five-digit zip code has been expanded by four digits and is called the ZIP+4 code (nine-digit zip code); this code is used by business mailers, not by individuals.
The five-digit code identifies every individual post office and metropolitan area delivery station in the USA. The zip code simplifies and expedites mail distribution.
Note: the names of American states are commonly abbreviated in two ways: the normal state abbreviation and the postal abbreviation (e.g. Massachusetts: Mass. and MA; Kansas: Kans. and KA).

Zipping Werbespoteliminierung aus TV-Videoaufnahme

The act of eliminating a commercial taped on a video cassette recorder (VCR), eg through fast forwarding.

Zone Zone, Gebiet

The area of a town or country marked off and used for a special reason or purpose, e.g. for administrative purposes.

Zone pricing Zonenpreissystem

Also called zone-delivered pricing or freight allowed system.

A pricing system which charges all customers who live within the same geographical area/zone the same price for the same delivered goods.

The charging of a buyer for delivery of the goods based on distance as defined by the geographic zones.

Zoning Gebietsaufteilung

The division of a larger territory into smaller areas or zones. At the beginning selling is confined to particular geographical or distribution areas, then it is gradually expanded to a larger area.

Deutsch-Englische Wortliste

German-English Glossary

10-Sekunden-Werbung	ten (:10)
20-Sekunden-Werbung	twenty (:20)
30-Sekunden-Werbung	thirty (:30)
50-50-Plan	fifty-fifty (50 : 50) plan

A

ABC-Kundeneinstufung	ABC classification
ABC-Methode (Aufmerksamkeit, Nutzen, Abschluß)	ABC method
ACORN (Wohngegendklassifikation)	ACORN
AIDA-Modell	AIDA model
AIDAS-Modell	AIDAS model
AIDCA-Modell	AIDCA model
AIDCAS-Modell	AIDCAS model
AIO-Aussagen	AIO statements
ATR-Modell (Bewußtsein, Probe, Wiederkauf)	ATR model
Abbestellung	countermand
Abbildung	illustration
Abendsendezeit, frühe	early fringe
Abendzeit, frühe, zu der Getränke in Lokalen reduziert sind	Happy Hour
Aberntestrategie	harvesting strategy
Abdeckung aller Marktsegmente	complete segmentation
Abfahrt	departure (dep)
Abfahrtszeit, voraussichtliche	estimated time of departure
Abfall	waste
Abfallpost	junk mail
Abfallprodukt	byproduct
Abfallwirtschaft	garbology
Abfertigungsschalter	checkin desk
Abflughalle	departure lounge
Abgabe von Angeboten	bidding
Abgabefrist	filing date
Abgaben	dues
Abgabepreis	selling price
Abgabepreis, empfohlener	suggested retail price
Abhängigkeitsrate	dependency ratio
Abhol- und Zustelldienst	pickup and delivery service
Abholgebühr	collection charge
Abholgroßhändler	cash and carry wholesaler
Abholgroßhändler	limited function wholesaler

Abholgrossist	**cash and carry wholesaler**
Abholmarkt	**box store**
Abholung	**collection**
Abkommen, bindendes, verbindliches	**binding agreement**
Abladen	**unloading**
Ablauf	**lapse**
Ablaufdatum, sichtbares	**open dating**
Ablehnung	**rejection**
Ablehnung, allgemeine	**blanket refusal**
Abliefertermin	**delivery date**
Ablieferung	**delivery**
Abnahme	**decrease**
Abnahme	**taking delivery**
Abnahmebescheinigung	**inspection certificate**
Abnehmer	**buyer**
Abnehmer	**customer**
Abnehmer	**purchaser**
Abnehmer	**taker**
Abnehmer, gewerblicher	**industrial buyer**
Abo-TV, bei dem nur Einschaltzeit bezahlt wird	**pay-per-view**
Abonnement	**standing order**
Abonnement	**subscription**
Abonnementsauflage	**subscription circulation**
Abonnementsfernsehen	**subscription television**
Abonnementsverlängerung	**renewal**
Abonnent/in	**subscriber**
Abrechnung	**statement**
Abrechnung	**invoicing**
Abrechnungstag	**prompt day**
Abreisetag	**departure date**
Abreißgutschein	**tear-off coupon**
Abreißgutschein, perforierter	**Ad-A-Card, ad-a-card**
Abruf nach Bedarf	**call off as required**
Abrufauftrag	**call purchase**
Abrufvertrag	**call-off purchase agreement**
Abrunden	**rounding off**
Absahnpreis	**skimming price**
Absahnpreisstrategie	**skim-the-cream pricing**
Absatz	**marketing**
Absatz	**sales**
Absatz	**selling**
Absatz(menge)	**sales volume**
Absatz durch ein Kartell	**pool selling**
Absatz, indirekter	**indirect marketing**
Absatzmix	**sales mix**
Absatzanalyse	**sales analysis**
Absatzbemühungen	**marketing efforts**
Absatzbudget	**sales budget**
Absatzchancen	**sales potential**

Absatzförderung	**sales promotion**
Absatzförderung beim Handel	**trade promotion**
Absatzförderung, informative	**informative promotion**
Absatzförderung, kombinierte	**cross merchandising**
Absatzforschung	**sales research**
Absatzgebiet	**outlet**
Absatzgebiet	**sales area**
Absatzgebiet	**trading area**
Absatzgeschwindigkeit	**rate of selling**
Absatzhandbuch	**sales manual**
Absatzkampagne	**sales campaign**
Absatzkampagne	**sales drive**
Absatzkanal	**marketing channel**
Absatzkartell	**sales cartel**
Absatzkartell	**syndicate**
Absatzkette	**sales chain**
Absatzkonferenz	**sales meeting**
Absatzkontrolle	**sales control**
Absatzkosten	**distribution cost(s)**
Absatzkostenanalyse	**marketing cost analysis**
Absatzlehre	**marketing**
Absatzmagnet	**anchor store**
Absatzmangel	**lack of sales**
Absatzmarkt	**sales market**
Absatzmarkt für industrielle Erzeugnisse	**business to business market**
Absatzmarkt, monopolistischer	**captive market**
Absatzmittler	**marketing intermediary**
Absatzmittler	**mercantile agent**
Absatzmöglichkeiten	**sales potential**
Absatzorganisation	**sales force**
Absatzorganisation, gemeinschaftliche	**joint sales organisation**
Absatzorientierung	**sales orientation**
Absatzorientierung	**marketing orientation**
Absatzplan	**marketing and sales plan**
Absatzplan	**sales budget**
Absatzplanung	**sales planning**
Absatzpolitik	**marketing policy**
Absatzpolitik	**sales policy**
Absatzpotential	**sales potential**
Absatzpotential eines Marktes	**market sales potential**
Absatzpotential, gesamtes	**total market potential**
Absatzprognose	**sales forecast**
Absatzprognose für ein Unternehmen	**company sales forecast**
Absatzprognose, internationale	**international sales forecast**
Absatzquote	**sales quota**
Absatzrückgang	**sales decline**
Absatzstrategie, offensive	**offensive market strategy**
Absatzvorbereitung	**merchandising**
Absatzweg	**channel of distribution**
Absatzweg	**distribution channel**

Absatzweg, direkter	**direct channel**
Absatzweg, dualer	**dual distribution channel**
Absatzwettbewerb	**sales contest**
Absatzwirtschaft	**distributive trade(s)**
Absatzzentrum	**distribution center**
Abschätzungsmethode (bei Werbeetatfestsetzung)	**assessment method**
abschicken	**consign**
Abschlagszahlung	**payment on account**
Abschlagszahlung	**progress payment**
Abschluß	**deal**
Abschluß eines Verkaufs(gesprächs)	**closing**
Abschluß eines Verkaufs(gesprächs)	**sales closing**
Abschluß, direkter	**direct close**
Abschlußtag	**contract date**
Abschlußtechnik	**closing technique**
Abschöpfungspreis	**skimming price**
Abschöpfungspreisbildung	**market skimming pricing**
Abschöpfungspreispolitik	**price skimming**
Abschöpfungspreisstrategie	**skim-the-cream pricing**
Abschrift	**copy**
Abschwungphase	**contractionary phase**
absenden	**forward**
Absenden	**forwarding**
Absender	**freighter**
Absender	**poster**
Absender	**sender**
Absender	**shipper**
Absender	**addresser**
Absender (von Waren)	**consignor**
Absenderanschrift	**return address**
Absetzbarkeit	**marketability**
Absicht	**intent**
Absichtserklärung, schriftliche	**letter of intent**
Absprache (geheime)	**collusion**
Abstinenz	**abstinence**
Abstinenztheorie des Zinses	**abstinence theory of interest**
Abstoßen	**divestment**
Abszisse	**abscissa**
Abteilung für Sonderangebote	**bargain basement**
Abteilungsleiter im Warenhaus	**floor manager**
Abtropfmatte	**drip mat**
Abwehrwerbung	**defensive advertising**
Abweichung	**variance**
Abweichung, mittlere (Stat)	**average deviation**
Abweichung, mittlere quadratische (Stat)	**standard deviation**
Abweisung, schroffe	**rebuff**
Abwicklungsvergütung	**handling allowance**
Abzahlungsgeschäft, Inhaber eines	**tallyman**
Abzahlungskauf	**buying on time**

Abzahlungskauf	**instal(l)ment buying**
Abzahlungsvertrag	**credit sale(s) agreement**
Abzahlungsvertrag	**deferred payment agreement**
Abziehbild	**transfer**
Abzug	**deduction**
Abzug, bar ohne	**net cash**
Achse	**axis**
Achtundvierzigerformat	**forty-eight sheet**
Achtzig/zwanzig (80/20) Regel	**eighty/twenty (80/20) rule**
Adaptierung	**adaptation**
Additiv	**additive**
Adoption	**adoption (of a product)**
Adoptionskurve(nlinie)	**adoption curve**
Adressantn	**addresser**
Adressat	**addressee**
Adressaten, Zahl der	**target audience**
Adreßbuch	**directory**
Adreßbuchwerbung	**directory advertising**
Adresse	**address**
Adressenliste	**mailing list**
Adressenverlag	**list broker**
Affidavitanzeige	**testimonial advertisement**
Agent/in	**agent**
Agentur	**agency**
Agentur, federführende	**agency of record**
Agenturprovision	**agency commission**
Agentursendung	**agency-produced program**
Agrarerzeugnisse	**produce**
Agrargenossenschaft	**agricultural cooperative**
Agrarsubventionen	**agricultural subsidies**
Agroindustrie	**agroindustry**
Ähnlichkeitsstrategie	**passing off**
Akkordprämie	**production bonus**
Akkulteration	**acculturation**
Akontozahlung	**payment on account**
Akquisiteur	**canvasser**
Akquisiteur	**solicitor**
Aktendeckel	**binder**
Aktiva, immaterielle	**intangible assets**
Aktualisierung	**update**
Akzelerationsprinzip	**acceleration principle**
Akzelerator	**accelerator**
Akzeptanz	**acceptance**
Akzeptanz	**adoption (of a product)**
Akzeptanztest einer Produktidee	**concept test**
Akzeptierender	**adopter**
Akzeptierender, früh	**early adopter**
All-we-can-afford Methode	**affordable method**
Alleinleser	**exclusive reader**
Alleinsponsor	**sole sponsor**

Alleinvertreter	**sole agent**
Alleinvertretung	**exclusive agency**
Alleinvertrieb	**exclusive distribution**
Allokationseffizienz	**allocative efficiency**
"Alte mit Schwung"	**grays on the go**
Alternativ-Verkaufsabschluß	**alternative closing**
Alternativbewertung	**alternative evaluation**
Alternativfrage	**closed question**
Alternativfrage	**dichotomous question**
Alternativkosten	**alternative cost(s)**
Alternativkosten	**opportunity cost**
Alters- und Lebenszyklusstadium	**age and life cycle stage**
Altersklasse	**age group**
Altindustrie	**sunset industry**
Amerikanischer Marketingverband	**American Marketing Association**
Amt für Verbraucherschutz (GB)	**Office of Fair Trading**
Analogiewerbung	**analogy advertising**
Analyse konkurrierender Produkte	**competitor analysis**
Analyse, eingehende	**in depth study**
Analyse, makrodynamische	**macro-dynamics**
Analysenzertifikat	**certificate of analysis**
Anbieter	**marketer**
Anbieter	**offeror/offerer**
Anbieter	**supplier**
Anbieter einer vollständigen Produktpalette	**full-line supplier**
Anbieter, etablierter	**in-supplier**
Anbieterabsprache	**collusive tendering**
Anbieterüberschuß	**sellers over**
Anchorman	**anchorman**
Änderung, erwartete	**anticipated change**
Änderung, redaktionelle	**editorial alteration**
Anerkennungsschreiben	**testimonial**
Anfang	**departure (dep)**
Anfangsbestand	**beginning inventory**
Anfangsbestand	**opening stock**
Anfordern, Vorlage auf ...	**on demand**
Anfrage	**enquiry/inquiry**
Anfrage, bestimmte	**special inquiry**
Anfragebrief	**letter of enquiry**
Anfragetest	**inquiry test**
Angabe, falsche	**false claim**
Angaben	**data**
Angaben	**particulars**
Angaben, wissentlich falsche	**fraudulent misrepresentation**
Angebot	**offer**
Angebot	**proposal**
Angebot	**quotation**
Angebot	**tender**
Angebot	**supply**

Angebot (Kostenvoranschlag)	**estimate**
Angebot und Nachfrage	**supply and demand**
Angebot und Nachfrage, Gesetz von	**law of supply and demand**
Angebot und Preis	**supply and price**
Angebot zur Rückerstattung des Kaufpreises bei Nichtgefallen der Ware	**refund offer**
Angebot, Erlöschen eines	**termination of offer**
Angebot, Ja/Nein	**alternative closing**
Angebot, Preiselastizität des	**price elasticity of supply**
Angebot, aggregiertes	**aggregate supply**
Angebot, bedingtes	**conditional offer**
Angebot, bestimmtes	**specific offer**
Angebot, elastisches	**elastic supply**
Angebot, festes, verbindliches	**firm offer**
Angebot, freibleibendes, unverbindliches	**offer subject to confirmation**
Angebot, freibleibendes, unverbindliches	**open offer**
Angebot, günstiges	**attractive offer**
Angebot, günstiges	**bargain offer**
Angebot, im	**on offer**
Angebot, inverses	**regressive supply**
Angebot, konkurrierendes	**competitive supply**
Angebot, konkurrierendes	**composite supply**
Angebot, offenes	**open bid**
Angebot, öffentliches	**general offer**
Angebot, unelastisches	**inelastic supply**
Angebot, unverlangtes	**unsolicited offer**
Angebot, unverlangtes	**voluntary offer**
Angebot, verbundenes, komplementäres	**joint supply**
Angebot, verlangtes	**solicited offer**
Angebot, verschlossenes	**sealed bid**
Angebot, verstecktes (in einem Werbeträger)	**blind offer**
Angebot, zusammengesetztes	**composite supply**
Angebote werden entgegengenommen	**open to offers**
Angebote, Abgabe von	**bidding**
Angebotsabgabe	**tendering**
Angebotsabgabe, Aufforderung zur	**request for proposal**
Angebotsänderung	**change in supply**
Angebotsannahme	**acceptance of proposal**
Angebotsannahme	**award**
Angebotsannahme	**acceptance of offer**
Angebotsarten	**offer types**
Angebotsbedingungen	**conditions of supply**
Angebotsbegrenzung	**termination of offer**
Angebotsdeterminanten	**determinants of supply**
Angebotseinholung	**proposal solicitation**
Angebotselastizität	**elasticity of supply**
Angebotsempfänger	**offeree**
Angebotsempfänger	**tenderee**
Angebotsexpansion	**expansion of supply**

Angebotsgesetz	**law of supply**
Angebotsinflation	**supply push inflation**
Angebotsinflation	**supply inflation**
Angebotskurs (Bö)	**asked price**
Angebotskurs (Bö)	**offer(ed) price**
Angebotskurve	**supply curve**
Angebotskurve, Verschiebung der	**shift of supply curve**
Angebotskurve, allgemeine	**general supply curve**
Angebotsmenge	**quantity supplied**
Angebotsoptimierung	**merchandise**
Angebotsoptimierung	**merchandising**
Angebotspreis	**bid price**
Angebotspreis	**offer(ed) price**
Angebotspreis	**quoted price**
Angebotspreis	**supply price**
Angebotsrückgang	**decrease in supply**
Angebotsschrumpfung	**contraction of (in) supply**
Angebotstabelle	**supply schedule**
Angebotsüberhang	**excess(ive) supply**
Angebotsüberschuß	**sellers over**
Angebotsüberschuß	**surplus**
Angebotsverschiebung	**supply shift**
Angebotszugang	**supply access**
Angriffsstrategie	**attack strategy**
Angstappeal in der Werbung	**fear appeal in advertising**
Angstkauf	**panic buying**
Anhänger	**follower**
Anhänger	**label**
Anhänger	**tag**
Anhängezettel	**tie-on label**
Anhäufung	**mountain**
Animateur	**animator**
Ankündigung	**notice**
Ankündigungseffekt	**announcement effect**
Ankunftsanzeige	**advice of arrival**
Ankunftszeit, geschätzte, voraussichtliche	**estimated time of arrival (ETA)**
Ankurbelung der Konjunktur/Wirtschaft	**pump priming**
Anlage	**installation**
Anlagegüter	**capital goods**
Anlagewerte, immaterielle	**intangible assets**
Anlaufkosten	**launching costs**
Anlieferung	**supply**
Anmeldeschluß	**closing date**
Anmerkung	**footnote**
Anmerkung	**note**
Annäherung, Art der	**approach**
Annahme	**acceptance**
Annahme	**hypothesis**
Annahme (eines Produktes)	**adoption (of a product)**
Annahme, eingeschränkte	**qualified acceptance**

Annahme, zur ... innerhalb x Tagen	**for acceptance within x days**
Annahmeerklkärung	**letter of acceptance**
Annahmeort	**place of acceptance (POA)**
Annahmeprozeß	**adoption process**
Annahmeschluß	**deadline**
Annahmeverweigerung	**nonacceptance**
Annahmeverweigerung	**rejection**
annoncieren	**insert**
Anordnung	**format**
Anpassung	**adaptation**
Anpassung, doppelte, duale	**dual adaptation**
Anpassung, kulturelle	**acculturation**
Anpassungsfähigkeit, Mangel an	**inelasticity**
Anpassungsinflation	**adaptive inflation**
Anpreisung, marktschreierische	**puffing**
Anrede	**greeting**
Anreiz, zusätzlicher	**sweetener**
Anreizmarketing	**incentive marketing**
Anruf, gebührenfreier	**freephone/freefone**
Anrufbeantworter	**telephone answering machine**
Anrufbeantworter	**answerphone**
Anrufer	**caller**
Ansager/in	**announcer**
Anschaffungen	**purchases**
Anschaffungskosten	**cost**
Anschaffungskosten	**original cost**
Anschaffungspreis	**cost price**
Anschaffungswert	**entry value**
Anschauungsmaterial	**illustration**
Anschlagfläche	**facing**
Anschlagtafel	**bulletin board**
Anschlagtafel	**hoarding**
Anschlagwerbemittelkontakt, Nettozahl der Personen mit ...	**net circulation**
Anschlußauftrag	**add-on sale**
Anschlußauftrag	**follow-up/on order**
Anschlußkauf	**rebuy**
Anschlußkauf, direkter	**straight rebuy**
Anschlußmarkt	**aftermarket**
Anschpruchsniveau	**aspiration level**
Anschrift	**address**
Anschriftenzeile	**address line**
Ansicht, zur	**on approval (on appro)**
Ansoff-Matrix	**Ansoff matrix**
Anstehzeit	**dwell time**
Anstieg	**rise**
Anstieg (scharfer)	**upswing**
Anteil der gelesenen Seiten einer Publikation	**page traffic**
Anteil gründlicher Leser	**read most**

Anteilspunkt	**share point**
Anthropologie (Lehre vom Menschen)	**anthropology**
Anti Dumping	**antidumping**
Anti Marketing	**demarketing**
Anti-Trust Gesetz (USA)	**Anti-Trust Law**
Antidumping-Gesetz	**Antidumping law**
Antwort	**response**
Antwort, geleitete, gestützte	**prompted response**
Antwort, schlagfertige	**comeback**
Antwort, spontane	**unprompted response**
Antwortfrist	**reply time**
Antwortinserat	**direct response advertising**
Antwortkarte	**reply card**
Antwortkarte, freigemachte, frankierte	**prepaid reply card**
Antwortmöglichkeiten, Frage mit vorgegebenen ...	**closed-end question**
Antwortquote	**response rate**
Antwortvorgabe	**fixed alternative**
Anwender	**user**
Anwerber	**bird dog**
anvertrauen	**consign**
Anzahl der Werbeempfänger	**exposure**
Anzahlung	**advance**
Anzahlung	**deposit**
Anzahlung	**downpayment/down payment**
Anzeige	**advertisement**
Anzeige	**insert**
Anzeige (Bildschirm)	**display**
Anzeige, Preis für ganzseitige	**page rate**
Anzeige, Tenor der	**advertising theme**
Anzeige, alleinstehende	**solus advertisement**
Anzeige, doppelseitige	**centrespread/centre spread**
Anzeige, doppelseitige	**double page spread**
Anzeige, doppelseitige	**spread**
Anzeige, doppelseitige	**two-page spread**
Anzeige, einspaltige	**single column advertisement**
Anzeige, ganzseitige	**full-page advertisement**
Anzeige, ganzseitige	**spread**
Anzeige, persönliche	**agony column**
Anzeige, redaktionell aufgemachte	**advertorial**
Anzeige, redaktionell aufgemachte	**editorial ad**
Anzeige, rubrizierte	**classified advertisement**
Anzeige, teilisolierte	**semi-solus advertisment**
Anzeige, versteckte, vergrabene	**buried advertisement**
Anzeigen(annahme)schluß	**copy date**
Anzeigen(ver)mittler	**space buyer**
Anzeigen-Split	**split run advertising**
Anzeigenabteilung	**advertising department**
Anzeigenabteilung, Leiter der	**advertisement manager**
Anzeigenagentur	**advertising representative**

Anzeigenagentur	**space broker**
Anzeigenannahme	**advertising office**
Anzeigenaquisiteur	**space salesperson**
Anzeigenauftrag	**insertion order**
Anzeigenauftrag	**space order**
Anzeigenbeilage (lose)	**freestanding insert**
Anzeigenbeilage	**stuffer**
Anzeigenblatt	**freesheet, free sheet**
Anzeigenblatt	**giveaway magazine**
Anzeigenblatt	**shopping newspaper**
Anzeigenblock	**clutter**
Anzeigenetat, -budget	**advertising budget**
Anzeigenexpediteur	**advertising space buyer**
Anzeigenfehler	**fudge**
Anzeigenfestpreis	**flat rate**
Anzeigenfläche	**space**
Anzeigengröße	**advertisement size**
Anzeigengrundpreis	**base rate**
Anzeigengrundtarif	**open rate**
Anzeigeninflation	**adflation**
Anzeigenkosten	**advertising costs**
Anzeigenkunde	**advertising customer**
Anzeigenkunde	**advertising space buyer**
Anzeigenkunde	**advertiser**
Anzeigenleiter	**advertisement manager**
Anzeigenmittler	**space buyer**
Anzeigenplazierung, feste	**fixed position**
Anzeigenposition (Druckmedien)	**advertising location**
Anzeigenposition gegenüber redaktionellem Text	**facing matter**
Anzeigenposition rechts gegenüber der Kommentarseite	**Campbell Soup position**
Anzeigenpositon links/rechts oben	**top left/right position**
Anzeigenpostion, textanschließende	**following reading matter**
Anzeigenpreis bei täglicher Inserierung	**daily rate**
Anzeigenpreisliste	**adrate card**
Anzeigenpreisliste	**rate card**
Anzeigenpretest	**advertising pretest**
Anzeigenraum	**advertising space**
Anzeigenraum	**lineage**
Anzeigenraum	**space**
Anzeigenraum, zuteilen von ... bei Nachfrageüberhang	**allotment**
Anzeigenreichweite	**advertising reach**
Anzeigenschaltplan	**advertising schedule**
Anzeigenseite	**adpage/ad page**
Anzeigenseite, Leserschaft einer	**adpage audience**
Anzeigenseite, ausschlagbare	**gatefold**
Anzeigenseitenkontakt	**adpage exposure**
Anzeigentarif	**advertising rate**

Anzeigenteil (einer Seite oder Zeitung)	**ad columns**
Anzeigenteil einer Zeitung	**advertising section**
Anzeigentext	**advertising copy**
Anzeigenvermittler	**space broker**
Anzeigenvertrag	**advertising contract**
Anzeigenvertreter	**advertising representative**
Anzeigetafel, elektronische	**electronic bulletin board**
Anziehungskraft	**appeal**
Anziehungskraft der Werbung	**advertising appeal**
Apothekerpreis	**fancy price**
Appeal, gefühlsbetonter	**emotional appeal**
Apperzeptionstest, thematischer (TAT)	**thematic apperception test**
Arbeit, vorausbezahlte	**dead horse**
Arbeiter, ungelernte	**shop floor/shopfloor**
Arbeiterklasse	**upper-lower class**
Arbeiterklasse	**working class**
Arbeitsauftrag	**shop order**
Arbeitsgemeinschaft	**syndicate**
arbeitsintensiv	**labour intensive**
Arbeitskosten	**labour cost(s)**
Arbeitskräfte, ungelernte	**shop floor/shopfloor**
Arbeitsrückstand	**backlog**
Arbeitswertlehre	**labour theory of value**
Arbitragegeschäft unter Ausnutzung von Preisdifferenzen auf verschiedenen Handelsplätzen zum gleichen Zeitpunkt	**space arbitrage**
Arena-Werbung	**arena advertising**
Armutsfalle	**poverty trap**
Armutsgrenze	**poverty line**
Art der Annäherung	**approach**
Art und Weise der Verkaufsanbahnung	**sales approach**
Art und Weise, ein Problem in Angriff zu nehmen	**approach**
Art-Direktor	**art director**
Artikel	**article**
Artikel, die immer auf Lager sein müssen	**never-outs**
Artikel, führender	**leader**
Artikel, kostenlos verteilter	**handout**
Artikelgruppenmarke	**category brand**
Artikelnummr, europäische	**European article number (EAN)**
Arzneimittel, nicht ethische	**over-the-counter**
Ärztevertreter	**medical rep**
Asch-Phänomen	**asch phenomenon**
Assistent, persönlicher	**personal assistant**
Assoziationstest	**association test**
Asymptote	**asymptote**
Atmosphäre	**atmosphere**
Attrappe	**dummy pack(age)**
Audienz	**audience**

Audimeter	**audimeter**
Aufdringlichkeit	**intrusiveness**
Aufforderung	**demand**
Aufforderung an Hörer, sich bei Sender zu melden	**hook**
Aufforderung an Leser, sich zu melden	**hook**
Aufforderung an Zuschauer, sich bei Sender zu melden	**hook**
Aufforderung, auf	**on demand**
Aufforderung zur Angebotsabgabe	**request for proposal**
Aufforderung, ein Vertragsangebot abzugeben	**invitation to treat**
Aufforderung, zahlbar bei	**payable on demand**
Aufführung	**performance**
Aufhänger, werblicher	**hook**
Aufhebung	**revocation**
Aufkauf (zwecks Monopolbildung)	**corner**
Aufkaufen großer Mengen zum Wiederverkauf zu überhöhten Preisen	**abbroachment**
Aufklärungswerbung	**informative advertising**
Aufklärungswerbung	**reason why advertising**
Aufklebeadresse	**gummed address label**
Aufkleber	**label**
Aufkleber	**sticker**
Aufkleber	**tip on**
Aufkleber für feuergefährliche oder explosionsgefährdete Stoffe	**red label**
Aufladen	**loading**
Auflage	**circulation**
Auflage	**edition**
Auflage (z.B. Buch)	**issue**
Auflage, kontrollierte, überprüfte	**audited circulation**
Auflagenhöhe	**circulation**
Auflagenprüfung	**audit**
Aufmacher	**hook**
Aufmachung	**format**
Aufmachung	**getup**
Aufmachung	**layout**
Aufmerksamkcit	**attention**
Aufmerksamkeit	**notice**
Aufmerksamkeit, unfreiwillige	**involuntary attention**
Aufmerksamkeitserreger	**attention getter**
Aufmerksamkeitswert	**attention value**
Aufpreis	**surcharge**
Aufreißer	**hook**
Aufrunden	**rounding off**
Aufschlag	**surcharge**
Aufschub	**abstinence**
Aufschub	**deferment**
Aufschwung	**recovery**

Aufschwung	**upswing**
Aufschwung, erwarteter	**anticipated economic upswing**
Aufschwung, starker	**boom**
Aufstellplakat	**counter card**
Aufstellplakat	**showcard**
Aufstellung	**display**
Aufstellung	**return**
Aufteilung einer Werbekampagne	**fragmentation**
Auftrag	**order**
Auftrag zu Festpreisen	**fixed price contract**
Auftrag, bedingter	**conditional order**
Auftrag, noch nicht ausgeführter	**unexecuted order**
Auftrag, offener, unerledigter	**open order**
Auftrag, unerledigter	**back order**
Auftrag, unerledigter	**outstanding order**
Auftragsabwicklung	**order processing**
Auftragsabwicklung, Kosten der	**order costs**
Auftragsannahme	**acceptance of order**
Auftragsannahme	**order taking**
Auftragsannahme- und Kündigungsschluß	**firm order date**
Auftragsarbeit	**contract work**
Auftragsarten	**order types**
Auftragsausführung	**execution of order**
Auftragsbearbeitung	**sales order processing**
Auftragsbeschaffer	**order getter**
Auftragsbeschaffung	**order getting**
Auftragsbestätigung	**acknowledg(e)ment of order**
Auftragsbestätigung	**confirmation of order**
Auftragsbuch	**order book**
Auftragseingang	**order intake**
Auftragserfüllung	**order fulfil(l)ment**
Auftragserteilung, Preisfestlegung bei	**preretailing**
Auftragserteilung, zahlbar bei	**cash with order**
Auftragsflut	**flood orders**
Auftragsnummer	**order number**
Auftragspooling	**pooling of orders**
Auftragsrückstand	**backlog**
Auftragsschwemme	**boom in orders**
Auftragsstornierung	**cancellation of order**
Auftragsstornierung	**order cancellation**
Auftragsvergabe	**award**
Auftragsverlust	**loss of order**
Auftragszyklusspanne	**order cycle time**
Aufwand	**cost**
Aufwand	**expenses**
Aufwärtsentwicklung	**uptrend**
Aufwärtstrend	**uptrend**
Aufwendungen	**expenses**
Aufzeichnung	**record**
Aufzeichungs- und Selbstwählgerät, automatisches	**auto-dial recorded message player**

Augenbewegung	**gaze motion**
Augenfälligkeitstest	**stand out test**
Augenkamera	**eye movement camera**
Augenwischerei	**eye-wash**
Auktion	**auction**
Auktion	**public sale**
Auktion	**sale by auction**
Auktion (Holländische)	**Dutch auction**
Auktionator/in	**auctioneer**
Auktionshaus	**auction house**
Auktionsmarkt	**auction market**
Auktionsposten	**odd lot**
Auktionsraum	**salesroom**
Auktionsverkauf	**auction sale**
Ausbringung	**output**
Ausdrucksmittel	**vehicle**
Ausdrucksweise, umgangssprachliche, ungepflegte	**jargon**
Ausfertigung	**copy**
Ausflug	**excursion**
Ausfuhrerklärung	**specification**
Ausfuhrhandel	**export trade**
Ausführer/in	**effector/effecter**
Ausführung	**implementation**
Ausführungsverzögerung	**implementation lag**
Ausführungsverzögerung, betriebliche	**inside lag**
Ausgabe	**copy**
Ausgabe	**edition**
Ausgabe(n)	**expense(s)**
Ausgabebereitschaft	**willingness to spend**
Ausgaben zur freien Verfügung	**discretionary spending**
Ausgaben, autonome	**autonomous expenditure(s)**
Ausgaben, autonome	**autonomous spending**
Ausgabenaufteilung der Marketingausgaben	**spending split**
Ausgabensteuer	**expenditure tax**
Ausgabenstruktur	**consumer spending patterns**
Ausgabenstruktur	**spending pattern**
Ausgangsfracht	**carriage outward(s)**
Ausgangspost	**outgoing mail**
Ausgangsrechnung	**outgoing invoice**
Ausgleichszahlung	**compensating payment**
Ausgliederung	**divestment**
Aushängeschild	**flagship**
Aushöhlungseffekt	**backwash effect**
Ausladen	**discharge**
Auslage verwandter Produkte	**related display**
Auslage, beleuchtete	**illuminated display**
Auslagekarton	**display outer**
Auslagekasten	**display cabinet**

Auslagen, kleine	**petties**
Auslagenbehälter	**display bin**
Auslagenkiste	**display bin**
Auslagenposition	**display position**
Auslagenstand	**display stand**
Auslagepackung	**display pack**
Auslageregal, beiderseitig offenes	**gondola**
Ausland, Handel mit dem	**overseas trade**
Auslandsauftrag	**indent**
Auslandsauftrag mit Herstellerspezifizierung	**closed indent**
Auslandsauftrag mit Herstellerspezi-fizierung	**open indent**
Auslandsbesuch	**overseas visit**
Auslandskonkurrenz	**foreign competition**
Auslandsmarkt, Segmentierung eines ...	**in-country segmentation**
Auslandsmarktzutritt	**foreign market entry**
Auslandsnachfrage	**external demand**
Auslandssektor	**foreign sector**
Auslandsverkaufsvertreter	**foreign sales agent (FSA)**
Auslandsversand	**overseas shipment**
Auslandsvertreter	**overseas agent**
Auslandswerbung	**foreign advertising**
Auslieferer	**distributor**
Auslieferung	**delivery**
Auslieferung, Kauf zur späteren ...	**forward purchase**
Auslieferungsauftrag	**delivery order**
Auslieferungslager	**distribution depot**
Auslieferungsschein	**delivery order**
Ausnahmen beim Nachfragegesetz	**exceptions to the law of demand**
Ausnahmetarif	**exception rate**
Aussage, pauschale	**blanket statement**
Ausschließlichkeitsvertrag	**exclusive dealing agreement**
Ausschließlichkeitsvertrag	**exclusive contract**
Ausschlußfrist	**time bar**
Ausschlußkauf	**preclusive buying**
Ausschreibungsunterlagen	**tender documents**
Ausschuß	**spoilage**
Ausschußteil	**reject**
Ausschußware	**rejects**
Ausschußware	**defective goods**
Ausschußware	**rummage**
Außendienst(verkaufs)personal	**field sales force**
Außendienst-Interviewer	**field interviewer**
Außendienstleiter	**field sales manager**
Außendienstmitarbeiter	**field staff**
Außendienstmitarbeiter	**sales force**
Außendienstmitarbeiter, der Auftrag/ Bestellung annimmt	**field order taker**
Außendienstverkäufer/in	**field salesperson**

Außendienstverkaufsbericht	**field sales report**
Außenhandel	**foreign trade**
Außenhandel	**trade**
Außenhandel	**overseas trade**
Außenhandel, Gewährung gegenseitig gleicher Bedingungen im ...	**fair trade**
Außenhandel, Preisangebote im	**foreign trade - price quotations**
Außenhändler	**trader**
Außenwerbung	**exterior advertising**
Außenwerbung	**outdoor advertising**
Außenwerbung, Zahl der an ... vorbeifahrenden Personen	**site passage**
Außenwerbung, alleinstehende	**solus site**
Außenwerbung, gigantische	**extension ad**
Außenwirtschaftspolitik (USA)	**commercial policy**
Außer-Haus-Verkauf, Restaurant für ...	**takeaway**
Ausstellen und Zusenden von Rechnungen	**billing**
Aussteller	**exhibitor**
Ausstellung	**fair**
Ausstellung	**exhibition**
Ausstellung	**exhibit**
Ausstellung	**show**
Ausstellung, mobile	**mobile exhibition**
Ausstellunggelände	**exhibition grounds**
Ausstellungsnachlaß	**display allowance**
Ausstellungsrabatt	**display allowance**
Ausstellungsraum	**exhibition hall**
Ausstellungsraum	**showroom/show room**
Ausstellungsstück	**display article**
Ausstellungsstück	**exhibit**
Ausstellungsstück	**showpiece**
Ausstellungsvitrine	**display case**
Ausstrahlungseffekt	**Halo effect**
Austausch	**exchange**
Austauschbeziehung	**tradeoff**
Austragungsort	**venue**
Ausverkauf	**bargain sale**
Ausverkauf	**closeout**
Ausverkauf	**clearance sale**
Ausverkauf	**sale**
Ausverkauf	**sellout/sell out**
ausverkauft	**out of stock**
Ausverkauf wegen Geschäftsaufgabe	**closing-down sale**
Ausverkaufsware	**bunches**
Ausverkaufsware(n)	**sales goods**
Auswahl	**choice**
Auswahl	**range**
Auswahl (Stat)	**sample**
Auswahl, bewußte	**judgement sampling**
Auswahlfrage	**multiple choice question**

Auswahlvertrieb	**selective selling**
Ausweichnachfrage	**alternate demand**
Auswertung, sekundärstatistische	**desk research**
Auszahlung	**payment**
Auszahlungsstrom	**cash outflow**
Auszeichnung	**label(l)ing**
Auszeichnung mit Verfalldatum	**code dating**
Auszeichnung mit gebrochenen Preisen	**odd pricing**
Autarkie	**self sufficiency**
Automatenverkauf	**automatic vending**
Autonomie	**autonomy**
Autoradio, Spitzennutzungszeit von	**evening drive (time)**
Autorenhonorar	**royalty**

B

Babyboomer	**baby boomers**
Bahnhofswerbung	**station poster**
Bahntransport	**rail transport**
Bahnwerbung	**railroad showing**
Baisse	**baisse**
Balkencode	**bar code**
Ballen (Warenmenge)	**bale**
Band	**volume**
Banderole	**package band**
Banderolenpackung	**banded pack**
Bandwagon-Effekt	**bandwagon effect**
Bankabwicklung vom privaten Haushalt	**home banking**
Bankett	**banquet**
Bankfeiertag	**bank holiday**
Bankmarketing	**bank marketing**
Bankschalterbeamter	**cashier**
Banner	**banner**
Bareinkauf	**cash purchase**
Bareinnahme	**cash receipt**
Bareinnahmen	**takings**
Barerstattungsangebot	**cash refund offer**
Bargeld	**cash**
Bargeld	**ready cash**
Bargeld(bestand)	**cash in/on hand**
Bargeldrückfluß, schneller	**early cash recovery**
Bargeschäft	**cash sale**
Barguthaben	**cash in/on hand**
Barmittelzufluß	**cash inflow**
Barpreis	**cash price**
Barrel (Hohlmaß)	**barrel**
Barvergütungsangebot	**cash refund offer**
Barverkauf	**cash dealing**
Barverkauf	**cash sale**
Barwert	**present value**

Barzahlung	**cash**
Barzahlung bei Auftragserteilung	**cash with order**
Barzahlung bei Lieferung	**cash on delivery**
Barzahlung bei Versand	**cash on shipment**
Barzahlung bei Verschiffung	**cash on shipment**
Barzahlung vor Lieferung	**cash before delivery**
Barzahlung vor Versand	**cash before shipment**
Barzahlung, Frist für	**discount period**
Barzahlung, nur gegen	**cash only**
Barzahlungs(kassen)beleg	**petty cash voucher**
Barzahlungs-Händler-Rabatt	**discount**
Barzahlungsangebot	**cash offer**
Barzahlungsauftrag	**cash order**
Barzahlungsbedingungen	**cash terms**
Barzahlungspreis	**cash price**
Barzahlungsrabatt	**cash discount**
Barzahlungsrabatt	**purchase discount**
Barzahlungsrabatt	**sales discount**
Barzahlungsrabatt	**settlement discount**
Basisjahr	**base year**
Basispreis	**basic price**
Basispreis	**basic rate**
Basis-Ziel-Marketing	**benchmarketing**
Bauteil	**component**
Bayessche Regel	**Bayes' rule**
Beachtung	**attention**
Beachtung, unfreiwillige	**involuntary attention**
Beachtungswert	**noting score**
Bearbeitungsgebühr	**service charge**
Bearbeitungszeit	**lead time**
Beauftragte(r)	**agent**
Bedarf	**demand**
Bedarf	**need**
Bedarf	**requirements**
Bedarf, aggregierter	**aggregate demand**
Bedarf, latenter	**latent demand**
Bedarfs(deckungs)wirtschaft	**subsistence economy**
Bedarfsanalyse	**demand analysis**
Bedarfsbefriedigung	**satisfaction of demand**
Bedarfsbeschreibung, allgmeine	**general need description**
Bedarfsmeldung	**purchase requisition**
Bedarfsprognose	**demand forecast**
Bedenken	**objection**
Bedenkzeit	**cooling-off period**
Bedienungsanleitung	**operating manual**
Bedienungsgeld	**service charge**
Bedienungsqualität	**service quality**
Bedienungstheorie	**queu(e)ing theory**
Bedienungstheorie	**waiting line theory**
Bedingungen	**terms**

Bedingungen, Rechtsgeschäft zu unfairen	catching bargain
Bedingungen, günstige	concessionary terms
Bedingungen, günstige	easy terms
Bedingungen, günstige	soft terms
Bedürfnis	need
Bedürfnisbefriedigung	need satisfaction
Bedürfnisbefriedigung	satisfaction of wants
Bedürfnishierarchie	hierarchy of wants
Bedürfnishierarchie	need hierarchy
Bedürfniskoinzidenz	coincidence of wants
Bedürfniskoinzidenz	double coincidence
Bedürfnisse	needs
Bedürfnisse	wants
Bedürfnisse, Hierarchie der	scale of preferences
Bedürfnisse, immaterielle	immaterial wants
Bedürfnisse, materielle	material wants
Bedürfnisse, soziale	social needs
Bedürfnisse, wiederkehrende	recurring wants
Beeinflusser	influencer
Beendigung	closure
befördern	forward
befördern	freight
Beförderung	carriage
Beförderung	conveyance
Beförderung	transport
Beförderung	haulage
Beförderung (PW)	promotion
Beförderungsart	mode of transport
Beförderungskosten	freight
Beförderungsmittel	conveyance
Beförderungsmittel	vehicle
Beförderungsunternehmen	carrier
Beförderungsunternehmer	private carrier
Beförderungszeit	transit time
Befrachter	freighter
Befrachtung	loading
Befrager	investigator
Befragte(r)	interviewee
Befragte(r)	respondent
Befragung	interview
Befragung	poll
Befragung unter zwei Paar Augen	one-to-one interview
Befragung, briefliche	mail interview
Befragung, briefliche	mail questionnaire
Befragung, computerunterstützte	computer-assisted interviewing
Befragung, halbstrukturierte	semistructured interview
Befragung, nichtdirektive	nondirective interview
Befragung, persönliche	face-to-face interviewing
Befragung, persönliche	one-to-one interview
Befragung, persönliche	personal interview

Befragung, strukturierte	**patterned interview**
Befragung, strukturierte	**structured interview**
Befragung, telephonische	**telephone survey**
Befragung, telephonische	**telephone interview**
Befragungsmethoden	**interviewing methods**
Befriedigung	**satisfaction**
Beglaubigung	**verification**
Begleichung	**settlement**
Begleitmusik	**incidental music**
Begleitschreiben	**covering letter**
Begrüßung	**greeting**
Behälter	**bin**
Behälter	**container**
Behälter, wiederverschließbarer	**reclos(e)able container**
Behälter, wiederverwendbarer	**reusable container**
Behauptung	**claim**
Beihilfe	**grant**
Beilage, eingeklebte	**tip in**
Beilage, farbige	**colour supplement**
Beilage, lose	**loose insert**
Beilegzettel mit Firmenaufdruck	**compliments slip**
Beitrag	**feature**
Beitrag	**subscription**
Beiträge	**dues**
Bekanntgabe	**publication**
Bekanntheitsgrad, höchster	**maximal awareness**
Bekanntmachung	**bulletin**
Bekanntsein	**publicity**
Beladen	**loading**
Beladen	**stuffing**
Belastungsanzeige	**debit note**
Beleg	**coupon**
Beleg	**receipt**
Belegbuch für Anrufe	**telephone calls record book**
Belegseite (für Werbungstreibende)	**tearsheet/tear sheet**
Belegungspreis	**space charge**
Belieferung	**supply**
Benchmarketing	**benchmarketing**
Benefit-Segmentation	**benefit segmentation**
Benutzer	**user**
Benutzerfreundlichkeit	**user friendliness**
Benutzerhandbuch	**user's guide**
Benutzungsgebühr	**user charge**
Beobachtung	**observation**
berechnen, zu viel	**overcharge**
Berechnung, ohne	**free of charge (foc)**
Berechnung, zu hohe	**overcharge**
Bereich	**field**
Bereich	**range**
Bereich	**sector**

Bereich, umsatzstarker	**hot selling area**
Berg	**mountain**
Bericht	**report**
Bericht	**return**
Bericht (nach außen)	**external report**
Berichterstattung über Teilbereiche	**segmental reporting**
Beruf	**trade**
Beschädigung	**damage**
Beschaffenheit	**quality**
Beschaffenheit und Güte, handelsübliche	**good merchantable quality and condition**
Beschaffung	**procurement**
Beschaffung	**purchasing**
Beschaffung, beständelose	**stockless buying**
Beschaffung, fertigungssynchrone	**just in time purchasing**
Beschaffung, fertigungssynchrone	**stockless buying**
Beschaffungsgruppe	**buying center**
Beschaffungskosten	**ordering cost(s)**
Beschaffungskosten	**procurement cost(s)**
Beschaffungsmarketing	**reverse marketing**
Beschaffungsmenge, optimale	**economic purchase quantity (EPQ)**
Beschaffungspreis	**purchase price**
Beschaffungswesen	**purchasing**
Beschaffungszeit	**lead time**
Beschleunigungsprinzip	**acceleration principle**
Beschreibung	**specification**
Beschwerde	**complaint**
Beschwerdebrief	**letter of complaint**
Besetztzeichen (Telefon)	**engaged tone**
Besitzeinkommen	**unearned income**
Bestand, eiserner	**base stock**
Bestand, eiserner	**minimum stock level**
Bestand, maximaler	**maximum stock level**
Bestände	**inventory**
Bestandsaufnahme	**stocktaking**
Bestandsermittlung	**stocktaking**
Bestandsfehlmenge	**stock shortage**
Bestandskontrolle	**inventory control**
Bestandsobergrenze	**maximum stock level**
Bestandsüberschuß	**overage**
Bestandsveränderung	**inventory change**
Bestandswerbung	**maintenance advertising**
Bestandteil	**component**
Bestätigung	**acknowledg(e)ment**
Bestätigung	**confirmation**
Bestätigung	**verification**
Bestätigungsschreiben	**letter of acknowledg(e)ment**
Bestechung	**bribery**
Bestechungsgeld	**bribe**
Bestechungsgeld	**graft**
Bestellbestand	**reorder quantity**

Bestellformular	**order form**
Bestellformular, vorgedrucktes	**preprint order form**
Bestellkarte	**order card**
Bestellkosten	**ordering cost(s)**
Bestellmenge	**order quantity**
Bestellmenge, optimale	**economic order quantity**
Bestellmenge, optimale	**optimum order quantity**
Bestellpunkt	**order timing**
Bestellsystem mit Fixgrößen	**fixed order system**
bestellt	**on order**
Bestellung	**order**
Bestellung	**purchase order**
Bestellung	**sales order**
Bestellung, auf ... gefertigt	**custom-made**
Bestellung, feste	**firm order**
Bestellung, Zusammenstellung einer	**order picking**
bestens	**at best**
Bestimmtheit	**certainty**
Bestimmungen	**terms**
Bestimmungsgröße, exogene	**exogenous factor**
Bestimmungsort	**destination**
Bestimmungsort	**place of destination**
Bestimmungsort, Fracht bezahlbar am ...	**freight forward**
Bestimmungsort, Lieferung frei ...	**free delivery**
Bestseller	**bestseller/best seller**
Besuch, kurzer	**call**
Besuch, unangemeldeter	**cold call**
Besucher	**audience**
Besucher	**caller**
Besucher, ungeladener	**walk-in**
Besucherfluß	**traffic**
Besuchsbericht	**call report**
Besuchshäufigkeit	**call frequency**
Besuchsplanung	**preapproach**
Besuchsrate	**call rate**
Besuchszyklus	**call cycle**
Betrachtungsweise	**approach**
Betrag, fälliger	**balance due**
Betrag, gerundeter, runder	**round figure**
Betrag, zu viel gezahlter	**overpayment**
Betrieb	**plant**
Betrieb	**shop floor/shopfloor**
Betrieb mit Kundenauftragsfertigung	**job shop**
Betriebs- und Hilfsstoffe	**consumable supplies**
Betriebsanlage	**plant**
Betriebsausgaben	**business expenses**
Betriebsbesichtigung	**works visit**
Betriebsergebnis, negatives	**trading loss**
Betriebsergebnis, positives	**trading profit**
Betriebsergebnisrechnung	**trading account**

Betriebsgeheimnis	**trade secret**
Betriebsgewinn	**operating profit**
Betriebsgewinn	**trading profit**
Betriebskapazität	**plant capacity**
Betriebskonto	**trading account**
Betriebskosten	**running cost(s)**
Betriebsoptimum	**ideal capacity**
Betriebsstillegung	**closure**
Betriebsstoffe	**operating supplies**
Betriebsverlust	**operating loss**
Betriebsverlust	**trading loss**
Betrug	**deceit**
Betrug	**fraud**
Beurteilung der Werbung	**advertising evaluation**
Beutel	**bag**
Beutel	**sachet**
Beutel, kartonierter	**bag-in-a-box**
Bevölkerung	**population**
Bevölkerung, alternde	**aging population**
Bevölkerung, nicht erwerbstätige	**dependent population**
Bevölkerung, rückläufige	**declining population**
Bevölkerungsdichte	**density of population**
Bevölkerungsstatistik	**demography**
Bevölkerungszahl, optimale	**optimum population**
Bevollmächtigte(r)	**agent**
Bevorschussung von Rechungen	**invoice discounting**
Beweggrund	**motive**
Beweis	**token**
Bewertung	**evaluation**
Bewertung der Werbung	**advertising evaluation**
Bewertungsfrage	**rating question**
Bewertungsindex	**weighted index**
Bewirtungsgewerbe	**catering trade**
Bewirtungskosten	**entertainment expenses**
Bezahlung	**payment**
Beziehungskauf	**direct purchase**
Bezirksdirektor	**district manager**
Bezirksleiter	**area manager**
Bezugsgruppe	**reference group**
Bezugskosten	**carriage inward(s)**
Bezugspreis, angekündigter	**advertised price**
Bezugsquelle	**source**
Bezugsquellennachweis	**dealer tie-in**
Bezugsquellennachweis	**trade directory**
Bezugsquellennachweis (in einer Anzeige)	**dealer listing**
Bezugsvertrag	**open-end contract**
Bezugszeitraum	**base year**
Bias	**bias**
Bierdeckel	**coaster**
Bieter	**tenderer**

Bieter	**bidder**
Bilanzgerade	**budget line**
Bilanzverlust	**net loss**
Bildkarte	**picture card**
Bildschirmanzeige	**display**
Bildschirmgerät	**visual display unit**
Bildschirmtelefon	**video phone**
Bildschirmtext	**videotext**
Bildschirmtext (Btx)	**teletext**
Bildschirmverkauf	**armchair shopping/buying**
Bildtext	**legend**
Bildüberschrift	**caption**
Bildunterschrift	**caption**
Bildunterschrift	**legend**
Billigangebot, Käufer eines	**bargain shopper**
Billigartikel	**catchpenny (article)**
Billigladen	**cut-price store**
Billigmarke	**cheap brand**
Billigpreisgeschäft	**bargain store**
billigst	**at best**
Bingo-Karte	**reader service card**
Binnenhandel	**home trade**
Binnenhandel	**domestic trade**
Binnenmarkt	**domestic market**
Binnenmarkt	**home market**
Binnenmarkt	**internal market**
Binnenmarkt	**local market**
Binnenmarkt, europäischer	**European domestic market (EDM)**
Binnenmarkt, europäischer	**Single European Market**
Binnenmarkt, gesättigter	**saturated home market**
Binnennachfrage	**domestic demand**
Binnenwasserstraßen	**inland waterways**
Biokost	**health food**
bis auf weiteres	**till forbid**
Blankoauftrag	**blanket order**
Blankoverkauf	**selling short**
Blatt	**folio**
Blickfang	**attention getter**
Blickfang	**eyecatcher**
Blickfang in Anzeige oder Verkaufsraum	**stopper**
Blickfang, werblicher	**hook**
Blickfänger	**flash pack**
Blickverlauf	**gaze motion**
Blickverlaufstest	**eye-movement test**
Blindtest	**blind test**
Blinzeltest	**eyeblink test**
Bodenfläche	**floor space**
Bodenverkaufsständer	**floor stand**
Bon	**voucher**
Bonus	**bonus**

Boom	**boom**
Bord, frei an ... plus frei von ...	**free on board free off board (fob/fob)**
Börse	**market**
Börse, feste	**firm market**
Börsenkurs	**market price**
Börsenstimmung	**undertone**
Börsentag	**market day**
Bösgläubigkeit	**bad faith**
Boston-Box	**Boston Box**
Boston-Matrix	**Boston Box**
Bote	**messenger**
Boulevardpresse	**popular press**
Boutique	**boutique**
Box-Jenkins-Methode	**Box-Jenkins method**
Boykott	**boycott**
Brainstorming	**brainstorming**
Branche	**business**
Branche	**line of business**
Branche	**trade**
Branchenadressbuch	**classified directory**
Branchenfernsprechbuch	**Yellow Pages**
Branchenklassifikation (GB)	**Standard Industrial Classification**
Branchenpublikation	**vertical publication**
Branchenverzeichnis	**Yellow Pages**
Branchenverzeichnis	**classified directory**
Branchenverzeichnis	**directory**
Branchenverzeichnis	**trade directory**
Brauch	**custom**
Break-Even-Analyse	**breakeven analysis**
Break-Even-Preisbildung	**breakeven pricing**
Breakeven-Preis	**breakeven price**
Breakeven-Punkt	**breakeven point**
Bremse, fiskalpolitische	**fiscal drag**
Brett, schwarzes	**bulletin board**
Brett, schwarzes	**noticeboard**
Brief (Bö)	**asked price**
Brief, kurzer	**note**
Brief, persönlicher	**personal letter**
Brief, unzustellbarer	**dead letter**
Briefchen	**sachet**
Briefform	**letter style**
Briefkasten	**letterbox/letter box**
Briefkasten	**mail box**
Briefkasten	**post**
Briefkasten, elektronischer	**electronic mail (e-mail)**
Briefkastenfirma	**bubble company**
Briefkastenfirma	**letterbox company**
Briefkastenmarketing	**letterbox marketing**
Briefkopf	**heading**
Briefkopf	**letterhead**

Briefkurs (Bö)	**asked price**
Briefkurs (Bö)	**offer(ed) price**
Briefkuvert	**envelope**
Briefstil	**letter style**
Briefumschlag	**cover**
Briefumschlag	**envelope**
Briefumschlag mit Werbung auf der Rückseite	**bangtail**
Briefumschlag ohne Fenster (je nach Format DIN C 6 oder DIN-lang)	**fullface envelope**
Briefumschlag, dessen Klappe als Bestellformular dient	**bangtail**
Briefumschlag, großer	**gusset envelope**
Briefverkehr, elektronischer	**electronic mail**
Briefwerbeaktion	**mail(ing) shot**
Briefwerbematerial	**mailer**
Britische Woche	**British week**
Broker	**broker**
Broschüre	**brochure**
Broschüre	**leaflet**
Broschüre	**pamphlet**
Bruchprobe	**torture testing**
brutto	**gross**
Brutto(anlagen)investitionen	**gross investment**
Bruttoallphasenumsatzsteuer	**turnover tax**
Bruttoausgaben (VGR)	**gross national expenditure**
Bruttobetrag	**gross amount**
Bruttoeinkommen	**income**
Bruttoeinkünfte	**gross income**
Bruttoeinnahmen	**gross receipts**
Bruttoerlös	**gross income**
Bruttogehalt	**gross income**
Bruttogewicht	**gross weight**
Bruttogewinn	**gross margin**
Bruttogewinn	**gross profit**
Bruttogewinn	**margin**
Bruttogewinnprozentsatz	**gross profit percentage**
Bruttoinlandsausgaben	**gross domestic expenditure**
Bruttoinlandsinvestitionen	**gross domestic capital formation**
Bruttoinlandsprodukt (BIP)	**gross domestic product**
Bruttokontaktsumme	**gross circulation**
Bruttokontaktwahrscheinlichkeit	**gross opportunity to see**
Bruttoproduktion	**gross output**
Bruttoreichweite	**gross circulation**
Bruttoreichweite	**gross audience**
Bruttosozialprodukt (BSP)	**gross national product**
Bruttosozialprodukt (BSP) Deflator	**gross national product (GNP) deflator**
Bruttosozialprodukt (BSP) zu Marktpreisen	**current gross national product**
Bruttosozialprodukt, nominales	**nominal gross national product**

Bruttoumsatz	**gross sales**
Bruttoumsatz	**gross turnover**
Bruttoumsatzerlös	**return**
Bruttoverdienst	**gross income**
Bruttoverlust	**gross loss**
Buch	**volume**
Bücherstand	**bookstand**
Buchhülle	**dust cover**
Buchrücken	**back cover**
Büchse	**can**
Buchstabiertafel	**telephone alphabet**
Buchung	**booking**
Buchung	**reservation**
Bude	**booth**
Budeninhaber	**stall holder**
Budget	**budget**
Budget, flexibles	**flexible budget**
Budget, starres	**fixed budget**
Budgetbeschränkung	**budget constraint**
Budgetgerade	**budget line**
Budgetrestriktion	**budget constraint**
Bulletin	**bulletin**
Bumerangeffekt	**boomerang effect**
Bund	**bundle**
Bündel	**bundle**
Bundeskartellamt (Deutschland)	**Federal Cartel Office**
Bürgerberatungsbüro	**Citizens Advice Bureau**
Bürgerinitiative	**public interest group**
Bürgerinitiative	**civic action group**
Bushel (Hohlmaß)	**bushel**

C

C-Klauseln	**C-terms**
Carryover-Effekt	**carryover effect**
Cash und Carry - Geschäft	**cash and carry**
Cash, electronic	**electronic funds transfer at the POS**
Cashflow-Prognose	**cash flow forecast**
Caterer	**caterer**
Catering	**catering**
Centstück (USA)	**penny**
Charakter	**character**
Charakteristikum	**feature**
Charge	**batch**
Chargennummer	**batch number**
Checkliste	**checklist**
Chef-Layouter	**art director**
Chiffre(nummer)	**key number**
Chiffreanzeige	**blind ad**
Chiffreanzeige	**keyed advertisement**

Clique	**clique**
Clusteranalyse	**cluster analysis**
Co-op (Gemeinschafts) Coupons	**co-op coupons**
Cobweb Theorem	**cobweb theorem**
Cocktail Party Marketing Theorie	**cocktail party theory of marketing**
Code	**code**
Combipack-Angebot	**banded offer**
Comeback	**comeback**
Competitive-Parity-Method (Methode zur Festlegung des Werbeetats, die sich an Konkurrenz orientiert	**competitive parity method**
Computer-Hardware	**hardware**
Container	**container**
Container(fracht)rate	**container rate**
Container, Entladen eines	**unstuffing**
Container, wiederverwendbarer	**reusable container**
Container, zylindrischer	**drum**
Container-Abnahmebescheinigung	**container inspection report**
Container-Bahnstation	**dry port**
Container-Frachtbrief	**container bill of lading**
Container-Frachtrate	**box rate**
Container-Komplettladung (volle)	**full container load (FCL)**
Containerbeladen	**stuffing**
Containerbeladung	**container stuffing**
Containerdepot	**container terminal**
Containerentladen	**stripping**
Containerfrachtladestelle	**container freight station (CFS)**
Containerschiff	**container ship**
Containerstapler	**container carrier truck**
Containerstellplatz	**slot**
Containerterminal	**container terminal**
Containerverkehr	**containerization**
Containerverkehr, Umstellung auf	**containerization**
Containerzug	**freightliner**
Copyright	**copyright**
Copytesten	**copytesting/copy testing**
Corporate Identity	**corporate identity**
Coupon	**in-pack coupon**
Couponanzeige	**coupon advertisement**
Couponwerbung	**admail**
Couponwerbung	**enquiry follow-up**
Courtage	**brokerage**
Courtage	**courtage**
Crash	**crash**
Crowding Out	**crowding-out**

D

D-Klauseln (Incoterms)	**D-terms**
DAGMAR-Modell	**DAGMAR model**
DIPADA	**DIPADA**

Dachmarke	**family brand**
Dachmarke	**umbrella brand**
Dachpreisstrategie	**umbrella pricing**
Darstellung, falsche	**misrepresentation**
Darstellung, grafische	**graph**
Databasemarketing	**database marketing**
Dateipflege	**file maintenance**
Daten	**data**
Daten(erfassungs)kasse	**point of sale system**
Daten, statistische	**statistics**
Daten-Matrix	**data matrix**
Datenanalyse	**data analysis**
Datenaustausch, elektronischer	**electronic data interchange**
Datenbank	**data bank**
Datenblatt	**data sheet**
Dateneingabe	**data entry**
Datenerfassung	**collection**
Datenerfassung	**data collection**
Datenkasse	**electronic point of sale (EPOS)**
Datenschutz	**data protection**
Datenschutzgesetz	**Data Protection Act**
Datensicherung	**data protection**
Datenspeicher	**data storage**
Datenträger	**data carrier**
Datenübermittler	**common carrier**
Datenverarbeitung	**data processing**
Datierung, offene, nicht kodierte	**open dating**
Dauerauftrag, langfristiger (mit laufendem Abruf)	**blanket order**
Datumsbedingungen	**date terms**
Dauerdumping	**persistent dumping**
Dauerinflation	**persistent inflation**
Dauernachfrage	**repeat demand**
Dauerniedrigpreis	**every day low price**
Dauerseher	**heavy viewer**
Day-After-Recall (DAR)	**day-after recall**
Deal-in	**deal-in**
Deal-out	**deal-out**
Dealer	**dealer**
Debitnote	**debit note**
Debitor	**debtor**
Debitorenbuch	**sales journal**
Debitorenverkauf	**factoring**
Deckenanhänger	**mobile**
Deckungsbeitrag	**contribution margin**
Deckungsbeitrag	**margin**
Deckungsbeitrag	**contribution**
Deckungsbeitrag pro Ausbringungseinheit	**unit contribution margin**
Deckungsbeitragsrechnung	**contribution costing**
Deckungsbeitragsrechnung	**direct costing**

Decoder	**decoder**
Defizit	**shortage**
Deflation	**deflation**
Deflation, galoppierende	**galloping deflation**
Deflationspolitik	**deflationary policy**
Degenerationsphase	**decline stage**
Dekodierer	**decoder**
Dekodierung	**decoding**
Delkredere	**del credere**
Delkredereagent	**del credere agent**
Delkredeprovision	**del credere commission**
Delphi-Befragung	**Delphi method**
Demand-Side-Economics	**demand side economics**
Demarketing	**demarketing**
Demassifizierung	**demassification**
Demo	**demonstration**
Demographie	**demography**
Denkmodell	**idea**
Denkweise, unorthodoxe	**lateral thinking**
Depot	**depot**
Depot eines Güterverkehrsunternehmens	**trucker-owned warehouse**
Depot, firmeneigenes	**company-owned warehouse**
Depression	**depression**
Depression	**slump**
Design	**design**
Designerprodukt	**designer product**
Desinflation	**disinflation**
Destinator	**consignee**
Detailhandelskette	**retail(ing) chain**
Determinanten der Konsumenten-/ Verbrauchernachfrage	**determinants of consumer demand**
Deutsche Mark	**mark**
Dia	**slide**
Diagramm	**chart**
Diagramm	**graph**
Diebstahl, geringfügiger	**pilferage**
Dienste und Güter, bezahlte, aber noch nicht gelieferte	**dead horse**
Dienste, geleistete	**services rendered**
Dienstgespräch	**business call**
Dienstleistung	**service**
Dienstleistung im gewerblichen Bereich	**business service**
Dienstleistung, nicht güterbezogene	**nongoods service**
Dienstleistungen	**services**
Dienstleistungen, erbrachte	**services rendered**
Dienstleistungen, erweitertes Marketingmix für ...	**extended marketing mix for services**
Dienstleistungen, kaufmännische	**commercial services**
Dienstleistungsbetrieb	**service provider**
Dienstleistungserbringer	**service provider**

Dienstleistungsindustrie	**service industry**
Dienstleistungsmarke	**service mark**
Dienstleistungsmarketing	**service marketing**
Dienstleistungsmarkt	**service market**
Dienstleistungssektor	**service sector**
Dienstleistungsverkehr	**invisible trade**
Dienstreise	**business trip**
Differenz	**difference**
Differenz zwischen zwei Preisen	**spread**
Differenzierung	**differentiation**
Diffusions-Prozeß	**diffusion process**
Direct-Response-Verkauf	**direct responce selling**
Direktabsatz	**direct marketing**
Direktansage	**live tag**
Direktantwort	**direct response**
direktbezogen (Wareneinkauf)	**first hand**
Direktbezug	**direct pruchase**
Direktdienste	**direct services**
Direkteinkauf	**buying round**
Direkteinkauf	**direct purchase**
Direktmarketingunternehmen	**direct mail house**
Direktverkauf	**direct marketing**
Direktverkauf	**factory outlet**
Direktverkauf	**nonstore retailing**
Direktverkauf (an Verbraucher)	**house-to-house selling**
Direktverkäufer	**house-to-house salesperson**
Direktversandwerbung	**direct mail advertising**
Direktwerbeaktion, Echo auf	**direct response**
Direktwerber	**canvasser**
Direktwerber	**mailer**
Direktwerber	**solicitor**
Direktwerbung durch die Post	**direct mail advertising**
Discount-Geschäft mit Vollsortiment	**full-line discount store**
Discounter	**discount house**
Discounter	**discounter**
Discountladen	**off-price shop**
Diskont(waren)haus mit Vollsortiment	**full-line discounter**
Diskont-Piraterie	**discount piracy**
Diskont/Rabatt, bar abzüglich ...	**cash less discount**
Diskonterträge	**discount(s) received**
Diskontgeschäft	**discount house**
Diskontpreis	**at a discount**
Diskonttabelle	**discount table**
Diskontwarenhaus	**discounter**
Diskussionskreis	**focus group**
Diskussionsrunde	**panel**
Dispatcher	**despatcher**
Dispersionstheorie	**dispersion theory**
Displayvergütung	**display allowance**
Disponent	**chaser**

Disponent	**expediter/expeditor**
Dissonanz, kognitive	**cognitive dissonance**
Distanzfracht	**distance freight**
Distanzfracht	**pro rata freight**
Distribution	**distribution**
Distribution, physische	**physical distribution (PD)**
Distributionsmix	**distribution mix**
Distributionsplanung	**distribution planning**
Diversifikation	**diversification**
Diversifikation, horizontale	**horizontal diversification**
Diversifikation, konglomerate, laterale	**conglomerate diversification**
Diversifikation, konzentrische	**concentric diversification**
Diversifikation, laterale, seitliche	**lateral diversification**
diversifizieren	**branch out**
Diversifizierung	**diversification**
Divisionskalkulation	**process costing**
Dokumente, handelsübliche, kaufmännische	**commercial documents**
Doppelpackung	**twin pack**
Doppelseite, halbe	**half-page (double) spread**
Doppelseitenanzeige, halbe	**half-page (double) spread**
Doppelverdiener, kinderlose	**Dinks**
Dose	**can**
Downsizing	**downsizing**
Draufgabe	**earnest (money)**
Draufgabe	**token payment**
Draufgeld	**earnest (money)**
Draufgeld	**token payment**
Drehbuch	**script**
Drehbuch	**storyboard**
Drehbuchannahme	**copy clearance**
Drehbuchautor	**scriptwriter**
Drehständer	**spinner**
Drei-Buchstaben-Abkürzung	**three-letter code**
drei L`s	**three Ls**
Drittland	**third country**
Drittleser	**tertiary reader**
Drive-in	**Drive-in**
Druckauflage	**gross circulation**
Drückergruppe	**group of solicitors**
Druckfehler	**literal (error)**
Druckfehler	**printer`s error**
Druckmedien, Kauf über die ...	**off-the-page buying**
Drucksache	**printed matter**
Drucksachenbeilage	**envelope stuffer**
Drucksachenumschlag	**postage saver**
Druckzeilenzahl	**lineage**
Dukatenesel	**cash cow**
Dumping	**dumping**
Dumping, gelegentliches	**sporadic dumping**
Dumping, negatives, umgekehrtes	**reverse dumping**

Dumping, räuberisches	**predatory dumping**
Dumping, räuberisches	**predatory pricing**
Duopol	**duopoly**
Duopson	**duopsony**
Duplizierung von Hörern/Lesern/ Zuschauern	**audience duplication**
Durchdringung	**penetration**
Durchfracht	**through rate**
Durchfrachttarif	**through rate**
Durchführbarkeitsstudie	**feasibility study**
Durchführung	**implementation**
Durchführung von lokalen Markttests	**test marketing**
Durchführungsverzögerung	**implementation lag**
Durchführungsverzögerung, betriebliche	**inside lag**
Durchlaufpreis	**carry-through rate**
Durchschnitt	**mean**
Durchschnitt, gleitender	**moving average**
Durchschnitts...	**average**
Durchschnittserlös	**average revenue**
Durchschnittskosten	**average costs**
Durchschnittspreis	**average price**
Durchschnittspreiskalkulation	**plateau pricing**
Durchwahl	**direct dial(l)ing**
Durckmedien, Werbung in	**press advertising**
Dutzend	**dozen**

E

E-Klausel	**E-term**
E-mail	**electronic mail (e-mail)**
EDV-Textanfertigung	**desktop publishing**
EDV-Überweisungsverkehr	**electronic funds transfer**
EFTPOS	**electronic funds transfer at the POS**
Echo auf Direktwerbeaktion	**direct response**
Eckplatzanzeige auf der Titelseite	**title corner**
Eckplatzanzeige auf der Titelseite	**ear**
Effekt, fiscal-drag	**fiscal drag**
Effekte, negative, externe	**external diseconomies**
Effekte, positive, externe	**external economies**
Effektivität	**effectiveness**
Effektivitätszuwachs	**economies of scale**
Effizienz	**efficiency**
Effizienz, ökonomische	**economic efficiency**
Ego	**ego**
Ehepaar mit doppeltem Einkommen ohne Kinder	**DINK**
Ehrenkodex, beruflicher	**code of ethics**
Eigenimage	**self image**
Eigeninserat	**house advertisement**
Eigenproduktion	**direct production**

Eigenschaft	**quality**
Eigenschaften, Gewährleistung für zugesicherte ...	**express warranty**
Eigenschaftverbesserung	**feature improvement**
Eigentum, gewerbliches	**industrial property**
Eigentumsübergabe	**delivery**
Eigentumsübertragung	**transfer of ownership**
Eigentumsübertragung	**transfer**
Eigentumsvorbehalt	**retention of ownership**
Eigentumsvorbehaltsklausel	**reservation of title (RT) clause**
Eigentumsvorbehaltsklausel in Teilzahlungsverträgen	**add-on clause**
Eigenwerbesendung	**house advertisement**
Eignungsstudie	**feasibility study**
Eignungstest für Verkaufspersonal	**sales aptitude test**
Eilauftrag	**pressing order**
Eilauftrag	**rush order**
Eilfracht	**fast freight**
Eilpost	**express post**
Eilzustellung	**express post**
Eilzustellung	**express delivery**
Eilzustellung	**special delivery**
Ein- und Verkaufsabteilung, Leiter der	**merchandise manager**
Ein-Produkt-Strategie	**single product strategy**
Einband	**cover**
Einchecken	**checkin**
Einfluß, normativer	**normative influence**
Einfluß, unzulässiger	**undue influence**
Einflußfaktoren, wirtschaftliche	**economic environment**
Einfühlungsvermögen	**empathy**
Einführung	**introduction**
Einführung	**launch**
Einführung (Produkt), landesweite	**national introduction**
Einführung neuer Produkte	**product pioneering**
Einführungsangebot	**introductory offer**
Einführungsparty	**launching party**
Einführungsphase	**introduction stage**
Einführungsphase	**pioneering stage**
Einführungsrabatt	**get-acquainted discount**
Einführungsrabatt	**introductory discount**
Einführungstest	**product placement test**
Einführungswerbung	**announcement advertising**
Einführungswerbung	**pioneer(ing) advertising**
Eingang	**receipt**
Eingangsanzeige	**advice of arrival**
Eingangsbenachrichtigung	**arrival notification form**
Eingangsdatum	**date of receipt**
Eingangsfracht	**carriage inward(s)**
Eingangsfracht und Ausgangsfracht	**freight in and out**
Eingangsrechnung	**purchase(s) invoice**

Einheit	**unit**
Einheitsbrief	**standard letter**
Einheitsladung	**unit(ised) cargo**
Einheitsladung	**unit load**
Einheitspreis	**uniform price**
Einheitspreisbildung	**unit pricing**
Einheitspreisgeschäft	**single price store**
Einheitspreispolitik	**one-price policy**
Einheitspreisstrategie	**single price strategy**
Einkauf	**purchasing**
Einkauf	**procurement**
einkaufen	**marketing**
Einkauf alles unter einem Dach	**one-stop shopping**
Einkauf im Einkaufszentrum	**one-stop shopping**
Einkauf(szentrale) vor Ort	**local buying office**
Einkauf, elektronischer	**electronic shopping**
Einkauf, zentraler	**central(ised) buying**
Einkauf/Verkauf durch Direkt/ Sofortbestellung	**direct response selling**
Einkäufe	**purchases**
Einkäufe	**shopping**
Einkaufen	**buying**
Einkaufen	**shopping**
Einkaufen, bargeldloses	**cashless shopping**
Einkaufen, preisbewußtes, wählerisches	**cherry picking**
Einkäufer	**buyer**
Einkäufer	**buying agent**
Einkäufer	**purchasing agent**
Einkäufer	**shopper**
Einkaufsabrechnung eines Kommissionärs	**account purchase**
Einkaufsabteilung	**buying department**
Einkaufsabteilung	**purchasing department**
Einkaufsagent	**purchasing agent**
Einkaufsbummel	**shopping spree**
Einkaufsbummel mit einem Parkhalt	**one-stop shopping**
Einkaufskanal	**shopping channel**
Einkaufskommissionär	**buying agent**
Einkaufskonto	**purchases account**
Einkaufskorb	**basket**
Einkaufskorb	**shopping basket**
Einkaufsleiter	**buyer**
Einkaufsleiter	**purchasing manager**
Einkaufsmarketing	**reverse marketing**
Einkaufsort	**point-of-purchase**
Einkaufsskonto	**purchase discount**
Einkaufsstraße	**shopping mall**
Einkaufssystem, kundenbedientes	**automatic checkout machine**
Einkaufstasche	**shopping bag**
Einkaufsverhalten	**buying behaviour**
Einkaufsviertel	**shopping precinct**

Einkaufswagen	**shopping trolley**
Einkaufswagen	**trolley/trolly**
Einkaufszentrum	**trading estate**
Einkaufszentrum (regionales)	**shopping center**
Einkaufszentrum, Einkauf im ...	**one-stop shopping**
Einkaufszentrum, lokales	**community shopping center**
Einkommen	**income**
Einkommen und Nachfrage	**income and demand**
Einkommen vor Steuerabzug	**pretax income**
Einkommen, (frei) verfügbares	**spendable earnings**
Einkommen, effektives	**real income**
Einkommen, frei verfügbares	**discretionary income**
Einkommen, pro Kopf	**per capita income**
Einkommen, verfügbares	**disposable income**
Einkommen, verfügbares, persönliches	**disposable personal income**
Einkommen-Hypothese, permanente	**permanent-income hypothesis**
Einkommenseffekt	**income effect**
Einkommenseffekt durch Preisänderung	**income effect of a price change**
Einkommenselastizität der Nachfrage	**income elasticity (of demand)**
Einkommenselastizität, negative	**negative income elasticity**
Einkommenselastizität, positive	**positive income elasticity**
Einkommensgefälle	**income differential**
Einkommenshypothese, relative	**relative income hypothesis**
Einkommenskreislauf	**flow of income**
Einkommenskreislaufgeschwindigkeit des Geldes	**income velocity of circulation**
Einkommensmobilität	**income mobility**
Einkommenspolitik	**incomes policy**
Einkommenssegmentierung	**income segmentation**
Einkommensteuer	**income tax**
Einkommensteuerfreibetrag	**income tax allowance**
Einkommensumverteilung	**income redistribution**
Einkommensumverteilung	**redistribution of income**
Einkommensverteilung	**income distribution**
Einkreisungsattacke	**encirclement attack**
Einkuvertieren	**stuffing**
Einlieferung	**delivery**
Einlösung	**redemption**
Einlösungsrate	**redemption**
Einnahme	**income**
Einnahme	**take**
Einnahmen	**gate money**
Einnahmen	**receipts**
Einnahmen	**takings**
Einnahmen aus unsichtbaren Leistungen	**invisible earnings**
Einpersonenhaushalt	**single-person household**
Einprägungszeit	**retention time**
Einreichungsfrist	**filing date**
Einreichungsschluß	**closing date**
Einrichtung, wohltätige	**charity**

Eins-zu-eins-Befragung	**one-to-one interview**
Einschaltprozentsatz, Kosten pro	**cost per rating point**
Einschaltquote	**audience rating**
Einschaltquote	**rating**
Einschaltquote	**share of audience**
Einschaltquote	**sets in use (SIU) rating**
Einschaltquote	**viewer rating**
Einschaltquote von Hörern, die bewußt ihr Lieblingsprogramm eingeschaltet haben	**Q rating**
Einschaltquote von Zuschauern, die bewußt ihr Lieblingsprogramm eingeschaltet haben	**Q rating**
Einschaltquote, durchschnittliche	**average audience rating**
Einschaltquote, gemessen von der A.C. Nielsen Company (USA)	**Nielsen rating**
Einschreiben mit Rückschein	**return receipt**
Einsendeabschnitt (Werbung)	**coupon**
Einsendeschluß	**deadline**
Einstandsgeld	**footing**
Einstandskosten der verkauften Ware	**cost of goods sold**
Einstandspreis	**cost price**
Einstandspreis der verkauften Ware	**cost of goods sold**
Einstellung	**attitude**
Einstellungsmessung	**attitude testing**
Einstellungsstudie	**attitude study**
Einstellungsveränderung	**attitude change**
Einstiegszeit	**access**
Eintausch	**exchange**
Eintritt	**footing**
Eintrittsgelder	**gate money**
Eintrittshäufigkeit	**frequency (freq)**
Eintrittskarte	**ticket**
Eintrittskarte	**voucher**
Eintrittssperrenpreis	**limit price**
Einwand	**objection**
Einwand, angegebener, erklärter	**stated objection**
Einwand, berechtigter	**valid objection**
Einwand, versteckter, verborgener	**hidden objection**
Einweg(ver)packung	**nonreturnable packing**
Einwegartikel	**one-way good(s)**
Einwegflasche	**one-way bottle**
Einwegpackung	**one-way package**
Einwegverpackung	**disposable pack(aging)**
Einwegverpackung	**nonreturnable packing**
Einwegware	**disposable product**
Einwohnerzahl	**population (Popn)**
Einzahlung	**payment**
Einzahlungsstrom	**cash inflow**
Einzel-Produkttest	**monadic product test**

Einzelanfertigung	**job production**
Einzelauslage von Waren	**spot display**
Einzelbezugsquelle	**single sourcing**
Einzelfertigung	**one-off production**
Einzelfertigung	**unit production**
Einzelfrachttarif	**commodity rate**
Einzelhandel	**retailing**
Einzelhandel	**retail trade**
Einzelhandel, elektronischer	**electronic retailing**
Einzelhandel, globaler	**global retailing**
Einzelhandels(einkaufs)genossenschaft	**retail(er) cooperative**
Einzelhandels(preis)index	**index of retail prices**
Einzelhandels-Fabrikladen für Endverbraucher	**factory outlet**
Einzelhandelsbestandsaufnahme	**store audit**
Einzelhandelsbetrieb	**trading business**
Einzelhandelsdiscountgeschäft	**retail discount house/store**
Einzelhandelseinkauf, elektronischer	**electronic retailing**
Einzelhandelsgeschäft	**outlet**
Einzelhandelsgeschäft	**retail outlet**
Einzelhandelskette	**multiple**
Einzelhandelskette	**retail(ing) chain**
Einzelhandelslebenszyklus	**retail life cycle**
Einzelhandelsmarketing	**retail marketing**
Einzelhandelsmix	**retail(ing) mix**
Einzelhandelspark	**retail park**
Einzelhandelspositionierung	**retail positioning**
Einzelhandelspreis	**retail price**
Einzelhandelspreisindex	**General Retail Price Index**
Einzelhandelspreisindex	**retail price index**
Einzelhandelsumsatzanalyse	**retail sales analysis**
Einzelhandelsverkauf	**retailing**
Einzelhandelsverkauf, elektronischer	**electronic retailing**
Einzelhandelsvertreter/in	**retail rep**
Einzelhandelsvertriebsform, bei der das Sortiment im Katalog präsentiert wird	**catalog(ue) showroom**
Einzelhandelswerbung	**retail advertising**
Einzelhandelverkäufer/in	**retail salesperson**
Einzelhändler	**merchant**
Einzelhändler	**retailer**
Einzelhändler mit beschränktem Sortiment	**limited line retailer**
Einzelhändler, Zusammenschluß von	**voluntary chain**
Einzelhändler, der seine Ware vermietet	**hire retailer**
Einzelhändler, selbständiger	**independent retailer**
Einzelhändlercoupon	**retailer coupon**
Einzelhändlerzeitschrift	**dealer magazine**
Einzelheiten	**particulars**
Einzelhonorar	**fee for service**
Einzelkosten	**prime cost**
Einzelperson, Werbung für eine	**person marketing**

Einzelverpackung	**unit pack(ing)**
Einzugsbereich	**catchment area**
Eisberg-Prinzip	**iceberg principle**
Eisenwaren	**hardware**
Elan	**drive**
Elastizität	**elasticity**
Elastizität = 1	**unitary elasticity**
Elastizität der Nachfrage	**elasticity of demand**
Elastizität des Angebots	**elasticity of supply**
Elastizität, unendliche	**perfect elasticity**
Elastizitätskoeffizient	**elasticity coefficient**
Elimination	**deletion**
Eliminierung	**deletion**
Eliminierung einer Produktgruppe	**line divestment**
Eltern, deren Kinder ausgezogen sind	**empty nesters**
Embargo	**embargo**
Emissionsanzeige	**tombstone advertising**
Emissionsprospekt	**prospectus**
Emissionsprospekt, vorläufiger	**red herring (prospectus)**
Empfang	**receipt**
Empfang	**reception**
Empfänger	**addressee**
Empfänger	**receiver**
Empfänger	**recipient**
Empfänger (von Waren)	**consignee**
Empfänger unbekannt	**addressee unknown**
Empfänger, Gebühr bezahlt ...	**freepost**
Empfangsdatum	**receiving date**
Empfangsort	**place of receipt (POR)**
Empfehlung, unverlangte	**unsolicited testimonial**
Empfehlungen als Briefschluß	**greetings**
Empfehlungskarte	**compliments slip (comp slip)**
Empfehlungskarte	**with compliments slip**
Empfehlungszettel	**compliments slip**
Empfehlungszettel	**with compliments slip**
empirisch	**empirical**
Endabnehmer	**end user**
Endbestand	**closing inventory**
Endbetrag	**grand total**
Enderzeugnis	**end product**
Enderzeugnis	**final product**
Endgewinn	**bottom line**
Endpreis	**final price**
Endprodukt	**end product**
Endprodukt	**final product**
Endscheidungsprozeß des Endverbrauchers	**final consumer`s decision process**
Endverbraucher	**consumer**
Endverbraucher	**end consumer**
Endverbraucher	**final consumer**
Endverbraucher	**ultimate user**

Endverbraucher, Endscheidungsprozeß des	**final consumer`s decision process**
Endverbraucherpreis	**consumer price**
Endverlust	**bottom line**
Engelsche Gesetz	**law of consumption**
Engelsches Gesetz	**Engel's law**
Engpaß	**bottleneck**
Engpaßbereich	**bottleneck**
Engpaßgebiet	**bottleneck area**
Engrosbezug	**bulk buying**
Entflechtung (Kartellgesetz)	**divestiture**
Entflechtung (Kartellgesetz)	**divestment**
Entgegenkommen	**accomodation**
Entgegenkommen	**concession**
Entgelt	**consideration**
Enthorten	**dishoarding**
Entladen	**discharge**
Entladen	**unloading**
Entladen eines Containers	**unstuffing**
Entlastung (einer Schuld/Verpflichtung)	**quittance**
Entscheider	**decider**
Entscheidung über Eigenfertigung oder Fremdbezug	**make or buy decision**
Entscheidung, versteckte	**hidden decision**
Entscheidungsbildung, extensive	**extensive decision making**
Entscheidungsträger	**decision maker**
Entscheidungsträger	**decider**
Entscheidungsunterstützungssystem	**decision support system**
Entscheidungsverzögerung	**decision lag**
Entsparen	**dissaving**
Entstaatlichung	**denationalisation**
Entstehungsperiode	**gestation period**
Entwicklung	**development**
Entwicklung, beschleunigte	**accelerated development**
Entwicklungland	**less developed country**
Entwicklungs-Fördergebiet	**development area**
Entwicklungsabteilung	**development department**
Entwicklungsaufwand	**development cost(s)**
Entwicklungsgebiet, besonderes	**special development area**
Entwicklungskosten	**development cost(s)**
Entwicklungsrichtung	**trend**
Entwurf	**design**
Entwurf	**draft**
Entwurf	**layout**
Ereignis	**event**
Ereignis, durch Werbung finanziertes	**sponsored event**
Ereignissegmentierung	**occasion segmentation**
Erfahrung	**experience**
Erfahrungsgut	**experience good**
Erfahrungskurve	**experience curve**
Erfahrungskurve, Preisbildung mittels der	**experience curve pricing**

Erfahrungsqualitäten	**experience qualities**
Erfindung	**invention**
Erfindung, bahnbrechende	**breakthrough product**
Erfolg	**profit**
Erfolgskennziffer	**operating ratio**
Erfolgskonto	**trading account**
Erfolgskontrolle	**rating**
Erfolgsquote	**hit rate**
Erfüllung	**fulfil(l)ment**
Erfüllung	**take-down**
Erfüllungsort	**place of fulfil(l)ment**
Erfüllungstag	**due date**
Ergänzungswerbung	**accessory advertising**
Ergebnis	**outcome**
Erhalt	**receipt**
Erhaltungswerbung	**maintenance advertising**
Erhebung (Stat)	**survey**
Erhebungsbogen	**questionnaire**
Erhebungsforschung	**observation research**
Erhöhung	**rise**
Erholung, markttechnische	**technical rally**
Erinnerung an den Inhalt einer Werbeanzeige	**ad playback**
Erinnerung, gestützte	**aided recall**
Erinnerung, gestützte	**prompted recall**
Erinnerung, spontane	**spontaneous recall**
Erinnerungswerbung	**reminder advertising**
Erkennungsmelodie	**sounder**
Erkennungsmelodie	**theme**
Erkennungsverzögerung	**recognition lag**
Erkundigung	**query**
erlaubt	**free**
Erlebnismarketing	**events marketing**
Erlös	**proceeds**
Erlöschen	**lapse**
Ermessensauswahl	**convenience sampling**
Ermessensauswahl	**judgement sampling**
Ermessensauswahl	**nonprobability sampling**
Ermittler	**investigator**
Erneuerung	**replacement**
Erneuerung	**renewal**
Erneuerung, laufende	**continuous innovation**
Erntebeschränkung	**crop restriction**
Eroberungsstrategie	**conquest strategy**
Eröffnung	**opening**
Erorberungsdumping	**predatory dumping**
Erregungsmethode	**galvanic skin response**
Ersatz(stück)	**replacement**
Ersatzbedarf	**replacement demand**

Ersatzinserat	**makegood**
Ersatzspot	**makegood**
Ersatzware	**replacement good**
Erscheinungsbild, einheitliches (eines Unternehmes)	**corporate identity**
Erscheinungsdatum	**publication date**
Erschließungsbedarf	**latent demand**
Ersparnis, negative	**dissaving**
Ersparnisse, positive, externe	**external economies**
Ersparnisse, volkswirtschaftliche	**aggregate savings**
Erstauftrag	**first order**
Erstauftrag	**first order**
Erstausrüster	**original equipment manufacturer**
Erstbesteller	**launch customer**
Ersterwerber	**first-time buyer**
Erstkauf	**initial purchase**
Erstkauf	**new buy**
Erstkauf	**trial purchase**
Erstkontakt	**initial approach**
Erstleser	**buyer-reader**
Erstleser	**primary reader**
Erstverkauf	**initial sale**
Ertrag	**yield**
Ertrag aus investiertem Kapital	**return on capital (employed)**
Ertrag, durchschnittlicher	**average revenue**
Erträge, zunehmende	**increasing returns**
Ertragsgesetz	**diminishing returns (law of)**
Ertragsgesetz	**law of diminishing returns**
Ertragsschwelle	**breakeven point**
Erwartungen	**expectations**
Erwartungen, wirtschaftliche	**economic expectations**
Erwartungselastizität	**elasticity of expectation**
Erwerber	**purchaser**
Erwerber	**vendee**
Erwerbsgesellschaft	**acquisitive society**
Erwiderung	**response**
Erzeuger	**manufacturer**
Erzeugerpreis	**producer price**
Erzeugerpreisindex	**producer price index**
Erzeugnis	**article**
Erzeugnis	**product**
Erzeugnis, artverwandtes	**related product**
Erzeugnis, bahnbrechendes	**breakthrough product**
Erzeugnis, veredeltes	**improved product**
Erzeugnisse, halbfertige	**semi-finished products**
Erzeugnisse, unfertige	**partly manufactured goods/products**
Erzeugnisse, unfertige	**work in process**
Essen	**fare**
Eßgeschirr	**flatware**
Etat	**budget**

Etatbeschränkung	budget constraint
Ethik	ethics
Etikett	docket
Etikett	label
Etikett	tag
Etikett	ticket
Etikett mit Inhaltsangaben	descriptive label
Etikett, produktorientiertes	descriptive label
Etikettierung	label(l)ing
Etikettierung, aufklärende	informative labelling
Eträge	proceeds
Euro-Markenartikel	Eurobrand
Euro-Markenprodukt	Eurobrand product
Euro-Werbung	Euro ad(vertisement)
Europäische Gemeinschaft (EG)	Common Market
Europäische Gemeinschaft (EG)	European Community
Europäische Union (EU)	European Union (EU)
Europäische Währungseinheit (ECU)	European Currency Unit
Europäischer Binnenmarkt	European domestic market (EDM)
Europäischer Wirtschaftsraum (EWR)	European Economic Area (EEA)
Eventmarketing	events marketing
Exemplar	copy
Exemplare, bestellte	request(ed) circulation
Existentialismus	existentialism
Existenzerhaltungspreisbildung	survival pricing
Existenzfähigkeit, wirtschaftliche	viability
Existenzgründungskredit	business startup loan
Existenzminimum	subsistence level
Existenzwert	existence value
Exklusivleser	exclusive reader
Exklusivvertrieb	exclusive distribution
Exkursion	excursion
Expansion	expansion
Expansionspreisbildung	expansion pricing
Expedient	despatcher
Expedition	despatch/dispatch
Expedition	forwarding
Expedition	mailroom
Experiment	experiment
Expertengruppe	panel of experts
Exponat	exhibit
Export, indirekter	indirect exporting
Export- und Inlandsmarketing	export and domestic marketing
Export-Basispreis	basic export price
Export-Marketing	export marketing
Export-Marketing Strategie	export marketing strategy
Export-Preisbildung	export pricing
Export-Preisliste	export price list
Exporterklärung	specification
Exportförderung	export promotion

Exporthandel	export trade
Exportlieferung	export delivery
Exportmarkt	export market
Exportpreis	export price
Exportpreisangebot	export price quotation
Express-Vertrieb	express distribution
Extraangebot	with-pack premium
Extraauflage	bonus circulation
Extras	optional extras
Extraware statt Nachlaß/Rabatt	free merchandise
Eyecatcher	flash pack

F

F-Klauseln	F-terms
FIO-Klausel	free in and out
Fabrik	factory
Fabrik	plant
Fabrikmarke	manufacturer(`s) brand
Fabrikverkauf	factory sale
Fabrikverkaufsstelle	factory outlet
Fachausstellung	trade fair
Fachgeschäft	specialist shop
Fachgespräch	shoptalk
Fachgroßhändler	specialty-merchandise wholesaler
Fachhändler	stockist
Fachhändler mit größeren Auslieferungslagern	stockist agency
Fachmesse	trade show
Fachpresse	trade press
Fachsprache	jargon
Fachverband	trade association
Fachzeitschrift	journal
Fachzeitschrift	professional journal
Fachzeitschrift	trade journal
Factor	factor
Factoring	factoring
Factoring, stilles, verdecktes	undisclosed factoring
Factoring-Provision	factorage
Factoringgeschäft	factoring
Factoringgesellschaft	factor
Fahrgast	fare
Fahrgeld	fare
Fahrkarte	ticket
Fahrkartenverkaufsstelle	ticket agency
Fahrlässigkeit	negligence
Fahrplan	schedule
Fahrpreis	fare
Fahrpreis, voller	full fare
Fahrrad-Bote	despatch rider

Fahrtstrecke	**route**
Fahrzeug	**vehicle**
Fahrzeug mit Hubladebühne	**high loader**
Fahrzeugzuschuß	**car allowance**
Faksimile	**facsimile**
Faktor, dispositiver	**entrepreneur**
Faktoranalyse	**factor analysis**
Faktoren, die Angebotsänderungen bewirken	**factors affecting changes in supply**
Faktoren, die Nachfrageänderungen bewirken	**factors affecting changes in demand**
Faktorgrenzkosten	**marginal factor cost**
Faktorkosten	**factor cost**
Faktornachfrage	**factor demand**
Faktura	**invoice**
Fakturierung	**sales invoicing**
Fakturierung	**invoicing**
Fakturierung, fortlaufende	**continuous billing**
Fallen	**fall**
Fälligkeitstag	**due date**
Falschdarstellung	**misrepresentation**
Fälschung	**imitation**
Fälschungen	**bogus merchandise**
Falschwerbung	**deceptive advertising**
Falschwerbung	**misleading advertising**
Falsifikat	**imitation**
Faltanzeige	**foldout**
Faltblatt	**folder**
Faltblatt, großes	**broadsheet**
Faltsprospekt	**leaflet**
Familien-Lebenszyklus	**family life cycle**
Familienbudget	**familiy budget**
Familienlebenszyklus	**family life cycle**
Familienmarke	**family brand**
Familienserie, rührselige	**soap opera**
Familienstand	**marital status**
Faq-Qualität	**fair average quality**
Farbbeilage	**colour supplement**
Farben und Verpackung	**colours and packaging**
Farbmusterkarte	**colour chart**
Faß	**barrel**
Faß	**cask**
Faß, großes	**hogshead**
Faß, kleines	**keg**
Fäßchen	**keg**
Fast-Nachahmung	**passing off**
Faxversand	**fax mailing**
Feedback	**feedback**
Fehlbestand	**stockout**
Fehlbetrag	**shortage**
Fehler	**error**

Fehler	**fault**
Fehler	**imperfection**
Fehler	**mistake**
Fehler, kleiner	**lapse**
Fehler, statistischer	**statistical error**
Fehler, systematischer (Stat.)	**bias**
Fehlerhaftigkeit	**imperfection**
Fehlerquote	**error rate**
Fehlersuche	**troubleshooter**
Fehlfracht	**dead freight**
Fehlmenge	**shortage**
Fehlmengenkosten	**out-of-stock costs**
Fehlmengenkosten	**stockout cost(s)**
Fehlschluß	**fallacy**
Fehlschluß der Verallgemeinerung	**fallacy of composition**
Fehlstreuung	**waste circulation**
Feilschen	**haggling**
Feilscher/in	**haggler**
Feingehalt	**fineness**
Feingehaltsstempel	**hall mark/hallmark**
Feldarbeit	**fieldwork**
Feldforschung	**field research**
Feldforschung	**fieldwork**
Fensteraufkleber	**window banner**
Fernfracht	**distance freight**
Ferngespräch	**national call**
Ferngespräch	**trunk call**
Fernseh- und Rundfunkfinanzierung, Übernahme durch Nichtwerbeträger	**underwriting**
Fernseh-/Radiosendung, kurze Absage am Ende	**tag**
Fernseheinschaltquote	**television rating**
Fernseheinschaltquote	**viewer rating**
Fernsehen, durch Werbung finanziertes	**sponsored television**
Fernsehhaushalt	**television household**
Fernsehmarketing	**television marketing**
Fernsehpause	**act break**
Fernsehprogramm mit Geschenken/Preisen	**giveaway/give away**
Fernsehsender, Werbung in lokalen	**spot television**
Fernsehwerbung	**television advertising**
Fernsehwerbung, lokale, regionale	**spot advertising**
Fernsehzeit	**time spent viewing**
Fernsehzuschauer	**viewer**
Fernsehzuschauer pro Haushalt	**viewers per household**
Fernsehzuschauer, Zahl der effektiven	**persons using television**
Fernsprechgebühr	**toll**
Fernsprechgebühren	**telephone rates**
Fertigerzeugnisse	**finished goods**
Fertigfabrikate	**finished goods**
Fertiggericht	**instant**

Fertiggericht(e)	**convenience good(s)**
Fertigmahlzeiten, Lieferung von	**catering**
Fertigprodukt	**final product**
Fertigprodukt	**readymade**
Fertigstellungsbescheinigung	**certificate of manufacture**
Fertigung	**manufacturing**
Fertigung	**production**
Fertigungsabteilung	**production department**
Fertigungsauftrag	**shop order**
Fertigungsauftrag	**manufacturing order**
Fertigungseinheit	**unit of production**
Fertigungseinzelkosten	**prime cost**
Fertigungsgemeinkosten	**manufacturing overhead**
Fertigungskapazität	**production capacity**
Fertigungskosten	**cost(s) of production**
Fertigungskosten	**manufacturing cost(s)**
Fertigungsstätte	**factory**
Fertigungswirtschaft	**manufacturing industry**
Fertigungszeit	**production cycle**
Fertigwarenlager	**finished goods inventory**
Fertiware	**readymade**
Fest(tag)	**festival**
Festangebot	**firm offer**
Festauftrag	**firm order**
Festessen	**banquet**
Festigungswerbung	**reinforcement advertising**
Festival	**festival**
Festpreis	**firm price**
Festpreismethode	**fixed-price technique**
Festsetzung des Werbeetats nach dem Gesichtspunkt, welche Ausgaben man sich leisten kann	**affordable method**
Festsetzung des Werbeetats, über den Daumen gepeilt	**arbitrary method**
Festsetzung von Prestigepreisen	**premium pricing**
Festspiele	**festival**
Festverkauf	**firm sale**
Fettdruck	**boldface/bold face**
Fifo-Methode	**first-in, first-out**
Fifty-fifty (50:50) Plan	**fifty-fifty (50:50) plan**
Filiale	**branch**
Filialkette	**chain store**
Filialkette	**retail(ing) chain**
Filialleiter	**branch manager**
Filmuntertitel	**caption**
Filterfrage	**filter question**
Finanz-Supermarkt	**financial supermarket**
Finanzierung eines Warenlagers	**floor plan (finance)**
Finanzierung eines Warenlagers	**floor plan(ning)**
Finanzierungs-Leasing	**finance lease**

Finanzkauf	**hire purchase**
Finanzwerbung	**financial advertising**
Finnmark	**mark**
Firmen-Goodwillwerbung	**institutional advertising**
Firmenansehen	**company image**
Firmeneinkauf	**organisational buying**
Firmengelände-Marketing	**business site marketing**
Firmengruppe	**group**
Firmenimage, Gestaltung des	**atmospherics**
Firmenimagewerbung	**corporate (image) advertising**
Firmenimagewerbung	**prestige advertising**
Firmenkennzeichen	**brand mark**
Firmenlogo	**brand mark**
Firmenname	**business name**
Firmenname	**company name**
Firmenname	**firm name**
Firmenname	**tradename**
Firmenreferenz	**trade reference**
Firmenschild	**facia**
Firmenwagen	**company car**
Firmenwerbung	**institutional advertising**
Firmenwert (immaterieller)	**goodwill**
Fixkosten	**fixed cost(s)**
Fixkosten	**unavoidable costs**
Fixkosten, durchschnittliche	**average fixed cost(s)**
Flächenstichprobe	**area sample**
Flaschenanhänger	**bottle hanger**
Flaute	**depression**
Flaute	**downswing**
Flaute	**lull**
Flaute	**stagnation**
Flaute	**slackness of business**
Flipchart	**flip chart**
Floaten (von Wechselkursen)	**float**
Flohmarkt	**flea market**
Flop	**flop**
Flugbegleiter	**flight attendant**
Flugblatt	**flier/flyer**
Flugblatt	**fly sheet**
Flugblatt	**giveaway/give-away**
Flugblatt	**handbill**
Flugblatt	**leaflet**
Fluggesellschaft	**carrier**
Flughafenhotel	**airtel**
Flughafensteuer	**departure tax**
Flugplan	**schedule**
Flugpreis	**fare**
Flugticket	**ticket**
Flugurlaub mit vorbestelltem Mietwagen	**fly-drive holiday**
Flugzeug, frei	**free on aircraft (foa)**

Fluktuation	**fluctuation**
Flüssigkeitsverlust	**ullage**
Flüssigware	**wet goods**
Fly and Drive	**fly-drive holiday**
Focusgruppe	**focus group**
Folge, arithmetische	**arithmetic(al) progression**
Folge, geometrische	**geometric progression**
Folgeleser	**pass-along/-on reader**
Folgeleser	**secondary reader**
Folgemarkt	**aftermarket**
Folgeprodukt, angepaßtes, erweitertes, verändertes	**adaptive new product**
Folie	**foil**
Folienverpackung	**blister pack(age)**
Folioblatt (einmal gefalteter Druckbogen)	**folio**
Förderer	**patron**
Fördergebiet	**special development area**
Forderung	**demand**
Forderungen (aus Lieferungen und Leistungen), Ankauf u Bevorschussung von	**factoring**
Förderungsgebiet	**enterprise zone**
Forderungsberechtigter	**debtee**
Format	**format**
Formelpreisbildung	**formula pricing**
Forschung und Entwicklung	**research and development**
Forschung, angewandte	**applied research**
Forschung, empirische	**empirical research**
Fortschrittsbericht	**progress report**
Fortschrittszahlung	**progress payment**
Fracht	**freight**
Fracht bezahlt	**carriage paid**
Fracht gegen/per Nachnahme	**freight forward**
Fracht mit niedrigem Staumaß	**low density cargo**
Fracht nach Gewicht/Maß	**weight/measurement (W/M) freight**
Fracht, von mehreren Spediteuren beförderte	**interline freight**
Fracht vorausbezahlt	**freight prepaid**
Fracht zahlbar am Bestimmungsort	**freight forward**
Fracht zahlt Empfänger	**carriage forward**
Fracht(gut)	**cargo**
Fracht(ver)stauung	**cargo stowage**
Fracht, heterogene	**heterogeneous cargo**
Fracht, homogene	**homogeneous cargo**
Fracht, von mehreren Spediteuren beförderte	**interline freight**
Frachtbasis	**basing point**
Frachtbasis, Preisfestsetzung auf	**basing-point pricing**
Frachtbeförderung	**freightage**
Frachtbrief	**waybill**

Frachteingangsbenachrichtigung	**arrival notification form**
Frachter	**cargo ship**
Frachter	**freighter**
Frachtflugzeug	**cargo plane**
Frachtflugzeug	**freighter**
frachtfrei	**carriage paid**
frachtfrei	**carriage free**
frachtfrei	**freight prepaid**
frachtfrei (bis) Grenze	**carriage paid to frontier**
Frachtfüher, Risiko des	**carrier's risk**
Frachtführer	**carrier**
Frachtführer, privater	**private carrier**
Frachtgebühr	**freight charge**
Frachtgut	**freightage**
Frachtgut, homogenes	**homogeneous cargo**
Frachtgut, nicht-containerfähiges	**non-containerizable cargo**
Frachtgutmarkierung	**cargo marking**
Frachtkosten	**carriage**
Frachtkosten	**freightage**
Frachtkosten	**freight costs**
Frachtkosten	**freight**
Frachtkosten (Bahn/LKW)	**truckage**
Frachtkosten nach Gewicht	**weight charge**
Frachtkosten, tarifunabhängig von Warenart	**freight all kind(s) (FAK, fak)**
Frachtkostenübernahme	**freight absorption**
Frachtliste	**manifest**
Frachtmanifest	**cargo manifest**
Frachtrate für Stückgut	**general cargo rate (GCR)**
Frachtrate, offene	**open rate**
Frachtraum	**space**
Frachtrechnung	**freight invoice**
Frachtrechnung	**freight note**
Frachtschiff	**cargo ship**
Frachtschiff	**freighter**
Frachttarif	**freight rate**
Frachtunterbietung	**rate cutting**
Frachtversicherer	**carriage underwriter**
Frachtvertrag	**freight contract**
Frachtvorauszahlung	**advance freight**
Frachtzahlung am Bestimmungsort	**freight payable at destination**
Frage	**query**
Frage mit begrenzter Antwortmöglichkeit	**limited response question**
Frage mit unvollendetem Satz	**sentence completion question**
Frage mit vorgegebenen Antwortmöglichkeiten	**closed-end question**
Frage, direkte	**direct question**
Frage, eindeutige, unzweideutige	**unambiguous question**
Frage, halbstrukturierte	**semistructured question**
Frage, nicht zu beantwortende	**unanswerable question**

Frage, offene oder frei beantwortbare	**open-ended question**
Frage, skalierte	**ranking (scale) question**
Frage, strukturierte	**structured question**
Frage, unstrukturierte	**unstructured question**
Frage, zwei-, mehrdeutige	**ambiguous question**
Frage-und-Antwortspiel	**question and answer**
Fragearten	**question types**
Fragebogen	**aide-memoire**
Fragebogen	**questionnaire**
Fragebogen zum Selbstausfüllen	**self completion questionnaire**
Fragebogen, postalischer	**postal questionnaire**
Fragebogen, schriftlicher	**self completion questionnaire**
Fragebogen, strukturierter	**structured questionnaire**
Fragebogen, unstrukturierter	**unstructured questionnaire**
Fragebogengestaltung	**questionnaire design**
Fragesteller(in)	**interviewer**
Fragezeichen(produkt)	**question mark**
Franchisegeber	**franchisor/franchiser**
Franchisenehmer	**fanchisee**
Franchising (Art von Filialsystem)	**franchising**
Frankaturvermerk	**freight prepayment mark**
frankiert	**post paid**
franko	**carriage free**
franko	**charges prepaid**
Frau, sehr geehrte	**Madam**
Frauenzeitschrift	**womens`s magazine**
frei	**franco**
frei Geschäft	**free in store (FIS)**
frei Haus	**franco domicile**
frei LKW (USA)	**free on truck (FOT, fot)**
frei Laden	**free in store (FIS)**
frei Waggon (GB)	**free on truck (FOT, fot)**
frei an Bord plus frei von Bord	**free on board free off board (fob/fob)**
frei ein und aus	**free in and out**
frei laden und löschen (Lieferklausel)	**free in and out**
frei, franko Waggon	**free on rail / free on truck**
freibleibend	**without engagement**
Freiexemplar	**sample copy**
Freiexemplar	**unpaid copy**
Freiexemplare	**request(ed) circulation**
freigemacht	**post paid**
Freigabebescheinigung	**release note (RN)**
Freihandel	**free trade**
Freihandelsbefürworter	**free trader**
Freihandelsgebiet	**free trade area**
Freihandelsgemeinschaft	**free trade association**
Freihandelszone	**free trade area**
Freihauslieferungszone	**free delivery area**
Freiheit, wirtschaftliche	**economic freedom**
Freikarte	**complimentary ticket**

Freistempelung	**franking**
Freiumschlag	**business reply envelope**
Freiumschlag	**reply paid envelope**
Freiumschlag	**stamped envelope**
Freiumschlag, adressierter	**stamped addressed envelope (SAE, sae)**
Freiversand	**controlled circulation**
Freizeit	**free trime**
Fremdenverkehr	**tourism**
Fremdenverkehrsamt	**information office**
Fremdenverkehrsmarketing	**tourist marketing**
Frequenzzuweisung	**allocation**
"Freßviertel"	**food court**
Freundschaftsvertrag	**sweetheart contract**
Frischhaltedatum	**pull date**
Frist	**time limit**
Frist für Barzahlung	**discount period**
Fristablauf	**lapse of time**
Frontwerbefläche	**front end**
Frühdispositionsrabatt	**early order discount**
Frühindikator	**leading economic indicator**
Frühindikator	**leader**
Fuhrpark	**fleet**
Fuhrunternehmer	**carter**
Fuhrunternehmer	**haulier**
Fuhrunternehmer	**haulage contractor**
Full-Service-Einzelhändler	**full-service retailer**
Full-Service-Werbeagentur	**full-service advertising agency**
Füllanzeige	**filler**
Füllen	**stuffing**
Füller	**filler**
Füllmaterial	**stuffing**
Fundbüro	**lost and found office**
Fungibilien	**fungibles**
Funkmedienkontakter	**time buyer**
Funktionsrabatt	**functional discount**
Für und Wider von Werbung	**advertising pros and cons**
Fusion	**merger**
Fusion(ierung)	**amalgamation**
Fuß	**foot**
Fußgängerzone	**pedestrian precinct**
Fußnote	**footnote**
Fußnote	**note**

G

Gabelstapler	**forklift (truck)**
Gag	**gag**
Gallone	**gallon**
Galvanometermethode	**galvanic skin response**
Gang	**aisle**

Garantie	**warrant**
Garantie(erklärung)	**warranty**
Garantie, erweiterte, verlängerte	**extended guaranty/guarantee**
Garantieerklärung	**guarantee/guaranty**
Garantiefonds	**guarantee fund**
Garantiepreis	**guaranteed price**
Garantievertreter	**del credere agent**
Garderobe	**check room**
Garderobenfrau	**checker**
Garderobenschein	**check**
Gast	**patron**
Gastfreundschaft	**hospitality**
Gastgeberland	**host country**
Gattungsbezeichnung	**generic term**
Gattungskauf	**sale by description**
Gattungsname	**generic term**
Gattungssachen	**generics**
Gattungssachen	**unascertained goods**
Gattungsware	**unascertained goods**
Gauß'sche Normalverteilung	**normal (Gaussian) distribution**
Gebiet	**field**
Gebiet	**zone**
Gebietsaufteilung	**zoning**
Gebietskartell	**market sharing cartel**
Gebietsleiter	**area manager**
Gebietsleiter	**territory manager**
Gebot	**bid**
Gebot, erstes (Versteigerung)	**opening bid**
Gebot, letztes	**closing bid**
Gebrauchsanleitung	**directions for use**
Gebrauchsanweisung	**directions for use**
Gebrauchsanweisung	**fly sheet**
Gebrauchsfähigkeit	**performance**
Gebrauchsfähigkeit, eines Produkts	**product performance**
Gebrauchsgüter	**consumer(s') goods**
Gebrauchsgüter	**consumer durables**
Gebrauchsgüter	**hard goods**
Gebrauchsgüter	**utility goods**
Gebrauchsgüter (langlebige)	**durables**
Gebrauchsgüter, teure	**big ticket items**
Gebrauchsmuster, eingetragenes	**registered design**
Gebrauchswert	**value in use**
Gebrauchswert	**value**
Gebrauchtwarenhändler	**secondhand dealer**
Gebühr	**charge**
Gebühr	**fee**
Gebühr bezahlt Empfänger	**freepost**
Gebühr(en)	**tariff**
Gebühren	**dues**
Gebühren	**terms**

Gebührenanzeiger	**call-charge indicator**
Gebührenliste	**scale of charges**
Gebührenrechnung	**bill of charges**
Geburtenrate	**birth rate**
Gedächtnistest	**recall test**
Gedächtnistest, reiner	**unaided recall test**
Gedanke	**idea**
Gefahr	**hazard**
Gefährdungshaftung	**absolute liability**
Gefährdungshaftung	**strict liability**
Gefahrgut	**hazardous cargo**
Gefahrgutschein	**dangerous goods note (DGN)**
Gefälligkeit	**service**
Gefeilsche	**haggling**
Gegenangebot	**counter offer**
Gegenangebot	**counterbid**
Gegendarstellung in der Werbung (freiwillige oder gesetzlich erzwungene)	**counteradvertising**
Gegengebot	**counter offer**
Gegengebot	**counterbid**
Gegengeschäft (AuW)	**counterpurchase**
Gegenkauf (AuW)	**counterpurchase**
Gegenmacht	**countervailing power**
Gegenofferte	**counter offer**
Gegenseitigkeitsgeschäft	**contra-deal**
Gegenseitigkeitsvereinbarung	**reciprocal dealing**
Gegenstand, in Zahlung gegebener	**trade-in**
Gegenwartswert	**present value**
Gelbe Seiten	**Yellow Pages**
Geld "waschen"	**laundering money**
Geld zurück, bei Nichtgefallen	**money back guarantee**
Geld, gehortetes zirkulieren lassen	**dishoarding**
Geldausgabe(n)	**expense(s)**
Geldbetrag, an Verkäufer gegebner zur Zahlung der Ware	**tender cash**
Geldbetrag, einbehaltener	**retention money**
Geldeinwurf (Automat)	**slot**
Gelder freigeben	**release**
Gelder, flüssige	**cash in/on hand**
Geldgeber	**backer**
Geldgeber	**sponsor**
Geldillusion	**money illusion**
Geldinstitut	**finance house**
Geldkassette	**till**
Geldkuh	**cash cow**
Geldmittelbewegung	**flow of funds**
Geldrückerstattung	**money refund**
Geldschein (USA)	**greenback**
Geldstrom	**flow of funds**
Geldüberschuß	**excess supply of money**

Geldwäsche	**laundering of money**
Geldwert	**money value**
Geldwert	**value**
Geldwert, realer	**real value of money**
Gelegenheitskauf	**bargain**
Gelegenheitskunde	**casual customer**
Gelegenheitskunde	**irregular customer**
Gelegenheitskunde	**occasional customer**
Gelegenheitspreis	**bargain price**
Gelegenheitssegmentierung	**occasion segmentation**
Gelieferte, das	**delivery**
Geltungskonsum	**conspicuous consumption**
Geltungskonsum	**ostentatious consumption**
gemäß	**as per**
Gemeinkosten	**indirect cost(s)**
Gemeinkosten	**overhead**
Gemeinschaft, europäische (EG)	**European Community**
Gemeinschafts(werbe)versand	**cooperative mailing**
Gemeinschafts-Vertrieb	**joint marketing**
Gemeinschaftsunternehmen	**joint venture**
Gemeinschaftswerbung	**cooperative advertising**
Gemeinschaftswerbung	**group advertising**
Gemeinschaftswerbung eines Herstellers mit seinen Händlerkunden	**vertical cooperative advertising**
Gemischtwarengeschäft	**general store**
Gemischtwarengroßhändler	**general merchandise wholesaler**
Gemischtwarenhandel	**scrambled merchandising**
Genehmigung	**licence**
Generalvertrag	**blanket contract**
Generalvertreter	**general agent**
Generalvertreter	**universal agent**
Generation X	**generation X**
Generika	**generics**
Genossenschaft	**cooperative society**
Genossenschaft, landwirtschaftliche	**agricultural cooperative**
Genußmensch	**hedonist**
Geozentrismus	**geocentrism**
Gepäckabfertigung	**parcel(s) office**
Gepäckaufbewahrer	**checker**
Gepäckaufbewahrung (Bahn)	**check room**
Gepäckausgabe	**luggage claim**
Gepäckschein	**check**
Gerechtigkeit	**fairness**
Geriatrika	**geriatric products**
Gesamtabschluß	**blanket purchasing contract**
Gesamtangebot	**aggregate supply**
Gesamtangebot	**composite supply**
Gesamtangebot	**total offer**
Gesamtangebotskurve	**aggregate supply curve**

Gesamtarbeitsvorgang, Zeit für	**cycle time**
Gesamtauflage	**total circulation**
Gesamtauftragszyklus	**total order cycle**
Gesamtausgaben der Inländer für Güter und Leistungen	**absorption**
Gesamtbetrag	**total**
Gesamtgeldbedarf	**aggregate monetary demand**
Gesamthörerschaft, Prozentsatz der	**share of audience**
Gesamtkosten	**total cost(s)**
Gesamtkosten, durchschnittliche	**average total cost(s)**
Gesamtnachfrage	**aggregate demand**
Gesamtnachfrage	**composite demand**
Gesamtnachfrage	**market demand**
Gesamtnachfrage, monetäre	**aggregate monetary demand**
Gesamtnachfragekurve	**aggregate demand curve**
Gesamtnutzen	**total utility**
Gesamtpreis	**all-in-price**
Gesamtpreis	**total price**
Gesamtproduktion	**aggregate production**
Gesamtsumme	**grand total**
Gesamtsumme	**total**
Gesamtumsatzerlös	**total revenue**
Gesamtvertriebskosten	**total distribution costs**
Gesamtzahl der Hörer	**total audience**
Gesamtzahl der Hörer, die Sender/ Programm hören	**individuals reached**
Gesamtzahl der Leser	**total audience**
Gesamtzahl der Zuschauer	**total audience**
Gesamtzahl der Zuschauer, die Sender/ Programm sehen	**individuals reached**
Gesamtzahl der erreichten Sendernetzhaushalte	**households reached**
Geschäft	**bargain**
Geschäft	**business transaction**
Geschäft	**deal**
Geschäft	**store**
Geschäft	**trade**
Geschäft	**transaction**
Geschäft auf Gegenseitigkeit	**reciprocity**
Geschäft für Bedarfsartikel mit langen Öffnungszeiten	**bantam store**
Geschäft im Geschäft	**shop within a shop**
Geschäft in einem Geschäft	**in-store shop**
Geschäft mit Bindung an eine Lieferfirma	**tied shop**
Geschäft mit beschränktem Sortiment	**box store**
Geschäft unter Freunden	**sweetheart contract**
Geschäft, faires	**fair deal**
Geschäft, frei	**free in store (FIS)**
Geschäft, kleines	**shop**
Geschäft, konjunkturabhängiges	**cyclic(al) business**

Geschäft, schlechtes	**bad bargain**
Geschäft, unabhängiges	**independent store**
Geschäfte, laufende	**current transactions**
Geschäfte, zu wenig haben	**understored**
Geschäftemacher	**profiteer**
Geschäftemacher	**racketeer**
Geschäftsabschluß	**commercial transaction**
Geschäftsabschluß ohne Gewinn u. Verlust	**breakeven**
Geschäftsadresse	**business address**
Geschäftsaufgabe	**closure**
Geschäftsaufgabe, Verkauf wegen	**forced sale**
Geschäftsbedingungen, allgemeine	**general terms and conditions**
Geschäftsbesuch	**business call**
Geschäftsbeziehung	**account**
Geschäftseinheit, strategische (SGE)	**strategic business unit (SBU)**
Geschäftsessen	**business lunch**
Geschäftsflaute	**slackness of business**
Geschäftsgeheimnis	**trade secret**
Geschäftsimage	**store image**
Geschäftsinhaber	**shopkeeper**
Geschäftskarte	**business card**
Geschäftskatalog	**trade catalog(ue)**
Geschäftskatalog	**trade list**
Geschäftskosten, feste	**fixed charge**
Geschäftsmann	**trader**
Geschäftspraktiken, restriktive	**restrictive business practices (RBPs)**
Geschäftsreise	**business trip**
Geschäftsschluß	**closing time**
Geschäftsstatistik	**business statistics**
Geschäftsstellenleiter	**branch manager**
Geschäftsstraße	**shopping mall**
Geschäftstreue	**store loyalty**
Geschäftsviertel	**downtown**
Geschäftsviertel	**shopping precinct**
Geschäftsviertel	**trading estate**
Geschäftsvorfall	**business transaction**
Geschäftswert	**goodwill**
Geschäftszeit	**business hours**
Geschäftszweig	**business**
Geschenk	**gift**
Geschenkartikelwerbung	**specialty advertising**
Geschenkgutschein	**gift voucher**
Geschenkpapier	**gift wrapping**
Geschenkpapier	**wrapping paper**
Geschenkverpackung	**gift wrapping**
Geschlechtssegmentierung	**sex segmentation**
Geschwätz	**eye-wash**
Gesellschaft, nachindustrielle	**postindustrial society**
Gesellschaft, transnationale	**transnational corporation**
Gesellschaften, Liste der 5OO größten in den USA	**Fortune 500**

Gesellschaftssystem	**social system**
Gesellschaftswerte	**social values**
gesetzwidrig	**illegal**
Gesetz der großen Zahlen	**law of large numbers**
Gesetz der steigenden (Grenz)Erträge	**law of increasing returns**
Gesetz des komparativen Vorteils	**law of comparative advantage**
Gesetz gegen Gefahren für Verbraucher/GB	**Consumer Safety Act**
Gesetz gegen Wettbewerbs-beschränkungen (GB)	**Fair Trading Act**
Gesetz über Vertragsrücktritt	**Cooling-off law**
Gesetz über Warenbeschreibung (GB)	**Trade Description Act**
Gesetz vom abnehmenden Ertrag(szuwachs)	**diminishing returns (law of)**
Gesetz vom abnehmenden Ertrag(szuwachs)	**law of diminishing returns**
Gesetz vom abnehmenden Grenznutzen	**law of diminishing marginal utility**
Gesetz von Angebot und Nachfrage	**law of supply and demand**
Gesetz, ökonomisches	**economic law**
Gesetze über den Warenverkauf (GB)	**Sale of Goods Acts**
Gesetze, Gossensche	**Gossen's laws**
Gespräch, freies	**in-depth interview**
Gestaltspsychologie	**Gestalt psychology**
Gestaltung	**design**
Gestaltung des Erscheinungsbildes des Unternehmens	**corporate design**
Gestaltung des Firmenimages	**atmospherics**
Gestell	**rack**
Gestell	**shelf**
Gesundschrumpfung	**shakeout**
Getränk im Karton	**bag-in-a-box**
Getränkeunterlage	**drip mat**
Gewährleistung	**guarantee/guaranty**
Gewährleistung	**warranty**
Gewährleistung für zugesicherte Eigenschaften	**express warranty**
Gewährleistung, vertragliche	**express warranty**
Gewährleistungsausschluß	**caveat emptor**
Gewährleistungspflicht des Verkäufers	**caveat vendor**
Gewalt, höhere	**force majeure**
Gewebe	**material**
Gewerbegebiet	**commercial district**
Gewichtsbescheinigung	**certificate of weight**
Gewichtsbescheinigung	**weight note**
Gewichtsfracht	**weight charge**
Gewichtsliste	**weight list**
Gewinn	**income**
Gewinn	**prize**
Gewinn	**profit**
Gewinn	**yield**
Gewinn vor Steuerabzug	**pretax profit**

Gewinn, außergewöhnlicher	**superprofit**
Gewinn, realisierter	**realized profit**
Gewinn, realisierter, verdienter	**earned income**
Gewinn- und Verlustrechnung	**operating statement**
Gewinnanteil	**rake off**
Gewinnaufschlag (in %)	**markup**
Gewinnaufschlag, variabler	**variable markup**
Gewinnberechnung	**calculation of profit(s)**
Gewinndruck	**profit squeeze**
Gewinne, kleine - schnelle Umsätze	**small profits, quick returns**
Gewinnermittlung	**calculation of profit(s)**
Gewinnmaximierung	**profit maximization**
Gewinnmaximierung, gegenwärtige	**current profit maximization**
Gewinnmitnahme	**profit taking**
Gewinnmitnahme, kleine	**scalp**
Gewinnmitnahmestrategie	**milking strategy**
Gewinnschwelle	**breakeven point**
Gewinnschwellenanalyse	**breakeven analysis**
Gewinnspanne	**margin**
Gewinnspanne	**profit margin**
Gewinnspiel	**sweepstake**
Gewinnsteuer	**profits tax**
Gewinnträchtigkeit einer Marktstrategie (PIMS)	**profit impact of market strategy**
Gewinnzielkalkulation	**target pricing**
Gewißheit	**certainty**
Gewohnheit	**habit**
Gewohnheiten, ausländische	**foreign customs**
Gewohnheitskauf	**habitual buying**
Ghostshopper	**ghost shopper**
Giffen Güter	**Giffen goods**
Glanzpunkt	**highlight**
Glaube, böser	**bad faith**
Glaube, guter	**good faith**
Glaubhaftmachung	**substantiation**
Gläubiger	**creditor**
Gläubiger	**debtee**
Glaubwürdigkeit der Werbung	**advertising believability**
Glaubwürdigkeit der Werbung	**believability of advertising**
Gleichgewicht	**equilibrium**
Gleichgewicht, allgemeines/totales (ökonomisches)	**general (economic) equilibrium**
Gleichgewicht, binnenwirtschaftliches	**internal balance**
Gleichgewicht, gestörtes	**disequilibrium**
Gleichgewichtsmenge	**equilibrium output**
Gleichgewichtsmenge	**equilibrium quanity**
Gleichgewichtspreis	**equilibrium price**
Gleichgewichtsproduktion	**equilibrium output**
Gleichgewichtspunkt	**equilibrium point**
Gleichheit	**equation**

Gleichung	**equation**
Gleichwertigkeit	**indifference**
Gleisanschluß, privater	**private siding**
Globalabkommen	**omnibus agreement**
Globalbewertung einer Werbekampagne	**holistic evaluation**
Globalisierung	**globalization**
Glücksspiel	**gamble**
Glücksspiel	**hazard**
Glücksspiel	**lottery**
Gold, schwarzes	**black gold**
Goodwill	**goodwill**
Goodwill-Werbung	**image advertising**
Gossensche Gesetze	**Gossen's laws**
Grad der Markdurchdringung	**achieved penetration**
Grafik	**chart**
Grafik	**graph**
Gramm	**gramme**
Graph	**graph**
gratis	**free of charge (foc)**
Gratisanzeige	**free advertisement**
Gratiserwähnung	**editorial mention**
Gratisexemplare	**request(ed) circulation**
Gratismuster	**free sample**
Gratisverteilung	**controlled circulation**
Gratisware	**free merchandise**
Gratiszeitung	**freesheet**
Graupappe	**chipboard**
Grenzbetrieb	**marginal firm**
Grenzerlös	**marginal revenue**
Grenzerlös	**marginal profit**
Grenzkauf	**marginal purchase**
Grenzkäufer	**marginal buyer**
Grenzkonsumneigung	**marginal propensity to consume**
Grenzkosten	**direct cost(s)**
Grenzkosten	**incremental cost**
Grenzkosten	**marginal cost**
Grenzkosten, steigende	**increasing marginal cost**
Grenzkostenpreisbildung	**marginal (cost) pricing**
Grenzleistungsfähigkeit des Kapitals	**marginal efficiency of capital**
Grenznachfrager	**marginal buyer**
Grenzneigung zum Sparen	**marginal propensity to save**
Grenznutzen	**marginal utility**
Grenznutzen, Gesetz vom abnehmenden	**law of diminishing marginal utility**
Grenznutzen, abnehmender, sinkender	**diminishing marginal utility**
Grenzprodukt	**marginal product**
Grenzproduktivität	**marginal productivity**
Grenzproduzent	**marginal firm**
Grenzrate der Substitution	**marginal rate of substitution**
Grenzverkäufer	**marginal seller**
Grenzvorteil	**marginal benefit**

Grenzwert	**margin**
Grenzwertanalyse	**marginal analysis**
Gros	**gross**
Großabschluß	**big-ticket sale**
Großanschlagsfläche	**supersite**
Großanzeige	**display advertisement**
Großanzeige	**display advertising**
Großanzeige, rubrizierte	**classified display advertisement**
Großanzeigenwerbung	**display advertising**
Großaufnahme	**extreme close-up**
Großbuchstabe(n)	**uppercase**
Größe, stets vorrätige/(lager)gängige	**stock size**
Größe, konstante	**constant**
Großeinkauf	**bulk buying**
Großeinkaufsgenossenschaft	**cooperative wholesale society**
Größendegression	**economies of scale**
Größenvorteile	**economies of scale**
Großfertigung	**large-scale production**
Großformat	**king size**
Großhandel	**wholesaling**
Großhandelspreis	**trade price**
Großhandelspreis	**wholesale price**
Großhandelsunternehmen	**merchant wholesaler**
Großhändler	**distributor**
Großhändler	**jobber**
Großhändler	**merchant**
Großhändler	**wholesaler**
Großhändler für Streckengeschäft	**drop shipper**
Großhändler mit Vollsortiment	**full-line wholesaler**
Großhändler mit beschränktem Sortiment	**specialty-merchandise wholesaler**
Großhändler mit keinem oder geringem Kundendienst	**limited function wholesaler**
Großindustrieller	**magnate**
Grossist	**distributor**
Grossist ohne eigenes Lager	**drop shipper**
Großkunde	**big ticket customer**
Großkunde	**key account**
Großkunde, potentieller	**key prospect**
Großmarkt	**hypermarket**
Großpackung	**bauded pack**
Großpackung	**economy size**
Großpackung	**jumbo pack**
Großschreibung	**uppercase**
Großverbraucher	**heavy user**
Growth-Share-Matrix	**growth-share matrix**
Grundbedürfnis	**need**
Grundbedürfnisse	**basic needs**
Grundgehalt	**straight salary**
Grundgesamtheit	**universe**
Grundlagenforschung	**basic research**

Grundpreis	**advertised price**
Grundpreis	**basic price**
Grundpreis	**basic rate**
Grundpreis	**base price**
Grundstoffe	**basic commodities**
Grundstoffe	**primary products**
Grundstoffindustrie	**extractive industry**
Grundstoffindustrie	**primary industry**
Grundstücksmakler	**house agent**
Gründung	**promotion**
Grundverpackung	**primary package**
Gruppe	**group**
Gruppen, sozioökonomische	**socioeconomic groups**
Gruppendiskussion	**group discussion**
Gruppenfrachttarif	**class rate**
Gruppennormen	**group norms**
Gruppenverhalten	**group behaviour**
Gruppenverkauf	**group selling**
Gruppenwerbung	**group advertising**
Gruppierung	**group**
Gruß	**greeting**
Grüße als Briefschluß	**greetings**
Guerilla-Attacke	**Guerrilla attack**
Gut, hochwertiges	**specialty good**
Gut, homogenes	**homogeneous commodity**
Gut, meritorisches	**merit good**
Gut, räumlicher Nutzen eines	**place utility**
Gut, substitutives	**substitute good**
Gut, superiores	**superior good**
Gutachten	**report**
Güte	**quality**
Güte und Beschaffenheit, handelsübliche	**good merchantable quality and condition**
Güteklasse	**grade**
Güteklasseneinteilung	**grading**
Güter	**goods**
Güter des nicht täglichen Bedarfs	**shopping goods**
Güter des täglichen Bedarfs	**necessaries**
Güter und Dienste, bezahlte, aber noch nicht gelieferte	**dead horse**
Güter(ladung), gefährliche	**hazardous cargo**
Güter, (auf)gestaute	**stowage**
Güter, Markt für hochwertige	**class market**
Güter, freie	**free goods**
Güter, heterogene	**heterogeneous commodities**
Güter, inferiore	**inferior goods**
Güter, komplementäre	**complementary goods**
Güter, lebensnotwendige	**essential commodities**
Güter, leicht verderbliche	**perishables**
Güter, nicht lebensnotwendige	**nonessential goods**
Güter, nicht lebensnotwendige	**discretionary goods**

Güter, nicht verladene	**shut outs**
Güter, öffentliche	**collective goods**
Güter, öffentliche	**public goods**
Güter, sensible	**sensitive products**
Güter, verdorbene	**perished goods**
Güter- und Dienstleistungsmarkt	**goods and services market**
Güter- und Leistungsstrom	**flow of goods and services**
Güterbahnhof	**freight station**
Güterdepot	**freight depot**
Güterdepot	**goods depot**
Güterkraftverkehr	**road transport**
Gütermarkt	**commodity market**
Gütermarktpotential	**product market potential**
Gütermarktstrategien	**product market strategies**
Güternahverkehr	**short haul**
Güterniederlage	**freight depot**
Gütersatz, unvollständiger	**broken lot**
Gütertarif	**freight rate**
Güterverladeanlagen	**freight handling facilities**
Güterwagen, offener	**truck**
Güterwaggon	**freight car**
Güterzug	**freight train**
Gütesiegel	**hallmark**
Gütesiegel	**kitemark**
Gütesiegel (auf Produkten)	**standard label**
Gütezeichen	**certification mark**
Güte(zu)sicherung	**quality assurance**
Gutgrenze	**acceptable quality level**
Guthaben	**credit balance**
Gutschein	**coupon**
Gutschein	**gift voucher**
Gutschein	**voucher**
Gutschein, Preisnachlaß mittels ...	**coupon price reduction**
Gutschein, der für ein anderes Produkt gilt	**cross couponing**
Gutschein, der im Geschäft eingelöst wird	**store-redeemable coupon**
Gutschein, eingepackter	**in-pack coupon**
Gutschein, nur einlösbar in bestimmtem Geschäft	**in-store coupon**
Gutscheinangebot	**coupon offer**
Gutscheineinlösung	**coupon redemption**
Gutscheineinlösung	**redemption**
Gutschrift	**credit note**
Gutschrift	**credit advice**
Gutschriftsanzeige	**credit note**
Gutschriftsanzeige	**credit advice**

H

Hab und Gut	**goods and chattels**
Haftpflicht, gesetzliche	**statutory liability**
Haftung, verschuldensunabhängige	**absolute liability**
Haftung, verschuldensunabhängige	**strict liability**
Haftungsausschluß	**exclusion of/from liability**
Haftungsschäden	**liability losses**
Halb-Container	**half-height (H/H) container**
Halberzeugnisse	**semi-finished products**
Halberzeugnisse	**work in process**
Halbfabrikate	**partly manufactured goods/products**
Halbfabrikate	**semi-finished products**
Halbfettdruck	**boldface**
Halbjahres-Betriebsergebnis	**first-half operating profit**
Halbpension	**half board**
Halbseite, hochformatige	**vertical half page**
Hälfte, gewichtige	**heavy half**
Halo-Effekt	**Halo effect**
Haltbarkeit	**shelf life**
Haltbarkeit, offene	**open dating**
Haltbarkeitsdatum	**pull date**
Haltbarkeitskodierung	**date code**
Haltestelle	**stand**
Haltestellenwerbung	**station poster**
Haltung	**attitude**
Hammer, unter den ... kommen	**hammer**
Hamsterer	**hoarder**
Handbuch	**handbook**
Handbuch	**manual**
Handel	**traffic**
Handel	**trading**
Handel	**trade**
Handel (Binnen- und Außen-)	**commerce**
Handel mit dem Ausland	**overseas trade**
Handel(sverkehr), unsichtbarer	**invisible trade**
Handel, computerunterstützter	**computer-assisted trading (CAT)**
Handel, gelenkter	**managed trade**
Handel, internationaler	**international trade**
Handel, multilateraler	**multilateral trade**
Handel, rund um die Uhr	**twenty-four-hour trading**
Handeln	**bargaining**
Handelsagent	**mercantile agent**
Handelsauskunft	**trade reference**
Handelsbedingungen	**trade terms**
Handelsbeschränkungen	**restrictions on trade**
Handelsbezeichnung	**brand name**
Handelsbrauch	**custom**
Handelsbrauch	**trade custom**

Handelsbrauch	**trade usage**
Handelsbrauch	**usage of the market**
Handelsfaktura	**commercial invoice**
Handelsgeschäft	**commercial transaction**
Handelsgewinn	**turn**
Handelsgut mittlerer Art und Güte	**fair average quality**
Handelshemmnisse, nichttarifäre, zollfremde	**nontariff barriers**
Handelshemmnisse, tarifäre	**tariff barriers**
Handelshemnisse	**barriers to trade**
Handelskette, freiwillige	**voluntary chain**
Handelsklauseln im Außenhandel	**Incoterms**
Handelsmakler	**agent middleman**
Handelsmarke	**trademark/trade mark**
Handelsmarketing	**retail marketing**
Handelsmesse	**trade show**
Handelsministerium (USA)	**Department of Commerce (US)**
Handelsmission	**trade mission**
Handelsname	**brand**
Handelsname	**trade name**
Handelspanel	**retail audit**
Handelspanel	**store audit**
Handelspartner	**trading partner**
Handelsplatz	**market**
Handelspolitik	**commercial policy**
Handelsrabatt	**functional discount**
Handelsrechnung	**commercial invoice**
Handelsrecht	**commercial law**
Handelsrecht	**mercantile law**
Handelsrestriktionen	**barriers to trade**
Handelsschiff	**merchant ship**
Handelsspanne	**margin**
Handelsspanne	**markup**
Handelsspanne	**spread**
Handelsstatistik	**trade statistics**
Handelsunternehmen	**business enterprise**
Handelsunternehmen, marktbestimmendes	**megadealer**
Handelsvertreter	**commercial agent**
Handelsvertreter	**manufacturer's agent**
Handelsvertreter	**mercantile agent**
Handelsvertreter	**sales agent**
Handelsware	**merchandise**
Handelsware	**trade**
Handelsware(n)	**commercial goods**
Handelswaren, Bestand an	**merchandise inventory**
Handelswaren-Mix	**merchandise mix**
Handelszentrum	**entrepot**
Handgepäck	**hand baggage/luggage**
Handhabung	**handling**

Handhubrollwagen	**hand pallet transporter**
Handkarren	**hand barrow**
Händler	**dealer**
Händler	**distributor**
Händler	**merchant**
Händler	**trader**
Händler, ambulanter	**itinerant trader**
Händler, ambulanter	**pedlar**
Händler, fliegender	**hawker**
Händleradresse, in Werbung eingedruckte	**dealer imprint**
Händlereindruck	**hooker**
Händlermarke	**distributor brand**
Händlermarke	**private brand**
Händlernachweis (in einer Anzeige)	**dealer listing**
Händlerprovision	**dealer commission**
Händlerrabatt	**trade discount**
Händlerwerbung	**trade advertising**
Händlerzeitschrift	**dealer magazine**
Handling	**handling**
Handlung, unerlaubte wirtschaftliche	**economic tort**
Handlung, unerlaubte, rechtswidrige	**unlawful act**
Handlungsprogramm	**action programme**
Handwerk	**trade**
Handzettel	**handbill**
Handzettel	**throwaway**
Handzettel, großformatiger	**broadsheet**
Happy Hour	**happy hour**
Hardware (DV)	**hardware**
Harmonisierung	**harmonization**
Hartpapier	**manil(l)a**
Häufigkeit	**frequency (freq)**
Häufigkeitsverteilung	**frequency distribution**
Hauptabsatzgebiet	**principal market area**
Hauptabsatzgebiet	**primary marketing area**
Hauptabsatzmarkt	**prime market**
Hauptauftraggeber	**key account**
Haupterfolgsfaktoren	**key success factors**
Hauptgeschäftsviertel	**central business district (CBD)**
Hauptgeschäftszeit	**peak business hours**
Haupthandelsplatz	**primary market**
Hauptmeinungsmacher	**key buying influencer**
Hauptpost(amt)	**General Post Office**
Hauptsendegebiet	**area of dominant influence**
Hauptsendezeit	**peak time**
Hauptsendezeit	**prime time**
Hauptverbreitungsgebiet	**primary marketing area**
Hauptverkaufsargument	**focus of sale**
Hauptwerbeargument	**advertising point**
Hauptzeiten, außerhalb der	**offpeak**

Haus, frei	**franco domicile**
Haus-zu-Haus-Lieferung	**door-to-door**
Hausfrau	**lady of the house**
Hausfrauensendezeit	**housewife time**
Hausgemeinschaft	**nonfamily household**
Haushalt	**household**
Haushaltsbuchforschung	**home audit**
Haushaltsgeräte	**domestic appliances**
Haushaltspackung	**bauded pack**
Haushaltsrechnung	**familiy budget**
Haushaltswaren	**hardware**
Hausherrin	**lady of the house**
haussieren	**rocket**
haussierend	**bullish**
Hausierer	**door-to-door salesman**
Hausierer	**hawker**
Hausierer	**itinerant trader**
Hausierer	**pedlar**
Hausmarke	**dealer brand**
Hausmarke	**ownbrand**
Hausmarke	**private brand**
Hausmitteilungen	**house magazine**
Hausse, auf eine hindeutend	**bullish**
Haussemarkt	**bull market**
Haussemarkt	**boom market**
Haussespekulant	**bull**
Haussier	**bull**
Hausstil	**house style**
Haustürverkauf	**door-to-door**
Haustürverkäufer	**house-to-house salesperson**
Hauszeitschrift	**house magazine**
Hawthorne-Effekt	**Hawthorne effect**
Heckreklame	**rear**
Hedonismus	**hedonism**
Hehler	**receiver**
Heile-Welt-Werbung	**rosy advertising**
Heimarbeit	**outwork**
Heimarbeit (industrielle)	**cottage industry**
Heimindustrie	**cottage industry**
Heimverkauf	**party plan**
Heimwerkerbedarf	**DIY goods**
Heimwerkerladen	**do-it-yourself (DIY) store**
Herabsetzung	**abatement**
Herangehen(sweise)	**approach**
Herantreten	**approach**
Herausforderer	**challenger**
Hereingefallene, der/die	**fall guy**
Herkunftsbezeichnung	**informative labelling**
Herkunftszeichen	**mark of origin**
Herstell- /Verfalldatum, Kennzeichnung mit	**date coding**

herstellen	**make**
Hersteller	**maker**
Hersteller	**producer**
Hersteller	**manufacturer**
Hersteller, Preisauszeichnung durch den	**prepricing**
Hersteller, der direkt an Endverbraucher verkauft	**direct marketing manufacturer**
Herstellererwähnung im redaktionellen Teil	**editorial mention**
Herstellergarantie	**manufacturer's guarantee**
Herstellergutschein	**in-ad coupon**
Herstellermarke	**manufacturer brand**
Herstellermarke	**national brand**
Herstellermarkt	**producer market**
Herstellerpreis, empfohlener	**manufacturer`s recommended price**
Herstellerwerbung	**producer advertising**
Herstellkosten	**cost(s) of production**
Herstellkosten	**product cost(s)**
Herstellung	**manufacturing**
Herstellung	**make**
Herstellung	**production**
Herstellungsetikett	**Made in label**
Herstellungskosten	**cost**
Herstellungskosten	**cost of goods manufactured**
Herstellungskosten	**cost(s) of production**
Herstellungskosten	**cost price**
Herstellungslizenz	**manufacturing licence**
Herstellungspreis	**cost price**
Herstellungsprozeß	**industrial process**
Herunterzeichnung, automatische	**automatic markdown**
Heuristik	**heuristics**
heute, von ... an	**forward**
High-Involvement-Produkt	**high involvement product**
Hilfs- und Betriebsstoffe	**consumable supplies**
Hilfsfunktionen des Handels	**aids to trade**
Himmelswerbung	**aerial advertising**
Himmelswerbung	**sky advertising**
Hineinverkauf in den Handel	**selling in**
Hintergrundmusik, stimmungsvolle	**mood music**
Hinweis	**tip**
Histogramm	**bar chart**
Histogramm	**histogram**
Hoch	**high**
Hochkonjunktur	**boom**
Hochkonjunktur	**prosperity**
Hochpreisstrategie	**high-price strategy**
Hochpreisstrategie	**skimming pricing**
Hochsaison	**high season**
Höchstgebot	**closing bid**
Höchstkurs	**peak price**

Höchstpreis	**ceiling price**
Höchstpreis	**maximum price**
Höchstpreis	**peak price**
Höchstpreis	**price ceiling**
Höchstpreis	**price plateau**
Höchstpreis	**premium price**
Höchstpreisgestaltung	**premium pricing**
Höchststand	**high**
Hochtechnologie	**high technology**
Hochtechnologieindustrie	**sunrise industry**
Höhepunkt	**highlight**
Hogshead, Flüssigkeitsmaß (bes. für alkoholische Getränke)	**hogshead**
Home Banking	**home banking**
Home-Shopping	**home shopping**
Homo oeconomicus/Wirtschaftsmensch (der Mensch als wirtschaftliches Wesen)	**economic man**
Honorar	**fee**
Honorar	**honarium**
Honorar	**remuneration**
Honorar	**terms**
Hörer(schaft)	**audience**
Hörer, Gesamtzahl der	**total audience**
Hörer, seltener	**light listener**
Höreranalyse	**audience measurement**
Hörerschaft	**listenership**
Hörerzahl, durchschnittliche	**average audience**
horten	**hoarding**
Hortung	**hoarding**
Hot Shop	**hot shop**
Hotel- und Gaststättengewerbe	**catering trade**
Hotelabreise	**checkout**
Hotelanmeldung	**checkin**
Hotline	**hotline/hot line**
Huckepackladung	**piggyback (service)**
Huckepackspot	**integrated commercial**
Huckepackspot	**piggyback commercial**
Huckepacksystem (AuW)	**piggyback export scheme**
Huckepackverkehr	**piggyback (service)**
Hülle	**cover**
Hülle	**envelope**
Hund, armer	**dog**
Hundertjahrfeier	**centenary**
Hundertstel	**cent**
Hundredweight (Gewichtseinheit)	**hundredweight**
Hyperinflation	**hyperinflation**
Hypermarkt	**hypermarket**
Hypothese	**hypothesis**

I

ISO 9000	ISO 9000
Ich	ego
Ich-Generation	me generation
Ich-auch Produkt	me-too product
Idealbestand	model stock
Idee	idea
Ideenfindung	brainstorming
Ideengestalter	visualizer
Ideenmarketing	idea marketing
Identifikation	identification
Identifikationseinblendung	identification commercial
Identifikator	identifier
Identifizierung	identification
illegal	illegal
Illustration	illustration
Image	image
Imagedifferenzierung	image differentiation
Imagepreisbildung	image pricing
Imagestudie	image study
Imageveränderung	image change
Imagewerbung	image advertising
Imbißstube	takeaway
Imitation	imitation
Imitationsstrategie	imitative strategy
Immobilien	immovables
Immobilienmakler	house agent
Import-Preisfestsetzung	import pricing
Importeur	importer
Importfirma	importer
Importland	importer
Impulskauf	impulse buying
Impulskäufer	impulse buyer
Impulsware	impulse good
in die Höhe schnellen (Preise)	rocket
Incentive-Marketing	incentive marketing
Incoterms	Incoterms
Incoterms	trade terms
Indent, bei dem der Indentgeber dem Indent-Nehmer die Wahl der Lieferquelle überläßt (AuW)	open indent
Indentgeschäft	indent
Index	index
Index der Industrieproduktion	index of industrial production
Index der Lebenhaltungskosten	index of retail prices
Index der Lebenshaltungskosten	cost-of-living-index
Indexbindung	index linking
Indexbindung	indexing
Indexierung	index linking

Indexierung	**indexing**
Indexzahl, -ziffer	**index number**
Indifferenz	**indifference**
Indifferenzkurve	**indifference curve**
Indikator	**indicator**
Indikator, volkswirtschaftlicher	**social indicator**
Industrie	**industry**
Industrie(güter)-Marketing	**industrial marketing**
Industrie, absterbende, niedergehende	**sunset industry**
Industrie, aufstrebende	**sunrise industry**
Industrie, junge, unterentwickelte	**infant industry**
Industrie, standortgebundene	**tied industry**
Industrie, verarbeitende	**manufacturing industry**
Industrie, verarbeitende	**secondary sector**
Industrie, verarbeitende	**secondary industry**
Industrie, verstaatlichte	**nationalised industries**
Industrieerzeugnis	**industrial product**
Industrieerzeugnisse	**manufactured goods**
Industrieförderungsgebiet	**enterprise zone**
Industrieforschung	**industrial research**
Industriegelände	**trading estate**
Industriegesellschaft	**industrial society**
Industriegüter	**heavy equipment**
Industriegüter	**manufactured goods**
Industriegüterkunden	**industrial product customers**
Industrie(güter)marketing	**industrial marketing**
Industriegütermarkt	**industrial market**
Industriegüterwerbung	**industrial advertising**
Industrieland	**industrial country**
Industriemagnat	**tycoon**
Industrien, rohstofforientierte	**resource-oriented industries**
Industrienation	**industrial nation**
Industriepark	**industrial park**
Industriepolitik	**industrial policy**
Industrieproduktion	**industrial production**
Industrieproduktion	**secondary production**
Industrieproduktion, Index der	**index of industrial production**
Industriesektor	**industrial sector**
Industriezweig	**industry**
Inelastizität	**inelasticity**
Inflation	**inflation**
Inflation durch Kreditaufnahme des Staates	**government inflation**
Inflation durch Nachfragestrukturveränderungen	**demand-shift inflation**
Inflation und Nachfrage	**inflation and demand**
Inflation, angebotsinduzierte	**supply push inflation**
Inflation, dezelerierte	**disinflation**
Inflation, erwartete	**anticipated inflation**
Inflation, galoppierende	**galloping inflation**

Inflation, import-induzierte	**import-push inflation**
Inflation, importierte	**import-push inflation**
Inflation, in Kauf genommene	**validated inflation**
Inflation, kosteninduzierte	**cost-push (inflation)**
Inflation, nachfrageinduzierte	**demand-pull inflation**
Inflation, rasende	**hyperinflation**
Inflation, schleichende	**creeping inflation**
Inflation, sich spiralenförmig nach oben bewegende	**spiralling inflation**
Inflation, strukturelle	**structual inflation**
inflation, trabende	**trotting inflation**
Inflation, verdeckte, versteckte	**hidden inflation**
Inflation, zunehmende	**accelerating inflation**
Inflation, zurückgestaute	**repressed inflation**
Inflation, zurückgestaute	**suppressed inflation**
Inflationsarten	**inflation types**
Inflationsrate	**inflation rate**
Inflationsrate	**rate of inflation**
Inflationsspirale	**inflationary spiral**
Information	**information office**
Information	**message**
Information	**notice**
Informationen	**data**
Informationsblatt	**fact sheet**
Informationsblatt	**newsletter**
Informationsbrief	**newsletter**
Informationsbuch/blatt	**fact book/sheet**
Informationsregulator	**gatekeeper**
Informationsschalter	**accomodation desk**
Informationsstop	**embargo**
Informationssuche	**information search**
Informercial	**infomercial**
Infrastruktur	**infrastructure**
Inhaber eines Abzahlungsgeschäfts	**tallyman**
Inhome-Befragung	**in-home interview**
Inhome-Einzelhandel	**in-home retailing**
Inhome-Einzelhandelsverkauf	**in-home retailing**
Initialwerbung	**pioneer(ing) advertising**
Inklusivpreis	**all-in price**
Inklusivpreisbildung	**optional-product pricing**
Inkrafttreten der Zahlungsbedingungen ab Warenannahme	**receipt of goods (ROG) dating**
Inlandsgeschäft	**home sales**
Inlandsmarketing	**domestic marketing**
Inlandsmarkt	**domestic market**
Inlandsmarkt	**home market**
Inlandsmarkt	**local market**
Inlandsumsätze	**home sales**
Inlandsverbrauch	**home consumption**
Inlandsware	**home produce**

Innenstadt	**downtown**
Innenwerbung	**indoor advertising**
Innovation	**innovation**
Innovation, permanente, stetige	**continuous innovation**
Innovationsmarketing	**innovative marketing**
Innovationsteam	**venture team**
Innovator	**innovator**
Inselanzeige	**solus advertisement**
Inserat	**insert**
Inserat, verstecktes	**buried advertisement**
Inserent	**advertiser**
Inserent	**advertising space buyer**
Inserent	**space buyer**
Insertionsanweisung	**insertion order**
Insertionshäufigkeit	**frequency (freq)**
Insertionsplan	**advertising schedule**
Inspektion vor dem Versand	**preshipment inspection (PSI)**
Instabilität	**instability**
Instandhaltung	**preventive maintenance**
Instrumente der Wirtschaftspolitik	**economic instruments**
Integration	**integration**
Integration, horizontale	**horizontal integration**
Integration, laterale	**lateral integration**
Intensivinterview	**depth interview**
Intensivinterview	**qualitative interview**
Intensivvertrieb	**intensive distribution**
Intensivwachstum	**intense growth**
Intensivwerbung	**intensive coverage**
Inter-Markt-Segmentierung	**intermarket segmentation**
Interesse, öffentliches	**collective interest**
Interessenkonflikt einer Werbeagentur	**account conflict**
Interessent	**potential customer**
Interessent	**prospect**
Interessentenliste	**prospect list**
Interessenverband	**association**
Interessenvertretung	**lobby**
Intermediavergleich	**intermedia comparison**
Internationale Regeln für die Auslegung von Handelsklauseln	**Incoterms**
Internationaler Normenausschuß (ISO)	**International Standards Organization (ISO)**
Internationaler Verband von Werbefachleuten	**International Advertising Association**
Interview	**interview**
Interview, offenes	**depth interview**
Interview, persönliches	**personal interview**
Interview, qualitatives	**qualitative interview**
Interview, quantitatives	**quantitative interview**
Interviewer	**interviewer**
Interviewer-Bias	**interviewer bias**

Interviewmethoden	**interviewing methods**
Interviewte(r)	**interviewee**
Inventar, totes	**dead stock**
Inventur, permanente, laufende	**perpetual inventory**
Investition, induzierte	**induced investment**
Investitionsgüter	**capital goods**
Investitionsgüter	**industrial goods**
Investitionsgüter	**investment goods**
Investitionsgüter	**producer goods**
Investitionsgüter, langfristige Vermietung von	**finance lease**
Investitionsgütermarketing	**industrial marketing**
Investitionsgüterwerbung	**industrial advertising**
Investitionslücke	**deflationary gap**
Inzahlungnahme (beim Kauf)	**part exchange**
Irreführung	**fallacy**
Irrtum	**error**
Irrtum	**lapse**
Irrtum	**mistake**
Isobudgetgerade	**budget line**

J

JIT-Beschaffung	**just in time purchasing**
JIT-Produktion	**just in time (JIT) production**
Ja/Nein-Angebot	**alternative closing**
Jahrbuch	**annual**
Jahrbuch	**yearbook**
Jahresbonus	**annual discount**
Jahresrabatt	**annual discount**
Jahrmarkt	**fair**
Jargon	**jargon**
Jetzt-Vorher-Preisschild	**off-price label**
Joint Marketing	**joint marketing**
Joint Venture	**joint venture**
Jollies (betuchte ältere Menschen)	**jollies**
Jubiläumsrabatt	**jubilee discount**
Jubiläumsverkauf	**anniversary sale**
Jugendlichkeit	**youthfulness**
Jugendmarkt	**youth market**
Junk Food	**junk food**
Just-in-Time-Beschaffung (JIT)	**stockless buying**

K

KISS-Formel	**KISS principle**
Kabelfernsehen	**cable television**
Kalkulationszuschlag	**markup**
Kalkulator	**estimator**

kalkulieren	**cost**
Kampagne	**campaign**
Kanister	**can**
Kannibalisierungseffekt	**cannibalisation**
Kapazität, freie	**excess capacity**
Kapazität, freie, ungenutzte	**idle capacity**
Kapazitätsoptimum	**ideal capacity**
Kapazitätsreserve	**idle capacity**
Kapital, Ertrag aus investiertem	**return on capital (employed)**
Kapitalabfluß	**cash outflow**
Kapitalfluß	**flow of funds**
Kapitalrentabilität	**return on capital (employed)**
Kapitalrentabilität	**return on investment (ROI)**
Kapitalwert	**net present value**
Karaoke	**karaoke**
Karat	**carat**
Kartell	**cartel**
Kartell	**pool**
Kartell	**ring**
Kartell	**trust**
Kartell, Absatz durch ein	**pool selling**
Kartellamt (USA)	**Federal Trade Commission**
Kartellaufsichtsbehörde (GB)	**Monopolies (and Mergers) Commission**
Kartellgesetz (GB)	**Restrictive Trade Practices Act**
Kartellgesetz (USA)	**Anti-Trust Law**
Kartellgesetz (USA)	**Sherman Antitrust Act**
Kartellverbot, formales (USA)	**Sherman Antitrust Act**
Kartentelefon	**cardphone**
Kassageschäft	**spot sale**
Kassakurs (Bö)	**spot price**
Kasse	**booking office**
Kasse	**box office**
Kasse	**cash desk**
Kasse	**checkout**
Kasse	**pay desk**
Kasse, kleine	**petty cash**
Kasse, netto	**net cash**
Kassenbeleg	**cash voucher**
Kassenbereich	**front end**
Kassenbestand	**cash**
Kassenbestand	**cash float**
Kassenbestand	**till money**
Kasseneingang	**cash receipt**
Kasseneinnahmebuch	**cash receipts journal**
Kassenerfolg	**draw**
Kassenhaltungseffekt, realer	**Pigou effect**
Kassenhaltungseffekt, realer	**real balance effect**
Kassenquittung	**cash receipt**
Kassenschalter	**pay desk**
Kassenschlager	**box success**
Kassenschlager	**draw**

Kassenschlager	**money spinner**
Kassensystem, elektronisches	**electronic point of sale system**
Kassenterminal	**point-of-sale terminal**
Kassenterminal, elektronischer	**electronic point of sale (EPOS)**
Kassenüberschuß	**overage**
Kassenzettel	**salescheck**
Kassenzettel (Beleg, Quittung)	**coupon**
Kassenzettel, meist handgeschrieben	**cash memo**
Kassierer/in	**cashier**
Kassierer/in	**checker**
Kasten	**box**
Kasten	**bin**
Katalog	**catalog(ue)**
Katalog, Kauf nach	**catalog(ue) buying**
Katalog, gegliedert nach Produkten/ Bereichen/Fachgebieten	**classified catagog(ue)**
Katalogausstellung	**catalog(ue) exhibition**
Kataloggeschäft	**catalog(ue) showroom**
Katalogmarketing	**catalog(ue) marketing**
Katalogverkauf	**armchair shopping/buying**
Katalogwarenhaus	**catalog store**
Kategorie	**category**
Kauf auf Abruf	**call purchase**
Kauf auf Abruf	**standing order**
Kauf auf Probe	**sale on approval**
Kauf auf Raten	**buying on time**
Kauf auf Raten	**instal(l)ment buying**
Kauf mit Rückgaberecht	**sale or return**
Kauf nach Beschreibung	**selling by description**
Kauf nach Katalog	**catalog(ue) buying**
Kauf nach Muster	**sale by sample**
Kauf nach Probe	**sale by sample**
Kauf über die Druckmedien	**off-the-page buying**
Kauf unter Inzahlungnahme	**part exchange**
Kauf von Werbesendezeit bei Lokalsender	**spot buy**
Kauf zur Ansicht	**sale on approval**
Kauf zur späteren Auslieferung	**forward purchase**
Kauf, bei Kauf eines Produkts, gibt es ein weiteres kostenlos	**buy one - get one free**
Kauf, schlechter	**bad bargain**
Kaufabschluß mittels Zusammenfassung aller Argument	**summative close**
Kaufabsicht	**buying intent**
Kaufabsicht	**intention to purchase**
Kaufanreiz	**buying incentive**
Kaufanreiz, käuferfreundlicher	**added buyer effect**
Kaufanreize	**buying stimuli**
Kaufanreize	**incentives to purchase**
Kaufanreize	**marketing stimuli**
Kaufauftrag	**purchase order**

Kaufauftrag für Abschnitte zu verschiedenen Kursen	**split order**
Kaufbereitschaft	**eagerness to buy**
Kaufbereitschaftsstadien	**buyer-readiness states**
Kaufbeweis	**proof-of-purchase**
Kaufeinwand	**objection**
Kaufen	**buying**
Kaufentscheid für ein Markenprodukt	**brand choice**
Kaufentscheider	**purchase decider**
Kaufentscheidung	**buying decision**
Kaufentscheidung	**purchase decision**
Kaufentscheidung, persönliche	**personal buying decision**
Kaufentscheidungsträger	**key buying influencer**
Kaufentschluß	**buyer decision**
Käufer	**buyer**
Käufer	**customer**
Käufer	**purchaser**
Käufer	**shopper**
Käufer	**taker**
Käufer	**vendee**
Käufer von Billigangeboten	**bargain shopper**
Käufer, abwechslungsuchender	**variety-seeking buyer**
Käufer, der Vergleiche anstellt	**comparison shopper**
Käufer, ehemaliger, früherer	**former buyer**
Käuferablehnung	**buyer rejection**
Käuferanteil, der Gutscheine nicht einlöst	**slippage rate**
Käuferbefragung (vor, beim oder nach dem Kauf) im Geschäft	**in-store interview**
Käuferdynamik	**buyer dynamics**
Käuferentscheidungsprozeß	**buyer-decision process**
Käufererwartungsmethode	**buyer`s expectation method**
Käufermarkt	**buyers' market**
Käuferreaktionen auf Preisänderungen	**buyers` reactions to price changes**
Käuferrechte	**buyer's rights**
Käuferrisiko	**buyer`s risk**
Käuferstreik	**buyer`s strike**
Käuferträgheit	**buyer's inertia**
Käuferverhalten	**buyer behaviour**
Käuferzielgruppe	**market target**
Käuferzufriedenheit	**consumer satisfaction**
Kaufgewohnheit	**custom**
Kaufhäufigkeit	**purchase frequency**
Kaufhaus	**department(al) store**
Kaufhaus mit Vollsortiment	**full-line department store**
Kaufhaus mit beschränktem Sortiment	**limited line department store**
Kaufhaus-Abteilungsleiter	**floor manager**
Kaufkraft	**purchasing power**
Kaufkraft	**spending power**
Kaufkraft	**value**

Kaufkraft, frei verfügbare	**discretionary buying power**
Kaufkraft, tatsächliche/echte	**real value of money**
Kaufkraft-Index	**buying power index (BPI)**
Kaufkraftparität	**purchasing power parity**
Kaufleser	**buyer-reader**
Kaufleser, tatsächlicher	**actual buyer-reader**
Kauflust	**eagerness to buy**
Kaufmann	**dealer**
Kaufmann	**merchant**
Kaufmann	**trader**
Kaufmann, technischer	**sales engineer**
Kaufmotive	**buying motives**
Kaufmotive, bewußte	**conscious buying motives**
Kaufmotive, rationale	**rational buying motives**
Kaufnachweis	**proof of purchase**
Kaufobjekt, günstiges	**bargain**
Kaufoption	**option to purchase**
Kaufpreis	**purchase price**
Kaufpreis	**purchase money**
Kaufprozeß	**buying process**
Kaufrisiko, wahrgenommenes	**perceived purchase risk**
Kaufsignale	**buying signals**
Kaufstruktur	**spending pattern**
Kaufstruktur der Verbraucher	**consumer spending patterns**
Kaufsumme	**purchase money**
Kaufunlust	**consumer resistance**
Kaufunlust	**sales resistance**
Kaufverhalten	**purchase pattern**
Kaufverhaltensrollen	**buying roles**
Kaufverhandlung	**sales negotiation**
Kaufvertrag	**bargain**
Kaufvertrag	**contract of sale**
Kaufvertrag	**purchase contract**
Kaufvertrag	**sales contract**
Kaufvertrag unter Eigentumsvorbehalt	**conditional sales contract**
Kaufvorgang	**purchasing activity**
Kaufwerbung, auf direkte Reaktion(en) zielende Werbung	**direct-action advertisement**
Kennmelodie	**theme**
Kennzeichen	**earmark**
Kennzeichen	**identifier**
kennzeichnen	**mark**
Kennzeichnung mit Herstell- oder Verfalldatum	**date coding**
Kennzeichnung	**label(l)ing**
Kennzeichnung, hergestellt in	**Made in label**
Kennziffer	**key number**
Kennziffernanalyse	**ratio analysis**
Kennziffernanzeige	**blind ad**
Kennziffernkarte	**reader service card**

Kernfamilie	**nuclear family**
Kettenladen	**chain store**
Key Account Manager	**key account manager**
Keynes' Investitionstheorie	**Keynes' theory of investment**
Keynes-Effekt	**keynes effect**
Keynesianismus	**Keynesianism**
King-Size-Plakat	**king size poster**
Kinowerbung	**cinema advertising**
Kinowerbung	**screen advertising**
Kinowerbung	**theater advertising**
Kiosk	**kiosk**
Kiste	**box**
Kiste	**bin**
Kiste	**case**
Kistenanhänger	**bin tag**
Kitsch	**kitsch**
Klappkarte	**tent card**
Klasse, unterpriviligierte	**underclass**
Klassifikation	**classification**
Klassiker	**classical economists**
Kleinanzeige	**classified advertisement**
Kleinanzeige	**small advertisement**
Kleinanzeige	**want ad**
Kleinanzeigenspalte, -rubrik	**classified section**
Kleinbuchstabe	**lowercase**
Kleinfusion	**minimerger**
Kleingeld	**change**
Kleingeld	**chickenfeed**
Kleinkram	**odds and ends**
Kleinpreisgeschäft	**variety store**
Kleinserie	**job lot**
Kleinserienfertigung (nach Kundenauftrag)	**jobbing production**
"Kleinvieh"	**peanuts**
Klotzwerbung, phasenweise	**burst advertising**
Klüngel	**clique**
Knappheit	**scarcity**
Knappheit	**shortage**
Knockoffs	**knockoffs**
Know-how	**know-how**
Know-how Lizenz	**know-how licence/license**
Köderwerbung	**switch selling**
Kollektivgüter	**collective goods**
Kollektivgüter	**public goods**
Kollo	**package**
Kombination von Hörern, Lesern, Zuschauern	**advertising-audience combination**
Kombinationsgeschäft	**combination store**
Kombinationspreis	**combination rate**
Kombinationswerbung	**tie-in advertisement**

Kombiverkehr	**piggyback (service)**
Komfort	**comfort**
Kommentar	**editorial**
Kommerzialisierung	**commercialization**
Kommissionär	**agent**
Kommissionär	**commission merchant**
Kommissionär	**commission agent**
Kommissionär	**mercantile agent**
Kommissionsagent	**sales agent**
Kommissionsbasis, Verkauf auf	**memorandum sale**
Kommissionskonto	**consignment account**
Kommissionslager	**consignment stock**
Kommissionsverkauf	**consignment trade**
Kommissionsverkauf	**consignment sale**
Kommissionsware	**consignment goods**
Kommissionsware	**goods on consignment**
kommissionsweise	**on consignment**
Kommittent	**consignor**
Kommunikation	**communication**
Kommunikation, einseitige	**one-way communication**
Kommunikation, interpersonelle	**interpersonal communication**
Kommunikation, mündliche	**oral communication**
Kommunikation, nichtverbale	**nonverbal communication**
Kommunikation, zweiseitige	**two-way communication**
Kommunikationseffekt der Werbung	**communication effect of advertising**
Kommunikationsmedien für ethnische Gruppen/Minderheiten	**ethnic media**
Kommunikationsmix	**communications mix**
Kommunikatorglaubwürdigkeit	**source credibility**
Kompensationsgeschäft	**reciprocal transaction**
Kompensationshandel	**countertrade**
Kompensationsmethode	**compensation method**
Komplementärgüter	**complementary goods**
Komplementärgüternachfrage	**complementary demand**
Kompromißbereitschaft	**give and take**
Konformist	**conformist**
Konglomerat	**conglomerate**
Königsformat	**king size**
Konjukturtief	**bottom**
Konjunktur, Ankurbelung der	**pump priming**
Konjunktur, florierende	**boom**
Konjunktur-Indikator	**economic indicator**
Konjunktur-Kennziffer	**economic indicator**
Konjunktur-Stabilisator, automatischer	**built-in (automatic) stabilizer**
Konjunkturabschwung	**downswing**
Konjunkturabschwung	**recession**
Konjunkturaufschwung	**upswing**
Konjunkturaufschwung	**recovery**
Konjunkturaufschwung, erwarteter	**anticipated economic upswing**
Konjunkturbarometer	**business barometer**

Konjunkturbericht	**economic report**
Konjunkturförderung, staatliche	**pump priming**
Konjunkturindikator	**cyclical indicator**
Konjunkturindikatoren	**business indicators**
Konjunkturklima	**economic climate**
Konjunkturphase	**business cycle**
Konjunkturphase	**cycle**
Konjunkturphase	**trade cycle**
Konjunkturpolitik	**economic policy**
Konjunkturprognose	**economic forecast(ing)**
Konjunkturprognose, langfristige	**long-term economic forecast**
Konjunkturrückgang	**slowdown in business**
Konjunkturrückgang, mäßiger	**shakeout**
Konjunkturrückgang, starker	**slump**
Konjunkturstabilisierung	**stabilisation ot the economy**
Konjunkturtief	**trough**
Konjunkturüberhitzung	**overheating (of the economy)**
Konjunkturverlauf	**economic development**
Konjunkturverlauf	**economic trend**
Konjunkturverlauf	**run of business**
Konjunkturzyklus	**business cycle**
Konjunkturzyklus	**cycle**
Konjunkturzyklus	**trade cycle**
Konkretisierung	**appropriation**
Konkretisierung einer Ware	**appropriation of goods**
Konkurrent	**competitor**
Konkurrent	**rival**
Konkurrent, neuer	**entrant**
Konkurrenten, verdrängen von	**freeze out**
Konkurrenz	**competition**
Konkurrenz, atomistische	**atomistic competition**
Konkurrenz, direkte	**direct competition**
Konkurrenz, freie	**free competition**
Konkurrenz, harte, scharfe	**keen competition**
Konkurrenz, monopolistische	**monopolistic competition**
Konkurrenz, oligopolistische	**oligopolistic competition**
Konkurrenz, polypolistische	**atomistic competition**
Konkurrenz, ruinöse	**cutthroat competition**
Konkurrenz, unvollständige	**imperfect competition**
Konkurrenz, vollkommen homogene	**pure competition**
Konkurrenz, vollständige	**perfect competition**
Konkurrenz, wirtschaftliche	**economic competition**
Konkurrenz, zeitabhängige	**time-based competition**
Konkurrenzanalyse	**competitor analysis**
Konkurrenzangebot	**competitive supply**
Konkurrenzerzeugnis	**rival commodity**
Konkurrenzfähigkeit	**competitiveness**
Konkurrenzkunde, treuer	**competitive loyal**
Konkurrenzmarkt	**competitive market**
Konkurrenznachfrage	**competitive demand**

Konkurrenzpreis	**competitive price**
Konkurrenzpreise	**competitors` prices**
Konkurrenzprodukt	**competing product**
Konkurrenzprodukt	**rival product**
Konkurrenzprodukt	**rival commodity**
Konkurrenzunternehmen	**competitor**
Konkurrenzwerbung	**competitive advertising**
Konservierungsmittel	**food additive**
Konsignant	**consignor**
Konsignatar	**commission merchant**
Konsignatar	**consignee**
Konsignation, in	**on consignment**
Konsignationshandel	**consignment trade**
Konsignationslager	**consignment stock**
Konsignationsverkauf	**consignment sale**
Konsignationsware	**consignment**
Konsignationsware	**goods on consignment**
Konsortium	**syndicate**
Konstante	**constant**
Konstenfunktion	**cost function**
Konsum, Verbrauch	**consumpiton (C)**
Konsum, autonomer	**autonomous consumption**
Konsum, induzierter	**induced consumption**
Konsumaufschub	**abstinence**
Konsument	**consumer**
Konsument, reifer	**mature consumer**
Konsumentenbefragung	**consumer survey**
Konsumentenkredit	**consumer credit**
Konsumentenkredite, Spezialinstitut für	**consumer finance company**
Konsumentennachfrage	**consumer demand**
Konsumentennachfrage, Determinanten der	**determinants of consumer demand**
Konsumentenpräferenz	**consumer's preference**
Konsumentenrechte	**consumer rights**
Konsumentenrente	**consumer's surplus**
Konsumentensouveränität	**consumer(s') sovereignty**
Konsumententreue	**consumer loyalty**
Konsumentenwerbung	**consumer advertising**
Konsumerismus	**Naderism**
Konsumerismus	**consumerism**
Konsumforschung	**consumer research**
Konsumfunktion	**consumption function**
Konsumgenossenschaft	**consumer cooperative (society)**
Konsumgesellschaft	**consumer society**
Konsumgesetz	**law of consumption**
Konsumgewohnheit	**habit of consumption**
Konsumgewohnheiten	**consumption patterns**
Konsumgüter	**consumer non-durables**
Konsumgüter	**consumer(s') goods**
Konsumgüter	**single-use goods**
Konsumgüter (kurzlebige)	**nondurable goods**

Konsumgüter, bei deren Auswahl und Kauf der Kunde kritische Vergleiche anstellt	**shopping goods**
Konsumgüter, dauerhafte	**consumer durables**
Konsumgüter, kurzlebige	**softs**
Konsumgüter, langlebige	**hard goods**
Konsumgüterklassifikation	**consumer product classification**
Konsumgütermarkt	**consumer market**
Konsumgüterpreisbildung	**pricing consumer goods**
Konsumgüterwerbung	**consumer goods advertising**
Konsumneigung	**propensity to consume**
Konsumquote	**propensity to consume**
Konsumquote, durchschnittliche	**average propensity to consume**
Konsumquote, marginale	**marginal propensity to consume**
Konsumstatistik	**consumption statistics**
Kontakhäufigkeit	**frequency (freq)**
Kontakmemorandum	**call report**
Kontaktbericht	**call report**
Kontaktchance/Kontaktwahrscheinlichkeit, etwas zu sehen	**opportunity to see**
Kontakter	**account executive**
Kontakter	**account manager**
Kontakter	**space broker**
Kontakter	**space buyer**
Kontaktgruppenleiter	**account manager**
Kontaktgruppenleiter	**account executive**
Kontaktgruppenleiter	**account supervisor**
Kontakthäufigkeit, durchschnittliche	**average frequency**
Kontaktwahrscheinlichkeit mit einer Radio(werbe)sendung	**opportunity to hear**
Konto, kreditorisch geführtes	**credit account**
Konto, offenes	**open account**
Kontoauszug	**statement**
Kontraktfracht	**contract rate**
Kontrolle	**check**
Kontrolle vor Warenabnahme	**pre-delivery inspection**
Kontrolleur	**checker**
Kontrollfrage	**control question**
Kontrollgruppe	**control group**
Kontrollinterview	**callback**
Kontrolliste	**checklist**
Kontrollsystem, anpassungsfähiges	**adaptive control system**
Konzentration, geographische	**geographical concentration**
Konzentrationsmaß	**concentration ratio**
Konzentrationsrate	**concentration ratio**
Konzept	**draft**
Konzern	**group**
Konzession	**concession**
Konzession	**licence**
Konzessionsgeber	**licensor/licenser**
Konzessionsinhaber	**licensee/licencee**

Kooperation	**cooperation**
Kooperation, verwaltete, vertikale	**administered vertical market system**
Kooperationsvertrag	**cooperation agreement**
Koordinatennullpunkt	**origin**
Kopf, pro	**per capita**
Kopf-an-Kopf Konkurrenz	**head-to-head competition**
Kopfsteuer	**head tax**
Kopie	**copy**
Kopie	**facsimile**
Kopie	**imitation**
Koppelanzeige	**dealer tie-in**
Koppelungsanzeige	**tie-in advertisement**
Koppelungsgeschäft	**tie-in sale**
Koppelungsvereinbarung	**tying contract**
Koppelungswerbung	**tie-in advertising**
Korb	**basket**
Korbflasche	**carboy**
Körpersprache	**body language**
Korrektheit	**correctness**
Korrelation	**correlation**
Kosten	**cost**
Kosten	**expenses**
Kosten decken	**clear**
Kosten der Auftragsabwicklung	**order costs**
Kosten der Auftragsabwicklung	**order filling costs**
Kosten der Kuppelproduktion	**joint cost**
Kosten der entgangenen Gelegenheit	**opportunity cost**
Kosten pro Anfrage	**cost per inquiry**
Kosten pro Auftrag	**cost per order**
Kosten pro Einschaltprozentsatz	**cost per rating point**
Kosten pro Kontakt	**cost per contact**
Kosten und Preisbildung	**costs and pricing**
Kosten vorausbezahlt	**charges prepaid**
Kosten, Fracht und Entladekosten bezahlt	**cost and freight, free out (C + F FO)**
Kosten, abnehmende	**decreasing cost(s)**
Kosten, aufgabenbezogene	**functional costs**
Kosten, beeinflußbare	**controllable costs**
Kosten, direkte	**direct cost(s)**
Kosten, direkte (variable)	**prime cost**
Kosten, effektive	**explicit cost(s)**
Kosten, feste	**fixed charge**
Kosten, feste, fixe	**fixed cost(s)**
Kosten, fixe	**unavoidable costs**
Kosten, in Rechnung gestellte	**billed cost(s)**
Kosten, indirekte	**indirect cost(s)**
Kosten, nicht beeinflußbare	**uncontrollable cost(s)**
Kosten, teilvariable	**mixed cost(s)**
Kosten, teilvariable	**semivariable (semi-variable) costs**
Kosten, variable, veränderliche	**variable cost(s)**
Kosten, zurechenbare	**traceable costs**

Kosten-Nutzen-Analyse	**cost-benefit analysis**
Kosten-Preis-Schere	**cost-price squeeze**
Kostenabweichung	**cost variance**
Kostenaufwand in Marktpreisen oder in Wiederbeschaffungspreisen	**current cost**
Kostendeckungspreis	**breakeven price**
Kostendeckungspunkt	**breakeven point**
Kostendegression	**decreasing cost(s)**
Kostenersparnisse durch Erhöhung der Produktionskapazitäten	**economies of scale**
Kosteninflation	**cost-push (inflation)**
Kosteninflation für Werbung	**adflation**
kostenlos	**free**
kostenlos	**free of charge (foc)**
kostenlos zur Probe	**free trial**
Kostentarif	**tariff**
Kostenvergleich	**cost comparison**
Kostenvoranschlag	**estimate**
Kostenvoranschlag	**quotation**
Kostenvorteil, absoluter	**absolute cost advantage**
Kostenzunahme	**diseconomy**
Kräfte, ökologische	**ecological forces**
Kraftfahrzeugzuschuß	**car allowance**
Kraftpapier	**kraft paper**
Kraftverkehrsunternehmen	**haulage contractor**
Kreativ(werbe)agentur	**creative boutique**
Kreativdirektor	**creative director**
Kreativstrategie	**creative strategy in advertising**
Kredit, auf	**on credit**
Kredit, auf ... kaufen/verkaufen	**credit**
Kredit, gegen	**on account**
Kredit, gesichert durch Warenlager	**field warehousing loan**
Kreditbedingungen	**terms of credit**
Kreditgeschäft	**credit transaction**
Kreditkarte	**credit card**
Kreditkarte	**plastic money**
Kreditkarte (zur direkten Abbuchung von Käufen)	**debit card**
Kreditkarte für Einkauf in bestimmtem Geschäft	**storecard**
Kreditkarten-Telefon	**credit call telephone**
Kreditkarten-Telefonat	**credit card call**
Kreditkauf	**credit buying**
Kreditkonditionen	**credit terms**
Kreditkonto	**credit account**
Kreditkonto (offenes)	**charge account**
Kreditkonto, "offenes"	**budget account**
Kreditkunde	**credit customer**
Kreditlaufzeit	**credit period**
Kreditor	**creditor**
Kreditor	**debtee**

Kreditstand	**credit(s) outstanding**
Kreditverkauf	**credit sale**
Kreditversicherung	**credit insurance**
Kreditvolumen, eingeräumtes	**credit(s) outstanding**
Kreisdiagramm	**pie chart**
Kreislauf	**cycle**
Kreuzpreiselastizität der Nachfrage	**cross elasticity of demand**
Krimskrams	**odds and ends**
Kündigungsklausel	**cancellation clause**
Kuhhandel	**horse trading**
Kultur	**culture**
Kulturgefälle	**culture lag**
Kultursponsoring	**arts sponsorship**
Kunde	**account**
Kunde	**buyer**
Kunde	**customer**
Kunde	**custom**
Kunde	**patron**
Kunde	**client**
Kunde, aktueller	**live customer**
Kunde, der in einem Geschäft ein Kreditkonto hat	**credit customer**
Kunde, ehemaliger	**former buyer**
Kunde, geschätzter	**valued customer**
Kunde, konkurrenztreuer	**competitive loyal**
Kunde, möglicher	**potential customer**
Kunde, potentieller	**key prospect**
Kunde, treuer	**current loyal**
Kunde, überregionaler	**national account**
Kunde, unentschlossener	**vacillating customer**
Kunde, wichtiger	**key customer**
Kunde, wirtschaftlich denkender	**economic shopper**
Kunden-Info	**visit brief**
Kundenabgänge	**loss of customers**
Kundenauftragsfertigung, Betrieb mit	**job shop**
Kundenbedarf	**demand**
Kundenbesuch, Instruktionen vor einem	**visit brief**
Kundenbesucher	**detailer**
Kundenbesuchsbericht	**call report**
Kundenbesuchshäufigkeit	**call frequency**
Kundenbesuchsrate	**call rate**
Kundenbesuchszyklus	**call cycle**
Kundenbesuchszyklus	**calling cycle**
Kundenbetreuer	**account manager**
Kundenbetreuung	**customer care**
Kundenbuch	**sales journal**
Kundendaten	**customer records**
Kundendienst	**after-sales service**
Kundendienst	**customer service**
Kundendienst	**serviceman**

Kundendienst	**service**
Kundendienst	**servicing**
Kundendienst (nach dem Verkauf)	**postsale service**
Kundendienst, absatzvorbereitender	**presale service**
Kundendienstabteilung	**customer service department**
Kundendienstabteilung	**service department**
Kundendienstschalter	**service desk**
Kundeneinzugsgebiet	**catchment area**
Kundenfahrzeug, Transport mit	**customer`s own transport (COT)**
Kundenfänger	**bird dog**
Kundenfluktuation	**customer turnover**
Kundenjäger	**bird dog**
Kundenkartei	**client list**
Kundenkasse am Ladenausgang	**front-end checkout**
Kundenkonto, "offenes"	**budget account**
Kundenkreditkarte	**charge card**
Kundenkreditkarte	**in-store card**
Kundenkreditkarte für Einkauf in bestimmtem Geschäft	**storecard**
Kundenkreditkonto	**charge account**
Kundenliste	**client list**
Kundenorientierung	**customer orientation**
Kundenpenetrationsrate	**account penetration ratio**
Kundenpflegemarketing	**relationship marketing**
Kundenprofil	**customer profile**
Kundenrabatt	**sales discount**
Kundenschalter	**accomodation desk**
Kundensegment, Preisgestaltung nach	**customer segment pricing**
Kundensegmentierung	**customer segmentation**
Kundenskonto (-skonti)	**discount(s) allowed**
kundenspezifisch	**purpose-designed**
Kundenverkehr	**store traffic**
Kundenverkehr	**traffic**
Kundenverlust(rate)	**attrition loss (rate)**
Kundenwerber	**bird dog**
Kundenwerbung, ungezielte	**cold canvassing**
Kundenwunsch, auf gefertigt	**custom-made**
Kundenziele	**account objectives**
Kundenzufriedenheitsindex	**customer satisfaction index**
Kündigungs- und Auftragsannahmeschluß	**firm order date**
Kundschaft	**clientele**
Kundschaft	**custom**
Kundschaft	**patronage**
Kundschaft	**trade**
Kunstsponsoring	**art(s) sponsorship**
Kunststück	**stunt**
Kupon, Verkaufsförderung mittels	**couponing**
Kuppelkalkulation	**joint costing**
Kuppelprodukt	**joint product**
Kuppelproduktion, Kosten der	**joint cost**

Kurier	**messenger**
Kurierdienst	**courier service**
Kurs	**quoted price**
Kursanstieg	**upstick/up stick**
Kursanstieg auf breiter Front	**buoyancy**
Kurse, Fallen der	**baisse**
Kursivschrift	**italics**
Kursrückgang, anhaltender (Bö)	**slump**
Kurssturz	**plunge in prices**
Kursstützung	**pegging**
Kursverfall	**collapse**
Kurswert (Bö)	**market price**
Kurve	**graph**
Kurzbericht	**brief**
Kurzbericht	**summary report**
Kybernetik	**cybernetics**

L

LKW	**truck**
LKW-Container, Lufttransport von ...	**birdyback**
LKW-Stückgut	**less-than-truckload (LTL)**
Labor-Testverfahren	**laboratory method**
Ladekosten	**handling charges**
Ladeliste	**freight list**
Ladeliste	**manifest**
Laden	**shop**
Laden	**store**
Laden an der Ecke	**corner shop**
Laden für zweite Wahl	**reject shop**
Laden, fahrender	**mobile shop**
Laden, frei	**free in store (FIS)**
Laden, im Laden vermieteter ...	**shop within a shop**
Laden, zollfreier	**duty-free shop**
Laden-Promotion	**in-store promotion**
Laden-Test	**placement test**
Ladenanordnung	**store layout**
Ladenaufsicht	**floorwalker**
Ladenbesucher	**shopper**
Ladendiebstahl	**shoplifting**
Ladendiebstahl	**shrinkage**
Ladendurchlauf	**store traffic**
Ladenfront	**shop front**
Ladenhüter	**cats and dogs**
Ladenhüter	**dead stock**
Ladenhüter	**drug in/on the market**
Ladenhüter	**nonseller**
Ladenhüter	**shelf warmer**
Ladenhüter	**sleeper**
Ladenhüter	**sticker**

Ladeninhaber	**shopkeeper**
Ladenkasse	**till**
Ladenpreis	**retail price**
Ladenpreis	**selling price**
Ladenpreis	**sticker price**
Ladenschluß	**closing time**
Ladenschluß, früher	**early closing**
Ladenstraße	**shopping mall**
Ladentisch	**counter**
Ladentreue	**store loyalty**
Ladenwerbung	**in-store promotion**
Laderampe	**ramp**
Laderaum	**space**
Laderaum	**stowage**
Laderost	**pallet**
Ladeverzeichnis	**manifest**
Ladezeit, gebührenfreie	**free time**
Ladung	**cargo**
Ladung	**freight**
Ladung	**lading**
Ladung	**shipment**
Ladung, (auf)gestaute	**stowage**
Ladung, gespaltene	**split load**
Ladung, nicht teilbare	**indivisible load**
Ladung, wertvolle	**valuable cargo**
Lag	**lag**
Lage	**location**
Lagebericht	**progress report**
Lagebericht	**situation report (sitrep)**
Lager	**store**
Lager	**warehouse**
Lager(haltungs)kosten	**inventory costs**
Lager(raum)	**storeroom**
Lager, ab	**ex warehouse (ex whse, X whse)**
Lager, ab	**ex stock**
Lager, auf	**in stock**
Lager, automatisiertes	**automated warehouse**
Lager, nicht am	**out of stock**
Lagerauffüllung, -aufstockung	**restocking**
Lagerbestand	**stock**
Lagerbestand, ausgewogener	**balanced stock**
Lagerbestand, kritischer	**reorder quantity**
Lagerbestand, maximaler	**maximum stock level**
Lagerbestände	**inventory**
Lager(bestands)kontrolle	**stock control**
Lagerbestandsobergrenze	**maximum stock level**
Lagerbestandvermarktung	**dishoarding**
Lagerfach	**bin**
Lagerfähigkeit	**shelf life**
Lagergebühr(en)	**storage charge(s)**

Lagergeld	demurrage
Lagergeld	storage
Lagergeld	storage charge(s)
Lagerhaltung	storage
Lagerhaltung	warehousing
Lagerhaus	depot
Lagerhaus	storehouse
Lagerhaus	warehouse
Lagerist	storekeeper
Lagerkapazität	storage capacity
Lagerkapazität	warehouse capacity
Lagerkontrolle	inventory control
Lagerkosten	carrying charges
Lagermiete	storage
Lagerplatz	yard
Lagerraum	store
Lagerraum	storage
Lagerretouren	returns to store
Lagerschein	warrant
Lagerumsatz	inventory turnover
Lagerumschlag	inventory turnover
Lagerumschlag	stockturn (rate)
Lagerumschlag	stock rotation
Lagerumschlag, mittlerer	turnround
Lagerung	storage
Lagerverwalter	storekeeper
Lagervorrat	stock
Lagerwirtschaft	inventory control
Lagerwirtschaft	inventory management
Lagerwirtschaft	stock control
Lagerzugänge	receipts
Laissez-faire	laissez-faire/laisser-faire
Land mit niedrigem Pro-Kopf-Einkommen	low income country
Landbevölkerung	rural population
Länder mit hohem pro-Kopf-Einkommen	high income countries
Ländergruppierung, geographische	geographic grouping of countries
Länderpotential	country potential
Landwirtschaftsausstellung	agricultural show
Langzeitliefervertrag mit Zahlung bei Lieferung	take-and-pay contract
Langzeitliefervertrag mit unbedingter Zahlungsverpflichtung	take-or-pay contract
Langzeittrend	secular trend
Langzeitwirkung der Werbung	advertising carryover
Lastkraftwagen (LKW)	truck
Lastschriftanzeige	debit note
Lastschriftkarte zur direkten Abbuchung von Einzelhandelskäufen	debit card
Lattenkiste	crate
Lattenverschlag	crate

Laufkunde	**casual customer**
Laufkunde	**irregular customer**
Laufkunde	**walk-in**
Laufzeit eines Kredits	**credit period**
laut	**as per**
Lawinensystem	**pyramid selling**
Layout	**layout**
Layouter	**layout person**
Layoutskizze	**visual**
Lean Design	**lean design**
Lean Marketing	**lean marketing**
Lean Production	**lean production**
Leasing	**leasing**
Leasing, offenes	**open-end lease**
Leasinggeber	**lessor**
Leasingnehmer	**lessee**
Lebenserwartung	**expectation of life**
Lebenserwartung	**life expectancy**
Lebenshaltungsindex	**index of retail prices**
Lebenshaltungskosten	**cost of living**
Lebenshaltungskosten-Index	**cost-of-living index**
Lebenshaltungskostenausgleich	**cost-of-living adjustment/allowance (COLA)**
Lebensmittelbehörde (USA)	**Food and Drug Administration**
Lebensmittelgeschäft	**grocery store**
Lebensmittelgesetz (GB)	**Food and Drugs Act**
Lebensmittelhändler	**grocer**
Lebensmittelkartenabschnitt	**coupon**
Lebensmittellieferant	**caterer**
Lebensmittelviertel	**food court**
Lebensmittelzusatz	**food additive**
Lebensqualität	**quality of life**
Lebensqualität, Segmentierung nach	**quality of life segmentation**
Lebensstandard	**standard of living**
Lebensstil	**lifestyle/life style**
Lebenszyklus	**life cycle**
Leckage	**leakage**
Leerfracht	**deadheading**
Leerfracht	**dead freight**
Leergewicht	**tare weight**
Leergewicht	**unladen weight**
Leergut	**returned empties**
Leerpackung	**dummy pack(age)**
Leerverkauf (Bö)	**selling short**
Legende	**caption**
Leichtindustrie	**light industry**
Leistung, pro Kopf	**per capita output**
Leistungsverkehr (AuW)	**current transactions**
Leitartikel	**editorial**
Leitartikel	**leader**

Leitbefehl	**routing order**
Leitbildwerbung	**endorsement advertising**
Leiter der Anzeigenabteilung	**advertisement manager**
Leiter der Ein- und Verkaufsabteilung	**merchandise manager**
Leiter der Einkaufsabteilung	**purchasing agent**
Leiter der Verkaufsförderungsabteilung	**promotion manager**
Leitfaden	**manual**
Leithammelwerbung	**bellwether advertising**
Leitstudie	**pilot study**
Leitung, fest geschaltete	**dedicated line**
Leporello	**accordion insert**
Leporellofalzbeilage	**accordion insert**
Lernen	**learning**
Lesedauer	**reading time**
Lesedauer	**time spent reading**
Lesen und Sehen	**reading and noting**
Leser einer Ausgabe	**issue reader**
Leser pro Expemplar (LpE)	**readers per copy**
Leser pro Nummer (LpN)	**readers per copy**
Leser(schaft)	**audience**
Leser, Anteil gründlicher	**read most**
Leser, Gesamtzahl der	**total audience**
Leser, seltener	**light reader**
Leser, unregelmäßiger	**nonregular reader**
Leser/in	**reader**
Leseranalyse	**audience measurement**
Leserkreis	**readership**
Leserprofil	**reader profile**
Leserreaktion	**reader response**
Leserschaft	**readership**
Leserschaft einer Anzeigenseite	**adpage audience**
Leserschaft, durchschnittliche einer Publikation	**average issue readership**
Leserschaftsuntersuchung	**readership study**
Lesertreue	**reader loyalty**
Leserzahl, durchschnittliche pro Ausgabe	**average issue audience**
Lesevorgänge	**page traffic**
letzter Termin	**closing date**
Letztverbraucher	**ultimate user**
Leuchtschriftnachrichten	**newscaster**
Leuchtwerbung	**illuminated advertising**
Lichthofeffekt	**Halo effect**
Lichtreklametafel	**electric spectacular**
Liebhaberpreis	**fancy price**
Liebhaberpreis	**lover price**
Lieferanschrift	**delivery address**
Lieferant	**supplier**
Lieferant	**vendor**
Lieferantenauswahl	**supplier selection**
Lieferantenbeurteilung	**supplier evaluation**

Lieferantenbeurteilung	**vendor rating**
Lieferantenkredit	**supplier credit**
Lieferantenkredit	**trade credit**
Lieferantenmanagement	**supplier management**
Lieferantensuche	**supplier search**
Lieferanzeige	**delivery notice**
Lieferauftrag	**delivery order**
lieferbar, sofort	**spot**
Lieferbedingungen	**delivery terms**
Lieferbedingungen	**terms of delivery**
Lieferbeziehung, wechselseitige	**reciprocity**
Lieferbuch	**delivery book**
Lieferdatum	**delivery date**
Lieferdienst	**package delivery service**
Lieferengpaß	**supply shortage**
Lieferer	**vendor**
Lieferfirma	**supplier**
Lieferfrist	**time of delivery**
Lieferklauseln im Außenhandel	**Incoterms**
Liefermonat	**delivery month**
Liefernachweis	**proof of delivery**
Lieferort	**place of delivery**
Lieferposten	**lot**
Lieferpreis	**delivered price**
Lieferpreis	**supply price**
Lieferschein	**delivery note**
Lieferschein	**delivery order**
Liefersperre	**refusal to deal/sell**
Liefertermin	**delivery date**
Liefertermin	**time of delivery**
Lieferung	**delivery**
Lieferung	**supply**
Lieferung frei Bestimmungsort	**free delivery**
Lieferung frei Haus	**delivery free**
Lieferung frei Haus	**direct store delivery**
Lieferung frei Haus	**store / door delivery**
Lieferung sofort nach Auftragseingang	**ready delivery**
Lieferung von Fertigmahlzeiten	**catering**
Lieferung, Preis für künftige	**forward price**
Lieferung, Zahlung nach	**payment after delivery**
Lieferung, sofortige	**prompt delivery**
Lieferung, sofortige (gegen Kasse)	**spot delivery**
Lieferung, unvollständige	**short delivery**
Lieferung, verspätete	**delayed delivery**
Lieferung, verspätete	**late delivery**
Lieferung, zahlbar bei	**cash on delivery**
Lieferung, zahlbar bei	**payable on delivery**
Lieferungskosten	**delivery expenses**
Lieferungsverzug	**default in/of delivery**
Lieferungsverzug	**delay in delivery**

Liefervertrag	**supply contract**
Liefervorschrift	**delivery instruction**
Lieferwagen	**delivery van**
Lieferzeit	**delivery time**
Lieferzeit	**time of delivery**
Lifestyle-Werbung	**lifestyle advertising**
Lifo-Methode der Vorratsbewertung	**last in, first out**
Likert-Skala	**Likert scale**
limitierter Auftrag	**limit**
Limitpreis	**limit price**
Limitpreis	**price ceiling**
Linienschaubild	**line chart**
Linzenzerteilung, -gewährung	**licencing**
Liquiditätsklemme trotz hoher Rendite	**overtrading**
Liste	**list**
Liste, schwarze	**blacklist**
Listenpreis	**list price**
Listenpreis für Werbung	**gross rate**
Listenpreis für einstündiges Programm während Hauptsendezeit	**gross night hour**
Litfaßsäule	**advertising pillar**
Litfaßsäule	**hoarding**
Live-Sendung	**live program(me)**
Lizenz	**licence**
Lizenzaustausch	**cross licensing**
Lizenzfertigung	**licensed production**
Lizenzgeber	**licensor/licenser**
Lizenzgebühr	**royalty**
Lizenzinhaber	**licensee/licencee**
Lizenzkonzessionserteilung	**franchising**
Lizenzvertrag	**license agreement**
Lobby	**lobby**
Lock(vogel)angebot	**bait**
Lockangebot	**switch selling**
Lockartikel	**bait**
Lockartikel	**call bird**
Lockartikel	**leader**
Lockartikel	**loss leader**
Lockartikel	**price leader**
Lockmittelwerbung	**switch selling**
Lockpreisstrategie	**leader pricing**
Lockvogel	**call bird**
Lockvogel	**lowball**
Lockvogel	**loss leader**
Lockvogel	**price leader**
Lockvogelangebot	**switch selling**
Lockvogelpreisbildung	**leader pricing**
Lockvogelpreisfestsetzung	**bait pricing**
Lockvogelwerbung	**bait advertising**
Lockvogelwerbung	**switch selling**

Loco-Preis	**loco price**
Logistik	**logistics**
Logo	**brand mark**
Logo	**logo**
Lohn-Preis-Spirale	**wage-price spiral**
Lohndruckinflation	**wage-push inflation**
Lohninflation	**wage-push inflation**
lohnintensiv	**labour intensive**
Lohnkosten	**labour cost(s)**
Lohn(kosten)inflation	**wage inflation**
Lohnpolitik	**incomes policy**
Lohnstückkosten	**unit labour cost(s)**
Lokalpresse	**local press**
Lokalsender	**home station**
Lokalsender	**local station**
Loko-Preis	**price loco**
Lokopreis (Bö)	**spot price**
Los	**batch**
Löschen (Ladung)	**unloading**
Löschen (Ladung)	**discharge**
Lösgericht	**instant**
Losgröße	**economic order quantity**
Losgröße, minimale	**minimum manufacturing quantity**
Losgröße, nicht handelsübliche	**broken lot**
Lotterie	**lottery**
Lotterie	**sweepstake**
Low-Involvement-Produkt	**low involvement product**
Lücke, deflatorische	**deflationary gap**
Lücke, inflatorische	**inflationary gap**
Lückenanalyse	**gap analysis**
Lückenbüßer	**filler**
Luftfracht	**air freight**
Luftfrachtbrief	**waybill**
Luftfrachtführer	**air carrier**
Luftpost	**airmail**
Lufttransport	**air transport**
Lufttransport von LKW-Containern	**birdyback**
Luftverkehrsgesellschaft	**air carrier**
Luftwerbung	**aerial advertising**
Luftwerbung	**sky advertising**
Luxussteuer	**luxury tax**
Luxuswaren	**luxury goods**

M

Machtmißbrauch	**abuse of power**
Made in label	**Made in label**
Magazin	**magazine**
Magazin	**magazine**
Magazin	**periodical**

Magnat	magnate
Magnetkarte	magnetic card
Magnetkartentelefon	cardphone
Mahnung, verdeckte	hidden reminder
Mail-Order	mail order
Mailing, personalisiertes	personalised mailing
Mailings, Antwortquote bei	response rate
Makler	broker
Makler	dealer
Makler	agent
Maklergebühr	brokerage
Maklergeschäft	brokerage
Maklergeschäft	broking
Maklerprovision	brokerage
Makromarketing	macromarketing/macro marketing
Makroökonomik	macroeconomics
Makrosegmentierung	macrosegmentation
Makroumwelt	macroenvironment
Malrabatt	frequency discount
Malrabatt	time discount
Malrabatt für Werbung	consecutive-weeks discount
Malrabatt für häufige Werbung in einer festgelegten Zeitperiode	vertical discount
Management nach Zielvorgabe und Zielkontrolle	management by objective(s)
Mangel	fault
Mangel	imperfection
Mangel	need
Mangel	scarcity
Mangel an Elastizität (Angebot, Nachfrage)	inelasticity
Mangel, offener	apparent defect
Mangel, verborgener, versteckter	hidden defect
Mangel, verborgener, versteckter	inherent vice
Mangel, vorborgener, versteckter	latent defect
Mängelausschluß des Verkäufers	caveat emptor
Mängelhaftungsgarantie	maintenance bond
Mängelrüge	claim
Mängelrüge	consumer complaint
Mängelrüge	complaint
Mangelwaren, hoher Preis für	scarcity value
Manifest	manifest
Mantelgesellschaft	bubble company
Manuskript	script
Manuskriptannahme	copy clearance
Marge	spread
Marge	turn
Marginalanalyse	marginal analysis
Markdurchdringung	sales penetration
Marke	make

Marke	**mark**
Marke X	**brand X**
Marke, Marktanteil einer	**brand share**
Marke, flankierende	**flanker brand**
Marke, für die geworben wird	**advertised brand**
Marke, gut eingeführte	**established product**
Markenakzeptanz	**brand acceptance**
Markenalternative, erinnerte	**evoked set**
Markenartikel	**brand**
Markenartikel	**branded good**
Markenartikel	**proprietary goods**
Markenartikelfälschung	**faking of brands**
Markenartikelpolitik, geozentrische	**geocentric branding policy**
Markenartikelwerbung	**brand advertising**
Markenbewußtsein	**awareness**
Markenbewußtsein	**brand awareness**
Markenbewußtsein	**brand recognition**
Markenbild (eines Produkts)	**brand image**
Markenerweiterung	**brand extension**
Markenerzeugnis hoher Qualität	**premium brand**
Markenetikett	**brand label**
Markenfamilienbranding	**blanket branding**
Markenführer	**brand leader**
Markenherstellerverband zur Abwehr von Plagiatprodukten	**Anticounterfeiting Coalition**
Markenindifferenz	**brand indifference**
Markenkampf	**battle of the brands**
Markenkennzeichnung, individuelle	**idividual branding**
Markenklasse	**brand category**
Markenkonsumindex	**brand development index**
Markenname	**brand name**
Markenname, willkürlich gewählter	**arbitrary mark**
Markennamenauswahl	**brand name selection**
Markenneupositionierung	**brand repositioning**
Markenpiraterie	**brand piracy**
Markenpiraterie	**trademark piracy**
Markenpräferenz	**brand preference**
Markenprodukt, Kaufentscheid für ein	**brand choice**
Markenprodukt-Management	**brand management**
Markenproduktpositionierung	**brand positioning**
Markentingstandardisierung, globale	**global marketing standardization**
Markentreue	**brand loyalty**
Markenwahl	**brand choice**
Markenwahl	**brand selection**
Markenwarendifferenzierung	**brand differentiation**
Markenwechsel	**brand switching**
Markenwettbewerb	**brand competition**
Markenzeichen	**brand mark**
Markt, freier, offener	**open market**
Marketing	**marketing**

Marketing für breite Zielgruppen	**mass marketing**
Marketing für gemeinnützige Zwecke	**nonprofit marketing**
Marketing, Werterhöhung durch	**value-added marketing**
Marketing, computergestütztes	**database marketing**
Marketing, das auf ähnliche Beziehungen zwischen Anbieter und Konsument aufbaut	**affinity marketing**
Marketing, differenziertes	**differentiated marketing**
Marketing, differenziertes, selektives	**selective marketing**
Marketing, flächendeckendes	**extensive marketing**
Marketing, gesamteuropäisches	**Pan-European marketing**
Marketing, getrenntes	**divergent marketing**
Marketing, gezieltes	**concentrated marketing**
Marketing, globales	**global marketing**
Marketing, horizontales	**horizontal marketing**
Marketing, innerbetriebliches	**internal marketing**
Marketing, innovatives	**innovative marketing**
Marketing, integriertes	**integrated marketing**
Marketing, internationales	**international marketing**
Marketing, konzentriertes	**concentrated marketing**
Marketing, koordiniertes, aufeinander abgestimmtes	**coordinated marketing**
Marketing, kundenspezifisches	**custom marketing**
Marketing, kundenspezifisches	**customised marketing**
Marketing, multinationales	**multinational marketing**
Marketing, nicht standardisiertes	**nonstandardized marketing**
Marketing, offensives	**offensive marketing**
Marketing, produktdifferenziertes	**product differentiated marketing**
Marketing, soziökologisches	**socioecological marketing**
Marketing, standardisiertes, genormtes	**standardized marketing**
Marketing, umweltfreundliches	**green marketing**
Marketing, undifferenziertes	**undifferentiated marketing**
Marketing, verbraucherorientiertes	**consumer-oriented marketing**
Marketing, vertikales	**vertical marketing**
Marketing, verwaltetes, vertikales	**administered vertical market system**
Marketing, zielorientiertes	**target marketing**
Marketing-Audit	**marketing audit**
Marketing-Datenbank	**marketing database**
Marketing-Informationssystem	**marketing information system**
Marketing-Infrastruktur	**marketing infrastructure**
Marketing-Umweltanalyse	**opportunity and threat analysis**
Marketingabteilung	**marketing department**
Marketingarten	**marketing types**
Marketingausgaben, Ausgabenaufteilung der ...	**spending split**
Marketingberater	**marketing consultant**
Marketingbudget	**marketing budget**
Marketingdienstleistungsagentur	**marketing service agency**
Marketingdreieck, magisches	**gem triangle**
Marketingentscheidungen	**marketing decisions**
Marketingfachmann	**marketing man**

Marketingfaktoren, wirtschaftliche	economic marketing factors
Marketingforschung	marketing research
Marketingkontrolle	marketing control
Marketingkonzept	marketing concept
Marketingmanagement	marketing management
Marketingmanager	marketing manager
Marketingmanager, nationaler	national marketing manager
Marketingmix	marketing mix
Marketingmix Entscheidungen	marketing mix decisions
Marketingmix, angepaßtes	adapted marketing mix
Marketingmix, erweitertes für Dienstleistungen	extended marketing mix for services
Marketingmix, standardisiertes	standardized marketing mix
Marketingplan	action programme
Marketingplan	marketing plan
Marketingplanung	marketing planning
Marketingspraktiken, unmoralische	unethical marketing practices
Marketingprozeß	marketing process
Marketingstrategie	marketing strategy
Marketingstrategie zur Schaffung von Verbrauchernachfrage	pull strategy
Marketingstrategie, Unternehmen mit breitgefächerter ...	middle-of-the-roader
Marketingstrategie, die den Handel zum Verkauf eines Produkts bewegen soll	push strategy
Marketingstrategie, offensive	offensive market strategy
Marketingsystem, vertikales	vertical marketing system
Marketingumfeld	marketing environment
Marketingverband, amerikanischer	American Marketing Association
Marketingziele	marketing objectives
markieren	mark
Markierung	label(l)ing
Markierung	mark
Markierungszeichen	shipping marks
Markt	fair
Markt	market
Markt	market place
Markt	mart
Markt	traffic
Markt der gehobenen Preisklasse	upmarket
Markt eines monopolistischen Anbieters	captive market
Markt für Käufer mit hohem Einkommen	high-end market
Markt für hochwertige Güter	class market
Markt mit nachgebenden Preisen	soft market
Markt mit stabiler Preisentwicklung	firm market
Markt mit steigendem Preisniveau	advancing market
Markt mit vollkommenem Wettbewerb	perfect market
Markt ohne Zutritts- und Austrittsschranken	contestable market

Markt, angestrebter	**target market**
Markt, aufnahmefähiger	**ready market**
Markt, begrenzter, enger	**narrow market**
Markt, begrenzter, enger	**thin market**
Markt, beschränkter	**restricted market**
Markt, bestens organisierter	**highly-organised market**
Markt, fester	**stable market**
Markt, fester	**steady market**
Markt, flauer, gedrückter	**depressed market**
Markt, flauer, lustloser	**sluggish market**
Markt, frei verfügbarer	**available market**
Markt, freier, offener	**competitive market**
Markt, gemeinnütziger	**not-for-profit market**
Markt, gesättigter	**mature market**
Markt, grauer	**grey/gray market**
Markt, horizontaler	**horizontal market**
Markt, lebhafter	**active market**
Markt, leicht (empfindlich) reagierender	**sensitive market**
Markt, lustloser	**narrow market**
Markt, organisierter	**market overt**
Markt, organisierter	**organised market**
Markt, örtlicher, lokaler	**local market**
Markt, potentieller	**potential market**
Markt, rückläufiger	**soft market**
Markt, schwacher	**weak market**
Markt, sich durch zu hohe Preise vom ... ausschließen	**price out of market**
Markt, stark schwankender	**jumpy market**
Markt, verfügbarer	**available market**
Markt, vertikaler	**vertical market**
Markt, vollkommener	**perfect market**
Markt, vorhandener	**available market**
Markt, zugänglicher	**available market**
Marktabdeckung	**coverage**
Marktabdeckung	**market coverage**
Marktabdeckung, globale	**global marketing standardization**
Marktabschöpfung(sstrategie)	**market skimming**
Marktakzeptanz	**market acceptance**
Marktanalyse	**market analysis**
Marktanteil	**market coverage**
Marktanteil	**market share**
Marktanteil	**penetration**
Marktanteil	**sales penetration**
Marktanteil einer Marke	**brand share**
Marktanteil, relativer	**relative market share**
Marktarten	**market types**
Marktanteil-/Marktwachstum-Portfolio	**growth-share matrix**
Marktausschluß durch zu hohe Preise	**price out of market**
Marktauswahl	**market selection**
Marktbeobachter	**business monitor**

Marktbeobachter	**ghost shopper**
Marktbericht	**market report**
Marktdichte	**market density**
Marktdiversifizierung	**market diversification**
Marktdurchdringung	**market penetration**
Marktdurchdringung	**penetration**
Märkte, entfernt gelegene	**distant markets**
Märkte, nahegelegene	**near markets**
Märkte, verstreute	**scattered markets**
Markteintrittsschranken, natürliche	**natural barriers to entry**
Marktentwicklung	**market development**
Markterweiterung	**market expansion**
Marktfähigkeit	**marketability**
Marktfähigkeit	**salability (saleability)**
Marktfaktorenanalyse	**market factor analysis**
Marktfolger	**follower**
Marktfolger	**market follower**
Marktformen	**market forms**
Marktformenlehre	**theory of market structure**
Marktforschung	**market research**
Marktforschung für Industriegüter	**industrial market research**
Marktforschung für Investitionsgüter	**industrial market research**
Marktforschung, gemeinsame	**syndicated market research**
Marktführer	**key product**
Marktführer	**market leader**
Marktführerfolger-Preisgestaltung	**follow-the-leader pricing strategy**
Marktgleichgewicht	**market equilibrium**
Marktgröße	**market size**
Marktherausforderer	**market challenger**
Marktherausforderer, Strategien eines	**market challenger strategies**
Marktinformationen	**marketing intelligence**
Marktkapazität	**market capacity**
Marktkonzentration	**market concentration**
Marktkonzentration, geographische	**geographic market concentration**
Marktkräfte	**market forces**
Marktkraft	**pulling power**
Marktleiter	**market manager**
Marktlücken-Kommunikation	**narrowcasting/narrow casting**
Marktlückenanalyse	**gap analysis**
Marktmacht	**market power**
Marktmacht, ausgleichende	**countervailing power**
Marktmechanismus	**market mechanism**
Marktnachfrage	**market demand**
Marktnische	**market niche**
Marktökologie	**market ecology**
Marktpenetrationsgrad	**achieved penetration**
Marktpositionierung	**market positioning**
Marktpotential	**market potential**
Marktpotential, gesamtes	**total market potential**
Marktpreis	**market price**

Marktpreis (angemessener)	**value**
Marktpreis, angemessener	**actual cash value**
Marktpreis, angemessener	**fair market value (FMV)**
Marktpreis, freier	**free market price**
Marktpreis-Mechanismus	**price mechanism**
Marktprofil	**market profile**
Marktprognose	**market forecast**
Marktsättigung	**saturation of a market**
Marktsättigungspunkt	**absorption point**
Marktsegment	**market segment**
Marktsegmente, Abdeckung aller	**complete segmentation**
Marktsegmentiertung, demographische	**demographic segmentation**
Marktsegmentierung	**market segmentation**
Marktsegmentierung auf Grund von Verhaltensmerkmalen	**behaviour segmentation**
Marktsegmentierung nach Markentreue	**brand loyalty segmentation**
Marktsegmentierung, psychographische	**psychographic segmentation**
Marktstand	**booth**
Marktstellung	**market position**
Marktstimmung	**undertone**
Marktstrategie, Gewinnträchtigkeit einer	**profit impact of market strategy (PIMS)**
Marktstruktur	**market structure**
Marktstrukturdarstellung	**market map**
Marktstrukturkarte	**market map**
Markttag	**market day**
Marktteilnehmer	**marketer**
Markttendenzen	**market trends**
Markttest	**market test(ing)**
Markttest	**product placement test**
Markttests, Durchführung von lokalen	**test marketing**
Marktumfrage	**market survey**
Marktverhalten	**market behaviour**
Marktverkäufer	**marketeer**
Marktwert	**current value**
Marktwert	**going value**
Marktwert	**market price**
Marktwert	**market value**
Marktwert	**present value**
Marktwiderstand	**market resistance**
Marktwirtschaft	**market economy**
Marktwirtschaft	**private enterprise**
Marktwirtschaft, System der freien	**free market system**
Marktwirtschaft, freie	**free economy**
Marktwirtschaft, freie	**unplanned economy**
Marktzerrüttung	**market disruption**
Marktzugang	**access to the market**
Marktzugänglichkeit	**accessibility**
Marktzugänglichkeit	**market accessibility**
Marktzutritt	**entry**

Marktzutritt	**market entry**
Marktzutrittshindernisse	**market entry barriers**
Marktzutrittsschranke	**barrier to entry**
Marotte	**fad**
Marschroute	**strategy**
Maslows Bedürfnishierarchie	**Maslow`s hierarchy of needs**
Maslows Bedürfnispyramide	**Maslow`s hierarchy of needs**
Massenabsatzstrategie	**mass marketing**
Massenauslage	**mass display**
Masseneinkauf	**bulk buying**
Massenerzeugnis	**staple**
Massenfertigung	**mass production**
Massenfertigung, Stückkostenrechnung für	**process costing**
Massenfrachtgut	**bulk cargo**
Massengeschäft	**bulk business**
Massengüter	**bulk goods**
Massengütertransport	**bulk shipment**
Massengutfrachter	**bulk carrier**
Massenkommunikation	**mass communication**
Massenmarkt	**mass market**
Massenmarktprodukt	**mass market product**
Massenmedium	**mass medium**
Massenmerchandising	**mass merchandising**
Massenproduktion	**large-scale production**
Massenproduktion	**mass production**
Massenproduktion	**volume production**
Massentourismus	**mass tourism**
Maßnahmen zur Ankurbelung der Nachfrage	**want creation**
Maßnahmen, ausgabedämpfende	**expenditure-dampening policies**
Material	**material**
Materialabfall	**spoilage**
Materialabfall	**waste**
Materialanforderung	**purchase requisition**
Materialaufbereitung	**data processing**
Materialbedarfsplanung	**materials requirements planning**
Materialeinkäufer	**materials buyer**
Materialkosten	**material costs**
Materialpreisabweichung	**materials price variance**
Materialtransport	**materials handling**
Materialwirtschaft	**materials management**
Materialwirtschaft	**materials handling**
Materialwirtschaft, fertigungssynchrone	**just in time**
Maut	**toll**
Mautgebühr	**road toll**
Maximalpreis	**maximum price**
Mäzenatentum	**sponsorship**
Me-too Produkt	**copycat product**
Me-too Produkt	**me-too product**

Media-Mix	**media mix**
Median	**median**
Medien	**media**
Medien für ethnische Gruppen/ Minderheiten	**ethnic media**
Medien, elektronische	**electronic media**
Medien, zuhause genutzte	**in-home media**
Medienauswahl	**media selection**
Medienbudget	**media budget**
Mediendatenbuch	**rate book**
Medienereignis	**media event**
Medienplan	**media plan**
Medienplan	**media plan**
Medienplaner	**media planner**
Medienplanung	**advertising planning**
Medienpräsentation	**media presentation**
Medienreichweite	**media reach**
Medienwerbung	**media advertising**
Medikamente, rezeptfreie, nicht verschreibungspflichtige	**over-the-counter drugs/products**
Medium	**vehicle**
Megaladen	**megastore**
Megamarketing	**megamarketing**
mehr als vier Kontakte	**four-plus cover**
Mehrfach-Säulen-Diagramm	**multiple bar chart**
Mehrfachleser	**multiple reader**
Mehrfachleserschaft	**multiple readership**
Mehrfachpackung	**multipack**
Mehrfachpackungsangebot	**multipack offer**
Mehrfachvertrieb	**multichannel distribution**
Mehrheit	**majority**
Mehrheit, frühe (bei Einführung neuer Produkte)	**early majority**
Mehrheit, späte	**late majority**
Mehrmarken-Produkt	**multiple branding**
Mehrprodukt-Unternehmen	**multi-product company**
Mehrproduktwerbung	**multiunit advertising**
Mehrstückpackung	**multiple pack**
Mehrstückpackung	**multipack**
Mehrthemenbefragung	**omnibus survey**
Mehrwegpackung	**multi-way packing**
Mehrwertprodukt	**added value product**
Mehrwertsteuer	**value added tax**
Mehrwertsteuer, einschließlich	**VAT included**
Mehrwertsteuerbefreiung	**zero rating**
Mehrwertsteuerbefreiung (GB)	**exemption from VAT**
Meinungsbildner	**opinion leader**
Meinungsforschung	**opinion research**
Meinungsführer	**opinion leader**
Meinungsmacher	**key buying influencer**

Meinungsumfrage	**opinion poll**
Meinungsverschiedenheit	**difference**
Meistbietende(r)	**highest bidder**
Meldebestand	**reorder quantity**
Melkstrategie	**milking strategy**
Menge	**batch**
Menge	**quantity**
Menge, angebotene	**quantity supplied**
Menge, nachgefragte	**quantity demanded**
Mengenabweichung	**volume discrepancy**
Mengenanpasser	**price taker**
Mengenrabatt	**bulk discount**
Mengenrabatt	**quantity discount**
Mengenrabatt auf Jahresbasis	**annual volume discount**
Mengenrabatt bei Funk und Fernsehen	**time discount**
Mengenrabatt, kumulativer	**cumulative quantity discount**
Mensch, haushälterischer, sparsamer	**economizer/economiser**
Merchandiser	**merchandiser**
Merchandising	**merchandising**
Merchandising, gemischtes	**scrambled merchandising**
Merkantilismus	**mercantilism**
Merkmal	**earmark**
Merkmale, demographische	**demographics**
Merkmalsanalyse, psychographische	**psychographics**
Merkmalsverbesserung	**feature improvement**
Meßbarkeit	**maesurability**
Messe	**exhibition**
Messe	**fair**
Messegelände	**exhibition grounds**
Messehalle	**exhibition hall**
Messestand	**booth**
Messestand	**stand**
Messung des Publikums	**audience measurement**
Metallwaren	**hardware**
Methode des erwarteten Umsatzes (bei Festetzung des Werbeetats)	**percent(age) of sales method**
Methode zur Festlegung des Werbeetats, die sich an Konkurrenz orientiert	**competitive parity method**
Mietbesitz	**leasehold**
Miete	**lease**
Mietkauf	**hire purchase**
Mietvertrag	**lease**
Mikromarketing	**micromarketing**
Mikroökonomie	**microeconomics**
Mikroökonomik	**microeconomics**
Mikrosegmentierung	**microsegmentation**
Mimicry	**passing off**
Mindererlös	**loss**
Minderjährige(r)	**infant**

Minderjährige(r)	**minor**
Minderung	**abatement**
Mindesrendite, erwartete	**hurdle rate of return**
Mindestanzeigenraum, der belegt werden muß	**backup space**
Mindestauftrag	**minimum order**
Mindestbestand	**minimum stock level**
Mindestbetrag	**minimum charge**
Mindesteinschaltquote	**guaranteed home impacts**
Mindestgebühr	**minimum charge**
Mindesthaltbarkeits(datum)	**best before date**
Mindestpreis	**floor**
Mindestpreis	**floor price**
Mindestpreis	**knocked-down price**
Mindestpreis	**minimum price**
Mindestpreis	**price floor**
Mindestpreis	**reserve price**
Mindestpreis (bei Versteigerungen)	**upset price**
Mindestpreiskalkulation	**price floor pricing**
Mindestverkaufspreis	**reservation price**
Miniaturisierung	**downsizing**
Minimalpreis	**minimum price**
Minimarkt	**minimarket**
Minimax-Regel	**minimax principle**
Minimumpreis	**price floor**
Minusbestand	**stock shortage**
Mischen	**blending**
Mischkonzern	**conglomerate**
Mischkosten	**mixed cost(s)**
Mischkosten	**semivariable/semi-variable costs**
Mischung der Werbemittel	**advertising mix**
Mischwirtschaft	**mixed economy**
mit Wirkung vom, ab	**as from**
Mitbewerber	**competitor**
Mitglied, neues	**entrant**
Mitgliedsbeiträge	**dues**
Mitläufereffekt	**bandwagon effect**
Mitläufereffekt	**demonstration effect**
Mitleser	**pass-along/ on reader**
"Mitreiten"	**passing off**
Mitteilungsblatt	**newsletter**
Mittel, arithmetisches	**arithmetic mean**
Mittel, flüssige	**cash**
Mittel, geometrisches	**geometric mean**
Mittelklasse, obere	**upper-middle class**
Mittelkurs	**mean price**
Mittelwert	**mean**
Mittelwert, arithmetischer	**average**
Mittelwert, gleitender	**moving average**
Mittler	**intermediary**

Mittler	middleman
Mobile	mobile
Mobilien	mov(e)ables
Mobilität, vertikale	upward mobility
Mode	fashion
Mode(torheit)	fad
Modeartikel	fancy article
Modell einer hierarchischen Abfolge von Wirkungen	hierarchy of effects model
Modell in Originalgröße	mockup
Modell, ökonomisches	economic model
Moderator	anchorman
Moderator	presenter
Modernisierung	facelift/face-lift
Modewelle	fad
Modewort	buzzword
Modezyklus	fashion cycle
Modifikation, funktionale	functional modification
Mogelpackung	deceptive packaging
Möglichkeit	chance
Molkereiprodukte	dairy products
Moment-Einschaltsquote	instantaneous audience rating
Monat, laufender	instant
Monatsumsatz	monthly sales
Monopol	monopoly
Monopol, bilaterales, zweiseitiges	bilateral monopoly
Monopol, natürliches	natural monopoly
Monopol, reines, echtes	pure monopoly
Monopol, reines, vollkommenes	absolute monopoly
Monopol, staatliches	government monopoly
Monopol, staatliches	statutory monopoly
Monopole, Zerschlagung von	trustbusting
Monopolentflechtung	divestment
Monopolisierung	monopolisation
Monopolist	monopolist
Monopolkommission (GB)	Monopolies (and Mergers) Commission
Monopolmacht	monopoly power
Monopson	monopsony
Montage	installation
Montagehalle	assembly shop
Moral	ethics
Morgenausgabe	bulldog edition
Motiv	motive
Motivation	motivation
Motivforschung	motivation research
Motorrad-Bote	despatch rider
Mülleimer	bin
Müllkunde	garbology
Multi-Marken-Strategie	multibrand strategy
Multiangebot	multiple offer

Multikonzern, weltweit tätiger	global player
Multimarkenstrategie	multibrand strategy
Multimedia	multimedia
Multimediawerbung	multimedia advertising
Multipack	multiple pack
Multisegmentstrategie	multisegment strategy
Mund-zu-Mund-Werbung	word-of-mouth-advertising
Mundreklame	word-of-mouth-advertising
Münzfernsehen	pay TV
Münzfernsprecher	payphone
Mußwarnung	mandatory blurb
Muster	design
Muster	pattern
Muster	sample
Muster(streifen)	swatch
Muster, käufliches	sal(e)able sample
Musterbuch	pattern book
Musterbuch	sample book
Musterhaus	show house
Musterkoffer	display case
Musterkoffer	sampling case
Musterprozeß	test case
Musterquote	free merchandise
Musterverkauf	sale by sample
Musterwohnung	show flat
Mystery Shopper	mystery shopper

N

Nachahmung	imitation
Nacharbeitung	rework
Nachbarschaftsladen	convenience store
Nachbarschaftsladen	neighbourhood shop
Nachbesprechung	debriefing
Nachbesserung	rework
Nachbestellung	repeat order
Nachbestellung	reorder
Nachbestellung, automatische	automatic reorder
Nacheinandersenden von zwei Werbespots	double spotting
Nachfaßaktion	follow-up
Nachfaßangebot	follow-up quotation
Nachfaßbesuch	follow-up
Nachfaßbrief	follow-up letter
Nachfaßinterview	callback
Nachfaßwerbung	follow-up
Nachfrage	market
Nachfrage (effektive)	demand
Nachfrage durch Wertzuwachs	regressive demand
Nachfrage in der Vorphase	incipient demand
Nachfrage und Angebot	demand and supply

Nachfrage und Preis	**demand and price**
Nachfrage, Elastizität = 1	**unitary elasticity (demand)**
Nachfrage, Kreuz(preis)elastizität der	**cross elasticity of demand**
Nachfrage, Maßnahmen zur Ankurbelung der	**want creation**
Nachfrage, Preiselastizität der	**price elasticity of demand**
Nachfrage, abgeleitete, derivative	**derived demand**
Nachfrage, anhaltende, stetige	**persistent demand**
Nachfrage, aufgeschobene	**deferred demand**
Nachfrage, beginnende	**incipient demand**
Nachfrage, diffuse	**diffused demand**
Nachfrage, direkte	**direct demand**
Nachfrage, effektive, tatsächliche	**effective demand**
Nachfrage, elastische	**elastic demand**
Nachfrage, geringe, schwache, stagnierende	**slack demand**
Nachfrage, homogene	**homogeneous demand**
Nachfrage, industrielle	**industrial demand**
Nachfrage, inverse	**inverse demand**
Nachfrage, inverse	**regressive demand**
Nachfrage, komplementäre, verbundene	**complementary demand**
Nachfrage, konkurrierende	**alternate demand**
Nachfrage, konkurrierende	**competitive demand**
Nachfrage, konkurrierende	**composite demand**
Nachfrage, konkurrierende	**rival demand**
Nachfrage, latente	**latent demand**
Nachfrage, laufende	**current demand**
Nachfrage, lebhafte	**strong market**
Nachfrage, monetäre oder effektive	**monetary demand**
Nachfrage, negative	**negative demand**
Nachfrage, potentielle (mögliche)	**potential demand**
Nachfrage, schwache	**weak demand**
Nachfrage, schwankende	**fluctuating demand**
Nachfrage, schwankende	**volatile demand**
Nachfrage, selektive	**selective demand**
Nachfrage, starke	**keen demand**
Nachfrage, tatsächliche	**existing demand**
Nachfrage, tief verwurzelte	**deep rooted demand**
Nachfrage, unelastische	**inelastic demand**
Nachfrage, unstete, launenhafte	**erratic demand**
Nachfrage, verbundene	**complementary demand**
Nachfrage, verbundene, komplementäre	**joint demand**
Nachfrage, vollkommen elastische	**perfectly elastic demand**
Nachfrage, vollkommen unelastische	**perfectly inelastic demand**
Nachfrage, zusammengesetzte	**composite demand**
Nachfrage-Duopol	**duopsony**
Nachfrage-Kosten-Inflation, gemischte	**mixed demand-cost inflation**
Nachfrageanalyse	**demand analysis**
Nachfragearten	**demand types**
Nachfrageänderung	**change in demand**

Nachfragebedingungen	**conditions of demand**
Nachfragedeckung	**satisfaction of demand**
Nachfragedeterminanten	**determinants of demand**
Nachfrageelastizität	**elasticity of demand**
Nachfrageexpansion	**expansion of demand**
Nachfragefaktoren	**demand factors**
Nachfragefluktuation	**demand fluctuation**
Nachfragefunktion	**demand function**
Nachfragegesetz	**law of demand**
Nachfragegesetz, Ausnahmen beim	**exceptions to the law of demand**
Nachfrageinflation	**demand-pull inflation**
Nachfrageinflation, nichtmonetäre	**demand-shift inflation**
Nachfrageinflation, nichtmonetäre	**bottleneck inflation**
Nachfragekurve	**demand curve**
Nachfragekurve, Verschiebung der	**shift of demand curve**
Nachfragekurve, allgemeine	**general demand curve**
Nachfragekurve, fallende	**downward sloping demand curve**
Nachfragekurve, geknickte	**kinky demand curve**
Nachfragemenge	**quantity demanded**
Nachfragemonopol	**monopsony**
Nachfragemonopolist	**monopsonist**
Nachfragepreis	**demand price**
Nachfrageprognose	**demand forecast**
Nachfragerückgang	**decrease in demand**
Nachfrageschaffung	**demand creation**
Nachfrageschöpfung	**demand creation**
Nachfrageschrumpfung	**contraction of (in) demand**
Nachfragesog	**demand pull**
Nachfragesteuerung	**demand management**
Nachfragetabelle	**demand schedule**
Nachfragetheory	**demand theory**
Nachfrageüberhang	**excess(ive) demand**
Nachfrageüberschuß	**overfull demand**
Nachfrageverschiebung	**demand shift**
Nachfrageverschiebungsinflation	**demand-shift inflation**
Nachfüllpackung	**refill pack**
Nachgebühr	**excess postage**
Nachkaufverhalten	**postpurchase behaviour**
Nachlaß	**abatement**
Nachlaß	**deduction**
Nachlaß	**reduction**
Nachlaß (vom Listenpreis)	**trade discount**
Nachlaß außerhalb der Saison	**seasonal discount**
Nachlaß, über 2 % Skonto	**trade discount**
Nachlaß, zusätzlicher	**anticipation**
Nachmittag, Stoßverkehrszeit am	**afternoon drive**
Nachnahme	**cash on delivery**
Nachnahme (per)	**charges forward**
Nachnahme, Fracht gegen/per	**freight forward**
Nachnahme, gegen	**collection on delivery (COD)**

Nachporto	**postage due**
Nachprüfung	**verification**
Nachricht	**message**
Nachrichtenagentur	**news agency**
Nachrichtenquelle	**source**
Nachrichtensender, reiner	**all news**
Nachrichtensprecher	**newscaster**
Nachsaison	**dead season**
Nachsaison	**low season**
Nachschlagewerk	**reference book**
Nachsendeadresse	**forwarding address**
Nachsendeantrag	**rerouting request**
Nachsendung	**forwarding**
Nachteile, externe	**external diseconomies**
Nachvollziehender, früh	**early adopter**
Nachzügler	**laggard**
Naderismus	**Naderism**
Nahaufnahme	**extreme close-up**
Nahaufnahme eines Produkts in der Fernsehwerbung	**beauty shot**
Nährstoffangabe	**nutritional labelling**
Nahrung	**fare**
Nahverkehr	**short haul**
Name	**name**
Namensgebung	**naming**
Naturaltausch	**barter**
Naturaltausch	**trade**
Naturalwirtschaft	**barter economy**
Nebenerzeugnis	**byproduct**
Nebenkasse	**petty cash**
Nebenkosten	**extras**
Nebenleistung	**peripheral service**
Nebenprodukt	**byproduct**
Nebenprodukt	**spinoff/spin-off**
Nebenproduktpreisbildung	**byproduct pricing**
Nebensaison	**off season**
Neckwerbung	**teaser ad(vertisement)**
Negativwerbung	**negative advertising**
Nennwert, unter	**at a discount**
Neoklassik (Lehrmethode)	**neo-classical economics**
netto	**net/nett**
netto Kasse	**net cash**
Netto-Leasing	**net lease**
Netto-Zahlungsbedingungen	**terms net**
Nettoauflage, effektive	**net circulation**
Nettobetrag	**net amount**
Nettobetriebsgewinn	**net operating profit**
Nettobetriebsverlust	**net operating loss**
Nettoeinkaufswert	**net purchases**
Nettoeinkommen	**disposable income**

Nettoeinkommen	**spendable earnings**
Nettoerlös	**net proceeds**
Nettogewicht	**net weight**
Nettogewinn	**net earnings**
Nettoinlandsprodukt	**net domestic product**
Nettoinvestition	**net investment**
Nettonutzerschaft	**net audience**
Nettopreis	**net price**
Nettopreis-System	**mill pricing**
Nettoproduktion	**net output**
Nettoreichweite	**audience accumulation**
Nettoreichweite	**net reach**
Nettoreichweite	**net cover(age)**
Nettoreichweite	**unduplicated audience**
Nettoreichweitenprozentpunkt	**net rating point**
Nettosozialprodukt	**net national product**
Nettosozialprodukt zu Faktorpreisen	**national income**
Nettotara	**net tare**
Nettoumsatz	**net turnover**
Nettoumsatzerlöse	**net turnover**
Nettoumsatzrendite	**net profit percentage**
Nettoverlust	**net loss**
Nettovolkseinkommen	**net national income**
Nettozahl der Personen mit Anschlagwerbemittelkontakt	**net circulation**
Neuanfang	**departure (dep)**
Neuanschaffung	**accession**
Neubenutzer/in	**new user**
Neuheit	**novelty**
Neukonsument	**new user**
Neupositionierung	**repositioning**
Neuproduktaufnahme	**new buy**
nicht am Lager	**out of stock**
nicht anderweitig spezifiziert	**not otherwise specified (NOS)**
nicht vorrätig	**out of stock**
Nicht-Grundgüter	**discretionary goods**
Nichtannahme	**nonacceptance**
Nichtbeantwortung	**nonresponse**
Nichterfüllung	**nonperformance**
Nichterfüllung	**nondelivery**
Nichtkauf-Leser, tatsächlicher	**acutal non-buyer reader**
Nichtlieferung	**nondelivery**
Nichtzahlung	**nonpayment**
Niederlassung	**branch**
Niedrigpreis	**cut price**
Niedrigpreis, täglicher	**everyday low price**
Niedrigpreis-Kaufhaus-Kette	**variety chain store**
Niedrigpreisgeschäft	**cut-price shop/store**
Niedrigpreisgeschäft	**variety store**
Niedrigpreisladen	**off-price shop**

Niedrigpreisverkauf	unloading
Niedrigpreisware	cut price merchandise
Nische	niche
Nischenanbieter	market nicher
Nischenanbieter	nicher
Nischenmarketing	niche marketing
Nischenstrategie	niche strategy
Nonprofit-Marketing	social marketing
Normalgut	normal good
Normalpreis	normal price
Normalverteilung (Gauß'sche)	normal (Gaussian) distribution
Normalzeit(verbrauch)	level(l)ed time
Normen	norms
Normen	standards
Normenkartell	standardization cartel
Normenverband, britischer	British Standards Institution
Normungs- und Typungskartell	standardization cartel
Notfalltelefon	hotline (hot line)
Notverkauf	distress sale
Notwendigkeit	need
Notwendigkeitsgüter	essential commodities
Notwendigkeitsgüter	necessaries
Null (Zahl oder Zeichen)	zero
Null-Basis-Budgetierung	zero-base(d) budgeting
Nullelastizität	zero elasticity
Nullwachstum	zero economic growth
Nutzen	benefit
Nutzen	utility
Nutzen	value
Nutzen	satisfaction
Nutzen, abnehmender	diminishing utility
Nutzen, negativer	disutility
Nutzen, räumlicher, eines Gutes	place utility
Nutzen, wirtschaftlicher	economic utility
Nutzen-Kosten-Analyse	benefit-cost (B-C) analysis
Nutzenfunktion	utility function
Nutzenmaximierung	utility maximization
Nutzenschwelle	breakeven point
Nutzensegmentierung	benefit segmentation
Nutzensegmentierung	benefit segmentation
Nützlichkeit	utility
Nutzungsdauer	service life
Nutzungsdauer, technologische	technological life
Nutzungsdauer, voraussichtliche	life expectancy
Nutzungsdauer, wirtschaftliche	economic life

O

Oberbegriff	**generic term**
Oberflächenbeschaffenheit	**finish**
Oberklasse, obere	**upper-upper class**
Oberschicht	**upper class**
Oberschicht, gehobene soziale	**upscale**
Off-Kommentar	**voiceover, voice over**
Offenlegung, vollständige	**full disclosure**
Offensivstrategie	**attack strategy**
Öffentlichkeitsarbeit	**public relations**
Öffentlichkeitsmitarbeiter	**public relations officer**
Offerent	**offeror/offerer**
Offerte	**tender**
Öffnungszeiten	**opening hours**
Öko-Design	**lean design**
Ökologie	**ecology**
Ökonomie, klassische	**classical economics**
Ökonomie, neoklassische	**neo-classical economics**
Ökosteuer	**green tax**
Ökosystem	**ecosystem**
Oligopol	**oligopoly**
Oligopol, bilaterales	**bilateral oligopoly**
Oligopol, homogenes	**perfect oligopoly**
Oligopol, unvollkommenes	**imperfect oligopoly**
Oligopolpreisbildung	**parallel pricing**
Oligopson	**oligopsony**
Omnibusbefragung	**omnibus survey**
One-Stop-Einkauf	**one-stop shopping**
Online-Einzelhandel	**online retailing**
Operating-Leasing	**operating leasing**
Operations Research	**operations research**
Operationsforschung	**operations research**
Opportunitätskosten	**alternative cost(s)**
Opportunitätskosten	**opportunity cost(s)**
Opportunitätspreis	**opportunity price**
Optimierer	**optimizer**
Optimierung	**optimization**
Ordinate	**ordinate**
Ordnung, marktwirtschaftliche	**free market system**
Organisation zur Förderung von Werbung für Angelegenheiten des öffentlichen Interesses (USA)	**Advertising Council of America**
Organisation, unabhängige, zur Kontrolle der Auflagenziffern von Zeitungen und Zeitschriften	**Audit Bureau of Circulations**
Original	**original**
Original Equipment Manufacturer	**original equipment manufacturer**
Original(werbe)film	**answer print**

Ort	**place**
Ort der Leistung	**place of fulfil(l)ment**
Ortsgespräch	**local call**
Ortshändler, franchisierter	**franchise outlet**
Ortszeit	**local time (lt)**
Österreichische (Grenznutzen)Schule	**Austrian School**
Output	**output**
Output	**production**
Outsourcing	**outsourcing**

P

P's, vier (des Marketingmix)	**four Ps**
PEST-Faktor	**PEST factor**
POISE-Formel	**POISE**
POP-Werbeauslage	**point-of-purchase (POP) display**
POS-System	**point of sale system**
POS-Terminal	**point-of-sale terminal**
POS-Werbung	**point-of-sale advertising**
Paarvergleich	**diadic (product) test**
Paarvergleichstest	**paired comparison test**
Paasche Index	**Paasche index**
Pacht	**lease**
Pachtbesitz	**leasehold**
Pachtvertrag	**lease**
Päckchen	**package**
Päckchen	**sachet**
Packer/in	**packer**
Packliste	**packing list**
Packliste	**specification**
Packmaterial	**dunnage**
Packpapier	**wrapping paper**
Packpapier, kräftiges	**kraft paper**
Packstelle	**packing station**
Packstück	**package**
Packung	**package**
Packung	**packet**
Packung, die durch Deckelabnahme zu Regalauslage wird	**tray pack**
Packung, wieder verschließbare	**reclosable pack**
Packungsanhänger	**package outsert**
Packungsbanderole	**package band**
Packungsbeilage	**package enclosure**
Packungswerbung	**on-pack promotion**
Packungszugabe	**in-pack premium**
Packzettel	**packing slip**
Paginierung	**folio**
Paket	**packet**
Paketannahme	**parcel(s) office**
Paketausgabe	**parcel(s) office**

Paketpost	parcel post
Paketsendung	parcel post
Paketzustelldienst	package delivery service
Paketzustellung	parcel delivery
Palette	pallet
Palette	range
Palettenbreite	width of product range
Palettenladung	pallet load
Panel	panel
Panelforschung	panel research
Panikkauf	panic buying
Papier mit Briefkopf	headed paper
Papierkorb	bin
Papierkorbwerbung	junk mail
Papierkorbwerbung	litter bin advertising
Papiermaße	paper sizes
Pappe	paperboard
Paradepferd	flagship
Parallelposition	parallel position
Parameter	parameter
Pareto-Effekt	Pareto`s law
Paretosches Gesetz	Pareto's law
Pari, unter	at a discount
Paritätspreisfestsetzung	parity pricing
Paritätsprodukte	parity products
Partie	lot
Partieware	job lot
Partyverkauf	party plan
Partyverkauf	hostess party selling
Passagier, festgebuchter, aber nicht mitfliegender/reisender	no show
Passagierliste	waybill
Passantenzählung	journey mapping
Patent	patent
Patentanmeldung	patent application
Patentaufgabe	abandonment
Patentgeber	patentor
Patentgewährung, gegenseitige	cross licensing
Patentinhaber	patentee
Patentschrift	specification
Patenturkunde	letters patent
Patentverletzung	patent infringement
Patzer	fluff
Pauschalangebot	package deal
Pauschalbetrag	lump sum
Pauschalfracht	lump sum freight
Pauschalgebühr	flat rate
Pauschalgeschäft	basket transaction
Pauschalpreis	flat rate
Pauschalreise	package holiday

Pay per View	**pay-per-view**
Pay-TV	**pay TV**
Peer Group	**peer group**
Peisfestsetzung, gewinnorientierte	**profit-oriented pricing**
Peisnachlaßangebot	**cents-off offer**
Penetration(sgrad)	**penetration**
Penetrationsgrad	**achieved penetration**
Penetrationspreisbildung	**market penetration pricing**
Penetrationspreispolitik	**penetration pricing**
Penny (Münze) (GB)	**penny**
Periode, latente	**gestation period**
Perronanschlag	**station poster**
Person, der etwas vorgelegt wird	**presentee**
Person, die Drucksachen beilegt	**envelope stuffer**
Person, die jemanden etwas vorlegt	**presenter**
Personal einer Werbeagentur	**agency personnel**
Personal, kundenorientiertes	**customer-oriented personnel**
Personalkosten	**labour cost(s)**
Personalrabatt	**employee discount**
Personen/Haushalte, die mit Werbemittel /-träger Kontakt haben	**audience**
Personenmarketing	**person marketing**
Persönlichkeit	**personality**
Pfandbesteller	**pawner/pawnor**
Pfandbesteller	**pledger/pledgor**
Pfandinhaber	**pledgee**
Pfandinhaber	**pawnee**
Pfandleiher	**pawnbroker**
Pfandrecht	**lien**
Pfandrecht des Verkäufers	**seller's lien**
Pfandware	**returned empties**
Pfennigbeträge	**peanuts**
Pflichtetikett	**descriptive label**
Pflichtwarnung	**mandatory blurb**
Pförtner	**gatekeeper**
Pfund	**pound**
Phantasiename	**arbitrary mark**
Phantasiepreis	**fancy price**
Phantasiepreisgestaltung	**fictitious pricing**
Phase, geozentrische	**geocentric stage**
Phasenwerbung	**flighting**
Phasenwerbung	**pulsing**
Phsychogramm	**psychographics**
Pigou-Effekt	**Pigou effect**
Pigou-Effekt	**real balance effect**
Pigou-Effekt	**wealth effect**
Pilotanlage	**pilot plant**
Pilotstudie	**pilot study**
Pint(e) (Flüssigkeits-/Trockenmaß)	**pint**
Pionier	**innovator**

Pionierpreisfestlegung	**pioneer pricing**
Plagiat	**copycat product**
Plakat	**bill**
Plakat	**poster**
Plakat, großformatiges	**king size poster**
Plakatanschlagfläche	**facing**
Plakatanschlagsposition frontal zum Verkehrsfluß	**head-on position**
Plakatanschlagstelle	**poster site**
Plakataufkleber	**snipe**
Plakatauswechslung	**renewal**
Plakattafel	**sandwich board**
Plakatwerbeunternehmen	**poster plant**
Plakatwerbung	**billing**
Plakatwerbung	**outdoor advertising**
Plan	**design**
Plan, Fifty-fifty (50:50)	**fifty-fifty (50:50) plan**
Plan, kurzfristiger	**short range plan**
Plankosten	**standard cost**
Plankostenrechnung	**standard costing**
Planung	**planning**
Planung, strategische	**strategic planning**
Planung, taktische	**tactical planning**
Planwirtschaft	**command economy**
Plastikgeld	**plastic money**
Platz	**place**
Platz	**slot**
Plausibilitätskontrolle	**editing**
Plazierungsvereinbarung, ohne	**run of paper**
Pleite	**flop**
Plunder	**borax**
Plus-minus-Null, arbeiten mit	**breakeven**
Polaritätsfrage	**semantic differential question**
Polaritätsprofil	**semantic differential**
Politik der offenen Tür (AuW)	**open-door policy**
Polypol	**polypoly**
Pool	**pool**
Populationsmerkmale	**population characteristics**
Portfolioanalyse	**portfolio analysis**
Porto	**postage**
Porto und Bearbeitung	**postage and handling**
Portobuch	**postage book**
Positionierung	**positioning**
Post	**post office**
Post	**post**
postlagernd	**general delivery**
postlagernd	**poste restante**
Post erster Klasse (bevorzugt abgefertigt)	**first class mail**
Post zweiter Klasse	**second class mail**
Post(sendung)	**mail**

Post, elektronische	electronic mail
Post, gewöhnliche	surface mail
Post, mit gleicher (gesonderter)	under separate cover
Postamt	post
Postamt für unzustellbare Briefe und Pakete	dead letter office
Postanschrift	postal address
Postbestellung	mail order
Posteinlieferungsschein	post office receipt
Poster	poster
Postfach	post office box
Postfachnummer	box number
Postgebühren	postal charges
Postgut dritter Klasse (USA)	third class mail
Postkasten	post
Postleitzahl (GB)	postcode
Postleitzahl (USA)	zip code
Postleitzahlenbuch	address coding guide
Postpaket	package
Postpaketempfangsschein	parcel post receipt
Post(schließ)fach	post office box
Poststelle	mailroom/mail room
Poststempel	postmark
Posttermini	postal terms
Posttest	posttest/post test
Postversand	mail shipment
Postversandauftrag	mail order
Postversandwerbung	direct mail advertising
Postwurfsendung	bulk mail
Postwurfsendung	direct mail advertising
Postwurfsendung	mailing piece
Präferenzen, bekundete oder offenbarte	revealed preferences
Präferenzfrage	preference question
Präferenzgut	preference item
Präferenzordnung	hierarchy of wants
Präferenzordnung	scale of preferences
Präferenzskala	preference scale
Praktiken, irreführende	deceptive practices
Prämie	hook
Prämie	prize
Prämie bei Verpackungsteileinsendung	boxtop offer
Prämiengutschein	premium coupon
Präsentation	getup
Präsentationsgestell	rack board
Präsentationspackung	display pack
Preis	charge
Preis	cost
Preis	premium
Preis	price
Preis	prize

Preis	**rate**
Preis FOB Bestimmungsort	**FOB destination price**
Preis FOB Fabrik	**FOB factory price**
Preis ab ...	**loco price**
Preis ab Werk	**ex factory price**
Preis aus Kundensicht	**perceived value pricing**
Preis frei Haus	**delivered price**
Preis für ganzseitige Anzeige	**page rate**
Preis für künftige Lieferung	**forward price**
Preis ohne Rabatte	**base price**
Preis und Nachfrage	**price and demand**
Preis und Wert	**price and value**
Preis(e) freibleibend, unverbindlich	**price(s) subject to change without notice**
Preis, abbröckelnder	**softening price**
Preis, angemessener	**fair price**
Preis, angemessener	**just price**
Preis, angestrebter	**target price**
Preis, ausgehandelter	**negotiated price**
Preis, äußerster	**bottom price**
Preis, äußerster, niedrigster	**rock-bottom price**
Preis, einschließlich aller Kosten	**all-in-price**
Preis, empfohlener	**recommended price**
Preis, ermäßigter	**reduced price**
Preis, erwarteter	**expected price**
Preis, gängiger	**popular price**
Preis, gebotener	**bid price**
Preis, geforderter	**asking price**
Preis, gegenwärtiger	**current price**
Preis, geltender	**going rate**
Preis, gesalzener	**loaded price**
Preis, gesalzener, saftiger	**fishy price**
Preis, gespaltener, unterschiedlicher (auf verschiedenen Märkten)	**split price**
Preis, gewöhnlicher	**customary price**
Preis, hochgeschraubter	**loaded price**
Preis, irreführender	**misleading price**
Preis, konkurrenzfähiger	**competitive price**
Preis, konkurrenzfähiger	**keen price**
Preis, marktüblicher	**normal price**
Preis, natürlicher	**natural price**
Preis, niedrigster	**bottom price**
Preis, niedrigster, äußerster	**knocked-down price**
Preis, optischer, psychologischer	**psychological price**
Preis, psychologischer, gebrochener	**penny-off or penny-down-price**
Preis, regulierter	**administered price**
Preis, relativer	**relative price**
Preis, scharf kalkulierter	**close price**
Preis, sehr niedriger	**bargain price**
Preis, sehr niedriger, scharf kalkulierter	**keen price**

Preis, subjektiver	**subjective price**
Preis, subventionierter	**pegged price**
Preis, subventionierter	**subsidised price**
Preis, tatsächlicher	**real price**
Preis, voller	**full price**
Preis, wirtschaftlicher	**economic price**
Preis-Kosten-Schere	**cost-price squeeze**
Preis-Scanner	**price scanner**
Preisabsprache	**common pricing**
Preisabsprache	**price fixing**
Preisabsprache bei der Abgabe von Angeboten	**collusive tendering**
Preisabsprache, horizontale	**horizontal price fixing**
Preisabtastgerät	**price scanner**
Preisabweichung	**price variance**
Preisänderung(en) vorbehalten	**price(s) subject to change wihtout notice**
Preisänderungen	**price changes**
Preisänderungsklausel	**price variation clause (PVC, pvc)**
Preisangabe	**quotation**
Preisangabe irreführende	**deceptive pricing**
Preisangabe, pauschale (ohne Etikett)	**item price removal**
Preisangebot	**price quotation**
Preisanhebung	**pricing up**
Preisanpassung	**price adjustment**
Preisanreiz	**price incentive**
Preisanstieg	**advance**
Preisanstieg, gradueller	**escalation of prices**
Preisarten	**price types**
Preisaufschlag, durchschnittlicher	**average markon**
Preisaufschlag, zusätzlicher	**additional markon**
Preisauszeichnung	**price marking**
Preisauszeichnung durch den Hersteller	**prepricing**
Preisauszeichnung mit gebrochenen/ ungeraden Preisen	**odd pricing**
Preisauszeichnung, doppelte (irreführende)	**double pricing**
Preisauszeichnungsgesetz	**Prices Act**
Preisbewußtsein	**price awareness**
Preisbewußtsein	**price consciousness**
Preisbildung	**pricing**
Preisbildung	**price fixing**
Preisbildung anhand des wahrgenommenen Wertes	**perceived value pricing**
Preisbildung auf Durchschnittskostenbasis	**average cost pricing**
Preisbildung durch Marktmechanismus	**market pricing**
Preisbildung für eine Sonderveranstaltung	**special event pricing**
Preisbildung für eine Produktgruppe	**product line pricing**

Preisbildung inklusive Extras	**optional-product pricing**
Preisbildung mittels der Erfahrungskurve	**experience curve pricing**
Preisbildung und Wettbewerb	**pricing and competition**
Preisbildung, absatzorientierte	**sales-based pricing**
Preisbildung, absatzorientierte, verkaufsorientierte	**sales-oriented pricing**
Preisbildung, die sich an der Kundschaft orientiert	**patronage-oriented pricing**
Preisbildung, ertragsorientierte	**revenue-oriented pricing**
Preisbildung, ethische, moralische	**ethical pricing**
Preisbildung, handelsübliche	**customary pricing**
Preisbildung, innovative	**innovative pricing**
Preisbildung, mathematische	**mathematical pricing**
Preisbildung, moralische	**moral pricing**
Preisbildung, nachfrageorientierte	**demand oriented pricing**
Preisbildung, räuberische	**predatory pricing**
Preisbildung, regierungsabhängige	**government and pricing**
Preisbildung, subjektive	**perceived value pricing**
Preisbildung, vertriebsorientierte	**distribution-based pricing**
Preisbildung, wettbewerbsorientierte	**competition orientated pricing**
Preisbildungsfaktor	**price determinant**
Preisbildungsmethoden	**pricing methods**
Preisbildungsorientierung	**pricing orientation**
Preisbildungsziele	**pricing objectives**
Preisbildungsziele, gewinnorientierte	**profit-based pricing objectives**
Preisbindung	**price control**
Preisbindung der zweiten Hand	**price maintenance**
Preisbindung (der zweiten Hand)	**resale price maintenance**
Preisbindung zweiter Hand	**vertical price fixing**
Preisbindung, vertikale	**resale price maintenance**
Preisbindung, vertikale	**vertical price fixing**
Preisbindung, vertikale (USA)	**fair trade**
Preisbündelung	**price bundling**
Preiscode	**price code**
Preisdifferenzierung	**multiple pricing**
Preisdifferenzierung	**price discrimination**
Preisdiskriminierung (Kartell)	**rate discrimination**
Preise	**terms**
Preise, Differenz zwischen zwei	**spread**
Preise, Fallen der	**baisse**
Preise, Theorie der administrativen ...	**administered price theory**
Preiseffekt	**price effect**
Preiseinwand	**price objection**
Preiselastizität	**price elasticity**
Preiselastizität der Nachfrage	**price elasticity of demand**
Preiselastizität des Angebots	**price elasticity of supply**
Preisempfehlung des Herstellers	**manufacturer's recommended price**
Preisentscheidung	**price decision**
Preisentwicklung, Markt mit stabiler	**firm market**
Preiserhöhung	**price increase**

Preiserhöhung, versteckte	**hidden price increase**
Preiserhöhungen, Zurücknahme von	**rollback**
Preisermittlung	**price determination**
Preiseskalation	**escalation of prices**
Preiskartell	**price cartel**
Preisfestlegung bei Auftragserteilung	**preretailing**
Preisfestlegung, gewinnmaximierende	**profit maximising pricing**
Preisfestsetzung	**pricing**
Preisfestsetzung	**price setting**
Preisfestsetzung	**price fixing**
Preisfestsetzung auf Frachtbasis	**basing-point pricing**
Preisfestsetzung auf Probe	**trial-and-error pricing**
Preisfestsetzung durch Submissionsangebot	**bid pricing**
Preisfestsetzung durch Produktvergleich	**comparison pricing**
Preisfestsetzung durch Verhandeln	**negotiated pricing**
Preisfestsetzung nach Standort	**location pricing**
Preisfestsetzung unter Berücksichtigung einer angemessenen Rendite	**rate of return pricing**
Preisfestsetzung, administrative	**administered pricing**
Preisfestsetzung, behördliche	**valorization**
Preisfestsetzung, bündelfreie, ungebündelte	**unbundled pricing**
Preisfestsetzung, die Konkurrenz vom Markt fernhält	**keep out pricing**
Preisfestsetzung, flexible	**flexible pricing**
Preisfestsetzung, geographische	**geographical pricing**
Preisfestsetzung, gewinnorientierte	**profit oriented pricing**
Preisfestsetzung, gleitende	**escalator pricing**
Preisfestsetzung, irreführende	**deceptive pricing**
Preisfestsetzung, probeweise	**trial and error pricing**
Preisfixierer	**price maker**
Preisfixierung	**price setting**
Preisforderung	**terms of sale**
Preisführer	**price leader**
Preisführerschaft	**price leadership**
Preisgarantie	**price guarantee**
Preisgestaltung nach Kundensegment	**customer segment pricing**
Preisgestaltung, flexible	**flexible pricing**
Preisgestaltung, freie, variable	**variable pricing**
Preisgestaltung, gleichgerichtete	**parallel pricing**
Preisgestaltung, käuferorientierte	**buyer-oriented pricing**
Preisgestaltung, marktorientierte	**market pricing**
Preisgestaltung, psychologische	**psychological pricing**
Preisgestaltung, verkaufsfördernde	**promotional pricing**
Preisgestaltungsziele	**pricing objectives**
Preisgleitklausel	**escalator clause**
Preisgleitklausel	**price escalator clause**
Preisgleitklausel	**price variation clause**
Preisgrenze, untere	**floor**

Preisherabsetzung	**pricing down**
Preisindex	**price index**
Preisindex für Lebenshaltungskosten	**retail price index**
Preisinformationsabsprache	**open price agreement**
Preisinformationsabsprache	**information agreement**
Preiskalkulation durch Gewinnzuschlag auf Selbstkosten	**cost-plus pricing**
Preiskalkulation, kostenorientierte	**cost-based pricing**
Preiskartell	**price ring**
Preisklasse, untere	**low end**
Preiskontrolle	**price control**
Preiskoppelung	**price bundling**
Preiskrieg	**cutprice war**
Preiskrieg	**price war**
Preiskrieg	**rate war**
Preislage	**price range**
Preislage, akzeptable	**acceptable price range**
Preislesepistole	**price scanner**
Preislinie	**price lining**
Preisliste	**price list**
Preismethode, variable	**floating-price technique**
Preismix	**price mix**
Preisnachahmer	**price follower**
Preisnachlaß	**allowance**
Preisnachlaß	**markdown**
Preisnachlaß	**rebate**
Preisnachlaß	**rake off**
Preisnachlaß	**sales allowance**
Preisnachlaß für Selbstabholer	**backhaul allowance**
Preisnachlaß mittels Gutschein	**coupon price reduction**
Preisnachlaß offeriert auf Produktetikett	**cents-off the label**
Preisnachlaß, nachträglich wegen Beanstandung gewährt	**purchase(s) allowance**
Preisnachlaßcoupon	**cents-off coupon**
Preisnachlaßangebot	**money-off offer**
Preisnachlaßangebot	**price off offer**
Preisnachlaßgutschein	**money-off coupon**
Preisneufestsetzung	**price repression**
Preisniveau	**price level**
Preisniveau, allgemeines	**general price level**
Preisniveau, hohes	**price plateau**
Preisniveau, stabiles	**stable price level**
Preisobergrenze	**price ceiling**
Preispolitik	**pricing policy**
Preispolitik, aggressive	**aggressive pricing**
Preispolitik, offene	**open pricing**
Preispolitik, populäre	**popular pricing**
Preispolitik, staatlich dirigierte	**government controlled pricing**

Preisreagibilität	**price sensitivity**
Preisrückgang, anhaltender (Bö)	**slump**
Preisschild	**price tag**
Preisschild mit Originalpreis und reduziertem Preis	**off-price label**
Preissenkung	**price cutting**
Preissenkung	**markdown**
Preissenkung	**price reduction**
Preissenkung, automatische	**automatic markdown**
Preissenkung, frühe	**early markdown**
Preisspanne	**price range**
Preisstabilität	**price stability**
Preisstellung mit Übernahme der Frachtkosten	**freight absorption pricing**
Preisstellung, einheitliche frei Haus	**uniform delivered pricing**
Preisstellung, einheitliche, frei Haus	**single-zone pricing**
Preisstrategie, konkurrenzangepasste	**equivalent-price strategy**
Preissturz	**break**
Preissturz	**plunge in prices**
Preisstützung	**pegging**
Preisstützung	**price maintenance**
Preisstützung	**price pegging**
Preisstützung	**price support**
Preissucher	**price searcher**
Preissystem	**price mechanism**
Preissystem, mehrstufiges	**multiple pricing**
Preistabelle	**scale of prices**
Preistheorie	**price theory**
Preisüberprüfung	**pricing review**
Preisüberwachung	**price control**
Preisunelastizität	**price inelasticity**
Preisunterbietung	**dumping**
Preisunterbietung	**price cutting**
Preisunterbietung	**underselling**
Preisunterbietung, ruinöse	**predatory pricing**
Preisuntergrenze	**price floor**
Preisveredelung	**glossing**
Preisverfall	**collapse**
Preisverhandlung	**price negotiation**
Preisverzeichnis	**price list**
Preisverzeichnis	**tariff**
Preiswettbewerb	**price competition**
Preiszugeständnis	**price shading**
Presse	**press**
Presse, nationale, überregionale	**national press**
Pressearbeit	**press relations**
Pressedienst	**news agency**
Pressekonferenz	**press conference**
Pressemitteilung	**handout**
Pressemitteilung	**press release**

Pressenotiz	**news release**
Pressereferent	**information officer**
Prestige-Preisgestaltung	**glossing**
Prestigeartikel	**prestigious product**
Prestigepreise, Festsetzung von	**premium pricing**
Prestigewerbung	**prestige advertising**
Prestigezeitschrift	**class magazine**
Pretest	**pretest/pre-test**
Primärbedürfnisse	**primary needs**
Primärdaten	**primary data**
Primärforschung	**fieldwork**
Primärforschung	**field research**
Primärleser	**primary reader**
Primärnachfrage	**primary demand**
Prinzip, ökonomisches	**efficiency rule**
Privatwirtschaft	**private enterprise (system)**
Pro-Kopf-Ausgaben	**per capita expenditure**
Pro-Kopf-Einkommen	**per capita income**
Pro-Kopf-Leistung	**per capita output**
Pro-Kopf-Verbrauch	**per capita consumption**
Proactive Marketing	**proactive marketing**
Proband	**respondent**
Proband	**interviewee**
Probe	**sample**
Probe	**trial**
Probe(ver)kauf	**sale on approval**
Probe, auf	**on approval (on appro)**
Probe, kostenlose	**free trial**
Probe-Mailing	**trial mailing**
Probeabonnement	**trial subscription**
Probeangebot	**trial offer**
Probeauftrag	**sampling order**
Probeauftrag	**trial order**
Probeerhebung	**pilot survey**
Probeexemplar	**sample copy**
Probekauf	**trial purchase**
Probekauf	**trial purchase**
Probenverteilung	**sampling**
Probepackungsgröße	**trial size**
Probestück	**trial sample**
Probeversand	**trial mailing**
Probewerbesendung	**animatic**
Product-Placement	**product placement**
Produkt	**product**
Produkt der zweiten Generation	**second generation product**
Produkt eines Herstellers, das sich am besten verkauft	**flagship brand**
Produkt in der Entwicklungsphase	**embryo (product)**
Produkt mit Zugabe	**with-pack premium**

Produkt mit geringem Marktanteil und schwachem Wachstum ("armer Hund")	**dog**
Produkt mit geringen Marktchancen	**dog**
Produkt oder Unternehmen mit starkem Wachstum und großem Marktanteil	**star**
Produkt von geringer Faszination	**low involvement product**
Produkt, Gebrauchsfähigkeit eines	**product performance**
Produkt, Reifephase eines	**maturity stage**
Produkt, abgeleitetes	**derivative product**
Produkt, attraktives	**sexy product**
Produkt, besondere Eigenschaften eines	**product feature**
Produkt, ein sich schnell verkaufendes	**runner**
Produkt, erfolgversprechendes, aber nicht auf den Markt gebrachtes	**vaporware**
Produkt, ertragsstarkes	**cash cow**
Produkt, erweitertes	**augmented product**
Produkt, für das keine Werbung gemacht wird	**unadvertised product**
Produkt, gut eingeführtes	**established product**
Produkt, lahmes	**lame duck**
Produkt, markenfreies	**no-name (product)**
Produkt, nachgemachtes	**me-too product**
Produkt, neues	**new product**
Produkt, neupositioniertes	**repositioned product**
Produkt, preiselastisches, -reagibles	**price sensitive product**
Produkt, sorgfältig ausgewähltes	**high involvement product**
Produkt, undifferenziertes	**undifferentiated product**
Produkt, verbessertes durch Zusatzleistung	**augmented product**
Produkt, wertfreies	**low involvement product**
Produkt-Markt-Matrix	**Ansoff matrix**
Produkt-Markt-Matrix	**product-market matrix**
Produktakzeptanz	**product acceptance**
Produktakzeptanztest	**product acceptance test**
Produktalternative, erinnerte	**evoked set**
Produktanalyse	**product analysis**
Produktannahmeprozeß	**adoption process**
Produktanpassung	**product adaptation/adaption**
Produktanwendervorteile	**customer values**
Produktaufgabe	**product deletion**
Produktausbreitung	**product proliferation**
Produktauswahl	**product selection**
Produktauswertung im voraus	**product screening**
Produktbeilage	**premium product**
Produktbeschreibung	**product specification**
Produktbestand	**product portfolio**
Produktbetreuung	**product management**
Produktbewußtsein	**brand awareness**
Produktbündelrechnung	**batch costing**
Produktdesign	**product design**

Produktdifferenzierung	**product differentiation**
Produktdifferenzierung, funktionale	**functional product differentiation**
Produkte, Analyse konkurrierender	**competitor analysis**
Produkte, Auslage verwandter	**related display**
Produkte, Einführung neuer	**product pioneering**
Produkte, generische	**generic products**
Produkte, gleichwertige	**parity products**
Produkte, landwirtschaftliche	**produce**
Produkteigenschaften	**product attributes**
Produkteinführung	**product launch**
Produkteinführung, landesweite	**national introduction**
Produkteinführung, schrittweise	**rollout**
Produkteinheit, letzte	**marginal unit**
Produkteinstellung zugunsten Fremdbezugs	**desintegration**
Produkteinwand	**product objection**
Produktelimination	**product elimination**
Produktenbörse	**produce exchange**
Produktenmakler	**produce broker**
Porduktentwicklung	**product development**
Produktentwicklung, beschleunigte	**accelerated development**
Produktentwicklung, innovative	**innovative product development**
Produkterwähnung im redaktionellen Teil	**editorial mention**
Produkterweiterung	**augmented product**
Produkterweiterung "nach unten"	**downward stretching**
Produkterweiterung in den Niedrigpreisbereich	**downward stretching**
Produktetikett, Preisnachlaß offeriert auf	**cents-off the label**
Produktevolution	**product evolution**
Produktfälschungen	**bogus merchandise**
Produktfamilie	**product family**
Produktforschung	**product research**
Produktforschung und -entwicklung	**product research and development**
Produktgruppe	**product line**
Produktgruppe, Eliminierung einer	**line divestment**
Produktgruppe, Preisbildung für eine	**product line pricing**
Produktgruppe, Rationalisierung einer	**line simplification**
Produktgruppenbreite	**product line breadth**
Produktgruppenerweiterung	**product line extension**
Produktgruppentiefe	**product line depth**
Produktgruppenverpackung	**family packaging**
Produktgruppenwerbung	**primary demand advertising**
Produktgruppierung	**assorting**
Produkthaftpflichtversicherung	**product liability insurance**
Produkthaftung	**manufacturer's liability**
Produkthaftung	**product liability**
Produkthaftungsgesetz	**product liability law**
Produktherabsetzung	**product disparagement**
Produktidee	**product idea**
Produktidee, Akzeptanztest einer	**concept test**

Produktideenbewertung	**product idea testing**
Produktimage	**product image**
Produktinformation/-info	**fact book**
Produktinformation/-info	**fact sheet**
Produktinhalt	**actual product**
Produktinnovation	**product innovation**
Produktion	**manufacturing**
Produktion	**make**
Produktion	**output**
Produktion	**production**
Produktion und Kosten	**output and costs**
Produktion, gesamtwirtschaftliche	**national output**
Produktion, nachfrageorientierte	**production oriented demand**
Produktion, schlanke	**lean production**
Produktionsabteilung	**production department**
Produktionsanlage	**plant**
Produktionsaufteilung	**production sharing**
Produktionsauftrag	**manufacturing order**
Produktionsausstoß	**production**
Produktionseinheit	**unit of production**
Produktionsfaktornachfrage	**factor demand**
Produktionsfunktion	**production function**
Produktionsgenossenschaft	**producers' cooperative**
Produktionsgüter	**investment goods**
Produktionsgüter	**producer goods**
Produktionskapazität	**production capacity**
Produktionskoeffizient	**production coefficient**
Produktionskosten	**cost(s) of production**
Produktionskosten	**production cost(s)**
Produktionskosten für Werbung	**above-the-line cost(s)**
Produktionskosten, durchschnittliche	**average cost(s) of production**
Produktionskostentheorie	**cost of production theory**
Produktionsmenge	**make**
Produktionsmöglichkeitskurve	**production possibility curve**
Produktionsumfang	**scale of production**
Produktionsverzögerung	**production lag**
Produktionszweige	**branches of production**
Produktivität	**efficiency**
Produktivitätsoptimum	**productive efficiency**
Produktkenntnisse	**product knowledge**
Produktkennzeichnung, ausführliche	**descriptive label(l)ing**
Produktkern	**actual product**
Produktklasse	**product class**
Produktklassifizierung	**product classification**
Produktkompatibilität	**product compatibility**
Produktkontrolle	**product control**
Produktlebenszyklus	**product life cycle**
Produktlebenszyklus und Rentabilität	**product life cycle (PLC) and profitability**
Produktlinie	**product line**

Produktlücke	**product gap**
Produktmanagement	**product management**
Produktmanager	**brand manager**
Produktmarketing	**product marketing**
Produktmerkmale	**product characteristics**
Produktmißerfolg	**product failure**
Produktmißerfolg, relativer	**relative product failure**
Produktmix	**product mix**
Produktmixbreite	**width of product mix**
Produktmixtiefe	**depth of product mix**
Produktmodifikation	**product modification**
Produktmodifikation, funktionale	**functional modification**
Produktorientierung	**product orientation**
Produktpalette, -linie	**line**
Produktpalette, Anbieter einer vollständigen	**full-line supplier**
Produktpalettenbreite	**width of product range**
Produktplazierung	**product placement**
Produktpolitik	**product policy**
Produktportfolio	**product portfolio**
Produktpositionierung	**product positioning**
Produktpotential, verstecktes	**unsought goods**
Produktpräsentation	**sales presentation**
Produktpräsentation, vorbereitete	**prepared sales presentation**
Produktproliferation	**product proliferation**
Produktqualität	**product quality**
Produktrentabilität, direkte	**direct product profitability**
Produktrückruf	**product recall**
Produktstandardisierung	**product standardisation**
Produktstellung	**product position**
Produktstrategie	**product strategy**
Produkttest	**product test**
Produktvergleichsanalyse	**comparative product analysis**
Produktversuch	**product trial**
Produktverwender, vorbildlicher	**lead user**
Produktvorprüfung	**product screening**
Produktwerbung	**competitive advertising**
Produktwerbung	**product advertising**
Produktwerbung, allgemeine	**generic advertising**
Produktwert	**product value**
Produzent	**manufacturer**
Produzent	**producer**
Produzentenhaftung	**manufacturer's liability**
Produzentenhandel	**direct distribution**
Produzentenkartell	**producer cartel**
Produzentenmarkt	**producer market**
Produzentenpreis	**producer price**
Produzentenrente	**producer's surplus**
Produzentenwerbung	**producer advertising**
produzieren	**make**

Profil	**personality**
Proforma-Rechnung	**pro forma invoice**
Prognose	**forecast**
Prognose	**prediction**
Prognose	**projection**
Prognose, unveränderte	**no change forecast**
Programm für häufigen Kunden	**frequent buyer programme**
Programm, angrenzendes	**adjacency**
Programmeinschaltquote eines Senders	**program station basis**
Programmunterbrechung für Werbung	**commercial break**
Projekt, schlüsselfertiges	**turnkey project**
Projektgruppe	**venture team**
Projektion	**projection**
Projektstudie	**feasibility study**
Promille	**per mille**
Prominentenwerbung	**personality promotion**
Promoter	**promoter**
Promotionmanager	**promotion manager**
Promotionmaterial am Verkaufsort	**point-of-sale (POS) material**
Prospekt	**brochure**
Prospekt	**catalog(ue)**
Prospekt	**handbill**
Prospekt	**leaflet**
Prospekt	**pamphlet**
Prospekt	**prospectus**
Prosperität	**prosperity**
Protektionismus	**protectionism**
Prototyp	**prototype**
Provision	**commission**
Provision auf Verkaufsbasis	**straight commission**
Provision, angepaßte, gleitende	**sliding commission**
Provision, regressive	**regressive commission**
Provision, widerrechtliche	**rake off**
Provisionsverkäufer	**contractual sales force**
Prozent	**per cent/percent**
Prozentsatz der Gesamthörerschaft	**share of audience**
Prozentsatz der Personen, denen eine Marke bekannt ist	**share of mind**
Prozentsatz der Zuschauerschaft	**share of audience**
Prozentsatzänderung	**percentage change**
Prüfung	**scrutiny**
Prüfung	**verification**
Ps, sieben	**seven Ps**
Public Relations	**public relations**
Publikation	**publication**
Publikation, Anteil der gelesenen Seiten einer ...	**page traffic**
Publikation, Umfang des Anzeigenteils einer ...	**advertising lineage/linage**
Publikation, Verkaufspreis einer	**cover price**

Publikum	**audience**
Publikum einer Werbesendung	**commercial audience**
Publikum, Messung des	**audience measurement**
Publikum, das Zuhause ist	**at/in-home audience**
Publikum, das nicht Zuhause ist	**away-from-home audience**
Publikum, dupliziertes	**duplicated audience**
Publikum, kumuliertes	**cumulative audience**
Publikum, potentielles	**potential audience**
Publikum, unfreiwilliges	**captive audience**
Publikumsabnahme	**audience loss**
Publikumsanteil	**audience share**
Publikumsfluß	**audience flow**
Publikumskumulierung	**audience accumulation**
Publikumsprofil	**audience profile**
Publikumsqualität	**audience quality**
Publikumsreaktion(en) auf Werbung	**advertising response**
Publikumszeitschrift	**consumer magazine**
Publikumszeitschrift	**general interest magazine**
Publikumszunahme	**audience gain**
Publikumszusammensetzung	**audience composition**
Publizität	**publicity**
Pull-Push-Strategie	**pull-push strategy**
Pull-Strategie	**pull strategy**
Pulvergericht	**instant**
Punkt, grüner	**green label**
Punktelastizität	**point elasticity**
Push-Strategie	**push strategy**

Q

Qualität	**quality**
Qualität und Preis	**quality and price**
Qualität, gängige, handelsübliche	**commercial quality**
Qualität, handelsübliche, marktgängige	**merchantable quality**
Qualität, mindere	**low-grade**
Qualität, von besonders guter	**premium**
Qualitätsabnahmebescheinigung des Lieferers	**supplier's quality inspection certificate**
Qualitätsbezeichnung	**grade**
Qualitätskennzeichen	**grade label**
Qualitätskontrolle	**quality control**
Qualitätskontrolleur	**quality controller**
Qualitätsmanagement, umfassendes	**total quality management**
Qualitätsmanagement-Zertifizierungsverfahren ISO 9000	**ISO 9000**
Qualitätsmarketing	**quality advertising**
Qualitätsmarkt	**quality market**
Qualitätsmodifikation	**quality modification**
Qualitätsniveau, ausreichendes	**acceptable quality level**
Qualitätssicherung	**quality assurance**

Qualitätswettbewerb	**quality competition**
Qualitätszeichen	**kitemark**
Qualitätszeitung	**quality newspaper**
Qualitätszeugnis	**quality certificate**
Quantität	**quantity**
Quantitätswerbung	**quantity advertising**
Quasieinzelhandel	**quasi retailing**
Quelle	**source**
Querdenken	**lateral thinking**
Quittung	**cash voucher**
Quittung	**coupon**
Quittung	**quittance**
Quittung	**receipt**
Quittung	**voucher**
Quizsendung	**gameshow/game show**
Quote	**quota**
Quotenauswahl	**quota sample**
Quotenkartell	**quota cartel**
Quotenstichprobenverfahren	**quota sampling**

R

R-Gespräch	**collect call**
R-Gespräch	**reverse charge call**
R-Gespräch	**transfer charge call**
Rabatt	**allowance**
Rabatt	**deduction**
Rabatt	**rebate**
Rabatt	**reduction**
Rabatt, verkaufsfördernder	**cash rebate**
Rabattangebot	**money-off offer**
Rabattarten	**discount types**
Rabattmarke	**stamp**
Rabattmarke	**trading stamp**
Radio/TV-Spielshow	**gameshow/game show**
Radioeinschaltquote	**radio rating point**
Radiohaushalt	**radio household**
Radiohörerschaft	**listenership**
Radiohörzeit	**time spent listening**
Radioprogramm mit Geschenken/Preisen	**giveaway/give-away**
Radioprogramm (ohne Werbung)	**package**
Radiosender, Werbung in lokalen	**spot radio**
Radiosender, breitgefächerter	**middle-of-the-roader**
Radiowerbetext	**radio copy**
Radiowerbung, lokale, regionale	**spot advertising**
Rampe	**ramp**
Ramsch	**catchpenny (article)**
Ramsch	**rummage**
Ramschladen	**junk shop**
Ramschverkauf	**job selling**

Ramschverkauf	**odds sale**
Ramschverkauf	**rummage sale**
Ramschware	**job lot**
Ramschware	**odds and ends**
Randwerbung	**accessory advertising**
Randzeit	**fringe time**
Rang	**grade**
Rangstufenfrage	**ranking question**
Rate	**instal(l)ment**
Raten, zahlbar in bequemen	**payable in easy terms**
Ratenkaufvertrag	**credit sale(s) agreement**
Ratenverkauf	**instal(l)ment selling**
Ratenzahlung	**deferred payment**
Ratenzahlung	**instal(l)ment**
Ratenzahlung, erste	**token payment**
Ratenzahlungskauf	**hire purchase**
Ratenzahlungsvertrag	**deferred payment agreement**
Rationalisierung	**rationalisation/rationalization**
Rationalisierung einer Produktgruppe	**line simplification**
Rationierung	**rationing**
räumen (Lager)	**clear**
Räumungsverkauf	**clearance**
Räumungsverkauf	**clearance sale**
Reaganomics	**Reaganomics**
Reaktion	**response**
Reaktion, verzögerte	**delayed response**
Reaktion, verzögerte	**lagged response**
Realeinkommen	**real income**
Realkasseneffekt	**wealth effect**
Realkosten	**real cost**
Realwert	**real value**
Rechnung	**bill**
Rechnung	**check**
Rechnung	**invoice**
Rechnung mit Sonderterminierung	**extra dating**
Rechnung mit Werbebeilage	**bill insert**
Rechnung, auf/für ... von	**for the account ...**
Rechnung, aufgegliederte, detaillierte	**itemized invoice**
Rechnung, für	**on account**
Rechnung, laut erteilter	**account rendered**
Rechnung, offene	**open account**
Rechnung, vorläufige	**pro forma invoice**
Rechnungen, Ausstellen und Zusenden	**billing**
Rechnungen, Bevorschussung von	**invoice discounting**
Rechnungsabzug	**off-invoice**
Rechnungsanschrift	**invoice address**
Rechnungsaufstellung	**statement**
Rechnungsaufstellung, über den Monat verteilte	**cycle billing**
Rechnungsbeleg	**voucher**

Rechnungsdatierung mit Extratagen	**extra dating**
Rechnungsdatum	**billing date**
Rechnungsdatum	**date of invoice**
Rechnungsdatum	**invoice date**
Rechnungsformular	**billhead**
Rechnungskopf	**billhead**
Rechnungsstellung	**sales invoicing**
Rechnungsstellung, ausführliche	**descriptive billing**
Rechnungsstellung, laufende	**continuous billing**
Rechte des Käufers	**buyer's rights**
Rechtsberater	**legal adviser**
Rechtsbeschränkungen	**legal constraints**
Rechtsgeschäft zu unfairen Bedingungen	**catching bargain**
Recognition-Test	**recognition test**
Redakteur im Studio	**presenter**
Reduktionsmarketing	**demarketing**
Reduzierung	**reduction**
Referenz, unverlangte	**unsolicited testimonial**
Reflation	**reflation**
Reformkost	**health food**
Regal	**rack**
Regal	**shelf**
Regalauffüller	**shelf filler**
Regalauszeichnung	**shelf pricing**
Regalfläche	**shelf space**
Regalfläche, zugewiesene	**space allocation**
Regalgebühr	**shelf fee**
Regalgroßhändler	**rackjobber/rack jobber**
Regalgroßhändler	**service merchandiser**
Regalleiste	**channel strip**
Regalpackung	**shelf pack**
Regalplakat, kleines	**shelf talker**
Regalpreisauszeichnung	**item price removal**
Regalpreisschild	**shelf marker**
Regalprospekt	**rack folder**
Regalschild	**shelf card**
Regalstreifen mit Werbung	**shelf strip**
Regenbogenpresse	**yellow press**
Regierung und Preisbildung	**government and pricing**
Region, geförderte	**assisted area**
Regionalausgabe	**regional issue**
Regionalsender	**local station**
Register	**register**
Registrierkasse	**cash register**
Regressionsanalyse	**regression analysis**
Reichtum	**wealth**
Reichweite	**reach**
Reichweite (eines Werbemediums)	**coverage**
Reichweite und Häufigkeit	**reach and frequency**
Reichweite, wirksame (Werbung)	**effective cover**

Reifephase eines Produkts	**maturity stage**
Reifezeit	**gestation period**
Reihenanschlag(swerbung)	**inside panel**
Reinfall	**flop**
Reingewicht	**net weight**
Reingewinn	**net margin**
Reingewinn	**net profit**
Reingewinn	**net earnings**
Reingewinn erzielen	**clear**
Reingewinn in Prozent	**net profit percentage**
Reinverlust	**net loss**
Reisebeilage	**travel supplement**
Reisebüro	**travel agency**
Reisebüro	**travel agent**
Reisegepäck	**luggage**
Reisekosten	**travel expenses**
Reisekostenzuschuß	**travel allowance**
Reisender	**commercial travel(l)er**
Reisender	**travelling salesman**
Reisespesen	**travel expenses**
Reiseveranstalter	**travel agent**
Reiz	**appeal**
Reklamation	**claim**
Reklamation	**complaint**
Reklamationsabteilung	**complaints department**
Reklame	**advertisement**
Reklame	**advertising**
Reklame	**publicity**
Reklame, wilder Anschlag von	**fly posting**
Reklamefläche	**billboard**
Reklamefläche	**space**
Reklamefläche, alleinstehende	**individual location**
Reklamesendung, unwerwünschte	**junk mail**
Reklametafel	**hoarding**
Reklamevieh	**admass**
Reklamezettel	**fly sheet**
Reklamezettel	**handout**
Reklamezettel	**throwaway**
Relaunch	**relaunch**
Remarketing	**remarketing**
Rendite	**rate of return**
Renner	**runner**
Rentabilität	**efficiency**
Rentabilität	**profitability**
Rentabilität	**rate of return**
Rentabilität der investierten Zeit	**return on time invested**
Rentabilitätsanalyse	**profitability analysis**
Repräsentant	**representative**
Repräsentanz	**representative office**
Repräsentationswerbung	**prestige advertising**

Repräsentativerhebung (Stat)	**sample survey**
Reprivatisierung	**denationalisation**
Reservierung	**booking**
Reservierung	**forward booking**
Reservierung	**reservation**
Ressourcen	**resources**
Ressourcen, natürliche	**natural resources**
Ressourcen, nicht ersetzbare	**non-renewable resources**
Ressourcen, ökonomische	**economic resources**
Ressourcenumgang, sparsamer	**economical use of resources**
Rest(bestand)	**remainder**
Restaurant für Außer-Haus-Verkauf	**takeaway**
Restbetrag	**remainder**
Restpartie	**odd lot**
Restpostenauslage	**jumble display**
Restwaren	**rummage**
Resultat	**outcome**
Retorsionsmaßnahme	**retaliation**
Retoure(n)	**return**
Retouren	**returns**
Retourenbuch	**sales returns book**
Revitalisierungsstrategie	**extension strategy**
Rezeption	**front desk**
Rezession	**recession**
Rezession, internationale	**international recession**
Rezessionslücke	**recessionary gap**
Rezessionsmarketing	**recession marketing**
Rezessionsphase	**contractionary phase**
Reziprozitätsvertrag (AuW)	**reciprocity**
Richtigstellungsanzeige	**corrective advertising**
Richtigstellungswerbung	**corrective commercial**
Richtlinien (ethische) für gute Werbung	**Code of Advertising Practice**
Richtpreis	**administered price**
Richtpreis	**recommended price**
Richtpreis	**target price**
Richtpreis, empfohlener	**suggested retail price**
Riesenbestellung	**outsize order (OS order)**
Rinnverlust	**leakage**
Risiko	**hazard**
Risiko, betriebswirtschaftliches	**commercial risk**
Risikogeschäft	**adventure**
Road Show	**road show**
Robinson-Patman-Gesetz (USA)	**Robinson-Patman Act**
Robinsonliste	**Robinson list**
Robinsonliste	**no direct mail list**
Robinsonliste (USA)	**Asterisk law**
Roboter	**robot**
Rohdaten	**raw data**
Rohentwurf	**rough**
Rohgewinn	**gross margin**

Rohlayout	**rough**
Rohlayout für den Kunden	**client rough**
Rohstoffe	**basic commodities**
Rohstoffe	**primary products**
Rohstoffe	**raw materials**
Rohstoffmarkt	**commodity market**
Rollenspiel	**role playing**
Rollgeld	**cartage**
Rollgeld	**carriage**
Rolltreppenplakat	**escalator panel**
Rolltreppenplakat	**escalator card**
Rolltreppenwerbung	**escalator card**
Route	**route**
Routenplanung	**territorial planning**
Rubrikanzeige	**want ad**
Rückantwort, bezahlte	**business reply card or envelope**
Rückantwortkarte, bezahlte	**business reply card**
Rückantwortschein	**reply coupon**
Rückantwortschein, internationaler	**international reply coupon**
Rückerstattung	**refund**
Rückerstattungsgarantie	**money back guarantee**
Rückerstattungsgarantie	**satisfaction**
Rückforderung(sanspruch)	**comeback**
Rückfracht	**backfreight**
Rückfracht	**return load**
Rückfracht, Preis für	**back-haul rate**
Rückfracht, Transport von	**backhauling**
Rückgabe	**redelivery**
Rückgaberecht mit Gelderstattung	**complete refund offer**
Rückgang	**decrease**
Rückgang	**drop**
Rückgang	**setback**
Rückkaufvereinbarung	**buy-back agreement**
Rückkoppelung	**feedback**
Rückladung	**backload**
Rückladung	**return load**
Rücklaufquote	**response rate**
Rücklieferung	**redelivery**
Rückruf	**callback**
Rückruf	**recall**
Rückruf	**return call**
Rückschlag	**setback**
Rücksein	**return receipt**
Rückseite	**back cover**
Rücksendung	**backfreight**
Rücksendung(en)	**return(s)**
Rücksendungen und Nachlässe	**returns and allowances**
Rücktrittsrecht (vom Vertrag)	**right of rescission**
Rücktrittsfrist	**cooling-off period**
Rückumschlag	**business reply envelope**

Rückumschlagsystem (ohne Wertzeichen)	**freepost**
Rückvergütung	**refund**
Rückvergütung von Verbrauchssteuern	**excise drawback**
Rückwärtsintegration	**backward integration**
Rufschädigung	**defamation**
Rundfunkhörer(schaft)	**radio audience**
Rundfunkpause	**act break**
Rundfunkwerbung	**radio advertising**
Rundschreiben	**circular letter**
Rundungsfehler	**rounding error**

S

SB-Warenhaus	**superstore**
SWOT-Analyse	**SWOT analysis**
Sachbearbeiter von Werbeetats	**account executive**
Sachen, bewegliche	**mov(e)ables**
Sachen, konkretisierte	**ascertianed goods**
Sachet	**sachet**
Sachleistung	**payment in kind**
Sachmangel	**fault**
Sack	**bag**
Sack	**sack**
Saison, außerhalb der	**off season**
Saison, tote	**dead season**
Saison, tote	**off season**
Saisonbereinigung	**seasonal adjustment**
Saisonbewegung	**seasonal fluctuation**
Saisonschwankung	**seasonal fluctuation**
Saisonware	**seasonal product**
Saisonwerbung	**seasonal advertising**
Sammelband	**omnibus book**
Sammelgutspediteur	**groupage agent**
Sammelgutunternehmen	**consolidator**
Sammelkarte	**picture card**
Sammelladung	**consolidated shipment**
Sammelladung	**groupage**
Sammelladung	**mixed cargo**
Sammelladung	**split consignment**
Sammelladungs-Frachtrate	**groupage rate**
Sammelrechnung	**unit billing**
Sammelwerbung	**multiunit advertising**
Sandwichplakat	**sandwich board**
Satisfizierung	**satisficing**
Sättigung	**saturation**
Sättigungspunkt	**saturation point**
Sättigungsreichweite	**blanket coverage**
Sättigungswerbung	**saturation advertising**
Saturierung	**saturation**
Satz, unvollständiger	**broken lot**

Satzumfangsberechnung (Druck)	**casting off**
Satzvervollständigungsfrage	**sentence completion question**
Säulendiagramm	**bar chart**
Säulendiagramm	**histogram**
Sauregurkenzeit	**dead season**
Sauregurkenzeit	**off season**
Saysches Theorem	**Say's law (of the market)**
Scanner	**scanner**
Scanner-Kassensystem, automatisches	**automatic checkout machine**
Schacherer	**haggler**
Schachtel	**case**
Schaden	**damage**
Schaden(sfall)	**loss**
Schaden, festgestellter	**known damage**
Schaden, immaterieller	**intangible damage**
Schaden, versteckter	**concealed damage**
Schaden, wirtschaftlicher	**economic loss**
Schadenquote (Vers)	**loss ratio**
Schadensabteilung	**claims department**
Schalter	**booking office**
Schalter (BaW)	**counter**
Schattenwirtschaft	**black economy**
Schattenwirtschaft	**informal economy**
Schätzer	**estimator**
Schätzung	**estimate**
Schätzung, grobe	**guesstimate**
Schätzwert	**estimate**
Schaubild	**graph**
Schaubild, klappbares	**flip chart**
Schaufensteraufkleber	**window banner**
Schaufensterauslage	**window dressing**
Schaufensterauslage	**window display**
Schaufensterbummel	**window shopping**
Schaufensterbummler	**windowshopper**
Schaufensterdekoration	**window dressing**
Schaufenstergestaltung	**window dressing**
Schaufensterplakat	**window banner**
Schaufensterplakat	**window poster**
Schaukarton	**tray pack**
Schaukasten	**display cabinet**
Schaukasten	**display case**
Schaukasten	**showcase**
Schaupackung	**display pack**
Schauplatz	**venue**
Scheffel	**bushel**
Scheinbieter	**by-bidder**
Scheinkauf	**mock purchase**
Scheinkunde	**mystery shopper**
Scheinpreisgestaltung	**fictitious pricing**
Schenkung	**donation**

Schenkung	**gift**
Schenkungssteuer	**gift tax**
Scherzartikel	**novelty**
Schienentransport	**rail transport**
Schiffsladung	**shipment**
Schild(chen)	**label**
Schirmherrschaft	**sponsorship**
Schlagwort	**buzzword**
Schlagwort	**catchphrase/catch phrase**
Schlagzeile	**headline**
Schleichhandel	**smuggling**
Schleichwerbung	**camouflaged advertising**
Schleichwerbung	**plug**
Schleuderpreis	**knockout price**
Schleuderpreis	**rock-bottom price**
Schleusenpreis	**price threshold**
Schlitz	**slot**
Schluß	**closure**
Schlußbestand	**ending inventory**
Schlüssel	**code**
Schlüsselentscheidungsträger	**key buying influencer**
Schlüsselindustrie	**key industry**
Schlüsselprodukt	**key product**
Schlüsselwerbung	**bellwether advertising**
Schlußprüfung vor Lieferung	**preaudit**
Schlußrechnung	**final invoice**
Schlußtermin	**deadline**
Schlußverkauf	**sales**
Schmalz	**schmal(t)z**
Schmiergeld	**bribe**
Schmiergeld	**graft**
Schmiergeld	**kickback**
Schmiergeld	**under-the-table money**
Schmuggel	**smuggling**
Schnäppchen	**bargain**
Schnäppchenjäger	**bargain hunter**
Schneeball-Vertriebs-System	**pyramid selling**
Schnelldreher	**fast selling merchandise**
Schnelldreher	**money spinner**
Schnelldreher	**runner**
Schnellgericht	**fast food**
Schnellgut	**fast freight**
Schnitzer	**fluff**
Schnupperauslage	**sniffer**
Schreibfehler	**literal (error)**
Schreibtischforschung	**desk research**
Schriftart	**font**
Schriftart	**typeface**
Schrumpfpackung	**shrink wrapping**
Schuldenerlaß	**quittance**

Schuldner	**debtor**
Schuldner, zahlungsunfähiger	**defaulter**
Schundnahrung	**junk food**
Schundware	**catchpenny (article)**
Schüttgutladung	**bulk cargo**
Schutzhandel, beschränkter	**fair trade**
Schutzumschlag	**jacket**
Schutzzoll	**protective duty**
Schwachstelle	**soft spot**
Schwankung	**fluctuation**
Schwankungen, konjunkturelle	**cyclical fluctuations**
Schwarzhandel	**black trading**
Schwarzmarkt	**black market**
Schwarzweiß	**black and white**
Schwellenpreis	**price threshold**
Schwemme	**glut**
Schwergut	**heavy lift (H/l)**
Schwerindustrie	**heavy industry**
Schwindelfirma	**bubble company**
Schwindler	**racketeer**
Schwund	**ullage**
Schwund	**leakage**
Schwung	**drive**
Screening	**screening**
Segementierung nach Schlüsselelementen	**key-element segmentation**
Segmentierung	**segmentation**
Segmentierung auf Grund von Verhaltensmerkmalen	**behaviour segmentation**
Segmentierung aufgrund des Absatzvolumens	**volume segmentation**
Segmentierung eines Auslandsmarkts	**in-country segmentation**
Segmentierung nach Alter- und Lebenszyklus	**age and life cycle segmentation**
Segmentierung nach Einkommen	**income segmentation**
Segmentierung nach Gebrauchsnutzen	**usage segmentation**
Segmentierung nach Geschlecht	**gender segmentation**
Segmentierung nach Geschlecht	**sex segmentation**
Segmentierung nach Lebensqualität	**quality of life segmentation**
Segmentierung nach Lebensstil	**lifestyle segmentation**
Segmentierung nach Markentreue	**brand loyalty segmentation**
Segmentierung nach der Verbrauchsrate	**usage rate segmentation**
Segmentierung, geodemographische	**geodemographic segmentation**
Segmentierung, geographische	**geographic segmentation**
Segmentierung, geographische	**spatial segmentation**
Segmentierung, regionale	**regional segmentation**
Segmentierung, religiöse	**religious segmentation**
Segmentierungsarten	**segmentation types**
Segmentierungsvariablen	**segmentation variables**
Seifenoper	**soap opera**
Seite, auf der eine Anzeige steht	**adpage/ad page**

Seite, gegenüberliegende	**facing page**
Seitenflächenposition	**side position**
Seitennumerierung	**folio**
Seitenpreis	**page rate**
Sektor, primärer	**primary sector**
Sektor, privater	**private sector**
Sektor, staatlicher, öffentlicher	**public sector**
Sektor, tertiärer	**tertiary sector**
Sekundärdaten	**secondary data**
Sekundärforschung	**secondary research**
Sekundärkunden	**fringe accounts**
Sekundärleser	**pass-along/-on reader**
Sekundärleser	**secondary reader**
Sekundärmarkt	**secondary market**
Selbst	**ego**
Selbstabholer, Preisnachlaß für	**backhaul allowance**
Selbstabholung gegen Kasse	**cash and carry**
Selbständigkeit	**autonomy**
Selbstbedienungsladen	**self-service store**
Selbstbild	**self image**
Selbstkontrolle, freiwillige	**self regulation**
Selbstkontrolle, freiwillige	**voluntary self-control**
Selbstkosten	**prime costs**
Selbstkostenpreis, Warenangebot zum	**self-liquidating offer**
Selbstkostenpreis, Warenauslage zum	**self liquidating display**
Selbstläufer	**fast selling merchandise**
Selbstversorgung	**direct production**
Selbstversorgung	**self sufficiency**
Selbstverwirklichungsbedürfnis	**self actualization need**
Selbstwähl- und Aufzeichungsgerät, automatisches	**auto-dial recorded message player**
Selbstwählferndienst	**subscriber trunk dialling**
Selling off-the-page	**sellin goff-the-page**
Seltenheitswert	**scarcity value**
Sendebeginn	**sign on**
Sendegebiet	**circulation area**
Sendeminute	**commercial minute**
senden	**consign**
senden	**forward**
Senden	**forwarding**
Sendepause	**station break**
Sender	**sender**
Sender (von Waren)	**consignor**
Senderabkürzung	**call letters**
Sendermelodie	**sounder**
Sendernetzhaushalte, Gesamtzahl der erreichten	**households reached**
Senderzeichen	**station identification**
Sendeschluß	**sign off**
Sendetermin	**air airdate/date**

Sendeunterbrechung für Werbung	**break**
Sendezeit	**airtime, air time**
Sendezeit	**running time**
Sendezeit am frühen Morgen	**early morning time**
Sendezeit von 23:00 Uhr bis Sendeschluß	**late fringe**
Sendezeit vor und nach der Hauptsendezeit	**fringe time**
Sendezeit(punkt) (Radio, TV)	**air date/airdate**
Sendezeit, morgendliche während der Fahrt zur Arbeit	**morning drive (time)**
Sendezeit, zuteilen von ... bei Nachfrageüberhang	**allotment**
Sendezeitkäufer	**airtime buyer**
Sendezeitsegment	**daypart/day part**
Sendezeitsegment	**time segment**
Sendezeitvereinbarung, ohne	**run of station**
Sendung	**consignment**
Sendung	**shipment**
Sendung läuft	**on the air**
Sendung, aktuelle	**live program(me)**
Sendung, auf	**on the air**
Sendung, die täglich oder werktäglich vom selben Sender zur selben Uhrzeit ausgestrahlt wird	**across the board (commercial)**
Senkrechtstarter	**shooting star**
Sensationspresse	**yellow press**
Serie	**batch**
Serienfertigung	**repetitive manufacture/production**
Serienkalkulation	**batch costing**
Seriennummer	**batch number**
Serienproduktion	**repetitive manufacture/production**
Service	**service**
Service 130	**freephone/freefone**
Service Merchandiser	**rackjobber/rack jobber**
Service, nicht güterbezogener	**nongoods service**
Servicegrad	**service level**
Servicemann	**serviceman**
Servicemarketing	**service marketing**
Servicequalität	**service quality**
Servicetelefon	**hootline/hot line**
Seufzerspalte	**agony column**
Sherman Antitrust Act (USA)	**Sherman Antitrust Act**
Sherman Gesetz von 1890 (USA)	**Sherman Antitrust Act**
Shooting Star	**shooting star**
Shopping Center	**shopping center**
Shopping Goods	**shopping goods**
Shortlanding Zertifikat	**shortlanding certificate**
Showbusiness	**showbusiness**
Showgeschäft	**showbusiness**
Showmarketing	**events marketing**

Sicherheit	**certainty**
Sicherheit	**safety**
Sicherheitsbedürfnis	**safety need**
Sicherheitsbestand	**inventory cushion**
Sicherheitsbestand	**safety stock**
Sicherheitsrückruf	**safety recall**
Sicht, bei	**on demand**
Sichtgerät	**visual display unit**
Sichtpackung	**blister pack(age)**
Sickerquote	**leakage**
Sickerverluste	**leakage**
Signalwirkung	**announcement effect**
Signum	**logo**
Single-Sourcing	**single sourcing**
Sinken	**fall**
Sitte	**custom**
Sitten, ausländische	**foreign customs**
Situationsanalyse	**situation analysis**
Sitz	**base**
Skala, bipolare	**bipolar scale**
Skalafrage	**ranking (scale) question**
Skalenertrag, konstanter	**constant returns to scale**
Skalenertrag, sinkender	**decreasing returns to scale**
Skizze	**layout**
Skonto	**cash discount**
Skonto	**discount**
Skonto	**purchase discount**
Skonto	**sales discount**
Skonto	**settlement discount**
Skontoerträge	**discount(s) received**
Skontofrist	**discount period**
Slogan	**catchphrase/catch phrase**
Slogan	**slogan**
Snapper	**Snapper**
Snob-Güter	**snob goods**
sofort lieferbar	**spot**
sofort zahlbar	**spot**
Sofortlieferant	**prompt supplier**
Sofortzahlung	**cash payment**
Sogwirkung	**bandwagon effect**
Sollkosten	**standard cost**
Sollkostenrechnung	**standard costing**
Sommerschlußverkauf	**summer sale**
Sommerzeit	**daylight saving time (DST)**
Sonderangebot	**bargain sale**
Sonderangebot	**bargain pack**
Sonderangebot	**bargain offer**
Sonderangebot	**deal**
Sonderangebot	**premium offer**
Sonderangebot	**sepcial offer**

Sonderangebote, Abteilung für	**bargain basement**
Sonderangebote, Theke für	**bargain counter**
Sonderangebote, Verkaufstisch für	**bargain counter**
Sonderangebote, jemand der ... sucht	**bargain hunter**
Sonderangebotsabteilung	**budget department**
Sonderangebotsauslage	**jumble display**
Sonderangebotskaufen (das Herauspicken von Rosinen)	**cherry-picking**
Sonderangebotspackung	**price pack**
Sonderangebotspreis	**bargain price**
Sonderangebotsware	**deal merchandise**
Sonderauftrag	**special order**
Sonderbeitrag	**feature**
Sonderbestellung	**special order**
Sondermodifikation	**special modification**
Sondernachlaß	**special discount**
Sonderpreis	**special price**
Sonderpreis für die Ausstrahlung einer Werbesendung in einem laufenden Programm	**commercial integration charge**
Sonderpreisverpackung	**flash pack**
Sondersendung	**special**
Sonderveranstaltung, Preisbildung für eine	**special event pricing**
Sonderzubehör	**optional extras**
Sonntagsbeilage	**sunday supplement**
Sorgenkind	**problem child**
Sorgenkind	**question mark**
Sorgfalt, gebührende, verkehrsübliche	**due diligence**
Sorgfaltspflicht	**duty of care**
Sorgfaltspflicht des Verkäufers	**caveat vendor**
Sorgfaltspflicht, Vernachlässigkeit der	**neglect of care**
Sortiment	**assortment of goods**
Sortiment	**line**
Sortiment	**product range**
Sortiment	**range**
Sortiment, Zwang zur Abnahme eines ganzen	**full line forcing**
Sortiment, breites	**broad assortment**
Sortiment, tiefes	**deep assortment**
Sortimentsaufbau	**assorting**
Sortimentsaufwertung	**trading up**
Sortimentsauslage	**assortment display**
Sortimentsbeschränkgung	**variety reduction**
Sortimentserweiterung	**diversification**
Sortimentserweiterung	**line extension**
Sortimentsstrategien	**assortment strategies**
Sortimentszusammenstellung	**assorting**
Souvenirladen	**gift shop**
Sozialhilfe	**welfare**
Sozialprodukt	**national product**

Sozialverhalten	**social performance**
Sozio-Marketing	**social marketing**
Sozio-Sponsoring	**social sponsoring**
Spätnachmittagssendezeit	**early fringe**
Sparen, autonomes	**autonomous saving**
Sparkampagne	**economy drive**
Sparpackung	**economy size**
Sparprogramm	**austerity**
Sparquote, durchschnittliche	**average propensity to save**
Sparquote, marginale	**marginal propensity to save**
Sparte	**line**
Spediteur	**carrier**
Spediteur	**common carrier**
Spediteur	**forwarding agent**
Spediteur	**shipper**
Spediteur, Risiko des	**carrier's risk**
Speditionskosten	**carrying charges**
Speise	**fare**
Speisekarte	**tariff**
Speisekarte, nach der	**à la carte**
Speisekartenfrage	**multiple choice question**
Speisen zum Mitnehmen	**takeaway**
Spekulationsgeschäft	**adventure**
Spekulationskauf	**speculative buying**
Spende	**donation**
Spende, karitative, wohltätige	**charitable donation**
Spendermarkt	**donor market**
Sperrzeit für Werbung	**blocked-out time**
Spesenkonto	**expense account**
Spesenpauschale	**expense allowance**
Spesenzuschuß	**expense allowance**
spezialangefertigt	**custom-made**
Spezialgeschäft	**single line store**
Spezialinstitut für Konsumentenkredite	**consumer finance company**
Spezialisierung (Unterscheidung)	**differentiation**
Spezialshop als Anziehungspunkt	**anchor store**
Spezialzeitschrift	**special interest magazine**
Speziessachen	**ascertained goods**
Spezifikation	**specification**
Spezifikationskauf	**buying by specification**
Spezifikationskauf	**sale by description**
Spiel	**game**
Spiel	**gamble**
Spinnwebtheorem	**cobweb theorem**
Spirituosenhandlung	**package store**
Spitzenartikel	**leader**
Spitzenbedarf	**topout**
Spitzenbekanntheit	**top of mind**
Spitzenerzeugnis	**premium brand**
Spitzenerzeugnis	**premium product**

Spitzenjahr	**peak year**
Spitzenmarke	**brand leader**
Spitzennachfrage	**peak demand**
Spitzennachfrage	**topout**
Spitzennutzungszeit von Autoradios	**evening drive (time)**
Spitzenpreis	**peak price**
Spitzenpreis	**premium price**
Spitzenpreisstrategie	**umbrella pricing**
Spitzenprodukt	**star**
Spitzentechnologie	**high technology**
Spitzenumsatz	**record sales**
Spitzenunternehmen	**star**
Spitzenware	**leader**
Spitzenzeit, bei der Autofahrer Radio hört	**drive time**
Spitzname	**secondary meaning**
Sponsor	**backer**
Sponsor	**sponsor**
Sponsoring	**sponsorship**
Spontanbefragung	**intercept interview**
Spontankauf	**impulse buying**
Spontankäufer	**impulse buyer**
Sporteinnahmen	**gate money**
Sportsponsoring	**sports sponsoring**
Spotkurs (Bö)	**spot price**
Spottpreis	**bargain price**
Sprechertext	**voiceover**
Spruchband	**banner**
sprunghaft ansteigen (Preise)	**rocket**
Staatsmonopol	**statutory monopoly**
Staatsverbrauch	**government purchases**
Stabdiagramm	**bar chart**
Stabdiagramm	**histogram**
Stabilisierungswerbung	**sustaining advertising**
Stadtrandstandort	**edge of town location**
Stagflation	**stagflation**
Stagnation	**stagnation**
Stammkunde	**long-standing customer**
Stammkunde	**live customer**
Stammkunde	**patron**
Stammkunde	**regular customer**
Stammkunde, treuer	**current loyal**
Stammkundenmarketing	**retention marketing**
Stand	**stand**
Standardabweichung	**standard deviation**
Standardbrief	**standard letter**
Standardmodell	**regular model**
Standardzeitung	**standard newspaper**
Ständerprospekt	**rack folder**
Standesordnung	**code of ethics**

Standgebühr	**market dues**
Standinhaber	**stall holder**
Standleitung	**dedicated line**
Standmiete	**market dues**
Standort	**base**
Standort	**location**
Standort, Werbewert eines	**space position value**
Standortmarketing	**place marketing**
Stapel	**batch**
Stapelung	**stacking**
Stapelware	**staple**
Statistik	**statistics**
Statistik, deskriptive	**descriptive statistics**
Status quo-Preisbildung	**status quo pricing**
Statusprodukt	**status product**
Statussymbol	**status symbol**
Stauen	**stowage**
Staugebühr	**stowage**
Staugeld	**stowage**
Staulücke	**broken stowage**
Staumaß, Fracht mit niedrigem	**low density cargo**
Staumaß, hohes	**high stowage factor**
Stauung	**stowage**
Stelle	**slot**
Stellenanzeige	**recruitment advertising**
Stellenanzeige	**want ad**
Stellvertretung	**representation**
Sterbeziffer	**death rate**
Sterblichkeitsziffer	**death rate**
Sternzeichen-Gesetz (USA) (vergleichbar mit Robinsonliste)	**Asterisk law**
Steuer, spezifische	**specific tax**
Steuer, versteckte	**hidden tax**
Steueraufkommen	**revenue**
Steuerbefreiung	**tax exemption**
Steuerbefreiung	**exemption form tax**
Steuergruppe (GB)	**schedule**
steuerlich absetzbar	**deductible**
Steuersatz	**tariff**
Steuersatz, durchschnittlicher	**average rate of taxation**
Steuerwirkung	**tax impact**
Stichprobe	**random check**
Stichprobe	**sample**
Stichprobe, adäquate	**adequate sample**
Stichprobe, geschichtete	**stratified sample**
Stichprobe, parallelisierte	**matched sample**
Stichprobe, repräsentative	**representative sample**
Stichprobenauswahl, bewußte	**judgement sampling**
Stichprobenentnahme	**breaking bulk**
Stichprobenentnahme	**sampling**

Stichprobenerhebung	**sample survey**
Stichprobenentnahme bei Warenannahme	**acceptance sampling**
Stichprobenfehler	**sampling error**
Stichprobenumfang	**sampling fraction**
Stichprobenumfang	**sample size**
Stichprobenverfahren mit Klumpenauswahl	**cluster sampling**
Stichprobenverfahren, sequentielles	**sequential sampling**
Stichtag	**call date**
Stichtag	**deadline**
Störungssucher	**troubleshooter**
Stoff	**material**
Stopp	**freeze**
Store-Test	**placement test**
Stornierung	**countermand**
Storyboard	**storyboard**
Stoßverkehrszeit am Nachmittag	**afternoon drive**
Stoßzeit	**peak period**
Strafe	**penalty**
Straßen- und Brückenbenutzungsgebühr	**toll**
Straßenbefragung	**intercept interview**
Straßengütertransport	**road transport**
Straßenhändler	**hawker**
Straßenmarkt	**street market**
Straßennutzungsgebühr	**road toll**
Straßenverkäufer	**vendor**
Strategie	**strategy**
Strategien eines Marktherausforderers	**market challenger strategies**
Strecke	**route**
Streckengeschäft	**drop shipment business**
Streubreite	**coverage**
Streudiagramm	**scatter diagram**
Streuplanung	**media buying**
Streuung (Stat)	**variance**
Streuung der Anlagepalette	**diversification**
Streuverluste	**waste circulation**
Strichcode	**barcode/bar code**
Strichcodeleser	**barcode reader**
Strohfeuer	**grass fire**
Strohmann	**dummy**
Stück	**unit**
Stück, angepaßtes, überarbeitetes	**adaptation**
Stück, fehlerhaftes	**reject**
Stückgut	**general cargo**
Stückgut	**part load**
Stückgut (Sendung)	**less than carload lot**
Stückgut(ladung)	**general cargo**
Stückgutfracht	**package freight**
Stückgutladung	**general cargo**
Stückgutladung, Waggon für	**package car**

Stückkalkulation	**product costing**
Stückkosten	**average costs**
Stückkosten	**unit cost(s)**
Stückkostenrechnung	**unit costing**
Stückkostenrechnung für Massenfertigung	**process costing**
Stückpreis	**unit price**
Studiomethode	**laboratory method**
Studioredakteur	**anchorman**
Studiotest	**in-theater test**
Studiotest	**theater test**
Stufe	**grade**
Stützungswerbung	**sustaining advertising**
Subkultur	**subculture**
Submissionsangebot	**bid**
Submissionsangebot	**tender**
Submissionsangebot in versiegeltem Umschlag	**sealed bid**
Submissionsangebot, Preisfestsetzung durch ...	**bid pricing**
Submissionsempfänger	**tenderee**
Submissionsverfahren	**competitive bidding**
Submittent	**tenderer**
Subskriptionspreis	**subscription price**
Substantiierung	**substantiation**
Substantiierung des Werbeinhalts	**advertising substantiation**
Substitution, Grenzrate der	**marginal rate of substitution**
Substitutionseffekt	**substitution effect**
Substitutionsgut	**substitute good**
Subunternehmer	**subcontractor**
Subunternehmervertrag	**subcontract/sub-contract**
Subvention	**grant**
Subventionswirtschaft	**sheltered economy**
Suchanzeige, rubrizierte	**classified advertisement**
Suggestivfrage	**leading question**
Sukzessivlieferungsvertrag	**open-end contract**
Summe, lächerliche	**peanuts**
Sündenbock	**fall guy**
Superette	**superette**
Superinflation	**hyperinflation**
Superlativwerbung	**puffery**
Supermarkt	**supermarket**
Superprodukt	**star piece**
Superstore	**superstore**
Supply-Side-Economics	**supply side economics**
Synchromarketing	**synchromarketing**
Synergy	**synergy**
Systemanbieter	**systems seller**
Systemverkauf	**systems selling**

T

TÜV-Plakette	**standard label**
TÜV-Zeichen	**standard label**
TV-Information, werbliche	**infomercial**
TV-Spielshow	**gameshow/game show**
Tabellarisierung	**tabulation**
Tabelle	**list**
Tabelle	**table**
Tabelle	**tabulation**
Tafel, weiße	**whiteboard**
Tafelgeschirr	**flatware**
Tag, an dem die Geschäfte nachmittags geschlossen sind	**early closing day**
Tag, jeden (Insertionsanweisung)	**every day**
Tag, jeden zweiten (Insertionsanweisung)	**every other day**
Tagegeld (für Geschäftsreisen)	**subsistence allowance**
Tagesbericht	**daily report**
Tageseinnahmen	**till money**
Tageskosten	**current cost**
Tagespreis	**current price**
Tagestätigkeitsbericht	**daily activities report**
Tagestour	**day trip**
Tageswert	**current value**
Tageswert	**going value**
Tageswert	**market value**
Tageswert	**market price**
Tageswert	**present value**
Tageszeitungen	**dailies**
Talkshow	**talk show**
Talsohle	**trough**
Talsohle, konjunkturelle	**economic tailspin**
Tante-Emma-Laden	**corner shop**
Tante-Emma-Laden	**mom and pop store**
Tara	**tare**
Taragewicht	**tare weight**
Tarif	**tariff**
Tasche	**bag**
Tastatur	**keyboard**
Tätiger, kreativ ...	**creative person**
Tätigkeit, Diversifikation der	**diversification**
Tätigkeit, jede wirtschaftliche	**business**
Tätigkeit, jede wirtschaftliche	**traffic**
Tätigkeitsbericht	**activity report**
Tatsachen, Vorspielung falscher	**false pretences**
Tauschabkommen	**barter agreement**
Tauschgeschäft	**exchange**
Tauschhandel	**barter**
Tauschhandel, internationaler	**countertrade**

Täuschung (arglistige)	**fraud**
Tauschwert	**value in exchange**
Tauschwert	**value**
Tauschwirtschaft	**barter economy**
Tauschwirtschaft	**exchange economy**
Tausend, vom	**per mille**
Tausenderpreis	**cost per thousand (CPM, CPT)**
Taxator	**estimator**
Teaser	**teaser ad(vertisement)**
Teaser	**teaser**
Technologie	**technology**
Technologie, kapitalintensive	**capital-intensive technology**
Technologie-Lizenzvergabe	**technology licensing**
Technologiebewertung	**technology assessment**
Technologiemonopol	**technological monopoly**
Teil-Containerladung	**less than container load (LCL)**
Teil-Sendefinanzierung	**partial sponsorship**
Teilauftrag	**part load**
Teilauftrag	**part order**
Teilausverkauf	**closeout**
Teile	**parts**
Teile, (fremd)bezogene	**bought-in parts**
Teile, vorgefertigte	**fabricated parts**
Teilkosten deckende Werbezusage	**semi-liquidator**
Teilkostenrechnung	**direct costing**
Teilladung	**part load**
Teillieferung	**part delivery**
Teillieferung	**part load**
Teillieferung	**part order**
Teilnehmer	**entrant**
Teilzahlung	**instal(l)ment**
Teilzahlung	**part payment**
Teilzahlung, als	**on account**
Teilzahlung, kleine	**token payment**
Teilzahlungskauf	**hire purchase**
Teilzahlungskauf	**instal(l)ment buying**
Teilzahlungskredit	**instal(l)ment credit**
Teilzahlungskreditinstitut	**finance house**
Teilzahlungskreditinstitut	**industrial bank**
Teilzahlungskreditinstitut	**hire purchase company**
Teilzahlungsverkauf	**instal(l)ment selling**
Telefon	**telephone**
Telefon mit Wahlwiederholung und Nummernspeicher	**X-press callmaker**
Telefon, schnurloses, tragbares	**cordless telephone**
Telefon-Kreditkarte	**calling card**
Telefonalphabet	**telephone alphabet**
Telefonanruf	**call**
Telefonat	**call**
Telefonauftrag	**telephone order**

Telefonbuch	directory
Telefonbuch	phone book
Telefonbuch	telephone directory
Telefonbuchwerbung	directory advertising
Telefonbuchwerbung	telephone directory advertising
Telefondurchwahl	direct dial(l)ing
Telefongebühren	telephone rates
Telefongebührenanzeiger	call-charge indicator
Telefongespräch, (vor)angemeldetes	fixed-time call
Telefonhörer	receiver
Telefonkarte	phonecard
Telefonkontakter	telemarketer
Telefonmarketer	telemarketer
Telefonmarketing	telephone marketing
Telefonmarketing	telemarketing
Telefonmarketing, aktives	outbound telemarketing
Telefonmarketing, passives	inbound telemarketing
Telefonrückruf	return call
Telefonverkauf	telephone marketing
Telefonvorwahl	dial(l)ing code
Telefonzelle	booth
Telefonzelle	kiosk
Teleeinkauf	teleshopping
Telekommunikation	telecommunication(s)
Telemarketing	Telemarketing
Teleshopping	home shopping
Teleshopping	teleshopping
Tenor der Anzeige/Werbung	advertising theme
Termin	time limit
Termin, letzter	deadline
Terminabteilung	traffic department
Termingeschäft	forward deal
Termingeschäft	forward transaction
Termingeschäft, Preis für	futures price
Termingeschäfte	futures
Terminhandel	forward deal
Terminhandel	futures trading
Terminierung	timing
Terminjäger	chaser
Terminjäger	expediter/expeditor
Terminkontrakt	forward contract
Terminkontrakte	futures
Terminkurs	futures price
Terminlieferung	forward delivery
Terminlieferung	future delivery
Terminmarkt	forward market
Terminmarkt	terminal market
Terminsicherung	forward cover
Terminüberwacher	traffic manager
Terminwaren	futures

Terminwerbung	**fixed spot**
Terminwerbung	**fixed break**
Test, anonymer	**blind test**
Test, kostenloser	**free trial**
Testbefragung	**opinion research**
Testeinkäufer	**ghost shopper**
Testfall	**test case**
Testgruppe	**panel**
Testimonialanzeige	**testimonial advertisement**
Testmarkt	**test market**
Testsiegel	**seal of approval**
Testwerbesendung	**animatic**
teuer, zu	**overpriced**
Teuerungsausgleich	**cost-of-living adjustment/allowance (COLA)**
Teuerungszulage	**cost of living allowance**
textanschließend	**next to reading**
Text, gegenüber (redaktionellem)	**facing matter**
Text, neben	**next to reading**
Text, redaktioneller	**editorial copy**
Texter	**copywriter**
Textgestaltung, computerunterstützte	**desktop publishing**
Textilien	**softgoods/soft goods**
Textilwaren	**dry goods**
Textilwaren	**softs**
Textteil (einer Anzeige)	**body copy**
Theaterwerbung	**theater advertising**
Theke für Sonderangebote	**bargain counter**
Theorie der Preisbestimmung	**theory of price determination**
Theorie der administrativen Preise	**administered price theory**
Theorie des Verbraucherverhaltens	**theory of consumer behaviour**
Tiefeninterview	**depth interview**
Tiefeninterview	**in depth interview**
Tiefpunkt	**bottom**
Tiefstand	**bottom**
Timing	**timing**
Tip	**tip**
Tippfehler	**literal (error)**
Tischkarte	**tent card**
Titel(zeile)	**heading**
Titel	**caption**
Titel	**title**
Titelboxanzeige	**ear**
Titelboxanzeige	**title corner**
Titelkopf einer Werbedrucksache	**masthead**
Titelmusik	**title music**
Titelseite	**cover**
Titelseite	**cover page**
Titelseite	**front cover**
Titelseite, ausschlagbare	**gatefold**

Titelüberschrift	**heading**
Titelüberschrift	**headline**
Titelzeile	**headline**
Tonne	**barrel**
Tonne	**cask**
Total Quality Management	**total quality management**
Totalverlust	**dead loss**
Tourismus	**tourism**
Tourismusmarketing	**tourist marketing**
Touristikmarketing	**tourist marketing**
Tradeoff	**tradeoff**
Trading-down	**trading down**
Trading-up	**trading up**
Tragetasche	**carrier bag**
Tragetasche	**shopping bag**
Trägheitsverkauf	**inertia selling**
Transaktion	**transaction**
Transaktionskosten	**transaction cost(s)**
Transfer	**transfer**
Transferpreis, Festsetzung von	**transfer pricing**
Transitlager	**entrepot**
Transparent	**banner**
Transparenz	**transparency**
Transport	**carriage**
Transport	**cartage**
Transport	**conveyance**
Transport	**haulage**
Transport	**transport**
Transport durch Bahn und LKW	**truckage**
Transport in Containern	**containerization**
Transport mit Kundenfahrzeug	**customer`s own transport (COT)**
Transport von Rückfracht	**backhauling**
Transport, auf dem	**in transit**
Transport, kombinierter, multimodaler	**intermodal transport**
Transport, multimodaler	**multi-modal transport**
Transportbehälter	**bin**
Transportflugzeug	**cargo plane**
Transportflugzeug	**freight plane**
Transportkosten	**carriage**
Transportkosten	**carriage outward(s)**
Transportkosten	**cartage**
Transportkosten	**haulage**
Transportkosten	**transportation charges**
Transportkostenrechnung	**freight note**
Transportmittel	**conveyance**
Transportpapiere	**shipping documents**
Transportunternehmen	**common carrier**
Transportunternehmer	**haulier**
Transportunternehmer/nehmen (LKW)	**haulage contractor**
Transportweg	**route**

Transportweg, Vorschrift(en) über den	**routing order**
Trend	**trend**
Trendanalyse	**trend analysis**
Trendwende	**turnaround**
Tresenaufsteller	**counter card**
Treueprämie bei Verpackungsteileinsendung	**boxtop offer**
Treuerabatt	**aggregated rebate**
Treuerabatt	**deferred rebate**
Treuerabatt	**loyalty rebate**
Treuerabatt	**patronage discount**
Treuerabatt	**patronage rebate**
Trickfilmzeichner	**animator**
Trinkgeld	**gratuity**
Trinkgeld	**tip**
Trockenware	**dry goods**
Trommel	**drum**
Tröpfelkampagne (Werbung)	**drip**
Trugschluß	**fallacy**
Trust	**trust**
Trusts, Zerschlagung von	**trustbusting**
Tüte	**bag**
TV-Programm (ohne Werbung)	**package**
Tycoon	**tycoon**
Typenbeschränkgung	**variety reduction**
Typenkartell	**standardization cartel**

U

U-Bahn-Plakat	**tube card**
U4	**back cover**
UPC-Strichcode	**universal product code**
Über(be)zahlung	**overpayment**
Überangebot	**excess(ive) supply**
Überangebot	**glut**
Überbestand	**excess stock**
überbewertet	**overpriced**
überbieten	**outbid**
Überblick	**survey**
Übereinkunft	**deal**
überfällig	**overdue**
Übergabe	**delivery**
übergeben	**consign**
Übergepäck	**excess baggage**
Übergewinn	**super-normal profit**
Überholung, technisch-wirtschafliche	**obsolescence**
Überkapazität	**excess capacity**
Überlandverkehr	**overland transport**
Überlappung von Hörern/Lesern/ Zuschauern	**audience duplication**

Überlebenspreisbildung	**survival pricing**
Übernachfrage	**excess(ive) demand**
Übernachfrage	**overfull demand**
Übernahme	**absorption**
Übernahmeperiode	**takeover time**
Überproduktion	**overrun**
Überproduktion	**overproduction**
Überprüfung der Werbung	**advertising control**
Überschneidung von Hörern/Lesern/ Zuschauern	**audience duplication**
Überschrift	**caption**
Überschrift	**heading**
Überschuß	**surplus**
übersenden	**consign**
übersenden	**forward**
Übersicht	**table**
Übersicht	**survey**
Überspartheorie	**oversaving theory**
Übertragung	**transfer**
Übertragung, zeitverschobene	**delayed broadcast**
Übertragungssperre	**blackout**
Übertragungswirkung	**carryover effect**
Überwachung	**follow-up**
Überzahlung	**overpayment**
Überzeugung	**belief**
Überzeugungswerbung	**competitive advertising**
Ultimoabrechung	**end-of-month-settlement**
Umbrella-Promotion	**umbrella promotion**
Umbruch	**make-up**
Umfang des Anzeigenteils einer Publikation	**advertising lineage/linage**
Umfeld, betriebliches	**business environment**
Umfeld, betriebliches	**external environment**
Umfeld, politisches	**political environment**
Umfrage	**poll**
Umfrage	**survey**
Umfrage einen Tag nach Werbemittelkontakt	**day-after survey**
Umfrage, briefliche	**mail interview**
Umladekosten	**handling charges**
Umladeplatz	**place of transshipment**
Umladeplatz	**terminal**
Umladung	**transhipment**
Umladung	**reshipment**
Umleitung	**detour**
Umleitung	**rerouting**
Umleitung einer Warensendung	**reconsignment**
Umpositionierung	**repositioning**
Umsatz	**sales**
Umsatz	**turn**

Umsatz	**turnover**
Umsatz einer Werbeagentur	**billing**
Umsatz, hoher, mit geringer Gewinnspanne	**buy turnover**
Umsatz, höheren... haben als	**outsell**
Umsatzanalyse	**sales analysis**
Umsatzbonus	**annual volume discount**
Umsatzbonus	**turnover bonus**
Umsätze, Erzielung zu niedriger	**undertrading**
Umsatzerlöse	**sales**
Umsatzgigant	**sales giant**
Umsatzmaximierung	**sales maximization**
Umsatzrendite	**profit percentage**
Umsatzrendite	**return on sales**
Umsatzrentabilität	**profit percentage**
Umsatzrentabilität	**return on sales**
Umsatzstatistik	**sales analysis**
Umsatzsteigerungsversuch durch Erhöhung der Preise	**trading up**
Umsatzsteigerungsversuch durch Senkung der Preise	**trading down**
Umsatzsteuer	**turnover tax**
Umsatzsteuer (GB)	**value added tax (VAT)**
Umsatzsteuer (USA)	**sales tax**
Umsatzsteuer, einschließlich	**VAT/sales tax included**
Umsatzvolumen	**sales volume**
Umsatzvolumen	**volume of business**
Umsatzvolumen	**volume**
Umsatzziel	**sales target**
Umschalten, häufiges (des TV-Kanals)	**zapping**
Umschlag	**binder**
Umschlag	**cover**
Umschlag	**envelope**
Umschlag	**jacket**
Umschlag	**turnover**
Umschlag, großer für Briefe	**gusset envelope**
Umschlag, neutraler	**plain cover**
Umschlagplatz	**terminal**
Umschlagsdepot	**entrepot**
Umschlagseite	**cover page**
Umschlagseite zwei	**inside front cover**
Umschlagseite, dritte	**inside back cover**
Umschlagseite, dritte	**third cover (3C)**
Umschlagseite, letzte, vierte	**back cover**
Umschlagseite, zweite	**inside front cover**
Umschlagshäufigkeit	**rate of turnover**
Umschlagshäufigkeit	**stockturn (rate)**
Umschlagshäufigkeit	**turnover rate**
Umschlagzeit	**turnaround time**
Umsteiger	**switcher**
Umtausch	**exchange**

Umtausch	**replacement**
Umtauschangebot	**swap offer**
Umweg	**detour**
Umwegproduktion	**indirect production**
Umwelt, interne	**internal environment**
Umwelt, kulturelle	**cultural environment**
Umwelt, natürliche	**natural environment**
Umweltabgabe	**environmental tax**
Umweltabgaben	**affluent charges**
Umweltanalyse	**environmental analysis**
Umweltbedingungen	**environmental conditions**
Umweltmanagement	**environmental management**
Umweltministerium (GB)	**Department of the Environment**
Umweltschutz(bewegung)	**environmentalism**
Umweltschutzbehörde (USA)	**Environmental Protection Agency**
Umweltschützer	**environmentalist**
Umweltsponsoring	**environmental sponsoring**
Umweltsteuer	**green tax**
Umweltverschmutzung	**environmental pollution**
Umweltverschmutzung	**pollution**
Umzingelungsattacke	**encirclement attack**
Unbeständigkeit	**instability**
Unbekannten, die jungen	**generation X**
uneingeschränkt	**free**
unentgeltlich	**free**
Unelastizität, unendliche	**perfect inelasticity**
unfrei	**carriage forward**
unfrei	**freight forward**
unfrei	**freepost**
Ungleichgewicht	**disequilibrium**
Uniform Commercial Code (UCC) (USA)	**Uniform Commercial Code**
Unit-Load	**unit load**
Unmenge	**quantity**
Unterauftrag	**subcontract/sub-contract**
Unterbezahlung	**underpayment**
Unterbrechung	**discontinuity**
Unterbringung	**accomodation**
Untergrundwirtschaft	**black economy**
Untergrundwirtschaft	**hidden economy**
Unterhaltungsindustrie	**entertainment industry**
Unterhaltungsindustrie	**showbusiness**
Unterhaltungskosten	**entertainment expenses**
Unterhaltungsmusik, leichte	**easy listening**
Unterklasse, obere	**upper-lower class**
Unterkonsumtheorie	**underconsumption theory**
Unterlagen	**data**
Untermalung, musikalische	**incidental music**
Unternehmen mit breitgefächerter Marketingstrategie	**middle-of-the-roader**
Unternehmen oder Produkt mit starkem Wachstum und großem Marktanteil	**star**

Unternehmen, Absatzprognose für ein	**company sales forecast**
Unternehmen, absatz-, marktorientiertes	**market-orientated firm**
Unternehmen, expandierendes	**growth company**
Unternehmen, führendes	**major**
Unternehmen, führendes ... in der Vertriebskette	**channel captain**
Unternehmen, gewagtes	**adventure**
Unternehmen, internationales	**global firm**
Unternehmen, lieferantengebundenes	**tied company**
Unternehmen, marktbeherrschendes	**dominant firm**
Unternehmen, multinationales (internationales)	**multinational**
Unternehmen, multinationales	**transnational corporation**
Unternehmen, nicht lebensfähiges	**lame duck**
Unternehmen, risikoreiches	**venture**
Unternehmen, riskantes	**gamble**
Unternehmensbereich ausgründen, ausgliedern, abstoßen	**hive off**
Unternehmensexpansion, zu starke	**overtrading**
Unternehmensimage	**corporate image**
Unternehmensimage	**company image**
Unternehmensindikatoren	**business indicators**
Unternehmensportfolio	**business portfolio**
Unternehmensprofil	**company profile**
Unternehmensprognose	**business forcast(ing)**
Unternehmenswachstum	**expansion**
Unternehmensziele	**objectives**
Unternehmenszusammenschluß	**amalgamation**
Unternehmenszusammenschluß	**combine**
Unternehmenszusammenschluß	**integration**
Unternehmenszusammenschluß	**merger**
Unternehmer/in	**entrepreneur**
Unternehmerverband	**trade association**
Untersatz	**coaster**
Unterscheidungskompetenz	**distinctive competence**
Unterscheidungstest	**discrimination test**
Unterschied	**difference**
Unterschied, kaum wahrnehmbarer	**just noticeable difference**
Untersuchung	**scrutiny**
Untersuchung, eingehende	**in depth study**
Untertitel	**caption**
Untertitel	**subhead(ing)**
Untervermietung	**sublease**
Untervermietung	**underlease/under-lease**
Unterverpachtung	**sublease**
Untervertreter	**subagent**
unterwegs	**in transit**
Unvollkommenheit	**imperfection**
Unze	**ounce**
Unzustellbarkeit	**undeliverability**

Urheberrecht	**copyright**
Urlaubsmarketing	**vacation marketing**
Urmaterial	**primary data**
Ursprung	**source**
Ursprungsbezeichnung	**mark of origin**
Ursprungszeugnis	**certificate of manufacture**
Usance	**trade usage**
Utilitarismus	**utilitarianism**

V

Variable	**variable**
Variable, abhängige	**dependent variable**
Variable, endogene	**endogenous variable**
Variable, nicht beeinflußbare	**uncontrollable variable**
Variable, unabhängige	**independent variable**
Variablen, sozioökonomische	**socioeconomic variables**
Varianz (Stat)	**variance**
Varieteevorstellung	**floor show**
Vebleneffekt	**Veblen effect**
Veralten, geplantes	**built-in obsolescence**
Veralten, geplantes	**planned obsolescence**
Veralten, wirtschaftliches	**economic obsolescence**
Veralten, vorzeitiges	**obsolescence**
Veralterung, geplante	**artificial obsolescence**
Veränderung, erwartete	**anticipated change**
Veranstalter	**promoter**
Veranstaltung	**event**
Veranstaltungsmarketing	**events marketing**
Verantwortung, soziale	**social responsibility**
Verarbeitung(squalität)	**finish**
Veräußerer	**seller**
Veräußerung	**divestment**
Veräußerung	**realization**
Veräußerung einer Beteiligung	**divestiture**
Verband	**association**
Verbindungsrente mit Übergang	**joint and survivor annuity**
Verbrauch, privater	**personal consumption expenditure**
Verbraucher	**consumer**
Verbraucher höherer Einkommensschichten	**upscale consumers**
Verbraucher und Preisbildung	**consumers and pricing**
Verbraucher, Kaufstruktur der	**consumer spending patterns**
Verbraucher, informationsaktiver	**information seeker**
Verbraucher, reifer	**mature consumer**
Verbraucherabholmarkt	**box store**
Verbraucheranalyse	**consumer research**
Verbraucherausgaben	**consumer expenditure**
Verbraucherbedürfnis	**consumer want**
Verbraucherbefragung	**consumer survey**

Verbraucherberatungsstelle	**consumer advice centre**
Verbraucherbeschwerde	**consumer complaint**
Verbraucherforschung	**consumer research**
Verbrauchergroßmarkt	**hypermarket**
Verbraucherkaufverhalten	**consumer buying behaviour**
Verbraucherkredit	**consumer credit**
Verbraucherkreditgesetz (GB)	**Consumer Credit Act**
Verbraucherkreditvertrag	**consumer credit agreement**
Verbrauchermarketing	**consumer marketing**
Verbrauchermarkt	**superstore**
Verbrauchermarkt, kleiner	**convenience store**
Verbrauchernachfrage	**consumer demand**
Verbrauchernutzen	**consumer benefit**
Verbraucherpanel	**consumer panel**
Verbraucherpräferenz	**consumer preference**
Verbraucherpreis	**consumer price**
Verbraucherpreisindex	**consumer price index**
Verbraucherprofil	**consumer profile**
Verbraucherpromotion	**consumer promotion**
Verbraucherrechte	**consumer rights**
Verbraucherschutz	**consumer protection**
Verbraucherschutzbewegung	**consumerism**
Verbrauchertestgruppe	**consumer panel**
Verbraucherunzufriedenheit	**consumer dissatisfaction**
Verbraucherverband	**consumer(s') association**
Verbraucherverhalten	**consumer behaviour**
Verbraucherverlosung	**consumer sweepstake(s)**
Verbrauchervortest	**consumer pretest**
Verbraucherwerbung	**consumer advertising**
Verbraucherwettbewerb	**consumer contest**
Verbrauchsfrist	**shelf life**
Verbrauchsgewohnheit	**habit of consumption**
Verbrauchsgut, schnell umschlagendes	**fast-moving consumer good/product**
Verbrauchsgüter	**convenience goods**
Verbrauchsgüter	**consumer(s') goods**
Verbrauchsgüter	**nondurable goods**
Verbrauchsgüter, kurzlebige	**softgoods/soft goods**
Verbrauchsort	**place of final use**
Verbrauchsrate	**usage rate**
Verbrauchssteuer	**consumption tax**
Verbrauchssteuer	**excise**
Verbrauchssteuer	**purchase tax**
Verbrauchssteuern, Rückvergütung von	**excise drawback**
Verbreitungsgebiet	**circulation area**
Verbundpackung	**banded pack**
Verbundwerbung	**cooperative advertising**
Verbundwerbung	**dealer tie-in**
Verbundwerbung	**tie-in advertising**
verdienen	**make**
Verdienstspanne	**spread**

Verdrängen von Konkurrenten	**freeze out**
Verdrängungswettbewerb	**predatory practices**
Verdrängungswettbewerb (des Staates)	**crowding-out**
Vereinbarung, mündliche	**verbal contract**
Verfall	**lapse**
Verfalldatum	**expiry date**
Verfalldatum (Lebensmittel)	**pull date**
Verfalldatum, Auszeichnung mit	**code dating**
Verfallsdatum (der Haltbarkeit)	**sell by date**
Verfalltag	**due date**
Verfalltag	**expiry date**
Verfälschung durch den Befrager/ Interviewer	**interviewer bias**
Verflechtung, vertikale	**vertical integration**
verfrachten	**freight**
Verfrachter	**freighter**
Verfrachtung	**freightage**
Verfügbarkeit	**availability**
Verführer, geheimer	**hidden persuader**
Vergeltungsmaßnahme	**retaliation**
Vergeßlichkeitsspanne	**forgetting rate**
Vergeudung	**wastage**
Vergeudung	**waste**
Vergleich, zwischenbetrieblicher	**interfirm comparison**
Vergleichspreis	**comparative price**
Vergleichspreis	**reference price**
Vergleichstest	**comparison test**
Vergnügungsreise als Dienstreise deklariert	**junket**
Vergnügungssteuer	**entertainment tax**
Vergrößerung	**enlargement**
Vergütung	**consideration**
Vergütung	**remuneration**
Verhälnis Gewinn zu Umsatz	**profit to sales ratio**
Verhalten	**attitude**
Verhalten, sparsames	**economizing behaviour**
Verhalten, wettbewerbsbeschränkende(s)	**restrictive practice(s)**
Verhalten, wettbewerbswidriges	**anticompetitive practice**
Verhalten, wirtschaftliches	**economic behaviour**
Verhaltensänderung	**behavioural change**
Verhaltensforschung	**behaviour(al) research**
Verhaltensmessung	**attitude testing**
Verhaltenssegementierung	**behaviour segmentation**
Verhaltensstudie	**attitude study**
Verhaltenswissenschaft(en)	**behavioural science**
Verhältnis	**ratio**
Verhältnis von Werbeaufwand zu Verkäufen/Absatz/Umsatz	**advertising-to-sales ratio**
Verhältnis, im umgekehrten	**inverse relationship**
Verhandeln	**bargaining**

Verhandlungsbasis (VB)	**asking price**
Verhandlungsbasis (VB)	**or near offer (ONO, ono)**
Verhandlungsposition	**bargaining position**
Verhandlungsstärke	**bargaining power**
Verhandlungstaktiken	**bargaining tactics**
Verhandlungsverkauf	**negotiation selling**
Verkauf	**marketing**
Verkauf	**realization**
Verkauf	**sale**
Verkauf	**sell**
Verkauf (als Vorgang)	**selling**
Verkauf an der Haustür	**door-to-door**
Verkauf auf Kommissionsbasis	**commission sale**
Verkauf auf Kommissionsbasis	**memorandum sale**
Verkauf auf Probe	**sale on approval**
Verkauf bei gleichzeitiger Rückvermietung an den Verkäufer	**sale and leaseback/lease back**
Verkauf durch Außendienstmitarbeiter	**field selling**
Verkauf gegen Barzahlung bei eigenem Transport	**cash and carry**
Verkauf im Ausland	**selling overseas**
Verkauf mit (gleichzeitiger) Rückmiete	**leaseback**
Verkauf mit Rückgaberecht	**on sale or return**
Verkauf nach Beschreibung	**sale by description**
Verkauf nach Muster	**sale by sample**
Verkauf nach Probe	**sale by sample**
Verkauf nach Weiterempfehlung	**referral selling**
Verkauf nach oben	**selling up**
Verkauf unter Umgehung der festgelegten Absatzwege	**backdoor selling**
Verkauf wegen Geschäftsaufgabe	**forced sale**
Verkauf zu herabgesetzten Preisen	**bargain sale**
Verkauf zu stark reduzierten Preisen	**bargain sale**
Verkauf, zum	**on offer**
Verkauf zur Ansicht	**sale on approval**
Verkauf, aggressiver	**high pressure selling**
Verkauf, aggressiver	**hard sell**
Verkauf, angepaßter	**adaptive selling**
Verkauf, beratender	**consultative selling**
Verkauf, extensiver	**extensive selling**
Verkauf, freihändiger (nicht durch Versteigerung)	**sale by private treaty**
Verkauf, kreativer	**creative selling**
Verkauf, leichter	**ready sale**
Verkauf, persönlicher	**face-to-face selling**
Verkauf, persönlicher	**personal selling**
Verkauf, problemlösungsorientierter	**problem-solving selling**
Verkaufen, anpassungsfähiges	**adaptive selling**
Verkaufen, dezentes, unaufdringliches	**low pressure selling**
Verkaufen, zurückhaltendes	**soft sell(ing)**

Verkäufer/in	**marketer**
Verkäufer/in	**seller**
Verkäufer/in	**shop assistant**
Verkäufer/in	**clerk**
Verkäufer/in	**vendor**
Verkäufer, an ... gegebner Geldbetrag zur Zahlung der Ware	**tender cash**
Verkäufer/in, die Bestellung im Geschäft annimmt	**inside order taker**
Verkäufer, stummer	**dispenser**
Verkäufer, stummer	**silent salesperson**
Verkäufer/in, technische(r)	**technical salesperson**
Verkäuferhandbuch	**rate book**
Verkäuferin	**saleslady**
Verkäufermarkt	**sellers' market**
Verkäuferpfandrecht	**seller's lien**
Verkäuflichkeit	**salability/saleability**
Verkaufs- und Lieferbedingungen	**terms and conditions**
Verkaufsabrechnung eines Kommissionärs	**account sales**
Verkaufsabschluß	**closing**
Verkaufsabschluß mit Zugeständnissen	**concession close**
Verkaufsabschluß mittels Entgegenkommen	**concession close**
Verkaufsabschluß, direkter	**direct close**
Verkaufsabschluß, stiller	**silent close**
Verkaufsabschlußtechnik	**closing technique**
Verkaufsabteilung	**sales department**
Verkaufsagentur	**sales agency**
Verkaufsaktion	**sales drive**
Verkaufsaktion	**sales campaign**
Verkaufsanbahnung, Art und Weise der ...	**sales approach**
Verkaufsangebot	**offer for sale**
Verkaufsanreiz	**sales incentive**
Verkaufsargument	**sales pitch**
Verkaufsargument, einzigartiges, einmaliges	**unique selling proposition**
Verkaufsargument, wichtigstes, prioritäres	**single selling proposition**
Verkaufsaufgabe	**selling task**
Verkaufsaußendienst	**field sales force**
Verkaufsausstellung auf Rädern	**road show**
Verkaufsautomat	**automatic vending machine**
Verkaufsautomat	**dispenser**
Verkaufsautomat	**slot machine**
Verkaufsautomat	**vending machine**
Verkaufsautomat	**vendor**
Verkaufsbedingungen	**conditions of sale**
Verkaufsbedingungen	**terms of sale**
Verkaufsbedingungen	**trade terms**
Verkaufsberater	**missionary salesperson**
Verkaufsbericht	**sales report**

Verkaufsbuch	**sales book**
Verkaufsbulletin	**sales bulletin**
Verkaufsbüro	**sales office**
Verkaufsdemonstration im Verkaufsladen	**in-store demonstration**
Verkaufseffizienz der Werbung	**sales effect of advertising**
Verkaufselastizität	**sales elasticity**
Verkaufserfolg, außergewöhnlicher	**blockbuster**
Verkaufserlöse	**sales**
Verkaufsexperte	**merchandiser**
Verkaufsfiliale	**branch store**
Verkaufsfiliale eines Herstellers	**factory outlet**
Verkaufsfläche	**shop floor/shopfloor**
Verkaufsfläche	**selling space**
Verkaufsförderung	**promotion**
Verkaufsförderung	**sales promotion**
Verkaufsförderung beim Konsumenten/ Verbraucher	**consumer promotion**
Verkaufsförderung direkt beim Einzelhandel/im Geschäft	**in-store promotion**
Verkaufsförderung durch normale Werbemaßnahmen	**above-the-line (promotion)**
Verkaufsförderung durch Preisnachlaß	**price off promotion**
Verkaufsförderung durch indirekte Werbemaßnahmen	**below-the-line (promotion)**
Verkaufsförderung im (Einzelhandels) Geschäft	**store promotion**
Verkaufsförderung im Geschäft	**in-store promotion**
Verkaufsförderung mittels Kupon	**couponing**
Verkaufsförderung, eingeleitet vom Außendienst	**field-activated promotion**
Verkaufsförderung, informative	**informative promotion**
Verkaufsförderung, irreführende	**deceptive promotion**
Verkaufsförderungsabteilung, Leiter der	**promotion manager**
Verkaufsförderungsaktivitäten	**promotional activities**
Verkaufsförderungsbudget	**promotional budget**
Verkaufsförderungsforschung	**promotion research**
Verkaufsförderungsmaterial am Verkaufsort	**point-of-sale (POS) material**
Verkaufsförderungsmittel	**promotional tools**
Verkaufsförderungsmix	**promotion mix**
Verkaufsförderungsnachlaß	**promotional discount**
Verkaufsförderungsprämie	**push money**
Verkaufsförderungsprämie	**spiff**
Verkaufsforschung	**sales research**
Verkaufsgespräch	**sales talk**
Verkaufsgespräch, Abschluß eines	**closing**
Verkaufsgespräch, Abschluß eines	**sales closing**
Verkaufsgespräch, emotionales Beenden eines ...	**emotional close**
Verkaufsgesprächsabschluß mit Kaufaufforderung	**urgency close**

Verkaufshilfe	**dealer aid**
Verkaufshilfen	**sales aids**
Verkaufshilfen, audiovisuelle	**audiovisual sales aids**
Verkaufshilfen, visuelle	**visual aids**
Verkaufshinweis	**sales lead**
Verkaufsingenieur	**sales engineer**
Verkaufsjournal	**sales journal**
Verkaufskartell	**syndicate**
Verkaufskolonne	**group of solicitors**
Verkaufskommissionär	**commission merchant**
Verkaufskommissionär	**consignee**
Verkaufskommissionär	**factor**
Verkaufskommissionär	**selling agent**
Verkaufskunst	**salesmanship**
Verkaufsleiter	**general sales manager**
Verkaufsleiter	**sales manager**
Verkaufsleiter für ein bestimmtes Produkt	**brand manager**
Verkaufsleiter, nationaler	**national sales manager**
Verkaufsleitung	**sales management**
Verkaufsmappe	**sales portfolio**
Verkaufsmaximierung	**sales maximization**
Verkaufsmethode	**selling technique**
Verkaufsmissionar	**missionary salesperson**
Verkaufsniederlassung	**sales branch**
Verkaufsoption	**option to sell**
Verkaufsorganisation	**sales force**
Verkaufsorientierung	**sales orientation**
Verkaufsort	**point-of-sale**
Verkaufspersonal	**sales staff**
Verkaufspersonal, Eignungstest für	**sales aptitude test**
Verkaufspersonal, firmeneigenes	**company salespeople**
Verkaufspolitik	**sales policy**
Verkaufsprämie	**push money**
Verkaufsprämie	**sales incentive**
Verkaufspreis	**selling price**
Verkaufspreis einer Publikation	**cover price**
Verkaufspreis, amerikanischer	**American Selling Price (ASP)**
Verkaufspreis, berichtigter	**adjusted selling price (ASP)**
Verkaufsprovision, angepaßte, gleitende	**sliding commission**
Verkaufsquote	**sales quota**
Verkaufsraum	**salesroom**
Verkaufsrechnung	**outgoing invoice**
Verkaufsrechnung	**sales invoice**
Verkaufsreihenbogen	**aisle arch**
Verkaufsrückgang	**sales decline**
Verkaufsschlager	**flagship brand**
Verkaufsschlager	**hot-selling line**
Verkaufsschlager	**seller**
Verkaufsschlager, potentieller	**sleeper**

Verkaufsskonto	**sales discount**
Verkaufsstab	**sales force**
Verkaufsstand	**stand**
Verkaufsständer aus Draht	**wire stand**
Verkaufsstelle, betriebseigene	**industrial store**
Verkaufsstelle, mobile	**mobile shop**
Verkaufssteuerung	**merchandise**
Verkaufssyndikat	**selling syndicate**
Verkaufstagung	**sales meeting**
Verkaufstalent	**sales aptitude**
Verkaufstechnik	**sales technique**
Verkaufstechnik, dezente, weiche, zurückhaltende	**soft sell(ing)**
Verkaufstisch für Sonderangebote	**bargain counter**
Verkaufstraining	**sales training**
Verkaufstraining, formales	**formal sales training**
Verkaufsunterlage	**business paper**
Verkaufsverfahren	**selling process**
Verkaufsvertreter	**sales representative**
Verkaufsvertreter	**selling agent**
Verkaufsvoraussage	**sales forecast**
Verkaufsvorführung, stereotype	**canned presentation**
Verkaufsvorgang	**sales process**
Verkaufswerbung	**sales advertising**
Verkaufswerbung, aggressive	**hard sell advertisement**
Verkaufswettbewerb	**sales contest**
Verkaufswiderstand	**sales resistance**
Verkaufswirkung (der Werbung)	**sales response (to advertising)**
Verkaufsziel	**sales objective**
Verkaufsziel	**sales target**
Verkehr (Güter, Personen)	**traffic**
Verkehr, multimodaler	**intermodal transport**
Verkehrsaufkommen	**traffic**
Verkehrsfähigkeit	**marketability**
Verkehrsfluß innerhalb des Markts	**in-the-market traffic**
Verkehrsmittel, Werbeplakatanschläge in	**inside transit advertising**
Verkehrsmittelposter	**car card**
Verkehrsmittelwerbung	**baby billboard**
Verkehrsmittelwerbung	**transit advertising**
Verkehrsunternehmen, öffentliches	**common carrier**
Verkehrszählung	**traffic count**
Verkleinerung	**downsizing**
Verladeliste	**freight list**
Verladen	**loading**
Verladepapiere	**shipping documents**
Verlader	**freighter**
Verlader	**shipper**
Verladungskosten	**cargo handling charges**
Verlängerung des Produktlebenszyklus	**life cycle extension**
Verlangen, auf	**on demand**

Verlangen, zahlbar bei	**payable on demand**
Verleumdung	**defamation**
Verleumdung	**slander**
Verlosung, Wettbewerb mit ...	**sweepstake**
Verlust	**damage**
Verlust	**loss**
Verlust, erkannter	**known loss**
Verlust, realisierter	**realized loss**
Vermietung	**lease**
Vermietung von Investitionsgütern, langfristige	**finance lease**
Vermittler	**broker**
Vermittler	**intermediary**
Vermittler	**middleman**
Vermittlungsprovision	**finder`s fee**
Vermögen	**wealth**
Vermögen, bewegliches	**mov(e)ables**
Vermögen, unbewegliches	**immovables**
Vermögenseinkommen	**estate income**
Vermögensschaden	**economic loss**
Vermögensumverteilung	**redistribution of wealth**
Vermögenswert	**value**
Vernachlässigung der Sorgfaltspflicht	**neglect of care**
Veröffentlichung	**issue**
Veröffentlichung	**publication**
Veröffentlichung	**release**
Verpachtung	**lease**
Verpacken	**packaging**
Verpackung	**packaging**
Verpackung	**package**
Verpackung, kundenresistente	**customer-unfriendly packaging**
Verpackungsabteilung	**boxing department**
Verpackungsbescheinigung	**packing certificate**
Verpackungsdesign	**packaging design**
Verpackungsetikettierung mit Inhaltsangaben und/oder Gebrauchsanleitung	**informative labelling**
Verpackungsgewicht	**tare weight**
Verpackungsgewicht	**tare**
Verpackungsgutschein	**boxtop offer**
Verpackungskosten	**packing charges**
Verpackungsmaschine	**packer**
Verpackungsmix	**packaging mix**
Verpackungs- und Auszeichnungs-vorschriften	**packaging and labelling regulations**
Verpackungsunternehmen	**packer**
Verpfänder	**pawner/pawnor**
Verpflichteter	**debtor**
Verpflichtung	**commitment**
Verrechnungspreis	**transfer price**

Verringerung	**reduction**
Versand	**consignment**
Versand	**despatch/dispatch**
Versand	**forwarding**
Versand	**shipping**
Versand	**shipment**
Versand, Barzahlung vor	**cash before shipment**
Versand(haus)handel	**mail order business**
Versand, Inspektion vor dem	**preshipment inspection (PSI)**
Versandabteilung	**despatch department**
Versandabteilung	**traffic department**
Versandanweisung	**forwarding instruction**
Versandanweisung	**delivery instruction**
Versandanzeige	**advice note**
Versandanzeige	**delivery note**
Versandanzeige	**despatch/dispatch note**
Versandanzeige	**letter of advice**
Versandanzeige	**shipping note**
Versandanzeige	**waybill**
Versandauftrag	**shipping order**
Versandavis	**advice note**
Versandbestellung	**mail order buying**
Versanddatum	**despatch date**
Versandeinzelhandel	**mail order retailing**
Versandgroßhändler	**mail order wholesaler**
Versandhaus	**mail order house**
Versandhauskatalog	**mail order catalog(ue)**
Versandkatalog	**mail order catalog(ue)**
Versandkosten	**delivery expenses**
Versandleiter	**traffic manager**
Versandliste	**mailing list**
Versandliste	**packing list**
Versandmarkierung	**shipping marks**
Versandrechnung	**shipping invoice**
Versandtag	**date of shipment**
Versandtermin	**date of shipment**
Verschiffung	**shipment**
Verschiffungsdokumente	**shipping documents**
Verschlechterung	**setback**
Verschleiß	**wastage**
Verschleiß, eingebauter	**artificial obsolescence**
Verschleiß, eingebauter	**built-in obsolescence**
Verschluß(vorrichtung)	**closure**
Verschlußauslage	**closed display**
Verschlüsselung	**encoding**
Verschmelzung	**merger**
Verschmutzung	**pollution**
Verschneiden	**blending**
Verschulden	**fault**
Verschwendung	**wastage**

Verschwendung	**waste**
Versehen	**error**
versenden	**consign**
versenden	**forward**
versenden	**post**
Versenden	**forwarding**
Versender (von Waren)	**consignor**
Versicherungsmarketing	**insurance marketing**
Versicherungsträger	**carrier**
Versorgung	**supply**
Versorgung(sdienst)	**service**
Versorgungsbetriebe	**utilities**
Versorgungsbetriebe, öffentliche	**public utilities**
Versorgungsgüter, Werbung für	**utility advertising**
Verstärkungswerbung	**reinforcement advertising**
Verstauung	**stowage**
Versteigerung (Holländische)	**Dutch auction**
Versteigerung	**auction sale**
Versteigerung	**hammer**
Versteigerung	**public sale**
Versteigerung mit Scheingeboten	**mock auction**
Versteigerung, jemand der auf einer ... zu wenig bietet	**underbidder**
Versteigerung, öffentliche	**auction**
Versteigerung, öffentliche	**sale by auction**
Versuch	**experiment**
Versuch	**trial**
Versuch, Kunden höherwertige Were zu verkaufen	**selling up**
Versuchsanlage	**pilot plant**
Vertagung	**deferment**
Verteidigungsstrategie	**defense strategy**
Verteiler	**distribution list**
Verteiler	**distributor**
Verteilerliste	**distribution list**
Verteilungstheorie	**distribution theory**
Vertrag auf der Basis Selbstkosten plus Gewinnaufschlag	**cost plus (contract)**
Vertrag, ausdrücklicher	**express contract**
Vertrag, ausgehandelter	**negotiated contract**
Vertrag, bilateraler, gegenseitiger, zweiseitiger	**bilateral contract**
Vertrag, der die vollständige Projektdurchführung verlangt	**turnkey/turn-key contract**
Vertrag, mündlicher	**verbal contract**
Vertrag, rechtsgültiger, rechtsverbindlicher	**valid contract**
Vertrag, stillschweigender, konkludent abgeschlossener	**implied contract**
Vertragsabschlußtag	**contract date**
Vertragsangebot, Aufforderung ein ... abzugeben	**invitation to treat**

Vertragsannahme	**acceptance of offer**
Vertragsdatum	**contract date**
Vertragshändler	**appointed dealer**
Vertragshändler	**authorized dealer**
Vertragshändler	**authorized distributor**
Vertragshändler	**concessionaire**
Vertragshändler	**distributor**
Vertragsklauseln, handelsübliche (Incoterms)	**trade terms**
Vertragspreis	**contract price**
Vertragsrücktritt, Gesetz über	**Cooling-off law**
Vertragsverlängerung	**extension of a contract**
Vertrautheitswerbung	**familiarity advertising**
Vertreter	**commercial travel(l)er**
Vertreter	**sales representative**
Vertreter	**representative**
Vertreter	**travelling salesman**
Vertreter	**agent**
Vertreter mit eigenem Lager	**stocking agent**
Vertreterauftrag	**journey order**
Vertreterbericht	**call slip**
Vertreterbesuch	**sales call**
Vertreterprovision	**agent`s commission**
Vertretung	**representation**
Vertretung kleiner Firmen durch große (AuW)	**piggyback export scheme**
Vertretungsvertrag	**agency agreement**
Vertrieb	**distribution**
Vertrieb	**marketing**
Vertrieb durch ausgewählte Händler	**selective selling**
Vertrieb, direkter	**direct channel**
Vertrieb, eingeschränkter	**limited distribution**
Vertrieb, indirekter	**indirect marketing**
Vertrieb, indirekter	**indirect selling**
Vertrieb, mehrkanäliger	**multichannel distribution**
Vertrieb, selektiver	**selective distribution**
Vertrieb, weltweiter	**global distribution**
Vertriebsabteilung	**marketing department**
Vertriebsdirektor	**general sales manager**
Vertriebsforschung	**distribution research**
Vertriebsgemeinkosten	**selling cost(s)**
Vertriebsgemeinkosten	**selling overhead**
Vertriebskanal	**marketing channel**
Vertriebskartell	**sales cartel**
Vertriebskosten	**distribution cost(s)**
Vertriebskosten	**selling cost(s)**
Vertriebskostenanalyse	**distribution cost analysis**
Vertriebskostenanalyse	**marketing cost analysis**
Vertriebsleiter	**distributions manager**
Vertriebsleiter	**sales manager**

Vertriebsleitung	**sales management**
Vertriebslücke	**distribution gap**
Vertriebsmanagement	**distribution management**
Vertriebsnetz	**distribution network**
Vertriebsplanung	**distribution planning**
Vertriebspolitik	**marketing policy**
Vertriebsstruktur	**distribution structure**
Vertriebsunternehmen	**distribution agent**
Vertriebsvereinbarung	**marketing agreement**
Vertriebsweg	**channel of distribution**
Vertriebsweg	**distribution channel**
Vertriebsweg, direkter	**direct channel**
Vertriebszentrum	**districentre**
Verweilzeit	**turnaround time**
Verzeichnis	**catalog(ue)**
Verzeichnis	**list**
Verzeichnis	**record**
Verzeichnis	**register**
Verzeichnis	**schedule**
Verzeichnis unsicherer Kunden	**blacklist**
Verzerrung	**bias**
Verzögerung	**lag**
Verzögerung, zeitliche	**time lag**
Videoausstellung	**video exhibition**
Videokonferenz	**video conference**
Videotext	**videotext**
Vielflieger	**frequent flyer**
Vielseher	**heavy viewer**
vier O`s für Marketing-Operation	**four Os**
Vierfarbenanzeige	**four colour (4/c) advertisement**
Vierfelder-Portfolio-Matrix	**Boston Box**
Vierteljahreszeitschrift	**quarterly**
Visitenkarte	**calling card**
Visitenkarte	**business card**
Visitenkarte	**visiting card**
Visualiser	**visualizer**
Vitrine	**display cabinet**
Vitrine	**showcase**
Volkseinkommen	**national income**
Volkseinkommen, reales	**real national income**
Volksfest	**fair**
volkstümlich, -verbunden	**grass roots**
Volksvermögen	**national wealth**
Volkswirtschaft	**economy**
Volkswirtschaft, reife	**mature economy**
Volkswirtschaftsplan	**national plan**
Volkszählung	**census**
Vollbringer/in	**effector/effecter**
Volljährige(r)	**major**
Volljährigkeit	**majority**

Vollkosten	**full cost**
Vollkosten-Preisgestaltung	**absorption pricing**
Vollkostenkalkulation	**full cost pricing**
Vollkostenkalkulation	**markup pricing**
Vollkostenrechnung	**absorption costing**
Vollpension	**full board**
Vollsortiment	**full line**
Vorsichtsmarkierungen	**caution marks**
Volumen	**volume**
Volumensegmentierung	**volume segmentation**
Volumenware	**high density freight**
von heute an	**forward**
Vorausbestellung	**advance order**
Vorausbesuch (von Einzelhändlern bei Werbekampagne)	**advance canvass**
Vorausbezahlung	**cash in advance**
Vorausbuchung	**forward booking**
Vorauskasse	**cash in advance**
Vorauskasse	**payment in advance**
Voraussage, suggestiv wirkende/sich nicht erfüllende	**self-fulfilling prophecy**
Vorauszahlung	**payment in advance**
Vorauszahlung	**prepayment**
Vorauszahlungsrabatt	**anticipating rebate**
Vorbehaltspreis	**fall-back price**
Vorbestellung	**forward booking**
Vorentwurf	**rough draft**
Vorfinanzierung	**prefinancing**
Vorführgerät	**demonstration model**
Vorführmodell	**demonstration model**
Vorführung	**demonstration**
Vorführung im Geschäft	**store demonstration**
Vorführung vor Ort	**on site demonstration**
Vorhersage	**forecast**
Vorhersage	**prediction**
Vorhersage, technische	**technical forecast**
Vorlage	**presentation**
Vorlage	**production**
Vorlage, bei Anfordern	**on demand**
Vorrat	**stock**
Vorrat	**supply**
Vorräte	**inventory**
Vorräte, Wertminderung von	**stock depreciation**
Vorräte, Wertsteigerung von	**stock appreciation**
vorrätig	**in stock**
Vorratsbewertung, Lifo-Methode	**last in, first out**
Vorratshaltung, zu hohe	**overstocking**
Vorratslager, Bildung von	**stockpiling**
Vorsaison	**dead season**
Vorsaison	**early season**

Vorsatz	**intent**
Vorschau	**preview**
Vorschlag	**proposal**
Vorschrift(en) über den Transportweg	**routing order**
Vorschriften, werberechtliche	**advertising regulations**
Vorsicht(smaßnahme)	**precaution**
Vorspielung falscher Tatsachen	**false pretences**
Vorstadtzentrum	**suburban center**
Vorstellung	**idea**
Vorstellung	**introduction**
Vorstellungsbild	**image**
Vorsteuer	**input tax**
Vorteil	**benefit**
Vorteil des zuerst Handelnden	**first mover advantage**
Vorteil, Gesetz des komparativen	**law of comparative advantage**
Vorteile, externe	**external economies**
Vorverkaufskasse	**booking office**
Vorverkaufsstelle	**ticket agency**
Vorwahl	**dial(l)ing code**
Vorzugsbedingungen	**concessionary terms**
Vorzugskonditionen	**concessionary terms**
Vorzugsplatz	**special position**
Vorzugsplazierung	**preferred position**
Vorzugsplazierung	**special position**

W

Wachstum	**expansion**
Wachstum	**growth**
Wachstum, diversifiziertes	**diversified growth**
Wachstum, exportinduziertes	**export-led growth**
Wachstum, horizontales	**horizontal expansion**
Wachstum, integriertes	**integrated growth**
Wachstum, reales	**real growth**
Wachstum, stetiges	**sustained growth**
Wachstum, ungleichgewichtiges	**unbalanced growth**
Wachstumsbereich	**growth area**
Wachstumsbranche	**growth industry**
Wachstumsindustrie	**growth industry**
Wachstumsmarkt	**growth market**
Wachstumsphase	**growth stage**
Wachstumsrate	**growth rate**
Wachstumsstrategien	**growth strategies**
Wachstumstheorie	**growth theory**
Wagenladung, weniger als	**less than carload lot**
Waggon für Stückgutladung	**package car**
Waggon, frei, franko	**free on rail / free on truck**
Wahl	**choice**
Wahl, zweite	**second(s)**
Wahlfreiheit	**freedom of choice**

Wahrnehmung	**perception**
Wahrnehmung, selektive	**selective perception**
Wahrnehmungslandkarte	**perceptual map**
Wahrscheinlichkeit	**chance**
Wahrscheinlichkeit	**probability**
Wahrscheinlichkeit, bedingte	**conditional probability**
Wahrscheinlichkeitsstichprobe	**probability sample**
Wahrscheinlichkeitsverteilung	**probability distribution**
Währungen, grüne	**green currencies**
Währungseinheit (Cent)	**cent**
Währungseinheit, europäische (ECU)	**European Currency Unit**
Wand-Spannplakat	**wall banner**
Wandlung (Rücktritt vom Vertrag)	**cancellation of sale**
Wandschaubild	**wall chart**
Wandübersicht(stafel)	**wall chart**
Ware	**commodity**
Ware auf Abruf	**merchandise on call**
Ware zu stark herabgesetzten Preisen	**distress merchandise**
Ware(n)	**merchandise**
Ware(n), sensible	**sensitive products**
Ware, Ausstellung von	**display**
Ware, Konkretisierung einer	**appropriation of goods**
Ware, beim Kauf mitgenommene	**carryouts**
Ware, beschädigte, mangelhafte	**defective goods**
Ware, billige, aber augenfällige	**borax**
Ware, braune	**browngoods/brown goods**
Ware, die sich gut verkauft	**seller**
Ware, effektive, physische	**actuals**
Ware, freie	**no-name (product)**
Ware, gehortete zirkulieren lassen	**dishoarding**
Ware, generische	**generics**
Ware, heimische	**home produce**
Ware, hochwertige	**specialty good/product**
Ware, kundeneigene	**customer-owned goods (cog)**
Ware, minderwertige	**inferior goods**
Ware, schnellverkäufliche	**fast selling merchandise**
Ware, schwer verkäufliche	**slow moving merchandise**
Ware, sofort lieferbare	**prompts**
Ware, spottbillige	**dead bargain**
Ware, unbeschädigte	**sound cargo**
Ware, unverkäufliche	**unmerchantable good(s)**
Ware, unverpackte	**nonpackaged good(s)**
Ware, verpackte	**packaged good(s)**
Ware, weiße	**generic products**
Ware, weiße	**white goods**
Ware, zu knapp gelieferte	**shortlanded cargo**
Ware, zurückgelegte	**layaway**
Waren	**goods**
Waren des täglichen Bedarfs	**convenience goods**
Waren des täglichen Bedarfs	**essential commodities**

Waren freigeben	**release**
Waren zur Ansicht / auf Probe	**goods on approval**
Waren zweiter Qualität	**seconds**
Waren, Einzelauslage von	**spot display**
Waren, an den Lieferanten zurückgegebene (nicht verkaufte)	**unsolds**
Waren, fungible, vertretbare	**fungibles**
Waren, halbfertige	**partly manufactured goods/products**
Waren, latent vorhandene	**unsought goods**
Waren, minderwertige	**Giffen goods**
Waren, nicht bewußte/bekannte	**unsought goods**
Waren, unaufgefordert zugesandte, unbestellte	**unsolicited goods**
Waren, unverkäufliche	**dead stock**
Waren, verdorbene	**perished goods**
Waren, zollfreie	**duty-free goods**
Waren, zollfreie	**free goods**
Waren- und Dienstleistungssteuer	**goods and services tax (GST)**
Warenabnahme, Kontrolle vor	**pre-delivery inspection**
Warenangebot mit Rücknahmegarantie und Rückerstattung des Kaufpreises bei Nichtgefallen	**refund offer**
Warenangebot zum Selbstkostenpreis	**self-liquidating offer**
Warenankunftsavis	**arrival notification form**
Warenannahme	**acceptance of goods**
Warenannahme	**acceptance**
Warenannahme	**goods receiving department**
Warenannahme	**receiving department**
Warenannahme	**receipt of goods (ROG, rog)**
Warenannahme, Stichprobenentnahme bei	**acceptance sampling**
Warenannahme, Wirksamwerden der Zahlungsbedingungen ab ...	**receipt-of goods dating**
Warenannahmeschein	**goods received note**
Warenauslage	**display**
Warenauslage außerhalb des Regals	**off shelf display**
Warenauslage unter Verschluß	**closed display**
Warenauslage zum Selbstkostenpreis	**self liquidating display**
Warenauslage, alleinstehende	**island display**
Warenauslageregal, beiderseitig offenes	**gondola**
Warenauslieferungsabteilung eines Warenhauses	**traffic department**
Warenauszeichnung	**label(l)ing**
Warenbegleitpapier	**shipping documents**
Warenbegleitschein	**docket**
Warenbehälter	**display bin**
Warenbeschreibung	**indentification of goods**
Warenbestand	**trading stock**
Warenbestand, ausgewogener	**balanced stock**
Warenbestandskonto	**stock account**
Warenbevorratung	**stockpiling**

Warenbewertungsmethode, zuerst eingekauft, zuerst verbraucht	**first-in, first-out**
Warenbezeichnung	**brand name**
Warenbörse	**commodity market**
Warenbörse	**commodity exchange**
Warenbörsenmakler	**commodity broker**
Warendarbietung	**merchandising**
Warendepot eines Güterverkehrsunternehmens	**trucker-owned warehouse**
Warendepot, firmeneigenes	**company-owned warehouse**
Wareneingangsabteilung	**receiving department**
Wareneingangsbescheinigung	**delivery receipt**
Wareneingangsbuch	**goods received register**
Wareneingangsbuch	**purchase(s) journal**
Wareneinkäufe	**merchandise purchases**
Wareneinkaufskonto	**purchase(s) account**
Wareneinsatz	**cost of goods sold**
Warenempfangsschein	**delivery receipt**
Warenendbestand	**closing inventory**
Warenerkennung, automatische	**automatic identification**
Warengeld	**commodity money**
Warenhaus	**department(al) store**
Warenhaus, Abteilungsleiter im	**floor manager**
Warenhauskette	**department store chain**
Warenkennzeichen	**brand mark**
Warenkette	**giant retailer**
Warenkonzern	**giant retailer**
Warenkorb	**basket of goods**
Warenkredit	**trade credit**
Warenlager	**depot**
Warenlager	**goods depot**
Warenlager	**magazine**
Warenlager	**warehouse**
Warenlager, Finanzierung eines	**floor plan (finance)**
Warenlieferung	**delivery of goods**
Warenlombard	**merchandise advance**
Warenmarkierung	**merchandise mark**
Warenmarkt	**commodity market**
Warenprobe	**sample**
Warenprobenverteilung	**sampling**
Warenprodukttest, anonymer	**anonymous product testing**
Warenprofil	**personality**
Warenpyramide	**floor pyramid**
Warenrechnung	**invoice**
Warenretouren	**merchandise returns**
Warenrücksendung (an den Lieferer)	**purchase return(s)**
Warenrücksendungen	**merchandise returns**
Warenrücksendungsbuch	**sales returns book**
Warensendung	**consignment**

Warensendung	**shipment**
Warensendung, Umleitung einer	**reconsignment**
Warensendung, Zerlegen einer	**breaking bulk**
Warensendung, die am Bestimmungsort an verschiedene Empfänger verteilt wird	**split consignment**
Warensendung, palletierte	**palletized consignment**
Warensonderangebot	**bargain pack**
Warensortiment	**assortment of goods**
Warensortiment, Verbesserung des	**upgrading**
Warenstapel	**floor pyramid**
Warenstapel	**pile of goods**
Warenstapel am Ende des Ganges	**end aisle display**
Warensteuer	**commodity tax**
Warentermingeschäft	**commodity futures contract**
Warentermingeschäft	**forward contract**
Warenterminmarkt	**terminal market**
Warentest, anonymer	**blind product test**
Warentest, vergleichender	**comparative product analysis**
Warenüberschuß	**overage**
Warenverkauf, Gesetze über den (GB)	**Sale of Goods Acts**
Warenverteilung	**physical distribution (PD)**
Warenverteilung, angemessene	**adequate distribution**
Warenvorrat	**trading stock**
Warenzeichen	**brand**
Warenzeichen	**trademark/trade mark**
Warenzeichen, eingetragenes, (gesetzlich) geschütztes	**registered trademark**
Warenzeichen, irreführendes	**deceptive mark**
Warenzeichenfälschung	**commercial counterfeiting**
Warenzeichenfigur	**trade character**
Warenzeichenimitation	**trademark imitation**
Warenzeichenpolitik	**branding**
Warenzugabe	**free merchandise**
Warenzusammenstellung	**assorting**
Warenzuteilung	**allocation**
Warnhinweis	**mandatory blurb**
Warteschlange	**queue**
Warteschlangentheorie	**queu(e)ing theory**
Warteschlangentheorie	**waiting line theory**
Warte(schlangen)zeit	**dwell time**
Wartung	**servicing**
Wartung	**service**
Wartung, vorbeugende	**preventive maintenance**
Wartungshandbuch	**maintenance manual**
Wartungsvertrag	**service agreement**
Wartungsvertrag	**contract maintenance**
Wasserzeichen	**watermark**
Wechselautomat	**change machine**
Wechselbeziehung	**correlation**
Wechselgeld	**change**

Wechselgeld falsch herausgeben	**fluff**
Wechselgeld in der (Laden)Kasse	**float**
Wegwerfpackung	**one-way package**
Wegwerfpost	**junk mail**
Wegwerfprodukt	**disposable product**
Weichwaren	**softs**
Weihnachtsfeiertag, erster	**Christmas Day**
Weiterverkauf	**resale**
Weiterverwender	**user customer**
Welthandel	**international trade**
Weltmarke	**world brand**
Weltmarke(nartikel)	**global brand**
Weltneuheit	**new-to-the-world product**
Weltpreis	**world price**
Weltunternehmen	**global company**
Weltwirtschaft	**global economy**
Weltwirtschaftskrise	**Great Depression**
Werbe(mittel)mix	**advertising mix**
Werbe(sende)zeit	**advertising time**
Werbeabteilung	**advertising department**
Werbeagentur	**advertiser**
Werbeagentur	**advertising agency**
Werbeagentur, Interessenkonflikt einer	**account conflict**
Werbeagentur, Personal einer	**agency personnel**
Werbeagentur, Umsatz einer	**billing**
Werbeagentur, kleine, kreative	**hot shop**
Werbeaktion, spektakuläre	**stunt**
Werbeansage	**advertising announcement**
Werbeansage, lokale	**local tag**
Werbeanschlag	**advertising bill**
Werbeanschlagfläche	**advertising hoarding**
Werbeanzeige, Erinnerung an den Inhalt einer	**ad playback**
Werbeanzeige, in der ein Konkurrenzprodukt diskreditiert wird	**knocking copy**
Werbeanzeige, ungünstig/abseits plazierte	**buried position**
Werbeappeal, gefühlsbetonter	**emotional appeal**
Werbeappeal, negativer	**negative appeal**
Werbeargument	**advertising point**
Werbearten	**advertising types**
Werbeartikel	**advertising specialty**
Werbeartikel	**advertising novelty**
Werbeartikel zum Selbstkostenpreis	**self-liquidator**
Werbeaufgaben	**advertising functions**
Werbeaufkleber	**tip on**
Werbeauftrag, schwebender	**abeyance order**
Werbeaufwand	**advertising expenditure**
Werbeausgaben	**advertising spending**
Werbeauslage am Verkaufsort	**point-of-purchase (POP) display**

Werbeaussage	**advertising message**
Werbeaussage, einseitige	**one-sided ad message**
Werbeautomat	**auto-dial recorded message player**
Werbebehauptung	**advertising claim**
Werbebehauptung	**claim**
Werbebeilage	**advertising supplement**
Werbebeilage	**freestanding insert**
Werbebeilage	**insert**
Werbebeilage	**stuffer**
Werbebeilage, eingeklebte	**tip in**
Werbebeilage, lose	**loose insert**
Werbebeipack	**insert**
Werbeblatt	**handbill**
Werbeblock	**clutter**
Werbebotschaft	**advertising message**
Werbebotschaft	**message**
Werbebrief	**sales letter**
Werbebudget, -etat	**advertising budget**
Werbedeckenanhänger im Schaufenster	**pelmet**
Werbedrucksache, Titelkopf einer	**masthead**
Werbedrucksache, unerwünschte	**junk mail**
Werbedurchdringung	**advertising penetration**
Werbedurchsage	**advertising announcement**
Werbedurchschlagskraft	**penetration**
Werbeeinblendung	**insert**
Werbeeinblendung	**spot announcement**
Werbeelastizität	**advertising elasticity**
Werbeempfänger, Zahl der	**exposure**
Werbeentscheidungsprozeß	**advertising decision process**
Werbeerfolg	**advertising effectiveness**
Werbeerfolgskontrolle durch Scannersystem	**behaviour scan**
Werbeerfüller	**adopter**
Werbeerinnerung einen Tag nach dem Werbespot oder der Anzeige	**day-after recall**
Werbeerinnerung nach max. 24 Stunden	**twenty-four hour recall**
Werbeetat, -budget	**advertisement budget**
Werbeetat, -budget	**advertising budget**
Werbeetat, Aufteilung des auf Werbegebiete	**area allocation**
Werbeetat, Festsetzung des ... nach dem Gesichtspunkt, welche Ausgaben man sich leisten kann	**affordable method**
Werbeetatfestsetzung, gewillkürte, über den Daumen gepeilte	**arbitrary method**
Werbeetatfestsetzung: Methode des erwarteten Umsatzes	**percent(age) of sales method**
Werbefachmann	**adman**
Werbefachverband (GB)	**Advertising Association**
Werbefachverband, amerikanischer	**American Advertising Federation**

Werbefeldzug, überregionaler	**national campaign**
Werbefilmdrehbuch	**storyboard**
Werbefläche	**billboard**
Werbefläche	**space**
Werbeförderung	**advertising promotion**
Werbeforschung	**advertising research**
Werbegag	**gag**
Werbegebiete, Aufteilung des Werbeetats auf ...	**area allocation**
Werbegeschenk	**advertising specialty**
Werbegeschenk	**door opener**
Werbegeschenk	**free gift**
Werbegeschenk	**giveaway/give-away**
Werbegeschenk, per Post angefordertes	**mail-in**
Werbegeschenk, unerlaubtes	**illegal gift**
Werbegraphik	**artwork/art work**
Werbegraphiker	**advertising artist**
Werbegraphiker	**commercial artist**
Werbegrundpreis	**advertised price**
Werbeidee, Verbildlichung einer	**visual**
Werbeinhalt, Substantiierung des	**advertising substantiation**
Werbekampagne	**advertising campaign**
Werbekampagne über beigefügten Coupon	**coupon (promotion) scheme**
Werbekampagne, Globalbewertung einer	**holistic evaluation**
Werbekampagne-Plan	**campaign plan**
Werbekontakter	**account executive**
Werbekontakter	**account manager**
Werbekontinuität	**continuity of advertising**
Werbekosten	**advertising expenditure**
Werbekosten	**advertising costs**
Werbekraft	**pulling power**
Werbekunde	**advertising customer**
Werbeleiste	**channel strip**
Werbeleistungsüberprüfung	**advertising audit**
Werbeleiter	**advertising manager**
Werbeleiter bei einem Werbeträger	**advertising manager**
Werbeleiter bei einem Werbeträger	**advertisement manager**
Werbemaßnahmen, die dem Verkauf vorausgehen	**pre-selling advertising**
Werbemaßnahmen, ergänzende	**accessory advertising**
Werbematerial	**sales literature**
Werbematerial, das Vertreter beim Kunden läßt	**leave piece**
Werbematerial, das einer Rechnung beiliegt	**bill insert**
Werbematerial, zusätzliches	**collateral material**
Werbemedien, alternative	**alternative advertising media**
Werbemittel	**advertising medium**
Werbemittel, Mischung der	**advertising mix**
Werbemittelbeachtung	**ad noting**

Werbemittelkontakt	**advertising exposure**
Werbemittelkontakt	**exposure**
Werbemittelkontakt, effektiver täglicher	**daily effective circulation**
Werbemittelkontakt, selektiver	**selective exposure**
Werbenachlaß	**advertising allowance**
Werbepaket	**package plan**
Werbepaket	**package**
Werbepenetration	**advertising penetration**
Werbeplakat	**advertising bill**
Werbeplakat	**showbill/show bill**
Werbeplakat fürs Showgeschäft	**showbill/show bill**
Werbeplakatanschläge in Verkehrsmitteln	**inside transit advertising**
Werbeplan	**advertising schedule**
Werbeplan	**media plan**
Werbeplanung	**advertising planning**
Werbepreis für lokale Werbungstreibende	**local rate**
Werbepreis für nationale Werbung	**national advertising rate**
Werbepreisliste	**adrate card**
Werbepreisliste	**grid card**
Werbepreisliste	**rate card**
Werbeprospekt	**handout**
Werbeprospekt, großformatiger	**broadsheet**
Werbepublikum	**advertising audience**
Werber	**bird dog**
Werber	**canvasser**
Werber	**solicitor**
Werberabatt	**advertising allowance**
Werberat	**Advertising Standards Authority (ASA)**
Werbereaktion	**advertising response**
Werbereaktionsfunktion	**advertising response function**
Werbereichweite	**advertising reach**
Werberfolg, außergewöhnlicher	**blockbuster**
Werberichtlinien	**Code of Advertising Practice**
Werbesache mit Rückantwort	**self mailer**
Werbeschild, beidseitiges	**sandwich board**
Werbeschrift	**pamphlet**
Werbeschwelle	**advertising threshold**
Werbesendeminute	**commercial minute**
Werbesendezeit	**spot**
Werbesendezeit	**time slot**
Werbesendezeit	**space**
Werbesendezeit, Kauf von ... bei Lokalsender	**spot buy**
Werbesendung	**announcement**
Werbesendung	**commercial**
Werbesendung	**mailing**
Werbesendung für mehrere Produkte	**multiple product announcement**
Werbesendung, Zeitdauer einer	**timelength**

Werbesendung, die täglich oder werktäglich vom selben Sender zur selben Uhrzeit ausgestrahlt wird	**across the board (commercial)**
Werbesendung, integrierte	**integrated commercial**
Werbesendungen, unmittelbar aufeinanderfolgende	**back-to-back commercials**
Werbesendungsplazierung, feste	**fixed position**
Werbesendungsplazierung, feste	**fixed spot**
Werbesendungsreichweite	**commercial delivery**
Werbeslogan	**advertising slogan**
Werbesong	**jingle**
Werbespot, kurzer, eingeblendeter	**spot announcement**
Werbespot	**announcement**
Werbespot	**commercial**
Werbespot	**spot**
Werbespot am Anfang oder Ende einer Programmsendung	**adjacency**
Werbespoteliminierung aus TV-Videoaufnahme	**zipping**
Werbespots mit eingeblendeter Telefon- oder Faxnummer, so daß Zuschauer sofort Kontakt aufnehmen kann	**direct response TV**
Werbespots, Nacheinandersenden von zwei	**double spotting**
Werbespruch	**slogan**
Werbestandort (Außenwerbung)	**advertising location**
Werbestrategie	**advertising strategy**
Werbetarif	**advertising rate**
Werbetest	**advertising test**
Werbetext	**advertising copy**
Werbetext	**copy**
Werbetext, produktbezogener	**product copy**
Werbetexter	**copywriter**
Werbethema	**advertising theme**
Werbeträger	**advertising medium**
Werbeträger	**media vehicle**
Werbeträger	**vehicle**
Werbeversand	**mail-out**
Werbevertrag	**advertising contract**
Werbeviereck	**advertising quadrangle**
Werbewand, große	**bulletin board**
Werbewert eines Standorts	**space position value**
Werbewirkung	**impact (of advertising)**
Werbewirkung	**message effect**
Werbewirkung, Nachlassen, Verfall der	**advertising wearout**
Werbezeit, günstigste	**best time available**
Werbezeitschrift	**giveaway magazine**
Werbezettel	**giveaway/give-away**
Werbezettel	**leaflet**
Werbezettel	**throwaway**
Werbeziel	**advertising objective**

Werbezielkonzeption	**creative strategy in advertising**
Werbezusage, Teilkosten deckende	**semi-liquidator**
Werbezuschuß	**advertising allowance**
Werbung	**advertising**
Werbung	**advertisement**
Werbung	**publicity**
Werbung am Verkaufsort	**point-of-sale advertising**
Werbung auf nationaler Ebene	**national advertising**
Werbung für Produktgruppe	**line advertising**
Werbung für ein neues Produkt	**plug**
Werbung für eine Einzelperson	**person marketing**
Werbung für eine neue Firma	**plug**
Werbung für Versorgungsgüter	**utility advertising**
Werbung in Druckmedien	**press advertising**
Werbung in den Gelben Seiten	**Yellow Page advertising**
Werbung in lokalen Fernsehsendern	**spot television**
Werbung in lokalen Radiosendern	**spot radio**
Werbung jede zweite Woche	**alternate weeks**
Werbung mit Gutschein, der für ein anderes Produkt gilt	**cross couponing**
Werbung mit bekannten, vertrauten Marken	**familiarity advertising**
Werbung mit ironischem Unterton	**facetious advertising**
Werbung mit kleinem Werbebudget	**low-budget advertising**
Werbung mit verzögerter Wirkung	**delayed-action advertisement**
Werbung ohne direkte Kaufaufforderung	**indirect advertising**
Werbung und Marktanteil	**advertising and market share**
Werbung und Nachfrage	**advertising and demand**
Werbung und der Verbraucher	**advertising and the consumer**
Werbung von Unternehmen zu Unternehmen	**business-to-business advertising**
Werbung zur Information der Öffentlichkeit	**public service advertising**
Werbung, 10-Sekunden	**ten (:10)**
Werbung, 20-Sekunden	**twenty (:20)**
Werbung, 30-Sekunden	**thirty (:30)**
Werbung, Anziehungskraft der	**advertising appeal**
Werbung, Dauer einer ... im Fernsehen/ Rundfunk	**commercial length**
Werbung, Für und Wider von	**advertising pros and cons**
Werbung, Glaubwürdigkeit der	**advertising believability**
Werbung, Glaubwürdigkeit der	**believability of advertising**
Werbung, Kosteninflation für	**adflation**
Werbung, Langzeitwirkung der	**advertising carryover**
Werbung, Malrabatt für	**consecutive-weeks discount**
Werbung, Neugier weckende	**teaser ad(vertisement)**
Werbung, Produktionskosten für	**above-the-line cost**
Werbung, Publikumsreaktion(en) auf	**advertising response**
Werbung, Regalstreifen mit ...	**shelf strip**
Werbung, Sperrzeit für	**blocked-out time**

Werbung, Tenor der	**advertising theme**
Werbung, Überprüfung der	**advertising control**
Werbung, Verkaufseffizienz der	**sales effect of advertising**
Werbung, Verkaufswirkung der	**sales response (to advertising)**
Werbung, Werbepreis für nationale	**national advertising rate**
Werbung, Zielsetzung der	**advertising objective**
Werbung, aggressive, kämpferische	**competitive advertising**
Werbung, aggressive, kämpferische überredende, überzeugende	**persuasive advertising**
Werbung, alleinstehende	**solus advertisement**
Werbung, antizyklische	**anticyclical advertising**
Werbung, appetitanregende	**appetizing advertising**
Werbung, audiovisuelle	**audiovisual advertising**
Werbung, auf direkte Reaktion(en) zielende	**direct-action advertisement**
Werbung, aufdringliche	**borax**
Werbung, bedürfnisweckende	**want creating advertising**
Werbung, begleitende, unterstützende	**accessory advertising**
Werbung, begründete, rationale	**reason why advertising**
Werbung, belehrende	**educational advertising**
Werbung, berichtigende	**corrective advertising**
Werbung, defensive	**defensive advertising**
Werbung, die Umworbenen zu Antwort/Reaktion veranlassen soll	**direct response advertising**
Werbung, die ein Stück wirklichen Lebens zeigt	**slice-of-life advertising**
Werbung, die so gut ist, daß sie die Aufmerksamkeit vom Produkt auf sich lenkt	**vampire video**
Werbung, die zu späterer/aufgeschobener Kaufhandlung führen soll	**delayed-action advertisement**
Werbung, die zwischen Programmsendung ausgestrahlt wird	**spot advertising**
Werbung, durch ... finanziertes Programm	**sponsored program**
Werbung, eingeblendete, integrierte	**integrated commercial**
Werbung, emotionale, gefühlsbetonte	**emotional advertising**
Werbung, engagierte	**advocacy advertising**
Werbung, extrem übertriebene	**knocking advertising**
Werbung, geschmacklose	**buckeye**
Werbung, geschmacklose	**tasteless advertising**
Werbung, gesperrte Sendezeit für	**airtime blocked to/for advertisers**
Werbung, gesungene, musikalische	**jingle**
Werbung, gezielte	**selective advertising**
Werbung, globale, internationale	**global advertising**
Werbung, grenzüberschreitende	**cross-national advertising**
Werbung, große, aufsehenerregende	**spectacular**
Werbung, herabsetzende	**disparaging advertising**
Werbung, herabsetzende	**knocking advertising**
Werbung, in der eine prominente Person ein Produkt demonstriert	**celebrity endorsement**

Werbung in einem Programmheft	**package advertising**
Werbung, indirekt vergleichende	**dangling comparatives**
Werbung, indirekte	**indirect advertising**
Werbung, informative	**informative advertising**
Werbung, internationale	**international advertising**
Werbung, irreführende	**deceptive advertising**
Werbung, irreführende	**false advertising**
Werbung, irreführende	**misleading advertising**
Werbung, jemand der Programme finanziert und dafür ... betreiben darf	**sponsor**
Werbung, kämpferische	**competitive advertising**
Werbung, kosmetische	**cosmetic marketing**
Werbung, kundenspezifische	**customised advertising**
Werbung, landesweite	**national advertising**
Werbung, lebensnahe	**slice-of-life advertising**
Werbung, lokale	**local advertising**
Werbung, marktschreierische, reisserische, übertriebene	**puffery**
Werbung, redaktionelle	**editorial publicity**
Werbung, reißerische, übertriebene	**hype**
Werbung, saisonale	**seasonal advertising**
Werbung, scherzhafte	**facetious advertising**
Werbung, standardisierte, genormte	**standardized advertising**
Werbung, stimmungserzeugende	**mood advertising**
Werbung, stoßweise	**burst (advertising)**
Werbung, umwelt- und verbraucherfreundliche	**soft advertising**
Werbung, unaufwendige	**soft advertising**
Werbung, unterschwellige	**subliminal advertising**
Werbung, vergleichende	**comparative advertising**
Werbung, verkaufsfördernde Wirkung der	**usage pull**
Werbung, versteckte	**camouflaged advertising**
Werbung, versteckte, verschleierte	**hidden persuader**
Werbung, witzige, sensationelle	**gimmick**
Werbungsevaluierung	**advertising evaluation**
Werbungspretest	**advertising pretest**
Werbungstreibender, lokaler	**local advertiser**
Werk	**factory**
Werk	**plant**
Werk, ab	**ex warehouse (ex whse, X whse)**
Werk, urheberrechtlich nicht geschütztes	**public domain**
Werkhalle	**shop**
Werkstatt	**shop**
Werksvertreter	**manufacturer's agent**
Werkszeitung	**house magazine**
Wert	**value**
Wert für den Kunden, wirtschaftlicher	**economic value to the customer (EVC)**
Wert und Preis	**value and price**
Wert, angemessener	**fair value**
Wert, angemessener	**reasonable value**

Wert, realer	**real value**
Wertanalyse	**value analysis**
Werte, dem ... nach	**ad valorem**
Werterhöhung durch Marketing	**value-added marketing**
Wertfracht	**ad valorem freight**
Wertgegenstände	**valuables**
Wertminderung von Vorräten	**stock depreciation**
Wertnachnahme	**delivery against payment (DAP)**
Wertpapiere, Abstoßen von	**unloading**
Wertpapierhandel	**trade**
Wertparadoxon	**value paradox**
Wertschöpfung	**value added**
Wertschöpfungskalkulation	**value-based pricing**
Wertsteigerung von Vorräten	**stock appreciation**
Werttheorie	**theory of value**
Wertverlust	**holding loss**
Wertvorstellungen	**values**
Wertvorstellungen und Lebensstil, Zielgruppeneinteilung nach	**values and lifestyles**
Wertzuwachs	**holding gain**
Wertzuwachs, unverdienter	**unearned increment**
Wesentlichste	**bottom line**
Wettbewerb	**competition**
Wettbewerb	**contest**
Wettbewerb mit Verlosung	**sweepstake**
Wettbewerb, außerpreislicher	**nonprice competition**
Wettbewerb, durch Werbung finanzierter	**sponsored event**
Wettbewerb, indirekter	**indirect competition**
Wettbewerb, lauterer	**fair trading**
Wettbewerb, nationaler	**national competition**
Wettbewerb, reiner	**pure competition**
Wettbewerb, ruinöser	**cutthroat competition**
Wettbewerb, ruinöser ... wegen zu hoher Ladendichte	**overshopping**
Wettbewerb, unlauterer	**illegal competition**
Wettbewerb, unlauterer	**unfair competition**
Wettbewerb, unvollständiger	**imperfect competition**
Wettbewerb, vollständiger	**perfect competition**
Wettbewerb, weltweiter	**global competition**
Wettbewerbsarten	**competition types**
Wettbewerbs-Aufsichtsbehörde (USA)	**Federal Trade Commission**
Wettbewerbsbeschränkung	**restraint of competition**
Wettbewerbsbeschränkungen	**barriers to competition**
Wettbewerbsbeschränkungen, Gesetz gegen (GB)	**Fair Trading Act**
Wettbewerbsfähigkeit	**competitiveness**
Wettbewerbsgesetz	**Competition Act**
Wettbewerbsgesetz	**competition law**
Wettbewerbshandlungen, unlautere	**fraudulent trading**
Wettbewerbshandlungen, unlautere	**unfair trade practices**

Wettbewerbshüter	**competition watchdogs**
Wettbewerbsmarkt	**competitive market**
Wettbewerbsposition	**competitive position**
Wettbewerbspreis	**competitive price**
Wettbewerbspreisbildung	**competitive pricing**
Wettbewerbspreisbildung	**equivalent-price strategy**
Wettbewerbsstrategie	**competitive strategy**
Wettbewerbsverbot	**tie out**
Wettbewerbsvorteil	**competitive advantage**
Wettsteuer	**betting tax**
Whiteboard	**whiteboard**
Wichtigste	**bottom line**
Widererkennungstest	**recognition test**
Widerruf	**revocation**
wie besichtigt	**as seen**
Wieder(holungs)kauf	**rebuy**
Wieder(holungs)kauf	**repeat purchase**
Wiederauszeichnung	**remarking**
Wiederbelebung	**recovery**
Wiederbeschaffungspreis	**replacement price**
Wiederbeschaffungsverzögerung	**replacement lag**
Wiedereinführung	**relaunch**
Wiedererkennungstest	**recognition test**
Wiederholungswerbung	**repeat advertising**
Wiederinbesitznahme	**repossession**
Wiederkauf	**repurchase (RP)**
Wiederkauf, modifizierter	**modified rebuy**
Wiederkauf, unmodifizierter	**straight rebuy**
Wiederkaufszyklus	**repurchase cycle**
Wiederverkauf	**resale**
Wiederverkäufer, der den Produktwert erhöht	**value adding reseller**
Wiederverkäufermarkt	**reseller market**
Wiederverkäuferpreis	**trade price**
Wiederverkäuferrabatt	**trade allowance**
Wiederverkäuferrabatt	**trade discount**
Wiederverkaufsbeschränkung	**resale restriction**
Wiederverkaufspreis	**dealer`s price**
Wiederverkaufsrecht	**right of resale**
Wiederverladung	**reshipment**
Wiederverschiffung	**reshipment**
Wildkatze	**question mark**
Wildkatze	**wildcat**
Windhandel	**selling short**
Windhundverfahren (wer zuerst kommt, wird zuerst bedient)	**first-come, first served method**
Windschattenmarketing	**ambush marketing**
Wink	**tip**
Winterschlußverkauf	**winter sale**
Wirksamkeitsverzögerung	**effectiveness lag**

Wirksamwerden der Zahlungsbedingungen ab Warenannahme	**receipt-of goods dating**
Wirkung, mit ... vom, ab	**as from**
Wirkungsverzögerung	**effect lag**
Wirkungsverzögerung	**impact lag**
Wirkungsverzögerung	**lag**
Wirkungsverzögerung	**time lag**
Wirtschaft	**economy**
Wirtschaft, Ankurbelung der	**pump priming**
Wirtschaft, freie	**unplanned economy**
Wirtschaft, gelenkte	**controlled economy**
Wirtschaft, marktwirtschaftlich gesteuerte	**market-driven economy**
Wirtschaft, nicht-marktwirtschaftlich orientierte	**nonmarket economy (NME)**
Wirtschaft, staatlich gelenkte	**state-planned economy**
Wirtschaft, statische	**static economy**
Wirtschaftkrise	**economic crisis**
Wirtschaftlichkeit	**economic efficiency**
Wirtschaftlichkeit	**efficiency**
Wirtschaftsberatungsunternehmen	**economic consultancy**
Wirtschaftsbericht	**economic report**
Wirtschaftsforschung, empirische	**empirical research**
Wirtschaftsgemeinschaften	**economic trading groups**
Wirtschaftsgut	**commodity**
Wirtschaftsgut	**economic good**
Wirtschaftsgut mit begrenzter Nutzungsdauer	**wasting asset**
Wirtschaftsgüter	**durables**
Wirtschaftskreismodell, erweitertes	**full economy**
Wirtschaftskrise mit Inflation	**slumflation**
Wirtschaftsliberalismus	**economic liberalism**
Wirtschaftsliberalismus	**laissez-faire/laisser-faire**
Wirtschaftsmacht	**economic power**
Wirtschaftsministerium (GB)	**Department of Trade and Industry**
Wirtschaftsministerium (USA)	**Department of Commerce**
Wirtschaftsordnung	**economic system**
Wirtschaftsplanung	**economic planning**
Wirtschaftspolitik	**commercial policy**
Wirtschaftspolitik	**economic policy**
Wirtschaftspolitik, Instrumente der	**economic instruments**
Wirtschaftspolitik, angebotsorientierte	**supply side economics**
Wirtschaftspolitik, antizyklische	**countercyclical economic policy**
Wirtschaftspolitik, nachfrageorientierte	**demand side economics**
Wirtschaftspolitik, nachfrageverändernde	**expenditure-changing policies**
Wirtschaftspresse	**business press**
Wirtschaftsproblem	**economic problem**
Wirtschaftsprognose	**economic forecast(ing)**
Wirtschaftsprozeß	**economic process**
Wirtschaftsrecht	**mercantile law**

Wirtschaftssystem	**economic system**
Wirtschaftssystem mit zentraler Planung	**command economy**
Wirtschaftssystem, gemischtes	**mixed economy**
Wirtschaftstätigkeit	**economic activity**
Wirtschaftsunternehmen	**business enterprise**
Wirtschaftswachstum	**economic expansion**
Wirtschaftswachstum	**economic growth**
Wirtschaftswachstum, beschleunigtes	**forced draught/draft expansion**
Wirtschaftswachstum, harmonisches	**balanced economic growth**
Wirtschaftswissenschaft, normative	**normative economics**
Wirtschaftswohlstand	**economic welfare**
Wirtschaftszeitung	**business paper**
Wirtschaftszweig	**industry**
Wirtschaftszweig	**trade**
Wirtschaftszweig, konjunkturabhängiger	**cyclic(al) industry**
Wirtschaftszweige, nicht standortgebundene	**footlose industries**
Witz	**gag**
Woche, im Laufe der ...	**run of week**
Wochenblatt	**weekly**
Wochenend(sonder)angebot	**weekend special**
Wohlergehen	**welfare**
Wohlstand	**prosperity**
Wohlstand	**wealth**
Wohlstandsgesellschaft	**affluent society**
Wohltätigkeit	**charity**
Wohltätigkeitsbasar	**rummage sale**
Wohltätigkeitsmarketing	**charity marketing**
Wohltätigkeitsverein	**charitable society**
Wohngemeinschaft (WG)	**nonfamily household**
Wortassoziation	**word association**
Wuchtplanung	**impact scheduling**
Wühlkiste	**jumble display**
Wühlkorb	**dump bin**
Wurfsendung	**door drop**

X Y Z

X-Achse	**X-axis**
X-Koordinate	**abscissa**
Y-Achse	**Y-axis**
Yard (Längenmaß)	**yard**
Yuppie	**Yuppie**
ZBB-Planung	**zero-base(d) budgeting**
Zahl der Anschlagtafeln, die Anschlagwerbeunternehmen einem Werbetreibenden anbietet	**allotment**
Zahl der Werbeempfänger	**exposure**

Zahl der an Außenwerbung Vorbeifahrenden	**site passage**
Zahl der effektiven Fernsehzuschauer	**persons using television**
zahlbar, sofort	**spot**
Zahlen, Gesetz der großen	**law of large numbers**
Zahlen, gerade	**even numbers**
Zahlenmaterial	**data**
Zahlenschlüssel	**figure code**
Zahler, säumiger	**defaulter**
Zahlung	**payment**
Zahlung bei Erhalt der Rechnung	**payment on invoice**
Zahlung bei Erhalt des Kontoauszugs	**payment on statement**
Zahlung bei Lieferung	**collection on delivery (COD)**
Zahlung in offener Rechnung	**payment on open account**
Zahlung in voller Höhe	**payment in full**
Zahlung in voller Höhe	**full payment**
Zahlung nach Lieferung	**payment after delivery**
Zahlung, gestundete	**deferred payment**
Zahlung, prompte	**prompt cash (payment)**
Zahlung, sofortige	**spot payment**
Zahlung, symbolische	**token payment**
Zahlungsanweisung	**draft**
Zahlungsaufschub	**days of grace**
Zahlungsaufschub	**deferred payment**
Zahlungsbedingungen	**payment terms**
Zahlungsbedingungen	**terms**
Zahlungsbedingungen	**terms of payment**
Zahlungsbedingungen, Inkrafttreten der ... ab Warenannahme	**receipt of goods (ROG) dating**
Zahlungsbeleg	**receipt**
Zahlungsdatum	**date of payment**
Zahlungserinnerung, verdeckte	**hidden reminder**
Zahlungsfrist, zusätzliche	**days of grace**
Zahlungsmittel, gesetzliches	**legal tender**
Zahlungsmodalitäten	**payment terms**
Zahlungsmodalitäten	**terms of payment**
Zahlungsort	**place of payment**
Zahlungstermin	**date of payment**
Zahlungstermin	**payment date**
Zahlungsverkehr, bargeldloser, elektronischer	**electronic funds transfer**
Zahlungsverkehr, elektronischer in Verbindung mit einem POS-System	**electronic funds transfer at the POS**
Zahlungsverzug	**default in (of) payment**
Zahlungsverzug	**delay in/of payment**
Zahlungsweise	**mode of payment**
Zahlungsziel	**credit**
Zahlungsziele	**terms of payment**
Zauderer	**laggard**
Zeichen, eingebranntes	**brand**

Zeilenabstand	**line spacing**
Zeilenpreis	**line rate**
Zeilenzahl	**lineage**
Zeit für Gesamtarbeitsvorgang	**cycle time**
Zeit, Rentabilität der investierten	**return on time invested**
Zeit, bei der Autofahrer Radio hört	**drive time**
Zeit, berechenbare	**billable time**
Zeit, zu der ein Hotelzimmer geräumt sein muß	**checkout**
Zeitablauf	**lapse of time**
Zeitabstand zwischen Werbung für Konkurrenzprodukte	**commercial protection**
Zeitbegrenzung	**time-out**
Zeitdauer einer Werbesendung	**timelength**
Zeitkarte	**season ticket**
Zeitlimit	**time limit**
Zeitlupe	**slow motion**
Zeitmanagement	**time management**
Zeitnutzen	**time utility**
Zeitplan	**schedule**
Zeitpräferenz	**time preference**
Zeitpräferenzrate, positive	**positive rate of time preference**
Zeitschrift	**magazine**
Zeitschrift	**periodical**
Zeitschrift, Anzeigenteil einer	**advertising section**
Zeitschrift, minderwertige	**low-class magazine**
Zeitschriftenwerbung	**magazine advertising**
Zeitsegment	**daypart/day part**
Zeitsegment	**time segment**
Zeitspanne	**lapse**
Zeitung	**newspaper**
Zeitung	**paper**
Zeitung im Normalformat	**standard newpaper**
Zeitung, Anzeigenteil einer	**advertising section**
Zeitung, kleinformatige	**tabloid**
Zeitungsbeilage	**newspaper insert**
Zeitungskiosk	**newsstand**
Zeitungskopf	**masthead**
Zeitungskopfanzeige	**title corner**
Zeitungsstand	**newsstand**
Zeitungswerbung	**newspaper advertising**
Zeitungswesen	**press**
Zeitvorteil	**time utility**
Zeitwahl	**timing**
Zeitwert	**current value**
Zeitwert	**going value**
Zeitwert	**market value**
Zeitwert	**present value**
Zentner, ca.	**hundredweight**
Zentralbank von England	**Bank of England**

Zentraleinkauf	**central purchasing**
Zentraleinkauf	**central(ised) buying**
Zentralgenossenschaft	**cooperative wholesale society**
Zentralwert	**median**
Zentrierung	**centring**
zerbrechlich	**fragile**
Zerlegen einer Warensendung	**breaking bulk**
zerlegt	**knocked down (KD, kd)**
zerlegt, vollständig	**completely knocked down**
Zertifizierungsverfahren ISO 9000	**ISO 9000**
Ziel	**target**
Ziel, auf ... kaufen/verkaufen	**credit**
Ziel-Aufgaben-Methode	**objective and task method**
Ziel-Aufgaben-Methode	**task method**
Ziele, makroökonomische	**macroeconomic aims**
Zielerreichung	**achievement of objectives**
Zielgruppe	**target group**
Zielgruppe, soziale	**aspirational group**
Zielgruppen, Marketing für breite	**mass marketing**
Zielgruppen-Kommunikation	**narrowcasting/narrow casting**
Zielgruppeneinteilung nach Wertvorstellungen und Lebensstil	**values and lifestyles**
Zielgruppenindex	**target group index**
Zielkonzeption	**creative strategy in advertising**
Zielmarkt	**target market**
Zielpreis	**target price**
Zielpublikum	**target audience**
Zielrealisierung	**achievement of objectives**
Zielsetzung der Werbung	**advertising objective**
Zielverkauf	**credit sale**
Zitrone	**lemon**
Zoll	**tariff**
Zolltarif	**tariff**
Zone	**zone**
Zonenpreissystem	**zone pricing**
Zubringer	**feeder**
Zudringlichkeit	**intrusiveness**
Zufallsauswahl	**random sampling**
Zufallsfehler	**random error**
Zufallsleser	**tertiary reader**
Zufallsstichprobenauswahl	**random sampling**
Zufallstreuung (Werbung)	**blanket coverage**
Zufallsvariable	**random variable**
Zufriedenheit	**satisfaction**
Zugabe	**gift**
Zugabe	**free merchandise**
Zugabe (Produkt)	**premium product**
Zugabe, eingepackte	**in-pack premium**
Zugabeartikel zum Selbstkostenpreis	**self-liquidating offer (SLO)**
Zugabeartikel zum Selbstkostenpreis	**self-liquidator**

Zugabepackung	**bonus pack**
Zugabepackung	**premium pack**
Zugänglichkeit	**accessibility**
Zugang durch Dritte	**third party access**
Zugangsbeschränkung	**barrier to entry**
Zugeständnis	**concession**
Zuhause-Publikum	**at/in-home audience**
Zuhausebefragung	**door to door interview**
Zuhausebefragung	**in-home interview**
Zukunftsforschung	**futurology**
Zukunftsindustrie	**sunrise industry**
Zukunftsschock	**future shock**
Zulassung	**licence**
Zulieferant	**component supplier**
Zulieferbetrieb	**commission manufacturer**
Zulieferbetrieb	**supplier**
Zulieferer	**commission manufacturer**
Zulieferer	**component supplier**
Zulieferer	**supplier**
Zulieferungen	**supplies**
Zuliefervertrag	**subcontract/sub-contract**
Zurückbehaltungsrecht	**lien**
Zurückbehaltungsrecht des Verkäufers	**vendor's lien**
Zurücknahme von Preiserhöhungen	**rollback**
Zurückstellung	**abstinence**
Zurückstellung	**deferment**
Zusage	**commitment**
Zusammenarbeit	**cooperation**
Zusammenbruch	**collapse**
Zusammenbruch	**crash**
Zusammenfassen von Aufträgen	**pooling of orders**
Zusammenprallplanung	**impact scheduling**
Zusammenschluß unabhängiger kommerzieller Fernsehstationen (GB)	**Independent Television**
Zusammenschluß, horizontaler	**horizontal integration**
Zusammenschluß, monopolistischer	**pool**
Zusammenstellung einer Bestellung	**order picking**
Zusatz	**additive**
Zusatzauflage	**bonus circulation**
Zusatzprodukt	**augmented product**
Zusatzservice	**supplementary service**
Zusatzsteuer	**surcharge**
Zuschauer	**viewer**
Zuschauer(schaft)	**audience**
Zuschauer, Gesamtzahl der	**total audience**
Zuschauer, potentieller	**potential viewer**
Zuschauer, seltener	**light viewer**
Zuschaueranalyse	**audience measurement**
Zuschauerschaft, Prozentsatz der	**share of audience**
Zuschauerzahl, durchschnittliche	**average audience**

Zuschauerzähler	**peoplemeter**
Zuschlag	**acceptance**
zusenden	**consign**
Zustandsbericht	**situation report (sitrep)**
Zustellbote	**carrier**
Zustellgebühr	**fee for service**
Zustellkosten	**delivery expenses**
Zustellung frei Haus	**delivery free**
Zustimmungspost	**applause mail**
Zutatenangabe	**nutritional labelling**
Zuteilung	**allocation**
Zuteilung	**rationing**
Zutrittsbarrieren	**access barriers**
Zuverlässigkeit	**reliability**
Zwang zur Abnahme eines ganzen Sortiments	**full line forcing**
Zwang zur Produktabnahme	**forcing**
Zwangssparen	**forced saving**
Zwangsverkauf	**forced sale**
Zwangsverkauf	**hammer**
Zwangsversteigerung	**forced sale**
Zwangswahlverfahren	**forced choice method**
Zweifarbenanzeige	**two colour (2C) advertisement**
Zweiggeschäft	**branch store**
Zweigniederlassung	**branch**
Zweigstelle	**branch**
Zweimonatspublikation	**bimonthly**
Zweiprodukttest	**diadic (product) test**
Zweitbest-Theorie	**theory of the second best**
Zweitbesuch	**follow-up**
Zweitinserat	**readvertisement**
Zweitleser	**actual non-buyer reader**
Zweitleser	**nonbuyer-reader**
Zweitleser	**secondary reader**
Zweitname	**secondary meaning**
Zweiwochenpublikation	**biweekly**
Zwischenhändler	**distributor**
Zwischenhändler	**intermediary**
Zwischenhändler	**middleman**
Zwischenprodukt	**intermediate product**
Zwischenverkauf vorbehalten, freibleibend	**subject to (prior) sale**
Zyklus	**cycle**

Abbreviations used in marketing:

A

A/C, A/c, a/c	account	Kunde, Geschäftsbeziehung, Konto
A/O, a/o	account of	auf Rechnung von
A/P	account purchase(s)	Einkaufs(ab)rechnung eines (Einkaufs)Kommissionärs
A/S	account sales	Verkaufs(ab)rechnung eines (Verkaufs)Kommissionärs
A/S ratio	advertising-to-sales ratio	Verhältnis von Werbeaufwand zu Verkäufen/Absatz/Umsatz
A/W, a/w	alternate weeks	Werbung jede zweite Woche
AA	Advertising Association	Werbefachverband (GB)
AA, aa	average audience	durchschnittliche Hörerzahl, Zuschauerzahl
AAD	at a discount	Diskontpreis, mit Rabatt/Skonto, unter Pari/Nennwert
AAF	American Advertising Federation	Amerikanischer Werbefachverband
ABC	American Broadcasting Company	ABC (große Radio- and Fernsegesellschaft, USA)
ABC	Audit Bureau of Circulation	unabhängige Organisation zur Kontrolle der Auflagenziffern von Zeitungen und Zeitschriften
AC	adult contemporary	Radioprogramm für nichtjugendliche bzw. ältere Erwachsene
AC	agency commission	Mittlerprovision für Werbeagentur (meist 15%) vom Anzeigen- oder Werbespotpreis
AC	average costs	Durchschnittskosten, Stückkosten
acc	acceptance	Akzeptanz, Zuschlag, (Waren)Annahme
acce	acceptance	Akzeptanz, Zuschlag, (Waren)Annahme
acct	account	Kunde, Geschäftsbeziehung
ACF	absolutely chlorine free	total chlorfrei
ACG	Address coding guide	Postleitzahlenbuch
ACK	acknowledg(e)ment	Bestätigung
acktg	acknowledg(e)ment	Bestätigung
ACM	automatic checkout machine	automatisches Scanner-Kassensystem, kundenbedientes Einkaufssystem

ACORN	A Classification Of Residential Neighbourhoods	ACORN (Wohngegendklassifikation)
AD	art director	Art-Direktor, Chef-Layouter
AD	aggregate demand	Gesamtnachfrage, aggregierter Bedarf
ad	advertisement	Anzeige, Werbung, Reklame
ad	advertising	Werbung, Reklame
ad val	ad valorem	dem Werte nach
ADD	address	Adresse, Anschrift
ADI	area of dominant influence	Hauptsendegebiet
ADOGA	attention, desire, organization, gift, address	Formel der Direktwerbung (Aufmerksamkeit erzeugen, Kaufwunsch wecken, Verkaufsorganisation, Geschenk anbieten, richtige Adresse)
ADRMP	auto-dial recorded message player	automatisches Selbstwähl- und Aufzeichnungsgerät, Werbeautomat
adv frt	advance freight	Frachtvorauszahlung
advert	advertisement	Anzeige, Werbung, Reklame
AE	account executive	(Werbe)Kontakter, Sachbearbeiter eines Werbeetats Kontaktgruppenleiter
AF	advance freight	Frachtvorauszahlung, Frachtvorschuß
AFA	Advertising Federation of America	amerikanische Organisation von Werbetreibenden
AFC	average fixed cost	durchschnittliche Fixkosten
AFS	audience flow system	Programmflußstrategie mit dem Ziel, die Empfänger am Sender zu halten
AGB	any good brand	eine/jede gute Qualität
agcy	agency	Agentur
AGL	acceptable quality level	ausreichendes Qualitätsniveau, Gutgrenze
agt	agent	Agent, Bevollmächtigter, Vertreter, Beauftragter, Makler, Kommissionär
agy	agency	Agentur
AI	artificial intelligence	künstliche Intelligenz (KI)
AIA	average issue audience	durchschnittliche Leserzahl pro Ausgabe
AIDAS	attention, interest, desire, satisfaction	AIDAS
AIDCA	awareness, interest, desire, conviction, action	AIDCA
AIDCAS	attention, interest, desire, conviction, action, satisfaction	AIDCAS
AIO	attitudes towards, interests in, and opinions of	AIO

AIR	average issue readership	durchschnittliche Leserzahl pro Ausgabe
AM	account manager	Account-/Kunden-Manager
AMA	American Marketing Association	American Marketing Association, amerikanischer Marketing Verband
AMD	aggregte monetary demand	monetäre Gesamtnachfrage, Gesamtgeldbedarf
amt	amount	Betrag, Summe, Menge
AN	advice note	Versandanzeige, -avis
ANF	arrival notification form	(Fracht)Eingangsbenachrichtigung, Warenankunftsavis
ANSI	American National Standards Institute	Institution des amerikanischen Normenverbandes (DIN vergleichbar)
AOR	agency of record	federführende Agentur
AP	answer print	Original(werbe)film
AP	aggregate production	Gesamtproduktion
APC	average propensity to consume	(durchschnittliche) Konsumquote (C/Y)
approx.	approximate(ly)	ungefähr, circa
APS	average propensity to save	(durchschnittliche) Sparquote (S/Y)
APX	adpage exposure	Anzahl der Werbekontakte oder Werbeanstöße, Anzeigenseitenkontakt
AR	advice of receipt	Rückschein
AR	average revenue	Durchschnittserlös, durchschnittlicher Ertrag
ARB	Advertising Review Board	amerikanischer Werberat
AS	aggregate supply	Gesamtangebot, aggregiertes Angebot
ASA	Advertising Standards Authority	Werberat, Selbstkontrollorgan der Werbewirtschaft (GB)
asap	as soon as possible	umgehend, baldmöglichst
ASP	American Selling Price	amerikanischer Verkaufspreis (US-Zollbewertung nach dem inländischen Verkaufspreis; nicht nach Incoterms)
ASP	adjusted selling price	berichtigter Verkaufspreis
assn	association	(Interessen)Verband
Assoc	association	(Interessen)Verband
ATC	average total cost	durchschnittliche Gesamtkosten
ATR	awareness-trial-repeat	ATR-Modell (Bewußtsein, Probe, Wiederkauf)
attn	attention	Aufmerksamkeit, Beachtung
AU	advertising unit	standardisierte Anzeigenvorlage (kann durch eingefügte Produkt/Firmennamen individualisiert werden

AV	ad valorem	dem Werte nach
av	average	arithmetischer Mittelwert, Durchschnitts...
av	audiovisual commercial	Standardwerbesendung, audiovisuelle Werbung
AVD	annual volume discount	Umsatzbonus, Mengenrabatt auf Jahresbasis
avg	average	arithmetischer Mittelwert, Durchschnitts...
AVR	agent`s vehicle record	Vertreterfahrtenbuch

B

B&W, b&w	black and white	Schwarzweiß
B/W, b/w	black and white	Schwarzweiß
BAM	bulk air mail	Massenluftpost
BB	bulletin board	Anschlag-, Anzeigenbrett
BC, b/c	bulk cargo	Massenfrachtgut, Schüttgutladung
BC, bc	back cover	(Buch)Rücken, letzte/vierte Umschlagseite, U4
BC	budgetary control	Budgetkontrolle
BCA	benefit-cost-analysis	Nutzen-Kosten-Analyse
BCU	big close-up	Großaufnahme, Nahaufnahme
BD	brand development	Marktanteil einer Marke, Markenkonsumanteil
BDI	brand development index	Markenkonsumindex
bdle	bundle	Bund, Bündel
BEP	breakeven point	Breakeven-Punkt, Gewinn- oder Ertragsschwelle, Kostendeckungspunkt, Nutzenschwelle
BF, bf	boldface	Halbfettdruck, Fettdruck
BG	background	Hintergrund, Zusammenhang; Kulisse
BIS	basis incentive system	kontinuierliches Anreiz-Verkaufsförderungssystem für Verkaufspersonal
Bkg	breakage	Bruch-Schaden, Refaktie
bkge	brokerage	Maklergebühr, Provision, Courtage, Maklergeschäft
bl	barrel	Faß, Tonne, Barrel (Hohlmaß)
BNF	Brand Names Foundation	Warenzeichenstiftung (USA)
BOGOF	buy one - get one free	bei Kauf eines Produkts, gibt es ein weiteres kostenlos
BPI	brand potential index	Index des Markenpotentials
BPI	buying power index	Kaufkraftindex

BPSR	big profits, slow returns	große Gewinne, langsame Umsätze; hohe Rendite, langsamer Umschlag
BRC	business reply card	(bezahlte) Rückantwort
BRE	business reply envelope	(bezahlte) Rückantwort, Freiumschlag, Rückumschlag
BRI	brand rating index	Markenbewertungsindex
brl	barrel	Faß, Tonne, Barrel (Hohlmaß)
BRM	business reply mail	Rückantwort, Freiumschlag
bsh	bushel	Scheffel, Bushel (Hohlmaß)
BSI	British Standards Institution	Britischer Normenverband, Normenausschuß (GB)
BTA	best time available	günstigste Werbezeit
bu	bushel	Scheffel, Bushel (Hohlmaß)
bush	bushel	Scheffel, Bushel (Hohlmaß)
bx	box	Kiste, Kasten
bxs	boxes	Kisten

C

C	consumption	Konsum, Verbrauch
c	case	Kiste
c	coupon	Bon, Gutschein
C + C	cash and carry	Verkauf gegen Barzahlung bei eigenem Transport, Selbstabholung gegen Kasse Cash und Carry - Geschäft
C + F FO	cost and freight, free out	Kosten, Fracht und Entladekosten bezahlt
C of C	chamber of commerce	(Industrie- und) Handelskammer
C/F, c/f	carriage forward	Fracht zahlt Empfänger, unfrei
C/N	credit note	Gutschriftsanzeige, Gutschrift
C/N	consignment note	Frachtbrief
C/nee	consignee	Empfänger, Konsignatar
c/o	care of	per Adresse, bei/in Firma
C/P	carriage paid	frachtfrei, Fracht bezahlt, Fracht vorausbezahlt
C/R	carrier`s risk	Risiko des Spediteurs, Frachtführers
c/w	commercial weight	Handelsgewicht
C/Y	propensity to consume	Konsumneigung, Konsumquote
c & a effect	cheap and awful effect	cheap and awful (billig und schrecklich) Effekt
CAAS	computer-aided advertising system	computergestützte Werbung
CAB	Citizens Advice Bureau	Bürgerberatungsbüro
CAI	computer-assisted interviewing	computerunterstützte Befragung

CAP	Code of Advertising Practice	Werberichtlinien, (ethische) Richtlinien für gute Werbung
CAPR	computer-aided public relations	computergestützte PR-Arbeit
carr fwd	carriage forward	Fracht zahlt Empfänger, unfrei
carr pd	carriage paid	frachtfrei, Fracht bezahlt
CAS	computer-aided selling	computergestützte Vertriebssteuerung mit Verkaufsmanagement
CASM	computer-aided space management	computergestützte Raumoptimierung bei Ladeneinrichtung und Warenpräsentation
CAT	computer-assisted trading	computergestützter Handel
cat	catalog(ue)	Katalog, Verzeichnis, Prospekt
CATI	computer-assisted telephone interview	computergestützte Telefonbefragung
CATS	computer-assisted trading system	computergestütztes Handelssystem
CATV	cable television	Kabelfernsehen
CB	container base	Containerfrachtladestelle
CBA	cost-benefit analysis	Kosten-Nutzen-Analyse
CBD	central business district	(Haupt)Geschäftsviertel, Innenstadt
CBD, cbd	cash before delivery	Barzahlung vor Lieferung
CBO	confirmation of broadcast order	Reservierungsbestätigung für Werbezeit
CBS	Columbia Broadcasting System	CBS (große Radio- und Fernsehgesellschaft, USA)
CBS	cash before shipment	Barzahlung vor Versand
CC	controlled circulation	kontrollierter Versand bei Mailings, unabhängige Auflagenkontrolle, Gratisverteilung, Freiversand
CC	cancellation clause	Kündigungsklausel
CCCC	cross-cultural consumer characteristics	kulturunabhängige Verbrauchermerkmale
CCTV	closed-circuit TV	Kabelfernsehen
CD	corporate design	einheitliches Unternehmensdesign, Gestaltung des Erscheinungsbildes des Unternehmens
CD	creative director	leitender Grafiker (in Verlag/Werbeagentur), Kreativdirektor
CD	cash discount	Skonto
CD-ROM	ready-only memory compact disc	Festspeicher-Datenträger für mulitimedialen Einsatz
CF	carriage free	frachtfrei, franko
CFS	container freight station	Containerfrachtladestelle

cge	carriage	Transport, Beförderung, Frachtkosten, Transportkosten, Rollgeld
cge paid	carriage paid	Transport bezahlt
CGI	computer generated images	Grafikgestaltung am Computer
cgo	cargo	Ladung, Fracht(gut)
ch	charge	Gebühr, Preis
ch fwd	charges forward	(per) Nachnahme, Gebühr bezahlt Empfänger
CHC	cargo handling charge(s)	Frachtladekosten
ch ppd	charges prepaid	franko, Kosten vorausbezahlt
CHR	contemporary hit radio	Radiosender, der aktuelle Popmusik/Schlagerhits spielt
CI	corporate identity	Corporate Identity (einheitliches äußeres Erscheinungsbild eines Unternehmens in der Öffentlichkeit
CIA, cia	cash in advance	Vorausbezahlung, Vorauskasse
CIS	consumer impact study	Werbeeindrucksstudie
ck	cask	Faß, Tonne
CKD, ckd	completely knocked down	vollständig zerlegt
cl	classification	Klassifikation
class	classification	Klassifikation
CLC	color laser copier	Farbkopierer
clk	clerk	Verkäufer(in)
CM	Common Market	Europäische Gemeinschaft (EG) gemeinsamer Markt
CM	contribution margin	Deckungsbeitrag
CMX	commodity exchange	Warenbörse
CNN	Cable News Network	CNN (Nachrichtensender, USA)
co	cash order	Bestellung mit vereinbarter Barzahlung
COD, cod	cash on delivery	Nachnahme, Barzahlung bei Lieferung, zahlbar bei Lieferung
COD, cod	collection on delivery	Zahlung bei Lieferung, (gegen) Nachnahme
COD, cod	collect on delivery	Zahlung bei Lieferung, (gegen) Nachnahme
cog	customer-owned goods	kundeneigene Ware
COGS, cogs	cost of goods sold	Einstandspreis (Kosten) der verkauften Ware, Wareneinsatz
COLA	cost-of-living adjustment	Lebenshaltungskostenausgleich, Teuerungsausgleich
com	commerce	Handel (Binnen- und Außenhandel)
com(m)	commission	Provision
comex	commodity exchange	Warenbörse
comi	commercial invoice	Handelsfaktura, Handelsrechnung

con	contract	Vertrag
consgt	consignment	(Waren)Sendung Konsignationsware
contr	contract	Vertrag
coop	cooperative society	Genossenschaft
COS, cos	cash on shipment	Barzahlung bei Versand, Verschiffung
COT	customer`s own transport	Transport mit Kundenfahrzeug
coty	commodity	Ware, Wirtschaftsgut
court	courtage	Courtage
cp	charges prepaid	franko, Kosten vorausbezahlt
cp	coupon	Gutschein, Einsendeabschnitt (Werbung), Kassenzettel (Beleg, Quittung), Lebensmittelkartenabschnitt
CPFF	cost-plus-fixed fee	Vertrag zu Istkosten plus fester (Gewinn)Zuschlag
CPI	cost per inquiry	Kosten pro Anfrage
CPI	consumer price index	Verbraucherpreisindex
CPM, CpM	cost per mill	Tausenderpreis (Werbung)
CPO, CpO	cost per order	Kosten pro Auftrag
CPR	cost per rating point	Kosten pro Einschaltprozentsatz
CPRP	cost per rating point	Kosten pro Einschaltprozentsatz
CPT	cost per thousand	Tausenderpreis (Werbung)
CPU	cost per unit	Stückkosten
Cr, cr	credit	Zahlungsziel, auf Kredit bzw. Ziel
cr	crate	Lattenkiste, (Latten)Verschlag, (Flaschen)Kasten
CSC	customer service center	Computerterminal zur Selbstbedienung (z.B. elektronischer Bankschalter)
CSF	critical success factors	wesentliche Erfolgsfaktoren (z.B. für Produkt oder Unternehmen)
CSI	customer satisfaction index	Kundenzufriedenheitsindex
csk	cask	Faß, Tonne
ctge	cartage	Rollgeld, Transportkosten Transport
CWD	consecutive-weeks discount	Malrabatt für Werbung
CWO, cwo	cash with order	Barzahlung bei Auftragserteilung, zahlbar bei Auftragserteilung
CWS	cooperative wholesale society	Zentral-, Großeinkaufs-genossenschaft
cwt	hundredweight	Hundredweight, (etwa) Zentner
CY	container yard	Containerterminal, Containerdepot

D

D	delivery	Ab-, Aus-, Ein-Lieferung, Lieferung (das Gelieferte) (Eigentums)Übergabe
D & O	directors and officers	Direktoren und Geschäftsführer
D/D	delivery date	Liefertermin, Lieferdatum, Abliefertermin
d/d	due date	Fälligkeitstag, Verfalltag
D/f	dead freight	Leerfracht, Fehlfracht
D/I	date of invoice	Rechnungsdatum
D/N	debit note	Debitnote, Lastschriftanzeige, Belastungsanzeige
D/O	delivery order	Lieferauftrag, Auslieferungsauftrag, -schein, Lieferschein
D/P	deferred payment	Zahlungsaufschub, gestundete Zahlung Ratenzahlung
d/s	days	Tage
DAB	digital audio broadcasting	digitaler Hörfunk in CD-Qualität, digitaler Satelliten-Rundfunk
DAGMAR	Defining Advertising Goals for Measured Advertising Results	DAGMAR
DAP	delivery against payment	Wertnachnahme
DAR	day-after recall	Day-After-Recall (DAR), Werbeerinnerung einen Tag nach dem Werbespot oder der Anzeige
DB	delayed broadcast	aufgezeichnete Sendung, zeitverschobene Übertragung
DbF	design by features	Markendesign, unverkennbares Design
dd	days after date	Verzugstage
dd	delivery date	Liefertermin
DEC	daily effective circulation	effektiver täglicher Werbemittelkontakt
def.	deferred	aufgeschoben
Dely, dely	delivery	Ab-, Aus-, Ein-Lieferung, Lieferung (das Gelieferte) (Eigentums)Übergabe
dft	draft	Zahlungsanweisung, Entwurf, Konzept
DGN	dangerous goods note	Gefahrgutschein
DI	disposable income	verfügbares Einkommen, Nettoeinkommen

DINKS, Dinks	double/dual income, no kids	Ehepaar mit doppeltem Einkommen ohne Kinder, kinderlose Doppelverdiener
DIPADA	definition, identification, proof, acceptance, desire, action	DIPADA
dir	directory	Adreßbuch, Telefonverzeichnis, Branchenverzeichnis, EDV-Inhaltsverzeichnis
dis	discount	Skonto, Rabatt, Preisnachlaß
disct	discount	Skonto, Rabatt, Preisnachlaß
DIY	do-it-yourself	Heimwerkerbedarf, Do-it-yourself
DJ	disc jockey	Diskjockey
DLO	dead letter office	Postamt für unzustellbare Briefe und Pakete
DM	direct marketing	Direktmarketing, Direktabsatz, Direktverkauf
DMA	designated market area	designiertes Marktgebiet
DMA	direct mail advertising	Post-/Direktversandwerbung, Direktwerbung durch die Post, Postwurfsendung
DMSP	dealer marketing support program	Händlermarketing-Unterstützungsprogramm
DoE	Department of the Environment	Umweltministerium (GB)
DP	data processing	Datenverarbeitung, Materialaufbereitung elektronische Datenverarbeitung
DP	dynamic positioning	dynamische Positionierung
DPI	disposable personal income	verfügbares persönliches Einkommen
DPP	direct product profit measuring	Gewinnrechnung für ein Einzelprodukt
DPP	direct product profitability	direkte Produktrentabilität
DPR	director of public relations	Leiter/in der Öffentlichkeitsarbeit
DPS	double page spread	doppelseitige Anzeige
DR	direct response	Direktantwort, Echo auf Direktwerbeaktion
Dr, dr	debtor	Schuldner, Debitor
DRTV	direct response TV	Werbespots mit eingeblendeter Telefon- oder Faxnummer, so daß Zuschauer sofort Kontakt aufnehmen kann
DRY	direct real income	reales verfügbares Einkommen
DSA	digital signature algorithm	Verschlüsselungssystem für eine rechtsgültige elektronische Unterschrift
DSD	direct store delivery	Lieferung frei Haus
DSI	dealer satisfaction index	Händler-Qualitätsindex
DSS	decision support system	Entscheidungsunterstützungs-system

DST	daylight saving time	Sommerzeit
dstn	destination	Bestimmungsort
DTI	Department of Trade and Industry	Wirtschaftsministerium (GB)
DTP	desktop publishing	Text- und Graphikgestaltug von Drucksachen am PC mit Drucker
DUP	directly unproductive profit seeking activities	direkt unproduktive auf Gewinn gerichtete Aktivitäten
DVD	digital video disc	multimediale CD
DVP	delivery versus payment	Nachnahme, Barzahlung bei Lieferung, zahlbar bei Lieferung, Wertnachnahme
Dy	delivery	Ab-, Aus-, Ein-Lieferung, Lieferung (das Gelieferte) (Eigentums)Übergabe
dz	dozen	Dutzend

E

E	effective demand	effektive, tatsächliche Nachfrage
E&OE	errors and omissions excepted	Irrtümer und Auslassungen vorbehalten
E-mail, email	electronic mail	elektronische(r) Post, Briefverkehr, E-mail
EA	editorial alteration	redaktionelle Änderung
EAAA	European Association of Advertising Agencies	Europäischer Verband der Werbeagenturen
EAN	European article number	europäische Artikelnummer
eaoe	errors and omissions excepted	Irrtümer und Auslassungen vorbehalten
EASA	European Alliance for Advertising Standards	Europäische Allianz der Werbeselbstkontrolle
EAT	European Advertising Tripartite	Europäische Dachorganisation der Werbewirtschaft (bestehend aus Werbemedien, Werbungstreibenden, Werbeagenturen)
EB	electronic book	elektronische Buch, CD-ROM
EC	European Community	Europäische Gemeinschaft (EG)
econ	economy	(Volks)Wirtschaft
ECU	extreme close-up	Großaufnahme, Nahaufnahme
ECU	European Currency Unit	Europäische Währungseinheit (ECU)
ED	every day	jeden Tag (Insertionsanweisung)
ED, Ed	elasticity of demand	Elastizität der Nachfrage, Nachfrageelastizität
ed	edition	Ausgabe
EDI	electronic data interchange	elektronischer Datenaustausch

EDLP	every day low price	Dauerniedrigpreis
EDM	European domestic market	Europäischer Binnenmarkt
EDMA	European Direct Marketing Association	Europäischer Direktwerbeverband
EDP	electronic data processing	Datenverarbeitung, Materialaufbereitung elektronische Datenverarbeitung
EE	errors excepted	Irrtümer (und Auslassungen) vorbehalten
EEA	European Economic Area	Europäischer Wirtschaftsraum (EWR)
EFS	environmental friendly strategy	umweltfreundliche Unternehmensstrategie
EFTPOS	electronic funds transfer at the point of sale	elektronischer Zahlungsverkehr in Verbindung mit einem POS-System (elektronische Abbuchung am Verkaufsortterminal, d.h. POS)
eg	exempli gratia/for example	zum Beispiel
EIA	environmental impact assessment	Umweltverträglichkeitsprüfung
EL	easy listening	leichte Unterhaltungsmusik
ELZ	economic lot size	optimale Bestellmenge, Losgröße
EM	electronic marketing	computergestütztes Marketing
EmMa	emerging market	Entwicklungsmarkt
EMR	electronic media rating	elektronische Zuschauerquotenbewertung (Radio/TV)
EMS	electronic mail system	elektronisches Postsystem (z.B. Telefon, Telefax, Btx)
EMS	express mail service	Schnellpost, Kurierdienst
EOD	every other day	jeden zweiten Tag (Insertionsanweisung)
EODTF	every other day till forbid	bis auf weiteres jeden 2. Tag
EOFA	eyes open in front of advertisement	Anzeigenbeachtung
EOI	every other issue	jede zweite Ausgabe
EOM	end-of-month	ultimo
EOQ	economic order quantity	optimale Bestellmenge, Losgröße
EOSTF	every other issue till forbid	bis auf weiteres jede zweite Ausgabe
EOW	every other week	jede zweite Woche
EOWTF	every other week till forbid	bis auf weiteres jede zweite Woche
EPA	Environmental Protection Agency	Umweltschutzbehörde (USA)
EPOS	electronic point of sale	Datenkasse, elektronischer Kassenterminal
EPQ	economic purchase quantity	optimale Beschaffungsmenge
EPT	electronic payment terminal	elektronisches Zahlungsterminal
ES, Es	elasticity of supply	Angebotselastizität, Elastizität des Angebots

ESL	electronic shelf label	elektronische Preisauszeichnung am Regal
est	estimate	Kostenvoranschlag
ETA	estimated time of arrival	geschätzte, voraussichtliche Ankunftszeit
ETD	estimated time of departure	voraussichtliche Abfahrtszeit
ETV	educational TV	Lehrfernsehprogramm
EU	European Union	Europäische Union (EU)
EVC	economic value to the customer	wirtschaftlicher Wert für den Kunden
EVR	electronic video recording	elektronische Bildaufzeichnung
ex	exchange	Aus-, Ein-, Umtausch, Tauschgeschäft
ex stk	ex stock	ab Lager
ex whse	ex warehouse	ab Lager, ab Werk
exch	exchange	Aus-, Ein-, Umtausch, Tauschgeschäft
exp	expenses	Kosten, Aufwand, Aufwendungen, (Geld) Ausgabe(n)

F

f/d	free delivery	Lieferung frei Haus
FACS	facial action coding system	Testverfahren zur Bewertung und Auswahl des Gesichtsausdrucks einer Person in einer Werbung
FAK, fak	freight all kind(s)	Frachtkosten tarifunabhängig von Warenart
FAP	field-activated promotion	Verkaufsförderung, eingeleitet vom Außendienst
FAQ, faq	fair average quality	Faq-Qualität, Handelsgut mittlerer Art und Güte
FAR	full attention rating	effektive Einschaltquote
FCL	full container load	(volle) Container-Komplettladung
fco	franco	frei, franko
FD	forward delivery	Terminlieferung
FD	free domicile	frei Haus
FDA	Food and Drug Administration	Lebensmittelbehörde (USA)
FDA	Food and Drugs Act	Lebensmittelgesetz (GB)
ffp	fit for printing	Druckfreivermerk
fgt	freight	Frachtkosten, Beförderungskosten, befördern, verfrachten
FIFO, fifo	first-in, first-out	Fifo-Methode, "zuerst eingekauft, zuerst verbraucht" (Methode zur Bewertung der Warenbestände)

FIO, fio	free in and out	frei ein und aus, frei laden und löschen (Lieferklausel/FIO-Klausel)
FIS	free in store	frei Laden, Geschäft
FLC	family life cycle	Familienlebenszyklus
FM	facing matter	Anzeigenposition gegenüber redaktionellem Text
fm	fair merchantable	gute Durchschnittsware
FMCG	fast-moving consumer good	schnell umschlagendes Verbrauchsgut
FMCP	fast-moving consumer product	schnell umschlagendes Verbrauchsgut
FMV	fair market value	angemessener Marktpreis
fo	firm offer	festes, verbindliches Angebot, Festangebot
fo	for orders	bei Aufträgen, für Aufträge
FOA	free on board at airport	FOB Flughafen, frei Flughafen
foa	free on aircraft	frei Flugzeug
fob/fob	free on board free off board	frei an Bord plus frei von Bord
FOBA	FOB airport	FOB Flughafen, frei Flughafen
foc	free of charge	ohne Berechnung, kostenlos, gratis
fod	free of damage	frei von Beschädigung
FOD abs	free of damage absolutely	frei von jeglicher Beschädigung
FOQ, foq	free on quay	frei (auf) Kai
FOR, for	free on rail	frei Waggon (GB)
FOR/FOT	free on rail/free on truck	frei (franko) Waggon
FOT, fot	free on truck	frei LKW (USA), frei Waggon (GB)
FOW	free on wag(g)on	frei (franko) Waggon
fp	fully paid	voll bezahlt
FPAD	freight payable at destination	Fracht zahlbar am Bestimmungsort
FPC	film production code	freiwillige amerikanische Filmselbstkontrolle
FRC	free of reported casualty	frei von bekannten Schäden
freq	frequency	Eintrittshäufigkeit, Häufigkeit (Stat), Kontakthäufigkeit, Insertionshäufigkeit
frt	freight	Frachtkosten, Beförderungskosten, befördern, verfrachten
frt fwd	freight forward	unfrei, Fracht gegen/per Nachnahme, Fracht zahlbar am Bestimmungsort
frt ppd	freight prepaid	Fracht vorausbezahlt, frachtfrei
FSA	foreign sales agent	Auslandsverkaufsvertreter
FSI, fsi	freestanding insert	Anzeigenbeilage, Werbebeilage

FSM	fast selling merchandise	Selbstläufer, Schnelldreher, schnellverkäufliche Ware
FTA	free trade area	Freihandelsgebiet, -zone
FTC	Federal Trade Commission	US-Wettbewerbs-Aufsichtsbehörde (Kartellamt)
FTZ	free trade zone	Freihandelsgebiet, -zone
fwd	forward	weiterleiten, befördern, übersenden, transportieren
FYI	for your information	zur Kenntnisnahme

G

g	gram(me)	Gramm
GA	general agent	Generalvertreter
gal	gallon	Gallone
gbo	goods in bad order	Ware in schlechtem Zustand
GCR	general cargo rate	Frachtrate für Stückgut
GDP	gross domestic product	Bruttoinlandsprodukt (BIP)
gds	goods	Güter, Waren
GE	general equilibrium	allgemeines Gleichgewicht
gfa	good fair average	mittlere Qualität, gute Durchschnittsqualität
GHIs	guaranteed home impacts/ impressions	Mindesteinschaltquote
GHRs	guaranteed home ratings	Mindesteinschaltquote
GIN	general interest newspaper	Zeitung/Zeitschrift mit breitgefächertem Redaktionsprogramm
GM	gross margin	Bruttogewinn, Bruttohandelsspanne, Bruttomarge
Gmq	good merchantable quality	gute Handelsqualität
GNE	gross domestic expenditure	Bruttoinlandsausgaben
GNH	gross night hour	Listenpreis für einstündiges Programm während Hauptsendezeit
GNP	gross national product	Bruttosozialprodukt (BSP)
gob	good ordinary brand	gute, gewöhnliche Sorte
GOTS	gross opportunity to see	Bruttokontaktwahrschein-lichkeit
GPO	General Post Office	Hauptpost(amt)
gr.wt.	gross weight	Bruttogewicht
GRN	goods received note	Warenannahmeschein
GRPs	gross rating points	Bruttoreichweite (Medienforschung)
GSR	galvanic skin response	Erregungsmethode
GST	goods and services tax	Waren- und Dienstleistungssteuer

H

H/H	half-height	Halb...
H/l	heavy lift	Schwergut
h.b.	hours of business	Geschäftszeiten
HBO	home box office	Heim-Kinokasse, gebührenpflichtiger TV-Kabelsender
HDTV	high definition television	hochauflösendes Fernsehen in Kinoqualität
HH	household	Haushalt
hhd	hogshead	großes Faß, Flüssigkeitsmaß
HoQ	house of quality	grafischer Stammbaum der Qualitätskriterien eines Produktes
HOT	home order television	Teleshopping, Kauf/Verkauf via Bildschirm
HP, hp	hire purchase	Ratenzahlungskauf, Teilzahlungskauf, Finanzkauf, Mietkauf
HPRP	homes per rating point	Zahl der Haushalte pro Prozentpunkt eingeschalteter Radio-/Fernsehgeräte
HQ	high quality	hohe Qualität(sstufe)
HRD	high rate discharge	hohe Ausstoßrate
HSN	homeshopping network	Verkauf per Bildschirm
HUR	households using radio	Zahl der effektiven Hörerhaushalte
HUT	households using television	Zahl der effektiven Fernsehhaushalte

I

i/c	in charge	zuständig
IAA	International Advertising Association	Internationaler Verband von Werbefachleuten
IBC	inside back cover	dritte Umschlagseite
IBI	invoice book inwards	Eingangsfakturenbuch
IBO	invoice book outwards	Ausgangsfakturenbuch
ID	identification	Identifizierung, Identifikation
IDI	idea development interview	Ideenentwicklungsinterview
ie	id est/that is	d.h.
IFC	inside front cover	zweite Umschlagseite
IMF	International Marketing Federation	Internationale Marketing-Förderation

incl	including, inclusive	einschließlich
info	information	Information
inst	instant	laufender Monat, Fertig-, Lös-, Pulvergericht
inv	inventory	Vorräte, (Lager)Bestände
inv	invoice	(Waren)Rechnung, Faktura
IRC	international reply coupon	internationaler Rückantwortschein
IRP	index of retail prices	Index der Lebenshaltungskosten, Einhelhandels(preis)index
IS	information seeker	informationsaktiver Verbraucher
ISO	International Standards Organization	Internationaler Normenausschuß (ISO)
ITV	Independent Television	Zusammenschluß unabhängiger kommerzieller Fernsehstationen (GB)
iv	invoice value	Rechnungswert, Fakturawert

J

JIT	just in time	fertigungssynchrone Materialwirtschaft
JND	just noticeable difference	kaum wahrnehmbarer Unterschied
JV	joint venture	Joint Venture, Gmeinschafts-unternehmen

K

KBI	key buying influencer	Schlüssel-Kaufentscheidungsträger, (Haupt)Meinungsmacher
KD, kd	knocked down	zerlegt
KDM	key decision maker	Schlüssel-Kaufenscheidungsträger, (Haupt)Meinungsmacher
KISS, kiss	keep it simple, stupid	KISS-Formel
KISS, kiss	keep it short and simple	Werbetheorie: Werbung muß kurz, einfach und leichtverständlich sein; KISS-Formel

L

l.g.	low-grade	mindere Qualität
LC, lc	lowercase	Kleinbuchstabe
LCL	less than carload lot	weniger als Wagenladung, Stückgut(Sendung)

LCL	less than container load	Teil-Containerladung
LDC	less developed country	Entwicklungsland
ldg	loading	Auf-, Be-, Verladen, Befrachtung
LFTV	less than fair value	weniger als der angemessene Wert
lg	low grade	mindere Qualität
LI	letter of intent	schriftliche Absichtserklärung
LIFO, lifo	last in, first out	zuletzt herein (eingkauft), zuerst hinaus (verbraucht); Lifo-Methode der Vorratsbewertung
LISH, lish	last in still here	Fifo-Methode, "zuerst eingekauft, zuerst verbraucht" (Methode zur Bewertung der Warenbestände)
lkg	leakage	Leckage, Rinnverlust, Sicherverluste, Sicherquote
Lkge + Bkge	leakage + breakage	Leckage und Bruch
LMT	limit	limitierter Auftrag
LoB	line of business	Branche, Sparte
loh	lady of the house	Hausherrin, Hausfrau
LOI	letter of intent	schriftliche Absichtserklärung
LPU	least publishable unit	kleinste veröffentlichungsfähige Einheit
lslf	looseleaf	Lose-Blatt ....
LT	last telecast	letzter Sendetermin
lt	local time	Ortszeit
LTL	less than truckload	LKW-Stückgut

M

M and E	music and sound effects	Musik- und Toneffekte
M.sh.	merchant ship	Handelsschiff
M/D, m/d	month(s) after date	Monat(e) nach Datum
M`dise	merchandise	Handelsware, Ware(n), Verkaufssteuerung, Angebotsoptimierung
manfr	manufacturer	Hersteller(firma), Erzeuger, Produzent
manufg	manufacturing	Fertigung, Herstellung, Produktion
MAT, mat	material	Material, Stoff, Gewebe
MBO	management by objective(s)	Management nach Zielvorgabe und Zielkontrolle (MBO)
MC	marginal cost	Grenzkosten
mcht	merchant	Kaufmann, (Groß-, Einzel-) Händler
MDI	market development index	Marktanteilindex einer Produktkategorie

mdse	merchandise	Handelsware, Ware(n), Verkaufssteuerung, Angebotsoptimierung
MEC	marginal efficiency of capital	Grenzleistungsfähigkeit des Kapitals
mf	manufacturer	Hersteller(firma), Erzeuger, Produzent
MFC	marginal factor cost	Faktorgrenzkosten
mfd	manufactured	hergestellt, produziert
mfg	manufacturing	Fertigung, Herstellung, Produktion
mfr	manufacturer	Hersteller, Produzent
MG	makegood	Ersatzsinserat, Ersatzspot
MHS	message handling systems	direkte persönliche Mitteilungssysteme (z.B. Fax)
MIS	Marketing information system	Marketing-Informationssystem
mkt	market	Markt, Handelsplatz, Börse, Nachfrage
ml	mail	Post(sendung)
MMC	Monopolies (and Mergers) Commission	Kartellaufsichtsbehörde, Monopolkommission (GB)
MMQ	minimum manufacturing quantity	minimale Losgröße
MO	mail order	Postversandauftrag, Postbestellung, Mail-Order
MOR	middle-of-the-roader	Unternehmen mit breitgefächerter Marketingstrategie, breitgefächerter Radiosender
MoR ware	middle-of-the-road ware	Massenware
mp	month(s) after payment	Monat(e) nach Zahlung
MPA	multiple product announcement	Werbesendung für mehrere Produkte
MPC	marginal propensity to consume	marginal Konsumquote, Grenzkonsumneigung
MPS	marginal propensity to save	marginale Sparquote, Grenzneigung zum Sparen
MR	marginal revenue	Grenzerlös
MR	manufacturer`s representative	Handelsvertreter, Werksvertreter
MR	motivation research	Motivforschung
MRP	manufacturer`s recommended price	Preisempfehlung des Herstellers, emphohlener Herstellerpreis
MRP	materials requirements planning	Materialbedarfsplanung
MRS	marginal rate of substitution	Grenzrate der Substitution
MS	manuscript	Manusskript
MS	market share	Marktanteil
MU	marginal utility	Grenznutzen
MV	merchant vessel	Handelsschiff
MV, mv	market value	Börsenwert, Kurswert, Markt-, Tages-, Zeitwert

N

n/a	not applicable	nicht zutreffend, entfällt (in Formularen)
n/a	nonacceptance	Ausnahmeverweigerung, Nichtannahme
N/C	no charge	kostenlos, gratis, gebührenfrei
N/o	no orders	keine Aufträge
N/R	no risk	kein Risiko
N/S	newsstand	Zeitungsstand, Zeitungskiosk
N/t	net terms	Nettokonditionen
N	new	neu
Na	nonacceptance	Ausnahmeverweigerung, Nichtannahme
NAB	National Association of Broadcasters	Verband der Rundfunk- und Fernsehstationen (USA)
NAC	net advertising circulation	effektive Nettoauflage, Nettozahl der Personen mit Anschlagwerbemittelkontakt
NARB	National Advertising Review Board	Werberat (USA)
NBC	National Broadcasting Company	NBC (große Radio- und Fernsehgesellschaft, USA)
NCV, ncv	no commercial value	ohne wirtschaftlichen Wert
ND	no discount	kein Nachlaß/Rabatt/Skonto
nd	non delivery	Nicht(aus)lieferung
NDP	net domestic product	Nettoinlandsprodukt
Nettaps	net ad produced purchases	durch Werbung ausgelöste Käufe
NFD	no fixed date	kein festes Datum, kein fester Termin
NI	national income	Volkseinkommen, Nettosozialprodukt zu Faktorpreisen
NL	no liability	keine Haftung
NME	nonmarket economy	nicht-marktwirtschaftlich orientierte Wirtschaft
NNI	net national income	Nettovolkseinkommen
NNP	net national product	Nettoinlandsprodukt
NO, no	number	Nummer
NOI	net operating income	Nettobetriebsgewinn
NOL	net operating loss	Nettobetriebsverlust
NOP	net orders processed	Nettoverkäufe, Nettoumsatz
NOP	net operating profit	Nettobetriebsgewinn
nop	not otherwise provided	vorbehaltlich anderweitiger/ anderslautender Bestimmungen
NOS	not otherwise specified	nicht anderweitig spezifiziert
not.	notice	Information, Aufmerksamkeit, Ankündigung

np	net proceeds	Nettoerlös
NPV	net present value	Kapitalwert
NR	next to reading	neben Text, textanschließend
NR	no risk	kein Risiko
NRM	next to reading matter	neben Text, textanschließend
NRP	net rating point	Nettoreichweitenprozentpunkt
NS	not specified	nicht spezifiziert
NT, nt	net terms	Nettokonditionen
nt wt	net weight	Netto-, Reingewicht
NTBs	nontariff barriers	nichttarifäre, zollfremde Handelshemmnisse

O

O	output	Output, Ausbringung, Produktion
O, o	order	Auftrag, Bestellung
O.D.	on demand	auf Anfordern
o.o.	on order	bestellt
o.s., o/s	out of stock	ausverkauft, nicht vorrätig, nicht am Lager
o/a	on account	gegen Kredit, für Rechnung, als Teilzahlung
O/A, o/a	open account	offenes Konto, offene Rechnung
o/c	overcharge	zu hohe Berechnung, zu viel berechnen
o/d	on demand	auf Anfordern
O/N	order number	Auftragsnummer
o/o	on order	bestellt
o/s	out of stock	ausverkauft, nicht vorrätig
o/t	on truck	auf LKW
o/tor	on truck or railway	auf LKW oder Bahn
OAT	on-air-test	Werbetest mit gesendeter Werbesendung
OBC	outside back cover	vierte Umschlagseite
OCR	optical character recognition	optische Zeichenerkennung durch elektronisches Lesegerät
OE	original equipment	Originalausstattung
OEM	original equipment manufacturing	Auftragsproduktion unter der Originalmarke eines anderen Herstellers
OEM	original equipment manufacturer	Erstausrüster, Original Equipment Manufacturer (OEM)
OFC	outside front cover	erste Umschlagseite, Titelseite
off	offer	Angebot
OFT	Office of Fair Trading	Amt für Verbraucherschutz (GB)
OMA	orderly marketing arrangements	Vereinbarungen über Vertrieb und Verkauf
on appro	on approval	zur Ansicht, auf Probe

ONO, ono	or near offer	Verhandlungsbasis (VHB, VB)
OOQ	optimum order quantity	optimale Bestellmenge
op	out of print	vergriffen
OPM	other peoples money	anderer Leute Geld
OR	operations research	Operations Research (OR), Operationsforschung
OR	operational research	Operations Research (OR), Operationsforschung
orb	owner`s risk of breakage	Bruchrisiko des Eigentümers
Ord, ord	order	Auftrag, Bestellung
os, o/s	out of stock	ausverkauft, nicht vorrätig
OTC	over the counter	rezeptfreie, nicht verschreibungspflichtige Medikamente; nicht ethische Arzneimittel, über den Tresen
OTH	opportunity to hear	Kontaktwahrscheinlichkeit mit einer Radio(werbe)sendung
OTO	one time only	einmal gesendete Programm- oder Werbesendung
OTS	opportunity to see	Kontaktchance/Kontaktwahr-scheinlichkeit mit einer Fernseh(werbe)sendung
oz	ounce	Unze

P

p	page	Seite
p	penny	Penny (Münze) (GB), Centstück (USA)
P & H	postage and handling	Porto und Bearbeitung
P&D	pick up and delivery	Übernahme und Auslieferung
p&p	postage and packing	Porto und Verpackung
P+H	postage and handling	Porto und Bearbeitung
P/C	per cent (percent)	Prozent
P/C	petty cash	kleine Kasse, Nebenkasse
P/C, p/c	price current	gültiger Preis, Preisliste, Preisverzeichnis
p/i	pro forma invoice	Proforma-Rechnung, vorläufige Rechnung
P/L	product liability	Produkthaftung
P/L	partial loss	Teilverlust, -schaden
P/O	purchase order	Kaufauftrag, Bestellung
P/S	public sale	Versteigerung, Auktion
PA	personal assistant	persönlicher Assistent
pa	per annum	jährlich, pro Jahr
PAT	product acceptance test	Akzeptanztest für ein Produkt, Produktakzeptanztest

pat	patent	Patent
patt	pattern	Muster
payt	payment	Zahlung (bezahlte Summe) (Be-, Ein-, Aus-)Zahlung
pc	per cent	Prozent
pc(t)	per cent	Prozent
PC, pc	prime cost	direkte (variable) Kosten, (Fertigungs)Einzelkosten
pchsr	purchaser	Käufer, Erwerber, Abnehmer
PD	public domain	urheberrechtlich nicht geschütztes Werk
PD	prompt delivery	sofortige Lieferung
PD	physical distribution	physische Distribution/Warenverteilung
pd	paid	bezahlt
PDI	pre-delivery inspection	Kontrolle vor Warenabnahme
PDM	physical distribution management	Vertriebsleitung
PDMS	Postal Direct Marketing Service	Vereinbarung europäischer Postverwaltungen zur Förderung der Direktwerbung
pdn	production	Produktion, Fertigung, Herstellung, Output, Produktionsausstoß, Vorlage
PE	printer`s error	Druckfehler
p.e.	probable error	wahrscheinliche(r) Fehler/Abweichung
PEST	political, economic, social, technological	PEST-Faktor
PI	per inquiry (advertising)	Werbung auf Anfragebasis
PIK	payment in kind	Sachleistung
PIMS	profit impact of market strategy	Gewinnträchtigkeit einer Marktstrategie, PIMS
pkg	package	Kollo, Packstück, Postpaket, Packung
PL & R	postal laws and regulations	Postgesetze und -vorschriften
PLC	product life cycle	Produktlebenszyklus
PM	push money	Verkaufsförderungsprämie
Pm, pm	premium	von besonders guter Qualität, Preis
PMA	primary marketing area	Hauptverbreitungsgebiet, Hauptabsatzgebiet
Pn	production	Produktion, Fertigung, Herstellung, Output, Produktionsausstoß, Vorlage
PNR	proved name registration	nachgeprüfte Werbeerinnerung, validierte Namenserinnerung
PO	Post Office	Post
POA	point of animation	Ort, der Spaß macht
POA	place of acceptance	Annahmeort

POB	post office box	Postschließfach
POD	point of decision	Ort der Kaufentscheidung
POD	place of delivery	Lieferort
POD	payment on delivery	zahlbar bei Lieferung, Wertnachnahme
pod	payable on delivery	zahlbar bei Lieferung
POF	point of fun	Ort, der Spaß macht
POI	point of information	Informationsort
POISE	profitable, offensive, integrated, strategic, effective	POISE-Formel
POJ	point of joy	Ort, der Spaß macht
POP	printing-out paper	Kopierpapier
POP	point-of-purchase	Einkaufsort, Verkaufsförderungsmaterial
POPA	point-of-purchase advertising	Werbung am Verkaufsort
Popn	population	Bevölkerung, Einwohnerzahl
POR	place of receipt	Empfangsort
POS	point-of-sale	Verkaufsort, Verkaufsförderungsmaterial
POSA	point-of-sale advertising	Werbung am Verkaufsort, POS-Werbung
POSS	POS system	Kassenterminal, POS-Terminal
POSS	point of sale system	Daten(erfassungs)kasse, Computerkasse, POS-System
POST	point of sale terminal	Kassenterminal, POS-Terminal
POST	POS terminal	Daten(erfassungs)kasse, POS-System
p.p.	postpaid	im voraus bezahlt, Porto bezahlt
ppd	prepaid	vorausbezahlt
PPI	producer price index	Großhandelspreisindex
PPP	purchasing power parity	Kaufkraftparität
PPR	performance price recognition	Preis-Leistungs-Verhältnis bei der Messung des Erinnerungswertes von Werbung
ppt	prompt	sofort
PPV	pay-per-view	Pay per View; Abo-TV, bei dem nur Einschaltzeit bezahlt wird
PR	public relations	Public Relations, PR-Arbeit, Öffentlichkeitsarbeit
pr	price	Preis
PRD	product research and development	Produktforschung und -entwicklung
Prem.	premium	von besonders guter Qualität, Preis
PRI	probability of receiving an impression	Kontaktwahrscheinlichkeit
PRO	public relations officer	Öffentlichkeitsmitarbeiter
PSA	public service announcement	nichtkommerzielle Werbeansage zur Öffentlichkeitsinformation

PSA	public service advertising	Werbung zur Information der Öffentlichkeit
PSB	program station basis	Programmeinschaltquote eines Senders
PSI	preshipment inspection	Inspektion vor dem Versand
PSS	professional selling skills	professionelle Verkaufsfertigkeiten
PT	purchase tax	Verbrauchssteuer
pt	payment	Zahlung (bezahlte Summe) (Be-, Ein-, Aus-)Zahlung
PTO, pto	please turn over	bitte wenden
pub	publicity	Werbung, Reklame, Publizität, Bekanntsein
PUT	persons using television	Zahl der effektiven Fernsehzuschauer
PV	potential viewer	potentieller Zuschauer
PV	present value	Marktwert, Zeitwert
PVC, pvc	price variation clause	Preisänderungsklausel
PVP	perceived value pricing	Preisbildung aus Kunden-sicht/anhand des wahrgenom-menen Wertes
PYT	payment	Zahlung (bezahlte Summe) (Be-, Ein-, Aus-)Zahlung

Q

Q	quality	Beschaffenheit, Eigenschaft, Güte, Qualität
Q	quantity	Menge, Quantität, Unmenge
Q	sales volume	Absatz(menge), Umsatzvolumen
q & a	question and answer	Frage- und Antwortspiel
QC	quality control	Qualitätskontrolle
qlty	quality	Beschaffenheit, Eigenschaft, Güte, Qualität
QM	quality measurement	Qualitätsbewertung
qnt	quantity	Menge, Quantität, Unmenge
qnty	quantity	Menge, Quantität, Unmenge
QSP	quality, service, pricing	erstklassige Qualität, zuvorkommender Kundendienst, kundenfreundliche Preisgestaltung
qt	quantity	Menge, Quantität, Unmenge
qty	quantity	Menge, Quantität, Unmenge
qu	quotation	Angebot, Kostenvoranschlag, Preisangabe
Quot	quotation	Angebot, Kostenvoranschlag, Preisangabe
Qy, qy	query	Frage, Erkundigung

R

R	return	Aufstellung, Bericht, Rücksendung, Retoure(n), Bruttoumsatzerlös
R & D	research and development	Forschung und Entwicklung
R + F	reach and frequency	Reichweite und Häufigkeit
R, r	receipt	Eingang, Empfang
r/c	return cargo	Rückladung, -fracht
RADI	radio area of dominant influence	Hörfunk-Vorherrschaftsgebiet
RBPs	restrictive business practices	restriktive Geschäftspraktiken
RC	reply coupon	Rückantwortschein
rcpt	receipt	Eingang, Empfang
rcvr	receiver	Empfänger
Re, re	with reference to	was .... betrifft
rec	receipt	Eingang, Empfang
Ref No, ref no	reference number	Bezugsnummer, Aktenzeichen
refd	refund	Rückerstattung, Rückvergütung
RELET	referring to letter	Bezugnahme auf Schreiben
rep	representative	Vertreter, Repräsentant
ret	return	Aufstellung, Bericht, Rücksendung, Retoure(n), Bruttoumsatzerlös
RFP	request for proposal	Aufforderung zur Angebotsabgabe
RFQ	request for quotation	Aufforderung zur Angebotsabgabe
rgds	regards	Grüße, Empfehlungen (bes. in Briefen)
RIC	readership involvement commitment	(Werbe)Texter-Regel: "Leser fesseln, festlegen und zur Handlung bewegen".
RICO Act	Racketeer Influenced and Corrupt Organizations Act	"Mafia-Gesetz", Gesetz, das falsche/irreführende Werbung strafbar macht (USA)
RMS	relative market share	relativer Marktanteil
RN	release note	Freigabebescheinigung
ROA	roll on advertising	Werbung an Transportfahrzeugen
ROB	run-of-book	ohne Plazierungsvereinbarung
ROCE	return on capital employed	Ertrag aus investiertem Kapital, Kapitalrentabilität
ROD	run-of-day	(Werbung läuft) im Laufe des Tages
ROG, rog	receipt of goods	Warenannahme
ROI	return on investment	Ertrag aus investiertem Kapital, Kapitalrentabilität

ROM	run-of-month	(Werbung läuft) im Laufe des Monats
ROP	run of paper	ohne Plazierungsvereinbarung
ROP	run of press	ohne Plazierungsvereinbarung
ROP	reorder point	Bestellbestand, Meldebestand
ROS	run of station	ohne Sendezeitvereinbarung
ROS	return on sales	Umsatzrentabilität, Umsatzrendite
ROTI	return on time invested	Rentabilität der investierten Zeit
ROW	run of week	(Werbung läuft) im Laufe der Woche
ROY	run of year	im Laufe des Jahres
RP	repurchase	Wiederkauf
RP	recommended price	empfohlener Preis, Richtpreis
RPC, rpc	readers per copy	Leser pro Nummer/Exemplar (LpN, LpE)
rpi	readers per issue	Leser pro Ausgabe (LpA)
RPI	General Retail Price Index	Einzelhandelspreisindex
RPI	retail price index	Einzelhandelspreisindex, Preisindex für Lebenshaltungskosten
RPM	resale price maintenance	Preisbindung der zweiten Hand, vertikale Preisbindung
RRP	radio rating point	Radioeinschaltquote
RRP	recommended retail price	empfohlener Abgabepreis, Richtpreis
RSVP	please reply (répondez s´il vous plait)	um Anwort wird gebeten (u.A.w.g.)
RT	reservation of title	Eigentumsvorbehalt
RT	retention of title	Eigentumsvorbehalt
rtn	return	Aufstellung, Bericht, Rücksendung, Retoure(n), Bruttoumsatzerlös
RTPA	Restrictive Trade Practices Act	Kartellgesetz (GB)

S

S	supply	Angebot, Lieferung, Be- und Anlieferung, Vorrat, Versorgung
s&he	sundays & holidays excepted	nicht an Sonn- und Feiertagen
s.o.	standing order	Abonnement, Kauf auf Abruf
s.o.	sine obligo	ohne Gewähr, Haftung
s/a	safe arrival	sichere Ankunft
S/n	shipping note	Versandanzeige
S/R	sale or return	Kauf mit Rückgaberecht
SAE, sae	stamped addressed envelope	adressierter Freiumschlag
SAQ	social advertising quality	soziale Qualität einer Werbung
SBU	strategic business unit	strategische Geschäftseinheit (SGE)

SC	single column	einspaltig
SC	service corporation	Dienstleistungsunternehmen
SD, sd	short delivery	unvollständige Lieferung
SD	standard deviation	Standardabweichung, mittlere quadratische Abweichung
SE	sound effect	Geräuscheffekt
SE	statistical error	statistischer Fehler
SGAs	Sale of Goods Acts	Gesetze über den Warenkauf
shpt	shipment	Versand, Verschiffung (Schiffs)Ladung, (Waren)Sendung
SI	sponsor identification	Ansage/Einblendung des Programmsponsors, Identifikationseinblendung
SI	station identification	Senderzeichen
SIC	Standard Industrial Classification	Branchenklassifikation, Produktklassifikation
SICS	Standard Industrial Classification System	Branchenklassifikation, Produktklassifikation
sitrep	situation report	Lagebericht, Zustandsbericht
SIU	sets in use	Gesamtzahl eingeschalteter Radio/TV-Geräte in bestimmtem Gebiet zu bestimmter Zeit
SKD	semi knocked down	transport- und montagegerecht zerlegt
SKU	stock-keeping unit	Einzelmarke einer Markenfamilie
SLO	self-liquidating offer	Zugabeartikel zum Selbstkostenpreis
SMP	single minded proposition	Werbebotschaft, die auf das Wesentliche reduziert ist
SO	standing order	Abonnement, Kauf auf Abruf
SoA	share of advertising	Anteil (in %) des Werbeetats vom Umsatz
SoD	service-on-demand	Inanspruchnahme von am TV-Bildschirm angebotenen Diensten
SOE	state-owned enterprise	Staatsbetrieb
SOHO	small office - home office	Markt der Kleinbetrieb-, Haus- und Privatbüros
SOL	standard of living	Lebensstandard
SOR	sale or return	Kauf mit Rückgaberecht
SPQR	small profits, quick returns	schmale Rendite, rascher Umschlag; kleine Gewinne, schnelle Umsätze
SPRGD	strategy planning for running ahead in global development	Strategie zur globalen Markführerschaft
SPV	space position value	Werbewert eines Standorts
SRP	suggested retail price	empfohlener Abgabepreis, Richtpreis

SSS	single-source-service	Alleinservice eines Lieferanten
ST	sales tax	Umsatzsteuer (USA)
STAS	short time advertising strength	Methode zur kurzfristigen Messung der Wirkung von TV-Werbung
Std	standard	Standard
STD	subscriber trunk dialling	Selbstwählferndienst
STO	standing order	Abonnement, Kauf auf Abruf
STV	subscription television	Abonnementsfernsehen
SWAT	sell what`s available today	verkaufen, was verfügbar oder vorrätig ist
sy	supply	Angebot, Lieferung, Be- und Anlieferung, Vorrat, Versorgung

T

TP&ND	theft, pilferage and non-delivery	Diebstahl, Beraubung und Nichtlieferung
t	ton/tonne	Tonne
t.o.	turnover	Umsatz, Umschlag
T/S	transhipment	Umladung
TA	total audience	Gesamtzahl der Hörer/Leser/Zuschauer
TA	trade association	Unternehmerverband, Fachverband
TAT	thematic apperception test	thematischer Apperzeptionstest (TAT)
TC	till countermanded	bis auf weiteres
TC	total cost(s)	Gesamtkosten
TC	trunk call	Ferngespräch
TCC	transfer charge call	R-Gespräch
TDA	Trade Description Act	Gesetz über Warenbeschreibung (GB)
TED	Tender`s Electronic Daily	Teledialogsystem für zeitgleiche telefonsiche TV-Zuschauerbefragungen
TEE	total effective exposure	Gesamtzahl der Werbemittelkontakte
tel	telephone	Telefon
TF	till forbid	bis auf weiteres
TGI	target group index	Zielgruppenindex
TM	trademark (trade mark)	Warenzeichen, Handelsmarke
TN	tradename	Firmenname
TNC	transnational corporation	transnationale Gesellschaft, mulitnationales Unternehmen
TOFC	trailer on flat car	Huckepackverkehr, Kombiverkehr

ToP	terms of payment	Zahlungsbedingungen, Zahlungsziele, Zahlungsmodalitäten im Außenhandel
TPA	third party access	Zugang durch Dritte
TPND	theft, pilferage and non-delivery	Diebstahl, Beraubung und Nichtlieferung
TQM	total quality management	Total Quality Management, umfassendes Qualitätsmanagement
TR	total revenue	Gesamtumsatzerlös
tr	tare	Tara, Verpackungsgewicht
TRF, trf	transfer	Transfer, Abziehbild
TSL	time spent listening	Radiohörzeit
TSR	time spent reading	Lesedauer
TST	time shifted television	zeitversetztes Fernsehen
TSV	time spent viewing	Fernsehzeit
TTO	Technology Transfer Office	Technologietransferbüro
TV	television	Fernsehen
TVHH	television household	Fernsehhaushalt
TVR	television recording	Fernsehaufzeichnung
TVR	television rating	Fernseheinschaltquote

U

u/c	undercharge	zu niedrig berechneter Betrag
UAP	unique advertising proposition	werbliche Alleinbehauptung/ Alleinstellung
UC, uc	uppercase (upper case)	Großbuchstabe(n), Großschreibung
uc	usual conditions	übliche Bedingungen
UCC	Uniform Commercial Code	Uniform Commercial Code (UCC) (USA)
UCE	unforeseen circumstances excepted	unvorhergesehene Umstände ausgeschlossen
UMP	unique marketing proposition	einzigartiger Marketingvorteil/Marketing-anspruch
UPC	universal product code	UPC-Strichcode
UPP	unique product position	einzigartiges Produktversprechen
USC	unique selling composition	einzigartige Gestaltung der Verkaufs- und Anbiettechnik
USP	unique selling proposition	einzigartiges, einmaliges Verkaufsargument
ut	usual terms	übliche Bedingungen

V

v/o	voiceover/voice over	Off-Kommentar (Werbetext des nicht sichtbaren Erzählers in TV- und Kinowerbung)
VA	value analysis	Wertanalyse
val	value	Wert, Tauschwert, Geldwert, Vermögenswert, Gebrauchswert, Nutzen, (angemessener) Marktpreis, Kaufkraft
VALS	values and life styles	Zielgruppeneinteilung nach Wertvorstellungen und Lebensstil
VAR	value adding reseller	Wiederverkäufer, der den Produktwert erhöht
VAT	value added tax	Mehrwertsteuer (MwSt)
VDU	visual display unit	Bildschirmgerät, Sichtgerät
VFM	value for money	das Geld wert sein
VIO	very important object	sehr wichtiges Objekt
VIP	very important person	Person, die wichtig ist oder dafür gehalten wird
VMS	vertical marketing system	vertikales Marketingsystem
VO	voiceover/voice over	Off-Kommentar (Werbetext des nicht sichtbaren Erzählers in TV- und Kinowerbung), Sprechertext
VoD	video-on-demand	Bildschirmangebot mit Abrufmöglichkeit zur direkten Überspielung
vol	volume	Umsatzvolumen, Volumen
vou	voucher	Gutschein, Quittung, Rechnungsbeleg, Bon, Eintrittskarte
VPH	viewers per household	Fernsehzuschauer pro Haushalt
VPVH	viewers per viewing household	durchschnittliche Personenzahl pro Fernsehhaushalt
VR	virtual reality	künstliche Realität durch audiovisuelle Computeranimation
VTR	videotape recorder	Videorekorder

W

W/B	waybill	Frachtbrief, Luftfrachtbrief, Versandanzeige, Passagierliste
W/C	week commencing	Woche beginnend ...
W/d	warranted	garantiert, zugesichert
W/M	weight/measurement	Fracht nach Gewicht/Maß

W/R	warehouse receipt	Lagerempfangsschein, Lagerschein
WB	waybill	Frachtbrief, Luftfrachtbrief, Versandanzeige, Passagierliste
wc	without charge	gebührenfrei
WEF	with effect from	mit Wirkung vom
WFA	World Federation of Advertisers	Internationaler Dachverband der Werber
wg	weight guaranteed	garantiertes Gewicht
wgt	weight	Gewicht
whse	warehouse	Lagerhaus, Lager, Warenlager
WIP	work in process	unfertige Erzeugnisse, Halberzeugnisse, Halbfabrikate
WIP	work in progress	unfertige Erzeugnisse, Halberzeugnisse, Halbfabrikate
WOM	word-of-mouth	Mund-zu-Mund
WPI	wholesale price index	Erzeugerpreisindex
wrt	with reference to	bezüglich
wt	weight	Gewicht
WWW	WorldWideWeb	Multimediales Informationssystem im Internet
WYSIWYG	what you see is what you get	originalgetreu, wie gesehen

X

X stk	ex stock	ab Lager, ab Werk
X whse	ex warehouse	ab Lager, ab Werk
XCU	extra-close up	Großaufnahme, Nahaufnahme

Y

Y	income	Einkommen
yd	yard	Yard (Längenmaß), Lagerplatz
yr	year	Jahr

Z

ZEG	zero economic growth	Nullwachstum
ZPG	zero population growth	Nullbevölkerungswachstum

Our best advertisement

is a satisfied customer.

Barry L. Bayus